21st EDITION

Government by the People

NATIONAL, STATE, AND LOCAL VERSION

David B. Magleby
Brigham Young University

David M. O'Brien
University of Virginia

Paul C. Light
New York University

James MacGregor Burns
University of Maryland, College Park
and Williams College

J.W. Peltason
University of California

Thomas E. Cronin
Whitman College

PEARSON
Prentice
Hall

Upper Saddle River, New Jersey 07458

Library of Congress Cataloging-in-Publication Data

Government by the people.—National, state, and local version, 21st ed./David B.
   Magleby . . . [et al.].
      p. cm.
   Includes bibliographical references and index.
   ISBN 0-13-192156-8 (alk. paper)
   1. United States—Politics and government—Textbooks. 2. State governments—United
States—Textbooks. 3. Local government—United States—Textbooks. I. Magleby, David B.

JK276.G68 2006b
320.473—dc22

2004054180

VP, Editorial Director: Charlyce Jones Owen
Acquisitions Editor: Glenn Johnston
Production Editor: Rob DeGeorge
Development Editor: Betty Gatewood
Editorial Assistant: Suzanne Remore
Director of Marketing: Heather Shelstad
Marketing Manager: Kara Kindstrom
Copy Editor: Sylvia Moore
**VP, Director of Production
   and Manufacturing:** Barbara Kittle
Prepress and Manufacturing Manager:
   Nick Sklitsis
Prepress and Manufacturing Buyer:
   Sherry Lewis
Creative Design Director: Leslie Osher
Interior and Cover Designer: Carmen
   DiBartolomeo
Director, Image Resource Center:
   Melinda Reo

Manager, Visual Research: Beth Brenzel
Manager, Rights and Permissions:
   Zina Arabia
**Manager, Cover Visual Research and
   Permissions:** Karen Sanatar
Image Permission Coordinator:
   Michelina Viscusi
Photo Researchers: Kathy Ringrose
   and Elaine Soares
Illustrations: Mirella Signoretto
Chapter Opening Layout: Bruce Killmer
Cover Art: EyeWire Collection/Getty
   Images–Photodisc
Composition: Pine Tree Composition
Printer/Binder: Courier Companies, Inc.
Cover Printer: The Lehigh Press, Inc.
Text: 9/12 Utopia

Credits and acknowledgments borrowed from other sources and reproduced, with permission,
in this textbook appear on appropriate page within text or, in the case of photographs, on p. C-1.

Pearson Education LTD.
Pearson Education Singapore, Pte. Ltd
Pearson Education, Canada, Ltd
Pearson Education—Japan
Pearson Education Australia PTY, Limited

Pearson Education North Asia Ltd
Pearson Educación de Mexico, S.A. de C.V.
Pearson Education Malaysia, Pte. Ltd
Pearson Education, Upper Saddle River,
   New Jersey

10 9 8 7 6 5 4 3 2
College: ISBN 0-13-192156-8
High School: ISBN 0-13-192491-5

BRIEF CONTENTS

CONTENTS

PART III Policy-Making Institutions

APPENDIX

A MESSAGE FROM THE AUTHORS

The United States emerged from the 2004 election divided not only on the war in Iraq and how best to pursue the war on terror, but also on issues like stem cell research, same-sex marriage, future funding for Social Security, and how to revitalize the economy. The country is also divided along party lines. The intensity of the partisan division is explained in part by the differing perceptions of the fairness of the vote count in the 2000 presidential election. Democrats won the popular vote and believe that the decision to deny them Florida's electoral vote was driven by partisanship. Republicans believe they won the presidency fairly. While the two sides in the 2004 election did not agree on much, they did and do agree that elections matter and that there are real policy consequences to elections. What is also undisputed is the importance of government and politics in people's lives.

The political parties and interest groups made voter registration and turnout—getting voters to the polls—a major priority in 2003 and 2004. While the surge in new-voter registration was most concentrated in the presidential battleground states, it was evident elsewhere as well. Some groups concentrated on getting young citizens to register and vote while other groups focused on other issues. Federal legislation was also a factor in this dynamic election environment since voters could cast provisional ballots if their registration was uncertain, a provision that resulted in multiple legal challenges. Ballot initiatives on minimum wage and same-sex marriage gave citizens additional reasons to exercise the franchise and vote. An enduring dispute in American government is how hard or easy the act of voting should be for citizens.

The war on terror not only has changed electoral politics but also has prompted recommendations about reform of our intelligence agencies, fostered a debate about defense priorities and expenditures, and led to the creation of a Department of Homeland Security. Citizens expect their government to provide security. How can government achieve this fundamental objective in light of the reality of terrorists who target America and Americans? To what extent do we pursue countries producing weapons of mass destruction? Is preemptive war a good idea given these potentially lethal weapons that could kill millions of Americans? Should the war on terror be waged by the United States alone if allies are not willing to join us? More broadly, what is the proper balance between providing security and protecting liberty? In many chapters of this edition we compare public opinion in the United States with opinions in other countries, including opinions on items like the institutions and policies of democracy in the United States. Why is the United States perceived in such a negative way in so many

countries? Are there ways the United States can improve its global image?

The economy is another policy area that illustrates the importance of government at all levels. At the national level the issue has centered on whether we could pursue a global war on terror and at the same time cut taxes. The alternative of funding the war through borrowing and raising the federal budget deficit poses its own tradeoffs. Additionally, there is dispute over what kinds of taxes are most fair and beneficial to the economy. Economic factors also impact state and local governments, who generally must balance their budgets by either cutting spending or raising taxes in difficult economic times.

Constitutional democracy—the kind we have in the United States—is exceedingly hard to achieve, equally hard to sustain, and often hard to understand without rigorous study. Our political history has been an evolution toward an enlarged role for citizens and voters. Citizens have more rights and political opportunities in 2005 and 2006 than they had in 1800 or 1900. The framers of our Constitution warned that we must be vigilant in safeguarding our rights, liberties, and political institutions. But to do this, we must first understand these institutions and the forces that have shaped them.

Many U.S. citizens take for granted civil liberties, civil rights, free and fair elections, the peaceful transfer of power, and economic freedom and prosperity. Yet many people live in places where these freedoms are nonexistent. This is a time of testing for new democracies as well as old ones. Contempt for government and politics is being expressed in the United States and abroad, yet politics and partisan competition are the lifeblood that enables free societies to achieve the ideal of government by the people.

Although we constantly turn to government and to our elected officials with problems and requests, we are critical of their shortcomings. A recurrent theme of this book is the absolute need for politics and politicians, despite the widespread tendency to criticize nearly everything political. In many chapters, we showcase examples of people in politics who have made a difference. These politically active individuals have divergent parties, ideologies, and agendas, but they share a common trait of engagement in democracy. The reality is that our political system should not be taken for granted, even as we seek ways in which it can be improved.

We want you to come away from reading this book with a richer understanding of American politics, government, and the job of politicians. We hope you will participate actively in making this constitutional democracy more vital and responsive to the urgent problems of the twenty-first century.

Reviewers

The writing of this book has profited from the informed, professional, and often sharp, critical suggestions of our colleagues around the country. This and previous editions have been considerably improved as a result of reviews by the following individuals, for which we thank them all:

James E. Anderson, Texas A&M University
Alan Balboni, Community College of Southern Nevada
Thad Beyle, University of North Carolina
Robert R. Bland, University of North Texas
Wendell S. Broadwell, Georgia Perimeter College
Mark Cassel, Kent State University
Ray Christensen, Brigham Young University
Douglas Crane, Georgia Perimeter College
James Decker, Macon State College
Veronica D. DiConti, American University
Cecile Durish, Austin Community College
Jeff Fox, Fort Lewis College

Russell Arben Fox, Arkansas State University
Earl H. Fry, Brigham Young University
Bill Gangi, St. Johns University
G. David Garson, North Carolina State University
John Green, University of Akron
Yoram Haftel, Ohio State University
Kenneth G. Hartman, Longview Community College
Paul Herrnson, University of Maryland
Heidi Hobbs, North Carolina State University
Terry Jack, Gulf Coast Community College
Ronald F. King, Tulane University

Joseph Lamb, Macon State College
Gary Moncrief, Boise State University
Ron Pettus, St. Charles Community College
John R. Phillips, Springfield College
Saundra J. Reinke, Augusta State University
Michael W. Sonnleitner, Portland Community College
Grier Stephenson, Franklin & Marshall College
Regina Swopes, Northeastern Illinois University
Robert A. Taylor, Florida Institute of Technology
Lois Duke Whitaker, Georgia Southern University
Frank L. Wilson, Purdue University

Acknowledgments

This book builds on a long tradition of clear and accessible writing, sound scholarship, and currency. James MacGregor Burns and Jack Peltason, the founding authors of the book, and Tom Cronin, who later joined them, set a high standard in these areas. As additional authors have joined the book we have worked hard to maintain this legacy while at the same time extensively revising each new edition to maintain its tradition of currency. Writing this book requires teamwork—first, among the coauthors, who converse often about the broad themes, features, and focus of the book and who read and rewrite each other's first drafts; then with our research assistants, who track down loose ends and give us the perspective of students; and with the editors and other professionals at Prentice Hall. Important to each revision are the detailed reviews by teachers and researchers, who provide concrete suggestions on how to improve the book. We are grateful to all who helped with this edition.

Research assistants for the current edition of *Government by the People* are Susan Christiansen, Stephanie Curtis, Yale Layton, Jeffrey R. Makin, Emily McClintock, Ryan Mehner, R. Chad Pugh, Dustin Slade, Peter Stone, and Paul V. Russell at Brigham Young University and Cindy Bolyes at the University of Virginia. Donna Jones and JoAnn Collins at Whitman College provided secretarial assistance. Shara Merchant at the Brookings Institution was also of assistance.

Books for major college courses like this feature state-of-the-art teaching and learning tools. Web-based items for students and instructors are some examples of these ancillaries. Learning is reinforced though simulations like those found in the "Make It *Real*" simulations at the end of each chapter. We thank the professionals who produced the supplements.

We gratefully acknowledge the professionalism and commitment of Political Science Editor Glenn Johnston. Our production editor, Rob DeGeorge, kept us on schedule and orchestrated the production of this edition. Currency has always been a hallmark of this book and Rob did a superb job of facilitating our updating of text and tables right up to the point of publication. Our thanks, too, to Suzanne Remore, who assisted Glenn Johnston in the numerous tasks involved in publishing a book of this scope. Others at Prentice Hall we wish to thank for their continued support are Yolanda de Rooy and Charlyce Jones Owen.

Many skilled professionals were important to the publication of this book. They include Pine Tree Composition for page layout, Kathy Ringrose for photo research, Mirella Signoretto for line art creation, Carmen DiBartolomeo for interior and cover design and design supervision, and Betty Gatewood for text development.

We also want to thank you, the professors and students who use our book, and who send us letters and e-mail messages with suggestions for improving *Government by the People*. We welcome feedback and suggestions from you. Please write us in care of the Political Science Editor at Prentice Hall, 1 Lake Street, Upper Saddle River, New Jersey 07458, or contact us directly:

David B. Magleby   Distinguished Professor of Political Science and Dean of FHSS, Brigham Young University, Provo, UT 84602 david_magleby@byu.edu

David M. O'Brien   Leone Reaves and George W. Spicer Professor, Department of Government and Foreign Affairs, University of Virginia, Charlottesville, VA 22903 dmo2y@virginia.edu

Paul C. Light   Paulette Goddard Professor of Public Service at New York University and Douglas Dillon Senior Fellow at the Brookings Institution pcl226@nyu.edu

James MacGregor Burns   Academy of Leadership, University of Maryland, College Park, MD 20742.

J. W. Peltason   School of Social Sciences, University of California, Irvine, CA 92717-5700 jwpeltas@uci.edu

Thomas E. Cronin   Office of the President, Whitman College, Walla Walla, WA 99362 cronin@whitman.edu

A MESSAGE FROM THE PUBLISHER

Always one step ahead . . .

Prentice Hall is extremely proud to publish the book that remains the most reliable, responsive, and respected text for use in colleges and universities in every state of the nation. For over fifty years, this is the book that has always remained one step ahead of all the others by anticipating your needs as an educator and your students' needs as learners. Now in its twenty-first edition, Magleby, O'Brien, Light, Burns, Peltason, and Cronin's *Government by the People* continues this tradition.

We are entering a very complex political era and there is no better text poised to take students from being simple onlookers to knowledgeable participants in the American political experience. The level of scholarship of the *Government by the People* author team, as well as the way in which they treat each new edition as a fresh challenge, is clearly represented in this latest edition. That is why, time and time again, *Government by the People* remains the most current, respected, and reliable book on the market and remains . . . one step ahead.

New to this Edition

- *New! Late-Breaking, Up-to-Date Content*   This new edition has been thoroughly updated and revised with coverage of the 2004 elections. Almost all chapters have undergone revisions to reflect the many changes and events in the last two years. This text is right on top of the demographic changes that are remaking society before our eyes. Special attention is given to presenting the key trends in diversity that matter in American politics, including a focus on the people in politics who are the movers and shakers that are making a difference on issues related to managing the increased diversity of America. There is an increased focus on comparative and global issues to introduce students to the increasing globalization of American politics. The rulings of the Supreme Court have been thoroughly updated and highlight changes and controversies over affirmative action, the separation of religion and government, the rights of homosexuals, searches and seizures, and the Rehnquist Court's recent rulings on federalism. There is also great coverage of the impact of campaign finance reform as well as coverage of the voter mobilization drive in 2004.

- *New! Global Perceptions Features*   This brand new feature utilizes the most current data from the Pew Research Center to show students how public opinion in various nations compares with public opinion in the United States as well as how people throughout the world view the United States. Topics covered include the spread of American ideas and customs throughout the world, attitudes throughout the world toward immigrants, and attitudes throughout the world toward unions.

- *New! Chapter Opening Time Lines*   Each chapter begins with a chapter-specific historical time line to help students place significant historical moments into context with what they are studying—as they are studying—making an otherwise difficult concept more manageable and, therefore, more meaningful.

Enduring Features of the Text

Among the many attributes of *Government by the People* are the features that have come to support the balanced presentation of topics within the text. Each of these features has been appropriately revised to reflect those issues that are most significant within our political environment today.

- *In Comparative Perspective*   This boxed feature uses data, maps, and figures to show students how the United States compares to other nations throughout the world with regard to a variety of topics, including: The British and American Systems: A Study in Contrasts, and Registration and Voting in the World's Democracies.

- *People and Politics: Making a Difference*   This thoroughly revised boxed feature provides students with short profiles of influential political figures, some of historical importance as well as some contemporary figures. Many focus on the positive contributions of America's public servants and ordinary citizens, including: Joan Blades and Wes Boyd of MoveOn, Stephen Moore and the Club for Growth, Blaise Hazelwood, Karl Rove, Sean Hannity, and Steve Rosenthal of America Coming Together.

- *You Decide/Thinking It Through*   Provides broader discussion on current topics. This participatory question-and-answer feature is designed to strengthen students' critical thinking skills as well as introduce interesting and challenging issues and ideas about American politics.

- *Changing Face of American Politics*   This feature addresses the diverse nature of the American political system. These unique boxes are designed to reflect the concerns and experiences of ethnic and minority groups in American politics, giving students tangible examples of the key trends in diversity on the American political landscape, including such topics as whether there is a relationship between race and trust.

Teaching and Learning Resources

- *Practice Tests* This study resource includes chapter outlines, study notes, a glossary, and practice tests designed to reinforce information in the text and help students develop a greater understanding of American government and politics.

- *Instructor's Resource CD-ROM* New from Prentice Hall, the Instructor's Resource CD-ROM allows you maximum flexibility as you prepare your lectures and manage your class. For presentation use, this CD-ROM contains a database that includes the Instructor's Resource Manual, Test Item File, line art from the text, video and audio segments of classical and contemporary political science footage, and Powerpoint™ presentations.

- *Instructor's Resource Manual with Test Item File* For each chapter, a summary, review of concepts, lecture suggestions and topic outlines, and additional resource materials—including a guide to media resources—are provided. An electronic version is also included on the Instructor's Resource CD-ROM.

    The **Test Item File** has undergone extensive review and revision, so instructors can have more confidence than ever in the quality of test questions. This edition presents the highest level of quality and accuracy, with over 2,000 questions in multiple choice, true/false, short answer, and essay format covering factual and conceptual material from the text.

- *Prentice Hall Test Manager* A computerized test bank contains the items from the Test Item File. The program allows for full editing of questions and the addition of instructor-generated items. Suitable for Windows and Macintosh operating systems.

- *Government by the People Transparencies* This set of full-color transparency acetates reproduces illustrations, charts, and maps from the text as well as from additional sources.

- *Prentice Hall Custom Video: How a Bill Becomes a Law* This 25-minute video chronicles an environmental law in Massachusetts—from its start as one citizen's concern to its passage in Washington, D.C. Students see the step-by-step process of how a bill becomes a law, complete through narrative and graphics. Available to qualified college adopters. Please contact your local Prentice Hall representative for details.

- *Films for the Humanities and Social Sciences* Qualified college adopters may select from a high quality library of political science videos from Films for the Humanities and Social Sciences. Please contact your local Prentice Hall representative for details on qualifying orders and a complete listing.

- *Choices: An American Government Custom Reader* Exercise freedom of expression by creating an American government reader that truly reflects your teaching style, your course goals, your perspective! *Choices: An American Government Custom Reader* delivers quality scholarship, pedagogy, and exceptional source materials. You choose the readings and the sequence. You can even add your own work or other favorite materials to create a reader that fits your course precisely. The price of your reader is determined by its length. Your students pay for what they need—no more. Over 250 articles, documents, book excerpts, and speeches—representing classic pieces as well as current articles and covering over 20 topical areas—are available. Visit the *Choices* Website: www.choices reader.com and learn about updates.

New and Improved Technology

As in previous editions, *Government by the People* leads the industry in providing creative, innovative electronic solutions for your classroom. Whether in the form of tools that enable more effective communication or by providing dynamic presentation of content via the World Wide Web, Prentice Hall continues to anticipate your needs.

- *New!* OneKey For instructors who would like to implement the use of course management software to organize their course and communicate with their students, Prentice Hall is pleased to offer access to *OneKey*, an exclusive new resource for instructors and students. *OneKey* provides you access to the best online teaching and learning tools—all available 24 hours a day, 7 days a week. *OneKey* means that all of your resources are in one place for maximum convenience, simplicity, and success. *OneKey* features a host of organizational tools for both students and instructors for Blackboard, WebCT, and CourseCompass. Students can be better prepared for class and instructors can save time preparing for lectures and managing their course by utilizing the available online resources such as multimedia, tests, quizzes, and research through *Research Navigator*™, as well as gradebooks for grading and tracking student progress and success. Access to *OneKey* is available to qualified college adopters. Please contact your local Prentice Hall representative for more information.

- *New!* **Make It Real** Available as part of *OneKey* or by itself, *Make It Real* is a new Web-based resource that enables students to take concepts discussed in the text and put them to practical use. Simulations based on real data give students a hands-on experience based on real election results; real demographics, including gender, age, education level, race, and income; real score cards from actual Senate members showing their votes on public interest issues; and real maps, including political persuasion in different regions. *Make It Real* also includes activities that enhance and promote civic participation and visual literacy. This program incorporates Census 2000 data and primary source documents. In addition, there are chapter-based assessments, flashcards, crossword puzzles, and interactive maps and time lines. Access codes are available free when packaged with *Government by the People*.

- **Evaluating Online Resources for Political Science with Research Navigator™** Our newest addition to the reliable Internet guide for political science, Prentice Hall's *Research Navigator*™ keeps instructors and students abreast of the latest news and information and helps students create top quality research papers. From finding the right articles and journals to citing sources, drafting and writing effective papers, and completing research assignments, *Research Navigator*™ simplifies and streamlines the entire process. Complete with extensive help on the research process and three exclusive databases full of relevant and reliable source material, including EBSCO's *ContentSelect*™ Academic Journal Database, *The New York Times* Search-by-Subject Archive, and *Best of the Web* Link Library.

A unique access code for *Research Navigator*™ is provided on the inside front cover of the booklet. *Evaluating Online Resources for Political Science with Research Navigator*™ is free for qualified college adoptions when packaged with *Government by the People* and available for stand-alone sale. Take a tour on the web at www.researchnavigator. com

■ **Companion Website**™   (www.prenhall.com/magleby) Students can take full advantage of the World Wide Web to enrich their study of American government through the *Government by the People Companion Website*™. The site features interactive practice tests, chapter objectives, and overviews. Web destinations provide a valuable source of supplemental information.

Supplemental Texts and Readings for American Government

The following books feature specialized topical coverage, allowing you to tailor your American government content to suit the needs of your course. Featuring contemporary issues or timely readings, any of the following books is available to qualified college adopters at a discount when bundled with

Government by the People. Please visit our online catalog at www.prenhall.com/magleby for additional details.

Government's Greatest Achievements: From Civil Rights to Homeland Security, 20th ed.
Paul C. Light, New York University
ISBN: 0-13-110192-7 © 2004

21 Debated: Issues in American Politics, 2nd ed.
Gregory Scott, University of Central Oklahoma
Loren Gatch, University of Central Oklahoma
ISBN: 0-13-184178-5 © 2005

Strategies for Active Citizenship
Kateri M. Drexler
Gwen Garcelon
ISBN: 0-13-117295-6 © 2005

The Political Science Student Writer's Manual, 4th ed.
Gregory M. Scott, University of Central Oklahoma
Stephen M. Garrison, University of Central Oklahoma
ISBN: 0-13-040447-0 © 2002

Real Politics in America Series

This series is another resource for contemporary instructional material that can be used to bridge the gap between research and relevancy. More descriptive than quantitative, more case study than data study, these books cut across all topics to bring students relevant details in current political science research. From exploring the growing phenomenon of direct democracy to who runs for the state legislature, these books show students that real political science is meaningful and exciting. Individual titles are available at a significant a discount when bundled with *Government by the People*. Please see your Prentice Hall representative or access www.prenhall.com for more details on the titles in the series. A complete listing of the titles in this series can be found on page xxii.

RELIABLE.
RESPONSIVE.
RESPECTED.
That's
GOVERNMENT
BY THE PEOPLE.

BUILDING ON A LONG TRADITION OF CLEAR AND accessible writing, sound scholarship, and currency, GOVERNMENT BY THE PEOPLE **has become the most reliable, responsive, and respected text for today's American Government course.** Its distinguished author team has revised each edition with one steadfast commitment—to address your needs and the needs of your students with the most innovative response to teaching trends, as well as trends in the discipline.

As students become active participants in the study of American government, they will learn to understand and appreciate the crucial role of government and politicians—as well as their own vital role as voters and contributors to America's constitutional democracy. With this essential foundation, students will be set to respond—as involved American citizens—to the political issues facing their country, and their world, in the twenty-first century.

■ *Changing Face of American Politics*

These boxed features appear in context with topics presented in every chapter, exemplifying the ever-increasing level of diversity in the American political landscape. By involving students on a personal level, this text engages them in a more meaningful, memorable study of politics as it affects their own lives.

CHANGING FACE OF AMERICAN POLITICS

PRESIDENTIAL APPOINTEES

Presidents Bill Clinton and George W. Bush both promised to appoint administrations that were as diverse as the country. Although both presidents came surprisingly close on race, neither approached the 50 percent mark on gender. According to detailed analysis of every executive branch appointee nominated for Senate confirmation in the first year of the first term of both administrations, 30 percent of the appointees in Clinton's first year were women, compared to just 23 percent in Bush's first year.

Although the numbers seem disappointing given the changing face of the federal bureaucracy discussed in the next chapter, both administrations did much better than their predecessors—less than 15 percent of the appointees in Carter's first year (1977) were women, compared to just 8 percent in Reagan's first year (1981).* And the fact that both Clinton and Bush were both able to recruit many women and minority appointees at lower levels suggests that future administrations will be even more successful. Past research shows that the higher-level jobs almost always go to appointees with prior appointee-service at lower levels. By increasing the numbers of women and minorities in the pipeline, the Clinton and Bush administrations increased the odds that there will be more women and minority candidates for the top jobs for future Democratic and Republican administrations alike.

*The Carter and Reagan numbers come from Gary King and Lynn Ragsdale, *The Elusive Executive: Discovering Elusive Statistical Patterns in the Presidency* (CQ Press, 1988), pp. 236–237.

	Clinton Administration, 1993	Bush Administration, 2001
Gender		
Women	30%	23%
Men	70	77
Race		
African-American	14%	9%
Hispanic	6	8
Asian-American	3	3
White	77	80

SOURCE: Data collected by the Presidential Appointee Initiative, analysis by authors.

■ *People & Politics: Making a Difference*

Politically active people represent divergent parties, ideologies, and agendas—but share the common trait of engagement in the political process. This feature reinforces the importance of being an active participant in—and contributor to—political change.

PEOPLE & POLITICS *Making a Difference* ★★★

GENERATION X IN CONGRESS (HAROLD FORD, JR., AND ADAM PUTNAM)

As the two youngest members of Congress, Adam Putnam (R.-Fla.) and Harold Ford, Jr. (D.-Tenn.) care deeply about reengaging young Americans in politics. Both were elected in part on promises to give young Americans a stronger voice in debates about the future of programs such as Social Security, and both continue to work hard to connect with their generation on jobs and access to education.

Putnam was just 26 years old when he was elected to Congress in 2000. "I want to energize a whole new generation of young people to reengage in politics," Putnam says. You, know, Kennedy did it, Reagan did it, probably Clinton '92 did it. We've got to do a better job talking across generational lines."

Ford was just 26, too, when he was elected to Congress in 1996. Young people were a central part of his first campaign. He visited more than 100 schools and spoke to an estimated 40,000 to 50,000 high school students en route to a landslide victory. "We've grown up in a different world," his chief of staff explained to reporters when asked about Ford's view of politics. "We're more comfortable with diversity, with change, with new ideas and new attitudes."

Age does not create a shared agenda, however Putnam opposes many of the issues that young Americans support, including abortion rights. He also rejected MTV's request to film his first campaign by saying he didn't want any "purple-hair yahoo" asking whether he wore "boxers or briefs." But he does support Social Security reform, which is a key issue for young Americans who do not believe the program will still be alive when they retire.

Putnam and Ford do believe they can make a difference in showing that age is no barrier to participation. "I'm not invited to a high school class to articulate the merits of permanent normal trade relations with China," Putnam says. "I'm invited to classes to talk about why it's important for young people to get involved and how they can do it." Ford agrees. "Once you get young people to pay attention, you find that you've turned on a faucet that's hard to turn off." The fact that these two Gen X'ers are in Congress is no small part of showing young Americans that age is not a barrier to involvement at the very top of American politics.

Adam Putnam

Harold Ford, Jr.

GLOBAL *Perceptions*

QUESTION: Is the influence of trade unions very good, somewhat good, somewhat bad, or very bad?

How do the views of people in other countries on unions compare with the views of people in the United States? The Pew Global Attitudes Project allows us to explore this question.

Unions are seen very positively in Vietnam, where 59 percent said they were a "very good" influence and 92 percent said they were a "very good" or "somewhat good" influence. People in Argentina had strongly negative views of unions, with 42 percent saying they were "very bad."

In addition to Vietnam, combining the "very good" and "somewhat good" responses found most people in these countries likely to see unions positively: Nigeria (82%), Phillipines (75%), Great Britain (67%), Uganda (67%), Bolivia (65%), Germany (65%), USA (63%), and South Korea (62%). In contrast, unions were seen as bad in Argentina (75%) and by two-out-of five respondents in Russia, Brazil, Mexico, Venezuela, Italy, Poland, Slovak Republic, Jordan, and Turkey.

Unions were seen as having a good influence on a country more than did multinational corporations in the United States, Canada, and Europe (excluding Italy), but not in other parts of the world. Countries like Great Britain, Slovak Republic, and several countries in South America, Africa, and Asia saw multinational corporations as having a good influence. The positive view of unions in Vietnam does not limit the enthusiasm for multinational corporations, where 93 percent said such corporations were a good influence.

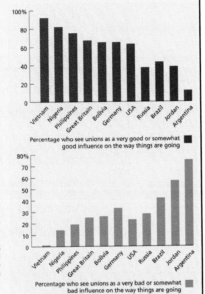

Percentage who see unions as a very good or somewhat good influence on the way things are going ■

Percentage who see unions as a very bad or somewhat bad influence on the way things are going ▨

SOURCE: The Pew Research Center. *Views of a Changing World*, 2003, pp. 100, T-43.

★★ IN COMPARATIVE PERSPECTIVE ★★

IMMIGRATION POLITICS IN CANADA

On a proportional basis, Canada has more immigrants each year than does the United States. Other differences between the United States and Canada in immigration policy include Canada's allowing more skilled immigrants to immigrate and the establishment of a special status for potential immigrants who are willing to invest money in a Canadian business and hire Canadian workers. Federalism is also part of Canadian immigration policy, with provincial governments having some say in whom they will allow as "independent immigrants" (not coming for family reunification or other purposes). Quebec has taken advantage of this policy because it wants to ensure that immigrants either already speak French or are willing to learn French.[*] As noted, Canadians are the most likely of any polity to view immigrants favorably.

The historic patterns of immigration to Canada and the United States also provide an interesting contrast. Both countries are world leaders in welcoming immigrants, and both countries until 1900 "absorbed large inflows from the British Isles."[†] The United States absorbed many more Irish Catholics than did Canada, while Protestants from Northern Ireland were more likely to immigrate to Canada. In the last half-century, Canada experienced a "massive demographic shift as hundreds of thousands of non-British, non-French—including many Asians—came in."[‡]

Following the terrorist attacks of September 11, 2001, Canada's immigration policies have drawn criticism as being too lax. United States and Canadian newspapers accused "the nation to the north" as being a "haven to terrorists."[§] The United States significantly tightened its immigration policies as part of the war on terrorism, but Canada was criticized by the United States, in part because Canada rarely detains refugees who cannot provide identificaton.[‖] The State Department criticized Canada in 2004 as having "lax immigration laws," with implications not only for terrorism but for human trafficking and prostitution.[¶]

[*]Information provided by Earl Fry, Political Science Department, Brigham Young University, February 27, 2004.
[†]Seymour Martin Lipset. *Continental Divide*, New York: Routledge, Chapman, and Hall, Inc., p. 182.
[‡]Seymour Martin Lipset, *Continental Divide*, New York: Routledge, Chapman, and Hall, Inc., p. 185.
[§]James Neff, "Few Resources Spent Guarding Canada Border," *The Seattle Times*, September 29, 2001, p. A1; see also Bob McDonald, "Bush Showing His Toughness," *The Toronto Sun*, September 26, 2001, p. 6.
[‖]Allan Thompson, "Is Canada Really the Weak Link?" *Toronto Star*, October 6, 2001, p. A1.
[¶]Sheldon Alberts, "U.S. Raps Canadian Immigration," Ottawa *Citizen*, February 26, 2004, p. A9.

■ *Global Perceptions*

Understanding America's global image in today's world is critical to understanding the impact of its policies on both a national and international level. New to this edition is *Global Perceptions*, with data from the Pew Research Center that shows students how citizens around the world view not only the United States, its policies, institutions, and leaders, but also issues that affect their daily lives, like the Internet and crime.

■ *In Comparative Perpective*

The emphasis on providing a global context for understanding American politics is reinforced with *In Comparative Perspective* boxes. Through this feature, students learn more about foreign political structure and process, and also how these similar and/or differing approaches can affect—and be affected by—American politics.

TIME LINE

CAMPAIGNS AND ELECTIONS

1781	John Hanson is elected "President of the United States in Congress Assembled"
1789	Constitution is ratified and George Washington is elected "President of the United States"
1800	House of Representatives chooses Thomas Jefferson over Thomas Pinckney
1824	House of Representatives chooses John Quincy Adams over Andrew Jackson when the electoral college fails to elect a president
1860	Southern secession following election of Abraham Lincoln
1876	Samuel Tilden wins the popular vote but loses the Electoral College to Rutherford B. Hayes
1932	Realigning election creates a "New Deal" coalition behind the Democratic Party
1951	Constitution amended limiting president to two terms
1960	First televised presidential debates benefit the Kennedy campaign
1974	"Watergate class" creates liberal majorities in both the House and the Senate
1992	Carol Mosley-Braun becomes the first African American woman elected to the Senate
2000	George W. Bush wins the electoral college in an outcome determined by the Supreme Court
2002	Congress passes Bipartisan Campaign Reform Act, doubling individual contribution limits

■ Timelines

New *time lines* at the beginning of each chapter trace the historical development of American politics and institutions by highlighting key people, events, and documents that helped shape them. Each time line focuses specifically on historical events that are pertinent to the content of the chapter. This historical context helps students appreciate the dynamics of politics and government today and how history will continue to shape government and politics of tomorrow.

These visually-clarifying *time lines* come to life with interactivity in **OneKey** for students who want to explore further as they learn to place significant historical moments into context with what they are studying, making an otherwise difficult concept more manageable and, therefore, more meaningful.

Also available with GOVERNMENT BY THE PEOPLE—

Introducing *Make It Real*

Students will experience the power of politics through multimedia simulations featuring real data in American government. With abundant— and authentic—material tied to the text and designed to bring every chapter to life, *Make It Real*, includes:

■ Civic participation activities and exercises.

■ Video clips of key events that shaped American government and politics.

■ Interactive maps.

■ Audio speeches.

■ Primary source documents.

■ Census data to illustrate real, recent statistics that have an effect on—or are affected by—government and politics.

Fully integrated activities and assessment tools in *Make It Real* tie its content to the text material and offer an easy way to test students' comprehension.

Make It Real is available FREE when packaged with GOVERNMENT BY THE PEOPLE. Please contact your local Prentice Hall sales representative for more information.

One Key *The new, all-inclusive online resource for students*

Designed and presented to accompany this new edition, Prentice Hall's exclusive **OneKey** is a unique website that offers students access to all of their learning resources—all in one place. A robust collection of study and application tools, **OneKey** enables students to enjoy a more in-depth learning experience.

■ *Students will study smarter and perform better.*

Chapter-by-chapter outlines, review quizzes, and essays, as well as interactive flashcard and crossword puzzle activities, reinforce text material. These tools are linked to an e-book version of the text, allowing students to immediately link to appropriate pages for help and feedback where they need it most.

■ *Students will experience the power of politics.*

Also included in **OneKey** is *Make It Real*. With activities, speeches, video, and documents directly tied to the text, *Make It Real* brings politics to life for your students by engaging them to become involved, active learners.

For more information, or to request **OneKey** for your students, please contact your local Prentice Hall sales representative or visit **www.prenhall.com**.

One**Key** *The new, all-inclusive online resource for instructors*

Prentice Hall's exclusive **OneKey** is a unique website that offers instructors free access to all of their teaching resources—all in one place. It contains all of the resources from the printed **Instructor's Manual** and **Test Item File**, as well as PowerPoint™ slides of all art and images from this text . . . and much more. With **OneKey** for instructors, preparing for lectures, testing, and communication with students will be easier and more convenient than ever before.

■ *Present more powerfully than ever before* using text-tied audio, video, and PowerPoint™ slides, organized by chapter of this text, to bring concepts to life for students.

■ *Assess your students' comprehension* of the major concepts and the specific chapters of this text using your choice of reliable test questions from the Test Item File.

■ *Assign your students* chapter-by-chapter, self-graded quizzes or choose essay questions and activities tied to each chapter for use as homework or relevant in-class activities.

Use the *Make It Real* simulations and activities in **OneKey**—all tied to the text—to reinforce material by involving students in the political process through active learning. Use these activities as homework assignments—or in class to spark debates among students as they experience real situations using real data from American government and politics.

Introducing **SafariX:** This new Pearson Choice offers students an online subscription to the same content online at a 50% savings. With the **SafariX WebBook**, students search the text, make notes online, print reading assignments that incorporate lecture notes, and bookmark important passages. Ask your Prentice Hall sales representative for details on available versions of this text, or **visit www.safarix.com.**

REAL POLITICS IN AMERICA

Paul S. Herrnson, Series Editor, *University of Maryland*

PRESIDENTIAL CAMPAIGN QUALITY:
Incentives and Reform
Buchanan
© 2004, 160 pp., paper (0-13-184140-8)

TRANSFORMING THE
AMERICAN POLITY:
The Presidency of George W. Bush and
the War on Terrorism
Conley
© 2005, 160 pp., paper (0-13-189342-4)

WOMEN'S PACS:
Abortion and Elections
Day/Hadley
© 2005, 160 pp., paper (0-13-117448-7)

THE MEDIUM AND THE MESSAGE:
Television Advertising and
American Elections
Goldstein/Strach
© 2004, 256 pp., paper (0-13-177774-2)

WAR STORIES FROM CAPITOL HILL
Campbell/Herrnson
© 2004, 160 pp., paper (0-13-028088-7)

REFORMING THE REPUBLIC:
Democratic Institutions for the
New America
Donovan/Bowler
© 2004, 224 pp., paper (0-13-099455-3)

NO HOLDS BARRED:
Negativity in U.S. Senate Campaigns
Kahn/Kenney
© 2004, 144 pp., paper (0-13-097760-8)

CONGRESS AND THE POLITICS OF
FOREIGN POLICY
Campbell/Rae/Stack
© 2003, 194 pp., paper (0-13-042154-5)

CONGRESS AND THE INTERNET
Thurber/Campbell
© 2003, 198 pp., paper (0-13-099617-3)

CITIES AND PRIVATIZATION:
Prospects for the New Century
Greene
© 2002, 178 pp., paper (0-13-029442-X)

STEALING THE INITIATIVE:
How State Government Responds to
Direct Democracy
Gerber/Lupia/McCubbins/Kiewiet
© 2001, 128 pp., paper (0-13-028407-6)

PLAYING HARDBALL:
Campaigning for the U.S. Congress
Herrnson
© 2001, 160 pp., paper (0-13-027133-0)

WHO RUNS FOR THE LEGISLATURE?
Moncrief/Squire/Jewell
© 2001, 144 pp., paper (0-13-026608-6)

CLICKER POLITICS:
Essays on the California Recall
Bowler/Cain
© 2006, paper (0-13-193336-1)

Prentice Hall is pleased to provide adopters with an opportunity to receive significant
discounts on these titles when packaged together with GOVERNMENT BY THE PEOPLE.
Please contact your local Prentice Hall sales representative for details.

ABOUT THE AUTHORS

David B. Magleby

David B. Magleby is nationally recognized for his expertise on direct democracy, voting behavior, and campaign finance. He is dean as well as Professor of Political Science at Brigham Young University and has taught at the University of California, Santa Cruz, and the University of Virginia. His writings include *Direct Legislation* (1984), *The Money Chase* (1990), and *Myth of the Independent Voter* (1992), and he is editor of *Financing the 2000 Election* (2002) and co-editor of *The Last Hurrah? Soft Money and Issue Advocacy in the 2002 Congressional Elections* (2004). He was president of Pi Sigma Alpha, the national political science honor society, has received numerous teaching awards, and was a Fulbright Scholar at Nuffield College, Oxford University.

David M. O'Brien

David M. O'Brien is the Leone Reaves and George W. Spicer Professor at the University of Virginia. He was a Judicial Fellow and Research Associate at the Supreme Court of the United States, a Fulbright Lecturer at Oxford University, held the Fulbright Chair for Senior Scholars at the University of Bologna, and a Fulbright Researcher in Japan, as well as a Visiting Fellow at the Russell Sage Foundation. Among his publications are *Storm Center: The Supreme Court in American Politics, 6th ed.* (2005); a two volume casebook, *Constitutional Law and Politics, 5th ed.* (2005); an annual *Supreme Court Watch;* and *Animal Sacrifice and Religious Freedom: Church of Lukumi Babablu Aye v. City of Hialeah* (2004). He received the American Bar Association's Silver Gavel Award for contributing to the public's understanding of the law.

Paul C. Light

Paul C. Light is currently the Paulette Goddard Professor of Public Service at New York University's Wagner School of Public Service and Douglas Dillon Senior Fellow at the Brookings Institution. Professor Light has a wide-ranging career in both academia and government. He has worked on Capitol Hill as a senior committee staffer in the U.S. Senate and as an American Political Science Association Congressional Fellow in the U.S. House. He has taught at the University of Virginia, University of Pennsylvania, and Harvard University's John F. Kennedy School of Government. He has also served as a senior adviser to several national commissions on federal, state, and local public service. He is the author of 15 books on government, public service, and public policy.

James MacGregor Burns

James MacGregor Burns is a Senior Scholar at the Academy of Leadership, University of Maryland, College Park. He has written numerous books, including *The Power to Lead* (1984), *The Vineyard of Liberty* (1982), *Leadership* (1979), *Roosevelt: The Soldier of Freedom* (1970), *The Deadlock of Democracy: Four-Party Politics in America* (1963), and *Roosevelt: The Lion and the Fox* (1956). With his son, Stewart Burns, he wrote *A People's Charter: The Pursuit of Rights in America* (1991); with Georgia Sorenson, *Dead Center: Clinton, Gore, and the Perils of Moderation* (2000); and with Susan Dunn, *The Three Roosevelts* (2001). Burns is a past president of the American Political Science Association and winner of numerous prizes, including a Pulitzer Prize in History.

J.W. Peltason

J.W. Peltason is a leading scholar on the judicial process and public law. He is Professor Emeritus of Political Science at the University of California, Irvine. As past president of the American Council on Education, Peltason has represented higher education before Congress and state legislatures. His writings include *Federal Courts in the Political Process* (1955), *Fifty-Eight Lonely Men: Southern Federal Judges and School Desegration* (1961), and with Sue Davis, *Understanding the Constitution* (2000). Among his awards are the James Madison Medal from Princeton University, the Irvine Medal from the University of California, Irvine, and the American Political Science Association's Charles E. Merriam Award.

Thomas E. Cronin

Thomas E. Cronin is a leading student of the American presidency, leadership, and policy-making processes. He teaches at and serves as president of Whitman College. He was a White House Fellow and a White House aide and has served as president of the Western Political Science Association. His writings include *The State of the Presidency* (1980), *U.S. v. Crime in the Streets* (1981), *Direct Democracy: The Politics of Initiative, Referendum, and Recall* (1989), *Colorado Politics and Government* (1993), and *The Paradoxes of the American Presidency* (1998). Cronin is a past recipient of the American Political Science Association's Charles E. Merriam Award.

CONSTITUTIONAL DEMOCRACY

The oldest constitutional democracy in the world, the United States of America, has survived for more than two centuries, yet it is still an experiment and a work in progress. We think of it as an enduring, strong government, but in a real sense, our constitutional political system is built on a fragile foundation. The U.S. Constitution and Bill of Rights survive not because the parchment they were written on is still with us but because each generation of Americans respects, renews, and works at understanding the principles and values found in these precious documents. Different generations have faced different challenges in preserving, protecting, and defending our way of government. Some have faced depressions, others world wars; most recently, Americans have confronted foreign attacks on domestic soil, terrorism around the world, and protracted war in Iraq and Afghanistan.

Terrorism on a global scale has become part of the daily news and a major concern of the American government. Before September 11, 2001, terrorist attacks seemed sporadic and far removed from the United States. The catastrophic attack on the World Trade Center in New York City and the Pentagon in Washington, D.C., made terrorism and security a preoccupation for many Americans. When asked to identify the most important problem facing our nation, terrorism and the economy are the most often mentioned problems. Voters are also concerned about moral values, as evidenced by the debate over same-sex marriage. But the war on terrorism and how best to wage it was the central theme of the 2004 election. The terrorist attacks of September 11, 2001, also changed our perceptions of domestic and international security. The government created the new Department of Homeland Security, increased spending on intelligence and security, and launched preemptive wars against terrorists and governments believed to pose a threat to the United States.

TIME LINE ★★

CREATING THE REPUBLIC

1620	Mayflower Compact established the first basis in the new world for written laws
1775	Revolutionary War begins with battles at Lexington and Concord
1776	Declaration of Independence
1781	Articles of Confederation ratified—establishing the United States
1783	Revolutionary War ends with peace treaty with Great Britain
1786	Annapolis Convention calls for revision of the Articles of Confederation
1786–1787	Shays' Rebellion—poor farmers defy courts and state militia
1787	Constitutional Convention in Philadelphia
1787	Delaware becomes first state to ratify the Constitution
1788	Constitution ratified, replacing the Articles of Confederation
1789	Congress proposes the first amendments: the Bill of Rights

Let us define some of the basic terms we'll be using throughout this book. *Government* refers to the procedures and institutions (such as elections, courts, and legislatures) by which a people govern and rule themselves. *Politics* is the process by which people decide, at least in our system of government, who shall govern and what policies shall be adopted. Such processes invariably involve discussions, debates, and compromises over tactics and goals. *Politicians* are the people who fulfill the tasks of an operating government. Some politicians—legislators, mayors, and presidents—come to office through an election. Nonelected politicians may be political party officials or aides, advisers, or consultants to elected officials. *Political science* is the study of the principles, procedures, and structures of government and the analysis of political ideas, institutions, behavior, and practices.

In the aftermath of September 11, 2001, the United States took the offensive against Al-Qaeda by attacking its bases as well as removing the Taliban government in Afghanistan, which had supported Osama bin Laden. The war in Afghanistan successfully eradicated most terrorist camps and captured or killed many of the organization's leaders, but it failed to kill or capture bin Laden. The ability of bin Laden to evade U.S. forces and to periodically issue video or audio tapes calling for continuing hostilities highlights the problems of fighting individuals and groups like Al-Qaeda.

President Bush, who gained stature and public approval in the aftermath of the September 11 attacks on the United States, linked those attacks to the war in Afghanistan. Less than two months after the attacks on New York and Washington, D.C., President Bush said, "I have called our military into action to hunt down the members of the Al-Qaeda organization who murdered innocent Americans. I gave fair warning to the government that harbors them in Afghanistan. The Taliban made a choice to continue hiding terrorists, and now they are paying a price."[1] In a later speech he broadened the international dimension of the war on terrorism by referring to an "Axis of Evil" consisting of Iraq, Iran, and North Korea. All three of these totalitarian governments were thought to possess weapons of mass destruction and, in the cases of Iraq and Iran, were believed to be sponsoring terrorism. The U.N. weapons inspectors had been trying to determine whether Iraq possessed weapons of mass destruction. Frustrated with their inability to gain U.N. support, the United States and Britain went to war with Iraq largely on their own. Whether the United States should have waited until it had the endorsement and support of the United Nations or several more nations before going to war in Iraq will be debated for years to come.

Both the tone and style of President Bush's leadership alienated some European leaders, most notably in France and Germany. Great Britain, especially Prime Minister Tony Blair, was steadfast in support of the American approach of preemptive war in Iraq. More important to President Bush than his popularity abroad was securing his reelection in 2004, and a cornerstone of his reelection campaign was national security and his efforts to enhance it.

For the Democrats, the terrorist attacks of September 11 made criticizing President Bush much more difficult. A bipartisan coalition enacted legislation creating a homeland security department, authorizing the president to take action in Afghanistan and later Iraq, and appropriating the many billions of dollars to fund the military and nation-building expenses in Afghanistan and Iraq. Democratic presidential candidates were faced with the challenge of criticizing President Bush's policies without seeming to criticize our troops. One tack was to criticize the president's priorities in pursuing Saddam Hussein in Iraq rather than Osama bin Laden and Al-Qaeda. Some expressed support for the removal of Hussein; others opposed the war in Iraq. A common criticism among all the Democratic candidates was that President Bush and his administration had badly underestimated the challenges of establishing order and installing a new democratic government in Iraq. The steady stream of attacks on American and allied forces after President Bush had prematurely declared, "In the battle of Iraq, the United States and our allies have prevailed," underscored the Democrats' criticisms.

The Bush doctrine of using preemptive war against governments believed to pose a substantial risk to the United States and doing so even when others in the international community oppose the action will be much debated in the future. Also debated will be the extent of risk posed by Iraq, especially since the much feared weapons of mass destruction supposedly held by Iraq could not be found after the war; the impact on civil liberties of legislation like the U.S.A. Patriot Act, passed soon after September 11, 2001; who was responsible for the prison abuse in Iraq and Afghanistan; and questions about how to treat foreign nationals captured in the war on terrorism are also important topics.

One challenge for the United States in the post-Iraq war period is the way much of the rest of the world perceives us. In this book we will incorporate our analysis of innovative surveys of citizens from a large number of countries around the world on how our government and country are perceived. Americans like to think of themselves as popular around the world, especially in places like Germany and France where our government played a substantial role in the liberation of France in 1945 and in the reconstruction of the economies of both countries following World War II. We now find, however, that the differences in foreign policy approach between the United States and what Defense Secretary Rumsfeld labeled "old Europe" are substantial and may be enduring. In the minds of citizens in large parts of the Middle East, we are closely linked to Israel and therefore seen as an enemy.

The role of the United States and other prosperous countries in the international economy has also engendered backlash and protest. Because the U.S. economy is the world's largest, it has been the primary target of those concerned over the loss of local economic independence and the growing power of U.S. corporations and their products. Globalization concerns also include workers' rights and compensation and lower environmental standards in the developing world. Globalization is linked in part to the thinking of Osama bin Laden, who sharply criticizes the growing Western/American influence in the Islamic world and the impact this influence has had on culture and beliefs.

The terrorist threat raises important questions for American government. Should the response to terrorism and the threat of terrorism involve the United Nations or at least several countries? Should there be a multilateral approach, or should the United States go it alone if other countries choose not to participate, i.e., a unilateral approach? The Bush administration took the unilateral approach until the going got tough in Iraq and then seemed to shift to a more multilateral approach. The problem with a multilateral approach is that the United States will not have as much control as it does when it acts unilaterally. The problem with a unilateral approach is that the United States is left with the entire burden and expense of the operation, and should it fail the United States will be blamed.

Another consequence of the wars in Iraq and Afghanistan is their cost. Deficit spending, which had become the norm in American politics, ended during the Clinton years, and in the 2000 presidential election the candidates debated how to spend the budget surplus. President Bush, who campaigned promising a tax cut if elected, delivered on that promise. The "Bush" tax cut lowered individual income taxes by 1.3 trillion dollars over ten years. The wisdom of cutting taxes at the same time the nation was fighting a costly global war on terrorism was much debated before the 2004 election. The growing budget deficit and whether to make the "Bush" tax cut permanent were also debated. President Bush campaigned on the idea of making his tax cuts permanent to keep the economy expanding, estimating that the deficit would be cut in half within five years. Democratic standard-bearer John Kerry promised tax relief for the middle class while rolling back the Bush tax cut for high-income individuals. He also promised to reduce the deficit by half in five years.

More generally, economic issues were central to the 2004 election. Here the Republicans and President Bush were put on the defensive about the loss of jobs and the overall state of the economy. Several of the most competitive states in 2004 had experienced severe job loss. Ohio, Pennsylvania, Wisconsin, and Iowa were competitive in part because of the job loss issue. On domestic issues, Democrats and Republicans see things quite differently and the country is evenly divided. Republicans took credit for their success in enacting in 2003 a prescription drug benefit for older Americans, a program many Democrats criticized for its limitations and costs to seniors. Both parties in recent years have pushed a social policy initiative, often one long claimed by the other party. Bill Clinton's 1996 campaign touted his role in enacting welfare reform, and George W. Bush did the same with his "No Child Left Behind" education legislation and prescription drug benefits for seniors in 2002 and 2004.

Social issues, which were important to American politics in the 1970s and 1980s, were also important in 2004. Abortion and gay marriage were galvanizing issues on both the left and right. These issues also served to underscore the importance of the Supreme Court, which has ruled in recent years on these questions, often by narrow majorities. With several Supreme Court justices possibly considering retirement, the Court's future composition was the subject of campaign communications by both conservative and liberal groups.

Events of the past few years have reinforced the importance of government in setting priorities and making policies. It is also clear that who holds power makes a substantial difference in what government does or does not do. At the same time, the country's sharp divisions in partisanship and ideology, and the presence of constitutional checks and balances, make abrupt changes in direction unlikely.

AMERICAN GOVERNMENT AND POLITICIANS IN CONTEXT

The American Republic, founded on enduring values, has shown resiliancy and adaptability. We have held 109 presidential and midterm elections (including the 2004 election), and we have witnessed the peaceful transfer of power from one party to another on dozens of occasions. The United States has succeeded in large part because Americans love their country, revere the Constitution, and respect the free enterprise system. We also believe that our differences are best reconciled by debate, compromise, and free elections. From an early age, we practice democracy in elementary school classrooms, and even though we may be critical of elected leaders, we recognize the need for political leadership. We also know that there are deep divisions and unsolved problems in the United States. Many people are concerned about the persistence of racism, about religious bigotry, about the gap in economic opportunities between rich and poor, and about the gun violence that disproportionately afflicts children and minorities. And we want our government, in addition to providing a defense against terrorism and foreign enemies, to provide basic health care and education as well as to address other domestic problems.

But what is this government of which we expect so much? The reality is that "government" is merely a shorthand term to refer to tens of thousands of our fellow Americans: the people we elect and the people they appoint to promote the general welfare, provide for domestic tranquillity, and secure the blessings of liberty for us.

More than any other form of government, the kind of democracy that has emerged under the U.S. Constitution requires active participation and a balance between faith and skepticism. Government by the people, however, does not require that *everyone* be involved in politics and policy making. Many citizens will always be too busy doing other things, and some people will always be apathetic toward government and politics. Government by the people does require a substantial segment of the public to be attentive, interested, involved, informed, and willing, when necessary, to criticize and change the direction of government.

Thomas Jefferson, one of our best-known champions of constitutional democracy, believed in the common sense of the people and in the flowering possibilities of the human spirit. Jefferson warned that every government degenerates when it is left only in the hands of the rulers. The people themselves, Jefferson wrote, are the only safe repositories of government. His was a robust commitment to popular control, representative processes, and accountable leadership. But he was no believer in the simple participatory democracy of ancient Greece or revolutionary France. The power of the people, too, must be restrained from time to time.

Government by the people requires faith concerning our common human enterprise, a belief that if the people are informed and caring, they can be trusted with their own self-government and an optimism that when things begin to go wrong, the people can be relied on to set them right. But a healthy skepticism is needed as well. Democracy requires us to question our leaders and never trust a group or institution that holds too much power. And even though constitutional advocates prize majority rule, they must remain skeptical about whether the majority is always right.

Constitutional democracy requires constant attention to protecting the rights and opinions of others, to ensure that our democratic processes are effectively serving the principles of liberty, equality, and justice. Thus a peculiar blend of faith and skepticism is warranted when dealing with the will of the people.

Thomas Jefferson.

Constitutional democracy is necessarily government by representative politicians. A central feature of democracy is that those who hold power do so only by winning a free election. In our political system, the fragmentation of powers requires elected officials to mediate among factions, build coalitions, and work out compromises among and within the branches of our government to produce policy and action.

We expect a lot from our politicians. We expect them to operate within the rules of democracy and to be honest, humble, patriotic, compassionate, sensitive to the needs of others, well informed, competent, fair-minded, self-confident, and inspirational. They must be candidates of all the people, not just of the ones with money.

Why does such a gap persist between our image of the ideal politician and our views about actual politicians? The gap exists in part because we have unrealistic expectations. We want politicians to be perfect, to have all the answers, and to have all the "correct" values (as we perceive them). We want politicians to solve our problems, yet we also want them to serve as scapegoats for the things we dislike about government: taxes, regulations, hard times, limits on our freedom. It is impossible for anyone to live up to these ideals. Like all individuals, politicians live in a world in which perfection may be the goal but compromise, ambition, fund raising, and self-promotion are necessary.

Americans will never be satisfied with their political candidates and politicians. The ideal politician is probably a fictional entity, for the perfect official would be able to please everyone, make conflict disappear, and not ask us to make any sacrifices. Politicians become "ideal" only when they are dead.

But the love of liberty invites disagreements of ideology and values. Politicians and candidates, as well as the people they represent, have different ideas about what is best for the nation. That's why we have politics, candidates, opposition parties, heated political debates, and elections.

"The Athenians are here, Sire, with an offer to back us with ships, money, arms, and men—and, of course, their usual lectures about democracy."

DEFINING DEMOCRACY

The word "democracy" is nowhere to be found in the Declaration of Independence or in the U.S. Constitution, nor was it a term used by the founders of the Republic. It is both a very old term and a modern one. It was used at the time of the founding of this nation to refer to various undesirables: mobs, lack of standards, and a system that encourages leaders to gain power by appealing to the emotions and prejudices of the rabble.

The distinguishing feature of democracy is that government derives its authority from its citizens. In fact, the word comes from two Greek words: *demos* (the people) and *kratos* (authority or power). Thus **democracy** means *government by the people,* not government by one person (a monarch, dictator, or priest) or government by the few (an oligarchy or aristocracy).

Ancient Athens and a few other Greek city-states had a **direct democracy** in which citizens came together to discuss and pass laws and select their rulers. These Greek city-states did not last. Most degenerated into mob rule and then resorted to dictators. When the word "democracy" came into use in English in the seventeenth century, it denoted this kind of direct democracy. It was a term of derision, a negative word, a reference to power wielded by an unruly mob.

James Madison, writing in *The Federalist,* No. 10, reflected the view of many of the framers of the U.S. Constitution when he wrote, "Such democracies [as the Greek and Roman] . . . have ever been found incompatible with personal security, or the rights of property; and have in general been as short in their lives, as they have been violent in their deaths" (*The Federalist,* No. 10, is reprinted in the Appendix at the back of this book).

Over time our democracy has become more and more of a combination of representative and direct democracy. The most important examples of direct democracy were added roughly a century ago and include the direct primary, which selects who may run for office; the initiative and referendum, which allow citizens to put to a vote of the people laws or constitutional amendments; and the recall, which allow voters to remove

democracy
Government by the people, either directly or indirectly, with free and frequent elections.

direct democracy
Government in which citizens vote on laws and select officials more directly.

elected officials from office between elections. There has been substantial growth in use of the initiative since the mid-1970s, and 2003 saw the first governor recalled in 82 years when California voters recalled Gray Davis and replaced him with Arnold Schwarzenegger.

Today it is no longer possible, even if desirable, to assemble the citizens of any but the smallest towns to make their laws or to select their officials directly from among the citizenry. Rather, we have invented a system of representation. Democracy today means **representative democracy**, or, to use Plato's term, a *republic,* in which those who have governmental authority get and retain authority directly or indirectly as a result of winning free elections in which all adult citizens are allowed to participate. The framers preferred to use the term "republic" to avoid any confusion between direct democracy, which they disliked, and representative democracy, which they liked and thought secured all the advantages of a direct democracy while curing its weaknesses. Today, as in this book, *democracy* and *republic* are used interchangeably.

In defining democracy, several other terms need to be clarified. **Constitutional democracy**, as used here, refers to a government in which the individuals who exercise substantial governmental powers do so as the result of winning free and relatively frequent elections. *It is a government in which there are recognized, enforced limits on the powers of all governmental officials.* It also generally involves a written set of governmental rules and procedures, a constitution.

Constitutionalism is a term we apply to arrangements—checks and balances, federalism, separation of powers, rule of law, due process, a bill of rights—that require our leaders to listen, think, bargain, and explain before they make laws. We then hold them politically and legally accountable for how they exercise their powers.

Like most political concepts, democracy encompasses many ideas and has many meanings. Democracy is a way of life, a form of government, a way of governing, a type of nation, a state of mind, and a variety of processes. We can divide these many meanings of democracy into three broad categories: a system of interacting values, a system of interrelated political processes, and a system of interdependent political structures.

Democracy as a System of Interacting Values

Belief in representative democracy may be as near a universal faith as the world has today. Respect for human dignity, freedom, liberty, individual rights, and other democratic values is widespread. The ideas of personal liberty, respect for the individual, equality of opportunity, and popular consent are at the core of democratic values. As the Taliban government in Afghanistan demonstrated, there are governments that not only suppress democratic values but find them threatening enough to terrorize governments that embrace them.

PERSONAL LIBERTY Liberty has been the single most important value in American history. It was for "life, liberty, and the pursuit of happiness" that independence was declared; it was to "secure the Blessings of Liberty" that the Constitution was drawn up and adopted. Even our patriotic songs extol the "sweet land of liberty." The essence of liberty is *self-determination,* meaning that all individuals must have the opportunity to realize their own goals. Liberty is not simply the absence of external restraint on a person (freedom *from*); it is the individual's freedom and capacity to act positively to reach his or her goals (freedom *to*). Moreover, both history and reason suggest that individual liberty is the key to social progress. The greater the people's freedom, the greater the chance of discovering better ways of life.

RESPECT FOR THE INDIVIDUAL Popular rule in a democracy flows from a belief that every individual has the potential for common sense, rationality, and fairness. Individuals have important rights; collectively, those rights are the source of all legitimate governmental authority and power. These concepts pervade all democratic thought. They are woven into the writings of Thomas Jefferson, especially in the Declaration of Independence: "All men . . . are endowed by their Creator with certain unalienable rights" (the Declaration of Independence is reprinted in the Appendix). Constitutional

representative democracy
Government that derives its powers indirectly from the people, who elect those who will govern; also called a *republic.*

constitutional democracy
A government that enforces recognized limits on those who govern and allows the voice of the people to be heard through free, fair, and relatively frequent elections.

constitutionalism
The set of arrangements, including checks and balances, federalism, separation of powers, rule of law, due process, and a bill of rights, that requires leaders to listen, think, bargain, and explain before they act or make laws. We then hold them politically and legally accountable for how they exercise their powers.

GLOBAL *Perceptions*

QUESTION: Which of these statements comes closer to your view: I like American ideas about democracy, OR I dislike American ideas about democracy?

C onstitutional democracy as we practice it is not universally valued or appreciated around the world. In 2002, the Pew Charitable Trusts supported a worldwide public opinion survey of how people think about democracy, government, and public policy, generally. These studies help us appreciate how people in many nations view freedom, liberties, and democracy as well as other related topics. The Pew Global Survey asked representative samples of people in 44 countries whether they liked or disliked American-style democracy (see question at the beginning of this box).

China and Egypt were the only countries in which the researchers were not allowed to ask the question. American-style democracy was most liked in Africa, where the proportion saying they liked it exceeded the proportion saying they disliked it in all countries surveyed. In Kenya and Nigeria over 86 percent said they liked it. People in most Asian countries also tended to like it more than dislike it. However, in France 53 percent said they disliked it, and in Europe as a whole, the public was split fairly evenly. U.S. citizens tend to assume that our democracy is the envy of the world. In fact that is not the case. Countries in which 50 percent or more of the public disliked American ideas about democracy include: Jordan (69), Pakistan (60), Bolivia (60), France (53), Brazil (51), Turkey (50), and Argentina (50).

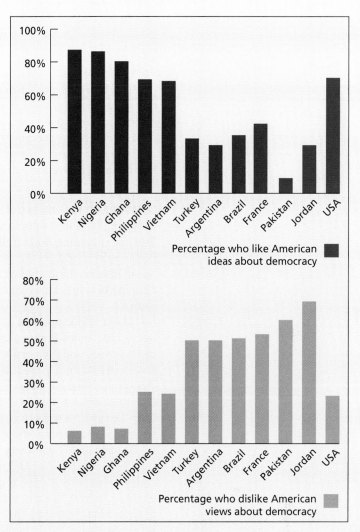

Source: Pew Research Center, *What the World Thinks in 2002*, p. T-55.

democracies make the *person*—rich or poor, black or white, male or female—the central measure of value.

Not all political systems put the individual first. Some promote **statism**, a form of government based on centralized authority and control, especially over the economy. Examples of countries with this approach include China and Cuba. In a modern democracy, the nation, or even the community, is less important than the individuals who compose it.

EQUALITY OF OPPORTUNITY   The importance of the individual is enhanced by the democratic value of *equality:* "All men are created equal and from that equal creation they derive rights inherent and unalienable, among which are the preservation of liberty and the pursuit of happiness." So reads Jefferson's first draft of the Declaration of Independence, and the words indicate the primacy of the concept. Alexis de Tocqueville and other international visitors who have studied American democracy were all struck by the strength of egalitarian thought and practice in our political and social lives.

statism
The idea that the rights of the nation are supreme over the rights of the individuals residing in that nation.

But what does equality mean? Equality for whom? For blacks as well as whites? For women as well as men? For Native Americans, descendants of the Pilgrims, and recent immigrants? And what kind of equality? Economic, political, legal, social, or some other kind of equality? Equality of opportunity? Does equality of opportunity simply mean that everyone should have the same place at the starting line? Or does it mean an effort should be made to equalize the factors that determine how well a person fares economically or socially? These enduring issues arise often in our study of American politics.

POPULAR CONSENT   The animating principle of the American Revolution, the Declaration of Independence, and the resulting new nation was **popular consent**, the idea that a just government must derive its powers from the *consent of the people it governs.* A commitment to democracy thus entails a community's willingness to participate and make decisions in government. These principles sound unobjectionable intellectually, but in practice they mean that certain individuals or groups may not get their way. A commitment to popular consent must involve a willingness to lose when most people vote the other way.

DEMOCRATIC VALUES IN CONFLICT   The basic values of democracy do not always co-exist happily. Individualism may conflict with the collective welfare or the public good. Self-determination may conflict with equal opportunity. For example, the right of a homeowner to add another floor to her home may conflict with the right of her neighbor to have an unobstructed view. Or the right of a person to smoke an after-dinner cigar in a restaurant may conflict with the right of others not to have to breathe tobacco smoke.

Much of our political combat revolves around how to strike a balance among democratic values, how to protect the Declaration of Independence's unalienable rights of life, liberty, and the pursuit of happiness while trying to "form," as the Constitution announces, "a more perfect Union, establish Justice, insure domestic Tranquility, provide for the common defence, promote the general Welfare, and secure the Blessings of Liberty to ourselves and our Posterity" (see the Preamble to the Constitution on page 46). Over the years, the American political system has moved, despite occasional setbacks, toward greater freedom and more democracy.

Expansion of democracy in the United States and elsewhere was in many ways a twentieth-century idea. Although on dozens of occasions in the past century, democracies collapsed and gave way to authoritarian regimes, even more democracies triumphed. Indeed, "the global range and influence of democratic ideas, institutions, and practices has made [the last century] far and away the most flourishing period for democracy."[2]

Democracy as a System of Interrelated Political Processes

Far more people dream about democracy than ever experience it, and many new democracies fail. To be successful, democratic government requires a well-defined political process as well as a stable governmental structure. To become reality, democratic values must be incorporated into a political process, most importantly in the form of free and fair elections, majority rule, freedom of expression, and the right to assemble and protest.

FREE AND FAIR ELECTIONS   Democratic government is based on free and fair elections held at intervals frequent enough to make them relevant to policy choices. Elections are one of the most important devices for keeping officials and representatives accountable.

We previously described representative democracy as a government in which those who have the authority to make decisions with the force of law acquire and retain this authority either directly or indirectly as the result of winning free elections in which the great majority of adult citizens are allowed to participate. Crucial to modern-day definitions of democracy is the idea that opposition political parties can exist, can run candidates in elections, and can at least have a chance to replace those who are currently

popular consent
The idea that a just government must derive its powers from the consent of the people it governs.

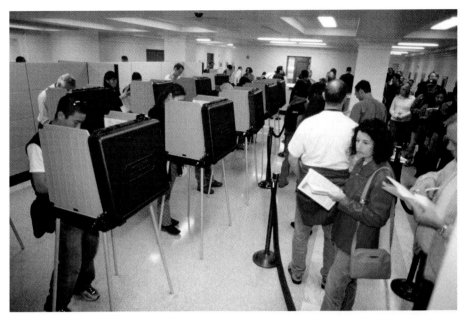

Free and fair elections are an important characteristic of democracies; however, participation requires time and patience, as is evident by these citizens standing in line to vote.

holding public office. Thus *political competition and choice* are crucial to the existence of democracy.

Although all citizens should have equal voting power, free and fair elections do not imply that everyone must or will have equal political influence. Some people, because of wealth, talent, or position, have more influence than others. How much extra influence key figures should be allowed to exercise in a democracy is frequently debated. But in an election, each citizen—president or plumber, corporate CEO or ditch digger—casts only one vote.

MAJORITY (PLURALITY) RULE Majority rule—governance according to the expressed preferences of the majority—is a basic rule of democracy. The **majority** candidate or party is the one that receives *more than half* the votes and so wins the election and takes charge of the government until the next election. In practice, however, majority rule is often **plurality** rule, in which the candidate or party with the *most* votes wins the election, even though it may not constitute a true majority of more than half the votes. About a third of our presidents have won with pluralities in the popular vote rather than majorities.[3] Once elected, officials do not have a right to curtail the attempts of political minorities to use all peaceful means to become the new majority. Even as the winners take power, the losers are at work to try to get it back at the next election.[4]

Should the side with the most votes prevail in all cases? Americans answer this question in a variety of ways. Some insist that majority views should be enacted into laws and regulations. However, an effective representative democracy involves far more than simply ascertaining and applying the statistical will of most of the people. In a constitutional democracy, the will of a majority of the people may not contradict the rights of individuals. For example, the Supreme Court stuck down a 1964 California initiative which would have allowed discrimination against minorities.[5] It is a more complicated and often untidy process in which the people and their agents debate, compromise, and arrive at a decision only after thoughtful deliberation.

The framers of the U.S. Constitution wanted to guard society against any one faction of the people acting unjustly toward any other faction of the people. The Constitution reflects their fear of tyranny by majorities, especially momentary majorities that spring from temporary passions. They insulated certain rights (such as freedom of speech) and institutions (such as the Supreme Court) from popular choice. Effective representation of the people, the framers insisted, should not be based solely on parochial interests or shifting breezes of opinion.

majority rule
Governance according to the expressed preferences of the majority.

majority
The candidate or party that wins more than half the votes cast in an election.

plurality
Candidate or party with the most votes cast in an election, not necessarily more than half.

FREEDOM OF EXPRESSION   Free and fair elections depend on access to information relevant to voting choices. Voters must have access to facts, competing ideas, and the views of candidates. Free and fair elections require a climate in which competing, nongovernment-owned newspapers, radio stations, and television stations can flourish. If the government controls what is said and how it is said, there is no democracy. Without free speech, there are no free and fair elections.

THE RIGHT TO ASSEMBLE AND PROTEST   Citizens must be free to organize for political purposes. Obviously, individuals can be more effective if they join with others in a party, a pressure group, a protest movement, or a demonstration. The right to oppose the government, to form opposition parties, and to have a chance of defeating incumbents is more than vital; it is a defining characteristic of a democracy.

Democracy as a System of Interdependent Political Structures

Democracy is, of course, more than values and processes. It also entails political structures that safeguard these values and processes. The Constitution and its first ten amendments (the Bill of Rights) set up an ingenious structure—one that both grants and checks government power. This constitutional structure is reinforced by a system of political parties, interest groups, media, and other institutions that intercede between the electorate and those who govern and thus help maintain democratic stability.

The U.S. constitutional system has five distinctive elements: *federalism,* the division of powers between the national and state governments; *separation of powers* among the

---

PEOPLE & POLITICS *Making a Difference* ★ ★ ★

JOAN BLADES AND WES BOYD AND MOVEON

One of the surprises of the 2004 election cycle was a group founded by a husband–wife team from Berkeley, California. The couple, Joan Blades and Wes Boyd, was not always politically active. Before founding MoveOn in 1998 as an e-mail campaign opposing the impeachment of President Clinton, the couple had been more concerned with software for handicapped persons and developing popular screen savers. In the 2000 campaign, MoveOn raised more than $2 million for Democratic candidates. But it was in the 2004 election cycle that MoveOn became more visible and important. As with the campaign of Howard Dean, Blades and Boyd tapped into a passionate public who were reachable through the Internet. Dean built his own Internet campaign on the MoveOn model.[*]

What Blades and Boyd demonstrated through MoveOn is that people could be organized for political purposes on a large scale through the medium of the Internet. The membership of MoveOn more than doubled during the months prior to the war in Iraq, a war MoveOn opposed, and continued to grow thereafter. MoveOn does not require a membership fee but does have a subscriber list which permits it to communicate messages and show its attention-getting ads. One major donor to MoveOn was George Soros, who pledged to provide the group with $2.5 million.[†] The group has fed off of controversy, including an ad criticizing President Bush that it tried unsuccessfully to run during the Super Bowl.[§]

Regardless of whether or not you agree with Boyd and Blades, their use of the Internet for organizing citizens, petitioning government, and raising political contributions has had an impact on American politics.

[*]Dan Gilgoff, "The Democrats' Internet Gain," *U.S. News and World Report,* October 6, 2003: p. 27.
[†]Editorial, "Mr. Soros' Millions," *The Washington Post,* November 23, 2003: p. B06.
[§]Jim Rutenberg, "Ad Rejections by CBS Raise Policy Questions," *The New York Times,* January 19, 2004: p. 7.

executive, judicial, and legislative branches; *bicameralism,* the division of legislative power between two institutions — the House of Representatives and the Senate; *checks and balances* in which each branch is given the constitutional means, the political independence, and the motives to check the powers of the other branches; and a judicially enforceable, written, explicit *Bill of Rights* that provides a guarantee of individual liberties and due process before the law.

Conditions Conducive to Constitutional Democracy

Although it is hard to specify the precise conditions that are essential for the establishment and maintenance of a democracy, here are a few things we have learned.

EDUCATIONAL CONDITIONS   The exercise of voting privileges takes some level of education on the part of the citizenry. But a high level of education does not guarantee democratic government, as the example of Nazi Germany readily illustrates. And there are some democracies, such as India, where large numbers of people are illiterate. Still, voting makes little sense unless a considerable number of the voters can read and write and express their interests and opinions. The poorly educated and illiterate often get left out in a democracy. Direct democracy puts a further premium on education. Better educated persons are more able to understand and participate in policy making through initiatives and referendums.[6]

ECONOMIC CONDITIONS   A relatively prosperous nation, with an equitable distribution of wealth, provides the best context for democracy. Starving people are more interested in food than in voting. Where economic power is concentrated, political power is likely to be concentrated. Well-to-do nations have a greater chance of sustaining democratic governments than those with widespread poverty do. The reality is that extremes of wealth and poverty undermine the possibilities for a healthy constitutional democracy. Thus the prospects for an enduring democracy are greater in Canada or France than in Rwanda, Zimbabwe, or Mongolia.

Some measure of private ownership of property and a relatively favorable role for the market economy are also related to the creation and maintenance of democratic institutions. Democracies can range from heavily regulated economies with public ownership of many enterprises, such as Sweden, to those in which there is little government regulation of the marketplace. But there are no democracies with a highly centralized government-run economy and little private ownership of property, although there are many nations with a market economy and no democracy. There are no truly democratic communist states, nor have there ever been any.

SOCIAL CONDITIONS   Economic development generally makes democracy possible, yet proper social conditions are necessary to make it real.[7] In a society fragmented into warring groups that differ fiercely on fundamental issues, government by discussion and compromise is difficult, as we have seen in the Balkans and more recently in Afghanistan and Iraq. When ideologically separated groups consider the issues at stake to be vital, they may prefer to fight rather than accept the verdict of the ballot box.

In a society that consists of many overlapping associations and groupings, however, individuals are not as likely to identify completely with a single group and give their allegiance to it. For example, Joe Smith is a Baptist, an African American, a southerner, a Democrat, an electrician, and a member of the National Rifle Association, and he makes $50,000 a year. On some issues, Joe thinks as a Baptist, on others as a southerner, and on still others as an African American. Sue Jones is a Catholic, a white Republican, an auto dealer, and a member of the National Organization for Women (NOW); she comes from a Polish background, and she makes $150,000 a year. Sometimes she acts as a Republican, sometimes as an American of Polish descent, and sometimes as a member of NOW. Jones and Smith differ on some issues and agree on others. In general, the differences between them are not likely to be greater than their common interest in maintaining a democracy.[8]

IDEOLOGICAL CONDITIONS   **Ideology** refers to basic beliefs about power, government, and political practices—beliefs that arise out of the educational, economic, and social

ideology
A consistent pattern of beliefs about political values and the role of government.

★ ★ **YOU DECIDE**

In 2003 California voters decided to remove Governor Gray Davis from office. Davis had been elected in 2002, only eleven months before the recall. The process of recall is triggered by voters signing petitions, and if enough valid signatures are gathered to meet a specified threshold, a recall election is held. U.S. Representative Darrell Issa, a wealthy conservative from Southern California, spent $2 million of his own money to hire signature collectors, which greatly helped the 2003 recall effort meet the signature threshold. Proponents of the recall contend that it provides a means for voters to maintain greater control over politicians while opponents of the recall contend that the normal election process provides ample opportunity to remove politicians from office. What do you think? Does the recall enhance or detract from constitutional democracy?

conditions individuals experience. Out of these conditions must also develop a general acceptance of the ideals of democracy and a willingness of a substantial part of the people to agree to proceed democratically. This acceptance is sometimes called the *democratic consensus.*

THE CONSTITUTIONAL ROOTS OF THE AMERICAN EXPERIMENT

Americans often take democracy for granted. Most of us probably consider it inevitable. We take pride in our ability to make it work, yet we have essentially inherited a functioning system. Its establishment was the work of others, nine or ten generations ago. The challenge for us is not just to keep it going but to improve it and make it adapt to the challenges of our times. To do so, however, we must first understand it, and this requires systematic consideration of our democratic and constitutional roots.

The Colonial Beginnings

There were many reasons one might have expected our democratic experiment to fail. The 13 original states (formerly colonies) were independent and could have gone their separate ways. Sectional differences based on social and economic conditions, especially the southern states' dependence on slavery, were an obvious problem. Religious, ethnic, and racial diversity, which challenges so many governments around the world today, existed to a substantial degree in the United States during its formative years.

Given these potential problems, how did democracy survive? How did this nation establish democratic principles for its government? How did it limit potential abuses? These questions are of importance not only to Americans but also to all others who value freedom and democracy. The United States has been a world leader in promoting the use of democratic institutions, in effect universalizing its successful experiment.

In 2003, Californians voted in a recall election to remove Democratic Governor Gray Davis from office and to replace him with Republican Arnold Schwartzenegger (left). U.S. Representative Darrell Issa (right) spent $2 million of his own money to spearhead the recall effort.

The framers of the U.S. Constitution had experience to guide them. For almost two centuries, Europeans had been sailing to the New World in search of liberty—especially religious liberty—as well as land and work. While still aboard the *Mayflower*, the Pilgrims drew up a compact to protect their religious freedom and to make possible "just and equal laws." In the American colonies, editors found they could speak freely in their newspapers, dissenters could distribute leaflets, and agitators could protest in taverns or in the streets.

But the picture of freedom in the colonies was mixed. The Puritans in Massachusetts soon established a **theocracy**, a system of government in which religious leaders claimed divine guidance and in which certain religious sects were denied religious liberty. Dissenters were occasionally chased out of town, and some printers were beaten and had their shops closed. In short, the colonists struggled with the balance between unity and diversity, stability and dissent, order and liberty. Puritans continued to worry "about what would maintain order in a society lacking an established church, an attachment to place, and the uncontested leadership of men of merit."[9] Nine of the 13 colonies eventually set up a state church. Throughout the 1700s, Puritans in Massachusetts barred certain men from voting on the basis of church membership. To the Anglican establishment in Virginia, campaigns for toleration were in themselves subversive. Women and slaves could not vote at all.

The Rise of Revolutionary Fervor

As resentment against British rule mounted during the 1770s and revolutionary fervor rose, Americans became determined to fight the British to win their rights and liberties. A year after the fighting broke out in Massachusetts, the Declaration of Independence proclaimed in ringing tones that all men are created equal, endowed by their Creator with certain unalienable rights; that among them are "life, liberty, and the pursuit of happiness"; that to secure those rights, governments are instituted among men; and that whenever a government becomes destructive of those ends, it is the right of the people to alter or abolish it. (Read the full text of the Declaration of Independence in the Appendix.)

We have all heard these great ideals so often that we take them for granted. Revolutionary leaders did not. They were deadly serious about these rights and willing to fight and pledge their lives, fortunes, and sacred honor for them. Indeed, by signing the Declaration of Independence they were effectively signing their own death warrants if the Revolution failed.[10] Bills of rights in the new state constitutions guaranteed free speech, freedom of religion, and the natural rights to life, liberty, and property. All their constitutions spelled out the rights of persons accused of crime, such as knowing the nature of the accusation, being confronted by their accusers, and receiving a timely and public trial by jury.[11] Moreover, these guarantees were set out *in writing*, in sharp contrast to the unwritten British constitution.

Toward Unity and Order

As the war against the British widened, the need arose for a stronger central government that could pull the colonies together and conduct a revolutionary war. For a time, the Continental Congress, which had led the way toward revolution, tried to direct hostilities against the British, but it took a man of George Washington's iron resolve to unify and direct the war effort. Sensing the need for more unity, Congress established a new national government under a written document called the **Articles of Confederation**. At first hardly worthy of the term "government," the Articles were not approved by all the state legislatures until 1781, after Washington's troops had been fighting for six years.

This new Confederation was a move toward a stronger central government, but a limited and inadequate one. Having fought a war against a strong central government in London, Americans were understandably reluctant to create another one, so the Articles established a fragile league of friendship rather than a national government. From

★★ **THINKING IT THROUGH**

The California recall effort and all the media attention to it highlighted the reality that large numbers of Californians, including many Democrats, were disappointed with Gray Davis and his lack of leadership. The high turnout demonstrated that voters will participate in a high-profile recall election held at a time different from other elections. While it placed a new governor in office it did not allow voters to change other elected offices at the same time, and thus the new governor must work with the previously elected legislature and other state officials.

One concern about the recall process is that it may make elected officials timid and indecisive because of the fear that if they act they might trigger a recall against them. Another concern is that interest groups on all sides that have resources can hire signature gatherers to force a recall election. But to be successful, a group must not only qualify a recall for the ballot, it must get a majority to vote to remove the incumbent.

Understanding the recall process and choosing from among so many possible candidates in an election like the 2003 California recall election is difficult and may have been confusing for some. The intense media coverage and the presence of a high-profile movie star candidate in 2003 mitigated these problems, but if recall elections become commonplace they could be a concern in the future.

theocracy
Government by religious leaders, who claim divine guidance.

Articles of Confederation
The first governing document of the confederated states, drafted in 1777, ratified in 1781, and replaced by the present Constitution in 1789.

WEAKNESSES OF THE ARTICLES OF CONFEDERATION

1. Congress had no direct authority over citizens but had to work through the states; it could not pass laws or levy taxes to carry out its responsibilities to defend the nation and promote its well-being.
2. Congress could not regulate trade between the states or with other nations. States taxed each other's goods and even negotiated their own trade agreements with other nations.
3. Congress could not forbid the states from issuing their own currencies, further complicating interstate trade and travel.
4. Congress had to handle all administrative duties because there was no executive branch.
5. The lack of a judicial system meant that the national government had to rely on state courts to enforce national laws and settle disputes between the states. In practice, state courts could overturn national laws.

Annapolis Convention
A convention held in September 1786 to consider problems of trade and navigation, attended by five states and important because it issued the call to Congress and the states for what became the Constitutional Convention.

Constitutional Convention
The convention in Philadelphia, May 25 to September 17, 1787, that framed the Constitution of the United States.

Shays' Rebellion
Rebellion by farmers in western Massachusetts in 1786–1787, protesting mortgage foreclosures; led by Daniel Shays and important because it highlighted the need for a strong national government just as the call for the Constitutional Convention went out.

1777 to 1788, Americans made progress under the Confederation, but with the end of the war in 1783, the sense of urgency that had produced unity began to fade. Conflicts between creditors and debtors in the various states grew intense. Foreign threats continued; territories ruled by England and Spain surrounded the new nation, which, internally divided and lacking a strong central government, made a tempting prize.

As pressures on the Confederation mounted, many leaders became convinced it would not be enough merely to revise the Articles of Confederation. To create a union strong enough to deal with internal diversity and factionalism as well as to resist external threats, a stronger central government was needed.

In September 1786, under the leadership of Alexander Hamilton, supporters of a truly national government took advantage of the **Annapolis Convention**—a meeting in Annapolis, Maryland, on problems of trade and navigation attended by delegates from five states—to issue a call for a convention that would have full authority to consider basic amendments to the Articles of Confederation. The delegates in Annapolis asked the legislatures of all the states to appoint commissioners to meet in Philadelphia on the second Monday of May 1787, "to devise such further provisions as shall appear to them necessary to render the Constitution of the Federal Government adequate to the exigencies of the Union." The convention they called for became the **Constitutional Convention**.

For a short time, all was quiet. Then, late in 1786, messengers rode into George Washington's plantation at Mount Vernon with the kind of news he and other leaders had dreaded. Farmers in western Massachusetts, crushed by debts and taxes, were rebelling against foreclosures, forcing judges out of their courtrooms, and freeing debtors from jails. Washington was appalled. "What, gracious God, is man?" he exclaimed. Ten years before, he had been leading Americans in a patriotic war against the British, and now Americans were fighting Americans!

Not all Americans reacted as Washington did to what became known as **Shays' Rebellion** after Daniel Shays, its leader. When Abigail Adams, the politically knowledgeable wife of John Adams, sent news of the rebellion to Thomas Jefferson, the Virginian replied. "I like a little rebellion now and then," noting also that the "tree of liberty must be refreshed from time to time with the blood of patriots and tyrants. It is its natural manure."[12]

Shays' Rebellion petered out after the farmers attacked an arsenal and were cut down by cannon fire. Yet this "little rebellion" sent a stab of fear into the established leadership. It also acted as a catalyst. The message was now plain: Action must be taken to strengthen the machinery of government. Seven states appointed commissioners to attend the Philadelphia convention to strengthen the Articles of Confederation. Congress finally issued a cautiously worded call to all the state legislatures to appoint delegates for the "sole and express purpose of revising the Articles of Confederation." The suspicious congressional legislators specified that no recommendation would be effective unless approved by Congress and confirmed by all the state legislatures, as provided by the Articles.

THE CONSTITUTIONAL CONVENTION OF 1787

The delegates who assembled in Philadelphia that May had to establish a national government powerful enough to prevent the young nation from dissolving but not so powerful that it would crush individual liberty. What these men did continues to have a major impact on how we are governed. It also provides an outstanding lesson in political science for the world.

The Delegates

Seventy-four delegates were appointed by the various states, but only 55 arrived in Philadelphia. Of these, approximately 40 actually took part in the work of the convention. It was a distinguished gathering. Many of the most important men of the nation were there: successful merchants, planters, bankers, lawyers, and former and present governors and congressional representatives (39 of the delegates had served in Congress). Most had read the classics of political thought. Most had participated vigorously in the practical task of constructing local and state governments. Many had also worked hard to create and direct the national Confederation of the states. And 8 of the 56 signers of the Declaration of Independence were present at the Constitutional Convention.

The convention was as representative as most political gatherings at the time: The participants were all white male landowners. These well-read, well-fed, well-bred, and often well-wed delegates were mainly state or national leaders, for in the 1780s, ordinary people were not likely to participate in politics. (Even today, farm laborers, factory workers, and truck drivers are seldom found in Congress, although a haberdasher, a peanut farmer, and a movie actor have made their way to the White House.)

Although active in the movement to revise the Articles of Confederation, George Washington had been reluctant to attend the convention. He accepted only when persuaded that his prestige was needed for its success. He was selected unanimously to preside over the meetings. According to the records, he spoke only twice during the

PEOPLE & POLITICS *Making a Difference* ★ ★ ★

ALEXANDER HAMILTON AND JAMES MADISON

In the Constitution of the United States, the framers offered perhaps the most brilliant example of collective intellectual genius (combining theory and practice) in the history of the Western world. How could such a sparsely populated country by today's standards produce several dozen men of genius in Philadelphia and probably another hundred or so equally talented political thinkers who did not attend? The lives of two prominent delegates, Alexander Hamilton and James Madison, help explain the origins of this collective genius.

Alexander Hamilton had been the engineer of the Annapolis Convention, and as early as 1778, he had been urging that the national government be made stronger. Hamilton had come to the United States from the West Indies and while still a college student had won national attention for his brilliant pamphlets in defense of the Revolutionary cause. During the war, he served as General Washington's aide, and his experiences confirmed his distaste for a Congress so weak it could not even supply the Revolution's troops with enough food or arms.

James Madison was only 36 years old at the time of the convention, yet he was

Alexander Hamilton.

James Madison.

one of its most learned members. He had helped frame Virginia's first constitution and had served both in the Virginia Assembly and in the Continental Congress. Madison was also a leader of those who favored the establishment of a stronger national government.

Like most of the other framers, Hamilton and Madison were superbly educated. Both had extensive private tutoring—a one-to-one teacher–student ratio. Like scores of other thinkers of the day, both combined extensive practical experience with their schooling. Both

were active in their political and religious groups; both took part in political contests and electoral struggles; both helped build political coalitions.

Both men were "moral philosophers" as well as political thinkers. They had strong views on the supreme value of liberty as well as on current issues. Instead of simply sermonizing about liberty, they analyzed it; they debated what kind of liberty, how to protect it, and how to expand it.

Representing different constituencies and different ideologies, the Constitutional Convention devised a totally new form of government that provided for a central government strong enough to rule but still responsible to its citizens and to the member states.

deliberations, yet his influence was felt in the informal gatherings as well as during the sessions. Everyone understood that Washington favored a more powerful central government led by a president. The general expectation that Washington would likely be the first president played a crucial role in the creation of the presidency. "No one feared that he would misuse power. . . . His genuine hesitancy, his reluctance to assume the position, only served to reinforce the almost universal desire that he do so."[13]

The proceedings of the convention were kept secret. To encourage everyone to speak freely, delegates were forbidden to discuss the debates with outsiders. It was feared that if a delegate publicly took a firm stand on an issue, it would be harder for him to change his mind after debate and discussion. The delegates also knew that if word of the inevitable disagreements got out, it would provide ammunition for the many enemies of the convention. There were critics of this secrecy rule, but without it, agreement might not have been possible.

Consensus

The Constitutional Convention is usually discussed in terms of its three famous compromises: the compromise between large and small states over representation in Congress, the compromise between North and South over the regulation and taxation of foreign commerce, and the compromise between North and South over the counting of slaves for the purpose of taxation and representation. There were many other important compromises; yet on many significant issues, most of the delegates were in agreement.

Although a few delegates might have privately favored a limited monarchy, all supported a republican form of government based on elected representatives of the people. This was the only form seriously considered and the only form acceptable to the nation. Equally important, all the delegates opposed arbitrary and unrestrained government.

The common philosophy accepted by most of the delegates was that of *balanced government*. They wanted to construct a national government in which no single interest would dominate. Because most of the delegates represented citizens who were alarmed by the tendencies of desperate farmers to interfere with the property rights of others, they were primarily concerned with balancing the government in the direction of protection for property and business.

Benjamin Franklin, the 81-year-old delegate from Pennsylvania, favored extending the right to vote to all white males, but most of the delegates believed that owners of land were the best guardians of liberty. James Madison feared that those without property, if given the right to vote, might combine to deprive property owners of their rights. Delegates agreed in principle on limited voting rights but differed over the kind and amount of property one must own in order to vote. Because states were in the process of relaxing qualifications for the vote, the framers recognized that they would jeopardize approval of the constitution if they made the qualifications to vote in federal elections more restrictive than those of the states. As a result, each state was left to determine the qualifications for electing members of the House of Representatives, the only branch of the national government that was to be elected directly by the voters.

Within five days of its opening, the convention—with only the Connecticut delegates dissenting—voted that "a national government ought to be established consisting of a supreme legislative, executive, and judiciary." This decision to establish a supreme national government profoundly altered the nature of the union from a loose confederation of states to a true nation.

Few dissented from proposals to give the new Congress all the powers of the old Congress plus all other powers necessary to ensure that the integrity of the United States would not be challenged by state legislation. The framers agreed that a strong executive, which had been lacking under the Articles of Confederation, was necessary to provide energy and direction. An independent judiciary was also accepted without much debate. Other issues, however, sparked considerable conflict.

Conflict and Compromise

There were serious differences among the various delegates, especially between those from the large and small states. The conflict between the large and small states ensued before the Constitutional Convention. With the success of the War of Independence, the United States gained the formerly British land west of the colonial borders. States with large western borders like Virginia claimed that their borders should simply be extended further west, as depicted in the accompanying map. Landlocked colonies like New Jersey and Connecticut took exception to the claims of colonies with western borders like Virginia, reinforcing the tension between the colonies. The matter was resolved in the Land Ordinance of 1785 and Northwest Ordinance of 1787 when all states agreed to cede the Western lands to the national government and permit the newly acquired land to become part of new states rather than expand the border of preexisting states. But the rivalries between the former colonies were very much a part of the politics at the Convention in Philadelphia in 1787. For example, the large states also favored a strong national government (which they expected they could dominate), while delegates from small states were anxious to avoid being dominated (see Figure 1–1).

This tension surfaced in the first discussions of representation in Congress. Franklin favored a single-house national legislature, but most states had had two-chamber legislatures since colonial times, and the delegates were used to the system. **Bicameralism**—the principle of the two-house legislature—reflected delegates' belief in the need for balanced government. The Senate, the smaller chamber, would represent the states, and to some extent the aristocracy, and offset the larger, more democratic House of Representatives.

THE VIRGINIA PLAN   The Virginia delegation took the initiative. Its members had met before the convention, and as soon as it was convened, they presented 15 resolutions. These resolutions, known as the **Virginia Plan**, called for a strong central government with a legislature composed of two chambers. The members of the more representative chamber were to be elected by the voters; those of the smaller and more aristocratic chamber were to be chosen by the larger chamber from nominees submitted by the state legislatures. Representation in both houses would be based on either wealth or

"*Remember, gentlemen, we aren't here just to draft a constitution. We're here to draft the best damn constitution in the world.*"

bicameralism
The principle of a two-house legislature.

Virginia Plan
Initial proposal at the Constitutional Convention made by the Virginia delegation for a strong central government with a bicameral legislature, the lower house to be elected by the voters and the upper chosen by the lower.

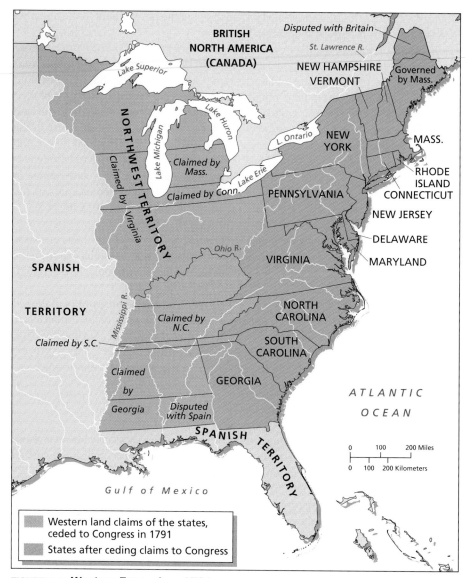

FIGURE 1-1 Western Expansion, 1791.

numbers, which would give the wealthier and more populous states—Massachusetts, Pennsylvania, and Virginia—a majority in the national legislature.

The Congress thus created was to be given all the legislative power of its predecessor under the Articles of Confederation, as well as the right "to legislate in all cases in which the separate States are incompetent." Further, it was to have the authority to veto state legislation that conflicted with the proposed constitution. The Virginia Plan also called for a national executive with extensive jurisdiction who would be chosen by the legislature. A national Supreme Court, along with the executive, was to have a qualified veto over acts of Congress.

THE NEW JERSEY PLAN The Virginia Plan dominated the discussion for the first few weeks. But by June 15, additional delegates from the small states arrived, and they began a counterattack. They rallied around William Paterson of New Jersey, who presented a series of resolutions known as the **New Jersey Plan**. Table 1-1 outlines the key features of both plans. Paterson did not question the need for a strengthened central government, but he was concerned about how this strength might be used. The New Jersey Plan would give Congress the right to tax and regulate commerce and to coerce states,

New Jersey Plan

Proposal at the Constitutional Convention made by William Paterson of New Jersey for a central government with a single-house legislature in which each state would be represented equally.

TABLE 1–1 THE VIRGINIA AND NEW JERSEY PLANS	
Virginia Plan	*New Jersey Plan*
Legitimacy derived from citizens, based on popular representation	Derived from states, based on equal votes for each state
Bicameral legislature	Unicameral legislature
Executive size undetermined, elected and removable by Congress	More than one person, removable by state majority
Judicial life-tenure, able to veto state legislation	No power over states
Legislature can override state laws	Government can compel obedience to national laws
Ratification by citizens	Ratification by states

and it would retain the single-house unicameral legislature (as under the Articles of Confederation) in which each state, regardless of size, would have the same vote.

The New Jersey Plan contained the germ of what eventually came to be a key provision of our Constitution: the *supremacy clause*. The national Supreme Court was to hear appeals from state judges, and the supremacy clause would require all judges—state and national—to treat laws of the national government and the treaties of the United States as superior to the constitutions and laws of each of the states.

To adopt the Virginia Plan—which would create a powerful national government dominated by Massachusetts, Pennsylvania, and Virginia and eliminate the states as important units of government—would guarantee that many of the other states would reject the new constitution. Still, the large states resisted, and for a time the convention was deadlocked. The small states believed that all states should be represented equally in Congress, especially in the smaller "upper house" if there were to be two chambers. The large states insisted that representation in both houses be based on population or wealth and that national legislators be elected by voters rather than by state legislatures. Finally, the so-called Committee of Eleven was elected to devise a compromise. On July 5, it presented its proposals.

THE CONNECTICUT COMPROMISE   Because of the prominent role of the Connecticut delegation in constructing this plan, it has since been known as the **Connecticut Compromise**. It called for one house in which each state would have an equal vote and a second house in which representation would be based on population and in which all bills for raising or appropriating money would originate. This proposal was a setback for the large states, which agreed to it only when the smaller states made it clear this was their price for union. After equality of state representation in the Senate was accepted, most objections to a strong national government dissolved.

NORTH-SOUTH COMPROMISES   Other issues split the delegates from the North and South. Southerners were afraid a northern majority in Congress might discriminate against southern trade. They had some basis for this concern. John Jay, secretary of foreign affairs for the Confederation, had proposed a treaty with Great Britain that would have given advantages to northern merchants at the expense of southern exporters. To protect themselves, the southern delegates insisted that a two-thirds majority be required in the Senate before the president could ratify a treaty.

Differences between the North and South were also evident on the issue of representation in the House of Representatives. The question was whether to count slaves for the purpose of apportioning seats in the House. The South wanted to count slaves, thereby enlarging its number of representatives; the North resisted. After heated debate, the delegates agreed on the **three-fifths compromise**. Each slave would be counted

Connecticut Compromise
Compromise agreement by states at the Constitutional Convention for a bicameral legislature with a lower house in which representation would be based on population and an upper house in which each state would have two senators.

three-fifths compromise
Compromise agreement between northern and southern states at the Constitutional Convention that three-fifths of the slave population would be counted for determining direct taxation and representation in the House of Representatives.

as three-fifths of a free person for the purposes of apportionment in the House and of direct taxation; this fraction was chosen because it maintained a balance of power between North and South. The issue of balance would recur in the early history of our nation as territorial governments were established and territories applied for statehood.

OTHER ISSUES   Delegates found other issues to argue about. Should the national government have lower courts, or would one federal Supreme Court be enough? This issue was resolved by postponing the decision. The Constitution states that there shall be one Supreme Court and that Congress may establish lower courts.

How should the president be selected? For a long time, the convention accepted the idea that the president should be chosen by Congress, but the delegates feared that Congress would dominate the president, or vice versa. Election by the state legislatures was rejected because the delegates distrusted the state legislatures. Finally, the electoral college system was devised. This was perhaps the most novel and most contrived contribution of the delegates and has long been one of the most criticized provisions in the Constitution.[14] (See Article II, Section 1, of the Constitution, which is reprinted between Chapters 2 and 3.)

After three months, the delegates stopped debating. On September 17, 1787, they assembled for an impressive ceremony of signing the document they were recommending to the nation. All but three of those still present signed; others who opposed the general drift of the convention had already left. Their work well done, delegates adjourned to the nearby City Tavern to celebrate.

According to an old story, Benjamin Franklin was confronted by a woman as he left the last session of the convention.

"What kind of government have you given us, Dr. Franklin?" she asked. "A republic or a monarchy?"

"A republic, Madam," he answered, "if you can keep it."

In Comparative Perspective

THE NEW CONSTITUTION IN AFGHANISTAN: BALANCING ISLAM AND DEMOCRACY

In December 2001, following the collapse of the Taliban regime in Afghanistan, several Afghan groups met under United Nations guidance to begin planning for democracy in Afghanistan. Their agreement, called the Bonn Agreement, set in motion the election of a transitional government, a nine-member Constitutional Drafting Commission and a larger Constitutional Commission of thirty-five members which revised the draft constitution and conducted hearings in the provinces and among refugees.

The new constitution ratified by Loya Jirga in 2004 combines Islamic and democratic values, and guarantees basic liberties, with elections to follow. Examples of the Islamic nature of the new constitution are that it declares Afghanistan an Islamic Republic and makes Islam the official religion of the country. The constitution mandates that laws under the new constitution may not be contrary to Islam. An example of

the pervasiveness of Islam in the new constitution is the mandate that a school curriculum must be "based on the provisions of the sacred religion of Islam, national culture, and in accordance with academic principles."[*]

At the same time, the new Afghan constitution guarantees fundamental rights and promises government "based on the people's will and democracy." It notes that Afghanistan is committed to the United Nations Charter and Universal Declaration of Human Rights. The new constitution ensures that women will make up at least 16.5 percent of the membership of the upper legislative house and otherwise guarantees women's rights against discrimination. While Islam is the official state religion, the constitution allows non-Muslims to practice their religion.

This blending of Islam and democracy breaks new ground in the Middle East. Turkey, which has a largely Muslim population, has a largely secular government. The lessons learned in Afghanistan may one day be applied elsewhere in the region.

[*]AfghanGovernment, n.d, "Afghan Draft Constitution: 2004," http://www.afghangovernment.com/2004constitution.htm. 30 December 2003.

TO ADOPT OR NOT TO ADOPT?

The delegates had gone far. Indeed, they had wholly disregarded Congress's instruction to do no more than revise the Articles. They had ignored Article XIII of the Articles of Confederation, which declared the Union to be perpetual and prohibited any alteration of the Articles unless agreed to by Congress and by *every one of the state legislatures*—a provision that had made it impossible to amend the Articles. The convention delegates, however, boldly declared that their newly proposed Constitution should go into effect when ratified by popularly elected conventions in nine states.

They turned to this method of ratification for practical considerations as well as for reasons of securing legitimacy for their newly proposed government. Not only were the delegates aware that there was little chance of winning approval of the new Constitution in all state legislatures; many also believed the Constitution should be ratified by an authority higher than a legislature. A constitution based on approval *by the people* would have higher legal and moral status. The Articles of Confederation had been a compact of state governments, but the Constitution was based on the people (recall its opening words: "We the People . . ."). Still, even this method of ratification would not be easy. The nation was not ready to adopt the Constitution without a thorough debate.

Federalists Versus Antifederalists

Supporters of the new government, by cleverly appropriating the name **Federalists**, took some of the sting out of charges they were trying to destroy the states and establish an all-powerful central government. By calling their opponents **Antifederalists**, they pointed up the negative character of the arguments of those who opposed ratification.

The split was in part geographic. Seaboard and city regions tended to be Federalist strongholds; backcountry regions from Maine (then a part of Massachusetts) through Georgia, inhabited by farmers and other relatively poor people, were generally Antifederalist. But as in most political contests, no single factor completely accounted for the division between Federalists and Antifederalists. Thus in Virginia, the leaders of both sides came from the same general social and economic class. New York City and Philadelphia strongly supported the Constitution, yet so did predominantly rural New Jersey.

The great debate was conducted through pamphlets, papers, letters to the editor, and speeches. The issues were important, but with few exceptions, the argument about the merits of the Constitution was carried on in a quiet and calm manner. Out of the debate came a series of essays known as *The Federalist*, written (using the pseudonym Publius) by Alexander Hamilton, James Madison, and John Jay to persuade the voters of New York to ratify the Constitution. *The Federalist* is still "widely regarded as the most profound single treatise on the Constitution ever written and as among the few masterly works in political science produced in all the centuries of history."[15] (Three of the most important *Federalist* essays, Nos. 10, 51, and 78, are reprinted in the Appendix of this book. We urge you to read them.) The great debate stands even today as an outstanding example of free people using public discussion to determine the nature of their fundamental laws.

The Antifederalists' most telling criticism of the proposed Constitution was its failure to include a bill of rights.[16] The Federalists believed a bill of rights was unnecessary because the proposed national government had *only* the specific powers delegated to it by the states and the people. Thus there was no need to specify that Congress could not, for example, abridge freedom of the press because the states and the people had not given it power to regulate the press. Moreover, the Federalists argued, to guarantee some rights might be dangerous, because it would then be thought that rights not listed could be denied. The Constitution already protected some important rights—trial by jury in federal criminal cases, for example. Hamilton and others also insisted that paper guarantees were weak supports on which to depend for protection against governmental tyranny.

The Antifederalists were unconvinced. If some rights were protected, what could be the objection to providing constitutional protection for others? Without a bill of rights,

Federalists
Supporters of ratification of the Constitution whose position promoting a strong central government was later voiced in the Federalist party.

Antifederalists
Opponents of ratification of the Constitution and of a strong central government generally.

The Federalist
Series of essays promoting ratification of the Constitution, published anonymously by Alexander Hamilton, John Jay, and James Madison in 1787 and 1788.

CHALLENGES FOR OUR CONSTITUTIONAL DEMOCRACY

1. *"All men are created equal":* What kinds of equality are—and should be—protected by the Constitution, and by what means?
2. *"Government by the people":* Does the evolving constitutional system, including political parties and interest groups, strengthen fair and effective representation of the people?
3. *Federalism:* Does the Constitution provide an efficient and realistic balance between national and state power?
4. *Checks and balances:* Does the constitutional separation of powers between the president and Congress lead too often to gridlock and stalemate?
5. *Minority rights:* Does the Constitution adequately protect the rights of women, African Americans, Native Americans, Hispanic Americans, other ethnic groups, and recent immigrants?
6. *Suspects' rights:* Can representative government uphold the rights of the criminally accused and yet protect its citizens?
7. *Individual liberties:* Are individual liberties adequately protected in the Constitution? Do big government and big business diminish the freedom of the individual?
8. *The judicial branch:* Is it too powerful? Are the federal courts exceeding their proper powers as interpreters of the Constitution?
9. *War and peace:* What are the responsibilities of the United States as the only superpower?
10. *Constitutional responsibilities:* Are Americans participating adequately in our democratic system? Do citizens have the social capital and understanding of our governmental processes to be heard and to make a difference?

what was to prevent Congress from using one of its delegated powers to abridge free speech? If bills of rights were needed in state constitutions to limit state governments, why was a bill of rights not needed in the national constitution to limit the national government? This was a government farther from the people, they contended, with a greater tendency to subvert natural rights.

The Politics of Ratification

The absence of a bill of rights in the proposed constitution dominated the struggle over its adoption. In taverns and church gatherings and newspaper offices up and down the eastern seaboard, people were muttering, "No bill of rights—no constitution!" This feeling was so strong that some Antifederalists, who were far more concerned with states' rights than individual rights, joined forces with bill of rights advocates in an effort to defeat the proposed Constitution.

The Federalists were first to begin the debate over the Constitution that opened as soon as the delegates left Philadelphia in mid-September 1787. The Federalists' tactic was to secure ratification in as many states as possible before the opposition had time to organize. The Antifederalists were handicapped. Most newspapers were owned by supporters of ratification. Moreover, Antifederalist strength was concentrated in rural areas, which were underrepresented in some state legislatures and difficult to arouse to political action. The Antifederalists needed time to perfect their organization and collect their strength, while the Federalists, composed of a more closely knit group of leaders throughout the colonies, moved in a hurry.

In most of the small states, now satisfied by equal Senate representation, ratification was gained without difficulty. Delaware was the first state to ratify, and by early 1788, Pennsylvania, New Jersey, Georgia, and Connecticut had also ratified (see Table 1-2). Reports were coming in from Massachusetts, however, that opposition was broadening. The position of such key leaders as John Hancock and Samuel Adams was in doubt. The debate in the ratifying convention in Boston pitched some of the most polished Federalist speakers against an array of eloquent but plainspoken Antifederalists. The debate raged for most of January 1788 into February. At times it looked as though the Constitution would lose, as Antifederalists raised the cry of "Why no bill of rights?" and other objections. But in the end, the Constitution was narrowly ratified in Massachusetts, 187 to 168.

The struggle over ratification continued through the spring of 1788. By June 21, Maryland, South Carolina, and New Hampshire had ratified, putting the Constitution over the top in the number (nine) required for ratification. But two big hurdles remained:

TABLE 1–2 RATIFICATION OF THE U.S. CONSTITUTION	
State	*Date*
Delaware	December 7, 1787
Pennsylvania	December 12, 1787
New Jersey	December 18, 1787
Georgia	January 2, 1788
Connecticut	January 9, 1788
Massachusetts	February 6, 1788
Maryland	April 28, 1788
South Carolina	May 23, 1788
New Hampshire	June 21, 1788
Virginia	June 25, 1788
New York	July 26, 1788
North Carolina	November 21, 1789
Rhode Island	May 29, 1790

Patrick Henry's famous cry of "Give Me Liberty or Give Me Death!" symbolizes the underlying spirit of optimism in the United States. This spirit has endured throughout this country's history, despite the many problems the country has experienced.

The Map of Freedom

New democracies often fail. It is one thing to espouse democratic values and quite another to put them into practice. In this Make It Real feature, you are asked to categorize the nations of the world in terms of freedom (free, partly free, or not free), based on the extent to which they have such rights as universal suffrage, free and fair elections, and political participation by racial minorities. When you encounter a country that is more or less free than you thought, you might want to read more about that country and learn about its political history. Also, determine what factors seem to predict which countries will be free and which will be less free.

Go to Make It Real: "The Map of Freedom."

Virginia and New York. It would be impossible to begin the new government without the consent of these two major states. Virginia was crucial. As the most populous state, the home of Washington, Jefferson, and Madison, it was a link between North and South. The Virginia ratifying convention rivaled the Constitutional Convention in the caliber of its delegates. Madison, who had only recently switched to favoring a bill of rights after saying earlier it was unnecessary, captained the Federalist forces. The fiery Patrick Henry led the opposition. In an epic debate, Henry cried that liberty was the issue: "Liberty, the greatest of earthly possessions . . . that precious jewel!" But Madison quietly rebutted him and then played his trump card, a promise that a bill of rights embracing the freedoms of religion and speech and assembly would be added to the Constitution as the first order of business once the new government was established. At a critical moment, Washington himself tipped the balance with a letter urging ratification. News of the Virginia vote, 89 for the Constitution and 79 opposed, was rushed to New York.[17]

The great landowners along New York's Hudson River, unlike their southern planter friends, were opposed to the Constitution. They feared federal taxation of their holdings, and they did not want to abolish the profitable tax New York had been levying on trade and commerce with other states. When the convention assembled, the Federalists were greatly outnumbered, but they were aided by Alexander Hamilton's strategy and skill and by word of Virginia's ratification. New York approved by a margin of three votes. Although North Carolina and Rhode Island still remained outside the Union (the former ratified in November 1789, the latter six months later), the new nation was created. In New York, a few members of the old Congress assembled to issue the call for elections under the new Constitution. Then they adjourned without setting a date for reconvening.

S U M M A R Y

1. The response to the terrorist attacks of September 11, 2001, expanded to wars in Afghanistan and Iraq. The cost of these wars and the domestic homeland security efforts is substantial and has helped, along with major tax cuts, to greatly expand the budget deficit and national debt. President Bush made national security a major theme of his 2004 election,

while Democrats criticized the president on the lack of planning for the aftermath of the war in Iraq and the inability to eliminate Al-Qaeda as a threat. Other important issues in 2004 included the economy, jobs, and such social issues as gay marriage.

2. Americans have long been skeptical of politicians and politics. Yet politics is a necessary activity for a democracy. Indeed, politics and politicians are indispensable to making our system of separated institutions and checks and balances work.

3. "Democracy" is an often misused term, and it has many different meanings. We use it here to refer to a system of interacting values, interrelated political processes, and interdependent political structures. The vital principle of democracy is that a just government must derive its powers from the consent of the people and that this consent must be regularly renewed in free and fair elections.

4. The essential democratic values are a belief in personal liberty, respect for the individual, equality of opportunity, and popular consent. Essential elements of the democratic process are free and fair elections, majority rule, freedom of expression, and the right to assemble and protest.

5. Stable constitutional democracy is encouraged by various conditions, such as an educated citizenry, a healthy economy, and overlapping associations and groupings within a society in which major institutions interact to achieve a certain degree of consensus.

6. There has recently been some concern about a decline in *social capital*—the experiences people gain in working together in community groups. Lessons about compromise, accommodation, and participation are important building blocks for democracy. Some observers say we have experienced a decline in civic engagement, while others see a healthy level of voluntary and charitable engagement that is making our communities and our nation better.

7. Constitutionalism is a general label we apply to arrangements such as checks and balances, federalism, separation of powers, rule of law, due process, and the Bill of Rights that force our leaders and representatives to listen, think, bargain, and explain before they act and make laws. A constitutional government enforces recognized and regularly applied limits on the powers of those who govern.

8. Democracy developed gradually. A revolution had to be fought before a system of representative democracy in the United States could be tried and tested. It took several years before a national constitution could be written and almost another year for it to be ratified. It took another two years before the Bill of Rights could be adopted and ratified. It has taken more than 200 years for democratic institutions to be refined and for systems of competition and choice to be hammered out. Democratic institutions such as free and fair elections and equal protection of the laws in the United States are still in the process of being refined and improved.

KEY TERMS

democracy	popular consent	Articles of Confederation	New Jersey Plan
direct democracy	majority rule	Annapolis Convention	Connecticut Compromise
representative democracy	majority	Constitutional Convention	three-fifths compromise
constitutional democracy	plurality	Shays' Rebellion	Federalists
constitutionalism	ideology	bicameralism	Antifederalists
statism	theocracy	Virginia Plan	*The Federalist*

FURTHER READING

BERNARD BAILYN, ED., *The Debate on the Constitution: Federalist and Antifederalist Speeches, Articles, and Letters During the Struggle over Ratification*, 2 vols. (Library of America, 1993).

LANCE BANNING, *The Sacred Fire of Liberty: James Madison and the Founding of the Federal Republic* (Cornell University Press, 1995).

WILLIAM J. CROTTY, ED., *The State of Democracy in America* (Georgetown University Press, 2001).

ROBERT A. DAHL, *On Democracy* (Yale University Press, 1998).

S.N. EISENSTADT, *Paradoxes of Democracy: Fragility, Continuity and Change* (Johns Hopkins University Press, 1999).

ALEXANDER HAMILTON, JAMES MADISON, AND JOHN JAY, *The Federalist Papers*, ed. Clinton Rossiter (New American Library, 1961). Also in several other editions.

SAMUEL P. HUNTINGTON, *The Third Wave: Democratization in the Late Twentieth Century* (University of Oklahoma Press, 1991).

DANIEL LESSARD LEVIN, *Representing Popular Sovereignty: The Constitution in American Political Culture* (State University of New York Press, 1999).

AREND LUPHART, *Patterns of Democracy: Government Forms and Performance in Thirty-Six Countries* (Yale University Press, 1999).

DREW R. McCOY, *The Last of the Fathers: James Madison and the Republican Legacy* (Columbia University Press, 1989).

RICHARD B. MORRIS, *Witnesses at the Creation: Hamilton, Madison, and Jay and the Constitution* (Holt, Rinehart and Winston, 1985).

PIPPA NORRIS, ED., *Critical Citizens: Global Support for Democratic Institutions* (Oxford University Press, 1999).

JACK N. RAKOVE, *Original Meanings: Politics and Ideas in the Making of the Constitution* (Vintage Books, 1997).

MICHAEL J. SANDEL, *Democracy's Discontent: America in Search of a Public Philosophy* (Belknap Press, 1996).

MICHAEL SCHUDSON, *The Good Citizen: A History of American Civic Life* (Harvard University Press, 1998).

THEDA SKOCPOL AND MORRIS P. FIORINA, EDS., *Civic Engagement in American Democracy* (Brookings/Russell Sage, 1999).

CASS R. SUNSTEIN, *Designing Democracy: What Constitutions Do* (Oxford University Press, 2001).

ALEXIS DE TOCQUEVILLE, *Democracy in America*, 2 vols. (1835).

GARRY WILLS, *A Necessary Evil: A History of American Distrust of Government* (Simon & Schuster, 1999).

GORDON S. WOOD, *The Creation of the American Republic, 1776–1787* (University of North Carolina Press, 1969).

See also the *Journal of Democracy* (Johns Hopkins University Press).

THE LIVING CONSTITUTION

2

The Constitution of the United States is the world's oldest written constitution and one of the shortest. The original, unamended Constitution, which went into effect in 1789, contains just 4,543 words. Yet it established the framers' experiment in free-government-in-the-making that each generation reinterprets and renews. The Constitution remains a document Americans revere. Optimists read it as expressing their hopes; pessimists put faith in its protections against tyranny and other abuses.

Why, after more than 218 years, have we not written another constitution—let alone two, three, or more, like other countries around the world? Part of the answer is the widespread acceptance of the Constitution by optimists and pessimists alike. But also part of the answer is the Constitution's brilliant structure for limited government and the facts that the framers built into the document the capacity for adaptability and flexibility.

As the Constitution won the support of citizens of the early years of the Republic, it took on the aura of **natural law**—law that defines right from wrong, law that is higher than human law. "The [Founding] Fathers grew ever larger in stature as they receded from view; the era in which they lived and fought became a Golden Age; in that age there had been a fresh dawn for the world, and its men were giants against the sky."[1] This early Constitution worship helped bring unity to the diverse new nation. Like the crown in Great Britain, the Constitution became a symbol of national loyalty, evoking both emotional and intellectual support from Americans, regardless of their differences. The framers' work became part of the American creed and culture.[2] It stood for liberty,

TIME LINE

THE LIVING CONSTITUTION

1788	*Federalist Papers* provide political arguments for ratifying the Constitution
1789	Judiciary Act establishes the structure of the federal judiciary
1801	Federalists relinquish control over the federal government
1803	*Marbury* v. *Madison* asserts the power of judicial review
1835	Chief Justice John Marshall dies—most influential Supreme Court Justice
1868	President Johnson impeached but not convicted over reconstruction
1920	19th Amendment grants women the right to vote
1972	Equal Rights Amendment (ERA) proposed
1974	Nixon becomes first president to resign
1982	Deadline passes and ERA fails
1998	President Clinton impeached but not convicted
2000	Supreme Court ends recount of presidential election.

"And there are three branches of government, so that each branch has the other two to blame everything on."

© Tribune Media Services. All rights reserved. Reprinted with permission.

natural law
God's or nature's law that defines right from wrong and is higher than human law.

separation of powers
Constitutional division of powers among the legislative, executive, and judicial branches, with the legislative branch making law, the executive applying and enforcing the law, and the judiciary interpreting the law.

equality before the law, limited government—indeed, for just about whatever anyone wanted to read into it.

Even today, Americans generally revere the Constitution, even though many do not know what is in it. A poll by the National Constitution Center found that nine out of ten Americans are proud of the Constitution and feel it is important to them. However, a third think the Constitution establishes English as the country's official language. One in six believes the Constitution establishes America as a Christian nation. Only one out of four could name a single First Amendment right. Although two out of three knew that the Constitution creates three branches of the national government, only one in three could name all three branches.[3]

The Constitution is more than a symbol, however. It is a supreme and binding law that both grants and limits powers. "In framing a government which is to be administered by men over men," wrote James Madison in *The Federalist*, No. 51, "the great difficulty lies in this: you must first enable the government to control the governed; and in the next place oblige it to control itself." (See *The Federalist*, No. 51, in the Appendix of this book, or go on the Web to www. law.ou.edu/hist/federalist/.) The Constitution is both a positive instrument of government, which enables the governors to control the governed, and a restraint on government, which enables the ruled to check the rulers. In what ways does the Constitution limit the power of the government? In what ways does it create governmental power? How has it managed to serve as a great symbol of national unity and at the same time as an adaptable instrument of government? The secret is an ingenious separation of powers and a system of checks and balances that check power with power.

CHECKING POWER WITH POWER

It may seem strange to begin by stressing the ways in which the Constitution *limits* governmental power, but keep in mind the dilemma the framers faced. They wanted a stronger and more effective national government than they had under the Articles of Confederation. At the same time, they were keenly aware that the people would not accept too much central control. Efficiency and order were important concerns, but they were not as important as liberty. The framers wanted to ensure domestic tranquillity and prevent future rebellions, but they also wanted to forestall the emergence of a homegrown King George III. Accordingly, they allotted certain powers to the national government and reserved the rest for the states, thus establishing a system of *federalism* (whose nature and problems we take up in Chapter 3). Even this was not enough. They believed they needed additional means to limit the national government.

The most important way they devised to make public officials observe the constitutional limits on their powers was through *free and fair elections;* voters would be able to throw out of office those who abuse power. Yet the framers were not willing to depend solely on political controls, because they did not fully trust the people's judgment. "Free government is founded on jealousy, and not in confidence," said Thomas Jefferson. "In questions of power, then, let no more be heard of confidence in man, but bind him down from mischief by the chains of the Constitution."[4]

No less important, the framers feared that a majority might deprive minorities of their rights. "A dependence on the people is, no doubt, the primary control on the government," Madison argued in *The Federalist*, No. 51, "but experience has taught mankind the necessity of auxiliary precautions." What were these "auxiliary precautions" against popular tyranny?

Separation of Powers

The first step was the **separation of powers**, the distribution of constitutional authority among the three branches of the national government. In *The Federalist*, No. 47, Madison wrote, "No political truth is certainly of greater intrinsic value, or is stamped with the authority of more enlightened patrons of liberty, than that . . . the accumulation of all powers, legislative, executive, and judiciary, in the same hands . . . may justly be pronounced the very definition of tyranny."[5] Chief among the "enlightened patrons of liberty" to whose authority Madison was appealing were John Locke and Montesquieu, whose works were well known to most educated Americans.

The intrinsic value of the principle of dispersion of power does not by itself account for its inclusion in our Constitution. Dispersion of power had been the general practice in the colonies for more than 100 years. Only during the Revolutionary period did some of the states concentrate authority in the hands of the legislature, and that unhappy experience confirmed the framers' belief in the merits of the separation of powers. Many attributed the evils of state government and the lack of energy in the central government to the fact that there was no strong executive both to check legislative abuses and to give energy and direction to administration.

Still, separating power was not enough. In the framers' view, there was the danger that different officials with different powers might pool their authority and act together. Separation of powers by itself might not prevent governmental branches and officials from responding to the same pressures—from the demand of an overwhelming majority of the voters to suppress an offensive book, for example, or to impose confiscatory taxes on rich people. If separating power was not enough, what else could be done?

Checks and Balances: Ambition to Counteract Ambition

The framers' answer was a system of **checks and balances**. "The great security against a gradual concentration of the several powers in the same department," wrote Madison in *The Federalist*, No. 51, "consists in giving to those who administer each department the necessary constitutional means and personal motives to resist encroachments of the others: . . . Ambition must be made to counteract ambition." Each branch therefore has a role in the actions of the others (see Figure 2–1). Congress enacts laws, but the president can veto them. The Supreme Court can declare laws passed by Congress and signed by the president unconstitutional, but the president appoints the justices and all the other federal judges, with the Senate's approval. The president administers the laws, but Congress provides the money. Moreover, the Senate and the House of Representatives have an absolute veto over each other in the enactment of laws, because both houses must approve bills.

Not only does each branch have some authority over the others, but each is politically independent of the others. Voters in each local district choose members of the House; voters in each state choose senators; the president is elected by the voters in all the states. With the consent of the Senate, the president appoints federal judges, who remain in office until they retire or are impeached.

The framers also ensured that a majority of the voters could win control over only part of the government at one time. Although in an off-year (nonpresidential) election a new majority might take control of the House of Representatives, the president still has at least two more years, and senators hold office for six years. Finally, independent federal courts, which exercise their own powerful checks, were also provided.

Modifications of Checks and Balances

Distrustful of both the elites and the masses, the framers deliberately built inefficiency into our political system. They designed the decision-making process so that the national government can act decisively only when there is a consensus among most groups and after all sides have had their say. "The doctrine of separation of powers was adopted by the convention of 1787," in the words of Justice Louis D. Brandeis, "not to promote efficiency but to preclude the exercise of arbitrary power. The purpose was not to avoid friction, but, by means of the inevitable friction incident to the distribution of the governmental powers among three departments, to save the people from autocracy."[6] Still,

THE EXERCISE OF CHECKS AND BALANCES, 1789–2003

vetoes The president has vetoed more than 2,500 acts of Congress. Congress has overridden presidential vetoes more than 100 times.

judicial review The Supreme Court has ruled some 174 congressional acts or parts thereof unconstitutional. Its 1983 decision striking down legislative vetoes (*INS* v. *Chadha*) affects another 200 provisions.

impeachment The House of Representatives has impeached two presidents and 15 federal judges; of these, the Senate has convicted seven judges but neither president.

confirmation The Senate has refused to confirm nine cabinet nominations, and many other cabinet and subcabinet appointments were withdrawn because of likely Senate rejection.

For additional resources on the Constitution, go to www.prenhall.com/burns.

checks and balances
Constitutional grant of powers that enables each of the three branches of government to check some acts of the others and therefore ensure that no branch can dominate.

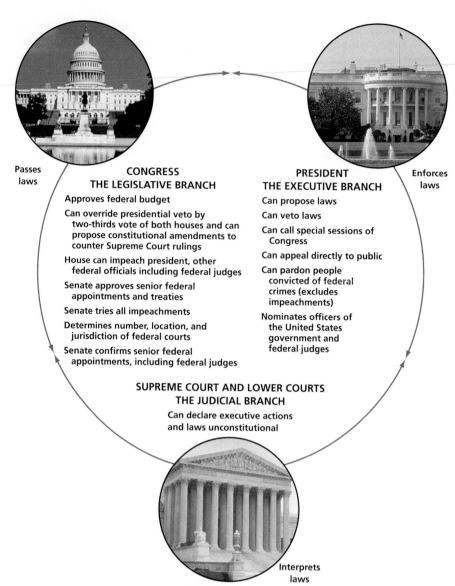

Passes laws

CONGRESS
THE LEGISLATIVE BRANCH

Approves federal budget

Can override presidential veto by two-thirds vote of both houses and can propose constitutional amendments to counter Supreme Court rulings

House can impeach president, other federal officials including federal judges

Senate approves senior federal appointments and treaties

Senate tries all impeachments

Determines number, location, and jurisdiction of federal courts

Senate confirms senior federal appointments, including federal judges

PRESIDENT
THE EXECUTIVE BRANCH

Can propose laws

Can veto laws

Can call special sessions of Congress

Can appeal directly to public

Can pardon people convicted of federal crimes (excludes impeachments)

Nominates officers of the United States government and federal judges

Enforces laws

SUPREME COURT AND LOWER COURTS
THE JUDICIAL BRANCH

Can declare executive actions and laws unconstitutional

Interprets laws

FIGURE 2–1 The Separation of Powers and Checks and Balances.

even though the fragmentation of political power written into the Constitution remains, several developments have modified the way the system of checks and balances works.

THE RISE OF NATIONAL POLITICAL PARTIES   Political parties can serve as unifying factors, at times drawing together the president, senators, representatives, and sometimes even judges behind common programs. When parties do this, they help bridge the separation of powers. Yet parties can be splintered and weakened by having to work through a system of fragmented governmental power, so they never become strong or cohesive. Moreover, when one party controls Congress or one of its chambers and the other controls the White House (**divided government**), as has generally been the case since the end of World War II, the parties may intensify checks and balances rather than moderate them, to the point that action on some important issues may be difficult.[7]

Divided government may lead to so much competition between the legislative and executive branches that we find "each institution protecting and promoting itself through a broad interpretation of its constitutional and political status, even usurping the other's power when the opportunity presents itself."[8] Thus we have had battles over presidential impoundment of funds appropriated by Congress, budget gridlock, and unseemly and angry confirmation hearings for the appointment of justices of the Supreme Court and even lower federal courts and members of the executive branch. Divided

divided government
Governance divided between the parties, especially when one holds the presidency and the other controls one or both houses of Congress.

government also makes it difficult for the voters to hold anybody or any party account-able. "Presidents blame Congress . . . while members of Congress attack the president. . . . Citizens genuinely cannot tell who is to blame."[9]

Still, when all the shouting dies down, political scientist David Mayhew concludes, there have been just as many congressional investigations and just as much important legislation passed when one party controls Congress and another controls the presidency as when the same party controls both branches.[10] And Charles Jones, a noted authority on Congress and the presidency, adds that not only is divided government not that important in determining how our government responds to crises, but divided government is precisely what the voters appear to have wanted through much of our history.[11]

EXPANSION OF THE ELECTORATE AND THE MOVE TOWARD MORE DIRECT DEMOCRACY The framers wanted the president to be chosen by the electoral college—wise, independent citizens free from popular passions and hero worship—rather than by ordinary citizens. Almost from the beginning, however, that is not the way the electoral college worked.[12] Rather, voters actually do select the president, because presidential electors chosen by the voters are pledged in advance to cast their electoral votes for their party's candidates for president and vice president. Nevertheless, presidential candidates may very occasionally win the national popular vote but lose the vote in the electoral college, as demonstrated in Al Gore's winning the popular vote in the 2000 presidential election but losing the electoral college with 266 votes to George W. Bush's 271.

The kind of people allowed to vote has expanded from white property-owning males to all citizens over 18 years of age. In addition, during the past century, American states have expanded the role of the electorate by adopting **direct primaries**, in which the voters elect party nominees for the House and Senate and even for president; by permitting the voters in about half the states to propose and vote on laws (**initiatives**); and by allowing voters to reconsider actions of the legislature (**referendums**) and even to remove elected state and local officials from office (**recall**). And with the passage of the Seventeenth Amendment, senators are no longer elected by state legislatures but are chosen directly by the people.

ESTABLISHMENT OF AGENCIES DELIBERATELY DESIGNED TO EXERCISE LEGISLATIVE, EXECUTIVE, AND JUDICIAL FUNCTIONS When the national government began to regulate the economy, it found that it was impossible to legislate precise and detailed rules on complex matters such as railroad safety, mass communications, the health and safety of working conditions, and environmental protection. Consequently, in assigning these regulatory responsibilities, Congress provides administrative agencies with the power to make and apply rules and to decide disputes. Beginning in 1887, Congress created *independent regulatory commissions* such as the Interstate Commerce Commission (which went out of business in 1995, although many of its functions were transferred to the Surface Transportation Board within the Department of Transportation) and later the Federal Communications Commission. More recently, it has established *independent executive agencies* such as the Environmental Protection Agency.

CHANGES IN TECHNOLOGY The system of checks and balances operates differently today from the way it did in 1789. Back then, there were no televised congressional committee hearings; no electronic communications; no *Larry King Live* talk shows; no *New York Times, Wall Street Journal, USA Today,* CNN, or C-SPAN; no nightly news programs with national audiences; no presidential press conferences; and no live coverage of wars and of Americans fighting in foreign lands. Nuclear bombs, television, computers, cellular telephones, fax machines, the Internet—these and other innovations create conditions today that are very different from those of two centuries ago. We also live in a time of instant communication and polls that tell us what people are thinking about public issues.

In some ways, these new technologies have added to the powers of presidents by permitting them to appeal directly to millions of people and giving them immediate access to public opinion. And these new technologies have also added leverage to

direct primary
Election in which voters choose party nominees.

initiative
Procedure whereby a certain number of voters may, by petition, propose a law or constitutional amendment and have it submitted to the voters.

referendum
Procedure for submitting to popular vote measures passed by the legislature or proposed amendments to a state constitution.

recall
Procedure for submitting to popular vote the removal of officials from office before the end of their term.

IN COMPARATIVE PERSPECTIVE

THE EUROPEAN UNION

The European Union grew out of a succession of alliances formed after World War II to promote economic integration and cooperation. Through a series of treaties, the union has grown to include 25 countries, with the addition of 10 Central and Eastern European countries in 2004. One of the most important institutions created by the union is the European Court of Justice (ECJ). The ECJ has the power to declare national laws invalid when they conflict with treaty obligations and has created a uniform system of law that takes precedence over national laws and constitutions. The member states of the European Union also signed the European Convention on Human Rights, which establishes a long list of civil liberties. They are subject to the jurisdiction of the European Court of Human Rights, which resolves allegations of human rights abuses and has invalidated national laws that contravene provisions of the convention.

For the most part, the issues coming before the ECJ have been economic and commercial in nature, but it has struck down laws based on gender discrimination and advanced the right to equal pay for equal work. Critics of the ECJ complain that it has become too activist and compare it to the U.S. Supreme Court in the early nineteenth century under Chief Justice John Marshall, whose rulings striking down state trade barriers promoted the growth of our unified economy.

Due to the success of economic integration, additional treaties, the introduction of the euro as the common currency, and the enlargement of the EU, a Treaty Establishing a Constitution for Europe was submitted for ratification by all 25 member states in 2004–2005. The Constitution strengthens the powers of the European Parliament, creates a President of the Council of Ministers, and includes a Charter of Fundamental Rights for EU citizens; it also clarifies the competences of other EU supranational institutions and those member states.

Membership in the European Union.

For more information on the European Union, go to www.userpage.chemie. fu-berlin.de/adressen/eu.html and www.lib.berkeley.edu/gssi/eugde.html. The ECJ maintains a site at www.europa.eu.int/cj/en containing recent decisions and other information.

organized interests by making it easier to target thousands of letters and calls at members of Congress, to organize the writing of letters to the editor, and to organize and mobilize on the Internet. New technologies have also given greater independence and influence to nongovernmental institutions such as the press. They have made it possible for rich people like Ross Perot and religious leaders like Pat Robertson, who have access to ample financial resources, to bypass political parties and carry their message directly to the electorate.

THE GROWTH OF PRESIDENTIAL POWER Today problems elsewhere in the world—Afghanistan, Israel, Pakistan, North Korea, Iraq—often create crises for the United States. The need to deal with perpetual emergencies has concentrated power in the hands of the chief executive and the presidential staff. The president of the United States has emerged as the most significant player on the world stage, and media coverage of summit conferences with foreign leaders enhance his status. Headline-generating events give the president a visibility no congressional leader can achieve. The office of the president has on occasion served to modify the system of checks and balances and provide some measure of national unity. Drawing on constitutional, political, and emergency powers, the president is sometimes able to overcome the restraints imposed by the Constitution on the exercise of governmental power—to the applause of some Americans and the alarm of others.

JUDICIAL REVIEW AND THE "GUARDIANS OF THE CONSTITUTION"

The judiciary has become so important in our system of checks and balances that it deserves special attention. Judges did not claim the power of **judicial review**—the power of a court to strike down a law or a government regulation that in the opinion of the judges conflicts with the Constitution—until some years after the Constitution was adopted. From the beginning, however, judges were expected to restrain legislative majorities. "The independence of judges," wrote Alexander Hamilton in *The Federalist*, No. 78 (which appears in the Appendix), "may be an essential safeguard against the effects of occasional ill humors in the society."

Judicial review is a major contribution of the United States to the art of government, a contribution that has been adopted at an increasing pace by other nations. In Germany, France, Italy, and Spain, constitutional courts are responsible for reviewing laws referred to them to ensure constitutional compliance, including compliance with the charter of rights that is now part of their constitutions.[13] (See also the box on the growth of judicial power in the European Union.)

Origins of Judicial Review

The Constitution says nothing about who should have the final word in disputes that might arise over its meaning. Whether the delegates to the Constitutional Convention of 1787 intended to give the courts the power of judicial review is a question long debated. The framers clearly intended that the Supreme Court have the power to declare state legislation unconstitutional, but whether they intended to give it the same power over *congressional* legislation and the president is not clear. Why then didn't the framers specifically provide for judicial review? Probably because they believed the power could be inferred from certain general provisions and the necessity of interpreting and applying a written constitution.

The Federalists—who urged ratification of the Constitution and controlled the national government until 1801—generally supported a strong role for federal courts and favored judicial review. Their opponents, the Jeffersonian Republicans (called Democrats after 1832), were less enthusiastic. In the Kentucky and Virginia Resolutions of 1798 and 1799, respectively, Jefferson and Madison (who by this time had left the Federalist camp) came close to the position that state legislatures—and not the Supreme Court—had the ultimate power to interpret the Constitution. These resolutions seemed to

judicial review
The power of a court to refuse to enforce a law or a government regulation that in the opinion of the judges conflicts with the U.S. Constitution or, in a state court, the state constitution.

CHANGING FACE OF AMERICAN POLITICS

THE CIVIL RIGHTS MOVEMENT AND JUSTICE THURGOOD MARSHALL

In 1909, the National Association for the Advancement of Colored People (NAACP) was founded to protest various forms of racial discrimination—discrimination in the criminal justice system, in voting rights, and in education and employment. In the 1920s and 1930s, one of the NAACP's major initiatives was to lobby Congress to enact a federal law against lynching, as well as to bring lawsuits challenging racial segregation. But, because the NAACP was involved in lobbying it was denied tax-exempt status, and in 1938 under the direction of Thurgood Marshall the NAACP's litigation activities were separated and carried forth with the formation of the NAACP Legal Defense and Education Fund, Inc. (LDF).

Justice Thurgood Marshall.

As a leader in the civil rights movement in the 1940s and 1950s, Thurgood Marshall was a crusading lawyer for the NAACP's LDF. He argued before the Supreme Court and won a companion case with the landmark ruling in *Brown* v. *Board of Education of Topeka* (1954), which held that segregated public schools were unconstitutional. President John Kennedy appointed him to the federal appellate bench in 1961. President Lyndon Johnson then persuaded Marshall to become solicitor general of the United States, and he was appointed to the Supreme Court in 1967. As the first African American on the Supreme Court, Justice Marshall served until 1991 and continued to champion the cause of civil rights throughout his career.

At the time of the Bicentennial of the Constitution, he spoke out in dissent and defended his view of our "living Constitution":

> I do not believe that the meaning of the Constitution was forever "fixed" at the Philadelphia Convention. Nor do I find the wisdom, foresight, and sense of justice exhibited by the framers particularly profound. To the contrary, the government they devised was defective from the start, requiring several amendments, a civil war, and momentous social transformation to attain the system of constitutional government, and its respect for the individual freedoms and human rights, that we hold as fundamental today. When contemporary Americans cite "The Constitution," they invoke a concept that is vastly different from what the framers barely began to construct two centuries ago.

> For a sense of the evolving nature of the Constitution we need look no further than the first three words of the document's preamble: "We the People." When the Founding Fathers used this phrase in 1787, they did not have in mind the majority of America's citizens. "We the People" included, in the words of the framers, "the whole Number of free Persons." On a matter so basic as the right to vote, for example, Negro slaves were excluded, although they were counted for representational purposes—at three-fifths each. Women did not gain the right to vote for over a hundred and thirty years. . . .

> And so we must be careful, when focusing on the events which took place in Philadelphia two centuries ago, that we not overlook the momentous events which followed, and thereby lose our proper sense of perspective. . . . If we seek, instead, a sensitive understanding of the Constitution's inherent defects, and its promising evolution through 200 years of history, the celebration of the "Miracle at Philadelphia" will, in my view, be a far more meaningful and humbling experience. We will see that the true miracle was not the birth of the Constitution, but its life, a life nurtured through two turbulent centuries of our own making, and a life embodying much good fortune that was not.[*]

[*]Remarks at the annual seminar of the San Francisco Patent and Trademark Law Association, Maui, Hawaii, May 16, 1987. In David M. O'Brien, ed., *Judges on Judging*, 2d ed. (C.Q. Press, 2004).

question whether the Supreme Court even had final authority to review state legislation, something about which there had been little doubt.

When the Jeffersonians defeated the Federalists in the election of 1800, it was still undecided whether the Supreme Court would actually exercise the power of judicial review. Logical reasons to support such a doctrine were at hand, and some precedents could even be cited; nevertheless, judicial review was not an established power. Then in 1803 came *Marbury* v. *Madison,* the most pathbreaking Supreme Court decision of all time.[14]

Marbury Versus *Madison*

The election of 1800 marked the rise to power of the Jeffersonian Republicans. President John Adams and fellow Federalists did not take their defeat easily. Indeed, they were greatly alarmed at what they considered to be the "enthronement of the rabble." Yet there was nothing much they could do about it before leaving office—or was there? The Constitution gives the president, with the consent of the Senate, the power to appoint federal judges to hold office during "good Behaviour"—basically, lifetime tenure, subject to removal only by impeachment. With the judiciary in the hands of Federalists, thought Adams and his associates, they could stave off the worst consequences of Jefferson's victory.

The outgoing Federalist Congress consequently created dozens of new federal judgeships. By March 3, 1801, Adams had appointed and the Senate had confirmed loyal Federalists to all these new positions. Adams signed the commissions and turned them over to John Marshall, his secretary of state, to be sealed and delivered. Marshall had just received his own commission as chief justice of the United States, but he continued to serve as secretary of state until Adams's term as president expired. Working right up until nine o'clock on the evening of March 3, Marshall sealed, but was unable to deliver, all the commissions. The only ones left were for the justices of the peace for the District of Columbia. The newly appointed chief justice left the delivery of these commissions for his successor, James Madison.

This "packing" of the judiciary angered Jefferson, now inaugurated as president. When he discovered that some of the commissions were still lying on a table in the Department of State, he instructed a clerk not to deliver them. Jefferson could see no reason why the District needed so many justices of the peace, especially Federalist justices.[15]

Among the commissions not delivered was one for William Marbury. After waiting in vain, Marbury decided to seek action from the courts. Searching through the statute books, he came across Section 13 of the Judiciary Act of 1789, which authorized the Supreme Court "to issue writs of mandamus." A **writ of mandamus** is a court order directing an official, such as the secretary of state, to perform a duty about which the official has no discretion, such as delivering a commission. So, thought Marbury, why not ask the Supreme Court to issue a writ of mandamus to force James Madison, the new secretary of state, to deliver the commission? Marbury and his companions went directly to the Supreme Court and, citing Section 13, they made the request.

What could Marshall do? On the one hand, if the Court issued the writ, Jefferson and Madison would probably ignore it. The Court would be powerless, and its prestige, already low, might suffer a fatal blow. On the other hand, by refusing to issue the writ, the judges would appear to support the Jeffersonian Republicans' claim that the Court had no authority to interfere with the executive. Would Marshall issue the writ? Most people thought so; angry Republicans even threatened impeachment if he did so.

On February 24, 1803, the Supreme Court delivered its opinion. The first part was as expected. Marbury was entitled to his commission, said Marshall, and Madison should have delivered it to him. Moreover, the proper court could issue a writ of mandamus, even against so high an officer as the secretary of state.

Then came the surprise. Section 13 of the Judiciary Act appears to give the Supreme Court the power to issue a writ of mandamus in cases of original jurisdiction, such as this one in question. But Section 13, said Marshall, is contrary to Article III of the Constitution, which gives the Supreme Court original jurisdiction only when an ambassador or other foreign minister is affected or when a state is a party. Even though this is a case of original jurisdiction, Marbury is neither a state nor a foreign minister. Under the Constitution, wrote Marshall, the Court had no power to issue a writ of mandamus in cases on original jurisdiction.

Marshall then posed the question in a more pointed way: Should the Supreme Court enforce an unconstitutional law? Of course not, he concluded. *The Constitution is the supreme and binding law,* and the courts cannot enforce any action of Congress that conflicts with it, even if it expands the power of the Court. Thus by limiting the Court's power to what is granted in the Constitution, Marshall gained the much more important power to declare laws passed by Congress unconstitutional. It was a brilliant move.

Chief Justice John Marshall (1755–1835), our most influential Supreme Court justice. Appointed in 1801, Marshall served until 1835. Earlier he had been a staunch defender of the U.S. Constitution at the Virginia ratifying convention, a member of Congress, and a secretary of state. He was one of those rare people who served in all three branches of government.

writ of mandamus
Court order directing an official to perform an official duty.

Two U.S. presidents, Andrew Johnson and Bill Clinton, have been impeached by the U.S. House of Representatives. In both cases the U.S. Senate did not muster a two-thirds majority vote, which would have been needed to convict these two presidents. President Richard Nixon almost surely would also have been impeached by the House of Representatives in 1974 but he resigned and left the presidency, and this decision preempted the House's action.

impeachment
Formal accusation against a public official, the first step in removal from office.

Marbury v. *Madison* might have been interpreted by subsequent generations in a very limited way. It could have been interpreted to mean that the Supreme Court had the right to determine the scope of its own powers under Article III, but Congress and the president had the authority to interpret their powers under Articles I and II. But over the decades, building on Marshall's precedent, the Court has taken the commanding position as the authoritative interpreter of the Constitution.

Several important consequences follow from the acceptance of Marshall's argument that judges are the official interpreters of the Constitution. The most important is that people can challenge laws enacted by Congress and approved by the president. Simply by bringing a lawsuit, those who lack the clout to get a bill through Congress can often secure a judicial hearing. And organized interest groups often find that goals unattainable by legislation can be achieved by litigation. Litigation thus supplements, and at times even takes precedence over, legislation as a way to make public policy.[16]

THE CONSTITUTION AS AN INSTRUMENT OF GOVERNMENT

As careful as the Constitution's framers were to limit the powers they gave the national government, the main reason they assembled in Philadelphia was to create a stronger national government. Having learned that a weak central government was a danger to liberty, they wished to establish a national government within the framework of a federal system with enough authority to meet the needs of all time. They made general grants of power, leaving it to succeeding generations to fill in the details and organize the structure of government in accordance with experience.

Hence our formal, written Constitution is only the skeleton of our system. It is filled out in numerous ways that must be considered part of our constitutional system in a larger sense. In fact, it is primarily through changes in the informal, unwritten Constitution that our system is kept up to date. These changes are found in certain basic statutes and historical practices of Congress, presidential practices, and decisions of the Supreme Court.

The Unwritten Constitution

CONGRESSIONAL ELABORATION Because the framers gave Congress authority to provide for the structural details of the national government, it is not necessary to amend the Constitution every time a change is needed. Rather, Congress can create legislation to meet the need. Examples of congressional elaboration appear in such legislation as the Judiciary Act of 1789, which laid the foundations for our national judicial system; in the laws establishing the organization and functions of all federal executive officials subordinate to the president; and in the rules of procedure, internal organization, and practices of Congress.

A dramatic example of congressional elaboration of our constitutional system is the use of the impeachment and removal power. An **impeachment** is a formal accusation against a public official and the first step in removal from office. Constitutional language defining the grounds for impeachment is sparse. Look at the Constitution (reprinted between this chapter and the next) and note that Article II (the Executive Article) calls for removal of the president, vice president, and all civil officers of the United States on impeachment for, and conviction of, "Treason, Bribery, or other High Crimes and Misdemeanors." It is up to Congress to give meaning to that language.

Article I (the Legislative Article) gives the House of Representatives the sole power to initiate impeachments and the Senate the sole power to try impeachments. In the event the president is tried, the chief justice of the United States presides, as Chief Justice William H. Rehnquist did in the impeachment of President Bill Clinton. Article I also requires conviction on impeachment charges to have the agreement of two-thirds of the senators present. Judgments shall extend no further than removal from office and disqualification from holding any office under the United States, but a person convicted

THE BRITISH AND AMERICAN SYSTEMS: A STUDY IN CONTRASTS

Our political system is based on the Constitution; the United Kingdom of Great Britain and Northern Ireland has no such single document. Yet both systems are "constitutional" in the sense that the rulers are subject to well-defined restraints. Parliament is the guardian of the British constitution. In the United States, it is the courts—ultimately, the Supreme Court—that are the keepers of the constitutional conscience, not Congress or the president. The limitations in our written Constitution and the practices in the unwritten British constitution rest on underlying national values and attitudes toward government.

In the British system, voters elect members of the House of Commons from districts, much as we elect members of our House of Representatives. Like us, the party with the most votes in a district wins the seat, so that even with three or more parties, a plurality of the popular vote usually results in a majority of the parliamentary seats. So long as the parliamentary majority stays together, it can enact into law the ruling party's program.

In British politics, parties are cohesive and disciplined; party members vote together and support their parliamentary leaders. In Britain, the party that wins an election has a very good chance of seeing its policies enacted. By contrast, our system depends on the agreement of many elements of society. The party that wins a presidential or congressional election or even one that controls both these branches may still have a tough time carrying out its campaign promises.

Leaders of the majority party in the House of Commons serve as executive ministers who collectively form the cabinet, with the prime minister at its head. The majority selects the prime minister. If the ruling party loses the support of the majority in the Commons on a major issue, it must resign or call for new elections. The House of Commons, when it chooses to act, has almost complete constitutional power. By tradition, there was no high court with the power to declare acts of Parliament unconstitutional, and the prime minister cannot veto them, although he or she may ask the crown to dissolve Parliament and call new elections.

In recent years, the British system has been substantially modified, however. In 2000, Britain forged sweeping constitutional reforms with the passage of the Human Rights Act, incorporating the European Convention on Human Rights as part of its domestic law and giving citizens their first American-style bill of rights. Besides introducing elements of federalism by devolving power to regional parliaments in Scotland, Wales,

Comparison of the British and American Systems.

and Northern Ireland, the House of Lords was stripped of its hereditary peers (members who served as a result of hereditary titles). The House of Lords now consists only of people appointed by the prime minister for their accomplishments in the arts, business, and public service. The 800-year-old office of the Lord Chancellor, who served as speaker of the House of Lords but also exercised executive and judicial powers in overseeing the administration of the courts, was abolished. A separate supreme court was proposed and the power to appoint justices and judges was to be given to an independent judicial appointments commission. The addition of a bill of rights, the devolution of power, and the judicial reforms creating a separation of powers are the most important changes in the British constitutional system in more than 300 years.

HOW SHOULD THE CONSTITUTION BE INTERPRETED?

Although we have the oldest written constitution in the world, we do not have an agreed-on theory of how it should be interpreted, nor does the document itself say how it should be read. Justices, no less than politicians and citizens, differ over how to interpret it. Some, like Justice Antonin Scalia, contend that judges should adhere to the "original intent" of the Constitution, while others, like Justice William J. Brennan Jr., view the Constitution as a "living document" that requires contemporary ratification.

may also be liable to indictment, trial, judgment, and punishment according to the law. Article I also exempts cases of impeachment from the president's pardoning power. Article III (the Judicial Article) exempts cases of impeachment from the jury trial requirement. That is all the relevant constitutional language about impeachment. We must look to history to answer most questions about the proper exercise of these and other powers.[17]

Fortunately, past experience has triggered few acute constitutional disputes about the interpretation of impeachment procedures, so there is little history to go on. The House of Representatives has investigated 67 individuals for possible impeachment and has impeached 15 (two presidents—Andrew Johnson and Bill Clinton—and 13 federal judges). The Senate has held 15 impeachment trials and convicted only seven, all federal judges.

Presidential Practices

Although the formal constitutional powers of the president have not changed, the office is dramatically more important and more central today than it was in 1789. Vigorous presidents—George Washington, Thomas Jefferson, Andrew Jackson, Abraham Lincoln, Theodore Roosevelt, Woodrow Wilson, Franklin Roosevelt, Harry Truman, Lyndon Johnson, Bill Clinton, and George W. Bush—have boldly exercised their political and constitutional powers, especially during times of national crisis like the current war against international terrorism. Their presidential practices have established important precedents, building the power and influence of the office.

A major practice involves **executive orders**, which carry the full force of law. They may make major policy changes, such as withholding federal contracts from businesses engaging in racial discrimination, or they may simply be formalities, such as the presidential proclamation of Earth Day.

Other practices include **executive privilege** (the right to confidentiality of executive communications, especially those that relate to national security), **impoundment** by a president of funds previously appropriated by Congress, the power to send our armed forces into hostilities, and most important, the authority to propose legislation and work actively to secure its passage by Congress.

Foreign and economic crises as well as nuclear age realities have expanded the president's role: "When it comes to action risking nuclear war, technology has modified the Constitution: the President, perforce, becomes the only such man in the system capable of exercising judgment under the extraordinary limits now imposed by secrecy, complexity, and time."[18] The presidency has also become the pivotal office for regulating the economy and promoting the general welfare. Plainly, the president has become a leader in sponsoring legislation as well as the nation's chief executive.

Custom and Usage

Custom and usage round out our governmental system. The development of structures outside the formal Constitution—such as national political parties and the expansion of suffrage in the states—has democratized our Constitution. Other examples of custom and usage are in televised press conferences and presidential and vice presidential debates. Through such developments, the president has become responsive to the people and has a political base different from that of Congress. Consequently, the constitutional relationship between the branches today is considerably different from that envisioned by the framers.

Judicial Interpretation

As discussed earlier, judicial interpretation of the Constitution, especially by the Supreme Court, plays an important role in keeping the constitutional system up to date. As social and economic conditions change and new national demands develop, the Supreme Court has changed its interpretation of the Constitution accordingly. Because the Constitution adapts to changing times, it does not require frequent formal amendment. The

executive order
Directive issued by a president or governor that has the force of law.

executive privilege
The power to keep executive communications confidential, especially if they relate to national security.

impoundment
Presidential refusal to allow an agency to spend funds authorized and appropriated by Congress.

advantages of this flexibility may be appreciated by comparing the national Constitution with the rigid and often overly specific state constitutions. Many state constitutions are so detailed that they tie the hands of public officials and must be amended or replaced frequently.

CHANGING THE LETTER OF THE CONSTITUTION

Many people are disturbed by the idea of a constantly changing system. How, they contend, can you have a constitutional government when the Constitution is constantly being twisted by interpretation and changed by informal methods? This view fails to distinguish between two aspects of the Constitution. As an expression of *basic and timeless personal liberties,* the Constitution does not, and should not, change. For example, a government cannot destroy free speech and still remain a constitutional government. In this sense, the Constitution is unchanging. But when we consider the Constitution as an *instrument of government* and a positive grant of power, we realize that if it does not grow with the nation it serves, it would soon be irrelevant and ignored.

The framers could never have conceived of the problems facing the government of a large, powerful, and wealthy nation of over 285 million people at the beginning of the twenty-first century. Although the general purposes of government remain the same—to establish liberty, promote justice, ensure domestic tranquillity, and provide for the common defense—the powers of government that were adequate to accomplish these purposes in 1787 are simply insufficient more than 218 years later. Through its remarkable adaptability, our Constitution has survived democratic and industrial revolutions, the turmoil of civil war, the upheavals of major depressions, and the dislocations of world wars.

The framers knew that future experiences would call for changes in the text of the Constitution and that some means for formal amendment was necessary. In Article V, they gave responsibility for amending the Constitution to Congress and to the states. The president has no formal authority over constitutional amendments; presidential veto power does not extend to them, although presidential political influence is often crucial in getting amendments proposed and ratified.

Proposing Amendments

The first method for proposing amendments—and the only one used so far—is by *a two-thirds vote of both houses of Congress.* Dozens of resolutions proposing amendments are introduced in every session. Thousands have been introduced since 1789, but few make any headway. Throughout our history, Congress has proposed only 31 amendments, of which 27 have been ratified—including the Twenty-Seventh, which was originally part of the Bill of Rights but took more than 200 years to be ratified (see Figure 2–2).

Recent decades have seen a flurry of congressional attempts at constitutional amendments.[19] Congress has considered more than 11,000 proposals and the states have filed close to 400 petitions for calling a constitutional convention to consider amendments. Why is proposing amendments to the Constitution so popular? In part because interest groups unhappy with Supreme Court decisions seek to overturn them. In part because groups frustrated by their inability to get things done in Congress hope to bypass Congress. And in part because scholars or interest groups (not necessarily mutually exclusive categories) seek to change the procedures and processes of government to make the system more responsive.

The second method for proposing amendments—*a convention called by Congress at the request of the legislatures in two-thirds of the states*—has never been used. Under Article V of the Constitution, Congress could call for such a convention without the concurrence of the president. This method presents some difficult questions.[20] First, can

★★ THINKING IT THROUGH

Justice Scalia, a staunch conservative, contends that departing from the original intent of the Constitution undermines the legitimacy of the Court and leads to judicial legislation. In his view: "A democratic society does not, by and large, need constitutional guarantees to insure that its laws will reflect 'current values.' Elections take care of that quite well. The purpose of constitutional guarantees—and in particular those constitutional guarantees of individual rights that are at the center of this controversy—is precisely to prevent the law from reflecting certain changes in original values that the society adopting the Constitution thinks fundamentally undesirable." "Originalism," according to Justice Scalia "establishes a historical criterion that is conceptually quite separate from the preferences of the judge himself."[*]

By contrast, Justice Brennan, a leading liberal on the Court from 1956 to 1990, emphasized the problems with appealing to original intent: "It is arrogant to pretend that from our vantage [point] we can gauge accurately the intent of the framers on application of principle to specific, contemporary questions. Typically, all that can be gleaned is that the framers themselves did not agree about the application or meaning of particular constitutional provisions and hid their differences in cloaks of generality." Moreover, Justice Brennan maintained that "current justices read the Constitution in the only way that we can: as [contemporary] Americans. We look to the history of the time of framing and to the intervening history of interpretation. But the ultimate question must be: What do the words of the text mean in our time? For the genius of the Constitution rests not in any static meaning it might have had in a world that is dead and gone, but in the adaptability of its great principles to cope with current problems and current needs."[**]

[*]Antonin Scalia, "Originalism: The Lesser Evil," *University of Cincinnati Law Review* 55 (1989), p. 894.

[**]William J. Brennan, Jr., "The Constitution of the United States: Contemporary Ratification," lecture delivered at Georgetown University, October 12, 1985.

THE AMENDING POWER AND HOW IT HAS BEEN USED

Leaving aside the first ten amendments (the Bill of Rights), the power of constitutional amendment has served a number of purposes:

To Add or Subtract National Government Power

The Eleventh took some jurisdiction away from the national courts.

The Thirteenth abolished slavery and authorized Congress to legislate against it.

The Sixteenth enabled Congress to levy an income tax.

The Eighteenth authorized Congress to prohibit the manufacture, sale, or transportation of liquor.

The Twenty-First repealed the Eighteenth and gave states the authority to regulate liquor sales.

The Twenty-Seventh limited the power of Congress to set members' salaries.

To Expand the Electorate and Its Power

The Fifteenth extended suffrage to all male African Americans over the age of 21.

The Seventeenth took the right to elect their United States senators away from state legislatures and gave it to the voters in each state.

The Nineteenth extended suffrage to women over the age of 21.

The Twenty-Third gave voters of the District of Columbia the right to vote for president and vice president.

The Twenty-Fourth outlawed the poll tax, thereby prohibiting states from taxing the right to vote.

The Twenty-Sixth extended suffrage to otherwise qualified persons 18 years of age or older.

To Reduce the Electorate's Power

The Twenty-Second took away from the electorate the right to elect a person to the office of president for more than two full terms.

To Limit State Government Power

The Thirteenth abolished slavery.

The Fourteenth granted national citizenship and prohibited states from abridging privileges of national citizenship; from denying persons life, liberty, and property without due process; and from denying persons equal protection of the laws. This amendment has come to be interpreted as imposing restraints on state powers in every area of public life.

(cont.)

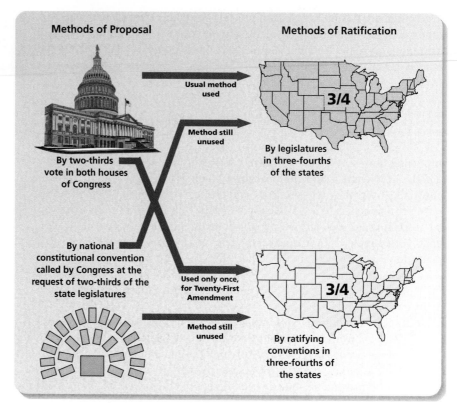

FIGURE 2–2 Four Methods of Amending the Constitution.

state legislatures apply for a convention to propose specific amendments on one topic, or must they request a convention with full powers to revise the entire Constitution? How long do state petitions remain alive? How should delegates be chosen? How should such a convention be run? Congress has considered bills to answer some of these questions but has not passed any, in part because most members do not wish to encourage a constitutional convention for fear that once in session it might propose amendments on any and all topics.

Under most proposals, each state would have as many delegates to the convention as it has representatives and senators in Congress. Finally—a crucial point—the convention would be limited to considering only the subject specified in the state legislative petitions and described in the congressional call for the convention. Scholars are divided, however, on whether Congress has the authority to limit what a constitutional convention might propose.[21]

Ratifying Amendments

After an amendment has been proposed, it must be ratified by the states. Again, two methods are provided by the Constitution: approval by the legislatures in three-fourths of the states or approval by specially called ratifying conventions in three-fourths of the states. Congress determines which method is used. All amendments except one—the Twenty-First (to repeal the Eighteenth, the Prohibition Amendment)—have been submitted to the state legislatures for ratification.

Seven state constitutions specify that their state legislatures must ratify a proposed amendment to the U.S. Constitution by majorities of three-fifths or two-thirds of each chamber. Although a state legislature may change its mind and ratify an amendment after it has voted against ratification, the weight of opinion is that once a state has ratified an amendment, it cannot "unratify" it.[22]

The Supreme Court has said that ratification must take place within a "reasonable time." When Congress proclaims an amendment to be part of the Constitution, it must decide whether the amendment has been ratified within a reasonable time so that it is "sufficiently contemporaneous to reflect the will of the people."[23] However, Congress approved ratification of the Twenty-Seventh Amendment, which had been before the nation for almost 203 years, so there seems to be no limit on what it considers a "reasonable time." Because of the experience with the Twenty-Seventh Amendment, Congress will probably continue the current practice of stipulating in the text of a proposed amendment that the necessary number of states must ratify it within seven years from the date of submission by Congress. In fact, ratification ordinarily takes place rather quickly (see Figure 2–3).[24]

Ratification Politics

The failure of the Equal Rights Amendment to be ratified provides a vivid example of the pitfalls of ratification. First introduced in 1923 and frequently thereafter, the Equal Rights Amendment (ERA) did not get much support until the 1960s. An influential book by Betty Friedan, *The Feminine Mystique* (1963), challenged stereotypes about the role of women. The National Organization for Women (NOW), formed in 1966, made passage of the ERA its central mission. By the 1970s, the ERA had overwhelming support in both houses of Congress and in both national party platforms. Every president from Harry Truman to Ronald Reagan, and many of their wives, endorsed the amendment; however, in 1980 the Republican party adopted a neutral stance on the ratification of the amendment. More than 450 organizations with a total membership of more than 50 million were on record in support of the ERA.[25] The ERA provided:

> ***Section 1.*** Equality of rights under the law shall not be denied or abridged by the United States or by any State on account of sex.
>
> ***Section 2.*** The Congress shall have power to enforce, by appropriate legislation, the provisions of this article.
>
> ***Section 3.*** This amendment shall take effect two years after the date of ratification.

Soon after passage of the amendment by Congress in 1972 and submission to the states, many legislatures ratified it quickly—sometimes without hearings—and by overwhelming majorities. By the end of that year, 22 states had ratified the amendment, and it appeared that the ERA would soon become part of the Constitution. But opposition organized under the leadership of Phyllis Schlafly, a prominent spokesperson for conservative causes, and the ERA became controversial.

THE AMENDING POWER AND HOW IT HAS BEEN USED (*CONT.*)

To Make Structural Changes in Government

The Twelfth corrected deficiencies in the operation of the electoral college that were revealed by the development of a two-party national system.

The Twentieth altered the calendar for congressional sessions and shortened the time between the election of presidents and their assumption of office.

The Twenty-Fifth provided procedures for filling vacancies in the vice presidency and for determining whether presidents are unable to perform their duties.

FIGURE 2–3 The Time for Ratification of the 27 Amendments to the Constitution.

PEOPLE & POLITICS *Making a Difference* ★ ★ ★

GREGORY WATSON

As a student at the University of Texas writing a paper on the Equal Rights Amendment in 1982, Gregory Watson came across an amendment proposed in 1789 as part of the Bill of Rights. It would prohibit a pay raise for members of Congress until the intervention of an election for members of the House. He also found that only six of the original 13 states had ratified it and that during the intervening years only three more states had done so.

Watson decided to start a ratification movement. He got some publicity for his efforts and, with the help of Texas Republican State Representative Don Mielke, persuaded six more state legislatures to ratify this long-forgotten proposed amendment. (By the way, Watson got only a C on his paper, although he is credited with starting a grass-roots movement to persuade 26 state legislatures to ratify the Twenty-Seventh Amendment.)[*]

After members of Congress tried unsuccessfully in 1989 to avoid public anger by delegating their decision to increase their own salaries to an independent commission, anti-Congress sentiment began to grow, and the ratification movement picked up steam. On May 7, 1992, the Michigan legislature became the thirty-eighth state to ratify the amendment.

The first reaction of some congressional leaders was to question this action because the Supreme Court had made it clear that amendments must be ratified within a "reasonable time." However, when members of Congress realized that the issue could be used against them in the next election, they declared the Twenty-Seventh Amendment to be "valid as part of the Constitution of the United States." The vote was 99 to 0 in the Senate, 414 to 3 in the House.

[*]Ruth Ann Strickland, "The Twenty-Seventh Amendment and Constitutional Change by Stealth," *PS: Political Science and Politics* (December 1993), p. 720.

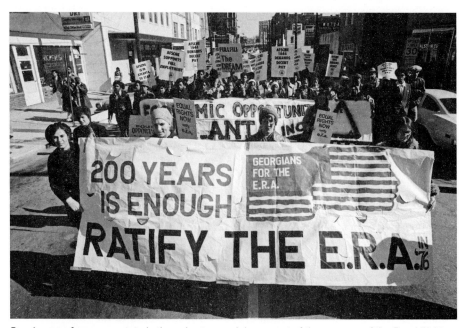

People came from every state in the union to march in support of the passage of the Equal Rights Amendment.

Opponents argued that "women would not only be subject to the military draft but also assigned to combat duty. Full-time housewives and mothers would be forced to join the labor force. Further, women would no longer enjoy existing advantages under state domestic relations codes and under labor law."[26] The ERA also became embroiled in the controversy over abortion. Many opponents contended that its ratification would jeopardize the power of states and Congress to regulate abortion and would compel public funding of abortions.[27]

After the ERA became controversial, state legislatures held lengthy hearings, and floor debates became heated. Legislators hid behind parliamentary procedures and avoided making a decision for as long as possible. Opposition to ratification arose chiefly in the same cluster of southern states that had opposed ratification of the Nineteenth Amendment, which gave women the right to vote. As the opposition grew more active, proponents redoubled their efforts.

In the autumn of 1978, it appeared that the ERA would fall three short of the necessary number of ratifying states before the expiration of the seven-year limit on March 22, 1979. After an extended debate, and after voting down provisions that would have authorized state legislatures to change their minds and rescind prior ratification, Congress, by a simple majority vote, extended the time limit until June 30, 1982. Nonetheless, by the final deadline, the amendment was still three states short of the 38 needed for ratification.

The framers intended that amending the Constitution should be difficult, and the ERA ratification battle demonstrates how well they planned. Still, through interpretation, practices, usages, and judicial decisions, the Constitution has proved an enduring and adaptable governing document.

THIS CONSTITUTION: WHAT IF YOU WERE A FOUNDING FATHER?

You have seen in this chapter that constitutions require trade-offs among competing principles and entail some form of checks and balances. The Make It Real feature for this chapter allows you to see how constitutional principles and changes that you favor would conflict with and require modifications of the Constitution.

Go to Make It Real: "The Constitution: What If You Were a Founding Father?"

S U M M A R Y

1. The U.S. Constitution, adopted in 1789, is the world's oldest. It has lasted because it is adaptable and flexible. It both grants and limits governmental power. The Constitution's separation of powers distributes authority among three branches of government: the legislative, executive, and judicial. Checks and balances limit the power of each branch.

2. Political parties may sometimes overcome the separation of powers, especially if the same party controls both houses of Congress and the presidency. Typically, this is not the case, however, and a divided government intensifies checks and balances. Presidential power, which has increased over time, has sometimes been able to overcome some restraints imposed by the Constitution.

3. Judicial review is the power of the courts to strike down acts of Congress, the executive branch, and the states as unconstitutional. It is one of the unique features of the U.S. constitutional system. The Supreme Court's power of judicial review was established in the 1803 case of *Marbury* v. *Madison.*

4. The Constitution is the framework of our governmental system. The constitutional system has been modified over time, adapting to new conditions through congressional elaboration, presidential practices, custom and usage, and judicial interpretation.

5. Although adaptable, the Constitution itself needs to be altered from time to time, and the framers provided a procedure for

its amendment. An amendment must be both proposed and ratified: proposed by either a two-thirds vote in each chamber of Congress or by a national convention called by Congress on petition of the legislatures in two-thirds of the states; ratified either by the legislatures in three-fourths of the states or by specially called ratifying conventions in three-fourths of the states.

6. The Constitution has been formally amended 27 times. The usual method has been proposal by a two-thirds vote in both houses of Congress and ratification by the legislatures in three-fourths of the states.

K E Y   T E R M S

natural law	direct primary	judicial review	executive privilege
separation of powers	initiative	writ of mandamus	impoundment
checks and balances	referendum	impeachment	
divided government	recall	executive order	

FURTHER READING

LANCE BANNING, *The Sacred Fire of Liberty: James Madison and the Founding of the Federal Republic* (Cornell University Press, 1995).

CAROL BERKIN, *A Brillant Solution: Inventing the American Constitution* (Harcourt, 2002).

JAMES BRYCE, *The American Commonwealth*, 2 vols. (Macmillan, 1889).

JAMES MACGREGOR BURNS, *The Vineyard of Liberty* (Knopf, 1982).

GERHARD CASPER, *Separation of Powers: Essays on the Founding Period* (Harvard University Press, 1997).

NEIL H. COGAN, *The Complete Bill of Rights: The Drafts, Debates, Sources, and Origins* (Oxford University Press, 1997).

CHRISTOPHER L. EISGRUBER, *Constitutional Self-Government* (Harvard University Press, 2001).

MICHAEL KAMMEN, *A Machine That Would Go of Itself: The Constitution in American Culture* (Knopf, 1986).

PHILIP B. KURLAND AND RALPH LERNER, *The Founders' Constitution*, 5 vols. (University of Chicago Press, 1987).

LIBRARY OF CONGRESS, CONGRESSIONAL RESEARCH SERVICE, *The Constitution of the United States of America: Analysis and Interpretation,* Senate Document 100–9 (U.S. Government Printing Office, 1991). Updated at www.findlaw.com/case_code.

WILLIAM NELSON, Marbury v. Madison: *The Origins and Legacy of Judicial Review* (University Press of Kansas, 2000).

J. W. PELTASON AND SUE DAVIS, *Understanding the Constitution,* 16th ed. (Wadsworth, 2004).

CHARLES H. SHELDON, *Essentials of the American Constitution: The Supreme Court and Fundamental Law,* ed. Stephen L. Wasby (Westview Press, 2002).

CASS SUNSTEIN, *Designing Democracy: What Constitutions Do* (Oxford University Press, 2001).

JOHN R. VILE, ED. *Proposed Amendments to the U.S. Constitution: 1787-2001* (The Lawbook Exchange, 2003).

On Reading the Constitution

More than 218 years after its ratification, our Constitution remains the operating charter of our republic. It is neither self-explanatory nor a comprehensive description of our constitutional rules. Still, it remains the starting point. Many Americans who swear by the Constitution have never read it seriously, although copies can be found in most American government and American history textbooks.

Justice Hugo Black, who served on the Supreme Court for 34 years, kept a copy of the Constitution with him at all times. He read it often. Reading the Constitution would be a good way for you to begin (and then reread again to end) your study of the government of the United States. We have therefore included a copy of it at this point in the book. Please read it carefully.

The Constitution of the United States

The Preamble

W e the People of the United States, in Order to form a more perfect Union, establish Justice, insure domestic Tranquility, provide for the common defense, promote the general Welfare, and secure the Blessings of Liberty to ourselves and our Posterity, do ordain and establish this Constitution for the United States of America.

Article I—The Legislative Article

Legislative Power

Section 1   All legislative Powers herein granted shall be vested in a Congress of the United States, which shall consist of a Senate and House of Representatives.

House of Representatives: Composition; Qualifications; Apportionment; Impeachment Power

Section 2

Clause 1.   The House of Representatives shall be composed of Members chosen every second Year by the People of the several States, and the Electors in each State shall have the Qualifications requisite for Electors of the most numerous Branch of the State Legislature.

Clause 2.   No Person shall be a Representative who shall not have attained to the Age of twenty five Years, and been seven Years a Citizen of the United States, and who shall not, when elected, be an Inhabitant of that State in which he shall be chosen.

Clause 3.   Representatives and direct Taxes[1] shall be apportioned among the several States which may be included within this Union, according to their respective Numbers, which shall be determined by adding to the whole Number of free Persons, including those bound to Service for a Term of Years, and excluding Indians not taxed, three fifths of all other Persons.[2] The actual Enumeration shall be made within three Years after the first Meeting of the Congress of the United States, and within every subsequent Term of ten Years, in such Manner as they shall by Law direct. The Number of Representatives shall not exceed one for every thirty Thousand, but each State shall have at least one Representative; and until each enumeration shall be made, the State of New Hampshire shall be entitled to chuse three, Massachusetts eight, Rhode-Island and Providence Plantations one, Connecticut five, New-York six, New Jersey four, Pennsylvania eight, Delaware one, Maryland six, Virginia ten, North Carolina five, South Carolina five, and Georgia three.

Clause 4.   When vacancies happen in the Representation from any State, the Executive Authority thereof shall issue Writs of Election to fill such Vacancies.

Clause 5.   The House of Representatives shall chuse their Speaker and other Officers; and shall have the sole Power of Impeachment.

Senate Composition: Qualifications, Impeachment Trials

Section 3

Clause 1.   The Senate of the United States shall be composed of two Senators from each State, chosen by the Legislature thereof,[3] for six Years; and each Senator shall have one Vote.

Clause 2.   Immediately after they shall be assembled in Consequence of the first Election, they shall be divided as equally as may be into three Classes. The Seats of the Senators of the first Class shall be vacated at the Expiration of the second Year, of the second Class at the Expiration of the fourth Year, and of the third Class at the Expiration of the sixth Year, so that one third may be chosen every second Year; and if Vacancies happen by Resignation, or otherwise, during the Recess of the Legislature of any State, the Executive thereof may make temporary Appointments until the next Meeting of the Legislature, which shall then fill such Vacancies.[4]

Clause 3.   No person shall be a Senator who shall not have attained to the Age of thirty Years, and been nine Years a Citizen of the United States, and who shall not, when elected, be an inhabitant of that State for which he shall be chosen.

Clause 4.   The Vice President of the United States shall be President of the Senate, but shall have no Vote, unless they be equally divided.

Clause 5.   The Senate shall chuse their other Officers, and also a President pro tempore, in the Absence of the Vice President, or when he shall exercise the Office of President of the United States.

Clause 6.   The Senate shall have the sole Power to try all Impeachments. When sitting for that Purpose, they shall be on Oath or Affirmation. When the President of the United States is tried, the Chief Justice shall preside: And no Person shall be convicted without the Concurrence of two thirds of the Members present.

Judgment in Cases of Impeachment shall not extend further than to removal from Office, and disqualification to hold and enjoy any Office of honor, Trust or Profit under the United States; but the Party convicted shall nevertheless be liable and subject to Indictment, Trial, Judgment and Punishment, according to law.

Congressional Elections: Times, Places, Manner

Section 4   The Times, Places and Manner of holding Elections for Senators and Representatives, shall be prescribed in each State by the Legislature thereof; but the Congress may at any time by Law make or alter such Regulations, except as to the Places of chusing Senators.

---

[1] Modified by the 16th Amendment
[2] Replaced by Section 2, 14th Amendment

[3] Repealed by the 17th Amendment
[4] Modified by the 17th Amendment

The Congress shall assemble at least once in every Year, and such Meeting shall be on the first Monday in December, unless they shall by Law appoint a different Day.[5]

Powers and Duties of the Houses

Section 5

Clause 1. Each House shall be the Judge of the Elections, Returns and Qualifications of its own Members, and a Majority of each shall constitute a Quorum to do Business; but a smaller Number may adjourn from day to day, and may be authorized to compel the Attendance of absent Members, in such Manner, and under the Penalties as each House may provide.

Clause 2. Each House may determine the Rules of its Proceedings, punish its Members for disorderly Behaviour, and, with the Concurrence of two thirds, expel a Member.

Clause 3. Each House shall keep a Journal of its Proceedings, and from time to time publish the same, excepting such Parts as may in their Judgment require Secrecy; and the Yeas and Nays of the Members of either House on any question shall, at the Desire of one fifth of those Present, be entered on the Journal.

Clause 4. Neither House, during the Session of Congress, shall, without the Consent of the other, adjourn for more than three days, nor to any other place than that in which the two Houses shall be sitting.

Rights of Members

Section 6

Clause 1. The Senators and Representatives shall receive a Compensation for their Services, to be ascertained by Law, and paid out of the Treasury of the United States. They shall in all Cases, except Treason, Felony and Breach of the Peace, be privileged from Arrest during their Attendance at the Session of their respective Houses, and in going to and returning from the same; and for any Speech or Debate in either House, they shall not be questioned in any other Place.

Clause 2. No Senator or Representative, shall, during the time for which he was elected, be appointed to any civil Office under the Authority of the United States, which shall have been created, or the Emoluments whereof shall have been encreased during such time; and no Person holding any Office under the United States, shall be a Member of either House during his Continuance in Office.

Legislative Powers: Bills and Resolutions

Section 7

Clause 1. All Bills for raising Revenue shall originate in the House of Representatives; but the Senate may propose or concur with Amendments as on other Bills.

Clause 2. Every Bill which shall have passed the House of Representatives and the Senate, shall, before it becomes a Law, be presented to the President of the United States; if he approve he shall sign it, but if not he shall return it, with his Objections to that House in which it shall have originated, who shall enter the Objections at large on their Journal, and proceed to reconsider it. If after such Reconsideration two thirds of that House shall agree to pass the Bill, it shall be sent, together with the Objections, to the other House, by which it shall likewise be reconsidered, and if approved by two thirds of that House, it shall become a Law. But in all such Cases the Votes of both Houses shall be determined by yeas and Nays, and the Names of the Persons voting for and against the Bill shall be entered on the Journal of each House respectively. If any Bill shall not be returned by the President within ten Days (Sundays excepted) after it shall have been presented to him, the Same shall be a Law, in like Manner as if he had signed it, unless the Congress by their Adjournment prevent its Return, in which Case it shall not be a Law.

Clause 3. Every Order, Resolution, or Vote to which the Concurrence of the Senate and House of Representatives may be necessary (except on a question of Adjournment) shall be presented to the President of the United States; and before the Same shall take Effect, shall be approved by him, or being disapproved by him, shall be repassed by two thirds of the Senate and House of Representatives, according to the Rules and Limitations prescribed in the Case of a Bill.

Powers of Congress

Section 8

Clause 1. The Congress shall have Power To lay and collect Taxes, Duties, Imposts and Excises, to pay the Debts and provide for the common Defence and general Welfare of the United States; but all Duties, Imposts and Excises shall be uniform throughout the United States.

To borrow Money on the Credit of the United States;

To regulate Commerce with foreign Nations, and among the several States, and with the Indian Tribes;

To establish an uniform Rule of Naturalization, and uniform Laws on the subject of Bankruptcies throughout the United States;

To coin Money, regulate the Value thereof, and of foreign Coin, and fix the Standard of Weights and Measures;

To provide for the Punishment of counterfeiting the Securities and current Coin of the United States;

To establish Post Offices and post Roads;

To promote the Progress of Science and useful Arts, by securing for limited Times to Authors and Inventors the exclusive Right to their respective Writings and Discoveries;

To constitute Tribunals inferior to the supreme Court;

To define and punish Piracies and Felonies committed on the high Seas, and Offences against the Law of Nations;

To declare War, grant Letters of Marque and Reprisal, and make Rules concerning Captures on Land and Water;

To raise and support Armies, but no Appropriation of Money to that Use shall be for a longer Term than two Years;

To provide and maintain a Navy;

To make Rules for the Government and Regulation of the land and naval Forces;

To provide for calling for the Militia to execute the Laws of the Union, suppress Insurrections and repel Invasions;

To provide for organizing, arming, and disciplining, the Militia, and for governing such Part of them as may be employed in the Service of the United States, reserving to the States respectively, the Appointment of the Officers, and the Authority of training the Militia according to the discipline prescribed by Congress;

Clause 2. To exercise exclusive Legislation in all Cases whatsoever, over such District (not exceeding ten Miles square) as may, by Cession of particular States, and the Acceptance of Congress, become the Seat of the Government of the United States, and to exercise like Authority over all Places purchased by the Consent of the Legislature of the State in which the Same shall be, for the Erection of Forts, Magazines, Arsenals, dock-Yards, and other needful Buildings;—And

Clause 3. To make all Laws which shall be necessary and proper for carrying into Execution the foregoing Powers, and all other Powers vested by this Constitution in the Government of the United States, or in any Department or Officer thereof.

Powers Denied to Congress

Section 9

Clause 1. The Migration of Importation of such Persons as any of the States now existing shall think proper to admit, shall not be prohibited by the Congress prior to the Year one thousand eight hundred and eight, but a Tax or Duty may be imposed on such Importation, not exceeding ten dollars for each Person.

Clause 2. The privilege of the Writ of Habeas Corpus shall not be suspended, unless when in Cases of Rebellion or Invasion the public Safety may require it.

---

[5]Changed by the 20th Amendment

Clause 3. No Bill of Attainder or ex post facto Laws shall be passed.

Clause 4. No Capitation, or other direct, Tax shall be laid, unless in Proportion to the Census or Enumeration herein before directed to be taken.[6]

Clause 5. No Tax or Duty shall be laid on Articles exported from any State.

Clause 6. No Preference shall be given by any Regulation of Commerce or Revenue to the Ports of one State over those of another; nor shall Vessels bound to, or from, one State, be obliged to enter, clear, or pay Duties in another.

Clause 7. No Money shall be drawn from the Treasury, but in Consequence of Appropriations made by Law; and a regular Statement and Account of the Receipts and Expenditures of all public Money shall be published from time to time.

Clause 8. No Title of Nobility shall be granted by the United States; And no Person holding any Office of Profit or Trust under them, shall, without the Consent of Congress, accept of any present, Emolument, Office, or Title, of any kind whatever, from any King, Prince, or foreign State.

Powers Denied to the States

Section 10

Clause 1. No State shall enter into any Treaty, Alliance, or Confederation; grant Letters of Marque and Reprisal; coin Money; emit Bills of Credit; make any Thing but gold and silver Coin a Tender in Payment of Debts; pass any Bill of Attainder, ex post facto Law, or Law impairing the Obligation of Contracts, or grant any Title of Nobility.

Clause 2. No State shall, without the Consent of the Congress, lay any Imposts or Duties on Imports or Exports, except what may be absolutely necessary for executing its inspection Laws: and the net Produce of all Duties and Imposts, laid by any State on Imports or Exports, shall be for the Use of the Treasury of the United States; and all such Laws shall be subject to the Revision and Controul of the Congress.

Clause 3. No State shall, without the Consent of Congress, lay any Duty of Tonnage, keep Troops, or Ships of War in time of Peace, enter into any Agreement or Compact with another State, or with a foreign Power, or engage in War, unless actually invaded, or in such imminent Danger as will not admit of Delay.

ARTICLE II—THE EXECUTIVE ARTICLE

Nature and Scope of Presidential Power

Section 1

Clause 1. The executive Power shall be vested in a President of the United States of America. He shall hold his Office during the Term of four Years and, together with the Vice President, chosen for the same Term, be elected as follows:

Clause 2. Each State shall appoint, in such Manner as the Legislature thereof may direct, a Number of Electors, equal to the whole Number of Senators and Representatives to which the State may be entitled in the Congress: but no Senator or Representative, or Person holding an Office of Trust or Profit under the United States, shall be appointed an Elector.

Clause 3. The Electors shall meet in their respective States, and vote by Ballot for two Persons, of whom one at least shall not be an Inhabitant of the same State with themselves. And they shall make a List of all the Persons voted for, and of the Number of Votes for each; which List they shall sign and certify, and transmit sealed to the Seat of the Government of the United States, directed to the President of the Senate. The President of the Senate shall, in the Presence of the Senate and House of Representatives, open all the Certificates, and the Votes shall then be counted. The Person having the greatest Number of Votes shall be the President, if such Number be a Majority of the whole Number of Electors appointed; and if there be more than one who have such Majority and have an equal Number of Votes, then the House of Representatives shall immediately chuse by Ballot one of them for President; and if no person have a Majority, then from the five highest on the List the said House shall in like Manner chuse the President. But in chusing the President, the Votes shall be taken by States, the Representation from each State having one Vote; A quorum for this Purpose shall consist of a Member or Members from two thirds of the States, and a Majority of all the States shall be necessary to a Choice. In every Case, after the Choice of the President, the person having the greatest Number of Votes of the Electors shall be the Vice President. But if there should remain two or more who have equal Vote, the Senate shall chuse from them by Ballot the Vice President.[7]

Clause 4. The Congress may determine the Time of chusing the Electors, and the Day on which they shall give their Votes; which Day shall be the same throughout the United States.

Clause 5. No Person except a natural born Citizen, or a Citizen of the United States, at the time of the Adoption of this Constitution, shall be eligible to the Office of President; neither shall any Person be eligible to that Office who shall not have attained to the Age of thirty five Years, and been fourteen Years a Resident within the United States.

Clause 6. In Case of the Removal of the President from Office, or of his Death, Resignation, or Inability to discharge the Powers and Duties of the said Office, the same shall devolve on the Vice President, and the Congress may by Law provide for the Case of Removal, Death, Resignation, or Inability, both of the President and Vice President, declaring what Officer shall then act as President, and such Officer shall act accordingly, until the Disability be removed, or a President shall be elected.[8]

Clause 7. The President shall, at stated Times, receive for his Services, a Compensation, which shall neither be encreased nor diminished during the Period of which he shall have been elected, and he shall not receive within that Period any other Emolument from the United States, or any of them.

Clause 8. Before he enter on the Execution of his Office, he shall take the following Oath or Affirmation:—"I do solemnly swear (or affirm) that I will faithfully execute the Office of President of the United States, and will to the best of my Ability, preserve, protect and defend the Constitution of the United States."

Powers and Duties of the President

Section 2

Clause 1. The President shall be the Commander in Chief of the Army and Navy of the United States, and of the Militia of the several States, when called into the actual Service of the United States, he may require the Opinion, in writing, of the principal Officer in each of the executive Departments, upon any Subject relating to the Duties of their respective Offices, and he shall have the Power to grant Reprieves and Pardons for Offences against the United States, except in Cases of Impeachment.

Clause 2. He shall have Power, by and with the Advice and Consent of the Senate to make Treaties, provided two thirds of the Senators present concur; and he shall nominate, and by and with the Advice and Consent of the Senate, shall appoint Ambassadors, other public Ministers and Consuls, Judges of the supreme Court, and all other Officers of the United States, whose Appointments are not herein otherwise provided for, and which shall be established by Law: but the Congress may by Law vest the Appointment of such inferior Officers, as they think proper, in the President alone, in the Courts of Law, or in the Heads of Departments.

Clause 3. The President shall have Power to fill up all Vacancies that may happen during the Recess of the Senate, by granting Commissions which shall expire at the End of their next Session.

---

[6]Modified by the 16th Amendment

[7]Changed by the 12th and 20th Amendments
[8]Modified by the 25th Amendment

Section 3 He shall from time to time give to the Congress Information of the State of the Union, and recommend to their Consideration such Measures as he shall judge necessary and expedient; he may, on extraordinary Occasions, convene both Houses, or either of them, and in Case of Disagreement between them, with Respect to the Time of Adjournment, he may adjourn them to such Time as he shall think proper; he shall receive Ambassadors and other public Ministers; he shall take Care that the Laws be faithfully executed, and shall Commission all the Officers of the United States.

Section 4 The President, Vice President and all civil Officers of the United States, shall be removed from Office on Impeachment for, and Conviction of, Treason, Bribery, or other High Crimes and Misdemeanors.

ARTICLE III—THE JUDICIAL ARTICLE

Judicial Power, Courts, Judges

Section 1 The judicial Power of the United States, shall be vested in one supreme Court, and in such inferior Courts as the Congress may from time to time ordain and establish. The Judges, both the supreme and inferior Courts, shall hold their Offices during good Behaviour, and shall, at stated Times, receive for their Services, a Compensation, which shall not be diminished during their Continuance in Office.

Jurisdiction

Section 2 The judicial Power shall extend to all Cases, in Law and Equity, arising under this Constitution, the Laws of the United States, and Treaties made, or which shall be made, under their Authority;—to all Cases affecting Ambassadors, other public Ministers and Consuls;—to all Cases of admiralty and maritime Jurisdiction;—to Controversies to which the United States shall be a Party;—to Controversies between two or more States; between a State and Citizens of another State;[9]—between Citizens of different States;—between Citizens of the same State claiming Lands under Grants of different States, and between a State, or the Citizens thereof, and foreign States, Citizens, or Subjects.

In all Cases affecting Ambassadors, other public Ministers and Consuls, and those in which a State shall be Party, the supreme Court shall have original Jurisdiction. In all the other Cases before mentioned, the supreme Court shall have appellate Jurisdiction, both as to Law and Fact, with such Exceptions, and under such Regulations as Congress shall make.

The Trial of all Crimes, except in Cases of Impeachment, shall be by Jury; and such Trial shall be held in the State where the said Crimes shall have been committed; but when not committed within any State, the Trial shall be at such Place or Places as the Congress may by Law have directed.

Treason

Section 3 Treason against the United States, shall consist only in levying War against them, or in adhering to their Enemies, giving them Aid and Comfort. No Persons shall be convicted of Treason unless on the Testimony of two Witnesses to the same overt Act, or on Confession in open Court.

The Congress shall have Power to declare the Punishment of Treason, but no Attainder of Treason shall work Corruption of Blood, or Forfeiture except during the Life of the Person attainted.

ARTICLE IV—INTERSTATE RELATIONS

Full Faith and Credit Clause

Section 1 Full Faith and Credit shall be given in each State to the public Acts, Records, and judicial Proceedings of every other State. And the Congress may by general Laws prescribe the Manner in which such Acts, Records and Proceedings shall be proved, and the Effect thereof.

Privileges and Immunities; Interstate Extradition

Section 2

Clause 1. The Citizens of each State shall be entitled to all Privileges and Immunities of Citizens in the several States.

Clause 2. A person charged in any State with Treason, Felony or other Crime, who shall flee from Justice, and be found in another State, shall on Demand of the executive Authority of the State from which he fled, be delivered up, to be removed to the State having jurisdiction of the Crime.

Clause 3. No person held to Service or Labour in one State, under the Laws thereof, escaping into another, shall, in Consequence of any Law or Regulation therein, be discharged from such Service or Labour, but shall be delivered up on Claim of the Party to whom such Service or Labour may be due.[10]

Admission of States

Section 3 New States may be admitted by the Congress into this Union; but no new State shall be formed or erected within the Jurisdiction of any other State; nor any State to be formed by the Junction of two or more States, or Parts of States, without the Consent of the Legislatures of the States concerned as well as of the Congress.

The Congress shall have Power to dispose of and make all needful Rules and Regulations respecting the Territory or other Property belonging to the United States; and nothing in this Constitution shall be so construed as to Prejudice any Claims of the United States, or of any particular State.

Republican Form of Government

Section 4 The United States shall guarantee to every State in this Union a Republican Form of Government, and shall protect each of them against Invasion; and on Application of the Legislature, or of the Executive (when the Legislature cannot be convened) against domestic Violence.

ARTICLE V—THE AMENDING POWER

The Congress, whenever two thirds of both Houses shall deem it necessary, shall propose Amendments to this Constitution, or, on the Application of the Legislatures of two thirds of several States, shall call a Convention for proposing Amendments, which, in either Case, shall be valid to all Intents and Purposes, as Part of this Constitution, when ratified by the Legislatures of three fourths of the several States, or by Conventions in three fourths thereof, as the one or the other Mode of Ratification may be proposed by the Congress; Provided that no Amendment which may be made prior to the Year One thousand eight hundred and eight shall in any Manner affect the first and fourth Clauses in the Ninth Section of the first Article; and that no State, without its Consent, shall be deprived of its equal Suffrage in the Senate.

ARTICLE VI—THE SUPREMACY ACT

Clause 1. All Debts contracted and Engagements entered into, before the Adoption of this Constitution, shall be as valid against the United States under the Constitution, as under the Confederation.

Clause 2. This Constitution, and the Laws of the United States which shall be made in Pursuance thereof; and all Treaties made, or which shall be made, under the Authority of the United States, shall be the supreme Law of the Land; and the Judges in every State shall be bound thereby, any Thing in the Constitution or Laws of any State to the Contrary notwithstanding.

Clause 3. The Senators and Representatives before mentioned, and the Members of the several State Legislatures, and all executive and judicial Officers, both of the United States and of the several States, shall

---

[9]Modified by the 11th Amendment

[10]Repealed by the 13th Amendment

50

be bound by Oath or Affirmation, to support this Constitution; but no religious Test shall ever be required as a Qualification to any Office or public Trust under the United States.

ARTICLE VII—RATIFICATION

The Ratification of the Conventions of nine States, shall be sufficient for the Establishment of this Constitution between the States so ratifying the Same.

Done in Convention by the Unanimous Consent of the States present the Seventeenth Day of September in the Year of our Lord one thousand seven hundred and Eighty seven and of the Independence of the United States of America the Twelfth In Witness whereof We have hereunto subscribed our Names.

AMENDMENTS

The Bill of Rights

[The first ten amendments were ratified on December 15, 1791, and form what is known as the "Bill of Rights."]

Amendment 1—Religion, Speech, Assembly, and Politics

Congress shall make no law respecting an establishment of religion, or prohibiting the free exercise thereof; or abridging the freedom of speech, or of the press; or the right of the people peaceably to assemble, and to petition the government for a redress of grievances.

Amendment 2—Militia and the Right to Bear Arms

A well-regulated Militia, being necessary to the security of a free State, the right of the people to keep and bear Arms, shall not be infringed.

Amendment 3—Quartering of Soldiers

No Soldier shall, in time of peace be quartered in any house, without the consent of the Owner, nor in time of war, but in manner to be prescribed by law.

Amendment 4—Searches and Seizures

The right of the people to be secure in their persons, houses, papers, and effects, against unreasonable searches and seizures, shall not be violated, and no Warrants shall issue, but upon probable cause, supported by Oath or affirmation, and particularly describing the place to be searched, and the persons or things to be seized.

Amendment 5—Grand Juries, Self-Incrimination, Double Jeopardy, Due Process, and Eminent Domain

No person shall be held to answer for a capital, or otherwise infamous crime, unless on a presentment or indictment of a Grand jury, except in cases arising in the land or naval forces, or in the Militia, when in actual service in time of War or public danger; nor shall any person be subject for the same offence to be twice put in jeopardy of life or limb; nor shall be compelled in any criminal case to be a witness against himself, nor be deprived of life, liberty, or property, without due process of law; nor shall private property be taken for public use, without just compensation.

Amendment 6—Criminal Court Procedures

In all criminal prosecutions, the accused shall enjoy the right to a speedy and public trial, by an impartial jury of the State and district wherein the crime shall have been committed, which district shall have been previously ascertained by law, and to be informed of the nature and cause of the accusation; to be confronted with the witnesses against him; to have compulsory process for obtaining Witnesses in his favor, and to have the Assistance of Counsel for his defense.

Amendment 7—Trial by Jury in Common Law Cases

In Suits at common law, where the value in controversy shall exceed twenty dollars, the right of trial by jury shall be preserved, and no fact tried by a jury shall be otherwise re-examined in any Court of the United States, than according to the rules of the common law.

Amendment 8—Bail, Cruel and Unusual Punishment

Excessive bail shall not be required, nor excessive fines imposed, nor cruel and unusual punishments inflicted.

Amendment 9—Rights Retained by the People

The enumeration in the Constitution, of certain rights, shall not be construed to deny or disparage others retained by the people.

Amendment 10—Reserved Powers of the States

The powers not delegated to the United States by the Constitution, nor prohibited by it to the States, are reserved to the States respectively, or to the people.

Amendment 11—Suits Against the States

[Ratified February 7, 1795]

The Judicial power of the United States shall not be construed to extend to any suit in law or equity, commenced or prosecuted against one of the United States by Citizens of another State, or by Citizens or Subjects of any Foreign State.

Amendment 12—Election of the President

[Ratified June 15, 1804]

The Electors shall meet in their respective states, and vote by ballot for President and Vice-President, one of whom, at least, shall not be an inhabitant of the same state with themselves; they shall name in their ballots the person voted for as President, and in distinct ballots the person voted for as Vice-President, and they shall make distinct lists of all persons voted for as President, and of all persons voted for as Vice-President, and of the number of votes for each, which lists they shall sign and certify, and transmit sealed to the seat of the government of the United States, directed to the President of the Senate;—The President of the Senate shall, in presence of the Senate and House of Representatives, open all the certificates and the votes shall then be counted;—The person having the greatest number of votes for President, shall be the President, if such number be a majority of the whole number of Electors appointed; and if no person have such majority, then from the persons having the highest numbers not exceeding three on the list of those voted for as President, the House of Representatives shall choose immediately, by ballot, the President. But in choosing the President, the votes shall be taken by states, the representation from each state having one vote; a quorum for this purpose shall consist of a member or members from two-thirds of the states, and a majority of all states shall be necessary to a choice. And if the House of Representatives shall not choose a President whenever the right of choice shall devolve upon them, before the fourth day of March next following, then the Vice-President shall act as President, as in the case of the death or other constitutional disability of the President.[11] The person having the greatest

---

[11]Changed by the 20th Amendment

number of votes as Vice-President, shall be the Vice-President, if such a number be a majority of the whole numbers of Electors appointed, and if no person have a majority, then from the two highest numbers on the list, the Senate shall choose the Vice-President; a quorum for the purpose shall consist of two-thirds of the whole number of Senators, and a majority of the whole number shall be necessary to a choice. But no person constitutionally ineligible to the office of President shall be eligible to that of Vice-President of the United States.

Amendment 13—Prohibition of Slavery

[Ratified December 6, 1865]

Section 1 Neither slavery nor involuntary servitude, except as a punishment for crime whereof the party shall have been duly convicted, shall exist within the United States, or any place subject to their jurisdiction.

Section 2 Congress shall have power to enforce this article by appropriate legislation.

Amendment 14—Citizenship, Due Process, and Equal Protection of the Laws

[Ratified July 9, 1868]

Section 1 All persons born or naturalized in the United States, and subject to the jurisdiction thereof, are citizens of the United States and of the State wherein they reside. No State shall make or enforce any law which shall abridge the privileges or immunities of citizens of the United States; nor shall any State deprive any person of life, liberty, or property, without due process of law; nor deny to any person within its jurisdiction the equal protection of the laws.

Section 2 Representatives shall be apportioned among the several States according to their respective numbers, counting the whole number of persons in each State, excluding Indians not taxed. But when the right to vote at any election for the choice of electors for President and Vice President of the United States, Representatives in Congress, the Executive and Judicial officers of a State, or the members of the Legislature thereof, is denied to any of the male inhabitants of such State, being twenty-one[12] years of age, and citizens of the United States, or in any way abridged, except for participation in rebellion, or other crime, the basis of representation therein shall be reduced in the proportion which the number of such male citizens shall bear to the whole number of male citizens twenty-one years of age in such State.

Section 3 No person shall be a Senator or Representative in Congress, or elector of President and Vice President, or hold any office, civil or military, under the United States, or under any State, who, having previously taken an oath, as a member of Congress, or as an officer of the United States, or as a member of any State legislature, or as an executive or judicial officer of any State, to support the Constitution of the United States, shall have engaged in insurrection or rebellion against the same, or given aid or comfort to the enemies thereof. But Congress may by a vote of two-thirds of each House, remove such disability.

Section 4 The validity of the public debt of the United States, authorized by law, including debts incurred for payment of pensions and bounties for services in suppressing insurrection or rebellion, shall not be questioned. But neither the United States nor any State shall assume or pay any debt or obligation incurred in aid of insurrection or rebellion against the United States, or any claim for the loss or emancipation of any slave; but all such debts, obligations and claims shall be held illegal and void.

Section 5 The Congress shall have power to enforce, by appropriate legislation, the provisions of this article.

Amendment 15—The Right to Vote

[Ratified February 3, 1870]

Section 1 The right of citizens of the United States to vote shall not be denied or abridged by the United States or by any State on account of race, color, or previous condition of servitude.

Section 2 The Congress shall have power to enforce this article by appropriate legislation.

Amendment 16—Income Taxes

[Ratified February 3, 1913]

The Congress shall have power to lay and collect taxes on incomes, from whatever source derived, without apportionment among the several States, and without regard to any census or enumeration.

Amendment 17—Direct Election of Senators

[Ratified April 8, 1913]

The Senate of the United States shall be composed of two Senators from each State, elected by the people thereof, for six years; and each Senator shall have one vote. The electors in each State shall have the qualifications requisite for electors of the most numerous branch of the State legislatures.

When vacancies happen in the representation of any State in the Senate, the executive authority of such State shall issue writs of election to fill such vacancies: Provided, That the Legislature of any State may empower the executive thereof to make temporary appointment until the people fill the vacancies by election as the legislature may direct. This amendment shall not be so construed as to affect the election or term of any Senator chosen before it becomes valid as part of the Constitution.

Amendment 18—Prohibition

[Ratified January 16, 1919. Repealed December 5, 1933 by Amendment 21]

Section 1 After one year from the ratification of this article the manufacture, sale, or transportation of intoxicating liquors within, the importation thereof into, or the exportation thereof from the United States and all territory subject to the jurisdiction thereof for beverage purposes is hereby prohibited.

Section 2 The Congress and the several states shall have concurrent power to enforce this article by appropriate legislation.

Section 3 This article shall be inoperative unless it shall have been ratified as an amendment to the Constitution by the legislatures of the several states, as provided in the Constitution, within seven years from the date of the submission hereof to the States by the Congress.[13]

Amendment 19—For Women's Suffrage

[Ratified August 18, 1920]

The right of the citizens of the United States to vote shall not be denied or abridged by the United States or by any State on account of sex.

Congress shall have power, by appropriate legislation, to enforce the provision of this article.

---

[12]Changed by the 26th Amendment

[13]Repealed by the 21st Amendment

Amendment 20—The Lame Duck Amendment

[Ratified January 23, 1933]

Section 1 The terms of the President and Vice President shall end at noon on the 20th day of January, and the terms of the Senators and Representatives at noon on the 3rd day of January, of the years in which such terms would have ended if this article had not been ratified; and the terms of their successors shall then begin.

Section 2 The Congress shall assemble at least once in every year, and such meeting shall begin at noon on the 3rd day of January, unless they shall by law appoint a different day.

Section 3 If, at the time fixed for the beginning of the term of the President, the President elect shall have died, the Vice President elect shall become President. If a President shall not have been chosen before the time fixed for the beginning of his term, or if the President elect shall have failed to qualify, then the Vice President elect shall act as President until a President shall have qualified; and the Congress may by law provide for the case wherein neither a President elect nor a Vice President elect shall have qualified, declaring who shall then act as President, or the manner in which one who is to act shall be selected, and such person shall act accordingly until a President or Vice President shall have qualified.

Section 4 The Congress may by law provide for the case of the death of any of the persons from whom the House of Representatives may choose a President whenever the right of choice shall have developed upon them, and for the case of the death of any of the persons from whom the Senate may choose a Vice President whenever the right of choice shall have devolved upon them.

Section 5 Sections 1 and 2 shall take effect on the 15th day of October following the ratification of this article.

Section 6 This article shall be inoperative unless it shall have been ratified as an amendment to the Constitution by the legislatures of three-fourths of the several States within seven years from the date of its submission.

Amendment 21—Repeal of Prohibition

[Ratified December 5, 1933]

Section 1 The eighteenth article of amendment to the Constitution of the United States is hereby repealed.

Section 2 The transportation or importation into any State, Territory, or Possession of the United States for delivery or use therein of intoxicating liquors, in violation of the laws thereof, is hereby prohibited.

Section 3 This article shall be inoperative unless it shall have been ratified as an amendment to the Constitution by conventions in the several States, as provided in the Constitution, within seven years from the date of the submission hereof to the States by the Congress.

Amendment 22—Number of Presidential Terms

[Ratified February 27, 1951]

Section 1 No person shall be elected to the office of the President more than twice, and no person who has held the office of President, or acted as President, for more than two years of a term to which some other person was elected President shall be elected to the Office of the President more than once. But this Article shall not apply to any person holding the office of President when this article was proposed by the Congress, and shall not prevent any person who may be holding the office of President, or acting as President, during the term within which this Article becomes operative from holding the office of President or acting as President during the remainder of such term.

Section 2 This Article shall be inoperative unless it shall have been ratified as an amendment to the Constitution by the legislatures of three-fourths of the several states within seven years from the date of its submission to the States by the Congress.

Amendment 23—Presidential Electors for the District of Columbia

[Ratified March 29, 1961]

Section 1 The District constituting the seat of Government of the United States shall appoint in such manner as the Congress may direct:
    A number of electors of President and Vice President equal to the whole number of Senators and Representatives in Congress to which the District would be entitled if it were a State, but in no event more than the least populous State; they shall be in addition to those appointed by the States, but they shall be considered, for the purposes of the election of President and Vice President, to be electors appointed by a State; and they shall meet in the District and perform such duties as provided by the twelfth article of amendment.

Section 2 The Congress shall have power to enforce this article by appropriate legislation.

Amendment 24—The Anti-Poll Tax Amendment

[Ratified January 23, 1964]

Section 1 The right of citizens of the United States to vote in any primary or other election for President or Vice President, for electors for President or Vice President, or for Senator or Representative in Congress, shall not be denied or abridged by the United States or any State by reason of failure to pay any poll tax or other tax.

Section 2 The Congress shall have power to enforce this article by appropriate legislation.

Amendment 25—Presidential Disability, Vice Presidential Vacancies

[Ratified February 10, 1967]

Section 1 In case of the removal of the President from office or his death or resignation, the Vice President shall become President.

Section 2 Whenever there is a vacancy in the office of the Vice President, the President shall nominate a Vice President who shall take the office upon confirmation by a majority vote of both houses of Congress.

Section 3 Whenever the President transmits to the President pro tempore of the Senate and the Speaker of the House of Representatives his written declaration that he is unable to discharge the powers and duties of his office, and until he transmits to them a written declaration to the contrary, such powers and duties shall be discharged by the Vice President as Acting President.

Section 4 Whenever the Vice President and a majority of either the principal officers of the executive departments, or of such other body as Congress may by law provide, transmit to the President pro tempore of the Senate and the Speaker of the House of Representatives their written declaration that the President is unable to discharge the powers and duties of his office, the Vice President shall immediately assume the powers and duties of the office as Acting President.
    Thereafter, when the President transmits to the President pro tempore of the Senate and the Speaker of the House of Representatives his

written declaration that no inability exists, he shall resume the powers and duties of his office unless the Vice President and a majority of either the principal officers of the executive departments, or of such other body as Congress may by law provide, transmit within four days to the President pro tempore of the Senate and the Speaker of the House of Representatives their written declaration that the President is unable to discharge the powers and duties of his office. Thereupon Congress shall decide the issue, assembling within forty-eight hours for that purpose if not in session. If the Congress, within twenty-one days after receipt of the latter written declaration, or, if Congress is not in session, within twenty-one days after Congress is required to assemble, determines by two-thirds vote of both houses that the President is unable to discharge the powers and duties of his office, the Vice President shall continue to discharge the same as Acting President; otherwise, the President shall resume the powers and duties of his office.

Amendment 26—Eighteen-Year-Old Vote

[Ratified July 1, 1971]

Section 1   The right of citizens of the United States, who are eighteen years of age, or older, to vote shall not be denied or abridged by the United States or by any State on account of age.

Section 2   The Congress shall have power to enforce this article by appropriate legislation.

Amendment 27—Congressional Salaries

[Ratified May 7, 1992]

No law, varying the compensation for the services of the Senators and Representatives, shall take effect, until an election of Representatives shall be intervened.

AMERICAN FEDERALISM

3

Responding to opposition to the Massachusetts supreme court's ruling that its state constitution forbids discrimination against same-sex couples seeking to marry, President George W. Bush said "if necessary" he would "support a constitutional amendment which would honor marriage between a man and a woman." But he added that the issue was basically a state matter, not a federal one, and he would not oppose "whatever legal arrangements people want to make."[1] That disappointed some of his conservative supporters because Vermont and California already recognize "civil unions" and "domestic partnerships" that confer the same legal benefits—health, insurance, and death benefits—for gay couples as for heterosexuals.

Although the Massachusetts court's decision may be overridden by a proposed state constitutional amendment in 2006, it renewed a national debate over the U.S. Constitution's full faith and credit clause. In 1996, Congress passed and President Bill Clinton signed the Defense of Marriage Act (DOMA), which relieves states of any obligation to recognize same-sex marriages even if they are recognized in other states and stipulates that the national government only recognizes heterosexual marriages for federal benefits such as Social Security.[2] Supporters of the law argue that the Constitution gives Congress the responsibility for prescribing the manner in which states are to comply with the full faith and credit clause. But the DOMA is likely to be challenged in the courts for going beyond the power of Congress to provide states with an exemption from their constitutional obligation under the full faith and credit clause.

The Supreme Court has not addressed the issue squarely and precedents provide no clear answer. The Court has held that states must comply with other states' judicial decisions,

TIME LINE

AMERICAN FEDERALISM

1781	Articles of Confederation establish state as preeminent over federal government
1788	Constitution ratified, replacing the Articles of Confederation
1791	Bill of Rights ratified by the states
1803	Louisiana Purchase greatly expands the size of the United States
1819	*McCulloch* v. *Maryland* interprets "necessary and proper" clause broadly
1824	*Gibbons* v. *Ogden* establishes congressional control over interstate commerce
1860	South Carolina is the first state to secede from the United States
1865	Civil War ends
1877	End of Reconstruction
1916	Federal Highway Act is first large-scale cash grant to states
1965	Voting Rights Act ends racial discrimination in voting practices in the states
1972	General revenue sharing increases funds available to state
1995	Congress prohibits "unfunded mandates," costing over $50 million
1996	Welfare reform reduces restrictions on states' use of welfare funds
2004	Massachusetts become first state to allow marriage of same-sex couples

devolution revolution
The effort to slow the growth of the federal government by returning many functions to the states.

but not necessarily with their other laws or administrative decisions. In light of recent Court rulings tilting toward states' rights and, as one scholar argues, "the fact that marriage has traditionally been an almost exclusive sphere of state authority, the Court would likely maintain the noncentralized and dual nature of American domestic relations that exist today, and allow the states to decide whether to recognize same-sex marriages."[3] However, similar DOMA laws in 38 states are likely to be challenged as well,[4] in light of the ruling in *Lawrence* v. *Texas*[5] invalidating state laws criminalizing homosexual sodomy, dissenting Justice Antonin Scalia has warned that states may no longer be able to ban same-sex marriages.

The controversy over same-sex marriages underscores the continuing debate over federalism. How do states interact with each other and with the national government? What is the proper balance of power between the national government and the states on providing homeland security, combating illegal immigration, improving education, and fighting corporate corruption and environmental pollution?

Since the founding of the Republic, Americans have debated the relationship of the national government to the states.[6] In 1787, the Federalists defended the creation of a strong national government, whereas the Antifederalists warned that a strong national government would overshadow the states. More recently, Republicans have led the charge against big government, urging the return of many functions to the states—a **devolution revolution**[7]—and they have had some success, such as when President Bill Clinton agreed to turn over more responsibilities for welfare to the states.

Federalism has recently emerged as a hot topic in other countries as well. Western European countries have formed the European Union (EU), with member nations giving up considerable authority over the regulation of businesses and labor, adopting a common monetary policy and currency (the euro), the addition in 2004 of ten Central and Eastern European countries, and debates over the ratification of a Treaty Establishing a Constitution for Europe.[8]

Heightened interest in federalism also comes from demands for greater autonomy for ethnic nationalities. The Canadian federal system strains under the demands of the French-speaking province of Quebec for special status and even independence. In the United Kingdom, devolution has occurred with Scotland, Northern Ireland, and Wales gaining their own parliaments or assemblies with considerable authority and, in the case of Scotland, limited power to tax. Belgium, Italy, and Spain have been devolving powers from their central governments to regional governments.

In contrast to some countries, the United States has had a relatively peaceful experience with the shifting balances of power under federalism. Since the New Deal in the 1930s, power and responsibility have drifted from the states to the national government. Although presidents from Richard Nixon to Bill Clinton slowed the growth of the national government, it was not until the late 1990s that the Republican-controlled Congress sought major reforms that heated the debate over federalism. As with welfare reform in 1996, Congress promoted decentralization in education with the Educational Flexibility Partnership Demonstration Act of 1999, authorizing the secretary of education to grant states waivers from federal rules setting educational goals. Still, in spite of such moves toward decentralization, Congress continues to expand federal law by making such offenses as the burning of churches, carjacking, and acts of terrorism federal crimes, even though they are already state and local crimes.

After more than half a century, the Supreme Court has placed some constraints on congressional powers in the name of federalism.[9] Like Congress, however, the Court's recent record on federalism is mixed. In spite of recent rulings holding that Congress exceeded its powers and may not authorize individuals to sue states to enforce federal laws,[10] the Court nevertheless ruled that state welfare programs may not restrict benefits to new residents to what they would have received in the states from which they moved[11] and that Congress may restrict states from selling drivers' personal information.[12]

Debates over federalism resemble those over whether "the glass is half-empty or half-full."[13] People who think they can get more of what they want from the national

Supporters applaud the announcement of a ruling by the Massachusetts Supreme Judicial Court on November 18, 2003, confirming that the state constitution does not bar same-sex couples from marrying. The issue of same-sex marriage illustrates how the debate over federalism is still a vital issue in the United States today. Proponents of same-sex marriage argue that the issue should remain in the hands of the individual states, whereas opponents want the federal government to propose an amendment to the Constitution defining marriage as a union specifically between a male and a female.

government usually advocate national action. Those who view states as more responsive and accountable argue for decentralization. Although Republicans generally favor action at the state level and Democrats tend to support action by the national government, neither party is consistent in its positions on the balance of power between the national government and the states. It depends on the issue at stake.

In this chapter, we first define federalism and its advantages. We then look at the constitutional basis for our federal system and how court decisions and political developments have shaped, and continue to shape, federalism in the United States.

DEFINING FEDERALISM

Scholars argue and wars (including our own Civil War) have been fought over what federalism means. One scholar counted 267 definitions.[14]

Federalism, as we define it, is a form of government in which a constitution distributes powers between a central government and subdivisional governments—usually called states, provinces, or republics—giving to both the national government and the regional governments substantial responsibilities and powers, including the power to collect taxes and to pass and enforce laws regulating the conduct of individuals.

The mere existence of both national and state governments does not make a system federal. What is important is that a *constitution divides governmental powers between the national government and the subdivisional governments,* giving clearly defined functions to each. Neither the central nor the subdivisional government receives its powers from the other; both derive them from a common source—the Constitution. No ordinary act of legislation at either the national or the state level can change this constitutional distribution of powers. Both levels of government operate through their own agents and exercise power directly over individuals.

federalism
Constitutional arrangement whereby power is distributed between a central government and subdivisional governments, called states in the United States. The national and the subdivisional governments both exercise direct authority over individuals.

At the official opening of Scotland's parliament on July 1, 1999, Queen Elizabeth was presented with the Scottish crown. The 129-member assembly is Scotland's first parliament in nearly 300 years.

Our definition of federalism is broad enough to include competing visions of it and the range of federal systems around the world. The following are some of the leading visions of federalism.

- *Dual federalism* views the Constitution as giving a limited list of powers—primarily foreign policy and national defense—to the national government, leaving the rest to sovereign states. Each level of government is dominant within its own sphere. The Supreme Court serves as the umpire between the national government and the states in disputes over which level of government has responsibility for a particular activity. During our first hundred years, dual federalism was the favored interpretation given by the Supreme Court.

- *Cooperative federalism* stresses federalism as a system of intergovernmental relations in delivering governmental goods and services to the people and calls for cooperation among various levels of government.

- *Marble cake federalism*, a term coined by political scientist Morton Grodzins, conceives of federalism as a marble cake in which all levels of government are involved in a variety of issues and programs, rather than a layer cake, or dual federalism, with fixed divisions between layers or levels of government.[15]

- *Competitive federalism*, a term first used by political scientist Thomas R. Dye, views the national government, 50 states, and thousands of other units as competing with each other over ways to put together packages of services and taxes. Applying the analogy of the marketplace, Dye emphasizes that at the state and local levels, we have some choice about which state and city we want to "use," just as we have choices about what kind of automobile we drive.[16]

- *Permissive federalism* implies that although federalism provides "a sharing of power and authority between the national and state government, the states' share rests upon the permission and permissiveness of the national government."[17]

GLOBAL *Perceptions*

QUESTION: Please indicate whether you completely agree, mostly agree, mostly disagree, or completely disagree with the following statement: The government controls too much of our daily lives.

The United States has more governments (federal, state, local, school districts, and special authorities) than any other country in the world. Yet, Americans are no more likely than citizens of other western democracies to believe that government in general controls too much of their daily lives. In fact, they have become less likely to agree with the statement since the early 1990s, even though the number of U.S. governments has increased.

The Pew survey suggests that people respond more to what government does by way of regulating their daily lives than the number of governments. Thus, Russians were the most likely to say that government has become less involved in their daily lives, which reflects the change from communism to a more democratic process.

SOURCE: Pew Global Attitudes Project, 2003

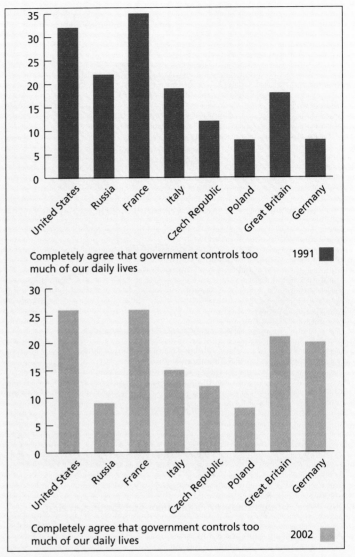

Completely agree that government controls too much of our daily lives — 1991

Completely agree that government controls too much of our daily lives — 2002

SOURCE: Pew Global Attitudes Project, p. 110

■ *"Our federalism,"* championed by Ronald Reagan, Justices Sandra Day O'Connor, Antonin Scalia, and Clarence Thomas, along with Chief Justice William Rehnquist, presumes that the power of the federal government is limited in favor of the broad powers reserved to the states.

Federal nations are diverse and include Australia, Canada, Germany, Russia, and Switzerland. Although their number is not large, they "cover more than half of the land surface of the globe and include almost half of the world's population."[18] Federalism thus appears well suited for large countries with large populations, even though only 21 of the world's approximately 185 nation-states claim to be federal.

Constitutionally, the federal system of the United States consists of only the national government and the 50 states. "Cities are not," the Supreme Court reminded us, "sovereign entities." But in a practical sense, we are a nation of almost 88,000 governmental units, from the national government to the school board district. This does not make for a tidy, efficient, easy-to-understand system; yet, as we shall see, it has its virtues.

Government Under the Articles of Confederation, 1781–1788

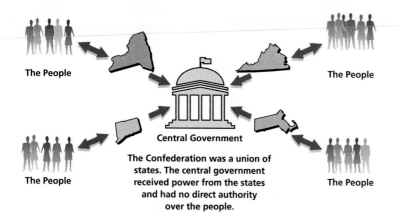

The People

The People

Central Government

The People

The People

The Confederation was a union of states. The central government received power from the states and had no direct authority over the people.

Government Under the U.S. Constitution (Federation) Since 1789

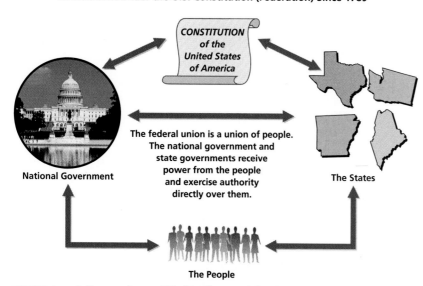

CONSTITUTION of the United States of America

National Government

The States

The federal union is a union of people. The national government and state governments receive power from the people and exercise authority directly over them.

The People

FIGURE 3–1 A Comparison of Federalism and Confederation.

Alternatives to Federalism

Among the alternatives to federalism are **unitary systems** of government, in which a constitution vests all governmental power in the central government. The central government, if it so chooses, may delegate authority to constituent units, but what it delegates it may take away. France, Israel, and the Philippines have unitary governments. In the United States, state constitutions usually create this kind of relationship between the state and its local governments.

At the other extreme from unitary governments are **confederations**, in which sovereign nations, through a constitutional compact, create a central government but carefully limit the power of the central government and do not give it the power to regulate the conduct of individuals directly. The central government makes regulations for the constituent governments, but it exists and operates only at their direction. The 13 states under the Articles of Confederation operated in this manner (see Figure 3–1), as did the southern Confederacy during the Civil War. The European Union is another example, though debates over its integration continue.[19]

Why Federalism?

In 1787, federalism was an obvious choice. Confederation had been tried but proved unsuccessful. A unitary system was out of the question because most people were too deeply attached to their state governments to permit subordination to central rule. Federalism was, and still is, thought to be ideally suited to the needs of a heterogeneous people spread over a large continent, suspicious of concentrated power, and desiring unity but not uniformity. Federalism offered, and still offers, many advantages for such a people.

FEDERALISM CHECKS THE GROWTH OF TYRANNY   Although in the rest of the world, federal forms have not always been notably successful in preventing tyranny, and many unitary governments are democratic, Americans tend to associate freedom with federalism.[20] As James Madison pointed out in *The Federalist,* No. 10: If "factious leaders . . . kindle a flame within their particular states," national leaders can check the spread of the "conflagration through the other states" (*The Federalist,* No. 10, appears in the Appendix of this book). Moreover, when one political party loses control of the national government, it is still likely to hold office in a number of states. It can then regroup, develop new policies and new leaders, and continue to challenge the party in power at the national level.

Such diffusion of power creates its own problems. It makes it difficult for a national majority to carry out a program of action, and it permits those who control state governments to frustrate the policies enacted by Congress and administered by federal agencies. To the framers, these obstacles were an advantage. They feared that a single interest group might capture the national government and suppress the interests of others. Of course, the size of the nation and the many interests within it are the greatest obstacles to the formation of a single-interest majority—a point often overlooked today

unitary system
Constitutional arrangement in which power is concentrated in a central government.

confederation
Constitutional arrangement in which sovereign nations or states, by compact, create a central government but carefully limit its power and do not give it direct authority over individuals.

but emphasized by Madison in *The Federalist,* No. 10. If such a majority were to occur, having to work through a federal system would check its power.

FEDERALISM ALLOWS UNITY WITHOUT UNIFORMITY   National politicians and parties do not have to iron out every difference on every issue that divides us, whether it be abortion, same-sex marriage, gun control, capital punishment, welfare financing, or assisted suicide. Instead, these issues are debated in state legislatures, county courthouses, and city halls. But this advantage of federalism is becoming less significant as many local issues become national ones and as events in one state immediately affect policy debates at the national level.

FEDERALISM ENCOURAGES EXPERIMENTATION   Supreme Court Justice Louis Brandeis pointed out that state governments provide great "laboratories" for public policy experimentation; states may serve as proving grounds. If they adopt programs that fail, the negative effects are limited; if programs succeed, they can be adopted by other states and by the national government. Georgia, for example, was the first state to permit 18-year-olds to vote; Wisconsin experimented with putting welfare recipients to work; California pioneered air pollution control programs; Oregon and Hawaii created new systems for the delivery of health care. Nevada is the only state, so far, to legalize statewide gambling, but aspects of legalized casino gambling are now found in more than half the states. Not all innovations, even those considered successful, become widely adopted. Nebraska is the only state to have a unicameral legislature, although in recent years both Minnesota and California considered adopting one.

CHANGING FACE OF AMERICAN POLITICS

MINORITIES AND WOMEN ARE GAINING GROUND IN THE WORKFORCE

In the last few decades minorities and women have made significant gains in prestigious professions, especially as physcians and lawyers, but white males still dominate in certain highly visible occupations like police and firefighters.

Civil Workforce by Gender and Race—As a Percentage of Total Occupation

Occupation	Year	Men	Women	White	Black	Hispanic	Other	Total
Lawyers	1980	86%	14%	95%	3%	2%	1%	468,378
	1990	76	24	93	3	2	1	697,272
	2000	71	29	89	4	3	2	871,115
Physicians	1980	87	13	83	3	4	10	421,985
	1990	79	21	81	4	5	11	571,319
	2000	73	27	74	4	5	17	705,960
Firefighters	1980	99	1	89	6	4	1	186,867
	1990	97	3	84	9	5	2	216,914
	2000	96	4	82	8	6	3	242,395
Police Officers	1980	93	7	85	9	4	1	379,758
	1990	87	13	79	12	7	2	492,107
	2000	87	13	76	12	9	4	597,925

SOURCE: Census Bureau, 2000 Census; D'Vera Cohn and Sarah Cohen, "Minorities, Women Gain Professionally," *The Washington Post* A1 (December 30, 2003).

**NUMBER OF GOVERNMENTS
IN THE UNITED STATES**

National	1
States	50
Counties	3,034
Municipalities	19,431
Townships or towns	16,506
School districts	13,522
Special districts	35,356
Total	87,900

SOURCE: U.S. Bureau of the Census, *Statistical Abstract of the United States,* available at http://wwwcensus.gov/prod/2003pubs/02statab/stlocgov.pdf.

FEDERALISM KEEPS GOVERNMENT CLOSER TO THE PEOPLE   By providing numerous arenas for decision making, federalism involves many people and helps keep government closer to the people. Every day, thousands of Americans are busy serving on city councils, school boards, neighborhood associations, and planning commissions. Since they are close to the issues and have firsthand knowledge of what needs to be done, they may be more responsive to problems than the experts in Washington.

We should be cautious, however, about generalizing that state and local governments are necessarily closer to the people than the national government. True, more people are involved in local and state politics than in national affairs, and confidence in state governments has increased while respect for national agencies has diminished. A majority of the public often appears dissatisfied with the federal government. Yet national and international affairs are on people's minds more often than state or local politics. And fewer voters participate in state and local elections than in congressional and presidential elections.

THE CONSTITUTIONAL STRUCTURE OF AMERICAN FEDERALISM

Dividing powers and responsibilities between the national and state governments has resulted in thousands of court decisions, hundreds of books, and endless speeches to explain them—and even then the division lacks precise definition. Nonetheless, a basic understanding of how the Constitution divides these powers and responsibilities and of what obligations are imposed on each level of government is helpful (see Table 3–1).

The formal constitutional framework of our federal system may be stated relatively simply:

1. The national government has only those powers delegated to it by the Constitution (with the important exception of the inherent power over foreign affairs).

2. Within the scope of its operations, the national government is supreme.

3. The state governments have the powers not delegated to the central government, except those denied to them by the Constitution and their state constitutions.

TABLE 3–1   THE FEDERAL DIVISION OF POWERS

Powers Delegated to the National Government	Some Powers Reserved for the States	Some Concurrent Powers Shared by the National and State Governments
• Express powers stated in the Constitution	• To create a republican form of government	• To tax citizens and businesses
• Implied powers that may be inferred from the express powers	• To charter local governments	• To borrow and spend money
• Inherent powers that allow the nation to present a united front to foreign powers	• To conduct elections	• To establish courts
	• To exercise all powers not delegated to the national government or denied to the states by the Constitution	• To pass and enforce laws
		• To protect civil rights

4. Some powers are specifically denied to both the national and state governments; others are specifically denied only to the states; still others are denied to the national government but not the states.

Powers of the National Government

The Constitution, chiefly in the first three articles, delegates legislative, executive, and judicial powers to the national government. In addition to these **express powers**, such as the power to regulate interstate commerce and to appropriate funds, Congress has assumed constitutionally **implied powers**, such as the power to create banks, which are inferred from the express powers. The constitutional basis for the implied powers of Congress is the **necessary and proper clause** (Article I, Section 8, Clause 3). This clause gives Congress the right "to make all Laws which shall be necessary and proper for carrying into Execution the foregoing Powers, and all other Powers vested . . . in the Government of the United States."

In the field of foreign affairs, the Constitution gives the national government **inherent powers**. The national government has the same authority to deal with other nations as if it were the central government in a unitary system. Such inherent powers do not depend on specific constitutional provisions. For example, the government of the United States may acquire territory by purchase or by discovery and occupation, though no specific clause in the Constitution allows such acquisition. Even if the Constitution were silent about foreign affairs—which it is not—the national government would still have the power to declare war, make treaties, and appoint and receive ambassadors.

Together, these express, implied, and inherent powers create a flexible system that allows the Supreme Court, Congress, the president, and the people to expand the central government's powers to meet the needs of a modern nation in a global economy and confronting threats of international terrorism. This expansion of central government functions rests on four constitutional pillars.

These four constitutional pillars—the *national supremacy article,* the *war power,* the *commerce clause,* and most especially, the *power to tax and spend* for the general welfare—have permitted a tremendous expansion of the functions of the national government, so much so that despite the Supreme Court's recent declaration that some national laws exceed Congress's constitutional powers, the national government has, in effect, almost full power to enact any legislation that Congress deems necessary, so long as it does not conflict with the provisions of the Constitution designed to protect individual rights and the powers of the states.

THE NATIONAL SUPREMACY ARTICLE   One of the most important pillars is found in Article VI of the Constitution: "This Constitution, and the Laws of the United States which shall be made in Pursuance thereof; and all Treaties made . . . under the Authority of the United States, shall be the supreme Law of the Land; and the Judges in every State shall be bound thereby; any Thing in the Constitution or Laws of any State to the Contrary notwithstanding." All officials, state as well as national, swear an oath to support the Constitution of the United States. States may not override national policies; this restriction also applies to local units of government, since they are agents of the states. National laws and regulations of federal agencies *preempt* the field so that conflicting state and local regulations are unenforceable.

THE WAR POWER   The national government is responsible for protecting the nation from external aggression, whether from other nations or international terrorism. The government's power to protect national security includes the power to wage war. In today's world, military strength depends not only on troops in the field but also on the ability to mobilize the nation's industrial might as well as to apply scientific and technological knowledge to the tasks of defense. The national government has the power to do whatever is necessary and proper to wage war successfully. Thus the national government has the power to do almost anything not in direct conflict with constitutional guarantees.

THE POWER TO REGULATE INTERSTATE AND FOREIGN COMMERCE   Congressional authority extends to all commerce that affects more than one state. Commerce includes

express powers
Powers specifically granted to one of the branches of the national government by the Constitution.

implied powers
Powers inferred from the express powers that allow Congress to carry out its functions.

necessary and proper clause
Clause of the Constitution (Article I, Section 8, Clause 3) setting forth the implied powers of Congress. It states that Congress, in addition to its express powers, has the right to make all laws necessary and proper for carrying out all powers vested by the Constitution in the national government.

inherent powers
The powers of the national government in the field of foreign affairs that the Supreme Court has declared do not depend on constitutional grants but rather grow out of the very existence of the national government.

AN EXPANDING NATION

A great advantage of federalism—and part of the genius and flexibility of our constitutional system—has been the way in which we acquired territory and extended rights and guarantees by means of statehood, commonwealth, or territorial status, and thus grew from 13 to 50 states, plus territories.

Louisiana Purchase	1803
Florida	1819
Texas	1845
Oregon	1846
Mexican Cession	1848
Gadsden Purchase	1853
Alaska	1867
Hawaii	1898
Philippines	1898–1946
Puerto Rico	1899
Guam	1899
American Samoa	1900
Canal Zone	1904–2000
U.S. Virgin Islands	1917
Pacific Islands Trust Territory	1947

commerce clause
The clause in the Constitution (Article I, Section 8, Clause 1) that gives Congress the power to regulate all business activities that cross state lines or affect more than one state or other nations.

the production, buying, selling, renting, and transporting of goods, services, and properties. The **commerce clause** (Article I, Section 8, Clause 1) packs a tremendous constitutional punch; it gives Congress the power "to regulate Commerce with foreign Nations, and among the several States, and with the Indian Tribes." In these few words, the national government has been able to find constitutional justification for regulating a wide range of human activity, since very few aspects of our economy today affect commerce in only one state and are thus outside the scope of the national government's constitutional authority.[21]

The broad authority of Congress over interstate commerce was affirmed in the landmark ruling of *Gibbons* v. *Ogden* in 1824. There, in interpreting the commerce clause, Chief Justice John Marshall asserted national interests over those of the states and laid the basis for the subsequent growth in congressional power over commerce and activities that affect interstate commerce.

Gibbons v. *Ogden* arose from a dispute over a monopoly to operate steamboats in New York waters that was granted to Robert Livingston and Robert Fulton. They in turn licensed Aaron Ogden to exclusively operate steamboats between New York and ports in New Jersey. Ogden sued to stop Thomas Gibbons from running a competing ferry. Gibbons countered that his boats were licensed under a 1793 act of Congress governing vessels "in the coasting trade and fisheries." New York courts sided with Ogden in holding that both Congress and the states may regulate commerce, just as each has the power to tax. Congress, therefore, had not preempted New York from granting the monopoly. Gibbons appealed to the Supreme Court.

The stakes were high in *Gibbons* v. *Ogden,* for at issue was the very concept of "interstate commerce." May both Congress and the states regulate interstate commerce? And when conflicts arise between national and state regulations, which prevails?

Chief Justice Marshall asserted that national interests prevail and astutely defined "interstate commerce" as "intercourse that affects more states than one." Unlike the power of taxation, Congress's power over interstate commerce is complete and overrides conflicting state laws.[22]

Gibbons v. *Ogden* was immediately heralded for promoting a national economic common market in holding that states may not discriminate against interstate transportation and out-of-state commerce. Chief Justice Marshall's brilliant definition of "commerce" as *intercourse among the states* provided the basis clause for national regulation of an expanding range of economic activities, from the sale of lottery tickets[23] to prostitution[24] to radio and television broadcasts,[25] and telecommunications and the Internet.

The commerce clause has also been used to sustain legislation that goes beyond commercial matters. When the Supreme Court upheld the Civil Rights Act of 1964, forbidding discrimination because of race, religion, gender, or national origin in places of public accommodation, it said: "Congress's action in removing the disruptive effect which it found racial discrimination has on interstate travel is not invalidated because Congress was also legislating against what it considers to be moral wrongs."[26] Discrimination restricts the flow of interstate commerce; therefore, Congress could legislate against discrimination. Moreover, the law applies even to local places of public accommodation because local incidents of discrimination have a substantial and harmful impact on interstate commerce. The Court, however, has recently limited congressional power to address some other similar harms because it did not find a substantial connection with interstate commerce.[27]

THE POWER TO TAX AND SPEND Congress lacks constitutional authority to pass laws solely on the grounds that they will promote the general welfare, but it may raise taxes and spend money for this purpose. For example, Congress lacks the power to regulate education or agriculture directly, yet it does have the power to appropriate money to support education or to pay farm subsidies. By attaching conditions to its grants of money, Congress may thus regulate what it cannot directly control by law.

When Congress puts up the money, it determines how the money will be spent. By withholding or threatening to withhold funds, the national government can influence or control state operations and regulate individual conduct. For example, Congress has stipulated that federal funds should be withdrawn from any program in which any person is denied benefits because of race, color, national origin, sex, or physical handicap. Congress also used its power of the purse to force states to raise the drinking age to 21 by tying such a condition to federal dollars for highways.

Congress frequently requires states to do certain things—for example, provide services to indigent mothers and clean up the air and water. These requirements are called **federal mandates**. Often Congress does not supply the funds required to carry out these mandates—called "unfunded mandates"—and its failure to do so has become an important issue as states face growing expenditures with limited resources. The Supreme Court has also ruled that Congress may not compel states through "unfunded mandates" to enact particular laws or require state officials to enforce federal laws, such as, requiring checks on the backgrounds of handgun purchasers.[28]

Powers of the States

The Constitution *reserves for the states all powers not granted to the national government,* subject only to the limitations of the Constitution. Powers not given exclusively to the national government by provisions of the Constitution or by judicial interpretation may be exercised concurrently by the states, as long as there is no conflict with national law. Such **concurrent powers** with the national government include the power to levy taxes and regulate commerce internal to each state.

In general, a state may levy a tax on the same item as the national government does, but a state cannot, by a tax, "unduly burden" commerce among the states, interfere with a function of the national government, complicate the operation of a national law, or abridge the terms of a treaty of the United States. Where Congress has not preempted the field, states may regulate interstate businesses, provided that these regulations do not cover matters requiring uniform national treatment or unduly burden interstate commerce.

Who decides what matters require "uniform national treatment" or what actions might place an "undue burden" on interstate commerce? Congress does, subject to final review by the Supreme Court. When Congress is silent or does not clearly state its intent, the courts—ultimately, the Supreme Court—decide if there is a conflict with the national Constitution or if there has been federal preemption by law or regulation.

Constitutional Limits and Obligations

In order to ensure that federalism works, the Constitution imposes certain restraints on both the national and the state governments. States are prohibited from:

1. Making treaties with foreign governments
2. Authorizing private persons to prey on the shipping and commerce of other nations
3. Coining money, issuing bills of credit, or making anything but gold and silver coin legal tender in payment of debts
4. Taxing imports or exports
5. Taxing foreign ships
6. Keeping troops or ships in time of peace (except the state militia, now called the National Guard)
7. Engaging in war, unless invaded or in such imminent danger as will not admit of delay

The national government, in turn, is required by the Constitution to refrain from exercising its powers, especially its powers to tax and to regulate interstate commerce, in such a way as to interfere substantially with the states' abilities to perform their responsibilities. Today, the protection states have from intrusions by the national government comes primarily from the political process because senators and

federal mandate
A requirement imposed by the federal government as a condition for the receipt of federal funds.

concurrent powers
Powers that the Constitution gives to both the national and state governments, such as the power to levy taxes.

representatives elected from the states participate in the decisions of Congress. However, the Court has held that Congress may not command states to enact laws to comply with or order state employees to enforce unfunded federal mandates; for example, as noted earlier, Congress may not require local law enforcement officials to make background checks prior to handgun sales.[29] It has also ruled that the Eleventh Amendment's guarantee of states' sovereign immunity from lawsuits forbids state employees from suing states in federal and state courts in order to force state compliance with federal employment laws.[30] Although Congress may not use those sticks, it may offer the carrot of federal funding if states comply with national policies, such as establishing a minimum drinking age.

The Constitution also requires the national government to guarantee to each state a "republican form of government." The framers used this term to distinguish a republic from a monarchy, on the one side, and from a pure, direct democracy, on the other. Congress, not the courts, enforces this guarantee and determines what is or is not a republican form of government. By permitting the congressional delegation of a state to be seated in Congress, Congress acknowledges that the state has the republican form of government guaranteed by the Constitution.

In addition, the national government is obliged by the Constitution to protect states against *domestic insurrection*. Congress has delegated to the president the authority to dispatch troops to put down such insurrections when so requested by the proper state authorities. If there are contesting state authorities, the president decides which is the proper one. The president does not have to wait, however, for a request from state authorities to send federal troops into a state to enforce federal laws.

Interstate Relations

Three clauses in the Constitution, taken from the Articles of Confederation, require states to give full faith and credit to each other's public acts, records, and judicial proceedings; to extend to each other's citizens the privileges and immunities of their own citizens; and to return persons who are fleeing from justice.

FULL FAITH AND CREDIT   The **full faith and credit clause** (Article IV, Section 1), one of the more technical provisions of the Constitution, requires state courts to enforce the civil judgments of the courts of other states and accept their public records and acts as valid.[31] It does not require states to enforce the criminal laws or legislation and administrative acts of other states; in most cases, for one state to enforce the criminal laws of another would raise constitutional issues. The clause applies especially to enforcement of judicial settlements and court awards.

INTERSTATE PRIVILEGES AND IMMUNITIES   Under Article IV, Section 2, states must extend to citizens of other states the privileges and immunities granted to their own citizens, including the protection of the laws, the right to engage in peaceful occupations, access to the courts, and freedom from discriminatory taxes. Because of this clause, states may not impose unreasonable residency requirements, that is, withhold rights to American citizens who have recently moved to the state and thereby have become citizens of that state. For example, a state may not set unreasonable time limits to withhold state-funded medical benefits from new citizens or to keep them from voting. How long a residency requirement may a state impose? A day seems about as long as the Supreme Court will tolerate to withhold welfare payments or medical care, 50 days or so for voting privileges, and one year for eligibility for in-state tuition for state-supported colleges and universities.

Financially independent adults who move into a state just before enrolling in a state-supported university or college may be required to prove that they have become citizens of that state and intend to remain after finishing their schooling by supplying such evidence of citizenship as tax payments, a driver's license, car registration, voter registration, and a continuous, year-round off-campus residence. Students who are financially dependent on their parents remain citizens of the state of their parents.

full faith and credit clause
Clause in the Constitution (Article IV, Section 1) requiring each state to recognize the civil judgments rendered by the courts of the other states and to accept their public records and acts as valid.

In Comparative Perspective

THREE DIFFERENT APPROACHES TO FEDERALISM

There is no single model for dividing authority between national and state governments or for power sharing in intergovernmental relations. The federal systems in Canada, Germany, and Switzerland are illustrative.

Canada combines a federal system with a parliamentary form of government that has authority to legislate on all matters pertaining to "peace, order, and good government." The system was established in 1867, in part to prevent conflicts similar to those between the states that led to the American Civil War. In each of the ten provinces, the lieutenant governor is appointed on the advice of the prime minister and must approve any provincial law before it goes into effect. The legislative powers of the provinces are thus checked and limited. However, the provinces retain residual powers, and unlike the U.S. Supreme Court, the Canadian judiciary has generally encouraged decentralization in recognition of its multicultural society. Thus Canadian provinces exercise greater power and the national government is weaker than in the United States. In addition, the special status claimed by French-speaking Quebec has led to intergovernmental relations that alternate between periods of centralization and decentralization.

The Federal Republic of Germany, whose Basic Laws of 1949 became the constitution with the reunification of East and West Germany in 1990, is often referred to as an example of cooperative federalism. Its 16 states, or Länder, exercise a great deal of power, far more than states do in the United States. The central government has a president and a bicameral parliament composed of an upper house, the Federal Council, and a lower house, the National Assembly, as well as an independent judiciary. The central government has exclusive authority over foreign affairs, money, immigration, and telecommunications. But the Länder retain residual powers over all other matters and have concurrent powers over civil and criminal law, along with matters related to education, health, and the public welfare. Moreover, national legislation does not become law unless approved by a majority of the Federal Council, whose members are selected by legislatures in the Länder, not by popular elections.

Switzerland established a confederation on the basis of regional governments (cantons). The cantons reflect the ethnic and linguistic differences of their German-, French-, and Italian-speaking populations. All three languages are officially recognized by the central government. But of the 22 cantons, there are 18 that are unilingual, three that are bilingual, and one that is trilingual. They exercise most lawmaking powers and are represented in the National Council, a bicameral legislature, and the Council of States. Recent constitutional reforms further entrenched a tripartite federalism by expressly recognizing the autonomy of cities and munipalities, along with that of cantons and the federal government. As a result, cities and municipalities, unlike in the United States where they are agents of the states, have constitutional status.

For more information on comparative federalism, go to the Web site of the International Political Science Association's Section on Comparative Federalism at www.iu.edu/~soeaweb/IPSA and to the site of the Forum on Federations at www.forumfed.org.

EXTRADITION In Article IV, Section 2, the Constitution asserts that when individuals charged with crimes have fled from one state to another, the state to which they have fled is to deliver them to the proper officials upon the demand of the executive authority of the state from which they fled. This process is called **extradition**. "The obvious objective of the Extradition Clause," the courts have claimed, "is that no State should become a safe haven for the fugitives from a sister State's criminal justice system."[32] Congress has supplemented this constitutional provision by making the governor of the state to which fugitives have fled responsible for returning them. Despite their constitutional obligation, governors of asylum states have on occasion refused to honor a request for extradition.

INTERSTATE COMPACTS The Constitution also requires states to settle disputes with one another without the use of force. States may carry their legal disputes to the Supreme Court, or they may negotiate **interstate compacts**. Interstate compacts often establish interstate agencies to handle problems affecting an entire region. Before most interstate compacts become effective, congressional approval is required. After a compact has been signed and approved by Congress, it becomes binding on all signatory states, and its terms are enforceable by the federal judiciary. A typical state may belong to 20 compacts dealing with such subjects as environmental protection, crime control, water rights, and higher education exchanges.[33]

extradition
Legal process whereby an alleged criminal offender is surrendered by the officials of one state to officials of the state in which the crime is alleged to have been committed.

interstate compact
An agreement among two or more states. The Constitution requires that most such agreements be approved by Congress.

★★ YOU DECIDE

DO WE NEED A MORE RESTRICTED GOVERNMENT IN WASHINGTON?

Whereas in the 1980s President Ronald Reagan pressed to abolish the Department of Education, President George W. Bush signed into law his "No Child Left Behind" education bill, which among other things mandates annual standardized testing of elementary school children by 2005–2006. Some states objected to this legislation. In the aftermath of 9/11 and continuing threats of international terrorism, the Bush administration also increased the government's role in the area of homeland security, including the expanded use of state agencies as "first responders," and in combating illegal immigration. Yet, many states object to the increased financial costs and to the burden of having to track down and report on illegal immigrants in their communities.

Do we need federal standards or can states and localities be trusted to handle most domestic problems in their own way? If the national government sets standards, should it provide the funds but leave the details to the states? Should responsibility for education and welfare be given back to the states? Should states be forced to assume a greater role in improving education, maintaining homeland security, and reporting on illegal immigrants?

THE ROLE OF THE FEDERAL COURTS: UMPIRES OF FEDERALISM

Although the political process ultimately decides how power will be divided between the national and the state governments, the federal courts—and especially the Supreme Court—are often called on to umpire the ongoing debate about which level of government should do what, for whom, and to whom. This role for the courts was claimed in the celebrated case of *McCulloch* v. *Maryland*.

McCulloch Versus *Maryland*

In *McCulloch* v. *Maryland* (1819), the Supreme Court had the first of many chances to define the division of power between the national and state governments.[34] Congress established the Bank of the United States, but Maryland opposed any national bank and levied a $10,000 tax on any bank not incorporated within the state. James William McCulloch, the cashier of the bank, refused to pay on the grounds that a state could not tax an instrument of the national government.

Maryland was represented before the Court by some of the country's most distinguished lawyers, including Luther Martin, who had been a delegate to the Constitutional Convention. Martin said that the power to incorporate a bank was not expressly delegated to the national government in the Constitution. He maintained that the necessary and proper clause gives Congress only the power to choose those means and to pass those laws absolutely essential to the execution of its expressly granted powers. Because a bank is not absolutely necessary to the exercise of its delegated powers, he argued, Congress had no authority to establish it. As for Maryland's right to tax the bank, the power to tax is one of the powers reserved to the states; they may use it as they see fit.

The national government was represented as well by distinguished counsel, including Daniel Webster. Webster conceded that the power to create a bank is not one of the express powers of the national government. However, the power to pass laws necessary and proper to carry out Congress's express powers is specif-

There have been times throughout U.S. history when federal law has superseded state and local law. One example of this in recent history is the Voting Rights Act of 1965, which enforced the voting rights of African Americans in the South. In this photo, African American citizens in Montgomery, Alabama, are registering to vote for the very first time following a march that took place during one of the many voter registration drives of 1964 and 1965.

ically delegated to Congress. Therefore, Congress may incorporate a bank as an appropriate, convenient, and useful means of exercising the granted powers of collecting taxes, borrowing money, and caring for the property of the United States. Although the power to tax is reserved to the states, Webster argued that states cannot interfere with the operations of the national government. The Constitution leaves no room for doubt; in cases of conflict between the national and state governments, the national government is supreme.

Speaking for a unanimous Court, Chief Justice John Marshall rejected every one of Maryland's contentions. He summarized his views on the powers of the national government in these now-famous words: "Let the end be legitimate, let it be within the scope of the Constitution, and all means which are appropriate, which are plainly adapted to that end, which are not prohibited, but consist with the letter and spirit of the constitution, are constitutional." Having thus established the doctrine of *implied national powers,* Marshall set forth the doctrine of **national supremacy**. No state, he said, can use its taxing powers to tax a national instrument. "The power to tax involves the power to destroy. . . . If the right of the States to tax the means employed by the general government be conceded, the declaration that the Constitution, and the laws made in pursuance thereof, shall be the supreme law of the land, is empty and unmeaning declamation."

The long-range significance of *McCulloch* v. *Maryland* in providing support for the developing forces of nationalism and a unified economy cannot be overstated. The contrary arguments in favor of the states, if they had been accepted, would have strapped the national government in a constitutional straitjacket and denied it powers needed to deal with the problems of an expanding nation.

Federal Courts and the Role of the States

The authority of federal judges to review the activities of state and local governments has expanded dramatically in recent decades because of modern judicial interpretations of the Fourteenth Amendment, which forbids states from depriving any person of life, liberty, or property without *due process of the law.* States may not deny any person the *equal protection of the laws,* including congressional legislation enacted to implement the Fourteenth Amendment. Almost every action by state and local officials is now subject to challenge before a federal judge as a violation of the Constitution or of federal law.

Preemption occurs when a federal law or regulation takes precedence over enforcement of a state or local law or regulation. State and local laws are preempted not only when they conflict directly with federal laws and regulations but also if they touch a field in which the "federal interest is so dominant that the federal system will be assumed to preclude enforcement of state laws on the same subject."[35] Examples of federal preemption include laws regulating hazardous substances, water quality, clean air standards and many civil rights acts, especially the Civil Rights Act of 1964 and the Voting Rights Act of 1965.

Over the years, federal judges, under the leadership of the Supreme Court, have generally favored the powers of the federal government over the states. In spite of the Supreme Court's recent bias in favor of state over national authority, few would deny the Supreme Court the power to review and set aside state actions. As Justice Oliver Wendell Holmes of the Supreme Court once remarked: "I do not think the United States would come to an end if we lost our power to declare an Act of Congress void. I do think the Union would be imperiled if we could not make that declaration as to the laws of the several States."[36]

The Great Debate: Centralists Versus Decentralists

From the beginning of the Republic, there has been an ongoing debate about the "proper" distribution of powers, functions, and responsibilities between the national government and the states. Did the national government have the authority to outlaw slavery in the territories? Did the states have the authority to operate racially segregated

---

★ ★ THINKING IT THROUGH

Centralists argue that state and local officials are often less competent than national officials and tend to be concerned only with the narrow interests of their constituents. State and local governments are more apt to reflect local racial and ethnic biases as well as the biases of dominant local industries. State and local governments are also unable or unwilling to raise the taxes needed to carry out vital governmental functions.

Decentralists counter that increased urbanization has made states more responsive to the needs of communities, and they have become as sensitive to the needs of the poor and minorities as the national government. In recent years, state and local governments have also shown a greater willingness to raise taxes than the national government, and they have reformed and modernized in order to become more effective.

The great debate over which level of government best performs functions continues to rage. The Republican party started its history as the party of the National Union, while the Democrats were then the champion of states' rights, but over the past several decades, there have been changes. After winning control of Congress in the mid-1990s, Republicans led the charge against Washington, demanding the return of functions to the states. Democrats were reluctant to remove all federal standards, especially with respect to regulation of the environment and the workplace, and they generally favored providing minimum standards for programs, especially welfare and health care. More recently, President Bush and Republican leaders in Congress have pushed for expanded federal powers to counter threats to national security, to improve educational standards, and to expand Medicare coverage to include some of the costs of prescription drugs. Democrats in turn have countered that some homeland security programs do not go far enough and others go too far, that funding for education remains inadequate, and that prescription drug coverage will fall short when it takes effect in 2006.

---

national supremacy
Constitutional doctrine that whenever conflict occurs between the constitutionally authorized actions of the national government and those of a state or local government, the actions of the federal government prevail.

preemption
The right of a federal law or regulation to preclude enforcement of a state or local law or regulation.

schools? Could Congress regulate labor relations? Does Congress have the power to regulate the sale and use of firearms? Does Congress have the right to tell states how to clean up air and water pollution? Even today, as in the past, such debates are frequently phrased in constitutional language, with appeals to the great principles of federalism. But they are also arguments over who gets what, where, when, and how.

During the Great Depression of the 1930s, the nation debated whether Congress had the constitutional authority to enact legislation on agriculture, labor, education, housing, and welfare. Only 40 years ago, some legislators and public officials—as well as some scholars—questioned the constitutional authority of Congress to legislate against racial discrimination. The debate continues between **centralists**, who favor national action, and **decentralists**, who defend the powers of the states and favor action at the state and local levels.

THE DECENTRALIST POSITION   Among Americans favoring the decentralist or **states' rights** interpretation were the Antifederalists, Thomas Jefferson, John C. Calhoun, the Supreme Court from the 1920s to 1937, and more recently, Presidents Ronald Reagan and George H.W. Bush, the Republican leaders of Congress, Chief Justice William H. Rehnquist, and Justices Sandra Day O'Connor, Antonin Scalia, and Clarence Thomas.

Most decentralists contend that the Constitution is basically a compact among sovereign states that created the central government and gave it very limited authority. As Justice Clarence Thomas, an ardent advocate of states' rights, wrote in a dissenting opinion supporting the argument that a state has the power to impose term limits on members of Congress, "The ultimate source of the Constitution's authority is the consent of the people of each individual State, not the consent of the undifferentiated people of the Nation as a whole."[37] Thus the national government is little more than an agent of the states, and every one of its powers should be narrowly defined. Any question about whether the states have given a particular function to the central government or have reserved it for themselves should be resolved in favor of the states.

Decentralists hold that the national government should not interfere with activities reserved for the states. The Tenth Amendment, they claim, makes this clear: "The powers not delegated to the United States by the Constitution, nor prohibited by it to the States, are reserved to the States respectively, or to the people." Decentralists insist that state governments are closer to the people and reflect the people's wishes more accurately than the national government does. The national government, they add, is inherently heavy-handed and bureaucratic; to preserve our federal system and our liberties, central authority must be kept under control.

THE CENTRALIST POSITION   The centralist position has been supported by Chief Justice John Marshall, Presidents Abraham Lincoln, Theodore Roosevelt, and Franklin Roosevelt, and throughout most of our history, the Supreme Court.

Centralists reject the whole idea of the Constitution as an interstate compact. Rather, they view the Constitution as a supreme law established by the people. The national government is an agent of the people, not of the states, because it was the people who drew up the Constitution and created the national government. They intended that the central government's powers should be defined by the national political process and is denied authority only when the Constitution clearly prohibits it from acting.

Centralists argue that the national government is a government of all the people, whereas each state speaks only for some of the people. Although the Tenth Amendment clearly reserves powers for the states, it does not deny the national government the authority to exercise, to the fullest extent, all of its powers. Moreover, the supremacy of the national government restricts the states, because governments representing part of the people cannot be allowed to interfere with a government representing all of them.

The Supreme Court and the Role of Congress

From 1937 until the 1990s, the Supreme Court essentially removed federal courts from what had been their role of protecting states from acts of Congress. The Supreme Court broadly interpreted the commerce clause to allow Congress to do whatever Congress thought necessary and proper to promote the common good, even if the federal laws and

centralists
People who favor national action over action at the state and local levels.

decentralists
People who favor state or local action rather than national action.

states' rights
Powers expressly or implicitly reserved to the states and emphasized by decentralists.

regulations infringed on the activities of state and local governments. The Court went so far as to tell the states that they should look to the political process to protect their interests, not to the federal courts.[38]

In the past decade, however, a bare majority of the Supreme Court has signaled that federal courts should no longer remain passive in resolving federalism issues.[39] The Court declared that a state could not impose term limits on its members of Congress, but it did so only by a 5 to 4 vote. Justice John Paul Stevens, writing for the majority, built his argument on the concept of the federal union as espoused by the great Chief Justice John Marshall, as a compact among the people, with the national government serving as the people's agent. By contrast, Justice Clarence Thomas, writing for the dissenters, espoused a view of federalism not heard from a justice of the Supreme Court since prior to the New Deal. He interpreted the Tenth Amendment as requiring the national government to justify its actions in terms of an enumerated power and granting to the states all other powers not expressly given to the national government.[40]

The Court also declared that the clause in the Constitution empowering Congress to regulate commerce with the Indian tribes did not give Congress the power to authorize federal courts to hear suits against a state brought by Indian tribes.[41] Unless states consent to such suits, they enjoy "sovereign immunity" under the Eleventh Amendment. The effect of this decision goes beyond Indian tribes. As a result, except to enforce rights stemming from the Fourteenth Amendment, which the Court explicitly acknowledged to be within Congress's power, Congress may no longer authorize individuals to bring legal actions against states in order to force their compliance with federal law in either federal or state courts.[42]

Building on those rulings, the Court continues to press ahead with its "constitutional counterrevolution"[43] in returning to an older vision of federalism not embraced since the constitutional crisis over the New Deal in the 1930s. Among other recent rulings, the Court struck down the Violence Against Women Act, which had given women who are victims of violence the right to sue their attackers for damages.[44] Congress had found that violence against women annually costs the national economy $3 billion, but the Court held that Congress exceeded its powers in enacting the law and intruded on the powers of the states.

These Supreme Court decisions—most of which split the Court 5 to 4 along ideological lines, with the conservative justices favoring states' rights—may signal a major shift in the Court's interpretation of the constitutional nature of our federal system. Chief Justice Rehnquist, joined by Justices Scalia, Thomas, O'Connor, and frequently Justice Anthony M. Kennedy, have pushed the Court back to a decentralist position. President Clinton's two appointees, Justices Ruth Bader Ginsburg and Stephen Breyer, joined by Justices David Souter and John Paul Stevens, are resisting this movement back to a states' rights interpretation of our federal system. Consequently, federalism issues are likely to come up in future Supreme Court confirmation hearings, and the outcome of presidential elections—which greatly influence who gets appointed to the Supreme Court—could well determine how these and other federalism issues will be decided.

REGULATORY FEDERALISM: GRANTS, MANDATES, AND NEW TECHNIQUES OF CONTROL

Congress authorizes programs, establishes general rules for how the programs will operate, and decides whether and how much room should be left for state or local discretion. Most important, Congress appropriates the funds for these programs and generally has deeper pockets than even the richest states. One of Congress's most potent tools for influencing policy at the state and local levels has been federal grants.

Federal grants serve four purposes, the most important of which is the fourth:

1. To supply state and local governments with revenue.
2. To establish minimum national standards for such things as highways and clean air.

PEOPLE & POLITICS *Making a Difference* ★ ★ ★

CHIEF JUSTICE WILLIAM H. REHNQUIST

When asked his career plans by his elementary school teacher, William H. Rehnquist recalls saying, "I am going to change the government."[*] After serving in the army during World War II, he majored in political science at Stanford University and later graduated first in his class from Stanford Law School. He then clerked for a Supreme Court justice and went into private legal practice, while becoming active in Republican politics.

As an assistant attorney general in the administration of President Richard M. Nixon, he was appointed associate justice of the Supreme Court in 1972. In his early years on the Court he emerged as a champion of federalism, limiting the power of the national government and returning power to the states. However, he could not persuade a majority to go along with his views and earned the nickname "Lone Ranger" for writing more dissenting opinions than any other justice at the time. In 1986, President Ronald Reagan elevated him to chief justice. With subsequent changes in the Court's composition, Chief Justice Rehnquist was able to command a bare majority for changing the direction of the Court and reinvigorating debates over federalism.

A major legacy of the Rehnquist Court (1986–) is how it has curbed Congress in defense of the states. Besides resur-recting the rhetoric of states' rights and the Tenth Amendment, Chief Justice Rehnquist has commanded a majority for holding that:

- Congress must make a "plain statement" of its intent to pre-empt state laws; otherwise the Court will defer to the states.[†]
- Congress's power over interstate commerce has inherent limits, and it may not compel states to enact laws in compliance with federal standards or compel them to enforce federal laws.[‡]
- Congress's power under the commerce clause permits it to regulate noneconomic activities but only if they "substantially affect interstate commerce."[§]
- Congress's power to enforce the Fourteenth Amendment's guarantee of equal protection of the law is limited to remedying violations that the Court recognizes and does not extend to creating rights.[‖]
- States' immunity from lawsuits, under the Eleventh Amendment, bars lawsuits against them, without their consent, in federal and state courts and by citizens of other states as well as of their own state who seek state com-

pliance with federal laws forbidding, for example, discrimination on the basis of age or disability.[¶]

In short, Chief Justice Rehnquist has presided over a Court that has curbed the expansion of congressional powers and federal regulations in a renewed defense of the boundaries of federalism.

[*] Quoted in Craig Bradley, "William H. Rehnquist," in Clare Cushman, ed., *The Supreme Court Justices* (C.Q. Press, 1993), p. 496.
[†] *Gregory* v. *Ashcroft,* 501 U.S. 452 (1991).
[‡] *New York* v. *United States,* 505 U.S. 144 (1992), and *Printz* v. *United States,* 521 U.S. 898 (1997).
[§] *United States* v. *Lopez,* 514 U.S. 549 (1995), and *United States* v. *Morrison,* 529 U.S. 598 (2000); but see *Nevada* v. *Hibbs,* 538 U.S. 721 (2003).
[‖] *City of Boerne* v. *Flores,* 521 U.S. 507 (1997), and *United States* v. *Morrison,* 529 U.S. 598 (2000).
[¶] See, e.g., *Alden* v. *Maine,* 527 U.S. 706 (1998).

3. To equalize resources among the states by taking money from people with high incomes through federal taxes and spending it, through grants, in states where the poor live.

4. To attack national problems yet minimize the growth of federal agencies.

Types of Federal Grants

Three types of federal grants are currently being administered: *categorical-formula grants, project grants,* and *block grants* (sometimes called *flexible grants*). From 1972 to 1987, there was also *revenue sharing*—federal grants to state and local governments to be used at their discretion and subject only to very general conditions. But when budget deficits soared in the second Reagan administration (1985–1989) and there was no revenue to share, revenue sharing was terminated—to the states in 1986 and to local governments in 1987.

CATEGORICAL-FORMULA GRANTS   Congress appropriates funds for specific purposes, such as school lunches or the building of airports and highways. These funds are allocated by formula and are subject to detailed federal conditions, often on a matching basis; that is, the local government receiving the federal funds must put up some of its own dollars. Categorical grants, in addition, provide federal supervision to ensure that the federal dollars are spent as Congress wants. There are hundreds of grant programs, but two dozen, including Medicaid, account for more than half of total spending for categoricals.

PROJECT GRANTS   Congress appropriates a certain sum, which is allocated to state and local units and sometimes to nongovernmental agencies, based on applications from those who wish to participate. Examples are grants by the National Science Foundation to universities and research institutes to support the work of scientists or grants to states and localities to support training and employment programs.

BLOCK GRANTS   These are broad grants to states for prescribed activities—welfare, child care, education, social services, preventive health care, and health services—with only a few strings attached. States have great flexibility in deciding how to spend block grant dollars, but when the federal funds for any fiscal year are gone, there are no more matching federal dollars.

This maternity clinic is funded in part by federal block grants, which provide federal money to states for various services, such as health care, education, and welfare. States have great flexibility in deciding how to spend block grant dollars.

The Politics of Federal Grants

Republicans "have consistently favored fewer strings, less federal supervision, and the delegation of spending discretion to the state and local governments."[45] Democrats are generally been less supportive of broad discretionary block grants, favoring instead more detailed, federally supervised spending. The Republican-controlled Congress in the 1990s gave high priority to the creation of block grants, but it ran into trouble by trying to lump together welfare, school lunch and breakfast programs, prenatal nutrition programs, and child protection programs in one block grant.

Republicans, however, with President Clinton's support, succeeded in making a major change in federal-state relations—a devolution of responsibility for welfare from the national government to the states. The Personal Responsibility and Work Opportunity Reconciliation Act of 1996 put an end to the 61-year-old program of Aid to Families with Dependent Children (AFDC), a federal guarantee of welfare checks for all eligible mothers and children. The 1996 act substituted for AFDC a welfare block grant to each state, with caps on the amount of federal dollars that the state will receive. It also put another big federal child care program into another block grant—the Child Care and Development Block Grant (CCDBG).

Welfare block grants give states flexibility in how they provide for welfare, but no federal funds can be used to cover recipients who do not go to work within two years, and no one can receive federally supported benefits for more than five years. In order to slow down the "race to the bottom" in which states may try to make themselves "the least attractive state in which to be poor,"[46] Congress also stipulated that in order for states to receive their full share of federal dollars, they must continue to spend at least 75 percent of what they had been spending on welfare.

The battle over the appropriate level of government to control funding and to exercise principal responsibility for social programs tends to be cyclical. As one scholar of federalism explains, "Complaints about excessive federal control tend to be followed by proposals to shift more power to state and local governments. Then, when problems arise in state and local administration—and problems inevitably arise when any organization tries to administer anything—demands for closer federal supervision and tighter federal controls follow."[47]

Federal Mandates

Fewer federal dollars do not necessarily mean fewer federal controls. On the contrary, the federal government has imposed mandates on states and local governments, often without providing federal funds. State and local officials complained, and protests from state and local officials against unfunded federal mandates were effective. The Unfunded Mandates Reform Act of 1995 requires the Congressional Budget Office (CBO) and federal agencies to issue reports about the impact of unfunded mandates. The act also imposed some mild constraints on Congress itself. A congressional committee that approves any legislation containing a federal mandate must draw attention to the mandate in its report and describe its cost to state and local governments. If the committee intends any mandate to be partially unfunded, it must explain why it is appropriate for the cost to be borne by state and local governments.

Whether the Unfunded Mandates Reform Act significantly slows down federal mandates remains to be seen. So far, it has had little effect. The Americans with Disabilities Act (1990), for example, called on state and local governments to build ramps and alter curbs—renovations that are costing millions of dollars. Environmental Protection Agency regulations require states to build automobile pollution-testing stations and take other actions to reduce pollution, but without corresponding federal dollars. Still, state officials praise the law for increasing congressional awareness of unfunded mandates. It has forced members of Congress to take into account how a bill would affect state and local governments.[48]

New Techniques of Federal Control

In recent decades, Congress has used several other techniques in establishing federal regulations, including *direct orders, cross-cutting requirements, crossover sanctions,* and *total and partial preemption.*

DIRECT ORDERS   In a few instances, federal regulation takes the form of direct orders that must be complied with under threat of criminal or civil sanction. An example is the Equal Employment Opportunity Act of 1972, barring job discrimination by state and local governments on the basis of race, color, religion, sex, and national origin.

CROSS-CUTTING REQUIREMENTS   Federal grants may establish certain conditions that extend to all activities supported by federal funds, regardless of their source. The first and most famous of these is Title VI of the 1964 Civil Rights Act, which holds that in the use of federal funds, no person may be discriminated against on the basis of race, color, or national origin. Other laws extend these protections to persons because of gender or disability status. More than 60 cross-cutting requirements concern such matters as the environment, historic preservation, contract wage rates, access to government information, the care of experimental animals, and the treatment of human subjects in research projects.

CROSSOVER SANCTIONS   These sanctions permit the use of federal money in one program to influence state and local policy in another. For example, a 1984 act reduced federal highway aid by up to 15 percent for any state that failed to adopt a minimum drinking age of 21.

TOTAL AND PARTIAL PREEMPTION   Total preemption rests on the national government's power under the supremacy and commerce clauses to preempt conflicting state and local activities. Building on this constitutional authority, federal law in certain areas entirely preempts state and local governments from the field.[49] Sometimes federal law provides for partial preemption in establishing basic policies but requiring states to administer them. Some programs give states an option not to participate, but if a state chooses not to do so, the national government steps in and runs the program. Even worse from the states' point of view is *mandatory partial preemption,* in which the national government requires states to act on peril of losing other funds but provides no funds to support state action. The Clean Air Act of 1990 is an example of mandatory partial preemption; the federal government set national air quality standards and required states to devise plans and pay for their implementation.[50] Homeland security legislation is another example of the national government providing some funds but requiring states to provide services as "first responders" that cost more than federal funds cover.

THE POLITICS OF FEDERALISM

The formal structures of our federal system have not changed much since 1787, but the political realities, especially during the past half-century, have greatly altered how federalism works. To understand these changes, we need to look at some of the trends that continue to fuel the debate about the meaning of federalism.

The Growth of Big Government

Over the past two centuries, power has accrued to the national government. "No one planned the growth, but everyone played a part in it."[51] How did this shift come about? For a variety of reasons. One is that many of our problems have become national in scope. Much that was local in 1789, in 1860, or in 1930 is now national, even global. State governments could supervise the relations between small merchants and their few employees, but only the national government can supervise relations between multinational corporations and their thousands of employees, many of which are organized in national unions.

As industrialization proceeded, powerful interests made demands on the national government. Business groups called on the government for aid in the form of tariffs, a national banking system, subsidies to railroads and the merchant marine, and uniform rules relating to the environment. Farmers learned that the national government could give more aid than the states, and they too began to demand help. By the beginning of the twentieth century, urban groups in general and organized labor in particular pressed their claims. Big business, big agriculture, and big labor all added up to big government.

The growth of the national economy and the creation of national transportation and communications networks altered people's attitudes toward the national government. Before the Civil War, the national government was viewed as a distant, even foreign, government. Today, in part because of television and the Internet, most people know more about Washington than they know about their state capitals. People are apt to know more about the president than about their governor and more about their national senators and representatives than about their state legislators or even about the local officials who run their cities and schools.

The Great Depression of the 1930s stimulated extensive national action on welfare, unemployment, and farm surpluses. World War II brought federal regulation of wages, prices, and employment, as well as national efforts to allocate resources, train personnel, and support engineering and inventions. After the war, the national government helped veterans obtain college degrees and inaugurated a vast system of support for university research. The United States became the most powerful leader of the free world, maintaining substantial military forces even in times of peace. The Great Society programs of the 1960s poured out grants-in-aid to states and localities. City dwellers who had migrated from the rural South to northern cities began to seek federal funds for—at the very least—housing, education, and mass transportation.

Although economic and social conditions created many of the pressures for expansion of the national government, so did political claims. Until federal budget deficits became a hot issue in the 1980s and early 1990s, members of Congress, presidents, federal judges, and federal administrators actively promoted federal initiatives. Even with the return of deficit spending in the 2000s, Congress appears willing to actively promote some federal programs, at least in the areas of homeland security and prescription drug coverage. True, when there is widespread conflict about what to do—how to reduce the federal deficit, adopt a national energy policy, reform Social Security, provide health care for the indigent—Congress waits for a national consensus. But when an organized constituency wants something and there is no counterpressure, Congress "responds often to everyone, and with great vigor."[52] Once established, federal programs generate groups with vested interests in promoting, defending, and expanding them. Associations are formed and alliances are made. "In a word, the growth of government has created a constituency of, by, and for government."[53]

The politics of federalism are changing, however, and Congress is being pressured to reduce the size and scope of national programs, but at the same time to deal with the demands for homeland security. Meanwhile, the cost of entitlement programs such as Social Security and Medicare are going up because there are more older people and they are living longer. These programs have widespread public support, and to cut them is politically risky. "With all other options disappearing, it is politically tempting to finance tax cuts by turning over to the states many of the social programs . . . that have become the responsibility of the national government."[54]

The Devolution Revolution: Rhetoric Versus Reality

Recent Congresses, like their predecessors, have increased the authority of the national government in many areas. To be sure, the Republican-controlled Congress in the 1990s returned some functions, especially welfare, to the states. President Clinton also proclaimed, "The era of big government is over," though he tempered his comments by saying, "But we cannot go back to the time when our citizens were left to fend for themselves." Congress and the president came together for a major overhaul of welfare and, to a lesser degree, education. Congress also freed the states to set their own highway speed limits, changed the Safe Drinking Water Act to allow states to operate certain programs, and gave states a greater role over how federal rural development funds may be used.

In the aftermath of the attacks on the World Trade Center and the Pentagon and in confronting the continuing threats of terrorism, the role of the federal government in defending homeland security has expanded. Congress also established national criteria for state-issued drivers' licenses, forbade states from selling drivers' personal information, ended state regulation of mutual funds, nullified state laws restricting telecommunications competition, and made a host of offenses federal crimes, including carjacking and acts of terrorism. Appropriation bills pressured states to keep criminals behind bars by threatening to take grants away from states that fail to meet federal standards. Indeed, the only two major achievements of the devolution revolution remain the 1996 reform of welfare and the repeal of a national speed limit.[55] As one reporter concluded, "The 'devolution' promised by Congressional Republicans . . . has mostly fizzled. Instead of handing over authority to state and local governments, they're taking it away."[56]

THE FUTURE OF FEDERALISM

In 1933, during the Great Depression, with state governments helpless, one writer stated, "I do not predict that the states will go, but affirm that they have gone."[57] Such prophets of doom were wrong; the states are stronger than ever. During recent decades, state governments have undergone a major transformation. Most have improved their governmental structures, taken on greater roles in funding education and welfare, launched programs to help distressed cities, expanded their tax bases, and are assuming greater roles in maintaining homeland security and fighting corporate corruption. Able men and women have been attracted to the governorship. "Today, states, in formal representational, policy making, and implementation terms at least, are more representative, more responsive, more activist, and more professional in their operations than they ever have been. They face their expanded roles better equipped to assume and fulfill them."[58]

After the civil rights revolution of the 1960s, segregationists feared that national officials would work for racial integration. Thus they praised local government, emphasized the dangers of centralization, and argued that the protection of civil rights was not a proper function of the national government. As one political scientist observed, "Federalism has a dark history to overcome. For nearly two hundred years, states' rights have been asserted to protect slavery, segregation, and discrimination."[59]

Today the politics of federalism, even with respect to civil rights, is more complicated than in the past. The national government is not necessarily more favorable to the claims of minorities than state or city governments are. Rulings on same-sex marriages and "civil unions" by state courts interpreting their state constitutions have extended more protection for these rights than has the Supreme Court's interpretation of the U.S. Constitution. Other states, however, are passing legislation that would eliminate such protections, and opponents are pressing for a constitutional amendment to bar same-sex marriages.

States are also increasingly aggressive in addressing economic and environmental matters. State attorneys general are prosecuting anticompetitive business practices, as they did in joining the suit against Microsoft and, more recently, as New York attorney general Eliot Spitzer did in suing the mutual fund industry and spammers. After the Bush administration abandoned 50 investigations into violations of the Clean Air Act and changed policy on the regulation of power plants, Spitzer and several other state attorneys general sued the Bush administration and power plant companies to force them to make pollution-control improvements.[60] Business interests have argued that conflicting state regulations unduly burden interstate commerce and have sought broader preemptive federal regulation in order to save them not only from stringent state regulations but also from the uncertainties of complying with 50 different state laws. As a lawyer representing trade groups in the food and medical devices industries observed: "One national dumb rule is better than 50 inconsistent rules of any kind."[61]

The national government is not likely to retreat to a pre-1930 posture or even a pre-1960 one. Indeed, the underlying economic and social conditions that generated the demand for federal action have been altered substantially by international terrorism, the war in Afghanistan and Iraq, and rising deficits. In addition to such traditional issues as helping people find jobs and preventing inflation and depressions—which still require national action—countless new issues have been added to the national agenda by the growth of a global economy based on the information explosion, e-commerce, advancing technologies, and combating international terrorism.

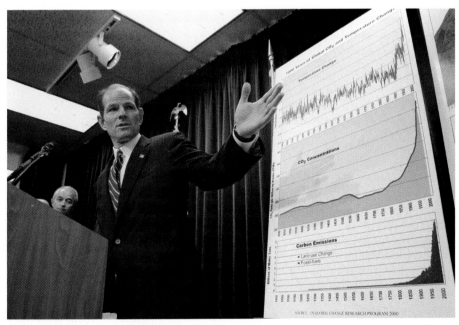

New York Attorney General Eliot Spitzer was one of several state attorneys general to sue the Bush administration and power plant companies over pollution control.

Most Americans have strong attachments to our federal system—in the abstract. They remain loyal to their states and show a growing skepticism about the national government. Yet, evidence suggests the anti-Washington sentiment "is 3,000 miles wide but only a few miles deep."[62] The fact is that Americans are pragmatists: We appear to prefer federal-state-local power sharing[63] and are prepared to use whatever level of government necessary to meet our needs and new challenges.

SUMMARY

1. A federal system is one in which the constitution divides powers between the central government and subdivisional governments—states or provinces. Alternatives to federalism are unitary systems, in which all constitutional power is vested in the central government, and confederations, which are loose compacts among sovereign states.

2. Federal systems check the growth of tyranny, allow unity without uniformity, encourage state experimentation, permit power sharing between the national government and the states, and keep government closer to the people.

3. The national government has the constitutional authority, stemming primarily from the national supremacy clause, the war powers, and its powers to regulate commerce among the states to tax and spend, to do what Congress thinks is necessary and proper to promote the general welfare and to provide for the common defense. These constitutional pillars have permitted tremendous expansion of the functions of the federal government.

4. States must give full faith and credit to each other's public acts, records, and judicial proceedings; extend to each others' citizens the privileges and immunities it gives its own; and return fugitives from justice.

5. The federal courts umpire the division of power between the national and state governments. The Marshall Court, in decisions such as *Gibbons* v. *Ogden* and *McCulloch* v. *Maryland,* asserted the power of the national government over the states and promoted a national economic common market. These decisions also reinforced the supremacy of the national government over the states.

6. Today, debates about federalism are less often about its constitutional structure than about whether action should come from the national or state and local levels. Recent Supreme Court decisions favor a decentralist position and signal shifts in the Court's interpretation of the constitutional nature of our federal system.

7. The major instruments of federal intervention in state programs have been various kinds of financial grants-in-aid, of which the most prominent are categorical-formula grants, project grants, and block grants. The national government also imposes federal mandates and controls some activities of state and local governments by other means.

8. Over the past 218 years, power has accrued to the national government, but recently Congress has been pressured to reduce the size and scope of national programs and to shift some existing programs back to the states. Although responsibility for welfare has been turned over to the states, the authority of the national government has increased in many other areas.

KEY TERMS

devolution revolution
federalism
unitary system
confederation
express powers

implied powers
necessary and proper clause
inherent powers
commerce clause
federal mandate

concurrent powers
full faith and credit clause
extradition
interstate compact
national supremacy

preemption
centralists
decentralists
states' rights

FURTHER READING

SAMUEL H. BEER, *To Make a Nation: The Rediscovery of American Federalism* (Harvard University Press, 1993).

CENTER FOR THE STUDY OF FEDERALISM, *The Federalism Report* (published quarterly by Temple University; this publication notes research, books and articles, and scholarly conferences).

CENTER FOR THE STUDY OF FEDERALISM, *Publius: The Journal of Federalism* (published quarterly by Temple University; one issue each year is an "Annual Review of the State of American Federalism"; and has a Web site at www.lafayette.edu/~publius).

TIMOTHY J. CONLAN, *From New Federalism to Devolution: Twenty-Five Years of Inter-governmental Reforms* (Brookings Institution, 1998).

DANIEL J. ELAZER AND JOHN KINCAID, *The Covenant Connection: From Federal Theology to Modern Federalism* (Lexington Books, 2000).

JOHN FEREJOHN AND BARRY WEINGAST, *The New Federalism: Can the States Be Trusted?* (Hoover Institute Press, 1998).

FRANK GOODMAN, ED., *The Supreme Court's Federalism: Real or Imagined?* (Sage, 2001).

NEIL C. MCCABE, ED., *Comparative Federalism in the Devolution Era* (Rowman & Littlefield, 2002).

FORREST MCDONALD, *States' Rights and the Union: Imperim in Imperio, 1776–1876* (Univeristy Press of Kansas, 2000).

KALYPSO NICOLAIDIS AND ROBERT HOWSE, EDS., *The Federal Vision: Legitimacy and Levels of Governance in the United States and the European Union* (Oxford University Press, 2001).

JOHN T. NOONAN, *Narrowing the Nation's Power: The Supreme Court Sides with the States* (University of California Press, 2002).

DAVID M. O'BRIEN, *Constitutional Law and Politics: Struggles for Power and Governmental Accountability,* 6th ed. (Norton, 2005).

LAURENCE J. O'TOOLE JR., *American Intergovernmental Relations,* 3d ed. (CQ Press, 2000).

PAUL J. POSNER, *The Politics of Unfunded Mandates: Whither Federalism?* (Georgetown University Press, 1998).

WILLIAM H. RIKER, *The Development of American Federalism* (Academic, 1987).

POLITICAL CULTURE AND IDEOLOGY

4

For many Americans, the first experience with democracy is a school election, often in an elementary school. What are the expectations of these young voters, and what do these expectations teach us about our political culture? Were we to observe such an election, we would see recurrent patterns. For example, it would be considered unfair if someone suggested that some students' votes count more than others' or that some students should not be allowed to vote at all. It is likely that the candidates will be asked to speak, and they may even make a few campaign promises. When the votes are counted, the young participants expect the person with the most votes to be elected. Many important elements of our political culture are widely shared, others are evolving, and some are in dispute. Our assumptions, beliefs, and values about politics, government, participation, freedom, and liberty are the central focus of this chapter.

The specifics of a nation's political culture can be discovered not only by what people believe and say but also by how they behave. A nation's political culture is the underlying

beliefs, assumptions, attitudes, and patterns of behavior people have toward government and politics. Political culture involves such fundamental issues as who may participate in political decisions, what rights and liberties citizens have, how decisions are made, and how people view politicians and government generally. Some elements of our political culture—like our fear of concentrated power and our reverence for individual liberty—have remained constant over time. In other respects, our political culture has changed from a belief that only property-owning white men should be allowed to vote to a conviction that all adults should have the right to vote, and that participation should include a wider range of political activities. Thus, citizens now vote in party primaries to select nominees for office, whereas previously, party leaders determined who would run for office. The surge in citizen activity on the Internet in the 2004 election may be a harbinger of a more interactive political culture in the future where citizens interact with candidates, contribute money, and mobilize each other to political action.

The idea of people coming together, listening to each other, exchanging ideas, learning to appreciate each other's differences, and defending their opinions is sometimes called deliberation and builds what has been called **social capital**. Such interaction is thought to build community and relationships in ways that do not happen when citizens only cast ballots. Political scientist Robert Putnam has defined social capital as "features of social organization such as networks, norms, and social trust that facilitate coordination and cooperation for mutual benefit."[1] Because of a decline in public participation in town council meetings, community groups, the PTA, labor unions, business associations, and other civic groups, Putnam believes that we as a people are losing the skills and learning people can develop in such settings. Not all political scientists agree with Putnam's assessment that social capital is in decline.[2] More recently, Putnam found evidence of expanded civic engagement in the weeks after the terrorist attacks of September 11, 2001, but not a growth in volunteering.[3]

The social capital debate has rekindled an interest in the nature and viability of the American political culture and has spurred an examination of how it is changing. Americans have conflicting ideas and beliefs about the proper role of government and where and how political power should be exercised. These attitudes and beliefs, when coherent and consistent, are what political scientists call *ideology*. In this chapter, we look at our political culture and ideology.

THE AMERICAN POLITICAL CULTURE

Political scientists use the term **political culture** to refer to the widely shared beliefs, values, and norms concerning the relationship of citizens to government and to one another.

American political culture centers on democratic values like liberty, equality, individualism, democracy, justice, the rule of law, patriotism, optimism, and idealism. There is no "official" list of American political values, however, and as we noted in Chapter 1, these widely shared democratic values overlap and sometimes conflict.

Shared Values

Before the American and French Revolutions of the late eighteenth century, discussions about individual liberty, freedom, equality, private property, limited government, and popular consent were rare. Europe had been dominated by aristocracies, had experienced centuries of political and social inequality, and had been ruled by governments that were often arbitrary in their exercise of power. Liberal political philosophers rebelled against these traditions and proclaimed the principles of classical liberalism. They claimed individuals have certain **natural rights**—the rights of all people to dignity and worth—and that government, as a primary threat to those rights, must be limited and controlled. During this same period, the economic system was changing from a mercantile to a free market system. People began to think they could improve their lot in life and own property. Radical new ideas like these influenced the thinking of the founders of our nation.

social capital
Democratic and civic habits of discussion, compromise, and respect for differences, which grow out of participation in voluntary organizations.

political culture
The widely shared beliefs, values, and norms concerning the relationship of citizens to government and to one another.

natural rights
The rights of all people to dignity and worth; also called *human rights*.

CHANGING FACE OF AMERICAN POLITICS

TRUST IN AMERICA

Not all Americans have the same level of social trust, an important element in social capital. With less time spent interacting with one another and more time in social isolation, social trust has declined.* Public perceptions about crime and concerns about personal safety are some reasons people are less trusting.[†] Political Scientist Wendy Rahn examined variations in the extent to which people trusted their fellow citizens across 49 communities.[‡] She defines generalized social trust "as a 'standing decision' to give most people—even those whom one does not know from direct experience—the benefit of the doubt."[§]

Across the 49 communities Rahn surveyed she found the mean level of social trust was 52 percent, with the high being 74 percent in Brown County, South Dakota, and the low being Camden, New Jersey, with 25 percent. The chart plots the percent expressing generalized social trust against the percent of non-Hispanic whites in the community. You will note there is a clear correlation be-

Samples from different communities were asked: "Generally speaking, would you say that most people can be trusted or that you can't be too careful in dealing with people?" Those that said you can trust most people were coded as trusting.

tween the racial composition of a community and the level of generalized social trust.

As the United States becomes more diverse, are we likely to have less trust in one another? Or is the level of trust related to socio-economic factors that are not directly related to racial diversity? As we discuss in this chapter and the next, there are other cultural forces that may pull us together.

*Robert D. Putnam, "The Decline of Civil Society: How Come? So What?" (presented at the Canadian Centre for Management Development, Ottawa, Ontario, February 1996), 11. www.collection.nlc-bnc.ca/100/200/301/ccmd-ccg/john_manion-e/jmlp66e.pdf.
[†]Francis Fukuyama, *The Great Disruption: Human Nature and the Reconstitution of Social Order* (New York: Touchstone, 1999).
[‡]Wendy Rahn, et al, *Geographies of Trust: Examining Variation in Generalized Social Trust Across Knight Communities* (American Institutes for Research, 2003). www.polisci.umn.edu/faculty/wrahn/KST7C473.doc.
[§]Rahn, Wendy M. and John E. Transue, "Social Trust and Value Change: The Decline of Social Capital in American Youth, 1976–1995," *Political Philosophy* 19 (March 1998): 545.

LIBERTY   No value in the American political culture is more revered than liberty. "We have always been a nation obsessed with liberty. Liberty over authority, freedom over responsibility, rights over duties—these are our historic preferences," wrote the late Clinton Rossiter, a noted political scientist. "Not the good man but the free man has been the measure of all things in this sweet 'land of liberty'; not national glory but individual liberty has been the object of political authority and the test of its worth."[4] This predominance of freedom and individualism over virtue and the public good is not universally accepted by students of American thought, and in reality both perspectives are built on some mix of the two views.[5]

EQUALITY   Jefferson's famous words in the Declaration of Independence express the primacy of our views of equality: "We hold these truths to be self-evident, that all men are created equal, that they are endowed by their Creator with certain unalienable rights, that among these are life, liberty, and the pursuit of happiness." Americans have always believed in social equality. In contrast to Europeans, our nation shunned aristocracy, and our Constitution explicitly prohibits governments from granting titles of nobility.

VALUES WE SHARE— NEW DATA BOX

The political values and attitudes of the American public provide insights into the American political culture. While there is some variability depending on how pollsters ask questions, these data are generally reflective of public opinion.

	Percent Agree
Elected officials in Washington lose touch with the people pretty quickly.	75%
Voting gives people like me some say about how government runs things.	73
Success in life is pretty much determined by forces outside our control.	30
I admire people who get rich by working hard.	90
As Americans we can always find a way to solve our problems and get what we want.	66
Our society should do what is necessary to make sure that everyone has an equal opportunity to succeed.	91
It is the responsibility of the government to take care of people who can't take care of themselves.	66
I am very patriotic.	91
Prayer is an important part of my daily life.	80

SOURCE: The Pew Research Center for the People and the Press, *Evenly Divided and Increasingly Polarized: 2004 Political Landscape.* Data collected in August, 2003.

In addition to social equality, Americans believe in *political equality*, the idea that every individual has a right to equal protection under the law and equal voting power. Although political equality has always been a goal, it has not always been a reality. In the past, African Americans, Native Americans, and women were denied the right to vote and otherwise participate in the nation's political life.

Equality encompasses the idea of *equal opportunity*, especially with regard to improving our economic status. Americans believe that social background should not limit our opportunity to achieve to the best of our ability, nor should race, gender, or religion. The nation's commitment to public education programs like Head Start for underprivileged preschool children, state support for public colleges and universities, and federal financial aid for higher education reflect this belief in equal opportunity.

INDIVIDUALISM The United States is characterized by a persistent commitment to the individual. Under our system of government, individuals have both rights and responsibilities. Policies that limit individual choice generate intense political conflict. The debate over legalized abortion is often framed in these terms. Although Americans agree with individual rights and freedoms, they also understand that their rights can conflict with another person's rights or with the government's need to maintain order.

RESPECT FOR THE COMMMON PERSON Most Americans have faith in the common sense and collective wisdom of ordinary people. Most prefer action to reflection. We are often anti-expert and sometimes anti-intellectual. The emphasis on practicality and common sense has become part of our national image. Poets like Walt Whitman and Carl Sandburg and storytellers like Mark Twain, Will Rogers, Eudora Welty, and Garrison Keillor have helped shape this tradition. This reverence for the common people helps explain our ambivalence toward power, politics, and government authority. Politicians from backgrounds of privilege often downplay their past in an effort to relate more to typical voters.

DEMOCRATIC CONSENSUS An important feature that binds most of us together is **democratic consensus**, a fairly widespread agreement on fundamental principles of

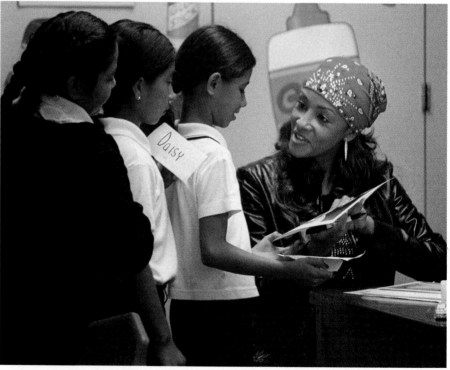

Vivica Fox autographs photographs for fifth-grade elementary school students in Lynwood, California, as part of Teach For America Week, an annual event in which successful Americans discuss their career with schoolchildren with the hope of inspiring them to realize their own goals and ambitions.

democratic consensus
Widespread agreement on fundamental principles of democratic governance and the values that undergird them.

Americorps National Service crew members remove tree limbs from the yard of a woman whose home was damaged after ice storms caused a tree to fall on it.

governance and the values that undergird them. We are a people from many different cultural and ethnic backgrounds, histories, and religions. Despite these differences, our political culture includes widely shared attitudes and beliefs about principles of government, procedures, documents, and institutions. Americans have strong opinions about who has power to do what, how people acquire power, and how they are removed from power. These are fundamental "rules of the game" in which widespread consensus is important. At the same time, this commitment to core elements of who has power and what limits exist on the exercise of that power does not necessarily mean people vote in elections, are current in public affairs, or believe government is always fair or just.

Elements of the democratic consensus are majority rule and popular sovereignty. We believe in **majority rule**—governance according to the expressed preferences of the majority at regular elections. Yet we also believe that people in the minority should be free to try to win majority support for their opinions. Despite the fact that large numbers of Americans lack strong party attachments, we favor a two-party system. Our institutions are based on the principles of representation and consent of the governed. We believe in **popular sovereignty**—that ultimate power resides in the people. Government, from this perspective, exists to serve the people rather than the other way around. The means by which the government learns the will of the people is through *elections,* perhaps the most important expression of popular consent. But there are instances when popular sovereignty and majority rule must be limited by other fundamental rights, as in the case of referendums limiting civil rights.[6] Examples include California's 1964 vote, subsequently overturned, to permit people to discriminate in the sale of residential housing and the same state's 1996 vote to prohibit affirmative action in state governmental bodies, including universities and colleges.

Many of the limits on governments are specified in the Constitution, especially in the first ten amendments (the Bill of Rights) and the Thirteenth, Fourteenth, Fifteenth, and Nineteenth amendments. The Constitution is revered as a national symbol, yet we often differ over the framers' original intentions. We honor many of these rights more in the abstract than in the particular. More than half of us, for instance, think that books with dangerous ideas should be banned from public school libraries (see Table 4–1). Intolerance of dissenting or offensive views is amply demonstrated in many public opinion polls and is observed on college and university campuses. Still, Americans can ordinarily be characterized as affirming support for democratic and constitutional values.

majority rule
Governance according to the expressed preferences of the majority.

popular sovereignty
A belief that ultimate power resides in the people.

TABLE 4–1 WHAT DO YOU MEAN BY RIGHTS AND FREEDOMS? IT DEPENDS . . .

	Agree	Disagree	Don't Know
Freedom of speech should apply to groups that are sympathetic to terrorists.	45%	50%	5%
There has been real improvement in the position of African Americans.	57	35	8
Books that contain dangerous ideas should be banned from public school libraries.	50	47	3
Protection rights should apply to the unborn.	72	24	4
The police should be allowed to search the houses of known drug dealers without a court order.	44	54	2
School boards ought to have the right to fire teachers who are known homosexuals.	33	62	5

SOURCE: The Pew Research Center for the People and the Press, *Evenly Divided and Increasingly Polarized: 2004 Political*. Data collected in August, 2003.

JUSTICE AND THE RULE OF LAW   Inscribed over the entrance to the U.S. Supreme Court are the words "Equal Justice Under Law." The rule of law means that government is based on a body of law applied equally and by just procedures, as opposed to rule by an elite whose whims decide policy or resolve disputes. Chief Justice John Marshall succinctly summarized this principle: "The government of the United States has been emphatically termed a government of laws, not of men."[7] Americans believe strongly in the principle of fairness: All individuals are entitled to the same legal rights and protections.

For government to adhere to the rule of law, its policies and laws should follow these five rules:

- *Generality:* Laws should be stated generally, not singling out any group or individual.

- *Prospectivity:* Laws should apply to the future, not punish something someone did in the past.

- *Publicity:* Laws cannot be kept secret and then enforced.

- *Authority:* Valid laws are made by those with legitimate power, and the people legitimate that power through some form of popular consent.

- *Due process:* Laws must be enforced impartially with fair processes.

PATRIOTISM, OPTIMISM, AND IDEALISM   Americans are highly nationalistic, sharing a sense of values and identity. This nationalism was reinforced by the terrorist attacks of 2001, which illustrated that unity under threat is a widely shared value. As President George W. Bush said, "We are a different country than we were on September 10th: sadder and less innocent; stronger and more united; and in the face of ongoing threats, determined and courageous."[8] We are proud of our past and our role in the world today. We are optimistic, though far more about people than about government.

We believe in opportunity, choice, individualism, and most of all, the freedom to improve ourselves and to achieve success with as little interference as possible from others or from government. As Table 4–2 indicates, U.S. citizens are more satisfied with their democratic government than are the citizens of other countries.

We know that our system is imperfect, yet we have an abiding faith in government by the people. We often grumble that elected officials have lost touch with us, we are disgusted by scandals, and we are impatient with the slowness of the system to solve problems like health care, crime, drug abuse, and terrorism. Despite the dissatisfactions, a remarkable belief persists that this nation is better, stronger, and more virtuous than other nations. Like every country, the United States has interests and motives that are selfish as well as generous, cynical as well as idealistic. Still, our support of human needs and rights throughout the world is evidence of an enduring idealism.

Where We Learn the American Political Culture

One important source of political culture in the United States, as in other nations, is the family. Children are taught from an early age what it means to be an American. They are curious about why people vote, what the president does, and whether Grandpa fought in World War II or Korea. The questions may vary somewhat from family to family, yet the themes of authority, freedom, equality, liberty, and partisanship are common. Families are the most important reference groups, and compared to families in other cultures, American families are much more egalitarian.[9]

Public schools are another source of the American political culture. Children and teachers often begin the school day by saluting the flag, reciting the Pledge of Allegiance, or singing the national anthem. Teaching American political and economic values is part of the curriculum. Not only are values taught in American history classes, but they are put into practice in school elections and newspapers and in encouraging students to participate in small-scale economic ventures.[10]

TABLE 4–2 SATISFACTION WITH THE WAY DEMOCRACY WORKS		
	Satisfied	*Dissatisfied*
United States	64%	27%
Canada	62	24
Germany	55	27
Iceland	54	23
Thailand	54	27
Costa Rica	52	25
Chile	43	31
France	43	32
Dominican Republic	40	38
United Kingdom	40	43
Japan	35	32
India	32	43
Spain	31	30
Venezuela	28	59
Taiwan	25	18
Hungary	17	50
Mexico	17	67

SOURCE: "People Throughout the World Largely Satisfied with Personal Lives," *Gallup Poll*, June 1995, p. 6.

Colleges and universities also play a role in fostering the American political culture. Students who attend college are often more confident than other persons in dealing with bureaucracy and politics generally, more likely to participate in politics and to vote, and more knowledgeable about government.[11] Many states require students at state colleges and universities to take courses in American government or state government, in part to instill a sense of civic duty while imparting knowledge about state and national governance.

Religious freedom and diversity have played a part in the formation and maintenance of the American political culture. American churches, synagogues, and mosques have long fostered a common understanding of right and wrong. Freedom, including freedom of religion, individualism, pluralism, and civic duty, have all been fostered by churches. As churches do not all take the same positions on political issues, their impact is sometimes mitigated, but they have been important to such major social and political movements as the abolition of slavery, the expansion of civil rights, and opposition to war. Civic organizations like the Boy Scouts, 4-H, League of Women Voters, Rotary Club, and Chamber of Commerce encourage citizen participation and pride in community and nation.[12]

In modern times, the mass media have taken over some functions previously performed by the family. By the time children leave high school, they will have spent more time watching television than in conversation with their parents. They may have had more political instruction from MTV than from their parents or their schools.[13] Finally, Americans educate each other about political values in the workplace, at the PTA meeting, or in more expressly political activities.

The American Dream

Many of our political values come together in the **American dream**, a complex set of ideas holding that the United States is a land of opportunity and that individual initiative and hard work can bring economic success. Whether realized or not, this American dream speaks to our most deeply held hopes and goals. The essence of the American dream can be found in our enthusiasm for **capitalism**, an economic system

American dream
The widespread belief that the United States is a land of opportunity and that individual initiative and hard work can bring economic success.

capitalism
An economic system characterized by private property, competitive markets, economic incentives, and limited government involvement in the production and pricing of goods and services.

GLOBAL *Perceptions*

QUESTION: Which of the following phrases comes closer to your view: It's good that American ideas and customs are spreading here, OR it's bad that American ideas and customs are spreading here?

American culture includes not only our democratic or political culture but also our popular culture, which includes such things as clothes, movies, food, and music. While the United States government may be unpopular abroad, our popular culture is ubiquitous. Blue jeans, Kentucky Fried Chicken, Starbucks, and the Terminator are international in popularity. While popular at one level, how do people respond when asked about the spread of American culture generally?

In other countries American popular culture is seen as a threat to the culture of that region, country or religion. The Pew Global Attitudes Project asked people their views on American popular culture. Interestingly, "people around the world object to the wide diffusion of American ideas and customs." Africa is the region most positive about American popular culture and the Middle East the least. Across all countries the range is wide, from 69 percent seeing American popular culture as good to only 2 percent having that view in Pakistan.

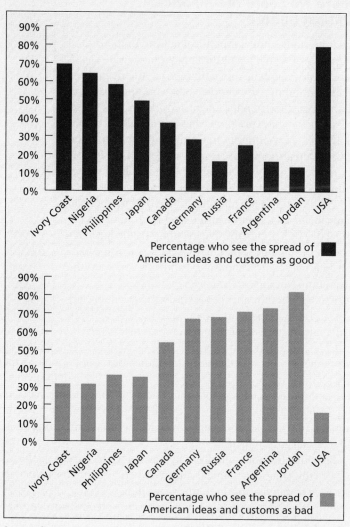

Percentage who see the spread of American ideas and customs as good

Percentage who see the spread of American ideas and customs as bad

SOURCE: The Pew Research Center for the People and the Press, *What the World Thinks in 2002.* Data collected in 2002, pp. 63, 67, T-54.

characterized by private property, competitive markets, economic incentives, and limited government involvement in the production and pricing of goods and services.

The concept of *private property* enjoys extraordinary popularity. In many European democracies, the state owns and operates transportation systems and other businesses that are privately owned and operated in the United States, although there has been some privatization of communications systems like telephone companies and broadcast media in Europe. Americans cherish the dream of acquiring property. Moreover, most Americans believe that the owners of property have the right to decide how to use it

The right to private property is just one of the economic incentives that cement our support for capitalism and fuel the American dream. This is the land of opportunity for the enterprising. Here the competitive, practical go-getter can make a fortune, build a dream home, and retire early. We assume that people who have more ability or who work extremely hard will get ahead, earn more, and enjoy economic rewards. We also believe that people should be able to pass most of what they have accumulated along to

In Comparative Perspective

POLITICAL CULTURE IN MEXICO

In the past decade Mexico experienced the first transfer of power from one party to another in 71 years when Vicente Fox of the National Action Party (PAN) won the 2000 election defeating the Institutional Revolutionary Party (PRI). Three years earlier PRI lost the majority in Congress as well. Given these changes and the limited experience with competitive elections in the past, how do Mexicans see democracy? Had their view changed with the peaceful transfer of power between parties? Alejandro Moreno and Patricia Mendez, drawing from data from the World Values Surveys from 1995–97 and 2000–01, attempt to answer these questions.*

The political culture of Mexico remains less supportive of democracy than in the more experienced democracies. Those surveyed in Mexico were roughly twice as likely to say having a strong leader is very good or fairly good (41 percent) compared to 22 percent in advanced democracies like Germany, Australia, Canada, and the United States. Even more revealing of enduring antidemocratic sentiments is the fact that one in four Mexicans say that having the army rule is very good or fairly good, compared to 6 percent in advanced

democracies. Obversely, just under two-thirds of Mexicans say democracy is the best system (65 percent) compared to 86 percent in advanced democracies. Finally, in terms of social trust, 24 percent of Mexicans surveyed felt most people could be trusted, compared to 41 percent in advanced democracies like Germany, Australia, Canada, and the United States.

This research on Mexico reminds us how popular support for democracy and democratic values like trust and tolerance take time to develop and how lingering tendencies to authoritarianism, like a preference for military rule, take time to dissipate. Moreno and Mendez conclude that Mexicans "aspire to live in a better, high-quality democracy. As they learn about it we should expect changes in democratic values and attitudes in the next years."[†]

*Alejandro Moreno and Patricia Mendez, "Attitudes Toward Democracy: Mexico in Comparative Perspective." This article and information on the World Values Survey can be found at www.worldvaluessurvey.org/library/index.html.
[†]Moreno and Mendez, p. 24.

their children and relatives. Even the poorest Americans generally oppose high inheritance taxes or limits on how much someone can earn. Americans believe that the free market system gives almost everyone a fair chance, that capitalism is necessary, and that freedom depends on it. We reject communism and socialism—a rejection fortified in recent decades as most communist nations shifted toward capitalism. In the United States, individuals and corporations have acquired wealth and, at the same time, exercised political clout. Their power has in turn been widely criticized. The Enron Corporation, for example, made over $2 million in political contributions in the 2000 elections, and between January 1, 1995, and June 30, 2001, Enron ranked among the top 15 political soft-money donors.[14] Enron later filed for bankruptcy and became a notorious example of corporate mismanagement and dishonest accounting.[15] Wealthy individuals have occasionally used their wealth to fund their campaigns for public office (Jon Corzine spent $60 million on his successful New Jersey Senate race in 2000)[16] or to influence elections or public policy (George Soros gave $27 million to organizations like America Coming Together, the Media Fund, MoveOn.org, Joint Victory Campaign, Young Democrats for America, and a few other groups working to defeat George W. Bush).[17]

The conflict in values between a *competitive economy,* in which individuals reap large rewards for their initiative and hard work, and an *egalitarian society,* in which everyone earns a decent living, carries over into politics. How the public resolves this tension changes over time and from issue to issue.

As important as the American dream is to the national consciousness, Americans know it remains unfulfilled. An underclass persists in the form of impoverished families, malnourished and poorly educated children, and people living on the streets.[18] Many cities are actually two cities, where some residents live in luxury while others live in squalor. The gap between rich and poor has grown in recent years, and a sharp difference between white and black income persists tenaciously.[19] For more people than we want to admit, chances for success still depend on the family you were born in, the neighborhood you grew up in, or the college you attended.

Coming from humble beginnings, Oprah Winfrey—television host, movie actress, and one of the highest-paid people in the country—epitomizes the American dream.

★★ **You Decide**

IS THE AMERICAN DREAM STILL ALIVE AND IMPORTANT?

Is the American dream alive? Is it important to people? Some would argue that the wealth and prosperity so many Americans have achieved means that for most the dream has been achieved and is therefore no longer important as a motivating force or a way to explain behavior. Others would contend that for people in poverty the hopelessness of their situauion would mean that talk of the American dream seems far fetched and unattainable. What do you think, is the American dream still an important element of the political culture of the United States?

Political and Economic Change

Political values are clearly affected by historical developments and by economic and technological growth. The Declaration of Independence and the Constitution identified such important political values as individual liberty, property rights, and limited government.[20] Early in our history, we emphasized separation of powers, checks and balances, states' rights, and the Bill of Rights. It took multiple generations before we also began to take seriously the expansion of suffrage and competitive nominations and elections. Notions of political equality and effective participation emerged during the presidency of Andrew Jackson and matured in the course of the nineteenth century. By the end of the nineteenth century, populists and suffragists turned ideals into action and formed large-scale movements to achieve more democratic forms of participation and more responsive forms of governance.

THE INDUSTRIAL TRANSFORMATION   By 1900, the agrarian society the framers knew had largely been replaced by industrial capitalism and the growth of giant corporations. With these changes, ideology was irreversibly transformed. Large privately owned corporations changed the economic order, including changes in the role of government and how people viewed each other. No one captures the implications of this shift better than political scientist Robert A. Dahl:

> One of the consequences of the new order has been a high degree of inequality in the distribution of wealth and income, and far greater inequality than had ever been thought likely or desirable under an agrarian order by Democratic Republicans like Jefferson and Madison, or had ever been thought consistent with democratic or republican government in the historic writings on the subject from Aristotle to Locke, Montesquieu, and Rousseau. Previous theorists and advocates had, like many of the framers of our own Constitution, insisted that a republic could exist only if the citizen body continued neither rich nor poor. Citizens, it was argued, must enjoy a rough equality of conditions.[21]

The success of the American economy led to the accumulation of great wealth in the hands of a few—the "robber barons" or tycoons. Many had taken great risks or earned their fortunes through inventions and efficient production practices. But as disparities of income grew, so did disparities in political resources. Economic resources can be converted into political resources, as when time is spent on political campaigns and money is contributed to parties and candidates.[22] At the beginning of the twentieth century, the rise of corporations and the concentration of individual wealth in the United States created divisions and resentment. Muckraking journalists charged that the huge corporations had become **monopolies**, using their dominance of their industry to exploit workers and limit competition. Unsafe working conditions led to regulation of the workplace by the states; however, it seemed that only the national government had the power to ensure fair treatment in the marketplace. This sentiment not only gave rise to the nation's first **antitrust legislation**—federal laws that try to prevent monopolies from dominating an industry and restraining trade—but also sowed the idea that the national government could—and should—as the Constitution asserts, "promote the general Welfare" by regulating working conditions, product safety, and labor-management disputes.

THE GREAT DEPRESSION AND THE NEW DEAL   Much of our thinking about the role of government in a capitalistic system was shaped by the Great Depression of the 1930s and the near collapse of the capitalistic system. Unrestrained capitalism and an unregulated market were faulted as causes of the Depression. The collapse of the stock market, massive unemployment, and a failed banking system caused widespread suffering among the nation's citizens. Americans had no unemployment compensation, no guarantee on bank savings, no federal regulation of the securities exchanges, and no Social Security. People turned to the government to improve the lot of millions of jobless and homeless citizens. Beginning with President Franklin D. Roosevelt's New Deal, the idea gradually gained widespread acceptance that governments, at both the national and

monopoly
Domination of an industry by a single company by fixing prices and discouraging competition; also, the company that dominates the industry by these means.

antitrust legislation
Federal laws (starting with the Sherman Act of 1890) that try to prevent a monopoly from dominating an industry and restraining trade.

state levels, should use their powers and resources to ensure some measure of equal opportunity and social justice.

Roosevelt's State of the Union Address in 1944 outlined a "Second Bill of Rights" for all citizens in which he declared that this nation must make a firm commitment to "economic security and independence." Included in his Second Bill of Rights were the following:

- The right to a useful and remunerative job in the industries, shops, farms, or mines of the nation

- The right to earn enough to provide adequate food and clothing and recreation

- The right of every farmer to raise and sell his products at a return that would give him and his family a decent living

- The right of every businessman, large and small, to trade in an atmosphere of freedom from unfair competition and domination by monopolies at home or abroad

- The right of every family to a decent home

- The right to adequate medical care and the opportunity to achieve and enjoy good health

- The right to adequate protection from the economic fears of old age, sickness, accident, and unemployment

- The right to a good education[23]

Roosevelt's policies and later efforts by Presidents John F. Kennedy and Lyndon B. Johnson in the 1960s to pass civil rights and voting rights legislation and launch a "war on poverty" defined the ideological and political fights of the second half of the twentieth century. Modern-day liberalism and conservatism turn, in large measure, on how much one believes in Roosevelt's Second Bill of Rights and how much government assistance one thinks is owed to minorities, women, and others who have suffered discrimination or have been left behind by the industrial or technological revolutions of the twentieth century. Today, free enterprise is no longer unbridled. Government regulations, antitrust laws, job safety regulations, environmental standards, and minimum wage laws try to balance freedom of enterprise against the rights of individuals. Most people today support a semiregulated or mixed free enterprise

★★★ THINKING IT THROUGH

The persistence of poverty in a land of plenty is perplexing, but it does not change the reality that some are able to escape it. Examples of individuals who have achieved at least a portion of the American dream arise often enough to reinforce acceptance that the dream can come true. While some achieve the dream because they win the lottery, more do so because of opportunities like an education.

More important than data on poverty is the belief that people can attain success and affluence. The American dream does not have to be achieved by everyone to be an important motivator. New immigrant groups have long been an incubator of the American dream, and they continue to be so today. Parents working multiple low-paying jobs while stressing education for their children provide an example of both the work and dream components of this aspiration. At the same time it is also clear that the American dream is less available to some than to others and that access to it can be limited by larger forces like recessions, unemployment, or illness. Some problems many middle-class individuals can take in stride can derail the hopes and aspirations of those without a safety net. The extent to which the American dream persists in our political culture, despite its limitations, is evidence of its power and importance.

Breadlines like this provided handouts of food to thousands of unemployed and destitute people during the Great Depression.

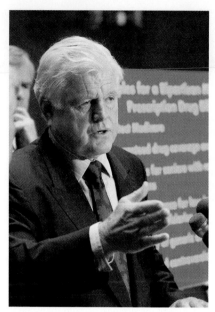

Senator Ted Kennedy (D.-Mass) has been a champion of liberal programs and legislation for many years. He is shown here at a press conference called by the consumer advocacy group Families USA to address the rising cost of the top fifty prescription drugs sold to senior citizens.

TABLE 4–3 ATTITUDES ON BUSINESS AND LABOR	
The strength of this country is mostly based on the success of American business.	75%
Government regulation of business usually does more harm than good.	53
Business corporations generally strike a fair balance between making profits and serving the public interest.	38
There is too much power concentrated in the hands of a few big companies.	77
Labor unions are necessary to protect the working person.	74

SOURCE: The Pew Research Center for the People and the Press, *Evenly Divided and Increasingly Polarized: 2004 Political Landscape.* Data collected in August, 2003.

system that checks the worst tendencies of capitalism, but they reject excessive government intervention (see Table 4–3). Much of American politics centers on how to achieve this balance. Currently, liberals and conservatives agree that some governmental intervention is necessary to assist Americans who fall short in the competition for education and economic prosperity.

POLITICAL IDEOLOGY AND ATTITUDES TOWARD GOVERNMENT

Political ideology refers to a consistent pattern of ideas or beliefs about political values and the role of government. It includes the views people have about how government should work and how it actually works. Ideology links our basic values to the day-to-day operations or policies of government.

Two major schools of political ideology dominate American politics: *liberalism* and *conservatism.* Three lesser schools of thought—*socialism, environmentalism,* and *libertarianism*—also help define the spectrum of ideology in the United States. Table 4–4 provides a general distribution of political ideology in the United States.

Liberalism

In the seventeenth and eighteenth centuries, classical liberals fought to minimize the role of government. They stressed individual rights and perceived government as the primary threat to rights and liberties. Classical liberals favored *limited government* and sought ample protections from governmental harassment. Over time, the emphasis on individualism remained constant, but the perception of the need for government changed.

CONTEMPORARY LIBERALS   In its current American usage, **liberalism** refers to a belief in the positive uses of government to bring about justice and equality of opportunity. Modern-day liberals wish to preserve the rights of the individual and the right to own private property, yet they are willing to have the government intervene in the economy to remedy the defects of capitalism. Liberals advocate equal access to health care, housing, and education for all citizens. They generally believe in affirmative action programs, workers' health and safety protections, tax rates that rise with income, and unions' rights to organize and strike.

On a more philosophical level, liberals generally believe in the probability of progress. They believe that the future will be better, that obstacles can be overcome. This positive set of beliefs may explain their willingness to trust government programs. Modern liberals contend that modern technology and industrialization cry out for government programs to offset the loss of liberties suffered by the poor and the weak. Liberals such as Edward Kennedy and Hillary Rodham Clinton frequently stress the need for an involved and affirmative government.

Liberals charge that conservatives usually act out of self-interest and follow the maxim "a rising tide will lift all boats." In contrast, liberals would agree with President

political ideology
A consistent pattern of beliefs about political values and the role of government.

liberalism
A belief in the positive uses of government to bring about justice and equality of opportunity.

TABLE 4–4 DIFFERENCES IN POLITICAL IDEOLOGY

	Conservative	*Moderate*	*Liberal*
Sex			
Male	44%	29%	26%
Female	47	20	32
Race			
White	47	28	26
Black	31	28	41
Age			
18–34	45	23	32
35–45	46	30	24
46–55	42	25	33
56–64	46	29	25
65+	46	32	22
Religion			
Protestant	50	27	23
Catholic	48	28	23
Jewish	17	40	43
Education			
Less than high school	39	39	39
High school diploma	43	35	35
Some college	47	27	27
Bachelor's degree	48	21	21
Advanced degree	42	25	25
Party			
Democrat	20	30	50
Independent	34	40	26
Republican	79	15	6

SOURCE: Center for Political Studies, University of Michigan, *2002 American National Election Study Guide to Public Opinion and Electoral Behavior.*

NOTE: We have combined with the moderates persons who do not know their ideology or had not thought much about it. For party identification, we have combined independent leaners with their respective parties. Rows may not add up to 100 percent due to rounding.

Harry Truman who said, "We have rejected the discredited theory that the fortunes of the nation should be in the hands of a privileged few. Instead, we believe that our economic system should rest on a democratic foundation and that wealth should be created for the benefit of all.... Every segment of our population and every individual has a right to expect from his government a fair deal."[24]

Equality of opportunity is viewed by liberals as essential, and to achieve that end, liberals believe that discriminatory practices must be eliminated. Some liberals favor the reduction of great inequalities of wealth that make equality of opportunity impossible. Most favor a certain minimum level of income. Rather than placing a cap on wealth, they want a floor placed beneath the poor. In short, liberals seek to lessen the impact of great inequalities of wealth and work to extend opportunities to all, regardless of their economic standing. If necessary they favor raising taxes to achieve these goals. If you are interested in learning more about the liberal ideology you may find www.prospect.org or www.turnleft.com/liberal.html helpful.

CRITICISMS OF LIBERALISM   Critics of liberalism say that liberals place too much reliance on governmental solutions, higher taxes, and bureaucracy. These opponents argue that somewhere along the line, liberals forgot that government, to serve our best interests, has to be limited. Power tends to corrupt, and too much dependence on government can corrupt the spirit, undermine self-reliance, and make people forget those cherished personal freedoms and property rights our Republic was founded to secure and protect. Too many governmental regulations, too much government bureaucracy, and too much taxation tend to undermine the self-help ethic that "made America great." In short, critics of liberalism contend that the welfare and regulatory state pushed by liberals will ultimately destroy individual initiative, the entrepreneurial spirit, and the very engine of economic growth that might lead to true equality of economic opportunity.

In recent elections, Republicans have made liberalism a villain while at the same time they have attempted to position their presidential candidates more in the mainstream. George H. W. Bush, in 1988, consistently referred to Michael Dukakis as from the "liberal Democratic party." Bill Clinton was careful not to label his program as liberal, focusing on the need for economic growth, jobs, and a lower budget deficit. He insisted he was a "New Democrat." Al Gore positioned himself in the tradition of Clinton as a centrist, not a liberal, but George W. Bush charged that Gore was an advocate of big government. The same charge was leveled against congressional Democratic candidates in 2002 by their Republican opponents and their allied interest groups.

The movement to the center by some Democrats and the conventional wisdom that liberal or progressive approaches are in decline is disputed by political commentator E. J. Dionne Jr., whose book on how progressives can regain power is aptly titled *They Only Look Dead.* Dionne contends that the current political upheaval should be defined less as a revolt against *big* government than as a rebellion against *bad* government—government that has proved ineffectual in grappling with the political, economic, and moral crises that have shaken the country. Dionne challenges the claims that big government is bad or even over. Pointing to past progressive or liberal successes, Dionne contends Americans want a government that eases economic transitions, helps "preserve a broad middle class," and "expands the choices available to individuals."[25]

The popularity of liberalism and conservatism and the importance of particular issues change with world events. For a time, we were preoccupied with budget deficits. With the end of the cold war, we became more concerned about domestic policy than about foreign policy. Policy concerns changed with the terrorist attacks of September 11, 2001, and the war on terrorism that followed. Budget deficits replaced projected surpluses, and Americans became focused on places like Iraq, Afghanistan, and North Korea.

The reelection of George W. Bush in 2004, along with a net loss of four U.S. Senate seats by the Democrats, was due in part to the importance of the national security issue but it also reflected public concerns with moral values. Enactment of referendums in thirteen states in 2004 defining marriage as between a man and a woman forced moral values questions onto the agenda of the presidential election. Efforts by liberals to define the same-sex marriage issue as primarily about rights failed.

Conservatism

Private property rights and belief in free enterprise are cardinal attributes of contemporary **conservatism**. In contrast to liberals, conservatives want to enhance individual liberty by keeping government small, especially the national government, except in the area of national defense. Conservatives take a more pessimistic view of human nature than liberals do. They maintain that people need strong leadership institutions, firm laws, and strict moral codes. Government, they think, needs to ensure order. Conservatives also believe that people who fail in life are in some way the architects of their own misfortune and must bear the main responsibility for solving their own problems. Conservatives prefer a reversal of laws on judicial rulings permitting abortion, affirmative action programs, and various worker protection laws.

TRADITIONAL CONSERVATIVES Traditional conservatives are emphatically pro-business. They favor tax cuts and resist all but the most necessary antitrust, trade, and environmental regulations on corporations. They believe that the functions of government should be to protect the nation from foreign enemies, preserve law and order,

conservatism
A belief that limited government ensures order, competitive markets, and personal opportunity.

enforce private contracts, foster competitive markets, encourage free and fair trade, and promote family values. Traditional conservatives favor dispersing power broadly throughout the political and social systems to avoid concentration of power at the national level. They favor having the market, rather than the government, provide services.

Until recent decades, conservatives opposed the New Deal programs of the 1930s, the War on Poverty in the 1960s, and many civil rights and affirmative action programs. Human needs, they say, can and should be taken care of by families and charities. Conservatives are more inclined to put their faith in the private sector and dislike the tendency to turn to government, especially the national government, for solutions to societal problems. Government social activism, they say, has been expensive and counterproductive. They prefer private giving and individual voluntary efforts targeted at social and economic problems rather than government programs. As noted, conservatives have come to see some social problems as needing a government response. They differ from liberals in the extent to which they see problems this way and in a preference for state and local government over national government activity when a government response is needed.

Conservatives, especially when in office, selectively advocate government activism, often while continuing to criticize government generally. Early in the 2000 presidential campaign, for example, George W. Bush said, "Too often, my party has confused the need for a limited government with a disdain for government itself." Love of country, he said, "is undermined by sprawling, arrogant, aimless government. It is restored by focused and effective and energetic government."[26] To learn more about conservative beliefs, go to www.aei.org or www.heritage.org.

SOCIAL CONSERVATIVES Some conservatives focus less on economics and more on morality and lifestyle. Social conservatives favor strong governmental action to protect children from pornography and drugs. They want stringent limits on abortions and oppose gay marriage. This brand of conservatism—sometimes called the New Right, ultraconservatism, or even the Radical Right—emerged in the 1980s. The New Right shares the traditional conservative's love of freedom and backs an aggressive effort to defend America's interests abroad. It favors the return of organized prayer in public schools and opposes policies like job quotas, busing, and tolerance of homosexuality. In sum, a defining characteristic of the New Right is a strong desire to impose various *social controls*.

A New Right or Religious Right group that supports social conservatism includes, among others, Pat Robertson, a minister who sponsors a nightly cable television program. Robertson's Christian Coalition was a major political force in the 1980s and early 1990s but has weakened in recent years.[27] Although ostensibly working in a bipartisan fashion, it is more at home in the Republican party. The Coalition endorses candidates who are profamily, antiabortion, and antigay. It favors a constitutional amendment that would guarantee the rights to organized prayer in public schools and religious symbols in public places. Without regard to denomination, nearly two-thirds (63 percent) of those who attend church regularly vote Republican, while those who do not vote just as disproportionately for the Democrats.[28]

Some conservatives are uncomfortable with the close association between the Republican party and the Christian Right. Former U.S. Senator Warren Rudman of New Hampshire has observed, "Politically speaking, the Republican Party is making a terrible mistake if it appears to ally itself with the Christian right. There are some fine, sincere people in its ranks, but there are also enough anti-abortion zealots, would-be censors, homophobes, bigots, and latter-day Elmer Gantrys to discredit any party that is unwise enough to embrace such a group."[29] Rudman's statement was later used to justify phone calls by Robertson to Christian Coalition members urging them to vote for George W. Bush in the 2000 South Carolina and Michigan primaries instead of for John McCain, whose campaign Rudman co-chaired.[30]

CRITICISMS OF CONSERVATISM Not everyone agreed with Ronald Reagan's statement that "government is the problem." Indeed, critics of conservatism point out that conservatives themselves urge more government when it serves their needs—regulating pornography and abortion, for example—but are opposed to it when it serves somebody else's. Conservatives may also have fewer objections to big government when

Grover Norquist, head of Americans for Tax Reform, is a major proponent of lowering federal, state, and local taxes. Conservatives believe that by lowering taxes, people will have more money to invest in the economy and to donate to charitable organizations.

individuals have a choice in determining how government will impact them. Vouchers for schools, choices in prescription drug benefit plans, and options to manage Social Security savings are examples of such choices proposed by President George W. Bush.[31] Critics of these proposals see conservatives as selective in their criticism of big government or supportive only when it fits their assumptions about what is the best approach.

Conservatives place great faith in the market economy—critics say too much faith. This posture often puts conservatives at odds with labor unions and consumer activists and in close alliance with businesspeople, particularly large corporations. Hostility to regulation and a belief in competition leads them to push for deregulation. This approach has not always had the intended positive effects, as the collapse of many savings and loan companies in the 1980s, the energy crisis in California in the early 2000s, and the business and accounting failures at Enron and other major corporations in 2002 revealed.[32] Conservatives counter that relying on market solutions and encouraging the free market are still the best course of action in most policy areas.

The policy of lowering taxes during the Reagan and George W. Bush administrations was consistent with the conservative hostility to big government. Many conservatives embraced the idea that if taxes are lowered on the rich, their increased economic activity will "trickle down" to the poor. This view was criticized by many Democrats, who pointed out that the growth in income and wealth in the 1980s was largely concentrated among the well-to-do.[33] They also pointed out that reduced taxes and increased government spending, especially for defense, tripled the deficit during the 1980s, when conservatives were in control. President George W. Bush pressed for tax cuts during his administration and pressed to make them permanent in his reelection campaign. Democrats and some conservative Republicans criticized Bush for wanting lower taxes at the same time the budget deficit was growing.

Liberals charge that some conservatives repeatedly fail to acknowledge and endorse policies that deal with racism and sexism. Their opposition to civil rights laws in the 1960s and to affirmative action more recently is cited. Not only have some conservatives opposed new laws in these areas, liberals charge, they have hampered the executive branch and sought to limit the courts' implementation of civil rights laws.

The selective application of government by liberals and social conservatives demonstrates the lack of consistency by some in both groups. Liberals favor vigorous governmental programs to help the poor but oppose governmental intrusion into people's private lives to protect our national security, while some social conservatives preach less government except when they consider it necessary to counter drugs, pornography, and other social evils.

Socialism

Socialism is an economic and governmental system based on public ownership of the means of production and exchange. Karl Marx once described socialism as a transitional stage of society between capitalism and communism. In a capitalist system, the means of production and most property are privately owned; in a communist system, property is controlled by the state in common for all the people, and the government is in charge of a single political party representing the working classes, with no opposition allowed. Communist countries like Cuba are ruled by one party, the Communist party. Some countries, like Sweden, have combined some aspects of government ownership and operation of business with democracy. Others have experimented with socializing medicine and telecommunications while keeping other economic sectors private.

In one of the most dramatic transformations in recent times, Russia, its sister republics, and its former eastern European satellites abandoned communism in the early 1990s and have been attempting to establish free markets. These countries had previously had a system of state ownership and centralized government planning of the economy. But political and economic failure in the Soviet Union resulted in the disintegration of its communist leadership and its empire. Once central power was loosened over the

socialism
An economic and governmental system based on public ownership of the means of production and exchange.

Soviet republics and satellites, a tide of political and economic reform left communism intact in only a few countries, such as Cuba and China. American socialists—of whom there are only a few prominent examples—favor a greatly expanded role for the government but argue that such a system is compatible with democracy. They would nationalize certain industries, institute a public jobs program so that all who want work would be put to work, place a much steeper tax burden on the wealthy, and drastically cut defense spending.[34] Most of the democracies of western Europe are more influenced by socialist ideas than we are in the United States, but they remain, like the United States, largely market economies. Many countries appear to be turning to market solutions for problems once assumed to be the responsibility of government. Debate will continue about the proper role of government and what the market can do better than government can.[35]

Environmentalism

An intense concern with the environment and related matters is **environmentalism**, an ideology that has taken root in several democracies in recent decades and led to the formation of Green parties in several countries. The Green movement has elected members of parliament in Finland, Germany, Switzerland, Sweden, Luxembourg, Austria, and the Netherlands and is part of the liberal-left coalition governing Germany today. In the United States, the Green party emphasizes such values as grassroots democracy, social justice, equal opportunity, nonviolence, respect for diversity, and feminism. In these areas, environmentalism is little different from liberalism, but it is in the emphasis on ecology and the environment that Greens are distinct.

The Web site of the U.S. Green party says, "We must practice agriculture which replenishes the soil; move to an energy-efficient economy; and live in ways that respect the integrity of natural systems."[36] Ralph Nader, the party's presidential candidate in 2000, enhanced the visibility of the party but still won less than 3 percent of the vote in the general election. In 2004, David Cobb, lacking the visibility or stature of Ralph Nader, received less than one-tenth of one percent of the vote. More broadly, the environment as an issue in 2004 was not as important as it had been in past elections and environmental groups focused less of their attention on congressional contests and more on the presidential contest. Most environmental groups supported John Kerry. The Green party endorsed gay marriage, a tougher stance on polluters, and slave reparations.

Libertarianism

Libertarianism is a political ideology that cherishes individual liberty and insists on sharply limited government. It carries some overtones of anarchism, of the classical English liberalism of the past, and of a 1930s-style conservatism. The Libertarian party has gained a small following among people who believe that both liberals and conservatives lack consistency in their attitude toward the power of the national government.

Libertarians preach opposition to almost all government programs. They favor massive cuts in government spending and an end to the Federal Bureau of Investigation, the Central Intelligence Agency, and most regulatory commissions. They oppose participation in the United Nations and favor a defense establishment that would defend the United States only if directly attacked. They oppose *all* government regulation, including, for example, mandatory seat-belt and helmet laws. Unlike conservatives, libertarians would repeal laws that regulate personal morality, including abortion, pornography, prostitution, and illicit drugs.

A Libertarian party candidate for president has been on the ballot in all 50 states in recent presidential elections, although never obtaining more than 1 percent of the vote. The Libertarian candidate for president in 2000, Harry Browne, ran on a platform that emphasized freedom from government. The 2000 Libertarian platform was committed to a smaller government, limited by the Constitution's specifications, and proposed immediate and complete removal of the federal government from education, energy,

Bernard Sanders, a self-described Socialist, represents Vermont in the U.S. House of Representatives as an Independent.

environmentalism
An ideology that is dominated by concern for the environment but also promotes grassroots democracy, social justice, equal opportunity, nonviolence, respect for diversity, and feminism.

libertarianism
An ideology that cherishes individual liberty and insists on a sharply limited government, promoting a free market economy, a noninterventionist foreign policy, and an absence of regulation in the moral and social spheres.

PEOPLE & POLITICS *Making a Difference* ★ ★ ★

RACHEL CARSON AND THE ENVIRONMENTAL MOVEMENT.

"There was once a town in the heart of America where all life seemed to live in harmony with its surroundings. . . . Then a strange blight crept over the area and everything began to change. . . . There was a strange stillness. . . . The few birds seen anywhere were moribund; they trembled violently and could not fly. It was a spring without voices."* These words of Rachel Carson, found at the beginning of her most famous work, *Silent Spring,* elicited a response that was anything but silent.

A gifted researcher and writer, Carson had worked with the U.S. Bureau of Fisheries (later the U.S. Fish and Wildlife Service) and was one of only two women then employed with the Bureau at a professional level. Her first book, *Under the Sea Wind,* demonstrated her ability to describe the natural world to her readers. During her years in government service she became alarmed by the widespread use of pesticides and their harmful effects on the

environment. She contacted *Reader's Digest* in hopes of writing an article on the subject, but was met with disinterest.[†] Not until many years later did alarming wildlife death rates in specific areas sprayed by pesticides serve as a catalyst for her to write and publish *Silent Spring.*

Without moral courage to go along with her academic abilities, it is doubtful that she could have made the impact that she did with *Silent Spring.* Carson overcame personal adversity, including the deaths of a niece and her mother and the discovery that she had terminal cancer.[‡] Carson's book has been criticized by the chemical industry, the Department of Agriculture, and many in the media. In response to these attacks she said, "I have felt bound by a solemn obligation to do what I could."[§] Carson's book made a difference, influencing lawmakers to pass legislation banning the use of DDT and establishing the Environmental Protection Agency.[||]

*Rachel Carson, *Silent Spring* (Houghton Mifflin, 1962), pp. 1, 2.
[†] Peter Matthiessen, "Rachel Carson," *Time Magazine,* March 29, 1999. www.time.com/time/time100/scientist/profile/carson02.html.
[‡] www.pbs.org/wgbh/aso/databank/entries/btcars.html.
[§] Matthiessen. www.time.com/time/time100/scientist/profile/carson03.html.
[||] For a more detailed biography of Rachel Carson see rachelcarson.fws.gov/carsonbio.html.

Libertarian Party

Michael Badnarik, Libertarian candidate for president in 2004. Badnarik received 380,000 votes in the 2004 election—just 20,000 less than Nader and the most of all official candidates for the minor parties.

regulation, crime control, welfare, housing, transportation, health care, and agriculture; repeal of the income tax and all other direct taxes; decriminalization of drugs and pardons for prisoners convicted of nonviolent drug offenses; and withdrawal of overseas military forces. Libertarian positions are rarely timid; at the very least, they prompt intriguing political debates.[37] The Libertarian party's 2004 candidate, Michael Badnarik, received 380,000 votes, just 20,000 behind Nader. Badnarik received the most votes of the official candidates for the minor parties (Brian Faler, "A Polling Sight: Record Turnout," *The Washington Post,* November 5, 2004, p. A7). In 2004, the Libertarian party endorsed same sex marriage, legalizing drugs, repealing the Patriot Act, withdrawing from Iraq, eliminating all gun control laws, retracting business regulations, and eliminating the FDA. To learn more about libertarianism, go to www.lp.org.

A Word of Caution

Political labels have different meanings across national boundaries as well as over time. To be a liberal in certain European nations is to be on the right; to be a liberal in the United States is to be on the left. In recent elections, the term "liberal"—which back in Franklin Roosevelt's day had been popular—became "the L-word," a label most politicians sought to avoid. But liberalism is more than a label. On big questions—such as the role of government in the economy, in promoting equality of opportunity, and in regulating the behavior of individuals or businesses—real differences separate conservative and liberal groups. This does not mean, however, that people who are conservative in one area are necessarily conservative in another or that liberals always hold similar views.

It is important to appreciate that ideology both causes events and is affected by them. Just as the Great Depression resulted in a tidal wave of ideological change, so did our involvement in World War II. The attacks on the World Trade Center and the Pentagon on September 11, 2001, may also have a lasting impact. For example, World War II, with its positive example of how government can work to defend freedom, strengthened positive views about the role of the national government. The Vietnam War probably had the opposite effect, producing disillusionment with government. The antigovernment sentiment in recent presidential elections is undoubtedly related to Vietnam, the Watergate scandal, and allegations of sexual misconduct by political leaders in recent years. The surge in patriotism and sense of national unity in the war against terrorism after September 11 stands in sharp contrast to the national mood during the final years of the Vietnam War. It also reflects, at least in the short term, a view that government has an important role to play in responding to a crisis (see Figure 4–1).

POLITICAL IDEOLOGY AND THE AMERICAN PEOPLE

For some people, ideological controversy today centers on the role of the government in improving schools, encouraging a stronger work ethic, and stopping the flow of drugs into the country. For others, ideology is centered on whether to permit openly gay people into the military or sanction same-sex marriages and on the best ways to instill moral values, build character, and encourage cohesive and lasting families.

Despite the twists and turns of American politics, the distribution of ideology in the nation has been remarkably consistent (see Figure 4–2). Conservatives outnumber liberals, but the proportion of conservatives did not increase substantially with the

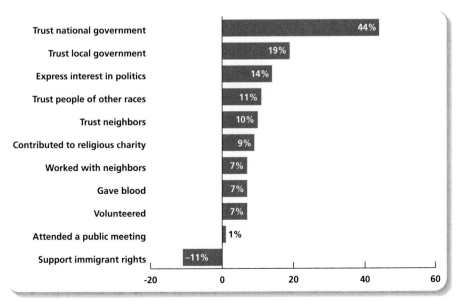

FIGURE 4–1 Net Changes in Civic Attitudes after September 11, 2001.
SOURCE: Robert D. Putnam, "Bowling Together," *American Prospect* 13 (February 11, 2002): 20–22.

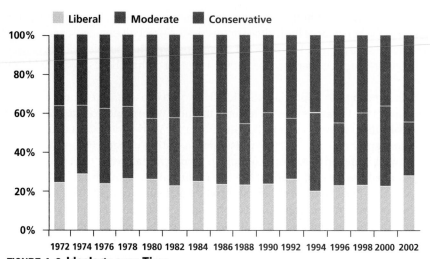

FIGURE 4–2 Ideology over Time.
Source: Center for Political Studies, University of Michigan, *2002 National Election Study Guide to Public Opinion and Electoral Behavior.*

FIGURE 4–3 Ideology Curve.
Source: Center for Political Studies, University of Michigan, *2002 National Election Study Guide to Public Opinion and Electoral Behavior.*

decisive Republican presidential victories of the 1980s or congressional victories of the 1990s.

Another important fact about ideology in the United States is that most people are moderates or not very ideological. In 2000 and 2002, only 2 percent of the population saw themselves as extreme liberals, while extreme conservatives ranged form 2–4 percent in these same years (see Figure 4–3). These percentages have changed very little over time. The tendency toward muted ideology is also demonstrated by the fact that more people consider themselves *slightly* liberal or *slightly* conservative than liberal or conservative. Despite claims by ideological extremes in both parties to move to the right or to the left, there are simply more votes in the middle.[38]

Both major parties targeted moderate or centrist voters in the 2000 presidential election, as reflected in the stands of the candidates on key issues, including their efforts to minimize ideological battles at the conventions. Governor Tommy Thompson of Wisconsin, who chaired the Republican Platform Committee, stated that their more conservative partisans did not push their issues because "they want to win."[39] In 2004, both presidential candidates again courted the "swing" or undecided voters in states where the race was close. But both parties also worked hard to activate more ideological voters, sometimes called the "base" vote. Kerry stressed jobs and a middle-class tax cut in an effort to secure support from working people. Bush emphasized reaching conservative Christian voters and Republicans who had moved in the last few years into outlying suburbs, sometimes called exurbs.

For those who have a liberal or conservative preference, ideology provides a lens through which to view candidates and public policies. It helps simplify the complexities of politics, policies, personalities, and programs. However, most Americans do not organize their political views systematically. A voter may want increased spending for defense but vote for the party that is for reducing defense spending because he or she has always voted for that party or prefers its stand on the environment. Or a person may favor tax cuts and balancing the budget while at the same time being unwilling to see government programs cut back substantially.

The degree to which people have ideologically consistent attitudes and opinions varies but is often relatively low. Much of the time, people view political issues as isolated matters and do not apply an overall standard of performance in evaluating parties or candidates. Indeed, many citizens find it difficult to relate what happens in one policy situation to what happens in another. This problem becomes more complex as government gets into more and more policy areas. Hence many people, not surprisingly, have difficulty finding candidates who reflect their ideological preferences across a wide range of issues.

The absence of widespread and solidified liberal and conservative positions in the United States makes for politics and policy-making processes that are markedly different from those in many European and other nations. Policy making in this country is characterized more by coalitions of the moment than by fixed alignments that pit one set of ideologies against another. Our politics is marked more by moderation, pragmatism, and accommodation than by a prolonged battle among two, three, or more competing philosophies of government. Elsewhere, especially in countries where a strong Socialist or Christian Democratic party exists, like Germany or Sweden, things are different. This does not, however, mean that policies or ideas are not important elements in American politics. There has been, for instance, a shift to strongly partisan and ideological voting in the House of Representatives. Part of the explanation for the increasing importance of ideology in Congress is Republican gains in the South, with remaining southern Democrats becoming more liberal[40]; in other parts of the country where moderate Republicans were once successful, liberal Democrats now hold many seats. Perhaps even more important, congressional districts are now being drawn in such a way as to make more of them safe for one or the other party, so Republican members of Congress tend to appeal to the more conservative wing of their party, while the more liberal Democratic members of Congress tend to appeal to the more liberal wing of their party.

IDEOLOGY AND TOLERANCE

Is there a connection between the ideologies of liberalism and conservatism and support for civil liberties and tolerance for racial minorities? Some political scientists assert that conservatives are generally less tolerant than liberals.[41] This view is stoutly contested by conservatives, who have charged liberals with trying to impose a "politically correct" position on faculty and students in universities, colleges, and the media. Liberals are usually more tolerant of dissent from some quarters and the expression of some unorthodox opinions. However, liberals, too, can be intolerant—of abortion foes, for example, or the National Rifle Association or the views of Sean Hannity. On the other side, some conservatives have worked to seek dismissal of faculty members and ministers who have been critical of the war against terrorism.

Most liberals are strongly opposed to crime and lawbreaking, yet they are also concerned about the causes of crime and trying to eliminate them. Perhaps for this reason, liberals exhibit somewhat greater concern than conservatives for the rights of the accused and are more willing to expand the rights of due process. Conservatives usually take a harder line and, in recent years, have won widespread popular support for their greater concern for the victims of crime than for the rights of the accused.

Such differences are most evident in the responses of liberals and conservatives to questions of civil rights and civil liberties. In the area of free speech, conservatives are usually seen as less willing to permit speech that is out of the political or cultural mainstream. Perhaps conservatives are less tolerant because those who claim to be exercising the right of free speech often attack established values. Liberals favor limiting speech in areas like cigarette advertising or campaign spending but favor fewer restrictions than conservatives do on countercultural individuals or groups.[42]

Conservatives believe that the United States has become morally too permissive. Many conservatives, especially in the New or Religious Right, are highly critical of homosexuals, drug users, prostitutes, unwed mothers, and pornographers. They worry about what they claim has been a decline in moral standards and, interestingly, call on government to help reverse these trends. Most liberals, by contrast, generally accept nonconformity in conduct and opinion as an inescapable byproduct of freedom.[43] In this regard, liberals are like libertarians.

"It's been hell! The breakfast bagels aren't toasted, I can't sleep with a nightlight, there's no "dry hair" formula shampoo in the showers, and the guard won't get close enough for me to stab him with a spoon!"

By Steve Stack, *Minneapolis Star-Tribune*. Reprinted with permission of Star Tribune.

POLITICAL SURVEY: WHAT DO YOU BELIEVE?

Political scientists measure ideology by asking people about their beliefs and values and then placing those individual responses in a context of a broader public. The Make it Real feature for this chapter provides a sample of these polling questions, allowing you to see how you would be categorized. You can also compare your views with those of the general public.

Go to Make it Real: "Political Survey: What Do You Believe?"

Ideologies have consequences. It is these sharp cleavages in political thinking that stir opposing interest groups into action. A wide variety of groups promote their views of what is politically desirable. It is also these differences in ideological perspectives that reinforce party loyalties and divide us at election time. Policy fights in Congress, between Congress and the White House, and during judicial confirmation hearings also have their roots in our uneasily coexisting ideological values.

Our hard-earned rights and liberties are never entirely safeguarded; they are fragile and are shaped by the political, economic, and social climate of the day. In later chapters, we examine the interest groups and political parties that are battling to advance their values and compete in the American political culture. But before turning to those topics, we examine the social and economic diversity of the American political landscape in Chapter 5 and see why agreement on shared democratic values is all the more remarkable.

SUMMARY

1. The United States, like every other nation or society, has a distinctive political culture. It consists of a widely held set of fundamental political values and accepted processes and institutions that help us manage conflict and resolve problems. In the United States, at least in the abstract, people respect the Constitution, the Bill of Rights, the two-party system, and the right to elect officials on the basis of majority rule. Our belief in social equality has fostered acceptance of the notion that government should guarantee equality of opportunity through programs like education and job training.

2. Americans share a widespread commitment to classical liberalism, which embraces the importance of individual liberty, equality, individualism, power to the people, private property, limited government, nationalism, optimism, idealism, the democratic consensus, and justice and the rule of law. They also believe that the American dream should be something we can all pursue.

3. American political values have been and continue to be affected by historical and economic developments. Among these have been the industrial revolution, the development of large corporations and other large institutions, the Great Depression, and a global economy.

4. The sources of the American political culture include the family, schools, religious and civic organizations, the mass media, and political activities.

5. Two broad schools of thought are important in American politics today: liberalism, a belief in the positive uses of government to bring about justice and equality of opportunity; and conservatism, a belief that limited government ensures order, competitive markets, and personal opportunity. Socialism, environmentalism, and libertarianism also attract a modest following in America.

6. Most Americans are nonideological and are guided primarily by moderate pragmatism. Few Americans are extremists.

7. Ideological orientation has a bearing on how tolerant we are of the views and conduct of others. Liberals tend to be more tolerant, whereas conservatives generally favor tradition, stability, and greater levels of social control. These differences have consequences for electoral contests and policy development in our political system.

KEY TERMS

social capital
political culture
natural rights
democratic consensus

majority rule
popular sovereignty
American dream
capitalism

monopoly
antitrust legislation
political ideology
liberalism

conservatism
socialism
environmentalism
libertarianism

Further Reading

H. W. BRANDS, *The Strange Death of American Liberalism* (Yale University Press, 2001).

JAMES W. CEASER, *Reconstructing America: The Symbol of America in Modern Thought* (Yale University Press, 1997).

E. J. DIONNE JR., *They Only Look Dead: Why Progressives Will Dominate the Next Political Era* (Simon & Schuster, 1996).

JEAN BETHKE ELSHTAIN, *Democracy on Trial* (Basic Books, 1995).

AMY GUTMANN AND DENNIS THOMPSON, *Democracy and Disagreement: Why Moral Conflict Cannot Be Avoided in Politics, and What Should Be Done About It* (Harvard University Press, 1996).

LAWRENCE E. HARRISON AND SAMUEL P. HARRINGTON, EDS., *Culture Matters: How Values Shape Human Progress* (Basic Books, 2000).

LOUIS HARTZ, *The Liberal Tradition in America* (Harcourt, 1955).

GEORGE KLOSKO, *Democratic Procedures and Liberal Consensus* (Oxford University Press, 2000).

IRVING KRISTOL, *Neoconservatism: The Autobiography of an Idea* (Free Press, 1995).

DAVID C. LEEGE, KENNETH D. WALD, BRIAN S. KRUEGER, AND PAUL D. MUELLER, *The Politics of Cultural Differences* (Princeton University Press, 2002).

HERBERT MCCLOSKY AND JOHN ZALLER, *The American Ethos: Public Attitudes Toward Capitalism and Democracy* (Harvard University Press, 1984).

LISA MCGIRR, *Suburban Warriors: The Origins of the New American Right* (Princeton University Press, 2001).

CHARLES MURRAY, *What It Means to Be a Libertarian: A Personal Interpretation* (Broadway Books, 1997).

MARCUS G. RASKIN, *Liberalism: The Genius of American Ideals* (Rowman and Littlefield, 2004).

JOHN RENSENBRINK, *Against All Odds: The Green Transformation of American Politics* (Leopold Press, 1999).

JONATHON M. SCHOENWALD, *A Time for Choosing: The Rise of American Conservatism* (Oxford University Press, 2001).

ROGER SCRUTON, *The Meaning of Conservatism* (St. Augustine Press, 2001).

ALEXIS DE TOCQUEVILLE, *Democracy in America*, 2 vols. (1835).

JOHN TOMASI, *Liberalism Beyond Justice: Citizens, Society, and the Boundaries of Political Theory* (Princeton University Press, 2001).

JOHN KENNETH WHITE, *The Values Divide* (Seven Bridges Press, 2003).

GARRY WILLS, *A Necessary Evil: A History of American Distrust of Government* (Simon & Schuster, 1999).

DANIEL YERGIN AND JOSEPH STAINSLAW, *The Commanding Heights: The Battle Between Government and the Marketplace That Is Remaking the Modern World* (Simon & Schuster, 1998).

The United States is a nation of immigrants, a fact that is a source of pride. Franklin D. Roosevelt once began a speech to the Daughters of the American Revolution by saying, "You and I, especially, are descended from immigrants and revolutionists."[1] Immigrants have long been drawn to America by the hope for prosperity and freedom. However, the American dream is rarely achieved in the first generation. There are notable exceptions. Take, for example, George Soros, an international financier who is among the most successful businesspeople in the United States. Soros was born in Hungary, educated in England, and then moved to the United States. Arte Moreno, the owner of the Anaheim Angels baseball team, is the first Hispanic to own a major U.S. sports franchise. Moreno started a billboard business with a partner during college. Over time the business grew, allowing expansion into similar businesses. The conglomerate was sold in 1999 for $8.3 billion.[2] Both George

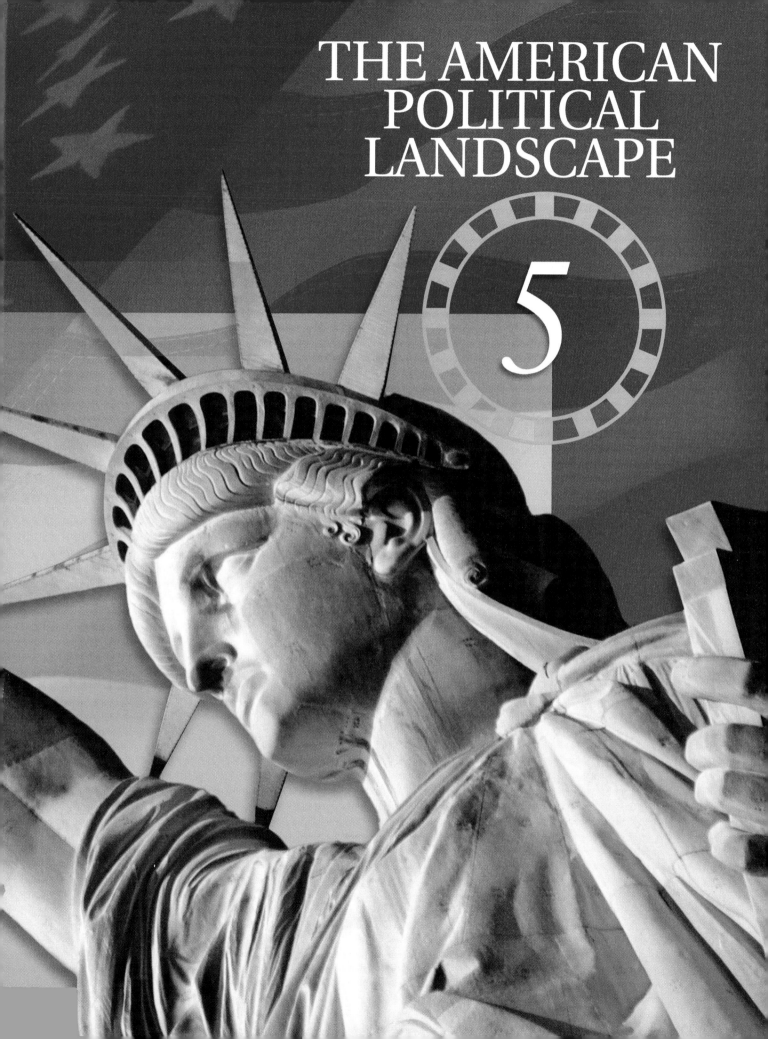

THE AMERICAN POLITICAL LANDSCAPE

5

TIME LINE

THE AMERICAN POLITICAL LANDSCAPE

1803	Louisiana Purchase greatly expands the size of the United States
1862	Congress allows for land grant colleges, fostering growth in higher education
1892	Ellis Island opens—the entry point for millions of immigrants to America
1920	19th Amendment gives women right to vote
1929	Stock Market Crash signals the Great Depression
1945	End of World War II begins economic and population booms
1960	Kennedy elected—first Catholic President
1971	Eighteen year olds given the right to vote
1994	Proposition 187 tries to discourage immigration to California
2000	Vermont becomes first state to recognize civil unions for same-sex couples

Soros and Arte Moreno illustrate the potential for fortunate and hardworking individuals to succeed in our political and economic system. Soros, an outspoken critic of President George W. Bush, gave $27 million in 2003–2004 to groups opposing Bush's reelection. Arte Moreno has been a contributor on a much smaller scale to predominantly Republican candidates and the Republican party. Our system not only permits immigrants and other individuals to accumulate wealth but also allows them to translate that wealth into political influence.

We have conflicting ideas about immigration. We celebrate our immigrant past and proudly recite the words of Emma Lazarus inscribed at the base of the Statue of Liberty: "Give me your tired, your poor, your huddled masses yearning to breathe free." And yet our borders are not open to all who wish to come here, and immigration is limited, with specific numbers of immigrants allowed to enter from each country each year. Hundreds of thousands avoid these limitations by crossing our borders illegally, seeking employment, refuge, and freedom.

After the terrorist attacks on the World Trade Center and the Pentagon in 2001, there was some anti-Arab and anti-Muslim sentiment, including some efforts in Congress to restrict student visas.[3] President Bush urged Americans to "treat each other with respect."[4] Disagreements about the admission of aliens into this country and about their rights and privileges have featured in political campaigns for more than two centuries. In 2004 President Bush proposed changes to the United States immigration policy that would allow illegal immigrants to receive legal status if they receive a temporary worker visa and are employed in the country.[5] His proposal and many others were debated in Congress and during the 2004 campaign.

Albert Einstein once said that most people are incapable of expressing opinions that differ much from the prejudices of their social upbringing.[6] This **ethnocentrism**—selective perception based on one's background, attitudes, and biases—is not uncommon, even among college students, who often assume that others share their economic opportunities, social attitudes, sense of civic responsibility, and self-confidence. In this chapter, we consider how our social environment explains, or at least shapes, our opinions and prejudices. We also look at our diversity as Americans and the implications of geographic, social, and economic divisions for politics and government. Specifically, this chapter explores the effects of regional or state identity on political perspectives; the implications of differences in race, ethnicity, gender, family structure, religion, wealth and income, occupation, and social class for opinions and voting choices; and the relationship between age and education and political participation.

A LAND OF DIVERSITY

Most nations consist of groups of people who have lived together for hundreds of years and who speak the same language, embrace the same religious beliefs, and share a common history. Most Japanese citizens are Japanese in the fullest sense of the word, and this sense of identity and oneness is generally the same in Germany, Sweden, Saudi Arabia, China, and France. The United States is different. We have attracted the poor and oppressed, the adventurous, and the talented from all over the world, and we have been more open to accepting these people than many other nations.

One reason so many people want to come to the United States is that it holds a promise of religious, political, and economic freedom. It is also a place of opportunity for the enterprising. Our economic system has provided widespread (but not universal) opportunity for individuals to improve their economic standing. The American dream—that anyone can find success in the United States—is widely shared.

Several elements of our diversity have political significance. Many Americans retain an identity with the native land of their ancestors, even after three or four generations. Holding on to such differences reflects socialization in families, churches, and other close-knit groups. **Political socialization** is the process by which parents and others teach children about political values, beliefs, and attitudes. This teaching occurs in the home, in school, on the playground, and in the neighborhood. In addition to fostering

ethnocentrism
Belief in the superiority of one's nation or ethnic group.

political socialization
The process by which we develop our political attitudes, values, and beliefs.

demographics
The study of the characteristics of populations.

political predisposition
A characteristic of individuals that is predictive of political behavior.

GLOBAL *Perceptions*

QUESTION: Is the influence of immigrants very good, somewhat good, somewhat bad, or very bad in your country?

Public opinion about the influence of immigrants on society varies dramatically across different countries. The chart shows how various countries responded to the question presented above.

Immigrants are viewed most favorably in Canada, where laws favorable to immigration have long been in place. In the United States, opinion is more evenly divided: 43 percent said immigrants have a bad influence and 49 percent said they have a good influence. Economics appears related to attitudes toward immigrants in some but not most places. Even in countries with a need for workers, like Germany, there is strong anti-immigrant sentiment.

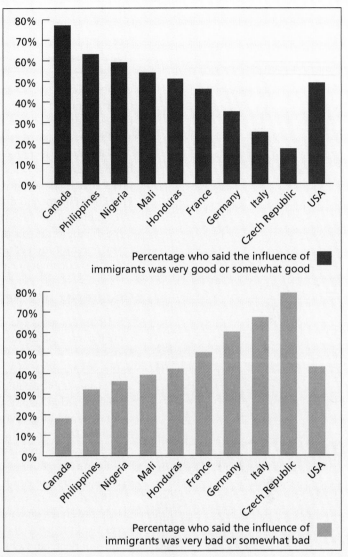

Percentage who said the influence of immigrants was very good or somewhat good

Percentage who said the influence of immigrants was very bad or somewhat bad

SOURCE: The Pew Research Center. *What the World Thinks in 2002.* p. T-36.

group identities, political socialization strongly influences how individuals see politics and which political party they prefer. Where we live and who we are in terms of age, education, religion, and occupation affect how we vote. Such characteristics of populations are called **demographics**. Persons in certain demographic categories tend to vote alike and to have certain **political predispositions** in common, and these characteristics sometimes predict political behavior. Although demographics can be important in both explaining and predicting political behavior, there are sometimes large individual differences within socioeconomic and demographic categories.

When social and economic differences coincide, they reinforce each other and make the differences between groups more important. Social scientists call these differences **reinforcing cleavages**; where these differences are reinforcing, political conflict becomes more intense and there is greater polarization in society. In Italy, for example, the regional divide between north and south is reinforced by the tendency of the north to lean toward the Socialist or Communist party and the south to be Christian Democratic and Catholic in orientation.

reinforcing cleavages
Divisions within society that reinforce one another, making groups more homogeneous or similar.

cross-cutting cleavages
Divisions within society that cut across demographic categories to produce groups that are more heterogeneous or different.

Nations can also have **cross-cutting cleavages**, instances where differences among people do not reinforce each other but rather pull in different directions. To illustrate, if all the rich individuals in a nation are of one religion and the poor of another, the nation would have reinforcing cleavages, and political conflict between the groups would be intensified. But if there are both rich and poor in all religions and if people sometimes vote on the basis of their religion and sometimes on the basis of their wealth, the divisions would be cross-cutting. American diversity has generally been more of the cross-cutting type than the reinforcing type, lessening political conflict because individuals have multiple allegiances.

In some societies, politics centers largely on passions over economic and religious differences. Although socioeconomic differences are important to understanding American government and politics, they are not as central to our politics as religion is in Bosnia or tribal identity in Rwanda. In Northern Ireland, the religious differences between Catholics and Protestants have produced centuries of violent strife that is yet to be resolved.

Despite the fact that America has been more hospitable to people from different religions, classes, and races than almost any other nation in the world, we Americans often prefer to associate only with people "like us" and are suspicious of people "like them." From hostility toward different religions in the early colonies to the anti-immigration movements of the late 1800s and early 1900s to the anti-immigration and anti–civil rights ballot initiatives of the last two decades, Americans have exhibited ethnocentrism, and for much of our history, minorities have been excluded from full participation in American political and economic life.

Geography and National Identity

The United States is a geographically large and historically isolated country. In the 1830s, French commentator Alexis de Tocqueville studied the early development of the United States and observed that the country had no major political or economic powers on its borders "and consequently no great wars, financial crises, invasions, or conquests to fear."[7] Geographic isolation from the major powers of the world during our government's formative period helps explain American politics. The Atlantic Ocean served as a barrier to foreign meddling, giving us time to establish our political tradition and develop our economy. The western frontier provided room to grow and avoid some of the social and political tensions that Europe experienced. Two great oceans also reinforced our sense of isolation from Europe and foreign alliances. American reluctance to become involved in foreign wars and controversies still emerges in debates over foreign policy.

Before the terrorist attacks of September 2001, only one foreign enemy had struck the United States on our own soil—England in the War of 1812. (The war against Mexico of 1846–1848 was fought almost entirely on Mexican land, some of which later became American land as a result of the war. The only other war fought on our soil was, of course, the Civil War.) By contrast, Poland has been invaded repeatedly and was partitioned by Austria, Prussia, and Russia in the eighteenth century and by Nazi Germany and the Soviet Union in the twentieth century. The difference is explained largely by location: Poland was surrounded by Europe's great powers. Had the United States been closer to Europe and not isolated by two oceans, it might have been overrun like Poland and our Constitution and institutions repeatedly changed or eliminated to suit the victorious invaders. The presence of powerful and aggressive neighbors impedes the development of democracy in relatively weak nations.

The ability of terrorists to promulgate war, especially if willing to die along with their enemies, as was the case with the attacks in 2001, means that isolation and national security have to be rethought. No longer does the United States have the luxury of developing our democracy behind the protection of two oceans; our newly recognized vulnerability to attacks on our own soil has changed the context in which we debate the balance between liberty and security. New York, San Francisco, and Chicago are now on the front line.

Size also confers an advantage. The landmass of the United States exceeds that of all but three nations in the world. In contrast, India has a population more than three

Slavery epitomizes the dark side of this country's national identity. During Reconstruction, some former slaves were able to purchase and work their own land while others moved north to take part in the industrial revolution of the late nineteenth century.

and a half times that of the United States on a landmass one-third the size. Geographic space gave the expanding population of the United States room to spread out. This possibility meant that some of the political conflicts arising from religion, social class, and national origin were defused because groups could isolate themselves from one another. This was what Madison hoped for in his concept of a "large republic" (see *The Federalist*, No. 10, in the Appendix). Moreover, the large and accessible landmass helped foster the perspective that the United States had a **manifest destiny** to be a continental nation reaching from the Atlantic to the Pacific oceans. Early settlers used the notion that the United States was "destined" to expand across the continent to justify taking land occupied by Native Americans and Mexicans, especially the land acquired following victory in the Mexican-American War.

The United States is also a land of abundant natural resources. We have rich farmland, which not only feeds our population but also makes us the largest exporter of food in the world.[8] We are rich in such natural resources as coal, iron, uranium, and precious metals. All these resources enhance economic growth, provide jobs, and stabilize government. As de Tocqueville observed long ago, "Yet what takes place in the United States is much less attributable to the institutions of the country than to the country itself."[9]

Geography also helps explain our diversity. Parts of the United States are wonderfully suited to agriculture, others to mining or ranching, and still others to shipping. These differences produce different regional economic concerns, which in turn influence politics. For instance, a person from the agricultural heartland may have a perception of foreign trade that is different from that of an automobile worker in Detroit. But if that automobile worker is African American, this fact may be more important to her politics than what she does or where she lives. To understand American politics, we must appreciate these differences and their relative importance.

Sectional Differences

Unlike many other countries, geography in the United States does *not* define an ethnic or religious division. All the Serbs in the United States do not live in one place, all French-speaking Catholics in another, and all German immigrants in another. Sectional differences in the United States are primarily geographic, not ethnic or religious.

The most distinct section of the United States remains the South, although the South's differences are diminishing. From the beginning of the Republic, the agricultural South differed from the North, where commerce and manufacturing were more significant. But the most important difference between the regions was the institution of slavery. Northern opposition to slavery, which grew increasingly intense by the middle of the nineteenth century, reinforced sectional economic interests. The 11 Confederate states, by virtue of their decision to secede from the Union, reinforced a common political identity, and after the Civil War, sectional differences were strengthened by the policy of Reconstruction and the problems of race relations.

The South is becoming less distinct from the rest of the United States. In addition to undergoing tremendous economic change, a large in-migration has diminished the sense of regional identity. The civil rights revolution eliminated roadblocks preventing African Americans from voting, opened up new educational opportunities, and helped integrate the South into the national economy. African Americans still lag behind whites in voter registration, but the gap is now no wider in the South than elsewhere and is explained more by differences in education than by race.[10] In economic terms, the South still falls below the rest of the country in per capita income and education, but much less so than 50 years ago. The religious and moral conservatism of the South remains notable.

Until the 1970s, political observers spoke of the "solid South"—a region that voted for Democrats at all levels. "The Civil War made the Democratic party the party of the South, and the Republican party, the party of the North."[11] The Democratic "solid South" remained a fixture of American politics for more than a century. Since 1968 that has changed dramatically, first at the presidential level and increasingly at the state and local levels. As two respected observers of the region comment, "The fall of the South

manifest destiny
A notion held by nineteenth-century Americans that the United States was destined to rule the continent, from the Atlantic to the Pacific.

Evidence of the persistent racial divide in this country can be found in the continued display of the flag of the Confederacy. Although many Southern states have finally removed this flag from state government buildings throughout the South, individuals within these states still prominently display this symbol of slavery on their vehicles and on their homes.

as an assured stronghold of the Democratic Party in presidential elections is one of the most significant developments in modern American politics."[12] "The decline of the South in the Democratic party would fundamentally reorder the American party system and realign the electorate."[13] The political alignment has shifted as African Americans have been enfranchised and become overwhelmingly Democrats and many whites have become Republicans. In 1992 and 1996, even with two southerners (Bill Clinton and Al Gore) on the ticket, Democrats won only 4 of the 11 former Confederate states. In 2000, George W. Bush carried all 11 southern states, including Al Gore's home state of Tennessee. Once again in 2004, George W. Bush carried all 11 former Confederate states, including vice presidential candidate John Edwards's home state of North Carolina.

What explains this dramatic reversal? Part of the explanation is that the Democrats' advocacy of aggressive action on civil rights in the 1960s alienated some southern whites. In addition, the debate within the Democratic party over Vietnam policy in the late 1960s and 1970s was "perceived by many southern voters as unpatriotic."[14] Democrats are aware of divisive or "wedge" issues; Howard Dean in 2004 expressed this concern "we have got to stop having the campaigns run in this country based on abortion, guns, God and gays."[15] Republican presidential candidates have more recently emphasized family values, opposition to taxes, same-sex marriage, and law-and-order issues that appeal to conservative southern voters. Republican success at the presidential level was slow to affect contests for Congress and state legislatures. Yet in recent years, Republicans had more than half of southern votes for the U.S. House of Representatives (see Table 5–1), and in 2004, they had 7 of the 11 governorships in the former Confederate states.[16] In the state legislatures of several southern states, remnants of the old "solid South" remain, but Republicans have made major inroads, and politics in the region is now predictably Republican, at least at the presidential level.

Both parties could point to successes in the South in 2002 and 2003. The Democrats picked up or retained the Governorships in Tennessee and Louisiana and the Republicans did the same in Georgia, Alabama, and Mississippi. In Georgia, this was the first GOP elected governor since Reconstruction, and in Alabama, the last Republican was elected in 1995. Overall, Republicans controlled more governorships than Democrats in the South after 2002 and 2003. In the U.S. Senate they have a much more commanding advantage, with at least 18 of the 22 U.S. Senate seats from the former confederate states in Republican hands. Because he was running for vice president, John Edwards did not run for reelection as U.S. senator in his home state of North Carolina and in November 2004, his Senate seat went to Republican Richard Burr.

Another sectional division is the Sun Belt—the 11 former Confederate states plus New Mexico, Arizona, Nevada, and the southern half of California. Sun Belt states are growing much more rapidly than the rest of the country. Arizona, California, Florida, Georgia, Nevada, North Carolina, and Texas gained 12 seats in the House of Representatives after the 2000 census.[18] Moreover, population growth in the South and West is occurring in different age groups. In the South, growth is largest among those over 65; in the West, younger persons provide the growth. Sun Belt states have also experienced greater economic growth as industries have headed south and southwest, where land and labor are cheaper and more abundant (see Figure 5–1). The shift of seats to the Sun Belt has helped Republicans as the states picking up additional seats have tended to be more Republican. That tendency was reinforced in 2003–2004 in Texas where the state legislature, after a protracted political battle, replaced the 2002 boundaries drawn by the courts with new districts aimed at defeating Democratic incumbents in the 2004 election.[19]

State and Local Identity

Different states have rather distinctive political traditions. Mention Utah, Mississippi, Oregon, New York, or Kansas, and a certain type of politics comes to mind. The same is true for many other states. Like most stereotypes, these images are often misleading, yet they reflect the fact that there is a sense of identity to states as political units that goes

TABLE 5–1   VOTING PATTERNS IN THE 11 FORMER CONFEDERATE STATES

Republican Vote for President

1980	50%
1984	62
1988	59
1992	43
1996	46
2000	54
2004	57

Republican Vote for U.S. Representatives

1980	40%
1982	39
1984	42
1986	41
1988	42
1990	43
1992	48
1994	58
1996	53*
1998	58
2000	53
2002	56
2004	55

Republican Share of State Legislators

	House	Senate
1980	18%	17%
1982	22	14
1984	23	17
1986	24	20
1988	27	24
1990	28	26
1992	31	31
1994	37	37
1996	44	44
1998	42	40
2000	44	42
2002	47	46
2004	50	49

SOURCE: U.S. Bureau of the Census, *Statistical Abstract of the United States,* 1993–2000. For 2004, CNN at www.cnn.com/ELECTION/2004; and *Congressional Quarterly Weekly Report,* November 11, 2000, pp. 2694–2703; and Todd Edwards, Council of State Governments, Southern Office, personal communication, December 22, 2000 and Doris Smith, Council of State Governments, Southern Office, November 10, 2004.

*The 1996 Texas runoff elections are not included.

beyond demographic characteristics and is supported by recent empirical evidence. States have distinctive political cultures that affect public opinion and policy outcomes.[20] Our electoral rules and other laws reinforce these state identities.

In American politics today, one state—California—stands out. More than one out of eight Americans is a Californian.[21] In terms of economic and political importance,

California is in a league by itself; its 53 members of the House of Representatives exceed the total number of representatives from the smallest 20 states. California's 55 electoral votes are key for any presidential candidate.[22] California's reputation for distinctive politics was reinforced in 2003 when voters replaced Governor Gray Davis with movie star Arnold Schwarzenegger in the first recall of a governor since North Dakota voters recalled Governor Lynn G. Frazier in 1921.[23]

WHERE WE LIVE

Four out of five Americans now live in central cities and their suburbs—what the Census Bureau calls *metropolitan areas*.[24] During the early twentieth century, the movement of population was from rural areas to central cities, but the movement since the 1950s has been from the central cities to their suburbs. Today the most urban state is California (over 94 percent of its population lives in cities or suburbs). Vermont is the least urban, with only 38 percent living in cities or suburbs.[25] Regionally, the West and Northeast are the most urban, the South and Midwest the most rural.

People move from cities to the suburbs for many reasons—better housing, new transportation systems that make it easier to get to work, the desire for cleaner air and safer streets. Another reason is white flight, the movement of whites away from the central cities so that children can avoid being bused for racial balance and attend generally better schools. White, middle-class migration to the suburbs has made American cities increasingly poor, African American, and Democratic. More than half of all African Americans now live in central cities, as opposed to only about one-fifth of whites, and the poverty level among blacks living in central cities is higher than among whites living in the same cities.[26] The proportions are very nearly reversed for the suburbs, where more than half of all white Americans reside. Approximately one-third of African Americans live in the suburbs, up from one-fifth in 1980.[27] In large cities such as Washington, D.C., Detroit, Baltimore, Atlanta, and New Orleans, the city population is now well over 50 percent African American (see Table 5–2). Hispanics constitute roughly three-fourths of the population of El Paso, Texas, and Santa Ana, California, and nearly two-thirds the population of Miami, Florida.[28]

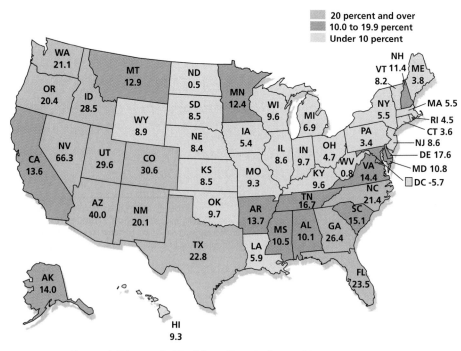

FIGURE 5–1 Percent Change in Resident Population, 1990–2000.
SOURCE: U.S. Bureau of the Census, www.census.gov/prod/2002pubs/01statab/pop.pdf.

As the better off have left the cities, the cities' problems have become more acute, and their tax base has not increased proportionate to their problems. Older suburban areas now face the same problems as the inner cities, as they too suffer from out-migration to newer cities and towns. High-tech and professional service companies frequently relocate to the suburbs to avoid traffic congestion and to be closer to the bedroom communities of their workers. Political boundaries, which define local governments and delineate responsibility for services, create understandable tensions among cities, suburbs, and rural areas. Tax revenues, legislative representation, zoning laws, and governmental priorities are hotly contested issues in most metropolitan areas.

WHO WE ARE

Sectional distinctions are less prominent today than they were a century or even a half-century ago. Today Americans are more likely to define themselves by a number of characteristics, each of which may influence how they vote or think about various candidates, issues, or policies.

Race and Ethnicity

Racial and ethnic differences have always had political significance. **Race** can be defined as a grouping of human beings with distinctive physical characteristics determined by genetic inheritance. **Ethnicity** is a social division based on national origin, religion, and language, often within the same race, and includes a sense of attachment to that group. In the United States, race and ethnicity issues focus on African Americans, Asian Americans, Native Americans, and Hispanics.

There are nearly 37 million African Americans in the United States, nearly 13 percent of the population. Asian Americans constitute about 4 percent of the population, and Native Americans, around 1.5 percent.[29] The Census Bureau classifies most American Hispanics as white, although Hispanics can be of any race. Hispanics are the fastest-growing ethnic group; the Census Bureau estimates that there are roughly 39 million American Hispanics, constituting over 13 percent of the population.[30] Because of differences in immigration and birthrates, whites in America will have declined to fewer than three-quarters of the population by the year 2050. The percentage of non-Hispanic whites will be about 50 percent by 2050.[31]

★★ THINKING IT THROUGH

Despite the homogenizing tendencies of national media like Fox and CNN and federal laws that have lessened state differences, an enduring set of state differences remains in American politics. People generally take pride in the state they are from.

Part of the reason for the enduring state identities is that we elect Congress and the President at the state level. States like Iowa and New Hampshire also play important roles in narrowing the field of presidential candidates seeking their party's nomination. And some states, such as Texas and Maine, cherish their ideas of themselves as home to independent thinkers who are somehow "different" from residents of other states.

Differences in state laws relating to driving cars, drinking, gambling, and taxes also reinforce the relevance of state identity. Colleges and universities may have the same effect while reinforcing competition between different states. State identities, which are stereotypes, can be relatively innocuous, but can also play into decisions about economic development and whether or not firms locate in one state over another.*

*Jerry D. Spangler and Bob Bernick, "Is Utah's Image a Liability?" *Deseret News*, February 12, 2004, p. A1.

TABLE 5–2 CITIES WITH POPULATIONS OF 100,000 OR MORE THAT ARE AT LEAST 50 PERCENT AFRICAN AMERICAN, 2000

City	Population	Percent African American
Atlanta, Ga.	416,474	61.4%
Baltimore, Md.	651,154	64.3
Birmingham, Ala.	242,820	73.5
Detroit, Mich.	951,270	81.6
Gary, Ind.	102,746	84
Jackson, Miss.	184,256	70.6
Memphis, Tenn.	650,100	61.4
Newark, N.J.	273,546	53.5
New Orleans, La.	484,674	67.3
Richmond, Va.	197,790	57.2
Savannah, Ga.	131,510	57.1
Washington, D.C.	572,059	60.0

SOURCE: U.S. Bureau of the Census, at www.census.gov/population/cen2000/phc-t6/tab05.pdf.

race
A grouping of human beings with distinctive characteristics determined by genetic inheritance.

ethnicity
A social division based on national origin, religion, language, and often race.

CHANGING FACE OF AMERICAN POLITICS

PERCENTAGE OF THE POPULATION BY RACE AND ORIGIN

	1990	2002	2025	2050
White	83.9%	80.7%	76.8%	72.1%
Non-Hispanic White	75.7	68.3	59.5	50.1
African American	12.2	12.7	13.7	14.6
American Indian, Inuit, Aleut	0.8	0.9	1.0	1.1
Asian and Pacific Islander	3.0	4.2	6.5	9.3
Hispanic	8.9	13.4	18.9	24.4

SOURCE: 1990 figures from U.S. Bureau of the Census, *Statistical Abstract of the United States, 2001* (Government Printing Office, 2001), pp. 16–17. All other figures from U.S. Bureau of the Census, *Statistical Abstract of the United States, 2003* (Government Printing Office, 2003), pp. 15, 18.
NOTE: Percentages do not equal 100 because Hispanics can be of any race. Figures for 2025 and 2050 are projections.

Vernon Robinson, the 2004 Republican congressional candidate for the Fifth District in Greensboro, North Carolina, was the first African American to run for a congressional seat on the Republican ticket since Oklahoma Representative J.C. Watts retired in 2002. Robinson lost the runoff election to Republican State Senator Virginia Foxx in August 2004.

AFRICAN AMERICANS   Most immigrants chose to come to this country in search of freedom and opportunity. In contrast, African Americans came against their will as slaves. Although they were freed as a result of the Civil War, racial divisions continue as one of the enduring issues of American politics. Until 1900, more than 90 percent of all African Americans lived in the South; a century later, that figure was 55 percent.[32] Many African Americans left the South hoping to improve their lives by settling in the large cities of the Northeast, Midwest, and West. The reality for many was urban poverty. More recently, some African Americans have been returning to the South, especially to its urban areas.

Most African Americans are economically worse off than most whites in the United States. African American median family income is close to $34,000, compared to about $54,000 for whites.[33] About one-quarter of African American incomes are below the poverty level, compared to about 9 percent of the incomes of whites.[34] Poverty among Native Americans and Alaskan Natives has averaged 26 percent in recent years, a proportion quite similar to that found among African Americans and Hispanics.[35] However, some African Americans have been doing better in recent years; one-third of African American households have earnings of over $50,000 (compared to 54 percent of white households).[36] Some African Americans, like Shaquille O'Neal, a basketball player with the Miami Heat, and Oprah Winfrey, a syndicated talk show host, have risen to top earnings in their professions.

Another way to measure economic well-being is in terms of assets or wealth. *Wealth* is the economic value of the things you own (savings, stocks, property), compared to *income*, which is how much money you make from your job or investments. As a group, the median net worth of African Americans is less than one-tenth that of whites, and the median net worth of Hispanics is only slightly more than that of African Americans (see Figure 5–2).[37] As a result, most African Americans and Hispanics have fewer resources to fall back on in hard times, and they are less likely to have the savings to help a child pay for college.

Middle-class African Americans, of whom there are a growing number, are role models for the young of all races, yet their still comparatively small number serves as a reminder that most African Americans remain behind whites in an economy that relies more and more on education and job skills. About 27 percent of whites graduate from college, whereas only about 17 percent of African Americans do.[38] Among recent high school graduates, 64 percent of whites go on to college, but only 55 percent of African Americans do.[39]

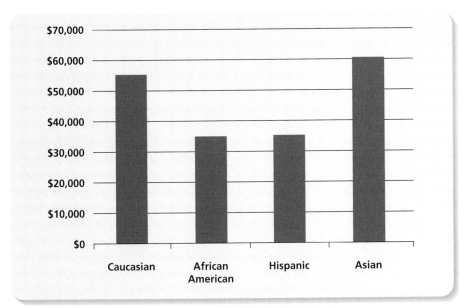

FIGURE 5–2 Wealth Distribution in the United States by Race.
SOURCE: U.S. Bureau of the Census, at www.census.gov/prod/2004pubs/03statab/income.pdf.

Barrack Obama, elected to the U.S. Senate from Illinois in 2004, is only the third African American senator in a century. Obama enjoyed the support of many Republicans as well as Democrats in his 2004 campaign, in part because his initial GOP opponent dropped out of the race. Obama delivered a passionate keynote address at the 2004 Democratic National Convention and is a rising star in the party.

Finally, the African American population is much younger than the white population; the median age for whites in 2002 was 37.1 years, compared to 30.5 for African Americans.[40] The combination of a younger African American population, a lower level of education, and their concentration in economically depressed urban areas has resulted in a much higher unemployment rate for young African Americans. Unemployment can in turn lead to social problems like crime, drug and alcohol abuse, and family dissolution.

African Americans had little political power until after World War II. Owing their freedom from slavery to the "party of Lincoln," most African Americans initially identified with the Republicans, but this loyalty started to change with Franklin Roosevelt, who insisted on equal treatment for African Americans in his New Deal programs.[41] After World War II, African Americans came to see the Democrats as the party of civil rights. The 1964 Republican platform position on civil rights espoused *states' rights*—at the time, the creed of southern segregationists—in what appeared to be an effort to win the support of southern white voters. Virtually all African Americans voted for Lyndon Johnson in 1964, and in presidential elections between 1984 and 2000, their Democratic vote averaged 86 percent.[42] In the 2004 election, 88 percent of African American voters voted for John Kerry.

Recently, African Americans have become much more important politically because of their increased voter participation and their concentrated population. African Americans constitute only 0.3 percent of the population in Montana and 0.5 percent in Idaho, but 37 percent in Mississippi, 33 percent in Louisiana, and 30 percent in South Carolina.[43] Southern senators and representatives cannot afford to ignore the African American vote.[44] Evidence of growing African American political power is the dramatic increase in the number of African American state legislators, which rose from 168 in 1970 to 584 in 2001.[45] Georgia has 47 African American state legislators, the most of any state. Alabama, Maryland, Mississippi, and South Carolina all have over 30.[46]

Ken Salazar, elected to the U.S. Senate from Colorado in 2004, is the fourth U.S. senator of Latino descent in U.S. history. Salazar replaced Ben Nighthorse Campbell, a Native American and Republican, who did not seek reelection. Salazar previously served two terms as Colorado attorney general.

HISPANICS (LATINOS) Hispanic Americans, who generally prefer to be called Latinos, are not a monolithic group, and while they share a common linguistic heritage, they often differ, depending on which country they or their forebears emigrated from. Cuban

Americans, for instance, tend to be Republicans, while Mexican Americans and Puerto Ricans are disproportionately Democrats.[47] Latinos are politically important in a growing number of states. Nearly two-thirds of Cuban immigrants live in Florida, especially in greater Miami; Puerto Rican immigrants are concentrated in and around New York City; and many Mexican American immigrants live in the Southwest and California. Almost 12 million Hispanics live in California.[48]

Cuban Americans are more in the upper-middle income levels, while Puerto Rican Americans and Mexican Americans are generally in lower and lower-middle income categories.[49] A recent study found differences among Latinos of Mexican, Puerto Rican, and Cuban descent in partisanship, ideology, and rates of participation, but widespread support for a liberal domestic agenda, including increased spending on health care, crime and drug control, education, the environment, child services, and bilingual education.[50] But since Hispanics are not politically homogeneous, they are not united as a voting block.

In the 1990s, America's Hispanic population grew by 58 percent.[51] This surge in growth has not, however, been accompanied by a similar surge in political participation or representation. Researchers cite many reasons for this, including redistricting, low rates of citizenship and voting, and a lack of common party commitment.

Hispanics have fared worse in redistricting than other groups. The large number of noncitizens and younger population among Hispanics diminishes their political power. For example, 9.5 million foreign-born Hispanics are not citizens, and more than half—5.4 million—are in this country illegally. This group of Hispanics cannot vote, nor can those under 18, which is a greater percentage of the Hispanic population than for others. Language problems also reduce Hispanic citizens' voter registration and turnout. Despite their huge increase in population, Hispanic groups were disappointed by the redrawing of legislative district boundaries after the 2000 census.[52] This has spurred some lawsuits as Hispanic activists seek to eliminate gerrymandering, the drawing of district boundaries to benefit a group or party.

Given the overall growth of the Latino population, it is not surprising that both major parties are aggressively cultivating Latino candidates. Three Latinos, all from New Mexico, have won election to the U.S. Senate, although none is currently serving. Several Hispanics have been cabinet members; in the George W. Bush administration, Mel Martinez resigned as secretary of Housing and Urban Development (HUD) to run successfully for the U.S. Senate from Florida in 2004. Ken Salazar, another Latino but a Democrat, was also elected to the senate in 2004 from Colorado. Alberto R. Gonzales left the Texas Supreme Court to join the Bush administration as White House counsel. After John Ascroft's resignation in November 2004, President George W. Bush nominated Gonzales as his new attorney general. Neither party has developed an effective strategy to mobilize the Hispanic vote. The Democrats, which have historically been the party of new immigrant groups, have done somewhat better among Hispanics than Republicans. Gore carried approximately 65 percent of the Latino vote in 2000, while Kerry only carried 56 percent in 2004. This was largely attributed to Latinos' high level of religiosity and Bush's appeal among highly religious people.

ASIAN AMERICANS Asian Americans are classified together by the Census Bureau for statistical purposes, but there are significant differences among them in culture, language, and political experience in the United States. Asian Americans include, among others, persons of Chinese, Japanese, Indian, Korean, Vietnamese, Filipino, and Thai origin, as well as persons from the Pacific Islands.

The United States is home to more than 12 million Asian Americans and Pacific Islanders, residing primarily in the western states, especially California, Hawaii, and Washington.[53] The numbers of Asian Americans grew during the 1970s and 1980s, largely as a result of immigration from Southeast Asia. Immigrants from China, India, Korea, the Philippines, and Vietnam account for five of the top ten leading countries of foreign-born persons living in this country.[54]

Many Asian Americans have done well both economically and educationally. 47 percent of Asian Americans have graduated from college, compared to 27 percent of white Americans and 17 percent of African Americans.[55] Asian Americans are becoming

Alberto Gonzales, who served as White House general counsel during George W. Bush's first term, has been a prominent advisor to the president. Bush picked Gonzales to serve as attorney general for his second term in office.

PEOPLE & POLITICS *Making a Difference* ★ ★ ★

BILL RICHARDSON: GOVERNOR OF NEW MEXICO

New Mexico Governor Bill Richardson served in Congress, as U.S. Ambassador to the United Nations, and as Secretary of Energy, before being elected governor in 2002. His breadth of experience and political drive have made him the most visible Hispanic politician in the United States. Richardson's father was American and his mother Mexican, and he grew up in Mexico City. He was drafted by the Kansas City Athletics to play baseball, but after an elbow injury, went on to college at Tufts University where he earned a B.A. and M.A. in diplomacy. Representing New Mexico in the House of Representatives, he rose to the position of chief deputy Democratic Whip, the first Hispanic to hold this positon.

Richardson has been nominated for the Nobel Peace Prize three times, in part for his work as United States Ambassador to the United Nations. Among his activities were negotiating with North Korea, Iraq, Cuba, and Sudan for the release of American hostages, mediation between Zaire's former president and rebel leaders, helping oversee a peaceful transition of power in the Congo, and working with the U.N. investigaton of ethnic massacres.

Richardson has used his tenure as governor of New Mexico to position himself as a leader of the Democratic party. In 2004, Richardson delivered the first opposition party response to a president's State of the Union message in Spanish.* He chaired the 2004 Democratic National Convention and was visible in this role. As governor of one of the battleground states in 2004, he cam-

paigned frequently with John Kerry in New Mexico, only to see the state go for President Bush, 50 percent to 49 percent for Kerry.

*www.democrats.org/news/200401210005.html

---

more politically important and more visible in politics. Gary Locke, the first Chinese American governor of a state in the continental United States, served two terms in Washington.

THE TIES OF ETHNICITY   Except for Native Americans and the descendants of slaves, all Americans have immigrant ancestors. Early settlers were generally English-speaking Protestants; even today, people of English, Scottish, and Welsh background are the largest "ethnic" group in the United States. Irish immigrants, largely Catholics, started coming before the potato famine in the 1840s and came in larger numbers after it. Upon their arrival, they experienced economic exploitation and religious bigotry. Irish Americans responded by retreating among themselves, forming a strong ethnic consciousness. Other ethnic groups that followed—Italians, Greeks, Chinese—each experienced a similar cycle: flight from their homeland and happy arrival here, then discrimination, exploitation, residential clustering, and the formation of a strong group identity.

The largest number of immigrants came between 1900 and 1924, when 17.3 million people relocated to the United States—by far the largest immigration to one country in any quarter-century in human history. From 1991 to 2000, the United States welcomed more than 9 million immigrants,[56] primarily from the Caribbean and Mexico and from Asian countries such as the Philippines, Vietnam, and China. The foreign-born proportion of the U.S. population has increased in recent years, rising from 14 million in 1980 to nearly 31 million in 2002, the largest number of foreign-born in U.S. history.[57] Recently, the proportion of Asian and Mexican immigrants has pulled even with or surpassed the number of Europeans.

Having large numbers of immigrants can pose challenges to any political and social system. Immigrants are often a source of social conflict as they compete with more established groups for jobs, rights, political power, and influence.

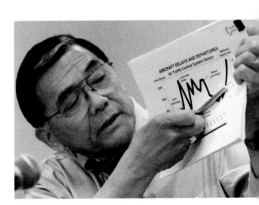

Transportation Secretary Norman Mineta is an Asian American, former Congressman, and the only Democrat in President George W. Bush's cabinet.

In Comparative Perspective

IMMIGRATION POLITICS IN CANADA

On a proportional basis, Canada has more immigrants each year than does the United States. Other differences between the United States and Canada in immigration policy include Canada's allowing more skilled immigrants to immigrate and the establishment of a special status for potential immigrants who are willing to invest money in a Canadian business and hire Canadian workers. Federalism is also part of Canadian immigration policy, with provincial governments having some say in whom they will allow as "independent immigrants" (not coming for family reunification or other purposes). Quebec has taken advantage of this policy because it wants to ensure that immigrants either already speak French or are willing to learn French.[*] As noted, Canadians are the most likely of any polity to view immigrants favorably.

The historic patterns of immigration to Canada and the United States also provide an interesting contrast. Both countries are world leaders in welcoming immigrants, and both countries until 1900 "absorbed large inflows from the British Isles."[†] The United States absorbed many more Irish Catholics than did Canada, while Protestants from Northern Ireland were more likely to immigrate to Canada. In the last half-century, Canada experienced a "massive demographic shift as hundreds of thousands of non-British, non-French—including many Asians—came in."[‡]

Following the terrorist attacks of September 11, 2001, Canada's immigration policies have drawn criticism as being too lax. United States and Canadian newspapers accused "the nation to the north" as being a "haven to terrorists."[§] The United States signfiicantly tightened its immigration policies as part of the war on terrorism, but Canada was criticized by the United States, in part because Canada rarely detains refugees who cannot provide identificaton.[‖] The State Department criticized Canada in 2004 as having "lax immigration laws," with implications not only for terrorism but for human trafficking and prostitution.[¶]

[*]Information provided by Earl Fry, Political Science Department, Brigham Young University. February 27, 2004.
[†]Seymour Martin Lipset, *Continental Divide,* New York: Routledge, Chapman, and Hall, Inc., p. 182.
[‡]Seymour Martin Lipset, *Continental Divide,* New York: Routledge, Chapman, and Hall, Inc., p. 185.
[§]James Neff, "Few Resources Spent Guarding Canada Border," *The Seattle Times,* September 23, 2001, p. A1; see also Bob McDonald, "Bush Showing His Toughness," *The Toronto Sun,* September 26, 2001, p. 6.
[‖]Allan Thompson, "Is Canada Really the Weak Link?" *Toronto Star,* October 6, 2001, p. A1.
[¶]Sheldon Alberts, "U.S. Raps Canadian Immigration," Ottawa *Citizen,* February 26, 2004, p. A9.

Gender

For most of U.S. history, politics and government were men's business. Women first gained the right to vote primarily in the western territories, beginning with Wyoming in 1869 and Utah in 1870, and then in Colorado and Idaho before the turn of the twentieth century.[58] The right was not extended nationally until 1920 with passage of the Nineteenth Amendment. The fears of some opponents and some proponents of *women's suffrage* (the right to vote)—that women would form their own party and vote largely for women or fundamentally alter our political system—have not been realized. During Susan B. Anthony's suffrage campaign, Jonas H. Upton, editor of the *Democratic Salem Monitor* in Salem, Oregon, contended that women, if given the right to vote, would combine to vote for war because they were exempt from the draft.[59] Others feared that women would unite to vote for prohibition.[60]

For a half-century after gaining the right to vote, American women voted at a lower rate than women in other Western democracies.[61] But in the past 20 years, slightly more women than men have voted in presidential elections, and there is no significant difference between the genders in rates of voting in midterm elections.[62] In the 2004 election, women comprised 54 percent of all voters and men comprised 46 percent. Because women outnumber men, there are more female than male voters.[63] Women have chosen to work within the existing political parties and do not overwhelmingly support female candidates, especially if they must cross party lines to do so.[64] Since 1917, less than 6 percent of representatives in the U.S. House have been women. A common way women have entered Congress have been through appointment after their husband's death. The number of women in the House of Representatives and U.S. Senate reached new highs in the 1990s. Following the 2000 elections, there were three female governors, 13 women serving in the Senate, and 58 in the U.S. House of Representatives. There were ten female major-party gubernatorial candidates in 2002, and on election day, four of them were elected. Three of the four successful candidates were Democrats. After the 2002 elections, 13 women served in the Senate during the 108th Congress. The proportion of women serving in the House of Representatives is about the same as in the Senate: below 15 percent. In contrast, some state legislative chambers are nearly 40 percent female. The number of female officeholders is rising in part because women are increasingly running in contests in which there is no incumbent.[65]

One group that has aggressively promoted female candidates is EMILY's List, a group that funds pro-choice Democrats. EMILY is an acronym for "Early Money Is Like Yeast," meaning that campaign contributions given to candidates early in their campaigns can help raise more money, just as yeast helps dough rise. EMILY's List supporters are proud of the fact that there are more women in the U.S. House than ever before. EMILY's List has also helped fund racial and ethnic female candidates, with roughly one-third of the candidates supported being African American or Latina. Republicans have duplicated EMILY's List with their own political action committee, Wish List, which gives to Republican female candidates who are pro-choice.

Is there a **gender gap**, or a persistent difference between men and women in voting and in attitudes on important issues? Women have typically divided their vote between the two major political parties. However, in recent elections, women have been more likely than men to vote for Democratic presidential candidates (see Figure 5–3). In the 2000 presidential election, Al Gore's share of the vote among women was 12 percent higher than among men.[66] In the 2004 election, Bush received 48 percent of the female vote to Kerry's 51 percent. Although women preferred Kerry over Bush by a small margin, Bush improved his standing among women by 5 percentage points compared to the 2000 election.

The women's movement in American politics encompasses a comprehensive agenda, including voting and political rights as well as extending the basic liberties of the Bill of Rights and the Fourteenth Amendment. In addition to rights and liberties, women seek equal opportunity, education, jobs, skills, and respect in what has been a male-dominated system.[67] Women are more likely than men to oppose violence in any form—the death penalty, new weapon systems, or the possession of handguns. Women, as a group, are more compassionate than men in that they are more likely to favor government that provides health insurance and family services. Women are generally more concerned than men about women's rights—enforcement of child support, punishment for sexual abuse and rape, and equal treatment in the legal system. They also identify work and family issues such as day care, maternity leave, and equal treatment in the workplace as important.[68] Other gender issues, some of them focal points in recent elections, include reproductive rights, restrictions on pornography, gun control, and sexual harassment.[69]

There are serious income inequalities between men and women. Nearly twice as many women than men have an annual income of $15,000 or less.[70] Because an increasing number of women today are the sole breadwinners for their families, the implications of this low income level are significant. Women earn on average less than men for the same work. Even among college graduates aged 25 to 34, women earn an average of 80 cents for every dollar earned by men of the same age and education. After controlling for characteristics such as job experience, education, occupation, and other measures of productivity, a U.S. Census Bureau study shows that wage discrimination is 76 cents on every dollar.[71] As age increases, the earnings gap widens. In law schools, women now constitute about half of entering classes,[72] but more generally women still lag behind men in income and opportunity.

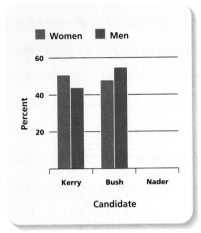

FIGURE 5–3 Gender and the Vote for President, 2004.
SOURCE: 2004 Exit Polls from Edison Media Research and Mitofsky International at www.cnn.com/ELECTION/2004/pages/results/states/US/P/00/epolls.o.htm.

gender gap
The difference between the political opinions or political behavior of men and of women.

Rosie O'Donnell, a gay parent, is a vocal advocate for gays who want to adopt children. O'Donnell and her partner were among many gay couples that traveled to San Francisco in early 2004 to obtain a marriage license.

Sexual Orientation

Differences in sexual orientation have become important politically in recent years. The modern movement for expanded rights for gays and lesbians traces its roots to 1969, when New York City police raided the Stonewall Inn in Greenwich Village and a riot ensued.[73] Precise data on the number of homosexuals in the United States are in dispute. The gay and lesbian communities talk in terms of 10 percent; other estimates come in much lower.[74] One source estimates that 2.8 percent of men and 1.4 percent of women identify themselves as homosexual or bisexual.[75] Regardless of its overall size, the homosexual community has become important politically in several cities, most notably San Francisco. Both parties have openly professed gay members of Congress.

In 2000, Vermont became the first state to enact legislation granting gay and lesbian couples "civil union" status, which confers many of the benefits of marriage. Before this law took effect, the Vermont Supreme Court had ruled that denying gay couples the same rights and benefits as heterosexual couples was unconstitutional. In 2003, the Massachusetts Supreme Judicial Court ruled that not allowing gay couples to marry was discriminatory, and that the only remedy was full marriage rights for both heterosexual and homosexual couples.[76] This decision pushed gay marriage onto the national agenda, spurring social conservatives to argue that traditional marriage, defined as marriage between a man and a woman, needed constitutional protection, a cause that was endorsed by President Bush. In the wake of the Massachusetts ruling, mayors in cities like San Francisco, California and New Paltz, New York authorized their cities to issue marriage licenses and perform same-sex marriages. San Francisco mayor Newsom justified his policy as constitutional in the sense that it removed a form of discrimination.[77]

The political agenda for gay and lesbian advocacy groups includes fighting discrimination, including the military's "Don't ask, don't tell" policy. On some fronts, the groups have been successful. In several cities and among some employers, gays and lesbians have been able to secure health care and other benefits for domestic partners. Antidiscrimination statutes protecting people from discrimination in housing and employment on the basis of sexual orientation have been passed in several cities and states. Groups like the Human Rights Campaign are visible advocates of eliminating restrictions based on sexual orientation. Hate crimes against gays and lesbians have led the Senate to include sexual orientation in federal hate crimes legislation.[78]

Conservative groups were successful in enacting initiatives in thirteen states in 2004 defining marriage as a union between a man and a woman. Among the groups that have been active in the protest movement have been some conservative Protestants, Catholics, and Mormons. The gay marriage issue appeared on the ballots of more than a dozen states in 2004 and Congress considered a proposed constitutional amendment defining marriage as a union between a man and a woman. Democrats accused Republicans of trying to exploit the marriage issue for partisan advantage. The courts have also been drawn into the battle over sexual orientation. In a 5-to-4 decision, the Supreme Court upheld the right of the Boy Scouts of America to bar homosexuals in its organization.[79]

Family Structure

Over the past half-century, the typical American family has been transformed from a "traditional family" (mother and father married, with children in the home) to a variety of living arrangements and varying family structures. Americans are much more likely to approve of premarital sex than in the early 1970s. From 1996 to 2002, the number of Americans who cohabit (live with someone of the opposite sex without being married) increased by 50 percent.[80] Cohabitation raises public policy questions such as whether the live-in partner is eligible for employment benefits and welfare payments. Contraception is widely used and accepted, and yet one-third of all births are now illegitimate.[81] These children will often be in need of social services and financial assistance.

People now marry later in life, with men marrying on the average at age 27 and women at age 25.[82] Yet marrying later has not improved the chances of avoiding divorce. The average marriage today lasts only about 7.2 years. Before World War II, only nine

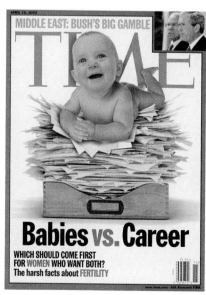

The risk of having children later in life has recently been the subject of cover stories in news magazines.

out of every 1,000 marriages ended in divorce; between 1950 and 1996, the divorce rate nearly doubled. Today it is estimated that about half of all marriages will end in divorce.[83]

Since the 1960s, birthrates have steadily declined in the United States. In the early 1960s, a woman statistically averaged about 3.5 children. By 2001, that number dropped to 2.1 children, barely meeting the 2.1 needed to replace the population. In other words, if the current trend continues, the American native-born population will actually decrease over time.[84]

Divorce is one reason why some women go to work and why the number of households headed by women has risen. Attitudes about the role of women in marriage and the family have also changed. In 1972, one-third of Americans thought that a woman belonged in the home and should not work outside the home, but in 1998, only one-sixth of all Americans felt this way.[85]

Religion

In many parts of the world, religious differences, especially when combined with disputes over territory or sovereignty, are a source of violent conflict. The conflict in Israel between Israelis and Palestinians escalated with suicide bombers willing to kill themselves while killing Israeli civilians and with Israeli troops and tanks rolling into Palestinian areas. In Iraq and Turkey, the Kurdish people have been subjected to expulsion and even genocide. The war between India and Pakistan over Kashmir is a religious and ethnic battle among Muslims and Hindus, as is the conflict between Muslims and Christians in Indonesia. Other countries like Afghanistan, Lebanon, Sri Lanka, and Sudan have also experienced intense religious conflicts in recent years. The Shi'ite–Sunni conflict in Iraq threatens the stability of the new government in Iraq.

Jews have often been the target of religious discrimination and persecution (anti-Semitism), which reached its greatest intensity in the Holocaust of the 1930s and 1940s, during which an estimated 6 million Jews were murdered.[86] The United States has not been immune from such hatred, despite its principle of religious freedom. In 1838, Governor Lilburn W. Boggs of Missouri issued an extermination order against the Mormons.[87]

Our government is founded on the premise that religious liberty is more likely when there is not one predominant or official faith, which is why the framers of our Constitution did not sanction a national church. In fact, James Madison wrote in *The Federalist*, No. 51, "In a free government the security for civil rights must be the same as that for religious rights. It consists in the one case in the multiplicity of interests, and in the other in the multiplicity of sects" (see the Appendix).

The absence of an official American church does not mean that religion is unimportant in American politics; indeed, there were established state churches in this country until the 1830s. Some observers contend that "the root of American political and social values . . . is the distinctive Puritanism of the early New England settlers."[88] Politicians frequently refer to God in their speeches or demonstrate their piety in other ways. In 2000, Democratic vice presidential candidate Joseph Lieberman, an observant Jew, made frequent references to God and religion in his speeches. George W. Bush concluded his 2004 State of the Union Address, in many ways the kickoff for his 2004 campaign, by saying "We can trust in that greater power who guides the unfolding of the years. And in all that is to come, we can know that His purposes are just and true. May God bless the United States of America. Thank you."[89] A more subtle use of religion by George W. Bush is the title he selected for his political memoir, *A Charge to Keep*. This title is also a Protestant hymn, allowing him to reinforce his connection to Protestants who will recognize the title as one of their hymns. The second verse of the hymn reads, "To serve the present age—My calling to fulfill—O may it all my powers engage—To do my Master's will."[90]

At one time, it was thought that a Catholic could not be elected president. With the election of 1960, that issue was resolved. John F. Kennedy directly confronted the question of whether a Catholic would put aside religious teachings if they conflicted with constitutional obligations. He said, "I am not the Catholic candidate for President. I am the

Democratic party's candidate for President who happens also to be Catholic. I do not speak for my church on public matters, and the church does not speak for me."[91] Nevertheless a candidate's religion may still become an issue today if the candidate's religious convictions on sensitive issues such as abortion threaten to conflict with public obligations.

During the 2004 Democratic party battle for the presidential nomination, Howard Dean initially contended that candidates should not interject religion into politics. In a town-hall meeting in New Hampshire, Dean criticized President Bush for his opposition to stem-cell research saying, "I think we ought to make scientific decisions, not theological and theoretical decisions."[92] When challenged on this comment, especially in light of the importance of religiosity in the South, he retreated to his original position. Dean's flip-flop on religion in 2004 is an example of the continuing importance of religion, at least in many parts of the country.

Religion also surfaces in political life as an important catalyst for change, as the Catholic church was in the overthrow of communism in central Europe and the leadership of black churches were in the American civil rights movement. As writer Taylor Branch explains, the black church "served not only as a place of worship but also as a bulletin board to a people who owned no organs of communication, a credit union to those without banks, and even a kind of people's court."[93] African American ministers, like the Reverend Martin Luther King Jr., became leaders of the civil rights movement; others, like the Reverend Jesse Jackson and more recently Al Sharpton, have run for national office. Hence religion can be important not only as a source of personal values and attitudes but also as a means of political activity and organization.

More recently, there has been an increase in political activity among fundamentalist Christians. Led by ministers like Jerry Falwell and Pat Robertson, they have supported political organizations such as the Moral Majority and the Christian Coalition. For two decades, they have sought to influence the national agenda, and Robertson taped telephone endorsements for George W. Bush in 2000. In 2004, Reverend Robertson generated some controversy in an interview he did on CNN when he said President Bush had originally assumed that there would be only limited casualties in the war in Iraq. They also focus their attention at the local level—school boards, city councils, mayorships, and local GOP leadership.[94] Their agenda includes the return of school prayer, the outlawing of abortion, restrictions on homosexuals, and opposition to gun control. To learn more about the Christian Coalition, go to www.cc.org. Many Americans take their religious beliefs seriously, more so than people of other industrial democracies.[95] Approximately a quarter of Americans attend houses of worship only a few times a year, 16 percent at least once a month, and 38 percent nearly every week.[96] Religion, like ethnicity, is a *shared identity*. People identify themselves as Baptist, Catholic, or Buddhist. To find out more information about religion in the United States, go to www.ipl.org/ref/RR/static/hum80.10.00.html. Sometimes church attendance or nonattendance is more important than differences between religions in explaining attitudes. "Among both Catholics and Protestants, opposition to abortion increases with frequency of church attendance, but the percentages expressing pro-choice and pro-life sentiments are quite similar for the Catholic and Protestant groups."[97]

One defining characteristic of religion in the United States is the tremendous variety of denominations. About half the people in the United States describe themselves as Protestant (see Figure 5–4). The largest Protestant denomination is Baptist, followed by Methodists, Lutherans, Presbyterians, Pentecostals, and Episcopalians. Because Protestants are divided among so many different churches, Catholics have the largest single membership in the United States, constituting nearly a quarter of the population.[98] Jews represent 2 percent of the population.[99] Followers of Islam number more than 1,100,000.[100] Protestants came to the United States first; most Catholics and Jews immigrated after the 1840s. It was not until 1960, however, that Americans elected a Catholic president.

Religion is important in American politics in part because of the concentrations of people of particular religions in a few states. Catholics, as noted, make up nearly a quarter of the U.S. population, yet they make up nearly two-thirds of the population of Rhode Island.[101] Baptists represent 16 percent of the U.S. population, yet they account for roughly a third of the population of Mississippi and Alabama.[102] Mormons represent only 2 percent of the U.S. population but constitute two-thirds of the population of

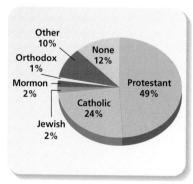

FIGURE 5–4 Religious Groups in America.
SOURCE: The Gallup Organization, at www.gallup.com/poll/focus/sr040302.asp.

Utah.[103] The state of New York has the highest percentage of Jews with 9 percent; New York City is 13 percent Jewish.[104]

In recent presidential elections, a majority of Protestants voted Republican, while majorities of Catholics and Jews voted Democratic.[105] However, in 2004, Bush received a majority of the Catholic vote and increased his majority among Protestants to 59 percent. Kerry received 75 percent of the Jewish vote. The perception among many Catholics and Jews that the Democratic party is more open to them helps explain the strength of their Democratic identification. Democrats won the loyalty of many Catholics by their willingness to nominate Al Smith for the presidency in 1928 and John Kennedy in 1960. Jewish voters' long-standing identification with the Democratic party may have been reinforced by Al Gore's selection of Joseph Lieberman to be his running mate in 2000. Southern Protestants have been Democrats for different reasons, having largely to do with the sectional issues discussed earlier. Religious groups vary in their rates of participation. Jews have the highest rate of reported voter turnout, 93 percent in 2000, while those who claim no religious affiliation have the lowest, 47 percent.[106] Catholics (62 percent) voted at a slightly higher rate than Protestants (59 percent).[107] Religion can be related to other politically important characteristics. For instance, Jews are the most prosperous and best educated of any ethnic or religious group. More than 46 percent of Jewish adults are college graduates, compared to 22 percent of Protestants and 20 percent of Catholics.[108] In this example, as in others, religion is a cross-cutting cleavage in American politics; the differences do not reinforce one another. On the basis of income and education, we might expect Jews to be Republicans, but 79 percent of American Jews voted for Al Gore in 2000.[109] Catholics had cross-pressures in 2004 because John Kerry is Catholic. This did not stop a majority of Catholics from voting for Bush. Catholics who attend church weekly were even more likely to vote against Kerry and for Bush; they gave 56 percent of their votes to Bush. Similarly, we might predict that southern Protestants would be heavily Republican, but many are Democrats.

Wealth and Income

The United States is a wealthy nation. Compared to other nations, our purchasing power is higher than that of any other advanced democracy.[110] Indeed, to some knowledgeable observers, "the most striking thing about the United States has been its phenomenal wealth."[111] Most Americans lead comfortable lives. They eat and live well and have first-class medical care. But the unequal distribution of wealth and income still results in important political divisions and conflicts.

Wealth (total value of possessions) is more concentrated than income (annual earnings). The wealthiest families hold most of the property and other forms of wealth like stocks and savings. Traditionally, one of the problems with concentrated wealth has been that it fosters an aristocracy. Thomas Jefferson sought to break up the "aristocracy of wealth" by changing from laws based on *primogeniture* (the eldest son's exclusive right to inherit his father's estate) to laws that encouraged people to divide their estates equally among all their children, resulting in smaller landholdings. Jefferson sought to encourage an "aristocracy of virtue and talent" through a public school system open to all for the primary grades and for the best students through the university level.[112]

Most college students come from the top quarter of American families in income—those earning $50,000 a year or more. Education is in turn one of the most important means to achieve upward economic and social mobility. People who go to college earn more than those who have not, and those from wealthier families are more inclined to get an education at nearly twice the rate as those positioned elsewhere on the socioeconomic ladder.[113]

College tuition and other costs have climbed substantially in recent years. Tuition, for example, climbed 113 percent, on average, at public colleges and universities and 93 percent at private institutions since 1990.[114] The impact of rising costs affects low-income students more than others. These students come from families that are less likely to be able to help with the rising costs. "College costs eat up 71% of earnings for low-income families but only 6% of the income of the top 25% of earners."[115] Low-income students have also been hurt by some college's shift away from a need-based system of scholarships.

Part of the problem for low-income students is also a success story. There are now more of them qualifying for admission, making the competition for support more intense.

The dangers of an unequal concentration of wealth were recognized in the earliest years of our history. "The most common and durable source of factions has been the various and unequal distribution of property," wrote James Madison in *The Federalist*, No. 10 (reprinted in the Appendix). "Those who hold, and those who are without property, have ever formed distinct interests in society." Madison was right. Economic differences often lead to conflict, and Americans remain divided politically along economic lines. Aside from race, income may be the single most important factor in explaining views on issues, partisanship, and ideology. Most rich people are Republicans, and most poor people are Democrats, and this has been true since at least the Great Depression of the 1930s. In terms of income, the Northeast is the most prosperous region and the South the least prosperous.

Between the 1950s and the 1970s inflation-adjusted income doubled. More recently, as shown in Figure 5–5, inflation-adjusted income has gone up and down.[116] What accounts for this pattern in contrast to the steady rise seen earlier? Economists debate the causes for this change; some cite higher energy costs, low levels of personal savings, and the worldwide slowdown in productivity growth.[117] More recent data, however, actually point to increased productivity, in part due to the more widespread use of computers and information technology.[118] While the long-term trend has been for income to rise, the bottom 10 percent of the population in terms of income has actually seen a decline in wages. At the same time, the top 10 percent has experienced substantial growth in income. Economists refer to this as *dispersion,* or the difference in growth patterns among income levels.

The bottom 12.1 percent in income is also the segment of the population that falls below the poverty line.[119] In 2003, the official poverty level for a family of four was an income below $18,660.[120] Families headed by a female are almost two times more likely to fall below the poverty line than families headed by a man, and 26.5 percent of all households headed by females fall below the poverty line.[121] Close to 16 percent of the poor are children under 18 years of age, and many appear to be trapped in a cycle of poverty (see Figure 5–6).[122] African American and Hispanic children are nearly three times as likely to be poor than white children.[123]

The definition of poverty is itself political, and a change in the definition of poverty can make it appear that there are more or fewer poor people than before. The poverty classification is intended to identify persons who cannot meet a minimum standard in such basics as housing, food, and medical care. Regardless of how one defines poverty, however, the poor are a minority who lack political power. The poor vote less than wealthier groups and are less confident and organized in dealing with politics and

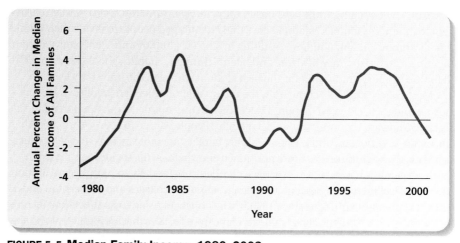

FIGURE 5–5 Median Family Income, 1980–2003.
SOURCE: Harold W. Stanley and Richard G. Niemi, *Vital Statistics on American Politics, 2003–2004* (CQ Press, 2000), p. 363–364.

government. Over the past two decades, inequality between rich and poor has been increasing, a trend quite different from the 1960s, when the gap between rich and poor narrowed.[124] Although the gap began to decrease under the first Bush administration (1989–1993), inequality between rich and poor has again been on the rise since then.[125]

The distribution of income in a society can have important consequences for democratic stability. If there is a perception that only the few at the top of the economic ladder can hope to earn enough for an adequate standard of living, domestic unrest and revolution may follow. Income is related to participation in politics. People who need the most help from government are the least likely to participate. They are also the most likely to favor social welfare programs.

Occupation

Americans at the time of Jefferson and for several generations thereafter worked primarily on farms, but by the end of World War I, the United States had become the world's leading industrial nation. This dramatic transformation also resulted in the expansion of American cities as workers moved to find jobs. Labor conditions, including child labor practices, became important political issues. Inventions and the application of technology, combined with abundant natural and human resources, meant that the U.S. **gross domestic product (GDP)** rose, after adjusting for inflation, by more than 297 percent over the period from 1960 to 2002.[126]

The United States several years ago entered what Daniel Bell, a noted sociologist, labeled the "postindustrial" phase of our development. "A post-industrial society, being primarily a technical society, awards less on the basis of inheritance or property . . . than on education and skill."[127] *Knowledge* is the organizing device of the postindustrial era. Postindustrial societies have greater affluence and a class structure less defined along traditional labor-versus-management lines.

The changing dynamics of the American labor force can be seen in Figure 5–7, which shows the percentage of the U.S. labor force in various occupations. There has been tremendous growth in the white-collar sector of our economy. This sector includes managers, accountants, and lawyers, as well as professionals and technicians in such rapid-growth areas as computers, communications, finance, insurance, and research. This shift has been accompanied by a dramatic decline in the number of people engaged in agriculture and a more modest decline in the number of people in manufacturing (the blue-collar sector). Today only 2.4 percent of working Americans are employed in agriculture, and only 13.3 percent are employed in manufacturing.[128] Governments are among the biggest employers in this country. Federal, state, and local governments produce more than 18 percent of our gross domestic product.[129]

Women and racial minorities have distinct occupational patterns. The majority of blue-collar jobs are held by men, while women hold over 62 percent of jobs in the service sector—especially in education, social services, and health care.[130] As noted earlier, women generally earn less than men of the same age and education. Occupations in which women predominate, like teaching and clerical work, are generally lower-paying than industrial or management jobs. And as women advance in their careers, especially in management, they encounter a barrier to advancement that has been referred to as the "glass ceiling."

Social Class

Why do Americans not divide themselves into social classes as Europeans do? American workers have not formed their own political party, nor does class seem to dominate our political life. Marxist categories of *proletariat* (those who sell their labor) and *bourgeoisie* (those who own or control the means of production) are far less important here than they are in Europe. Still, we do have social classes and what social scientists call **socioeconomic status (SES)**—a division of the population based on occupation, income, and education.

Most Americans, when asked what class they belong to, say "middle class." Very few see themselves as lower class or upper class. In many other industrial democracies, large proportions of the population think of themselves as "working class" rather than middle

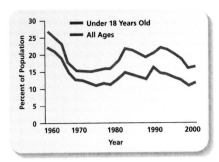

FIGURE 5–6 Percentage of Americans Living in Poverty, by Age, 1959–2000.
SOURCE: U.S. Bureau of the Census, *Statistical Abstract of the United States, 2003* (Government Printing Office, 2003), p. 22, 28.

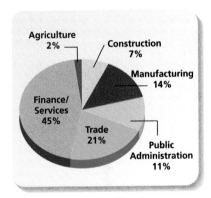

FIGURE 5–7 Occupational Groups 2002.
SOURCE: U.S. Bureau of the Census, *Statistical Abstract of the United States, 2003* (Government Printing Office, 2003), p. 404.

gross domestic product (GDP)
The total output of all economic activity in the nation, including goods and services.

socioeconomic status (SES)
A division of population based on occupation, income, and education.

"It's like this. If the rich have money, they invest. If the poor have money, they eat."

class.[131] In England, nearly three out of five persons identify themselves as working class.[132] But Americans rarely use that designation.

What constitutes the "middle class" in the United States is highly subjective. For instance, some individuals perform working-class tasks (such as plumbing), but their income places them in the middle class or even the upper-middle class. A schoolteacher's income is below that of many working-class jobs, but in terms of status, the job ranks among middle-class fields.

One explanation for Americans' responses may be the elements of the American dream that involve upward mobility. Or their responses may reflect the hostility many feel toward organized labor. In any case, compared to many countries, class divisions in the United States are less defined and less important to politics. As political scientist Seymour Martin Lipset has written, "The American social structure and values foster an emphasis on competitive individualism, an orientation that is not congruent with class consciousness, support for socialist or social democratic parties, or a strong union movement."[133]

Age

Americans are living longer, a phenomenon that has been dubbed the "graying of America" (Figure 5–8). This demographic change is having important consequences; it has increased the demand for medical care, retirement benefits, and a host of other age-related services. Persons over the age of 65 constitute less than 13 percent of the population yet account for 31 percent of the total medical expenditures.[134] With the decreasing birthrate discussed earlier, there is some concern about maintaining an adequate workforce in the future.

Older Americans are politically aware, and they vote. Past legislative victories have changed the lives of older citizens. For instance, the poverty rate among this group dropped from 15.7 percent in 1980 to 10.1 percent in 2001, a change partly due to improved medical benefits passed during the 1960s.[135] As a group, older Americans fight to ensure that Social Security is protected; they value Medicare and favor prescription drug coverage. Despite their desire for services that benefit themselves, they also favor tax cuts.

Their vote is especially important in western states and in Florida, the state with the largest proportion of people over 65. The "gray lobby" not only votes in large numbers but also has four other political assets not found in other age groups that make it politically powerful: disposable income, discretionary time, a clear focus on issues, and effective organization. When older Americans compete for their share of the budget pie, the young, minorities, and the poor often lose out.[136] Congressional passage of a limited prescription drug benefit in 2003 is an example of the political power of the "gray lobby." While the measure was not popular with some conservative Republicans, the Bush administration pushed and cited it as an accomplishment in the 2004 campaign. Conservatives were not alone in criticizing the Bush prescription drug plan. Liberals and Democratic candidate John Kerry criticized the plan as not going far enough. The American Association for Retired Persons (AARP), which had backed the plan over the protest of some members, ran ads aimed at informing seniors about how to make use of the benefit.

Age is important to politics in two additional ways: life cycle and generational effects. *Life-cycle effects* have shown that as people become middle-aged, they become more politically conservative, less mobile, and more likely to participate in politics. As they age further and rely more on the government for services, they tend

FIGURE 5–8 Percent of Population over Age 65, 1900–2000.
SOURCE: U.S. Bureau of the Census, at www.census.gov/statab/hist/HS-03.pdf.

to grow more liberal.[138] Young people, in contrast, are more mobile and less concerned about the delivery of government services.

Several groups made getting younger voters registered and to the polls a high priority in 2004. Exit polls from the 2004 election found that turnout among those 18–29 years old rose from 42 percent in 2000 to 51 percent in 2004. An estimated 4.6 million more 18–29 year olds voted in 2004. Because overall turnout was higher in 2004, the proportion of the voters aged 18–29 remained constant at 17 percent.[137]

There are also *generational effects* in politics that arise when a particular generation has had experiences that make it politically distinct. An example is the experience of those who lived through the Great Depression of the 1930s, which shaped their lifelong views of parties, issues, and political leaders. Some members of this generation saw Franklin Roosevelt as the leader who saved the country by pulling it out of the Depression; others felt he sold the country down the river by launching too many government programs. More recently and to a lesser extent, the baby boomers shared a common and distinctive political experience. These Americans came of age politically in the 1960s and 1970s during the civil rights movement and the Vietnam War.

Education

Differences in education affect not only economic well-being but political participation and involvement as well. Thomas Jefferson wrote of education, "Enlighten the people generally, and tyranny and oppressions of body and mind will vanish like evil spirits at the dawn of day."[139] The vast majority of people in the United States are educated in public schools. Nine out of every ten students in kindergarten through high school attend public schools, and more than three out of four students in college are in public institutions.[140]

Only recently has the number of college graduates in America surpassed the number of persons who did not graduate from high school.[141] Just over half of all Americans

---

TABLE 5–3 EDUCATIONAL ATTAINMENT IN THE UNITED STATES

Percent of Population—Highest Educational Level Attained

	Population (1,000)	Not a High School Graduate	High School Graduate	Bachelor's Degree	Advanced Degree
Age					
18 to 24 years old	27,313	24	68	8	—
25 to 34 years old	38,670	13	56	23	7
35 to 44 years old	44,284	12	60	20	9
45 to 54 years old	39,545	11	59	18	12
55 to 64 years old	25,874	16	57	15	11
65 to 74 years old	18,123	27	55	12	7
75 years old or over	15,647	34	51	9	5
Sex (Persons 25 years old and over)					
Male	86,996	16	55	18	10
Female	95,146	16	59	17	8
Race (Persons 25 years old and over)					
White	151,942	15	58	18	9
Black	20,359	21	62	12	5
Hispanic	19,670	43	46	8	3
Asian/Pacific Islander	7,866	13	40	31	16

SOURCE: U.S. Census Bureau, *Educational Attainment in the United States: March 2002*, at www.census.gov/population/www/socdemo/education/pp1–169.html, June 24, 2004.

Note: Percentages may not add up to 100 percent due to rounding error. "High school graduate" percentages and "some college" percentages are combined.

THE GREAT AMERICAN DIVIDE

This Make It Real feature examines the demographic makeup of the two major parties. The cross-cutting nature of American politics is more evident among some groups, while others are strongly inclined toward one party. Based on your reading of this chapter and your political experience, test your knowledge about which types of people identify with the Republican or Democratic party.

Go to Make It Real: "The Great American Divide."

have not gone to college, though many college students assume that the college experience is widely shared. A little over 27 percent of whites are college graduates, compared to 17 percent of African Americans and 11 percent of Hispanics; roughly 21 percent of African Americans and 43 percent of all Hispanics stopped their schooling before completing high school (see Table 5–3).[142]

Education is one of the most important variables in predicting political participation, confidence in dealing with government, and awareness of issues. Education is also related to the acquisition of democratic values. People who have failed to learn the prevailing norms of American society are far more likely to express opposition to democratic and capitalist ideals than those who are well educated and politically knowledgeable.[143]

UNITY IN A LAND OF DIVERSITY

As remarkable as American diversity is, the existence of a strong and widely shared sense of national unity and identity may be even more remarkable. Writing about the United States some years ago, a famous reporter, John Gunther, summarized his insights from extensive travels:

> Whoever invented the motto *E Pluribus Unum* [out of many, one] has given the best three-word description of the United States ever written. The triumph of America is the triumph of a coalescing federal system. Complex as the nation is almost to the point of insufferability, it interlocks. Homogeneity and diversity—these are the stupendous rival magnets. . . . Think of the United States as an immense blanket or patchwork quilt solid with different designs and highlights. But, no matter what colors burn and flash in what corners, the warp and woof, the basic texture and fabric, is the same from corner to corner, from end to end.[144]

Social scientists sometimes speak of the "melting pot," meaning that as various ethnic groups associate with other groups, they are assimilated into American society and come to share democratic values like majority rule, individualism, and the notion that America is the land of opportunity. The melting pot idea has been criticized as assuming that differences between groups are to be discouraged. In its place, critics propose the notion of the "salad bowl," in which "though the salad is an entity, the lettuce can still be distinguished from the chicory, the tomatoes from the cabbage."[145]

As this chapter has demonstrated, regional, social and economic differences have important political consequences. They influence public opinion, participation, voting, interest groups and political parties. At the same time our country has achieved a sense of unity despite our remarkable diversity.

S U M M A R Y

1. The character of a political society and its social environment are important to understanding our politics and government.

2. As a nation of immigrants, Americans are more diverse than the citizens of most other nations. Diversity in race and ethnicity are reflected in different family structures and religions. The nation's citizens also differ in wealth and income, occupation, social class, age, and education. Divisions by gender and sexual orientation have recently become more important. This diversity is often significant in our politics, though most divisions cut across demographic categories rather than reinforce them.

3. Geography, room to grow, abundant natural resources, wealth, and relative isolation from foreign entanglements help explain American politics and traditions, including the notions of manifest destiny, ethnocentrism, and isolationism.

4. Until recently, the South was a very distinct region in the United States, in large part because of its agricultural base and its history of slavery and troubled race relations. With in-migration and the impact of the civil rights movement, it is no longer solidly Democratic. Recently, the most significant migration has been from cities to suburbs. Today large cities are increasingly poor, African American, and

Democratic, surrounded by suburbs that are primarily middle class, white, and Republican.

5. Race has been among the most important of the differences in our political landscape. Although we fought a civil war over freedom for African Americans, racial equality was largely postponed until the latter half of the twentieth century. Race remains an important issue in our politics and government. Ethnicity, including the rising numbers of Hispanics, continues to be a factor in politics.

6. Gender is important in American politics. Women have gradually acquired political rights. They now play important

roles in our government, and they differ from men in their attitudes on some issues. Sexual orientation policies, especially relating to same-sex marriage, are among the most contentious in our society.

7. Since World War II, attitudes toward sexuality, marriage, and family have changed in important ways. People cohabit at much higher rates, and those who marry are older. Divorce has also become much more commonplace. Changing family structures and attitudes affect our tax policies, child care, parental leave, and gender equality. They are also important political issues.

8. The United States has a large variety of religious denominations, and these differences help explain public opinion and political behavior. Important differences also exist between Americans who are religious and those who are not.

9. Although the United States is a land of wealth with a large middle class, not everyone has an adequate share in the American economic success. Poverty has grown over the past two decades, and it is most concentrated among African Americans, Native Americans, Hispanics, and single-parent households. Women as a group continue to earn less than men, even in the same occupations. Differences in income and wealth remain important.

10. The United States has shifted from an agricultural to an industrial and now to a postindustrial society, with consequences for occupations and politics. Governments are a major source of employment. Social class is less important in America than in other industrialized democracies.

11. Age and education are important to understanding American politics. Older citizens participate much more than young voters and are a potent political force. Education not only opens up economic opportunities in America but also explains many important aspects of political participation.

12. Despite our diversity, Americans share an important unity. We are united by our shared commitment to democratic values, economic opportunity, work ethic, and the American dream.

K E Y   T E R M S

ethnocentrism	**political predisposition**	**manifest destiny**	**gender gap**
political socialization	**reinforcing cleavages**	**race**	**gross domestic product (GDP)**
demographics	**cross-cutting cleavages**	**ethnicity**	**socioeconomic status (SES)**

F U R T H E R   R E A D I N G

DOUGLAS L. ANDERSON, RICHARD BARTNETT, AND DONALD BOGUE, *The Population of the United States*, 3d ed. (Free Press, 1996).

DAVID H. BENNETT, *The Party of Fear* (University of North Carolina Press, 1990).

EARL BLACK AND MERLE BLACK, *The Rise of Southern Republicans* (Belknap Press, 2002).

URIE BRONFENBRENNER ET AL., *The State of Americans: The Disturbing Facts and Figures on Changing Values, Crime, the Economy, Poverty, Family, Education, the Aging Population, and What They Mean for Our Future* (Free Press, 1996).

DAVID T. CANON, *Race, Redistricting, and Representation: The Unintended Consequences of Black Majority Districts* (University of Chicago Press, 1999).

MAUREEN DEZELL, *Irish America: Coming Into Clover* (Anchor Books, 2000).

LOIS LOVELACE DUKE, ED., *Women in Politics: Outsiders or Insiders?* 2d ed. (Prentice Hall, 1995).

SARAH H. EVANS, *Born for Liberty: A History of Women in America* (Free Press, 1989).

GEOFFREY FOX, *Hispanic Nation: Culture, Politics and the Constructing of Identity* (Birch Lane Press, 1996).

RODOLFO O. DE LA GARZA, LOUIS DE SIPIO, F. CHRIS GARCIA, JOHN GARCIA, AND ANGELO FALCON, *Latino Voices: Mexican, Puerto Rican, and Cuban Perspectives on American Politics* (Westview Press, 1992).

JOHN C. GREEN, MARK J. ROZELL, AND CLYDE WILCOX, EDS., *The Christian Right in American Politics: Marching to the Millenium* (Georgetown University Press, 2003).

DONALD R. KINDER AND LYNN M. SANDERS, *Divided by Color: Racial Politics and Democratic Ideals* (University of Chicago Press, 1996).

JAN E. LEIGHLEY, *Strength in Numbers? The Political Mobilization of Racial and Ethnic Minorities* (Princeton University Press, 2001).

PEL-TE LIEN, M. MARGARET CONWAY, AND JANELLE WONG, *The Politics of Asian Americans* (Routledge, 2004).

SEYMOUR MARTIN LIPSET, *Continental Divide: The Values and Institutions of the United States and Canada* (Routledge, 1990).

JEREMY D. MAYER, *Runing On Race: Racial Politics in Presidential Campaign, 1960–2000* (Random House, 2002).

NANCY E. McGLEN AND KAREN O'CONNOR, *Women, Politics, and American Society*, 2d ed. (Prentice Hall, 1998).

KEVIN PHILLIPS, *The Politics of Rich and Poor: Wealth and the American Electorate in the Reagan Aftermath* (Random House, 1990).

STANLEY A. RENSHON, ED., *One America? Political Leadership, National Identity, and the Dilemmas of Diversity* (Georgetown University Press, 2001).

RUBEN G. RUMBAUT AND ALEJANDRO PORTES, *Ethnicities: Children of Immigrants in America* (University of California Press, 2001).

ARTHUR M. SCHLESINGER JR., *The Disuniting of America* (Norton, 1992).

PETER H. SCHUCK, *Diversity In America* (Belknap Press, 2003).

JEFFREY M. STONECASH, *Class and Party in American Politics* (Westview Press, 2000).

ALEXIS DE TOCQUEVILLE, *Democracy in America*, ed. J. P. Mayer, trans. George Lawrence (Doubleday, 1969). Originally published 1835.

KENNETH D. WALD, *Religion and Politics in the United States*, 3d ed. (CQ Press, 1996).

The 2004 presidential election featured not only ads from the candidates but also ads from interest groups opposing and, less frequently, supporting one of the candidates. During the Democratic convention, John Kerry and his advocates emphasized his preparation to be Commander-in-Chief and his Vietnam War heroism. Shortly after the convention, a group called Swift Boat Veterans for Truth started running ads questioning Kerry's heroism and patriotism. The group also released a book titled *Unfit for Command*,[1] which accused Kerry of lying about his record and exaggerating the atrocities committed by U.S. troops in Vietnam. Kerry responded by calling their claims "categorically false," arguing that the Bush campaign was behind the attacks, and calling on Bush to repudiate them.[2] Bush in turn suggested that both candidates urge all interest groups to stop running ads.[3]

Individuals closely connected to key Bush political advisors or family provided early funding and support for the Swift Boat Veterans for Truth. Bob J. Perry, a longtime associate of Karl Rove, the chief political strategist for President Bush, provided $200,000 to help launch the group.[4] The veterans group also had the same attorney as the Bush campaign. A candidate campaign and interest group using the same attorney was not limited to the Bush campaign nor was it illegal, but these facts did not diffuse the Kerry campaign's claim that the Swift Boat Veterans for Truth was a front for the Bush campaign.[5]

Swift Boat Veterans for Truth was not the only interest group to run ads critical of candidates in 2004. In fact, it spent far less on ads than liberal groups opposing President Bush.[6]

INTEREST GROUPS
THE POLITICS OF INFLUENCE

6

TIME LINE

INTEREST GROUPS

1833	Anti-Slavery Society founded
1890	National American Woman Suffrage Association formed
1893	Anti-Saloon League formed
1910	Passage of Federal Corrupt Practices Act (revised 1925, replaced 1971)
1912	U.S. Chamber of Commerce is created
1920	American Civil Liberties Union is founded
1955	AFL and CIO merge to form the largest labor union
1958	AARP is created but growth comes with the aging of Baby Boomers
1961	President Eisenhower warns against the "military-industrial complex"
1971	Federal Election Campaign Act passed
1974	Common Cause represents the interests of middle-class reformers
1976	*Buckley* v. *Valeo* ruling upholds public financing of presidential elections and contribution limits in congressional elections
2002	McCain–Feingold Bipartisan Campaign Reform Act limits "soft money"

Early in the primary season, a liberal group called MoveOn ran ads critical of President Bush. Some of these ads ran even before the Democrats had selected their nominee, reflecting the strong anti-Bush sentiment of the group. Both Swift Boat Veterans for Truth and MoveOn demonstrated that comparatively modest media buys could capture the interest of the media and greatly expand the impact of an ad. The Media Fund—a group with much more substantial advertising expenditures—also had defeating Bush as its primary objective.

All three of these interest groups were organized under Section 527 of the Internal Revenue Code. As so-called "527" organizations, these groups could raise and spend unlimited amounts of money as long as the expenditures were independent of the candidates or parties and did not use corporate or union treasury funds within thirty days of a primary election or within sixty days of a general election. Interest groups like these have long been important in electing and defeating candidates, in providing information to officeholders, and in setting the agenda of American politics. In some important respects the power and influence of interest groups has been enhanced by recent campaign finance legislation. Americans have long been concerned about the power of what some call "special interests" and the tendency of groups to pursue self-interest at the expense of less organized groups or the general public. Restraining the negative tendencies of interest groups while protecting liberty is not an easy task. Efforts to reform campaign finance and limit the potential for interest-group corruption of that process while also safeguarding electoral competition are examples of this balancing. In this chapter we examine the full range of interest-group activity as well as efforts to limit their potentially negative influences.

INTEREST GROUPS PAST AND PRESENT: THE "MISCHIEFS OF FACTION"

What we call interest groups today, the founders of the Republic called **factions**. (They also thought of political parties as factions.) For the framers of the Constitution, the daunting problem was how to establish a stable and orderly constitutional

Interest groups often use advertising to promote issues that they consider important. This advertisement, created by the National Rifle Association, is a caricature of John Kerry as a dog that "don't hunt." Judging from the animal's appearance, this dog was obviously not bred to be a hunting dog. This mailer attacks Kerry's positions on gun-related issues.

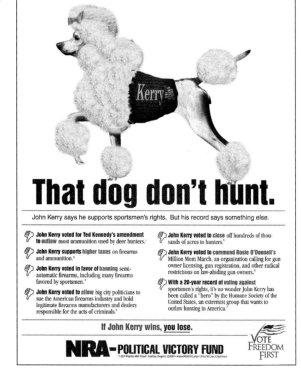

That dog don't hunt.

John Kerry says he supports sportsmen's rights. But his record says something else.

- John Kerry voted for Ted Kennedy's amendment to outlaw most ammunition used by deer hunters.
- John Kerry supports higher taxes on firearms and ammunition.
- John Kerry voted in favor of banning semi-automatic firearms, including many firearms favored by sportsmen.
- John Kerry voted to allow big city politicians to sue the American firearms industry and hold legitimate firearms manufacturers and dealers responsible for the acts of criminals.
- John Kerry voted to close off hundreds of thousands of acres to hunters.
- John Kerry voted to commend Rosie O'Donnell's Million Mom March, an organization calling for gun owner licensing, gun registration, and other radical restrictions on law-abiding gun owners.
- With a 20-year record of voting against sportsmen's rights, it's no wonder John Kerry has been called a "hero" by the Humane Society of the United States, an extremist group that wants to outlaw hunting in America.

If John Kerry wins, **you lose.**

NRA-POLITICAL VICTORY FUND

VOTE FREEDOM FIRST

faction
A term used by the founders of this country to refer to political parties and special interests or interest groups.

system that would also respect the liberty of free citizens and prevent the tyranny of the majority or of a single dominant interest. As a good practical politician and a brilliant theorist, James Madison offered both a diagnosis and a solution in *The Federalist*, No. 10 (reprinted in the Appendix). He began with a basic proposition: "The latent causes of faction are thus sown in the nature of man." All individuals pursue their self-interest, seeking advantage or power over others. Acknowledging that Americans live in a maze of group interests, Madison went on to argue that the "most common and durable source of factions has been the various and unequal distribution of property."

A Nation of Interests

As we noted in Chapter 5, some Americans identify with groups distinguished by race, gender, ethnic background, age, occupation, or sexual orientation. Others form groups based on issues like gun control or tax reduction. When such associations seek to influence government in some way, they are **interest groups**.

Interest groups are sometimes called "special interests." Politicians and the media often use this term in a pejorative way. What makes an interest group a "special" one? The answer is highly subjective. One person's special interest is another's public interest. Some interest groups claim to speak for the "public interest," yet so-called public interest groups like Common Cause or the League of Women Voters support policies that not everyone agrees with. Politics is best seen as a clash among interests with differing concepts of what is in the public interest rather than a battle between the special interests on one side and "the people" or the public interest on the other.

When political scientists call something an "interest group" or a "special interest," they are not calling it names. These are analytic terms to describe a group that speaks for some but not all of us. Much of our politics focuses on arguments about what is in the national interest. In a democracy, there are many interests and many organized interest groups. The democratic process exists to decide among those competing interests. Part of the politics of interest groups is to persuade the general public that your group's interest is better, broader, more beneficial, and more general than other groups' and at the same time label groups that oppose yours as "special interests." The term "special interest" conveys a selfish or narrow view, one that may lack credibility. For this reason, we use the neutral term "interest groups."

Social Movements

Interest groups sometimes begin as movements. A **movement** consists of a large body of people who are interested in a common issue, idea, or concern that is of continuing significance and who are willing to take action. Examples include the abolitionist, temperance, civil rights, environmental, antitax, animal rights, and women's rights movements. Each movement represents groups who have felt unrepresented by government. Such groups often arise at the grassroots level and evolve into national groups. Movements tend to see their causes as morally right and the positions of the opposition as morally wrong.

To a marked degree, our Constitution protects the liberties and independence of movements. The Bill of Rights guarantees movements, whether popular or unpopular, by supporting free assembly, free speech, and due process. Consequently, those who disagree with government policies do not have to engage in violence or other extreme activities in the United States, as they do in some countries, and they need not fear persecution for demonstrating peacefully. In a democratic system that restricts the power of government, movements have considerable room to operate *within* the constitutional system.

TYPES OF INTEREST GROUPS

Interest groups vary widely. Some are formal associations or organizations like the National Rifle Association; others have no formal organization, like Bubba's List, a group from Austin, Texas (Bubba stands for Brothers United for Building a Better America).

interest group
A collection of people who share some common interest or attitude and seek to influence government for specific ends. Interest groups usually work within the framework of government and employ tactics such as lobbying to achieve their goals.

movement
A large body of people interested in a common issue, idea, or concern that is of continuing significance and who are willing to take action. Movements seek to change attitudes or institutions, not just policies.

Some are organized primarily to lobby for limited goals such as restrictions on gun ownership, conducting research, or broadly influencing public opinion by publishing reports and mass mailings.

Interest groups can be categorized into several broad types: (1) economic, including both business and labor; (2) ideological or single-issue; (3) public interest; (4) foreign policy; and (5) government itself. Obviously, these categories are not mutually exclusive. The varied and overlapping nature of interest groups in the United States has been described as *interest group pluralism,* meaning that competition among open, responsive, and diverse groups helps preserve democratic values and limits the concentration of power in any single group.

Most Americans are represented by a number of interest groups, some of which they are aware of and others of which they may not be and often with which they differ. For instance, citizens over 50 may not be aware that the AARP (which began as the American Association of Retired Persons) claims to represent their interests, and now is open to anyone over fifty years of age. Others may not know that when they join the American Automobile Association (AAA), they are not only purchasing travel assistance and automobile towing when needed but also joining a group that lobbies Congress and the Federal Highway Administration on behalf of motorists.

Economic Interest Groups

There are thousands of economic interests: agriculture, consumers, plumbers, northern businesses, southern businesses, labor unions, the airplane industry, landlords, truckers, bondholders, property owners, and on and on.

BUSINESS   The most familiar business institution is probably the large corporation. Corporations range from one-person enterprises to vast multinational entities. Large corporations—General Motors, AT&T, Microsoft, Coca-Cola, McDonald's, Phillip Morris, and other large companies—exercise considerable political influence, as do hundreds of smaller corporations (see Tables 6–1 and 6–2). Corporate power and the implications of a changing domestic and global economy make business practices important political issues. As Microsoft and Wal-Mart have come under heightened government and public scrutiny, their political contributions have grown substantially. Wal-Mart contributed $450,000 in 2001–2002 to federal candidates or parties compared with $75,000 in 1999–2000.[7] Microsoft also donated roughly three times the amount in the 2000 and 2002 cycles than in the '98 cycle.[8]

Small business also is an important interest and can have an important voice in public policy. Within the Commerce Department there is a Small Business Administration. Small businesses are also organized into groups. An example is the National

---

TABLE 6–1   PACs THAT GAVE THE MOST TO FEDERAL CANDIDATES, 2000–2004 (MILLIONS OF DOLLARS)

	2004	*2002*	*2000*
National Association of Realtors	3.77	3.65	3.42
Wal-Mart Stores	1.65	1.08	0.46
National Association of Home Builders	2.06	1.92	1.85
Association of Trial Lawyers of America	2.17	2.81	2.66
International Brotherhood of Electrical Workers	2.33	2.22	2.62
National Auto Dealers Association	2.58	2.58	2.50
Laborers Union	2.63	2.26	1.79
Carpenters and Joiners Union	1.88	2.09	1.72
United Parcel Service	2.14	1.62	1.76
SBC Comunications	1.95	1.47	1.29

SOURCE: www.opensecrets.org/pacs/topacs.asp?strid=&cycle=2004&type=C&filter=P&txt=A&Format=Print.

TABLE 6–2   TOP TEN ALL-TIME DONORS 1989–2004

	Total
American Federation of State, County & Municipal Employees	$35,408,631
National Association of Realtors	$26,276,380
National Education Association	$24,170,353
Association of Trial Lawyers of America	$24,094,416
Communications Workers of America	$22,601,816
Service Employees International Union	$22,486,475
International Brotherhood of Electrical Workers	$22,122,055
Laborers Union	$21,899,082
American Medical Association	$21,774,021
Carpenters and Joiners Union	$21,567,447

Based on data released by the FEC on October 25, 2004.

SOURCE: Opensecrets.org at www.opensecrets.org/index.asp.

Federation of Independent Business, which is involved in electing pro-business candidates, and lobbying national government on behalf of this constituency.

TRADE AND OTHER ASSOCIATIONS   Businesses with similar interests in government regulations and other issues join together as *trade associations,* which are as diverse as the products and services they provide. In addition, businesses of all types are organized into large nationwide associations such as the National Mining Association, the National Association of Realtors, and the National Federation of Independent Business.

The broadest business trade association is the Chamber of Commerce of the United States. Organized in 1912, the Chamber is a federation of several thousand local Chambers of Commerce representing tens of thousands of firms. Loosely allied with the Chamber on most issues is the National Association of Manufacturers, which, since its founding in the wake of the depression of 1893, has tended to speak for the more conservative elements of American business.

LABOR   Workers' associations have a range of interests, from professional standards to wages and working conditions. Labor unions are one of the most important groups representing workers. The American work force is the least unionized of almost any industrial democracy (see Figure 6–1).

Probably the oldest unions in the United States were farm organizations. The largest farm group now is the American Farm Bureau Federation, which is especially strong in the Corn Belt. Originally organized around government agents who helped farmers in rural counties, the federation today is almost a semigovernmental agency, but it retains full freedom to fight for such goals as price supports and expanded credit. As farming has grown in scale and workers are less and less likely to be members of the farmer's family, there have been efforts to organize farm workers into unions. Noteworthy here have been the efforts of the late César Chávez and others to organize migrant farm workers.

Throughout the nineteenth century, workers organized political parties and local unions. Their most ambitious effort at national organization, the Knights of Labor, claimed 700,000 members. By the beginning of the twentieth century, the American Federation of Labor (AFL), a confederation of strong and independent-minded national unions mainly representing craft workers, was the dominant organization. During the ferment of the 1930s, unions more responsive to industrial workers broke away from the AFL and formed a rival national organization organized by industry, the Congress of Industrial Organizations (CIO). In 1955, the AFL and CIO reunited into the organization that exists today.

Union membership is optional in states whose laws permit the **open shop**, in which union membership cannot be required as a condition of employment. In states with the **closed shop**, union membership may be required as a condition of employment if most employees so vote. In both cases, the unions conduct negotiations with management, and the benefits the unions gain will be shared with all workers. In open-shop states, many

open shop
A company with a labor agreement under which union membership cannot be required as a condition of employment.

closed shop
A company with a labor agreement under which union membership can be a condition of employment.

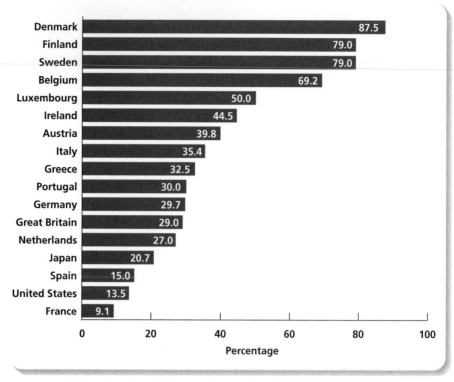

FIGURE 6–1 Union Membership in the United States Compared to Other Countries (Estimated Percentage of the Work Force).
SOURCE: European Industrial Observatory On-line, "Industrial Relations in the EU, Japan, and the US, 2001," at www.eiro.eurofound.eu.int/2002/12/feature/tn0212101f.html.

workers choose not to affiliate with a union, as they can secure the same benefits without incurring the costs associated with union membership. When a person benefits from the work or service of an organization like a union (or even a public TV or radio station) without joining or contributing, this condition is referred to as the **free rider** problem.

The AFL-CIO speaks for about 80 percent of unionized labor, but unions represent only about 14 percent of the nation's work force (see Figure 6–2).[9] The drop in the proportion of the work force belonging to unions is explained in part by the shift from an industrial to a service and information economy. Dwindling membership limits organized labor's political and lobbying muscle, and its prospects for increasing influence in the future are dim. Recently there has been growth in public sector unions, however, and even some doctors have unionized.

For some years, the Committee on Political Education (COPE) of the AFL-CIO was one of the most respected—and most feared—political organizations in the country. In the Kennedy and Johnson years, it won a reputation for political effectiveness. It encouraged and supervised grassroots political activity, and at the national level, it prepared and adopted a detailed platform that spelled out labor's position on issues. Labor contributed money to candidates, ran registration and get-out-the-vote campaigns, and otherwise supported its favorites. In recent elections, COPE has had a fairly successful record of wins for its endorsed House and Senate candidates.[10] Labor unions invested heavily in the fight against the North American Free Trade Agreement (NAFTA), claiming it would cost jobs. Labor's defeat in this battle was compounded by the 1994 election, which put Republicans in charge of the House of Representatives for the first time in forty years.

Unions have been effective in communicating with their members and organizing them for political purposes. In the 1998 elections and again in 2000 and 2002, unions sent mailings to their members, organized get-out-the-vote drives, and paid for television advertising. In the 2004 presidential primaries unions were divided; most supported former Missouri Congressman Dick Gephardt, but some—like the Service Employees International Union (SEIU) and the American Ferderation of State, County, and

free rider
An individual who does not join a group representing his or her interests yet receives the benefit of the influence the group achieves.

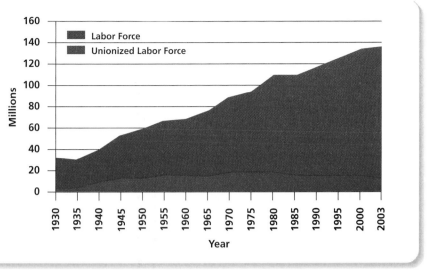

FIGURE 6–2 Labor Force and Union Membership, 1930–2003.
SOURCE: *The World Almanac and Book of Facts, 2000.* Copyright © 1999 Primedia Reference, Inc. Reprinted with permission; all rights reserved. U.S. Bureau of Labor Statistics, at www.stats.bls.gov/news.release/union2.toc.htm and www.bls.gov/cps/cpsaat40.pdf. 2003 data taken from Department of Labor, Bureau of Labor Statistics. "Press Release," January 21, 2004, at www.bls.gov/news.release/pdf/union2.pdf.

IN COMPARATIVE PERSPECTIVE

UNIONS IN SWEDEN

Interest groups are stronger in some countries and weaker in others. Organized labor, or unions, are a common feature of advanced democracies and industrial and postindustrial economies, but that does not mean that unions exercise the same influence over policy or politics in all countries.

In Sweden, unions are large and cohesive.* Nearly four out of five (79 percent) of the Swedish workforce is unionized,[†] compared with the United States, where less than one-seventh are unionized.[‡] In Sweden, moreover, unions form a single large labor federation, the Swedish Trade Union Confederation, which provides a powerful and cohesive voice in public policy. American unions are fragmented into several federations, and even within federations there are tensions between particular unions.

The Swedish Trade Union Confederation has a close relationship with the Social Democratic Party (SDP), with union leaders among the party leadership. One scholar has observed that in Sweden the Confederation supports the SDP with "money, manpower, and influence with the rank and file."[§] In the United States, most, but not all, unions support the Democratic party, and they are not as central to the Democratic coalition as unions are to Sweden's SDP.

Swedish unions are also more powerful in collective bargaining. In 2004, four industrial sectors agreed to a new three-year deal that would provide generally for a 6.8 percent pay raise, plus working time cuts worth a further 0.5 percent.[||] Swedish unions are also working to further reduce the statutory normal work week, which is presently 40 hours per week.[¶] Because of the close relationship the unions have with the governing party, they can significantly influence legislation. In the United States, labor unions opposed the re-election of George W. Bush, whose administration was seen by them as hostile.** With Republicans in control of both houses of Congress and the White House in recent years, labor unions in the United States were much less involved in policy making than were Swedish unions.

*Michael Roskin, *Countries and Concepts: Politics, Geography, Culture,* 8th ed. (Upper Saddle River, N.J.: Prentice Hall, 2004), p. 205.
[†]European Industrial Relations Observatory On-line, "Overall Union Membership Declines," at www.eiro.eurofound.eu.int/2001/06/feature/se0106105f.html.
[‡]European Industrial Relations Observatory On-line, "2001–2 Annual Review for the USA," at www.eiro.eurofound.eu.int/2002/11/feature/us0211101f.html.
[§]Michael Roskin, *Countries and Concepts: Politics, Geography, Culture,* 8th ed. (Upper Saddle River, N.J.: Prentice Hall, 2004), p. 205.
[||]European Industrial Relations Observatory On-line, "First Agreements in 2004 bargaining round concluded in Industry," at www.eiro.eurofound.ie/2004/03/feature/se0403103f.html.
[¶]European Industrial Relations Observatory On-line, "Working Time Developments–2003," at www.eiro.eurofound.eu.int/2004/03/update/tn0403104u.html.
**Steven Greenhouse, "A.F.L.-C.I.O. Plans to Spend $44 Million to Unseat Bush," *The New York Times,* March 11, 2004, p. A26.

Municipal Employees—supported former Vermont Governor Howard Dean. Finally, the firefighters supported Massachusetts Senator John Kerry. Unlike 2000, where unions were seen as important to Al Gore's securing the nomination, in 2004 they did not play that role in the Iowa caucus or other primaries.[11]

Traditionally identified with the Democratic party, unions have not enjoyed a close relationship with Republican administrations. Given labor's limited resources, one option for unions is to form temporary coalitions with consumer, public interest, liberal, and sometimes even with industry groups, especially on issues related to foreign imports. Few of labor's recent legislative initiatives have been successful, and turning to the courts has yielded mixed results.[12]

In recent elections, the AFL-CIO has mounted vigorous campaigns to elect a Democratic president and majority in Congress. Some foes of labor have proposed legislation and ballot initiatives called "paycheck protection," which would require annual authorization by union members for portions of their dues to be used for political purposes. Labor unions have successfully defeated these measures.

GLOBAL *Perceptions*

QUESTION: Is the influence of trade unions very good, somewhat good, somewhat bad, or very bad?

How do the views of people in other countries on unions compare with the views of people in the United States? The Pew Global Attitudes Project allows us to explore this question.

Unions are seen very positively in Vietnam, where 59 percent said they were a "very good" influence and 92 percent said they were a "very good" or "somewhat good" influence. People in Argentina had strongly negative views of unions, with 42 percent saying they were "very bad."

In addition to Vietnam, combining the "very good" and "somewhat good" responses found most people in these countries likely to see unions positively: Nigeria (82%), Phillipines (75%), Great Britain (67%), Uganda (67%), Bolivia (65%), Germany (65%), USA (63%), and South Korea (62%). In contrast, unions were seen as bad in Argentina (75%) and by two-out-of five respondents or more in Russia, Brazil, Mexico, Venezuela, Italy, Poland, Slovak Republic, Jordan, and Turkey.

Unions were seen as having a good influence on a country more than did multinational corporations in the United States, Canada, and Europe (excluding Italy), but not in other parts of the world. Countries like Great Britain, Slovak Republic, and several countries in South America, Africa, and Asia saw multinational corporations as having a good influence. The positive view of unions in Vietnam does not limit the enthusiasm for multinational corporations, where 93 percent said such corporations were a good influence.

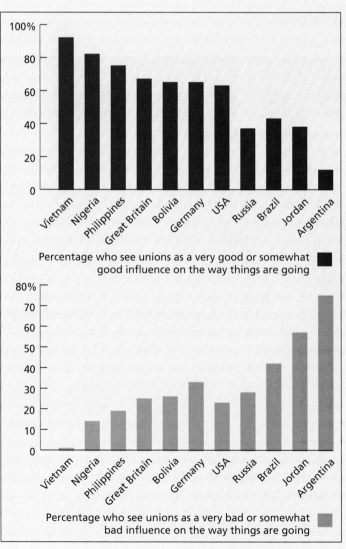

Percentage who see unions as a very good or somewhat good influence on the way things are going

Percentage who see unions as a very bad or somewhat bad influence on the way things are going

SOURCE: The Pew Research Center. *Views of a Changing World,* 2003, pp. 100, T-43.

PROFESSIONAL ASSOCIATIONS Professional people have organized some of the strongest unions in the nation. Some are well known, such as the American Medical Association and the American Bar Association. Others are divided into many subgroups. Teachers, for example, are organized into large groups such as the National Education Association, the American Federation of Teachers, and the American Association of University Professors and also into subgroups based on specialties, such as the Modern Language Association and the American Political Science Association.

Government, especially at the state level, regulates many professions. Lawyers, for example, are licensed by states, which, often as a result of pressure from lawyers themselves, have set up certain standards of admission to the state bar. Professional associations also use the courts to pursue their agendas. In the area of medical malpractice, for example, doctors lobby hard for limited liability laws, while the trial lawyers resist such efforts. Teachers, hairstylists, and marriage therapists work for legislation or regulations of concern to them. It is not surprising, then, that among the largest donors to political campaigns through political action committees are those representing professional associations such as the American Medical Association and the American Realtors Association.

Ideological or Single-Issue Interest Groups

Ideological groups behave very much like economic interest groups, although they are usually not driven by a desire to make money. Some of these groups are *single-issue groups*, often highly motivated and seeing politics primarily as a means to pursue their one issue. Such groups are often adamant about their position and unwilling to negotiate compromises. Right-to-life and pro-choice groups on abortion fit this description, as does the National Rifle Association.

Countless groups have organized around other specific issues, such as civil liberties, environmental protection, nuclear energy, and nuclear disarmament.[13] Such associations are not new. The Anti-Saloon League of the 1890s was single-mindedly devoted to barring the sale and manufacture of alcoholic beverages, and it did not care whether legislators were drunk or sober, as long as they voted dry. One of the best-known ideological groups today is the American Civil Liberties Union (ACLU), with roughly 250,000 members committed to the protection of civil liberties.[14] Religious groups are thriving in the otherwise pragmatic, pluralistic politics of today; an example is the Christian Coalition, which distributes voter guides before elections, although it has had less of a presence in recent years than it had in the 1990s.[15] African American churches have long been important politically and continue to encourage voter participation.

Public Interest Groups

Out of the political ferment of the 1960s came groups that make a specific claim to promote "the public interest." For example, Common Cause, founded in 1970 by independent Republican John W. Gardner and later led by noted Watergate prosecutor Archibald Cox, campaigns for electoral reform and for making the political process more open. Its Washington staff raises money through direct-mail campaigns, oversees state chapters, issues research reports and press releases on current issues, and lobbies on Capitol Hill and in major government departments.

Ralph Nader started a conglomerate of consumer organizations that investigates and reports on governmental and corporate action—or inaction—relating to consumer interests. Public Interest Research Groups (PIRGs) founded by Nader are among the largest interest groups in the country. PIRGs have become important players on Capitol Hill and in several state legislatures, promoting environmental issues, safe energy, consumer protection, and good government. Nader ran for president in 2000 as the nominee of the Green party and in 2004 as an independent. Despite his reputation as an advocate for consumers, he received only 3 percent of the popular vote in 2000 and one-third of 1 percent in 2004.

A specific type of public interest group is the tax-exempt public charity. Examples include the American Heart Association, the Girl Scouts of the U.S.A., and the American Cancer Society. These organizations must meet certain conditions, such as educational or philanthropic objectives, to qualify for this preferred status. Not only are public charities

The Women's Christian Temperance Union, a movement dedicated to the prohibition of drinking liquor, succeeded in passing the Eighteenth Amendment, which outlawed the manufacture and sale of alcoholic beverages. It was later repealed by the Twenty-first Amendment.

tax-exempt, but donations to these organizations are tax-deductible, and the organizations are not required to disclose information about their donors publicly. These organizations cannot participate in elections or support candidates, nor can they benefit an individual or small group. Despite these limitations, tax-exempt charitable organizations have been very active in voter registration efforts and in advertising campaigns designed to influence public opinion.

Foreign Policy Interest Groups

Domestic policy is not the only matter of concern to interest groups. Groups also organize to promote or oppose certain foreign policies. Among the most prestigious foreign affairs groups is the Council on Foreign Relations in New York City. Other groups, devoted to narrower areas of American foreign policy, exert pressure on members of Congress and the president to enact specific policies. For example, interest group pressure influenced U.S. policy toward South Africa and played a role in South Africa's decision to abandon apartheid. Groups ranging from student organizations to national lobbies like the American Committee on Africa urged divestment, sanctions, or other policy measures that ultimately promoted change in South Africa. Other groups support or oppose free trade.

The American-Israel Political Action Committee (AIPAC) has more than 50,000 members and has been very successful. Because AIPAC's primary focus is lobbying and not distributing campaign funds, it is not required to disclose where its money comes from or goes. Included in the long list of AIPAC lobbying successes are enactment of aid packages to Israel, passage of the 1985 United States–Israel Free Trade Agreement, and emergency assistance to Israel in the wake of the 1992 Gulf War. Its counterpart, the National Association of Arab Americans, lobbies for action in support of Arab causes. Efforts to secure a negotiated settlement between the Palestinians and Israel have meant that American interest groups on both sides of the dispute remain visible and important.

Public Sector Interest Groups

Governments are themselves important interest groups. Many cities and most states retain Washington lobbyists, and cities also hire lobbyists to represent them at the state legislature. Governors are organized through the National Governors Association, cities through the National League of Cities, and counties through the National Association of Counties. Other officials have their own national associations.

Government employees form a large and well-organized group. The National Education Association (NEA), for example, claims 2.7 million members.[16] Bush Administration Secretary of Education Rod Paige created controversy when he labeled the NEA a terrorist organization, a remark for which he later apologized.[17] Paige was at odds with teachers' unions because they disagreed with some of his agenda. His characterization, which caused ire among teachers, may have helped motivate teachers to participate even more in 2004 than they had in the past. Public employees are also important to organized labor, and they are the fastest-growing unions.

Other Interest Groups

Americans are often emotionally and financially involved in a variety of groups: veterans' groups such as American Legion or Veterans of Foreign Wars; nationality groups such as the multitude of German, Irish, Hispanic, Palestinian, and Korean organizations; or religious organizations such as the Knights of Columbus or B'nai B'rith. More than 150 nationwide organizations are based on national origin alone. In recent years,

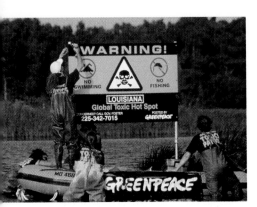

Interest groups such as Greenpeace stage demonstrations to call attention to environmental issues.

there has been a virtual explosion in the number and variety of interests and associations. This is especially true for environmental groups (see Table 6–3).

CHARACTERISTICS AND POWER OF INTEREST GROUPS

Groups vary in their goals, methods, and power. Among the most important group characteristics are size, resources, cohesiveness, leadership, and techniques.

Size and Resources

Obviously, size is important to political power; an organization representing 5 million voters has more influence than one speaking for 5,000. Perhaps even more important than size is the extent to which members are actively involved and fight for policy objectives. Often people join an organization for reasons that have little to do with its political objectives. They may want to secure group insurance, take advantage of travel benefits, participate in professional meetings, or get a job.

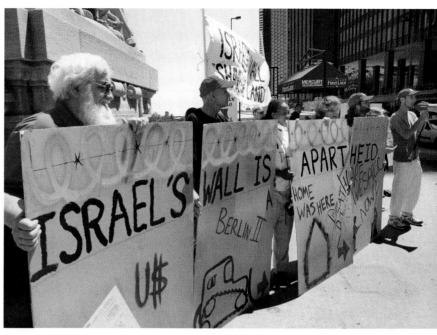

Some interest groups focus on foreign policy issues, such as U.S. aid to Israel in light of Israel's construction of a separation wall along the West Bank. Opponents argue that the wall is tantamount to apartheid and the Israeli government argues that it is a necessary security measure.

How do associations motivate potential members to join them? Organizations must provide incentives, material or otherwise, that are compelling enough to attract the potential free rider.[18] Unions are organized not just for lobbying but also to perform other important services for their members. They derive much of their strength from their negotiating position with corporations, which they use to obtain wage increases or improved safety standards. Similarly, the AARP, in addition to lobbying for prescription drug benefits and speaking out on other issues of concern to older citizens, offers incentives such as a free subscription to one of its magazines and member discounts at certain hotels. This combination of size and strength sets these groups apart from other large organizations in their effectiveness, since members derive numerous benefits from joining. The AARP was part of the coalition pushing the partial prescription drug for seniors bill that President Bush signed into law in 2003. Some AARP members, as well as former allies in Congress, expressed irritation at AARP supporting this partial benefit, which they thought was inadequate.[19]

TABLE 6–3   SOME ENVIRONMENTAL GROUPS AND HOW THEY DO BUSINESS

Group	Membership	Issues	Activities
Greenpeace USA	250,000	Forests, global warming, genetically engineered foods, oceans, persistent organic pollutants, nuclear weapons	Media events; mass mailings; grassroots activity; does not lobby government
Natural Resources Defense Council	1,000,000	Resources, energy, global warming, pollution, nuclear weapons	Lobbying; litigation; watchdog; its scientists compete with experts from agencies and industry
Sierra Club	700,000	Wilderness, pollution, global warming, human rights, population, suburban sprawl	Grassroots action; litigation; news releases
Wilderness Society	250,000	Wilderness areas, public lands, energy development	Scientific studies; analysis; advocacy group

SOURCE: Greenpeace USA at www.greenpeaceusa.org; Natural Resources Defense Council at www.nrdc.org; Sierra Club at www.sierraclub.org; Wilderness Society at www.wilderness.org.

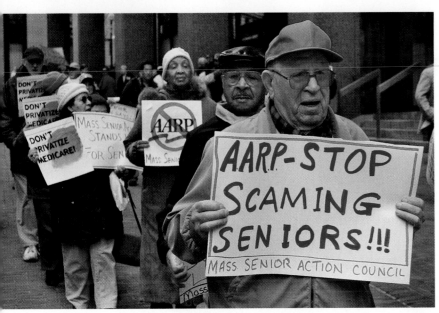

In 2003, the AARP successfully lobbied for passage of a prescription drug plan that many seniors argued would ultimately increase the cost of their prescription medications. To protest the AARP's position, some people burned their AARP cards.

While the size of an interest group is often important, so, too, is its *spread*—the extent to which membership is concentrated or dispersed. Automobile manufacturing is concentrated in Michigan and a few other states, and as a result, the auto industry's influence does not have the same spread as that of the American Medical Association, which has an active chapter in virtually every congressional district. An association consisting of 3 million supporters concentrated in a few states will usually have less influence than another group consisting of 3 million supporters spread out in a large number of states.

Interest groups also differ in the extent to which they preempt a policy area or share it with other groups. Doctors and the AMA have effectively preempted the health care policy area because they play such an important role in the delivery of health care. But in the transportation policy area, railroads must compete with interstate trucking and even air freight companies.

Groups also differ in their *resources*, which include money, volunteers, expertise, and reputation. Some groups can influence many centers of power—both houses of Congress, the White House, federal agencies, the courts, and state and local governments—while others cannot.

Cohesiveness

Usually, a mass membership organization is made up of three types of members: (1) a relatively small number of formal leaders who may hold full-time, paid positions or devote much time, effort, and money to the group's activities; (2) people intensely involved in the group who identify with the group's aims, attend meetings, faithfully pay dues, and do a lot of the legwork; and (3) people who are members in name only, do not participate actively, and cannot be depended on to vote in elections or otherwise act as the leadership wants.[20] In a typical large organization, for every top leader there might be a few hundred hard-core activists and thousands of essentially inactive members.

Another factor in group cohesiveness is its *organizational structure.* Some associations have a strong formal organization; others are local organizations that have joined together in a loose state or national federation in which they retain a measure of separate power and independence. Separation of powers may be found as well: The national assembly of an organization establishes, or at least ratifies, policy; an executive committee meets more frequently; a president or director is elected to head and speak for the group; and permanent paid officials form the organization's bureaucracy. Power may be further divided between the organization's main headquarters and its Washington office. An organization of this sort tends to be far less cohesive than a centralized, disciplined group such as some trade unions, trial lawyers, and realtors.

Leadership

Closely related to cohesion is the nature of the leadership. In a group that embraces many attitudes and interests, leaders may either weld the various elements together or sharpen their disunity. The leader of a national business association, for example, must tread cautiously between big business and small business, between exporters and importers, between chain stores and corner grocery stores, and between the producers and the sellers of competing products. The group leader is in the same position as a president or a member of Congress; he or she must know when to lead followers and when to follow them.

Techniques

Interest groups seeking to wield influence choose from a variety of political weapons and targets. They present their case to both houses of Congress, the White House staff, state and local governments, and federal agencies and departments. They also become involved in litigation. Other techniques include protest, election activities, establishing political parties, and lobbying.

PUBLICITY AND MASS MEDIA APPEALS   Interest groups exploit the communications media—television, radio, newspapers, leaflets, signs, direct mail, and word of mouth—to influence voters during elections and to motivate constituents to contact their representatives between elections. Business enjoys a special advantage in this arena, and businesspeople have the money and staff to use propaganda machinery. As large-scale advertisers, they know how to deliver their message effectively or can find an advertising agency to do it for them. But organized labor is also effective in communicating with its membership through shop stewards, mail, and phone calls.

The NRA is a large, powerful interest group with considerable political clout, dedicated to fighting all gun control legislation and to electing candidates who oppose any form of gun control.

As people communicate more and more via e-mail, this technology will become an important means of political mobilization. Howard Dean effectively used e-mail in the 2004 primary campaign to turn out crowds in Iowa, New Hampshire, and other states.[21] He also did well in raising money via the Internet.[22] John Kerry and George W. Bush also had success raising campaign funds in this way and used the Internet in their voter mobilization efforts.[23] Candidates at all levels used e-mail for fund raising and to motivate supporters. E-mail will likely become part of political communication at the workplace as management communicates information to its workers about the candidates and ballot issues.

MASS MAILING   One means of communication that has increased the reach and effectiveness of interest groups is computerized and targeted mass mailing.[24] Before computers, interest groups had to cull from telephone directories and other sources lists of people to contact, and managing these lists was time-consuming. As a result, some groups sent out mailings indiscriminately. Today the computer permits easy data storage and efficient management of mailing lists. Mass mailing is now used by all kinds of interest groups. Today's technology can produce personalized letters targeted to specific groups. Such targeted direct mail can also appeal to people who share a common concern, such as environmental groups.

INFLUENCE ON RULE MAKING   Organized groups have ready access to the executive and regulatory agencies that write the rules implementing laws passed by Congress. Government agencies publish proposed regulations in the ***Federal Register*** and invite responses from all interested persons before the rules are finalized. The *Federal Register* is published every weekday. You can find it at the library or on the Internet at www.gpoaccess.gov. Well-staffed associations and corporations peruse the *Register,* ever alert for actions that will affect their interests. Lobbyists prepare written responses to the proposed rules, draft alternative rules, and appear at the hearings to make their case. These lobbyists seek to be on good terms with the staff of the agencies so that they can learn what rules are being considered long before they are released publicly and thus have input in the early stages. Administrative rules are defined over time through legal cases and agency modifications, so even if an interest group fails to get what it wants, it can fight the rules in court or press for a reinterpretation when the agency leadership changes hands.

Finally, an interest group can seek to modify rules it does not like by pressuring Congress to change the legal mandate for the agency or have the agency's budget

Federal Register
Official document, published every weekday, that lists the new and proposed regulations of executive departments and regulatory agencies.

Taylor clipped the taxpayers by abusing student loans.

Mike Taylor made a fortune in the hair care industry. He also made up his own rules for awarding student loans.

— *Michael Taylor, Beauty Corner, Denver, Colorado.*

Abusing Student Loans

In a hair-raising scheme to ensure the success of his "Institute of Hair Design," Mike Taylor improperly gave out thousands of dollars in federal student loan funds. Mike Taylor's "Institute of Hair Design" profited from the misuse of money that was meant for educational purposes.[1]

Ability to Directly Issue Student Loans Revoked

In 1998, based on "repeat findings" of violations, the U.S. Department of Education revoked Mike Taylor's authority to directly disperse federal student loan monies.[2] In 1999, the U.S. Department of Education followed up on this action by assessing the Institute of Hair Design about $159,000 for the numerous violations uncovered by department investigators.[3]

With Mike Taylor,
There's no telling who will get clipped.

The use of both conventional and electronic mail is an effective way of reaching a large number of people during political campaigns. The Montana Democratic Party sent this ad to potential voters informing them of Republican candidate Mike Taylor's misuse of student loan money several years prior when he operated a beauty school in another state. The ad prompted Taylor to withdraw from the race.

reduced, making enforcement of existing rules difficult. In short, interest groups and lobbyists never really quit fighting for their point of view.

LITIGATION   When groups find the political channels closed to them, they may turn to the courts.[25] The Legal Defense and Education Fund of the National Association for the Advancement of Colored People (NAACP), for example, initiated and won numerous court cases in its efforts to end racial segregation and to protect the right to vote for African Americans. Urban interests and environmental groups, feeling underrepresented in state and national legislatures, turned to the courts to influence the political agenda.[26] Women's groups, such as the National Organization for Women and the American Civil Liberties Union's Women's Rights Project, also used the courts to pursue their objectives.[27] Conservative religious groups like the Washington Legal Foundation and groups identified with the Religious Right have also actively used litigation as a strategy to pursue their objectives.[28]

In addition to initiating lawsuits, associations can gain a forum for their views in the courts by filing *amicus curiae briefs* (literally, "friend of the court" briefs) in cases in which they are not direct parties. Despite the general impression that associations achieve great success in the courts, groups are no more likely than individuals to win their cases at the district court level.[29]

PROTEST Movements arise around particular issues but often lack widespread support. To generate interest and support for their cause, movements often use protest demonstrations. An example of a movement that used protest demonstrations to call attention to its

amicus curiae brief
Literally, a "friend of the court" brief, filed by an individual or organization to present arguments in addition to those presented by the immediate parties to a case.

concerns is the diverse set of interest groups that opposed the labor, environmental, and trade practices fostered by the World Trade Organization (WTO). The 1999 protest against a WTO meeting in Seattle turned into a riot.[30] Peaceful groups like Public Citizen and the AFL-CIO were brushed aside by more violent protesters, such as the Ruckus Society and the Direct Action Network. The Seattle police, unable to contain the situation and fearful that they would be unable to protect delegates from 135 countries, resorted to riot control tactics, including tear gas, rubber bullets, and pepper spray. They also arrested more than 400 protesters.[31] Newspapers and television broadcasts around the world showed the confrontations, arrests, and destruction.

The protesters succeeded in forcing the topic of globalization and the negative consequences of increased international trade onto the political agenda. Other movements or groups that have used protest include the civil rights movement, antiwar groups, and environmental groups.[32]

ELECTION ACTIVITIES Although nearly all large organizations say they are nonpolitical, almost all are politically involved in some way. What they usually mean when they say they are nonpolitical is that they are *nonpartisan*. A distinguishing feature of organized interest groups is that they often try to work through *both* parties. Another regularity is that they want to be friendly with the winners, which often means that they contribute to incumbents. But as competition for control of both chambers of Congress has intensified and with presidential contests also up for grabs, interest groups have generally invested more in one party or the other.

Labor usually favors Democrats. The AFL-CIO has supported every Democratic candidate for president since the New Deal, although the Teamsters Union has often endorsed Republicans. In 2004, the Teamsters joined most other unions in backing John Kerry. Business groups occasionally endorse Democratic incumbents but generally favor Republicans. Some organizations are prevented from taking a firm position because of the differing views of their members. A local retailers' group, for example, might be composed equally of Republicans and Democrats, and many of its members might refuse to openly support a candidate for fear of losing business.

Ideological groups target certain candidates, seeking to change a candidate's positions or, failing that, to influence voters to vote against that candidate. Americans for Democratic Action and the American Conservative Union publish ratings of members of Congress's voting records on liberal and conservative issues; so do the U.S. Chamber of Commerce, the AFL-CIO, and other groups.

How effective is electioneering by interest groups? In general, mass membership organizations fail to mobilize their full membership in elections. Although when a group's interests are directly attacked, as was the case with the anti-union "paycheck protection" ballot initiatives in 1998 and 2000, these groups can effectively mobilize their membership.[33] More typically, there are too many cross-pressures operating in the pluralistic politics of the United States for any one group to assume a commanding role. Some groups reach their maximum influence only by allying themselves closely with one of the two major parties. They may place their members on local, state, and national party committees and help send them to party conventions as delegates, but such alliances mean losing some independence.

Numerous groups sought to mobilize their membership in the 2004 presidential election. Groups created Web sites for members to obtain information on their organization's view of candidates and provided voter registration materials and absentee ballot request forms. They also solicited contributions to help fund these efforts. One group that was especially active in this effort was the Business and Industry Political Action Committee (BIPAC).[34] Organized labor, long perceived to be the leader in voter mobilization, was also especially active in 2004, as was the National Rifle Association. The Republican party and allied groups, having learned from the techniques used by labor unions, mounted a successful voter mobilization effort in 2004.

FORMING A POLITICAL PARTY Another interest group strategy is to form a political party. These parties are organized less with the intent to win elections than to publicize a cause. The Free Soil party was formed in the mid-1840s to work against the spread of slavery into the territories, and the Prohibition party was organized two decades later to ban the sale of liquor. Farmers have formed a variety of such parties. More often, however, interest groups prefer to work through existing parties.

Today, environmental groups and voters for whom the environment is a central issue must choose between supporting the Green party, which has yet to elect a person to federal office, an independent candidate like Ralph Nader in 2004, or one of the two major parties. Sometimes minor party candidates can spoil the chances of a major party candidate. In a New Mexico congressional special election in 1997, the Green party candidate won 17 percent of the vote, taking some votes from the Democrat and thereby helping elect a Republican to what had been a Democratic seat. In the 1998 election, environmental groups campaigned aggressively for the Democrat, who obtained 53 percent of the vote, while all minor parties combined got only 4 percent.[35] In South Dakota's 2002 Senate race between Tim Johnson (D) and John Thune (R), the Libertarian candidate got more than three thousand votes. Johnson defeated Thune by just over 500 votes. In the 2000

PEOPLE & POLITICS *Making a Difference* ★ ★ ★

STEPHEN MOORE, CLUB FOR GROWTH

An interest group that first appeared on the scene in the late 1990s and became visible in 2002 in some competitive contests is the Club for Growth. One of the three cofounders of Club for Growth is Stephen Moore. Known for his candor, Moore described contributing to candidates and parties as "spitting into an ocean of money," citing contributing to his Club as a much more effective way to influence policy and "get rid of Republicans in Name Only (RINOs)."[*] Moore is a graduate of the University of Illinois with a master's degree in economics from George Mason University. Prior to his activity at Club for Growth he directed fiscal policy studies at the Cato Institute and worked on the Joint Economic Committee under House Republican Whip Dick Armey. He was drawn into politics by his mentor and professor, Julian Simon. Moore sees the Club as more politically involved than the "think tanks," and has patterned the Club after EMILY's List, a successful pro-Choice Democratic group that helps connect donors and candidates."[†]

Congressional Quarterly Today said of Moore's group, "When the supply-siders at the Club for Growth decide to back a candidate who favors the economic policies of the Reagan era, donations don't just trickle down, they gush."[‡] In 2004, Club for Growth invested $2 million in the

Pennsylvania U.S. Senate primary election against long-term Republican incumbent Arlen Specter and for Pat Toomey, his opponent. The group also ran ads attacking Howard Dean in the weeks before the Iowa caucuses, describing Dean's campaign as a "tax hiking, government expanding, latte drinking, sushi eating, Volvo driving, *New York Times* reading, body piercing, Hollywood loving, left wing freak show."[§] The Club for Growth also invests in general elections, sometimes channeling hundreds of thousands of dollars into U.S. House or U.S. Senate races."[‖]

The Club for Growth seeks to pursue the "vision of limited government and lower taxes," as articulated by Ronald Reagan. The Club's home page has a photo of Reagan. Candidates endorsed by the Club support this vision and have a strong chance for electoral success. The Club invests in only a few contests where they believe they can make a difference. They do this by selecting candidates and then contacting donors who make the checks out directly to the candidate, then route the checks through the Club to enhance the Club's reputation with the candidate.[¶] Electoral involvement is then linked to lobbying. Speaking of the lobbying power of the Club for Growth, Stephen Moore said, "I think we have 30

or 40 members [of Congress] who are very grateful for the help we've given them, and we've got another 30 or 40 members of Congress who think that we're a very dangerous organization that could jeopardize their political careers."[**]

[*]Stephen Moore, phone interview by David Magleby, July 21, 2004.
[†]Ibid.
[‡]Jonathan Allen, "Club for Growth Becoming a Bigger Player in Republican-on-Republican Primary Races," *Congressional Quarterly Today*, February 6, 2003.
[§]*National Journal Online* at nationaljournal.com/members/adspotlight/2004/01/0108cfg1.htm.
[‖]See Kelly Patterson, "When Redistricting Means Never Having to Say You're Sorry: Utah's Second District," David Magleby and J. Quin Monson, eds., *The Last Hurrah* (Brookings Institution Press, 2004), pp. 252–253.
[¶]www.clubforgrowth.org/about.php?from=about.
[**]www.clubforgrowth.org/what.php.

presidential election, most environmental groups supported A1 Gore over Green party nominee Ralph Nader. Many Democrats, however, blame Nader for diverting votes from Gore in such battlegrounds as Florida and New Hampshire, thereby costing him the election. Democrats again worried that Nader would cost them the White House in 2004 but explicit appeals from the party and from interest groups may have helped reduce Nader's impact. Early in the campaign, Nader described Democrat John Kerry as very presidential but he later said that a vote for Kerry is "a vote for war—an endless, Vietnam-type quagmire" (see Joshua Weinstein, "Angry Ralph Nader: Scorn, Anger, and Resolve Sustain Nader," *Portland Press Herald,* October 6, 2004).

COOPERATIVE LOBBYING Like-minded groups often join together as cooperative groups. In 1987, the Leadership Conference on Civil Rights and People for the American Way brought together many groups in the battle to defeat the nomination of outspoken federal judge Robert Bork to the U.S. Supreme Court.[36] Different types of environmentalists work together, as do consumer and ideological groups on the right and on the left. Women continue to be represented by a large variety of groups that reflect diverse interests, but the larger the coalition, the greater the chance that members may divide over such issues as abortion. Another example of a cooperative group is the Business Roundtable (BRT), an association of chief executive officers of the 200 largest U.S. corporations. The BRT, which has been in existence for more than 30 years, promotes policies that help large businesses, such as free trade and less government regulation of business.

Personal contact with and access to decision makers continue to be key elements of lobbying today, as they were at the time of President Grant's administration.

THE INFLUENCE OF LOBBYISTS

The terms "lobbying" and "lobbyist" were not generally used until around the middle of the nineteenth century in the United States. The root in these words refers to the lobby or hallway outside House and Senate chambers in the U.S. Capitol. It also refers to those who hung around the lobby of the old Willard Hotel when presidents dined. The noun "lobby" has been turned into a verb in this political context. Thus "to lobby" is to seek to influence legislators and government officials, and we call this **lobbying** even if there is no lobby in sight.

Despite their negative public image, lobbyists perform useful functions for government. They provide information for the decision makers of all three branches of government, they help educate and mobilize public opinion, they help prepare legislation and testify before legislative hearings, and they contribute a large share of the costs of campaigns. Yet many people are concerned that lobbyists have too much influence on government and add to legislative gridlock by being able to stop action on pressing problems.

Who Are the Lobbyists?

The typical image is of powerful, hard-nosed lobbyists who skillfully employ a combination of knowledge, persuasiveness, personal influence, charm, and money to influence legislators and bureaucrats. **Lobbyists** are the employees of associations who try to influence policy decisions and positions in the executive and especially in the legislative branches of our government. They are experienced in the ways of government, often having been public servants before going to work for an organized interest group, association, or corporation. They might start as staff in Congress, perhaps on a congressional committee. Later, when their party wins the White House, they gain an administration post, often in the same policy area as their congressional committee work. After a few years in the administration, they are ready to make the move to lobbying, either by going to work for one of the interests they dealt with while in the government or by obtaining a position with a lobbying firm.

Moving from a government job to one with an interest group is quite common, a practice called the **revolving door**. Despite the fact that it is illegal for former national government employees to directly lobby the agency from which they came, their contacts made during government service are helpful to interest groups. Many former members of Congress make use of their congressional experience as full-time lobbyists.

lobbying
Engaging in activities aimed at influencing public officials, especially legislators, and the policies they enact.

lobbyist
A person who is employed by and acts for an organized interest group or corporation to try to influence policy decisions and positions in the executive and legislative branches.

revolving door
Employment cycle in which individuals who work for governmental agencies regulating interests eventually end up working for interest groups or businesses with the same policy concern.

The revolving-door tendency between government and interest groups produces networks of people who care about certain issues. These networks have been called **iron triangles**, consisting of mutually dependent relationships among interest groups, congressional committees and subcommittees, and the government agencies that share a common policy concern. Sometimes these relationships become so strong and mutually beneficial that the iron triangle becomes very powerful, a sort of subgovernment. A former senior staff person from a House or Senate agriculture committee now working for an agricultural corporation as a lobbyist who has ongoing friendships with his former staff colleagues, including some who now work at the Department of Agriculture, is an example of how personal relationships work within iron triangles. Powerful iron triangles may serve to enhance the policy preferences of narrow interests and not those of the broader public interest.

Legal and political skills, along with specialized knowledge, have become so crucial in executive and legislative policy making as to become a form of power in themselves. Elected representatives increasingly depend on their staffs for guidance, and these issue specialists know more about "Section 504" or "Title IX" or "the 2002 amendments"—and who wrote them and why—than most political and administrative leaders, who are usually generalists. It is in this gray area of policy making that many interest groups and lobbyists play a vital role, as people move freely from congressional or agency staff to association staff and perhaps back again. These groups of experts are sometimes called *issue networks* and are discussed in greater detail in Chapter 18, Economic and Regulatory Policy. Like iron triangles, issue networks are made up of people with similar policy concerns; however, they differ in two important ways. First, issue networks can include more players, such as the media, than iron triangles. Second, because members of issue networks are less dependent on one another than members of iron triangles are, organization is more amorphous and less structured.[37]

What Do Lobbyists Do?

Thousands of lobbyists are active in Washington, but few are as glamorous or as unscrupulous as the media suggest, nor are they necessarily influential. One limit on their power is the competition among interest groups. Rarely does any one group have a policy area all to itself. For example, transportation policy involves airplanes, trucks, cars, railroads, consumers, suppliers, state and local governments—the list goes on and on.

To members of Congress, the single most important thing lobbyists provide is money for their next reelection campaign. "Reelection underlies everything else," writes political scientist David Mayhew.[38] Money from interest groups has become instrumental in this driving need among incumbents. Interest groups also provide volunteers for campaign activity. In addition, their failure to support the opposition can enhance an incumbent's chances of being reelected.

Some people defend lobbyists as a kind of "third house" of Congress. Whereas the Senate and House are set up on a geographical basis, lobbyists represent people on the basis of interests and money. Small but important groups can sometimes get representation in the "third house" when they cannot get it in the other two. In a nation of vast and important interests, this kind of functional representation, if it is not abused, can be a useful supplement to geographical representation.

Beyond their central role in campaigns and elections, interest groups provide another essential commodity to legislators: information of two important types, political and substantive. The *political information* provided by lobbyists includes such matters as who supports or opposes legislation and how strongly they feel.[39] *Substantive information,* such as the impact of proposed laws, might not be available from any other source. Lobbyists often provide technical assistance on the drafting of bills and amendments, identify persons to testify at legislative hearings, and formulate questions to ask of administration officials at oversight hearings.

The battle over providing a prescription drug benefit for senior citizens illustrates how lobbyists influence the electoral and legislative process. The pharmaceutical industry invested over $10 million in the 2000 election and a similar amount in 2002 in limited and disclosed contributions to candidates and parties,[40] and another $15 to $20

iron triangle
A mutually dependent relationship among interest groups, congressional committees and subcommittees, and government agencies that share a common policy concern.

million in unlimited contributions to the parties in both of these elections.[41] In addition, an estimated $65 million was spent by "Citizens for Better Medicare" in 2000 on issue ads targeted to battleground states. In 2002 "The United Seniors Association" spent an estimated $9 to $13 million on issue ads in competitive contests.[42] Lobbying was also part of the pharmaceutical industry strategy. In 2002 they spent an unprecedented $94 million on lobbying activities, hiring almost 700 lobbyists from 138 different firms."[43] Congress enacted a prescription drug benefit for seniors that had the support of the pharmaceutical industry and the largest seniors organization, the AARP. The new benefit was criticized by some as being too costly,[44] and by others as not being comprehensive enough.[45] The intense electioneering and lobbying helped define the issue and set the stage for the legislation that was enacted.

MONEY AND POLITICS

As the battle over prescription drug benefits for seniors illustrates, interest groups have several ways they can seek to influence election outcomes and policy outcomes. They can seek to mobilize voters, especially the members of the group and their families and friends. They can loan staff to candidate campaigns. They can contribute money to candidates and parties through committees they form, which are called **political action committees (PACs)**, or they can urge their members and friends to contribute directly to candidates or parties or send their checks to the group and have them delivered in a bundle, a process called **bundling**. They can raise and spend money independently through what are called **independent expenditures**. When interest groups or individuals give money to a candidate or party committee, those contributions are limited and must be disclosed to the Federal Election Commission; they are sometimes referred to as **hard money**.

Until the 2004 election cycle individuals and groups could give unlimited amounts of money to party committees. This so-called **soft money** was for many years spent only on generic party activity like get-out-the-vote drives or broad party appeals. Corporations and unions, long banned from giving to candidates and parties from their general funds for election-specific purposes, were permitted to give soft money, and they did so in large amounts. Starting in the 1996 election cycle, the party committees used this money for specific candidate attack or promotion, a topic we will explore more later. By the 2000 and 2002 election cycles, soft money had climbed to around $500 million. Soft money was banned for the 2004 election cycle.

In 1996, interest groups found another way to circumvent disclosure and contribuiton limits through **issue advocacy**. Exploiting a definition in the court case defining the kinds of communication regulated by the Federal Election Campaign Act of 1971 (FECA) as those that used words like "vote for" or "vote against," groups simply made election ads without those words and then spent millions attacking or promoting particular candidates. Corporations and unions could and did spend millions of their general funds, which otherwise would have been banned from use in elections on issue ads in 1996–2002.

The Bipartisan Campaign Reform Act of 2002 (BCRA) redefines electioneering communications to include ads aimed at a particular population (state or district) that mention a candidate by name, show the image or likeness of a candidate, or mention the election within sixty days before a general election or thirty days before a primary election. BCRA bans corporations and unions from giving general funds to parties as soft money and from using those funds to buy electioneering ads during the period before a primary and general election, and requires more disclosure of this activity. BCRA does not regulate what any of these groups may do on the phone, through the mail, or in person.

Helping elect candidates helps create a relationship between the interest group and the elected official that then is exploited in the policy process. At a minimum, substantial involvement in the election process helps provide access to policy makers.[46] Interest groups retain political and policy professionals who provide information to policy makers, individuals that are generally called *lobbyists*. We begin our exploration of the role of money and politics by examining PACs, a primary means for groups to help elect and reelect public officials.

political action committee (PAC)
The political arm of an interest group that is legally entitled to raise funds on a voluntary basis from members, stockholders, or employees in order to contribute funds to favored candidates or political parties.

bundling
A tactic of political action committees whereby they collect contributions from like-minded individuals (each limited to $2,000) and present them to a candidate or political party as a "bundle," thus increasing their influence.

independent expenditures
The Supreme Court has ruled that individuals, groups, and parties can spend unlimited amounts in campaigns for or against candidates as long as they operate independently from the candidates. When an individual, group, or party does so, they are making an independent expenditure.

hard money
Political contributions given to a party, candidate, or interest group that are limited in amount and fully disclosed. Raising such limited funds is harder than raising unlimited funds, hence the term "hard money."

soft money
Money raised in unlimited amounts by political parties for party-building purposes. Now largely illegal except for limited contributions to state and local parties for voter registration and get-out-the-vote efforts.

issue advocacy
Unlimited and undisclosed spending by an individual or group on communications that do not use words like "vote for" or "vote against," although much of this activity is actually about electing or defeating candidates.

The Growth of PACs

A PAC is the political arm of an interest group that is legally entitled to raise funds on a voluntary basis from members, stockholders, or employees in order to contribute funds to favored candidates or political parties. PACs link two vital techniques of influence—giving money and other political aid to politicians and persuading officeholders to act or vote "the right way" on issues. Thus PACs are the means by which interest groups seek to influence which legislators are elected and what they do once they take office.[47] PACs can be categorized according to the type of interest they represent: corporations, trade and health organizations, labor unions, ideological organizations, and so on.

Surprisingly, considering the explosion of PACs that has occurred mainly in the business world, it was organized labor that invented this device. In the 1930s, John L. Lewis, president of the United Mine Workers, set up the Non-Partisan Political League as the political arm of the newly formed Congress of Industrial Organizations. When the CIO merged with the American Federation of Labor, the new labor group established the Committee on Political Education (COPE), whose activities we have already described. This unit came to be the model for most political action committees: "From the outset, national, state, and local units of COPE have not only raised and distributed funds, but have also served as the mechanism for organized and widespread union activity in the electoral process, for example, in voter registration, political education, and get-out-the-vote drives."[48] Some years later, manufacturers formed the Business and Industry Political Action Committee, but the most active business PAC is the one affiliated with the U.S. Chamber of Commerce.[49]

The 1970s brought a near revolution in the role and influence of PACs—ironically, as the result of reforms intended to reduce the influence of money in elections. The number of PACs increased dramatically, from about 150 to nearly 4,000 today.[50] Corporations and trade associations contributed most to this growth; today their PACs constitute the majority of all PACs. Labor PACs, by contrast, increased only slightly in number, representing less than 10 percent of all PACs.[51] But the increase in the number of PACs is less important than the intensity of recent PAC participation in elections and in lobbying.

The BCRA campaign finance reforms that took effect in the 2004 election cycle increased the role of PACs in funding candidates and parties. Because PAC contributions are limited, they were not as attractive a means to invest in elections for those who wanted to direct a lot of money to a particular race, which groups could do with soft money before BCRA. With that option closed in 2004, interest groups made PAC fundraising and contributions a higher priority. Members of Congress also increased their efforts to raise PAC dollars, including an expanded emphasis on leadership PACs. A Leadership PAC is a PAC a member of Congress can form to raise money from individuals or other PACs, which in turn can make contributions to others. Leadership PACs were once largely a tool used by congressional leaders or those aspiring to be leaders. In 2003–2004 almost a third of all lawmakers on the hill had formed a leadership PAC.[52] Because there were again so few competitive congressional contests in 2004, safe-seat incumbents with leadership PACs were pressed by their party leaders to contribute to their party candidates in the competitive contests. Member-to-member giving has become a more important part of campaign finance in competitive races as a result of BCRA.

How PACs Invest Their Money

PACs take part in the entire election process, but their main influence lies in their capacity to contribute money to candidates. Candidates today need a lot of money to wage their campaigns. It is no longer uncommon for House candidates to spend more than $1 million and for many senators and would-be senators to spend several times that amount.[53] And as PACs contribute more, their influence grows. What counts is not only the amounts they give but also to whom they give. PACs give to the most influential incumbents, to committee chairs, to party leaders and whips, and to the Speaker. PACs give not only to the majority party but also to key incumbents in the minority party as well, because they understand that today's minority could be tomorrow's majority.

PACs, like individuals, are limited by law in the amount of money they can contribute to any single candidate in an election cycle. The Federal Election Campaign Act of 1971 (FECA) as amended in 2002 limits PACs to $5,000 per election or $10,000 per election cycle (primary and general elections). Individuals have a limit of $4,000 per candidate per election cycle. PACs have found some creative ways around this limit. They can host fundraisers attended by other PACs to boost their reputation with the candidate, or they can collect money from several persons and give it to the candidate as a bundle. Through bundling, PACs and interested individuals can increase their clout with elected officials. Two of the most important groups doing bundling in 2003–2004 were EMILY's List and Club for Growth. EMILY's List, which stands for "Early Money Is Like Yeast," raises money from individuals committed to electing pro-choice, Democratic women. It identifies candidates that fit its criteria and then solicits checks for them at an early stage in the campaign. Club for Growth, a conservative group, sees itself as applying the same bundling techniques as EMILY's List but for pro-growth and anti-tax candidates (see the box on Stephen Moore on page 146).

Soft Money and Issue Advocacy

The 1996 election was a watershed in the involvement of interest groups and individuals in financing campaigns. That year the Clinton/Gore campaign on the advice of a consultant began to use party soft money for candidate-specific electioneering. Previously soft money had been reserved for generic ads or party-building activities like building voter lists, staffing the party, and so forth. Corporations and unions were allowed to give general funds as well as PAC funds to the party soft money accounts, and there were no contribution limits on soft money. Some of the largest PAC soft money contributors were labor unions, trial lawyers, corporations, and some individuals.

Party committees had limits on how much hard money they could spend on a particular race, but there were no such limits on soft money. With soft money as an option for the party committees, they quickly started spending it in competitive settings like presidential battleground states or highly contested House or Senate contests. In some of these races, they would expend millions of dollars of soft money. We discuss the use of soft money by the political parties in greater detail in Chapter 7.

The 1996 election was a watershed in a second respect as well. The AFL-CIO decided to test the limits of the definition of what fell under the regulation of the FECA, spending an estimated $35 million against most Republican candidates.[54] The union ads avoided words such as "vote for," "elect," "support," "cast your ballot for," "Smith for Congress," "vote against," "defeat," or "reject"—the definition for what constituted a communication subject to FECA regulation according to a footnote in the *Buckley* v. *Valeo* decision.[55] Other interest groups and their consultants discovered that they also could effectively communicate an electioneering message without using words like "vote for" or "vote against." Ads that avoided these words but that were clearly about electing or defeating particular candidates became a staple in competitive elections after 1996. Groups like the pharmaceutical industry, truckers, unions, and supporters of term limits would direct hundreds of thousands of dollars or more to particular contests for Congress or presidential battleground states. These groups mounted parallel campaigns in such locales, running ads on radio and television and investing heavily in phone calls, mail, and get-out-the-vote efforts.[56] In these competitive races the noncandidate campaign generally rivaled the candidate campaign in spending.[57] For example, in one hotly contested House race in 2000, the California 27th District race, candidates spent over $11.5 million[58] while the parties through soft money and interest groups through issue advocacy spent $7.5 million.[59]

Groups especially involved in issue advocacy included groups like the AFL-CIO, Citizens for Better Medicare, National Right to Work, United Seniors Association, Americans for Job Security, U.S. Chamber of Commerce, and Planned Parenthood. The heavy investment of interest groups in these unlimited electioneering efforts became controversial in the late 1990s and through the 2002 election cycle and helped motivate passage of BCRA.

BCRA and Interest Group Electioneering

In addition to restoring the ban on corporations and unions using their general funds for election ads through soft money or issue advocacy, BCRA attempted to follow court decisions with respect to ideological interest groups. It excludes from regulation some

★★ YOU DECIDE

**SHOULD CORPORATIONS AND UNIONS
BE UNLIMITED IN FUNDING PARTIES
AND IN RUNNING ISSUE ADS?**

Does limiting the ability of corporations or unions to use their general or "treasury" funds for election-related expenditures violate the constitutional guarantee of freedom of speech? Corporations and unions, like other groups, are free to form political action committees to make contributions to candidates and parties. What was at dispute was whether they could take their profits or general funds and spend those on electing or defeating candidates or in support of party efforts. For more than a century, federal law had banned unions and corporations from spending general or treasury funds on electoral politics. Was the Supreme Court correct in upholding that precedent?

527 group
A political group organized under section 527 of the IRS Code that may accept and spend unlimited amounts of money on election activities so long as they are not spent on broadcast ads run in the last 30 days before a primary or 60 days before a general election where a clearly identified candidate is referred to and a relevant electorate is targeted. 527 groups were important to the 2000 and 2004 elections.

interest groups that were not established by a business or labor union, or that are funded by individuals whose purpose is to "promote political ideas and cannot engage in business activities."[60] In 2004 there were four groups that had this special status and therefore could spend unlimited amounts of money raised from individuals on competitive races. These groups were NARAL Pro-Choice America, Planned Parenthood, League of Conservation Voters, and Defenders of Wildlife. While all of these groups were active in 2004, their legal status did not have a significant impact because other groups were allowed to raise and spend unlimited individual contributions. Interest groups that had previously taken union or corporate money could not claim this status.

Although BCRA made new rules restricting how funds could be spent for advertising, it left individuals and groups free to make unlimited contributions to groups that engaged in efforts to elect or defeat candidates through the mail, on the phone, or in person. These groups are called **527 groups**, a name that is derived from the section of the Internal Revenue Code that refers to political committees, not all of which have election activity as their primary purpose. The most notable example of one of these "527" groups is America Coming Together (ACT), founded by former political director of the AFL-CIO Steve Rosenthal and former president of EMILY's List Ellen Malcolm. One of the most visible donors to this group was financier George Soros. ACT launched reportedly the largest voter mobilization project in American history,[61] utilizing voter lists and door-to-door canvassing to target voters for mobilization on election day. Their stated purpose was to "defeat George W. Bush and elect Democrats in federal, state, and local elections in 2004."[62] Another group, also partially funded by George Soros, The Media Fund, ran broadcast ads before the time frame covered by BCRA (sixty days before a general election) and then used hard money to run ads closer to the election. This group was headed by Harold Ickes, who had been assistant to the president for political affairs and deputy chief of staff to President Clinton.

During the 2004 election cycle, 527 groups were much more active on the liberal or Democratic side than on the conservative or Republican. There are several reasons for this. Democratic party activists and allied interest groups understood that the BCRA ban on soft money would leave the party and its presidential candidate at a disadvantage against the fundraising prowess of President Bush and the Republican party. They thus started early and invested heavily in their 527 groups. Republicans and conservatives were less inclined to put money behind their Section 527 groups, in part because they controlled the government and had experienced so much success in fundraising in the past. There was also real doubt on the Republican side that BCRA or the new 527 groups would survive the court challenge and Federal Election Commission review process. When both occurred, they had lost valuable time in organizing and funding their 527 organizations.

Interest groups also utilized other sections of the tax code to involve themselves in the election. Section 501 of the tax code permits groups to organize and, in the case of Section 501-C-3, donations to the group are tax deductible. Because of their tax deductible status, 501-C-3 groups avoid candidate endorsements but can be involved in voter registration and other nonpartisan activity. For groups whose contributions are not tax deductible there is wider license in what they can do in elections. In 2004 several groups were involved in the election through their 501-C-4 and 501-C-6 groups. Examples of groups active in this way and of what they did in 2004 include, but are not limited to, the National Rifle Association sending direct mail to their members, the U.S. Chamber of Commerce creating a Web site for voteforbusiness.com, and the AFL-CIO spending money on internal communications. There were examples of 501-C groups supporting both parties, but unlike the 527 groups, Republicans found more allies in the 501-C organizations.[63]

Republican-allied 527 groups were slower to start campaigning but they were visible and important later in the campaign. One group, the Swift Boat Veterans for Truth, discussed earlier in this chapter, took Kerry "off message." Another pro-Bush group, Progress for America, ran an ad, which was shown extensively in the final days of the campaign, focused on how President Bush helped the daughter of a person killed in the attacks of September 11, 2001. The anti-Bush 527 organizations spent more money and focused their efforts on voter mobilization and on ads in the period between March and August when Bush had campaign money and Kerry did not.

The heavy reliance of both parties on 527 organizations and wealthy individual 527 donors raised questions about undue influence over elections from these individuals and what they expected in return if their side won the election. Regulation of 527 organizations is a topic President Bush and Senators John McCain and Russ Feingold pledged to pursue after the election.

THE EFFECTIVENESS OF INTEREST GROUP ACTIVITY IN ELECTIONS

The strong tendency of PACs to give more money to incumbents has meant that challengers face real difficulties in getting their campaigns funded. Challengers have to rely more on individual contributors. Even with the larger individual contribution limits allowed in 2004, most challengers still were largely underfunded compared to their incumbent opponents.

How much does interest group money influence election outcomes, legislation, and representation? Former U.S. Senator Alan Simpson (R-WY) testified in the court case to decide the constitutionality of BCRA that "too often, members' first thought is not what is right or what they believe, but how it will affect fundraising. Who, after all, can seriously contend that a $100,000 donation does not alter the way one thinks about—and quite possibly votes on—an issue?"[64] Another former U.S. Senator, Warren Rudman, said in the same court case that "you can't swim in the ocean without getting wet; you can't be part of this system without getting dirty."[65] In this area, as in others, money obviously talks. But it is easy to exaggerate that influence. Although a candidate may receive a great amount of interest group money, only a fraction of that total comes from any single interest. In addition, it is debatable how much campaign contributions affect election outcomes and uncertain that winning candidates will be willing and able to "remember" their financial angels or that the money in the end produces a real payoff in legislation.

Much depends, however, on the context in which money is given and received. Many campaigns—especially state and local campaigns—are small-scale undertakings in which a big contribution makes a difference. Amid all the murk of campaigning, a candidate may feel grateful for so tangible and convertible a contribution as money. Studies demonstrate a significant relationship between the frequency of lobbying contacts and favorable treatment in the Ways and Means and House Agriculture committees. Campaign contributions were found to predict lobbying patterns.[66]

One result of the recent campaign finance reforms was a surge in 2004 of interest groups communicating with voters via the mail and on the telephone. By closing down party soft money and limiting issue advocacy in television and radio ads in the weeks leading up to an election, the most recent reform makes issue advocacy via mail and telephone more attractive to individuals and groups. Examples of groups with substantially enlarged issue advocacy efforts in 2004 included the U.S. Chamber of Congress, NARAL Pro-Choice America, the National Rifle Association, and the Sierra Club. In selected

Campaign fund-raisers such as this one often charge donors $1,000 a plate or more for the privilege of meeting the candidates and mingling with influential policy makers.

The Court cited a long list of precedents in upholding the limitation on unions and corporations using their general funds to influence elections. The economic power of corporations like Microsoft or major unions could, if unconstrained, drown out the voices of other participants and corrupt the electoral processs. The opinion of the majority quoted corporate executives who made illegal donations in the early '70s/late '60s saying "they were motivated by the perception that this was a 'calling card, something that would get us in the door and make our point of view heard.'"*

But unions and corporations have a point in arguing that constraints on them are unfair when compared with the ability of wealthy individuals to spend unlimited amounts of their own money on politics via independent expenditures, one of the holdings of the Court in its prior landmark decision, *Buckley* v. *Valeo.*† Corporations and unions would also contend that soft money contributions were not bribes nor were they corrupting. Finally, they would agree with Justice Scalia's dissent in *McConnell* v. *FEC,* that restricting how much a group "can spend to broadcast his political views is a direct restriction on speech."‡

* *McConnell* v. *FEC,* 124 S.Ct. 533 (2003).

† *Buckley* v. *Valeo,* 96 S.Ct. 760 (1976).

‡ Justice Antonin Scalia, dissenting in *McConnell* v. *FEC,* 124 S.Ct. 618 (2003).

Republican primaries, the NRA did issue advocacy with a higher success rate. In the 2004 general election, the most active new group was America Coming Together, also known as ACT, who spent over $55 million in 2003 and 2004. ACT spent most of their resources on a massive get-out-the-vote campaign in all key states.

CURING THE MISCHIEFS OF FACTION— TWO CENTURIES LATER

If James Madison were to return today, he would not be surprised by the existence of interest groups, nor would he be surprised by their variety. He might be surprised, however, by the varied weapons of group influence, the deep involvement of interest groups in the electoral process, and the vast number of lobbyists in Washington and the state capitals. And doubtless Madison, were he alive today, would still be concerned about the power of faction, especially its tendency toward instability and injustice.

One of the main arguments against factions is that people are not represented equally. For example, fewer interest groups represent young or low-income people than represent corporations. Further, some groups are better organized and better financed, allowing them a decided advantage over more general groups. Another problem with factions is that the existence of a multiplicity of interests often leads to incoherent policies, inefficiency, and delay as lawmakers try to appease conflicting interests. In addition, the propensity of interest groups to support incumbents in elections increases their advantage, which is often seen as undesirable. Finally, the ability of interest groups to supply needed and accurate information to government officials increases their power. Providing inaccurate information spells trouble for interest groups.

Concern about the evils of interest groups has been a recurrent theme throughout U.S. history. President Ronald Reagan in his Farewell Address warned of the power of "special interests,"[67] and President Dwight Eisenhower used his Farewell Address to warn against the "military–industrial complex."

Single-issue interest groups organized for or against particular policies—abortion, handgun control, tobacco subsidies, animal rights—have aroused much concern in recent years. "It is said that citizen groups organizing in ever greater numbers to push single issues ruin the careers of otherwise fine politicians who disagree with them on one emotional issue, paralyze the traditional process of governmental compromise, and ignore the common good in their selfish insistence on getting their own way."[68] But which single issues reflect narrow interests? Women's rights—even a specific issue such as sexual harassment—are hardly "narrow," women's rights leaders contend, because they would help over half the population. Peace groups, too, claim that they represent the whole population, as do those who support prayer in schools. These issues may seem quite different from those related to subsidies to dairy farmers, for example.

What—if anything—should be done about factions? For decades, Americans have tried to find ways to keep interest groups in check. They have agreed with James Madison that the "remedy" of outlawing factions would be worse than the disease. It would be absurd to abolish liberty simply because it nourished faction. And the existence and activity of interest groups and lobbies are solidly protected by the Constitution. But by safeguarding the value of liberty, have Americans allowed interest groups to threaten equality, the second great value in our national heritage? The question remains: How can interest groups be regulated in a way that does not threaten our constitutional liberties?

Federal and State Regulation

Americans have generally responded to this question by seeking to regulate lobbying in general and political money in particular. Concern over the use of money—especially corporate funds—to influence politicians goes back well over a century, to the Crédit Mobilier scandals during the administration of Ulysses S. Grant, when members of Congress promoted the Crédit Mobilier construction company in exchange for the right to buy shares of the company's stock below market value, on which they made huge profits.

In the "progressive" era during the first two decades of the twentieth century, Congress legislated against corporate contributions in federal elections and required disclosure of the use of the money.

In 1921, Warren G. Harding's administration allowed private companies to secretly lease naval oil reserve lands. In response to this event, known as the Teapot Dome scandal, Congress passed the Federal Corrupt Practices Act. It required disclosure reports, both before and after elections, of receipts and expenditures by Senate and House candidates and by political committees that sought to influence federal elections in more than one state. Note that these were *federal* laws applying to *federal* elections; regulation of state lobbying and elections was left to the states.

Federal legislation, including the 1925 Federal Corrupt Practices Act and the 1946 Federal Regulation of Lobbying Act, was not very effective. It was, in fact, largely unenforced. Many candidates filed incomplete reports or none at all. The reform mood of the 1960s brought basic changes. The upshot was the Federal Election Campaign Act of 1971 (FECA), which supplanted the earlier legislation.

FECA, which was amended three times, established reporting or disclosure requirements for all candidates for the U.S. House of Representatives, the Senate, and the presidency, as well as their political parties and campaign committees. It also required disclosure of the amounts spent to influence federal elections by others, including individuals and political action committees. The act established partial public financing for presidential candidates, financed by a voluntary checkoff on federal income tax forms. If candidates opted not to take the partial public funds they had no spending limitations; those who accepted the funds in the primaries had state-by-state spending limits for the primary elections. Candidates could opt out of the partial public funding for the primaries but still accept public funding and spending limits in the general election. This is what George W. Bush did in 2000 and what he and John Kerry did in 2004.[69] Bush and Kerry, like all presidential general election candidates since 1976, accepted the general election public funding and spending limit.[70]

FECA had its critics, and Congress frequently debated reforming campaign financing. In 2002, as we have seen, it enacted the Bipartisan Campaign Reform Act. There have also been significant attempts to regulate interest-group activity in elections at the state level. Some states, including Maine, Wisconsin, Minnesota, Arizona, and Hawaii, provide for public financing of state offices and state legislative races; others, including Michigan, New Jersey, and Massachusetts, provide partial public financing of gubernatorial elections; a dozen more help underwrite parties with public funds.[71]

During President Bill Clinton's first term, and after the Republicans won control of the House in 1994, Congress passed the first major overhaul of lobbying laws since 1946. Under the Lobbying Disclosure Act of 1995, the definition of a lobbyist was significantly expanded to include part-time lobbyists, those who deal with congressional staff or executive branch agencies, and those who represent foreign-owned companies and foreign entities. This act was expected to increase the number of registered lobbyists to as much as ten times its then current level.[72] In fact, the number of registered "clients" nearly doubled eight years after enactment of the act.[73] The act also included specific disclosure and information requirements.

The Effects of Regulation

Reformers for more than a century sought disclosure of money in politics. This is consistent with efforts to have more complete disclosure of conflicts of interest in potential executive branch appointees and among legislators and judges. In campaigns and elections, disclosure was often incomplete, and groups quickly found ways to avoid it. However, the disclosure provisions of the 1971 Federal Election Campaign Act, as amended in 1974, were quite effective. Until the mid-1990s, citizens, journalists, and scholars had quite a complete picture of who was giving what to whom, and who was spending money and in what ways, to influence elections. That changed with the discovery of issue advocacy as an electioneering tool in the 1996 election cycle. Disclosure of a possible **quid pro quo** between an interest group and a politician was also diminished by soft money. A large donor could give millions to a party with the expectation that it was going to a

quid pro quo
Something given with the expectation of receiving something in return.

particular U.S. Senate campaign, but such a connection is not traceable because the soft money is passed through the party before going to candidates.

The 2002 reforms enhance disclosure first by banning soft money and then by broadening the definition of electioneering to capture much more of the issue advocacy of recent election cycles. The former test for whether a communication was or was not about an election was a language test, the so-called "magic words" test, included in the *Buckley* v. *Valeo* decision discussed earlier. The new legislation defines election communication targeted to a specific audience and which includes mentioning a candidate by name, mentioning an election, or showing the image or likeness of a candidate within 60 days of a general election and within 30 days of a primary election and which makes such communications subject to disclosure.

The FECA reforms of the 1970s sought to limit the influence of large donors in federal elections. Individuals and groups were limited in what they could contribute to parties, PACs, and candidates. The Supreme Court in 1976 declared that limits on independent expenditures were unconstitutional when they were truly independent of a party or candidate. The level of independent expediture activity has always been relatively modest, and FECA had as its intended effect reducing the influence of large contributors. That changed with the surge in unlimited soft money contributions and issue advocacy in the 1996–2002 period. BCRA restores limits on large donors by banning party soft money and requiring broadcast issue advocacy in the period before primaries and general elections that targets a particular audience and mentions a particular candidate to be funded by limited contributions from individuals and groups, not from general funds of unions or corporations. Interest groups can continue to skirt disclosure should they communicate with voters through the mail, in newspaper ads, on billboards, on the phone, and by e-mail—even in the period leading up to the election.

Can groups and individuals still seek to influence the electoral process through financial contributions? BCRA permits them to make contributions to a federal candidate for a primary election and for a general election, with additional contributions allowed if runoffs become necessary. For each of these types of elections, individuals can contribute $2,000. Individuals have an aggregate two-year federal election cycle limit of $94,500 in contributions to parties or candidates. Individuals can make unlimited contributions to interest groups and other types of political actors.

The 2004 election cycle saw more invidual contributions, in part because of the larger individual contribution limits. One of the beneficiaries of these higher limits was the re-election campaign of President George W. Bush. In 2000, Bush raised about one-fifth of his total funds from two hundred individuals, who in turn raised funds from other individuals.[74] The Bush approach was similar to that of direct marketing companies that build networks of personal contacts around individuals. In the case of the Bush efforts in 2000, a person who raised $100,000 from other individuals was designated a Pioneer. In 2004, with the higher contribution limits, an individual who raised $200,000 from individuals was designated a Ranger. Overall in 2004 the Bush campaign raised $266,476,243 from individuals.

TABLE 6–4   TOP SOFT MONEY DONORS, 2001–2002

Donor (Industry)*	Republicans	Democrats	Total
Saban Capital Group	0	$9,280,000	$9,280,000
Newsweb Corp.	0	7,390,000	7,390,000
Shangri-La Entertainment	0	6,700,000	6,700,000
American Federation of State/County/Municipal Employees	500	6,586,000	6,586,500
Service Employees International Union	41,622	4,821,117	4,862,739
Freddie Mac	2,335,615	1,687,500	4,023,115

Source: Opensecrets.org at www.opensecrets.org/bigpicture/softtop.asp?cycle=2002.

*Includes contributions from subsidiaries and/or executives.

Interest groups under BCRA will continue to participate through PACs. As noted, many members of Congress thrive on the present arrangements, and the leaders and members of both parties actually compete for PAC dollars (see Table 6–4). Although Republicans have generally received larger amounts, Democrats in recent election cycles put pressure on the pharmaceutical and insurance industries to give more to Democratic candidates.[75] More pragmatic PACs contribute to both parties to be in a favored position with whichever party wins the majority. One reason members of Congress become entrenched in their seats is that PACs fund them. The PAC contribution limits were not changed by BCRA, remaining at $5,000 per candidate for each of up to three elections (primary, general, and runoff).

One consequence of BCRA was that interest groups are spending more in issue advocacy. Many interest groups have already been diversifying their investment strategy. An example of diversification before BCRA is the pharmaceutical industry, whose PACs donated an estimated $5.2 million to federal candidates in 2000 and then also gave another $15.2 million in soft money to the political parties.[76] Beginning in 1999, the pharmaceutical industry contributed heavily to a group named Citizens for Better Medicare, which reported it would spend $40 million in issue advertising in 2000.[77] It ran ads in states with competitive Senate races.[78] The industry was also active in 2002.

Interest groups typically made the presidential campaign their highest priority in 2004. Some groups, like the League of Conservation Voters (LCV), in the past had invested some of their resources in presidential races but made House and Senate races higher priorities. LCV did just the opposite in 2004. With the presidential race so competitive and with so much passion behind supporting or opposing the incumbent president, the decision by interest groups to emphasize the presidential contest is not surprising.

One example of an interest group that diversified its approach in 2004 is the United States Chamber of Commerce. The Chamber did not endorse a candidate for president but strongly supported the reelection of President Bush—a position that was only strengthened when John Kerry chose as his running mate a former trial lawyer, John Edwards. But the Chamber also invested heavily in state races for state attorney general, state supreme court, and state congress in an effort to win friendlier state policies and court decisions involving business.

Some corporations had complained prior to passage of BCRA about the "shake down" by elected officials for large corporate soft money contributions. The BCRA ban on soft money gave corporations an excuse to spend less overall on politics in 2004. As noted, BCRA left other avenues open to corporations and unions. These alternative avenues included organizing the PACs, sending internal communications to members, and encouraging their employees to make individual contributions to the campaigns. It is important to remember that BCRA has only been in effect for one election and history teaches us that groups adapt over multiple elections to new rules.

What have been the effects of past reforms on interest groups? Ironically, one has been to increase the number and importance of such groups. The strategy of FECA in 1971 law was to authorize direct and open participation by both labor and corporate organizations in elections and lobbying in the hope that a visible role for interest-group activity, backed by effective enforcement, would be constitutional under the First Amendment. FECA allowed unions and corporations to communicate on political matters to members or stockholders, to conduct registration and get-out-the-vote drives, and to spend union and company funds to set up "separate segregated funds" (PACs) to use for political purposes.

TABLE 6–5 TOTAL PAC CONTRIBUTIONS TO FEDERAL CANDIDATES, 1990–2002

	2002	2000	1998	1996	1994	1992
Millions Contributed	282.0	259.8	219.9	217.8	189.6	188.9

Source: FEC, "PAC Activity Increases For 2002 Elections", at www.fec.gov.

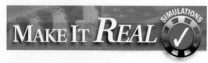

LOBBYING AMERICA

In this simulation, you will lobby on behalf of a fictional interest group. Your goal is to get legislation passed for your interest group. To accomplish this goal, you will research different members of Congress and finally disburse your limited resources of time and money (campaign contributions). Only if you use your resources efficiently will the legislation be passed.

Go to Make It Real "Lobbying America."

Corporations, trade associations, and unions made PACs a central part of their government relations strategy. But what changed the rules of the game for corporate interests was passage in 1974 of limits on individual contributions, something not part of the 1971 act. An explosion of corporate PACs followed this 1974 amendment.[79] In 1978, there was little difference in the level of campaign activity of PACs representing corporations, labor unions, or trade associations.[80] But that has changed, with corporate PACs spending more than the others and ideological PACs at roughly half the level of spending of trade and labor PACs.

Even with the surge in issue advocacy and party soft money contributions by interest groups in elections between 1996 and 2002, all three major types of PACs remained active in making PAC contributions to candidates. Interest groups gave PAC money to retain relationships with incumbents and candidates in relatively safe seats of parties they favored in what has long been the typical contest. PAC contributions are especially aimed at committee chairs and party leaders. To reinforce this relationship the Republicans have developed a strategy, the "K Street Project," to do even better in getting PAC contributions. K Street in Washington, D.C., houses many of the lobbying and law firms that represent trade associations and corporations that make contributions. House Republican Leader Tom DeLay, a prime mover in the K Street project, once said, "If you want to play in our revolution you have to live by our rules."[81]

With soft money largely banned in 2004 and with the uncertain legal status of some issue advocacy, many groups returned to the strategy of using their PAC as the primary means of investing in elections (see Table 6–5).

A centerpiece of past efforts to regulate interest group activity was disclosure of how politicians fund their campaigns. Disclosure permits the press and public to assess the implications of how candidates finance their campaigns. BCRA requires that the sponsors of all election-related advertising be identified in the communication, with this disclosure made prominently. This is why ads in 2004 featured the line, "I am candidate X and I approved of this ad," or something to that effect. Furthermore, BCRA requires that everything filed with the Federal Election Commission be made available to the public within 48 hours.

Candidates and some appointed officials must also disclose their personal finances, permitting voters and the press to see what investments and resources candidates have that may affect their ability to be impartial. Such public disclosure of personal assets, the value of property owned, and outstanding debts no doubt discourages some persons from entering public life, but it also makes officeholders accountable for certain obligations and actions once they enter office.

S U M M A R Y

1. Interest groups exist to make demands on government. The dominant interest groups in the United States are economic or occupational, but a variety of other groups—ideological, public interest, foreign policy, government itself, as well as ethnic, religious, and racial—have memberships that cut across the big economic groupings; thus their influence is both reduced and stabilized.

2. Movements of large numbers of people who are frustrated with government policies have always been with us in the United States. Blacks, women, and the economic underdogs have at various times organized themselves into movements.

3. Elements in interest-group power include size, resources, cohesiveness, leadership, and techniques, especially the ability to contribute to candidates and political parties as well as the ability to fund lobbyists. But the actual power of an interest group stems from the manner in which these elements relate to the political and governmental environment in which the interest group operates.

4. For many decades, interest groups have engaged in lobbying, but these efforts have become far more significant as groups become more deeply involved in the electoral process, especially through the expanded use of political action committees (PACs). Interest groups also take their

messages directly to the public through mass mailings and advertising campaigns. Other interest-group techniques include influencing rule making, litigation, election activities, and cooperative lobbying.

5. Concern about PACs centers on their ability to raise money and spend it on elections on behalf of endorsed candidates, typically incumbents. This concern has led to proposals to ban PACs or more strictly limit their activities. Yet their existence and rights are protected by the First Amendment.

6. Reforms of interest group excesses often include regulations that seek fairness, disclosure, and balance. All reform efforts must operate so as not to infringe on the

basic constitutional rights of individuals. The key issue today in "controlling factions" is whether to allow groups to proliferate and so balance each other, to try to regulate groups, or to seek reforms outside the groups by fostering balanced power in political parties or elsewhere.

7. Congress has enacted laws attempting to regulate and reform excesses of interest groups in electoral democracy. The Federal Election Campaign Act was passed in the 1970s in response to the Watergate scandal and the Bipartisan Campaign Reform Act was passed in 2002 in response to the soft money abuses by political parties and interest groups. The impact of these laws is debated and is often criticized for infringing on such rights as freedom of speech and freedom of association. Defenders of the reforms point to the success in removing large contributors from federal elections, at least for a couple of decades until groups found ways to circumvent the laws.

K E Y   T E R M S

faction	*Federal Register*	political action committee (PAC)	527 group
interest group	*amicus curiae brief*	bundling	quid pro quo
movement	lobbying	independent expenditures	
open shop	lobbyist	hard money	
closed shop	revolving door	soft money	
free rider	iron triangle	issue advocacy	

F U R T H E R   R E A D I N G

SCOTT H. AINSWORTH, *Analyzing Interest Groups: Group Influence on People and Policies* (Norton, 2002).

JEFFREY M. BERRY, *New Liberalism: The Rising Power of Citizen Groups* (Brookings Institution Press, 1999).

ROBERT BIERSACK ET AL., EDS., *After the Revolution: PACs, Lobbies, and the Republican Congress* (Addison-Wesley, 1999).

JEFFREY H. BIRNBAUM, *The Money Men: The Real Story of Fund-Raising's Influence on Political Power in America* (Crown, 2000).

WILLIAM P. BROWNE, *Groups, Interests, and Public Policy* (Georgetown University Press, 1998).

ALLAN J. CIGLER AND BURDETT A. LOOMIS, EDS., *Interest Group Politics*, 6th ed. (CQ Press, 2002).

MARTHA A. DERTHICK, *Up in Smoke* (CQ Press, 2002).

KENNETH M. GOLDSTEIN, *Interest Groups, Lobbying, and Participation in America* (Cambridge University Press, 1999).

GENE GROSSMAN AND ELHANAN HELPMAN, *Special Interest Politics* (MIT Press, 2001).

PAUL S. HERRNSON, RONALD G. SHAIKO, AND CLYDE WILCOX, *The Interest Group Connection: Electioneering, Lobbying, and Policymaking in Washington* (Chatham House, 1998).

ALLEN D. HERTZKE, *Representing God in Washington: The Role of Religious Lobbies in the American Polity* (University of Tennessee Press, 1988).

KEVIN W. HULA, *Lobbying Together: Interest Group Coalitions in Legislative Politics* (Georgetown University Press, 1999).

DAVID LOWERY AND HOLLY BRASHER. *Organized Interests and American Government* (McGraw-Hill, 2004).

DAVID B. MAGLEBY AND J. QUIN MONSON, EDS., *The Last Hurrah? Soft Money and Issue Advocacy in the 2002 Congressional Elections* (Brookings Institution Press, 2004).

MICHAEL J. MALBIN, ED., *Life After Reform: When the Bipartisan Campaign Reform Act Meets Politics* (Rowman & Littlefield, 2003).

ANTHONY J. NOWNES, *Pressure and Power: Organized Interests in American Politics* (Houghton Mifflin, 2001).

MANCUR OLSON, *The Logic of Collective Action* (Harvard University Press, 1965).

DAVID VOGEL, *Kindred Strangers: The Uneasy Relationship Between Politics and Business in America* (Princeton University Press, 1996).

JACK L. WALKER, JR., *Mobilizing Interest Groups in America: Patrons, Professions, and Social Movements* (University of Michigan Press, 1991).

DARRELL M. WEST AND BURDETT A. LOOMIS, *The Sound of Money: How Political Interests Get What They Want* (Norton, 1999).

S ome years ago, a community college district in Los Angeles held a nonpartisan election for its trustees in which any registered voter could run if he or she paid the $50 filing fee and gathered 500 valid signatures on a petition. A total of 133 candidates ran, and each voter could cast up to seven votes in the election. Political parties were not allowed to nominate candidates, and party labels did not appear on the ballot to help orient voters to the candidates.

How did people vote in an election without parties? Candidates were listed alphabetically, and those whose names began with the letters A to F did better than those later in the alphabet. Being well known helped. Endorsements by the *Los Angeles Times* also influenced the outcome, as did campaigning by a conservative group. A Mexican American surname also helped. In this election, an important voting cue was absent: incumbency. Because the board of trustees was newly created, none of the candidates were incumbents. Candidates who are incumbents have an advantage because they are generally better known and have developed an identity related to the position by providing services or generating activity.[1]

Rarely do American voters face such unorganized and plentiful choices, because parties give structure to national and state elections. E. E. Schattschneider, a noted political scientist, once said, "The political parties created democracy, and modern democracy is

POLITICAL PARTIES
ESSENTIAL TO DEMOCRACY

7

TIME LINE
POLITICAL PARTIES

1796	Thomas Jefferson guides creation of "Democratic-Republican party"
1824	First partisan realigning election, others in 1860 and 1896
1828	Andrew Jackson, the first Democrat to be elected president, ushers in the first party based on popular support
1836	Martin Van Buren is the second Democrat to be elected president
1860	Abraham Lincoln is the first Republican to be elected president
1903	Wisconsin creates the first primary election
1912	Theodore Roosevelt's "Bull Moose party" splits the Republican vote—a Democrat is elected
1932	Last partisan realigning election
1948	Strom Thurmond creates States' Rights party to combat desegregation
1968	Democratic convention in Chicago is overrun by protests and riots
1971	Libertarian party is created
1984	Geraldine Ferraro is the first woman nominated as vice president by a major party
1992	Billionaire Ross Perot creates United We Stand, predecessor of the Reform party
1994	Republicans regain control of the House of Representatives for first time in 40 years
2002	Soft money for federal party committees banned by Bipartisan Campaign Reform Act (BCRA)

political party
An organization that seeks political power by electing people to office so that its positions and philosophy become public policy.

unthinkable save in terms of the parties."[2] This provocative statement is true, but such a favorable evaluation of political parties runs counter to a long-standing and deep-seated American fear and distrust of them. Experience has taught us that free people create political parties to promote their own goals. Even though our founders hoped to discourage them, political parties quickly became an integral part of our political system.

Parties serve many functions, including the important one of narrowing the choices for voters.[3] They are both a consequence of democracy and an instrument of it. Parties need not be strong and cohesive like those in Britain and most European democracies, but there are few, if any, democratic systems that do not have political parties. Elections serve the vital task of deciding who can legitimately exercise political power, and parties are an integral part of making national and state elections work. We Americans take for granted the peaceful transfer of power from one elected official to another and from one party to another, yet in new democracies, the transfer of power following an election is often problematic. In such democracies, the holding of power may be more important than the principle of democratic competition. Well-established parties help stabilize democracy.

This chapter begins by examining the purposes parties serve that make them so vital to the functioning of democracy. We then examine the evolution of American political parties. Although American political parties have changed over time, they remain important in three different settings: as institutions, in government, and in the electorate. It is important to understand how parties facilitate democracy in all three settings. Finally, we turn to a discussion of the strength of parties today and the prospects for party reform and renewal.

WHAT PARTIES DO FOR DEMOCRACY
Party Functions

Political parties are organizations that seek political power by electing people to office so that their positions and philosophy become public policy. American political parties serve a variety of political and social functions, some obvious and some not so obvious. They perform some functions well and others not so well, and how they perform them differs from place to place and time to time.

ORGANIZE THE COMPETITION   One of the most important functions of parties is to organize the competition by designating candidates to run under their label. Parties exist primarily as an organizing mechanism to win elections and thus win control of government. For some races, parties recruit and nominate candidates for office; they register and activate voters; and they help candidates by training them, raising money for them, providing them with research and voter lists, and enlisting volunteers to work for them.[4] For more visible contests, especially ones where there is a real chance of winning, multiple candidates often compete with each other for the nomination, often without party efforts to recruit them. Recently, campaign consultants rather than party officials have taken over some of these responsibilities; we explore this topic at some length in Chapter 10.[5]

The ability of parties to influence the selection of candidates varies by the type of nominating system used in the state. A few states use a *caucus* or *convention system*, which permits party leaders to play a role in the selection of nominees by placing their selection in the hands of people willing to attend party meetings called caucuses or conventions. Most people are not willing to invest this much time in a nomination process. Other states hold *primary elections* where voters cast ballots on who the party nominees should be. As more and more states turn to primary elections, the ability of party leaders to influence who runs under their party label is reduced. Candidates with little party experience but with well-known names or ample personal funds can often win in a primary over a person with a known track record of prior party service or success in a less visible office. New Jersey Senator Jon Corzine had never run for office and was not well known in the state before spending $60 million in his successful 2000 campaign. Not all little-known, self-financed candidates win; in fact, they are often defeated. For example, Steve Forbes spent a combined $129 million in unsuccessful bids for the Republican presidential nomination in 1996 and 2000. Examples of former athletes who made successful candidates include Jim Bunning, a former baseball player and now Senator from Kentucky; Univeristy of Nebraska football coach Tom Osborne, now in the House of Representatives; and former NFL football player Jack Kemp, who served in the House of Representatives and was the Republican nominee for vice president in 1996.

A party's ability to organize the competition is also influenced by how states organize their ballots. In many states, candidates are listed in party columns—on a **party column ballot**—which makes it easier for voters to vote a *straight ticket* for all the party candidates. Straight-ticket voting is also more likely in voting systems that permit flipping one switch or punching one spot on the computer card to vote for all candidates from one party. Other states organize the ballot by office—the **office block ballot**—which makes straight-ticket voting harder. Even though many voters cast votes for candidates in more than one party, the party label of a candidate means something to most voters and is important in their voting decision.

Local and judicial elections in most states are **nonpartisan elections**, which means no party affiliation is indicated. Such systems make it more difficult for political parties to operate—precisely why many jurisdictions have adopted this reform. Proponents of nonpartisan local and judicial elections contend that party affiliation is not important to being a good judge or school board member. As with our example of the community college board at the beginning of this chapter, many voters in these nonpartisan elections rely more on how recognizable the name of a candidate is, or whether he or she now holds office (incumbency).

UNIFY THE ELECTORATE   Parties are often accused of creating conflict, but they actually help unify the electorate and moderate conflict, at least within the party. There is a strong incentive in both parties to fight out their differences inside the party but then come together to take on the opposition. Moreover, in order to win elections, parties need to reach out to voters outside their party and gain their support. This action also helps unify the electorate, at least into the two large national political parties in our system.

Parties have great difficulty building coalitions on controversial issues like abortion or gun control. Not surprisingly, candidates and parties generally try to avoid defining themselves or the election in single-issue terms. Rather, they hope that if voters disagree with the party's stand on one issue, they will still support the party because they agree with it on other issues. Deemphasizing single issues in this way helps defuse conflict and unify the electorate.

HELP ORGANIZE GOVERNMENT   Although political parties in the United States are not as cohesive as in some other democracies, parties are important when it comes to organizing our state and national governments. Congress is organized along party lines. The political party with the most votes in each chamber elects the officers of that chamber, selects the chair of each committee, and has a majority on all the committees. State legislatures, with the notable exception of Nebraska, are also organized along party lines. The 2004 election enlarged the Republican majorities in the U.S. Senate and U.S. House of Representatives. In the Senate, the GOP rose from 51 to 55 members, but this number remained below the number needed to override a filibuster. Republicans continued to control all committee chairs, but due to party rules, there was some rotation among Republicans. The Senate Judiciary Committee chairmanship, for example, switched in 2005 from Orrin Hatch (R.–Utah) to Arlen Specter (R.–Penn.).

The party that controls the White House, the governor's mansion, or city hall gets **patronage**, which means it can select party members as public officials or judges. Such appointments are limited only by civil service regulations that restrict patronage typically to the top posts, but these posts, which number about 4,000 in the federal government, are also numerous at the state and local levels. Patronage provides an incentive for people to become involved in politics and gives the party leaders and elected politicians loyal partisans in key positions to help them achieve their policy objectives. Patronage has declined dramatically over time in the United States.

party column ballot
Type of ballot that encourages party-line voting by listing all of a party's candidates in a column under the party name.

office block ballot
Ballot on which all candidates are listed under the office for which they are running, making split-ticket voting easier.

nonpartisan election
A local or judicial election in which candidates are not selected or endorsed by political parties and party affiliation is not listed on ballots.

patronage
The dispensing of government jobs to persons who belong to the winning political party.

TRANSLATE PREFERENCES INTO POLICY   One of the great strengths of our democracy is that even the party that wins an election usually has to moderate what it does in order to win reelection. For that reason, public policy does not change dramatically with each election. Nonetheless, the party that wins the election has a chance to enact its policies and implement its campaign promises.

American parties have had only limited success in setting the course of national policy, especially when compared with countries with strong parties. The European model of party government, which has been called a *responsible party system*, assumes that parties discipline their members through their control over nominations and campaigns. Officeholders in such party-centered systems are expected to act according to party wishes or they will not be allowed to run again under the party label. Moreover, candidates run on fairly specific party platforms and are expected to implement those policies if they win control in the election.

Although we lack a European-type party system, most but not all Democrats in Congress vote together, as do most but not all Republicans. There are times, however, when a president of one party receives more congressional votes from the opposing party than from his own, as President Bill Clinton did in 2000 on legislation granting China permanent normal trade relations status with the United States.[6] And when the House passed the Enhanced Border Security and Visa Entry Reform Act of 2002, which President Bush wanted, nearly twice as many Democrats voted yes—182, compared to 92 yes votes from the Republicans.[7]

Because American parties do not control nominations, they are less able to discipline members who express views contrary to those of the party.[8] The American system is largely *candidate-centered;* politicians are nominated largely on the basis of their qualifications and personal appeal, not party loyalty. In fact, it is more correct to say that in most contests, we have *candidate* politics rather than *party* politics. As a consequence, party leaders cannot guarantee passage of their program, even if they are in the majority.

Even though parties cannot exert tight control over candidates, their ability to raise and spend money has had a significant influence. Through the 2002 election, parties played an important role in competitive federal elections through their **soft money** expenditures.[9] In the 2002 South Dakota Senate race, for example, the party committees and allied interest groups spent a combined $12 million, equaling what the two major party candiates spent in that race.[10]

The Bipartisan Campaign Reform Act (BCRA), which took effect in the 2003–04 election cycle, abolished soft money donations to political parties at the federal level. Soft money consisted of contributions given to the political parties by individuals, corporations, labor unions, and political action committees (PACs) for "party-building" purposes that came to be used for candidate promotion. Because such contributions were unlimited, parties put a premium on raising them. The ads soft money paid for were often candidate centered and focused on themes important to that race.[11]

Political parties responded to the soft money ban by raising more of the limited **hard money** from individuals and political action committees. BCRA made this easier by raising the contribution limits for individuals from $1,000 to $2,000.[12] In an election cycle, an individual who wanted to give the maximum possible to candidates and parties could give $95,000, up from $50,000.[13] Both parties raised record-setting amounts of hard money in 2003–2004, surpassing what they had raised in hard and soft money combined in 1999–2000 or 2001–2002. Party hard money in 2004 was spent on a range of activities including get-out-the-vote efforts, contributions to candidates, and advertising. Parties are also allowed to contribute $5,000 of hard money to House candidates and $35,000 to Senate candidates per election cycle, and additional money in hard money coordinated expenditures. Political partes are also allowed to spend limited amounts of hard money on campaign activities that are coordinated with the candidate and in which the candidate pays part of the cost. Between 1996 and 2004, parties had scaled back their coordinated spending and contributions to candidates, instead focusing on soft money.

Political parties also could spend unlimited amounts of hard money on **independent expenditures** for or against candidates. The Supreme Court gave parties and groups the same right to independent expenditures in a 1996 Supreme Court Decision,

soft money
Money raised in unlimited amounts by political parties for party building purposes. Now largely illegal except for limited contributions to state or local parties for voter registration and get-out-the-vote efforts.

hard money
Political contributions given to a party, candidate, or interest group that are limited in amount and fully disclosed. Raising such limited funds is harder than raising unlimited funds, hence the term "hard" money.

independent expenditure
The Supreme Court has ruled that individuals, groups, and parties can spend unlimited amounts in campaigns for or against candidates as long as they operate independently from the candidates. When an individual, group, or party does so, they are making an independent expenditure.

Colorado Republican Federal Campaign Committee v. *FEC.*[14] In 2003–04, with soft money not an option and with more success in raising hard money, both parties made substantial independent expenditures. For example, in the 2004 special election in South Dakota, the two parties combined spent nearly $3 million, mostly in independent expenditures.[15]

PROVIDE LOYAL OPPOSITION Accountability in a democracy comes from the party out of power closely monitoring and commenting on the actions of the party in power. When national security issues are involved or the country is under attack, parties restrain their criticism, as the Democrats in Congress did for some time after September 11, 2001. There is usually a polite interval following an election—known as the **honeymoon**—after which the opposition party begins to criticize the party that controls the White House, especially when the opposition party controls one or both houses of Congress.[16] The length of the honeymoon depends in part on how close the vote was in the election, on how contentious the agenda of the new administration is, and on the leadership skills of the new president. Early success in enacting policy can prolong the honeymoon; mistakes or controversies can shorten it.

The Nomination of Candidates

From the beginning, parties have been the mechanism by which candidates for public office are chosen. The **caucus** played an important part in pre-Revolutionary politics. Elected officials organized themselves into groups or parties and together selected candidates to run for higher office, including the presidency. This method of nomination operated for several decades after the United States was established.

As early as the 1820s, however, charges of "secret deals" in "smoke-filled rooms" were made against this method. Moreover, it was not representative of people from areas where a party was in a minority or nonexistent, since only officeholders took part in the caucus. Efforts were made to make the caucus more representative of rank-and-file party members. The *mixed caucus* brought in delegates from districts in which the party had no elected legislators.

Then, during the 1830s and 1840s, a system of **party conventions** was instituted. Delegates, usually chosen directly by party members in towns and cities, selected the party candidates, debated and adopted a platform, and built party spirit by celebrating noisily. But the convention method soon came under criticism that it was subject to control by the party bosses and their machines.

To involve more voters and reduce the power of the bosses to pick party nominees, states adopted the **direct primary**, in which people could vote for the party's nominees for office. Primaries spread rapidly after Wisconsin adopted them in 1905—in the North as a Progressive era reform and in the South as a way to bring democracy to a region that had seen no meaningful general elections since the end of Reconstruction, due to one-party rule by the Democrats. By 1920, direct primaries were the norm for some offices in almost all states.

Today the direct primary is the typical method of picking party candidates. Primaries vary significantly from state to state. They differ in terms of (1) who may run in a primary and how one qualifies for the ballot; (2) whether the party organization can or does endorse candidates before the primary; (3) who may vote in a party's primary—that is, whether a voter must register with a party in order to vote; and (4) how many votes are needed for nomination—a plurality, a majority, or some other number determined by party rule or state law. The differences among primaries are not trivial; they have an important impact on the role played by party organization and on the strategy used by candidates.

In states with **open primaries**, any voter, regardless of party, can participate in whichever primary he or she chooses. This kind of primary permits **crossover voting**—Republicans and Independents helping determine who the Democratic nominee will be, and vice versa. Other states use **closed primaries**, in which only persons already registered in that party may participate. Some states, like Washington and California, experimented with *blanket primaries*, in which all voters could vote for any candidate, regardless of party. Blanket primaries permitted voters to vote for a candidate of one party for one office and for a candidate from another party for another office, something that is not

honeymoon
Period at the beginning of a new president's term during which the president enjoys generally positive relations with the press and Congress, usually lasting about six months.

caucus
A meeting of local party members to choose party officials or candidates for public office and to decide the platform.

party convention
A meeting of party delegates to vote on matters of policy and in some cases to select party candidates for public office.

direct primary
Election in which voters choose party nominees.

open primary
Primary election in which any voter, regardless of party, may vote.

crossover voting
Voting by a member of one party for a candidate of another party.

closed primary
Primary election in which only persons registered in the party holding the primary may vote.

permitted under either closed or open primaries. In 2000, the Supreme Court held that California's blanket primary violated the free association rights of political parties, in part because blanket primaries permit people who have "expressly affiliated with a rival" party to have a vote in the selection of a nominee from a different party.[17] In a detailed study of California's blanket primary, political scientists found that fewer than 5 percent of voters associated with one party actually voted for nominees from another party. More broadly, they concluded that the rules of a primary are important in determining the winner.[18]

Along with modern communications and fund-raising techniques, direct primaries have diminished the influence of leaders of political parties. Many critics believe that this change has had more undesirable than desirable consequences. Party leaders now have less influence over who gets to be the party's candidate, and candidates are less accountable to the party both during the election and after it.

Direct primaries are used to nominate most party candidates for most offices. Yet in some states, local caucuses choose delegates to attend regional meetings, which in turn select delegates to state and national conventions, where they nominate party candidates for offices. The Iowa presidential caucuses, in which 122,000 Iowans participated in 2004,[19] are highly publicized as the first important test of potential presidential nominees.[20]

In a few states, conventions still play a role in the nominating process for state and federal candidates. In Connecticut, for example, convention choices become the party nominees unless they are challenged. Candidates who attain at least 15 percent of the vote in the convention have an automatic right to challenge the winner at the convention, but they do not always exercise this right.[21] In Utah, if a candidate gets 60 percent of the delegate vote at the convention, there is no primary election vote for that office. Should no candidate reach 60 percent, only the top two candidates are listed on the primary ballot. In other states, convention nominees are designated as such on the primary ballot; they may or may not receive help from the party organization. Conventions are also used to invigorate the party faithful by enabling them to meet with their leaders.

In most states, candidates can get their names on the ballot as an Independent or minor party candidate by securing the required number of signatures on a nomination petition. This is hard to do, but it can be done, as Ross Perot demonstrated in 1992. He spent his own money to build an organization of volunteers who put his name on the ballot in all 50 states. Minor party gubernatorial candidates like the Minnesota Reform party's Jesse Ventura in 1998 or the Green party's presidential candidate Ralph Nader in

A precinct captain takes a head count during the caucus in Burlington, Iowa, on January 19, 2004. John Kerry easily won the precinct.

2000 secured their nominations as candidates of existing minor parties. Ralph Nader was on the ballot in 34 states and the District of Columbia as an independent candidate in 2004. Democrats successfully challenged his efforts to qualify for the ballot in Ohio, Arizona, and Pennsylvania. Some Republicans supported Ralph Nader's efforts to be on the ballot in more states, a move Democrats suspected was intended to draw support from John Kerry. Ballot access remains a major hurdle for minor party candidates.

Party Systems

Ours is a two-party system; most other democracies have a multiparty system. Although we have many minor parties, only the two major parties have much of a chance to win elections. Multiparty systems are almost always found in countries that have a parliamentary government, in contrast to our presidential system. This is, however, not always

GLOBAL *Perceptions*

QUESTION: How important is it to you to live in a country where honest elections are held regularly with a choice of at least two political parties? Is it very important, somewhat important, not too important, or not important at all?

An idea that citizens of the United States take for granted, like the need for at least two political parties, is not seen as important in all countries. For example, in countries like Bolivia, South Korea, and Jordan, less than half of the public thinks having two parties is very important. In the United States, by contrast, 84 percent say having a choice between at least two parties is important.

In the Pew Global Attitudes Project, respondents were also asked how they felt about American ideas about democracy (see Chapter 1 box). In most cases the attitudes on one question predict the attitudes in the other. But in the Philippines, Turkey, Argentina, Brazil, and Pakistan, much higher proportions say "having two parties is important" than say they "like American ideas about democracy." In Turkey, for example, 75 percent think having two parties is very important but only 33 percent like American ideas about democracy. The reverse is true in Ghana, where 80 percent like American ideas about democracy but only 58 percent think having two parties is important. This reinforces the point that in the minds of people in some countries democracy is distinguishable from their views of democracy in the United States.

SOURCE: The Pew Research Center, *Views of a Changing World,* 2003, p. T-67.

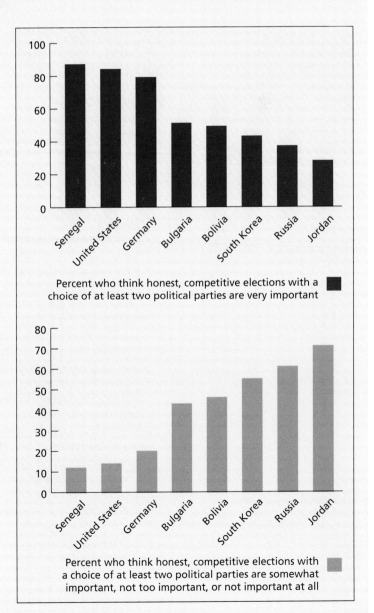

Percent who think honest, competitive elections with a choice of at least two political parties are very important

Percent who think honest, competitive elections with a choice of at least two political parties are somewhat important, not too important, or not important at all

IN COMPARATIVE PERSPECTIVE

ISRAEL'S COALITION GOVERNMENT

Israel has a multiparty system. Though Israelis vote for prime minister and parliament separately, the prime minister must still have the support of the majority of the members of parliament. If he doesn't, he is in danger of facing a parliamentary vote of no confidence. A vote of no confidence leads to new elections for prime minister and parliament. Because there are many parties, it is difficult—if not impossible—for any one party to gain a majority of the seats in the Knesset, the Israeli parliament. Usually one party can get only a plurality of the seats. A party with only a plurality of seats must form a coalition with other parties in order to maintain power. Certain concessions must be made to those parties to convince them to join. If the ruling party loses the support of its coalition partners, the prime minister and his party must form a new coalition, or else their government will be toppled by a parliamentary vote of no confidence.

The conflict with the Palestinians and disagreement over how best to coexist with them has been a source of destabilization to Israeli coalition governments. In July 2000, Prime Minister Ehud Barak, after upsetting rightist parties within his coalition by having peace talks with the Palestinians, exercised his authority to call an early election for prime minister

in order to avoid a vote of "no confidence." Ariel Sharon, an outspoken critic of Barak, soundly defeated him in the election.

The conflict between Israel and the Palestinians has escalated since 2002 and, ironically, Sharon is in a plight similar to Barak's. In early 2004, Sharon shocked rightist members of his coalition by making known that he would unilaterally withdraw all Israeli settlements from the Gaza strip along with some other settlements on the West Bank. As a result, he has faced heated opposition not only from members of the Knesset within his coalition but even within his cabinet.* In order to save his faltering government, Sharon invited the leftist Labour party to join what had been a rightist coalition.† Sharon's own Likud party voted against letting Labour into their coalition in August 2004. Sharon continued to seek help from Labour to implement his disengagement policy. This illustrates the scrambling and compromise that often occur within countries that have a multiparty system.

*Gil Hoffman, "Sharon: Settlements in Gaza Cannot Remain," *The Jerusalem Post*, February 3, 2004, p. 1.
†Greg Myre, "Sharon Invites His Favorite Dove to Help Build a Coalition," *The New York Times*, July 13, 2004, p. 4.

true. For example, England has a parliamentary system but also a strong two-party system.

Parliamentary systems usually have a *head of the nation,* often called the president, but they also have a *head of the government,* often called the prime minister or chancellor, who is the leader of one of the large parties in the legislature. In democracies with multiparty systems, such as Israel and Italy, because no one party has a majority of the votes, *coalition* governments are necessary. Minor parties can gain concessions—positions in a cabinet or support of policies they want implemented—in return for their participation in a coalition. Major parties need the minor parties and are therefore willing to bargain. Thus the multiparty system favors the existence of minor parties by giving them incentives to persevere.

In some multiparty parliamentary systems, parties run slates of candidates for legislative positions, and winners are determined by **proportional representation**, in which the parties receive a proportion of the legislators corresponding to their proportion of the vote. In our **winner-take-all system**, only the candidate with the most votes in a district or state takes office.[22] Because a party does not gain anything by finishing second, minor parties in a two-party system can rarely overcome the assumption that a vote for them is a wasted vote.[23] Even if a third-party candidate can keep either major party candidate from receiving more than 50 percent (a *majority*) of the vote, the candidate with the most votes (a *plurality*) wins.

In multiparty systems, parties at the extremes are apt to have more influence than in our two-party system, and in nations with a multiparty system, their legislatures more accurately reflect the full range of the views of the electorate. Political parties in multiparty systems can be more doctrinaire than ours because they do not have to appeal to masses of people. Even though parties that do not become part of the governing coalition may have little to say in setting government policy, they survive because they appeal

proportional representation
An election system in which each party running receives the proportion of legislative seats corresponding to its proportion of the vote.

winner-take-all system
An election system in which the candidate with the most votes wins.

to some voters. Under such a system, an incentive exists for third, fourth, or additional parties to run because they may win some seats. In contrast, our two-party system tends to create *centrist* parties that appeal to moderate elements and suppress the views of extremists in the electorate. Moreover, once elected, our parties do not form as cohesive a voting bloc as ideological parties do in multiparty systems.

Multiparty parliamentary systems often make governments unstable as coalitions form and collapse. In addition, swings in policy when party control changes can be quite dramatic. In contrast, two-party systems produce governments that tend to be stable and centrist, and as a result, policy changes occur incrementally.

Minor Parties: Persistence and Frustration

Although we have a primarily two-party system in the United States, we also have **minor parties**, sometimes called *third parties.* Those that arise around a candidate usually disappear when the charismatic personality does. Examples of such parties are Theodore Roosevelt's Bull Moose party and George Wallace's American Independent party. Wallace's party polled more than 13 million votes and won 46 electoral votes in 1968. Ross Perot won 19 million votes, 19 percent of the total vote in 1992.[24] He did only about half as well in 1996, despite having organized a political party. Without Ross Perot to lead it, the Reform party was badly divided in 2000. Its presidential candidate, Pat Buchanan, failed to reach 1 percent of the national popular vote and thus lost the Reform party much of the ground it had gained under Ross Perot in terms of ballot access and federal campaign funding. More visible than the Reform party was the Green party, which, although not on the ballot in seven states, mounted a major effort to reach 5 percent of the popular vote for presidential candidate Ralph Nader and thereby qualify the party for federal funding in the 2004 elections. The effort failed. The Green party mustered only 3 percent of the popular vote. In 2004, Nader, running as an independent, but endorsed by the Reform party, received one-third of 1 percent of the vote.

Minor parties that are organized around an *ideology* usually persist over a longer time than those built around a particular leader. Communist, Prohibition, Libertarian, Right to Life, and Green parties are of the ideological type. Minor parties of both types come and go, and there are usually several minor parties running in any given election.[25] Some parties arise around a single issue, like the Right to Life party active in states like New York.

Minor parties have been criticized by major parties as "spoilers," diverting votes away from the major party candidate and costing that candidate the election. Green party candidate Ralph Nader was accused of doing this to Al Gore in 2000. Interest groups identified with environmental issues ran ads urging voters not to waste their vote on Nader, who could not win the election. The closeness of the 2000 election and the perception that Nader may have cost Al Gore the White House meant that Democrats aggressively tried to block access to the ballot for Nader in 2004 and stressed his potential to be a spoiler again in 2004. Early in the campaign, John Kerry and Ralph Nader met and the candidates were on good terms. This later dissipated as Nader criticized the Democratic party and lack of differences between the major party candidates.

Minor parties have had an indirect influence in our country by drawing attention to controversial issues and by organizing such groups as the antislavery and the civil rights movements.[26] Ross Perot, for example, elevated the importance of balanced budgets in 1992 and made it more difficult for George Bush to attack Bill Clinton on character issues.[27] However, they have never won the presidency or more than a handful of congressional seats (see Table 7–1).[28] They have done somewhat better in gubernatorial elections.[29] They have never shaped national policy from *inside* the government, and their influence on national policy and on the platforms of the two major parties has been limited.[30]

Examples of minor parties operating in recent elections include the Libertarian, Green, and Reform parties. The **Libertarian party** (www.lp.org) places heavy emphasis on individual liberties, personal responsibility, and freedom from government. Its agenda calls for an end to the federal government's role in education and crime control. Libertarians believe that "if government's role were limited to protecting our lives, rights and property, then America would prosper and thrive as never before." Libertarians also

In 2004, independent presidential candidate Ralph Nader received one-third of 1 percent of the popular vote.

minor party
A small political party that rises and falls with a charismatic candidate or, if composed of ideologies on the right or left, usually persists over time; also called a *third party*.

Libertarian party
A minor party that believes in extremely limited government. Libertarians call for a freemarket system, expanded individual liberties such as drug legalization, and a foreign policy of non-intervention, free trade, and open immigration.

Green party
A minor party dedicated to the environment, social justice, nonviolence, and a foreign policy of nonintervention. Ralph Nader ran as the Green party's nominee in 2000.

Reform party
A minor party founded by Ross Perot in 1995. It focuses on national government reform, fiscal responsibility, and political accountability. It has recently struggled with internal strife and criticism that it lacks an identity.

believe that "every service supplied by the government can be provided better *and* cheaper by private business." Libertarians favor, in their terms, "re-legalizing" drugs and prostitiuton and also support open immigration. In 2004, a total of 278 Libertarians ran for office.[31]

The **Green party** (www.greenpartyus.org) takes its name from other pro-environment parties throughout Europe. In the United States, the Greens not only embrace pro-environment positions but are also committed to social justice, decentralization, respect for diversity, community-based economics, nonviolence, feminism, ecological wisdom, grassroots democracy, and personal and global responsibility. The party's 2004 presidential candidate, David Cobb, called for public campaign financing, greater environmental protection, and affordable housing. The party seeks to achieve social justice, eliminate discrimination, and promote self-reliance.

The **Reform party** (www.reformparty.org) was organized in 1995 by Ross Perot. It focuses on national government reform, fiscal responsibility, and political accountability. In 1996, Perot won 9 percent of the popular vote in the presidential election and qualified the party for official party status. In 2000, Pat Buchanan ran as the Reform party's presidential nominee and managed to win only 1 percent of the vote. Recently, the Reform party has been characterized by internal strife; a number of state organizations withdrew from the party, and many of the top party leaders resigned in 2002. As noted, the Reform party endorsed Ralph Nader for president in 2004.

A BRIEF HISTORY OF AMERICAN POLITICAL PARTIES

Our First Parties

To the founders of the young Republic, parties meant bigger, better-organized, and fiercer factions, and they did not want that. Benjamin Franklin worried about the "infinite mutual abuse of parties, tearing to pieces the best of characters." In his Farewell

TABLE 7–1 MINOR PARTIES IN THE UNITED STATES

Year	Party	Presidential Candidate	Percentage of Popular Vote Received	Electoral Votes
1832	Anti-Masonic	William Wirt	8%	7
1856	American (Know-Nothing)	Millard Fillmore	22	8
1860	Democratic (Secessionist)	John C. Breckinridge	18	72
1860	Constitutional Union	John Bell	13	39
1892	People's (Populist)	James B. Weaver	9	22
1912	Bull Moose	Theodore Roosevelt	27	88
1912	Socialist	Eugene V. Debs	6	0
1924	Progressive	Robert M. La Follette	17	13
1948	States' Rights (Dixiecrat)	Strom Thurmond	2	39
1948	Progressive	Henry A. Wallace	2	0
1968	American Independent	George C. Wallace	14	46
1980	National Unity	John Anderson	7	0
1992	Reform	Ross Perot	19	0
1996	Reform	Ross Perot	8	0
2000	Reform	Pat Buchanan	0	0
2000	Green	Ralph Nader	3	0
2004	Reform	Ralph Nader	0	0

Address, George Washington warned against the "baneful effects of the Spirit of Party." And Thomas Jefferson said, "If I could not go to heaven but with a party, I would not go there at all."[32]

How, then, did parties get started? Largely out of practical necessity. The same early leaders who so frequently stated their opposition to political parties also recognized the need to organize officeholders who shared their views so that government could act. To get its measures passed by Congress, the Washington administration had to fashion a coalition among factions. This job fell to Treasury Secretary Alexander Hamilton, who built an informal Federalist party, while Washington stayed "above politics."

Secretary of State Jefferson and other officials, many of whom despised Hamilton and his aristocratic ways as much as they opposed the policies he favored, were uncertain about how to deal with these political differences. Their overriding concern was the success of the new government; personal loyalty to Washington was a close second. Thus Jefferson stayed in the cabinet, despite his opposition to administration policies, during most of Washington's first term. When he left the cabinet at the end of 1793, many who joined him in opposition to the administration's economic policies remained in Congress, forming a group of legislators opposed to Federalist fiscal policies and eventually to Federalist foreign policy, which appeared "soft on Britain." This party was later known as Republicans, then as Democratic-Republicans, and finally as Democrats.[33]

Realigning Elections

American political parties have evolved and changed over time, but some underlying characteristics have been constant. Historically, we have had a two-party system with minor parties. Our parties are moderate and accommodative, meaning that they are open to people with diverse outlooks. Political scientist V. O. Key and others have argued that our party system has been shaped in large part by **realigning elections**, turning points that define the agenda of politics and the alignment of voters within parties during periods of historic change in the economy and society. Realigning elections are characterized by intense electoral involvement by the voters, disruptions of traditional voting patterns, changes in the relations of power within the community, and the formation of new and durable electoral groupings. They have occurred cyclically, not randomly. These elections tend to coincide with expansions of the suffrage or changes in the rate of voting.[34] We focus here on four realigning elections: 1824, 1860, 1896, and 1932.

1824: ANDREW JACKSON AND THE DEMOCRATS Party politics was invigorated following the election of 1824, in which the leader in the popular vote—the hero of the battle of New Orleans, Democrat Andrew Jackson—failed to achieve the necessary majority of the electoral college and was defeated by John Quincy Adams in the runoff election in the House of Representatives. Jackson, brilliantly aided by Martin Van Buren, a veteran party builder in New York State, later knitted together a winning combination of regions, interest groups, and political doctrines to win the presidency in 1828. The Whigs succeeded the Federalists as the opposition party. By the time Van Buren, another Democrat, followed Jackson in the White House in 1837, the Democrats had become a large, nationwide movement with national and state leadership, a clear party doctrine, and grassroots organization. The Whigs were almost as strong; in 1840, they put their own man, General William Henry Harrison ("Old Tippecanoe"), into the White House. A two-party system had been born, and we have had that two-party system ever since—one of few such systems worldwide.

1860: THE CIVIL WAR AND THE RISE OF THE REPUBLICANS Out of the crisis over slavery evolved a new party: the second Republican party—ultimately dubbed the "Grand Old Party" (GOP).[35] Abraham Lincoln was elected in 1860 with the support not only of financiers, industrialists, and merchants but also of large numbers of workers and farmers. For 50 years after 1860, the Republican coalition won every presidential race except

★★ THINKING IT THROUGH

How you answer this question depends on what you want to accomplish with your vote. For those who see the vote as a largely symbolic exercise, then voting for a minor party candidate with little chance of winning provides that opportunity. The problem is that the more electable candidate who is clearly preferred over the other more competitive alternative may not win office at all if a voter does not consider electability. The winner-take-all system makes this trade-off more consequential. In a system where proportional representation is possible, a voter is more likely to be able to translate policy preferences into a vote for representatives. But in our system, voters must often vote for their second choice in order to avoid their third choice winning office. Interest groups, like environmental groups, often find themselves not endorsing a minor party candidate who may be closer to their views because they want to avoid helping elect a competitive alternative candidate whose views they abhor.

One alternative that would lessen the influence of these candidates would be requiring a run-off election if no candidate got a majority, with only the top two vote getters in the run-off. While this would force another election in some instances, it would force people who vote to decide among the more viable options. A counterargument is that many people who support minor party candidates would opt out of an election without this chance to express their preferences, and so such a run-off is already accomplished with the plurality winner system we already have.

realigning election
An election during periods of expanded suffrage and change in the economy and society that proves to be a turning point, redefining the agenda of politics and the alignment of voters within parties.

FACTS ABOUT AMERICAN POLITICAL PARTIES

- Parties began in this country as soon as people started taking sides in the debate over ratifying the U.S. Constitution, although it took a few years for them to organize into formal bodies.
- Political parties, and especially our two-party system, have persisted over the course of our history.
- Ours has almost always been a two-party system, differentiating us from most nations, which have a one-party or multiparty system.
- Since 1830, we have witnessed reasonably effective competition in our national party system.
- Our parties have historically been decentralized and fragmented. Parties are organized around states, congressional districts, counties, and cities, with state parties the most important units.
- Winning office and power has been more important to party leaders than specific issues or platforms; political parties in the United States are primarily organized to win and hold political power.
- Our parties can be characterized as moderate, centrist, and pragmatic, with only modest ideological cohesion and voting discipline, especially when compared to European political parties.

laissez-faire economics
Theory that opposes governmental interference in economic affairs beyond what is necessary to protect life and property.

Keynesian economics
Theory based on the principles of John Maynard Keynes, stating that government spending should increase during business slumps and be curbed during booms.

for Grover Cleveland's victories in 1884 and 1892. The Democratic party survived with its durable white male base in the South.

1896: A PARTY IN TRANSITION   The Republican party's response to industrialization and hard times for farmers changed it in the late 1800s. A combination of western and southern farmers and western mining interests sought an alliance with workers in the East and Midwest to "recapture America from the foreign moneyed interests responsible for industrialization. The crisis of industrialization squarely placed an agrarian-fundamentalist view of life against an industrial-progress view."[36] The two parties also differed over whether U.S. currency should be tied to a silver or gold standard, with Republicans favoring gold and Democrats silver. William Jennings Bryan, the Democratic candidate for president in 1896, was a talented orator but lost the race to William McKinley.[37] The 1896 realignment differs from the others, however, in that the party in power did not change hands. In that sense it was a *converting realignment* because it reinforced the Republican majority status that had been in place since 1860.[38]

The Progressive era, the first two decades of the twentieth century, was a period of political reform led by the Progressive wing of the Republican party. Much of the agenda of the Progressives focused on the corrupt political parties. Civil service reforms shifted some of the patronage out of the hands of party officials. The direct primary election took control of nominations from party leaders and gave it to the rank-and-file. And in a number of cities, nonpartisan governments were instituted, totally eliminating the role of a party. With the ratification of the Seventeenth Amendment to the Constitution in 1913, U.S. senators came to be popularly elected. Women obtained the right to vote when the Nineteenth Amendment was ratified in 1920. Thus within a short time, the electorate changed, the rules changed, and even the stakes of the game changed. Democrats were unable to build a durable winning coalition during this time and remained the minority party until the early 1930s, when the Hoover administration was overwhelmed by the Great Depression.

1932: FRANKLIN ROOSEVELT AND THE NEW DEAL ALIGNMENT   The 1932 election was a turning point in American politics. In the 1930s, the United States faced a devastating economic collapse. Between 1929 and 1932, the gross national product fell over 10 percent per year, and unemployment rose from 1.5 million to more than 15 million, with millions more working only part time. Herbert Hoover and the Republican majority in Congress had responded to the Depression by arguing that the problems with the economy were largely self-correcting and that their long-standing policy of following **laissez-faire economics**, a hands-off approach, was appropriate.

Voters wanted more. Franklin D. Roosevelt and the Democrats were swept into office in 1932 by a tide of anti-Hoover and anti-Republican sentiment. Roosevelt rode this wave and promised that his response to the Depression would be a "New Deal for America." He rejected laissez-faire economics and instead relied on **Keynesian economics**, which asserted that government could influence the direction of the economy through fiscal and monetary policy. After a century of sporadic government action, the New Dealers stepped in and fundamentally altered the relationship between government and society.

The central issue on which the Republicans and Democrats disagreed in the New Deal period was the role of government with respect to the economy. Roosevelt Democrats argued that the government had to take action to pull the country out of the Depression, but Republicans objected to enlarging the scope of government activity and intruding it into the economy. This basic disagreement about whether the national government should play an active role in regulating and promoting our economy remains one of the most important divisions between the Democratic and Republican parties today, although, with time, the country and both parties accepted many of the New Deal programs.

For the two decades following the 1932 election, the Republican party was relegated to watching the majority Democrats—a new coalition of union households, immigrant workers, and people hurt by the Great Depression—implement their domestic policies. During World War II, both parties cooperated in embracing a bipartisan foreign policy.

We have gone a long time since the last critical or realigning election. You will note that each realignment lasted roughly 36 years, or a couple of generations. Some political scientists anticipated that we were ripe for realignment in 1968 or 1972, but it did not happen. A shift in party allegiances among many southern whites, from the Democratic to the Republican party, coincided with the enfranchisement of southern blacks, who largely identify with the Democratic party. But this was more important regionally and did not constitute a national realignment. Now, as memories of the New Deal fade and the agenda of American politics shifts, the alignments of the 1930s and 1940s hold less and less relevance. Yet, to a surprising degree, the parties are stable and closely competitive, as recent elections demonstrated. Whether one party can seize the agenda of politics and fashion itself as the new majority party is one of the interesting political questions for the future.

Divided Government

Major shifts in the demographics of the parties have occurred in recent decades. The once "Solid South" that the Democrats could count on to bolster their legislative majorities and help win the White House has now become the "Solid Republican South" in presidential and increasingly in congressional elections as well. Republican congressional leaders—House Majority Leader Tom DeLay of Texas and Senate Majority Leader Bill Frist of Tennessee—came from states that once rarely elected Republicans. Further evidence of partisan change in the South is the sweep of U.S. Senate victories Republicans had in 2004 in Florida, North Carolina, South Carolina, and Georgia, picking up seats that had been held by Democrats going into the 2004 elections. This shift in the South is explained by the movement of whites out of the Democratic party, largely as a result of the party's position on civil rights. The rise of the Republican South reinforced the shift to conservatism in the Grand Old Party. This shift, combined with the diminished ranks of conservative southern Democrats, made the Democratic party, especially the congressional Democrats, more unified and more liberal than in the days when more of its congressional members had "safe" southern seats.

Since 1953, **divided government**, with one party controlling Congress and the other the White House, has been in effect twice as long as one-party control of both legislative and executive branches, and at other times Congress has had divided control with one party having a majority in the House and the other in the Senate. Until the 1992 and 1994 elections, the Republicans' strength had been in presidential elections, where they often won with landslide margins. Part of the explanation was their ability to attract popular candidates like Dwight Eisenhower and Ronald Reagan, but Republicans also reaped the rewards of Democratic party divisiveness and generally weaker Democratic presidential candidates. Evidence that voters are inclined to favor divided government came in the 1990s, when voters elected a Republican congressional majority in 1994 and then retained it in 1996 and 1998. Building on the Republicans' securing unified party control of government in 2002, the GOP in 2004 expanded its congressional majorities. This was especially the case in 2005 when the Republican majority in the U.S. Senate climbed to 55 Republicans versus 44 Democrats, and 1 Independent.

Republican victories in presidential elections between 1952 and 1992 were achieved with the support of some elements of Roosevelt's New Deal coalition. New Deal programs that benefited these voters had expanded the middle class and made possible the conservative "hold onto what we've got" thinking of voters in the 1980s, 1990s, and 2000. One way to interpret the closeness of the 2000, 2002, and national elections is that the country is evenly divided.

The 2000, 2002 and 2004 Elections: Into the New Century

Neither party could claim a mandate after the tightly contested 2000 elections, which resulted in a 50–50 partisan tie in the Senate, a slim Republican majority in the House, and a presidential contest whose outcome was unresolved for weeks as ballots were recounted in Florida. Although the outcome was essentially a tie, the breakdown of the vote was anything but random. The 2000 presidential results and exit polls revealed a divided nation. Al Gore carried the Northeast and Pacific states and a few urban states in

divided government
Governance divided between the parties, as when one holds the presidency and the other controls one or both houses of Congress.

the nation's midsection. George W. Bush carried the South and interior of the country, minus a few states like New Mexico. Demographically, the Democrats received large majorities of votes from African Americans, Hispanics, union households, Jews, and gays. Republicans did well among white males, religious conservatives, gun owners, and higher-income voters.[39]

The 2002 election departed from historic patterns in several respects. First, the long-standing pattern had been for the party of the president to lose seats in the House of Representatives. Since 1934, in only two elections—1998 and 2002—have the president's party gained seats. In 2002, the Republicans picked up seats in both the House and Senate, returning to the majority in the Senate and expanding their majority in the House. President George W. Bush campaigned aggressively for Republican candidates. In the last five days before the election, President Bush traveled 10,000 miles to 17 cities in 15 states. Bush and his White House political team had been deeply involved in 2002: They recruited some candidates and urged others not to run or to seek other office, they traveled to key districts and states and hosted fundraisers, and they raised party soft money for the competitive races. The net effect was a more Bush-friendly Congress, heightened political credibility, and better reelection chances in 2004. Not everything went the Republicans' way in 2002. Democrats won some key gubernatorial elections, making the number of Democratic and Republican governors nearly equal.

George W. Bush not only secured reelection in 2004 but his party picked up seats in the Senate and House. Most of the open and competitive seats in 2004 were in predictably Republican states in terms of presidential voting, such as Alaska, Oklahoma, and South Dakota. Bush carried all of these states by wide margins. In all of these states, the Senate Republican candidate won, including in South Dakota, where Senate Democratic Leader, Tom Daschle, was defeated by John Thune. Republicans also swept the open Senate seats in Florida, South Carolina, Georgia, and North Carolina. All of these seats were held by Democrats going into 2004. Democrats picked up a Republican Senate seat in 2004 with the election of Ken Salazar. Democrats also picked up a net gain of three state legislative majorities in 2004.

AMERICAN PARTIES TODAY

Americans typically take political parties for granted.[40] If anything, most people are critical or even fearful of the major parties. Parties are, in a word, distrusted. Some see parties as corrupt institutions, interested only in the spoils of politics. Critics charge that the parties evade the issues, they fail to deliver on their promises, they have no new ideas, they follow public opinion rather than lead it, or they are just one more special interest.

Still, Americans understand that parties are necessary. They want party labels kept on the ballot, at least for congressional and presidential elections as well as for statewide offices. Most voters think of themselves as Democrats or Republicans and typically vote for candidates from their party. They even contribute millions of dollars to the two major parties. Far more individual contributions go to the Republicans than to the Democrats.[41] Thus Americans appreciate, at least vaguely, that you cannot run a big democracy without parties.

Both the Democratic and Republican national parties and most state parties are moderate in their policies and leadership.[42] Successful party leaders must be diplomatic; to win presidential elections and congressional majorities, they must find a middle ground among more or less hostile groups. Members of the House of Representatives, in order to be elected and reelected, have to appeal to a majority of the voters from their own district. As more House districts have become "safe" for incumbents, the House of Representatives has become less moderate and the home of partisan ideological clashes to a greater extent than the Senate or the White House.

Although each party usually takes its extremist supporters more or less for granted and seeks out the voters in the middle, both parties retain some ideological diversity. The Democratic coalition includes the conservative Coalition for a Democratic Majority, the moderate Democratic Leadership Council (dominated by an array of southern governors and senators), a new group in 2004 called "Democrats for the West" composed of moderate western Democrats, and the liberal Americans for Democratic Action. The Democratic coalition embraces activists in the civil rights and other liberal-left movements. Republicans, while more homogeneous, have their contentious factions as well. On the more conservative side are the Religious Right, staunch supporters of the right to bear arms, and antitax activists, but also young professionals who are conservative economically but moderate or liberal on social issues like abortion and gay marriage.

As noted in Chapter 5, a gender gap exists in voting in presidential and congressional elections, with women voting Democratic more than men. As political scientist Virginia Sapiro has written, "Women and men may still be socialized to think about politics somewhat differently, or at least some groups of women and men are. The two sexes play different kinds of roles in society and family life and thus have different kinds of experiences."[43] Some interest groups also seek to reinforce the gender gap, emphasizing issues like reproductive rights, gun control, or the environment as they relate to women and often urging women to vote Democratic. Some individual Republican candidates have been successful in narrowing the gender gap.

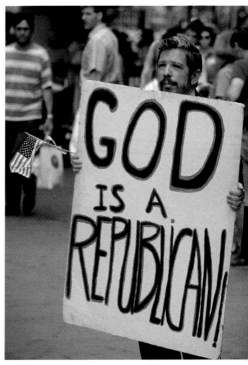

Religion is sometimes linked to partisanship. In reality, devoutly religious people are found in both major parties.

Among Republican elected officials, the split has been between more liberal northeastern Republicans like Senator Lincoln Chafee of Rhode Island and Governor George Pataki of New York and the dominant conservative wing. Democratic officeholders also have substantial policy differences. Examples include a group of U.S. House members who are called "Blue Dog Democrats." The moniker is derived from the old reference to "yellow dog Democrats," a description of party loyalty, where a person would supposedly vote for a yellow dog before voting for a Republican. The "blue dogs" were representatives whose "moderate-to-conservative-views had been 'choked blue' by their party in the years leading up to the 1994 election."[44] Former Georgia Governor and U.S. Senator Zell Miller, also a conservative Democrat, endorsed President George W. Bush and gave an impassioned speech at the 2004 Republican National Convention. He described the Democrats running for president in a *Wall Street Journal* article as indistinguishable. He said, "Look closely, there's not much difference among them. I can't say there's 'not a dime's worth of difference' because there's actually billions of dollars' worth of difference among them. Some want to raise our taxes a trillion, while the others want to raise our taxes by several hundred billion. But, make no mistake, they all want to raise our taxes."[45]

Parties as Institutions

Like other institutions of American government—Congress, the presidency, and the courts—political parties have rules, procedures, and organizational structure. What are the institutional characteristics of political parties?

NATIONAL PARTY LEADERSHIP   The supreme authority in both major parties is the **national party convention,** which meets every four years for four days to nominate candidates for president and vice president, to ratify the party platform, and to adopt rules.

In charge of the national party when it is not assembled in convention is the *national committee.* In recent years, both parties have strengthened the role of the national committee and enhanced the influence of individual committee members. The committees are now more representative of the party rank-and-file. But in neither party is the national committee the center of party leadership.

Each major party has a *national chair* as its top official. The national committee formally elects the chair, but in reality it is the choice of the presidential nominee. For the party that controls the White House, the chair actually serves at the pleasure of the president and does the president's bidding. Party chairs often change after elections. During the 2004 election cycle the Republican National Committee (RNC) Chair was Ed Gillespie. Mr. Gillespie had been an important staff person for House Republicans, was the strategist for the Elizabeth Dole Senate campaign in North Carolina in 2002, and was the Bush spokesperson during the contentious recount in Florida in 2000.[46] He was a visible and frequently cited leader of the Republicans in 2004.

national party convention
A national meeting of delegates elected in primaries, caucuses, or state conventions who assemble once every four years to nominate candidates for president and vice president, ratify the party platform, elect officers, and adopt rules.

2004 Democratic National Committee Chairperson Terry McAuliffe.

Terry McAuliffe, the Democratic National Committee (DNC) Chair, was elected after the Democratic presidential election defeat in 2000. McAuliffe had previously served as Finance Director at both the DNC and the Democratic Congressional Campaign Committee (DCCC), the party committee for House Democratic candidates. McAuliffe chaired the Clinton/Gore reelection committee in 1996 and also chaired the 2000 Democratic National Convention. As the head of a party out of power, he was a visible spokesperson for the Democrats. He also led efforts to rebuild the party headquarters and expand its hard money fundraising base.[47]

The chair of the party without an incumbent president has considerable independence yet works closely with the party's congressional leadership. The national committee often elects a new head after an electoral defeat. Although chairs are the heads of their national party apparatus, they remain largely unknown to the voters. The chair may play a major role in running the national campaign; after the election, the power of the national chair of the victorious party tends to dwindle.

National party organizations are often agents of an incumbent president in securing his renomination. When there is no incumbent president seeking reelection, the national party committee is generally neutral until the nominee is selected. Although heated primary contests often preclude having a united party in the general election, national and state parties can attempt to dissuade candidates but in the end cannot prevent them from running.[48]

In addition to the national party committees, there are also congressional and senatorial *campaign committees*. In recent years, congressional and senatorial campaign committees have become much more active—recruiting candidates, training them, and assisting with campaign finance.[49] Senatorial campaign committees are composed of senators chosen for two-year terms by their fellow party members in the Senate; congressional campaign committees are chosen in the same manner by the House. Chairs of campaign committees are nominated by their party leadership and typically ratified by their party caucus. For information on the party committees and their leadership, go to www.nrcc.org, www.nrsc.org, www.dccc.org, and www.dscc.org. These committees have a lot of say about which candidates get party campaign funds. With the abolition of soft money, the power of the party committees was presumed to lessen. In fact, the party committees continued to be active in competitive races and battleground states through independent expenditures. While this spending did not rival the old soft money, it was substantial in 2004.

PARTY PLATFORMS While national party committees exist primarily to win elections and gain control of government, policy goals are also important. Every four years each party formulates and adopts a platform at the national nominating convention. The typical party platform—the official statement of party policy—is often a vague and ponderous document that hardly anyone reads. Platforms are ambiguous by design, giving voters few obvious reasons to vote against the party. This generalization about party platforms does not mean that political parties do not stand for anything. Most business and professional people believe the Republican party best serves their interests, while working people tend to look to the Democrats to speak for them. The proportion of voters discerning important differences between the parties has increased sharply as the parties have become more polarized (See Figure 7–1).[50]

Many politicians contend that platforms rarely help elect anybody, but platform positions can hurt a presidential candidate. Because the platform-writing process is not always controlled by the nominee, it is possible for presidential candidates to disagree with their own party platform. But the platform-drafting process gives partisans, especially those motivated by particular issues, an opportunity to express their views, and it serves to identify the most important values and principles on which the parties are based. Once elected, politicians are rarely reminded of what their platform position was on a given issue. One major exception to this was former President George Bush's promise not to raise taxes if elected in 1988 with his memorable quote, "Read my lips— no new taxes." He was forced to eat those words when taxes were raised.[51] In reality, the winning party actually seeks to enact much of its party platform.[52]

Party platforms in 2004 were carefully controlled by the Bush and Kerry campaigns. The Republican platform played to the conservative base of the party on such issues as

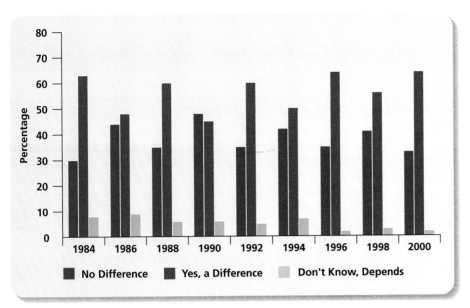

FIGURE 7–1 Important Difference in What Democratic and Republican Parties Stand for, 1984–2000.
SOURCE: *2002 National Election Study,* "Important Difference in What Democratic and Republican Parties Stand for, 1952–2000," (Center for Political Studies, University of Michigan, 2002).

abortion, gay marriage, and taxes. The Democratic platform, like the Democratic convention, sought to reassure the country that the party was strong on national security while also retaining its longstanding commitment to seniors, education, and social justice.

PARTIES AT THE STATE AND LOCAL LEVELS   The two major parties are decentralized, organized around elections in states, cities, or congressional districts. They have organizations for each level of government, national, state, and local. Party organization at the state and local levels is structured much like the national level. Each state has a *state committee* headed by a *state chair.* State law determines the composition of the state committees and sets rules regulating them. Members of state committees are usually elected from local areas. Party auxiliaries such as the Young Democrats or the Federation of Republican Women are sometimes represented as well. In many states, these committees are dominated by governors, senators, or coalitions of locally elected business and ethnic leaders. State chairs are normally elected by the state committees, although in approximately one-quarter of the states they are chosen at state conventions. When the party controls the governorship, chairs are often agents of the governor.[53]

Some powerful state parties have developed in recent years. Despite much state-to-state variation, the trend is toward stronger state organizations, with Republicans typically being much better funded.[54] In some states, third and fourth parties play a role in local elections. New York, for instance, has both a Liberal party and a Conservative party in addition to the Democratic and Republican parties. The role minor parties play in statewide elections can be important, even though they rarely win office themselves.

Below the state committees are *county committees,* which vary widely in function and power. The key role of these committees is recruiting candidates for such offices as county commissioner, sheriff, and treasurer. The recruiting job often involves finding a candidate for the office, not deciding among competing contenders. For a party that rarely wins an election, the county committee has to struggle to find someone willing to run. When the chance of winning is greater, primaries, not the party leaders, usually decide the winner.[55] Many county organizations maintain a significant level of activity, distributing campaign literature, organizing telephone campaigns, putting up posters and lawn signs, and canvassing door-to-door. Other county committees do not function at all, and many party leaders are just figureheads.

Through the 2002 election, state party organizations were the means by which millions of dollars in soft money were spent. Rulings of the Federal Election Commission made it advantageous for national parties to spend their soft money through the state parties. The focus of these expenditures was candidate promotion. In many instances, broadcast ads paid for with soft money did not even mention the party.[56] Soft money was largely banned by the BCRA enacted in 2002.

It is not clear that soft money helped build stronger parties at the state and local levels. Some soft money spending may have enhanced such party activities as building a list of active partisans in the state or district or improving the computer technology of the party offices or may have had secondary benefits when party supporters were mobilized for a U.S. Senate or House race. But for most soft money spending, state parties simply became local bank accounts for national party committee candidate-centered campaign communications. Even after the scores of millions of dollars of soft money spent by party committees, strong local party organization is rare at the city, town, ward, and precinct levels. Most local party committees are poorly financed and inactive except during the few weeks before election day.[57] In a few places, local ward and precinct leaders still do favors for constituents, from getting more police patrols in a neighborhood to organizing clambakes or obtaining horse-racing passes in a state like Arkansas.

What then was the impact of BCRA on party activity in 2004? The Democrats, who were more dependent on soft money and who had been slower to build a large hard money donor base, were the most affected. While their hard money fundraising was more successful than ever, it did not make up for the loss of soft money. Party committees for both parties spent some of their hard money in 2004 as independent expenditures in the relatively few competitive races that existed. What did make up for much of the difference was nonparty groups that raised and spent money on advertising, mail, phones, and voter mobilization. These groups, often called **527 organizations**, after the section of the tax code under which they are organized, were especially active on the Democratic side in 2004. (See Chapter 6 for a fuller disscussion of these and related groups.) Republicans had fewer allied groups campaigning for them, but they also had more hard money, which they deployed on the full range of campaign tactics, especially voter registration and mobilization. The Republican voter mobilization effort in 2002, called the 72 Hour Task Force, built on the successful mobilization effort in 2000.[58] The impact of the soft money ban was even more pronounced for the congressional campaign committees in both parties, but especially for the Democrats.

Parties in Government

Political parties are central to the operation of our government. They help bridge the separation of powers and facilitate coordination between levels of government in a federal system.

IN THE LEGISLATIVE BRANCH   Members of Congress take their partisanship seriously, at least while they are in Washington. Their power and influence are determined by whether their party is in control of the House or Senate; they also have a stake in which party controls the White House. The chairs of all standing committees in Congress come from the majority party, as do the presiding officials of both chambers. Members of both houses sit together with fellow partisans on the floor and in committee.

Members of congressional staffs are also partisan. From the volunteer intern to the senior staffer, members of Congress expect their staff to be loyal first to them and then to their party. Should you decide to go to work for a representative or senator, you would be expected to identify yourself with that person's party, and you would have some difficulty working for the other party later. Employees of the House and Senate—from elevator operators to the Capitol Hill police and even including the chaplain—hold patronage jobs. With few exceptions, such jobs go to persons from the party that has a majority in the House or the Senate.

IN THE EXECUTIVE BRANCH   Presidents select almost all senior White House staff and cabinet members from their own party. Presidents, however, typically surround themselves with advisers who have campaigned with them and have proved their party loyalty.

Partisanship is also important in presidential appointments to the highest levels of the federal bureaucracy. The party that wins the White House has around 5,000 noncareer positions to fill.[59] Included in these positions are cabinet-level appointments and

527 organization
Interest groups organized under Section 527 of the Internal Revenue Service code may advertise for or against candidates. If their source of funding is corporations or unions, they have some restrictions on broadcast advertising. 527 organizations were important in the 2000 and 2004 elections.

PEOPLE & POLITICS *Making a Difference* ★ ★ ★

BLAISE HAZELWOOD

During the highly contested 2004 elections the Republican National Committee (RNC) political director was Blaise Hazelwood. Her involvement in politics began at the age of 10 when she canvassed door-to-door for her father, who was running for precinct committeeman. Her interest in "grassroots" politics continued in the 2000, 2002, and 2004 election cycles, in which she was a leader in organizing the Republican voter mobilization efforts.

Hazelwood's work at the Republican National Committee began soon after she graduated from Vassar College. Ironically, after the 1994 election she and other staff were urged to seek more permanent employment. "Blaise had set her mind to stay at the RNC and began arriving at work at 6:00 A.M. and briefing Anderson (Curt Anderson, the Political Director at the time) on the news and current events. This display of determination convinced Anderson to keep her."[*] Hazelwood has played a variety of roles at the RNC, including Deputy Chief of Staff and

Director of Coalitions for Victory 2000, which included work with pro-life groups, Latinos, Catholics, and many ethnic American groups.

Republicans came out of the 2000 election feeling a need to counteract the Democrats' voter mobilization strategy. Hazelwood has been instrumental in that effort. She and others organized the "72 Hour Task Force" in 2002 and 2004. This effort deployed large numbers of people, including what Hazelwood calls "paid volunteers," into key districts. Hazelwood described her approach as "fewer leaflets and more volunteers."[†] These individuals delivered person-to-person contact in the critical final phases of the 2002 and 2004 elections. In some areas the task force increased voter turnout by 2 to 3 percent.[†] According to her husband and direct mail consultant, Dan Hazelwood, "Blaise brought back the culture of grassroots campaigns into the Republican party making grassroots campaigns as important as TV, mail, and phone."[§] The Republican

ground game was widely seen as having been important to the reelection of President Bush in 2004.

[*] Dan Balz, "Getting the Votes—And the Kudos: Hazelwood Helped GOP to Victory with an Emphasis on Shoe Leather." *Washington Post,* January, 1 2003, p. A17.

[†] www.abcnews.go.com/sections/politics/TheNote/TheNote_July25.html.

[‡] Dan Balz and David S. Broder, "Close Election Turns on Voter Turnout," *The Washington Post,* November 1, 2002, page A01.

[§] Dan Hazelwood, phone interview by David Magleby, August 3, 2004.

ambassadorships around the world. Party commitment, including making campaign contributions, is expected of those who seek these positions.

IN THE JUDICIAL BRANCH   The judicial branch of the national government, with its lifetime tenure and political independence, is designed to operate in an expressly non-partisan manner. Judges, unlike Congress, do not sit together by political party. But the appointment process for judges has been partisan from the beginning. The landmark case establishing the principle of judicial review, *Marbury* v. *Madison* (1803), concerned the efforts of one party to stack the judiciary with fellow partisans before leaving office.[60] Today party identification remains an important consideration in the naming of federal judges. Although the party affiliation of a judicial nominee is not called for on any form, the individuals responsible for screening and evaluating candidates do take party and ideology into account. Appointees must be acceptable to certain power centers in the party. For example, Republicans in the Ronald Reagan and George Bush administrations insisted on conservative judges; Bill Clinton, although nominating Democrats, placed more importance on gender and race than on ideology in selecting judges. The confirmation process has also become increasingly partisan. Republicans claimed that Democrats were delaying hearings for George W. Bush's judicial nominees, and Democrats countered that they were responding in kind to what Republicans did to Clinton nominees when the GOP controlled the Senate.

AT THE STATE AND LOCAL LEVELS   The importance of party in the operation of local government varies among states and localities. In some states, such as New York and Illinois, local parties play an even stronger role than they do at the national level. In others, such as Nebraska, parties play almost no role. In Nebraska, the state legislature is expressly nonpartisan, though factions perform like parties and still play a role. Parties are likewise unimportant in the government of most city councils. But in most states and many cities, parties are important to the operation of the legislature, governorship, or mayoralty. Judicial selection in most states is also a partisan matter. Much was made by the 2000 Bush campaign of the fact that six of the seven Florida Supreme Court justices deciding the 2000 ballot-counting case in favor of Gore were Democrats. Democrats noted that the five U.S. Supreme Court justices who decided the election in favor of Bush were Republicans.

Parties in the Electorate

Political parties would be of little significance if they did not have meaning to the electorate. Adherents of the two parties are drawn to them by a combination of factors, including their stand on the issues; personal or party history; religious, racial, or social peer grouping; and the appeal of their candidates. The emphases among these factors change over time, but they are remarkably consistent with those identified by political scientists more than 40 years ago.[61]

PARTY REGISTRATION   For citizens in most states, "party" has a particular legal meaning—**party registration**. At the time voters register to vote in these states, they are asked to state their party preference. They then become registered Democrats, Republicans, Libertarians, or whatever. Voters can subsequently change their party registration. The purpose of party registration is to limit the participants in primary elections to members of that party and to make it easier for parties to contact people who might vote for their party.

PARTY ACTIVISTS   Activists tend to fall into three broad categories: party regulars, candidate activists, and issue activists. *Party regulars* place the party first. They value winning elections and understand that compromise and moderation may be necessary to reach that objective. They also realize that it is important to keep the party together as much as possible, because a fractured party only helps the opposition.

Candidate activists are followers of a particular candidate who see the party as the means to place their candidate in power. Candidate activists are often not concerned with the other operations of the party—with nominees for other offices or with raising money for the party. For example, people who supported Pat Buchanan in his unsuccessful run for the presidency as a Reform party candidate in 2000 would be classified as candidate activists. Buchanan, a television commentator and unsuccessful candidate for the Republican nomination in 1996, built a personal following. Reform party members who traced their roots in the party to Ross Perot found Buchanan so repellent that they split from him and nominated their own candidate for president. Buchanan fared poorly in the 2000 election, getting less than 1 percent of the vote and as a result losing millions of dollars in federal subsidies for the 2004 elections.

Issue activists wish to push the parties in a particular direction on a single issue or a narrow range of issues: the war in Iraq, abortion, taxes, school prayer, the environment, or civil rights. To issue activists, the party platform is an important battleground because they seek party endorsement for their position. Issue activists are also often candidate activists if they can find a candidate willing to embrace their position.

Both issue activists and candidate activists insist on making their "statement" regardless of the electoral consequences. They would rather lose the election than compromise. Party activists thus include a diverse group of people who come to the political party with different objectives. It is not surprising, then, that some of the most interesting politics are over candidate selection and issue positions within the political parties. Fights over strategy and party position are conducted in open meetings and under democratic procedures. Political parties foster democracy not only by competition *between* the parties but *within* the parties as well.

party registration
The act of declaring party affiliation; required by some states when one registers to vote.

CHANGING FACE OF AMERICAN POLITICS

PORTRAIT OF THE ELECTORATE

	Republican	Democrat	Independent	Other
Sex				
Male	32%	32%	32%	4%
Female	31	35	26	7
Race				
White	36	29	30	6
Black	7	70	20	3
Hispanic	23	38	35	4
Age				
18–34	30	32	32	6
35–45	37	30	25	7
46–55	28	36	30	6
56–64	29	36	31	4
65+	32	37	27	5
Income				
$0–$14,999	20	47	27	10
$15,000–$34,999	25	41	30	17
$35,000–$49,999	29	31	33	17
$50,000–$64,999	35	31	28	12
$65,000–$84,999	36	30	26	25
$84,999+	40	27	29	16
Religion				
Protestant	46	29	22	3
Catholic	30	37	31	2
None/Atheist/Agnostic	13	38	38	13
Other/Jewish	19	40	28	13
Ideology				
Liberal	9	55	30	5
Moderate	20	35	20	5
Conservative	48	20	28	4
Region				
Northeast	30	34	33	3
North-Central	33	33	27	7
South	32	35	28	5
West	32	32	29	8
Total	31	33	28	7

SOURCE: *2002 National Election Study* (Center for Political Studies, University of Michigan, 2002). *Note: Numbers may not add up to 100 due to rounding.*

Party Identification

Party registration and party activists are important, but many voters are not officially registered with a political party. Most Americans are mere spectators of party activity. They lack the partisan commitment and interest needed for active party involvement. This is not to say that parties are irrelevant or unimportant to them. For them, partisanship is

"Very Republican. I love it."

what political scientists call **party identification**—an informal and psychological attachment with a political party that most people acquire in childhood, a standing preference for one party over another.[62] This type of voter may sometimes vote for a candidate from the other party, but in the absence of a compelling reason to do otherwise, most will vote according to their party identification. Peers and early political experiences reinforce party identification, generally acquired from parents. It is part of the political socialization process described in Chapter 4.

Party identification is the single best predictor of how people will vote. Unlike candidates and issues, which come and go, party identification is a long-term element in voting choice. The strength of party identification is also important in predicting participation and political interest. Strong Republicans and strong Democrats participate more actively in politics than any other groups and are generally more knowledgeable and informed. Pure Independents are just the opposite; they vote at the lowest rates and have the lowest levels of interest and awareness of any of the categories of party identification. This evidence runs counter to the notion that persons who are strong partisans are unthinking party adherents.[63]

Partisan Realignment and Dealignment

With the exception of the shift of southern whites to the Republican party and the enfranchisement of blacks who remain Democrats, the current system of party identification is built on a foundation of the New Deal and the critical election of 1932, events that took place nearly three-quarters of a century ago. How can events so removed from the present still be important in shaping our party system? When will there be another realignment—an election that dramatically changes the voters' partisan identification? Or has such a realignment already occurred? The question is frequently debated in the literature of political science. Most scholars believe that we have not experienced a major realignment since 1932.[64] Partisan identification has been stable for more than four decades, and even though new voters have been added to the electorate—minorities and 18- to 21-year-olds—the basic nature of the party system has trended slightly Republican but not changed dramatically. Table 7–2 presents the party identification breakdown for the period from the 1950s to 2002.

Evidence of a possible voting realignment came in the early 1980s, when Republicans won several close Senate elections and gained a majority in that body.[65] Democrats, however, won back the Senate in 1986, and until 1994 they appeared to have a permanent majority in the House. All that changed with the 1994 election, as Republicans were swept into office on a tidal wave of victories. Republicans made major inroads in the South and strengthened their share of the vote among white males.

In presidential voting, Republicans have done well, winning seven of the last ten presidential elections. Their success ratio masks a much more evenly divided electorate. Indeed, in recent years, the country has been evenly divided in partisan preferences. Democrats would also be quick to point out that their party won the popular vote in 2000, only reinforcing the point that the country is evenly divided. Why have the Republicans done better than Democrats in winning presidential elections? The answer is that they have been more effective in activating their core supporters and those few undecided voters in recent elections. Republicans also have a larger set of states they can predictably count on, forcing Democrats to win most of the populous states, which are often more competitive. The fact that Republicans have won more than they have lost in the last forty years is not yet an indication of a realignment toward the GOP.

We may therefore conclude from recent national elections that American voters overall have no consistent preference for one party over the other. In a time of such electoral volatility and low turnout, the winners and losers are determined by the basics of politics: who attracts positive voter attention, who strikes themes that motivate voters to participate, who does a better job in communicating with voters. Party identification remains important for those voters who come out to vote, and strength of partisanship remains positively correlated with turnout.

party identification
An informal and subjective affiliation with a political party that most people acquire in childhood.

TABLE 7–2 PARTY IDENTIFICATION, 1950s–2002

Decade	Strong Democrat	Weak Democrat	Independent-Leaning Democrat	Independent	Independent-Leaning Republican	Weak Republican	Strong Republican	Apolitical
1950s*	23%	23%	8%	7%	7%	15%	13%	4%
1960s	22	25	8	10	7	15	12	2
1970s	17	24	12	14	10	14	9	2
1980s	18	26	11	12	11	14	11	2
1990s	18	19	13	10	12	15	13	1
2000s	18	16	14	9	13	14	15	1

SOURCE: *2000 and 2002 National Election Study* (Center for Political Studies, University of Michigan, 2002).

NOTE: Data may not sum to 100 percent due to averaging.

*1950s percentages based on years 1952, 1956, and 1958.

Thus there are few signs of voter realignment but stronger signs of voter disengagement. Some observers feel that we are experiencing a rejection of partisanship in favor of becoming Independents, and there has indeed been an increase in the number of persons who characterize themselves as Independents. Journalist Hedrick Smith expresses a widespread view: "The most important phenomenon of American politics in the past quarter century has been the rise of independent voters, who have at times outnumbered Republicans."[66]

The **dealignment** argument—that people have abandoned both parties to become Independents—would be more persuasive were it not that two-thirds of all self-identified Independents are really partisans in their voting behavior and attitudes. One-third of those who claim to be Independents lean toward the Democratic party and vote Democratic in election after election. Another third of Independents lean toward Republicans and just as predictably vote Republican. The remaining third, who appear to be genuine Independents and who do not vote predictably for one party, turn out to be people with little interest in politics. Despite the reported growth in Independents, there are proportionately about the same number of Pure Independents now as there were in 1956.[67] There are, in short, at least three types of Independents, and most of them are predictably partisan. Table 7–3 summarizes voting behavior in recent contests for president and the House of Representatives.

Why has realignment moved so slowly? Why aren't all conservatives now happily ensconced in the Republican party and all liberals gladly lodged in the Democratic party?

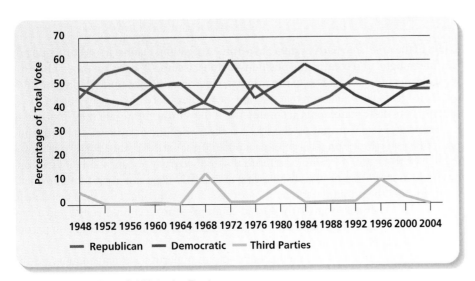

FIGURE 7–2 Presidential Vote by Party.
SOURCE: Data obtained from CQ Voting and Elections Collections, at library.cqpress.com/elections/.

dealignment
Weakening of partisan preferences that points to a rejection of both major parties and a rise in the number of Independents.

HOW PARTY IDENTIFICATION IS MEASURED

Party identification is commonly measured by political scientists and political pollsters using the answers to the following questions:

- Generally speaking, in politics do you usually think of yourself as a Republican, a Democrat, an Independent, or what?

Persons who answer Republican or Democrat to this question are then asked:

- Would you call yourself a strong or a not very strong Republican/Democrat?

Persons who answered Independent to the first question are asked this follow-up question:

- Do you think of yourself as closer to the Republican or the Democratic party?

Persons who do not indicate Democrat, Republican, or Independent to the first question rarely exceed 2 percent of the electorate and include those who are apolitical or who identify with one of the minor political parties. Because of their consistently small numbers, they are typically not important to election outcomes. In a close race, like the 2000 presidential contest, Green party supporters became an important target for both Al Gore and Ralph Nader.

The party identification questions produce seven categories of persons: strong Democrats, weak Democrats, Independent-leaning Democrats, Pure Independents, Independent-leaning Republicans, weak Republicans, and strong Republicans. Over the nearly 50-year period during which political scientists have been conducting such surveys, the partisan preferences of the American public have remained remarkably stable.

TABLE 7–3 VOTING BEHAVIOR OF PARTISANS AND INDEPENDENTS, 1992–2002

| | *Percent Voting Democratic* | | | | | | | |
| | President | | | U.S. House | | | | |
	1992	1996	2000	1994	1996	1998	2000	2002
Strong Democrats	93%	96%	97$	88%	87%	77%	90%	89%
Weak Democrats	68	82	89	73	70	57	73	71
Independent-leaning Democrats	70	76	72	68	69	63	73	67
Pure Independents	41	35	44	55	41	41	50	35
Independent-learning Republicans	11	20	13	25	21	24	26	27
Weak Republicans	14	20	14	21	21	25	18	25
Strong Republicans	3	5	2	7	3	7	12	8

SOURCE: *2002 National Election Study* (Center for Political Studies, University of Michigan, 2002).

Americans do not casually cross party lines. If you grew up in a conservative New Hampshire family whose forebears voted Republican for a century, you are pretty much conditioned to stay with the GOP. Even if that party took a direction you disliked, you might continue to register as a Republican but quietly vote Democratic to avoid friction in the family. Or if you come from a "yellow dog" Democratic family in Texas, you might continue to vote for Democrats locally even though you disliked various Democratic candidates for president or senator. This pattern was once common throughout the South.[68]

Another reason for slow realignment is the local nature of the parties. For decades, conservative Democrats in the South have been voting for Republican candidates for president—not just George W. Bush and Ronald Reagan but also Richard Nixon and even Dwight Eisenhower—without changing their identification from the Democratic Party to the Republican.[69] Why? Partly because they still see themselves as Democrats, but also because the Democratic party remains stronger at the state and local levels in many southern states. So if candidates and voters want to have an impact on local politics, in which the only meaningful elections may be in the Democratic primaries, they retain their Democratic affiliation.

ARE THE POLITICAL PARTIES DYING?

Critics of the American party system make three allegations against it: (1) parties do not take meaningful and contrasting positions on most issues, (2) party membership is essentially meaningless, and (3) parties are so concerned with accommodating the middle of the ideological spectrum that they are incapable of serving as an avenue for social progress. Are these statements accurate? And if they are accurate, are they important?

Some analysts fear that parties are in a severe decline or even mortally ill. They point first to the long-run adverse impact on political parties of the Progressive movement reforms early in this century, reforms that robbed party organizations of their control of the nomination process by allowing masses of independent and "uninformed" voters to enter the primaries and nominate candidates who might not be acceptable to party leaders. They also point to the spread of nonpartisan elections in cities and towns and the staggering of national, state, and local elections that made it harder for parties to influence the election process.

Legislation limiting the viability and functions of parties was bad enough, say the party pessimists, but parties suffer from additional ills. The rise of television and electronic technology and the parallel increase in the number of campaign, media, and direct-mail consultants have made parties less relevant in educating, mobilizing, and organizing the electorate. Television, radio, the Internet, and telephones have strengthened the role of candidates and lessened the importance of parties. (See Chapter 10 for more on the media in this role.)

Advocates of strong parties concede that parts of this diagnosis may be correct: the demise of political machines at the local level, the decline in strong partisan affiliations, the weakness of grassroots party membership. Yet they also see signs of party revival, or at least the persistence of party. The national party organizations—the national committees and the congressional and senatorial campaign committees—are significantly better funded than they were in earlier days; they even own permanent, modern headquarters buildings in Washington, D.C., located a few blocks from the U.S. Capitol. Moreover, the parties through 2002 were capable of providing assistance to candidates in competitive races and to state and local party organizations because of their financial base, especially from soft money contributions. However, the new campaign finance reforms will likely lessen party activity. Advocates hope that strong national parties will exercise some leverage over the positions that candidates and officeholders take on party issues.[70]

Since the first years of the Reagan administration, both the Republican and Democratic parties have demonstrated a remarkable cohesiveness in Congress. This trend can be measured by the *party unity score,* defined as the percentage of members of a party who vote together on roll call votes in Congress on which a majority of the members of one party vote against a majority of the members of the other party. During the 107th Congress (2001), House and Senate Republicans voted together 90 percent of the time. Democrats were only slightly less united at 85 percent, tying their previous unity record.[71] These numbers demonstrate the growing partisanship within the two chambers. Thus while rank-and-file voters do not display strong partisan ties, party organizations and the party in government do show significant signs of strength.[72]

Reform Among the Democrats

In Chicago in 1968, the Democratic National Convention saw disputes inside the hall and riots outside, largely because of protests against the country's policy in Vietnam. Responding to the disarray and to disputes about the fairness of delegate selection procedures, members of the party agreed to a number of reforms. They established a process that led to greater use of direct primaries for the selection of delegates to the national convention and greater representation of younger voters, women, and minorities as elected delegates. Another reform was the abolition of the rule that a winner of a state's convention or primaries got all the state's delegates (the *unit rule*). This rule was replaced by a system of *proportionality* in which candidates won delegates in rough proportion to the votes they received in the primary election or convention in each state.

Chicago's former mayor Richard J. Daley, father of the current mayor of Chicago, and many other party stalwarts argued that these reforms would make the party reflective of the views of minorities within the party, such as college professors and intellectuals who would have time and resources to invest in the political process, and not working-class people, unionists, the elderly, and elected officials who depend more on group leaders to make their case. The new process also meant that elected officials who wanted a voice in determining presidential candidates had to run for delegate to the national convention. Responding to this criticism, the party created "superdelegate" positions for elected officials and party leaders who were not required to run for election as delegates.

Reform Among the Republicans

Republicans have not been immune to criticism that their party conventions and party procedures were keeping out the rank-and-file. They did not make changes as drastic as those made by the Democrats, but they did give the national committee more control over presidential campaigns, and state parties were urged to encourage broader participation by all groups, including women, minorities, youth, and the poor.

The Republican party has long had a party organization superior to that of the Democrats. In the 1970s, the GOP emphasized grassroots organization and membership recruitment. Seminars were held to teach Republican candidates how to make speeches and hold press conferences, and weekend conferences were organized for training young party professionals. The Democrats have become better organized and more professional. Both parties now conduct training sessions for candidates on campaign planning, advertising, fund raising, using phone banks, recruiting volunteers, and campaign scheduling.[73] But Republicans have cultivated a larger donor base and have been less reliant on the large-donor soft money contributions that became so controversial in recent elections.

Campaign Finance Reform and Political Parties

Following the 1976 election, both parties pressed for amendments to the Federal Election Campaign Act, claiming that campaign finance reforms resulted in insufficient money for generic party activities like billboard advertising and get-out-the-vote drives. The 1979 amendments to the act and the interpretations of this legislation by the Federal Election Commission permitted unlimited contributions to the parties by individuals and PACs for these party-building purposes. Corporations and unions could also give the parties soft money from their general funds, something they could not do in support of candidates or other party activities. With the 1996 election cycle, both parties found ways to spend this soft money in unlimited amounts to promote the election or defeat of specific candidates, effectively circumventing the campaign finance reform rules.[74]

In the 1998, 2000, and 2002 elections, congressional campaign committees, following the lead of the national party committees in the 1996 presidential election, raised unprecedented amounts of soft money. In 2000 all party committes combined raised $500 million in soft money, a figure equaled in 2002, a year without a presidential election. Soft money was spent in the most competitive races where it could help determine which party controlled Congress or the most competitive states in the 1996 and 2000 contests for the White House. This is why banning soft money became such a dedicated cause for Arizona Senator John McCain, a cosponsor of the McCain-Feingold campaign finance reform legislation. McCain, who beat George W. Bush in the New Hampshire presidential primary, in part on the basis of his challenging the party establishment on soft money, eventually lost to Bush in the 2000 nomination fight. Despite repeated defeats in one or both houses of Congress over 15 years, Congress passed the BCRA in 2002. Table 7–4 shows the effects of BCRA on the parties.

What were the implications of this surge in soft money in presidential and congressional elections? First, because soft money contributions were unlimited, the priority given to raising soft money elevated the importance of large contributors. Parties came to rely heavily on these large donors. Among the largest soft money donors to the Democrats were the Affiliated Federal State County and Municipal Employees (AFSCME), the Service Employees International Union, and the Communications Workers of America. The largest Republican soft money donors were Phillip Morris and AT&T.

Central to the arguments for BCRA was the contention that the ability of individuals and groups to donate unlimited amounts of money to the parties gives these donors extraordinary access to and influence over elected officials. Since party leaders often were the ones asking for the unlimited soft money contributions, the potential for corruption was cited by a majority of the Supreme Court as justification to uphold the 2002 BCRA legislation. The Court majority noted, "there is substantial evidence in these cases to support Congress' determination that such contributions of soft money give rise to corruption and the appearance of corruption. For instance, the record is replete with examples of national party committees' peddling access to federal candidates and officeholders in exchange for large soft-money donations."[75]

One uncertainty following BCRA was whether soft money donors would attempt to find another way to spend money on electing or defeating candidates. Some donors abandoned large donations altogether, instead making the limited and disclosed PAC or individual contributions. As we noted in Chapter 6, 2004 saw growth in PAC contributions. Other donors and some new contributors, however, pursued an alternative way to spend unlimited sums on the 2004 elections. As we have seen, they typically did this through groups formed under Section 527 of the tax code or other groups, which allowed

TABLE 7–4 EFFECTS OF THE 2002 CAMPAIGN FINANCE REFORMS

	Before 2002 Reform	After 2002 Reform
Party contributions to candidates	$5,000 per election or $10,000 per election cycle	National Party Committees are limited to $5,000 per election, although there are special limits for Senate candidates. National committees and Senate campaign committees share a contribution limit of $35,000 per campaign.
Party-coordinated expenditures with candidates	*Senate:* State voting age population times 2 cents, multiplied by the cost-of-living adjustment (COLA), or $20,000 multiplied by the COLA, whichever is greater *House:* $10,000 multiplied by the COLA; if only one representative in the state, same as the Senate limit	*Senate:* State voting age population times 7.462 cents, multiplied by the COLA, or $74,620 multiplied by the COLA, whichever is greater. *House:* $37,310 multiplied by the COLA; if only one representative in the state, the spending limit for the House nominee is $74,620, the same as the Senate limit.
Party soft money contributions to the national party committee	Unlimited	Banned
Soft money to national or state and local parties for voter registration and get-out-the-vote drives	Unlimited	Limit of $10,000 per group to each state or local party committee (Levin Amendment)
Contributions to parties for buildings	Unlimited	Banned
Party-independent expenditures	Unlimited	Unlimited, except if ad falls under "electioneering communications definition." Then source of funding is subject to FECA regulations and limits, and the ad may not be broadcast within 30 days of a primary or 60 days of a general election. Parties may choose either independent expenditures or coordinated but not both.
Individual contributions to candidates per two-year election cycle	$2,000	$4,000
Aggregate individual contribution limit to candidate or parties per two-year election cycle	$50,000	$95,000

SOURCE: www.fec.gov/pages/bcra/bcra_update.htm.

Senators John McCain (left) and Russ Feingold (right) hold a news conference to announce Senate approval of the McCain-Feingold Campaign Finance bill, aimed at reducing the influence of soft money on political campaigns.

THE POLITICAL HORIZON

This simulation examines party ideologies and the changes that have occurred in America's political parties. People affiliate with a party in part because of their stands on particular issues. Based on your beliefs and opinions, find out with which political party you agree most.

Go to Make It Real, "The Political Horizon."

them to spend unlimited amounts on voter registration, mobilization, mail and phone communications, and in the period prior to the two months before the general election or one month before the primary election to run ads on television. Section 527 group activity was more pronounced on the Democratic side of the 2004 election. Democratic 527 groups like the Media Fund and MoveOn advertised heavily against President Bush, especially in the period between March and September 2004. Republican groups like Swift Boat Veterans for Truth and Progress for America advertised later but were highly visible. Other groups like America Coming Together (ACT) were geared toward voter registration and mobilization of Democratic voters. Although these outside groups were more important to the Democratic effort, in the end they were important to both sides. A lot of the funding for these groups came from wealthy individuals.

Critics of BCRA had long contended that banning soft money would drive soft money to groups with less disclosure of their activity. It was clearly the case in 2004 that following Section 527 group activity was more difficult than following soft money had been in the past. Voters tend to assume that candidates are responsible for all communications in their election contests. Whether it made much difference to them if an ad was from the Ohio Democratic Party or America Coming Together is doubtful. In both cases they would have assumed that the Democratic candidate was responsible.[76]

It is unclear whether soft money had a positive effect on the parties. In competitive contests, parties have become major players, mounting their own campaigns, often against the other party's candidate. Most party spending has been on ads placed on television and radio, sent through the mail, or delivered over the telephone. To a lesser extent, parties have worked to register voters and mobilize them on election day. This latter type of activity is the only one to have an enduring effect on state and local parties. BCRA provides for limited contributions to state and local party committees; individuals and groups may donate up to $10,000 per party committee. This provision has the potential to encourage parties to continue to invest in mobilizing voters.

While the particular role parties play in financing elections may be changing, the broader roles of organizing electoral competition, simplifying voter choices, and providing an enduring psychological identification for voters have not changed. Parties are also remarkably permeable organizations that provide citizens who want to influence the course of their government an accessible and often consequential way to get involved. Finally, parties continue to reinforce federalism through the distinctive nature of many state parties.

S U M M A R Y

1. Political parties are essential to democracy—they simplify voting choices, organize the competition, unify the electorate, help organize government by bridging the separation of powers and fostering cooperation among branches of government, translate public preferences into policy, and provide loyal opposition.

2. Political parties help structure voting choice by nominating candidates to run for office. Before the advent of direct primaries, in which voters determine the party nominees, the parties had more control over who ran under their label. States determine the nomination rules. While most states employ the direct primary, some use a caucus or mixed caucus system where more committed partisans have a larger role in the decision of who gets nominated. Recently,

some states adopted a blanket primary in which voters could vote for a candidate from any party. These primaries were declared unconstitutional.

3. American parties are moderate. Bringing factions and interests together, they are broad enough to win the presidency and other elections. Third parties have been notably less successful. One reason for this is our single-member-district, winner-take-all election rules. In systems with proportional representation or multimember districts, there is a greater tendency for more parties to form and consequently a need to assemble governing coalitions of several parties.

4. American parties have experienced critical elections and realignments. Most political scientists agree that the last realignment occurred in 1932. In recent years, there has been divided government

and an increase in the number of persons who call themselves Independents. This trend is sometimes called dealignment, but most Independents are closet partisans who vote fairly consistently for the party toward which they lean.

5. For half a century, it has been routine to have divided government, with one party in control of the presidency and the other in control of one or both houses of Congress. Successful presidents have found ways to cope with divided government and enact important parts of their agenda. The 2002 election gave Republicans unified government with control of both houses of Congress and the White House. Republican control of national government was strengthened by the 2004 elections.

6. Parties are governed by their national and state committees, and the focal points of

party organization are the national and state party chairs. When the party controls the executive branch of government, the executive (governor or president) usually has a determining say in selecting the party chair. With the rise of soft money in recent elections, parties had more resources to spend on politics. In 2002, Congress banned soft money except for some narrowly defined and limited activities.

7. Party platforms are vague and general by design, giving the other party and voters little to oppose.

8. Parties are vital in the operation of government. They are organized around elected offices at the state and local levels. Congress is also organized around parties, and judicial and many executive branch appointments are based in large part on partisanship.

9. Parties are also active in the electorate, seeking to organize elections, simplify voting choices, and strengthen party identification.

10. Frequent efforts have been made to reform our parties. The Progressive movement saw parties, as then organized, as an impediment to democracy and pushed direct primaries as a means to reform them. Following the 1968 election, the Democratic party took the lead in pushing primaries and stressing greater diversity among the individuals elected as delegates. Republicans have also encouraged broader participation, and they have improved their party structure and finances.

11. The Bipartisan Campaign Reform Act (BCRA) significantly changed the role of party committees by banning soft money and raising hard money contribution limits to the parties. One consequence of BCRA was a renewed emphasis on building a large individual donor base. Donors wanting to spend more than the BCRA limits did so in 2004 through a range of interest groups, many of which were allied 527 groups that ran parallel campaigns with the candidates and parties in 2004.

12. Compared to some European parties, ours remain organizationally weak. There has been some party renewal in recent years as party competition has grown in the South and the parties themselves have initiated reforms.

K E Y   T E R M S

political party	honeymoon	winner-take-all system	divided government
party column ballot	caucus	minor party	national party convention
office block ballot	party convention	Libertarian party	party registration
nonpartisan election	direct primary	Green party	party identification
patronage	open primary	Reform party	dealignment
soft money	crossover voting	realigning election	527 organization
hard money	closed primary	laissez-faire economics	
independent expenditures	proportional representation	Keynesian economics	

F U R T H E R   R E A D I N G

JOHN H. ALDRICH, *Why Parties? The Origin and Transformation of Party Politics in America* (University of Chicago Press, 1995).

PAUL ALLEN BECK AND MARJORIE RANDON HERSHEY, *Party Politics in America*, 10th ed. (Longman, 2002).

JOHN F. BIBBY *Politics, Parties, and Elections in America*, 5th ed. (Wadsworth, 2002).

DAVID BOAZ, *Libertarianism: A Primer* (Free Press, 1998).

MARY C. BRENNAN, *Turning Right in the Sixties: The Conservative Capture of the GOP* (University of North Carolina Press, 1995).

BRUCE E. CAIN AND ELISABETH R. GERBER, EDS., *Voting at the Political Fault Line: California's Experiment with the Blanket Primary* (University of California Press, 2002).

LEON EPSTEIN, *Political Parties in the American Mold* (University of Wisconsin Press, 1986).

DONALD GREEN, BRADLEY PALMQUIST, AND ERIC SCHICKLER, *Partisan Hearts and Minds* (Yale University Press, 2002).

JOHN C. GREEN AND RICK FARMER, EDS., *The State of the Parties: The Changing Role of Contemporary American Parties*, 4th ed. (Rowman & Littlefield, 2003).

JOHN C. GREEN AND PAUL S. HERRNSON, EDS., *Responsible Partisanship?: The Evolution of American Political Parties Since 1950* (University Press of Kansas, 2002).

PAUL S. HERRNSON AND JOHN C. GREEN, EDS., *Multiparty Politics in America: Prospects and Performance*, 2d ed. (Rowman & Littlefield, 2002).

WILLIAM J. KEEFE AND MARC J. HETHERINGTON, *Parties, Politics, and Public Policy in America*, 9th ed. (Congressional Quarterly Press, 2003).

BRUCE E. KEITH, DAVID B. MAGLEBY, CANDICE J. NELSON, ELIZABETH ORR, MARK C. WESTLYE, AND RAYMOND E. WOLFINGER, *The Myth of the Independent Voter* (University of California Press, 1992).

DAVID B. MAGLEBY, ED., *Financing the 2000 Election* (Brookings Institution Press, 2002).

DAVID B. MAGLEBY AND J. QUIN MONSON, EDS., *The Last Hurrah? Soft Money and Issue Advocacy in the 2002 Congressional Electons* (Brookings Institution Press, 2004).

L. SANDY MAISEL AND KARA Z. BUCKLEY *The Electoral Process*, 4th ed. (Rowman & Littlefield, 2005).

KELLY D. PATTERSON, *Political Parties and the Maintenance of Liberal Democracy* (Columbia University Press, 1996).

STEVEN J. ROSENSTONE, ROY L. BEHR, AND EDWARD H. LAZARUS, *Third Parties in America: Citizen Response to Major Party Failure*, 2d ed. (Princeton University Press, 1996).

JEFFREY M. STONECASH, MARK D. BREWER, AND MACK D. MARIANI, *Diverging Parties: Social Change, Realignment, and Party Polarization* (Westview Press, 2003).

JAMES SUNDQUIST, *Dynamics of the Party System: Alignment and Realignment of Political Parties in the United States*, rev. ed. (Brookings Institution Press, 1983).

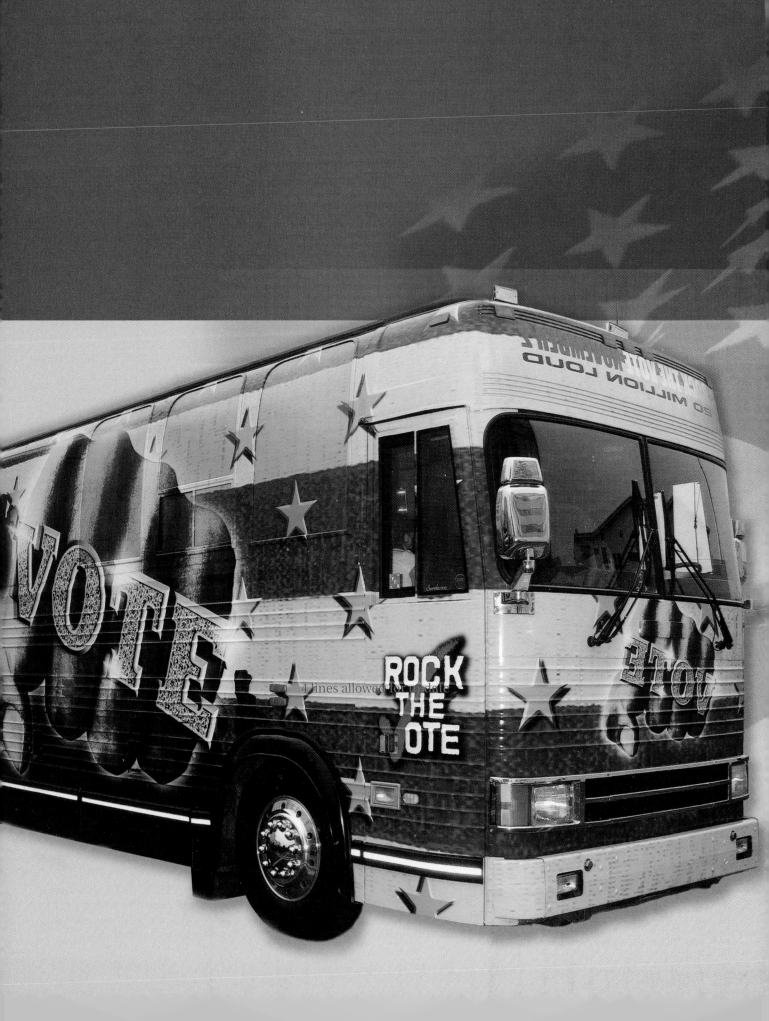

PUBLIC OPINION, PARTICIPATION, AND VOTING

8

Undecided or "swing voters" received a lot of attention in competitive states in the 2004 presidential election. In June 2004, well before either party held its nominating convention, the proportion of undecided voters was very small compared to the same time period in earlier elections, with fewer than one-in-ten voters undecided.[1] The closeness of the 2000 presidential election in states like Florida and New Mexico reinforced the urgency of finding and converting undecided voters in 2004. Undecided voters in competitive states were courted by both sides, receiving multiple campaign communications. The 2004 election cycle saw a renewed emphasis on person-to-person contact and also targeted communications through the mail and on the telephone. In the battleground states, undecided voters received many communications about the election, often from both sides. Groups and parties were also part of this "ground war." Part of the 2004 effort included registering new voters. Republicans also concentrated on activating voters who had infrequently voted in the past. The result was a much higher turnout, especially in the competitive states, with some voters standing in line for two or more hours waiting to vote.

In a nation as evenly divided as the United States is now, candidates must also effectively mobilize their most loyal supporters, or what is often called the "base." To do this they reaffirm their support for issues or groups that matter to the base. President Bush did this by supporting a constitutional amendment defining marriage as between a man and a woman. He also committed himself to further budget and tax cuts. John Kerry had an unusually unified base, in part because four years out of power motivated

Democratic voters to unify in hopes of winning. Kerry also sent clear signals to blacks, Hispanics, union members, people who are pro-choice on abortion, and others that he was the better candidate for them.

At the individual level, likely voters in states where the outcome was close and who had already made up their minds were bombarded with postcards reminding them to vote and phone calls reminding them that it was election day and that their vote was needed. For example, in 2004, the candidates and parties mobilized voters to vote early in states where that was possible. This effort, sometimes called "banking the vote," reduced the list of people the campaigns needed to mobilize on election day. On election day, poll watchers would track who had not yet voted and those who had pledged support were again called and urged to vote.

Campaigns learn about the candidate preferences and the issue positions of potential voters through interviews conducted on the telephone or in person, a process called a *canvass*. Individuals who are undecided and probable voters in competitive races are likely to receive communications that persuade them to vote for one particular candidate and motivate them to vote. Interest groups and political parties may also conduct a canvass, followed by mail and phone calls, often reinforcing the same themes expressed by the candidates. In 2004, the Republican party took the lead for the Bush/Cheney campaign in mobilizing voters.

On the Democratic side a consortium of interest groups working together under the name "America Votes" shared data from the canvass and coordinated follow-up contacts. Among the groups participating in America Votes were America Coming Together (ACT), the AFL-CIO, Sierra Club, League of Conservation Voters, Planned Parenthood, NARAL-Pro Choice America, and more than 25 other groups. The focus of both the Republican Party and America Votes was highly competitive states in the 2004 presidential election, sometimes called battleground states. There were relatively few competitive Senate or House contests in 2004 and most of these were not in presidential battlegrounds. Overall, less than 10 percent of House races and only about twice that proportion of Senate races were competitive. Some of these were highly contested, such as the Senate races in South Dakota and Alaska. Most races for the Senate and House in 2004 saw much less activity.

The volume of communication in presidential battleground states was extraordinary. Voters in battleground states received unprecedented levels of contact in the 2004 presidential election. One household in Akron, Ohio, received 15 phone calls in the 24 hours before the polls closed. One home in Tallmadge, Ohio, received 11 unique pieces of mail from the Republican National Committee alone in 2004. Groups, candidates, and the parties all sent mail to voters they thought needed reinforcement or persuasion.

We learned from recent elections that a few hundred votes can determine an election outcome. Candidates cannot take any votes for granted, so in close contests voter mobilization is critical. In this chapter, we look at the nature and level of political participation in the United States, and why people vote as they do. We begin by exploring the related topic of public opinion, how to measure it, and the factors that affect the formation of opinions.

PUBLIC OPINION

All governments in all nations must be concerned with public opinion. Even in nondemocratic nations, unrest and protest can topple those in power. And in a constitutional democracy, citizens can express opinions in a variety of ways, including demonstrations, letters to their elected representatives and to newspaper editors, and voting in free and regularly scheduled elections. There are clear and direct connections between what voters want and what our governments do. In short, democracy and public opinion go hand in hand.

What Is Public Opinion?

Politicians frequently talk about what "the people" think or want. But social scientists use the term more precisely: We define **public opinion** as the distribution of individual preferences for, or evaluations of, a given issue, candidate, or institution within a specific population. *Distribution* means the proportion of the population that holds a particular opinion, compared to people with opposing opinions or those with no opinion at all. Public opinion is most commonly studied by systematic measurement through polls or survey. For instance, final preelection polls in 2004 by the Gallup Organization found that among potential voters, 49 percent reported they would vote for George W. Bush, 49 percent for John Kerry, and 1 percent for Ralph Nader. The actual vote was Bush 51 percent, Kerry 48 percent, and Nader .35 percent.

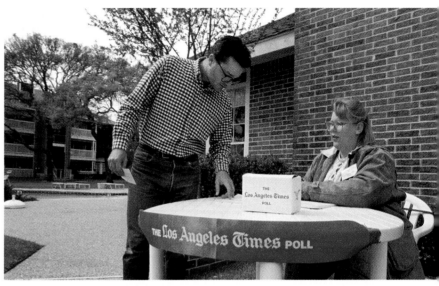

In addition to polls conducted by Gallup, Pew, and other such organizations, newspapers and TV networks conduct polls on election preferences and numerous other subjects.

TAKING THE PULSE OF THE PEOPLE   In a public opinion poll, a relatively small number of people can accurately represent the opinions of a larger population through the use of random *sampling* of people to survey. In a *random sample,* every individual has a known chance of being selected. The sample of randomly selected respondents should be appropriate for the questions being asked. For instance, a survey of 18- to 24-year-olds should not be done solely among college students, since roughly three-quarters of the members of this age group do not attend college. Even with proper sampling, surveys have a *margin of error,* meaning that the sample accurately reflects the population within a certain range—usually plus or minus 3 percent for a sample of at least 1,500 individuals. The final preelection survey results in 2004 were indeed within this margin of error for the actual vote.

The *art of asking questions* is also important to scientific polling. The wording of questions can influence the answers. Question order can also alter the responses. Good questions have to be pretested to be sure that the way a question is asked does not bias how it is answered. Questions should be delivered by trained and professional interviewers, who read them exactly as written and without any bias in their voices. Questions can be worded in different ways to measure factual knowledge, opinions, the intensity of opinion, or views on hypothetical situations. Sometimes *open-ended questions* are asked to permit respondents to answer in their own words rather than in set categories. Open-ended questions are harder to record and compare, but they allow respondents to express their views more clearly and may provide deeper insight into their thinking.

In addition to random sampling and clearly worded questions, thorough *analysis and reporting of the results* are required of scientific polls. Scientific polls inform the public of the sample size, the margin of error, and when and where the poll was conducted. It is also important to realize that public opinion can change from day to day and hour to hour. Polls are really snapshots of opinion at a point in time rather than moving pictures of opinions over time.

Individual preference emphasizes that when we measure public opinion, we are asking *individuals*—not groups—about their opinions. The *universe or population* is the relevant group of people for the question. When a substantial percentage of a sample agrees on an issue—for example, that we should honor the American flag—there is a *consensus.* But on most issues, opinions are divided. When two opposing sides feel intensely about an issue, the public is said to be *polarized.* The Vietnam War in the 1960s is an example of a polarizing issue. A recent example of a polarizing issue is gay marriage. One characteristic of such issues is that it is difficult to compromise or find a middle ground. An example of a contemporary issue with polarized opinions is gay marriage. Neither those who favor legalizing gay marriage nor those who unequivocally oppose see

public opinion
The distribution of individual preferences for or evaluations of a given issue, candidate, or institution within a specific population.

HOW YOU ASK THE QUESTION MATTERS

How you ask a polling question makes a lot of difference in the responses people give, as demonstrated in five different polls that asked about a proposed constitutional amendment defining marriage. The first two questions were part of national surveys conducted by CBS. The third question was part of an ABC/*Washington Post* poll. The fourth question was asked by the Pew Research Center for the People and the Press.

1. Would you favor or oppose an amendment to the U.S. Constitution that would allow marriage ONLY between a man and a woman?

Favor	60%
Oppose	37%
Don't Know	3%

2. Would you favor or oppose an amendment to the U.S. Constitution that would allow marriage only between a man and a woman, and outlaw marriages between people of the same sex?

Favor	51%
Oppose	42%
Don't Know	7%

3. Would you support amending the U.S. Constitution to make it illegal for homosexual couples to get married anywhere in the United States, or should each state make its own laws on homosexual marriage?

Amend Constitution	44%
State Laws	53%
Don't Know	3%

4. Do you strongly favor, favor, oppose, or strongly oppose allowing gays and lesbians to marry legally? IF OPPOSE GAY MARRIAGE ASK: There has been a proposal to change the U.S. Constitution to ban gay marriage. Do you think amending the Constitution to ban gay marriage is a good idea or a bad idea?

Total Favor	32%
Total Oppose	59%
(For those opposed) Good idea / favor Const. amendment	36%
Bad idea / oppose Const. amendment	21%
Don't Know / Refused	2%
Don't Know / Refused	9%

Source: The Pew Research Center for the People and the Press, "Reading the Polls on Gay Marriage and the Constitution," July 13, 2004, at www.people-press.org/commentary/display.php3?AnalysisID=92.

political socialization
The process most notably in families and schools by which we develop our political attitudes, values, and beliefs.

much room for compromise. The exception is those who oppose it but would favor some legal rights going to gay couples through "civil unions." (See Table 8–1.)

INTENSITY The factor called *intensity* produces the brightest and deepest hues in the fabric of public opinion. The fervor of people's beliefs varies greatly. For example, some individuals mildly favor gun control legislation and others mildly oppose it, some people are emphatically for or against it, and some have no interest in the matter at all; still others may not have even heard of it. People who lost their jobs or retirement savings because of corporate scandals likely feel more intensely about enhanced regulation of corporations and accounting firms than people who have not been directly affected by the scandals. Intensity is typically measured by asking people how strongly they feel about an issue or about a politician. Such a question is often called a *scale*.

LATENCY *Latency* refers to political opinions that exist but have not been fully expressed; they may not have crystallized, yet they are still important, for they can be aroused by leaders and converted into political action. Latent opinions set rough boundaries for leaders who know that if they take certain actions, they will trigger either opposition or support from millions of people. If leaders have some understanding of latent opinions—people's unexpressed wants, needs, and hopes—they will know how to mobilize people and draw them to the polls on election day. Many who lived in communist Poland, East Germany, Czechoslovakia, or Yugoslavia must have had latent opinions favorable to democracy—opinions supporting majority rule, freedom, and meaningful elections. The speed with which these countries embraced democratic reforms was possible when leaders encouraged widespread expression of such ideas. A more recent example of a latent opinion is the desire for security from foreign enemies, which had not been a concern before the terrorist attacks of September 11, 2001. Wanting homeland security has now became a manifest opinion.

SALIENCE By *salience* we mean the extent to which people believe issues are relevant to them. Most people are more concerned about personal issues like paying their bills and keeping their jobs than about national issues, but if national issues somehow threaten their security or safety, salience of national issues rises sharply. Saliency and intensity, while different, are often correlated on the same issue.

The salience of issues may change over time. During the Great Depression of the 1930s, Americans were concerned mainly about jobs, wages, and economic security. By the 1940s, foreign affairs came to the forefront. In the 1960s, problems of race and poverty aroused intense feelings. In the 1970s, Vietnam and then Watergate became the focus of people's attention. By the 2000s, concern about Social Security, health care, education, terrorism, and national security had become salient issues. Events like terrorist attacks or ongoing strife in Iraq tend to reinforce or elevate the importance of an issue.

How Do We Get Our Political Opinions and Values?

No one is born with political views. We learn them from many mentors and teachers. The process by which we develop our political attitudes, values, and beliefs is called **political socialization**. This process starts in childhood, and the family and the schools are usually the two most important political teachers. Children learn the content of our culture in childhood and adolescence but reshape it as they mature.[2] Socialization lays the foundation for political beliefs, values, ideology, and partisanship.

A common element of political socialization in all cultures is *nationalism,* a consciousness of the nation-state and of belonging to that entity. Robert Coles describes it this way:

> As soon as we are born, in most places on this earth, we acquire a nationality, a membership in a community. . . . A royal doll, a flag to wave in a parade, coins with their engraved messages—these are sources of instruction and connect a young person to a country. The attachment can be strong, indeed, even among children yet to attend school, wherever the flag is saluted, the national anthem sung. The attachment is as parental as the words imply—homeland, motherland, fatherland. . . . Nationalism works its way into just about every corner of the mind's life.[3]

TABLE 8–1 DIFFERING OPINIONS ON GAY MARRIAGE

	Opposed to Legalizing Gay Marriage	Opposed to Legalizing Gay Marriage but Favor Civil Unions*	Favor Legalizing Gay Marriage
Total	**61%**	**34%**	**30%**
Gender			
Men	67	32	24
Women	54	36	36
Region			
Northeast	52	46	34
Midwest	62	28	29
South	66	26	24
West	61	45	35
Age			
18–29	50	34	42
30–44	60	34	32
45–64	58	37	30
65+	81	31	12
Church Attendance			
More than once a week	82	20	10
Once a week	69	30	24
Once or twice a month	58	31	31
A few times a year	55	42	33
Never	45	50	45
Race			
Whites	62	35	31
African Americans	59	28	19
Latinos	61	37	30
Party			
Republican	74	27	18
Democrat	54	37	33
Independent	58	40	36
Political Philosophy			
Conservative	79	23	16
Moderate	57	48	32
Liberal	38	38	51
Marital Status			
Married or living as married	65	34	26
Others	54	36	35
Education			
High school or less	68	28	21
Some college	60	40	33
College degree or more	49	44	42

*Asked only of respondents who said "opposed" to legalizing gay marriage.

SOURCE: *National Annenberg Election Survey 2004*, "American Public Remain Opposed to Same-Sex Marriages as They Begin in Massachusetts, Annenberg Data Show," May 17, 2004, www.annenbergpublic policycenter.org/naes/2004_03_corrected-gay-marriage-update_05-17_pr.pdf.

"It should be 'yes' or 'no' or 'undecided'—
we don't accept a 'don't give a damn'
answer!"

Cartoon Features Syndicate.

The sources of our views are immensely varied in the pluralistic political culture of the United States. Political attitudes may stem from religious, racial, gender, ethnic, or economic beliefs and values. But we can make at least one generalization safely: We form our attitudes through participation in *groups,* and not only in groups such as families, schools, social organizations, and more political ones like the National Rifle Association or Planned Parenthood, but especially in close-knit groups like the family. When we identify closely with the attitudes and interests of a particular group, we tend to see politics through the "eyes" of that group.[4] Group affiliation does not necessarily mean that individual members do not think for themselves. Each member brings his or her own emotions, feelings, memories, and resistance to groups.

Children in the United States tend at an early age to adopt common values that provide continuity with the past and that legitimate the American political system. Young children know what country they live in, and their loyalty to the nation develops early. Although the details of our political system may still elude them, most young Americans acquire a respect for the Constitution and for the concept of participatory democracy, as well as an initially positive view of the most visible figure in our democracy, the president.[5]

FAMILY   Most social psychologists agree that family is the most powerful socializing agent.[6] American children typically show political interest by the age of ten, and by the early teens their interest may be fairly high. Consider your own political learning process. You probably formed your picture of the world by listening to a parent at dinner or by absorbing the tales your older brothers and sisters brought home from school. Perhaps you also heard about politics from grandparents, aunts, and uncles. You, in turn, influenced your family, if only by bringing some of your own hopes and concerns home from school. What we first learn in the family is not so much specific political opinions as basic *attitudes* that shape our opinions—attitudes toward our neighbors, political parties, other classes or types of people, particular leaders (especially presidents), and society in general.

Studies of high school students indicate a high correlation between the political party of the parents and the partisan choice of their children. This relatively high degree of correspondence continues throughout life. Such a finding raises some interesting questions: Does the direct influence of parents create the correspondence? Or does living in the same social environment—neighborhood, church, socioeconomic group—influence parents and children? The answer is *both,* and one influence often strengthens the other. For example, a daughter of Democratic parents growing up in a small southern town with strong Democratic leanings will be affected by friends, by other adults, and perhaps by youngsters in a church group, all of whom may reinforce the attitudes of her parents.[7] What happens when a young person's parents and friends disagree? Young people tend to go along with parents rather than friends on underlying political attitudes such as party affiliation, with friends rather than parents on some specific issues like the death penalty or gun control, and somewhere in between in their actual political behavior such as votes in presidential elections.[8]

SCHOOLS   Schools also mold young citizens' political attitudes. American schools see part of their purpose as preparing students to be citizens and active participants in governing their communities and nation. At an early age, schoolchildren begin to pick up specific political values and acquire basic attitudes toward our system of government. Education, like the family, prepares Americans to live in society.

From kindergarten through college, students generally develop political values consistent with the democratic process and supportive of the American political system. In their study of American history, they are introduced to our nation's heroes and heroines, the important events in our history, and the ideals of our society. Other aspects of their experience, such as the daily Pledge of Allegiance and occasional programs or assemblies, seek to reinforce respect of country. Children also gain practical experience in the workings of democracy through elections for class or school officers and student government. In some high schools and colleges, the state legislature or college trustees require students to take courses in U.S. history or American government to graduate.

Do school courses and activities give young people the skills needed to participate in elections and democratic institutions? A study of 18- to 24-year-olds commissioned

American children learn early the importance
of participatory democracy.

by the National Association of Secretaries of State found that young people "lack any real understanding of citizenship . . . information and understanding about the democratic process . . . and information about candidates and political parties."[9] "Furthermore, the Secretaries of State report noted that most young people do not seek out political information and that they are not very likely to do so in the future."[10] You and your classmates are not a representative sample in part because you are taking this course and therefore have more interest and knowledge than most people.

The debate about whether there is peer pressure on college campuses to conform to certain acceptable ideas or to use particular language highlights the role higher education can play in shaping attitudes and values. How does college influence political opinions? One study suggests that college students are more likely than people of the same age who are not attending college to be knowledgeable about politics, more in favor of free speech, and more likely to talk and read about politics.[11] Is this the influence of the professors, the curriculum, the students, or the background of people attending collge? It is difficult to generalize. Parents sometimes fear that professors have too much influence on their college-age children; however, most professors doubt that they have a significant influence on the political views of their students.

MASS MEDIA   Like everybody else, young people are exposed to a wide range of media—school newspapers, national newspapers, the Internet, movies, radio, television—all of which influence what they think. They, like adults, often pick and choose the media with which they agree, so their exposure is *selective*. The mass media also serve as agents of socialization by providing a link between individuals and the values and behavior of others. The popular media help shape the attitudes and opinions of the people who watch, listen to, or read them. News broadcasts present information about our society; events that get intensive media coverage often focus our attention on certain issues. For example, the hours of TV coverage of the war in Iraq directed widespread attention to the ethnic groups there and to the difficulty of establishing a lasting peace. Similarly, many Americans turned their attention to Islamic fundamentalism in the aftermath of the terrorist attacks of September 11, 2001.

OTHER INFLUENCES   Religious, ethnic, and racial attitudes also shape opinions, both within and outside the family. Generalizations about how people vote are useful, but we have to be careful about stereotyping people. For example, not all African Americans vote Democratic and not all Catholics agree with their church's position against abortion. It is a mistake to assume that because we know a person's religious affiliation or racial background, we know his or her political opinions.

Stability and Change in Public Opinion

Adults are not simply the sum of all their early experiences, but few change their opinions very often. Even if the world around us changes rapidly, we are slow to shift our loyalties or to change our minds about things that matter to us. In general, people who remain in the same place, in the same occupation, and in the same income group throughout their lives tend to have stable opinions. People often carry their attitudes with them, and families who move from cities to suburbs often retain their big-city attitudes for at least a time after they have moved. Political analysts are becoming more interested in the ways in which adults modify their views. A harsh experience—a war, economic depression, or loss of a job—may be a catalyst for change in attitudes and opinions

The September 11, 2001, terrorist attacks on the World Trade Center in New York, on the Pentagon in Washington, D.C., and on Flight 93 that crashed in Pennsylvania had at least a short-term impact on public trust and confidence in government. Political Scientist Robert D. Putnam has for several years been studying how the public views political institutions and community interaction. Putnam conducted a national survey in the summer of 2000. Following the terrorist attacks, he reinterviewed the same respondents to see how their views had changed. Table 8–2 shows the changes in selected dimensions. Putnam found that more than half of his sample expressed greater confidence in government after the attacks. Interest in public affairs grew by 27 percent among

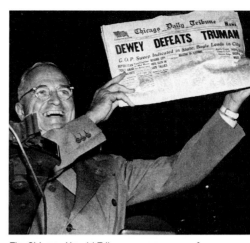

The Chicago Herald Tribune *was so sure of its polling data in the 1948 election, they predicted a win for Republican Thomas Dewey before the results were final. A victorious Harry Truman displays the mistaken headline.*

GLOBAL *Perceptions*

QUESTION: Please tell me if you think that the Internet represents a change for the better, a change for the worse, or it hasn't made much difference.

The Internet is becoming a more important part of political participation. People not only learn about news, but they can engage in political conversations; contribute money to candidates, causes, and parties; and in some places even vote via the Internet. But as the Pew Global Attitudes survey data demonstrate, the world has very different attitudes toward the Internet. Some places, like Vietnam, China, Canada, and the United States, have overwhelmingly positive views of the Internet. In these places some people have ready access to this tool, while in others like China and Vietnam access is more limited. Despite this limited access, people in China and Vietnam view the Internet positively.

But the Pew data are revealing in another way as well. In many less developed countries a large number of people, and in some places a majority of people, don't know much about the Interent. There this potential democratic tool has not become familiar. Places like Uganda and Pakistan lag behind more developed countries in public awareness of the Internet. This is a helpful reminder that not everyone in the world has access to the modern tools of democracy.

SOURCE: Pew Global Attitudes Project, *Views of a Changing World* (Washington, D.C.: The Pew Research Center for the People and the Press, 2003), p. T-15.

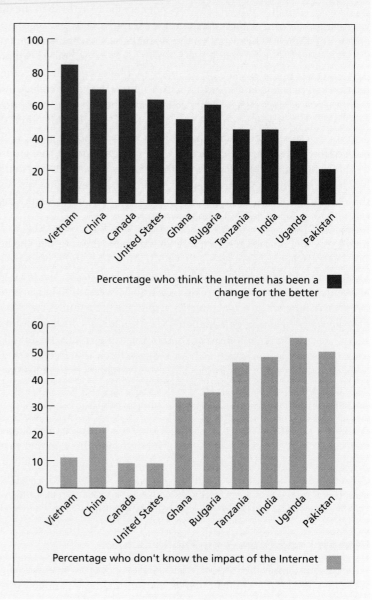

Percentage who think the Internet has been a change for the better

Percentage who don't know the impact of the Internet

younger people (age 35 and under) and 8 percent among older respondents. Putnam concludes, "Americans don't only trust political institutions more: We also trust one another more, from neighbors and co-workers to shop clerks and perfect strangers. Following the attacks, Americans express confidence that people in their community would cooperate, for example, with voluntary conservation measures in an energy or water shortage." The events of September 11 also appear to have led people to be "somewhat more generous."[12] How enduring these changes are is not yet clear and may be more consequential in people's private lives than in their public activities like voting, volunteering, or becoming more involved in politics. Putnam's subsequent research found that trust in community leaders, neighbors, other races, etc., declined by spring 2002, but it remained higher than before 9/11. Confidence in community cooperation also "tended to fade over time." On the other hand, civic engagement has continued at its post-9/11 level and maybe even gotten stronger.[13]

TABLE 8–2   CHANGES IN PUBLIC PERCEPTION AFTER TERRORIST ATTACKS OF SEPTEMBER 11, 2001

	Increased	Decreased	Net Change
Trust national government	51%	7%	44%
Trust local government	32	13	19
Hours watching TV	40	24	16
Interest in politics	29	15	14
Trust local police	26	12	14
Inter-racial trust	31	20	11
Trust shop-clerks	28	17	11
Support for unpopular book in library	28	18	10
Trust neighbors	23	13	10
Contributions to religious charity	29	20	9
Expect crisis support from friends	22	14	8
Trust "people running my community"	32	24	8
Worked with neighbors	15	8	7
Trust local news media	30	23	7
Gave blood	11	4	7
Volunteered	36	29	7
Expect local cooperation in crisis	23	17	6
Worked on community project	17	11	6
Attend political meeting	11	6	5
Newspaper readership	27	24	3
Visit with relatives	43	40	3
Attended club meeting	29	26	3
Attended public meeting	27	26	3
Contributions to secular charity	28	27	1
Attend church	20	19	1
Organizational memberships (number)	39	39	0
Had friends visit your home	39	45	− 6
Support for immigrants rights	21	32	−11

SOURCE: The Saguaro Seminar: Civic Engagement in America, January 15, 2002, www.ksg.harvard.edu/saguaro/press.html.

Some of our political opinions change very little because they are part of our core values. An example might be our attitudes toward abortion. Thus our views on abortion, the death penalty, and doctor-assisted suicide remain relatively stable over time. On issues that are less central to our values, such as our view of how a president is performing his job, opinions can show substantial change over time. Figure 8–1 contrasts the public opinion on President Bush with their views on abortion over time. On many issues, public opinion can change once the public learns more about the issue or perceives that there is another side to the question. It is on these issues that politicians can help shape attitudes. The decisions by Dwight Eisenhower, John Kennedy, and Lyndon Johnson to enforce school desegregation are examples of leadership of public opinion, as were the positions of Jimmy Carter on the Panama Canal Treaty and George H. W. Bush and Bill Clinton on the North American Free Trade Agreement (NAFTA).[14]

Public Opinion and Public Policy

For much of human history, it has been difficult to measure public opinion. "What I want," Abraham Lincoln once said, "is to get done what the people desire to be done, and the question for me is how to find that out exactly."[15] Politicians in our day do not face such uncertainty about public opinion; far from it.[16] Polling informs them of public

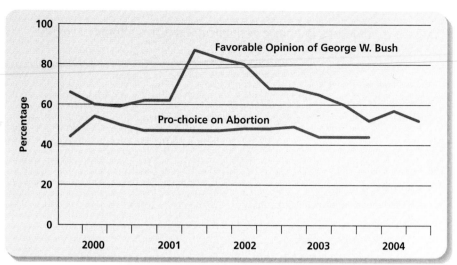

FIGURE 8–1 Comparison of Opinion of President George Bush and Attitude on Abortion Over Time.

SOURCE: Abortion/Pro-choice: Polling Report, at www.pollingreport.com/abortion.htm; Opinion of George W. Bush: Polling Report, at www.pollingreport.com/BushFav.htm9; USA Today/CNN/Gallup Poll reports, at www.usatoday.com/news/politicselections/nation/polls/usatodaypolls.htm.

opinion on all major policy issues. Politicians can commission polls themselves, or they can turn to public or media polls. More than 80 percent of newspapers and half of all television stations conduct or commission their own polls.[17]

Here are some examples of how public opinion can shape policy and in turn how policies shape opinion. During the Vietnam War, antiwar demonstrations on college campuses spread to cities all over the country. "Public opinion had a substantial impact on the rate of troop withdrawals."[18] In the Persian Gulf War, opposition to the use of U.S. forces was greatly reduced after a few days of success in the air and ground war. When American forces were dispatched to Somalia in Operation Restore Hope in January 1993, fully 79 percent of the public approved of the use of troops to ensure the delivery of humanitarian aid, food, and medical provisions. But when U.S. soldiers were killed and dragged through the streets of Mogadishu, support fell to only 17 percent in October of the same year.[19] On May 3, 2003, the day after Bush announced "Mission Accomplished" in the Iraq War on an aircraft carrier, 72 percent of Americans approved of the way Bush had handled the situation with Iraq. About a year later, after the Abu Ghraib prison torture and repeated attacks on American forces in Iraq, the Bush approval rating had fallen to 34 percent.[20]

Typically, elected officials focus on issues of importance to the public.[21] In a sense they follow public opinion. They use polls to learn how to talk about issues in ways that resonate with the public. Winning reelection is a strong motive for members of Congress.[22] "Legislators show greater attention to public opinion as election day looms," and the closeness of the fit between constituent opinion and roll call voting reflects that connection.[23] Candidates use polls to determine where to campaign, how to campaign, and even whether to campaign. The decision about which states John Kerry and George W. Bush most aggressively campaigned in was driven by the polls and a preoccupation with securing 270 electoral votes. Both campaigns lavished time and attention on Ohio, Florida, Wisconsin, Iowa, and Pennsylvania. Even smaller states like New Hampshire and New Mexico received substantial attention. Large states like New York, California, and Texas were taken for granted because one side or the other was ahead. A secondary objective was a plurality in the popular vote.

Surely polls are no substitute for elections. With a ballot before them, voters must translate their opinions into concrete decisions. They must decide what is important and what is not. Democracy is more than the expression of views, more than a simple mirror of opinion. It also involves choosing among leaders, taking sides on certain issues, and selecting the governmental actions that may follow. Democracy is the thoughtful participation of people in the political process. Elections, despite their failings, still establish the link between the many opinions "We the People" hold and the selection of our leaders.

Awareness and Interest

For most people, politics is of secondary importance to earning a living, raising a family, and having a good time; some Americans are more concerned about which team wins the World Series or the Super Bowl than they are about who wins the school board elections, who gets to be mayor, or even who gets to be president of the United States. Most people find politics complicated and difficult to understand. And they should, for democracy *is* complicated and difficult to understand. But it helps to understand the mechanics and structures of our government such as how the government operates, how the electoral college works, how Congress is set up, and the length of terms for the president and for members of the Senate and House of Representatives.

These college students feel responsible to vote and line up on campus to fill out absentee ballots.

Details about how the government works are typically best known by younger adults, who remember learning them in school. The general adult public, however, fares poorly when quizzed about their elected officials.[24] Just over 15 percent of Americans are able to recall the name of the congressional candidates from their district.[25] With so many voters not knowing who represents them in Congress, it is not surprising that "on even hotly debated congressional issues, few people know where their Congress member stands."[26]

Although the public's knowledge of institutional and candidate issues is poor, its knowledge of important public policy issues is worse. In 1982, after approximately 59 years of debate over ratification of the Equal Rights Amendment, nearly one-third of the adults in the United States indicated they had never heard of it. The same is true for many issues.[27] In 2004, only 31.7 percent were able to correctly identify William Rehnquist as the Chief Justice of the U.S. Supreme Court, 8.6 percent incorrectly identified him, and 59.7 percent didn't know.[28] Fortunately, not all Americans are uninformed or uninterested. About 25 percent of the public is interested in politics most of the time. This is the **attentive public**, people who know and understand how the government works. They vote in most elections, read a daily newspaper, and "talk politics" with their families and friends. They tend to be better educated and more committed to democratic values than other Americans.

At the opposite end of the spectrum are *nonvoters,* people who are rarely interested in politics or public affairs and who rarely vote. About 67 percent of Americans have indicated that they are interested "some of the time," "only now and then," or "hardly at all."[29] A subset of this group might be called *political know-nothings.* These individuals not only avoid political activity but also have little interest in government and limited knowledge about it.

Between the attentive public and the political know-nothings are the *part-time citizens,* roughly 40 percent of the American public. These individuals participate selectively in elections, voting in presidential elections but usually not in others. Politics and government do not greatly interest them; they pay only minimal attention to the news, and they rarely discuss candidates or elections with others.

Democracy can survive even when a large number of citizens are passive and uninformed, as long as a substantial number of people serve as opinion leaders and are interested and informed about public affairs. Obviously, these activists will have much greater influence than their less active fellow citizens.

attentive public
Those citizens who follow public affairs carefully.

When the student pro-democracy protest was stopped by Chinese government tanks in Tiananman Square on June 5, 1989, one man stood up in defiance until he was pulled to safety by bystanders.

PARTICIPATION: TRANSLATING OPINIONS INTO ACTION

Americans influence their government's actions in several ways, many of which are protected by the Constitution. They vote in elections, join interest groups, go to political party meetings, ring doorbells, call friends urging them to vote for issues or candidates, sign petitions, write letters to the editors of newspapers, and make calls to radio talk shows.

Protest is also a form of political participation. Our political system is remarkably tolerant of protest that is not destructive or violent. Boycotts, picketing, sit-ins, and marches are all legally protected. Rosa Parks and Martin Luther King Jr. used nonviolent protest to call attention to what they saw as unfair laws (see Chapter 17). The number of Americans who participate in protests is small, but the impact of their actions in shaping public opinion can be substantial.

A distinguishing characteristic of a democracy is that citizens can influence government decisions by participating in politics. When the citizens of Belgrade turned out night after night to protest the nullification of their election, they forced Slobodan Milosevic to permit the victorious candidate, Vojislav Kostunica, to take power. But protests and demonstrations are not always peaceful or successful. In totalitarian societies, participation is very limited, forcing people who want to influence government to resort to violence or revolution. The protest of Chinese students in Tiananmen Square in 1989 failed to stop the onslaught of tanks and the repression that followed. Americans sometimes forget that our democracy was born of revolution but that maintaining a constitutional democracy after the revolution is difficult and demands public participation.

Even in an established democracy, people may feel so strongly about an issue that they would rather fight than accept the verdict of an election. The classic example is the American Civil War. Following the election of 1860, in which Lincoln, an antislavery candidate who did not receive a single electoral vote from a slave state, won the presidency, the South took up arms. The ensuing war marked the breakdown of democracy. Examples in our own time include antiabortion or animal rights groups that use violence to press their political agenda and militia groups that arm themselves for battle against government regulations.

Participation can also include less intense activity and even engaging in patriotic rituals. For example, large numbers of Americans routinely sing the national anthem or recite the Pledge of Allegiance. They communicate their views about government and politics to their representatives in Washington and the state capitol. They serve as jurors in courtrooms and enlist in the military. They express concern about the involvement of American military forces in foreign hostilities. They complain about taxes and government regulations. And many families feel it important that their children visit Washington, D.C., and other historic sights.

For most people, politics is a private activity. Some still consider it impolite to discuss politics at dinner parties. To say that politics is private does not mean people do not have opinions or will not discuss them when asked by others, including pollsters. But often politics is avoided in discussions with neighbors, work associates, even friends and family, as too divisive or upsetting. Typically, less than one person in four attempts to influence how another person votes in an election. An even smaller number actually work for a candidate or party. Only about 11 percent make a contribution to a candidate,[30] and only 11 percent of taxpayers designate $3 of their taxes to the fund that pays for presidential general elections (see Table 8–3).[31] Few individuals attempt to influence others by writing letters to elected officials or to editors of newspapers for publication. Even smaller numbers participate in protest groups or activities. Despite the small number of persons who engage in these activities, it would be a mistake to assume that small numbers of individuals cannot make a difference to politics and government. An individual or small group can generate media interest in an issue and expand the impact. Peaceful protests for civil rights, about environmental issues, and both for and against abortion have generated public attention and even changed opinions.[32]

COUNTING VOTES

Until the 2000 election, Americans took the counting of ballots for granted. But with the closeness of that election and the controversy surrounding election administration in Florida, the public became aware that counting votes is not a simple matter.

Votes are counted in the United States according to state law as administered by local officials. There has been great variability in the technology used in voting. In Florida in 2000, some counties used paper ballots, others voting machines, others punch-card ballots, and at least one used ballots that could be scanned by a computer. More recently Florida and other states have moved to computerized voting systems with touch

TABLE 8–3 POLITICAL PARTICIPATION AND AWARENESS IN THE UNITED STATES

Watched Campaign on TV	62%
Vote in presidential elections	55
Vote in congressional elections	42
Try to persuade vote of others	29
Display campaign button, sticker, or sign	9
Give money to help a campaign	11
Attend dinner, meeting, or rally for candidate	5

SOURCE: U.S. Bureau of the Census, *Statistical Abstract of the United States: 2003* (U.S. Government Printing Office, 2003), p. 269; The 2002 National Election Study, Center for Political Studies, University of Michigan. The NES Guide to Public Opinion and Electoral Behavior, at www.umich.edu/~nes/nesguide/gd-index.htm#6; See also www.census.gov.

PEOPLE & POLITICS *Making a Difference* ★★★

STEVE ROSENTHAL AND AMERICA COMING TOGETHER

One of the most important developments of the 2004 election cycle was the growth of Section 527 organizations (see Chapter 7), and the most visible and important of these groups was America Coming Together (ACT).* This group was headed by Steve Rosenthal, who previously had been the political director of the American Federation of Labor-Congress of Industrial Organizations (AFL-CIO) and Ellen Malcom, formerly of EMILY'S List, a pro-choice group that supports female Democratic candidates. The funding for ACT came from several individuals and groups who shared a commitment to defeating George W. Bush in 2004.

Rosenthal, who says he "barely made it out of High School," has deep roots in the labor movement. As a child a brick was thrown through the front window of his home to warn his father not to form a union.† Rosenthal himself became a member of the Communications Workers of America and worked for the union for twelve years. He also has consulted with numerous political candidates. During the Clinton administration he served as Associate Deputy Secretary of Labor. He has also held positions in the Democratic National Committee.

Rosenthal is best known as having returned the labor movement to its roots of person-to-person communication at the workplace, on the phone, and at the doorstep. Rosenthal describes his method as follows: "what I do when I am thinking about an election is I break it down person by person, name by name, every single voter that we talk to, and who they talk to, to connect them to what we need to do in this state."‡ During the 2004 election cycle ACT, under Rosenthal's direction, targeted more than a dozen states with a concerted effort to register and then turn out voters. ACT registered large numbers of new voters, many of whom voted in 2004. But it was the Republican voter mobilization that carried the day, an effort in many ways patterned after what Rosenthal had done at the AFL-CIO.

*Jeffrey H. Birnbaum, "The New Soft Money: Campaign-Finance Reform Didn't Kill Big Political Donations, It Just Changed the Rules of the Game. Meet the Players." *Fortune*, November 10, 2003, p. 155.
†Ann Gerhart, "Ground War: Steve Rosenthal Wages a $100 Million Battle to Line Up Democratic Votes," *The Washington Post*, July 6, 2004, p. C1.
‡Ibid.

screens. Another lesson reinforced by the recent ballot-counting controversies is that in every election, in every jurisdiction, and with every technology there are imperfections in voting. Touch screens are vulnerable to manipulation of the software, paper ballots are subject to human error in counting, punch cards may not always have the punches perforate, and so on. The goal in election administration is to minimize errors and eliminate bias as much as possible.

But counting votes is more complicated than the means by which we vote. There are also judgment calls that election officials have to make about incomplete or flawed ballots. In the Florida controversy of 2000, substantial attention was devoted to punch-card ballots in which the ballot did not have a completely perforated "chad" or portion of the ballot the stylus was to punch. Did a dangling chad or one that protruded but was not perforated count? These decisions mattered in an election as close as Florida's was in 2000. With the growth in absentee voting and with the law allowing military and civilians living abroad to cast their ballots and return them by mail, election officials face the possibility of a close election not being decided until days after the ballots are cast.

The issue of who may vote on election day is also important to how elections are administered. Some groups contend that the voting rolls in states like Florida were incomplete in 2000 and voters who had registered were not on the rolls. In 2004 there was some confusion, for voters who only voted in presidential elections had their voting place or precinct changed as a result of the 2002 redistricting. Voters who think they should be allowed to vote but who are not on the rolls are allowed to cast what are called provisional ballots. These ballots are only counted if it is determined that the voter was in fact registered to vote.

Congress and state legislatures in the wake of the 2000 election have invested billions of dollars in new voting technology, new rules on provisional ballots, and an effort to modernize voting methods. Florida acted soon after 2000 allocating $32 million[33] to upgrade voting machinery and banning the punch card and paper ballots. The federal government enacted the Help America Vote Act (HAVA) and authorized $3.9 billion to assist states in making voting more reliable and accessible.[34]

Interest groups, political parties, and candidates made the integrity of the 2004 voting process a high priority. Thousands of individuals were poll watchers. Groups established toll free hot lines for voters to call if they felt they were not being fairly treated, and lawyers were on call to file immediate challenges in key jurisdictions. The monitoring of voting was most intense in Ohio, where Republicans charged that Democratic-allied groups had registered Daffy Duck and Mary Poppins. Republicans also threatened to challenge the registration of many of the newly registered voters as they voted. Florida also had controversy in the period before the election regarding newly registered voters and the voting status of felons who had served their jail terms. While there were some delays on election day, they were more the result of insufficient voting booths and machines and not a large-scale challenge to the voting lists.

Voting

Americans' most typical political activity is voting. The United States is a constitutional democracy with more than 200 years of free and frequent elections and a tradition of the peaceful transfer of power between competing groups and parties.

Originally, the Constitution left it to the individual states to determine the crucial question of who could vote, and the qualifications for voting differed considerably from state to state. All states except New Jersey barred women from voting, many did not permit African Americans to vote, and until the 1830s, property ownership was often a requirement. By the time of the Civil War, the franchise had been extended to all white male citizens in every state. Since that time, eligibility standards for voting have been expanded seven times by legislation and constitutional amendments (see Table 8–4).

The civil rights movement in the 1960s, which made voting rights a central issue, secured adoption of the Twenty-Fourth Amendment and passage of the 1965 Voting Rights Act. The Voting Rights Act banned literacy tests, eased registration requirements, and provided for the replacement of local election officials with federal registrars in areas

TABLE 8–4   CHANGES IN VOTING ELIGIBILITY STANDARDS SINCE 1870

Timeline	Change
1870	Fifteenth Amendment forbade states from denying the right to vote because of "race, color, or previous condition of servitude."
1920	Nineteenth Amendment gave women the right to vote.
1924	Congress granted Native Americans citizenship and voting rights.
1961	Twenty-Third Amendment permitted District of Columbia residents to vote in federal elections.
1964	Twenty-Fourth Amendment prohibited the use of poll taxes in federal elections.
1965	Voting Rights Act removed restrictions that kept African Americans from voting.
1971	Twenty-Sixth Amendment extended the vote to citizens age 18 and older.

where the denial of the right to vote had been most blatant. Its passage resulted in a dramatic expansion of black registration and voting. Once African Americans were permitted to register to vote, "the focus of voting discrimination shifted . . . to preventing them from winning elections."[35] In southern legislative districts where blacks are in the majority, however, there has been a "dramatic increase in the proportion of African American legislators elected" (see Figure 8–2).[36]

Registration

One peculiarly American legal requirement—**voter registration**—arose in response to concerns about voting abuses, but it also discourages voting. Most other democracies have automatic voter registration. Average turnout in the United States is more than 30 percentage points lower than in countries like Australia, Austria, Belgium, Denmark, Germany, and Italy.[37] This was not always the case. In fact, in the 1800s, turnout in the United States was much like that of Europe today. Turnout began to drop significantly around the turn of the twentieth century, in part as a result of election reform (see Figure 8–3). Voter registration requirements have a substantial impact on rates of voting.[38]

American elections in the 1800s were different from those of today. Ballots were prepared by the parties, often using different colors of paper that allowed party officials to monitor how people had voted. In some areas, charges of multiple voting generated a reform movement that substituted the **Australian ballot**, a secret ballot printed by the state, for the party printed ballots This same reform period also pressed for voter

FIGURE 8–2 Percentage of African Americans Registered to Vote, 1980–2000.
SOURCE: U.S. Bureau of the Census, *Statistical Abstract of the United States*, 2001 (U.S. Government Printing Office, 2001), p. 251.

voter registration
System designed to reduce voter fraud by limiting voting to those who have established eligibility by submitting the proper form.

Australian ballot
A secret ballot printed by the state.

FIGURE 8–3 Voter Turnout in Presidential Elections, 1800–2004.
SOURCE: Howard W. Stanley and Richard G. Niemi, *Vital Statistics on American Politics, 1999–2000* (CQ Press, 2000). See also "National Voter Turnout in Federal Elections, 1996–2000," at www.infoplease.com/ipa/A0781453.html. 2004 update by authors.

registration to reduce multiple voting and limit voting to those who had previously established their eligibility.

Registration laws vary by state, but in every state except North Dakota, registration is required in order to vote. Six states permit election day voter registration: Idaho, Maine, Minnesota, New Hampshire, Wisconsin, and Wyoming. The most important provision regarding voter registration may be the closing date. Through the early 1970s, it was not uncommon for closing dates to be six months before the election; now, by federal law, no state can stop registration more than 30 days before a federal election.[39] Voter registration places a responsibility on voters to take an extra step—usually filling out a form at the country courthouse, when renewing a driver's license, or with a roving registrar— some days or weeks before the election and every time they move to a new address. Other important provisions include places and hours of registration.[40]

Motor Voter

The burdens of voter registration were eased a bit when, on May 20, 1993, President Bill Clinton signed the National Voter Registration Act—called the "Motor Voter" bill because it allows people to register to vote while applying for or renewing a driver's license. Offices that provide welfare and disabled assistance can also facilitate voter registration. States have the option to include public schools, libraries, and city and county clerks' offices as registration sites. The law also requires states to allow registration by mail using a standardized form. Motor Voter requires that a questionnaire be mailed to registered voters every four years to purge for death and change of residence but forbids purging for any other reasons, such as nonvoting.

The law has been successful, at least in terms of numbers of new voters registered.[41] Early data on the impact of Motor Voter suggest that neither Democrats nor Republicans are the primary beneficiaries because most who have registered claim to be Independent.[42] Yet even with the increase in registration, Motor Voter does not appear to have increased turnout.

Turnout

Americans hold more elections for more offices than the citizens of any other democracy. In part because there are so many elections, American voters tend to pick and choose which elections to vote in. Americans elect officeholders in *general elections,* determine party nominees in *primary elections,* and replace senators who have died or left office in *special elections.*

Elections held in years when the president is on the ballot are called *presidential elections,* elections held midway between presidential elections are called *midterm elections,* and elections held in odd-numbered calendar years are called *off-year elections.* Midterm elections (like the ones in 2002 and 2006) elect about one-third of the U.S. Senate, all members of the House of Representatives, and most governors and other

IN COMPARATIVE PERSPECTIVE

Registration and Voting in the World's Democracies

	Average Voter Turnout*	Compulsory Voting†	Automatic Registration‡
Australia	82.7%	Yes	No
Austria	85	No	Yes
Belgium	85	Yes	Yes
Canada	68	No	Yes
Denmark	84	No	Yes
Finland	79	No	Yes
France	67	No	No
Germany	81	No	Yes
Greece	80	Yes	No
Ireland	75	No	Yes
Israel	80	No	Yes
Italy	93	Yes	Yes
Japan	69	No	Yes
Netherlands	85	No	Yes
New Zealand	86	No	No
Norway	80	No	Yes
Spain	77	No	Yes
Sweden	83	No	Yes
Switzerland	49	No	Yes
United Kingdom	75	No	Yes
United States	48	No	No

SOURCE: Richard S. Katz, *Democracy and Elections* (New York: Oxford University Press, 1997), pp. 234–235; International Institute for Democracy and Electoral Assistance, "Voter Turnout from 1945 to Date: A Global Report on Political Participation," at www.idea.int/voter_turnout/voter_turnoutl .html.

*Percentage of turnout for total voting age population (VAP).

†In a *compulsory voting* system, registered voters are required to turn out to vote.

‡Automatic registration uses another form of citizen identification, such as an identity card or a driver's license.

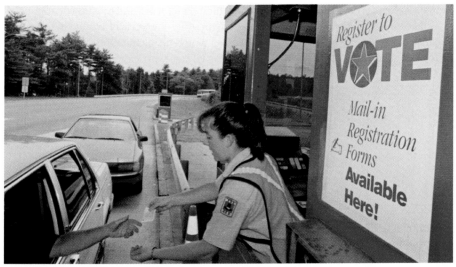

In an effort to make registration easier, states have made registration forms available at motor vehicle stations, schools, public buildings, and even highway tollbooths.

statewide officeholders as well as large numbers of state legislators. Many local elections to elect city councils and mayors are held in the spring of odd-numbered years.

Turnout—the proportion of the voting-age public that votes—is highest in presidential general elections (see Figure 8–4). When examining turnout across states and over time it is best to use as the standard against which you measure turnout the Census Bureau's estimate of population over the age of 18. Because states have different voter registration requirements, the Census Bureau's estimate of eligible voters is the better baseline from which to compare state differences in turnout. Turnout is higher in general elections than in primary elections and higher in primary elections than in special elections. Turnout is higher in presidential general elections than in midterm general elections, and higher in presidential primary elections than in midterm primary elections.[43] This is due to greater interest in and awareness of presidential elections. Turnout is higher in elections in which candidates for federal office are on the ballot (U.S. senator, member of the House of Representatives, president) than in state elections in years when there are no federal contests. Some states elect their governor and other state officials in odd-numbered years to separate state from national politics. The result is generally lower turnout. Finally, local or municipal elections have lower turnout than state elections, and municipal primaries generally have the lowest rates of participation.

Turnout peaked in 1960 at more than 65 percent of persons eligible to vote, but it has since declined to just under 60 percent in 2004.[44] In midterm elections, turnout was 39 percent nationally in 2002, up 3 percent from 1998. Competition tends to encourage turnout, as was the case in Ohio and Florida in 2004 and in states like Minnesota and South Dakota in 2002. More competitive elections generate more interest in the public and more spending by the candidates which in turn stimulate participation. The number of potential voters has increased since the 1960s because the Voting Rights Act of 1965 added large numbers of African Americans to the pool of registered voters. Younger voters were also given the right to vote with the Twenty-Sixth Amendment in 1971. Our electorate has also grown richer and more educated since the 1960s. Since wealth and education are related to voting, we should have seen an increase instead of a decrease in voting. However, over 80 million eligible Americans failed to vote in the 2004 presidential election; the nonvoting figures are even higher for congressional, state, county, and local elections.[45]

Who Votes?

The extent of voting varies widely among different groups. Level of education especially helps predict whether people will vote; as education increases, so does the propensity to vote. "Education increases one's capacity for understanding complex and intangible subjects such as politics," according to one study, "as well as encouraging the ethic of civic responsibility. Moreover, schools provide experience dealing with a variety of bureaucratic problems, such as coping with requirements, filling out forms, and meeting deadlines."[46]

Race and ethnic background are linked with different levels of voting, in large part because they correlate with education. In other words racial and ethnic minorities with college degrees vote at about the same rate as whites with college degrees. Blacks in

FIGURE 8–4 Voter Turnout in Presidential and Midterm Elections, 1990–2004.
SOURCE: U.S. Bureau of the Census, *Statistical Abstract of the United States*, 1998 (U.S. Government Printing Office, 1998), p. 97; Louis V. Gerstner, "Next Time, Let Us Boldly Vote as No Democracy Has Before," *USA Today*, November 16, 1998, p. A15; www.infoplease.com/ipa/A0781453.html; National Voter Turnout in Federal Elections: 1960–2000. 2004 update by authors.

turnout
The proportion of the voting-age public that votes, sometimes defined as the number of registered voters that vote.

CHANGING FACE OF AMERICAN POLITICS

VOTER TURNOUT BY DEMOGRAPHIC FACTORS

	1992	1994	1996	1998	2000	2002
Sex						
Men	60.2%	44.4%	52.8%	41.4%	53.1%	41.4%
Women	62.3	44.9	55.5	42.4	56.2	43.0
Race						
White	63.6	46.9	56.0	43.3	56.4	44.1
Black	54.0	37.0	50.6	39.6	53.5	39.7
Hispanic	28.9	19.1	26.7	20.0	27.5	18.9
Education						
Some high school	41.2	27.0	33.8	25.0	33.6	23.3
High school graduate	57.5	40.5	49.1	37.1	49.4	37.1
Some college	68.7	49.1	60.5	46.2	60.3	45.8
College graduate	81.0	63.1	73.0	57.2	72.0	58.5
Age						
18 to 24	42.8	20.1	32.4	16.6	32.3	17.2
25 to 34	53.2	32.2	43.1	28.0	43.7	27.1
35 to 44	63.6	46.0	54.9	40.7	55.0	40.2
45 to 64	70.0	56.0	64.4	53.6	64.1	53.1
65 and over	70.1	60.7	67.0	59.5	67.6	61.0

SOURCE: U.S. Census Bureau, *Statistical Abstract of the United States, 2003* (U.S. Government Printing Office, 2003), p. 269; U.S. Census Bureau, "Voting and Registration in the Election of November 2002: Detailed Tables for Current Population Report," at www.census.gov/prod/2004pubs/p20-552.pdf.

general turn out at lower rates than whites, although this is beginning to change. African American participation in the 2004 election increased by 25 percent from the 2000 election but this still only counted for 11 percent of the electorate. Turnout among black voters surged in many states in 2000. Although nationwide, African Americans accounted for 10 percent of the total vote, the same percentage as in 1996, some states experienced exceptional increases. For example, in Florida, African American turnout increased by 68 percent, from 530,000 in 1996 to 893,000 in 2000. Missouri and Illinois also experienced exceptional turnout among black Americans. One of the major reasons was an unprecedented voter mobilization effort mounted by the National Association for the Advancement of Colored People. The NAACP's National Voter Fund spent $10 million on a get-out-the-vote campaign. Mobilization efforts can affect election outcomes in races as close as those of 2000 and 2004. In 2004, groups like America Coming Together, the NAACP, and others were especially active. Both candidates spoke to African American groups but President Bush declined the invitation to speak to the NAACP

In 2004 both parties mounted major efforts to register and mobilize Hispanic voters, a group likely to be of growing importance. Candidates, parties, and allied interest groups, anticipating another very close election in 2004, made voter mobilization a high priority. Their efforts included personal appeals, often at the doorstep, where people were invited to register to vote, efforts to get people to vote early by absentee ballot, and offers of rides to the polls on election day. The intensity of the voter mobilization in 2004 was high compared to other recent elections.

Women, another historically underrepresented group, have increased their voting levels to the point that since 1984 more women than men vote.[47] Women's recent higher turnout is generally attributed to increasing levels of education and employment.

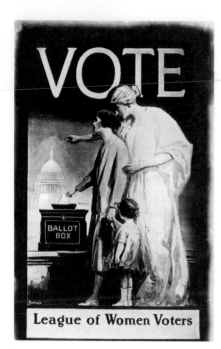

This poster, published by the League of Women Voters, urged women to use the vote the Nineteenth Amendment had given them.

A major initiative to register young persons and encourage them to vote was undertaken in 2004. The mobilization effort appeared to work, with more than 4.6 million more voters aged 18–29 voting in 2004 than in 2000. While an impressive gain, because of generally higher turnout, young voters as a percentage of all voters did not increase in 2004. Studies of young voters before the 2004 election found that 57 percent of young adults said that the election would have a "great deal" or "quite a bit" of impact on the country's future, in contrast to the 33 percent of young adults who responded this way during the 2000 election.[48]

Income and age are also important factors in voting. Those with higher family incomes are more likely to vote than those with lower incomes. Income, of course, corresponds to occupation, and those with higher-status careers are more likely to vote than those with lower-status jobs. Poor people are less likely to feel politically involved and confident, and their social norms tend to deemphasize politics.[49] Older people, unless they are very old and infirm, are more likely to vote than younger people. The greater propensity of older persons to vote will only amplify the importance of this group as baby boomers age and retire.

How Serious Is Nonvoting?

Although Americans can hardly avoid reading or hearing about political campaigns, especially during an election as intensely fought as that of 2004, about 40 percent of all Americans fail to vote. Who are they? Why don't they vote? Is the fact that so many Americans choose not to vote a cause for alarm? If so, what can we do about it?

The simplest explanation for low turnout is that people are lazy, but there is more to it than that. Of course, some people are apathetic, but the vast majority of Americans are not. Paradoxically, we compare favorably with other nations in political interest and awareness, but for a variety of institutional and political reasons, we fail to convert these qualities into votes (see Table 8–5).

The difficulty of voting in the United States, the cost in time and effort, is higher than in other democracies. In our system, people are required to register to vote, and they must decide how to vote for a large number of offices, and in many states how to vote on ballot questions relating to public policy or constitutional amendments. Elections in the United States are held on weekdays rather than holidays or weekends as they often are elsewhere. Another factor in the decline of voter turnout since the 1960s is the Twenty-Sixth Amendment, which lowered the voting age to 18. It increased the number of eligible voters, but that group is the least likely to vote. With ratification of the amendment in 1971, turnout fell from 62 percent in 1968 to 57 percent in 1972.[50]

Some political scientists argue that nonvoting is not a critical problem. "Nonvoting is not a social disease," contends Austin Ranney, a noted scholar of politics. He points

TABLE 8–5 WHY PEOPLE DON'T VOTE	
Too busy, conflicting schedule	27.1%
Illness or disability (own or family's)	13.1
Not interested, felt vote would not make a difference	12
Out of town or away from home	10.4
Other reason, not specified	9
Did not like candidates or campaign issues	7.3
Refused or don't know	7.5
Registration problems	4.1
Forgot to vote (or send in absentee ballot)	5.7
Inconvenient polling place or hours or lines too long	1.4
Transportation problems	1.7
Bad weather conditions	0.7

SOURCE: U.S. Bureau of the Census, "Reasons for Not Voting, by Sex, Age, Race and Hispanic Origin, and Educational Attainment: November 2002," at www.census.gov.

out that legal and extralegal denial of the vote to African Americans, women, Hispanics, persons over 18, and other groups has now been outlawed, so nonvoting is voluntary. He quotes the late Senator Sam Ervin of North Carolina: "I don't believe in making it easy for apathetic, lazy people to vote."[51] Some might even contend that nonvoting is a sign of voter satisfaction.

Those who argue that nonvoting is a critical problem cite the "class bias" of those who do vote. The social makeup and attitudes of nonvoters differ significantly from those of voters and hence greatly distort the representative system. "The very poor . . . have about two-thirds the representation among voters than their numbers would suggest." Thus the people who need help the most from the government lack their fair share of electoral power to obtain it. And, it is argued, this situation is growing worse.[52]

Declining participation through voting and other political acts has puzzled some political scientists because voting rates have continued to decline even as level of education, a strong predictor of voting, has increased—part of the answer to the puzzle may be that political parties and other groups have done less voter mobilization over time. In other words, some people don't vote because no one asks them to. Furthermore, advances in technology allow parties and campaigns to narrowly target their appeals to people who are already likely to turn out.[53]

Low voting, according to those who see a class bias in voting, reflects "the underdevelopment of political attitudes resulting from the historic exclusion of low-income groups from active electoral participation."[54] In short, part of the problem of nonvoting among low-income, less-educated people is their failure to be conscious of their interests. Dynamic leadership or strong party organization, or both, would not only attract the poor to the polls but also make clear their "class grievances and aspirations."[55] Others reject this class bias argument. They admit that nonvoters are demographically different but cite polls showing that nonvoters' attitudes are not much different from voters' attitudes. One study, comparing the party identification of voters with that of all Americans, found that the proportion of Democrats was nearly identical (51.4 percent of all citizens and 51.3 percent of voters), while Republicans as voters were slightly overrepresented (36 percent of citizens and 39.7 percent of voters). All other political differences are considered to be much smaller than this 3.7 percent gap. Further, voters are not "disproportionately hostile" to social welfare policies.[56]

What effect might increased voter turnout have in national elections? It might make a difference, since there are partisan differences between different demographic groups, and candidates would have to adjust to the demands of an expanded electorate. A noted political scientist, while acknowledging that no political system could achieve 100 percent participation, pointed out that the entire balance of power in the political system could be overturned if the large nonvoter population decided to vote.[57] However, others contend more persuasively that the difference may not be as pronounced. Nonvoters are not more in favor of government ownership or control of industry, and they are not more egalitarian. Nonvoters are, however, more inclined to favor additional spending on welfare programs.[58]

Another way to think of low voter turnout is to see it as a sign of approval of things as they are, whereas high voter turnout would signify disapproval and widespread desire for change. Even on the subject of how to interpret low turnout there is disagreement.

VOTING CHOICES

Why do people vote as they do? Political scientists have identified three main elements of the voting choice: party identification, candidate appeal, and issues. These elements often overlap.

Voting on the Basis of Party

Party identification is the subjective sense of identification or affiliation that a person has with a political party (see Chapter 7). Party identification often predicts a person's stand on issues. It is part of our national mythology that Americans vote for the

party identification
An informal and subjective affiliation with a political party that most people acquire in childhood.

★ YOU DECIDE

SHOULD WE ALLOW VOTING BY MAIL AND ON THE INTERNET?

During the past two centuries of constitutional government, this nation has gradually adopted a more expansive view of popular participation. Not only has the right to vote been extended to more people, but the decisions made in the voting booth have been expanded as well to include primary elections to nominate party candidates and ballot referendums in which state constitutional amendments and state laws are adopted.

It seems logical that the next step in our democratic progress is permitting voters to cast ballots through the mail or via the Internet. Not only would such a reform make voting easier, but it would permit us to have more elections. For example, when a city council wants voters to decide whether to build a new football stadium or when there is need for a special election to fill the term of a member of Congress who has died or resigned, election officials could mail out the ballots and then in two or three weeks count up those that have been returned. The state of Oregon has already conducted several general elections by mail, and other states are considering adopting the Oregon system.

What do you think? Should we move toward a system in which we replace the ballot box with the mailbox or the computer? What arguments would you make for and against such an idea?

person and not the party, but as you will see, the person we vote for is most often from the party we prefer.

As discussed, partisanship is typically acquired in childhood or adolescence as a result of the socialization process in the family and then reinforced by peer groups in adolescence. In the absence of reasons to vote otherwise, people depend on party identification to simplify their voting choices. Party identification is not the same as party registration; it is not party membership in the sense of being a dues-paying, card-carrying member, as in some European parties. Rather, it is a psychological sense of attachment to one party or another.

There has been a dramatic increase in the number of self-declared Independents since the mid-1970s. Nominally, there are more Independents in the electorate today than there are Republicans. But two-thirds of all Independents are, in fact, partisans in their voting behavior. Independent-leaning Democrats are predictably Democratic in their voting behavior, and Independent-leaning Republicans vote heavily Republican. Independent leaners are thus very different from each other and from the Pure Independents. Pure Independents have the lowest rate of turnout but generally do side with the eventual winner in presidential elections. These data on Independents only reinforce the importance of partisanship as an explanation of voting choice, because when we consider Independent-leaning Democrats and Independent-leaning Republicans as Democrats and Republicans, respectively, there were only 11 percent Pure Independents or others without a party in 2000,[59] and that proportion dropped in 2002 to 7 percent. These proportions are consistent with earlier election years. In short, the number of genuinely independent voters is relatively small and has remained so over time.

Although party identification has fluctuated somewhat in the past 40 years, it remains more stable than attitudes about issues or political ideology. Fluctuations in party identification appear to come in response to economic conditions and political performance, especially of the president. The more information voters have about their choices, the more likely they are to defect from their party and vote for a candidate from the other party.

Voting on the Basis of Candidates

While long-term party identification is important, it is clearly not the only factor in voting choices; otherwise the Democrats would have won every presidential election since the last realignment in 1932. In fact, since 1952, Republicans have been more successful in winning the White House than Democrats. The answer to this puzzle is largely found in a second major explanation of voting choice—**candidate appeal**.

The elections of the 1980s marked a critical threshold in the emergence of the candidate-centered era in American electoral politics. This change in focus from parties to candidates is an important historical trend that has been gradually taking place over the past several decades.[60] Candidate centered politics means that rather than rely on groups or parties to build a coalition of supporters for a candidate, the candidates make their case directly to the voters. In many races, the parties and groups have also made the candidate the major focus of attention, minimizing partisanship or group identification.[61]

Candidate appeal often involves an assessment of a candidate's character. Is the candidate honest? Is the candidate consistent? Is the candidate dedicated to "family values"? Does the candidate have religious or spiritual commitments? The press in recent elections has sometimes played the role of "character cop," asking questions about private lives and lifestyles. The press asks these questions because voters are interested in a political leader's background—perhaps even more interested in personal character than in a political position on hard-to-understand health care or regulatory policy issues.

Ronald Reagan's effort to generate positive candidate appeal was successful. His opponent in 1980, President Jimmy Carter, had hoped that Reagan would behave more like Barry Goldwater, who in his speech accepting the nomination in 1964 had said, "Extremism in the defense of liberty is no vice. . . . Moderation in the pursuit of justice is no virtue."[62] Lyndon Johnson, Goldwater's opponent, benefited from public perception

candidate appeal
How voters feel about a candidate's background, personality, leadership ability, and other personal qualities.

that Goldwater and those who nominated him were out of the mainstream of American politics, an idea reinforced by Goldwater's acceptance speech.

Like Barry Goldwater in 1964, George McGovern, who ran as the Democratic candidate for president in 1972, had negative appeal. He was perceived by many as too liberal, a view bolstered by images of his supporters, who by their dress and manner appeared out of the mainstream of American politics. In addition to ideological extremism, McGovern raised doubts about his judgment and leadership by how he handled his choice of a vice president. McGovern named Missouri Senator Tom Eagleton as his running mate, only to discover that Eagleton had once been hospitalized for emotional exhaustion and depression and had received electric shock therapy. McGovern initially stood behind Eagleton, but as press coverage and criticism of McGovern's lack of investigation into Eagleton's past grew, McGovern dropped Eagleton and named a new running mate, Sargent Shriver. In the end, "only about one-third of the public thought McGovern could be trusted as president."[63]

Candidate appeal or the lack of it—in terms of leadership, experience, good judgment, integrity, competence, strength, and energy—is sometimes more important than party or issues. Bill Clinton and John Edwards represent the regular working-class person rising against the odds. Dwight Eisenhower had great candidate appeal. He was a five-star general, a legendary hero of the Allied effort in World War II. His unmilitary manner, his moderation, his personal charm, and his lack of a strong party position made him appealing across the ideological spectrum. Ronald Reagan generated positive candidate appeal in part by asserting characteristics the public found lacking in Jimmy Carter—leadership and strength. In the 2004 presidential primaries, Howard Dean was initially perceived in positive terms, but that changed with his speech following the Iowa caucus. "The Scream," as it was labeled, called into question his self control.[64]

Increasingly, campaigns today focus on the negative elements of candidates' history and personality. Opponents and the media are quick to point out the limitations or problems of any given candidate. Bush was attacked in 2004 for his policies in Iraq, his failure to build broader coalitions with other countries, his tax cuts which lowered taxes for rich people as well as for others, and for rising deficits. Bush's record in the National Guard became a focus of a CBS "60 Minutes" segment, only to have CBS admit that the documents used in this critical story on Bush could not be authenticated. Kerry was attacked for flip-flopping over issues and his liberal voting record in the Senate. Kerry was also attacked for his war record by an outside group called Swift Boat Veterans for Truth. This attack put the Kerry campaign on the defensive for several days. (See Figure 8–5 for a list of which qualities mattered most to votes in 2004.)[65]

Voting on the Basis of Issues

Most political scientists agree that issues, while important, are not as central to the decision process as party identification and candidate appeal.[66] Part of the reason is that candidates often intentionally obscure their positions on issues—an understandable strategy.[67] Richard Nixon said he had a plan to end the Vietnam War in 1968, clearly the most important issue in that year, but he would not reveal the specifics. By not detailing his plan, he stood to gain votes from those who wanted a more aggressive war effort as well as those who wanted a cease-fire.

For issue voting to become of major significance, the issue must be important to a substantial number of voters, opposing candidates must take opposing stands on the issues, and voters must know these positions and vote accordingly. Rarely do candidates focus on only one issue. Voters often will agree with one candidate on one issue and with the opposing candidate on another. In such an instance, issues will likely not be the determining factor. But lack of interest by voters in issues does not mean candidates can take any issue position they wish.[68]

More likely than *prospective issue voting* (voting based on what a candidate pledges to do in the future about an issue if elected) is *retrospective issue voting* (holding incumbents,

---

★★ **THINKING IT THROUGH**

One of the problems with making elections more frequent is that voters will tire. Americans already vote more frequently and for more offices than citizens of any other democracy. Asking them to make voting choices even more frequently could result in lower turnout and less rational consideration. Many voters may be unaware that an election is going on. Yet the advantage of the vote-by-mail system employed by Oregon and some cities and counties is that it increases turnout, at least initially. What political scientists dispute is whether such increases in participation will continue when the novelty wears off.

Some critics of voting by mail or electronic democracy worry about fraud. Even when voters are required to sign their mailed-in ballots, the possibility of forgery still exists. Also, voting by mail or computer has the possibility of allowing people to pressure or harass voters. Another concern is late returns. Concerns about electronic voting have been reinforced by claims that the computer software is not secure and that some electronic voting fails to count all votes.*

Another criticism is that mail and electronic voting could be skewed toward participation by better-educated and higher-income voters, who routinely pay their bills by mail, make purchases on their computer, and own a personal computer with Internet access. Advocates of these new voting procedures contend that voters who do not own computers can drop off their ballots in some public building and that eventually computers will be available widely enough that access will not be a problem.†

However, if voting can be made easier and more convenient, why not do it? If the integrity of the vote can be protected and the new ways of voting become widely accessible, such changes are probably inevitable.

*E.J. Dionne Jr., "Election Dangers to be Avoided," *Washington Post*, May 25, 2004.

†Adam J. Berinsky, Nancy Burns, and Michael W. Tarugott, "Who Votes By Mail? A Dynamic Model of the Individual-Level Consequences of Voting-by-Mail Systems," *Public Opinion Quarterly* 65 (Summer 2001), pp. 178–197.

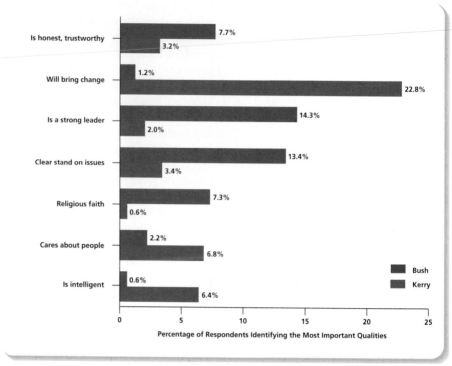

FIGURE 8–5 Which Quality Mattered Most in the 2004 Vote for President?
SOURCE: 2004 Exit Polls from Edison Media Research and Mitofsky International at www.cnn.com/
ELECTION/2004/pages/results/states/US/P/00/epolls.0.html.

usually the president's party, responsible for past performance on issues such as the economy or foreign policy).[69] In times of peace and prosperity, voters will reward the incumbent; if the nation falls short on either, voters are more likely to elect the opposition.

But good economic times do not always lead to the retention of an administration, as Al Gore learned in 2000. Part of Gore's problem in 2000 was that only half the public saw their family's financial situation as having gotten better. Of these voters, Gore received 61 percent of the vote.[70] But his inability to effectively claim credit for the good economic times hurt him, especially when Republicans contended that it was the American people, not the government, that produced the strong economy. A similar debate arose in 2004 over the state of the economy and the extent to which President Bush's policies or the terrorist attacks of September 11, 2001, had resulted in job loss and other economic problems. Democrats argued that the tax cut had been irresponsible, especially when the country was at war. The Republicans countered that the tax cuts had helped stimulate the economy.

The state of the economy is often the central issue in midterm elections as well as presidential ones. Several studies have found a positive relationship between the state of the economy and "out" party gains and "in" party losses in congressional seats.[71] Political scientists have been able to locate the sources of this effect in individual voters' decision making. Voters tend to vote against the party in power if they perceive a decline or standstill in their personal financial situations.[72]

Voters see responsibility for the economy as resting with the president and Congress more than with governors or local officials.[73] In 2004, the electorate was divided over the economy, jobs, and Bush's tax cut. More voters felt the economy was "not good or poor" than felt it was "excellent or good." The view of the economy appeared to be influenced by which candidate one preferred, with Bush supporters more positive and Kerry supporters more negative.[74] Kerry often tried to make the election about the economy and jobs but the issues of security and terrorism were seen as more vital.

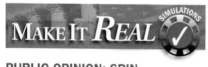

PUBLIC OPINION: SPIN DETECTION

Public opinion is important in a democracy because the government depends on the consent of the governed. This simulation describes survey techniques and identifies possible problems with surveys. Test your knowledge about survey research and attempt to identify problems with which surveyors deal.

Go to Make it Real, "Public Opinion: Spin Detection."

S U M M A R Y

1. Public opinion is a complex combination of views and attitudes individuals acquire through various influences from childhood on. Public opinion takes on qualities of intensity, latency, consensus, and polarization—each of which is affected by people's feelings about the salience of issues.

2. The American public has a generally low level of interest in politics, and most people do not follow politics and government closely. The public's knowledge of political issues is poor.

3. Americans who are interested in public affairs can participate by voting; joining interest groups and political parties; working on campaigns; writing letters to newspaper editors or elected officials; attempting to influence how another person will vote; donating money to a candidate, party, or group; or even protesting.

4. Better-educated, older, and party- and group-involved people tend to vote more; the young tend to vote the least. Voter turnout tends to be higher in national than in state and local elections, higher in presidential than in midterm elections, and higher in general than in primary elections.

5. Counting ballots has generated substantial controversy in recent elections. The Florida controversy in 2000 was resolved by the U.S. Supreme Court and Congress subsequently passed HAVA. In 2004, voter turnout soared, in part because of a close election and in part because of successful voter mobilization efforts.

6. Party identification remains the most important element in the voting choice of most Americans. It represents a long-term attachment and is a "lens" through which voters view candidates and issues as they make their voting choices. Candidate appeal, including character and record, is another key factor in voter choice. Voters decide their vote less frequently on the basis of issues.

K E Y   T E R M S

public opinion
political socialization

attentive public
voter registration

Australian ballot
turnout

party identification
candidate appeal

F U R T H E R   R E A D I N G

R. MICHAEL ALVAREZ AND JOHN BREHM, *Hard Choices, Easy Answers: Values, Information, and American Public Opinion* (Princeton University Press, 2002).

HERBERT ASHER. *Polling and the Public: What Every Citizen Should Know,* 6th ed. (CQ Press, 2004).

BARBARA A. BARDES AND ROBERT W. OLDENDICK, *Public Opinion: Measuring the American Mind* (Wadsworth, 2003).

M. MARGARET CONWAY, *Political Participation in the United States,* 4th ed. (CQ Press, 2000).

ROBERT M. EISINGER, *The Evolution of Presidential Polling* (Cambridge University Press, 2002).

ROBERT S. ERIKSON AND KENT L. TEDIN, *American Public Opinion: Its Origins, Content and Impact,* updated 6th ed. (Longman, 2002).

WILLIAM H. FLANIGAN AND NANCY H. ZINGALE, *Political Behavior of the American Electorate,* 10th ed. (CQ Press, 2002).

DONALD P. GREEN AND ALAN S. GERBER, *Get Out the Vote!: How to Increase Voter Turnout* (Brookings Institution Press, 2004).

ROBERT HUCKFELDT AND JOHN SPRAGUE, *Citizens, Politics, and Social Communication: Information and Influence in an Election Campaign* (Cambridge University Press, 1995).

LAWRENCE R. JACOBS AND ROBERT Y. SHAPIRO, *Politicians Don't Pander: Political Manipulation and the Loss of Democratic Responsiveness* (University of Chicago Press, 2000).

KATHLEEN HALL JAMIESON, *Everything You Think You Know About Politics and Why You're Wrong* (Basic Books, 2000).

BRUCE E. KEITH, DAVID B. MAGLEBY, CANDICE J. NELSON, ELIZABETH ORR, MARK C. WESTLYE, AND RAYMOND E. WOLFINGER, *The Myth of the Independent Voter* (University of California Press, 1992).

V. O. KEY JR., *Public Opinion and American Democracy* (Knopf, 1961).

JAN E. LEIGHLEY, *Strength in Numbers? The Political Mobilization of Racial and Ethnic Minorities.* (Princeton University Press, 2001).

MICHAEL B. MACKUEN AND GEORGE RABINOWITZ, EDS., *Electoral Democracy* (University of Michigan Press, 2004).

MICHAEL MARGOLIS AND DAVID RESNICK, *Politics as Usual: The Cyberspace 'Revolution,'* 6th ed. (Sage Publications, 2000).

MICHAEL NELSON, ED., *The Elections of 2000* (CQ Press, 2001).

RICHARD G. NIEMI AND HERBERT F. WEISBERG, *Classics in Voting Behavior* (CQ Press, 1993).

RICHARD G. NIEMI AND HERBERT F. WEISBERG, *Controversies in Voting Behavior,* 4th ed. (CQ Press, 2001).

FRANK R. PARKER, *Black Votes Count: Political Empowerment in Mississippi After 1965* (University of North Carolina Press, 1990).

THOMAS E. PATTERSON, *The Vanishing Voter: Public Involvement in the Age of Uncertainty* (Vintage, 2003).

GERALD M. POMPER, ED., *The Election of 2000: Reports and Interpretations* (Seven Bridges Press, 2001).

JAMES A. THURBER AND CANDICE J. NELSON, EDS., *Campaigns and Elections American Style,* 2d ed. (Westerview Press, 2004).

MICHAEL W. TRAUGOTT AND PAUL J. LAVRAKAS, *The Voter's Guide to Election Polls,* 3d ed. (Rowman & Littlefield, 2004).

MARTIN P. WATTENBERG, *Where Have All the Voters Gone?* (Harvard University Press, 2002).

JOHN ZALLER, *The Nature and Origins of Mass Opinion* (Cambridge University Press, 1992).

See also *Public Opinion Quarterly, The American Journal of Political Science,* and *American Political Science Review.*

CAMPAIGNS AND ELECTIONS

DEMOCRACY IN ACTION

9

S ome cynics contend that elections do not matter and there is little point
in voting. Strong evidence to the contrary comes from
the 2000 elections, in which Al Gore won the popular vote by 539,947 votes, or only slightly more than
180 votes per county! The contest was especially close in
Florida and New Mexico, where the statewide margins were
537 and 366 votes, respectively. The contest for the presidency was not the only one that required recounts. In Michigan, Mike Rogers won election to the House by 88 votes. In
the 2000 election, you could truthfully say that every vote
counted. In 2002, the Colorado Seventh district Congressional
race was decided by 121 votes and the South Dakota Senate
race was won by only 524 votes. In 2004, there were again some
close elections. Senate Minority Leader Tom Daschle, a Democrat, lost by 4,535 votes in South Dakota. In the presidential race, Bush carried New Mexico by only 8,000
votes. At the state and local level, there are often
races decided by only a few votes.

In the United States, citizens vote more
often and for more offices than citizens of
any other democracy. We hold
thousands of elections for
everything

from community
college directorsto county
sheriffs. About half a million
persons hold elected state and local
offices.[1] In 2004, we elected a president,
34 U.S. senators,[2] all 435 members of the U.S.
House of Representatives, 11 state governors, about a dozen state treasurers, nine
secretaries of state, and, in many states, judges.

In addition to electing people, voters in 27 states vote on laws or constitutional amendments proposed by initiative petitions or on popular referendums put on the ballot by petition. In all states except Delaware, voters must approve all changes in the state constitution.

In this chapter, we explore our election rules. We note four important problems: the lack of competition for some offices, the complexities of nominating presidential candidates, the distortions of the electoral college, and the influence of money in our elections. We also discuss proposed reforms in each of these areas.

ELECTIONS: THE RULES OF THE GAME

The rules of the game—the electoral game—make a difference. Although the Constitution sets certain conditions and requirements, most electoral rules remain matters of state law.

Regularly Scheduled Elections

In our system, elections are held at fixed intervals that cannot be changed by the party in power. It does not make any difference if the nation is at war, as we were during the Civil War, or in the midst of a crisis, as in the Great Depression; when the calendar calls for an election, the election is held. Elections for members of Congress occur on the first Tuesday after the first Monday in November of even-numbered years. Although there are some exceptions (for special elections or peculiar state provisions), participants know *in advance* just when the next election will be. In many parliamentary democracies, such as Great Britain and Canada, the party in power calls elections at a time of its choosing. The predetermined timing of elections is one of the defining characteristics of democracy in the United States.

Fixed, Staggered, and Sometimes Limited Terms

Our electoral system is based on *fixed terms,* meaning that the length of a term in office is specified, not indefinite. The Constitution has set the term of office for the U.S. House of Representatives at two years, the Senate at six years, and the presidency at four years.

Our system also has *staggered terms* for some offices; not all offices are up for election at the same time. All House members are up for election every two years, but only one-third of the senators are up for election at the same time. Since presidential elections occur two or four years into a senator's six-year term, senators can run for the presidency without fear of losing their seat, as John Kerry did in 2004. But if their Senate term expires the same year as the presidential election, the laws of many states require them to give up their Senate seat to run for president or vice president or any other position. An example of a state that permits a candidate to run for election to two offices is Connecticut, where Joseph Lieberman was reelected to the U.S. Senate in 2000 while being narrowly defeated in his race for vice president. Had he been victorious in both campaigns, he would have resigned his Senate seat.

Term Limits

The Twenty-Second Amendment to the Constitution, adopted in 1951, limits presidents to two terms. Knowing that a president cannot run again changes the way members of Congress, the voters, and the press regard the president. A politician who cannot, or has announced he or she will not, run again is called a *lame duck.* Efforts to limit the terms of other politicians have become a major issue in several American states. The most frequent targets have been state legislators. One consequence of term limits is more lame ducks.

Term limits are popular. Voters in 15 states have enacted them for their state legislature, and in two states, the legislature imposed term limits on themselves. Even more states limit the term of governors.[3] Three-fourths of all voters favor term limits, including 9 out of 10 strong Republicans and 7 out of 10 strong Democrats.[4] Still, despite their popularity, proposals for term limits have repeatedly been defeated when they have come to a vote in Congress.

The Supreme Court, by a vote of 5 to 4, declared that a state does not have the constitutional power to impose limits on the number of terms for which its members of the U.S. Congress are eligible, either by amending its own constitution or by state law.[5] Congress has refused to propose a constitutional amendment to impose a limit on congressional terms.

Winner Take All

An important feature of our electoral system is the **winner-take-all system,** or what is sometimes referred to as "first past the post" in other countries.[6] In most American electoral settings, the candidate with the most votes wins. The winner does not need to have a *majority* (more than half the votes cast); in a multicandidate race, the winner may have only a *plurality* (the largest number of votes). In 2000, three senators and seven House members were elected by pluralities. In 2002, again there were seven House races and three Senate races decided by a plurality. One senator and one House member were elected on pluralities in 2004. Winner-take-all electoral systems have the effect of reinforcing moderate and centrist candidates because they are more likely to secure a plurality or a majority. Candidates in a winner-take-all system often stress that a vote for a minor party candidate is a "wasted vote" and that it might have the effect of helping elect the voter's least desired candidate.

Most American electoral districts are **single-member districts**, meaning that in any district for any given election—senator, governor, U.S. House, state legislative seat—the voters choose *one* representative or official.[7] When the single-member-district and winner-take-all systems are combined, minor parties find it hard to win. For example, even if a third party gets 25 percent of the vote in several districts, it still gets no seats.

The combination of single-member districts and winner-take-all is different from a **proportional representation** system, in which political parties secure legislative seats and power in proportion to the number of votes they receive in the election. Let us assume that a state has three representatives up for election. In each of the three contests, the Republican defeats the Democrat, but in one district by only a narrow margin. If you add up the statewide vote, the Republicans get 67 percent and the Democrats 33 percent. Under our single-member-district and winner-take-all system, the Republicans get all three seats. But under a system of proportional representation, in which the three seats represent the whole state, the Democrats would receive one seat because they got roughly one-third of the vote in the entire state. Proportional representation thus rewards minor parties and permits them to participate in government. Countries that practice some form of proportional representation include Germany, Israel, and Japan.

The Electoral College

We elect our president and vice president not by a national vote but by an indirect device known as the **electoral college**. The framers of the U.S. Constitution devised this system because they did not trust the choice of president to a direct vote of the people. Under this system, each state has as many electors as it has representatives and senators. California therefore had 55 electoral votes (53 House seats and two Senate seats) and Vermont three electoral votes for the election of 2004.

Each state legislature is free to determine how its electors are selected. Each party nominates a slate of electors, usually longtime party workers. Electors are expected to cast their electoral votes for the party's candidates for president and vice president. In our entire history, no "faithless elector"—an elector who does not vote for his or her state's popular vote winner—has ever cast the deciding vote. There was one faithless elector in 2000 from the District of Columbia who abstained rather than cast her vote for Al Gore in order to protest the lack of congressional representation for Washington D.C.[8] The electoral college vote in 2004 had one faithless elector: an elector from Minnesota who voted for John Edwards instead of John Kerry. This happened in spite of both parties naming party faithful on the assumption that the election would be close.

The Twelfth Amendment requires electors to vote separately for president and vice president. To demonstrate how this works, if you voted for the Republican candidate in 2000, you actually voted for the Republican slate of electors in your state who pledged

IMPORTANT FACTORS IN WINNING AN ELECTION

Uncontrollable Factors

- Incumbent running
- Strength of party organization
- National tides or landslide possibility
- Socioeconomic makeup of district

Organizational Factors

- Registration drives
- Fund-raising
- Campaign organization
- Volunteers
- Media campaign
- Direct-mail campaign efforts
- Get-out-the-vote efforts

Candidate's Personal Factors

- Personal appeal
- Knowledge of issues
- Speaking and debating ability
- Commitment and determination
- Ability to earn free, positive media coverage

winner-take-all system
An election system in which the candidate with the most votes wins.

single-member district
An electoral district in which voters choose one representative or official.

proportional representation
An election system in which each party running receives the proportion of legislative seats corresponding to its proportion of the vote.

electoral college
The electoral system used in electing the president and vice president, in which voters vote for electors pledged to cast their ballots for a particular party's candidates.

ADVANTAGES AND DISADVANTAGES OF PROPORTIONAL REPRESENTATION

The winner-take-all rule of most American elections has some advantages but also means that substantial minorities go unrepresented. In cases where there are multiple candidates and the winner only has a plurality, it means that a majority goes unrepresented.

A system of proportional representation could be applied to the allocation of electoral votes by state, or in states with more than one member of the House of Representatives, it could be applied to the allocation of seats as it is in many democracies.

Proportional representation has some advantages. It more accurately reveals the preferences of voters and gives those who do not vote for the winning candidate a sense that they have some influence as a result of their vote. In this sense, proportional representation may encourage greater turnout for people who identify with parties that rarely win elections, like Democrats in Utah or Wyoming. Proportional representation may also encourage issue-oriented campaigns and enhance the representation of women and minorities.

But there are some problems with proportional representation. It may make it harder to have a clear winner. This problem is even greater if minor parties are likely to receive representation as well. In this sense, it may encourage minor parties. Opponents of proportional representation worry that it can contribute to political instability and ideological extremism. For another example of this see the comparative perspective box on Israel in Chapter 7.

to vote for George W. Bush for president and Dick Cheney for vice president in the electoral college.

Candidates who win a plurality of the popular vote in a state secure all that state's electoral votes, except in Nebraska and Maine, which allocate electoral votes to the winner in each congressional district plus two electoral votes for the winner of the state as a whole. Winning electors go to their state capital on the first Monday after the second Wednesday in December to cast their ballots. These ballots are then sent to Congress, and early in January, Congress formally counts the ballots and declares who won the election for president and vice president.

It takes a majority of the electoral votes to win. If no candidate gets a majority of the electoral votes for president, the House chooses among the top three candidates, with each state delegation having one vote. If no candidate gets a majority of the electoral votes for vice president, the Senate chooses among the top two candidates, with each senator casting one vote.

When there are only two major candidates for the presidency, the chances of an election being thrown into the House are remote. But twice in our history the House has had to act: In 1800, before the Twelfth Amendment was written, the House had to choose in a tie vote between Thomas Jefferson and Aaron Burr; and in 1824, the House picked John Quincy Adams over Andrew Jackson and William Crawford. Henry Clay, who was forced out of the race when he came in fourth in the electoral college, threw his support behind Adams. When Adams was elected, he made Clay his secretary of state. The 1824 vote in the House was especially contentious. Jackson, winner of the popular vote, was not elected when the decision passed to the House. This outcome infuriated Jackson, who won the electoral college vote by a wide margin four years later.

As we were reminded in 2000, our electoral college system makes it possible for a presidential candidate to receive the most popular votes, as Al Gore did, and yet not get enough electoral votes to be elected president. Al Gore won the popular vote by over 500,000 votes but lost the electoral college 271 to 266.[9] This also happened in 1824, when Andrew Jackson won 12 percent more of the vote than John Quincy Adams; in 1876, when Samuel Tilden received more popular votes than Rutherford B. Hayes; and in 1888, when Benjamin Harrison won in the electoral college despite Grover Cleveland's receiving more popular votes. It almost happened in 1960 and 1976, when the shift of a few votes in a few key states could have resulted in the election of a president without a popular majority. In a year with a serious minor party candidate, the result could be the

The Electoral Commission of 1877 met in secret session to decide the controversial presidential election between Rutherford B. Hayes and Samuel Tilden. After many contested votes the presidency was eventually awarded to Hayes.

election of a president without a plurality of the vote, as some believe happened with the Nader vote in 2000. (See Chapter 7)

In two of the four elections in which winners of the popular vote did not become president, the electoral college did not decide the winner. The 1824 election was decided by the U.S. House of Representatives. In 1876, the electoral vote in three southern states and Oregon was disputed, resulting in the appointment of an electoral commission to decide how those votes should be counted. In 1888 and 2000, the electoral college awarded the presidency to the candidate with fewer popular votes.

Concern about the electoral college is renewed every time there is a serious third-party candidate for the presidency. People began to ask, if no candidate receives a majority in the electoral college and the decision is left to Congress, which Congress casts the vote, the one serving during the election or the newly elected one? The answer is the new one, the one elected in November and taking office the first week in January. Since each state has one vote in the House, what happens if a state's delegation is tied in its vote, 2 to 2 or 3 to 3? The answer is its vote does not count. Would it be possible to have a president of one party and a vice president of another? Yes, if the election were thrown into the House and Senate and each chamber were controlled by a different party.

The electoral college sharply influences presidential politics. To win a presidential election, a candidate must appeal successfully to voters in populous states like California, Texas, Ohio, Illinois, Florida, and New York. California's electoral vote of 55 in 2004 exceeded the combined electoral votes of the 14 least populous states plus the District of Columbia. The map inside the back cover of this book provides a visual comparison of state size based on electoral votes. When the contest is close, as it was in 2000, every state's electoral votes count, and so greater emphasis is given to states in which the contest is close, even less populated states.[10]

Presidential candidates do not ordinarily waste time campaigning in a state unless they have at least a fighting chance of carrying that state; nor do they waste time in a state in which their party is a sure winner. Richard Nixon in 1960 was the last candidate to campaign in all 50 states, but he lost valuable time traveling to and from Alaska, while John Kennedy focused on the more populous states in which he had a chance to win. The contest usually narrows down to the medium-sized and big states, where the balance between the parties tends to be fairly even. In 2000 and 2004, all competitive contests received extraordinary attention from the candidates, parties, and allied groups (see Table 9–1).

TABLE 9–1   2004 BATTLEGROUND STATES

State	Electoral Votes	% Difference in 2004 Popular Vote
Wisconsin	10	.39% Kerry
New Mexico	5	.80% Bush
Iowa	7	.91% Bush
New Hampshire	4	1.36% Kerry
Pennsylvania	21	2.27% Kerry
Ohio	20	2.49% Bush
Nevada	5	2.62% Bush
Michigan	17	3.40% Kerry
Oregon	7	3.90% Kerry
Florida	27	5.02% Bush
Missouri	11	7.31% Bush

SOURCE: www.cbsnews.com/htdocs/politics/campaign2004/03%20battleground.pdf, and "2004 Battleground," at usinfo.state.gov/dhr/democracy/elections/battleground_states.html.

RUNNING FOR CONGRESS

How candidates run for Congress differs, depending on the nature of their district or state, on whether candidates are incumbents or challengers, on the strength of their personal organization, on how well known they are, and on how much money they have to spend on their campaign. We can also note several similarities in House and Senate elections.

First, most congressional elections are not close. In districts where most people belong to one party or where incumbents are popular and enjoy fund-raising and other campaign advantages, there is often little competition (see Figure 9–1).[11] Congressional districts have become less competitive on the whole in the 2000s, in large part because of the way district boundaries have been drawn by state legislatures. Districts in the 2002 redistricting were often drawn in ways that enhanced the reelection prospects of incumbents or one party, a processs called *partisan gerrymandering*. We explore this process in greater detail in Chapter 11, which deals with Congress. Those who believe that competition is essential to constitutional democracy are concerned that so many officeholders have **safe seats**. When officeholders do not have to fight to retain their seat, elections are not performing their proper role.[12]

safe seat
An elected office that is predictably won by one party or the other, so the success of that party's candidate is almost taken for granted.

GLOBAL *Perceptions*

QUESTION: Please indicate if you think that corrupt political leaders are a very big problem, a moderately big problem, a small problem, or not a problem at all.

In the vast majority of countries where the public was surveyed as part of the Pew Global Attitudes project, a large fraction of the people feel that corrupt political leaders are a "very big problem." In only a handful of countries did something less than a majority hold this view: the United States, Canada, Germany, Great Britain, Uzbekistan, and Jordan. The more prevailing response was for more than two-thirds of the public to report that corrupt political leaders were a large problem. In some cases, like Bangladesh and Argentina, nine-out-of-ten people said corruption was a very big problem. Even in the United States, nearly half of the respondents held this view. Places where perceived corruption is much less were once governed by monarchs and now have democracy and clean government or still have a monarchy (like Great Britain and Jordan). Countries that previously had totalitarian governments, such as Russia and Poland, have about the same distribution of opinon as countries in Africa and Asia. In short, most people in the world assume that their political leaders are corrupt.

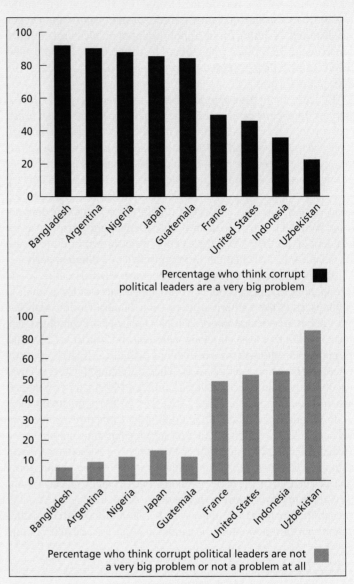

Percentage who think corrupt political leaders are a very big problem

Percentage who think corrupt political leaders are not a very big problem or not a problem at all

SOURCE: Pew Global Attitudes Project, *What the World Thinks in 2002* (Washington, D.C.: The Pew Research Center for the People and the Press, 2002), p. T-20.

Competition is more likely when funding is adequate for both candidates, which is not often the case in U.S. House elections (see Figure 9–1). Elections for governor and for the U.S. Senate are more seriously contested and more adequately financed than those for the U.S. House of Representatives.

Presidential popularity affects both House and Senate elections during presidential election years as well as midterm elections. The impact of presidential candidate popularity in a presidential election is known as the **coattail effect**, the boost candidates from the president's party get from a popular presidential candidate running in the same election. But winning presidential candidates do not always provide such a boost. The Republicans suffered a net loss of six House seats in 1988, even though George H. W. Bush won the presidency, and the Democrats suffered a net loss of ten house seats in 1992 when Bill Clinton won the presidential election. Democrats fared better in 1996,

coattail effect
The boost that candidates may get in an election because of the popularity of candidates above them on the ballot, especially the president.

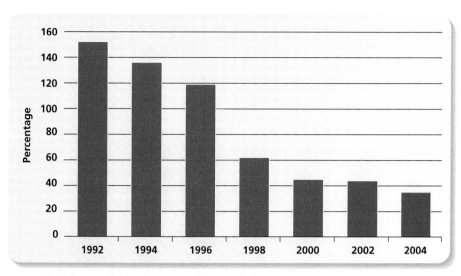

FIGURE 9–1 Competitive House Seats, 1992–2004.
SOURCE: Charlie Cook, "National Overview," *The Cook Political Report,* October 4, 2002, p. 6; "2004 Races at a Glance," *The Cook Political Report,* July 22, 2004. www.cookpolitical.com.
NOTE: Competitive races are those classified by Cook as "toss ups" or leaning toward one party.

registering a net gain of nine house seats. There were no discernible coattails in the 2000 elections. In 2004, Republicans picked up U.S. Senate seats in states carried by Bush, such as South Dakota, North Carolina, and South Carolina, and held contested seats in Oklahoma and Alaska. Overall, "measurable coattail effects continue to appear," according to congressional elections scholar Gary Jacobson, but they are "erratic and usually modest" in their impact.[13]

In midterm elections, presidential popularity and economic conditions have long been associated with the number of House seats a president's party loses.[14] These same factors are associated with how well the president's party does in Senate races, but the association is not as strong.[15] Figure 9–2 shows the number of seats in the House of Representatives and U.S. Senate gained or lost by the party controlling the White House in midterm elections since 1938. Republicans did better in 1994 than in any midterm election since 1946, picking up 53 seats. The Republican tide was not limited to the House but included a net gain of nine Senate seats.[16] In all of the midterm elections between 1934 and 1998, the party controlling the White House lost seats in the House. The range of losses, however, is quite wide, from a low of four seats for the Democrats in 1962 to a high of 71 seats for the Democrats in 1938. But in 2002, as in 1998, the longstanding pattern of the president's party losing seats did not hold. Republicans picked up a net gain of 2 seats in the Senate and 6 seats in the House. As noted, there were comparatively few competitive races in 2002, the most recent midterm election, especially for a year following redistricting.

When presidential landslides occur, as they did with Lyndon Johnson in 1964, the victorious party is especially vulnerable and likely to lose seats in the next midterm election, as the Democrats did in 1966. Given the historic pattern of the president's party's losing seats and the close party balance resulting from the 2000 elections, Democrats believed they were well positioned in 2002 to recapture control of both houses of Congress. The Democrats' hopes were dashed by a set of strong Republican candidates for the House and

Democratic Senator Barbara Boxer (center) from California debates Republican challenger Bill Jones (right) in her successful bid for reelection to the U.S. Senate in 2004.

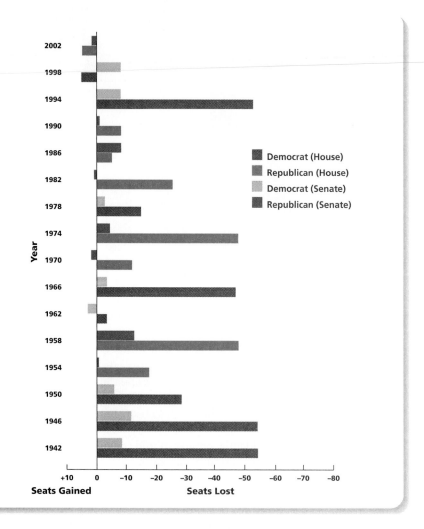

FIGURE 9–2 Seats Lost by the President's Party in Midterm Elections for the House of Representatives and the Senate, 1938–2002.

Senate, recruited in part with the assistance of the White House. President Bush invested a great deal of time and effort in helping Republican candidates in competitive races, with early visits to their states and districts to help with fundraising and an intense series of campaign stops in the last five days that more resembled the close to a presidential election than the close to a midterm election. Despite this heavy investment by President Bush, many 2002 contests revolved around more local issues. Arkansas voters rejected Republican Tim Hutchinson for another term in the Senate in part because of his private life, and South Dakota returned Democrat Tim Johnson despite five visits to the state by Bush. Johnson closely linked himself to fellow South Dakota Democrat Tom Daschle, whose power as Senate Majority Leader was at stake in 2002. In 2004, the White House was not as succesful in "clearing the field" for preferred candidates. In the Pennsylvania, Colorado, and Florida Senate races the Republicans had the kind of contested primaries they worked hard to avoid in 2002. Republicans went on to hold their seats in Pennsylvania and Florida but lost in Colorado, where the divisive primary helped the Democratic candidate.

The House of Representatives

Every two years, as many as 1,000 candidates—including approximately 400 incumbents—campaign for Congress. Incumbents are rarely challenged for renomination from within their own party, and when they are, the challenges are seldom serious. In the 1990s, for example, on average only two House incumbents were denied renomination in each election, and in 2002, 71 percent of all U.S. Representatives and 69 percent of all U.S.

Senators had no opponent in the primaries.[17] Challengers from other parties running against entrenched incumbents rarely encounter opposition in their own party.[18]

MOUNTING A PRIMARY CAMPAIGN The first step for would-be challengers is to raise hundreds of thousands of dollars (or even more) to mount a serious campaign. This requires asking friends and acquaintances as well as interest groups for money. Candidates need money to hire campaign managers and technicians, buy television and other advertising, conduct polls, and pay for a variety of activities. Parties can sometimes help, but they shy away from giving money in primary contests. The party organization usually stays neutral until the nomination is decided.

Another early step is to build a *personal organization.* A candidate can build an organization while holding another office, such as a seat in the state legislature, by serving in civic causes, helping other candidates, and being conspicuous without being controversial.

A candidate's main hurdle is gaining visibility. Candidates work hard to be mentioned by the media. In large cities with many simultaneous campaigns, congressional candidates are frequently overlooked, and in all areas, television is devoting less time to political news.[19] Candidates rely on personal contacts, on hand shaking and door-to-door campaigning, and on identifying likely supporters and courting their favor—the same techniques used in campaigns for lesser offices. Despite these efforts, the turnout in primaries tends to be low, except in campaigns in which large sums of money are spent on advertising.

CAMPAIGNING FOR THE GENERAL ELECTION As we have mentioned, most incumbent members of Congress win reelection.[20] Since 1970, over 95 percent of incumbent House members seeking reelection have won, and in 2000, 98 percent of incumbent House members running for reelection were successful (see Figure 9–3).[21] In 2002, again 98 percent of incumbents running in the general election won. In 2004, 99 percent of incumbents running in the general election were returned to office. Of the seven incumbents defeated, two ran against other incumbents.

One reason incumbents win so often is that they are able to outspend their challengers by roughly 3 to 1 in the House; in the Senate the difference is closer to 1.75 to 1.[22] Most challengers spend little money, run campaigns that are not significantly more visible than primary campaigns, contact few voters, and lose badly. Serious challengers in House races are hard to find. Many are scared away by the prospect of having to raise more than $1 million in campaign funds, others realize that the district has been drawn with fewer persons from their party than the incumbent's, and some do not want to face the media scrutiny that comes with a serious race for Congress. Nonetheless, in each election, a few challengers mount serious campaigns because of the incumbent's perceived vulnerability, the challengers' own wealth, party or political action committee efforts, or other factors.

Another reason most incumbents win so frequently is that their districts are predominantly Republican or Democratic. The 2002 redistricting process largely protected

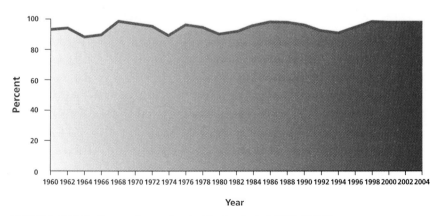

FIGURE 9–3 U.S. House Incumbents Reelected, 1946–2004.
SOURCE: Harold W. Stanley and Richard G. Niemi, eds., *Vital Statistics on American Politics 2001–2002* (CQ Press, 2001), pp. 53–55. 2004 update by authors.

"My former opponent is supporting me in the general election. Please disregard all the things I said about him in the primary."

Dunagin's People. Tribune Media Services.

incumbents in both parties by making districts less competitive. Few incumbents were seriously challenged. Retirements and redistricting create *open seats,* which can result in more competitive elections. Potential candidates, as well as political action committees and political party committees, all watch open-seat races closely. If, however, the district is heavily partisan, the predominant party is likely to retain the seat, and once elected the incumbent then reaps the other incumbency advantages as well. But as noted, most races have incumbents and most incumbents win, lending credibility to the charge that we have a "permanent Congress." Occasionally, one party has a big victory, as the Republicans did in 1994, with a 57-seat gain in the House, securing the majority for the first time in 40 years. Large shifts like 1994 are rare in part because state legislatures through redistricting have created fewer competitive districts.

Why is keeping a House seat so much easier than gaining it? Incumbents have a host of advantages that help them win reelection. These perquisites, or "perks," come with the job of communicating with constituents and include free mailings (the *franking privilege*) and telephone calls to constituents, the free use of broadcast studios to record radio and television tapes to be sent to local media outlets, and, perhaps most important of all, a large staff to perform countless favors for constituents and send a stream of press reports and mail back to the district.[23] Representatives also try to win committee posts, even on minor committees, that relate to the needs of their districts and build connections with constituents.[24]

The Senate

Running for the Senate is big-time politics. The six-year term and the national exposure make a Senate seat a glittering prize, so competition is usually intense. Senate campaigns generally feature state-of-the-art campaign techniques; a race normally costs millions of dollars (see Figure 9–4).[25] The essential tactics are to raise lots of money, get good people involved, make as many personal contacts as possible (especially in the states with smaller populations), avoid giving the opposition any positive publicity, and have a clear and consistent campaign theme. Incumbency is an advantage for senators, although not as much as for representatives.[26] Incumbent senators are widely known, but so are their opponents, who often raise and spend significant amounts of money.[27]

When one party controls the Senate by only a few seats, as has been the case in recent years, more good candidates run, and the number of competitive elections increases. Going into the 2002 elections, the Senate had 50 Democrats, 49 Republicans, and one Independent. Jim Jeffords of Vermont was reelected as a Republican in 2000

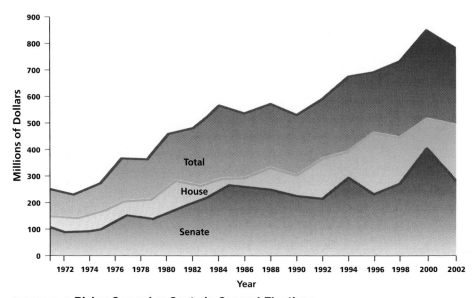

FIGURE 9–4 Rising Campaign Costs in General Elections.
SOURCE: Federal Election Commission, "Congressional Campaign Expenditures Total $772 Million," January 2, 2003, at www.fec.gov.

but switched parties in 2001, putting the Democrats in control of Senate leadership and all standing committees. The narrow margin of Democratic control meant that a net loss of one seat would put the Republicans back in the majority. The GOP mounted a major effort to reclaim the Senate in 2002, picking up a net gain of two seats and returning the Senate and all of the elected federal government to Republican control.[28] Competitive U.S. Senate races in 2004 were waged largely on Republican turf. Democrats won in Illinois and Colorado, picking up what had been Republican seats, but lost seats they had held in Florida, Georgia, North Carolina, South Carolina, and South Dakota. President Bush carried South Dakota by 60 percent to 39 percent, creating a difficult challenge for Democrats like Tom Daschle. Overall, Republicans enjoyed a net gain of four seats in the Senate, increasing their majority to 55 to 45.

The cost of Senate campaigns can vary greatly. California has nearly 70 times the number of potential voters as Wyoming; not surprisingly, running for a seat from Wyoming is much cheaper than running for a seat from California. As a result, interest groups and parties direct more money to competitive races in small states when the stakes for control of the Senate are high.[29]

RUNNING FOR PRESIDENT

Presidential elections are major media events, with candidates seeking as much positive television coverage as possible and trying at the same time to avoid negative coverage. The formal campaign has three stages: winning the nomination, campaigning at the convention, and mobilizing support in the general election.

Stage 1: The Nomination

Presidential hopefuls must make a series of critical tactical decisions. The first is when to start campaigning. For the presidential election of 2004, some candidates, like John Kerry, John Edwards, and Howard Dean, began soon after the 2000 presidential election.[30] Early decisions are increasingly necessary for candidates to raise the money and assemble an organization. Campaigning begins well before any actual declaration of candidacy as candidates try to line up supporters to win caucuses or primaries in key states and to raise money for their nomination effort.

One of the hardest jobs for candidates and their strategists is calculating how to deal with the complex maze of presidential primaries and caucuses that constitutes the delegate selection system. The system for electing delegates to the national party convention varies from state to state and often from one party to the other in the same state. In some parties in some states, for example, candidates must provide lists of delegates supporting them months in advance of the primary. The presidential campaign finance system provides funds to match small individual contributions during the nomination phase of the campaign for candidates who agree to remain within spending limitations. George W. Bush declined the federal funds in the 2000 and 2004 nomination phase, as did Democrats John Kerry and Howard Dean in 2004. Foregoing the public matching funds allows greater flexibility in when and where campaign money is spent and removes the overall limit for this phase of the process.

PRESIDENTIAL PRIMARIES State presidential primaries, unknown before 1900, have become the main method of choosing delegates to the national convention. A delegate is a person selected by local partisans to represent them in selecting nominees, party leaders, and party positions. Today, more than three-fourths of the states use presidential primaries. In 2000, some 84 percent of the Democratic delegates and 89 percent of the Republican delegates were chosen in the primaries.[31] The rest of the delegates were chosen by state party caucuses or conventions, or were party leaders who serve as "super delegates." In 2004, 85 percent of Democratic delegates and 69 percent of GOP delegates were chosen in the primaries. Several states (Arizona, Colorado, Delaware, Maine, Michigan, South Carolina, Utah, Virginia, and Washington) that held GOP primaries in 2000 switched to state caucuses or other methods in 2004 (see www.thegreenpapers.com/P04/tally.phtml).

The Iowa caucuses are an important first step in terms of media exposure for candidates running for president. Here, Democrat John Kerry speaks at a caucus site in Muscatine, Iowa, on January 12, 2004.

Presidential primaries often have two features: a *beauty contest,* or popularity vote, in which voters indicate which candidate they prefer but do not actually elect delegates to the convention, and *actual voting* for delegates pledged to a candidate. Since 1996, the Democrats require primary votes to be linked to delegate election. The Republicans allow states to separate a popularity vote from delegate selection. States which use this system include Montana, Nebraska, Illinois, New Jersey, Pennsylvania, and West Virginia.[32]

Candidates may win the beauty contest but find their opponents doing better in actual delegates elected because they failed to put a full slate of delegates on the ballot or because local notables were listed on the ballot as delegates pledged to another candidate. Different combinations of these two features have produced the following systems[33]:

■ *Proportional representation:* Delegates to the national convention are allocated on the basis of the percentage of votes candidates win in the beauty contest. This system has been used in most of the states, including several of the largest ones. The Democrats mandate proportional representation for all their primaries.[34] In some states, Republicans use this same system, but Republicans are much more varied in their delegate selection processes.[35]

■ *Winner take all:* Whoever gets the most votes wins all that state's delegates. To win all the delegates of a state like California is an enormous bonus to a candidate. Republicans still use the winner-take-all system at the state level, and in 2004, most states used this rule at either the state or congressional district levels.[36]

■ *Delegate selection without a commitment to a candidate.* New York Republicans allow the state committee to select 12 at-large delegates who are officially unpledged, as are the party chair and national committee representatives.[37]

■ *Delegate selection and separate presidential poll:* In several states, voters decide twice: once to indicate their choice for president and again to choose delegates pledged, or at least favorable, to a presidential candidate.

Voters in states like Iowa and New Hampshire, which are the first states to pick delegates, bask in media attention for weeks and even months before they cast the first ballots in the presidential sweepstakes. Because these early contests have had the effect of limiting the choices of voters in states that come later in the process, there has been a tendency for states to move their primaries up. This process is called "front loading."

California, which traditionally held its primary in June, moved it to March in 2000 so that its voters would play a more important role in selecting the nominee. Other states did the same thing. Front loading was even more prominent in 2004,[38] with Democratic National Committee Chair Terry McAuliffe's hope that the nominee would be chosen by March 2004, allowing time for the party to assist with fundraising and building party unity.[39]

In both 2000 and 2004 the nomination in both major parties was decided by March. This had the effect of compressing the nomination battle into several weeks of intense activity in the spring followed by months of much less activity before the fall general election campaign. For 2004, as in the past, states that felt overlooked in 2000 pushed for revision to the schedule, including possibly having four regional groupings (East, South, Midwest, and West).[40] States that gain visibility and importance through early primaries continue to want to maintain that advantage.

CAUCUSES AND CONVENTIONS A **caucus** is a meeting of party members and supporters of various candidates. In about a dozen states one or both parties use a caucus or convention system (or both) for choosing delegates.[41] Each state's parties and legislature regulate the methods used. The caucus or convention is the oldest method of choosing delegates and differs from the primary system in that it centers on party organization.

Delegates who will attend the national party conventions are chosen by delegates to state or district conventions, who themselves are chosen earlier in county, precinct, or town caucuses. The process starts at local meetings open to all party members, who discuss and take positions on candidates and issues and elect delegates to represent their views at the next level. This process is repeated until national nominating convention delegates are chosen by conventions of delegates throughout a district or state.

The best-known example of a caucus is in Iowa, because Iowa has held the earliest caucuses in the most recent presidential nominating contests. Every January or February in a presidential election year, Iowans have the opportunity to attend Republican and Democratic precinct meetings. Large numbers of voters attend these small town meetings and have a chance to meet and exchange views on issues and candidates, rather than merely pulling a lever in a voting booth or marking a ballot.[42]

Presidential hopefuls face a dilemma: To get the Republican nomination, you have to appeal to the more intensely conservative Republican partisans, those who vote in primaries and support campaigns. Democratic hopefuls have to appeal to the liberal wing of their party as well as minorities, union members, and environmental activists. But to win the general election, candidates have to win support from moderates and pragmatic voters, many of whom do not vote in the primaries. If candidates position themselves too far from the moderates in their nomination campaign, they risk being labeled extreme in the general election and losing these votes to their opponent.

STRATEGIES Strategies for securing the nomination have changed over the years. Some candidates think it wise to skip some of the earlier contests and enter first in states where their strength lies. John McCain pursued such a strategy in 2000, ignoring Iowa and concentrating on New Hampshire. In 2004 retired General Wesley Clark also bypassed Iowa, but unlike McCain he did not win in New Hampshire and dropped out of the race only a few weeks later. Most candidates choose to run hard in Iowa and New Hampshire, hoping that early showings in these states, which receive a great deal of media attention, will move them into the spotlight for later efforts.

During this early phase, especially important is the ability of candidates to manage the media's expectations of their performance in order to generate momentum. Lyndon Johnson actually won the New Hampshire primary in 1968, yet because his challenger, Eugene McCarthy, did better than the press had predicted, McCarthy was interpreted as the "winner." Both John Kerry and John Edwards did better than expected in Iowa in 2004, giving them momentum for New Hampshire and beyond.

Winning in the primaries thus becomes a game of expectations, and candidates may intentionally downplay their expectations so that "doing better than expected" might generate momentum for their campaign. It is also important to maintain a presidential bearing even in the primaries. In 2004, the front runner going into Iowa was Vermont Governor Howard Dean. In a speech to supporters after losing the Iowa

caucus
A meeting of local party members to choose party officials or candidates for public office and to decide the platform.

PEOPLE & POLITICS *Making a Difference* ★★★

KARL ROVE

Presidents have long had political advisors, both on their paid staff and more informally. Karl Rove has long been the chief political advisor to President George W. Bush. Rove has described his job as paying "attention to the things that affect his [Bush's] political future."* Another Bush confidant has described Rove as "the Bobby Fischer of politics," continuing that "he not only sees the [chess] board, he sees about 20 moves ahead."[†] Bush himself described Rove as the "boy genius."[‡]

Rove left the University of Utah before graduating to become chairman of the College Republicans. His interest in politics had started at an early age, when he helped campaign for Richard Nixon against John F. Kennedy. His political activism continued during high school, where he also developed an interest in debate and U.S. History. His involvement in the College Republicans helped him establish connections and enlarged his interest in politics. He was executive director of the College Republicans when George H.W. Bush was chair of the Republican National Committee. George H.W. Bush later hired Rove to help him run for president in 1980.

Rove formed his own consulting firm in Austin, Texas, where he did political and campaign consulting, including work on the successful campaign of Bill Clements, the first Texas Republican governor. Another Texas Governor became his most successful client, George W. Bush. Rove and Bush have a close working relationship. Rove, while heading the political affairs office in the White House, played an important role in recruiting candidates to run in 2002 and in talking others out of running. He also was the primary architect of the Bush 2004 reelection campaign.[§] Rove heavily emphasized playing to Bush's conservative base, an effective strategy in the wake of same-sex marriage initiatives in eleven states.

*James Carney and John F. Dickerson, "The Busiest Man in the White House: As Bush Hits 100 Days in Office, His Top Strategist, Karl Rove, Is Already Eyeing 2004." *Time,* April 22, 2001, at www.time.com/time/magazine/article/subscriber/0,10987,1101010430-107220,00.html.
[†]Dana Milbank, "'Background' Checks," *The Washington Post,* January 28, 2003, p. A19; Dan Balz, "Team Bush; The Governor's 'Iron Triangle' Points the Way to Washington," *The Washington Post,* July 23, 1999, p. C01.
[‡]David B. Magleby and J. Quin Monson, eds., *The Last Hurrah?: Soft Money and Issue Advocacy in the 2002 Congressional Elections* (Brookings Institute Press., 2004), p. 102.
[§]www.abcnews.go.com/sections/politics/DailyNews/rove_profile001228.html.

caucuses, placing third after Kerry and Edwards, an animated Dean, attempting to rally his followers, uttered what came to be called the "Dean scream," or "I have a scream" speech.[43] As Dean learned, such a mistake, when replayed countless times on cable and broadcast news and when made the brunt of jokes elsewhere on television, becomes a defining moment and makes it difficult for the candidate to reestablish a positive campaign agenda. While Dean's ascendancy and sudden demise were both notable features of the 2004 election, a more enduring aspect of his candidacy was his extensive use of the Internet, especially for fundraising, and his demonstrating to the other Democrats the depth of anti-Bush passion among Democratic voters.[44]

Stage 2: The National Party Convention

The delegates elected in primaries, caucuses, or state conventions assemble at their **national party convention** in the summer before the election to pick the party's presidential and vice presidential candidates. In the past, delegates arrived at national nominating conventions with differing degrees of commitment to presidential candidates; some delegates were pledged to no candidate at all, others to a specific candidate for one or two ballots, and others firmly to one candidate only. Recent conventions have merely ratified decisions already made in the primaries and caucuses, in part because delegates are required to pledge themselves to a specific presidential hopeful (in the Democratic party) or because one candidate has been able to amass a majority of delegates. And because of reforms encouraging delegates to stick with the person to whom they are pledged,

national party convention
A national meeting of delegates elected in primaries, caucuses, or state conventions who assemble once every four years to nominate candidates for president and vice president, ratify the party platform, elect officers, and adopt rules.

there has been no room to maneuver at conventions. National party conventions used to be events of high excitement because they determined who would be the party nominee, but in every election since the Republican convention of 1948 and the Democratic convention of 1952, the party primaries have decided who would be the nominee.

As recently as 1988, Democratic and Republican national conventions were given gavel-to-gavel coverage by the major networks, meaning that from the beginning of the first night to the end of the fourth night, television covered the conventions. Now the major networks leave comprehensive coverage to C-SPAN and CNN. National nominating conventions have ceased to dominate the national news, for the very good reason that they are no longer the place where candidates are selected.[45] The long-term trend of declining viewership and reduced hours of coverage has altered the parties' strategies. In 2004, the parties featured their most important speakers and highlighted their most important messages in the limited time given them by the networks. There were slight increases in viewership of the conventions in 2004.

Conventions follow standard rules, routines, and rituals. Usually, the first day is devoted to a keynote address and other speeches touting the party and denouncing the opposition; the second day, to committee reports, including party and convention rules and the party platform; the third day, to presidential and vice presidential balloting; and the fourth day, to the presidential candidate's acceptance speech, although in 2004 with both parties' nominees having only limited broadcast television time the foucs was on major speeches each night.[46] For sample coverage of the 2004 Republican convention go to www.2004nycgop.org, and for the Democrats see www.dems2004.org.

Because the choice of the party nominees has been decided well before the convention, there has been relatively little controversy on the floor of the conventions in recent years. The parties have turned to theatrics and celebrities in an effort to boost the audience watching the televised conventions. The networks have also shortened the proceedings on network television to only an hour or so per night of the convention.

THE PARTY PLATFORM   Delegates to the national party conventions decide on the *platform,* a statement of party perspectives on public policy. Why does anyone care what is in the party platform? Critics have long pointed out that the party platform is binding on no one and is more likely to hurt than to help a candidate. But presidential candidates as well as delegates take the platform seriously because it defines the direction a party wants to take. Also, despite the charge that the platform is ignored, most presidents make an effort to implement it.[47] For example, when President George W. Bush signed an education bill into law, he pointed to his party's commitment to "leave no child behind."[48] Neither party had a platform fight in 2004.

THE VICE PRESIDENTIAL NOMINEE   The choice of the vice presidential nominee garners widespread attention. Rarely does a person actually "run" for the vice presidential nomination, because only the president's vote counts. But there is a good deal of maneuvering to capture that one vote. Sometimes the choice of a running mate is made at the convention—not a time conducive to careful and deliberate thought. But usually the choice is made before the convention, and the announcement is timed to enhance media coverage and momentum going into the convention. The last time a presidential candidate left the choice of vice president to the delegates was for the Democrats in 1956.

Traditionally, the presidential nominee chooses a running mate who will "balance the ticket." Democratic presidential nominee Walter Mondale raised this tradition to a dramatic new height in 1984 by selecting a woman, New York Representative Geraldine A. Ferraro, to run with him. Mondale's bold decision was an effort to strengthen his appeal to women voters. But presidential candidates can also ignore the idea of a balanced ticket, as George W. Bush did when he chose another Texan from the oil industry to be his running mate. Dick Cheney moved his official residence to Wyoming and registered to vote there so that if the Bush-Cheney ticket won the popular vote in Texas, Republican Texas electors could vote for him, since the Constitution (Article II, Section 1) prohibits electors from voting for more than one person for president and vice president from their own state.

John Kerry's selection of John Edwards for his running mate in 2004 helped energize the Democratic campaign. Edwards was seen as appealing to young, rural, Southern, and moderate voters.[49] On most issues his positions were identical to Kerry's, but the two had fought aggressively against each other in the primaries despite these similarities. During the primaries, Kerry had criticized Edwards for his inexperience, especially in defense and foreign policy. Edwards helped motivate trial lawyers to contribute even more substantially to the Democratic ticket, but some parts of the business community was activated even more against Kerry because of its desire to enact limitations on damages in law suits.

THE VALUE OF CONVENTIONS   Why do the parties continue to have conventions if the nominee is known in advance and the vice presidential nominee is the choice of one person? What role do conventions play in our system? For the parties, they are a time of "coming together" to endorse a party program and to build unity and enthusiasm for the fall campaign. For candidates as well as other party leaders, conventions are a chance to capture the national spotlight and further their political ambitions. For nominees, they are an opportunity to define themselves in positive ways. The potential exists to heal wounds festering from the primary campaign and move into the general election united, but the potential is not always achieved. Conventions can be potentially divisive, as the Republicans learned in 1964 when conservative Goldwater delegates loudly booed New York Governor Nelson Rockefeller and as the Democrats learned in 1968 when the convention spotlighted divisions within the party over Vietnam as well as ugly battles between police and protesters near the convention hotels.

NOMINATION BY PETITION   There is a way to run for president of the United States that avoids the grueling process of primary elections and conventions—if you are rich enough or well known enough. John Anderson in 1980 and H. Ross Perot in 1992 met the various state requirements and made it onto the ballot in all 50 states. In 2000, Patrick Buchanan, candidate of the Reform party, was able to get his name on the ballot in all but one state and the District of Columbia, and Ralph Nader, candidate of the Green party, in all but seven states.[52] In 2004, the petition process was as simple as submitting the signatures of 1,000 registered voters in Washington State,[50] or by paying $500 in Colorado or Louisiana,[51] or as difficult as getting the signatures of currently registered voters equal to 2 percent of total votes cast in the last election in North Carolina (100,532 signatures).[53] In 2004, independent candidate Ralph Nader made the ballot in 34 states and the District of Columbia. He was excluded from 16 states, including Ohio and Pennsylvania.

Stage 3: The General Election

The national party convention adjourns immediately after the presidential and vice presidential candidates deliver their acceptance speeches to the delegates and the national television audience. Traditionally, the time between the conventions and Labor Day was a time for resting, binding up wounds from the fight for the nomination, gearing up for action, and planning campaign strategy. In recent elections, however, the candidates have not paused after the convention but launched directly into all-out campaigning. In 2004, both major party candidates campaigned aggressively from March through the general election. The intensity of the early campaign was noteworthy, with Bush spending in excess of $80 million on advertising between March and June and Kerry over $60 million.[54] Anti-Bush interest groups spent an estimated $32 million during this critical early period,[55] meaning that the Anti-Bush/Pro-Kerry spending exceeded the Bush spending during this time period. The early going in battleground states was unusually intense.

PRESIDENTIAL DEBATES   Televised presidential debates are a major feature of presidential elections. The 1960 debate between John Kennedy and Richard Nixon boosted Kennedy's campaign and elevated the role of television in national politics.[56] In 1976, President Gerald Ford debated Jimmy Carter and mistakenly said that each country in eastern Europe "is independent, autonomous, it has its own territorial integrity, and the United States does not conceive that those countries are under the domination of the Soviet Union."[57] That mistake damaged his credibility. Ronald Reagan's performance in the 1980 and 1984 debates confirmed the public view of him as decent, warm, and dignified. Bill Clinton's skirmishes with George Bush in 1992 and Bob Dole in 1996 showed him to be a skilled performer.

The 2004 presidential debates were widely watched and largely reinforced the candidate preferences of the viewers. Neither candidate made a major mistake and both candidates were able to state their positions and draw contrasts with their opponent. Challengers generally benefit more from debates and in 2004, Kerry was seen as the "winner" in public opinion surveys following all three debates. the vice pesidential debate followed the same pattern as the presidential debates, with no major mistake and few surprises. During both the presidential and vice presidential debates, mention was made by the Democrats of Vice President Cheney's daughter being a lesbian. The Republicans, and especially Mrs. Cheney, criticized the Democrats after the debate for drawing the daughter's sexual orientation into the campaign.

Since 1988, the nonpartisan Commission on Presidential Debates has sponsored and produced the presidential and vice presidential debates. The commission includes representatives from such neutral groups as the League of Women Voters. Before the commission became involved, there was often a protracted debate about debates. No detail seemed too small to the candidate managers—whether the candidates would sit or stand, whether they would be able to ask each other questions, whether they would be allowed to bring notes, and whether the questions would be posed by a single journalist, a panel of reporters, or a sample of citizens. By negotiating in advance many of the contentious details and arranging for debate locations, the commission now facilitates the presidential and vice presidential debates. In 2000, George W. Bush proposed alternative formats and locations, only to back down as it appeared he was avoiding debates.[58] The 2004 debates were again run by the Commission on Presidential Debates. The candidates again negotiated such things as whether they would be standing or sitting. An important departure from the presumed format was the use of split screens by the networks where one candidate was seen reacting while the other was speaking. President Bush, especially during the first debate, reacted with what was widely described as a "scowl" to some of the criticisms leveled by Senator Kerry. In a later debate, Bush made mention of his "scowl." The president seemed more comfortable in the format where questions came from the audience.

Minor party candidates often charge that the commission is biased in favor of the two major parties. To be included such candidates must have an average of 15 percent or higher in the five major polls used by the commission for this purpose and be legally eligible and be on the ballot in enough states to be able to win at least 270 electoral votes.[59] In 2004 Ralph Nader failed to meet these criteria for inclusion as did both he and Patrick Buchanan in 2000. In 1992, Ross Perot and his running mate, James Stockdale, had been included in the presidential and vice presidential debates, which generated large viewing audiences, averaging more than 80 million for each debate. The issue of excluding minor party candidates remains contentious. Including them takes time away from the major party candidates, especially if two or more minor party candidates are invited. Including them may also reduce the likelihood of both major parties' candidates' participating. But excluding them raises issues of fairness and free speech.

Although some critics are quick to express their dissatisfaction with presidential candidates for being so concerned with makeup and rehearsed answers, and although the debates have not significantly affected the election outcomes, they have provided important opportunities for candidates to distinguish themselves and for the public to weigh their qualifications. Candidates who do well in these debates are at a great advantage. They have to be quick on their feet, seem knowledgeable but not overly rehearsed, and project a positive image. Most presidential candidates are adept at all of these skills.

THE OUTCOME Though each election is unique, politicians, pollsters, and political scientists have collected enough information to agree broadly on a number of basic factors that they believe affect election outcomes. Whether the nation is prospering probably has the most to do with who wins a presidential election, but as we have noted, most voters vote on the basis of party and candidate appeal.[60] Who wins depends on voter turnout. The Democrats' advantage in the number of people who identify themselves as Democrats is

Presidential debates give candidates an opportunity to show how quickly and accurately they can respond to questions and outline their goals. In the debates of the 2004 elections, the consensus was that John Kerry outperformed George W. Bush in all three presidential debates; however his performance did not propel Kerry to victory in the election.

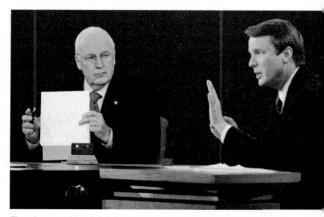

The vice presidential debate tends to be a more contentious exchange than presidential debates, providing each running mate with an opportunity to assail the opposition on various issues without the constraints that govern the presidential debates. The Iraq war, terrorism, and the economy all figured prominently in the 2004 vice presidential debate between John Edwards and Dick Cheney.

mitigated by higher voter turnout among Republicans. Republicans also usually have better access to money, which means they can run more television ads in more places and more often.

After the votes are cast, as we saw in the last chapter, they must be counted. And the way they are counted can be a critical factor in close races. Even before the votes were counted in 2004, both parties had deployed thousands of lawyers to observe the voting and ballot counting and to launch legal challenges if necessary. The Bush victory was large enough that these challenges did not materialize. As we have been reminded, the popular vote is not necessarily the deciding vote in presidential elections. The electoral college has an important role to play and courts may have to determine if state and federal laws have been fairly applied. The peaceful transfer of power from one individual or party to another, especially after such contested elections, is the culminating event in electoral democracy.

MONEY IN U.S. ELECTIONS

Election campaigns cost money, and the methods of obtaining the money have long been controversial. Campaign money can come from a candidate's own wealth, political parties, interested individuals, or interest groups. Money is contributed to candidates for a variety of reasons, ranging from altruism to self-interest. Individuals or groups, in hopes of influencing the outcome of an election and subsequently influencing policy, give **interested money**. Concern about campaign finance stems from the possibility that candidates or parties, in their pursuit of campaign funds, will decide that it is more important to represent their contributors than their conscience or the voters. The potential corruption that results from politicians' dependence on interested money concerns many observers of American politics.

Scandals involving money's influence on policy are not new. In 1925, responding to the Teapot Dome scandal, in which a cabinet member was convicted of accepting bribes, Congress passed the Corrupt Practices Act, which required disclosure of campaign funds but was "written in such a way as to exempt virtually all [members of Congress] from its provisions."[61]

The 1972 Watergate scandal—an illegal break-in at Democratic party headquarters by persons associated with the Nixon campaign to steal campaign documents and plant listening devices—led to discoveries by news reporters and congressional investigators that large amounts of money from corporations and individuals were "laundered" in secret bank accounts outside the country for political and campaign purposes. Nixon's 1972 campaign spent more than $60 million, more than twice what it had expended in 1968. Investigators discovered that wealthy individuals and corporations made large contributions to influence the outcome of the election or secure ambassadorships and administrative appointments.

In the early 1990s, Charles Keating and his failed Lincoln Savings and Loan spotlighted the possibility that undue influence comes with large contributions. Keating had asked five U.S. senators, all of whom had received substantial campaign contributions or other perks from him, to intervene on his behalf with federal bank regulators looking into his savings and loan business. These senators came to be called the Keating Five. One of the senators was John McCain, who later became a strong advocate of campaign finance reform. The 1996 election saw aggressive fundraising by the Clinton/Gore campaign, including opportunities for donors to have meetings with the President, to fly with him on Air Force One, and to spend the night in the White House Lincoln Bedroom. A congressional investigation into these and related concerns about campaign finance in the 1996 cycle reinforced the case for reform.[62]

Efforts at Reform

Reformers have tried three basic strategies to prevent abuse in political contributions: (1) imposing limitations on giving, receiving, and spending political money; (2) requiring public disclosure of the sources and uses of political money; and (3) giving governmental

interested money
Financial contributions by individuals or groups in the hope of influencing the outcome of an election and subsequently influencing policy.

In Comparative Perspective

THE SOFT MONEY LOOPHOLE IN JAPAN

The Japanese strategy to combat corruption and money politics has been to create some of the most stringent campaign regulations in the world:

- Door-to-door campaigning is banned.
- Candidates may not run campaign advertisements in the media, although parties may.
- Candidates may produce only two versions of their campaign brochure, and only a limited number may be distributed; the number varies according to the number of registered voters in a district.
- Campaign posters are allowed only on government-provided poster boards that are set up in several locations across a district during the campaign.
- Direct mailing of campaign literature that mentions a specific candidate is not allowed except for a specified number of government-provided campaign postcards.

- The number of campaign offices, employees, and vehicles is restricted by law.

These regulations should make it impossible for candidates to raise and spend large sums of money in a campaign, but Japanese candidates have found a giant loophole in these restrictions by avoiding "official" campaign activities. A candidate will go door to door or mail out literature to voters or put up posters advertising a speech to be given before the official campaign period. In these precampaign activities, the candidates will be very careful never to mention the upcoming election, so their efforts are not covered by law.

Attempts to limit these activities have run into constitutional concerns. If a campaign has not begun and a person has not declared his or her candidacy, how can the Japanese government restrict the right of a citizen to speak at a meeting, discuss issues with people, mail information to people, or put up posters advertising such activities?

subsidies to presidential candidates, campaigns, and parties. Recent campaign finance laws have tended to use all three strategies.

THE FEDERAL ELECTION CAMPAIGN ACT   In 1971, Congress passed the Federal Election Campaign Act (FECA), which limited amounts that candidates for federal office could spend on advertising, required disclosure of the sources of campaign funds as well as how they are spent, and required political action committees to register with the government and report all major contributions and expenditures. This law also provided a checkoff that allowed taxpayers to contribute $1 to a fund to subsidize presidential campaigns by checking a box on their income tax form. The checkoff option is now $3.

In 1974, Congress passed and President Gerald Ford signed the most sweeping campaign reform measure in U.S. history. These amendments to the Federal Election Campaign Act established somewhat more realistic limits on contributions and spending, tightened disclosure, and provided for public financing of presidential campaigns.

The 1974 law was again extensively amended after the Supreme Court's 1976 *Buckley* v. *Valeo* decision, which overturned several of its provisions on grounds that they violated the First Amendment.[63] The *Buckley* decision emphasized limitations on contributions and full and open disclosure of all fund-raising activities by candidates for federal office, as well as the system of public financing for presidential elections.[64] The Supreme Court made a distinction between campaign spending and campaign contributions, holding that the First Amendment protects spending; therefore, legislatures may not limit how much of their own money people spend on elections, but Congress may limit how much people contribute to somebody else's campaign. Later modifications of the law and interpretations by the Federal Election Commission sought to encourage volunteer activities and party building by permitting national political parties, corporations, labor unions, and individuals to give unlimited amounts, called **soft money**, to state parties, provided that the funds were used for party-building purposes.

One of the success stories of FECA was that presidential candidates of both parties for 20 years accepted the limitations on fundraising and campaign spending that were part of the public financing provisions. In recent presidential elections the public subsidy of presidential candidates has broken down. Until 2000, presidential candidates

soft money
Contributions to a state or local party for party-building purposes.

★★ YOU DECIDE

WHEN IS AN AD ABOUT AN ELECTION?

Political ads have many different purposes. Some are about issues, attempting to persuade the audience to a point of view; others are about a candidate's qualifications; and still others are about both issues and candidates. Groups in past elections spent many millions of dollars on election ads that fell outside the disclosure and other limitations of federal law. How would you define an election ad?

Assume you are watching an ad on TV or listening to one on the radio. Ask yourself if what you are seeing or hearing is only about issues, or if it is about electing or defeating a candidate.

- Does it feature the image or likeness of a candidate?
- Does it mention a candidate by name?
- Does it mention an election?
- Does it use words like "vote for," "vote against," or "support"?
- Is it shown in the weeks before an election?

The answers to questions like these can determine whether this is a campaign communication and therefore subject to the disclosure and other requirements of federal law.

(except wealthy, self-financed candidates) accepted the voluntary limitations that come with partial public financing of presidential nomination campaigns. George W. Bush, who raised more than $125 million for his campaign, declined federal matching funds in the 2000 primaries. In 2004, having raised over $366 million, he again turned down the matching funds in the primaries as did two of the Democrats, Howard Dean and John Kerry (Kerry raised over $322 million). In 2000 and 2004, Bush accepted the federal general election grant of roughly $75 million, along with the general election spending limit. John Kerry also accepted the public funding and spending limit in the 2004 presidential general election. Whether future candidates will also pass up some federal funds depends on how well funded their opponents are and their own ability to raise money. Beyond the problem of candidates' passing up federal funds, the number of taxpayers checking the campaign subsidy on their income tax forms has been declining, although enough did so to cover all the costs of the 2000 and 2004 elections.[65]

THE BIPARTISAN CAMPAIGN REFORM ACT (BCRA) One of the most serious problems with the campaign finance system was soft money—funds given to national parties by individuals or political action committees ostensibly for party-building registration drives, mailings, and advertising. No limits were set on the amount of such contributions. The money was called "soft" because federal law did not limit how much individuals or groups could contribute or how much parties could spend. Although soft money was supposed to benefit only parties, it was used by the parties to influence the election of federal candidates. Both parties made raising soft money a high priority, and soft money spending rose dramatically. All national party committees combined raised over $509 million of soft money in the 1999–2000 election cycle, up from $110 million adjusted for inflation in 1991–1992[66] (see Figure 9–5). In 2001–2002, all party committees combined raised over $495 million in soft money.

Soft money brought back the large donors as major players in campaign finance. It also strengthened the power of the national party committees, which allocate the money to state parties and indirectly to candidates. To the Supreme Court, which upheld the BCRA soft money ban, one of the major problems with soft money was that it

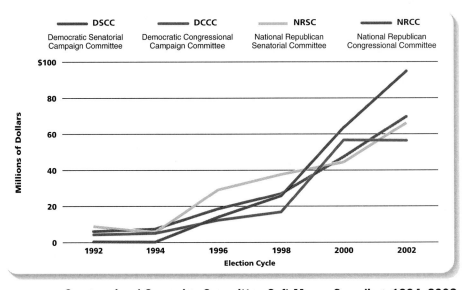

FIGURE 9–5 Congressional Campaign Committee Soft Money Spending, 1994–2002.
SOURCE: Federal Election Commission, "Party Committees Raise more than $1 Billion in 2002–2003," press release, March 20, 2002, at www.fec.gov, April 29, 2003. Adjusted by CPI, at ftp://ftp.bls.gov/pub/special.requests/cpi/cpiai.txt, January 15, 2003.
NOTE: The totals for each party do not equal the sum of the party committee receipts because the numbers provided by the FEC have been adjusted to account for transfers between party committees so as not to double count money in the total receipts.

purchased access to elected officials and with that access came influence and the possibility or appearance of corruption.[67]

In the past, soft money had been more important in presidential than in congressional contests, but that changed in a dramatic way with the 1998 and 2000 congressional elections. The most dramatic growth in 2000 and 2002 came among Senate Democrats. Figure 9–5 plots the surge in soft money funds for the four congressional campaign committees. The 2002 election cycle also saw extraordinary soft money activity by all party committees. Overall, the parties raised nearly as much soft money in 2001–2002 as they raised in 1999–2000, which was a presidential election year. When we compare 2002 with the last midterm year, 1998, we see soft money more than doubling in four years. With President Bush leading the way, the Republican National Committee raised nearly $114 million, up from $74 million in 1998. Again in 2002, the Democratic Senatorial Campaign Committee outpaced all other committees, raising more than $95 million.

BCRA banned most forms of soft money. All soft money contributions to national party committees were banned, as was soft money spending by state parties for or against federal candidates. However, BCRA permits state and local party committees to raise and spend limited amounts of soft money for voter registration and get-out-the-vote efforts. Such activities may be funded with soft money contributions of no more than $10,000 per individual or group as permitted by state law. This provision in BCRA is called "Levin Funds," so named after Michigan Senator Carl Levin, who sponsored this as an amendment.

ISSUE ADVOCACY ADVERTISING The 1996 election saw a surge in **issue advocacy**. Money spent on issue advocacy ads is unlimited and undisclosed because it presumably deals with issues, not candidates. Issue ad spending in some U.S. House races exceeded $1 million in recent elections; for example, in 2000, one group, the Alliance for Quality Nursing Home Care, spent more than $1 million on issue ads in the Delaware U.S. Senate race.[68] In the 1998, 2000, and 2002 elections, businesses, labor unions, health maintenance organizations, environmental groups, the Business Roundtable, pro- and anti-gun groups, pro- and anti-abortion groups, and the pharmaceutical industry ran issue ads (see Table 9–2).

★★ THINKING IT THROUGH

Until BCRA, groups relied on a distinction in the *Buckley* v. *Valeo* Supreme Court decision, which defined communications that use words such as "vote for" or "vote against" as election ads and those that did not use such words as "issue ads." This distinction was not meaningful in actual campaigns, however.* BCRA defines an electioneering communication as "a communication that refers to a clearly identified candidate, is publicly distributed shortly before an election for the office that candidate is seeking, and is targeted to the relevant electorate (U.S. House and Senate Candidates only)."†

BCRA's new electioneering definition had only a limited impact in 2004 because the campaign started so early, well before the 60 days before the general election. Some groups simply shifted to a strategy of doing independent expenditures which are unlimited but fully disclosed. Finally, BCRA's new definition did not apply to mail, phone, or personal contact, which was a major part of the process in 2004.

Critics of the new BCRA definition point out that Congress is often in session until a few days before an election, and interest groups need to be able to inform the public about important issues that are being considered. To limit issue ads during this period may stifle the free speech of groups with a more legislative than electoral agenda. Critics also see any restriction or limitation on electioneering as a restriction on First Amendment rights, and this includes limits on corporations and unions using their general funds for these purposes.

*David B. Magleby, "Dictum Without Data: The Myth of Issue Advocacy and Party Building," at csed.byu.edu/ publications/dictum.doc.

†Federal Elections Commission, "Electioneering Communications," June 2004, at www.fec.gov.

TABLE 9–2   SOME FREQUENT ISSUE ADVERTISERS

Advertiser	*Amount Spent**
Citizens for Better Medicare	$64
AFL-CIO	45
Coalition to Protect America's Health Care	30
National Rifle Association	25
U.S. Chamber of Commerce	15
Planned Parenthood Action Fund	14
Business Roundtable	13
Federation for American Immigration Reform	12
NAACP National Voter Fund	11
Americans for Job Security	10

SOURCE: Data from David B. Magleby, ed., *Election Advocacy: Soft Money and Issue Advocacy in the 2000 Congressional Elections* (Center for the Study of Elections and Democracy, Brigham Young University, 2001); Erika Falk, "Issue Advocacy Advertising Through the Presidential Primary, 1999–2000 Election Cycle," Annenberg Public Policy Center, press release, September 20, 2000.

*The numbers estimate total spending on issue advocacy and express advocacy; however, a large proportion went to issue advocacy.

---

issue advocacy
Promoting a particular position or an issue paid for by interest groups or individuals but not candidates. Much issue advocacy is often electioneering for or against a candidate, and until 2004 had not been subject to any regulation.

WHAT BCRA DOES

Federal campaign finance legislation passed in 2002 does all of the following:

- Keeps the Federal Election Commission, appointed by the president with the advice and consent of the Senate, to regulate the campaign financing of candidates for president, senator, and representative
- Retains the public financing of presidential general election campaigns with funds from the income tax checkoff
- Retains partial public financing of presidential nominating campaigns on a matching basis
- Retains subsidies to the two national parties for their convention expenses and to any minor party that polled 5 percent of the total vote in the previous presidential election
- Keeps limits on spending by candidates for presidential nominations (on a state-by-state basis and in total) and in the presidential general elections for those candidates who accept public funding
- Keeps limits on the amounts that national parties may spend on presidential campaigns and on individual congressional and senatorial campaigns
- Sets a limit of $2,000 on the amount that any individual can give to a candidate for the U.S. Senate or for the U.S. House of Representatives in the primary election; a limit of $2,000 per candidate in the general election; and a limit of $5,000 per candidate in the primary and $5,000 in the general election for political action committees
- Sets an overall limitation of $95,000 for individuals over a two-year election cycle
- Sets no limit on the amount of their own money candidates can spend on their campaign
- Sets no limit on the amount that individuals or groups can spend independently
- Bans soft money except for $10,000 per state and local party committee for voter registration and activation
- Bans the use of corporate and union treasury funds for all electioneering, including issue advocacy
- Redefines such "issue advocacy" as electioneering and makes its disclosure more consistent with independent expenditure disclosure.

The 2002 election saw an expansion of seniors' groups doing issue advocacy. Among those involved were 60 Plus, Seniors Coalition, United Seniors Association, and the American Association for Retired People (AARP). The AARP, by far the largest and best known of seniors' groups, urged voters to study the issues. The seniors' group that spent the most money was United Seniors, a group largely funded by the pharmaceutical industry. By masking its identity, the pharmaceutical industry could present its message without a stigma. Voters have an unfavorable impression of the pharmaceutical industry but know very little about United Seniors.[69] Other groups that engaged in substantial issue advocacy in 2002 included the Sierra Club, Planned Parenthood, and Club for Growth. These ads not only help the candidate that interest groups prefer or punish the candidate they oppose but also force candidates to discuss the interest group's agenda. Although these ads do not specifically say to vote for or against a candidate, they may contain candidates' images and names, and for voters they are indistinguishable from candidate or party ads.[70]

BCRA bans broadcast ads that show the image or likeness of a candidate, mention a candidate's name, and occur in the 60 days before a general election or 30 days before a primary election not paid for with disclosed money. This act also bans unions and corporations from using treasury funds for electioneering ads.

The use of issue ads and the growth in soft money meant that competitive congressional elections shifted from candidate-centered elections to party-centered and interest-group-centered campaigns. Soft money spending combined with interest group

Issue ads, such as this one placed by the U.S. Chamber of Commerce to promote pro-business candidates, try to influence voters to support candidates with favorable positions on the issues that are important to their sponsors.

issue advocacy spending exceeded the candidate campaigns in radio and television advertising by a margin of 2 to 1 in many of the most competitive congressional races of 2000 and 2004.[71] Parties and interest groups also spent large sums of money on mailings and telephone calls. For example, in some congressional races in 2000, targeted voters received as many as 12 pieces of political mail per day as election day approached. The intensity of issue advocacy and soft-money-funded communications in competitive races in 2002 was again extraordinary. In contests like the South Dakota Senate race, an hour of programing often had only political commercials. Because television time was sold out, some groups purchased radio time. Others turned to mail. Many groups with membership lists used these for personal contact and get-out-the-vote efforts.[72]

One of the problems with issue ads is accountability. Since interest groups using this form of electioneering are not required to disclose how much they spend or how they raise their money, voters have a hard time knowing the source of the funds. Ads by these groups also tend to be more negative.[73] Often candidates get blamed for the attacks made by these groups because voters assume that the ads are run by the candidates.

One predictable consequence of BCRA's ban on soft money was increased interest group electioneering via issue advocacy in 2004. The most visible of these new electioneering groups, sometimes called **527 groups**, is America Coming Together (ACT) which raised and spent an estimated $76 million in presidential battleground states in 2004. Much of the early money for ACT came from the wealthy investor George Soros. The advent of groups like ACT, while benefiting John Kerry and the Democrats, constitutes a shift in power toward groups and away from candidates and parties.

Republicans, in part because they were in power and had the fundraising skills of President Bush, did not see as many allied 527 groups as did the Democrats. Some examples of Republican 527 groups in 2004 included Progress for America, Leadership Forum, and the Republican Governors Association. The 527 group that may have had the greatest impact on the campaign was the Swift Boat Veterans for Truth, who attacked Senator Kerry's war record. The modest initial budget for ads generated news coverage. The message of the ads cut to the core of the persona that Kerry had presented at the Democratic National Convention. President Bush was not drawn into the controversy but former Senator Bob Dole's assertion that there may be something to the charges added to the attention the group received. Some Republican allied groups did not organize as 527 organizations but instead operated under a different section of the tax code (Section 501-C), which requires even less disclosure.[74] But it was on the Democratic side that 527 groups were most important. ACT, for example, helped organize many other interest groups in its voter registration and mobilization efforts. A related group, The Media Fund, spent $54 million in ads against President Bush up until 60 days before the election.

There are several important campaign finance-related issues that BCRA does not address. For example, it leaves intact the fund-raising advantages enjoyed by incumbents. It is not only the source of campaign money that is a problem but the pattern of unequal distribution as well. The high costs of television advertising diminish the ability of challengers to mount visible campaigns, resulting in declining competition. Only months after passage of the 2002 reforms, John McCain announced his support and sponsorship of legislation creating a "broadcast bank" where political parties would be given vouchers for free advertising time, with one-third of the time to go to challengers. Television stations, under McCain's proposal, are required to devote at least two hours per week to political coverage in which the candidates are on camera during the last month of the general election campaign.[75] For more information on broadcast time proposals, see The Alliance for Better Campaigns at www.bettercampaigns.org.

CANDIDATES' PERSONAL WEALTH Campaign finance legislation cannot constitutionally restrict rich candidates—the Rockefellers, the Kennedys, the Perots—from spending heavily on their own campaigns. Big money can make a big difference, and wealthy candidates can afford to spend big money. In presidential politics, this advantage can be most meaningful in the period before the primaries begin. There may be no constitutional way to limit how much money people can spend on their own campaigns. The 2000 New Jersey U.S. Senate race, for example, set new records for a candidate's personal spending in an

Candidates willing to spend personal wealth on their campaign enjoy important advantages. They are not subject to the contribution limitations imposed on other individuals. New Jersey Senator Jon Corzine spent $60 million of his own money on his 2000 race. Corzine was selected by the Democratic leadership to head the Democratic Senatorial Campaign Committee for 2003–2004.

527 Groups
Interest groups organized under Section 527 of the Internal Revenue Code may advertise for or against candidates. If their source of funding is corporations or unions, they have some restrictions on broadcast advertising. 527 organizations were important in recent elections.

IN COMPARATIVE PERSPECTIVE

CAMPAIGN FINANCING IN BRITAIN AND CANADA

United States election campaigns go on for months or even years and are very expensive. In contrast, Canadian general election campaigns are limited by law to about five weeks. Public opinion polls cannot be published during the last three days of a campaign, and the media are prohibited by law from reporting results from earlier time zones on the evening of the election in any district where voting is still taking place.

Expenditures are strictly limited for Canadian political parties and individual candidates. During the 1997 general election campaign to fill the 301 seats in the House of Commons, political parties that fielded candidates in all districts were limited by law to spending no more than approximately $8 million each for the entire election, and individual candidates could spend about $35,000 to $45,000, depending on the number of voters per district. In return, media outlets were required to sell a certain amount of airtime to the parties, and national and regional television and radio networks had to donate some free airtime to these parties. If individual candidates received more than 15 percent of the vote in their districts, the government reimbursed 50 percent of their election-related expenses. Political parties receiving at least 2 percent of the national vote or at least 5 percent of the votes cast in electoral districts where they ran candidates were reimbursed 22.5 percent of their expenses.

In the June 1997 Canadian elections, 1,672 candidates ran for office, and ten political parties received registered status. Total spending by the parliamentary candidates and political parties was approximately $70 million—less than half the $157 million spent by candidates in the United States during the 1996 election campaign ($29 million on seats in the House of Representatives and $128 million on seats in the Senate).

British general elections also offer an interesting contrast to elections in the United States. The election campaign lasts only three weeks. Candidates for the House of Commons, the most critical election in Britain, are allowed to raise and spend only $15,000. If they spend more, they are disqualified. Each candidate gets the same amount of free airtime, and each candidate is allowed one free election leaflet mailed to each voter in the constituency. About 75 percent of voters turn out, and about 95 percent of eligible voters are registered to vote. At the voting booth, the voter is handed a slip of paper with the names of three or four candidates for the House of Commons. No other offices or ballot questions are presented at the same time.

SOURCE: Adapted from Dudley Fishburn, "British Campaigning—How Civilized!" *The New York Times*, April 14, 1992, p. 25. See also, Alexancer Macleod, "Britain Leads in Campaign Finance Reform," *Christian Science Monitor*, July 30, 1999, Section: World; p. 6.

---

election. Wall Street investment banker Jon Corzine, a newcomer to elections, spent a total of $60 million, $35 million of it on the primary alone.[76] Corzine was elected. BCRA includes a millionaire's provision that was upheld by the Supreme Court in *McConnell* v. *FEC*. The provision allows candidates running against self-financed opponents who expend large amounts of their own wealth to have higher contribution limits for their donors.

INDEPENDENT EXPENDITURES BCRA does not constrain **independent expenditures** by groups, political parties, or individuals, as long as the expenditures by those individuals, parties, or groups are independent of the candidate and fully disclosed to the Federal Election Commission (FEC). A group or party that does independent expenditures within a month of a primary or two months of a general election must use hard money, that is, disclosed and limited contributions to the party or group. Any 527 organization wishing to broadcast an electioneering communication within one month of a primary or two months of a general election must not use corporate or union treasury funds, it must report the expenditures associated with the broadcast, and it must disclose all funding sources since the first day of the preceeding calendar year. While contribution sources are restricted in this case, contribution amounts are not. Individuals spending their own money and not coordinating with others are also not limited. This exemption was permitted by the Supreme Court on free speech grounds. In the 1999–2000 election cycle, interest groups spent a total of $22 million on independent expenditures. The National Rifle Association (NRA) led all other interest groups with $4.2 million, mostly for Republicans, but the League of Conservation Voters ($3.2 million), the National Education Association (NEA) ($2.4 million), and the National Abortion and Reproductive Rights Action League ($2.2 million) all combined to spend $7.8 million, mostly on behalf of Democrats. Individuals can also engage in

independent expenditures
Money spent by individuals or groups not associated with candidates to elect or defeat candidates for office.

independent expenditures. In the 2000 presidential election, Stephen Adams, owner of an outdoor advertising firm, spent $2 million in support of Governor George W. Bush.[77] In 2004, billionaire George Soros, who gave millions to 527 organizations opposed to the re-election of George Bush, also spent 2.3 million in independent expenditures against the president. He used the money to run full-page newspaper ads against Bush and to fund a speaking tour during which he expressed his opposition to Bush's reelection. In addition, he maintained a Web site and sent mailings to voters in key states.

Continuing Problems with Campaign Finance

The continuing problems with federal election fund raising are easy to identify: dramatically escalating costs, a growing dependence on PAC money, decreasing visibility and competitiveness of challengers (especially in the House), and the ability of wealthy individuals to fund their own campaigns. The danger of large contributions influencing lawmakers directly or indirectly through political parties was reduced by BCRA. Large contributons, however, can still influence the outcome of elections, as the 527 and other groups [since there were groups organized under other rules, too] demonstrated in the 2004 election.

RISING COSTS OF CAMPAIGNS   The American ideal that anyone—even a person of modest wealth—can run for public office and hope to win has become more a myth than a reality.[78] And rising costs also mean that incumbents spend more time raising funds and therefore less time legislating and representing their districts. Since the Federal Election Campaign Act (FECA) became law in 1972, total expenditures by candidates for the House of Representatives have more than doubled after controlling for inflation, and they have risen even more in Senate elections (see Table 9–3). One reason

TABLE 9–3   AVERAGE CAMPAIGN EXPENDITURES OF CANDIDATES FOR THE HOUSE OF REPRESENTATIVES, 1988–2002 GENERAL ELECTION (IN THOUSANDS OF 2004 DOLLARS)

	Incumbent	Challenger	Open Seat
Republican			
1988	$603.1	$148.0	$1,201.8
1990	531.1	147.8	1,109.1
1992	660.7	234.6	778.2
1994	541.7	281.4	1,189.3
1996	820.3	234.9	699.0
1998	715.5	262.2	758.6
2000	944.5	331.7	1,283.6
2002	860.9	188.3	1,080.0
Democrat			
1988	$528.0	$211.9	$658.9
1990	536.2	147.4	714.3
1992	751.6	199.8	599.2
1994	711.3	186.3	684.2
1996	635.1	329.4	698.0
1998	577.1	249.1	759.3
2000	787.0	485.6	1,176.7
2002	785.1	313.4	1,020.6

SOURCE: Federal Election Commission, "Congressional Fundraising and Spending Up Again in 1996," press release, April 14, 1997, p. 13; Federal Election Commission, "1998 Congressional Financial Activity Declines," press release, December 29, 1998, p. 5; Federal Election Commission, at www.ftp.fec.gov/fec.

for escalating costs is television. Organizing and running a campaign is expensive, limiting the field of challengers to those who have resources of their own or are willing to spend more than a year raising money from interest groups and individuals.

DECLINING COMPETITION   Unless something is done to help finance challengers, incumbents will continue to have the advantage in seeking reelection. Nothing in BCRA addresses this problem. Challengers in both parties are typically underfunded. House Democratic challengers averaged $198,330 in spending in 2004. In 2000 and 2002 the average for House Democratic challengers was around $350,000, while Republican challengers averaged between around $200,000 in 2002 and $250,000 in 2000.[79] In today's expensive campaigns, candidates are invisible if they only have this amount to spend.

The high cost of campaigns dampens competition by discouraging individuals from running for office. Potential challengers look at the fund-raising advantages enjoyed by incumbents—at incumbents' campaign war chests carried over from previous campaigns, which can reach $1 million or more, and at the time it will take for them to raise enough money to launch a minimal campaign—and they decide to direct their energies elsewhere. Moreover, unlike incumbents, who are being paid while campaigning and raising money, most challengers have to support themselves and their families throughout the campaign, which for a seat in Congress lasts roughly two years.

INCREASING DEPENDENCE ON PACS AND WEALTHY DONORS   Where does the money come from to finance these expensive election campaigns? For most House incumbents, it comes from political action committees (PACs), which we discussed in Chapter 6. In recent years more than two-out-of-five incumbents seeking reelection raised more money from PACs than from individuals (see Figure 9–6).[80] Senators get a smaller percentage of their campaign funds from PACs, but because they spend so much more, they need to raise even more money from PACs than House incumbents do. PACs are pragmatic, giving largely to incumbents. Challengers receive little from PACs because PACs do not want to offend politicians in power. BCRA raised the individual contribution limit to a candidate in the two-year campaign cycle to $4,000, still well below the PAC contribution limit for an election cycle of $10,000. Some individuals who formerly gave $2,000 will now double their contribution to particular candidates, but politicians will continue to rely on PACs because relatively few individuals have the means to give this much money. It also often takes less time to raise money from PACs than from individuals.

To be sure, PACs and individuals spend money on campaigns for many reasons. Most of them want certain laws to be passed or repealed, certain funds to be

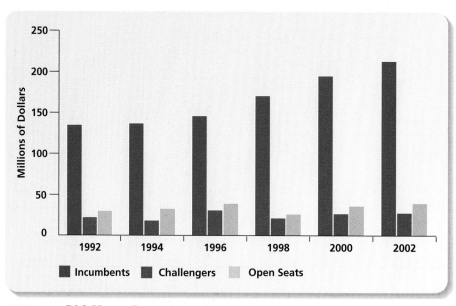

FIGURE 9–6 PAC Money Favors Incumbents.
SOURCE: FEC, "PAC Activity Increases for 2002 Elections," March 27, 2003, at www.fec.gov.

appropriated, or certain administrative decisions to be rendered. At a minimum, they want access to officeholders, a chance to talk with members before key votes.

Defenders of PACs point out that there is no demonstrable relationship between contributions and legislators' votes. But influence in the legislative process depends on access to staff and members of Congress, and most analysts agree that campaign contributions give donors extraordinary access. PACs influence the legislative process in other ways as well. Their access helps them structure the legislative agenda with friendly legislators and influence the drafting of legislation or amendments to existing bills. These are all advantages that others do not have.

IMPROVING ELECTIONS

A combination of party rules and state laws determines how we choose nominees for president. Reformers agree that the current process is flawed but disagree over which aspects require change. Concern over how we choose presidents now centers on four issues[81]: (1) the number, timing, and representativeness of presidential primaries; (2) the role of the electoral college, including the possibility that a presidential election might be thrown into the House of Representatives; (3) how we vote; and (4) how we fund presidential elections.

Reforming The Nominating Process

As noted, in 2004 once again the choice of presidential nominees was most influenced by the voters in early primary or caucus states like Iowa and New Hampshire. The fact is that most citizens do not have a say in who the nominees are. Moreover, these early states are not broadly representative of the country or of their respective parties. Participation in primaries has been low in recent years (see Figure 9–7). In the 2004 primaries, turnout was generally under 17 percent of the voting-age population, and it declined as the primary season progressed and the field of candidates narrowed.[82] Voters in primaries also tend to be more ideological than voters generally, a further bias in the current nominating process.

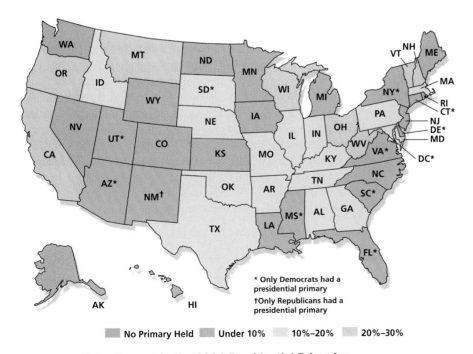

FIGURE 9–7 Voter Turnout in the 2004 Presidential Primaries.
Source: Curtis B. Gans, Director, Committee for the Study of the American Electorate, facsimile to author, September 22, 2004.

None of these concerns are new. What would the critics substitute for state presidential primaries? Some argue in favor of a *national presidential primary* that would take the form of a single nationwide election, probably held in May or September, or separate state primaries held in all the states on the same day.[83] Supporters contend that a one-shot national presidential primary (though a runoff might be necessary) would be simple, direct, and representative. It would cut down the wear-and-tear on candidates, and it would attract a large turnout because of media coverage. Opponents argue that such a reform would make the present system even worse. It would enhance the role of showmanship and gamesmanship, and being enormously expensive, it would hurt the chances of candidates who lack strong financial backing.

A more modest proposal is to hold *regional primaries,* possibly at two- or three-week intervals across the country. Regional primaries might bring more coherence to the process and encourage more emphasis on issues of regional concern. But such primaries would retain most of the disadvantages of the present system—especially the emphasis on money and media. Clearly, they would give an advantage to candidates from whatever region held the first primary, and this advantage would encourage regional candidates and might increase polarization among sections of the country.

A different proposal is to drastically reduce the number of presidential primaries and make more use of the caucus system. The turnout of voters in the Iowa caucuses in recent elections shows that participation can be high, and the time participants spent discussing candidates and issues shows that such participation can be thoughtful and informed. In caucus states, candidates are less dependent on the media and more dependent on convincing political activists. By centering delegate selection in party meetings, the caucus system would also, some say, enhance the role of the party.[84]

Still another idea—used by Colorado for nominations to state offices and by Utah for nominations to federal and state offices—would turn the process around. Beginning in May, local caucuses and then state conventions would be held in every state. They would then send delegates—a certain percentage of whom would be unpledged to any presidential candidate—to the national party conventions, which would be held in the summer. The national conventions would select two or three candidates to compete in a national primary to be held in September. In this plan, voters registered by party would be allowed to vote for their party nominee in the September primaries.[85] Such a plan would likely add voter engagement in the party process but also be more expensive since candidates would mount two national campaigns, one in September and another in November.

Given the problems with the current nomination process, why has it not been reformed? Part of the answer is strong resistance from the states that benefit from the current system. In our federal system, imposing a national or regional primary is difficult.

While many voters are effectively denied a vote in determining their party's nominee, news coverage of the primaries allows them to evaluate the candidates' political qualities and their abilities to organize campaigns; communicate through the media; stand up under pressure; avoid making mistakes (or recover if they do make them); adjust their appeals to shifting events and to different regions of the country; control their staffs as well as make good use of them, and be decisive; articulate, resilient, humorous, informed, and ultimately successful in winning votes. In short, supporters of the current system claim, primaries test candidates on the very qualities they must exhibit in the presidency.[86]

Reforming the Electoral College

The Florida ballot counting and recounting after the 2000 election and the fact that the popular vote winner did not become president prompted a national debate on the electoral college. The most frequently proposed reform is *direct popular election* of the president. Presidents would be elected directly by the voters, just as governors are, and the electoral college and individual electors would be abolished. Such proposals usually provide that if no candidate receives at least 40 percent of the total popular vote, a *runoff election* would be held between the two contenders with the most votes. Supporters argue that direct election would give every voter the same weight in the presidential balloting in accordance with the one-person, one-vote doctrine. Winners would take on more legitimacy because their victories would reflect the will of the voters.

Opponents contend that the plan would further undermine federalism, encourage unrestrained majority rule and hence political extremism, and hurt the most populous and competitive states, which would lose some of their present influence. Others fear that the plan would make presidential campaigns more remote from the voters; candidates might stress television and give up their forays into shopping centers and city malls.[87]

From time to time, Congress considers proposals for a constitutional amendment to elect presidents directly. Such proposals, however, seldom get far because of the strong opposition of various interests that believe they may be disadvantaged by such a change, especially small states and minority groups whose role is enlarged by the electoral college. Groups such as African Americans and farmers, for example, fear they might lose their swing vote power—their ability to make a difference in key states that may tip the electoral college balance.

Another alternative to the electoral college is sometimes called the National Bonus Plan. This plan adds to the current 538 electoral college members another 102 electoral votes, to be awarded on a winner-take-all basis to the candidate with the most votes, so long as that candidate received more than 40 percent of the popular vote. This system would avoid elections' being thrown into the House of Representatives and would help the popular vote winner take over the White House. The most serious liabilities of the plan are that it is complicated and that it requires a runoff election if there is no winner.

Finally, two states, Maine and Nebraska, have already modified the electoral college, adopting a district system in which the candidate who carries each congressional district gets that electoral vote and the candidate who carries the state gets the state's two additional electoral votes. This quasi-proportional representation system has the advantage of not shutting out a candidate who is strong in some areas of a state but not others, but otherwise it does not address the larger concerns with the electoral college.

The failure of attempts to change the system of elections points to an important conclusion about procedural reform: Americans normally do not focus on procedures. Even after the intense focus on the outcome of the 2000 election, including the role of the electoral college, reform was not seriously considered.

Reforming How We Vote

The 2000 presidential election ended with a monthlong controversy over ballots and how to count them. While Florida became the focal point of attention with its problems with punch-card ballots, dangling chads, voter confusion over ballot formats, and when to count or not count absentee ballots, such problems are common to all 50 states. As we noted earlier, election administration is a state and local matter.

Following the 2000 election, Florida enacted legislation modernizing its election process and establishing minimum standards for polling places and voting machines. These standards include certification of electronic voting machines and requirements for the use and storage of these machines. Despite this legislation and the purchase of more than $30 million worth of new electronic machines, their first use in the 2002 primary reminded many of the problems with punch-card ballots in 2000. Some new machines failed to record votes, others had too many votes, and precinct workers were not adequately prepared to help voters with the new technology.

At the national level, both houses of Congress passed the Help America Vote Act (HAVA) providing $3.9 billion in federal funds to modernize American voting procedures, mandating that states maintain accurate statewide voter registration lists.[88] The legislation also permits voters to cast provisional ballots if there is uncertainty about their registration. Advocates of the new voting technology hope that it will improve accuracy and make voting more accessible for persons who have disabilities or who do not speak English.[89] Opponents of the changes see the funding as inadequate to the need and worry about the accuracy and security of the new systems.[90] In the days just before the 2004

The touch-screen voting machine is an example of a new way for voters to register their choice. This computerized machine prevents voters from choosing more than one candidate, as many did erroneously during the 2000 election in Florida; however, there is considerable controversy over the fact that these machines are not required to produce a paper receipt for each vote cast, making recounts impossible should they become necessary.

ELECTION IN ACTION: 2004 PRESIDENTIAL ELECTION

Try your hand as the campaign manager for either major party candidate in the 2004 presidential campaign. You will make the strategic decisions that guide your candidate to victory. As you travel through the virtual process of coordinating campaign advertisements, budgeting the available funds through election day, and deciding which states to travel to, you will better understand the impact of the electoral college and the work that goes into electing a president of the United States.

Go to Make It Real, "Election in Action: 2004 Presidential Election."

election, both parties were preparing for legal challenges to the voting process. Issues included whether or not felons could vote and whether the parties could challenge the registration of new voters at the polls. The implementation of HAVA provisional ballots was also a source of likely litigation. States like Florida and Ohio were the likely battlegrounds for this legal battle, which did not materialize because of Bush's victory margin.

The HAVA is just the start of a broader effort to modernize democracy. It is likely that state legislatures and Congress will eventually debate permitting people to vote via the Internet. The argument will be that if people can make purchases over the Internet, why not let them vote electronically as well? Some states experimented with "e-voting" on a small scale in presidential primaries in 2000 and some counties in California have also experimented with it since then. A shift to e-voting is in some respects an extension of the Oregon vote-by-mail experience since 1996. Oregon elections are now largely conducted using mail ballots, a process which reduces costs and to date has increased participation. Yet critics worry that important elements of community and democracy are lost when people do not vote collectively at the local schoolhouse or fire station. Another concern with e-voting is that it may encourage a proliferation of elections and direct democracy. If we can vote from home, why not vote on more things and more often? E-voting could also foster a political culture of more and more ballot referendums.

Reforming Campaign Finance

The incremental reforms of BCRA and the Supreme Court decision in *McConnell* v. *FEC* upholding them have not resolved the issues of campaign finance. Among the unresolved issues are how presidential campaigns will be financed, the role of interest groups campaigning as Section 527 and 501-C groups, the adequacy of disclosure, and the strength and viability of the political parties. More broadly, the inability of the Federal Election Commission to reach decisions because of its partisan deadlock, as demonstrated by its inaction on Section 527 groups, has helped generate growing pressure to reform that agency.

The 2004 election cycle, with its substantial interest group activity through Section 527 and 501-C organizations, will be seen by those who favor deregulation of campaign finance as another example of the impossibility of limiting money in elections. This school of thought will continue to push for disclosure as the regulatory aim of government in this area.

Another group of reformers will press for more aggressive reforms than those found in BCRA. Included in this agenda will be reining in the 527 and 501-C groups, restructuring the public financing of presidential elections to sustain this element of FECA, and possibly extending public financing of congressional elections. Both sides are likely to agree that change is needed at the FEC but will not agree on how to change it.

S U M M A R Y

1. American elections, even presidential elections, are largely governed by state law and administered by local election officials. Following the 2000 elections, governments at all levels began to look for ways to improve the system.

2. Our electoral system is based on winner-take-all rules, with typically single-member-district or single-officeholder arrangements. These rules encourage a moderate, two-party system. That we have fixed and staggered terms of office adds predictability to our electoral system.

3. The electoral college is the means by which presidents are actually elected. To win a state's electoral votes, a candidate

must have a plurality of votes in that state. Except in two states, the winner takes all. Thus candidates cannot afford to lose the popular vote in the most populous states. The electoral college also gives disproportionate power to the largest and smallest states, especially if they are competitive. It also has the potential to defeat the popular vote winner.

4. Many congressional, state, and local races are not seriously contested. The extent to which a campaign is likely to be hotly contested varies with the importance of the office and the chance a challenger has of winning. Senate races are more likely to be contested, though most incumbents win.

5. The race for the presidency actually takes place in three stages: winning enough delegate support in presidential primaries and caucuses to secure the nomination, campaigning at the national party convention, and mobilizing voters in enough states for a win in the electoral college.

6. Even though presidential nominations today are usually decided weeks or months before the national party conventions, these conventions still have an important role in setting the parties' direction, unifying their ranks, and firing up enthusiasm.

7. Because large campaign contributors are suspected of improperly influencing

public officials, Congress has long sought to regulate political contributions. The main approaches to reform have been (1) imposing limitations on giving, receiving, and spending political money; (2) requiring public disclosure of the sources and uses of political money; and (3) giving governmental subsidies to presidential candidates, campaigns, and parties, including incentive arrangements. Present regulation includes all three approaches.

8. Loopholes in federal law—including soft money and issue advocacy—led to the passage of BCRA. These loopholes grew in size and importance with the 1996 election cycle and have persisted since.

9. The rising costs of campaigns have led to declining competition for congressional seats and increasing dependence on PACs and wealthy donors.

10. The present presidential selection system is under criticism because of its length and expense, because of uncer-

tainties and biases in the electoral college, and because it seems to test candidates for media skills less needed in the White House than the ability to govern, including the capacity to form coalitions and make hard decisions.

11. Reform efforts center on presidential primaries and the electoral college as well as on voting methods and campaign finance.

K E Y   T E R M S

winner-take-all system
single-member district
proportional representation
electoral college

safe seat
coattail effect
caucus

national party convention
interested money
soft money

issue advocacy
527 groups
independent expenditures

F U R T H E R   R E A D I N G

R. MICHAEL ALVAREZ, *Information and Elections* (University of Michigan Press, 1998).

LARRY M. BARTELS, *Presidential Primaries and the Dynamics of Public Choice* (Princeton University Press, 1988).

EARL BLACK AND MERLE BLACK, *The Vital South: How Presidents Are Elected* (Harvard University Press, 1992).

DAVID W. BRADY, JOHN F. COGAN, AND MORRIS P. FIORINA, EDS., *Continuity and Change in House Elections* (Stanford University Press, 2000).

BRUCE BUCHANAN, *Presidential Campaign Quality: Incentives and Reform* (Pearson Education, 2004).

ANN N. CRIGLER, MARION R. JUST, AND EDWARD J. MCCAFFERY, EDS., *Rethinking the Vote: The Politics and Prospects of American Election Reform* (Oxford University Press, 2004).

RONALD KEITH GADDIE, *Born to Run: Origins of the Political Career* (Rowman & Littlefield, 2004).

RONALD KEITH GADDIE AND CHARLES S. BULLOCK III, EDS., *Elections to Open Seats in the U.S. House: Where the Action Is* (Rowman & Littlefield, 2000).

PAUL GRONKE, *The Electorate, the Campaign, and the Office: A Unified Approach to Senate and House Elections* (University of Michigan Press, 2000).

RODERICK P. HART, *Campaign Talk* (Princeton University Press, 2000).

PAUL S. HERRNSON, *Playing Hardball: Campaigning for the U.S. Congress* (Prentice Hall, 2000).

PAUL S. HERRNSON, *Congressional Elections: Campaigning at Home and in Washington*, 4th ed. (CQ Press, 2004).

GARY C. JACOBSON, *The Politics of Congressional Elections*, 6th ed. (Longman, 2003).

KATHLEEN HALL JAMIESON, *Everything You Think You Know About Politics . . . and Why You're Wrong* (Basic Books, 2000).

KIM F. KAHN AND PATRICK J. KENNEDY, *The Spectacle of U.S. Senate Campaigns* (Princeton University Press, 1999).

LOUIS SANDY MAISEL AND KARA Z. BUCKLEY, *Parties and Elections in America: The Electoral Process*, 4th ed. (Rowman & Littlefield, 2004).

DAVID B. MAGLEBY, ED., *Financing the 2000 Election* (Brookings Institution Press, 2002).

DAVID B. MAGLEBY AND J. QUIN MONSON, EDS., *The Last Hurrah?: Soft Money and Issue Advocacy in the 2002 Congressional Elections* (Brookings Institution Press, 2004).

MICHAEL J. MALBIN, ED., *Life After Reform: When the Bipartisan Campaign Reform Act . . . Meets Politics* (Rowman & Littlefield, 2003).

JEREMY D. MAYER, *Running on Race: Racial Politics in Presidential Campaigns, 1960–2000* (Random House, 2002).

WILLIAM G. MAYER AND ANDREW E. BUSCH, *The Front-Loading Problem in Presidential Nominations* (Brookings Institution Press, 2004).

STEPHEN K. MEDVIC, *Political Consultants in U.S. Congressional Elections* (Ohio State University Press, 2001).

NELSON W. POLSBY AND AARON B. WILDAVSKY, *Presidential Elections: Strategies and Structures of American Politics*, 11th ed. (Rowman & Littlefield, 2004).

SAMUEL L. POPKIN, *The Reasoning Voter: Communication and Persuasion in Presidential Campaigns*, 2d ed. (University of Chicago Press, 1994).

PAUL D. SCHUMAKER AND BURDETT A. LOOMIS, EDS., *Choosing a President: The Electoral College and Beyond* (Seven Bridges Press, 2002).

JAMES A. THURBER, ED., *The Battle for Congress: Consultants, Candidates, and Voters* (Brookings Institution Press, 2001).

JAMES A. THURBER AND CANDICE J. NELSON, EDS., *Campaign Warriors: Political Consultants in Elections* (Brookings Institution Press, 2000).

STEPHEN J. WAYNE, *The Road to the White House 2004* (Wadsworth, 2004).

See also *Public Opinion Quarterly*, the *American Journal of Politics*, and *American Political Science Review*.

THE MEDIA
AND AMERICAN
POLITICS

10

At their final
number in the
2004 Super
Bowl half-time
show, Justin Timberlake and
Janet Jackson sang "Rock
Your Body." At the conclu-
sion of this song, Timberlake removed part of Jackson's costume, exposing her left
breast to 90 million viewers.[1] This incident, described by some as a "wardrobe
malfunction,"[2] created substantial controversey. CBS, the network broadcasting
the super bowl, claimed no advance knowledge of what occurred,[3] but was still
widely criticized for not exercising more control over the half-time entertainment. The Federal Communications Commission (FCC), which regulates broadcast media, received more than 200,000 viewer complaints in eight days,[4] and
FCC Chair Michael Powell stated, "We have a very angry public on our hands."[5]

Some thought too much was made of this fleeting moment, either because they did not
think it so outrageous or because they thought some of the commercials aired during the
Super Bowl were even more offensive. Referring to complaints that parents were blind-
sided by the event and citing the offensive commercials preceding it, Frank Rich of *The
New York Times* said, "What signal were these poor, helpless adults waiting for before pulling
their children away from the set? Apparently nothing short of a simulated rape would do."[6]
Others responded that what happened in the half-time show was not all that different than
what appears with some regularity on MTV or other cable networks.

Moreover, the same content on cable would not have been subject to indecency
regulations. Jane D. Brown, a media researcher at the University of North Carolina at
Chapel Hill and editor of *Sexual Teens, Sexual Media*, said, "For some children, this won't

TIME LINE ★★

THE MEDIA AND AMERICAN POLITICS

1780s	Founders use the press to advocate ratification of the Constitution; Hamilton, Jefferson, and others establish partisan newspapers
1820s	Press begins to shift its appeal toward larger masses of less educated people
1923	Coolidge delivers first broadcast State of the Union address over the radio
1933	FDR begins "fireside chats," the first informal communications over mass medium
1934	Federal Communications Commission (FCC) established to regulate rapidly expanding radio media
1947	Truman's State of the Union address is televised
1960	First televised presidential debates benefit Kennedy campaign
1963	Two largest television networks at the time, CBS and NBC, expand evening news to 30 minutes
1971	Supreme Court rules against censorship—*The New York Times* publishes the "Pentagon Papers"
1982	*USA Today* created by Gannett Corporation as national newspaper
1987	Fairness doctrine repealed
1992	Bill Clinton plays saxophone on late-night television
1998	Internet site "Drudge Report" breaks story of Clinton's affair with Monica Lewinsky
2004	CBS admits error in reports of President Bush's service record in the National Guard

mass media
Means of communication that reach the mass public, including newspapers and magazines, radio, television (broadcast, cable, and satellite), films, recordings, books, and electronic communication.

news media
Media that emphasizes the news.

have been anything out of the ordinary. If they're watching MTV, dating shows, or reality programming, this is pretty much what they see all the time."[7] One rationale for the different standards for indecency in broadcast and cable television is that broadcast television uses the airwaves and is free to the recipient, while cable broadcasts are purchased by consumers who willingly pay for them.

The controversy about the Super Bowl ads and halftime show led to action by the FCC and Congress. The FCC imposed a fine of $27,500 on each of the twenty stations owned by CBS, resulting in a total fine of $550,000. This fine was well below the $1.2 million fine levied against Fox for indecency shown on *Married by America.* The FCC did not fine CBS stations now owned by the network. It also reversed its previous ruling on Bono's use of an obscenity during the Golden Globes.[8] Subsequent to the Super Bowl incident, the House of Representatives passed legislation authorizing the FCC to impose fines up to $500,000 for indecency.[9] The media also responded to the controversy. Clear Channel Communications removed "shock jock" Howard Stern from its programming in some major markets.[10] This controversy about indecency in the media illustrates the delicate balance between free speech and broadcasters' use of the public airwaves.

THE INFLUENCE OF THE MEDIA ON POLITICS

The media, in particular the print media, have been called the "fourth estate," and the "fourth branch of government."[11] Evidence that the media influence our culture and politics is plentiful. The **mass media**—newspapers and magazines, radio, television (broadcast, cable, and satellite), the Internet, films, recordings, books, and electronic communication—are the means of communication that reach the mass public.[12] The **news media** are the mass media vehicles that emphasize the news, although the distinctions between entertainment and news

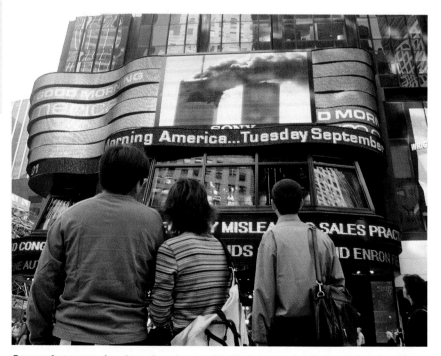

For over forty years, Americans have been getting their news primarily from television. Whenever there is a crisis, most people turn first to television for information. No event in recent history has done more to underscore the importance of television as the primary source of news in contemporary U.S. society than the terrorist attacks that took place on September 11, 2001.

are sometimes blurred. News programs often have entertainment value, and entertainment programs often convey news. Programs in this latter category include TV newsmagazines such as *60 Minutes* and *Dateline,* and talk shows with hosts like Larry King, Oprah Winfrey, Hannity and Colmes, and Jon Stewart.

By definition, the mass media disseminate messages to a large and often heterogeneous audience. Because they must have broad appeal, their messages are often simplified, stereotyped, and predictable. The mass media make money by appealing to large numbers of people. But do large audiences equal political clout? Two factors are important in answering this question: the media's pervasiveness and their role as a linking mechanism between politicians and government officials and the public.

Where do Americans get their news? Until 1960, most people got their news from newspapers. Today, although many people use several sources, they rely primarily on television. Whenever there is a crisis—from the assasination of John F. Kennedy to the *Challenger* explosion to the terrorist attacks on September 11, 2001—people are glued to their TV sets.

The Internet is becoming an increasingly important source of news for Americans, taking its place alongside print, radio, and television. The number of Americans going online for election news is growing dramatically and promises to become even more important as candidates and issue advocates pay increasing attention to the Internet as

PEOPLE & POLITICS *Making a Difference* ★ ★ ★

SEAN HANNITY

For more than a decade talk radio has been dominated by conservatives like Rush Limbaugh and more recently by Bill O'Reilly and Sean Hannity. In 2004, liberals responded by promoting Al Franken's new radio show as an alternative to the conservatives. An example of a personality who has used talk radio and cable television successfully is Sean Hannity.

Hannity attended college at New York University intermittenly because of limited resources but became interested in radio in part through his involvement with college radio stations. He placed a "Job Wanted" ad in the *R&R,* a weekly newspaper covering the music industry, billing himself as "the most talked about college radio host in America."[*] His professional involvement in radio began with a station in Huntsville, Alabama. He later moved to Atlanta, where his strong local ratings attracted the attention of WABC in New York City and the Fox News Channel. He moved to New York, where he launched "Hannity and Colmes" on the Fox News Channel (cable television), reaching an estimated

audience of over one million.[†] Hannity also hosts *The Sean Hannity Show,* which is carried by 400 radio stations, reaching an estimated audience of 12 million.[‡] *Talker Magazine* has rated his radio program the second most listened to talk radio show in America.[§] Hannity is also the author of two books, *Let Freedom Ring,*[‖] and *Deliver Us From Evil.*[¶]

Hannity is outspoken and aggressive in his interviews and interactions with those who call into his program. He has interviewed most leading conservatives and Republicans like Dick Cheney and Donald Rumsfeld. Hannity also frequently observes that liberals like Bill Clinton have refused to appear on his program. Evidence of the impact of conservative media personalities like Sean Hannity is found in the push by liberals to have their own talk shows. Comedian Al Franken in his first broadcast described this sentiment when he said, "The radical right wing has taken over the White House, Congress, and increasingly, the courts . . . and most insidiously, the airwaves."[**]

[*] www.hannity.com/story.php?content=/about_hannity.
[†] Ibid.
[‡] Ibid.
[§] Ibid.
[‖] Sean Hannity, *Let Freedom Ring: Winning the War of Liberty over Liberalism* (Regan Books, 2002).
[¶] Sean Hannity, *Deliver Us from Evil: Defeating Terrorism, Despotism, and Liberalism* (Regan Books, 2004).
[**] Allessandra Stanley, "Talk Network Makes Debut, with Rage a No-Show," *The New York Times,* April 1, 2004, p. A20.

a way to get their messages to the voting public.[13] Using the Internet as a news source permits the user to obtain information on only the topics or issues desired and from multiple sources. It also means the user can access the news from multiple locations and at convenient times. It also means that some people may turn to unreliable sources, which are plentiful on the Internet.

The Pervasiveness of Television

Television has changed American politics more than any other invention. Most Americans watch some kind of television news every day. The average American watches television four and one-half hours a day, and most homes have more than two sets.[14] Television provides instant access to news from around the country and the globe, permitting citizens and leaders alike to observe firsthand the capture of Saddam Hussein, a kidnapping in Southern California, or a refugee crisis in Indonesia. This instant coverage increases the pressure on world leaders to respond quickly to crises, permits terrorists to gain widespread coverage of their actions, and elevates the role played by the president in both domestic and international politics.

The growth of around-the-clock cable news and information shows is one of the most important developments in recent years. Until the late 1980s, the network news programs on CBS, NBC, and ABC captured more than 90 percent of the audience for television news at set times in the morning and early evening hours. Owing to the rise of cable television and the advent of the Internet, the broadcast networks now attract only about 40 percent of the viewing public,[15] and half of the public are regular viewers of CNN, CNBC, MSNBC, or Fox News.[16]

Satellites, cable television, computers using Internet search engines like Google or Yahoo, and DVDs make vast amounts of political information available 24 hours a day. These technologies eliminate the obstacles of time and distance and increase the volume of information that can be stored, retrieved, and viewed. They have also reduced the impact of single sources of broadcast or cable news. Competition from cable stations for viewing has put pressure on broadcast networks to remain profitable, which has meant reduced budgets for news coverage and a tendency to look for ways of boosting the entertainment value of broadcast news.

One of the biggest changes in American electoral politics of the last half-century is that most voters now rely more on television commercials for information about candidates and issues and less on news coverage. Although debates and speeches by candidates generate coverage, the more pervasive battleground for votes is radio and TV ads. As a result, electoral campaigns now focus on image and slogans rather than on substance. Successful candidates must be able to communicate with voters through this medium. To get their message across to TV audiences, politicians increasingly rely on media advisers to define their opponent as well as themselves. These consultants also seek positive news coverage, but in many congressional campaigns, news coverage is fleeting.

Candidates are not the only ones who have used television and radio to communicate electioneering messages to voters. Political parties and interest groups in competitive elections between 1996 and 2002 have expended approximately as much as candidates in competitive races urging voters to reject one candidate or support another. The use of party soft money, which was unlimited, and "issue advocacy," which was not only unlimited but undisclosed, allowed noncandidate entities to become major factors in the most competitive contests for Congress and in presidential battleground states.[17] **Issue advocacy**, which was a way for individuals and groups to avoid contribution limitations and disclosure requirements, was curtailed somewhat by the campaign finance reforms that took effect in 2004, aimed at broadcast ads aired during the period before elections. To voters, the messages from the parties and interest groups were indistinguishable from the messages from the candidates,[18] except that the tone was generally more negative.[19]

Passage of the Bipartisan Campaign Reform Act (BCRA) in 2002 and the Supreme Court's subsequent upholding of the act substantially changed the way parties and interest groups behaved in 2004. BCRA banned soft-money-funded electioneering by

issue advocacy
Promoting a particular position or an issue paid for by interest groups or individuals but not candidates. Much issue advocacy is often electioneering for or against a candidate and, until 2004, had not been subject to any regulation.

parties, which had been the largest noncandidate source of broadcast and cable ads. BCRA also banned corporations and unions from using their general funds for electioneering communications, defined as "broadcast ads" that mention a federal candidate by name, occur within 30 days of a primary election and 60 days of a general election, and are targeted to a particular electorate (50,000 people or more in the district or state where the named candidates are running). Consistent with past Supreme Court decisions, BCRA exempted from this limitation nonprofit organizations that do not receive corporate or union funds. Examples of groups like this that were able to run ads within the 60 days before the 2004 election are the League of Conservation Voters and NARAL Pro-Choice America. While these groups were active in 2004, others were even more active, in part because the Federal Election Commission did not strictly define what constituted a political committee under BCRA. Examples of very active groups include the Media Fund, America Coming Together, Progress for America, and Swift Boat Veterans for Truth.

The amount of television news devoted to politics has been declining and now constitutes less than one minute per half-hour broadcast.[20] A major effort to get local television stations to devote a few minutes to candidate debate in their nightly local news ended up with stations averaging 45 seconds a night, or as one observer put it, just enough time to "let candidates clear their throats."[21] Stations also often ignored campaigns in 2002 with a majority (56 percent) of local news broadcasts airing in the weeks leading up to the election making no mention of the campaign.[22]

In large urban areas, it is rare for viewers to see stories about their member of Congress, in part because there are several congressional districts in that media market. Newspapers do a better job of covering politics and devote more attention to it than television stations. The decline in news coverage of elections and voting, especially on television, has only amplified the importance of political advertising on television, through the mail, and on the telephone.

In referendum elections, advertising is the most important source of information in voter decision making.[23] The campaign finance reforms enacted in 2002 will likely only increase the amount of issue advocacy, especially through the mail and on the telephone. As previously noted, BCRA bans issue advocacy on television or radio that mentions a candidate by name in the two months before a general election or one month before a primary election. But it does not limit what groups can do through the mail, on the phone, or in person. In 2004, a wide range of groups communicated directly with voters through the mail, on the phone, and in person. This "ground war" had been growing in importance before passage of BCRA but the reforms accelerated the groups' use of these techniques. In battleground states or districts, voters were often canvassed by groups and then received mail and phone calls reinforcing the message in the initial call. Even more effective are face-to-face conversations, especially with people the voter knows.

The Persistence of Radio

Television and the newer media have not displaced radio. On the contrary, radio continues to reach more American households than television does. Only one household in 100 does not have a radio, compared with four in 100 without a TV.[24] More than 9 out of 10 people listen to the radio every week, and 8 out of 10 do so every day.[25] Many Americans consider the radio an essential companion when driving. Americans get more than "the facts" from radio: They also get analysis and opinion from their favorite commentators and talk show hosts.

The Continuing Importance of Newspapers

Despite vigorous competition from radio and television, Americans still read newspapers. Daily newspaper circulation has been declining for the past 30 years to about 55 million nationwide—or just under one copy for every five people.[26] The circulation figures for newspapers reflect a troubling decline in readership among younger persons: About 30 percent fewer young people read newspapers on a regular basis.[27]

In addition to metropolitan and local newspapers, we now have national ones. Created in 1982 by the Gannett Corporation, *USA Today,* with a circulation of more than

Extensive use of computers by young children has left them vulnerable to sexual predators and commercial fraud, opening the issue of whether government regulation is needed. Parental supervision remains the best protection.

2.1 million, recently replaced *The Wall Street Journal* as America's top-circulating newspaper.[28] *The Wall Street Journal,* with a circulation of over 2 million, has long acted as a national newspaper specializing in business and finance. *The New York Times* has a national edition that is read by more than one million people.

The Internet

From its humble beginnings as a Pentagon research project in the 1960s,[29] the World Wide Web has blossomed into a global phenomenon. There are now more than one billion documents on the Web,[30] and more than 15 million unique domains have been registered worldwide. Many people mistakenly think the Internet and the World Wide Web are the same thing. The truth is that the Internet was the original "giant international plumbing system" for accessing information. It permits information to travel between computers. The World Wide Web is now the most popular way of using the Internet because it transmits pictures, data, and text. However, the WWW incorporates all of the Internet services and much more.

The Internet opens up resources for citizens in dramatic ways. One study found that nearly half of Americans go online to search for news on a particular topic; somewhat smaller proportions go online for updates on stock quotes and sports scores. For about 20 percent of people, the Internet is a primary source of news.[31] Internet users can also interact with other people or politicians about politics through electronic mail and chat rooms. Younger people, including teenagers, use the Internet extensively for schoolwork and nearly three in four prefer it to the library.[32]

Candidates are now using the Web for fund raising. Once a candidate gains recognition, as Howard Dean did, it is possible to raise money quickly and inexpensively via the Web. In fact, in the third quarter of 2003, Dean broke the record for money raised in a quarter by a Democratic presidential candidate, a record he would set again the following quarter. Internet fundraising was integral to his success; half of the estimated $40 million he raised in 2003 came through the Internet.[33] Ironically, Dean himself didn't use a computer until 1998 and had initially refused to have a government e-mail address.[34] John Kerry also found the Internet to be a boon to his fundraising in the general election campaign. The success of the parties and candidates in Internet fundraising may significantly change the way politics is financed. As people gained confidence in making credit card transactions via the Internet, it has opened up the possibility of people contributing to parties and candidates in this way.

The Web provides an inexpensive way to communicate with volunteers, contributors, and voters and promises to become an even larger component of campaigns in the future, as illustrated by several presidential and congressional campaigns in 2004. Candidates maintain home pages where voters can learn about office seekers or ballot referendums.

THE CHANGING ROLE OF THE AMERICAN NEWS MEDIA

The controversy over the 2004 Super Bowl half-time show discussed earlier in this chapter itself became a major media story. Media coverage of this incident demonstrates the public's tremendous appetite for instant news and analysis, at least when it comes to a crisis or major controversy. Americans spend on average an hour a day consuming news, and the older they are, the more time they devote to it.[35] Yet people are quick to criticize the media. Writes journalist James Fallows, "Americans have never been truly fond of their press. Through the last decade, however, their disdain for the media establishment has reached new levels. Americans believe that the news media have become too arrogant, cynical, scandal-minded, and destructive."[36]

How often have you or your friends blamed the media for being biased, criticized the frenzy that surrounds a particular story, or denounced the "if it bleeds, it leads" mentality of nightly television news? Yet the content and style of news coverage is driven by market research in which viewers and readers are asked what they want to see reported and how they want it presented. Advertising revenue is directly linked to the number of readers or viewers a media outlet has.

Media bashing has become something of a national pastime. Americans blame the media for everything from increased tension between the races, biased attacks on public officials, sleaze and sensationalism, increased violence in our society, and for being more interested in making money than in conveying information. Many in the media even agree with these charges.[37] But complaints about the media may simply be a case of criticizing the messenger in order to avoid dealing with the message. Comments like "It's the media's fault that we have lost our social values" or "The media's preoccupation with the private lives of politicians turns Americans off to politics" are overly broad assertions. Americans tend to blame far more problems on the media than are warranted.

There are also occasional examples of fabrication or plagiarism, as in the case of Jayson Blair of *The New York Times,* who plagiarized stories including the writing from a Texas newspaper about the family of Iraqi prisoner of war Jessica Lynch[38]; and Jack Kelley, a top reporter for *USA Today* who fabricated parts of numerous stories including one article that made him a Pulitzer Prize finalist.[39] Cases like these have prompted these newspapers and the media in general to evaluate editorial review and standards of integrity, but they also provoked criticism of the media.

The news media has changed dramatically over the course of U.S. history. At the time of the ratification of the Constitution, newspapers consisted of a single sheet, often printed irregularly by store owners to hawk their services or goods. Newspapers rarely stayed in business more than a year, due to delinquent subscribers and high costs.[40] But the framers understood the important role the press should play as a watchdog of politicians and government, and they included freedom of the press in the Bill of Rights.

Political Mouthpiece

The new nation's political leaders, including Alexander Hamilton and Thomas Jefferson, recognized the need to keep voters informed. Political parties as we know them did not exist, but the active role of the press in supporting the Revolution had fostered a growing awareness of the political potential of newspapers. Hamilton recruited staunch Federalist John Fenno to edit and publish a newspaper in the new national capital of Philadelphia. Jefferson responded by attracting Philip Freneau, a talented writer and editor and a loyal Republican, to do the same for the Republicans. (Jefferson's Republicans later became the Democratic party.) The two papers became the nucleus of a network of competing partisan newspapers throughout the nation.

Although the two newspapers competed in Philadelphia for only a few years, they served as a model for future partisan newspapers. The early American press served as a mouthpiece for political leaders. Its close connection with politicians and political parties offered the opportunity for financial stability—but at the cost of journalistic independence.

Financial Independence

During the Jacksonian era of the 1820s and 1830s, the right to vote was extended to all white adult males through the elimination of property qualifications. The press began to shift its appeal away from elite readers and toward large masses of less educated and less politically interested readers. The rising literacy rate reinforced this popularization of newspapers. These two forces—increased political participation by the common people and the rise of literacy among Americans—began to alter the relationship between politicians and the press.

Some newspaper publishers began to experiment with a new way to finance their newspapers. They charged a penny a paper, paid on delivery, instead of the traditional annual subscription fee of $8 to $10, which was beyond the ability of most readers to pay. The "penny press," as it was called, expanded circulation and put more emphasis on advertising, enabling newspapers to become financially independent of the political parties.

MAINE EXPLOSION CAUSED BY BOMB OR TORPEDO?

Capt. Sigsbee and Consul-General Lee Are in Doubt---The World Has Sent a Special Tug, With Submarine Divers, to Havana to Find Out---Lee Asks for an Immediate Court of Inquiry---Capt. Sigsbee's Suspicions.

The New York World a day after

As the nineteenth century progressed, literacy grew among the U.S. masses and more people began to get their news from newspapers. The popularization of the print media forced politicians and public officials to devote growing attention to their relationship with the press.

The changing finances of newspapers also affected the definition of news. Before the penny press, all news was political—speeches, documents, editorials—directed at politically interested readers. The penny press reshaped the definition of news as it sought to appeal to less politically aware readers with human interest stories and reports on sports, crime, public trials, and social activities.

"Objective Journalism"

By the early decades of the twentieth century, many journalists began to argue that the press should be independent of the political parties. *New York Tribune* editor Whitelaw Reid eloquently expressed this sentiment: "Independent journalism! That is the watchword of the future in the profession. An end of concealments because it would hurt the party; an end of one-sided expositions . . .; an end of assaults that are not believed fully just but must be made because the exigency of party warfare demands them."[41]

Journalists began to view their work as a profession and established professional associations with journals and codes of ethics. This professionalization of journalism reinforced the notion that journalists should be independent of partisan politics. Further strengthening the trend toward objectivity was the rise of the wire services, such as the Associated Press and Reuters, which deliberately remained politically neutral so as to attract more customers.

The Impact of Broadcasting

Radio and television nationalized and personalized the news. People could follow events as they were happening and not have to wait for the publication of a newspaper. From the 1920s, when radio networks were formed, radio carried political speeches, campaign advertising, and coverage of political events such as national party conventions.[42] Radio provided a means to bypass the screening of editors and reporters, since politicians could now speak directly to listeners. It also increased interest in national and international news because events outside a listener's local area could be followed as if one were actually there.

President Franklin Roosevelt used radio with remarkable effectiveness. Before 1933, most radio speeches were formal orations, but Roosevelt spoke to his audience on a personal level, seemingly in one-on-one conversations. These "fireside chats" established a standard still followed today. When Roosevelt began speaking over the microphone, he would visualize a tiny group of average citizens in front of him. Roosevelt "would smile and light up as though he were actually sitting on the front porch or in the parlor with them."[43]

Television added a dramatic visual dimension, which contributed to rising audience interest in national events and permitted viewers to witness lunar landings and the aftermath of political assassinations, as well as more mundane news events. By 1963, the two largest networks at the time, CBS and NBC, had expanded their evening news programs from 15 to 30 minutes. Today news broadcasting has expanded to the point that many local stations provide 90 minutes of local news every evening as well as a half-hour in the morning and at noon. Programs such as *20/20* and other newsmagazine shows are among the most popular in the prime-time evening hours.

Cable television brought round-the-clock news coverage. During the Clinton impeachment hearings and the 2000 Florida ballot-counting controversy, American cable news was watched at home and around the world for its instantaneous coverage. C-SPAN now provides uninterrupted coverage of congressional deliberations, the courts, and state and local governments.

Investigatory Journalism

Contemporary news reporters do more than convey the news; they investigate it, and their investigations often have political consequences. Notable examples of influential investigatory reporters include Seymour Hersh of *The New York Times,* who exposed what became known as the *Pentagon Papers,* revealing how the United States became involved in the Vietnam War; Robert Woodward and Carl Bernstein of *The Washington Post,* who

Franklin D. Roosevelt was the first president to recognize the effectiveness of radio to reach the public. His fireside chats were the model for later presidents.

played an important role in uncovering the Watergate conspiracy; Nina Totenberg of National Public Radio, whose reporting on sexual harassment charges against Clarence Thomas helped force the Senate Judiciary Committee to extend the hearings on his confirmation to the U.S. Supreme Court; and Michael Isikoff of *Newsweek,* who broke the story of Bill Clinton's alleged perjury involving sexual misconduct with Monica Lewinsky.

Media Conglomerates

If a few owners corner the market on newspapers and television stations, is the free flow of information to the public endangered? As in other sectors of the economy, media companies have merged and created large conglomerates. When television was in its infancy, radio networks and newspapers were among the first to purchase television stations. These mergers established cross-ownership patterns that persist today. The Gannett Corporation, for example, owns 101 daily newspapers and 22 television stations and cable television systems—assets that provide news coverage to nearly 18 percent of the United States.[44] The *Chicago Tribune* substantially expanded its reach of newspapers and television stations by purchasing Times-Mirror, publisher of the *Los Angeles Times* and ten other newspapers, 22 TV stations, four radio stations, and a growing online business.[45]

Australian-born Rupert Murdoch owns the Fox network, dozens of U.S. television stations, magazines, publishing organizations, and movie studios.

Local firms used to own the local newspapers, radio, and television stations. Today large conglomerates, some of them foreign, have acquired ownership of many newspapers and broadcasting stations. Rupert Murdoch, founder of the Fox network, owns 35 television stations in the United States, 20th Century-Fox, HarperCollins publishers, and *TV Guide,* which has the largest magazine circulation in America. Murdoch's News Corporation recently purchased DirecTV and has moved its corporate headquarters to the United States.[46] The Federal Communications Commission (FCC) and the courts are reinforcing the trend toward media conglomeration by relaxing and striking down regulations that limit cable and television network ownership by the same company.[47] Congress responded by passing resolutions opposing the more lax FCC ownership limitations, prompting a compromise between the Bush administration and Congress increasing the maximum population reachable by conglomerates but not as much as the FCC had proposed.[48] An appeals court has ruled against even these modified relaxations, however, calling them "arbitrary and capricious."[49]

When reporting national news, local outlets depend heavily on news that is gathered, edited, and distributed by national organizations like the Associated Press. As a result, some people contend that information these days is more diluted, homogenized, and moderated than it would be if the newspapers and broadcast stations were locally owned and the news was gathered and edited locally.[50]

Regulation of the Media

Regulation of the broadcast media has existed in some form since their inception. Because of the limited number of television and radio frequencies, the national government oversees matters like licensing, financing, and even content. Once regulation required "fairness" in news programming.[51] As written into law and interpreted by the FCC, the **fairness doctrine** imposed an obligation on radio and television license holders to ensure that differing viewpoints were presented regarding controversial issues or persons. With the advent of cable television and the Reagan administration's antiregulatory campaign, much of the fairness doctrine was repealed in 1987, and the final remnants of it were repealed in 2000. Will broadcasters provide fair and balanced news coverage in the absence of regulation? Proponents of deregulation who pushed for repeal think so.[52]

MEDIATED POLITICS

When dramatic events like the terrorist attacks on the World Trade Center and the Pentagon on September 11, 2001, occur, we realize the power television has in bringing world events into our lives. Osama bin Laden, the purported mastermind behind the

fairness doctrine
Federal Communications Commission policy that required holders of radio and television licenses to ensure that different viewpoints were presented about controversial issues or persons; largely repealed in 1987.

IN COMPARATIVE PERSPECTIVE

A LESS THAN FREE PRESS IN RUSSIA

An example of a country struggling to establish a free press is Russia. After the fall of Communism and its state-controlled media, Russia saw multiple print and broadcast media take root. Over time these outlets have declined in number and in the ability to communicate. NTV, an independent television channel, had been critical of President Vladimir Putin, Boris Yeltsin, and the Russian war in Chechnya. Russian government officials, claiming the station was corrupt,[*] took over the channel in 2001. The government appointed Boris Jordan to head NTV after the takeover, only to fire him two years later after the channel had provided extensive coverage of a theater takeover by independence-seeking Chechen terrorists, with the Russian government's aggressive response and resulting loss of life. The moves by Putin's government against NTV have had a chilling impact on stations that are critical of the Putin government.[†] By June 2003, TVS, the last independent national network, went under, but more for financial than political reasons.[‡] Harassment of the media has not been limited to television. The weekly paper *Versiya*, which had reported the death toll to be higher than government reports at the Chechen theater incident and that the gas used to suppress the terrorists had been military and not civilian gas, found its offices ransacked and its computers and servers taken.[§]

Muzzling the media or putting them out of business helped Putin's United Russia Party to monopolize media coverage in the 2003 and 2004 elections, giving Putin's party even more seats in Parliament and reelecting Putin to the presidency. Putin justifies his policies regarding the media as efforts to not allow media moguls to become "king makers."[||] The difficulties Russia has had in maintaining a free press illustrate the difficulty new democracies encounter as they develop.

[*] "Media Muzzle," *The Economist,* April, 21, 2001.
[†] Erin E. Arvedlund, "News Corp. Said to Seek Russia Satellite T.V.," *The New York Times,* November 10, 2003, p. C2.
[‡] "Unplugged," *The Economist,* U.S. Edition, June 28, 2003.
[§] Christian Caryl and Eve Conant, "The Dead and the Silent," *Newsweek,* November 11, 2002, p. 39.
[||] "Russia—Looking East," *Campaign,* September 27, 2002, p. 16.

attacks, understood the power of the media both inside and outside the United States, as evidenced by his release of videotapes of himself through the Al-Jazeera network in the Middle East in the weeks and months after the attacks.

The pervasiveness of newspapers, magazines, radio, and television places the individuals who determine what we read, hear, and see in a position of great influence because they can reach so much of the American public so quickly. With a large population scattered over a continent, both the reach and the speed of the modern media elevate the importance of the people in charge of them. The main source of campaign news in 2004 for more than two-thirds of Americans was television (68 percent), a proportion that has held relatively constant since 1992. Newspapers were mentioned as the most important source by 15 percent. All other media trailed these two.[53]

Political parties and interest groups have long been political mediators that help organize the world of politics for the average citizen. Their role is less important today because the media now serve that function and political parties have largely lost control over the nominating process (see Chapters 7 and 9). Greater attention is now given to judging candidates not so much in terms of party affiliation and platform but in terms of character and competence. The press, not the parties, performs this evaluative function.

The news media have also assumed the role of "speaking for the people." Journalists report what "the people" want and think, and then they tell the people what politicians and policy makers are doing about it. Politicians realize how dependent they are on the media for getting their message out to voters, and they are well aware that a hostile press can hurt them. That explains why today's politicians spend so much of their time developing good relations with the press.

The Media and Public Opinion

The ability of television to present images and communicate events has influenced American public opinion. Television footage of the violence done to blacks during the civil rights revolution of the 1950s and 1960s made the issue more real and immediate.

News coverage of the war in Vietnam galvanized the antiwar movement in the United States because of the horrible images news shows brought into people's homes. The testimony of White House staff before the Senate Watergate and later House Judiciary committees intensified the crisis of confidence in the Nixon administration. The repeated television coverage of the terrorist attacks on the World Trade Center and Pentagon left an indelible impression on all who saw them.

For a long time, analysts tended to play down the influence wielded by the media in American politics relative to the influence wielded by political leaders. The impact of Franklin D. Roosevelt's fireside chats came to symbolize the power of the politician over that of the news editor. Roosevelt spoke directly to his listeners over the radio in a way and at a time of his own choosing, and no network official was able to block or influence that direct connection. President John Kennedy's use of the televised press conference represented a similar direct contact with the public. President Ronald Reagan was nicknamed the "Great Communicator" because of his ability to talk persuasively and often passionately about public policy issues with the people through television.

GLOBAL *Perceptions*

QUESTION: Is the influence of news organizations very good, somewhat good, somewhat bad, or very bad in your country?

How do people in other countries perceive the role of news organizations and the media? The Pew Global Attitudes Project asked people in many countries the question that begins this box. Africa is the region with the most positive assessment of the news media. In contrast, the Middle East is the region most likely to believe that the news media has a "very bad" influence on their countries. The proportion saying news organizations and the media have a very bad influence on their country ranged from a low of 2 percent in Asia and 3 percent in Africa to 10 percent in the Middle East. More than one in four Middle Easterners saw the news media as a very bad influence or somewhat bad influence.

Source: Pew Research Center for the People and the Press, "2002 Global Attitudes Survey: Final Top-line Results," p. T-34.

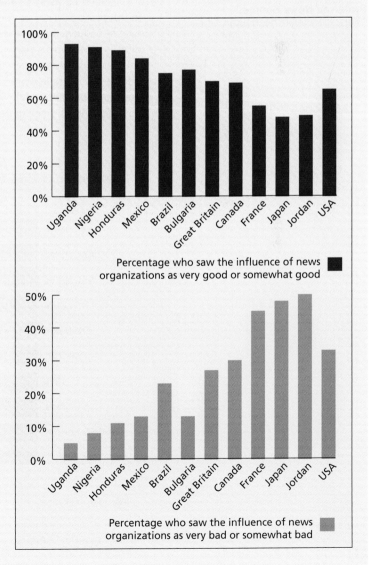

Percentage who saw the influence of news organizations as very good or somewhat good

Percentage who saw the influence of news organizations as very bad or somewhat bad

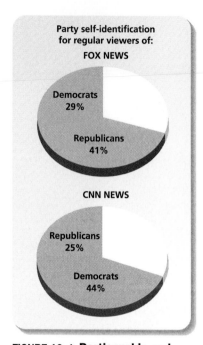

FIGURE 10–1 Partisanship and Preferred News Source.
SOURCE: *The New York Times,* July 18, 2004.

However, broadcasters and journalists are now so important to the political process that elected officials and politicians spend considerable time trying to learn how to use them to their advantage. Presidential events and "photo opportunities" are planned with the evening news and its format in mind.[54] Members of Congress use Capitol Hill recording studios to tape messages for local television and radio stations. White House press briefings are frequently included in the evening news.

Factors That Limit Media Influence on Public Opinion

People are not just empty vessels into which politicians and journalists pour information and ideas. How people interpret political messages depends on a variety of factors: political socialization, selectivity, needs, and the individual's ability to recall and comprehend the message.

POLITICAL SOCIALIZATION The media, particularly television, although not as important as family, play a role in socializing, influencing our values and attitudes.[55] The media shape public perceptions and knowledge. Television, with its concreteness and drama, has an emotional impact that print cannot hope to match.[56] Television cuts across age groups, educational levels, social classes, and races. Newspapers provide more detail about the news and often contain contrasting points of view, at least on the editorial pages, that help inform the public.

We develop our political attitudes, values, and beliefs through an education process that social scientists call **political socialization**.[57] (See Chapters 4 and 8 for more detail on this process.) Face-to-face contacts with friends and business associates (*peer pressure*) often have far more impact than the impersonal television or newspaper. Strong identification with a party also acts as a powerful filter.[58] A conservative Republican from Arizona might watch the "liberal eastern networks" and complain about their biased news coverage while sticking to her own opinions. A liberal from New York will often complain about right-wing talk radio, even if he listens to it some nights on the way home from work (see Figures 10–1 and 10–2).

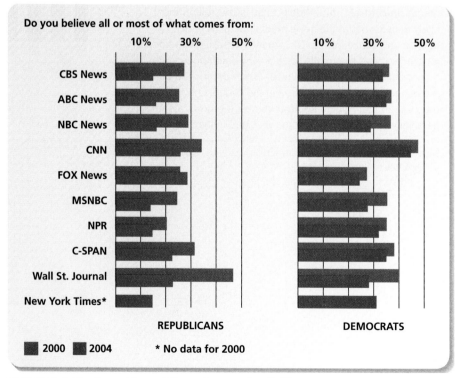

FIGURE 10–2 Partisanship and News Source Credibility.
SOURCE: *The New York Times,* July 18, 2004.

political socialization
The process by which we develop our political attitudes, values, and beliefs.

SELECTIVITY People practice **selective exposure**—screening out messages that do not conform to their own biases. They subscribe to newspapers or magazines that support their views. People also practice **selective perception**—perceiving what they want to in media messages.[59] One dramatic example was the differing reactions of Democrats and Republicans to reports of President Clinton's sexual misconduct with Monica Lewinsky, a former White House intern, and the possibility that he encouraged her to lie under oath. In the first weeks after the story broke, Republicans were four times more likely than Democrats to believe that Clinton had been sexually involved with Lewinsky.[60] More than two-thirds of Republicans and Democrats agreed that Clinton committed perjury before the grand jury, but they had dramatically different opinions on whether Clinton should remain in office. Nearly two-thirds of Republicans wanted Clinton out of office, while 63 percent of Independents and 87 percent of Democrats felt that Clinton should continue as president.[61]

NEEDS People read newspapers, listen to the radio, or watch television for very different reasons, often out of habit or because they want information.[62] People who seek information and cultivate an interest in politics are affected by what they read and see differently from those who use media primarily for entertainment.[63] For those seeking entertainment, gossip about politicians' peccadilloes is more important than those politicians' opinions or voting patterns. Members of the broader audience are also more likely to pay attention to news that directly affects their lives, such as interest rate changes or the price of gasoline.[64]

RECALL AND COMPREHENSION Still another limitation of media influence on public opinion is the extent to which the audience can recall the stories or comprehend their importance. Candidates and officials send out vast amounts of information designed to influence what people think and do, and especially how they vote, but people forget or fail to comprehend much of it.[65] The fragmentary and rapid mode of presentation of television news contributes to the problem. Most television news stories, for example, last less than 90 seconds.

Given the abundance of information available about politics and government, it is not surprising that most people pick and choose which media source—television, radio, newspapers, cable, the Web—they pay attention to and which news stories they consider important.[66] The best predictor of retention of news stories is political interest. People tend to fit today's news stories into their general assumptions or beliefs about government, politicians, or the media itself.

AUDIENCE FRAGMENTATION With the growth of cable television and new media like the Web, the influence of any one media source is weakened. Because people are scattered across a larger number of press outlets and these outlets cover politics in varied ways, the impact of the press will be more disparate. People can now tailor their news to their preferred point of view. In a study of the 2004 election it was observed that "today's fractionalized media environment has taken the heaviest toll on local news, network news, and newspapers."[67] Fragmentation of the media audience tends to counteract the impact of media conglomeration. As media giants move to both cable and broadcast (NBC, CNBC, MSNBC, for example), the trends may converge.

Are the Media Biased?

Americans tend to blame the media for lots of things. Conservatives complain, "The media are too liberal." Radio talk show host Rush Limbaugh even once said, "They all just happen to believe the same way. . . . They are part of the same culture as Bill Clinton."[68] Extreme liberals contend that the ruling class controls the mainstream press, and they charge that government propaganda distorts the facts. Conservatives say the press is too liberal in its selection of news covered and the interpretation of events. Liberals point to newspaper endorsements of Republican presidential candidates to support their claim that newspapers are biased in favor of conservative policies and candidates.

"Hey, do you want to be on the news tonight or not? This is a sound bite, not the Gettysburg Address. Just say what you have to say, Senator, and get the hell off."

selective exposure
The process by which individuals screen out messages that do not conform to their own biases.

selective perception
The process by which individuals perceive what they want to in media messages.

Newspapers, magazines, and television stations are business corporations concerned about profits. They work to boost circulation and ratings and must please their advertisers, sponsors, and stockholders. Reporters and editors pride themselves on impartial reporting of the facts.[69] Yet some liberal critics contend that the media reflect a conservative bias not only in what they report but also in what they choose to ignore. Political scientist Michael Parenti states that journalists "rarely doubt their own objectivity even as they faithfully echo the established political vocabularies and the prevailing politico-economic orthodoxy."[70]

Newspapers and television management go to some lengths to insulate reporters from their advertising and business operations, in part to reduce criticism about favorable treatment of large advertisers or the corporate owners. When the management of the *Los Angeles Times* attempted to foster closer relations between the business and news divisions, it was criticized for insensitivity to this concern.[71] Another internal check on media bias is the fact that news coverage involves many reporters and a host of editors, all of whom have input into what is covered and how it is presented.

Some commentators have suggested that a possible bias flows from the fact that reporters and editors become too friendly with the people and organizations they write about. David Broder of *The Washington Post* voices his concern about the confusion of roles by journalists who have served in government. According to Broder, a line should divide objective journalism from partisan politics, but many members of the print and television media have crossed this line. Broder opposes the idea of journalists' becoming government officials and vice versa.[72] Others argue that journalists with previous government service have close working relationships with politicians and can give us a valuable perspective on government without losing their professional neutrality.

A frequent criticism is the media's alleged political bias, whether liberal or conservative (see Table 10–1). But to whom are these critics referring? To reporters, writers, editors, producers, or owners of TV stations and newspapers? Do they assume that a journalist's personal politics will be translated into biased reporting? And does the public think so? Journalists are usually more liberal than the population as a whole; editors tend to be a bit more conservative than their reporters are; and media owners are more conservative still. Elite journalists—those who work for national news media organizations—tend to share a similar culture: cosmopolitan, urban, upper-class. Their

TABLE 10–1 THE CHANGING FACE OF JOURNALISTS

	Journalists	Policy Makers	Public
Party Identification			
Democrat	27%	43%	34%
Republican	4	24	28
Independent	55	26	21
Other	5	5	12
Don't Know/Refused	9	2	2
Self-Described Ideology			
Liberal	25%	25%	21%
Moderate	59	52	37
Conservative	6	18	35
Don't Know/Refused	11	5	7

SOURCE: The Kaiser Foundation, *The Role of Polls in Policy Making*, Combined Topline Results, June 2001, p. 27. www.kff.org/kaiserpolls/loader.cfm?url=/commonspot/security/getfile.cfm&PageID=13842.

approach to the events and issues they cover is governed by their common worldview, which may be derived from their professional training.[73] The result, some critics contend, is that elite journalists give greater weight to the side of issues that corresponds to their own version of reality.[74]

One bias of the media that does not have a particular partisan or ideological slant is the bias toward sensationalism. Scandals of all types happen to liberals and conservatives, Republicans and Democrats. Once the province of tabloids like the *National Enquirer,* stories about scandal have recently become commonplace in the mainstream media. For years, the media have seemed to gravitate to stories involving celebrities, sex, or both. From the O. J. Simpson murder trial to the coverage of a missing intern who had been involved in an affair with a congressman, we have seen what some observers have called a media "feeding frenzy."[75] The intense and unrelenting focus on the scandal involving former President Bill Clinton and White House intern Monica Lewinsky is a clear example of the media's fondness for sensational coverage.

Newspapers and television news often set a tone of dissatisfaction with the performance of the national government and cynicism about politics and politicians. A critical tone may be an inevitable element of the mind-set of the press, but to whose benefit does that critical tone work? The media are accused of having an antireligion bias, a bias in favor of young viewers, and a bias fostering continuing crises.[76] The question is not whether the press is biased but whether a press bias—whatever the direction—seeps into the content of the news. The answer to that question is still not settled.

Public Opinion

Two important influences of print and broadcast media on public opinion are *agenda setting* and *issue framing.*

AGENDA SETTING[77]   By calling public attention to certain issues, the media help determine what topics will become subjects of public debate and legislation.[78] However, the agenda-setting function of the media is not uniformly pervasive. The audience and the nature of the issue limit it.[79] According to former Vice President Walter Mondale, "If I had to give up . . . the opportunity to get on the evening news or the veto power, . . . I'd throw the veto power away. [Television news] is the President's most indispensable power."[80] Ronald Reagan, more than any president before him, effectively used the media to set the nation's agenda. Reagan and his advisers carefully crafted the images and scenes of his presidency to fit television. Thus television became an "electronic throne."

Communicating through the media works especially when it is natural and unscripted. When President Bush first visited the scene of the demolition of the World Trade Center in New York City, taking a bullhorn, he said, "I can hear you. The rest of the world hears you, and the people who knocked these buildings down will hear all of us soon."[81] This action projected leadership and empathy on the part of the president.

ISSUE FRAMING   Politicians, like everybody else, try to frame issues to win arguments, and they try to influence the "spin" the media will give to their actions or issues. Examples abound. Opponents of U.S. intervention in Bosnia tried to portray such action as another Vietnam. Objectors to permanent normal trade relations with China framed the granting of that status as a human rights travesty. When Bill Clinton wanted to forestall a Republican tax cut, he decried the resulting need to dip into the budget surplus to "rescue Social Security." People who favor abortion define the issue as one of freedom of choice; those who oppose it define it as murder. In referendum campaigns, the side that wins the battle of interpreting what the referendum is about wins the election.[82]

In the 2004 election, voters indicated that the Iraq war and terrorism, the economy and jobs, and moral values were the most important issues. All of these issues had received a lot of attention in the media except "moral values," which prompted intense discussion after the election about what people meant by this response. The fact that gay marriage was on the ballot in eleven states and frequently mentioned in the campaign may help explain why moral values was mentioned by one in five voters.

THE MEDIA AND ELECTIONS

News coverage of campaigns and elections is greatest in presidential contests, less in statewide races for governor and U.S. senator, and least for other state and local races. Generally, the more news attention given the campaign, the less likely voters are to be swayed by any one source. Hence news coverage is likely to be more influential in a city council contest than in an election for president or the Senate. For most city elections, there are only one or two sources of information about what candidates say and stand for; for statewide and national contests, there are multiple sources.

Diversification of the news media lessens the ability of any one medium to influence the outcome of elections. Newspaper publishers who were once seen as key figures in state and local politics are now less important because politicians and their media advisers are no longer so dependent on newspapers and other news media to communicate their messages. Candidates can use ads on radio and television, direct mail, phone, the Web, and cable television to communicate with voters. In local contests, or even some larger settings like the Iowa caucuses or the New Hampshire primary, personal contact can also be very important.[83]

Choice of Candidates

The extensive use of television has made looking and sounding good on television much more important. It has also fostered growth in the political consulting industry and made visibility the watchword in politics. Television greatly affects the public's idea of what traits are important in a candidate. A century ago, successful candidates needed a strong pair of lungs; today it is a telegenic appearance, a pleasing voice, and no obvious physical impairments. Back in the 1930s, the press chose not to show Franklin Roosevelt in his wheelchair or using braces, whereas today the country knows every intimate detail of the president's health. The importance of the public's perception of these traits is evident in the ridicule often directed at candidates. In 2004, Kerry was described as "French-looking"[84] and flip-flopping on issues, and Bush as stubborn and frequently smirking as Kerry spoke in the televised debates.

Although the media insist that they pay attention to all candidates who have a chance to win, they also influence who gets such a chance. Consequently, candidates have to come up with creative ways to attract media attention. The late Paul Wellstone, in his 1996 Minnesota Senate campaign, said in his advertisements that he did not have much money to pay for ads, so he would have to talk fast to cram what he had to say into fewer commercials. His witty commercial became a news event itself—it got Wellstone additional coverage.

In another bid for media attention, some candidates in states bordering Canada have organized bus trips to Canada for people to purchase prescription drugs at Canadian prices, which were sharply lower than in the United States. Candidates in both parties have recently made hunting a pastime, in part to reassure voters that they support the Second Amendment. In 2004, John Kerry went duck hunting in camouflage attire one day during the final week of the campaign. House and Sentate candidates have also included in recent campaign literature photos of them shooting rifles.

Campaign Events

Candidates schedule events—press conferences, interviews, and "photo ops"—in settings that reinforce their verbal messages and public image. A much publicized example of such a staged event was President Bush landing on the aircraft carrier USS Lincoln to announce the end of "major combat operations" in Iraq. While the event provided a dramatic backdrop for the president in his flight jacket, a debate ensued about the cost of the carrier remaining at sea an extra day,[85] and, more fundamentally, as the resistance

"I'm still undecided—I like Leno's foreign policy, but Letterman makes a lot of sense on domestic issues."

to American forces in Iraq continued and intensified, Bush's declaration on the Lincoln seemed more and more premature. Many events organized by campaigns fail to receive attention from reporters because of competing news stories and a sense that the events were staged primarily to generate news coverage.

The parties' national conventions used to capture national attention. However, since candidates are now selected in party primaries, the conventions no longer provide much suspense or make news except perhaps over who will be the vice presidential nominee. This is one reason why the networks have dramatically cut back their coverage of presidential nominating conventions. In 1952, the average television set was tuned to the political conventions for 26 hours, or an average of more than three hours a night for the eight nights of convention coverage.[86] During the 2000 presidential conventions, by contrast, the major networks provided only one or two hours of prime-time coverage each evening. Political parties have sought, in vain, to regain audience interest by relying on "movie stars, entertainment routines, and professionally produced documentaries to spice up their conventions."[87]

Technology

Although the expense associated with television has contributed to the skyrocketing costs of campaigning, it has also made politics more accessible to more people. Thanks to satellites, candidates can conduct local television interviews without actually traveling to local studios. Specific voter groups can be targeted through cable television or low-power television stations that reach homogeneous neighborhoods and small towns. Videocassettes with messages from the candidates further extend the campaign's reach.[88] All serious candidates for Congress and governor in 2000 and 2002 made themselves and their positions available through a home page on the World Wide Web.

The Internet and e-mail have primarily been used to reinforce voter preferences or help answer questions more than to reach and persuade more passive citizens. But with the Web, citizens now have the opportunity to interact with each other on a wide range of political topics. In this sense, the Web is something like a town meeting, but without people leaving their homes or offices. In chat rooms on the Internet people express ideas and respond to each other's opinions. Examples of chat rooms include Abortion Chat, Democrat Chat, Environment Chat, Republican Chat, and Congress Chat. Most chat rooms offer group discussions in which anyone in the group can read and send messages, but some chat rooms also permit private messages to be sent. As discussed earlier, the Internet has also become a way for candidates and groups to raise funds.

Younger voters are much more likely to use the Internet to get campaign news than middle aged and older voters. In a study of the 2004 election, nearly three times as many 18- to 29-year-olds said they used the Internet for news (20 percent), compared with only 7 percent of those over age 50. Persons between 30 and 49 years of age were in between, with 16 percent citing the Internet as a source of campaign news. Younger voters also reported a much greater reliance on comedy TV shows as a source of campaign news.[89]

Image Making and Media Consultants

Candidates recognize that their messages about issues are often ignored. The press tends to emphasize goofs and gossip or tension among party leaders. Candidates in turn try to spin the news. Attempts to shape the news and to portray candidates in the best possible light are not new. Presidential campaign sloganeering such as "Tippecanoe and Tyler Too" in 1840, "Abe the Rail Splitter" in 1860, and "I Like Ike" in 1952 conveyed the candidate's image. Radio, television, and the Web have expanded the ability to project

★ ★ **THINKING IT THROUGH**

Proponents of free air time cite the fact that broadcast stations use public airwaves and that stations therefore have an obligation to provide free air time to candidates as a public service. Broadcasters, they argue, generate over $60 billion a year in advertising revenue.[*] Proponents of free air time also refer to studies that show how television stations charge candidates and politicians inflated rates to run advertisements in the days before an election. Finally, proponents point to the fact that television stations provide little news of federal elections, making advertising and free air time even more important.

Opponents of free air time argue that the media are already required to charge candidates the lowest rate for that time segment (i.e., prime time between 7 and 10 P.M.). They say the current system provides both sides equal access and forces the candidates and parties to have real support from voters and financial contributors. They argue that the media covers campaigns in sufficient depth and that requiring stations to provide free time will mean they lose viewers or listeners because people will switch stations because they are turned off to politics. Finally, they point out that broadcasters are being unfairly singled out from other means of communicating with voters. Businesses that produce mail, make phone calls, or even cable television would not be forced to provide access to resources for free.

[*] www.bettercampaign.org/freeairtime/factsheets/sweetheartdeal.pdf.

A candidate's image often takes precedence over that candidate's message in the mass media. This was as true in the mid-nineteenth century as it is today. This is why image makers and media consultants have been in such high demand for so long. On the top, we see a portrait of Abraham Lincoln as "Abe the Rail Splitter." On the bottom, we see George W. Bush riding a mountain bike.

horse race
A close contest; by extension, any contest in which the focus is on who is ahead and by how much rather than on substantive differences between the candidates.

images, and that expansion has in turn affected candidates' vote-getting strategies and their manner of communicating messages. Television is especially important because of the power of the visual image.

Television has contributed to the rise of new players in campaign politics: *media consultants,* campaign professionals who provide candidates with advice and services on media relations, advertising strategy, and opinion polling.[90] For example, candidates regularly receive consultants' advice on what colors work best for them, especially on television. Male U.S. Senators often appear in light blue shirts with red ties, sometimes called "power ties." A primary responsibility of a campaign media consultant is to present a positive image of the candidate and to reinforce negative images of the opponent.

Some media consultants have been credited with propelling candidates to success. Dick Morris was seen as important to Clinton's resurgence after the 1994 congressional election defeats, until he had to resign from the campaign following a personal scandal. Republican consultant Mark McKinnon produced ads for President Bush's 2000 and 2004 campaigns, and John Kerry's media was done by Bob Shrum and Jim Margolis. Both parties have scores of media consultants who have handled congressional and gubernatorial campaigns as well as campaigns over ballot questions. While sometimes credited with helping elect or defeat candidates and referendums, they have also been blamed for the negativity of recent campaigns.

Media consultants have taken over the role formerly played by party politicians. Before World War II, party professionals groomed candidates for office at all levels. Such leaders made judgments about possible candidates on the basis of their chances of victory and observation of the candidates' performance under fire, decisiveness, conviction, political skill, and other leadership qualities. Party professionals advised candidates which party and interest group leaders to placate, which issues to stress, and which topics to avoid.

Today consultants coach candidates about television technique, appearance, and subject matter. Consultants report the results of *focus groups* (small sample groups of people who are asked questions about candidates and issues in a discussion setting) and *public opinion polls,* which in turn determine what the candidate says and does. Some critics allege that political consultants have become a new "political elite" who can virtually choose candidates by determining in advance which men and women have the right images or at least images that can be restyled for the widest popularity.[91] But political consultants who specialize in media advertising and image making realize their own limitations in packaging candidates. As one media consultant put it, "It is a very hard job to turn a turkey into a movie star; you try instead to make people like the turkey."[92]

The Media and Voter Choice

As television has become increasingly important to politics, and as the political parties have been weakened with such reforms as primary elections, news coverage of candidates has taken on added significance. Although some critics think reporters pay too much attention to candidates' personality and background, others say character and personality are among the most important characteristics for readers and viewers to know about. What is not in dispute is the central role the news media play in our democratic process.

THE HORSE RACE   A common tendency in the media is to comment on a candidate's position in the polls compared with other candidates—what is sometimes called the **horse race**—than they are about policy issues.[93] "Many stories focus on who is ahead, who is behind, who is going to win, and who is going to lose, rather than examining how and why the race is as it is."[94] Reporters focus on the tactics and strategy of campaigns because they perceive that the public is interested and influenced by such coverage.[95]

The media's propensity to focus on the "game" of campaigns displaces coverage of issues.

NEGATIVE ADVERTISING   Political advertising has always contained negative remarks about opponents, but recent campaigns have taken on an increasingly negative tone. A rule of thumb in the old politics was to ignore the charges of the opposition and thus to accord one's rival no importance or standing. That practice has changed as today's candidates trade charges and countercharges.

Voters say they are turned off by the attack style of politics, but the widespread perception among campaign consultants is that negative campaigning works. This seeming inconsistency may be explained by evidence suggesting that campaigns that foster negative impressions of the candidates contribute to lower turnout.[96] Negative advertising may thus discourage some voters who would be inclined to support a candidate (a phenomenon known as *vote suppression*) while reinforcing the inclination of committed supporters to come out to vote.

INFORMATION ABOUT ISSUES   In recent elections, the media have experimented with a more issues-centered focus, what has been called *civic journalism*. With funding from charitable foundations, some newspapers have been identifying the concerns of community leaders and talking to ordinary voters and then writing campaign stories from their point of view.[97] Some newspaper editors and reporters disagree with this approach; they believe the media should stick to responding to newsworthy events. Advocates of civic journalism counter that important concerns of the community are often overshadowed by news events like murders and violence.

MAKING A DECISION   Newspapers and television seem to have more influence in determining the outcome of primaries than of general elections,[98] probably because voters are less likely to know about the candidates and have fewer clues about how they stand in a primary. By the time of the November general election, however, party affiliation, incumbency, and other factors moderate the impact of media messages. The mass media are more likely to influence undecided voters who, in a close election, can determine who wins and who loses.

ELECTION NIGHT REPORTING   Does TV coverage on election night affect the outcome of elections? Election returns from the East come in three hours before the polls close on the West Coast. Because major networks often project the presidential winner well ahead of poll closings in western states, some western voters have been discouraged from voting. As a result, voter turnout in congressional and local elections has been affected. In a close presidential election, however, such early reporting may well stimulate turnout because voters know their vote could determine the outcome. In short, it is only in elections in which one candidate appears to be winning by a large margin that television reporting makes voters believe their vote is meaningless.[99]

At 7:50 P.M. (EST) on election night, November 7, 2000, television networks projected Al Gore as the winner of Florida, but they soon had second thoughts and revoked their announcement. Hours later Fox News projected Bush as winning Florida. The truth was that the vote in Florida was by every measure too close to call, and no network should have called the race. In the days and weeks after the election, the Voter News Service admitted that its Florida sample was flawed, that it underestimated the Florida absentee vote, and that it relied on incomplete actual vote totals. The mistaken projections by the networks were embarrassing. Tom Brokaw of NBC said, "That's not 'an egg' on our faces; that's 'an omelet.' "[100]

In 2002, the media exit polls failed again. On election day, the networks that sponsor the Voter News Service (VNS), which conducts the media exit polling, announced that they would not be releasing exit poll numbers nor would they be projecting winners. Following the 2000 election and the controversy over the Florida exit polling,

VNS invested in new computers and software and developed new models to project winners. They gathered data on election day but did not have confidence in their ability to accurately predict contests. Viewers on election night 2002 thus got what many had wanted, a night with only local exit polling. The absence of exit polling data, however, meant it was hard to assess the national mood and which types of people actually voted.

THE MEDIA AND GOVERNANCE

The press rarely follows the policy process to its conclusion. Rather, it leaves the issue at the doorstep of public officials. By the time a political issue reaches the stages of policy formulation and implementation, the press has moved on to another issue. When policies are being formulated and implemented, decision makers are at their most impressionable, yet the press has little impact at this stage.[101]

Lack of press attention to policy implementation explains in part why we know less about how bureaucrats go about their business than we do about heated legislative debates or presidential scandals. Only in the case of a policy scandal, such as the lax security surrounding nuclear secrets at Los Alamos, does the press take notice. "Most executives would be satisfied with a press strategy of no surprises. All their press officers need do to be doing their job is provide a rudimentary early warning system [for crises] and issue routine announcements."[102]

Some media critics contend that the media's pressuring policy makers to provide immediate answers forces them to make untimely decisions. Foreign policy may be in particular danger from such quick responses:

> If an ominous foreign event is featured on TV news, the president and his advisers feel bound to make a response in time for the next evening news broadcast. . . . If he does not have a response ready by the late afternoon deadline, the evening news may report that the president's advisers are divided, that the president cannot make up his mind, or that while the president hesitates, his political opponents know exactly what to do.[103]

Political Institutions and the News Media

Presidents have become the stars of the media, particularly television, and have made the media their forum for setting the public agenda and achieving their legislative aims. Presidential news conferences command attention (see Table 10–2). Every public activity, both professional and personal, is potentially newsworthy; a presidential illness can become front-page news, as can presidential vacations and family pets.

A president attempts to manipulate news coverage to his benefit. Speeches are used to set the national agenda or spur congressional action. Travel to foreign countries usually boosts popular support at home, thanks to the largely favorable news coverage. Better yet for the president, most coverage of the president—either at home or abroad—is favorable to neutral.[104] President Clinton's trip to Israel during the height of the furor surrounding his impeachment may have helped distract attention from his domestic problems in both senses of that word.

Congress is a fragmented body usually unable to act quickly. It is also more likely to get negative coverage than either the White House or the Supreme Court. Unlike the executive branch, it lacks an ultimate spokesperson, a single individual who can speak for the whole institution.[105] Congress does not make it easy for the press to cover it. Whereas the White House engages in attentive care and feeding of the press corps, Congress does not arrange its schedule to accommodate the media; floor debates, for example, often compete with committee hearings and press conferences.[106] Singularly dramatic actions rarely occur in Congress; the press therefore turns to the president to describe federal government activity on a day-to-day basis and treats Congress largely as a foil to the president. Most coverage of Congress is of its reaction to the initiatives of the president.[107]

The federal judiciary is least dependent on the press. The Supreme Court does not rely on public communication for political support. Rather, it relies indirectly on public opinion for continued deference to or compliance with its decisions.[108] The Court does not allow television cameras to cover oral arguments, rarely allows audiotaping, and has no reporters present when it votes. The Court has strong incentives to avoid the perception of manipulating the press, so it retains an image of aloofness from politics and public opinion. The justices' manipulation of press coverage is far more subtle and complex than that of the other two institutions.[109] For example, the complexity of the Supreme Court's decision in 2000's Florida vote recount case, with multiple dissents and concurrences and no press release or executive summary, made broadcast reporting on the decision difficult.

The news media's most influential role may be at the local level.[110] Most of us have multiple sources for finding out what is happening in Washington that act as a check on the biases and limitations of reporters who cover national government and policy. But when it comes to finding out about the city council, the school board, or the local water district, most of us are dependent on the work of a single reporter. Consequently, the media's influence is much greater when there are fewer news sources.

Not all who think the media are powerful agree that their power is harmful. After all, they argue, the media perform a vital educational function. Almost 70 percent of the public thinks the press is a watchdog that keeps government leaders from doing bad things.[111] At the very least, the media have the power to mold the agenda of the day; at most, in the words of the late Theodore White, they have the power to "determine what people will talk and think about—an authority that in other nations is reserved for tyrants, priests, parties, and mandarins."[112]

TABLE 10–2   PRESIDENTIAL PRESS CONFERENCES: JOINT AND SOLO SESSIONS, 1913–2004

President	Total	Solo	Joint	Joint as Percentage of Total	Months in Office	Solo Sessions per Month	Solo Sessions per Year
Wilson	157	157	0	0	96	1.6	19.6
Harding	No Transcripts Available				29		
Coolidge	521	521	0	0	67	7.8	93.4
Hoover	268	267	1	0.4	48	5.6	66.8
Roosevelt	1020	984	33	3.2	145.5	6.8	81.1
Truman	324	311	13	4.0	94.5	3.3	39.5
Eisenhower	193	192	1	0.5	96	2.0	24.0
Kennedy	65	65	0	0	34	1.9	23.0
Johnson	135	118	16	11.9	62	1.9	22.8
Nixon	39	39	0	0	66	0.6	7.1
Ford	40	39	1	2.5	30	1.3	15.6
Carter	59	59	0	0	48	1.2	14.8
Reagan	46	46	0	0	96	0.5	5.8
G. H. W. Bush	143	84	59	41.3	48	1.8	21.0
Clinton	193	62	131	67.9	96	0.7	7.8
G. W. Bush	85	16	69	81.2	46	0.4	4.2

Note: A joint press conference is one where the president answers questions along with someone else, most often a foreign leader. In a solo session, only the president answers questions. There are three missing transcripts for Roosevelt and one for Johnson, which makes it impossible to determine whether those sessions were solo or joint ones.

SOURCE: Chart from Martha Joynt Kumar, "Presidential Press Conferences: The Evolution of an Enduring Forum,"*Presidential Studies Quarterly*, vol. 35, no. 1, March 2005.

SUMMARY

1. The news media include newspapers, magazines, radio, television, films, recordings, books, and electronic communications, in all their forms. These means of communication have been called the "fourth branch of government."

2. The news media are a pervasive feature of American politics and generally help define our culture. The rise of new communications technologies has made the media more influential throughout American society. The news media serve as a link between politicians and government officials and the public.

3. Our modern news media emerged from a more partisan and less professional past. Autonomy of the media from political parties is one of the important changes. Now journalists strive for objectivity and see themselves as important to the political process. They also engage in investigative journalism.

4. Broadcasting on radio and television has changed the news media, and most Americans use television and radio as primary news sources. The role of corporate ownership of media outlets, especially media conglomerates, raises questions about media competition and orientation.

5. The influence of the mass media over public opinion is significant but not overwhelming. People may not pay much attention to the media or may not believe everything they read or see or hear. They may be critical or suspicious of the media and hence resistant to it. People tend to filter the news through their political socialization, selectivity, needs, and ability to recall or comprehend the content of the news.

6. The media are criticized as biased both by conservatives (who charge that the media are too liberal) and by liberals (who claim that the media are captives of corporate interests and major advertisers). Little evidence exists of actual, deliberate bias in news reporting.

7. A major effect of mass media news is agenda setting—determining what problems will become salient issues for people to form opinions about and to discuss. The media are also influential in defining issues for the general public.

8. Presidential campaigns are dominated by media coverage both before and after the national convention. One effect of media influence is that most people seem more interested in the contest as a game or "horse race" than as an occasion for serious discussion of issues and candidates. Another effect has been the rise of image making and the media consultant.

9. The press serves as both observer and participant in politics, as a watchdog, agenda setter, and check on the abuse of power, but it rarely follows the policy process to its conclusion.

KEY TERMS

mass media	issue advocacy	political socialization	selective perception
news media	fairness doctrine	selective exposure	horse race

FURTHER READING

STEPHEN ANSOLABEHERE AND SHANTO IYENGAR, *Going Negative: How Attack Ads Shrink and Polarize the Electorate* (Free Press, 1996).

BRUCE BIMBER AND RICHARD DAVIS, *Campaigning Online: The Internet in U.S. Elections* (Oxford University Press, 2003).

SIMONE CHAMBERS AND ANNE COSTAIN, EDS., *Deliberation, Democracy, and the Media* (Rowman & Littlefield, 2000).

TIMOTHY E. COOK, *Making Laws and Making News: Press Strategies in the U.S. House of Representatives* (Brookings Institution Press, 1990).

TIMOTHY E. COOK, *Governing with the News: The News Media as a Political Institution* (University of Chicago Press, 1998).

RICHARD DAVIS, *The American Press and American Politics: The New Mediator* (Prentice Hall, 2001).

ROBERT M. ENTMAN AND W. LANCE BENNETT, EDS., *Mediated Politics: Communication in the Future of Democracy* (Cambridge University Press, 2000).

JAMES FALLOWS, *Breaking the News: How the Media Undermine American Democracy* (Pantheon Books, 1996).

STEPHEN J. FARNSWORTH AND S. ROBERT LICHTER, *The Nightly News Nightmare: Network Television's Coverage of U.S. Presidential Elections, 1988–2000* (Rowman & Littlefield, 2003).

DORIS A. GRABER, *Mass Media and American Politics*, 6th ed. (CQ Press, 2002).

RODERICK P. HART, *Campaign Talk: Why Elections Are Good for Us* (Princeton University Press, 2000).

KATHLEEN H. JAMISON, *The Press Effect: Politicians, Journalists, and the Stories That Shape the Political World* (Oxford University Press, 2003).

PHYLISS KANISS, *Making Local News* (University of Chicago Press, 1991).

HOWARD KURTZ, *Spin Cycle: Inside the Clinton Propaganda Machine* (Free Press, 1998).

S. ROBERT LICHTER, STANLEY ROTHMAN, AND LINDA S. LICHTER, *The Media Elite* (Adler & Adler, 1986).

PIPPA NORRIS, *A Virtuous Circle: Political Communications in Post-Industrial Societies* (Cambridge University Press, 2000).

TOM ROSENSTEIL, *Strange Bedfellows: How Television and the Presidential Candidates Changed American Politics, 1992* (Hyperion, 1993).

MARK J. ROZELL, ED., *Media Power, Media Politics* (Rowman & Littefield, 2003).

JAMES A. THURBER, CANDICE J. NELSON, AND DAVID A. DULIO, EDS., *Crowded Airwaves: Campaign Advertising in Elections* (Brookings Institution Press, 2000).

DARRELL M. WEST, *Air Wars: Television Advertising in Election Campaigns, 1952–1992* (CQ Press, 1993).

CONGRESS
THE PEOPLE'S BRANCH

11

The United States Congress is one of the world's greatest democratic institutions. Members fight hard on behalf of their states and districts, are free to introduce any legislation they wish, even if there is no chance of passage, have seemingly endless opportunities to voice their opinions on the issues of the day, and provide a constant stream of information back home.

This openness also makes Congress one of the world's most frustrating institutions. Senators are free to talk as long as they can stand; committee chairs can delay legislation for months and years; very few proposals ever receive a hearing, let alone a final vote, and the competition among members for media attention can make Congress look more like a three-ring circus than a deliberative body.

The tension between representation and action has existed from the very first Congress in 1789. Because Congress is divided into two houses, each with its own calendar, rules, and electoral base, action requires broad agreements both within anad across the institution as a whole. As a result, members of Congress often agree to disagree about major legislation, even when the public wants action.

Frustration has a purpose in the constitutional system. It forces majorities to make their case to the entire nation, not just to their passionate supporters, and gives opponents an opportunity to fight legislation they believe is wrong.

There is growing evidence, however, that Congress has become less able to reach consensus over the past half century as moderate Democrats and Republicans have been steadily replaced with more ideological members of their parties.[1] The trend is likely to continue in the future. In 2004, for example, five moderate Southern Democrats retired—

TIME LINE

CONGRESS

1811	Elbridge Gerry is immortalized by his salamander-shaped reapportionment plan—the "gerrymander"
1870	Hiram Revels is elected as the first African American senator
1890	Insurgent Republicans join Democrats to defeat Speaker of the House Thomas Reed
1913	Seventeenth Amendment provides for direct election of senators
1917	Senate rules changed to permit cloture; previously, a filibuster could only be terminated if every member agreed
1955	Lyndon Johnson becomes one of the all-time most powerful Senate Majority Leaders
1974	In reaction to the Watergate scandal, voters elect large majorities of liberal Democrats to Congress
1994	Democrats lose control over the House of Representatives after being in the majority for over 40 years
2003	After serving in the Senate for 48 years, Strom Thurmond retires at age 100

John Breaux of Louisana, John Edwards of North Carolina, Bob Graham of Florida, Ernest Hollings of South Carolina, and Zell Miller of Georgia. All five were replaced by much more conservative Republicans. The victories left just four of the south's 26 seats still in Democratic hands, two of which are at the fringe of the south in Arkansas. In 1970, Republicans held just seven of the 26.

The loss of moderate Democrats and Republicans increases the odds that Congress will be less able to act. Moderates are often key to finding compromises across the party lines, and frequently soften the intense arguments that arise between more ideological members of Congress. Thus, Breaux often joined with other moderates in both parties to find compromises on issues such as the Bush Administration's 2001 tax cut and the more recent legislation giving presciption drug coverage to senior citizens in 2003, while Miller and Hollings often provided needed votes for compromise on issues such as education reform and homeland security.

Congress can still pass legislation with sharp divisions between the two parties, as it did with the prescription drug bill in 2003. But the votes on such legislation are often close, and can involve intense conflict. The prescription bill only passed on a razor-thin 220 to 215 vote in the House and a 55 to 44 margin in the Senate.

In this chapter, we examine how Congress organizes itself to make laws and represent the people. We also look at how the framers designed the institution to work. We will ask how Congress can remain open and accessible, yet still make the deals needed to pass important legislation in the national interest. Before turning to these questions, however, it is first important to ask how members of Congress are elected to office and to consider the ways in which congressional elections often act to insulate individual members from their own constituents.

CONGRESSIONAL ELECTIONS

There is only one Congress described in the Constitution, but there are two very different electoral calendars for entering office. Each of the 435 members of the House of Representatives is elected to a two-year term in even-numbered years, while only a third of the Senate's 100 members are chosen for six-year terms every two years. The number of House members was finally capped at 435 when Congress ordered states to stop drawing new districts in 1910.

There are also somewhat different requirements for becoming members of the House and Senate. At minimum, members of the House must be 25 years old and have been citizens for seven years, whereas senators must be 30 years old and have been citizens for nine years. House and Senate candidates must be residents of the states from which they are elected.

By setting the Senate's requirements higher and giving its members a six-year term, the framers hoped the Senate would act as a check against what they saw as the less predictable House. Concerned about the "fickleness and passion" of the House of Representatives, James Madison in particular saw the Senate as "a necessary fence against this danger."[2]

The framers did not limit the number of terms a House member or senator could serve. The term limits imposed by the Articles of Confederation had forced several talented members out of office, leaving the Continental Congress less effective and souring the framers on the idea.[3]

Regardless of differences between the two houses of Congress, representatives and senators are all politicians who enter office by winning an election. Ironically, it is often good politics for them to deny that they are politicians and to lead the charge against the institution in which they serve. The willingness of "House members to stand and defend their own votes or voting record contrasts sharply with their disposition to run and hide when a defense of Congress might be called for," writes political scientist Richard F. Fenno Jr. "Members of Congress run *for* Congress by running *against* Congress. The strategy is ubiquitous, addictive, cost-free, and foolproof. . . . In the short run, everybody plays and nearly everybody wins. Yet the institution bleeds from 435 separate cuts."[4]

Who Elects the Congress?

Members of the House and Senate represent different populations. According to the Constitution, every state has two U.S. senators, each of whom represents the entire state.

Seats in the House of Representatives are distributed or apportioned among the states according to population. There are 435 House districts, each composed of about 650,000 people. No matter how small its population, every state is guaranteed at least one House member.

The exact apportionment among the states is determined by a national census of the population that is required by the Constitution every ten years. As a result of the 2000 census, Congress had to reallocate seats based on population shifts through a process called **reapportionment**. New York and Pennsylvania lost two House seats; Ohio, Indiana, Illinois, Wisconsin, and Michigan all lost one seat. Florida, Georgia, Texas, and Arizona gained two seats; Colorado, Nevada, North Carolina, and California gained one seat each.

While census figures dictate how House districts are apportioned across the nation, each state determines where those districts lie within its own boundaries. State legislatures nearly always control this **redistricting** process, subject to final approval by the governor or redistricting commissions in states such as Arizona and Iowa. By tradition, redistricting occurs in the state legislative session following the census.

When a single party controls both the legisative and executive branches in a state, it often draws the new map to increase the number of House districts that its own candidates are likely to win. In extreme cases, this process is known as **gerrymandering**, after Governor Elbridge Gerry who approved a Massachusetts redistricting plan that created a salamander-shaped district drawn for distinctly partisan purposes following the 1810 census.

Gerrymandering has become more sophisticated with the computer age. Both parties have developed redistricting software that allows majorities to "pack" and "crack" legislative districts to help their party. Packing is designed to concentrate a minority party's voters in the smallest number of districts possible, thereby weakening their influence in other races, while cracking is designed to disperse a party's voters into as many districts as possible, also weakening their influence.

As noted, redistricting has generally occurred in the state legislative session following the census. With a divided legislature in charge in 2001, Texas left the state congressional map mostly unchanged, yielding a 17 to 15 Democratic edge. But with a Republican legislature and a Republican governor in charge in 2003, Texas decided to redistrict the state again, hoping for a 22 to 10 Republican edge. When all the votes were counted, Republicans had defeated four sitting Democrats, producing a 21 to 11 Republican edge. In two districts, the 19th and the 32nd, Democratic incumbents lost their reelection bids to Republican incumbents who had been placed in the same district.

State legislatures may also draw districts in which a majority of voters are members of minority groups. Such racial gerrymandering is legal unless the legislature considered race and ignored traditional redistricting concerns, such as keeping communities together and reelecting incumbents.[5] Furthermore, a party attacking a majority-minority district must show that the legislature could have achieved the same political result with a significantly different racial balance. A challenge to a North Carolina congressional district failed because Republicans could not show that the district could include more white voters and still be drawn as favorably to Democratic interests.[6]

The principle of equal representation does not apply to the Senate. Because each state has two senators regardless of population, the Senate represents constituencies that are more rural, white, and conservative than would be the case if the one-person, one-vote norm applied to Senate elections.

The word "gerrymander" comes from the name of the governor of Massachusetts, Elbridge Gerry, and the salamander-shaped district that was created to favor his party in 1811.

reapportionment
The assigning by Congress of congressional seats after each census. State legislatures reapportion state legislative districts.

redistricting
The redrawing of congressional and other legislative district lines following the census, to accommodate population shifts and keep districts as equal as possible in population.

gerrymandering
The drawing of legislative district boundaries to benefit a party, group, or incumbent.

Betty Castor, the Democratic candidate for U.S. Senate in Florida, greets supporters on a campaign stop. State campaigns such as this are important as both parties struggle to gain control of the Senate. Castor lost her bid by less than 100,000 votes out of just over 7 million cast.

Such disparities make the Senate the most malapportioned elected legislature in the democratic world, giving the advantage to residents of the smaller states. Frances Lee and Bruce Oppenheimer concluded that the size of a state's population affects senator-constituent relationships, fund raising and elections, strategic behavior within the Senate, and ultimately policy decisions.[7] The late Senator Daniel Patrick Moynihan (D.-N.Y.), who knew firsthand how citizens of larger states fared less well in U.S. Senate policy battles, predicted that "some time in the next century the United States is going to have to address the question of apportionment in the Senate,"[8] but the prospects for changing the two-senators-per-state constitutional rule are highly unlikely in the near future.

Predicting Congressional Elections

The outcome of any congressional election depends on many factors, including campaign financing, local and national policy issues, and each candidate's skills. But all congressional elections start with the nature of the seat at stake. Some House campaigns involve a **safe seat**—one that is predictably won by one party or the other. Others involve a competitive seat that draws strong candidates from both major parties, while still others involve an open seat that has been vacated by a sitting member who retires or runs for higher office.

Because only a third of Senate seats are up for election every two years, Senate elections tend to be highly competitive and better financed than House elections. They also tend to turn on national, not local, issues, particularly in states with substantial media coverage. Although contests in large states often involve the largest amounts of money, even small states such as South Dakota, where former Senate Majority Leader Tom Daschle lives, can play host to very expensive campaigns.

In contrast, House elections tend to be local affairs. Although current members of Congress are sometimes judged by what they do in Washington, particularly on nationally visible issues such as prescription drug coverage, the war in Iraq, or education, most citizens have a favorable view of their own member of Congress. They might not recognize their member on the street, but they will recognize their member's name on the ballot. Because **incumbents**, or sitting members of Congress, have such significant advantages in campaigns, they are almost always reelected if they decide to run. As a result, less than 10 percent of congressional districts are considered competitive in any given election.

In the Senate, incumbents also enjoy significant advantages, and the number of competitive contests has declined. But Senate elections can also turn into national contests depending upon the incumbent's visibility. Because there are fewer Senate contests in any given election year, money tends to concentrate on a relatively small number of competitive contests, which can draw the kind of national media attention to convert them into national, not local, contests.[9]

The last thing most candidates want to do is "nationalize" an election. They would much rather have the campaign be about how well they served the local community through constituent service.

The 2004 Congressional Elections

The 2004 congressional elections are best understood for what did not happen rather than for what did. Despite Democratic hopes for a surge in House seats and Republican hopes for a dramatic gain, the House campaigns produced a shift of only four seats for a balance of 232 to 202, with one independent reelected and the last two races decided in runoffs on December 4, 2004 (see table on page 277).

Also, despite Democratic hopes for a gain of enough Senate seats to recapture a majority and despite Republican hopes for a gain of enough seats to create the 60 votes needed to prevent filibusters, which are discussed later in this chapter, the Senate campaigns produced a net gain of four Republican seats for a balance of 55 to 44, with one independent who usually votes with the Democrats.

safe seat
An elected office that is predictably won by one party or the other, so the success of that party's candidate is almost taken for granted.

incumbents
The current holders of elected office.

The elections were hardly uneventful, however, particularly in the Senate, where the Democrats had 19 seats to defend and the Republicans had 15. Republicans took six seats from the Democrats, including the seat held by Senate minority leader Tom Daschle (D.-S.D.), who was defeated by 8,000 votes in the most expensive Senate race in the nation, and the last five Southern seats still held by Democrats, four of which were vacated through Democratic retirements. In turn, Democrats took two seats from the Republicans, including the Illinois seat won by Barack Obama, who had established a national presence with his keynote address at the Democratic National Convention in July 2004, and the Colorado seat occupied by Native American Ben Nighthorse Campbell, who had entered the Senate a Democrat but who retired after having switched to the Republican party.

THE RESULTS Beyond the Daschle upset and several tight contests in both chambers, the congressional elections produced little overall turnover. Voters reelected 18 of the 19 Senate incumbents who ran, and 394 of the 403 House incumbents who ran. Even including the Texas incumbents who lost, 98.2 percent of incumbents won reelection, marking the third highest rate in fifty years; without the Texans, the rate hit 99.2 percent.

Freshmen House of Representatives of the 108th Congress, who took office in January 2003, on the steps of the U.S. Capitol for their "class" picture.

Indeed, many Senators and Representatives faced token opposition at best. Even before the election, only 9 of the 33 Senate seats up for election were rated as competitive, six of which involved an open seat where an incumbent had retired; while 371 House districts were rated as "safe," including 28 Democrats and 34 Republicans who ran unopposed. "In more than half the states with Senate races, voters are being denied the experience of seeing their senators seriously tested on their records or their plans," Washington Post veteran columnist David Broder wrote just before election day, "The situation in the House of Representatives is similar—but worse." (See David Broder, "What Democracy Needs: Real Races," *The Washington Post*, October 31, 2004, p. B07.) As if to prove the point, four of the nine incumbents who were defeated came from Texas, where two of the losing Democratic incumbents were matched up against Republican incumbents in newly-created districts.

Much of the incumbency advantage involved campaign financing. According to the nonpartisan Campaign Finance Institute, candidates for the 435 House seats spent nearly $450 million in 2004, while candidates for the 33 Senate seats spent nearly $225 million. On average, the House campaigns cost more than $1 million per seat, up almost 20 percent from the winners in 2002, while the Senate campaigns cost more than $6.5 million, up nearly 50 percent from 2002 and almost 60 percent from 1998 when the same 33 seats were last up for election (see Campaign Finance Institute, "House Winners Average $1 Million for the First Time; Senate Winners Up 47%," news release, Washington, D.C., November 5, 2004).

More importantly, winners outspent their challengers by large margins. House incumbents who were reelected by 60 percent or more of the vote outspent their challengers by four to one, or $900,000 to $170,000; while Senate incumbents who won by similar margins outspent their challengers by a margin of five to one, or $4.9 million to $900,000. As of September 30, 2004, incumbent Senator George Voinovich (R.-Ohio) had $4.2 million in cash on hand against an opponent with just $93,000, while incumbent senator and future minority leader Harry Reid (D.-Nev.) had $3.3 million in hand against an opponent with just $15,000.

CONGRESSIONAL ELECTION RESULTS, 2004

SENATE		
	2002	**2004**
Republican	51	55
Democrat	48	44
Independent	1	1

HOUSE		
	2000	**2004**
Republican	229	232
Democrat	205	202
Independent	1	1

ADVANTAGES OF INCUMBENCY

■ Incumbents are better known than their challengers, and to be known at all is generally to be known favorably.

■ Except for the 90 days before an election, incumbents do not have to pay postage for mailings back home, and they are allowed to send bulk e-mails any time.*

■ Incumbents have greater access to the media, especially on local or state issues.

■ Incumbents can raise campaign money more easily than challengers—donors like to put their support behind winners.

■ Incumbents usually have more campaign experience than their challengers, and they are usually better campaigners.

■ Incumbents often help constituents solve problems with government, and they often take credit for federal spending in their districts or state.

* For a discussion of how members have evaded federal legislation against bulk e-mails, or spam, see Jennifer S. Lee, "We Hate Spam, Congress Says (Except When It's Sent by Us)," *The New York Times,* December 18, 2003, p. A1.

Given its national importance to both Democrats and Republicans, South Dakota had the most expensive Senate campaign at $33 million. But high spending was not always tied to competitiveness. Despite the lack of strong opposition, New York had the second most expensive Senate campaign at $28 million, followed by California at $23 million, and Pennsylvania at $20 million.

Texas had the most expensive House race at $8.4 million in a Dallas-Fort Worth contest between two incumbents, Democrat Martin Frost and Republican Pete Sessions, which Sessions won, while South Dakota came in with the second most expensive contest at almost $6 million as Democrat Stephanie Herseth outlasted Republican Larry Diedrich in a rematch of their special election battle only six months earlier.

Although incumbency and the campaign money that goes with it help explain the 2004 results, there were a number of unpredictable contests in which candidate conduct contributed to the uncertainty. In the Senate elections, Illinois Democrat Obama won his seat after the initial Republican candidate quit following reports that he had taken his wife to a sex club in Paris; Kentucky Republican incumbent and former major league Hall-of-Fame pitcher, Jim Bunning, survived despite having described his opponent as resembling one of Iraqi dictator Saddam Hussein's sons; Oklahoma Republican candidate Tom Colburn won his election after saying that physicians who perform abortions should be subject to the death penalty; and Alaska Republican Lisa Murkowski won her first election after having been appointed to her seat by her father, who was governor at the time. (For a complete summary of the 2004 congressional campaigns, see *Congressional Quarterly Weekly,* November 6, 2004.)

In the House, Illinois Democratic challenger Melissa Bean defeated the dean of the Republican majority, Philip Crane, who had been in the House since 1969 when she was just seven years old; while a Colorado Democrat and brother of the state's new senator won an open seat once held by a Republican.

If there was a single winner in the elections, it was House majority leader Tom DeLay, who designed the Texas redistricting strategy that gave the Republicans the four added seats. DeLay positioned himself as the heir-apparent when the current Speaker of the House, J. Dennis Hastert, retires. DeLay is not without enemies, however, and may yet face an indictment surrounding allegations that he directed corporate funding into the 2002 Texas state legislative campaigns that produced the new majority stemming from the redistricting.

GOVERNING IN THE NEW CONGRESS   The Senate clearly emerged as the new battleground in governing. Several of the new Republican senators are deeply conservative and have promised to bring issues such as abortion and gay marriage to the floor for votes as soon as possible, while veterans in both chambers have already signaled their intention to press for Democratic concessions on social and economic issues. "I earned capital in the campaign, political capital, and now I intend to spend it," President Bush said in November 2004, and he clearly hopes that his dual majorities in Congress will do much of the spending.

However, as Democrats learned when they had similar majorities in both chambers, 55 votes in the Senate is still five votes shy of the 60 needed to shut down filibusters and 11 short of the number needed to ratify treaties.

THE STRUCTURE AND POWERS OF CONGRESS

The framers made two critical decisions about Congress early in the Constitutional Convention. First, they agreed to create a legislature as the first branch of government. Next, they divided that legislature into two chambers, the House of Representatives and the Senate. In doing so, the framers created one of the single most important obstacles to making laws. Worried about the tendency for the legislative branch to dominate government, they diluted the power of Congress by creating two chambers "as little connected with each other as the nature of their common functions and their common

Members of Congress are expected to fight for federal funding of projects in their district. Here Representative Nancy Pelosi (Democrat, 8th Congressional District in San Francisco) takes part in an official groundbreaking for the new Federal Building in San Francisco.

dependence on the society will admit."[10] Not only would Congress be balanced by the presidency and judiciary, but it would also be balanced against itself.

A Divided Branch

Bicameralism remains the most important organizational feature of the U.S. Congress. Each chamber meets in separate wings of the Capitol Building (see Figure 11–1); each has offices for its members on separate ends of Capitol Street; each has its own committee structure, its own rules for considering legislation, and its own record of proceedings (even though the records are published together as the *Congressional Record*); and each sets the rules governing its own members (each establishes its own legislative committees, for example).[11]

Bicameral legislatures were common in most of the colonies, and the framers believed that the arrangement was essential for preventing strong-willed majorities from oppressing individuals and minorities.[12] As James Madison explained in *The Federalist*, No. 51, "In order to control the legislative authority, you must divide it." (*The Federalist*, No. 51, is reprinted in the Appendix.) Although the Seventeenth Amendment to the Constitution (1913) provided for direct election of U.S. senators (senators were originally chosen by state legislatures), the two chambers remain very different (see Table 11–1).

Defenders of bicameralism point to its moderating influence on partisanship or possible errors in either chamber. This constitutionally mandated structure also guarantees that many votes will be taken before a policy is finally approved. The arrangement also provides more opportunities for bargaining and allows legislators with different policy goals a role in the shaping of national laws.

The Powers of Congress

The framers gave the longest list of **enumerated powers** to Congress. Because the Revolutionary War had been sparked by unfair taxation, the framers listed the power "to lay and collect Taxes" as the very first duty of Congress. They then gave Congress the power to borrow and coin money, regulate citizenship, build post offices and postal roads, and establish the lower courts of the federal judiciary, meaning every court below the Supreme Court. The framers also gave Congress the power to protect the nation against

bicameralism
The principle of a two-house legislature.

enumerated powers
The powers explicitly given to Congress in the Constitution.

HOUSE OF REPRESENTATIVES · SENATE

FIGURE 11–1 The Capitol Building.

foreign threats by declaring war, raising armies, and building navies; and the power to protect the nation from domestic threats by regulating commerce and immigration.

Just in case the list was not enough to allow Congress to do its job, the framers gave Congress the catchall power to "make all Laws which shall be necessary and proper for carrying into Execution the foregoing Powers, and all other Powers vested by this Constitution in the Government of the United States, or in any Department or Officer thereof." This clause is sometimes called the *elastic clause* because it stretches to cover much of what Congress might do. The Constitution also gave Congress complete authority to set its own rules for its proceedings.

Finally, the Constitution gave Congress several nonlegislative functions, such as participating in the process of constitutional amendment and impeachment (given to the House) and trying an impeached federal officer (given to the Senate). The Constitution stipulates that the grounds for impeachment that can lead to the removal from office of a president or vice president or other federal officers, including federal judges,

TABLE 11–1   DIFFERENCES BETWEEN THE HOUSE OF REPRESENTATIVES AND THE SENATE

House	Senate
Two-year term	Six-year term
435 members	100 members
Elected in districts	Elected by states
Fewer personal staff	More personal staff
Tighter rules	Looser rules
Decision to act made by majority	Decision to act made by unanimous consent
Tax bills must come from the House	Foreign treaties must be ratified by the Senate
Less media coverage	More media coverage
Less prestige	More prestige
More powerful committee leaders	More equal distribution of power
Nongermane amendments (riders) not allowed	Nongermane amendments (riders) not allowed
Rules Committee sets terms of debate	Senate as a whole sets terms of debate
Limited debate	Extended debate
Some bills permit no floor amendments (closed rule)	Amendments generally allowed
No filibuster allowed	Filibuster allowed

are the commission of "High Crimes and Misdemeanors" (never clearly defined). The House sits to determine whether or not an official's actions reach the level of impeachable offenses, and if so, it can impeach by a majority vote. The Senate sits as a court to decide if the impeached official should be convicted and whether the nature of the offense warrants removal from office. A two-thirds vote is needed to convict; thus a minority of just 34 senators can block the conviction of an impeached official.

As the impeachment power shows, the Constitution gives different duties to each chamber. The Senate has the power to confirm many presidential nominations. The Senate must also play a crucial "advise and consent" role in making treaties—formal agreements between the United States and other countries. All treaties must be approved by a two-thirds vote in the Senate before they can be ratified by the president.

The House has some of its own responsibilities, too, but they are not as important as those given to the Senate. For example, although all revenue bills must originate in the House, this practice does not give the House much advantage, because the Senate can freely amend spending bills even to the point of changing everything except the title.

Despite its position as the first branch of government and its substantial powers, Congress has difficulty keeping pace with its great rival, the presidency. The president's national security responsibilities, preparation of the budget, media visibility, and agenda-setting influence have all enhanced the position of the presidency relative to Congress.

MAKING CONGRESS WORK

Today's Congress bears the unmistakable imprint of the bicameralism created more than 200 years ago. The Senate prides itself on being an incubator of ideas, a place in which individual members can take the floor to defend an intense minority and delay action until at least 60 senators vote to end the debate; the House prides itself on being the voice of the people.

The two chambers are no more complex, however, than the society they have come to represent and the executive branch they must oversee. It was far easier to control the 59 House members and 22 senators who represented white male property owners in 1789 when the First Congress was gaveled to order than it is to control the 435 House members and 100 senators who represent the diverse United States today. It was far easier to write legislation for the small government in 1789 than for today's 15 departments

IN COMPARATIVE PERSPECTIVE

THE NIGERIAN ASSEMBLY

As one of the world's largest suppliers of oil, Nigeria has extraordinary wealth. It has also long been divided by political and ethnic conflict. Nigeria adopted a new constitution in 1999 after nearly 16 years of brutal military rule. Under its new constitution, Nigeria adopted a variation of America's divided government, opting for a separately elected president and a bicameral legislature. Both chambers of the National Assembly are elected by popular vote for four-year terms.

In its first four years in office, the Nigerian Assembly showed both strengths and weaknesses. It has been a reluctant participant in efforts to reduce the corruption and bribery that emerged after military rule, and it has been unable to control human rights abuses against civilians. The assembly has also shown little willingness to challenge the president.

Building an effective legislature takes time and experience, however. According to recent newspaper reports, the Nigerian Assembly is increasingly aware of its need for greater independence, especially in the wake of spring 2003 elections. As Representative Ganiyu Solomon argued in July 2003, "Nigerians should just give us time to settle down and pick up our work tools, then they will never regret they voted us as their representatives. It is just barely three months we got in here, so, we hardly could have done anything astonishing. . . . Ours will never be called a rubber stamp legislature, we will not drag our reputation and the trust of our people into the mud for compromise sake."[*]

[*] "Nigeria: What Role for the National Assembly," *Africa Today,* July 18, 2003, Nexis.com.

GLOBAL *Perceptions*

QUESTION: Some feel that we should rely on a democratic form of government to solve our country's problems. Others feel that we should rely on a leader with a strong hand to solve our country's problems. Which comes closer to your opinion?

When given a choice between the delays that sometimes come with democratic government and a strong leader who makes the key decisions, citizens around the world come to very different judgments.

SOURCE: The Pew Global Attitudes Project, June 2003, p. 87.

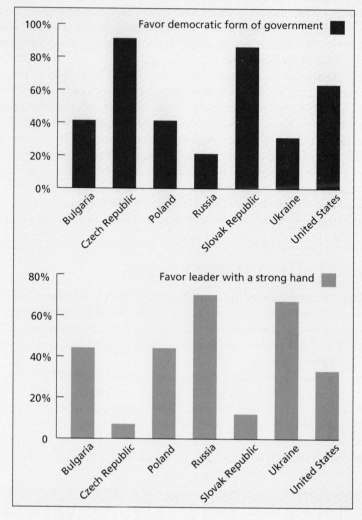

and 2.6 million employees. In the 1790s, a handful of permanent committees could handle the entire task of making the laws and checking government.

Leading the House of Representatives

The organization and procedures in the House are different from those in the Senate, largely because the House is more than four times larger than the Senate. A larger membership requires more rules, which means that *how* things are done affects *what* is done. The House assigns different types of bills to different calendars. For instance, financial measures—tax or appropriations bills—are put on a special calendar for quicker action.

The House has other ways to speed up lawmaking, including electronic voting. Ordinary rules may be suspended by a two-thirds vote, or immediate action may be taken by *unanimous consent* of the members on the floor. By acting as a *committee of the whole,* the House is able to operate more informally and more quickly than under its regular rules. A *quorum* in the committee of the whole requires only 100 members, rather than a majority of the whole chamber, and voting is quicker and simpler. Members are limited in how long they can speak, and debate may be cut off simply by majority vote.

These differences are based in part on how well each government has done in solving economic and social problems over the past decade. Russia and the Ukraine have been in nearly constant economic turmoil since the end of the Cold War, while the Czech Republic has made significant progress in strengthening its economy. Moreover, the Czech Republic was one of the leaders in the effort to overthrow communism in the late 1980s, which may help explains its support for democratic rule.

THE SPEAKER OF THE HOUSE The **Speaker** is the presiding officer in the House of Representatives.[13] The Constitution mandates that the House of Representatives shall choose its Speaker, yet it does not say anything about the duties or powers of the office. The Speaker is formally elected by the entire House yet is actually selected by the majority party. As the highest-ranking officer in Congress, the Speaker represents the legislative branch on ceremonial occasions. The Speaker is second in the line of succession to the presidency (after the vice president) in case of the death, resignation, or impeachment of the president and must keep the White House informed about his or her whereabouts.

The Speaker has the power to recognize members who rise to speak, rule on questions of parliamentary procedure, and appoint members to temporary committees (but not the major committees that help make the laws). In a sentence, the Speaker directs business on the floor of the House. More significant, of course, is the Speaker's political and behind-the-scenes influence.

When the Republicans won control of the House in 1994, they elected Representative Newt Gingrich of Georgia as Speaker. As the first Republican Speaker in 40 years, he was a novelty in Washington. "I had set out to do a very unusual job," said Gingrich, as "part revolutionary, part national political figure, part Speaker, part intellectual."[14]

Gingrich established his authority—reorganizing House committees, naming committee chairs, bypassing the seniority rule to appoint his allies to leadership posts, reorganizing House committees, and reducing perks and committee staffs. He pushed through some of the legislation outlined in the long list of campaign promises called the "Contract with America." He delegated considerable power to fellow Republican leaders yet claimed for himself the main role as spokesperson for major policy initiatives. He published books detailing his ideas about government and his party, and he cheerfully took on the White House and the national press.[15]

After a long investigation into the Speaker's use of tax-exempt funds, the House Ethics Committee concluded that Gingrich had violated its standards of conduct. He insisted that there was little overlap between his political activities and his nonpartisan educational endeavors, but the committee recommended, and the House of Representatives quickly passed, a reprimand of Gingrich and imposed a fine of $300,000 for misusing charitable deductions for political purposes and for misleading the House Ethics Committee. This was an unprecedented rebuke for a Speaker.

Following his party's poor showing in the midterm election of 1998, Gingrich retired both as Speaker and as a member of Congress. Republicans soon selected Illinois Representative J. Dennis Hastert as Speaker. Hastert, a former high school teacher and wrestling coach, had served for six years in the Illinois state legislature and 12 years in the U.S. House of Representatives before becoming Speaker of the House. "It's a calling that I have not sought," said Hastert about the Speakership. "However, it is a duty that I cannot ignore."[16] Hastert displays a low-key, quiet self-confidence that has pleased most Republicans and has earned praise from Democrats.[17] He has been particularly effective in holding Republicans together on key party votes in the chamber while drawing extra votes from Democrats who belong to the "Blue Dog" coalition, a group of mostly southern conservatives.

OTHER HOUSE OFFICERS The Speaker is assisted by the **majority leader**, who helps plan party strategy, confers with other party leaders, and tries to keep members of the party in line. The minority party elects the **minority leader**, who usually steps into the Speakership when his or her party gains a majority in the House. (These positions are also sometimes called majority and minority *floor leaders*.) Assisting each floor leader are the party **whips**. (The term comes from *whipper-in,* the huntsman who keeps the hounds

Republican Dennis Hastert, Speaker of the House of Representatives.

Speaker
The presiding officer in the House of Representatives, formally elected by the House but actually selected by the majority party.

majority leader
The legislative leader selected by the majority party who helps plan party strategy, confers with other party leaders, and tries to keep members of the party in line.

minority leader
The legislative leader selected by the minority party as spokesperson for the opposition.

whip
Party leader who is the liaison between the leadership and the rank-and-file in the legislature.

CHANGING FACE OF AMERICAN POLITICS

DIVERSITY IN CONGRESS

Although the Constitution does not mention race, gender, or wealth among the qualifications for office, the framers expected members of Congress to be white male property owners. After all, women and slaves could not vote, let alone hold office.

The framers would therefore be surprised at the face of Congress today. Recent Congresses have had record numbers of women and minorities. In 2004, Illinois voters elected only the third African American senator since the 1870s, Barack Obama, while Florida voters elected the first Cuban American, Mel Martinez, and Colorado voters elected the first Hispanic in thirty years, Ken Salazar. Voters also reelected all five women senators and added ten women and minority members to the list of U.S. representatives.

The changing face of Congress reflects the growing effectiveness of women and minority candidates in running for office, as well as increased participation by minority voters. The Voting Rights Act of 1965 allowed millions of African Americans to register and vote in the South. In Mississippi, for example, only 14 percent of African Americans were registered to vote in 1960. By 1968, the number had increased to 64 percent. As the number of African American voters increased, so did the number of African American legislators.

Congress is becoming more diverse by race and gender, but it still remains very different from the rest of America on income and occupation. Almost one-third of the senators who served in the 108th Congress were millionaires, and more than half were lawyers. Moreover, old customs die hard. Even with the Democratic senator from Washington, Patty Murray, sitting on his Appropriations Committee, Chairman Robert Byrd still addressed committee members as "Gentlemen." At the current rate of change in the number of women, for example, it

U.S. Senator Barbara Mikulsi (D-Md), shown at the podium, with the other female Democratic senators on stage at the 2004 Democratic National Convention in Boston.

Number of Women in U.S. Congress.
SOURCE: *Congressional Quarterly Weekly*, November 6, 2004, p. 263.

will take another 400 years before women constitute a majority in the House.[*]

[*]See the United States Capitol Historical Society, "Outstanding African-American Members of Congress" and "Women Members of Congress" at www.uschs.org/04_history/subs_articles/04e.html.

bunched in a pack during a fox hunt.) The whips serve as liaisons between the House leadership of each party and the rank-and-file. They inform members when important bills will come up for a vote, prepare summaries of the bills, do vote counts for the leadership, exert pressure (sometimes mild and sometimes heavy) on members to support the leadership, and try to ensure maximum attendance on the floor for critical votes.

At the beginning of the session and occasionally afterward, each party holds a **party caucus** of all its members (called a *conference* by the Republicans) to elect party officers, approve committee assignments, elect committee leaders, discuss important legislation, and perhaps try to agree on party policy.

THE HOUSE RULES COMMITTEE   The House has a powerful Rules Committee that regulates the time of floor debate for each bill and sets limitations on floor amendments.

party caucus
A meeting of the members of a party in a legislative chamber to select party leaders and to develop party policy. Called a *conference* by the Republicans.

By refusing to grant a *rule,* which describes the conditions of debate, the Rules Committee can delay consideration of a bill. A **closed rule** prohibits amendments altogether or provides that only members of the committee reporting the bill may offer amendments; closed rules are usually reserved for tax and spending bills. An **open rule** permits debate within the overall time allocated to the bill.

From the New Deal era in the mid-1930s until the mid-1960s, a coalition of Republicans and conservative Democrats used the Rules Committee to block significant legislation on civil rights, health care, and poverty. Liberals denounced it as unrepresentative, unfair, and dictatorial. More recently, the Rules Committee membership has come to reflect the views of the general makeup of the majority party. It has become much less an independent obstacle to legislation and more a place to design rules that help advance the general goals of the majority party.

Senator Bill Frist of Tennessee, Republican majority leader, holds a sample drug discount card that will soon be available to Medicare recipients as a result of major changes in the Medicare program made late in 2003.

Leading the Senate

The Senate has the same basic committee structure, elected party leadership, and decentralized power as the House, but because the Senate is a smaller body, its procedures are more informal, and it permits more time for debate. It is a more open, fluid, and decentralized body now than it was a generation or two ago. Indeed, it is often said that the Senate has 100 separate power centers and is so splintered that the party leaders have difficulty arranging the day-to-day schedule.[18]

The Senate is led by the Senate majority leader, who is elected by the majority party in the Senate. When the majority leader is from the president's party, the president is the party's most visible leader. However, when the majority leader and the president are from different parties, the majority leader is considered his or her party's national spokesperson.

As the Senate's power broker, the majority leader has the right to be the first senator heard on the floor. In consultation with the Senate minority leader, the majority leader controls the Senate's agenda and recommends committee assignments for members of the majority party. But the position confers less authority than the Speakership in the House, and its influence depends on the person's political and parliamentary skills and on the national political situation.[19] Senate majority leaders have to be persuaders and negotiators, not only working closely with the minority leader but also working with a number of powerful majority and minority senators and the White House.

Nevertheless, the majority leader does have substantial influence over the legislative agenda in the Senate. Senator Lott proved this point in the session of Congress immediately following the 2002 election. Although his party was not technically in the majority until the new Congress was sworn into office in January 2003, Lott worked with the president to make sure that the new Department of Homeland Security became law. (Chapter 13 provides more details on the new department.)

Lott was not to be majority leader for long, however. He soon became embroiled in a controversy surrounding remarks he made at the 100th birthday party for retiring South Carolina Senator Strom Thurmond. In congratulating Thurmond for his 48 years of Senate service, Lott remarked that the nation would have been better off had Thurmond won the presidency as the candidate of the Dixiecrat Party in 1948. The Dixiecrat Party was formed to oppose racial integration, and fought civil rights throughout the 1950s and into the 1960s. Lott was forced to resign his post on December 20, 2002, and was replaced by Tennessee Senator Bill Frist, a former heart surgeon who had been in the Senate for just eight years.

Party machinery in the Senate is similar to that in the House. There are party caucuses (conferences), majority and minority floor leaders, and party whips. Each party has a *policy committee,* composed of party leaders, which is theoretically responsible for the party's overall legislative program. In the Senate, the party policy committees assist the leadership in monitoring legislation and provide policy expertise. Unlike the House party committees, the Senate's party policy committees are formally provided for by law, and each has a regular staff and a budget. Although the Senate party policy committees have some influence on legislation, they have not asserted strong legislative leadership or managed to coordinate policy.

Former U.S. Senate minority leader Tom Daschle making a point on NBC's Meet the Press. Daschle was defeated for reelection in 2004, becoming the first senate leader of either party to lose his seat in over fifty years. Nevada's Harry Reid became the Senate Minority leader in January 2005.

closed rule
A procedural rule in the House of Representatives that prohibits any amendments to bills or provides that only members of the committee reporting the bill may offer amendments.

open rule
A procedural rule in the House of Representatives that permits floor amendments within the overall time allocated to the bill.

The president of the Senate (the vice president of the United States) also has little influence over Senate proceedings. A vice president can vote only in case of a tie. The Senate elects a **president pro tempore**, usually the most senior member from the majority party, who acts as chair in the absence of the vice president. Presiding over the Senate on most occasions is a thankless chore, so the president pro tempore regularly delegates this responsibility to junior members of the chamber's majority party.

Despite these various leaders and offices, the Senate is far less structured than the House. It has always operated under rules that vest great power in the individual senator. Extended debate allows senators to hold the floor as long as they wish unless a supermajority of 60 colleagues votes to end debate. Moreover, the Senate's rules allow individual senators to offer amendments on virtually any topic to a pending bill, allowing them to amend a bill to death.[20]

One relatively recent expression of this individualism is a practice called the **hold**. Holds were originally designed to give individual senators a short period to prepare for a debate or delay a vote for personal reasons. Over time, however, they have become a powerful device for blocking action on legislation and nominations.

Although successful Senate leadership still depends on personal relationships, individual members have become more partisan in recent decades. "Senators known for compromise, moderation and institutional loyalty," observe political scientists Nicol Rae and Colton Campbell, "have been replaced with more ideological and partisan members who see the chamber as a place to enhance their party fortunes."[21] Partisanship in the Senate was vehement during the Bill Clinton impeachment proceedings and to a lesser extent in the confirmation battle of George W. Bush's nominee, John Ashcroft, as his attorney general.

THE FILIBUSTER   Because of its smaller size and looser rules, debate is more open in the Senate. A senator who gains the floor may go on talking until he or she relinquishes the right to talk voluntarily or through exhaustion. This right to unlimited debate, known as the **filibuster**, may be used by a small group of senators to delay Senate proceedings by talking continuously so as to postpone or prevent a vote. At one time, the filibuster was a favorite weapon of southern senators intent on blocking civil rights legislation. More recently, the filibuster has been used for a wider range of issues, including efforts to stop judicial nominations and prevent passage of campaign finance reform.

A filibuster, or the threat of a filibuster, is typically most potent at the end of a congressional session, when a date has been fixed for adjournment, because it could mean that many bills that have otherwise made it through the legislative process will die for lack of a floor vote. The knowledge that a bill might be subject to a filibuster is often enough to force a compromise satisfactory to its opponents. Sometimes the leaders, knowing that a filibuster will tie up the Senate and keep it from enacting other needed legislation, do not bring a controversial bill to the floor.

A filibuster can be defeated. Until 1917, the Senate could terminate a filibuster only if every member agreed. That year, however, the Senate adopted its first debate-ending rule, or **cloture**. The rule specifies that the question of curtailing debate must be put to a vote two days after 16 senators sign a petition asking for cloture. If three-fifths of the total number of the Senate (60 of the 100 members) vote in favor of cloture, no senator may speak on the measure under consideration for more than one hour. Once invoked, cloture requires that the final vote on the measure be taken after no more than 30 hours of debate.

There has been an increase in the use and threat of filibusters in recent years, and these tactics have often been used for partisan and parochial purposes. Indeed, as noted, senators usually anticipate a filibuster on controversial measures, and the threat is often sufficient to force the majority to compromise and modify its position.[22] Both parties have learned to use the filibuster when they are in the minority. The Senate has averaged almost two dozen filibusters each year since 2001. Of the 45 cloture votes taken in 2001–2003, just 12 succeeded, 10 in 2001–2002, and two in 2003.[23]

THE POWER TO CONFIRM   The Constitution leaves the precise practices of the confirmation process somewhat ambiguous: "The President . . . shall nominate, and by and with the Advice and Consent of the Senate, shall appoint Ambassadors, other public

president pro tempore
Officer of the Senate selected by the majority party to act as chair in the absence of the vice president.

hold
A procedural practice in the Senate whereby a senator temporarily blocks the consideration of a bill or nomination.

filibuster
A procedural practice in the Senate whereby a senator refuses to relinquish the floor and thereby delays proceedings and prevents a vote on a controversial issue.

cloture
A procedure for terminating debate, especially filibusters, in the Senate.

Ministers and Consuls, Judges of the Supreme Court, all other officers of the United States." The framers of the Constitution regarded the confirmation process—the Senate's "advise and consent" power—as an important check on executive power. Alexander Hamilton viewed it as a way for the Senate to prevent the appointment of "unfit characters."

As with other legislative business, the confirmation process starts in committees, with the relevant committee that oversees the particular function or activity involved. For example, the Judiciary Committee considers federal judges and Supreme Court nominees; the Foreign Relations Committee considers ambassadorial appointments. Nominees appear before the committee to answer questions, and they typically meet individually with key senators before the hearing.

Presidents have never enjoyed exclusive control over hiring and firing in the executive branch. The Senate jealously guards its right to confirm or reject or even delay major appointments; during the period of strong Congresses after the Civil War, presidents had to struggle to keep their power to appoint and dismiss. But for most of the past century, presidents have gained a reasonable amount of control over top appointments, in part because a growing number of people in and out of Congress believe that chief executives without compatible cabinet-level appointees of their choice cannot be held accountable. The Senate's advise and consent powers sometimes force presidents to make compromises, plainly constraining their ability to use the presidential appointment power.

The Senate's role in the confirmation process was never intended to prevent a president from taking political considerations into account when appointments are made. Rather, the Senate was given the power to protect the judicial branch against weak or controversial nominees. During the Bush administration, conservatives complained that Senate Democrats were interfering with the executive power of the president by rejecting nominees because of their political beliefs. Only years before during the Clinton administration, however, liberals complained that Senate Republicans were doing the same thing.

In recent years, the Senate has taken a tough stand on some presidential appointments and spent more time evaluating and screening presidential nominations. The Senate rejected several nominees of Presidents Ronald Reagan and George Bush, and Presidents Bill Clinton and George W. Bush withdrew several nominees in the face of Senate opposition. In November, 2003, for example, Senate Republicans staged a 39-hour debate designed to break a Democratic filibuster of four controversial Bush administration judicial nominees. The debate began on a Wednesday night at 6 P.M. and continued until 9 A.M. Friday, but ended on 53 to 43 votes for all four nominees, seven votes short of the 60 needed to move ahead. During the debate, Democratic Senator Edward Kennedy (D.-Mass.) promised to "continue to resist any Neanderthal that is nominated by this president," while Republican Senator Orrin Hatch (R.-Utah) described the filibusters as "petty politics . . . cheap politics. . . ."[24]

There is an important distinction between *judicial* appointments, especially those to the Supreme Court, and *executive branch* or *administrative* appointments. For the most part, the Senate gives the president the benefit of the doubt in selecting executive appointees, but plays a greater role in judicial appointments because federal judges serve for life and constitute an independent check on both Congress and the executive branch.[25]

Even here, however, the Senate and the president often work closely to reach agreement, especially on district court judges. Under the tradition of **senatorial courtesy**, presidents confer with the senator or senators in their own political party from the state where a judge is to work, or "sit." Occasionally, a president has to take into account the views of a politically powerful senator in the opposition party. A nomination is less likely to secure Senate approval against the objection of these senators, especially if these senators are members of the president's party.

As part of her confirmation process, Labor Secretary Elaine Chao answered questions for congressional committee members on Capitol Hill.

Congressional Committees

It is sometimes said that Congress is a collection of committees that come together in a chamber every once in a while to approve one another's actions. Congress has long relied on committees to get its work done. Woodrow Wilson, a political science professor before he became president, expressed a similar thought: "Congress in session is

senatorial courtesy
Presidential custom of submitting the names of prospective appointees for approval to senators from the states in which the appointees are to work.

Members of the Senate Armed Services Committee hear testimony from Secretary of Defense Donald Rumsfeld on allegations of prisoner abuse in Iraq.

Congress on display. Congress in committee is Congress at work."[26] More precisely, Congress in subcommittee is Congress at work, because the initial struggle over legislation takes place in subcommittees.[27]

TYPES OF COMMITTEES   In theory, all congressional committees are created anew in each new Congress. In reality, however, most continue with little change from Congress to Congress. **Standing committees** are the most durable and are the sources of most bills, while **special or select committees** come together to address temporary priorities of Congress such as aging or taxes and rarely author legislation. **Joint committees** have members from both the House and the Senate and exist either to study an issue of interest to the entire Congress or to oversee congressional support agencies such as the Library of Congress or the U.S. Government Printing Office. Almost all standing committees have subcommittees that help handle the legislative workload.

Of the various types of committees, standing committees are the most important for making laws and representing constituents, and they fall into four types: authorizing, appropriations, rules, and revenue. There are more than three dozen standing committees in the House and Senate.

Authorizing committees   These committees pass the laws that tell government what to do. The House and Senate education and labor committees, for example, are responsible for setting the rules governing the Pell Grant student loan program, including who can apply, how much they can get, where the loans come from, and how defaults are handled. Simply stated, authorizing committees make the most basic decisions about who gets what, when, and how from government. In 1999–2000, there were 15 authorizing committees in the House and 17 in the Senate. The number of committees remained unchanged in 2003–2004.

Authorizing committees are also responsible for oversight of the federal bureaucracy. Some of this oversight is designed to ask whether programs are working well, and some is designed to reduce fraud, waste, or abuse in an agency of government. The amount of congressional oversight is increasing. Political scientist Joel Aberbach found, for example, that just 8 percent of all legislative hearings focused on oversight in 1961, compared to over 25 percent just two decades later.[28]

Appropriations committees   These committees make decisions about how much money government will spend on its programs and operations. Although there is just one appropriations committee in each chamber, each appropriations committee has one

standing committee
A permanent committee established in a legislature, usually focusing on a policy area.

special or select committee
A congressional committee created for a specific purpose, sometimes to conduct an investigation.

joint committee
A committee composed of members of both the House of Representatives and the Senate; such committees oversee the Library of Congress and conduct investigations.

subcommittee for each of the 13 appropriations bills that must be enacted each year to keep government running. Because they decide who gets how much from government, these subcommittees have great power to undo or limit decisions by the authorizing committees.

Rules and administration committees determine the basic operations of the two houses—for example, how many staffers individual members get. Again because of the number of members it must control, the House Rules Committee is more powerful than its twin in the Senate. As noted earlier, the House Rules Committee has special responsibility for giving each bill a rule, or ticket, to the floor of the House and determines what, if any, amendments to a bill will be permitted.

Revenue and budget committees These committees deal with raising the money that appropriating committees spend while setting the broad targets that shape the federal budget. The House Ways and Means Committee is arguably the single most powerful committee in Congress, for it both raises and authorizes spending. As the only committee in either chamber that can originate tax and revenue legislation, it is also responsible for making basic decisions on the huge Social Security and Medicare programs.

CHOOSING COMMITTEE MEMBERS The political parties control the selection of standing committee members. The chair and a majority of each standing committee come from the majority party. The minority party is represented on each committee roughly in proportion to its membership in the entire chamber, except on some powerful committees on which the majority may want to enhance its position.

Getting on a politically advantageous committee is important to members of Congress. A representative from Kansas, for example, would rather serve on the Agriculture Committee than on the Banking and Financial Services Committee. Members usually stay on the same committees from one Congress to the next, although junior members who have had less desirable assignments often seek better committees when places become available.

The House and Senate choose committee members in different ways, and actually rank committees in different ways. (See Table 11–2 for the differences.)

Republicans in the House choose committee members through their Committee on Committees, which is composed of one member from each state that has Republican representation in the House. Because each member has as many votes in the committee as there are Republicans in the delegation, the group is dominated by senior members from the large state delegations. Democrats in the House choose committee members through the Steering and Policy Committee of the Democratic caucus in negotiation with senior Democrats from the state delegations.

Veteran party members also dominate the Senate assignment process, where both parties have small Steering Committees that make committee assignments. In making assignments, leaders are guided by various considerations: how talented and cooperative a member is, whether his or her region is already well represented on a committee, and whether the assignment will aid in reelecting the member. Sometimes fierce battles erupt within these committees, reflecting ideological, geographical, and other differences.

One way Congress copes with its legislative workload is to organize its committees and subcommittees by subject matter. This specialization allows members to develop technical expertise in specific areas and to recruit skilled staffs. Thus Congress is often able to challenge experts from the bureaucracy. Interest groups and lobbyists realize the great power a specific committee has in certain areas and focus their attention on its members. Similarly, members of executive departments are careful to cultivate the committee and subcommittee chairs and members of "their" committees.

How each chamber in Congress uses committees is critical in its role as a partner in policy making, both with the other house and with the executive branch. In recent years, progress has been made in opening hearings to the public and improving the quality of committee staffs, but it is difficult to restructure committee jurisdictions so that they do not overlap. Consequently, a dozen different committees deal with energy, education, and the war on drugs. Efforts to make the committee system more efficient are often considered threats to the delicate balance of power within the chamber.

TABLE 11–2 RULES ON COMMITTEE SERVICE IN THE HOUSE AND SENATE

House	Senate
Exclusive Committees	**"A" Committees**
Members can usually serve on just one exclusive committee:	Members can usually serve on no more than two A committees:
Appropriations	Agriculture, Nutrition, and Forestry
Rules	Appropriations
Ways and Means	Banking, Housing, and Urban Affairs
Commerce	Commerce, Science, and Transportation
	Energy and Natural Resources
	Environment and Public Works
	Finance
	Foreign Relations
	Governmental Affairs
	Health, Education, Labor, and Pensions Judiciary
Nonexclusive Committees	**Super "A" Committees**
Members can usually serve on just two nonexclusive committees:	Members can serve on no more than one of the Super A Committees:
Agriculture	Appropriations
Armed Services	Armed Services
Banking and Financial Services	Finance
Education and the Workforce	Foreign Relations
International Relations	
Judiciary	
Resources	
Science	
Small Business	
Transportation and Infrastructure	
Veterans' Affairs	
Exempt Committees	**"B" Committees**
Members may serve on one exempt committee regardless of their other service:	Members may serve on one B Committee:
House Administration	Budget
Select Intelligence	Rules and Administration
Standards of Official	Small Business
	Veterans' Affairs
	Special Aging
	Select Intelligence
	Joint Economic Committee
	"C" Committees
	Members may serve on one or more C Committee:
	Select Ethics
	Indian Affairs
	Joint Taxation
	Joint Library
	Joint Printing

NOTE: Senate and House party rules have further restrictions on committee service that may affect these rules.

THE ROLE OF SENIORITY   Forty years ago, committee chairs determined the workload of committees, hired and fired staff, formed subcommittees, and assigned them jurisdictions, members, and aides. Chairs also managed the most important bills assigned to their committees. Since the mid-1970s, however, junior members have insisted on being given more authority. Subcommittee chairs have also become more independent. In recent years, there have also been moves to strengthen the powers of the party leaders and caucuses at the expense of committee chairs.

Most chairs are selected on the basis of the **seniority rule**; the member of the majority party with the longest continuous service on the committee becomes chair upon the retirement of the current chair or a change in the party in control of Congress. The seniority rule gives power to representatives who come from safe districts where one party is dominant and a member can build up years of continuous service. Conversely, the seniority rule lessens the influence of states or districts where the two parties are more evenly matched and where there is more turnover.

Although it is not uncommon for the party leadership to reward a junior member with a prestigious committee assignment, seniority has long been respected in Congress for several reasons: It encourages members to stay on a committee, it encourages specialization and expertise, and it reduces the interpersonal politics that would arise if several members of a committee sought to become chair. Under new rules adopted in the mid-1990s, however, both House and Senate Republicans agreed to limit committee chairs to serving no more than three consecutive terms.[29]

INVESTIGATIONS AND OVERSIGHT   Committees do more than produce legislation. They also have two additional roles in making government work.

The first is the power to *investigate.* Congress conducts investigations to determine if legislation is needed, to gather facts relevant to legislation, to assess the efficiency of executive agencies, to build public support, to expose corruption, and to enhance the image or reputation of its members.[30] Hearings by standing committees, their subcommittees, or special select committees are an important source of information and opinion. They provide an arena in which experts can submit their views.

The second is the *oversight* power—the responsibility to question executive branch officials to see whether their agencies are complying with the wishes of the Congress and conducting their programs efficiently. Authorization committees regularly hold oversight hearings, and appropriations committees, exercising "the congressional power of the purse," often use appropriations hearings to communicate committee members' views about how agency officials should conduct their business. Cabinet members and agency heads have been known to dread the loaded questions of hostile members of Congress and to hate having to watch themselves on the evening news trying to explain why their agency made some mistakes.

THE SPECIAL ROLE OF CONFERENCE COMMITTEES   Given the differences between the House and the Senate, it is not surprising that the version of a bill passed by one chamber may differ substantially from the version passed by the other. Only if both houses pass an absolutely identical measure can it become law. Most of the time, one house accepts the language of the other, but about 10 to 12 percent of all bills passed, usually major ones, must be referred to a **conference committee**—a special committee of members from each chamber that settles the differences between versions.[31] Both parties are represented, but the majority party has more members.

The proceedings of a conference committee are usually an elaborate bargaining process. When the revised bill is brought back to the two chambers, the conference report can be accepted or rejected (often with further negotiations ordered), but it cannot be amended. Conference members of each chamber must convince their colleagues that any concessions made to the other chamber were on unimportant points and that nothing basic to the original version of the bill was surrendered.

Conference committees have considerable leeway in reaching agreement, prompting President Ronald Reagan to note, "You know, if an orange and an apple went into conference consultations, it might come out a pear."[32] Ordinarily, members are expected to end up somewhere between the different versions. On matters for which there is no

Senator Orrin Hatch (R-Utah), shown on the right, left his post as Chair of the Senate Judiciary Committee at the end of his third term in 2005.

seniority rule
A legislative practice that assigns the chair of a committee or subcommittee to the member of the majority party with the longest continuous service on the committee.

conference committee
Committee appointed by the presiding officers of each chamber to adjust differences on a particular bill passed by each in different form.

clear middle ground, members are sometimes accused of exceeding their instructions and producing an entirely new bill. For this reason, the conference committee has been called a "third house" of Congress and one of the most significant congressional institutions.[33]

It is not clear whether the House or the Senate wins more often in conference committees. On the surface, it appears that the Senate's version wins more often, but this is partly because the Senate often acts on its legislation after the House. But by approving the initial bill first and thereby setting the agenda on an issue, the House often has more of an impact on the final outcome than the Senate.

CAUCUSES   In contrast to conference committees, which are appointed by the House and Senate leadership to perform a specific legislative role, caucuses are best defined as informal committees that allow individual members to promote shared legislative interests. There are caucuses for House members only, for senators only, and for members of both chambers together. By the 1990s, according to one count, House members actually served on more informal caucuses than on committees and subcommittees.[34]

The growing diversity of the caucuses parallels the rest of society. They include the Black Caucus, Hispanic Caucus, Women's Issues Caucus, Rural Health Caucus, Children's Caucus, Cuba Freedom Caucus, Pro-Life Caucus, Homelessness Task Force, Urban Caucus, and Ethiopian Jewry Caucus. The diversity also parallels the fragmentation of interest groups, with caucuses on nearly every business and public interest issue—including steel, beef, wheel bearings, the Internet, mushrooms, mining, gas, sweeteners, wine, footwear, soybeans, animal rights, Chesapeake Bay, clean water, drug enforcement, adoption, the arts, energy, military reform, AIDS, and antiterrorism. There are also caucuses composed of friends of the Caribbean Basin, animals, human rights monitors, and Ireland.

THE JOB OF THE LEGISLATOR

Membership in Congress was once a part-time job. Members came to Washington for a few terms, averaged less than five years of continuous service, and returned to their careers. Congressional pay was low, and Washington was no farther than a carriage ride from home.[35]

Congress started to meet more frequently in the late 1800s, pay increased, and being a member of Congress became increasingly attractive.[36] In the 1850s, roughly one-half of all House members retired or were defeated at each election; by 1900, the number who left at the end of each term had fallen to roughly one-quarter; by the 1970s, the number had fallen to barely a tenth. Even in the 1994 congressional elections, when Republicans won the House majority for the first time in 40 years, 90 percent of House incumbents who ran for reelection won.[37]

By the 1950s, being a member of Congress had become a full-time job and a long-term career. Members came to Washington to stay and began to exploit the natural advantages that come with running for reelection as an incumbent: name recognition, service to citizens back home, copious campaign funding, nearly unlimited access to the media, and free postage under the *franking privilege* for mailings back home. In 1954, for example, members of Congress sent 44 million pieces of mail back home. Fifty years later, the number will easily pass 500 million pieces. Include the amount of e-mail, and the average member of Congress is in touch with his or her district almost daily.[38]

The workday also got longer. According to a 1998 survey, most members reported that they worked more than 70 hours a week, dividing their time among committee and subcommittee hearings, floor debates, meetings with citizens and interest groups, and raising money for the next election. Members do not seem to think the job is too tough, at least not the 402 members who ran for reelection in 1998. Nor has job satisfaction declined: 96 percent of members reported that they were very or mostly satisfied with their jobs in 1998, and only 15 percent said the job had gotten less satisfying since they first entered Congress. There appears to be little softening of interest in holding these jobs, despite the high levels of public distrust in Congress as an institution.[39]

As members of Congress became attached to their careers, they began to abandon many of the norms that once guided their behavior in office.[40] The old norms were simple.

PEOPLE & POLITICS *Making a Difference* ★ ★ ★

GENERATION X IN CONGRESS (HAROLD FORD JR., AND ADAM PUTNAM)

As the two youngest members of Congress, Adam Putnam (R.-Fla.) and Harold Ford, Jr. (D.-Tenn.) care deeply about reengaging young Americans in politics. Both were elected in part on promises to give young Americans a stronger voice in debates about the future of programs such as Social Security, and both continue to work hard to connect with their generation on jobs and access to education.

Putnam was just 26 years old when he was elected to Congress in 2000. "I want to energize a whole new generation of young people to reengage in politics," Putnam says. You, know, Kennedy did it, Reagan did it, probably Clinton '92 did it. We've got to do a better job talking across generational lines."

Ford was just 26, too, when he was elected to Congress in 1996. Young people were a central part of his first campaign. He visited more than 100 schools and spoke to an estimated 40,000 to 50,000 high school students en route to a landslide victory. "We've grown up in a different world," his chief of staff explained to reporters when asked about Ford's view of politics. "We're more comfortable with diversity, with change, with new ideas and new attitudes."

Age does not create a shared agenda, however, Putnam opposes many of the issues that young Americans support, including abortion rights. He also rejected MTV's request to film his first campaign by saying he didn't want any "purple-hair yahoo" asking whether he wore "boxers or briefs." But he does support Social Security reform, which is a key issue for young Americans who do not believe the program will still be alive when they retire.

Putnam and Ford do believe they can make a difference in showing that age is no barrier to participation. "I'm not invited to a high school class to articulate

Adam Putnam

Harold Ford, Jr.

the merits of permanent normal trade relations with China," Putnam says. "I'm invited to classes to talk about why it's important for young people to get involved and how they can do it." Ford agrees. "Once you get young people to pay attention, you find that you've turned on a faucet that's hard to turn off." The fact that these two Gen X'ers are in Congress is no small part of showing young Americans that age is not a barrier to involvement at the very top of American politics.

Members were supposed to specialize in a small number of issues (the norm of specialization), defer to members with longer tenure in office (the norm of seniority), never criticize anyone personally (the norm of courtesy), and wait their turn to speak and introduce legislation (the norm of apprenticeship). As longtime House Speaker Sam Rayburn once said, new members were to go along in order to get along, and to be seen and not heard.

The new norms are equally simple. New members are no longer willing to wait their turn to speak or introduce legislation and now have enough staff to make their opinions known on just about any issue at just about any point in the legislative process. Although the norm of courtesy still lives on as members refer to each other with great respect, the new congressional career allows little time for the old norms of specialization, seniority, and apprenticeship. Members must take care of their electoral concerns first.

Legislators as Representatives

Congress has a split personality. On the one hand, it is a *lawmaking institution* that writes laws and makes policy for the entire nation. In this capacity, all the members are expected to set aside their personal ambitions and perhaps even the concerns of their own constituencies. Yet Congress is also a *representative assembly,* made up of 535 elected officials who serve as links between their constituents and the national government (see Table 11–3). The dual roles of making laws and responding to constituents' demands force members to balance national concerns against the specific interests of their states or districts.

TABLE 11–3 PROFILE OF THE 108TH CONGRESS, 2003–2005

	Senate (100)	*House (435)*
Party Affiliation		
Republican	51	229
Democratic	48	205
Independent	1	1
Sex		
Male	86	373
Female	14	62
Religion		
Catholic	25	124
Jewish	11	26
Protestant	63	278
Other	1	7
Average Age	60	54
Racial/Ethnic Minorities	3	64
Occupational Field		
Law	60	161
Education	12	88
Business, banking	25	165
Agriculture	5	26
Journalism	6	11
Engineering	1	8
Real estate	3	30

SOURCE: *Congressional Quarterly Weekly*, January 25, 2003, pp. 190–193.

Individual members of Congress perceive their roles differently. Some believe they should serve as **delegates** from their districts. These legislators believe it is their duty to find out what "the folks back home" want and act accordingly. Other members see their role as that of **trustee**. Their constituents, they contend, did not send them to Congress to serve as mere robots or "errand runners." They act and vote according to their own view of what is best for their district or state as well as the nation.

Most legislators shift back and forth between the delegate and trustee roles, depending on their perception of the public interest, their standing in the last and next elections, and the pressures of the moment. Most also view themselves more as free agents than as instructed delegates for their districts. And recent research suggests that they often *are* free, since about 50 percent of citizens are unaware of how their representatives voted on major legislation and often believe their representative voted in accordance with constituent policy views. Still, nearly everyone in Congress spends a lot of time building constituency connections, mending political fences, reaching out to swing voters, and worrying about how a vote on a controversial issue will "play" back home.[41]

Legislators as Lawmakers

About 5,000 bills are introduced in the House every two years and as many as 3,000 in the Senate. Members of Congress cast as many as 1,000 votes each year.[42] When they vote, members of Congress are influenced by their own philosophy and values, their perceptions of their constituents' interests, the views of their trusted colleagues and staff, their partisan ties, and party leaders, lobbyists, and the president.

delegate
An official who is expected to represent the views of his or her constituents even when personally holding different views; one interpretation of the role of the legislator.

trustee
An official who is expected to vote independently based on his or her judgment of the circumstances; one interpretation of the role of the legislator.

CHANGING FACE OF AMERICAN POLITICS

COMPARING MEMBERS

The *National Journal* is not the only publication to rate individual members of Congress. Interest groups often publish scorecards on key votes on important issues to their constituents. Consider how the U.S. Chamber of Commerce (conservative), the American Federation of Labor (AFL-CIO) (liberal), the National Right to Life Committee (conservative), and the National Abortion and Reproductive Rights Action League (NARAL) (liberal) rated four members of Congress on votes taken leading up to the 2002 election:

	Senator Richard Lugar (R.-Ind.)	Senator Mark Dayton (D.-Minn.)	Representative David Dreier (R.-Calif.)	Representative Barney Frank (D.-Mass.)
Chamber of Commerce	95%	45%	100%	26%
AFL-CIO	31	100	11	100
National Right to Life	33	0	100	0
NARAL	0	100	0	100

SOURCE: *Congressional Quarterly Weekly,* April 19, 2003, p. 925.

POLICY AND PHILOSOPHICAL CONVICTIONS   Members are influenced by their ideological beliefs most of the time. Their experiences and their attitudes about the role of government shape their convictions and help explain a lot of the differences in voting patterns.[43] A liberal on social issues is also likely to be a liberal on tax and national security issues. On controversial issues such as Social Security reform, tax cuts, or defense spending, knowing the general philosophical leanings of individual members provides a helpful guide both to how they make up their minds and how they will vote.

In 2003, the widely respected weekly report *National Journal* rated Barbara Boxer (D.–Calif.) as the most liberal senator and Pat Roberts (R.–Kansas) as the most conservative and rated John Conyers (D.–Mich.) and Pete Stark (D.–Calif.) as the most liberal representatives, while 13 members of the House tied as the most conservative. Although Democrats are more likely to be liberals and Republicans more likely to be conservatives, there are centrists in both parties. Almost all of the most liberal Democrats in the House and Senate come from western states, while almost all of the most conservative Republicans come from southern states.

VOTERS   Rarely does a legislator consistently and deliberately vote against the wishes of the people back home, but a paradox is evident here. Members of Congress sometimes think that what they do and how they vote make a lot of difference to voters back home, even though most voters do not follow Congress closely.[44] Aside from periodic polls, members hear most often from the **attentive public**—citizens who follow public affairs carefully—rather than the general public. Nearly 70 percent of constituents say they have not visited, faxed, phoned, e-mailed, or written their member of Congress in the past four years.[45] Still, members of Congress are generally concerned about how they will explain their votes, especially as election day approaches. Even if only a few voters are aware of their stand on a given issue, this group might make the difference between victory and defeat.

COLLEAGUES   Legislators are often influenced by the advice of their close friends in Congress. Their busy schedules and the great number of votes force them to depend on the advice of like-minded colleagues. In particular, they look to respected members of the committee who worked on a bill.[46] Legislators find out how their friends stand on an issue, listen to the party leadership's advice, and take the various committee reports into account. Sometimes members are influenced to vote one way merely because they know

attentive public
Those citizens who follow public affairs carefully.

a colleague is on the other side of the issue. For some legislators, the state delegation (senators and representatives from their home state) reinforces a common identity.

A member may also vote with a colleague in the expectation that the colleague will later vote for a measure about which the member is concerned—called **logrolling**. Some vote trading takes place to build coalitions so that members can "bring home the bacon" to their constituents. Other vote trading reflects reciprocity in congressional relations or deference to colleagues' superior information or expertise.

CONGRESSIONAL STAFF   Representatives and senators used to be at a distinct disadvantage in dealing with the executive branch because they were overly dependent on information supplied by the White House or lobbyists. The complexity of the issues and increasingly demanding schedules created pressures for additional staff. Congress responded and gradually expanded its staffs, and this expansion has strengthened the role of Congress in the public policy process.

Because both chambers have roughly equal amounts of money for staff, Senate members and committees have much larger staffs than their House counterparts. About one-third of the House of Representatives staff and one-fourth of the Senate staff are based back home, where they help their bosses communicate with voters and provide constituency services and casework. (Helping people with a misplaced Social Security check or helping them qualify for veterans' benefits are examples of casework provided by congressional offices.) Much of the work done in district offices is akin to a continuous campaign effort: generating favorable publicity, arranging for local appearances and newspaper interviews, scheduling, and contacting important civic and business leaders in the region.

Members rely heavily on the advice of congressional staffers. Staff members draft bills, do research, and are often involved in negotiating and coalition building. Staff specialists in policy areas sometimes deal on a day-to-day basis with their counterparts in the executive branch departments and with interest groups. With their direct access to the members of Congress they serve, these staff aides are often among the most influential people in Washington.

PARTY   Members generally vote with their party. Whether as a result of party pressure or natural affinity, on major bills there is a tendency for most Democrats to be arrayed against most Republicans. Partisan voting has increased in the House since the early 1970s and has intensified even more since the 1994 elections. Indeed, party-line voting has been greater in recent years than at any time in recent decades. Party differences are stronger over domestic, regulatory, and welfare reform measures than over foreign policy or civil liberties issues. Ninety-eight percent of House Republicans, for example, voted to impeach Bill Clinton in a historic vote in late 1998; the same percentage of House Democrats voted *against* impeachment.

Congressional redistricting has helped increase partisanship in congressional voting. "Advances in computer-driven mapping capabilities have made an art form of the old-fashioned gerrymandering that occurs where congressional districts are redrawn after each decennial census." Party operatives in the states can with great precision draw district lines to create relatively safe Democratic or Republican districts, "increasing the number of secure members answerable to only their own party's primary votes."[47]

As redistricting has created more safe seats, the House of Representatives has become more polarized. House Republicans have become more politically conservative and House Democrats more liberal. The House is more politically partisan than the Senate not because of personalities but largely because of these constitutional-political procedures. As House districts have become more distinctly and safely Republican or Democratic, the incentives for compromise have declined.

Party leaders in both chambers do their best to get their members to vote together. Republican leaders claim that cohesive voting is the only way Republicans can implement their party platform and satisfy the majorities who elected them in recent years. Senators are usually more independent, so party leaders in the Senate have a harder time maintaining party discipline than leaders in the House do.

logrolling
Mutual aid and vote trading among legislators.

U.S. Senator James Jeffords of Vermont, on the steps of the Capitol with prominent Democrats the day before he left the Republican Party to become an Independent. Jeffords's decision gave the Democrats control of the Senate until 2003. He left the Republican Party because he believed it had grown too conservative and was putting undue pressure on him to vote the party line.

INTEREST GROUPS   Interest groups use Political Action Committees (PACs) to contribute campaign funds to congressional candidates. These PACs give disproportionately to incumbents; at least 70 percent of PAC contributions have gone to incumbents in recent years.[48] In addition to their role as financiers of elections, interest groups provide important information for making laws.

Interest groups not only watch and try to influence national legislators but also monitor one another. If a member of Congress tries to insert a "special interest" measure into an appropriations bill that is especially favorable to a particular interest, for example, opposing interest groups are almost certain to lobby for the measure's defeat. "The result," says Senator Joe Lieberman of Connecticut, "is that everyone on Capitol Hill is keeping a close eye on everyone else, creating a self-adjusting system of checks and balances."[49]

Interest groups can also be effective when they mobilize grassroots activists and rally various constituencies to lobby their home state members of Congress. For example, higher education lobbying groups have effectively mobilized students and educators to write and call members of Congress on behalf of student aid and related provisions in various measures before Congress.[50] And tobacco companies spent large sums to fight taxes on cigarettes. Although most members of Congress reject the popular perception that interest groups "buy" their votes, political contributions certainly do influence the parties and help provide access to members of Congress.

THE PRESIDENT   Through effective use of their constitutional and political powers, presidents are usually partners with Congress in the legislative process. In fact, the president is often the single most important (though not always decisive) force in determining the course of legislation.

Members of Congress, however, are invariably reluctant to admit that they are influenced by pressure from the White House. On domestic issues, legislators generally say they are more likely to be influenced by their own convictions or by their constituents than by what the White House wants. But presidents and their aides work hard to influence public opinion and to win members over to the president's point of view. For example, despite a Democratic majority in the Senate and a razor-thin Republican majority in the House, George W. Bush won an impressive 87 percent support from Congress on the 120 votes on which he took a clear position in 2001. That was the best success mark since 1965, when Lyndon Johnson won 93 percent of the key votes.[51]

Bush set the mark in part by taking fewer strong positions on legislation. Whereas Bill Clinton took a position on an average of 86 House votes a year during his eight years in office, Bush took a position on only 43 House bills in 2001. Moreover, when Bush did take a position, it was mostly in favor of bills that Congress was about to pass. Nevertheless, Bush's support scores remained high; in 2002, he won 88 percent of his votes, while in 2003, he won 78 percent.

For a variety of reasons, especially because of the tendency of the nation to rally around the president in time of foreign crisis, presidents have more influence on how members of Congress vote on foreign policy or national security issues than on domestic policy.[52] President George W. Bush benefited from a bipartisan coalition that passed the resolution authorizing the use of military force against terrorist forces in Afghanistan, for example.

THE LEGISLATIVE OBSTACLE COURSE

Congress operates under a system of multiple vetoes. The framers intentionally dispersed powers so that no would-be tyrant or majority could accumulate enough authority to oppress the nation. Follow a bill through the legislative process, and this dispersal of power is clear (see Figure 11–2). The procedures and rules of the Senate differ somewhat from those of the House, but in each chamber, power is fragmented and decentralized.

How Ideas Become Bills

Members introduce bills for different reasons. Although many bills are introduced to help win reelection or higher office, members of Congress do care about the national interest. As Democratic representative Tim Penny of Minnesota said of his decision to run for Congress, "I was young and idealistic. . . . I wanted to show people that government can work and that partisanship doesn't have to be the dominant force in politics, that interest groups don't have to be a deciding factor on every vote."[53]

Members also care about making a personal difference. "Politicians are human beings," said Massachusetts representative Joe Kennedy II, whose father was assassinated with a handgun during the 1968 presidential campaign and whose cousin suffered from bone cancer. "When there is a degree of very personal pain that one feels toward an issue—it might be gun control or my uncle's interest in fighting cancer—commitment level is higher and your willingness to compromise is lower."[54]

FIGURE 11–2 How a Bill Becomes a Law.

How Bills Become Laws

The odds against a bill's becoming a law are great, but Congress still produces an extraordinary amount of legislation. In 2003, a typical year, members of Congress introduced a total of 7,000 bills (4,600 in the House and 2,400 in the Senate). Of those, committees in one or the other chamber sent 727 bills to the floor for further consideration, of which the Senate passed 590 and the House passed 674; 174 of those were approved by both chambers and signed into law. Congress is obviously very selective about which bills survive.[55]

A bill must win many small contests on the way to final passage. There are four broad steps from beginning to end: (1) introduction, which involves putting a formal proposal before the House or the Senate; (2) committee review, which involves holding a hearing and "marking up" the bill; (3) floor debate and passage, which means getting on the legislative calendar, passing once in each chamber, surviving a conference to iron out any differences between the House and Senate versions, and passing once again in each chamber; and (4) presidential approval.

INTRODUCING A BILL House members introduce a bill by placing it into a mahogany box (called the hopper) on a desk at the front of the House chamber; senators introduce a bill by either handing it to the clerk of the Senate or by presenting it to their colleagues in a floor speech. In the more informal Senate, members sometimes short-circuit the formalities by offering a bill as an amendment to pending legislation. A bill that comes from the House is always designated H.R. (House of Representatives) followed by its number, and a bill from the Senate is always designated S. (Senate) followed by its number. Although presidents often recommend legislation to Congress, all bills must be introduced by a member of the House or Senate.

COMMITTEE REVIEW Once a bill is introduced in either chamber, it is "read" into the record as a formal proposal and referred to the appropriate committee—tax bills to Ways and Means or Finance; farm bills to Agriculture; technology bills to Science, Space, and Technology; small business to Small Business; and so forth. The parliamentarian in each chamber decides where to send each bill.

WHO CAN KILL A BILL

The complexity of the congressional system provides a tremendous built-in advantage for opponents of any measure. Multiple opportunities to kill a bill exist because of the dispersion of influence. At a dozen or more points, a bill may be stopped or allowed to die (inaction is the same as killing a bill). Sponsors of a bill must win at every step; opponents need to win only once. Whether good or bad, a proposal can be delayed or rejected by any one of the following:

1. The chair of the House subcommittee
2. The House subcommittee as a whole
3. The chair of the House standing committee
4. The House standing committee as a whole
5. The House Rules Committee
6. The majority of the House
7. The chair of the Senate subcommittee
8. The Senate subcommittee as a whole
9. The chair of the Senate standing committee
10. The Senate standing committee as a whole
11. A senator or senators who mount a filibuster
12. The majority of the Senate
13. The floor leaders in both chambers
14. The House-Senate conference committee, if the chambers disagree
15. The president (by veto)

BELOW THE BELTWAY

★★ YOU DECIDE

SHOULD ALL PRESIDENTIAL NOMINEES GET A VOTE?

Under current Senate rules, there are times when an executive or judicial appointee can be stalled indefinitely through personal holds and the threat of a filibuster. Both the Clinton and Bush administrations argued that all nominees, no matter how controversial, should have the right to receive a final up-or-down majority vote by the Senate. Holds and filibusters are particularly visible during periods in which the White House and Senate are controlled by different parties, but there are occasions when senators stall nominations from their own president. Having gone through the rigors of the appointments process, which is described in more detail in Chapter 13, nominees often argue that simple fairness requires a final vote one way or the other.

discharge petition
Petition that, if signed by a majority of the members of the House of Representatives, will pry a bill from committee and bring it to the floor for consideration.

rider
A provision attached to a bill—to which it may or may not be related—in order to secure its passage.

pocket veto
A veto exercised by the president after Congress has adjourned; if the president takes no action for ten days, the bill does not become law and is not returned to Congress for a possible override.

override
An action taken by Congress to reverse a presidential veto, requiring a two-thirds majority in each chamber.

The Referral Decision   Although most bills are referred to a single committee, particularly complex bills may be referred simultaneously or sequentially to multiple committees. President Bush's proposed department of homeland security bill was so complicated and touched so many agencies that it was managed by a temporary special committee in the House. The bill was referred to at least ten committees, including Judiciary, Ways and Means, and Government Reform, all of which held hearings on specific provisions of the largest government reorganization since the Department of Defense was created in 1947. The bill went into the House as a 35-page proposal and came out almost 500 pages long. Committees and their subcommittees are responsible for building a legislative record in support of a given bill. This *legislative record* also helps the president and federal courts interpret what Congress intended.

Markup   Once a committee or subcommittee decides to pass the bill, it "marks it up" to clean up the wording or amend its version of the bill. The term *markup* refers to the pencil marks that members make on the final version of the bill. Once markup is over, the bill must be passed by the committee or subcommittee and forwarded to the next step in the process. If it is passed by a subcommittee, for example, it is forwarded to the full committee; if it is passed by a full committee in the House, it is then forwarded to the House Rules Committee for a rule that will govern debate on the floor; if it is passed by a full committee in the Senate, it is forwarded to the full chamber.

Discharge   Although most bills die in committee without a hearing or further review, a bill can be forced to the floor of the House through a **discharge petition** signed by a majority of the membership. In 2002, for example, House members were able to collect enough signatures to discharge the Rules Committee on a campaign finance reform bill that had been stalled for six months. Because most members share a strong sense of reciprocity, or mutual respect, toward the work of other committees, few discharge petitions are successful. The Senate does not use discharge petitions.

FLOOR DEBATE AND PASSAGE   Once reported to the full chamber directly from committee in the Senate or through the Rules Committee in the House, a bill will either be scheduled for floor action or dropped entirely, depending on the party leadership and the amount of time left in the session. The busiest time of the year occurs just before the end of a session, usually in late September or early October, when bills must be passed or die.

In the Senate, it is not uncommon for members to propose **riders**, or amendments, that are unrelated to the bill on which they want to ride. Senators use riders to force the president to accept legislation attached to a bill that was otherwise popular, because the president has to either accept the *entire* bill or to veto it. The number of riders attached to appropriations bills has increased in recent years. Democrats and Republicans alike use riders to increase spending in their states and districts.[56]

Except for tax bills, the House and Senate discuss bills simultaneously rather than waiting for one to act first. If only one chamber passes a bill at the end of the two years that comprise each Congress, it is dead and must be reintroduced in the next Congress. If both houses pass bills on the same subject but there are differences between the bills—and there often are—the two versions must go to a conference committee for *reconciliation*. If a bill does not make it through both chambers in identical form in the same two-year Congress, it must begin the entire process again in the next Congress.

When a bill has passed both houses in identical form, it goes to the president, who may *sign* it into law or *veto* it. If Congress is in session and the president waits ten days (not counting Sundays), the bill becomes law *without* his signature. If Congress has adjourned and the president waits ten days without signing the bill, it is defeated by what is known as a **pocket veto**. After a pocket veto, the bill is dead. Otherwise, when a bill is vetoed, it is returned to the chamber of its origin by the president with a message explaining the reasons for the veto. Congress can vote to **override** the veto by a two-thirds vote in each chamber, but assembling such an extraordinary majority is often difficult.

The Importance of Compromise

Since it takes a majority vote in two chambers of Congress and the signature of the president before a bill becomes a law, sponsors of new legislation have to be willing to compromise. One tactical decision at the start is whether to push for action in the Senate first, in the House first, or in both simultaneously. For example, if it appears that the Senate is not likely to approve a bill, its sponsors may seek passage in the House and hope that a sizable victory there will spur the Senate into action. Another tactic concerns the committee that will consider a bill. Normally, referral to a committee is automatic, but sometimes sponsors have discretion. A bill that involves more than one jurisdiction can be written in such a way that it may go to a committee that will look on it more kindly.[57]

AN ASSESSMENT OF CONGRESS

More than two centuries after its creation, Congress is a larger, more vital, and very different kind of institution from the one the framers envisioned. Yet most of its major functions remain the same, and their effective exercise is crucial to the health of our constitutional democracy. Even in the twenty-first century, we still look to Congress to make laws, raise revenues, represent citizens, investigate abuses of power, and oversee the executive branch.

Although most incumbents are easily reelected, most campaign constantly to stay in office, creating what some observers have called the "permanent campaign." Members appear driven by their desire to win reelection, so that much of what takes place in Congress seems mainly designed to promote reelection. These efforts usually pay off for members of Congress: Members who seek reelection almost always win. At the same time, these efforts also pay off for our democracy. Members' concern with reelection fosters *accountability* and the desire to please the voters.

Yet, the permanent campaign clearly hinders legislative progress. In an institution where most members act as individual entrepreneurs and consider themselves leaders,

★ ★ ★ **THINKING IT THROUGH**

The Constitution requires the Senate to give its advice and consent on nominations, but not a final vote. Senators argue that controversial nominees demand particularly close attention because of the potential harm they could do once in office, particularly if they hold lifetime appointments in the federal courts. Moreover, they argue that holds and filibusters do not prevent an up-or-down vote if the Senate can muster the 60 votes to remove a hold and end a filibuster. These ten extra votes are more difficult to find, especially when the Senate is closely divided between the two parties, but the process ensures that controversial nominees face an additional check before taking their posts.

On Tuesday, September 11, 2001, the leadership of the House of Representatives and the Senate gathered on the steps of the Capitol with other congressional members in a gesture of unity after the terrorist attacks.

RUNNING FOR CONGRESS

Deciding to run for Congress involves a variety of calculations. Potential candidates need to decide whether they want to take on an entrenched incumbent (difficult), run for an open seat (easier), or take on a vulnerable incumbent (easier still). They also need to ask whether they have enough funding, name recognition, and campaigning ability to mount a credible campaign, and whether their beliefs fit the prevailing opinions of their district. Once they have made the decision to run, candidates must also decide where to spend their money, how to spend their time, and what issues to emphasize. As the simulation on running for Congress shows, winning against incumbents is not easy, which helps explain why so many incumbents are reelected.

Go to Make It Real: Running for Congress.

the task of providing institutional leadership is increasingly difficult. With limited resources, and only sometimes aided by the president, congressional leaders are asked to bring together a diverse, fragmented, and independent institution. The congressional system acts only when majorities can be achieved. That the framers accomplished their original objective—creating a body that would not move with imprudent haste—has been generally well realized.

Newly elected presidents and members of Congress always arrive in Washington enthusiastically ready to enact the people's wishes. But they find that governing is invariably tougher and slower than they expected because government deals with complex issues about which there is often little consensus. Building policy majorities is hard because complex problems generate complex solutions, and the structure of Congress requires supermajorities to agree to serious changes. Thus the president's veto, the filibuster, and the use of holds and legislative riders all make consensus more difficult to find.

Criticism of Congress—its alleged incompetence, its overresponsiveness to organized interests, its inefficiencies, its partisan character—is difficult to separate from the context of policy preferences and democratic procedures. Sometimes criticism tells us more about the critic than it does about the effectiveness of Congress. Constitutional democracy is not the most efficient form of government. Congress was never intended to act swiftly; it was not created to be a rubber stamp or even a cooperative partner for presidents. Its greatest strengths—its diversity and deliberative character—also weaken its position in dealing with the more centralized executive branch.

The framers would not be troubled by the lack of action, however. By dividing power, they hoped to control it. The odds against action are high precisely because the framers did not want any one branch of the government to become a threat to individual liberty.

SUMMARY

1. Congress plays a crucial role in our system of shared powers, controlling key decisions and constraining presidents. Yet over time, Congress has lost some influence as the presidency has gained influence. In recent decades, however, Congress has become more capable as a policy-making competitor for presidents. Redistricting and reapportionment have shaped a Congress that somewhat more accurately reflects the population.

2. The most distinctive feature of Congress is its bicameralism, which the framers intended as a moderating influence on partisanship and possible error. Each chamber has a few distinctive functions. The organization and procedures of the two houses also differ slightly, as do their political environments.

3. Congress performs these functions: representation, lawmaking, consensus building, overseeing the bureaucracy, policy clarification, and investigating. The Senate also confirms or denies presidential appointments and participates in the ratification of treaties.

4. Congress manages its workload through a leadership system that is different in both chambers. The House is led by the Speaker, a majority and a minority

leader, and whips in each party, while the Senate is led by a majority and a minority leader. The Senate is more difficult to lead because of its greater individualism, which is sometimes expressed through the use of holds and filibusters to control the legislative process.

5. Most of the work in Congress is done in committees and subcommittees. Congress has attempted in recent years to streamline its committee system and modify its methods of selecting committee chairs. Seniority practices are still generally followed. Subcommittees are important. They can prevent or delay legislation from being enacted. But there are numerous other stages where bills can be killed, making it easier to stop legislation than to enact it.

6. As a collective body, Congress must attempt to accomplish its tasks even as most of its members serve as delegates or trustees for their constituents. When they vote, members are influenced by their philosophy and values, their perceptions of constituents' interests, and the views of trusted colleagues and staff, partisan ties and party leaders, lobbyists, and the president.

7. The members of Congress do an excellent job of representing the values and views of most of their constituents. But they are cautious about enacting proposed measures by their own colleagues or the legislative agenda put forward by presidents. Most proposed legislation dies for lack of majority support.

8. Members of Congress are motivated by the desire to win reelection, and much of what Congress does is in response to this motive. Members work hard to get favors for their districts, to serve the needs of constituents, and to maintain a high visibility in their districts or states. Incumbents have advantages that help explain their success at reelection: They have greater name recognition, they have large staffs, they are much better able to raise campaign money, and they have greater access to the media.

9. A bill becomes a law through a process that involves many opportunities for defeat. Although all formal bills are referred to committees for consideration, very few receive a hearing, even fewer are marked up and sent to the floor, and fewer still are enacted by both chambers and signed into law by the president. In

addition, the legislative obstacle course sometimes involves filibusters, riders, holds, and the occasional override of a presidential veto.

10. Individual members of Congress are more popular than the institution. Congress is criticized for being inefficient, unrepresentative, unethical, and lacking in collective responsibility. Yet criticisms of Congress are difficult to separate from the context of policy preference and democratic procedures. Congress's greatest strengths—its diversity and its deliberative character—also contribute to its weaknesses.

K E Y   T E R M S

reapportionment	majority leader	filibuster	delegate
redistricting	minority leader	cloture	trustee
gerrymandering	whip	senatorial courtesy	attentive public
safe seat	party caucus	standing committee	logrolling
incumbents	closed rule	special or select committee	discharge petition
bicameralism	open rule	joint committee	rider
enumerated powers	president pro tempore	seniority rule	pocket veto
Speaker	hold	conference committee	override

F U R T H E R   R E A D I N G

JOEL D. ABERBACH, *Keeping a Watchful Eye: The Politics of Congressional Oversight* (Brookings Institution Press, 1990).

E. SCOTT ADLER, *Why Congressional Reforms Fail: Reelection and the House Committee System* (University of Chicago Press, 2002).

SARAH A. BINDER AND STEVEN S. SMITH, *Politics or Principles? Filibustering in the United States Senate* (Brookings Institution Press, 1997).

SARAH A. BINDER, *Stalemate: Causes and Consequences of Legislative Gridlock* (Brookings Institution Press, 2003).

BILL BRADLEY, *Time Present, Time Past: A Memoir* (Knopf, 1996).

DAVID W. BRADY AND CRAIG VOLDEN, *Revolving Gridlock: Politics and Policy from Carter to Clinton* (Westview Press, 1998).

ADAM CLYMER, *Edward M. Kennedy: A Biography* (Morrow, 1999).

ROGER H. DAVIDSON AND WALTER J. OLESZEK, *Congress and Its Members*, 8th ed. (CQ Press, 2002).

CHRISTOPHER J. DEERING AND STEVEN S. SMITH, *Committees in Congress*, 3d ed. (CQ Press, 1997).

LAWRENCE C. DODD AND BRUCE J. OPPENHEIMER, EDS., *Congress Reconsidered*, 5th ed. (CQ Press, 1993).

RICHARD F. FENNO JR., *Home Style: House Members in Their Districts* (Little, Brown, 1978).

RICHARD F. FENNO JR., *Learning to Govern: An Institutional View of the 104th Congress* (Brookings Institution Press, 1997).

RICHARD F. FENNO JR., *Senators on the Campaign Trail: The Politics of Representation* (University of Oklahoma Press, 1996).

MORRIS P. FIORINA, *Congress: Keystone of the Washington Establishment*, 2d ed. (Yale University Press, 1989).

PAUL HERRNSON, *Congressional Elections*, 3d ed. (CQ Press, 2000).

JOHN R. HIBBING AND ELIZABETH THEISS-MORSE, *Congress as Public Enemy: Public Attitudes Toward American Political Institutions* (Cambridge University Press, 1995).

GODFREY HODGSON, *The Gentleman from New York: Daniel Patrick Moynihan* (Houghton Mifflin, 2000).

LINDA KILLIAN, *The Freshmen: What Happened to the Republican Revolution?* (Westview Press, 1998).

FRANCES E. LEE AND BRUCE I. OPPENHEIMER, *Sizing Up the Senate: The Unequal Consequences of Equal Representation* (University of Chicago Press, 1999).

JOSEPH I. LIEBERMAN, *In Praise of Public Life* (Simon & Schuster, 2000).

TOM LOFTUS, *The Art of Legislative Politics* (CQ Press, 1994).

JANET M. MARTIN, *Lessons from the Hill: The Legislative Journey of an Education Program* (St. Martin's Press, 1993).

DAVID R. MAYHEW, *America's Congress: Actions in the Public Sphere, James Madison Through Newt Gingrich* (Yale University Press, 2002).

BARBARA MIKULSKI ET AL., *Nine and Counting: The Women of the Senate* (Morrow, 2000).

WALTER J. OLESZEK, *Congressional Procedures and the Policy Process*, 4th ed. (CQ Press, 1995).

NORMAN J. ORNSTEIN, THOMAS MANN, AND MICHAEL MALBIN, *Vital Statistics on Congress, 2000–2002* (AEI Press, 2002).

RONALD M. PETERS JR., ED., *The Speaker: Leadership in the U.S. House of Representatives* (CQ Press, 1995).

DAVID E. PRICE, *The Congressional Experience: A View from the Hill* (Westview Press, 1993).

NICOL RAE AND COLTON CAMPBELL, EDS., *New Majority or Old Majority: The Impact of Republicans on Congress* (Rowman & Littlefield, 1999).

WARREN B. RUDMAN, *Combat: Twelve Years in the U.S. Senate* (Random House, 1996).

BARBARA SINCLAIR, *Unorthodox Lawmaking: New Legislative Processes in the U.S. Congress*, 2d ed. (CQ Press, 2000).

DARVELL M. WEST, *Patrick Kennedy: The Rise to Power* (Prentice Hall, 2001).

THE PRESIDENCY
THE LEADERSHIP BRANCH

12

The framers of the Constitution both admired and feared centralized leadership. Although they knew the country needed a more effective national government led by a single executive, they worried about the potential abuse of power if it were invested in a single executive. Having lived under the tyranny of the English monarchy, they had every right to worry. They wanted a president powerful enough to lead the nation during periods of domestic and international crisis, but they also wanted checks on his power.

Americans saw both sides of presidential power in the months and weeks leading up to the war with Iraq. President Bush began making the case for war in the summer of 2002 when he accused Saddam Hussein of hiding weapons of mass destruction that could be used against the United States. "If we wait for threats to fully materialize, we will have waited too long," Bush warned in a speech to graduates of West Point. "The war on terror will not be won on the defensive. We must take the battle to the enemy, disrupt his plans, and confront the worst threats before they emerge."

Congress eventually gave Bush authority to lauch a preemptive attack against Iraq. However, support was far from unanimous. Although Bush's request passed 296 to 133 in the House, and 77 to 23 in the Senate, many members of Congress urged the president to build the same broad multinational coalition of support that his father had rallied before the first Gulf War in 1991. Some also questioned the need for urgency, demanding hard evidence that the weapons of mass destruction, or WMD, actually existed.

TIME LINE
THE PRESIDENCY

1789	First president elected: George Washington, who was also the first to invoke executive privilege
1861	Lincoln suspends *Habeas corpus* for secessionists
1868	Johnson impeached but acquitted by one vote in the Senate
1901	McKinley assassinated by an anarchist
1932	FDR is elected to the first of a record four terms
1945	FDR casts the last of 635 vetoes—the most by any president
1963	JFK assassination shocks the nation
1970	OMB created to centralize presidential control over bureaucracy
1973	War Powers Act limits president's authority to commit troops without a declaration of war by Congress
1974	Nixon resigns before impeachment over Watergate scandal
1983	Supreme Court rules legislative vetoes unconstitutional
1986	Iran-Contra scandal exposes illegal diversion of secret funds
1998	Clinton impeached by House but acquitted by Senate in 1999
2000	Supreme Court rules that Florida can certify George W. Bush as the winner of the state's electoral votes, thereby securing his election as president

Americans were far from unanimous about the war, too. Although they initially gave the president strong support for action, their doubts increased as the nation moved closer to war. In August 2002, for example, 64 percent of Americans favored military action against Iraq, while only 21 percent were opposed; just before the war began in March 2003, 59 percent still favored action, while 30 percent were opposed. Moreover, of the 59 percent who favored war in March, more than a third supported action only if the United States had international support.[1]

Although Americans did rally behind the president when the war actually began, and rallied again after Saddam Hussein's capture the following December, they continued to worry about the cost of the war in both lives and money. So did Congress. Less than a year after the start of the war, Congress had launched a major investigation of the failure to find any weapons of mass destruction, asking hard questions about why the president and vice president could have been so sure Iraq actually posed an immediate threat to the United States.

These concerns clearly acted as a check on the Bush administration's plans. The administration accelerated its timetable for turning over power to the Iraqi people in response to public pressure, and it eventually created a national commission to investigate the questionable intelligence that had led to war. Thus, even though opponents of the war had been in the minority, they had been able to check the president's power, which is exactly how the framers intended the system to act.

This chapter will explore the presidential balancing act in more detail. We will start by reviewing the structure and powers of the presidency, then ask what Americans expect from the president, examine how presidents manage the presidency, outline the presidential job description, and conclude with a discussion of the ingredients of presidential greatness.

THE STRUCTURE AND POWERS OF THE PRESIDENCY

Just as the Constitution gives Congress the lawmaking power of the United States in the first sentence of Article I, it gives the president the executive power in the first sentence of Article II. The executive power includes everything from the president's role as commander in chief of the army and navy to broad responsibility for faithful execution of the nation's laws. It also provides the basic authority the president needs to oversee the federal bureaucracy, develop recommendations for spending money, and select the senior appointees of government.

Having given this executive responsibility to a single person, the framers insulated the presidency from public passions. To this day, for example, presidents are not elected by the public, but by electors who are selected in winner-take-all systems in all but two states, Maine and Nebraska. As a result, presidents often claim to speak for the entire nation, not a single district or state.

At the same time, the framers created a presidency of limited powers. They wanted a presidential office that would steer clear of parties and factions, enforce the laws passed by Congress, handle communications with foreign governments, and help states put down disorders. They wanted a presidency strong enough to match Congress yet not so strong that it would overpower Congress.

Separate Powers

The framers created a system of separate powers that prevents any one branch from controlling all of government. However, merely having three branches of national government—legislative, executive, and judicial—does not by itself create a pure system of separated powers; the United Kingdom also has legislative and executive branches, but both are automatically headed by the same political party.

In the United States, the legislative, executive, and judicial branches are all independent from one another. Although there are times when the legislative and executive branch are headed by the same political party, there is nothing automatic about unified government—it can exist only if voters in enough states and districts vote for the same party over enough elections to control the House, Senate, and presidency.

The United States is one of the few world powers that is neither a parliamentary democracy nor a wholly executive-dominated government. Our Constitution plainly invites both Congress and the president to set policy and govern the nation. Leadership and policy change are encouraged only when Congress and the president, and sometimes the courts along with them, concur on the desirability of new directions.

The president and Congress are legitimate participants in a whole range of policy activities. Triumphs for a president acting alone in a system of separated powers are rare. "Whenever powers are shared, attention must be devoted to the other decision makers," writes political scientist Charles O. Jones. "How do they view the problem? What are their present commitments? On what basis will they compromise? The test in a separated system is not simply one of presidential success. It is rather one of achievement by the system, with presidents and members of Congress inextricably bonded and similarly judged."[2]

Defining the Presidency

The framers' most important decision about the presidency was also their first. Meeting on June 1, 1787, the Constitutional Convention decided that there would be a single executive. Despite worries that a single president might lay the groundwork for a future monarchy, the framers also believed that the new government needed energy in the executive. They were willing to increase the risk of tyranny in return for some efficiency.

IN COMPARATIVE PERSPECTIVE

THE MEXICAN PRESIDENT

Mexican President Vicente Fox.

The Mexican president is one of the most powerful executives in the democratic world. Under the constitution of 1917, which was adopted after a decade of civil war, the president was given sweeping powers to run the country, including authority to hire and fire most government employees. Unlike the U.S. system, the Mexican legislature and judiciary have little power to check the presidency.

Elected by popular vote, the president holds the titles of chief of state, head of government, and commander in chief of the armed forces, and serves without a vice president. The president must be at least 35 years old on election day and cannot have been on active duty in the military during the six months preceding election. This latter provision was designed to prevent military officers from taking control of the government.

Because Mexican presidents can serve only for one six-year term, they have sometimes been called the most powerful "six-year monarchs" in the world. If the office becomes vacant during the first two years of a *sexenio,* or term, the congress appoints an interim president and holds a special election; if it becomes vacant in the final four years, the congress appoints a provisional president to serve out the term.

For 71 years from 1929 to 2000, the presidency was controlled by a single political party that the Mexican government created itself, the Institutional Revolutionary Party, or PRI. With party control ensured from term to term, presidents controlled the right to select their own successors through the *dedazo,* or tap. Although PRI candidates often faced opposition in the general election, the party earned a well-deserved reputation as the world's most efficient election machine.

Mexico took a dramatic step toward a more democratic system in 2000 when the nation elected Vicente Fox as president. A former Coca-Cola executive who ousted Pepsi as Mexico's favorite soft-drink, Fox drew upon his populist roots as a rancher from the rural state of Guanajuato, saying he was the only candidate who had ever milked a cow. But he also drew upon Mexico's desire for a change from one-party rule. "From today forward, we need to unite," he said at a victory rally in 2000. "Let's celebrate today, because beginning tomorrow there's a lot of work to do." Fox will have all the powers of the presidency to do so.

The Bush–Gore election in 2000 was so close that the role of the electoral college was brought into focus for the first time in years. On December 18, 2000, Alabama's nine Republican electors cast their votes for President-elect Bush.

Once past this first decision, the framers had to decide just how independent that executive would be from the rest of the national government, which in turn meant finding an appropriate method of selection or election. Had they wanted Congress to select the president from among its members, the framers would have created a **parliamentary system** of government that would look more like the English system.

The convention was initially divided on how the president would be selected. A small number of delegates favored direct election by the people, which Pennsylvania's James Wilson thought would ensure that the president was completely independent of Congress. Convinced that the nation was too diverse to handle direct election and afraid that states might join together to support regional candidates who would favor their part of the country, the delegates never seriously considered direct election. A larger number of delegates favored selection by Congress, tying the president more closely to the legislative branch.

Eventually, the framers compromised by creating an electoral college: Voters would cast their ballots for competing slates of electors, who would in turn cast their electoral votes for president. It might be called a form of indirect direct election. The framers also gave the executive a four-year term of office, further balancing the House (two-year term) and Senate (six-year term). Although they were silent on the number of terms a president could serve, the nation's first president, George Washington, quickly established a two-term precedent, which held until Franklin Roosevelt's historic four-term presidency from 1932 to 1945. The Twenty-Second Amendment to the Constitution, ratified in 1951, restored Washington's precedent by limiting presidents to two terms.

The framers also created the position of vice president just in case the president left office before the end of the term. With little debate, the founders decided to give the vice president the power to break tie votes in the Senate. Otherwise, the vice president has no constitutional duties but to wait for the president to be incapacitated or otherwise unable to discharge the powers and duties of the presidency.

The framers also established three simple qualifications for both offices. Under the Constitution, the president and vice president must be (1) at least thirty-five years old; (2) natural-born citizens of the United States, as opposed to immigrants who become

parliamentary system
A system of government in which the legislature selects the prime minister or president.

citizens by applying to the U.S. government for naturalization; and (3) residents of the United States for the previous fourteen years. The citizenship and residency requirements were designed to prevent a popular foreign-born citizen from capturing the office.

The Presidential Ticket

With this basic structure in place, the framers had to decide how the vice president would be selected. Once again, they created a remarkable electoral arrangement: The candidate who received the most electoral college votes would become president, and the candidate who came in second would become vice president.

It did not take long for the framers to discover the problem with this runner-up rule. The 1796 election produced Federalist President John Adams and Democratic-Republican Vice President Thomas Jefferson. Because the two disagreed so sharply about the future of the country, Jefferson was rendered virtually irrelevant to government.

This rule created a constitutional crisis in 1800. The election could not have been more important, for it occurred during a time of rising public anger about the nation's direction. With the Federalist party fading quickly in the wake of the Alien and Sedition Acts and growing anti-British sentiments, two Democratic-Republicans, Thomas Jefferson and Aaron Burr, emerged from the 1800 election with exactly 73 electoral votes each, leaving Federalist John Adams behind with just 63. With the election now thrown to the House of Representatives under the Constitution's tie-breaking rules, the nation teetered on the edge of a constitutional crisis for 36 ballots before Jefferson was finally elected. His vice president was none other than Aaron Burr, the candidate whom he had just defeated.

The problem was solved under the Twelfth Amendment, which was ratified in 1804. Under the new process, electors are allowed to cast two votes, one for president and one for vice president, thereby encouraging the two candidates to run together as a **presidential ticket.**

Presidential Powers

Article II of the Constitution begins even more simply than Article I: "The executive Power shall be vested in a President of the United States of America." Some experts argue that the executive power covers almost everything not granted to the legislature or judiciary, while others believe that the president's relatively short list of enumerated powers suggests that the framers wanted a more limited executive.[3] Although short, Article II does address foreign threats and the day-to-day operations of government, establishing the president's authority to play three central roles in the new government: (1) commander in chief, (2) diplomat in chief, and (3) administrator in chief.

COMMANDER IN CHIEF   The Constitution explicitly states that the president is to be commander in chief of the army and navy. It is a fundamental expression of the president's role in protecting the nation as a whole. The framers saw the president as the commander in chief but were divided over which branch would both declare and make war.[4]

The framers initially agreed that Congress would make war, raise armies, build and equip fleets, enforce treaties, and suppress and repel invasions, but eventually changed the phrase "make war" to "declare war." But they limited the presidential war power by giving to Congress as a whole the power to appropriate money for the purchase of arms and military pay, and to the Senate, responsibility to approve higher-level military promotion. Although they also gave Congress sole authority to declare war, recent presidents have used their power as commander in chief to order U.S. troops into battle without formal declarations dozens of times over the past century, including the recent wars in Afghanistan and Iraq.

DIPLOMAT IN CHIEF   Article II also makes the president negotiator in chief of treaties with foreign nations, which must be presented to the Senate and approved by a two-thirds vote. A **treaty** is a binding and public agreement between the United States and one or more nations that requires mutual action on the part of the signatories. Although

presidential ticket
The joint listing of the presidential and vice presidential candidates on the same ballot as required by the Twelfth Amendment.

treaty
A formal, public agreement between the United States and one or more nations that must be approved by two-thirds of the Senate.

President Bush meets with his national security advisors in the Situation Room of the White House soon after September 11, 2001.

presidents cannot make treaties without Senate approval, past presidents have argued that they have the power to terminate treaties without Senate consent.

Presidents can also make **executive agreements** with the leaders of foreign nations. Unlike treaties, which last beyond the end of any given administration and are between nations, executive agreements are generally between the chief executives of two or more nations, are sometimes secret, and can expire when one of the chief executives leaves office.

ADMINISTRATOR IN CHIEF By giving the president the power to require the opinion of the principal officer in each of the executive departments "upon any subject relating to the duties of their respective offices," the Constitution puts the president in charge of the day-to-day operation of the federal bureaucracy. As we shall see, the president also has the responsibility to appoint ambassadors, judges, and all other officers of the United States, including the heads of executive departments, with the advice and consent of a majority of the Senate. Together, these powers give presidents the instruments needed to supervise and control the day-to-day operations of the federal bureaucracy.

ADDITIONAL EXECUTIVE POWERS Alongside the specific powers associated with being commander, diplomat, and administrator in chief, the Constitution also gives the president five additional powers to lead government: (1) the power to appoint judges and officers of government; (2) the power to veto legislation, which serves as a check on Congress; (3) the power to grant pardons to individuals convicted of federal, but not state, crimes, thereby providing a check against the judiciary; (4) the power to take care that the laws are faithfully executed; and (5) the power to inform and convene Congress.

1. *The Appointment Power.* The Constitution gives the president authority to appoint judges, ambassadors, and other officers of the executive branch subject to the advice and consent of the Senate. Presidents choose appointees on the basis of party loyalty, interest group pressure, and management ability. Although the appointments process has become more controversial in recent years, the vast majority of judicial and executive appointees are easily confirmed—the Senate has rejected only eight nominations for cabinet positions since the first Congress, and just 29 out of 145 nominations to the Supreme Court.

    Moreover, roughly 2,000 executive branch appointees serve entirely at the pleasure of the president, including the chiefs of staff to cabinet secretaries, who keep track of each department's political agenda. Because these jobs are not

executive agreement
A formal but often secret agreement between the U.S. president and the leaders of other nations that does not require Senate approval.

GLOBAL *Perceptions*

QUESTION: Why do you have an unfavorable view of the United States? Is it mostly because of President George W. Bush, or is it a more general problem with America?

Strong presidents often evoke strong views from citizens in other nations, especially when they take highly visible positions on world issues such as terrorism or international trade. Although many citizens around the world have a favorable view of the United States, citizens in the Middle East are sharply divided about both our nation and its president. Interviewed in 2002, 79 percent of Israelis said they were favorable toward the United States, compared to just 6 percent of citizens in the Palestinian Authority and 18 percent of Jordanians. When asked why they had an unfavorable view, citizens across the globe tended to blame George W. Bush more than the United States in general.

SOURCE: The Pew Global Attitudes Project, June 2003, pp. 134–135.

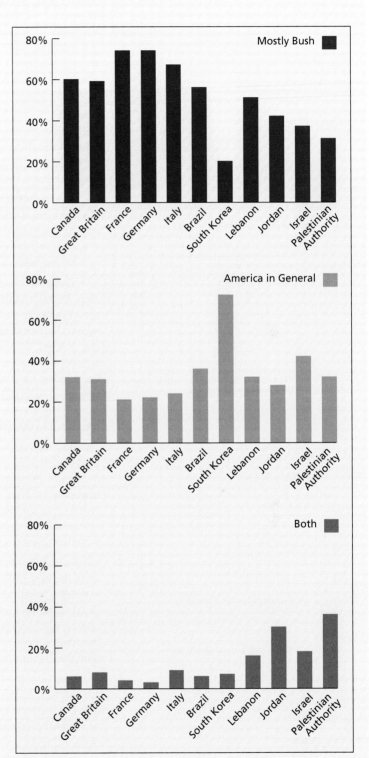

subject to Senate confirmation, they are often filled by campaign supporters, who act as the president's closest allies in the bureaucracy. All executive branch positions are considered "plums" for presidential friends, and are listed in a publication informally known as the "Plum Book." Because judges can serve for life, presidents view judicial appointments as a way to have influence far beyond the end of their term. Chief Justice Earl Warren was just such an influential figure. Nominated by President Dwight Eisenhower, Warren served for more than 15 years and presided over vast changes in civil rights and civil liberties. Presidents Clinton and Bush both nominated hundreds of federal judges who may have a similar impact, perhaps even as future Supreme Court justices.

2. *The Veto Power.* The Constitution provides that bills passed by the U.S. House of Representatives and Senate "shall be presented to the President of the United States," and the president can then approve the measure or issue a **veto**. If a bill is vetoed by a president, it can be enacted only if the veto is overridden, which requires a two-thirds vote in each chamber of Congress.

A variation of the veto is the **pocket veto**. In the ordinary course of events, if a president does not sign or veto a bill within ten days after receiving it (not counting Sundays), the bill becomes law without the president's signature. But if Congress adjourns within the ten days, the president, by taking no action, can kill the bill.

The power of a veto lies in the difficulty of overriding a president's decision. Recall that two-thirds of both houses must vote to overturn a veto. Historically, Congress has overridden fewer than 10 percent of presidents' regular vetoes. This requirement gives presidents a vital bargaining chip in the legislative process, where the mere threat of a veto, announced publicly or through legislative aides, can strengthen a president's hand in persuading Congress to accommodate his wishes. A president may also threaten to veto a bill that Congress wants unless action is taken on another bill that the president wants. Powerful though it is, the veto is essentially a negative weapon, more useful to presidents who want to block legislation than for those who seek programmatic changes.

Because the Constitution is straightforward about the veto power, its regular use by presidents stirs little controversy. Franklin Roosevelt holds the record with 635 vetoes, Ronald Reagan issued 78 vetoes in his two terms, and Bill Clinton vetoed only 37 times in his eight years. In late 1999, Clinton vetoed a Republican-backed appropriations bill and threatened to veto it again and again until Congress made major compromises with him. His use of the veto worked; Congress eventually went along on about two-thirds of the spending items that Clinton wanted.

3. *The Pardon Power.* The pardon power can be traced directly to the royal authority of the king of England, and is probably the most delicate power presidents exercise. The pardon power can be used to shorten prison sentences, correct judicial errors, and protect citizens from future prosecution. It can also be used to address national controversies. On his first full day in office in 1977, for example, President Jimmy Carter issued a pardon to any American who had avoided the draft during the Vietnam War by either not registering or leaving the country.

4. *The Take Care Power.* Presidents are also responsible to take care that the laws are faithfully exercised under the **take care clause**. Located near the end of Article II is the simple statement that the president "shall take Care that the Laws be faithfully executed." This clause makes the president responsible for implementing the laws that Congress enacts, even ones that are enacted through the override of a presidential veto.

Presidents sometimes use the take care clause to claim **inherent powers**, meaning powers they believe are essential to protecting the nation. Although Jefferson drew on this broad notion in making the Louisiana Purchase in 1804, Abraham Lincoln extended the concept early in the Civil War to suspend the rights of prisoners to seek judicial review of their cases, impose a blockade of Confederate shipping, and expand the size of the army beyond authorized

veto
A formal decision to reject a bill passed by Congress.

pocket veto
A formal decision to reject a bill passed by Congress after it adjourns—if Congress adjourns during the ten days that the president is allowed in order to sign or veto a law, the president can reject the law by taking no action at all.

take care clause
The constitutional requirement (in Article II, Section 3) that presidents take care that the laws are faithfully executed, even if they disagree with the purpose of those laws.

inherent powers
Powers that grow out of the very existence of government.

George W. Bush greets navy personnel after landing on the deck of the USS Abraham Lincoln in May 2003. Bush claimed inherent powers to justify the detention of Americans suspected of involvement with terrorism, arguing that they should be treated as a security threat to the nation.

ceilings, all without prior congressional approval as required under the Constitution's lawmaking power.

5. *The Power to Inform and Convene Congress.* Under Article II, presidents are required "from time to time [to] give to the Congress Information of the State of the Union, and recommend to their Consideration such Measures as he shall judge necessary." Over the years, the phrase "from time to time" has evolved to mean a constant stream of presidential messages, as well as the annual **State of the Union Address**. This power gives presidents a significant platform for presenting their legislative agenda to both Congress and the American people.

The president also has the power to convene Congress in extraordinary circumstances and recommend "such Measures as he shall judge necessary and expedient." Those suggestions can range from simple ideas presented in a letter or news conference to the proposals President George W. Bush made in his speech before a joint session of Congress following September 11, 2001.

Presidential Succession

Having decided how a president would enter office, the framers also decided how a president would leave. In addition to impeachment, reelection defeat, retirement, resignation, or death, the Constitution now contains two other ways to remove a president from office. Under the Twenty-Second Amendment, presidents must leave office after completion of two elected terms in office.

Under the Twenty-Fifth Amendment, presidents can also be forced from office temporarily if the vice president and a majority of either Congress or the president's own cabinet secretaries declares that the president is unable to discharge the powers and duties of the office. In such a case, the vice president becomes the acting president until the duly elected president returns to office. The amendment also allows a president to appoint a new vice president in the event of the vice president's own resignation, death, impeachment, or rise to the presidency.

Under the Constitution, the vice president is the next in line if the president leaves office prematurely. Once past the vice president, Congress is responsible for determining the line of succession. Under current law, the Speaker of the House of Representatives would

State of the Union Address
The president's annual statement to Congress and the nation.

be next in line, followed by the Senate president pro tempore, the secretary of state, secretary of the treasury, secretary of defense, and on down through the list of 15 cabinet secretaries by the date each department was established. The framers gave Congress exclusive power to remove the president through the **impeachment** process. Under the process, the House drafts articles of impeachment that charge the president with treason, bribery, or other high crimes and misdemeanors. If the articles are approved by a majority vote, the Chief Justice of the Supreme Court oversees a trial before the entire Senate. If convicted by a two-thirds vote of the Senate, the president is removed immediately from office.

The impeachment process has been used only twice in history, first in 1868 against Andrew Johnson and second in 1998 against Bill Clinton. Both Senate trials resulted in acquittals. Richard Nixon resigned from office in 1974 before the House could finish drafting the articles of impeachment regarding his role in the Watergate cover-up. Nixon almost certainly would have been both impeached and convicted had he stayed in office.

CONTROVERSIES IN PRESIDENTIAL POWER

The Constitution is not always clear on which branch of government has what power, leading to a system of what political scientists often call separate institutions sharing power. Many of the ambiguities have provoked intense controversy in recent decades as Congress and the courts have tried to determine whether presidents actually have the powers they sometimes assert, particularly during periods of internal crisis.

The War Power

The Constitution divides the war power between the president and Congress. Article I states that Congress has the power to declare war, but Article II gives the president the power to wage war as commander in chief. The framers recognized that declaring war was both one of the most important powers of government and one of the most easily abused. Writing as a young member of Congress, Abraham Lincoln expressed the founders' intent as follows:

> The provision of the Constitution giving the war-making power to Congress was dictated, as I understand it, by the following reasons. Kings had always been involving and impoverishing their people in wars, pretending generally, if not always, that the good of the people was the object. This our convention understood to be the most oppressive of all kingly oppressions, and they resolved to so frame the Constitution that no one man should hold the power of bringing this oppression upon us.[5]

Over the past half century, U.S. presidents have ordered troops into battle in Korea, Vietnam, Grenada, Panama, Iraq (twice), Kosovo, and Afghanistan, all without asking Congress for a formal declaration of war. If they ask for congressional approval at all, they usually seek broad resolutions of support.

In 2002, for example, Bush merely asked Congress to give him authority to deploy U.S. forces as "he determines to be necessary and appropriate" to defend national security against the threat posed by Iraq. Even as he made the request, the White House also argued that the president already had the authority to act with or without congressional approval.[6]

Presidents defend such actions by arguing that they have better information, much of it secret, than Congress. They also argue that presidents need the flexibility and secrecy to respond quickly to military threats to the nation's security interests. One State Department official described the president's warmaking authority as follows: "The Constitution leaves to the President the judgment to determine whether the circumstances of a particular armed attack are so urgent and the potential consequences so threatening to the security of the U.S. that he should act without formally consulting the Congress."[7]

Presidents and some scholars also blame Congress for abdicating its constitutional authority to the presidency. Constitutional scholar Louis Fisher holds that Congress has repeatedly given up its fundamental war powers to the president. The framers knew what monarchy looked like and rejected it, writes Fisher. "Yet especially in matters of the

impeachment
Formal accusation against the president or other public official, the first step in removal from office.

war power, the United States is recreating a system of monarchy while it professes to champion democracy and the role of law abroad."[8] Fisher calls on members of Congress to reeducate themselves on their constitutional prerogatives.

Congress tried to reassert its role and authority in the use of military force at the end of the Vietnam War. In 1973, Congress enacted the War Power Resolution over Richard Nixon's veto. The law, which is still in place, declares that a president can commit the armed forces of the United States only (1) after a declaration of war by Congress, (2) by specific statutory authorization, or (3) in a national emergency created by an attack on the United States or its armed forces. After committing the armed forces under the third circumstance, the president is required to report to Congress within 48 hours. Unless Congress declares war, the troop commitment must be ended within 60 days.

This resolution signaled a new determination by Congress to take its prerogatives seriously, yet presidents have generally ignored it. And many leading scholars now believe that this earnest and well-intentioned effort by Congress to reclaim its proper role actually gave away more authority than previous practices had already done. They say it was ill conceived and badly written, full of tortured ambiguity and self-contradiction. As one critic has written, "The statute further subordinates Congress to presidential war initiatives and should be repealed in its entirety."[9]

Most observers believe the United States is best served when both president and Congress are fully engaged partners in foreign and defense policy making. Congressman Lee Hamilton sums up the virtues of joint action by these rival branches: "I believe that a partnership, characterized by creative tension between the president and the Congress, produces a foreign policy that better serves the American national interest—and better reflects the values of the American people—than policy produced by the president alone."[10]

Executive Privilege

The Constitution does not give presidents the explicit power to withhold information from Congress or the public. However, courts have recognized that presidents have the power, or **executive privilege**, to keep secrets, especially if doing so is essential to protect jeopardized national security.

Some experts argue that executive privilege has no constitutional basis.[11] Yet presidents have withheld documents from Congress at least as far back as 1792, when President George Washington temporarily refused to share sensitive documents with a House committee studying an Indian massacre of federal troops. Although he later shared the information with Congress, Washington set the precedent for the use of executive privilege. Thomas Jefferson and the primary author of the Constitution, James Madison, also withheld information during their presidencies.

Most scholars, the courts, and even members of Congress agree that a president does have the implicit, if not constitutionally explicit, right to withhold information that could harm national security. Presidents must keep secrets, and they often fight hard to do so. However, executive privilege cannot be asserted in either congressional or judicial proceedings when the issue is basically one of refusing to cooperate in investigations of personal wrongdoing.

Although the formal term "executive privilege" was first used in the 1950s during the Eisenhower administration, Richard Nixon created the controversy over the term.[12] In an effort to hide his own role in the Watergate scandal, President Nixon refused to release secret tapes of the Oval Office meetings that followed the failed burglary of Democratic party headquarters in the Watergate building. He and his lawyers went so far as to claim that the decision to invoke executive privilege was not subject to review by Congress or the courts.

In its complicated decision, the Supreme Court acknowledged for the first time that presidents do indeed have the power to claim executive privilege if the release of certain information would be damaging to the nation's security interests. At the same time, the Court held that such claims are not exempt from review by the courts, and that national security was not threatened in the Watergate case. And so the Court ordered that Nixon had to yield his tapes, effectively dooming his presidency.[13]

Twenty-five years later, Congress asked the Bush administration to disclose the names of energy industry executives who had met with Vice President Dick Cheney's

executive privilege
The right to keep executive communications confidential, especially if they relate to national security.

2001 energy task force. The White House refused, arguing that Congress has no constitutional right to investigate the process by which the president or his advisers make decisions about public issues. Although the White House never formally invoked executive privilege in the case, the refusal was clearly modeled on the notion that presidents have the right to keep secrets. Congress eventually sued Cheney for the information, but dropped the case in 2003 after losing the first round in a federal district court.

The president's right to keep secrets will be revisited in each administration and tested by presidents and by the legislative branch. On occasion, courts will try to settle the ongoing dispute about the limits and conditions under which a president can invoke this well-established, if sometimes abused, presidential practice.

Executive Orders

Presidents execute the laws and direct the federal bureaucracy in part through **executive orders**, which are formal directives to departments and agencies that are just as strong as laws and can be challenged in the courts.

Although executive orders are not mentioned in the Constitution, they are considered essential to the faithful execution of the laws. According to past Supreme Court decisions, executive orders are generally accepted as the supreme law of the land unless they are in conflict with the Constitution or a federal law.

Beginning with George Washington, presidents have issued more than 13,000 executive orders. These orders have been used to declare American neutrality in the war between France and England (1793), to intern Japanese Americans during World War II, and to protect large tracts of federal land as "national monuments" in Arizona, Colorado, Oregon, Utah, and Washington in the Clinton Administration. President George W. Bush has been just as active as recent presidents in using executive orders to manage government. He issued an order in October 2001 to create a White House Office of Homeland Security to coordinate the federal government's efforts to protect its borders, another in January 2003 to create a White House Council on Service and Civic Participation to encourage more Americans to volunteer, and still another in February 2004 to create a commission to investigate why the United States had been so wrong regarding Iraq's weapons of mass destruction. In his first four years Bush issued roughly 40 orders per year.[14]

The Budget and Spending Power

Battles over budgets and spending have been at the heart of national politics since the beginning of the Republic. The Constitution explicitly gives Congress the power to appropriate money; presidents are charged with implementing and administering the spending.

Congress dominated the budget-making process until 1921, when it approved the Budget and Accounting Act. That law required the president to submit annual budgets to Congress, and it established the Bureau of the Budget, which in 1970 became the Office of Management and Budget. Although the 1921 act also created the General Accounting Office as an auditing and oversight arm of Congress, presidents have played an increasingly powerful role in shaping the federal budget.

President Nixon, however, overplayed his hand when his White House developed legal theories that justified a bold change in the traditional definition of **impoundment**. Under the traditional definition, presidents were allowed to change the purpose of a spending bill to accommodate emergencies such as war or international crisis. Under the Nixon definition, impoundment was broadened to allow changes in a spending bill based on the president's ideology. Thus, if the president did not want appropriated funds to be spent for purposes he did not like, he could impound, or withhold, the money. In 1974, Congress approved the Congressional Budget and Impoundment Control Act, which sharply curtailed the president's use of impoundment. Enacted over Nixon's veto, the law gave Congress new powers to control its own budget process, created the Congressional Budget Office (CBO) to give the institution its own sources of economic and spending forecasts, and required the president to submit detailed requests to Congress for any proposed *recission* (cancellation) of congressional appropriations.

executive orders
A formal order issued by the president to direct action by the federal bureaucracy.

impoundment
A decision by the president not to spend money appropriated by Congress, now prohibited under federal law.

Every budget cycle witnesses a new round of clashes between the branches. In recent years, Congress has almost always failed to pass all of the appropriations bills by the beginning of the fiscal year. Instead, the two branches have relied on *continuing resolutions,* proclamations extending the authority for federal spending a few days, weeks, or months.

In an effort to control its own tendency to overspend, Congress in 1996 voted to give the president greater budget power through the **line item veto**. Presidents were allowed to strike out specific sections of an appropriations bill while signing the rest into law. Although many governors have the line item veto, the Supreme Court decided that the law had disturbed the "finely wrought" procedure for making the laws, and declared it unconstitutional in a 6 to 3 vote. If Congress wanted a new procedure for making the laws, Justice John Paul Stevens wrote for the majority, it would have to pursue a constitutional amendment.[15]

EVOLUTION OF THE PRESIDENCY

By and large, the history of presidential power is one of steady, if uneven, growth. Of the individuals who have filled the office, about one-third have enlarged its powers. Andrew Jackson, Abraham Lincoln, and both Roosevelts, for example, redefined both the institution and many of its powers by the way they set priorities and responded to crises.

Nevertheless, today's presidency reflects precedents established by the nation's very first chief executive, George Washington. The framers could not have anticipated the kinds of foreign and domestic threats that now preoccupy the office, but they would recognize the importance of the presidency in protecting the nation in times of trouble.

The First Presidency

The framers designed the presidency hoping that George Washington would be the first to occupy the post. Washington commanded the public's trust and respect and was unanimously elected as the first president of the new Republic in 1789. He understood that the people needed to have confidence in their fledgling government, a sense of continuity with the past, and a time of calm and stability free of emergencies and crises. He also knew that the new nation faced both domestic and foreign threats to its future.

Washington's presidency set important precedents for the future, not the least of which was how the president would be addressed in public. Vice President John Adams argued that the president should be called "His Highness the President of the United States and protector of Their Liberties," a title the popularly elected House immediately rejected. The president of the United States would be called "the President of the United States."[16]

Washington's presidency also produced a model against which to measure future presidents. Not only did he establish the legitimacy and basic authority of the office, Washington negotiated the new government's first treaty, appointed its first judges and department heads, received its first foreign ambassadors, vetoed its first legislation, and signed its first laws, thereby demonstrating just how future presidents should execute and influence the laws.

Washington also established a host of lesser precedents for running the presidency that still hold today. He started by assembling the first White House staff. It was hardly large, composed of just two clerks, but it was an office nonetheless. Indeed, it was so small that Washington paid for staff and office expenses from his own pocket. Washington also appointed the first department secretaries, appointing Thomas Jefferson as secretary of state and Alexander Hamilton as secretary of the treasury.

Washington may have set his most important precedent in establishing the president's sole authority for supervising the executive branch. He was absolutely clear about the division of executive and legislative powers. Congress could appropriate money, confirm appointees, conduct oversight hearings, and always change the laws, but it could not run the departments. That was to be the president's job.

Washington's final contribution to the presidency involved his retirement after serving two terms. Although he would have been easily reelected to a third term, Washington believed that two terms were enough and returned to his Mount Vernon estate in

line item veto
Presidential power to strike, or remove, specific items from a spending bill without vetoing the entire package, declared unconstitutional by the Supreme Court.

1796. It was a precedent that held until Roosevelt's four terms, and was finally enshrined in constitutional language under the Twenty-Second Amendment.

The First Modern Presidency

Designed in part to check what the founders thought would be a more powerful Congress, the presidency has evolved over the past two hundred years into a powerful institution in its own right. Thomas Jefferson, Abraham Lincoln, and Theodore and Franklin Roosevelt all extended the president's authority to meet foreign and domestic threats through the use of inherent powers.

However, the expansion of the presidency has involved more than inherent powers. It has also reflected a growing government role in regulating the U.S. economy and protecting national interests abroad, which has increased the size and mission of government, which in turn has increased the demand for presidential leadership.

Although the modern presidency was not formed by any single president, most historians and political scientists agree that Franklin Roosevelt was the first president to exploit the institution's inherent and enumerated powers to their fullest impact. Although conservatives do not always endorse the use of these powers to expand the federal bureaucracy, they agree with liberals that Roosevelt left an indelible mark on the institution of the presidency itself.

Over his 12 years in office, Roosevelt created an extraordinary record of achievement. He expanded the role of the president as commander, diplomat, and administrator in chief, while dominating Congress in both shaping and making the laws. Inaugurated for the first of four terms at the height of the nation's deepest economic crisis, Roosevelt's first one hundred days in office in 1933 still stand as the most significant moment of presidential leadership in modern history. Most of his New Deal agenda for helping working and poor Americans is still on the statute books today, including Social Security for the aged, unemployment insurance and a guaranteed minimum wage for workers, banking and stock market regulation for investors, price supports for farmers, and a host of federal agencies that continue to deliver everything from electric power to schoolbooks.

Roosevelt clearly moved the presidency to the center of the legislative process. He created a new clearance process for sending specific legislative proposals to Congress, and used the State of the Union to focus the nation's attention on a specific list of presidential priorities. Although previous presidents had expressed their opinions about pending legislation, Roosevelt created new lobbying techniques that are still used to this day, the most notable of which involved the use of media to build public support for his program.

Roosevelt's impact extended well beyond the legislative agenda, however. He also exploited the powers of the presidency to build a highly personal relationship with the American public, using his "fireside chats" on radio to calm the public during the darkest days of the economic depression, while calling the nation to action during the early days of World War II. In doing so, he became the nation's communicator-in-chief, starting each broadcast with the simple phrase "My friends."

Roosevelt also changed the president's relationship with the federal bureaucracy, which grew from 600,000 employees before the New Deal to well over 1 million just before World War II. Not only did the New Deal produce a host of new federal agencies, it also demanded a larger White House staff to oversee the implementation of the laws. By 1937, Roosevelt's small White House staff was so overwhelmed that a national study group opened a report on the need for a stronger White House staff with the words: "The President needs help."

The Presidency Today

The formal powers the U.S. Constitution vests in a president have not been changed for more than 200 years, but the influence of modern presidents is considerably greater today than it has ever been, particularly at this moment in world history.

But even before September 11, several factors had strengthened the presidency. The danger of war and the destructive potential of new weaponry plainly increased the president's influence. The cold war—with its enormous standing armies, nuclear weapons, and widespread intelligence and alliance operations—invited presidential leadership in national security matters.

The end of the cold war in 1989 did not reduce the need for presidential leadership, however. As the 2003 Iraq War and continuing unrest in the Middle East show, the world is just as dangerous as it was at the height of the cold war—perhaps even more so. As weapons of mass destruction become more easily available, the president's role in protecting the nation from terrorism has become more pronounced.

Increased federal involvement in economic and social issues and the rise of complex public issues such as genetic engineering, global warming, and international terrorism have all enhanced public demands for strong presidential leadership. Problems not easily delegated to any one department often get pulled into the White House. When new programs involve several federal agencies, someone near the president is often asked to reconcile conflicts and set a consistent policy. White House aides, with some justification, claim that the presidency is the only place in government where it is possible to establish and coordinate national priorities. Presidents set up central review and coordination units that help formulate new policies, settle jurisdictional disputes among departments, and provide access for the well-organized interest groups that want their views to be given weight in decision making.

Nevertheless, some experts believe that presidential influence has declined in recent years, in part because of political scandals such as Watergate (Nixon), Iran-Contra (Reagan), and Whitewater and Monica Lewinsky (Clinton). Richard Nixon's resignation clearly diminished public respect for the presidency, Bill Clinton's impeachment clearly distracted the nation from more pressing problems such as the rising tide of anti-American sentiment in the Middle East, and the controversy over the 2000 election raised questions about the legitimacy of the electoral process.

MANAGING THE PRESIDENCY

Without help, presidents could not manage crises, build morale, set priorities and agendas, build legislative and political coalitions, mold public opinion, lead their parties, and otherwise take care that the laws are faithfully executed. Although some of that help

President George W. Bush and former Presidents Bill Clinton, George Bush, Jimmy Carter, and Gerald Ford, along with their wives, attending the state funeral for former President Ronald Reagan. Also pictured here are Vice President Dick Cheney and his wife.

comes from their *inner circle,* which is composed of their closest advisers including the first lady, presidents could not do their job without a vast array of support that extends well beyond 1600 Pennsylvania Avenue to include the executive branch as a whole.

The White House Staff

Presidents have come to rely heavily on their personal staffs. Nowhere else—not in Congress, not in the cabinet, not in the party—can presidents find the loyalty and single-mindedness that often develops among their closest White House aides.[17] Cabinet heads are often perceived as staunch advocates of their departments and the constituencies their departments serve and so cannot be assumed to give objective advice. By contrast, presidents presume that their aides will provide them with sound and unbiased policy guidance. But there are sometimes substantial costs to listening only to one's closest associates.

THE WHITE HOUSE ORGANIZATION   The White House staff grew steadily from the early 1900s through the early 1990s, then stabilized at roughly 400 today. The staff is headed by the **chief of staff**, who is considered the president's most loyal assistant. The White House staff also includes the president's chief lawyer, speechwriters, legislative liaison staff, and press secretary. The chief of staff supervises all other White House staff and is considered a member of the president's inner circle.

Most of these advisers have offices in the West Wing of the White House or the Old Executive Office Building. Once used to house all the federal departments in the early 1800s, the Old Executive Office Building now holds mostly presidential and vice presidential staff.

White House staff members sometimes insist that they are simply the eyes and ears of the president, that they make few important decisions, and that they never intrude between the chief executive and the heads of departments. But the inevitable emergence of a few strong White House advisers such as Karl Rove and Karen Hughes in the Bush White House renders this traditional picture inaccurate.[18]

RUNNING THE WHITE HOUSE   Over the past three decades, presidents have used three very different models for running the White House staff: competitive, collegial, and hierarchical. Among modern presidents, Franklin Roosevelt and Lyndon Johnson both used the competitive approach, a "survival of the fittest" situation in which the president allows aides to fight each other for access to the Oval Office. Johnson sometimes gave different staffers the same assignment, hoping that the competition would produce a better final decision.

In contrast, John Kennedy, Jimmy Carter, and Bill Clinton all used the collegial approach, in which presidents encourage aides to work together toward a common position. It is a much friendlier way to work than the competitive approach but may have the serious drawback of producing what some social psychologists call *groupthink.* Groupthink is the tendency of small groups to stifle dissent in the search for common ground.[19]

Finally, Dwight Eisenhower, Richard Nixon, Ronald Reagan, and George H. W. Bush all used the hierarchical model, in which the president establishes tight control over who does what in making decisions. A hierarchy is a form of organization that looks very much like a pyramid: one leader at the top, two right underneath, three or more right underneath those two, and so on down the organization. The chief advantage of a hierarchy is that it reduces the number of people the leader has to deal with—the tighter the hierarchy, the fewer the contacts. Most hierarchies depend on a "gatekeeper" near the very top, usually the chief of staff, to enforce tight control over access to the leaders.

George W. Bush has used a hierarchical approach in organizing the White House. He has used clear lines of authority to minimize chaos and has expected his staff to be loyal above all else. Most decisions have been made through tightly controlled discussions led by the president, his top staff aides, or Vice President Cheney.

The Executive Office of the President

Created in 1939, the **Executive Office of the President** consists of the Office of Management and Budget, the Council of Economic Advisers, and several other staff units (see Figure 12–1). It also contains the White House staff.

chief of staff
The head of the White House staff.

Executive Office of the President
The cluster of presidential staff agencies that help the president carry out his responsibilities. Currently the office includes the Office of Management and Budget, the Council of Economic Advisers, and several other units.

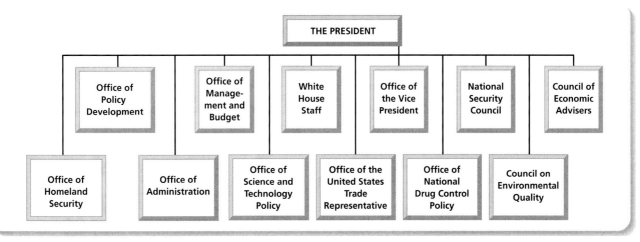

FIGURE 12–1 Executive Office of the President.
Source: *United States Government Manual, 2000–2001* (Government Printing Office, 2000), p. 87.

The **Office of Management and Budget (OMB)** is the central presidential staff agency. Its director advises the president in detail about the hundreds of government agencies—how much money they should be allotted in the budget and what kind of job they are doing. OMB seeks to improve the planning, management, and statistical work of the agencies. It makes a special effort to see that each agency conforms to presidential policies in its dealings with Congress; each agency has to clear its policy recommendations to Congress through OMB first.[20]

Through the long budget-preparation process, presidents use OMB as a way of conserving and centralizing their own influence. A budget is more than just a financial plan because it reflects power struggles and indicates national priorities (and wishful thinking). To the president, the budget is a means of control over administrators who may be trying to join ranks with other politicians or interest groups to thwart presidential priorities.

The Cabinet

It is hard to find a more unusual institution than the president's **cabinet**. The cabinet is not specifically mentioned in the Constitution, yet since George Washington's administration, every president has had one. Washington's consisted of his secretaries of state, treasury, and war, plus his attorney general.

SELECTING THE CABINET Selecting the cabinet today is the first major job for the president-elect. The cabinet consists of the president, the vice president, the heads of the 15 executive departments, and a few others a president considers cabinet-level officials. The cabinet has always been a loosely designated body, and it is not always clear who belongs in it. In recent years, certain executive branch administrators and White House counselors have been accorded cabinet rank. Nineteen officials have had cabinet status in the George W. Bush administration, including the 15 cabinet secretaries, the vice president, the chief of staff, and the director of Homeland Security.

CABINET GOVERNMENT Cabinet government is generally defined as a system of advice in which the voice of individual cabinet members is of major importance. As such, cabinet government does not exist in the United States.[21] In fact, an American president is not required by the Constitution to form a cabinet or to hold regular meetings. Presidents John Kennedy, Lyndon Johnson, and Richard Nixon all preferred small conferences with individuals specifically involved in a problem and rarely held cabinet meetings. Kennedy saw no reason, for example, to discuss Defense Department matters with his secretaries of agriculture and labor, and he thought cabinet meetings wasted valuable time. Both Jimmy Carter and Ronald Reagan tried to revive the cabinet, and both met often with their cabinets during their first two years. But the longer they remained in office, the less frequently they met with their cabinets as a whole.

Office of Management and Budget (OMB)
Presidential staff agency that serves as a clearinghouse for budgetary requests and management improvements for government agencies.

cabinet
Advisory council for the president, consisting of the heads of the executive departments, the vice president, and a few other officials selected by the president.

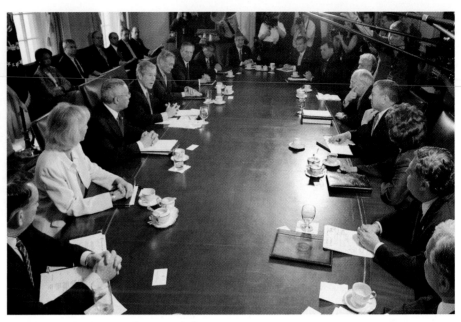

President George W. Bush with his cabinet.

CHANGING FACE OF AMERICAN POLITICS

PRESIDENTIAL APPOINTEES

Presidents Bill Clinton and George W. Bush both promised to appoint administrations that were as diverse as the country. Although both presidents came surprisingly close on race, neither approached the 50 percent mark on gender. According to detailed analysis of every executive branch appointee nominated for Senate confirmation in the first year of the first term of both administrations, 30 percent of the appointees in Clinton's first year were women, compared to just 23 percent in Bush's first year.

Although the numbers seem disappointing given the changing face of the federal bureaucracy discussed in the next chapter, both administrations did much better than their predecessors—less than 15 percent of the appointees in Carter's first year (1977) were women, compared to just 8 percent in Reagan's first year (1981).* And the fact that both Clinton and Bush were both able to recruit many women and minority appointees at lower levels suggests that future administrations will be even more successful. Past research shows that the higher-level jobs almost always go to appointees with prior appointee service at lower levels. By increasing the numbers of women and minorities in the pipeline, the Clinton and Bush administrations increased the odds that there will be more women and minority candidates

for the top jobs for future Democratic and Republican administrations alike.

*The Carter and Reagan numbers come from Gary King and Lynn Ragsdale, *The Elusive Executive: Discovering Elusive Statistical Patterns in the Presidency* (CQ Press, 1988), pp. 236–237.

	Clinton Administration, 1993	Bush Administration, 2001
Gender		
Women	30%	23%
Men	70	77
Race		
African American	14%	9%
Hispanic	6	8
Asian American	3	3
White	77	80

Source: Data collected by the Presidential Appointee Initiative, analysis by authors.

Bill Clinton, like those he followed, seldom called for full cabinet meetings, holding just 18 such meetings in his first term and even fewer during his second.[22] George W. Bush has also shown limited interest in full cabinet meetings, preferring to assemble small groups of cabinet members on an as-needed basis.

Presidential advisers and the heads of various White House–based cabinet-level councils, such as the National Security Council and the Office of Management and Budget, have gained equal or even superior status to many cabinet secretaries. This shift occurred in part because these advisers are physically located in or next door to the White House (see Figure 12–2). Further, presidents are aware that some cabinet members adopt narrow "advocate" views: the Agriculture Department secretary is a strong advocate for farmers; the Housing and Urban Development Department secretary is an ambassador for the housing industry and, to some extent, also for big city mayors; and so on through much of the cabinet, especially in departments occupied primarily with domestic policy matters.

CABINET DIFFERENCES   As the next chapter will discuss in more detail, cabinet departments vary by the number of employees (the Department of Defense has nearly a million employees, while the Department of Education has barely 5,000) and size of budget (the Department of Health and Human Services had a budget of well over $575 billion in 2005, while the Department of State barely hit $10 billion).

The departments also vary in their influence with the White House. Presidents tend to pay the greatest attention to the oldest and most visible of the departments: Defense, Justice, State, and Treasury. These four departments are often called the *inner cabinet* because they are so important to the president's foreign and domestic success. The economy (Treasury), crime (Justice), and international affairs (State and Defense) are rarely far from the top of the president's list of policy concerns. Presidents almost always appoint very close allies to the inner cabinet posts, even if those allies do not always have the best credentials for the jobs.

The other departments are generally called the *outer cabinet,* largely because they are more distant from the day-to-day worries that occupy the president and White House staff. The Department of Veterans Affairs, for example, is rarely in the headlines, even though its 250,000 full- and part-time employees make it the second-largest department in the federal bureaucracy.

The Vice Presidency

Despite Vice President Dick Cheney's visible role today, the vice presidency has not always been an important job. For most of American history, the vice president was at best seen as an insignificant officer and at worst a political rival who sometimes connived

In response to the terrorist attacks on September 11, 2001, President Bush used his presidential authority to appoint former Pennsylvania Governor Tom Ridge the director of Homeland Security. Ridge was later appointed as the first secretary of the Department of Homeland Security. In November 2004, Ridge announced that he would not continue as secretary of the Department of Homeland Security during President Bush's second term.

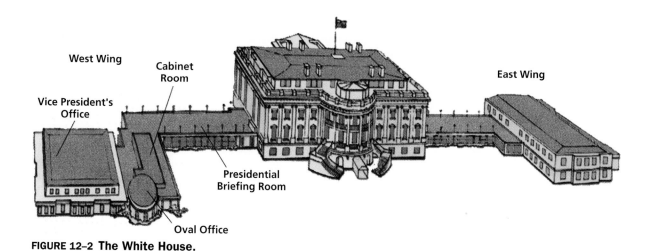

FIGURE 12–2 The White House.

While the vice president's primary responsibility is to take the oath of office should the president become unable to carry out his or her term, some vice presidents have wielded more power and influence than others.

against the president. The office was often dismissed as a joke. One reason for the vice president's posture as an outsider was that presidential nominees usually chose running mates who were geographically, ideologically, demographically, and in other ways likely to "balance the ticket."

No matter how influential they become, vice presidents have only one major responsibility, to be ready to take the oath of office in case the president cannot. Vice presidents are not mere replacement parts, however. President Jimmy Carter included Walter Mondale in the daily processes of decision making in the White House; President Clinton used Al Gore as an important adviser and confidant on domestic as well as foreign policy matters and key appointments. Even when recent presidents have mostly ignored their vice presidents, as the first President Bush did with his vice president, Dan Quayle, vice presidents enter office with substantial access, including an office just down the hall from the president in the West Wing of the White House, a substantial staff of their own, and access to all of the information flowing into the Oval Office.

Vice President Dick Cheney had more than just access to the second President Bush, however. He also had considerable influence. As a former member of Congress and secretary of defense during the first Bush administration, Cheney brought significant credibility to the Bush–Cheney ticket, reassuring voters that the younger Bush was ready for the presidency, and was a trusted advisor to the Bush family. It is no surprise, therefore, that Cheney soon became one of the most influential, visible, and popular vice presidents in history.

But Cheney also became one of the administration's strongest advocates of war with Iraq. Although he shared the president's high public approval immediately after the war began, his approval fell much faster than the president's as the war lingered on and the search for weapons of mass destruction turned futile. By February 2004, Americans were evenly divided on whether Cheney should even remain on the presidential ticket—even 28 percent of Republicans said the president should make a change.[23] Cheney remained highly popular among social conservatives, however, and was reelected in November 2004.

Although the sorts of tensions between president and vice president that existed in the past rarely affected Clinton and Gore or Bush and Cheney, tension between a president and a vice president is natural. After all, except for the vice president, everybody who works closely with a president can be fired. It is almost certain that vice presidents will continue to have an undefined ad hoc set of assignments, subject more to the goodwill and mood of the president than to any fixed description.[24]

The First Lady

The president's inner circle of close advisers has always included the first lady. Eleanor Roosevelt was particularly visible as an advocate for a strong national government during the economic depression of the 1930s. In recent decades, however, the first lady has steadily become more prominent as a policy adviser to the president, in part because the media have become so aggressive in covering the White House. Lady Bird Johnson was a tireless and persuasive advocate for the beautification of America, Betty Ford for cancer research, Rosalyn Carter for the Equal Rights Amendment, Nancy Reagan for drug control, and Barbara Bush for literacy programs. Hillary Clinton clearly drew on these role models in setting her own White House course.

What made Hillary Clinton different from her predecessors was her highly visible role in actually shaping important presidential proposals. As head of the president's health care reform task force, she played a major role in designing a top legislative initiative and soon emerged as a key player on a host of other issues. She clearly had the experience and the credentials for the job: She attended Wellesley College, where she was elected president of the student body; graduated first in her class at Yale Law School, just ahead of the future president; and was headed for a career in law and public service long before her husband entered public life.

PEOPLE & POLITICS *Making a Difference* ★★★

CONDOLEEZZA RICE

As the president's national security advisor, Condoleezza Rice was a natural for one of the toughest foreign policy jobs in Washington. The national security advisors sit only a few doors away from the president and are always on call during crises. They must also resolve the often public disputes among the president's foreign policy team, which can involve a host of political heavyweights that include the vice president; the secretaries of commerce, defense, homeland security, state, and treasury; the attorney general; the director of Central Intelligence; the U.S. trade representative; and senior military officers.

Rice had a nearly perfect résumé for the job. She earned her bachelor's degree in political science from the University of Denver at 19 and received her Ph.D. from the Graduate School of International Studies at Denver seven years later. Already a full professor at Stanford University, she joined the first Bush administration in 1989 as the director, then senior director, of the Soviet and East European desk at the National Security Council, then returned to Stanford as provost, the second most im-

portant administrative post at the university.

That resume would have been more than enough to qualify her for almost any foreign policy job in the second Bush administration. She earned the White House job by almost never leaving the president's side as he crisscrossed the nation during the 2000 presidential campaign. By paying her dues on the campaign trail, she earned the president's trust. During the hours and days after the terrorist attacks, President Bush often asked her to remain silent at key meetings so she could later give her private reading on the right course of action. Her service in this top job has not been without controversy. She came under fire for endorsing the claim that Saddam Hussein had tried to buy the ingredients for nuclear weapons, even though that claim had been discredited by the Central Intelligence Agency well before the president used it as part of his case for war. But the president never wavered from her side.

All this is by way of noting that her appointment had absolutely nothing to do with her being the first woman to serve as national security advisor. Nor did it

have anything to do with the fact that she is African American; the granddaughter of an Alabama sharecropper; that she was born in 1954, the year that the Supreme Court ruled that racial segregation of public schools was unconstitutional; that a nursery-school classmate was one of four girls killed by white extremists in a 1963 Birmingham church bombing; or that she has said she had to be "twice as good" to get ahead. Condoleezza Rice made it to the top by believing her parents when they told her that "you may not be able to have a hamburger at Woolworth's but you can be president of the United States."

Rice became secretary of state in 2005.

THE PRESIDENT'S JOB

Presidents are asked to perform roles not explicitly defined in the Constitution. Americans want the chief executive to be an international peacemaker as well as a national morale builder, a politician in chief as well as a commander in chief. They want the president to provide leadership on foreign, economic, and domestic policy. Americans also want presidents to be crisis managers and role models of a kind. They want them to be able to connect with ordinary Americans and be honest, yet be smarter, tougher, and more honest than the rest of us. (See Table 12–1 for what Americans say they care about most in picking a president.)

Presidents as Crisis Managers

The framers designed the president's job as commander in chief as a limited role. Congress, not the president, declares war, makes the rules for the army and navy, and controls the funding of wars. Yet the president is still in charge of the military as commander in chief.

The president's role is based on the principle of *civilian control over the military,* a central condition of a constitutional democracy.[25] Civilian control means that all soldiers

The first lady can be an important influence on a president. In recent decades, the first lady has evolved into a prominent policy adviser to the president as well as a champion of many important causes of her own choosing.

TABLE 12–1 WHAT AMERICANS WANT TO KNOW ABOUT THEIR CANDIDATES

Percentage of Americans who said it is very important to know the following about a presidential candidate:

	2000 Campaign	2004 Campaign
How well a candidate connects with average people	67%	71%
A candidate's voting record or policy positions he or she previously held	60	64
A candidate's reputation for honesty	84	88
A candidate's major campaign contributors	42	39
A candidate's military background	19	21
Whether a candidate is an active churchgoer	25	27

SOURCE: Pew Research Center for the People and the Press, "Democratic Primary Campaign Impresses Voters," February 19, 2004, p. 1.

and sailors, from the newest recruit to every general and admiral, take their orders from and owe their allegiance to the one person elected by all the people. The professional military, no matter what their own personal political views and values, take their military orders from the president and his chief civilian agent, the secretary of defense.

Presidents are expected to be crisis managers in the domestic sphere as well. Presidents or their surrogates in the cabinet are often the first on the scene in national disasters such as hurricanes and floods and are expected to play a significant role in reassuring the nation. In turn, the public often responds to presidential leadership with a temporary surge in support. These **rally points** are particularly strong when a military action, such as an invasion or a bombing, is both short and successful. Rally points do not necessarily last long, however. Although George W. Bush's ratings jumped dramatically following the capture of Saddam Hussein, they fell back quickly as questions emerged about the quality of the intelligence leading up to the war. (See Table 12–2 for examples of recent rally points.)

Not all rally points involve foreign crises, however. Clinton's approval rose after the Oklahoma City bombing in 1995 in large part because Americans turned to him for leadership in the crisis. Presidential approval can also rise during periods of great national pride. Reagan's public approval (and reelection chances) jumped during the 1984 Olympic Games as the United States won one gold medal after another, in part because the Soviet Union and its eastern European allies boycotted the event.

TABLE 12–2 RECENT RALLY POINTS

President and Event	*Approval Before*	*Approval After*	*Change in Approval*
George W. Bush			
Saddam Hussein's capture	50%	57%	+7%
Iraq War begins	55	67	+12
September 11 terrorist attacks	51	80	+29
Bill Clinton			
Oklahoma City bombing	46	51	+5
George H. W. Bush			
1991 Gulf War	59	79	+20

rally point
A rise in public approval of the president that follows a crisis as Americans "rally 'round the flag" and the chief executive.

Presidents as Morale Builders

As chief of state, the president must project a sense of national unity and authority as the country's chief ceremonial leader. The framers of the Constitution did not fully anticipate the symbolic and morale-building functions a president must perform. Certain magisterial functions, such as receiving ambassadors and granting pardons, were conferred. But over time, the presidency has acquired enormous symbolic significance.

Presidents are the nation's number one celebrities; almost anything they do is news. Presidents command attention merely by jogging, fishing, golfing, or going to church. By their actions, presidents can arouse a sense of hope or despair, honor or dishonor.

The morale-building job of the president involves much more than just ceremonial cheerleading or quasi-chaplain duties. Presidential leadership, at its finest, radiates national self-confidence and helps unlock the possibility for good that exists in the nation. Our best leaders have been able to provide this special and often intangible element. That is certainly what George W. Bush intended in the days and weeks that followed September 11, 2001. By his words and deeds, he sought to simultaneously calm the nation and warn the rest of the world that the United States would not tolerate further terrorist attacks.

Presidents as Agenda Setters

By custom and circumstance, presidents are now responsible for proposing initiatives in foreign policy and economic growth and stability. This was not always the case. But beginning with Woodrow Wilson, and especially since the New Deal, a president has been expected to propose reforms to ensure domestic progress. New ideas are seized on by a presidential candidate searching for campaign issues, and they are later refined and implemented by the executive office staff, by special presidential task forces, and by Congress.[26]

NATIONAL SECURITY POLICY   The framers foresaw a special need for speed and unity in dealing with other nations. As a result, presidents generally have more leeway in foreign policy and military affairs than they have in domestic matters. The Constitution vests in the president command of the two major instruments of foreign policy—the diplomatic corps and the armed services. It also gives the president responsibility for negotiating treaties and commitments with other nations, although the Senate must consent to treaty ratifications, and almost all international agreements require congressional action for their implementation.

Congress has granted presidents discretion in initiating foreign policies, for diplomacy frequently requires quick action. The Supreme Court has upheld strong presidential authority in this area. In *United States* v. *Curtiss-Wright* (1936), the Court referred to the "exclusive power of the president as the sole organ of the federal government in the field of international relations—a power which does not require as a basis for its exercise an act of Congress, but which, of course, like every other governmental power, must be exercised in subordination to the applicable provisions of the Constitution."[27] These are sweeping and much-debated words.[28] Still, a determined Congress that knows what it wants does not lack power in foreign relations. Congress must authorize and appropriate the funds that back up the president's policies abroad.

ECONOMIC POLICY   Ever since the New Deal, presidents have been expected to promote policies to keep unemployment low, fight inflation, keep taxes down, and promote economic growth and prosperity. The Constitution did not specify these duties for the executive, yet presidents know that when the nation is not prosperous and jobs are scarce, they may suffer the fate of Herbert Hoover, who was denounced for his inaction at the beginning of the Great Depression. The growth and complexity of economic problems since the Depression of the 1930s have placed more economic responsibility in the president's hands. The delicate balancing required to keep a modern economy operating means that presidents must make key fiscal and budgetary policy decisions.[29] The presidential elections in 1980 and 1992 turned largely on the economy, and the election of 2000 involved a debate about which candidate would be better able to keep the economic boom going. Although terrorism, social issues, and Iraq were top issues for Bush/Cheney supporters in 2004, economic issues were particularly inportant for Kerry/Edwards.

Although presidents sometimes get their economic advice elsewhere, their chief advisers on economic policy are the secretary of the treasury, the three members of the Council of Economic Advisers, and the director of the Office of Management and Budget. The chair of the Federal Reserve Board of Governors is also an influential, if independent, adviser on the economy.

DOMESTIC POLICY   Some experts believe that a leader is one who knows where the followers are. Abraham Lincoln did not invent the antislavery movement. John Kennedy and Lyndon Johnson did not begin the civil rights movement. Bill Clinton was not the first leader to notice the unfairness of health care and welfare policies, nor was George W. Bush the first to note the skyrocketing price of prescription drugs. But they all, in their respective times, became embroiled in these controversies, for a president cannot long ignore what divides or inspires a nation.

At the same time, presidents sometimes take highly unpopular positions for the good of the country. The vast majority of Americans opposed Harry Truman's decision to integrate the armed services, and many southerners bolted the Democratic party when Lyndon Johnson demanded action on civil rights. Similarly, many Americans opposed George W. Bush's 2001 decision to limit fetal stem-cell research, which he believed might increase abortion.

Presidents as Persuaders

Presidents must build political coalitions if they are to have any chance of winning passage of their legislative programs. As candidates, they make promises to the people and assemble an electoral coalition of supporters. To get things done and to get reelected, however, they must work with interest groups and people who have differing loyalties and responsibilities. Inevitably, presidents become embroiled in legislative, bureaucratic, and lobbying politics, and their approval ratings often suffer as a consequence.

Despite their formal powers, presidents spend most of their time *persuading* people. As Richard Neustadt argues, the power to persuade is the president's chief resource, and that power comes through bargaining.[30] Bargaining, in turn, comes primarily through getting others to believe it is in their self-interest to cooperate. Presidents and their aides spend a lot of time dispensing favors to various members of Congress from whom they are seeking votes and political support. Hence the skill of a president in communicating and winning others over is the necessary energizing factor in moving the institutions of the national government to action.

Presidents have been communicating with the public from the very beginning of the Republic, using press conferences, speeches, and public events to maintain contact with the country. Although much of the communication is designed to support other presidential roles, today's presidents are making more prime-time television appearances, giving more speeches, and spending more time outside of Washington in efforts to influence the country. According to political scientist Samuel Kernell, the number of major and minor presidential addresses has grown from just a dozen or so in the first three years of the Hoover administration (1929–1931) to well over 100 in the first three years of the Bush presidency almost 60 years later. The greatest growth came in the number of minor addresses before specialized audiences—trade associations, college graduations, advocacy groups.[31]

At the same time, presidents have been spending less time holding press conferences. Whereas Franklin Roosevelt averaged almost seven press conferences a month during his dozen years in office, Reagan, Bush, and Clinton averaged barely one a month. Presidents would much rather be interviewed by local reporters outside Washington than by members of the experienced White House press corps, much rather give exclusive interviews to a sympathetic interviewer than face a roomful of unpredictable reporters, and much rather use live satellite feeds to remote stations to get their message across than deal with the *Washington Post, New York Times*, or *Wall Street Journal*.

(Presidential press conferences are covered in more detail in Chapter 10.) This strategy is often labeled as "going public."

Going public clearly fits with changes in the electoral process. Presidents now have the staff, the technology, and the public opinion research to tell them how to target their message and the nearly instant media access to go public easily. And as elections have become more image-oriented and candidate-centered, presidents have the incentive to use these tools to operate a permanent White House campaign. Presidents are still welcome to bargain and persuade, to focus congressional attention and twist arms, but members of Congress may pay attention only when pressure is coming from the voters back home. (See Figure 12–3 for presidential approval trends over the past half century). Bush became the first incumbent in modern history to win reelection despite starting his campaign with an approval rating below 50 percent.

ELECTION 2004: AN ANALYSIS

George W. Bush started the 2004 campaign with a long list of liabilities. His public approval rating was falling; the economy was still sluggish; the war in Iraq was anything but the "mission accomplished" that the president had celebrated the previous May; and Democrats were well-funded, highly motivated, and still angry about the 2000 election, which Bush had won in the courts, not in the popular vote count.

Yet, Bush also had significant assets. He was a likable wartime president with a stubborn commitment to the war in Iraq. Bush also had all the perquisites of the presidency, including Air Force One, a powerful political machine, some of the cleverest political strategists in the country, and a plainspoken persistence that just might appeal to undecided voters. If Bush could get all of his supporters to the polls, shift the public's focus from the economy to terrorism, and win enough of the swing voters who had voted for Vice President Al Gore in 2000, he just might be able to win.

Bush also needed the right opponent. If Democrats nominated someone with just enough inconsistency in his record, just enough of a Boston accent in his voice, and just enough mistakes in his strategy, the president might be able to argue that he was the safer choice in an uncertain world. If Bush could make the 2004 election a referendum on his opponent, not on his record, he might erase the doubts about his own record on jobs, the war in Iraq, and health care.

The Results

Remarkably, Bush did all of the above and more. Despite pink slips for workers in "battleground" states such as Ohio and Pennsylvania, rising Medicare premiums for the elderly, worries about a draft for the young, and rising casualties and a prison-abuse scandal in Iraq, Bush won both the electoral and popular vote on Tuesday, November 2, 2004. At 10:00 a.m. on Wednesday morning, Senator John Kerry called to concede the election—"We cannot win the election," he would tell supporters who had waited all night at Boston's Faneuil Hall. With Bush's 286–252 electoral margin, and a 4-million popular-vote cushion, there would be no repeat of the agonizing recount that had paralyzed the country in 2000 (see Adam Nagourney, "Bush Celebrates Victory," The New York Times, November 4, 2004, p. A1).

Yet, if Bush's victory was firm, it was also surprisingly familiar. Although Bush earned 9 million more votes in 2004 than 2000, only three states actually switched sides: New Hampshire "flipped" from the Republican to the Democratic column, while Iowa and New Mexico flipped from the Democratic column to the Republican. The other 47 states remained exactly where they had been four years earlier, with the Republican "red" states concentrated in the South and Midwest and most of the Democratic "blue" states in the Northeast and on the West Coast.

BUSH V. KERRY		
	Bush	*Kerry*
Men	55	44
Women	48	51
18–29 years old	45	54
30–44 years old	53	46
45–59 years old	51	48
60 years old or over	54	46
White	58	41
Black	11	88
Hispanic/Latino	44	53
Asian	44	56
Republican	93	6
Independent	48	49
Democratic	11	89
White evangelical or born again Christian	78	21
Gay, lesbian, or bisexual	23	77

SOURCE: "Survey of Voters: Who They Were . . . ," The New York Times, Novemeber 4, 2004, p. P4.

Moreover, Bush and Kerry did well in 2004 exactly where Bush and Vice President Al Gore had done well in 2000. Bush ran ahead of Kerry among men, older Americans, whites, Republicans, and white born-again Christians; while Kerry ran ahead of Bush among women, younger Americans, minority voters, Democrats, and gays.

The obvious question is what changed. Simply put, how did George W. Bush win?

A first answer is that Bush's supporters were more committed than Kerry's, in part because the Bush campaign was able to rally religious conservatives who had stayed home in 2000. Anti-gay-marriage initiatives were on the ballot in eleven states, including Ohio, which some pundits argue brought large numbers of passionate conservatives to the polls.

However, Bush's winning margin did not come from these groups alone. Indeed, of the 9 million votes that Bush gained between 2000 and 2004, the largest share came from two groups that were distinctly non-evangelical and not opponents of gay marriage. His share of the vote among white women surged from 49 percent in 2000 to 55 percent in 2004, and among Hispanic/Latino voters from 36 percent to 44 percent (see table on page 330). Put together, the gains produced exactly 3.5 percent of the popular vote, or roughly the 4 million votes that gave Bush the deciding margin.

A second answer is that Bush was a much better candidate than John Kerry, which helps explain at least some of his surge. He was always judged the more likeable candidate—although voters had significant concerns about his policies, particularly his management of the economy and the war in Iraq, they saw him as more approachable. Kerry never fully connected with the public as an individual—he was generally viewed as distant, even snobbish.

It is no surprise, for example, that Bush ran well among voters who said they cared most about each candidate's religious faith—Bush won 91 percent of that group. But Bush also won 70 percent of those who wanted an honest, trustworthy president; 87 percent of those who wanted a strong leader; and 79 percent of those who wanted a president who takes a clear stand on issues. Although Kerry ran well among those who wanted a president that cares about people, his greatest strength came from those who wanted an intelligent leader who would bring change to the country.

A third answer is simply that Bush ran a better campaign. In spite of all the bad news coming into the campaign from Iraq, including the last-second revelation that the U.S. military had somehow misplaced almost 400 tons of dangerous explosives that Iraqi dictator Saddam Hussein had stockpiled just outside Baghdad, the Bush campaign kept Kerry on the defensive. Bush operatives were particularly effective in exploiting Kerry's own statements and creating an image of him as a "flip flopper" who could not be trusted to run the nation during war. As a Bush aide said of Kerry's oft-quoted statement that he voted for an $87-billion bill to arm the troops in Iraq just before he voted against it, "As soon as we saw it, we knew that was exactly what we wanted to say, but he said it for us. That's something he couldn't undo."

A fourth and final answer involves issues. When asked what issue most influenced their vote, 22 percent of Americans referred to moral issues such as abortion and gay marriage, another 20 percent said the economy and jobs, 19 percent said terrorism, 15 percent said the war in Iraq, and 8 percent said health care. Bush won 80 percent of the votes among those who focused on moral issues and 86 percent of the votes among those who focused on terrorism, while Kerry did exceptionally well among the rest.

A Mandate to Govern?

No matter how close the actual results, Bush began preparing for his second term as if he had won a sweeping mandate. The fact that Republicans picked up seats in the Senate and House gave him additional ammunition for the case. After all, this was the first time since 1924 that an incumbent president won reelection and gained seats in both chambers.

But claiming a mandate and having one are two different things. Second-term presidents have very little time to set the legislative agenda, in part because the modern

President John F. Kennedy understood the importance of direct communication with the American people and often addressed the public with television broadcasts.

campaign system forces candidates in both parties to start planning for the next election early. Because Bush refused to pick an heir-apparent as his vice presidential running mate, Republicans were already lining up for the 2008 election even before the 2004 election was over.

CONGRESS AND THE PRESIDENCY

Tensions between Congress and presidents go back to the origins of American government. Alexander Hamilton, General George Washington's chief aide, complained about the political stalemate that faced the the Continental Congress more than 200 years ago.

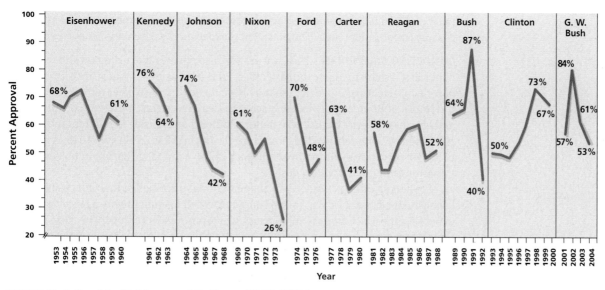

FIGURE 12–3 Presidential Approval Ratings, 1945–2004.
SOURCE: Gallup Organization, at www.gallup.com. Updated by the authors.

★ ★ YOU DECIDE

SHOULD PRESIDENTS BE LIMITED TO TWO TERMS IN OFFICE?

Before he left office, former President Ronald Reagan called for the repeal of the Twenty-Second Amendment to the Constitution, the one that limits a president to two terms. Why do you think he opposed the amendment? What additional reasons could be put forth to persuade people to repeal this relatively new (1951) provision in the Constitution? What are the best reasons for retaining the Twenty-Second Amendment?

Yet it was the intention of the framers of the U.S. Constitution to create a government of sharply limited powers and separated institutions that would both share and compete for power. The framers saw the separation of powers not necessarily as a weakness but as a source of strength and especially as a way to ensure deliberation and to prevent tyranny.

The Constitutional Framework

Article I of the Constitution grants Congress "all legislative Powers" but limits those powers to those "herein granted." It then sets forth in some detail the powers vested in Congress. In contrast, Article II vests in the president "the executive Power" without limiting it to such powers as are "herein granted" and then proceeds to describe those powers in very general terms.

Some scholars and most presidents have argued that Article II gives each president a general and undefined power to act to promote the well-being of the United States, subject only to precise constitutional limits. Therefore, they contend, a president is *not* limited to the specific powers spelled out in the Constitution, as Congress is, but has all the executive powers of the United States. Other scholars and many members of Congress contend that the president either has no such inherent power or has it only in extraordinary circumstances.[32]

Whatever the intent of the Constitution, the president has often exercised powers not expressly granted by it. These powers have been given a variety of names: *implied, inherent,* or *emergency powers.* For example, Bill Clinton found a way to lend Mexico billions of dollars in 1995 to stabilize its currency, even though Congress had essentially refused to do so. Similarly, George W. Bush ordered the armed services to start preparing for the war in Iraq well ahead of congressional authorization. Actions like these prompt many in Congress to criticize presidents, even if they believe that in certain emergencies a president must act promptly without clear constitutional or statutory support.

COMPETING CONSTITUENCIES   The Constitution also guarantees that Congress and the president will represent different constituencies. Members of Congress represent state and local districts, and hence they reflect specific geographic, ethnic, and economic interests. James Madison and other framers of the Constitution anticipated that legislators would often be pressured by local and state interests to adopt a narrow or parochial view, as opposed to a national view, on certain policy issues, and presidents and their aides often think Madison was right. Members of Congress, of course, see sensitivity to state and local concerns as essential to their job as representatives and to their prospects for reelection. As a result, members of Congress—even those from the president's own party and own region—may look at problems and solutions somewhat differently from the way the president does. The president is expected to take a national perspective.

COMPETING CALENDARS   The Constitution also ensures that Congress and the president will not share the same terms of office. Presidents serve for four years with a chance of reelection to a second term; senators have the luxury of six-year terms; members of the House of Representatives are elected to two-year terms. Different constituencies and lengths of service make these national officials responsive to different moods and points of view. Different electoral forces are at work in different election years. A majority of the voters can win control over only part of the national government at a time, and this arrangement, too, was by design.

Presidents often act quickly to shape national priorities in their first months following their electoral victory, to win support for their agendas before a possible decline in public approval. Congress, by contrast, usually moves more slowly "because it represents a vast array of local interests."[33] Another obvious difference in the speed of their two branches has to do with numbers: There is one president, but there are 435 members of the House and 100 senators.

COMPETING CAMPAIGNS   Finally, the Constitution ensures that Congress and the president will run different kinds of election campaigns. Most members of Congress finance their election campaigns with only minimal assistance from their national political party.

They customarily respond to local conditions and run their campaigns independently of their party's presidential candidate or national platform. And changes in the electorate in recent years that enhance an incumbent's chances of reelection weaken the connection between the president and fellow partisans in Congress.

Members of the president's party have typically run well ahead of their president in elections in their home districts, and thus they are less fearful of punishment for ignoring occasional party appeals for loyalty. They are more likely to go along with the president when a measure converges with their own political philosophy and is in the interest of their home district or state. Although parties have become vigorously partisan within Congress, especially in the House of Representatives, there are always several independent thinkers who will at times—sometimes crucial times for the White House—go their own way rather than cooperate with the White House, even when the president is a member of the same party.[34]

Influencing Congress

Presidents are clearly much more than faithful executors of the laws passed by Congress. They have long had a substantial, if not always dominant, role in shaping what Congress does. Their primary vehicle for doing so is the president's agenda, which is an informal list of top legislative priorities. Whether through the State of the Union address or through other messages and signals, presidents make clear what they think Congress should do.[35]

It is one thing to proclaim a presidential priority, however, and quite another to actually influence congressional action. As Richard Neustadt argued in *Presidential Power*, a president's constitutional powers add up to little more than a job as America's most distinguished office clerk. It is a president's ability to persuade others that spells the difference between being a clerk and being a national leader.[36] This power to persuade rests in the resources a president brings to office and the skills that he or she uses in making the most of those resources. (Figure 12–4 compares recent presidents on their ability to influence Congress on key votes. Bush's support scores remained remarkably high through his first three years. His third year score, while lower than his first and second, showed surprising strength.

Although Bush lost a number of votes on his judicial nominees in the Senate and refused to bargain with Congress over post-war aid to Iraq, his third-year score reflects a sharp increase in the number of votes on which he took a position. Whereas he took a position on 120 issues in 2001 and 98 in 2002, he took a position on 174 votes in 2003,

★★ **THINKING IT THROUGH**

Reagan felt that the people should be able to reelect a president as many times as they want, just as they now reelect House and Senate members. He also hinted that the Twenty-Second Amendment might weaken a president late in his second term by making him a lame duck, less powerful because everyone knows he will not be around in a year or so. Advocates of repeal also say we may sometimes need to keep a veteran president in office during a crisis period, much as we retained Franklin Roosevelt in 1940. Others say eight years may not be enough time to resolve certain major problems.

The Twenty-Second Amendment is not only a limit on the incumbent but also on the electorate, the first since the ratification of the Constitution to restrict the power of the electorate rather than expand it. It is based, advocates of repeal suggest, on the assumption that the voters cannot be trusted.

Advocates of the Twenty-Second Amendment argue that it acts as an additional check against presidential power by encouraging both parties to seek out effective candidates to take office, while discouraging dependence on a single ruler. In addition, few presidents are likely to have the health, the intellectual energy, and the new ideas needed to perform the demanding responsibilities of the presidency beyond eight years in office.

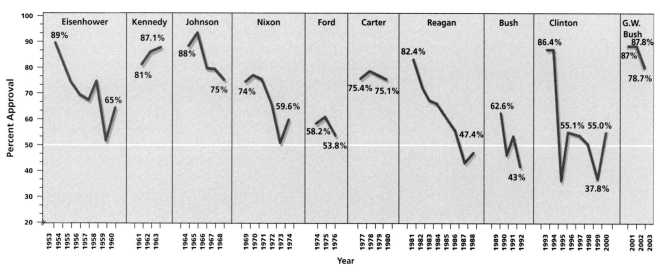

FIGURE 12–4 Presidential Legislative Support from Congress, 1953–2004.
Source: *Congressional Quarterly Weekly,* January 12, 2002, p. 110. Updated by the authors.
Note: Percentages represent average scores for both chambers of Congress.

creating more opportunities for defeat. It was the largest numbr of votes since 1995. Bush's score was inflated somewhat by several issues that produced repeated victories for the president, including eight votes on legislation to prohibit federal funding for an abortion procedure called "partial-birth" abortion. The increase also reflected increased division between the two parties in the Senate, where the Republican majority sought party-line victories that could be used against the future Democratic presidential candidate, John Kerry.

Presidential Resources

There are two kinds of resources that shape both the size of a president's agenda and its ultimate impact on Congress. The first involves the political resources needed to convince Congress to support the president, while the second involves the decision-making resources that help presidents decide what they want.

POLITICAL RESOURCES A president's external influence comes from three sources: (1) the mandate provided by his election, (2) the level of public approval, and (3) the number of party seats in Congress. New presidents usually begin with at least some of each.

Presidents who enter office with a large electoral margin, high public approval, and a party majority in Congress often claim a **mandate** to govern. As noted in Chapter 9, the winner-take-all nature of the electoral college system tends to make the president's popular vote look larger than it truly is. In 1984, for example, Ronald Reagan set the modern record by winning every state but Massachusetts and the District of Columbia, rolling up 98 percent of the electoral votes with a popular total of 59 percent.

Mandates also reside in public approval for either the president or some policy issue. In 1993, for example, Clinton claimed a mandate for national health insurance, arguing that the issue was at the core of much of his public support. The claim would have been more plausible, however, had Clinton won with a popular vote larger than 43 percent. George W. Bush made a similar claim for a broad agenda in 2001, arguing that the American public wanted action in Washington. Again, the claim would have been more plausible had he won the popular vote.

PERSONAL RESOURCES Presidents can hardly claim mandates or invest their political resources if they do not have the time, energy, and information to actually set the agenda, or the political skills to focus congressional attention on their priorities. The first two of these personal resources, time and energy, run out over the course of the term and are difficult to replace. Presidents have only so much time to make their mark. Since they can only serve for two consecutive terms under the Twenty-Second Amendment, they must make every day count.

Presidents have only so much energy to give to the job. One need only compare pictures of presidents at the start and end of their terms to see the impact of the long hours and constant stress. As Gerald Ford once remarked, "It's a hard job being president. . . . Anybody who walks in there thinking he can punch a time clock at 9 in the morning and leave at 5 has got another think coming. We do not elect presidents who want that kind of a life."

The third personal resource, information, actually increases over time as presidents learn their jobs. In a sense, the presidency is the nation's most intense American government course. One way presidents can increase their learning is to take "prerequisites" before entering office—that is, by holding other executive offices, such as the vice presidency or a governorship, that are similar to the presidency or by studying issues as a senator or member of the House that are central to the president's constitutional duties.

The final personal resource is the president's skill at legislative timing and lobbying. Timing involves a president's ability to win congressional attention at key points in the legislative process, while lobbying involves the president's personal skill at persuading individual members of Congress.[37] Lobbying can involve everything from invitations to special White House events to giving members of Congress extra help with government projects back home.

mandate
A president's claim of broad public support.

JUDGING PRESIDENTS

Historians, political scientists, and the American public generally agree that Lincoln, Washington, Franklin Roosevelt, and Jefferson were the nation's greatest presidents. These four became great in part by expanding the presidency, while stretching the Constitution to address great crises and war. Sometimes this is called the "doctrine of necessity"—doing what needs to be done. These presidents often exercised powers that were thought to be solely or primarily congressional, and occasionally challenged Congress and the Supreme Court as well.

There are several sources of greatness. President Washington, more than any other person, converted the paper notions outlined in the Constitution into an enduring, practical governing process. With extraordinary character, he set the precedents that balanced self-government and leadership, chief of state and chief executive, constitutionalism and statesmanship.

Thomas Jefferson, a genius in his generation, was a skilled organizer and a resourceful party leader and chief executive. He made mistakes, yet he adapted the presidency to the new realities of his day. His expansions of territory with the Louisiana Purchase, his sponsorship of the Lewis and Clark expedition, and similar bold ventures ensure him a revered status among presidents. President Lincoln is remembered for saving the Union and is revered as the nation's foremost symbol of democracy and tenacious leadership in the nation's ultimate crisis. President Franklin Delano Roosevelt is viewed as guiding the nation through its worst economic crisis and for leading the "greatest generation" to victory in World War II. These presidential accomplishments are part of the legend of America. Yet this heroic view of presidents raises a good many questions. If presidents alone were responsible for these and similar feats, it is little wonder that our expectations are so high concerning what current and future presidents should accomplish. (See Table 12–3 for a comparison of two different ratings of presidents, one by the *New York Times/Chicago Sun Times* of leading presidential historians, who tend to be more liberal, and the other by the *Wall Street Journal* designed to include more conservative historians.)

In fact, a variety of people and institutions contributed to the achievements credited to past presidents. History seldom adequately honors the reformers and leaders who provided behind-the-scenes leadership. The best presidents surround themselves with talented advisers and administrators. Great leadership depends on situation, resources, opportunity, and teams of leaders. Being at the right place at the right time also helps.

PRESIDENTIAL GREATNESS: HOW DO WE JUDGE THEM?

Presidents rise and fall in the historical rankings based on a number of factors. Some rise because they led the nation through periods of intense domestic or international crisis; others rise because they had a distinctive vision of where the nation should go on issues such as civil rights, social policy, or the economy. Rankings also involve at least some assessment of how presidents did as political and moral leaders of the nation. Some fall because of political or personal scandal, others because they failed to grapple with a big issue such as national health insurance or economic crisis. In the end, rankings involve the overall measure of a president's impact in meeting the public's expectations.

Go to Make It Real "Presidential Greatness: How Do We Judge Them?"

TABLE 12–3 RANKING PRESIDENTS

Ten Best		Ten Worst	
New York Times/ Chicago Sun Times	**Wall Street Journal**	**New York Times/ Chicago Sun Times**	**Wall Street Journal**
1. Abraham Lincoln	1. George Washington	1. Warren Harding	1. James Buchanan
2. George Washington	2. Abraham Lincoln	2. James Buchanan	2. Warren Harding
3. Franklin Roosevelt	3. Franklin Roosevelt	3. Franklin Pierce	3. Franklin Pierce
4. Thomas Jefferson	4. Thomas Jefferson	4. Ulysses Grant	4. Andrew Johnson
5. Theodore Roosevelt	5. Theodore Roosevelt	5. Andrew Johnson	5. Millard Fillmore
6. Woodrow Wilson	6. Andrew Jackson	6. Millard Fillmore	6. John Tyler
7. Harry Truman	7. Harry Truman	7. Richard Nixon	7. Richard Nixon
8. Andrew Jackson	8. Ronald Reagan	8. John Tyler	8. Ulysses Grant
9. James Polk	9. Dwight Eisenhower	9. Calvin Coolidge	9. Zachary Taylor
10. Dwight Eisenhower	10. James Polk	10. Herbert Hoover	10. Jimmy Carter

Sources: Steve Neal, "Putting Presidents in Their Place," *Chicago Sun-Times*, November 19, 1995, pp. 30–31; Arthur M. Schlesinger Jr., "The Ultimate Approval Rating," *New York Times Magazine*, December 15, 1996, pp. 46–51; James Lindgren and Steven Calabresi, "Ranking the Presidents," *Wall Street Journal*, November 16, 2000, p. 13.

Many of the great presidents made mistakes, sometimes great mistakes. And the great presidents typically look better some years later than they did while they were at the helm. Harry Truman is a prime example of a presidential leader who was viewed in a lesser light while in office but was later recognized as great.

The nation can learn from those presidents judged as failures. Experts rank some presidents at or near the bottom because of political corruption while placing others near the bottom because they lacked a compelling program, vision, political skill, or integrity. Although Richard Nixon was respected for his foreign policy initiatives, especially for his recognition of the People's Republic of China, he is nonetheless viewed as one of the lesser presidents because he lied to the American public, plotted a cover-up of illegal and unconstitutional activities, resigned in disgrace, and, in the eyes of many, sullied the dignity of the Oval Office.

It is too early to guess where George W. Bush will be ranked by history. His early response to September 11 was steady and reassuring, and Americans rallied to his side in the early months of the war in Iraq. At the same time, soaring budget deficits and questions about the missing weapons of mass destruction undermined both his credibility and his public support.

Ultimately, a president's place in history is determined years, even decades, after the president has left office. By remembering that there is a future accounting, presidents can find some inspiration for making the hard and sometimes unpopular choices that have led to greatness among their predecessors. Thus the judgment of history may be one of the most important sources of accountability that the nation has on its presidents. Bush's reelection in 2004 provides four more years in which to shape that judgment, whether through Supreme Court appointments or through bold legislative reforms of national programs such as Social Security.

S U M M A R Y

1. The framers created a presidency with limited powers. To enact government business, the president must cooperate with Congress, but powers are divided among the branches, and the politics of shared power has often been stormy. In general, however, both the role and the influence of presidents have increased over the course of the nation's history.

2. The framers gave the president three central roles in the new government: commander in chief, diplomat in chief, and administrator in chief. Presidents have expanded their powers in several ways over the decades. Crises, both foreign and economic, have enlarged these powers. When there is a need for decisive action, presidents are asked to supply it. Congress, of course, is traditionally expected to share in the formulation of national policy. Every president must learn anew the need to work closely with the members of Congress.

3. The Constitution is not always clear on which branch has what powers, which creates controversies over the president's war power, authority to assert executive privilege, issue executive orders, and control the budget and spending process. Congress has made several attempts in recent decades to clarify the president's war and spending power.

4. Presidents manage the executive branch with the assistance of a White House staff composed of roughly 400 individuals and a cabinet of department secretaries that oversees the civil servants. The vice president is also involved in helping the president manage government.

5. The presidency has evolved over the past two centuries to become one of the world's most powerful institutions. This evolution began with George Washington, who set many of the precedents for presidential leadership that exist to this day. It continued with the first modern president, Franklin Roosevelt, who built the presidency into an instrument for sweeping national policy.

6. Americans expect a great deal from their presidents. They want them to be crisis managers, morale builders, and agenda setters, yet also want them to be able to connect with average Americans.

7. The president and Congress often have a tense relationship because of different constitutional expectations and party divisions. Presidents have a variety of tools for influencing Congress, however, and use their political and personal resources to gain support for their policy proposals.

8. Presidential greatness is hard to define. Historians, political scientists, and the American public consider Lincoln, Washington, Jefferson, and Franklin Roosevelt as their greatest presidents, and Harding and Buchanan as their worst. Greatness depends in part on how presidents deal with crisis and war.

KEY TERMS

parliamentary system
presidential ticket
treaty
executive agreement
veto
pocket veto

take care clause
inherent powers
State of the Union address
impeachment
executive privilege

executive orders
impoundment
line item veto
chief of staff
Executive Office of the President

Office of Management and
   Budget (OMB)
cabinet
rally point
mandate

FURTHER READING

DAVID GRAY ADLER AND LARRY N. GEORGE, EDS., *The Constitution and the Conduct of American Foreign Policy: Essays on Law and History* (University Press of Kansas, 1996).

PAUL BRACE AND BARBARA HINCKLEY, *Follow the Leader: Opinion Polls and the Modern Presidents* (Basic Books, 1992).

JOHN P. BURKE AND MICHAEL NELSON, *The Institutional Presidency: Organizing and Managing the White House from FDR to Clinton*, 2d ed. (Johns Hopkins University Press, 2000).

THOMAS E. CRONIN, ED., *Inventing the American Presidency* (University Press of Kansas, 1989).

THOMAS E. CRONIN AND MICHAEL A. GENOVESE, *The Paradoxes of the American Presidency*, 2d ed. (Oxford University Press, 2004).

TERRY EASTLAND, *Energy in the Executive* (Free Press, 1992).

MICHAEL A. GENOVESE, *The Power of the American Presidency, 1989–2000* (Oxford University Press, 2000).

DAVID GERGEN, *Eyewitness to Power: The Essence of Leadership, Nixon to Clinton* (Simon & Schuster, 2000).

STEPHEN HESS, *Organizing the Presidency*, 2d ed. (Brookings Institution Press, 2003).

FRED GREENSTEIN, *The Presidential Difference* (Free Press, 2000).

ERWIN C. HARGROVE, *The President as Leader: Appealing to the Better Angels of Our Nature* (University Press of Kansas, 1998).

CHARLES O. JONES, *Passages to the Presidency: From Campaigning to Governing* (Brookings Institution Press, 1998).

SAMUEL KERNELL, *Going Public: New Strategies of Presidential Leadership* (CQ Press, 1997).

GARY KING AND LYN RAGSDALE, *The Elusive Executive: Discovering Statistical Patterns in the Presidency*, 2d ed. (CQ Press, 2002).

MARK LANDY AND SIDNEY M. MILKIS, *Presidential Greatness* (University Press of Kansas, 2000).

LEONARD W. LEVY AND LOUIS FISHER, EDS., *Encyclopedia of the American Presidency* (Simon & Schuster, 1994).

JOHN A. MALTESE, *Spin Control: The White House Office of Communications and the Management of the Presidential News* (University of North Carolina Press, 1992).

SIDNEY M. MILKIS, *The President and the Parties: The Transformation of the American Party System Since the New Deal* (Oxford University Press, 1993).

SIDNEY M. MILKIS AND MICHAEL NELSON, *The American Presidency: Origins and Development, 1976–2000*, 4th ed. (CQ Press, 2003).

MICHAEL NELSON, ED., *The Presidency and the Political System*, 6th ed. (CQ Press, 2000).

RICHARD E. NEUSTADT, *Presidential Power and the Modern Presidents* (Free Press, 1991).

HUBERT S. PARMET, *George Bush: The Life of a Lone Star Yankee* (Scribner, 1998).

STEPHEN PONDER, *Managing the Press: Origins of the Media Presidency* (Palgrave, 2000).

BRADLEY H. PATTERSON, JR., *The White House Staff: Inside the West Wing and Beyond* (Brookings Institution Press, 2000).

JAMES P. PFIFFNER, *The Strategic Presidency: Hitting the Ground Running*, 2d ed. (University Press of Kansas, 1996).

GLENN A. PHELPS, *George Washington and American Constitutionalism* (University Press of Kansas, 1993).

LYN RAGSDALE, *Vital Statistics on the Presidency*, rev. ed. (CQ Press, 1998).

SHELLEY LYNNE TOMKINS, *Inside OMB: Politics and Process in the President's Budget Office* (Sharpe, 1998).

KENNETH T. WALSH, *Feeding the Beast: The White House Versus the Press* (Random House, 1996).

SHIRLEY ANNE WARSHAW, *Powersharing: White House–Cabinet Relations in the Modern Presidency* (State University of New York Press, 1996).

THE FEDERAL BUREAUCRACY
EXECUTING THE LAWS

13

Whether they know it or not, Americans interact with the federal bureaucracy every day. Their air and water is guarded by the Environmental Protection Agency and Department of Interior, their food is protected by the Food and Drug Administration and Department of Agriculture, threats to their health are being studied by the National Institutes of Health and Centers for Disease Control and Prevention, their college loans are either funded or insured by the Department of Education, at least part of their retirement income is being sheltered by the Social Security Administration, their workplaces are inspected by the Occupational Health and Safety Administration, and their roads are smoothed in part by the Department of Transportation.

Despite its reach, and perhaps because of it, Americans have a love-hate relationship with the federal bureaucracy. They want more of virtually everything government delivers, from health care to national parks, from faster drug approval to home loans, yet they often complain that government is too big and wasteful. A majority of Americans believe that the federal government creates more problems than it solves and that it controls too much of daily life.[1] In October 2003, for example, 93 percent of Americans said that the federal government wastes a great deal or fair amount of money.[2]

When problems arise, however, Americans often ask the federal government to respond. This is certainly what happened immediately after September 11, 2001. Confidence in the president and vice president rose dramatically in the days following the terrorist attacks on New York City and Washington, as did confidence in elected officials such as members of Congress. The number of Americans who said they trusted the federal government

TIME LINE

THE FEDERAL BUREAUCRACY

1776	Board of War and Ordnance created (becomes Secretary of War in 1781)
1781	Department of Foreign Affairs created (becomes Department of State in 1789)
1789	Departments of War, State, and Treasury created
1789	Office of the Attorney General created (becomes Department of Justice in 1870)
1849	Department of Interior created
1862	Department of Agriculture created
1862	Commission of Internal Revenue created
1865	United States Secret Service created
1867	Office of Education created (becomes part of the newly created Department of Health, Education, and Welfare in 1953; becomes Department of Education in 1979)
1914	Federal Trade Commission is created
1939	Hatch Act restricts political activity among federal employees
1958	NASA is created to compete with the Soviet space program
1966	Freedom of Information Act opens many government records to citizens
1970	Environmental Protection Agency created in response to demand for cleaner air, water, and land
1977	Department of Energy created in reaction to the energy crisis of the early 1970s
1989	Veterans Affairs elevated to a cabinet-level department
2003	Department of Homeland Security is created

to do the right thing almost always or most of the time jumped from 29 percent in July 2001 to 57 percent in October.

Yet, even as confidence went up, Americans remained skeptical about big government. Interviewed three weeks after the 2001 terrorist attacks, 70 percent of Americans assumed that most federal employees chose to work for the government because of the job security, and 68 percent cited the salary and benefits. Even at a time when Americans accepted the need for a strong federal government, they doubted the basic motivations of the people who work for it.[3]

Moreover, what goes up must eventually come down. As the intense emotions of September 11 faded, so did the newfound trust in government. By May 2002, the number of Americans who said they trusted the government in Washington to do the right thing just about always or most of the time had fallen to 40 percent, which is where it stood two years later in July 2004. Although trust was still above its pre-September 2001 levels, Americans still viewed the federal government as wasteful and its employees as more motivated by the pay, benefits, and job security than the chance to make a difference, serve the country, and pride. Americans also believe that the president's own appointees are driven more by interest in making connections and making money than serving the people.

In this chapter, we examine the origins, functions, and realities of our national public bureaucracy. We also explore how government agencies are held accountable to the president, Congress, and the American public, and ask how government might make public service more attractive to its most talented citizens.

UNDERSTANDING THE FEDERAL BUREAUCRACY

The framers believed that differences of opinion and what Alexander Hamilton called the "jarring of parties" were healthy for protecting the nation from "excesses in the majority." However, once the laws were made, the framers expected the disagreements to end. As Hamilton explained in *The Federalist*, No. 70, "a government ill executed, whatever it may be in theory, must be, in practice, a bad government."[4]

The Undefined Branch

The framers spent little time worrying about the administrative structure of government and left most of the details to the first Congress and president. They believed the first bureaucracy would be relatively small, and they expected Congress to establish the same departments that had existed under the Articles of Confederation.[5] They also expected George Washington to be the government's first chief executive and believed he would lead the new government with the same skill that he had led the Continental Army.

Nevertheless, the framers made two key decisions about who would be responsible for executing the laws.

First, they prohibited members of the House and Senate from holding executive branch positions. They drew a sharp line on the issue in Article I, Section 6, of the Constitution: "No Senator or Representative shall, during the Time for which he was elected, be appointed to any civil Office under the Authority of the United States, which shall have been created, or the Emoluments whereof shall have been increased during such time, and no Person holding any Office under the United States, shall be a Member of either House during his Continuance in Office."

This provision prevented members of Congress from creating jobs for themselves in the executive branch, a common form of corruption in England prior to the Revolutionary War.[6] The founders also worried that simultaneous service in both branches would weaken the separation of powers.

Second, the framers decided not to give Congress the power to appoint the treasurer of the United States (now called the secretary of the treasury). For much of the summer of 1787, appointing the treasurer was first on the list of the legislature's enumerated powers, reflecting the framers' concern about the financial stability of the new nation.

It was not until the third-to-last working day of the convention that the founders deleted the provision in an effort to reaffirm the president's authority to appoint and supervise the officers of government. Having already made the president commander in chief of the armed services, the founders reaffirmed the president's power to run the government as a whole. Under Article II, it is up to the president, not Congress or the judiciary, to require the opinion of the "principal officer" of each executive department. And it is up to the president, not Congress or the judiciary, to fill any vacancies in those jobs without Senate review when the Senate is in recess. Although Article I does give Congress the power to create the departments of government and the Senate the power to confirm presidential appointees by a two-thirds vote, the president emerged from the final days of the Constitutional Convention as the nation's administrator in chief.

These decisions did not give the president unlimited authority to execute the laws, however. The framers gave Congress, not the president, the power to create the departments and agencies of government in the first place, and the responsibility for appropriating the money to administer programs and hire government employees. They also gave the Senate the power to confirm presidential appointees and clearly expected both houses to monitor executive implementation.

The Federal Bureaucracy Today

More than two hundred years later, the federal bureaucracy is anything but small. Almost 2.7 million Americans work for the federal government today, whether in the 15 cabinet-level departments, the U.S. Postal Service, or in the more than 50 independent agencies. Another 1.4 million Americans serve in the armed forces.

The vast majority work in six agencies: the Departments of the Army, the Navy, and the Air Force (all three in the Department of Defense); the Department of Veterans Affairs; the Department of Homeland Security; and the U.S. Postal Service. Although most agencies are directly responsible to the president, some, like the Postal Service, are partly, or quasi-, independent. Moreover, all federal agencies are created by acts of Congress; Congress can abolish them either by passing a new law or by withholding funds.

The terms "bureaucrat" and "bureaucracy" date from the early nineteenth century. Originally, the word "bureau" referred to a cloth covering the desks of French government officials in the eighteenth century; eventually it came to be applied to the desk itself. The term was soon linked with the suffix "-ocracy" (as in "democracy" or "aristocracy") to describe government (essentially, "rule by people at desks").

At one time in history, the term **bureaucracy** actually mean fast, effective, and rational. In its ideal form, a bureaucracy made sure that every job was carefully designed to ensure faithful performance by well-trained, highly-motivated **bureaucrats**, or employees. Over time, however, the term came to mean slow, confusing, and self-serving. Although this chapter uses "bureaucracy" and "bureaucrats" in neutral terms, the terms are often invoked to criticize red tape and waste.

In theory, government bureaucracies are designed to hold every employee in the organization accountable to the president through a chain of command that describes who is responsible for every decision. Most jobs are highly specialized and are filled on the basis of merit, not political connections or favoritism.[7] Also in theory, bureaucracies are designed to increase efficiency and lower costs.

In reality, governmental bureaucracies are particularly difficult to manage because of their size, interest group connections, and political history. First, duplication and overlap across departments and agencies can create confusion about which agencies are responsible for a problem such as mad cow disease, which can be transmitted to human beings by eating diseased meat. The Department of Agriculture's Animal and Plant Health Inspection Service keeps diseased cattle out of the United States, which is the best way to prevent the disease; the Department of Health and Human Services' Food and Drug Administration is supposed to monitor cattle feed, which is another way to prevent

bureaucracy
A form of organization that operates through impersonal, uniform rules and procedures.

bureaucrat
A career government employee.

the disease, and the Department of Agriculture's Food Safety and Inspection Service inspects cattle as they go to slaughter, which is the last defense against letting diseased meat enter the food supply. All three may have failed in 2003 when the meat from a diseased cow entered the U.S. food supply.

Second, even within a single agency, bureaucracy often creates dense layers of management that keep information from moving up and down the organization quickly. Just consider the reporting relationships that lead down to the Food Safety and Inspection Service, which employs the 8,000 federal workers who actually inspect the cattle that go to slaughter. Each cattle inspector reports to (1) a local supervisor who reports to (2) a deputy district office director who reports to (3) the district office director who reports to (4) an executive assistant administrator for regulatory operations in Washington who reports to (5) the deputy assistant administrator for field operations who reports to (6) the assistant administrator for field operations who reports to (7) a deputy administrator who reports to (8) the administrator of the Food Safety Inspection Service who reports to (9) the deputy undersecretary and undersecretary for food safety who reports to (10) the deputy secretary of agriculture who reports to (11) the deputy chief of staff to the secretary who reports to (12) the chief of staff who reports to (13) the secretary of agriculture who reports to (14) the president. Like the childhood game of telephone in which messages are distorted as they are whispered from one child to another, there are many places in the food safety reporting chain where information can get lost or misunderstood.

These problems have led some advocates to call for the creation of a single food safety organization with the resources and authority to regulate and oversee all aspects of the food chain. Such a reorganization would not only give consumers and producers a single point of contact, it would allow a winnowing of the needless layers of management that get in the way of accountability, and a streamlining of responsibilities. Under current law, for example, the Food and Drug Administration is responsible for the safety of cheese pizzas, while the Department of Agriculture is responsible for meat pizzas.

How the Federal Government Is Organized

The federal bureaucracy contains a wide variety of organizations. Some, such as the Department of Defense, are collections of huge agencies in their own right, which can create duplication and overlap. The Defense Department and its 2 million employees contains the Departments of the Army, Navy, and Air Force, each with its own separate duties (as if to confirm how Congress sometimes divides responsibilities, the Army has its own air force, and the Navy has its own army called the Marine Corps). Others, such as the Department of Education and its 5,000 employees, are tiny by comparison, but they spend huge amounts of money through grants to students. Public management scholars classify the organizations of government into four broad categories: (1) *departments*, (2) *independent agencies*, (3) *independent regulatory commissions*, and (4) *government corporations*.

Departments tend to be the largest federal organizations of all and have the broadest missions. **Independent agencies** tend to be smaller and have more focused responsibilities. **Independent regulatory commissions** are similar to agencies but are designed to be free from direct presidential control. Finally, **government corporations** are designed to operate much like private businesses.

Departments   Cabinet departments are the most visible organizations in the federal bureaucracy. Today's 15 departments of government employ more than 70 percent of all federal civil servants and spend 93 percent of all federal dollars—the rest is spent by the other kinds of agencies to be described. Fourteen of the departments are headed by secretaries; the fifteenth, the Justice Department, is headed by the attorney general. (See Figure 13–1 for the structure of the Department of Homeland Security, which was created in 2002 by merging 22 separate agencies.)

Measured by the total number of employees, the Defense Department is by far the largest department, followed by the Department of Veterans Affairs, which helps veterans return to civilian life after military service; the Department of Homeland Security, which was created to protect the nation from terrorism; the Department of the Treasury,

department
Usually the largest organization in government; also the highest rank in federal hierarchy.

independent agency
A government entity that is independent of the legislative, executive, and judicial branches.

independent regulatory commission
A government agency or commission with regulatory power whose independence is protected by Congress.

government corporation
A government agency that operates like a business corporation, created to secure greater freedom of action and flexibility for a particular program.

CHANGING FACE OF AMERICAN POLITICS

A REPRESENTATIVE BUREAUCRACY?

One way to make the federal bureaucracy more accountable to the public is to make it look more like the public. By creating a representative bureaucracy, at least in terms of race and gender, the federal government can strengthen its connection to the people it serves.

The federal government is clearly more representative of the public now than it was in the 1950s, when most of its employees were white and most women were clerk-typists. Women now occupy 45 percent of all federal jobs; minorities occupy nearly 30 percent.

Even though the number of women and minorities in the federal workforce is at an all-time high, they still face barriers in rising to the top. First, women and minorities are not equally represented in all departments and agencies. They tend to concentrate in departments with strong social service missions such as Education, Health and Human Services, Housing and Urban Development, and Veterans Affairs (which runs the VA hospital system, with its mostly female nursing corps), all of which have more than 50 percent female employees. Military and technical departments such as Defense, Energy, NASA, and Transportation have far fewer women. Health and Human Services has 65 percent women, while Transportation has just 25 percent; 50 percent of the Department of Education's employees are minorities, compared to just 16 percent of Agriculture's.

Second, women and minorities are not represented at all levels of the federal bureaucracy. In 2003, women held only 35 percent of the professional and administrative jobs, where the higher-paying management posts are, but 70 percent of the lower-paying technical and clerical positions. Minorities were also heavily represented in the lower-paying jobs. Together, women and minorities held almost half the jobs at the bottom level of the federal pay system in 2000 and just 10 percent of the posts at the top.

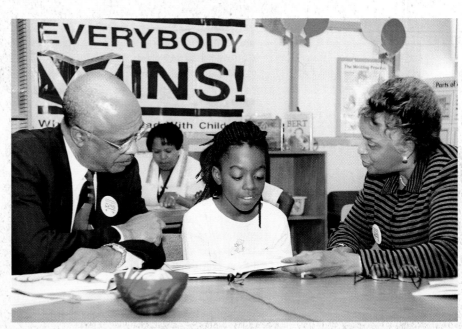

Education Department employee Claudia Gaines and Education Secretary Rod Paige work with a fourth grade student during National Volunteer Week.

The Face of the Federal Workforce, 2003

Gender	
Men	55%
Women	45
Race	
White	70
African American	17
Hispanic	7
Asian and Pacific Islander	5
American Indian	2
Education	
High school or some college	60
College graduate	40

SOURCE: Office of Personnel Management, *The Fact Book, 2003 Edition* (U.S. Government Printing Office, 2003).

THE FIFTEEN EXECUTIVE BRANCH DEPARTMENTS

Department of State
Department of the Treasury
Department of Defense
Department of Justice
Department of the Interior
Department of Agriculture
Department of Commerce
Department of Labor
Department of Health and Human Services
Department of Housing and Urban Development
Department of Transportation
Department of Energy
Department of Education
Department of Veterans Affairs
Department of Homeland Security

which manages the economy and raises revenues through the Internal Revenue Service; and the Department of Justice, which enforces the laws through the federal courts and investigates crime through the Federal Bureau of Investigation.

Measured by budget, the Department of Health and Human Services comes first, followed by the Department of Defense. The Department of Health and Human Services provides health insurance to the elderly through the huge Medicare program, helps states cover health care for the poor through the Medicaid programs, covers the cost of health insurance for children through the Children's Health Insurance Program (CHIP), and administers a variety of programs to help poor Americans. It also contains the Food and Drug Administration, the National Institutes of Health, and the Centers for Disease Control and Prevention, all of which protect Americans from disease.

These 15 departments represent two very different approaches to department building. One approach is to create an umbrella department by combining a number of related programs. The Department of Homeland Security was created by combining elements of 22 separate agencies, including the Coast Guard, Immigration and Naturalization Service, Customs Service, Federal Emergency Management Agency, Secret Service, and the Animal and Plant Health Inspection Service. The Departments of Health and Human Services, Commerce, and Defense also reflect a conglomerate approach.

The other approach is to create a single-purpose department that owes much of its survival to the strength of a constituency group. Congress created the Department of Veterans Affairs in 1989 under pressure from veterans' groups such as the American Legion, who wanted their own advocate in the president's cabinet. It was hardly the first time that Congress yielded to such pressure. One can easily argue that the Departments of Agriculture, Commerce, Education, and Labor were all created in response to interest group pressure.

Creating a department does not necessarily guarantee greater performance. Three years after its creation, the Department of Homeland Security is still working to make the merger work. It took two years for the department to decide on a common uniform for customs agents, immigration inspectors, and passenger screeners, for example, and it is still looking for a permanent space for its Washington headquarters.

Independent Regulatory Commissions Size and age are not the only ways to compare units within the federal bureaucracy. Power, or impact on daily life, is also important. Indeed, when Americans complain about bureaucracy being on their backs, they

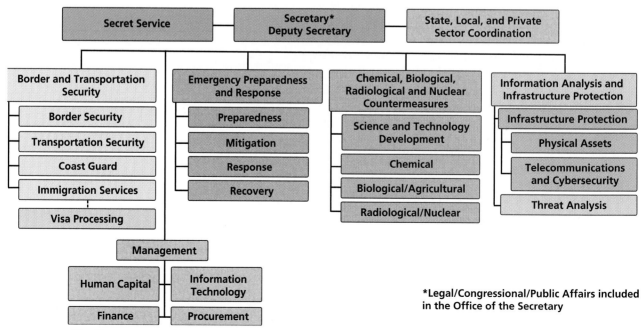

FIGURE 13-1 The Department of Homeland Security.

are often talking about the federal government's independent regulatory commissions.

Yet that is exactly why Congress and the president created the federal government's independent regulatory commissions. All were designed to "get on the backs" of people and corporations, whether to protect consumers (the Consumer Product Safety Commission), regulate stock markets (the Securities and Exchange Commission), oversee federal election laws (the Federal Election Commission), monitor television and radio (the Federal Communications Commission), regulate business (the Federal Trade Commission), control the supply of money (the Federal Reserve Board), or watch over nuclear power plants (Nuclear Regulatory Commission).

The commissions may be small in budget and employees (just $70 million and 1,200 employees for all the independent commissions combined), but their influence over American life is large. Many experts contend that the Federal Reserve Board chair is the second most influential person in making economic policy, and others would argue that the current chair, Alan Greenspan, is the most important leader in influencing public confidence about the economy.[8]

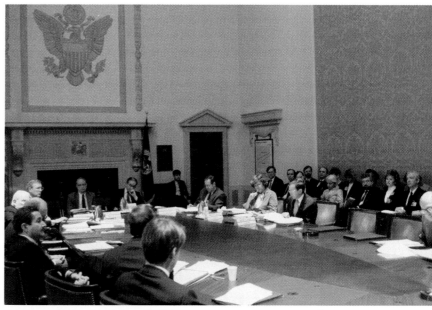

The Federal Reserve Board meets in Washington, D.C., under the seal of the U.S. Supreme Court.

Although independent regulatory commissions are part of the federal bureaucracy, they have a measure of independence from both Congress and the president through their leadership structure. By definition, these commissions are headed not by a single executive but by a small number of commissioners who are appointed by the president, with Senate confirmation, for fixed terms of office. Unlike other presidential appointees, commissioners cannot be removed from office without cause, which is defined by law to mean "inefficiency, neglect of duty, or malfeasance in office." As a result, independent regulatory commissions are less responsive to political pressure from either end of Pennsylvania Avenue.

Independent regulatory commissions are not completely independent, however. Their commissioners are appointed by the president and subject to Senate confirmation, their annual budgets must be approved by Congress, and their decisions are subject to judicial review. Nevertheless, most independent regulatory commissions operate with great freedom and public support. Any effort to reduce the independence of the Federal Reserve Board, Securities and Exchange Commission, or Federal Communications Commission would be seen as a threat to the economic vitality of the nation.

Moreover, the commissioners who lead these agencies often disagree on key issues, even to the point of being unable to reach majority decisions. Some have argued that the six-member Federal Election Commission was actually designed *not* to enforce the election laws. By law, three of its members are Democrats and three are Republicans, which often results in tie votes on key regulations.

Independent regulatory commissions tend to be much less visible than departments, at least until an issue such as corporate fraud becomes hot. The Securities and Exchange Commission was on the front pages for three years, for example, as one corporation after another disclosed accounting fraud in their annual reports to their investors. The SEC was created in the 1930s to restore investor confidence in the stock market, but it was accused of being negligent in monitoring accounting practices at big companies such as Enron and WorldCom in the early 2000s. It is currently rebuilding its staff and taking a much more aggressive stand on accounting standards.

Independent Agencies The word "independent" means at least two things in the federal bureaucracy. Applied to a regulatory commission, it means that the agency is outside the president's control. Applied to an agency or administration, it merely means "separate" or "standing alone." Whereas independent regulatory commissions do not report to the president, independent agencies do.

As a general rule, independent agencies are small federal bureaucracies that serve specific groups of Americans or work on specific problems. Becoming an agency is often the first step toward becoming a department. The Veterans Administration was created in 1930, but only became a department in 1988.

Independent agencies are usually headed by an administrator, which is the second most senior title in the federal bureaucracy behind secretary or attorney general. There are roughly 60 such agencies today, including the Environmental Protection Agency (EPA), the Central Intelligence Agency (CIA), the National Aeronautics and Space Administration (NASA), the National Security Agency (NSA), and the Small Business Administration (SBA).

Although independence increases each agency's ability to focus on its mission, independence also weakens its willingness to cooperate. The spread of independent agencies can also increase confusion about who is responsible for what in the federal government. Early in 2002, for example, White House homeland security "czar" and former Pennsylvania Governor, Tom Ridge, complained about the dozens of agencies involved in guarding the nation's borders:

"There is no line of accountability," he said. "As you take a look at twenty-first-century borders, you have got to have somebody in charge."[9] Congress eventually put Ridge in charge when it created the Department of Homeland Security.

Independent agencies come in many sizes, from small to very large. The National Aeronautics and Space Administration, for example, has an annual budget of over $11 billion and a workforce of more than 23,000 employees, not to mention several hundred thousand employees who work for the private companies that run the United Space Alliance, which is responsible for managing the space shuttle. NASA's budget ranks it ahead of four cabinet departments (Justice, Interior, State, and Commerce).

Moreover, independent agencies can be more important politically to the president than some cabinet departments. There are times, for example, when the director of the CIA or the administrator of the EPA gets a higher place on the president's agenda than the secretary of HUD or agriculture, particularly when an issue such as international spying or global warming is in the headlines.

The term "agency" does not just apply to independent agencies. Many highly visible agencies actually exist within departments, including the Forest Service (located in the Agriculture Department), the National Park Service (located in the Department of the Interior), the Occupational Safety and Health Administration (located in the Labor Department), and the Census Bureau (located in the Commerce Department). Unlike independent agencies, which report directly to the president, these agencies report to a department secretary, who, in turn, reports to the president.

Government Corporations   Government corporations are perhaps the least understood organizations in the federal bureaucracy. Because they are intended to act more like businesses than like traditional government departments and agencies, they generally have more freedom from the rules that control traditional government agencies. They often have greater authority to hire and fire employees quickly, and are allowed to make money through the sale of services such as train tickets, stamps, or home loans.[10]

Ultimately, no two government corporations are alike. The term is so loosely used that no one knows exactly how many corporations the federal bureaucracy has. What experts do know is that the number is between 31 and 47, including the Corporation for Public Broadcasting (which runs PBS television), the U.S. Postal Service, the National Railroad Passenger Association (better known as Amtrak), and Americorps (which runs a national service program created by the Clinton administration), along with a host of financial enterprises that make loans of one kind or another.

Once again, the fact that these organizations are not departments does not mean they are small or insignificant. The U.S. Postal Service employs almost 800,000 people, making it the second-largest organization in the federal bureaucracy. It also lost $1.5

billion in 2002, bringing the amount of money it has borrowed from the federal government over the years to more than $12 billion. Unlike private firms such as United Parcel Service or FedEx, the Postal Service is required to deliver mail anywhere in the country, which means that it often loses money.

Leading the Bureaucracy

Every department and agency of the federal bureaucracy is headed by a presidential appointee, who is either subject to confirmation by the Senate or appointed on the sole authority of the president. As political officers, presidential appointees serve at the pleasure of the president and generally leave their posts at the end of that president's term in office. There are roughly 3,000 presidential appointees who run the federal government, including 600 administrative officers who are subject to Senate confirmation, and another 2,400 who serve entirely "at the pleasure of the president." The president also appoints roughly 1,000 U.S. marshals, U.S. attorneys, and ambassadors to foreign nations.

Becoming a Presidential Appointee Presidential appointees have some of the toughest jobs in the world. They work long hours, resolve complex disputes, and make important decisions about how the laws will be executed. Secretary of Defense Donald Rumsfeld made many of the key decisions about the war in Iraq, for example, including which military units would be assigned to the battle.

All presidential appointees who must be confirmed by the Senate are appointed through a four-step process, none of which is automatic (see Figure 13–2). The first step is to be selected as a candidate. Except for individuals who are extraordinarily close to the president, candidates are selected by the White House Office of Presidential Personnel, which often turns to senators and representatives for names. Although the Bush administration received more than 100,000 resumes by mail and through the Internet in 2001, almost all successful candidates had political connections of some kind. Not surprisingly, most presidential appointees are members of the president's party, and many contributed either time or money to the president's campaign.

The second step in becoming an appointee is to survive the White House clearance process, which is designed to ensure that candidates are legally qualified for office and pose no potential embarrassment to the president. All candidates receive a packet of

In Comparative Perspective

THE JAPANESE BUREAUCRACY

Until 2001, the Japanese bureaucracy was one of the strongest in the world. Created immediately after the Japanese surrendered at the end of World War II, the bureaucracy was given sweeping powers to run the country. The Japanese emperor became a ceremonial position, and the national parliament was given little authority to regulate the bureaucracy.

With no checks and balances, the bureaucracy made a series of disastrous economic decisions over the decades and failed to anticipate the economic downturn that fueled a financial crisis through Asia in the late 1990s. The bureaucracy also turned out to be riddled with corruption. Under Japanese custom, senior bureaucrats often negotiated high-paying jobs with large private corporations before they retired.

On January 1, 2001, the legislature finally acted to reform the bureaucracy. It cut government employment by 25 percent and reduced the number of departments and agencies almost in half, from 24 to 13. At the same time, it gave the prime minister and the ministers of departments new powers to control the bureaucracy. Although the reforms are still under way, the bureaucracy is no longer unchecked.

The bureaucracy is still considered a prestigious place to work, however. Many college students still think of the bureaucracy as the best place to start their careers, and they can qualify for jobs only through rigorous training and highly competitive exams.

forms that require detailed disclosure on every aspect of their personal and professional life, including job history, drug use, personal counseling, financial investments, and even traffic fines of more than $150. They must list every job they have held over the past 15 years, including the name of a supervisor, as well as every place of residence they have lived, including the names of neighbors who might remember them, and every school they have attended, including the name of a high-school classmate who can vouch for them. Some candidates withdraw from consideration at this stage, either because they see potential problems in their past or simply do not have the time to fill out the forms.

In turn, every answer is subject to further review by the White House, Federal Bureau of Investigation, Internal Revenue Service, Office of Government Ethics, and the Senate Committee that is responsible for confirming a given candidate.

The third step in the process is the simplest: The president submits the name of a nominee on parchment paper to the clerk of the Senate. The document is placed in a special envelope, sealed with wax, and hand-delivered to the Senate when it is actually in session.

The fourth step involves Senate confirmation. The Senate refers each nomination to the appropriate committee, which conducts its own review of each candidate. Depending on the position and nominee, the Senate may ask to review the entire file developed by the White House, including the FBI's investigation. Once the review is complete, the committee holds a hearing on the nomination and usually sends the

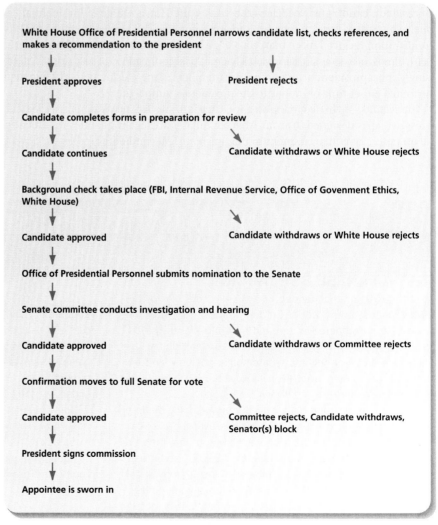

FIGURE 13–2 The Presidential Appointments Process.

nomination to the floor of the Senate with a favorable recommendation. In turn, most nominations are approved by the Senate on voice votes.

There are times, however, when the Senate uses nominations to send signals to the White House about political concerns. In late 2003, for example, Senator Hillary Clinton (D.-N.Y.) blocked the nomination of a new EPA admnistrator as a way to express her anger regarding air quality in New York City. Although she later withdrew her objections, she was able to delay the nomination long enough to force the Bush administration to make a promise to study air quality more closely in the future.

The Senior Leadership Corps   Presidential appointees work closely with the 7,000 members of the **Senior Executive Service**, which includes roughly 6,400 career executives who are appointed through a rigorous review process, and another 600 political executives who are appointed by the president without Senate confirmation. Career senior executives continue in their posts regardless of who happens to be president and are selected on the basis of merit, not political history or campaign contributions.

Together with the president's political appointees, there are 10,000 senior executives who sit atop the federal bureaucracy. The number has grown dramatically over the past three decades as the federal government has "thickened" with more layers of leadership and more leaders at each layer.[11]

Some political scientists argue that Congress created the pressure for thickening by creating highly complex programs that demand close supervision, while others believe that thickening is driven in part by a competition for power among competing organizations. According to this *theory of public bureaucracy,* bureaucratic organizations constantly seek to enhance their power, whether by creating new titles, adding more staff, or increasing their budgets.[12]

How the Bureaucracy Evolved

As already noted, the federal bureaucracy started out small. As public administration scholar Leonard White once wrote, the entire federal bureaucracy of 1790 consisted of nothing more than a "foreign office with John Jay and a couple of clerks to deal with correspondence from John Adams in London and Thomas Jefferson in Paris;…a Treasury Board with an empty treasury;…a 'Secretary at War' with an authorized army of 840 men;…[and] a dozen clerks whose pay was in arrears."[13] (See Table 13–1 for measures of the federal government's size since 1940.)

Creating the first departments was not easy, however. Congress fought to restrict the president's authority to fire appointees, and briefly considered creating a board to run

TYPES OF GOVERNMENT EMPLOYEES

1. Senior presidential appointees confirmed by the Senate: 550
2. Ambassadors, U.S. attorneys, and U.S. marshals also confirmed by the Senate: 600
3. Presidential appointees selected by the president and not confirmed by the Senate: 2,000
4. Senior career executives: 2,400
5. Middle-level managers and supervisors: 120,000
6. Middle-level employees: 600,000
7. Lower-level employees: 600,000
8. Postal Service employees: 850,000
9. Blue-collar employees: 250,000
10. Part-time/seasonal employees: 250,000
11. Military personnel: 1,400,000

In November 1995, the vast bureaucracy of the federal government shut down for lack of funds.

Senior Executive Service
Established by Congress in 1978 as a flexible, mobile corps of senior career executives who work closely with presidential appointees to manage government.

TABLE 13–1 MEASURING THE SIZE OF GOVERNMENT, 1940–2005

Year	Employment (in thousands)	Budget (in billions of current dollars)	Budget (in 1996 dollars)	Budget as a Percentage of Gross Domestic Product
1940	699	$ 9.5	$ 94.3	9.9%
1945	3,370	92.7	804.1	43.7
1950	1,439	42.6	312.5	16.0
1955	1,860	68.4	431.3	17.8
1960	1,808	92.2	493.0	18.3
1965	1,901	118.2	575.6	17.6
1970	2,203	195.6	761.6	19.9
1975	2,149	332.3	909.3	22.0
1980	2,161	590.9	1,092.5	22.3
1985	2,252	946.4	1,304.7	23.9
1990	2,250	1,253.2	1,483.6	21.9
1995	2,018	1,788.8	1,551.5	21.9
2000	1,784	1,788.8	1,659.5	18.2
2005	1,875	2,396.7	1,810.0	16.9

SOURCE: Office of Management and Budget, *Budget of the U.S. Government, Fiscal Year 2005, Historical Tables* (U.S. Government Printing Office, February 2004).

the new Department of the Treasury. President Washington won the arguments, however, and settled any remaining worries about his judgment by appointing Thomas Jefferson as Secretary of State, Alexander Hamilton as Secretary of the Treasury, and Henry Knox as Secretary of War. All three were easily confirmed and quickly went about the business of running their departments. At roughly the same time, Congress also created the Post Office Department and allowed for the appointment of a U.S. attorney general.

Even though the federal bureaucracy was but the tiniest fraction of its current size, it was not long before presidential candidates began promising smaller government. Indeed, Jefferson made waste in government a centerpiece of his first Inaugural Address in 1801, promising "a wise and frugal government, which shall restrain men from injuring one another, shall leave them otherwise free to regulate their own pursuits of industry and improvement, and shall not take from the mouth of labor what it has earned." Jefferson wanted a government that taxed lightly, paid its debts on time and in full, and sought "economy in the public expense." Jefferson set aside his promise long enough to make the Louisiana Purchase, which doubled the size of the nation and laid the groundwork for a vast expansion of America's economy.

Unfortunately, Jefferson's purchase also set off a wave of corruption at the federal government's General Land Office, where corrupt federal clerks reserved the best pieces of land to sell for themselves. The corruption eventually ignited the western anger that swept Andrew Jackson—and a new era in two-party competition—into office in 1828. Jackson soon introduced a **spoils system** into government—as in "to the victor belong the spoils."

Under Jackson's system, federal jobs were filled on the basis of political connections. Actual ability to do the work had almost nothing to do with obtaining an appointment. As such, the spoils system gave the president's party complete control over almost every government job, from cabinet secretaries all the way down to post office clerks. This political job system became known as *patronage*—individuals would patronize, or support, the president's party with money before an election, and get a job in government after.

The civil service was created in 1883 to end corruption in the spoils system. Indeed, it was a disappointed job seeker who started the federal bureaucracy down the road toward today's civil service system. Unfortunately for President James Garfield, that job seeker happened to be both disappointed and a good shot. Garfield's assassination

spoils system
A system of public employment based on rewarding party loyalists and friends.

prompted Congress to pass the Pendleton Act of 1883, which created an independent Civil Service Commission to assure that most federal jobs were awarded under a **merit system**, meaning on the basis of an individual's ability to do the work, not political connections. Federal service was placed under the control of a three-person bipartisan board called the Civil Service Commission, which functioned from 1883 to 1978.[14]

By the 1950s, coverage under the merit system had grown from 10 percent of all federal employees, when it was first established, to about 90 percent in 1950. In 1978, the Civil Service Reform Act abolished the Civil Service Commission and split its functions between two new agencies. This split was made to eliminate the possible conflict of interest in an agency that recruits, hires, and promotes employees and also passes judgment on employee grievances about fairness and discrimination.

Today, the **Office of Personnel Management (OPM)** administers civil service laws, rules, and regulations. The independent Merit Systems Protection Board is charged with protecting the integrity of the federal merit system and the rights of federal employees. It conducts studies of the merit system, hears and decides charges of wrongdoing, considers employee appeals against adverse agency actions, and orders corrective and disciplinary actions against an agency executive or employee when appropriate. (A sampling of current federal job offerings can be found at www.usajobs.opm.gov.)

The Centers for Disease Control and Prevention (CDC) has been very successful in educating the public about the importance of immunization for children.

WORKING FOR GOVERNMENT

Americans believe a number of myths about the federal bureaucracy. Polls show that many of us think that most federal employees work in Washington, D.C., and that the federal government spends much more on welfare and assistance for the poor than it does on Social Security or defense.

The realities are much different:

- Only about 15 percent of the career civilian employees work in the Washington area. More federal employees work in California, Georgia, and Texas, for example, than in Washington.

- More than 25 percent of the civilian employees work for the Army, the Navy, the Air Force, or some other defense agency; another 30 percent work for the U.S. Postal Service.

- Welfare may consume a sizable portion of the U.S. budget, yet the federal bureaucracy that administers it is relatively small. Fewer than 10 percent of the bureaucrats work for welfare agencies such as the Social Security Administration or the Department of Veterans Affairs.

- Federal civilian servants are much more likely to look like the rest of the nation in terms of race, sex, religion, education, and disability than the political appointees or members of Congress who make the laws they execute.

- Although the civil service includes more than 450 different kinds of jobs, the vast majority of workers occupy white-collar jobs such as lawyers, contract managers, budget analysts, engineers, inspectors, and auditors.

Although the public believes most bureaucrats come to work for the security, paycheck, and benefits, most care deeply about making a difference for their country. According to surveys conducted in 2001 and 2002, the vast majority of federal employees say they contribute to their agency's mission, and half say their organizations are very good at helping people. Most federal employees also say the people they work with are open to new ideas, willing to help other employees learn new skills, and concerned about their organization's mission.[15]

Nevertheless, there are reasons to worry about the health of the federal civil service. Substantial minorities of federal employees say their organizations do not provide the information, technological equipment, and training to do their jobs well, and a majority believes their organizations do not have enough employees to succeed. In addition, many federal employees believe that their organizations do not do well at

merit system
A system of public employment in which selection and promotion depend on demonstrated performance rather than political patronage.

Office of Personnel Management (OPM)
Agency that administers civil service laws, rules, and regulations.

disciplining poor performers. They also describe the federal hiring process as slow and confusing, and often complain that their senior leaders are not qualified for their jobs.

The Hiring Process

Unlike presidential appointees who are selected by the president, the vast majority of federal employees are recruited through the civil service. The civil service system was designed to reduce political corruption by promoting merit in the hiring process. But hiring on the basis of merit is not the only way government seeks to reduce corruption. As we shall see, it also regulates the political activities of civil servants.

As already noted, the Office of Personnel Management sets the federal government's rules for recruiting, hiring, promoting, and disciplining civil servants. However, individual agencies have the actual responsibility for hiring new personnel, subject to agency standards. Individual agencies may promote people from within or transfer a civil servant from another agency in the government. If, however, they wish to consider an "outsider," they request that OPM certify possible candidates from its roster of applicants. OPM typically certifies the top three applicants for the opening, and the agency normally selects one of these. However, the agency can decide to make no appointment or to request other applicants if it thinks none of the three is suitable.

These procedures are intended to protect the merit principle and to meet agencies' needs for qualified personnel. In practice, the two objectives sometimes come into conflict. Trade-offs have to be made, particularly between central control by OPM and delegation of discretionary authority to the agencies. And sometimes the pursuit of both objectives is undermined by other goals, such as giving military veterans extra credit in the hiring process.

Regulating the Civil Service

In 1939, Congress passed the Act to Prevent Pernicious Political Activities, usually called the **Hatch Act** after its chief sponsor, Senator Carl Hatch of New Mexico. The act was designed to neutralize the danger of a federal civil service being able to shape, if not dictate, the election of presidents and members of Congress. In essence, the Hatch Act permitted federal employees to vote in government elections but not to take an active part in partisan politics. The Hatch Act also made it illegal to dismiss federal officials below cabinet and subcabinet rank for partisan reasons.[16]

In 1993, Congress, with the encouragement of the Clinton administration, overhauled the Hatch Act and made many forms of participation in partisan politics permissible. The revised Hatch Act still bars federal officials from running as candidates in partisan elections, but it does permit most federal civil servants to hold party positions and involve themselves in party fund raising and campaigning. This new law was welcomed by those who believed the old Hatch Act discouraged political participation by 3 million people who might otherwise be vigorous political activists.[17]

The new Hatch Act spells out many restrictions on federal bureaucrats; they cannot raise campaign funds in their agencies, and those who work in such highly sensitive federal agencies as the CIA, FBI, Secret Service, and certain divisions of the IRS are specifically barred from nearly all partisan activity. Those who work in the U.S. military have stricter rules regulating their political involvement. On the one hand, federal employees *may* register and vote as they choose; assist in voter registration; express opinions about candidates and issues; contribute money to political organizations; attend political fund-raising functions; wear or display political badges, buttons, or stickers; attend political rallies and meetings; and join political parties. On the other hand, they *may not* be candidates for public office in partisan elections, use their jobs or authority to interfere with or affect the results of an election, collect contributions or sell tickets to political fund-raising functions from subordinate employees, or solicit funds or discourage the political activity of any person who has business before the employee's office.

Hatch Act
Federal statute barring federal employees from active participation in certain kinds of politics and protecting them from being fired on partisan grounds.

The Role of Government Employee Unions

Since 1962, federal civilian employees have had the right to form unions or associations that represent them in seeking to improve government personnel policies, and about one-third of them have joined such unions. Some of the most important unions representing federal employees today are the American Federation of Government Employees, the National Treasury Employees Union, the National Association of Government Employees, and the National Federation of Federal Employees.

Unlike unions in the private sector, federal employee unions lack the right to strike and are not able to bargain over pay and benefits. But they can attempt to negotiate better personnel policies and practices for federal workers, they can represent federal bureaucrats at grievance and disciplinary proceedings, and they can lobby Congress on measures affecting personnel changes. They can also vote in elections. This is why members of Congress from districts that have large numbers of federal workers often sit on the House and Senate civil service subcommittees.

THE BUREAUCRACY'S JOB

Whatever their size or specialty, all federal organizations share one job: to faithfully execute, or implement, the laws. **Implementation** covers a broad range of bureaucratic activities, from writing checks at the Social Security Administration to inspecting job sites at the Occupational Health and Safety Administration, swearing in new citizens at the Immigration and Naturalization Service, or monitoring airline traffic at the Federal Aviation Administration. Some agencies implement the laws by spending money, others by raising revenues or by issuing rules that govern what private citizens and businesses do, and still others by collecting information or conducting research. Whatever tool government uses, implementation is the act of converting a law into action.

Because Congress and the president could never pass laws that are detailed enough to execute themselves, they give federal departments and agencies a certain amount of **administrative discretion** to implement the laws in the most efficient and effective manner possible. This freedom often varies from agency to agency, depending on both past performance and congressional politics. Political scientist Theodore Lowi believes that Congress often gives the federal bureaucracy vague directions because it is unable or unwilling to make the tough choices needed to resolve the conflicts that arise in the legislative process. Congress gets the credit for passing a law, while the federal bureaucracy gets the challenge of implementing an unclear law.[18]

Whether a law is clear or ambiguous, most agencies implement the law through two means: administrative *regulations,* which are formal instructions for either running an agency or for controlling the behavior of private citizens and organizations, or *spending,* which involves the transfer of money to and from government.

Making Regulations

Regulations, or rules, are designed to convert laws into action. They tell people what they can and cannot do, as well as what they must or must not do. It is an Agriculture Department rule that tells meat and poultry processors how to handle food, an Environmental Protection Agency rule that tells automobile makers how much gasoline mileage their cars must get, a Social Security Administration rule that tells Americans how long they must work before they are eligible for a federal retirement check, an Immigration and Naturalization Service rule that tells citizens of other nations how long they can stay on a student visa, and a Justice Department rule that tells states what they must do to ensure that every eligible citizen can vote. Although all these rules can be traced back to legislation, they provide the details that most laws leave out.

Rules are drafted and reviewed through a quasi-legislative **rule-making process** that is governed by the Administrative Procedure Act. Enacted in 1946 to make sure that all rules are made visible to the public, the act requires that all proposed rules be

implementation
The process of putting a law into practice through bureaucratic rules or spending.

administrative discretion
Authority given by Congress to the federal bureaucracy to use reasonable judgment in implementing the laws.

regulations
The formal instructions that government issues for implementing laws.

rule-making process
The formal process for making regulations.

published in the *Federal Register.* Publication in the federal government's newspaper marks the beginning of what is known as the "notice and comment" period in which all parties affected by the proposed regulation are encouraged to make their opinions known to the agency. Because rules have the force of law and can become the basis for legal challenges, the process can take years from start to finish and can involve thousands of pages of records. Some agencies even hold hearings and take testimony from witnesses in the effort to build a strong case for a particularly controversial rule.

The rule-making process does not end with final publication and enforcement. All rules are subject to the same judicial review that governs formal laws, thereby creating a check against potential abuse of power when agencies exceed their authority to faithfully execute the laws.

Moreover, rules, like laws, can be changed by future action. In late 2003, for example, the Bush administration anounced plans to change the rules governing coal-burning electric power plants. Under a Clinton administration rule, mercury had been declared extremely dangerous to public health. As a result of the ruling, power plants were about to be forced to install expensive new technology to reduce the amount of mercury released to the mimimum amount possible. Under the new rules, power plants would have more freedom to release larger amounts of mercury, and save billions. Environmentalists charged that the new EPA administrator, former Utah governor Mike Leavitt, had been forced by the White House to accept the change in policy. Although Leavitt admitted that the proposal had been discussed within the administration, he argued that "the rules are ultimately made and signed here."[19] It was a nearly perfect statement of just how important making the rules can be to society.

Spending Money

The federal bureaucracy also implements laws through spending, whether by writing checks to more than 35 million Social Security recipients a year, buying billions of dollars' worth of military equipment, or making grants to state governments and research universities. Viewed in relative terms as a percentage of gross domestic product (GDP), federal spending more than doubled over the past half-century but began to shrink with the end of the cold war in 1989. Viewed in constant dollars to adjust for inflation, however, federal spending continues to rise each year, driven in part by the cost of caring for a rapidly aging population.

Most of this spending goes to what political scientists and budget experts call **uncontrollable spending**, defined as spending for (1) **entitlement programs** that provide financial benefits for any American who is eligible, such as Social Security for older Americans, college loans for poor students, or help for the victims of natural disasters such as floods and hurricanes (in these programs, everyone who is eligible and applies automatically gets the help), and (2) programs that require more federal spending each year automatically through cost-of-living increases or interest on the national debt.

Uncontrollable spending sharply limits the amount of the federal budget that is actually subject to debate in any given year. Even funding for programs such as defense, which is technically subject to yearly control, is almost impossible to cut without controversy, especially during a time of high public concerns about terrorism.

The largest share of uncontrollable spending comes from Social Security and Medicare, which are guaranteed to any American who has paid taxes into the program for enough years. The aging of the American population means that more older people than ever will qualify for Social Security and Medicare, so uncontrollable spending will almost certainly rise over the next few decades. In total, uncontrollable spending accounted for more than $1.36 trillion in 2005, accounting for over half of the federal government's $2.4 trillion budget.

A much smaller share of the uncontrollable budget involves welfare for the poor, which is linked to economic performance. More unemployment, for example, means more federal unemployment insurance; more poverty means more food stamps, job training, temporary financial assistance, and other income support programs.

The uncontrollable budget is not growing just because more people are eligible for entitlements, however. Many of these entitlements are subject to **indexing**—that is, they

uncontrollable spending
The portion of the federal budget that is spent on programs, such as Social Security, that the president and Congress are unwilling to cut.

entitlement program
Programs such as unemployment insurance, disaster relief, or disability payments that provide benefits to all eligible citizens.

indexing
Providing automatic increases to compensate for inflation.

GLOBAL *Perceptions*

QUESTION: Please tell me if you completely agree, mostly agree, mostly disagree, or completely disagree with the following statements: When something is run by the government it is usually inefficient and wasteful. Generally government is run for the benefit of the people.

Americans are not the only citizens who believe their government is inefficient and wasteful. A majority of citizens in all but six of the 49 nations surveyed by the Pew Global Attitudes survey said government is usually inefficient and wasteful. At the same time, a majority of citizens in all but seven of the 49 nations also said that government is run for the benefit of all people. Government may be inefficient, but at least it is inefficient for the benefit of all.

In theory, governments that are viewed as both inefficient *and* run for the benefit of a few would be under the greatest pressure to change, which has been the case in Japan, Russia, and Brazil. Using these two measures, Uzbekistan has the most respected bureaucracy in the world: Just 32 percent of its citizens characterized it as wasteful and inefficient, while 85 percent said it was run for the benefit of all the people.

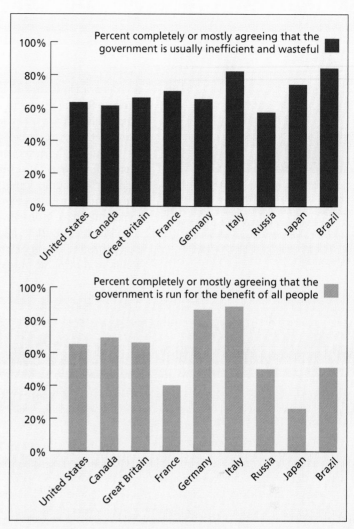

SOURCE: The Pew Global Attitudes Project, June, 2003, p. 109.

grow automatically with inflation, regardless of how the economy is doing. Indexing affects a growing list of federal programs, again leaving Congress and the president little control over year-to-year increases. The number of programs indexed to automatic cost-of-living adjustments (COLAs) grew from 17 in 1966 to almost 100 by 2004.[20]

HOLDING THE BUREAUCRACY ACCOUNTABLE

Every president enters office promising to make the federal bureaucracy work better. Indeed, Jimmy Carter, Ronald Reagan, Bill Clinton, and George W. Bush all made bureaucratic reform a central part of their presidential campaigns. Carter promised to create a government as good as the American people, Reagan promised to reduce waste in government, Clinton and Vice President Al Gore promised to reinvent government, and Bush promised to make government more friendly to citizens.

Yet presidents leave office frustrated by their lack of success. As political scientist James Q. Wilson noted, "Presidents see much of the bureaucracy as their natural enemy

Cabinet members, such as former Attorney General John Ashcroft, often have to answer questions Congress has regarding the bureaucratic and financial needs of their particular department. Ashcroft was one of the first Bush cabinet members to resign after the 2004 election.

and always are searching for ways to bring it to heel."[21] And presidents are not the only ones who want to control the bureaucracy. Congress, too, clearly worries about making bureaucracy work better. Together, both complain that the federal bureaucracy can be more accountable to interest groups and itself than either branch.

Accountability to the President

Modern presidents invariably contend that the president should be firmly in charge of the bureaucracy, for the chief executive is responsive to the broadest constituency. A president, it is argued, must see that popular needs and expectations are converted into administrative action. When the nation elects a conservative president who favors cutbacks in federal programs and less governmental intervention in the economy, for example, his policies must be carried out by the bureaucracy. The voters' wishes can be translated into action only if the bureaucrats support presidential policies.

Yet under the American system of checks and balances, the party winning the presidency does not acquire total control of the national government. Under our Constitution, the president is not even the undisputed master of the executive structure. Presidents come into an ongoing system over which they have little control and within which they have little leeway to make the bureaucracy responsive.

Still, the president has some control over the bureaucracy through the powers of appointment, reorganization, and budgeting. More specifically, a president can attempt to control the bureaucracy by appointing or promoting sympathetic personnel,

PEOPLE & POLITICS *Making a Difference* ★★★

DENISE JOHNSON

The federal government depends on talented employees like Denise Johnson to fulfill the promises Congress, presidents, and the judiciary make. As a senior executive at the U.S. Centers for Disease Control and Prevention in Atlanta, Georgia, Johnson is responsible for the U.S. part of the international effort to eliminate polio from the world.

The U.S. defeated polio in the 1950s and 1960s through an aggressive vaccination program funded by the federal government. Now it is trying to eliminate it around the world. Working through the United Nation's Children Fund, Johnson and her colleagues are part of the Global Polio Eradication Initiative, which seeks to educate foreign governments about the value of vaccination. In 2002 alone, Johnson traveled to India, where she helped India's eradication team organize a national immunization day, as well as to Ethiopia, Zimbabwe, and Nigeria.

Johnson has been at the Centers for Disease Control and Prevention for 25 years and has held assignments in Cincinnati; Kansas City; Baltimore; Harrisburg, Pennsylvania; New York; and most recently, Atlanta. Her career has spanned a long list of projects, including efforts to prevent sexually transmitted diseases, reduce domestic and sexual violence, and clean up toxic waste dumps. As deputy director of the Polio Eradication Branch of CDC, she has managed more than $300 million in grants to immunize more than 500 million children around the globe.

The international campaign against polio appears to be paying off. In 1988, polio still plagued 125 nations and infected more than 350,000 people a year. The rates are now falling so fast that polio may well be completely eradicated by 2008.

Johnson's commitment to making the world a safer place to live earned her a

2003 Service to America medal and $3,000 from *Government Executive Magazine*. When told of her award, Johnson refused to consider herself a hero: "I'm sitting here in my air-conditioned office. In India right now, there are people on the ground tromping through villages, going house to house, looking for kids to give them the vaccine. Those are real heroes."

mobilizing public opinion and congressional pressure, changing the administrative apparatus, influencing budget decisions, using extensive personal persuasion, and if all else fails, shifting a bureaucracy's assignment to another department or agency (although such a shift requires tacit if not explicit congressional approval).[22]

Recall that presidents appoint about 3,000 people to top positions within the executive branch, only a small number of which are subject to Senate confirmation. Some scholars suggest that presidents would be more effective chief executives if they were able to make many more appointments, while others argue that the large number of appointees, and the cumbersome appointments process that goes with it, weakens the president's ability to control the front lines of government.

Accountability to Congress

Congress has a number of ways to exercise control over the bureaucracy, whether by establishing agencies, formulating budgets, appropriating funds, confirming personnel, authorizing new programs or new shifts in direction, conducting investigations and hearings, or even terminating agencies.

Much of this authority is used to help constituents as they battle federal red tape. Members of Congress earn political credit by interceding in federal agencies on behalf of their constituents. Still, Congress deserves at least some of the blame for having created the red tape in the first place, whether by enacting pet programs, refusing to give federal agencies greater flexibility, delaying presidential appointments, or placing limits on bureaucratic discretion to protect some constituents but not others. Moreover, by demanding special attention for their constituents, members of Congress may undermine the fairness of the entire process. Like cutting into line at a movie theater, they slow the progress for everyone but the special few who get their attention.

The brutal fact is that only a small minority of our 535 members of Congress would trade the present bureaucratic structure for one that was an efficient, effective agent of the general interest—the political payoffs of the latter are lower than those of the former. Congressional talk of inefficient, irresponsible, out-of-control bureaucracy is typically just that—talk—and when it is not, it usually refers to agencies under the jurisdiction of other legislators' committees. Congress can abolish or reorganize an agency. Congress can limit or expand an agency's jurisdiction or allow its authority to lapse entirely. Congress can slash an agency's appropriations. Congress can investigate. Congress can do all these things, but individual members of Congress generally find reasons not to do so.[23]

It is not Congress as a whole that shares direction over the bureaucracy with the president. More accurately, individual members and committees specialize in the appropriations and oversight processes. They oversee policies of a particular cluster of agencies—often the agencies serving constituents in their own districts. Some legislators stake out a claim over specific areas. Members of Congress, who see presidents come and go, come to think they know more about particular agencies than the president does (and often they do). Some congressional leaders prefer to seal off "their" agencies from presidential direction and maintain their influence over public policy. Sometimes their power is institutionalized; the Army Corps of Engineers, for example, is given authority by law to plan public works and report to Congress without going through the president.

The Role of Oversight

Congress and the president spend a great deal of energy monitoring the federal bureaucracy. The hope is that **oversight**, the process of monitoring day-to-day activities, will somehow encourage agencies to perform better or at least deter them from worse performance.

Presidents have a number of tools for keeping a watchful eye. They can put loyal appointees, such as Attorney General John Ashcroft, into the top jobs at key agencies; they can direct White House aides, such as homeland security chief Tom Ridge or Vice

RECENT EFFORTS TO MAKE GOVERNMENT WORK

Since 1945, Congress has passed 177 major laws to make government work better. Some of these laws were designed to make government more efficient by combining independent agencies into new departments such as the Department of Health and Human Services or Homeland Security. Other laws were designed to make government more open to citizen review through freedom of information and other "sunshine in government" rules. Still other laws were designed to cut costs by reducing fraud, waste, and abuse.[*]

Patterns in the 177 laws show just how important the Watergate scandal was in changing political control of the bureaucracy. Prior to Watergate, Congress allowed the president to make most of the decisions about improving government. After Watergate, Congress became much more involved in drafting laws to improve how government works. Further review of the 177 laws reveals important patterns in how Congress, the president, and the judiciary have tried to improve government performance:

- The number of laws has increased over time, suggesting growing frustration with the inability to actually improve performance. One-third of the 177 laws were enacted before the Watergate scandal, two-thirds after.
- Congress has become more involved in shaping the laws, suggesting that it is less willing to let the president decide how to run the executive branch. Whereas 61 percent of pre-Watergate reforms originated in the White House, 82 percent of post-Watergate reforms originated in Congress.
- Finally, the laws have become less trusting toward federal employees. Whereas 56 percent of the pre-Watergate reforms had a trusting view of government employees, 81 percent of the post-Watergate reforms were distrusting.

[*]For an introduction to the laws, see Paul C. Light, *The Tides of Reform: Making Government Work, 1945–1995* (Yale University Press, 1998).

oversight
Legislative or executive review of a particular government program or organization. Can be in response to a crisis of some kind or part of routine review.

According to federal statistics, roughly half of all federal employees will be eligible to retire by 2010. This means a dramatic increase in the need for employees at all levels of the bureaucracy. Unfortunately, a 2003 survey of 1,002 seniors shows that the federal government will have difficulty selling the jobs to graduates.* A majority of seniors saw government as the most difficult sector to enter and viewed its hiring process as by far the slowest and most confusing. Even seniors who would prefer a government job said they did not know how to get one.

* Paul C. Light, "In Search of Public Service," Brookings Institution Press, June 2003.

Among its proposed reforms of the bureaucracy in 1995, Congress wanted to end support of public broadcasting, claiming that programs like Sesame Street could support themselves on commercial television. The public, however, disagreed, and Big Bird, Oscar the Grouch, and other childhood favorites still receive government subsidies.

central clearance
Review of all executive branch testimony, reports, and draft legislation by the Office of Management and Budget to ensure that each communication to Congress is in accordance with the president's program.

President Dick Cheney, to oversee the work of certain agencies; and they can always call cabinet meetings to learn more about what is happening in the bureaucracy.

However, presidents tend to use the Office of Management and Budget for most routine oversight. Departments and agencies must get the president's approval before testifying before Congress on pending legislation, making legislative proposals, or answering congressional inquiries about their activities. Under this **central clearance** system, OMB forwards communications to Congress in three categories: "in accordance" with the president's program (reserved for the president's top priorities), "consistent with" the president's program (indicating the president's second-tier priorities), or "no objection." If the president objects to any communication, OMB simply does not forward the legislation to Congress. OMB also conducts oversight on all federal departments and agencies as it assembles the president's budget plan.

Congress also has a number of tools for overseeing the federal bureaucracy, not the least of which consists of the individual members of Congress themselves, who are free to ask agencies for detailed information on just about any issue. However, most members and committees tend to use the General Accounting Office or the Congressional Budget Office (both discussed in Chapter 11) to conduct a study or investigation of a particular program.

Congress uses these and other sources of information as a basis for committee and subcommittee hearings on specific agencies or programs. Today, Congress holds more oversight hearings than ever before. In the 1960s, for example, both chambers held a total of 157 days of oversight hearings per two-year Congress; by the early 1980s, the number had more than tripled, to 587 days. The greatest increase occurred in the 1970s, fueled in part by the increasing number of legislative committees and subcommittees. More committees and more staff meant more time and energy to hold oversight hearings.[24]

Together, Congress and the president conduct two basic types of oversight. One is what can be called "police patrol" oversight, in which the two branches watch the bureaucracy through a routine pattern. They read key reports, watch the budget, and generally pay attention to how the departments and agencies are running. If they happen to see a "crime" in progress, all the better. But the general goal of the patrol is to deter problems before they arise. The other can be called "fire alarm" oversight, in which the two branches wait for citizens, interest groups, or the press to find a major problem and pull the alarm. The media play a particularly important role in such oversight, often uncovering a scandal before a routine "police patrol" can spot it.[25]

The Problem of Self-Regulation

Career administrators are in a good position to know when a program is not operating properly and what action is needed. But many Americans believe that federal employees, whether selected on merit or not, fail to make things better. The problem is that many career employees act as if the expansion of their organization is vital to the public interest. They sometimes become more skillful at building political alliances to protect their own organization than at building political alliances to ensure their programs' effectiveness.

Career administrators usually try hard to be nonpartisan, yet they are inevitably involved in politics. Some of them have more bargaining and alliance-building skills than the elected and appointed officials to whom they report. In one sense, agency leaders are at the center of action in Washington. Over time, administrative agencies may come to resemble entrenched pressure groups in that they operate to advance their own interests. The growth of federal programs from the 1930s through the 1970s brought an increase in the number of policy aides on Capitol Hill, of Washington law firms that specialize in assisting clients who are interested in policy development, and of lobbyists (some say at least 40,000) who work with Congress and the federal bureaucracy to advance various economic and professional interests.

Special-interest groups that perceive real or potential harm to their interests cultivate the bureau chiefs and agency staffs who have jurisdiction over their programs. They also work closely with the committees and subcommittees of Congress that authorize, appropriate, and oversee programs run by these key bureaucracies. Recognizing the power of interest groups, bureau chiefs frequently recruit them as allies in pursuing common goals. What these bureau officials have in common with interest groups and their allies in Congress is a shared view that more money should be spent on federal programs run by the bureau in question. These alliances among bureaucrats, interest groups, and subcommittee members and their staffs on Capitol Hill are sometimes described as *iron triangles,* a topic discussed in Chapter 6.

GOVERNMENT'S ACHIEVEMENTS

Despite these and other flaws, Americans are reluctant to support cutbacks in what government does. To the contrary. The vast majority say the federal government's big problem is not the wrong priorities, but inefficiency, and few support a drastic reduction in federal responsibilities. Americans may complain about the red tape and waste in Washington, but the federal bureaucracy continues to make progress in solving some of the most difficult problems of modern society.

The federal government helped rebuild Europe after the devastation of World War II, won the cold war against communism, strengthened voting rights for all Americans, reduced workplace discrimination, ended racial segregation in public schools, and won the race to the moon. The list of objective success goes on and on:

- Poverty among older Americans has fallen to modern lows.
- Air and water quality have improved.
- More women are graduating from college and professional school, and more are competing in college sports.
- Food and drugs have become safer, the drug approval process has become faster, and older Americans will soon receive prescription drugs at reduced cost through Medicare.
- More poor children are getting a head start in preschool.
- More pregnant women are receiving proper medical care.
- Home ownership rates have risen to their highest levels ever.
- Americans are living longer with greater financial security and a new prescription drug benefit.
- Polio and tuberculosis have been virtually eliminated.
- The Internet (originally developed by the Defense Department) has revolutionized communications.
- Crime rates are much lower today than they were two decades ago.
- More Americans are completing high school and attending college.

Many of these achievements depend on making sure the federal government can recruit the next generation of civil servants. None of the laws on which these achievements are based can be faithfully executed without the help of talented public employees.

Moreover, not every federal endeavor has produced success. Too many American children still go to bed hungry, too many people are still homeless, too many workers are unable to make ends meet with minimum-wage jobs, and too many citizens have too little access to health care. But if the mark of a great society is what it asks its government to achieve, Americans can be proud of the federal bureaucracy today.

★★ THINKING IT THROUGH

If the federal government wants to hire talented employees, these seniors had a clear recommendation: Make the jobs as challenging as possible. Although salaries and benefits are important considerations in choosing a job, especially for students with large college loans, these students were not saying "Show us the money," but "Show us the work." Students can see the kind of work the federal government does by visiting www.usajobs.gov and can learn more about working for government through the Partnership for Public Service at www.ourpublicservice.org.

MAKE IT *REAL*

BUREAUCRACY: A PLACE WHERE IDEALS MEET REALITY

The more senior the position in government, the more difficult the policy choices. In this simulation, the assistant director of the Census Bureau must make a series of choices regarding the future of the agency. Each memo produces consequences and feedback, sometimes positive, other times negative.

Go to Make It Real "Bureaucracy: A Place Where Ideals Meet Reality."

SUMMARY

1. The chief characteristics of bureaucracy are continuity, predictability, impartiality, standard operating procedures, and "red tape." Federal bureaucratic agencies reflect the ways in which the political system attempts to identify our most important national goals and how policies are implemented.

2. The framers made two key decisions about the structure of government. First, they prohibited members of Congress from serving in the executive branch, thereby guaranteeing some independence in executing the laws. Second, they gave the president the power to appoint the officers of government, albeit with the advice and consent of the Senate. These two decisions ensured that the president would be the nation's administrator in chief.

3. Most of the 2.7 million civilian employees of the federal government serve under a merit system that protects their independence of politics. They work in one of the 15 cabinet departments or elsewhere in a long list of government corporations, independent agencies, and independent regulatory boards or commissions. The bureaucracy is led by presidential appointees and senior career executives.

4. The federal government's Office of Personnel Management sets policy for recruiting and evaluating federal workers. Various restrictions on federal workers prevent them from running for political office or engaging in political fundraising activities. The federal bureaucracy generally prizes continuity, stability, and following the rules more than risk taking or innovation.

5. The bureaucracy generally uses regulations or spending to implement the laws. The rule-making process is governed by the Administration Procedure Act, while the spending process is governed by the federal budget. Most of the federal budget is uncontrollable, whether because of indexing to inflation or because Congress and the president are unwilling to cut highly popular programs such as Social Security.

6. The American bureaucracy has at least two immediate bosses: Congress and the president. It must pay considerable attention as well to the courts and their rulings and to well-organized interest groups and public opinion. In many ways, the bureaucracy is a semi-independent force—a fourth branch of government—in American politics.

7. Debates and controversy over big government and big bureaucracy, and over how to reorganize and eliminate waste in them, are never-ending. Compared with many other nations and their centralized bureaucracies, the hand of bureaucracy rests more gently and less oppressively on Americans than on citizens elsewhere.

KEY TERMS

bureaucracy
bureaucrat
department
independent agency
independent regulatory commission

government corporation
Senior Executive Service
spoils system
merit system
Office of Personnel Management (OPM)

Hatch Act
implementation
administrative discretion
regulations
rule-making process

uncontrollable spending
entitlement programs
indexing
oversight
central clearance

FURTHER READING

JOEL D. ABERBACH, *Keeping a Watchful Eye: The Politics of Congressional Oversight* (Brookings Institution Press, 1990).

DAN BAUM, *Smoke and Mirrors: The War on Drugs and the Politics of Failure* (Little, Brown, 1996).

ROBERT D. BEHN, *Rethinking Democratic Accountability* (Brookings Institution Press, 2001).

BARRY BOZEMAN, *Bureaucracy and Red Tape* (Prentice Hall, 2000).

COUNCIL FOR EXCELLENCE IN GOVERNMENT AND THE PRESIDENTIAL APPOINTEE INITIATIVE, *The Survivor's Guide for Presidential Nominees* (Brookings Institution Press, 2001).

SHELLEY L. DAVIS, *Unbridled Power: Inside the Secret Culture of the IRS* (HarperBusiness, 1997).

JOHN J. DiIULIO JR., ED., *Deregulating the Public Service: Can Government Be Improved?* (Brookings Institution Press, 1994).

JAMES W. FESLER AND DONALD F. KETTL, *The Politics of the Administrative Process* (Chatham House, 1991).

JANE E. FOUNTAIN, *Building the Virtual State: Information Technology and Institutional Change* (Brookings Institution Press, 2001).

CHARLES T. GOODSELL, *The Case for Bureaucracy*, 3d ed. (Chatham House, 1994).

AL GORE, *The Best Kept Secrets in Government: How the Clinton Administration Is Rein-venting the Way Washington Works* (Random House, 1996).

AL GORE, *Creating a Government That Works Better and Costs Less: The Report of the National Performance Review* (Plume-Penguin, 1993).

PHILIP K. HOWARD, *The Death of Common Sense: How Law Is Suffocating America* (Random House, 1994).

RONALD N. JOHNSON AND GARY D. LIBECAP, *The Federal Civil Service System and the Problem of Bureaucracy* (University of Chicago Press, 1994).

HERBERT KAUFMAN, *The Administrative Behavior of Federal Bureau Chiefs* (Brookings Institution Press, 1981).

ANDREW KOHUT, ED., *Deconstructing Distrust: How Americans View Government* (Pew Research Center for the People and the Press, 1998).

PAUL C. LIGHT, *The New Public Service* (Brookings Institution Press, 1999).

PAUL C. LIGHT, *Thickening Government: Federal Hierarchy and the Diffusion of Accountability* (Brookings Institution Press, 1995).

PAUL C. LIGHT, *The Tides of Reform: Making Government Work, 1945–1995* (Yale University Press, 1997).

AREND LIJPHART, *Patterns of Democracy: Government Forms and Performance in Thirty-Six Countries* (Yale University Press, 1999).

G. CALVIN MAKENZIE AND MICHAEL HAFKIN, *Scandal Proof: Do Ethics Laws Make Government Ethical?* (Brookings Institution Press, 2002).

DAVID OSBORNE AND TED GAEBLER, *Reinventing Government: How the Entrepreneurial Spirit Is Transforming the Public Sector* (Addison-Wesley, 1992).

DAVID OSBORNE AND PETER PLASTRIK, *Banishing Bureaucracy: The Five Strategies for Reinventing Government* (Addison-Wesley, 1997).

JAMES Q. WILSON, *Bureaucracy: What Government Agencies Do and Why They Do It* (Basic Books, 1989).

Four useful journals are the *Journal of Policy Analysis and Management, National Journal, Public Administration Review,* and *Government Executive.*

THE JUDICIARY
THE BALANCING BRANCH

14

oreign visitors are often amazed at the power of American judges. They also marvel at the majesty of the Supreme Court building and other courthouses, compared with those in other countries. As French aristocrat Alexis de Tocqueville, after his visit to the United States in 1834, observed: "If I were asked where I place the American aristocracy, I should reply without hesitation . . . that it occupies the judicial bench and bar. . . . Scarcely any political question arises in the United States that is not resolved, sooner or later, into a judicial question."[1] A century later, British political scientist Harold J. Laski observed, "The respect in which federal courts and, above all, the Supreme Court are held is hardly surpassed by the influence they exert on the life of the United States."[2] Only in recent decades have national courts in Europe and elsewhere asserted their power in a similar way, and there is an emerging trend toward the "globalization of judicial power."[3]

Why do judges play such a central role in our political life? As discussed in Chapter 2, Chief Justice John Marshall in 1803 successfully claimed for judges the power of **judicial review**, that is, the power to authoritatively interpret the Constitution. Only a constitutional amendment or a later Supreme Court can modify the Court's doctrine. Justice Felix Frankfurter suggested tersely: "The Supreme Court is the Constitution."

Judges—and not just those on the Supreme Court—are also asked to resolve disputes involving billions of dollars, decide conflicts among competing interest groups, supervise the criminal justice system, and make rules affecting the lives of millions of people. They not only settle legal conflicts but in some cases have overseen the operation of schools,

judicial review
The power of a court to refuse to enforce a law or government regulation that in the opinion of the judges conflicts with the U.S. Constitution or, in a state court, the state constitution.

adversary system
A judicial system in which the court of law is a neutral arena where two parties argue their differences.

justiciable dispute
A dispute growing out of an actual case or controversy and that is capable of settlement by legal methods.

class action suit
Lawsuit brought by an individual or a group of people on behalf of all those similarly situated.

prisons, mental hospitals, and complex businesses. Sometimes they decide the details of how these institutions should be run. Still, the scope and nature of judicial power limit the role of judges.

THE SCOPE OF JUDICIAL POWER

The American judicial process rests on an **adversary system**. A court of law is a neutral arena in which two parties argue their differences and present their points of view before an impartial arbiter. The adversary system is based on the *fight theory*, which holds that arguing over law and evidence, which may or may not arrive at the truth, guarantees fairness in the judicial system.[4] The adversary system thus imposes restraints on the exercise and scope of judicial power.

Judicial power is essentially *passive* and *reactive*. Judges cannot instigate cases. Moreover, not all disputes are within the scope of judicial power. Judges decide only **justiciable disputes**—lawsuits that grow out of actual controversies and are capable of judicial resolution. Judges do not use their power unless there is a real case or controversy. It is not enough for a judge merely to have a general interest in a subject or to believe that a law is unconstitutional.

The party bringing a lawsuit (the *plaintiff*) must have *standing to sue*. Plaintiffs must have sustained or be in immediate danger of sustaining a direct and personal injury. Plaintiffs may not raise hypothetical issues; they must have a real dispute and opposing interests with another party. Traditionally, individuals had to show an actual monetary damage in order to gain standing to sue. But in recent decades, the Supreme Court has granted standing to individuals who claim nonmonetary injuries that are shared by others. In a classic statement, the Court observed, "Aesthetic and environmental well-being, like economic well-being, are important ingredients of the quality of life in our society, and the fact that particular environmental interests are shared by the many rather than the few does not make them less deserving of legal protection through the judicial process."[5] Individuals still must claim a personal injury—the violation of a constitutional or other legal right—and show a "personal stake in the outcome." But they may now bring suits over environmental damages, defective consumer products, and other matters that affect interest groups and large numbers of people.[6]

A related and increasingly important development is the use of **class action suits**, in which a small number of persons represent all other people similarly situated—a suit on behalf of all students in a university, for example, or all persons who smoke a particular brand of cigarettes. "Would-be class action litigants must show that they are proper representatives for the class of persons they seek to champion [and] that the types of issues they wish to raise are common to the class, and they must be able to demonstrate how a remedy can be formed that will meet the needs of the class."[7] These lawsuits may force major changes in public policy—governing, for example, the operation of schools and prisons—and business practices, such as the marketing of defective or harmful products. In recent years, tobacco companies, drug manufacturers, and financial institutions have confronted a series of class action lawsuits and been ordered to pay damages.

When individuals sue each other over a traffic accident, for instance, they file suits under *civil law* and seek monetary awards for the injuries they suffered or the damages to their property. The government may also bring civil lawsuits against individuals and business. But only the government may prosecute individuals accused of crimes, such as carjacking and robbery, as defined in state and federal *criminal law*. As discussed further in Chapter 16, persons accused of crimes are guaranteed certain rights in the Bill of Rights and must be accorded the due process of law, but if convicted, they face imprisonment, and for murder, may be sentenced to death.

Judges decide cases; they do not prosecute persons for allegedly committing crimes. *Prosecutors* decide whether to charge an offense and which offense to charge. They have largely unreviewable discretion, so long as they have probable cause to believe that the accused has committed an offense.[8] Prosecutors negotiate with the lawyers for **defendants** (those accused of an offense) and often work out a **plea bargain**, whereby defendants agree to plead guilty to a lesser offense to avoid having to stand trial and face a sentence for a more serious offense. Prosecutors also make recommendations to judges about what sentences to impose.

On the federal level, the job of prosecution falls to the Department of Justice: the attorney general, the solicitor general, 94 U.S. attorneys, and some 1,200 assistant attorneys. The president, with the consent of the Senate, appoints a U.S. attorney for each district court. U.S. attorneys serve four-year terms but may be dismissed by the president at any time. These appointments are of great interest to senators, who exercise significant influence over the selection process. Because U.S. attorneys are almost always members of the president's political party, it is customary for them to resign if the opposition party wins the White House.

The attorney general, in consultation with the U.S. attorney in each district, appoints assistant attorneys. Some districts have only one; the largest, the Southern District of New York, has more than 65. These attorneys, working with the U.S. attorney and assisted by the Federal Bureau of Investigation and other federal law enforcement agencies, begin proceedings against those alleged to have broken federal laws. They also represent the United States in civil suits.

The state and federal governments provide lawyers for poor defendants in criminal trials. Traditionally, private attorneys have been appointed to provide assistance, but many state and federal courts employ a **public defender system**. Salaried public defenders operate in the federal courts under the general supervision of the Administrative Office of the United States Courts. The Judicial Conference of the United States, consisting of circuit and district court judges from around the country, has said that the most important problem confronting the public defender program is lack of money. The Legal Services Corporation also provides financial assistance to 323 organizations that assist the poor in noncriminal legal matters.

Courts cannot resolve all disputes. Some raise **political questions** that would require the use of methods not suitable for a court, for which there is no legal remedy, or which the Constitution explicitly assigns to Congress or the president to decide. Such is the case with many questions arising from the conduct of foreign affairs. Which of two competing state governments is the proper one? Which group of officials of a state or foreign nation should the United States recognize as the government?[9] When the president sends the military into international conflicts without congressional authorization, has the constitutional provision that only Congress may "declare war" been violated? These are political questions.

The political question doctrine is admittedly circular, and the Supreme Court ultimately decides what is and is not a "political question." In 2000, for instance, most observers thought that the Supreme Court would refuse to become involved in deciding which votes from Florida should be counted in the presidential election. There is hardly anything more political than this, and the Constitution specifically charges Congress with the responsibility for counting electoral votes. Nonetheless, the Supreme Court accepted the case in *Bush* v. *Gore*, deliberated promptly, and by a 5-to-4 majority stopped the recount of votes; the four dissenters contended that the matter should have been left to the political branches to decide.[10] In short, as political scientist John Roche observed, "Political questions are matters not soluble by the judicial process; matters not soluble by the judicial process are political questions. As an early dictionary explained, 'violins are small cellos, and cellos are large violins.'"[11]

Judicial Federalism: State and Federal Courts

Most countries have a single, unitary judiciary, but the United States has a dual judicial system of federal and state courts. Alongside the federal judiciary, each state maintains a judiciary of its own, and many large municipalities have judicial systems as complex as those of the states. Within both federal and state systems, judicial power is further

defendant
In a criminal action, the person or party accused of an offense.

plea bargain
Agreement between a prosecutor and a defendant that the defendant will plead guilty to a lesser offense to avoid having to stand trial for a more serious offense.

public defender system
Arrangement whereby public officials are hired to provide legal assistance to people accused of crimes who are unable to hire their own attorneys.

political question
A dispute that requires knowledge of a non-legal character or the use of techniques not suitable for a court or explicitly assigned by the Constitution to Congress or the president; judges refuse to answer constitutional questions that they declare are political.

GLOBAL *Perceptions*

QUESTION: How important is it to you to live in a country where there is a judicial system that treats everyone the same? Is it very important?

In the United States, 89 percent of the public think that a fair judiciary is very important. That is one of the highest percentages around the world—on par with Bangladesh (89) and slightly above that in Kenya and Turkey (88); Germany (87); and Argentina, Brazil, and the Czech Republic (84). But independent courts are ranked even higher in Senegal (91). The countries with the lowest percentages include South Korea (57), Bolivia (56), Angola (51), and Jordan (33).

SOURCE: Pew Global Attitudes Survey, 2003, pp. T73–74.

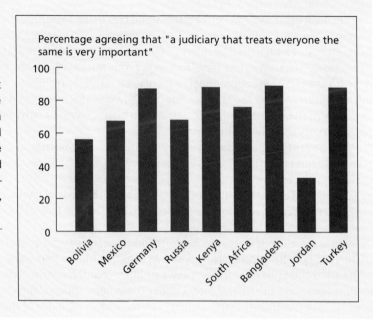

Percentage agreeing that "a judiciary that treats everyone the same is very important"

TYPES OF LAWS

Statutory Law

Law that comes from authoritative and specific lawmaking sources, primarily legislatures but also including treaties and executive orders.

Common Law

Judge-made law that originated in England in the twelfth century, when royal judges traveled around the country settling disputes in each locality according to prevailing custom. The common law continues to develop according to the rule of *stare decisis*, which means "let the decision stand." This is the rule of precedent, which implies that a rule established by a court is to be followed in all similar cases.

writ of habeas corpus
A court order requiring explanation to a judge why a prisoner is being held in custody.

divided between trial courts (and other lesser courts such as traffic courts) and one or more levels of appellate courts, which hear appeals from the lower courts.

The federal and state court systems are related, but not in a superior-inferior hierarchy. State courts primarily interpret and apply their state constitutions and law. When their decisions are based solely on state law, their rulings may not be appealed to or reviewed by federal courts. Only decisions that raise a federal question, involving the application of the Bill of Rights or other federal law, are federal courts able to review. Federal courts have **writ of habeas corpus** jurisdiction (the power to release persons from custody if a judge determines that they are not being detained constitutionally) and may review criminal convictions in state courts for violations of the federal constitutional and legal rights of the accused. Except for habeas corpus jurisdiction, the Supreme Court is the only federal court that may review state court decisions, and only in cases involving a conflict with federal law. Other than the original jurisdiction the Constitution vests directly in the Supreme Court, no federal court has any jurisdiction except that granted to it by an act of Congress. Congress also determines whether the judicial power of the United States is exercised exclusively by federal courts or concurrently by both federal and state courts.

Most litigation occurs in state courts, which annually face about 90 million civil and criminal cases. The type of litigation in state courts also tends to differ from that in federal courts. Apart from criminal cases, the largest portion of state court cases involves economic issues—state regulation of public utilities, zoning and small business, labor relations, natural resources, energy, and the environment. Litigation varies from state to state as well, depending on the size of the population, urbanization, and the economy.[12] (For more information on state courts and links to state court Web sites, go to the site of the National Council of States Courts at www.ncsconline.org.)

THE FEDERAL JUDICIAL SYSTEM

"The judicial Power of the United States," says Article III of the Constitution, "shall be vested in one supreme Court, and in such inferior courts as the Congress may from time to time ordain and establish." Courts created to carry out this judicial power are called

Article III or *constitutional courts.* Congress may also establish *Article I* or *legislative courts*—courts, for instance, to handle bankruptcies, claims involving property damage and contract disputes with the federal government, military appeals, and veterans' appeals—to carry out the legislative powers the Constitution has granted to it. The main difference between a legislative and a constitutional court is that the judges of a legislative court need not be appointed to "hold their Offices during good Behavior" and are appointed for fixed terms; they may be assigned other than purely judicial duties, such as supervising tax collections. Article III judges basically have lifetime appointments, subject only to removal by impeachment; only 11 federal judges have been impeached by the House of Representatives and seven convicted and removed by the Senate.[13]

The Constitution requires a Supreme Court. It is a necessity if the national government is to have the power to make and enforce laws that take precedence over those of the states. The lack of such a court to maintain national supremacy, ensure uniform interpretation of national legislation, and resolve conflicts among the states was one of the glaring defects of government under the Articles of Confederation.

Congress decides whether there will be other courts in addition to the Supreme Court. The First Congress divided the nation into circuits (geographical areas) and created lower courts for each. Today the hierarchy of federal courts of general jurisdiction consists of district courts, courts of appeals, and the Supreme Court (see Figure 14–1). In cases affecting ambassadors, other public ministers, and consuls, and in cases in which a state is a party, the Supreme Court has **original jurisdiction**, the authority of a court to hear a case "in the first instance." In all other cases, the Supreme Court has **appellate jurisdiction**—power to review decisions of other federal courts and agencies, as determined by Congress, and appeals from state supreme court decisions that raise questions of federal law. In general, federal courts may decide only cases or controversies arising under the Constitution, a federal law, a treaty, or admiralty and maritime law; cases brought by a foreign nation against a state or the federal government; and diversity suits—lawsuits between citizens of different states—if the amount of the controversy exceeds $50,000.

District Courts

Although the Supreme Court and its justices receive most of the attention, the workhorses of the federal judiciary are the district courts in the states, the District of Columbia, and U.S. territories. They hear more than 270,000 civil cases and 67,000 criminal cases annually.[14]

FIGURE 14–1 Structure of the Federal Courts.

original jurisdiction
The authority of a court to hear a case "in the first instance."

appellate jurisdiction
The authority of a court to review decisions made by lower courts.

In Comparative Perspective

CONSTITUTIONAL COURTS IN EUROPE

Historically, European countries rejected "American-style" judicial review. European courts remain subordinate to legislatures. After World War II, however, separate constitutional courts were created and set apart from national judiciaries in several countries in Western Europe. Austria was the first in 1945 and other constitutional courts were established in Italy (1948), the Federal Republic of Germany (1949), France (1958), Portugal (1976), Spain (1978), and Belgium (1985). Following the collapse of the former Soviet Union in 1989, constitutional courts were likewise established in the former communist countries of Central and Eastern Europe, including the Czech Republic, Hungary, Poland, Romania, Russia, Slovakia, the Baltics, and the countries of the former Yugoslavia.

A new European model of constitutional judicial review thus emerged. In contrast to the U.S. federal judiciary, which has general jurisdiction over issues of constitutional and statutory law, regular courts in Europe still have no jurisdiction over constitutional matters. Only constitutional courts may decide constitutional issues. That was an innovation,

but it is not all that separates the European model of judicial review from the American one.

In addition, unlike the U.S. federal judiciary's jurisdiction over only actual cases and controversies, European constitutional courts may exercise abstract and concrete review of legislation. Abstract constitutional review of legislation is initiated by elected officials or national and regional governmental bodies with respect to legislation that has been recently adopted but that either has not yet been put into force, as in France; or has not yet been enforced, or has been suspended, pending review by the constitutional court, as in Germany, Italy, and Spain. By contrast, concrete constitutional review arises from challenges to legislation in the courts when regular judges are uncertain about the constitutionality or the application of a statute or ordinance; they refer such cases to the national constitutional court for decision.

For further reading see Carlo Guarnieri and Patrizia Pederzoli, translated by C. A. Thomas, *The Power of Judges: A Comparative Study of Courts and Democracy* (Oxford University Press, 2002); and Ann-Marie Slaughter, Alec Stone Sweet, and J.H.H. Weiler, eds., *The European Court and National Courts—Doctrine and Jurisprudence* (Hart Publishing, 2000).

Each state has at least one federal district court. Larger states have as many as the demands of judicial business and the pressure of politics require, although no state has more than four. There are 665 judgeships in 94 district courts, located in each of the 50 states, the District of Columbia, and the Commonwealth of Puerto Rico. Each federal circuit has at least one district court judge but may have as many as 99.

District courts are the trial courts of original jurisdiction. They are the only federal courts that regularly employ **grand juries**, which are used to secure criminal indictments, and **petit juries**, used in trials. When cases tried before district judges involve citizens of different states, judges apply the appropriate state laws. Otherwise, district judges are concerned with federal laws. For example, they decide cases involving crimes against the United States—suits under the national revenue, postal, patent, copyright, trademark, bankruptcy, and civil rights laws.[15]

District judges normally sit separately and hold court by themselves; however, they sit in three-judge panels in cases involving reapportionment and voting rights. They are appointed by the president, subject to confirmation by the Senate, and hold office for life. District judges appoint and are assisted by clerks, bailiffs, stenographers, law clerks, court reporters, and probation officers.

District court judges also appoint **magistrate judges**, who are increasingly important because of rising caseloads. After being screened by panels composed of residents of the judicial districts, full-time magistrates are appointed for eight-year renewable terms and part-time magistrates for four-year renewable terms. There are 486 full-time and 51 part-time federal magistrate judges. Magistrates look and act like judges. Most wear robes and since 1990 are addressed as "Judge." They issue arrest warrants, hold hearings to determine whether arrested persons should be held for action by the grand jury, and if so, set bail. They hear motions subject to varying kinds of review by their district judges. They preside over civil trials—jury and nonjury—with the consent of both

grand jury
A jury of 12 to 23 persons who, in private, hear evidence presented by the government to determine whether persons shall be required to stand trial. If the jury believes there is sufficient evidence that a crime was committed, it issues an indictment.

petit jury
A jury of 6 to 12 persons who determine guilt or innocence in a civil or criminal action.

magistrate judge
An official who performs a variety of limited judicial duties.

parties and over nonjury trials for misdemeanors and petty offenses with the consent of the defendants. Under the supervision of the district judge, and with the consent of the accused, a magistrate may preside over preliminary hearings and the selection of a jury for a felony trial.[16]

Courts of Appeals

The decisions of federal district courts may be appealed and reviewed by federal **courts of appeals**, although reapportionment and voting rights cases decided by three-judge panels are taken directly to the Supreme Court. District judges are bound by the precedents of higher courts, but they have considerable discretion in applying them. Courts of appeals are located geographically in 11 *judicial circuits* that include all the states and U.S. territories (see Figure 14–2). A twelfth is located in the District of Columbia and hears the largest number of cases challenging federal statutes, regulations, and administrative decisions. The thirteenth appellate court is the Court of Appeals for the Federal Circuit, which is located in the District of Columbia and has national jurisdiction, though it deals primarily with appeals in patent, copyright, and international trade cases. The largest circuit is the ninth, with 28 circuit judges and 99 district judges. It is geographically the size of western Europe and contains 20 percent of the U.S. population.

Each circuit court of appeals consists of 6 to 28 permanent judgeships (179 in all). These courts normally hear cases in panels of three judges. But in especially important and controversial cases, all judges may be present; that is, they sit *en banc.* They annually hear about 57,000 appeals.

Although courts of appeals have only appellate jurisdiction, they are powerful policy makers. Fewer than 1 percent of their decisions are appealed to the Supreme Court. As the policy-making role of federal courts has become a prominent political issue, more attention has focused on these courts and the judges who serve on them.[17] One current controversy involves the growing failure of appellate courts to publish their opinions, due to their growing caseloads, and whether unpublished opinions are binding precedents.[18] Another controversy revolves around whether the number of judges should be increased to keep pace with rising caseloads. (For more information about the federal judiciary, go to the Web site of the Administrative Office of the U.S. Courts at www.uscourts.gov.)

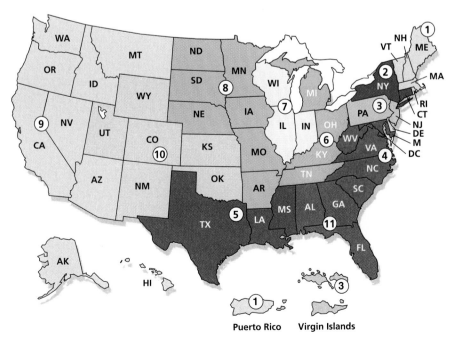

FIGURE 14–2 The Eleven U.S. Circuit Courts of Appeals.

court of appeals
A court with appellate jurisdiction that hears appeals from the decisions of lower courts.

THE POLITICS OF APPOINTING FEDERAL JUDGES

The selection of federal judges has always been a significant part of the political process. It makes a difference who serves on the federal courts. As the courts play an even more important role in the political process and as more and more interests—African Americans and women, for example—participate in that process, judicial selection politics has come front and center on the political stage.

Article II of the Constitution gives the president the power to appoint federal judges with the advice and consent of the Senate. Political reality imposes constraints on the president's discretion, so the selection of a federal judge is actually a complex bargaining process. The principal figures involved are the candidates, the president, and the "subpresidency for judicial selection,"[19] consisting of key members of the Department of Justice, U.S. senators, the American Bar Association, party leaders, and, increasingly, interest groups. In addition, recent presidents have inserted the White House much more directly into the process than their predecessors did.

Department of Justice officials and key White House staff meet often to review proposed candidates. Since the Reagan administration, the assistant attorney general in charge of the Office of Legal Policy in the Department of Justice oversees the screening of potential judicial nominees. After candidates' backgrounds and judicial philosophies have been checked, they are discussed by a White House working group that includes the legal counselor to the president and the attorney general. This group recommends to the president whom to nominate to the federal bench. (For more information about the Office of Legal Policy and current judicial nominations, go to its Web site at www.usdoj.gov/olp.)

In practice, before the White House submits names of nominees for the federal district and appeals courts, it observes the practice of **senatorial courtesy**—the custom of submitting the names of prospective appointees for approval to the senators from the states in which the appointees are to work. If negotiations are deadlocked between the senators or between the senators and the Department of Justice, a seat may stay vacant for years.[20] The custom of senatorial courtesy does not apply to Supreme Court appointments, since they have national jurisdiction; nevertheless, President Clinton consulted with Republican Senator Orrin Hatch, who at the time chaired the Senate Judiciary Committee because the Senate was controlled by Republicans, so as to avoid a confirmation battle over his nominees to the Supreme Court, Justices Ruth Bader Ginsburg in 1993 and Stephen Breyer in 1994.

In addition, liberal interest groups, such as People for the American Way and the Alliance for Justice, as well as conservative groups, such as the Heritage Foundation and a coalition of 260 conservative organizations called the Judicial Selection Monitoring Project, monitor potential judicial candidates. These organizations used to wait until after the president sent the name of a nominee to the Senate, but now they are active in the preliminaries, making known their views even before the names of nominees are released to the public or sent to the Senate Judiciary Committee.

The American Bar Association's Standing Committee on the Federal Judiciary once played a special role in evaluating candidates. Presidents were hesitant to submit for Senate confirmation a candidate rated "not qualified" by the ABA. In recent years, conservative groups mounted an attack on the ABA's role, contending that it reflects a liberal bias and has given low ratings to some conservative nominees. In response to this criticism, shortly after taking office, President George W. Bush announced in March 2001 that the ABA would no longer be asked to evaluate judicial candidates before nomination. But senators on the Judiciary Committee continue to receive the ABA's evaluations of judicial nominees.

senatorial courtesy
Presidential custom of submitting the names of prospective appointees for approval to senators from the states in which the appointees are to work.

Senate: Advice and Consent

The normal presumption is that the president should be allowed considerable discretion in the selection of federal judges. Despite this presumption, the Senate takes seriously its responsibility in confirming judicial nominations, especially when the party controlling the Senate is different from that of the president, as has been the case in recent years.

When the Senate receives the name of a judicial nominee, it sends the nomination to the Judiciary Committee for consideration. Before the committee holds a hearing on the nominee, it sends to the senators of the nominee's home state a letter—called a "blue slip" because of its color—asking whether they approve. If one of the senators declines to return the slip, the nomination is dead, and no hearing will be held. During the last two years of Clinton's presidency, Republican senators delayed and defeated confirmation of many of his judicial nominees in this way. With Democrats in control of the Senate during his first two years, they retaliated and stalled the confirmation of a number of President George W. Bush's nominees. After Republicans regained control of the Senate following the 2002 midterm elections, Democrats continued to oppose some of Bush's most conservative nominees and in several cases held filibusters in order to prevent a Senate vote on their confirmation.[21] If both home-state senators approve of a nominee, the committee holds a hearing, votes on the nominee, and sends its recommendation to the full Senate for consideration and confirmation based on a majority vote.

Prior to 1955, the common practice was for the Senate to look into candidates' qualifications and background but not to interview the person. But since then, the committee has asked judicial nominees a wide range of questions, since their judicial and political philosophy is a major factor in determining how they might vote on particular cases and controversies. Except for Robert Bork, nominated by President Ronald Reagan in 1987, most judicial nominees have refused to answer questions that might reveal how they would decide a case. But Judge Bork had written so many articles, made so many speeches, and decided so many cases that he thought he had to clarify his constitutional views. His candor may well have contributed to the Senate's rejection of him, and that has made subsequent nominees even more reluctant to respond to similar questions.

Until recently, most judicial appointments, especially those for the lower federal courts, were processed without much controversy. However, "now that lower court judges are more commonly viewed as political actors, there is increasing Senate scrutiny of these nominees."[22] The battle over judicial confirmations ordinarily takes place before the Senate Judiciary Committee. The Senate usually goes along with the recommendations of its Judiciary Committee without much debate, although floor debates are not all that rare. Overall, the Senate has refused to confirm 29 of the 138 presidential nominations for Supreme Court justices.[23]

The Role of Party, Race, and Gender

Presidents so seldom nominate judges from the opposing party (around 90 percent of judicial appointments since the time of Franklin Roosevelt have gone to candidates from the president's party) that partisan considerations are taken for granted, and partisan affiliation is rarely mentioned. Today more attention is paid to other characteristics, such as ideology, race, and gender.[24]

President Jimmy Carter, who had no opportunity to make an appointment to the Supreme Court, selected more African Americans, Hispanics, and women for the lower federal courts than all other prior presidents combined—40 women, 37 African Americans, and 16 Hispanics. President Ronald Reagan, although the first to appoint a woman to the Supreme Court, appointed fewer minority members or women than Carter did, perhaps in part because fewer minorities and women could pass the Reagan administration's ideological screening.[25] Twenty percent of George H.W. Bush's appointees were women, 7 percent African Americans, and 4 percent Hispanics.[26]

Bill Clinton promised to appoint federal judges who would be more representative of the ethnic makeup of the United States. "We don't have litmus tests or judicial-philosophy tests," insisted Assistant Attorney General Eleanor Dean Acheson, who oversaw judicial selection during the Clinton administration, "but I do think we've put people on the bench who are interested in people and their problems"[27] and brought diversity to the federal bench. Clinton lived up to his pledge by naming more women and minorities to the bench than his predecessors had; 182 of his 367 appointees were women and minorities, 49 percent of his appointees.

George W. Bush appointed a number of women and minorities in his first year in office but fewer thereafter. About 37 percent of his judicial nominees were women and minorities; 41 women (20 percent), 14 African Americans (7 percent), 18 Hispanics (9 percent), one Arab American, and one Asian American were appointed.[28]

The Role of Ideology

Finding a party member is not enough; presidents want to pick the "right" kind of Republican or "our" kind of Democrat to serve as judges. By and large, they have been able to achieve this goal. Judges picked by Republican presidents tend to be judicial conservatives (with some notable exceptions, such as President Dwight Eisenhower's appointments of Chief Justice Earl Warren and Justice William J. Brennan Jr., President Gerald Ford's appointment of Justice John Paul Stevens, and President George H. W. Bush's appointment of Justice David H. Souter). Judges picked by Democratic presidents are more likely to be liberals. Both of these orientations are tempered by the fact that judges must go through a senatorial confirmation process that during recent administrations has been rigorous and driven by opposition to the White House.[29]

President Ronald Reagan's two terms made it possible for him to join Presidents Franklin D. Roosevelt and Dwight D. Eisenhower as the only presidents in the last century to appoint a majority of the federal bench. All told, Reagan appointed 368 lifetime judges. His administration acted carefully to nominate only those whose views about the role of the courts and constitutional issues were consistent with Reagan's own.[30] Not only were a large number of judicial conservatives appointed, but many of them—because they were comparatively young—will continue to have an effect on judicial policy well into the twenty-first century.

Because President George H. W. Bush was less committed to conservatism than Reagan, conservative organizations—the Heritage Foundation, the Pacific Legal Foun-

PEOPLE & POLITICS *Making a Difference* ★ ★ ★

JUSTICE SANDRA DAY O'CONNOR

Appointed to the Supreme Court by Republican President Ronald Reagan in 1981, Justice Sandra Day O'Connor is the first woman to serve on the high bench. After graduating at the top of her class from Stanford Law School, she found it difficult to find a job in her home state of Arizona. She eventually entered politics, serving first as assistant attorney general and then winning election to the Arizona state senate, where she served until her appointment to a state trial court and later to a state intermediate court of appeals.

On the Supreme Court, Justice O'Connor is conservative but less hardline than the other Reagan appointees. She casts the deciding vote on contro-versial issues such as abortion, affirmative action, minority-majority voting districts, and some disputes involving the separation of church and state.

Because Justice O'Connor is at the center of the Rehnquist Court and casts so many deciding votes, when she retires a controversy over the appointment of her successor may arise and the balance of power on the Court is certain to change.

Justice O'Connor and her brother, H. Alan Day, published a book on their growing up in rural Arizona in the early twentieth century, *Lazy B: Growing Up on a Cattle Ranch in the American Southwest* (Random House, 2002). More recently, Justice O'Connor published a book of es-

says on law and her approach to constitutional interpretation, *The Majesty of the Law: Reflections of a Supreme Court Justice* (New York: Random House, 2003).

CHANGING FACE OF AMERICAN POLITICS

DIVERSITY ON THE FEDERAL BENCH

The federal judiciary has long been dominated by white males. But diversity on the federal bench has been increasing during the last several decades, largely due to the judicial appointments of Democratic Presidents Jimmy Carter and Bill Clinton.

Although the number of women and minorities appointed to the federal courts has only recently increased significantly, the first woman, Judge Florence Allen, was appointed in 1934 by President Franklin D. Roosevelt. President Harry Truman named the first African American, Judge William Henry Hastie, in 1950. President John F. Kennedy appointed the first Hispanic, Judge Reynaldo G. Garza, in 1961, and President Richard M. Nixon in 1971 appointed the first Asian American, Judge Herbert Choy. The first Native American, Judge

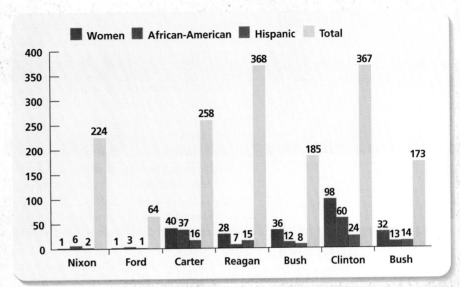

Legend: ■ Women   ■ African-American   ■ Hispanic   ▢ Total

Nixon: 1, 6, 2, 224
Ford: 1, 3, 1, 64
Carter: 40, 37, 16, 258
Reagan: 28, 7, 15, 368
Bush: 36, 12, 8, 185
Clinton: 98, 60, 24, 367
Bush: 32, 13, 14, 173

SOURCE: David M. O'Brien, "Ironies and Disappointments: Bush and Federal Judgeships," in Colin Campbell and Bert A. Rockman, eds., *The George W. Bush Presidency: Appraisals and Prospects* 147 (CQ Press, 2004); as updated through May 6, 2004, based on the data of the Federal Judicial Center at http://fcj.gov/newweb/ jnetweb.nsf/hisj.

Billy Michael Burrage, was appointed in 1994 by President Clinton.

dation, and the Federalist Society—focused more attention on his judicial nominees. Bush appointed 148 district judges, 37 appellate judges, and two Supreme Court justices—David Souter and Clarence Thomas. It turned out that his appointees, with the exception of Justice Souter, were among the most conservative in recent history.[31] His appointment of Justice Thomas helped consolidate the Court's "turn to the right."[32]

President Clinton gave Democratic senators "clear guidelines about the kind of judges he wants"[33]—competent professionals who would bring diversity to the bench. But after the Republicans took control of the Senate in 1994, Clinton instructed his advisers to consult closely with Republican Senator Orrin Hatch, chair of the Senate Judiciary Committee. Clinton abandoned or declined to nominate several judicial candidates opposed by conservative interest groups and had to reach compromises with Republican senators. In his second term, Clinton faced increasing opposition from the Republican-controlled Senate, which slowed down confirmations to such an extent that Chief Justice Rehnquist, in his annual reports on the federal judiciary, scolded the Senate for jeopardizing the ability of the federal courts to do their work. Despite the slowdown in Senate confirmations, by the time Clinton left office, he had named 367 of the 849 authorized federal judges and brought greater diversity to the federal bench.[34]

President George W. Bush likewise confronted increasing difficulties over his judicial nominees from the Democrats in the Senate. Democrats delayed Bush's most conservative nominees and held filibusters in order to prevent confirmation votes on ten appellate court nominees. In retaliation Bush bypassed the Senate by naming two—Judges Charles W. Pickering and William H. Pryor—to recess appointments, which they will hold until the next session of Congress in 2005; recess appointments, which go into

Justice David Souter was confirmed by an overwhelming vote in 1990, despite a dearth of information on his ideological orientation.

Justice Ruth Bader Ginsburg, a moderate nominated by President Clinton, was easily confirmed by the Senate in 1993.

Justice Stephen Breyer, another moderate Clinton nominee, was confirmed without fanfare in 1994.

judicial self-restraint
Philosophy proposing that judges should interpret the Constitution to reflect what the framers intended and what its words literally say.

judicial activism
Philosophy proposing that judges should interpret the Constitution to reflect current conditions and values.

effect without confirmation, have been made in only a handful of instances in the last 30 years.[35] Finally, five months before the 2004 presidential election the impasse was broken by a bipartisan deal. Democrats agreed to allow votes on the confirmation of 20 district court nominees and five appellate court nominees. In return, Bush agreed not to make any more recess appointments.[36]

The Role of Judicial Philosophy

What about a candidate's judicial philosophy? Does a candidate believe that judges should interpret the Constitution to reflect what the framers intended and what its words literally say; that is, does the candidate believe in **judicial self-restraint?** Or does the candidate believe that the Constitution should be adapted to reflect current conditions and philosophies; that is, does the candidate believe in **judicial activism?**

Throughout most of our history, federal courts have been more conservative than Congress, the White House, or state legislatures. Prior to 1937, judicial self-restraint was the battle cry of liberals who objected to judges' interpreting the due process clauses of the Fifth and Fourteenth Amendments to strike down many laws passed to protect labor and women and to keep the national and state governments from regulating the economy. These judges broadly construed the words of the Constitution to prevent what they thought to be unreasonable regulations of property.

With Presidents Richard Nixon, Ronald Reagan, George H. W. Bush, and George W. Bush, however, the judicial shoe was on the other foot, and it was conservatives who were advocates of judicial self-restraint. What is needed, they argued, are judges who will let Congress, the president, and the state legislatures regulate or forbid abortions, permit prayer in public schools, impose capital punishment, and not hinder law enforcement.

Still, it would be wrong to assume that judicial philosophy is nothing more than another way to argue about political ideology. Some conservatives, for example, favor judicial activism because they want current judges to reverse the last half-century of precedents on civil rights and to protect property rights from government regulation. The conservative majority on the Rehnquist Court has invited criticisms from liberals for its judicial activism in overturning precedents and striking down state and federal laws promoting affirmative action, for example, and invalidating congressional enactments for infringing on states' rights. In these areas, liberals favor judicial restraint because they believe that judges should defer to the democratic process and that democratic self-governance will flourish if judges stay out of such policy debates.

Hence the debate over the role of the Supreme Court and the federal judiciary today is less about activism and restraint than about competing conceptions of the proper balance between government authority and individual rights, between the power of democratically accountable legislatures and that of courts and unelected judges. The debate is also about whether and on what basis judges should make law.

Do Judges Make Law?

"Do judges make law? 'Course they do. Made some myself."[37] That was the candid response of New Hampshire Justice Jeremiah Smith. Most judges are less candid. Judges obviously make law, but to admit it is somehow disturbing. Such statements do not conform to popular notions of what judges do.

Why do people think judges should not make law? Many people equate a judge's role with that of a referee in a prizefight, because of their role in trials and the adversary system. We expect referees to be impartial and disinterested, treating both parties as equals. We expect them to apply rules, not make them. Laws are not made, however, in the same way as the rules of a sport, and therein lies the answer to our question. Not only *do* judges make law, but they *must.*

Legislatures make law by enacting statutes, but judges must apply the statutes to concrete situations. Statutes are drawn in broad terms: Drivers shall act with "reasonable care"; no one may make "excessive noise" in the vicinity of a hospital; employers must maintain "safe working conditions." Such broad terms must be used because legislators cannot know exactly what will happen in every circumstance. Courts must judge their application in concrete cases. In the words of Justice Felix Frankfurter, "Legislatures make law wholesale, judges retail."[38]

The problems of interpreting and applying law are intensified when judges are required—as American judges are—to apply our almost 220-year-old Constitution. The Constitution is full of generalizations: "due process of law," "equal protection of the laws," "unreasonable searches and seizures," "Commerce . . . among several States." Recourse to the intent of the framers or to the words of the Constitution may not help judges facing cases involving thermal imaging and other new forms of governmental surveillance, the Internet, reproductive rights, or same-sex marriages.

Adherence to Precedent

Just because judges make policy, they are not free to do whatever they wish. They are subject to a variety of limits on what they decide—some imposed by the political system of which they are a part and some imposed by higher courts and the legal profession. Among these constraints is the policy of ***stare decisis***, the rule of precedent.

Stare decisis pervades our judicial system and promotes certainty, uniformity, and stability in the law. Judges are expected to abide by previous decisions of their own courts and by rulings of superior courts. Although adherence to precedent is the norm, the doctrine of *stare decisis* is not very restrictive.[39] Judges may distinguish between precedents because of differences in the context of cases, and many questions of law have conflicting precedents that can be used to support a decision for either party.

The doctrine of *stare decisis* is even less controlling in the field of constitutional law. Because the Constitution itself, rather than any one interpretation of it, is binding, the Court can *reverse* a previous decision it no longer wishes to follow, as it has done hundreds of times. Supreme Court justices are therefore not seriously restricted by *stare decisis*. Liberal Justice William O. Douglas, for one, maintained that *stare decisis* "was really no sure guideline because what did the judges who sat there in 1875 know about, say, electronic surveillance? They didn't know anything about it."[40] Chief Justice William H. Rehnquist is no less candid in holding that precedents dealing with civil rights that were handed down on a 5-to-4 vote should always be open for reconsideration, since they were decided by only a bare majority of the Court. Since 1789, the Supreme Court has reversed 218 of its own decisions and overturned more than 174 acts of Congress, more than 967 pieces of state legislation and state constitutional provisions, and more than 115 city ordinances.[41]

Judicial Longevity and Presidential Tenure

Ideology and judicial philosophy affect not only presidents' nominations for the federal courts but also when sitting judges choose to retire. Because federal judges serve for life, they may be able to schedule their retirement to allow a president whose views they approve to nominate their successors. Chief Justice Roger B. Taney stayed on the bench long after his health began to fail to prevent President Abraham Lincoln from nominating a Republican. In 1929, Chief Justice William Howard Taft wrote: "I am older and slower and less acute and more confused. However, as long as things continue as they are, and I am able to answer in my place, I must stay on the court in order to prevent the Bolsheviki [Herbert Hoover, a conservative Republican, was in the White House] from getting control."[42]

Although Chief Justice Warren Burger denied that he retired in 1986 in order to permit President Ronald Reagan to replace him with a conservative, his retirement gave Reagan an opportunity to rejuvenate the conservative wing of the Court by promoting William H. Rehnquist to the chief justiceship. Reagan then picked another conservative, Antonin Scalia, to take the seat vacated by Rehnquist. Liberal Supreme Court Justices William J. Brennan Jr. and Thurgood Marshall held on to their seats well into their eighties, and many assumed that they were doing so in the hope that they might be able to stay on the Court until a president more congenial to their views might be in the

stare decisis
The rule of precedent, whereby a rule or law contained in a judicial decision is commonly viewed as binding on judges whenever the same question is presented.

After a contentious confirmation process in 1987, the Senate rejected Judge Robert Bork by a vote of 58 to 42.

Despite extensive controversy surrounding his nomination, the Senate narrowly confirmed Justice Clarence Thomas in 1991.

White House. They did not make it. Republican President George H. W. Bush, rather than a Democrat, appointed their successors. It should be noted, however, that personal and institutional factors other than partisan concerns are the main reason justices retire.[43]

Reform of the Selection Process

The televised confirmation hearings of Robert Bork in 1987 and Clarence Thomas in 1991, which were lengthy and embattled, aroused considerable criticism from both liberals and conservatives and called forth widespread complaints that "something is wrong with the process." Subsequently, several task forces and studies recommended that attempts be made to constrain the partisan politics surrounding the confirmation process for Supreme Court justices and lower federal court judges. They proposed that "Supreme Court nominees should no longer be expected to appear as witnesses during the Senate Judiciary Committee's hearings on their confirmation" and that the Senate should return to the practice of judging nominees on their written record and on the testimony of legal experts.[44] A bipartisan commission on judicial selection from the Miller Center of Public Affairs at the University of Virginia recommended that the time between nominations and Senate confirmation be shortened.[45] But the problems of delaying and blocking confirmation of judicial nominees remain, as both Presidents Clinton and George W. Bush found, particularly when the Senate is controlled by the party in opposition to the president.[46]

The politics of judicial selection may shock those who like to think judges are picked strictly on the basis of legal merit and without regard for ideology, party, gender, or race. But as a former Justice Department official observed, "When courts cease being an instrument for political change, then maybe the judges will stop being politically selected."[47] Moreover, as another scholar put it, "Supreme Court Justices have always been appointed for political reasons by politicians, and their confirmation process has always been dictated by politicians for political purposes. . . . In fact," he concluded, "not despite the politicization of the appointment and confirmation process, but because of it, the Supreme Court has endured as a flexible, viable force in the American democracy for over 200 years."[48]

CHANGING THE NUMBERS One of the first actions a political party takes after gaining control of the White House and Congress is often to increase the number of federal judgeships. With divided government, however, when one party controls Congress and the other holds the White House, a stalemate is likely to occur, and relatively few new judicial positions will be created. During Andrew Johnson's administration, Congress went so far as to reduce the size of the Supreme Court to prevent the president from filling two vacancies. After Johnson left the White House, Congress returned the Court to its former size to permit Ulysses S. Grant to fill the vacancies.

In 1937, President Franklin Roosevelt proposed an increase in the size of the Supreme Court by one additional justice for every member of the Court over the age of 70, up to a total of 15 members. Ostensibly, the proposal was aimed at making the Court more efficient. In fact, Roosevelt and his advisers were frustrated because the Court had declared much of the early New Deal legislation unconstitutional. Despite Roosevelt's popularity, his "court-packing scheme" aroused intense opposition. Roosevelt's proposals to change the Court's size failed. He lost the battle but won the war, as the Court began to sustain some important New Deal legislation, and subsequent retirements from the bench enabled him to make eight appointments to the Court.

CHANGING THE JURISDICTION Congressional control over the structure and jurisdiction of federal courts has been used to influence the course of judicial policy making. Although unable to get rid of Federalist judges by impeachment, the Jeffersonians abolished the circuit courts created by the Federalist Congress just before they lost control. In 1869, radical Republicans in Congress altered the Supreme Court's appellate jurisdiction in order to snatch from the Court a case it was about to review involving the constitutionality of some Reconstruction legislation.[49]

Each year, a number of bills are introduced in Congress to eliminate the jurisdiction of federal courts over cases relating to abortion, school prayer, and school busing or to eliminate the appellate jurisdiction of the Supreme Court over such matters. These attacks on federal court jurisdiction spark debate about whether the Constitution gives Congress authority to take such actions. And Congress has not yet decided to do so, because it would amount to a fundamental shift in the relationship between Congress and the Supreme Court. As one scholar concluded, "History suggests the public has seen such attempts for precisely what they are, as attacks on judicial independence, and such attacks have been resisted."[50]

THE SUPREME COURT AND HOW IT OPERATES

The Supreme Court's term runs from the first Monday in October through the end of June. The justices listen to oral arguments for two weeks each month from October to April and then adjourn for two weeks to consider the cases and to write opinions. By agreement, six justices must participate in each decision. Cases are decided by a majority vote. In the event of a tie vote, the decision of the lower court is sustained, although on rare occasions the case may be reargued.

At 10:00 A.M. on the days when the Supreme Court sits, the eight associate justices and the chief justice, dressed in their robes (Chief Justice Rehnquist has four gold stripes on each sleeve of his robe), file into the courtroom. As they take their seats—arranged according to seniority, with the chief justice in the center—the clerk of the Court introduces them as the "Honorable Chief Justice and Associate Justices of the Supreme Court of the United States." Those present in the courtroom, asked to stand when the justices enter, are seated, and counsel take their places along tables in front of the bench. The attorneys for the Department of Justice are at the right. The other attorneys are dressed conservatively; sport coats are not considered proper. Dress and ceremony are all part of the high ritual of the Court (see Figure 14–3).

1. Courtyards
2. Solicitor General's Office
3. Lawyers' Lounge
4. Marshall's Office
5. Main Hall
6. Court Room
7. Conference and Reception Rooms
8. Justices' Conference Room
9. Chief Justice's Chambers
10. Justices' Chambers

FIGURE 14–3 The Supreme Court Building.

DOES THE NUMBER OF FEDERAL JUDGES NEED TO BE INCREASED IN ORDER TO ENSURE ACCESS TO JUSTICE?

The Committee on Long-Range Planning of the Judicial Conference of the United States has studied the increasing caseload of federal courts and projects a continued growth in cases and a need for more judges. In 1950 the federal judiciary handled a caseload of 93,835 cases with 289 judges. Thirty years later, in 1980, the case filings more than doubled to 219,957 cases and the number of judges had grown to 648. With continued growth in the size of the federal caseload, it is estimated that in 2010 the lower federal courts will face 814,100 cases and require 2,350 judges. By 2020, it is projected that federal district courts alone will confront over 1 million cases and require over 2,400 judges, while the appellate courts will require more than 1,500 judges in order to handle the projected 325,100 appeals.*

*Committee on Long-Range Planning, Judicial Conference of the United States, *Proposed Long-Range Plan for the Federal Courts* (Judicial Conference of the United States, 1995), pp. 14–15.

The Powers of the Chief Justice

The chief justice of the United States is appointed by the president upon confirmation by the Senate, like other federal judges. Yet the chief justice heads the entire federal judiciary; as a result, he (in our history, all have been men) has greater visibility than if selected by rotation of fellow justices, as is the practice in the state supreme courts, or by seniority, as is the practice in the federal courts of appeals. The chief justice has special administrative responsibilities in overseeing the operation of the judiciary, such as assigning judges to committees, responding to proposed legislation that affects the judiciary, and delivering the Annual Report on the State of the Judiciary.

But within the Supreme Court, the chief justice is only "first among equals," even though periods in Court history are often named after the chief justice. As Chief Justice Rehnquist said when he was still an associate justice, the chief deals not with "eight subordinates whom he may direct or instruct, but eight associates who, like him, have tenure during good behavior, and who are as independent as hogs on ice."[51] As political scientist David Danelski observed, "The Chief Justiceship does not guarantee leadership. It only offers its incumbent an opportunity to lead." Yet the chief justice "sets the tone, controls the conference, assigns the most opinions, and usually, takes the most important, nation-changing decisions for himself."[52]

The ability of the chief justice to influence the Court has varied considerably. Chief Justice Charles Evans Hughes ran the conferences like a stern schoolmaster, keeping the justices on the point, moving the discussion along, and doing his best to work out compromises in order to achieve unanimous decisions, which carry greater weight. By contrast, Chief Justice Harlan F. Stone encouraged justices to state their own points of view and let the discussions wander. Chief Justice Warren Burger was not very successful in leading conferences. He devoted much of his time to judicial reform, speaking to bar associations and trying to build political support for modernizing the judicial process.

William H. Rehnquist had 15 years of Court experience prior to his elevation to chief justice. Unlike his predecessor, he moves conferences along quickly with a dry sense of humor and concise statements of the cases. Moroever, as the Reagan–Bush justices became a majority, his constitutional views on federalism, crime control, and affirmative action, formerly expressed in his dissenting opinions, became the opinions of the Court.

Which Cases Reach the Supreme Court?

When citizens vow to take their cases to the highest court of the land even if it costs their last penny, they underestimate the difficulty of securing Supreme Court review and misunderstand the Court's role. The rules for appealing a case are established by the Supreme Court and Congress. Until 1988, when Congress enacted the Act to Improve the Administration of Justice, the Supreme Court was obliged by law to review a large number of appeals. Today, however, almost all appeals come to the Court by means of a discretionary ***writ of certiorari***, a formal petition used to bring a case before the Court that may be denied. Since the Supreme Court's docket is now largely discretionary, it has the power to set its own agenda and to select which cases it wishes to review. As a result, the justices decide fewer than 100 of the over 9,000 cases appealed to them annually. That is half the number of cases decided annually two decades ago (see Figure 14–4).[53]

The crucial factor in determining whether the Supreme Court reviews a case is its importance to the operation of the governmental system as a whole. The Supreme Court will review a case only if the claim involves a substantial question of federal law that has broad public significance—what kinds of affirmative action programs are permissible, whether individuals have a right to doctor-assisted suicide, or under what conditions women may have abortions. The Court also tends to review cases in which rulings among the courts of appeals are in conflict, and by deciding a case, the Supreme Court establishes which ruling is to be followed. Or a case may raise a constitutional issue on which a state supreme court has presented an interpretation with which the Court disagrees.

writ of certiorari
A formal writ used to bring a case before the Supreme Court.

The Court grants cases based on the *rule of four.* If four justices are sufficiently interested in a petition for a *writ of certiorari,* it will be granted and the case brought up for review. The justices' law clerks read the petitions and write a memorandum on each, recommending whether a review should be granted. These memos circulate to all the justices except Justice John Paul Stevens, whose law clerks review the petitions for him, and he reads a few of them himself.[54]

Denial of a *writ of certiorari* does not mean that the justices agree with the decision of the lower court, nor does it establish precedent. Refusal to grant a review may indicate all kinds of possibilities. The justices may wish to avoid a political "hot potato," or the Court may be so divided on an issue that it is not yet prepared to take a stand, or it may want to let an issue "percolate" in the federal courts so that the Court may benefit from their rulings before it decides. The Court tends to take cases on which two or more appellate courts have rendered conflicting rulings on an issue, in order to resolve their conflict and to provide uniformity to the law.[55]

After a case is granted review, each side prepares written *briefs* presenting legal arguments, relevant precedents, and historical background for the justices and their law clerks to study and on the basis of which to render their decisions.

The Role of the Law Clerks

Beginning in the 1920s and 1930s, federal judges began hiring the best recent graduates of law schools to serve as clerks for a year or two. As the judicial workload increased, more law clerks have been appointed. Today each Supreme Court justice is entitled to four clerks. These are young people who have graduated from a leading law school and have previously clerked for a federal or state court.

Each justice picks his or her own clerks and works closely with them throughout the term. Clerks screen writs of certiorari and prepare draft opinions for the justices. Some observers and former law clerks claim that the justices now depend too much on their clerks and that the Court is "clerk-driven."[56] As the number of law clerks and computers has increased, so has the number of concurring and dissenting opinions. Today's opinions are longer and have more footnotes and elaborate citations of cases and law review articles. This is the result of the greater number of law clerks and that the justices' chambers operate like "nine little law firms," often practicing law against each other.[57]

The Solicitor General

Attorneys in the Department of Justice and from other federal agencies participate in more than half of the cases that the Supreme Court agrees to decide and therefore play a crucial role in setting its agenda. Of special importance is the *solicitor general* (SG), who represents the federal government before the Supreme Court and is sometimes called the "tenth justice."[58]

When the SG petitions the Supreme Court to review a decision of a lower court, the Court is likely to do so. That is in part because no appeal may be taken on behalf of the United States to any appellate court without the approval of the solicitor general. Hence the SG's office may pick which cases to appeal. Although an appointee of the president, the SG has considerable independence from the White House. The SG also relies on deputy attorneys general, who are experienced career attorneys and enjoy a reputation for the high quality of their work.

FIGURE 14–4 Supreme Court's Increasing Caseload.
SOURCE: David M. O'Brien, *Storm Center: The Supreme Court in American Politics,* 7th ed. (Norton, 2005).

The solicitor general also files *amicus curiae* (Latin for "friend of the court") **briefs** in cases in which the federal government is not a party. The practice of filing *amicus curiae* briefs guarantees that the Department of Justice is represented if a suit questions the constitutionality of an act of Congress or the executive branch. The solicitor general may also use these briefs to bring to the Court's attention the views of the current administration.[59] On occasion, though, solicitors general appear to compromise their independence, as during the administrations of Ronald Reagan and George H. W. Bush, in too aggressively asking the Court to overturn precedents.[60] Still, when the SG appears before the Supreme Court, only respectful formal attire is worn—dark vest, tails, and striped pants. (Briefs filed by the solicitor general may be found on the Web at www.usdoj.gov/osg.)

Amicus Curiae Briefs

Individuals, interest groups, and organizations may also file *amicus curiae* briefs if they claim to have an interest in the case and to have information of value to the Court.[61] An *amicus* brief may help the justices by presenting arguments or facts that the parties to the case have not raised. In recent decades, interest groups have increasingly filed such briefs in an effort to influence the Court and to counter the positions of the solicitor general and the government.

In *Webster* v. *Reproductive Health Services,* dealing with a Missouri law regulating abortions and asking the Court to reverse *Roe* v. *Wade,* 78 *amicus* briefs were filed.[62] In *United States* v. *Lopez,* which challenged congressional authority to ban guns in and around schools, more than 40 parties filed a dozen *amicus* briefs. Ohio, New York, and the District of Columbia argued in favor of federal power, as did associations of police and school officials. On the other side were some conservative public interest firms, the National Governors Association, and the National League of Cities.[63]

Interest groups once filed *amicus curiae* briefs before the Supreme Court granted a *writ of certiorari* in order to encourage the Supreme Court to review the case. Their doing so enhanced the probability that the Court would take the case for review but has almost no influence on how the case is decided.[64] More typically, these briefs are filed after the Court has granted a case review to urge the Court to reach a particular decision.

Oral Arguments

Once the justices receive printed briefs from each side, a case is set for oral arguments—usually in three to four months. Lengthy oratory before the Supreme Court, once lasting for several days, is a thing of the past. As a rule, counsel for each side is now allowed only 30 minutes. Lawyers use a lectern with two lights: A white light flashes five minutes before time is up. When the red light goes on, the lawyer must stop, even in the middle of a sentence.

The entire procedure is informally formal. Sometimes, to the annoyance of attorneys, justices talk among themselves or consult briefs or books during oral arguments. Other times, if justices find a presentation particularly bad, they will tell the attorneys so. Justices freely interrupt the lawyers to ask questions and request additional information. In recent years, "the justices seem barely able to contain themselves, often interrupting the answer to one question with another query."[65] Hence the 30-minute limit is problematic, especially when the solicitor general participates, since his 10 minutes come out of the time of the two parties before the Court.

If a lawyer is having a difficult time, the justices may try to help out with a question. Occasionally, justices bounce arguments off a hapless attorney and at one another. Justice Antonin Scalia is a harsh questioner. "When Scalia prepares to ask a question, he doesn't just adjust himself in his chair to get closer to the microphone like the others; he looks like a vulture, zooming in for the kill. He strains way forward, pinches his eyebrows, and poses the question, like '. . . do you want us to believe?' "[66] Justice Ruth Bader Ginsburg is a particularly persistent questioner, frequently rivaling Justice Scalia in asking the most questions.[67] Justice Clarence Thomas almost never asks a question. Justice David Souter has a thick New England accent. He once asked an attorney during oral arguments in an affirmative action case, "What's the floor?" The attorney hemmed and hawed until, with a smile, Souter explained he meant, "What's the flaw?"[68] (Oral

amicus curiae brief
Literally, a "friend of the court" brief, filed by an individual or organization to present arguments in addition to those presented by the immediate parties to a case.

arguments in landmark cases may be listened to on the Web by going to www.oyez.nwu.edu.)

Behind the Curtains: The Conference

On Wednesday afternoons and Fridays, the justices meet in private conference. They have heard the oral arguments and studied the briefs. Each brings to the meeting a book in which the cases and the votes of the justices are recorded. These conferences are held in secret. They are usually a collegial but vigorous give-and-take.

The chief justice presides, usually opening the discussion by stating the facts, summarizing the questions of law, and suggesting how to dispose of each case. Each justice, in order of seniority, then gives his or her views and conclusions. Chief Justice Rehnquist tries to see to it that "everybody [speaks] once before the vote is taken."[69] Recently, the justices have not bothered with casting formal votes because their votes are clear from their discussion of the case.[70]

Opinions

The Supreme Court announces and explains its decisions in **opinions of the Court**. Opinions generally state the facts, present the issues, and explain the reasoning of the Court. These opinions are the Court's principal method of expressing its views to the world. Their primary function is to instruct judges of state and federal courts how to decide similar cases in the future.

Opinions of the Court are delivered by a justice but do not reflect his or her thinking alone. They must explain the reasoning of the majority of the justices. Consequently, opinions of the Court are negotiated documents that require the author to compromise and at times bargain with other justices to attain agreement on an opinion.[71]

Judicial opinions may also be directed at Congress or at the president. If the Court regrets that "in the absence of action by Congress, we have no choice but to . . . ." or insists that "relief of the sort that petitioner demands can come only from the political branches of government," it is asking Congress to act.[72] Justices also use opinions to communicate with the public. A well-crafted opinion may increase support for a policy the Court favors.

ASSIGNING OPINIONS When voting with the majority, the chief justice decides who will draft the opinion of the Court. When the chief justice is in the minority, the senior justice among the majority makes the assignment. The justice assigned to write the opinion must give persuasive reasons for the outcome, for no vote in conference is final until the opinion of the Court has been agreed to. Justices are free to change their minds if not persuaded by draft opinions.

A justice is free to write a **dissenting opinion** if desired. Dissenting opinions are, in Chief Justice Charles Evans Hughes's words, "an appeal to the brooding spirit of the law, to the intelligence of a later day."[73] Dissenting opinions are quite common, as justices hope that someday these dissenting opinions will command a majority of the Court. If a justice agrees with the majority on how the case should be decided but differs on the reasoning, that justice may write a **concurring opinion**.

CIRCULATING DRAFTS Writing the opinion of the Court is an exacting task. The document must win the support of at least four—and more, if possible—intelligent, strong-willed persons. Assisted by the law clerks, the assigned justice writes a draft and sends it to colleagues for comments. If the justice is lucky, the majority will accept the draft, perhaps with only minor changes. If the draft is not satisfactory to the other justices, it must be redrafted and recirculated until a majority reaches agreement.

The two weapons justices can use against their colleagues are their votes and the threat of writing dissenting opinions attacking the majority's opinion. Especially if the Court is closely divided, one justice may be in a position to demand that a certain point or argument be included in, or removed from, the opinion of the Court as the price of his or her vote. Sometimes such bargaining occurs even though the Court is not closely

Then it went to the U.S. Supreme Court.

opinion of the court
An explanation of a decision of the Supreme Court or any other appellate court.

dissenting opinion
An opinion disagreeing with the majority in a Supreme Court ruling.

concurring opinion
An opinion that agrees with the majority in a Supreme Court ruling but differs on the reasoning.

divided. An opinion writer who anticipates that a decision will invite critical public reaction may want a unanimous Court and will therefore compromise to achieve unanimity. For this reason, the Court delayed declaring school segregation unconstitutional, in *Brown* v. *Board of Education,* until unanimity was secured.[74] The justices understood that any sign of dissension on the bench on this major social issue would be an invitation to evade the Court's ruling.

RELEASING OPINIONS TO THE PUBLIC   In the past, justices read their entire opinions from the bench on "opinion days." Now they give only brief summaries of the decision and their opinions. Copies are immediately made available to reporters and the public and published in the official *United States Supreme Court Reports*. Since April 2000, the Court has made its opinions immediately available on its Web site (www.supremecourtus.gov).

After the Court Decides

Victory in the Supreme Court does not necessarily mean that winning parties get what they want. The Court does not implement its own decision but *remands* the case, sending it back to the lower court with instructions to act in accordance with its opinion. The lower court often has considerable leeway in interpreting the Court's mandate as it disposes of the case.

Decisions whose enforcement requires only the action of a federal agency usually become effective immediately. Thus when the Supreme Court held that President Richard M. Nixon had to turn over confidential White House materials,[75] the president promptly complied.

The impact of a particular Supreme Court ruling on the behavior of individuals who are not immediate parties to a lawsuit is more uncertain. The most important rulings require a change in the behavior of thousands of administrative and elected officials. Sometimes Supreme Court pronouncements are simply ignored. For example, despite the Court's holding that it is unconstitutional for school boards to require students to pray within a school, some schools continue this practice.[76] And for years after the Supreme Court held public school segregation unconstitutional, many school districts remained segregated.[77]

The most difficult Supreme Court decisions to implement are those that require the cooperation of large numbers of officials. For example, a Supreme Court decision announcing a new standard for warrantless searches is not likely to have an impact on the way police make arrests for some time, since not many police officers subscribe to *United States Supreme Court Reports*. The process is more complex. Local prosecutors, state attorneys general, chiefs of police, and state and federal trial court judges must all participate to give meaning to Supreme Court decisions. The Constitution may be what the Supreme Court says it is, but a Supreme Court opinion, for the moment at least, is what a trial judge or police officer or prosecutor or school board or city council says it is.

JUDICIAL POWER IN A CONSTITUTIONAL DEMOCRACY

An independent judiciary is one of the hallmarks of a constitutional democracy and a free society. As impartial dispensers of equal justice under the law, judges should not be dependent on the executive, the legislature, parties to a case, or the electorate. But judicial independence, essential to protect judges in their role as legal umpire, encounters problems when a democratic society decides—as ours has—also to allow these same judges to make policy. Perhaps in no other society do the people resort to litigation as a means of making public policy as much as they do in the United States. For example, the National Association for the Advancement of Colored People (NAACP) turned to litigation to get relief from segregation practices in the 1930s, 1940s, and 1950s. More recently, an increasing number of women's organizations, environmental groups, and religious and conservative organizations have also turned to the courts.[78]

The involvement of courts in politics exposes the judiciary to political criticism. Throughout our history, the Supreme Court has been attacked for engaging in "judicial legislation." This is nothing new. Yet the active role of the federal courts on behalf of liberal causes since 1937 and Republican attacks on that role have returned these issues to the forefront of public debate.

Whereas in earlier times judges occasionally told public officials what they could *not* do, today they often tell them what they *must* do. For example, federal judges, responding to class action complaints, have told Congress, state legislatures, and local officials that they must provide attorneys for the poor, ensure adequate care for mental patients, modernize prisons, and even break up the telephone system. Often judges retain jurisdiction for years as they preside over the implementation of the decrees they have issued.[79] Judges have always been policy makers; that role is not a matter of choice but flows from the roles they play in deciding cases.

The Great Debate over the Proper Role of the Courts

Some people contend that the courts have a duty to protect the interests of the public. Defenders of this *activist* judicial role argue that if Congress, the White House, and the state legislatures are unwilling or unable to resolve pressing problems when people are denied justice and their constitutional rights, then the courts must address those problems. The Supreme Court, they say, should be "a leader in a vital national seminar that leads to the formulation of values for the American people."[80]

Critics of judicial activism contend that for the past half-century, the federal courts, in their zeal to protect people, have become unhinged from their political moorings in the political and constitutional system. Even if courts make the "right" decisions, these critics argue, it is still not right for them to take over the legislative function of elected representatives. Courts should exercise self-restraint and defer to elected representatives and the political process.

Others claim that the debate between those who favor judicial activism and those who favor judicial restraint oversimplifies the choices. Judges, they argue, should take a leadership role in some areas but a restrained role in others. They stand with Chief Justice Harlan F. Stone, who argued that courts have a special duty to intervene (1) whenever legislation restricts the political process by which decisions are made or (2) whenever legislation restricts the rights of "discrete and insular minorities" and (3) when guarantees of the Bill of Rights are violated. In all other areas, the political process should be allowed to work, and judges should not set aside legislation or interfere with administrative agencies merely because they would prefer some other policy or even some other interpretation of the Constitution.[81]

The People and the Court

Whether judges are liberal or conservative, defer to legislatures or not, try to apply the Constitution as they think the framers intended, or interpret it to conform to current values, there are linkages between what judges do and what the people want done. The linkages are not direct, and the people never speak with one mind, but these linkages are the heart of the matter.[82] In the first place, the president and the Senate are likely to appoint justices whose decisions reflect their values. Therefore, elections matter, because the perspectives of the people who nominate and confirm the judges are reflected in the composition of the courts. For instance, in 1992, the Supreme Court, by a 5-to-4 vote in *Planned Parenthood* v. *Casey,* refused to overturn *Roe* v. *Wade* and upheld its core holding—that the Constitution protects the right of a woman to an abortion—although upholding state regulations that do not "unduly burden" that right.[83] This close vote on abortion made it clear that presidential elections could determine whether that right would continue to be protected, depending on whether there are retirements from the bench and new appointments to the Court.

Scholars debate how public opinion influences what judges decide, whether it is direct or indirect through presidential selection and Senate confirmation of judges, but there is little question that there is a correlation between public opinion and judicial decisions.[84] Judicial opinions that reflect what the people want have the greatest survival value. When a new political coalition takes over the White House or Congress, the old regime may stay on in the federal courts. New electoral coalitions eventually take over

"Do you ever have one of those days when nothing seems constitutional?"

The Wall Street Journal, August 3, 1998. By permission of Cartoon Features Syndicate.

the federal courts, and before long, new interpretations of the Constitution reflect the dominant political ideology.[85]

Judges have neither armies nor police to execute their rulings. Although Congress cannot reverse Supreme Court decisions that relate to constitutional interpretations, and only six Supreme Court decisions have been reversed by formal constitutional amendment, the political system alters judicial policy in more subtle ways. Decisions are binding on the parties to a particular case, but the policies that result from judicial decisions are effective and durable only if they are supported by the electorate. To win a favorable Supreme Court decision is to win something of considerable political value.

"American courts are not all-powerful institutions."[86] If the Court's policies are too far out of step with the values of the country, the Court is likely to be reversed. In Chief Justice William H. Rehnquist's words, "No judge worthy of his salt would ever cast his vote in a particular case simply because he thought the majority of the public wanted him to vote that way, but that is quite a different thing from saying that no judge is ever influenced by the great tides of public opinion that run a country such as ours."[87]

"The people" speak in many ways and with many voices. The Supreme Court also hands down rulings on controversies—abortion, affirmative action, and the rights of homosexuals—on which the public is deeply divided. And the justices are often likewise split in deciding those cases. The Supreme Court—and the other courts—thus generally represent and reflect the competing values of the people. Whether they agree or disagree with particular rulings, the public generally holds the Supreme Court in high regard. Notably, the Court's public approval rating remained high and virtually unchanged after its controversial decision in *Bush* v. *Gore* (2000), contrary to predictions by the four dissenting justices and critics that the Court's reputation would be badly damaged by the bare majority's ruling assuring George W. Bush's election.[88]

Although the Court is not the defenseless institution portrayed by some commentators, and its decisions are as much shapers of public opinion as reflections of it, ultimately the power of the Supreme Court in a constitutional democracy rests on retaining the support of most of the people most of the time. The Court's power rests, as Chief Justice Edward White observed, "solely upon the approval of a free people."[89] No better standard for determining the legitimacy of a governmental institution has been discovered.

S U M M A R Y

1. The American judicial process is based on the adversary system. Judges in the United States play a more active role in the political process than they do in most other democracies. Unlike other countries, the United States has a dual judiciary—federal and state court systems. In both federal and state courts, individuals must have standing to sue and must assert a personal injury. Courts decide only justiciable disputes—actual cases or controversies—and not political questions.

2. Except for the Supreme Court, federal courts are established by and receive their jurisdiction directly from Congress, which must decide the constitutional division of responsibilities among federal and state courts. District courts are the trial courts of the federal judicial system,

and their decisions may be reviewed by courts of appeals. Federal judges apply federal criminal and civil law but in doing so exercise discretion. Their decisions are subject to reversal by the Supreme Court, which resolves conflicts and tries to promote stability and uniformity in the law.

3. The Supreme Court has almost complete control over the cases it chooses to review as they come up from the state courts, the courts of appeals, and district courts. Law clerks and the solicitor general play important roles in determining the kinds of cases the Supreme Court agrees to decide. Its nine justices dispose of thousands of cases, but most of their time is concentrated on the fewer than 100 cases per year that they accept for review. The Court's decisions and opinions

establish guidelines for lower courts and the country.

4. Partisanship and ideology are important factors in the selection of federal judges, and these factors ensure a linkage between the courts and the rest of the political system, so that the views of the people are reflected, even if indirectly, in the work of the courts. In recent decades, candidates for the presidency and the Senate have made judicial appointments an issue in their election campaigns.

5. The president's judicial nominees must be confirmed by the Senate, and the confirmation process tends to be stalled or to erupt into bitter political battles when the majority of the Senate and the president are from opposing political parties.

6. A continuing concern of major importance is the reconciliation of the role of judges—especially those on the Supreme Court—as independent and fair dispensers of justice with their vital role as interpreters of the Constitution. This is an especially complex problem in our democracy because of the power of judicial review and the significant role courts play in making public policy.

7. The debate about how judges should interpret the Constitution is almost as old as the Republic. Almost 220 years after the Constitution was adopted, the argument between those who contend that judges should interpret the document literally and those who believe they cannot and should not remains in the headlines. Both liberals and conservatives have attacked judicial activism and urged judicial self-restraint.

K E Y   T E R M S

judicial review	public defender system	petit jury	*stare decisis*
adversary system	political question	magistrate judge	*writ of certiorari*
justiciable dispute	writ of habeas corpus	court of appeals	*amicus curiae* brief
class action suit	original jurisdiction	senatorial courtesy	opinion of the court
defendant	appellate jurisdiction	judicial self-restraint	dissenting opinion
plea bargain	grand jury	judicial activism	concurring opinion

F U R T H E R   R E A D I N G

HENRY J. ABRAHAM, *Justices, Presidents, and Senators: A History of U.S. Supreme Court Appointments from Washington to Clinton* (Rowman & Littlefield, 1999).

ROBERT A. CARP AND RONALD STIDHAM, *The Federal Courts* (CQ Press, 2001).

CORNELL CLAYTON AND HOWARD GILMAN, EDS., *Supreme Court Decision Making: New Institutionalist Approaches* (University of Chicago Press, 1999).

CLARE CUSHMAN, *The Supreme Court Justices: Illustrated Biographies, 1789–1995,* 2d ed. (CQ Press, 1996).

DEL DICKSON, *The Supreme Court in Conference, 1940–1995* (Oxford University Press, 2001).

LEE A. EPSTEIN, JEFFREY A. SEGAL, HAROLD SPAETH, AND THOMAS WALKER, EDS., *The Supreme Court Compendium,* 2d ed. (CQ Press, 2001).

HOWARD GILLMAN, *The Votes That Counted: How the Court Decided the 2000 Presidential Election* (University of Chicago Press, 2001).

SHELDON GOLDMAN, *Picking Federal Judges: Lower Court Selection from Roosevelt Through Reagan* (Yale University Press, 1997).

KERMIT L. HALL, ED., *The Oxford Companion to the Supreme Court of the United States* (Oxford University Press, 1992).

PETER IRONS, *A People's History of the Supreme Court* (Viking, 1999).

RANDOLPH JONAKAIT, *The American Jury System* (Yale University Press, 2003).

DAVID KLEIN, *Making Law in the U.S. Courts of Appeals* (Cambridge University Press, 2002).

LISA KLOPPENBERG, *Playing It Safe: How the Supreme Court Sidesteps Hard Cases and Stunts the Development of the Law* (New York University Press, 2001).

ROBERT G. MCCLOSKEY, *The American Supreme Court,* 3d ed. (University of Chicago Press, 2001).

DAVID M. O'BRIEN, ED., *Judges on Judging: Views from the Bench,* 2d ed. (CQ Press, 2004).

DAVID M. O'BRIEN, *Storm Center: The Supreme Court in American Politics,* 7th ed. (Norton, 2005).

J. W. PELTASON, *Federal Courts in the Political Process* (Doubleday, 1955).

TERRI JENNINGS PERETTI, *In Defense of a Political Court* (Princeton University Press, 1999).

GERALD N. ROSENBERG, *The Hollow Hope: Can Courts Bring About Social Change?* (University of Chicago Press, 1991).

C. K. ROWLAND AND ROBERT A. CARP, *Politics and Judgment in Federal District Courts* (University Press of Kansas, 1996).

PETER RUSSELL AND DAVID M. O'BRIEN, EDS., *Judicial Independence in the Age of Democracy: Critical Perspectives from Around the World* (University Press of Virginia, 2001).

ELLIOT E. SLOTNICK, *Judicial Politics: Readings from Judicature,* 3d ed. (American Judicature Society, 2005).

DONALD R. SONGER AND SUSAN B. HAIRE, *Continuity and Change on the United States Courts of Appeals* (University of Michigan Press, 2000).

FIRST AMENDMENT FREEDOMS

15

The First Amendment declares, "Congress shall make no law respecting an establishment of religion, or prohibiting the free exercise thereof, or abridging the freedom of speech, or of the press, or the right of the people peaceably to assemble, and to petition the Government for a redress of grievances." In this one sentence, our Constitution lays down the fundamental principles of a free society: freedom of conscience and freedom of expression. These freedoms are essential to our individual self-determination and to our collective self-governance—to government by the people. Yet they are also vulnerable during times of war and now with recent security measures put into place to combat international terrorism.[1]

These freedoms were not constitutionally guaranteed, though, until the addition in 1791 of the first ten amendments, the Bill of Rights. For that reason, we begin this chapter by discussing the rights in the original Constitution and in the Bill of Rights as applied to both the national and state governments before turning to the "first freedoms" of religion, speech, press, and assembly. Before doing so, though, it may be helpful to clarify certain terms—*liberties, freedoms, rights,* and *privileges*—that are often used interchangeably in discussions of rights and freedoms. We offer these definitions. *Civil liberties* are the constitutionally protected freedoms of all persons against governmental restraint: the freedoms of conscience, religion, and expression, for example, which are secured by the First Amendment. These civil liberties are also protected by the due process and equal protection clauses of the Fifth and Fourteenth Amendments. *Civil rights* are the constitutional

writ of habeas corpus
Court order requiring explanation to a judge why a prisoner is being held in custody.

ex post facto law
Retroactive criminal law that works to the disadvantage of an individual; forbidden in the Constitution.

bill of attainder
Legislative act inflicting punishment, including deprivation of property, without a trial, on named individuals or members of a specific group.

rights of all persons, not just citizens, to due process and the equal protection of the laws: the constitutional right not to be discriminated against by governments because of race, ethnic background, religion, or gender. These civil rights are protected by the due process and equal protection clauses of the Fifth and Fourteenth Amendments and by the civil rights laws of national and state governments; they are discussed further in Chapters 16 and 17. *Legal privileges* are granted by governments and they may be subject to conditions or restrictions, for example, the right to welfare benefits or to a driver's license.

RIGHTS IN THE ORIGINAL CONSTITUTION

Even though most of the framers did not think a bill of rights was necessary, they considered certain rights important enough to be spelled out in the Constitution. These rights included the writ of habeas corpus and protection against *ex post facto* laws and bills of attainder.

Foremost among constitutional rights is the **writ of habeas corpus**. Literally meaning "produce the body," this writ is a court order directing any official holding a person in custody to produce the prisoner in court and explain why the prisoner is being held. As originally used, the writ was merely a judicial inquiry to determine whether a person in custody was held as the result of the action of a court with proper jurisdiction. But over the years, it developed into a remedy for any illegal confinement. People who are incarcerated may appeal to a judge, usually through an attorney, stating why they believe they are held unlawfully and should be released. The judge then orders the jailer or a lower court to show cause of why the writ should not be issued. If a judge finds a petitioner is detained unlawfully, the judge may order the prisoner's immediate release. Although state judges lack jurisdiction to issue writs of habeas corpus to find out why federal authorities are holding persons, federal district judges may do so to find out if state and local officials are holding people in violation of the Constitution or national laws.

In recent years, the use of the writ of habeas corpus by federal courts to review convictions by state courts has been widely criticized. Some people believe the writ has been abused by state prisoners to get an endless and expensive round of reviews, which sometimes lead to convictions being set aside by a federal judge after the matter has been reviewed by two or more state courts. Partly because of concerns about maintaining the principles of federalism and partly because of the growing caseloads of federal courts, the Supreme Court and Congress have restricted the habeas corpus jurisdiction of federal judges. The Antiterrorism and Effective Death Penalty Act of 1996, for example, restricts the number of times a person may be granted a habeas corpus review, stops appeals for most habeas petitions at the level of the U.S. Court of Appeals, and calls for deference by federal judges to the decisions of state judges unless they are clearly "unreasonable."[2]

The Supreme Court nonetheless underscored the fundamental nature of the right to a writ of habeas corpus in two 2004 decisions rejecting the position of President George W. Bush's administration that it could hold indefinitely foreign nationals and U.S. citizens deemed "enemy combatants" in its war against terrorism. The Court held that detainees have a right to a review of the basis for their detention by an independent tribunal.[3]

An *ex post facto law* is a retroactive criminal law making a particular act a crime that was not a crime when an individual committed it, increasing punishment for a crime after the crime was committed, lessening the proof necessary to convict for a crime after it was committed, or permitting prosecutions from crimes that were previously barred by statutes of limitations.[4] This prohibition does not prevent the retroactive application of laws that work to the benefit of an accused person—a law decreasing punishment, for example—or prevent the retroactive application of civil law, such as an increase in income tax rates applied to income already earned.

Bills of attainder are legislative acts inflicting punishment, including deprivation of property, on named individuals or members of a specified group without a trial. For example, when Congress adopted a rider to an appropriations bill denying payment of the salaries of three federal employees for "disloyalty," the Supreme Court struck down the rider for being a bill of attainder.[5]

THE BILL OF RIGHTS AND THE STATES

Although it was the framers who wrote the Constitution, in a sense it was the American people who drafted our basic charter of rights. The Constitution drawn up in Philadelphia included guarantees of a few basic rights but lacked a specific bill of rights similar to those in most state constitutions. The Federalists argued that the Constitution established a limited government that would not threaten individual freedoms, and therefore a bill of rights was unnecessary. The Antifederalists were not persuaded, and the omission aroused widespread suspicion. As a result, to persuade delegates to the state ratification conventions to vote for the Constitution, the Federalists promised to correct this deficiency. In its first session, the Congress made good on that promise by proposing 12 amendments, ten of which were promptly ratified and became part of the Constitution.[6]

The guarantees of the Bill of Rights originally applied *only to the national government,* not state governments.[7] Why not the states? The framers were confident that citizens could control their own state officials, and most state constitutions already had bills of rights. It was the new and distant central government the people feared. As it turned out, those fears were largely misdirected. The national government has generally shown less tendency to curtail civil liberties than state and local governments have.

When the Fourteenth Amendment, which applies to the states, was adopted in 1868, supporters contended that its **due process clause**—which states that no person shall be deprived by a state of life, liberty, or property without due process of law—limits states in precisely the same way the Bill of Rights limits the national government. But for decades, the Supreme Court refused to interpret the Fourteenth Amendment in this way. Then in *Gitlow* v. *New York* (1925), the Court announced that it assumed "that freedom of speech and of the press—which are protected by the First Amendment from abridgment by Congress—are among the fundamental personal rights and 'liberties' protected by the due process clause of the Fourteenth Amendment from impairment by the States."[8]

Gitlow v. *New York* was a revolutionary decision. For the first time, the U.S. Constitution protected freedom of speech from abridgment by state and local governments. In the 1930s and continuing at an accelerated pace during the 1960s, through the **selective incorporation** of provision after provision of the Bill of Rights into the due process clause, the Supreme Court applied the most important of these rights to the states.[9] Today the Fourteenth Amendment imposes on the states all the provisions of the Bill of Rights except those of the Second and Third Amendments, the Fifth Amendment provision for indictment by a grand jury, the Seventh Amendment right to a jury trial in civil cases, and the Ninth and Tenth Amendments (see Table 15–1).

Selective incorporation of most provisions of the Bill of Rights into the Fourteenth Amendment is probably the most significant constitutional development since the writing of the Constitution. It has profoundly altered the relationship between the national government and the states. It made the federal courts, under the guidance of the Supreme Court of the United States, the most important protectors of our liberties.

Recently, however, there has been a renewal of interest in state constitutions as independent sources of additional protections for civil liberties and civil rights.[10] Advocates of what has come to be called the *new judicial federalism* contend that the U.S. Constitution should set minimum but not maximum standards for protecting our rights. State bills of rights sometimes provide more protection of rights—the rights to equal education and personal privacy, for instance—than the national Bill of Rights or the Supreme Court's rulings on its guarantees. Despite the revival of interest in state bills of rights, the U.S. Supreme Court and the national Bill of Rights remain the dominant protectors of civil liberties and civil rights.

RIGHTS IN THE ORIGINAL CONSTITUTION

1. Habeas corpus
2. No bills of attainder
3. No *ex post facto* laws
4. No titles of nobility
5. Trial by jury in national courts
6. Protection for citizens as they move from one state to another, including the right to travel
7. Protection against using crime of treason to restrict other activities; limitation on punishment for treason
8. Guarantee that each state has a republican form of government
9. No religious test oaths as a condition for holding a federal office
10. Protection against the impairment of contracts

due process clause
Clause in the Fifth Amendment limiting the power of the national government; similar clause in the Fourteenth Amendment prohibiting state governments from depriving any person of life, liberty, or property without due process of law.

selective incorporation
The process by which provisions of the Bill of Rights are brought within the scope of the Fourteenth Amendment and so applied to state and local governments.

TABLE 15–1 SELECTIVE INCORPORATION AND THE APPLICATION OF THE BILL OF RIGHTS TO THE STATES

Right	Amendment	Year
Public use and just compensation for the taking of private property by the government	5	1897
Freedom of speech	1	1925
Freedom of the press	1	1931
Fair trial	6	1932
Freedom of religion	1	1934
Freedom of assembly	1	1937
Free exercise of religion	1	1940
Separation of religion and government	1	1947
Right to a public trial	6	1948
Right against unreasonable searches and seizures	4	1949
Freedom of association	1	1958
Exclusionary rule	4	1961
Ban against cruel and unusual punishment	8	1962
Right to counsel in felony cases	6	1963
Right against self-incrimination	5	1964
Right to confront witness	6	1965
Right of privacy	1,3,4,5,9	1965
Right to an impartial jury	6	1966
Right to a speedy trial and compulsory process for obtaining witnesses	6	1967
Right to a jury trial in nonpetty cases	6	1968
Protection against double jeopardy	5	1969

FREEDOM OF RELIGION

The first words of the First Amendment are emphatic and brief: "Congress shall make no law respecting an establishment of religion, or prohibiting the free exercise thereof." Note that there are *two* religion clauses: the *establishment* clause and the *exercise* clause. The Supreme Court has struggled to reconcile these two clauses, both of which are cast in absolute terms, and either of which, if expanded to a logical extreme, would clash with the other. Does a state scholarship for blind students given to a college student who decides to attend a college to become a minister violate the establishment clause by indirectly aiding religion? Or would denying the scholarship violate the student's free exercise of religion? The Supreme Court has held that giving such benefits does not violate the establishment clause, but also that the free exercise clause does not entitle individuals to receive such benefits or compel states to make them available.[11]

The Establishment Clause

establishment clause
Clause in the First Amendment that states that Congress shall make no law respecting an establishment of religion. It has been interpreted by the Supreme Court as forbidding governmental support to any or all religions.

In writing what has come to be called the **establishment clause**, the framers were reacting to the English system, wherein the crown was the head not only of the government but also of the established church—the Church of England—and public officials were required to take an oath to support the established church as a condition of holding office. The establishment clause goes beyond merely separating government from religion by forbidding the establishment of a state religion. It is designed to prevent three evils: government sponsorship of religion, government financial support of religion, and government involvement in religious matters. However, the clause does not prevent governments from "accommodating" religious needs. To what extent and under

GLOBAL *Perceptions*

QUESTION: Does the statement "you can practice your religion freely" describe your country "very well"?

I n spite of talk of "culture wars," most U.S. citizens (69 percent) believe very strongly that they may practice their religon freely. The only region of the world that compares as highly is Africa, where perceptions of religious freedom are higher than in the United States, except for Ghana (57), Nigeria (54), and Angola (52). Perceptions of the freedom of religious practice also rank higher in India (78). Public perceptions of the freedom of religion are lowest in Poland (39), Russia (35), and Bolivia and Turkey (29).

SOURCE: The Pew Global Attitudes Project, 2003, T-82–T83.

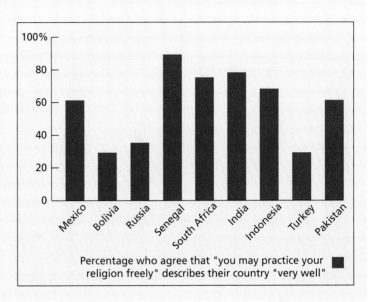

Percentage who agree that "you may practice your religion freely" describes their country "very well"

---

which conditions governments may accommodate these needs are at the heart of much of the debate in the Supreme Court and the country over interpreting the clause.

Controversies over the establishment clause are not easy to resolve. They stir deep feelings and frequently divide the justices among themselves. The prevailing interpretation stems from the decision in *Everson* v. *Board of Education of Ewing Township* (1947) that the establishment clause creates a "wall of separation" between church and state and prohibits any law or governmental action designed to specifically benefit any religion, even if all religions are treated the same.[12] That decision, though, was decided by a bare majority and upheld state support for transportation of children to private religious schools as a "child benefit."

The separation of church and state was further elaborated in *Lemon* v. *Kurtzman* (1971), which laid down a three-part test: (1) A law must have a secular legislative purpose, (2) it must neither advance nor inhibit religion, and (3) it must avoid "excessive government entanglement with religion."[13] This so-called *Lemon test* is often, but not always, used because the justices remain divided over how much separation between government and religion is required by the First Amendment.

Another test, championed by Justice Sandra Day O'Connor, is the *endorsement test.* Justice O'Connor believes that the establishment clause forbids governmental practices that a reasonable observer would view as endorsing religion, even if there is no coercion.[14] The endorsement test has been honed in a series of decisions as the Court struggled with the question of whether governments may allow religious symbols to be displayed on, in, or near public properties and in public places. For example, the Court concluded that when a nativity scene was displayed in a shopping district together with Santa's house and other secular and religious symbols of the Christmas season, there was little danger that a reasonable person would conclude that the city was endorsing religion.[15] But the Constitution does not permit a city government to display the nativity scene on the steps of the city hall, because in this context, the city gives the impression that it is endorsing the display's religious message.[16]

The Court's three most conservative justices—Chief Justice William Rehnquist and Justices Antonin Scalia and Clarence Thomas—support a *nonpreferentialist test.*[17] They believe the Constitution prohibits favoritism toward any particular religion but does not prohibit government aid to *all* religions. In their view, government may accommodate religious activities and even give nonpreferential support to religious or-ganizations so long as individuals are not legally coerced into participating in religious activities and religious activities are not singled out for favorable treatment.[18]

By contrast, the more liberal justices—Justices David H. Souter, John Paul Stevens, Ruth Bader Ginsburg, and Stephen Breyer—usually maintain that there should be *strict separation* between religion and the state.[19] They generally hold that even indirect aid for religion, such as scholarships or teaching materials and aids for students attending private religious schools, crosses the line separating the government from religion.

Applying these generalizations, we find that the establishment clause forbids states—including state universities, colleges, and school districts—from introducing devotional exercises into the public school curriculum, including school graduations and events before football games.[20] However, the Supreme Court has not, as some peo-ple assume, entirely prohibited prayer in public schools. It is not unconstitutional for stu-dents to pray in a school building. What is unconstitutional is sponsorship or encouragement of prayer *by public school authorities.*[21] Devotional reading of the Bible, recitation of the Lord's Prayer, and posting of the Ten Commandments on the walls of classrooms in public schools have also been ruled to be unconstitutional. A state may not forbid the teaching of evolution or require the teaching of "creation science"—the belief that human life did not evolve but rather was created by a single act of God.[22]

Tax exemptions for church properties, similar to those granted to other nonprofit institutions, are constitutional. State legislatures and Congress may also hire chaplains to open each day's legislative session—a practice that has continued without interrup-tion since the first session of Congress. But if done in a public school, this practice would be unconstitutional. Apparently, the difference is that legislators, as adults, are not "sus-ceptible to religious indoctrination or peer pressure."[23] Also, as the joke goes, legisla-tors need the prayer more.

A continuing controversy centers on whether requiring school children to recite the words "under God" in the Pledge of Allegiance violates the First Amendment. The Court avoided ruling on the issue in *Elk Grove Unified School District* v. *Newdow* (2004) by denying standing to Michael A. Newdow, an atheist, to sue on behalf of his daughter because he was not her legal guardian.[24] However, Chief Justice Rehnquist and Justices O'Connor and Thomas would have granted review and held that the Pledge does not violate the freedom of religion; Justice Scalia agrees with them but had to recuse him-self because in an earlier speech he had criticized the lower court's ruling that the First Amendment was violated. Americans United for the Separation of Church and State and other supporters of Newdow plan other lawsuits; they also oppose the efforts of the American Family Association, an evangelical Christian group, to get states to require the display of the national motto, "In God We Trust," in public schools. The controversy over the Pledge and national motto is certain to continue in the courts and to return to the Supreme Court in another case.

Vouchers and State Aid for Religious Schools

Another troublesome area involving the separation of religion and government has re-volved around states' providing financial assistance to parochial and other religious schools. The Supreme Court has tried to draw a line between permissible tax-provided aid to schoolchildren and impermissible aid to religion.

At the college level, the problems are relatively simple. Tax funds may be used to construct buildings and operate educational programs at church-related schools as long as the money is not spent directly on buildings used for religious purposes or on teach-ing religious subjects. Even if students choose to attend religious schools and become ministers, government aid to these students is permissible, because such aid has a sec-ular purpose. Its effect on religion is the result of individual choice "and it does not con-fer any message of state endorsement of religion."[25]

At the level of elementary and secondary schools, however, the constitutional prob-lems are more complicated. Here the secular and religious parts of institutions and in-struction are much more closely interwoven. Also, students are younger and more susceptible to indoctrination, so the chances are greater that aid to church-operated schools aids religion in violation of the establishment clause.

Despite the constitutional obstacles, some states have provided tax credits or deductions for parents who send their children to private, largely religious-run schools. Such deductions or credits available *only* to parents of children attending nonpublic schools are unconstitutional, but allowing taxpaying parents to deduct or take a credit from their state income taxes for what they paid for tuition and other costs to send their children to school—public or private—is constitutional, even if most of the benefit goes to those sending their children to private religious schools.[26]

The Supreme Court has also approved using tax funds to provide students who attend primary and secondary church-operated schools (except those that deny admission because of race or religion) with textbooks, standardized tests, lunches, transportation to and from school, diagnostic services, sign language interpreters, and teachers for remedial and enrichment classes, as well as computers and software for both public and parochial schools.[27]

One hot controversy that the Supreme Court avoided for years involved whether states may also use tax money to give parents **vouchers** for the tuition of children to attend schools of their choice, including religious schools. Maine and Vermont have long had voucher programs for students living in rural areas. Cleveland, Milwaukee, and the state of Florida experimented with voucher programs, permitting the payment of tuition at religious schools, and faced challenges in the courts. Opponents argue that such programs violate the establishment clause, while supporters counter that they do not and argue that the denial of vouchers for attending religious schools violates the free exercise clause and denies parents the freedom of school choice in opting out of dysfunctional public schools.

The Supreme Court finally addressed the constitutionality of voucher programs in *Zelman* v. *Simmons-Harris* (2002),[28] and by a 5-to-4 vote found Ohio's program to be neutral and permissible. Ohio's law provides low-income families in Cleveland with vouchers of up to $2,250 per child to put toward the cost of their children's attending public or private schools outside of the failing inner-city school district, and 96 percent of the vouchers went to religious schools. As a result of this ruling, Congress authorized a $14 million voucher program for students of low-income families in the District of Columbia. In its first year of operation, however, there were not enough applications from public school students to fill all of the slots available. Officials with the Washington Scholarship Fund, a nonprofit organization that runs the program awarding grants of $7,500 per student, pushed to recruit more in the 2005–2006 academic year.[29] There may be increased pressure on state legislatures and school boards to adopt voucher programs.

The Free Exercise Clause

The right to hold any or no religious belief is one of our few absolute rights. The **free exercise clause** affirms that no government has authority to compel us to accept any creed or to deny us any right because of our beliefs or lack of them. Requiring religious oaths as a condition of public employment or as a prerequisite to running for public office is unconstitutional. In fact, the original Constitution states, "No religious Test shall ever be required as a Qualification to any Office or public Trust under the United States" (Article VI).

Although carefully protected, the right to practice a religion has had less protection than the right to hold particular beliefs. Prior to 1990, the Supreme Court carefully scrutinized laws allegedly infringing on religious practices and insisted that the government provide some compelling interest to justify actions that might infringe on somebody's religion. In other words, the First Amendment was thought to throw a "mantle of protection" around religious practices, and the burden was on the government to justify interfering with them in the least restrictive way.

Then, in *Employment Division* v. *Smith* (1990), the Rehnquist Court significantly altered the interpretation of the free exercise clause by discarding the compelling

vouchers
Money provided by the government to parents for payment of their children's tuition in a public or private school of their choice.

free exercise clause
Clause in the First Amendment that states that Congress shall make no law prohibiting the free exercise of religion.

CHANGING FACE OF AMERICAN POLITICS

GROWING RELIGIOUS INTENSITY AND POLARIZATION

The United States is an intensely religious country, and the trend during the last two decades has been toward stronger religious belief. According to a study by The Pew Research Center for the People and the Press, eight of ten (81%) say that prayer is an important part of their daily lives, and even more (87%) agree with the statement "I never doubt the existence of God."*

The growing religious intensity is evident in how citizens characterize their religious faith. In the late 1980s, 41% of Protestants and 24% of the population identified themselves as "born-again or evangelical" Christians, whereas today 54% of Protestants and 30% of the population descibe themselves in that way. The trend is especially marked with respect to African Americans; 50% now describe themselves that way, compared with 36% earlier. Fewer than one in ten (9%) report that they have no religion.

Moreover, recent generations are becoming more religious as they age. Almost two decades ago 61% of people in their late teens and twenties expressed deep religious faith, but 71% of people in these generations now in their thirties and forties do.

In addition, during the last two decades religion and religious faith have grown more aligned with partisan and ideological identification. Republicans and Democrats remain equally likely to express strong religious attitudes, but Republicans have become increasingly united in that belief, with a widening gap between the parties (78% versus 71% of Democrats). While religiosity and conservatism have always been correlated, that relationship has increased substantially among self-identified conservatives (81% today compared to 73% in the late 1980s), while liberals have become somewhat less religiously oriented (54% express strong religious belief today, compared to 59% in the late 1980s).

*The Pew Research Center for the People and the Press, *The 2004 Political Landscape: Evenly Divided and Increasingly Polarized* (November 3, 2003), at people-press.org/reports/display.php3?reported=196.

governmental interest test for overriding the interests of religious minorities.[30] As long as a law is generally applicable and does not single out and ban religious practices, the law may be applied to conduct even if it burdens a particular religious practice.[31]

The ruling in *Employment Division* v. *Smith* was controversial and led Congress to enact the Religious Freedom Restoration Act of 1993 (RFRA), which aimed to override the *Smith* decision and to restore the earlier test prohibiting the government—federal, state, or local—from limiting a person's exercise of religion unless the government demonstrates a compelling interest that is advanced by the least restrictive means. Congress asserted its power to pass the RFRA because the Fourteenth Amendment gives it the authority to enforce rights secured by that amendment, including the right to free exercise of religion.

However, when the Catholic archbishop of San Antonio was denied a building permit in 1997 to enlarge a church in Boerne, Texas, because the remodeling did not comply with the city's historical preservation plan, he claimed that the city's denial of a building permit interfered with religious freedom as protected by the Religious Freedom Restoration Act. The Supreme Court then ruled the RFRA to be unconstitutional because Congress was attempting to define, rather than enforce or remedy, constitutional rights and was thereby assuming the role of the courts, which contradicted "vital principles necessary to maintain separation of powers and the federal balance."[32]

Tensions between the establishment and free exercise clauses have recently become more prominent. On the one hand, the University of Virginia denied a Christian student group funds to pay for the printing of its newspaper, *Wide Awake*, because it interpreted the establishment clause to forbid allocating student fee money to a newspaper that "primarily promotes a belief in or about a deity." The students argued that the university deprived them of their freedom of speech, including religious speech, and the Supreme Court agreed with the students.[33] On the other hand, some Christian students at the University of Wisconsin objected to the use of mandatory student activity fees for funding groups they deemed offensive and contrary to their religious beliefs.

They argued that they should be exempt from paying that portion of their fees, but the Supreme Court rejected their claim.[34]

FREE SPEECH AND FREE PEOPLE

Government by the people is based on every person's right to speak freely, to organize in groups, to question the decisions of the government, and to campaign openly against them. Only through free and uncensored expression of opinion can government be kept responsive to the electorate and political power transferred peacefully. Elections, separation of powers, and constitutional guarantees are meaningless unless all persons have the right to speak frankly and to hear and judge for themselves the worth of what others have to say. As Justice Oliver Wendell Holmes observed, "The best test of truth is the power of the thought to get itself accepted in the competition of the market. . . . That at any rate is the theory of our Constitution. It is an experiment, as all life is an experiment."[35]

Free speech is not simply the personal right of individuals to have their say; it is also the right of the rest of us to hear them. John Stuart Mill, whose *Essay on Liberty* (1859) is the classic defense of free speech, put it this way: "The peculiar evil of silencing the expression of opinion, is that it is robbing the human race. . . . If the opinion is right, they are deprived of the opportunity of exchanging error for truth; if wrong, they lose what is almost as great a benefit, the clearer perception and livelier impression of truth, produced by its collision with error."[36]

Reverend Anthony Cummins, pastor of St. Peter the Apostle Church, in front of his church in Boerne, Texas, after a battle with city officials who denied the church permission to build an addition to the historic structure.

PEOPLE & POLITICS *Making a Difference* ★ ★ ★

ERNESTO PICHARDO

A Cuban-born immigrant, Ernesto Pichardo, cofounded with other family members the first church of the Santeria religion, the Church of the Lukumi Babalu Aye, in Hialeah, Florida. Slaves brought to Cuba in the eighteenth and nineteenth centuries worshipped African gods alongside Catholic saints, and their religion became known as Santeria—"the way of the saints." Followers of Santeria came to the United States in great numbers after Fidel Castro's rise to power in 1959 and again with the 1980 Mariel "boatlift" that followed Castro's deportation of some 125,000 Cubans.

The founding of the church created a major controversy. In Cuba, the practice of Santeria was illegal and done in secret. Pichardo wanted to give the religion legitimacy, to institutionalize it, and to publicly perform rituals, including ritual animal sacrifice. Not only did leaders of various religions in Hialeah oppose the

church, but so did animal rights organizations.

Within weeks, the Hialeah city council passed ordinances making ritual animal sacrifice, except in slaughterhouses, a crime. The ordinances were defended as health and safety measures, as well as aimed at preventing animal cruelty. But Pichardo challenged them for violating the First Amendment free exercise clause. The ordinances specifically targeted a religious practice, and Hialeah did not criminalize hunting, fishing, and other kinds of killing of animals.

In *Church of the Lukumi Babalu Aye, Inc. and Ernesto Pichardo* v. *City of Hialeah,** the Court struck down Hialeah's ordinances banning ritual animal sacrifice. The Court unanimously held that the city had targeted and discriminated against a particular religion, thereby violating the First Amendment. Pichardo thus won an important victory

in the Court's reaffirming that government may not overtly discriminate against religious minorities.

*Church of the Lukumi Babalu Aye, Inc. and Ernesto Pichardo v. City of Hialeah, 508 U.S. 530 (1993); see also David M. O'Brien, Animal Sacrifice and Religious Freedom (University Press of Kansas, 2004); and more generally, Melvin Urofsky, ed., 100 Americans Making Constitutional History (CQ Press, 2004).

Police arrest Scott Tyler of Chicago after he set fire to an American flag on the steps of the Capitol building in Washington. The Supreme Court ruled that freedom of speech covers even "symbolic speech" like burning the U.S. flag.

Americans overwhelmingly support the principle of freedom of expression in general. Yet some who say they believe in free speech draw the line at ideas they consider dangerous or when speech attacks them or is critical of their race, religion, or ethnic origin. But what is a dangerous idea? Who decides? In the realm of political ideas, who can find an objective, eternally valid standard of right? The search for truth involves the possibility—even the inevitability—of error. The search cannot go on unless it proceeds freely in the minds and speech of all. This means, in the words of Justice Robert Jackson, that "freedom to differ is not limited to things that do not matter much. That would be a mere shadow of freedom. The test of its substance is the right to differ as to things that touch the heart of the existing order."[37]

Even though the First Amendment explicitly denies Congress the power to pass any law abridging freedom of speech, the amendment has never been interpreted in absolute terms. Like almost all rights, the freedoms of speech and of the press are limited. In discussing the constitutional power of government to regulate speech, it is useful to distinguish among *belief, speech,* and *action.*

At one extreme is the right to *believe* as we wish. Despite occasional deviations in practice, the traditional American view is that government should not punish a person for beliefs or interfere in any way with freedom of conscience. At the other extreme is *action,* which may be subject to governmental restraint. As has been said, "The right to swing your fist ends where my nose begins."

Speech stands somewhere between belief and action. It is not an absolute right, like belief, but neither is it as exposed to governmental restraint, like action. Some kinds of speech—libel, obscenity, fighting words, and commercial speech—are not entitled to constitutional protection. But many problems arise in distinguishing between what does and does not fit into the categories of nonprotected speech. People disagree, and it usually falls to the courts to decide and to defend the free speech of individual and minority dissenters.

Judging: Drawing the Line

Plainly, questions of free speech require that judges weigh a variety of factors: What was said? In what context? How was it said? Which level of government is attempting to regulate the speech—a city council speaking for a few people, or Congress, speaking for many? (The Supreme Court is much more deferential to acts of Congress than to those of a city council or state legislature.) How is the government attempting to regulate the speech—by prior restraint (censorship) or by punishment after the speech? Why is the government doing so—to preserve the public peace or to prevent criticism of the people in power? These and scores of other considerations are involved in the never-ending process of determining what the First Amendment permits and what it forbids.

Historical Constitutional Tests

It is useful to start with the three constitutional tests used in the first part of the twentieth century: the bad tendency test, the clear and present danger test, and the preferred position doctrine. Although they are no longer applied, they provide a background for the current judicial approach to governmental regulation of speech and to the courts' expanding protection for free speech.

THE BAD TENDENCY TEST   This test was rooted in English common law. According to the **bad tendency test**, judges presumed it was reasonable to forbid speech that has a tendency to corrupt society or cause people to engage in illegal acts. The test was abandoned because it swept too broadly and ran "contrary to the fundamental premises underlying the First Amendment as the guardian of our democracy."[38] Some legislators still appear to hold this position today, and it also seems to be the view of some college students, who want to see their institution punish student colleagues or faculty who express "hateful" or "offensive" ideas.

THE CLEAR AND PRESENT DANGER TEST   This is perhaps the most famous test. The **clear and present danger test** was formulated by Justice Oliver Wendell Holmes Jr. in *Schenck* v. *United States* (1919) as an alternative to the bad tendency test. In the words of

bad tendency test
Interpretation of the First Amendment that would permit legislatures to forbid speech encouraging people to engage in illegal action.

clear and present danger test
Interpretation of the First Amendment that holds that the government cannot interfere with speech unless the speech presents a clear and present danger that it will lead to evil or illegal acts. To shout "Fire!" falsely in a crowded theater is Justice Oliver Wendell Holmes's famous example.

Justice Holmes, "The question in every case is whether the words are used in circumstances and are of such a nature as to create a clear and present danger that they will bring about substantive evils that Congress has a right to prevent."[39] A government should not be allowed to interfere with speech unless it can prove, ultimately to a skeptical judiciary, that the particular speech in question presents an immediate danger—for example, speech leading to a riot, the destruction of property, or the corruption of an election.

Supporters of the clear and present danger test concede that speech is not an absolute right. Yet they believe free speech to be so fundamental to the operations of a constitutional democracy that no government should be allowed to restrict speech unless it can demonstrate a close connection between the speech and an imminent lawless action. To shout "Fire!" falsely in a crowded theater is the most famous example of unprotected speech.

THE PREFERRED POSITION DOCTRINE   This was advanced in the 1940s when the Court applied all of the guarantees of the First Amendment to the states. The **preferred position doctrine** came close to the position that freedom of expression—the use of words and pictures—should rarely, if ever, be curtailed. This interpretation of the First Amendment gives these freedoms, especially freedom of speech and of conscience, a preferred position in our constitutional hierarchy. Judges have a special duty to protect these freedoms and should be most skeptical about laws trespassing on them. Once that judicial responsibility was established, judges had to draw lines between nonprotected and protected speech, as well as between speech and nonspeech.

NONPROTECTED AND PROTECTED SPEECH

Today the Supreme Court holds that all speech is protected unless it falls into one of four narrow categories—*libel, obscenity, fighting words,* and *commercial speech.* Such **nonprotected speech** lacks social redeeming value and has been deemed not essential to democratic deliberations and self-governance.

Still, the fact that nonprotected speech does not receive First Amendment protection does not mean that the constitutional issues relating to these kinds of speech are simple. How we prove libel, how we define obscenity, how we determine which words are fighting words, and how much commercial speech may be regulated remain hotly contested issues.

Libel

At one time, newspaper publishers and editors had to take considerable care about what they wrote for fear they might be prosecuted for **libel**—published defamation or false statements—by the government or sued by individuals. Today, as a result of gradually rising constitutional standards, it has become more difficult to win a libel suit against a newspaper or magazine.

Seditious libel—defaming, criticizing, and advocating the overthrow of government—was once subject to criminal penalties but no longer is. Seditious libel was rooted in the common law of England, which has no First Amendment protections. In 1798, only seven years after the First Amendment had been ratified, Congress enacted the first national law against **sedition**, the Sedition Act of 1798. Those were perilous times for the young Republic, for war with France seemed imminent. The Federalists, in control of both Congress and the presidency, persuaded themselves that national safety required some suppression of speech. But popular reaction to the Sedition Act helped defeat the Federalists in the elections of 1800, and the Sedition Act expired in 1801. The Federalists had failed to grasp the democratic idea that a person may criticize the government, oppose its policies, and work for the removal of the individuals in power yet still be loyal to the nation. They also failed to grasp the distinction between *seditious speech* and *seditious action*—conspiring to commit and engaging in violence against the government, which can be prosecuted and punished.

preferred position doctrine
Interpretation of the First Amendment that holds that freedom of expression is so essential to democracy that governments should not punish persons for what they say, only for what they do.

nonprotected speech
Libel, obscenity, fighting words, and commercial speech, which are not entitled to constitutional protection in all circumstances.

libel
Written defamation of another person. Especially in the case of public officials and public figures, the constitutional tests designed to restrict libel actions are very rigid.

sedition
Attempting to overthrow the government by force or to interrupt its activities by violence.

★ ★ **YOU DECIDE**

SHOULD THE BILL OF RIGHTS BE AMENDED TO PROHIBIT FLAG BURNING?

The American flag arouses patriotic emotions in Americans, many of whom fought and saw friends die under that banner. It is understandable that they would be angry to see that flag burned by protesters. Do you think the Constitution should be amended to give Congress the right to prohibit desecration of the American flag? Or would a constitutional amendment to prohibit flag burning be an unconstitutional violation of free speech?

Hustler *publisher Larry Flynt agrees to a plea bargain in which obscenity charges were dropped and a fine imposed if Flynt removed X-rated videos from a downtown store.*

obscenity
Quality or state of a work that taken as a whole appeals to a prurient interest in sex by depicting sexual conduct in a patently offensive way and that lacks serious literary, artistic, political, or scientific value.

Another attempt to limit political criticism of the government was the Smith Act of 1940. That law forbade advocating the overthrow of the government, distributing material advocating the overthrow of government by violence, and organizing any group having such purposes. In 1951, during the cold war, the Supreme Court agreed that the Smith Act could be applied to the leaders of the Communist party who had been charged with conspiring to advocate the violent overthrow of the government.[40]

Since then, however, the Court has substantially modified constitutional doctrine, giving all political speech First Amendment protection. In *New York Times* v. *Sullivan* (1964), seditious libel was declared unconstitutional.[41] Now neither Congress nor any government may outlaw mere advocacy of the abstract doctrine of violent overthrow of government: "The essential distinction is that those to whom the advocacy is addressed must be urged to do something now or in the future, rather than merely to believe in something."[42] Moreover, advocacy of the use of force may not be forbidden "except where such advocacy is directed to inciting or producing imminent lawless action and is likely to incite or produce such action."[43]

In the landmark ruling in *New York Times* v. *Sullivan* and subsequent cases, the Supreme Court established guidelines for libel cases and severely limited state power to award monetary damages in libel suits brought by public officials against critics of official conduct. Neither public officials nor public figures can collect damages for comments made about them unless they can prove with "convincing clarity" that the comments were made with "actual malice." *Actual malice* means not merely that the defendant made false statements but that the "statements were made with a knowing or reckless disregard for the truth."[44]

Public figures cannot collect damages even when subject to outrageous, clearly inaccurate parodies and cartoons. Such was the case when *Hustler* magazine printed a parody of the Reverend Jerry Falwell; the Court held that parodies and cartoons cannot reasonably be understood as describing actual facts or events.[45] Nor does the mere fact that a public figure is quoted as saying something that he or she did not say amount to a libel unless the alteration in what the person said was made deliberately, with knowledge of its falsity, and "results in material change" in the meaning of the quotation.[46]

Constitutional standards for libel charges brought by private persons are not as rigid as those for public officials and figures. State laws may permit private persons to collect damages without having to prove actual malice if they can prove the statements made about them are false and were negligently published.[47]

Obscenity and Pornography

Obscene publications are not entitled to constitutional protection, but members of the Supreme Court, like everybody else, have great difficulty in defining obscenity. As Justice Potter Stewart put it, "I know it when I see it."[48] Or, as the second Justice John Marshall Harlan explained, "One man's vulgarity is another man's lyric."[49]

In *Miller* v. *California* (1973), the Court finally agreed on a constitutional definition of **obscenity**. A work may be considered legally obscene if (1) the average person, applying contemporary standards of the particular community, would find that the work, taken as a whole, appeals to a prurient interest in sex; (2) the work depicts or describes in a patently offensive way sexual conduct specifically defined by the applicable law or authoritatively construed; and (3) the work, taken as a whole, lacks serious literary, artistic, political, or scientific value.[50]

Before *Miller,* the distinction between *pornography* and *obscenity* was not clear. The *Miller* standard clarified that only hard-core pornography is constitutionally unprotected. X-rated movies and adult theaters that fall short of the constitutional definition of obscenity are entitled to some constitutional protection, but less protection than political speech, and they are subject to greater government regulation. Cities may, as New York City has done, also regulate where adult theaters may be located by zoning laws,[51] and they may ban totally nude dancing in adult nightclubs.[52] Under narrowly drawn statutes, state and local governments can also ban the sale of "adult" magazines to minors, even if such materials would not be considered legally obscene if sold to adults.

The Court has also held that *child pornography*—sexually explicit materials either featuring minors or aimed at them—is not protected by the First Amendment.[53] Just as the government may protect minors, so apparently may it protect members of the armed forces. The Supreme Court left standing a ruling of a lower court upholding an act of Congress forbidding the sale or rental on military property of magazines or videos whose "dominant theme" is to portray nudity "in a lascivious way."[54]

Pressure for regulating pornography came primarily from political conservatives and religious fundamentalists concerned that it undermines moral standards. Some feminists have joined them, however, arguing that pornography is degrading and perpetuates sexual discrimination and violence. They argue that just as sexually explicit materials featuring minors are not entitled to First Amendment protection, so should there be no protection for pornographic materials. They contend that pornography promotes the sexual abuse of women and maintains the social subordination of women as a class. Some feminists define pornographic materials more broadly than the Court has and would include sexually explicit pictures or words that depict women as sexual objects enjoying pain and humiliation or that present abuse of women as a sexual stimulus for men.[55]

Not all feminists favor antipornography ordinances, yet those who do have joined social conservatives in a battle over regulating pornography. For this antipornography coalition to be successful, a substantial alteration in constitutional doctrine will be required. Unlike the Canadian Supreme Court, which redefined obscenity to include materials that degrade women,[56] the U.S. Supreme Court does not appear willing to substantially change current doctrine.

Fighting Words

Fighting words were held to be constitutionally unprotected because "their very utterance may inflict injury or tend to incite an immediate breach of peace."[57] That the words are abusive, offensive, and insulting or that they create anger, alarm, or resentment is not sufficient. Thus a four-letter word worn on a sweatshirt was not judged to be a fighting word in the constitutional sense, even though it was offensive and angered some people.[58] In recent years, the Court has overturned convictions for uttering fighting words and struck down laws that criminalized "hate speech"—insulting racial, ethnic, and gender slurs.[59] The Court, though, has indicated that cross-burning by the Klu Klux Klan may be punished because it has historically been associated with intimidation.[60]

Commercial Speech

Commercial speech—such as advertisements and commercials—used to be unprotected because it was deemed to have lesser value than political speech. But in recent years, the Court has reconsidered and extended more protection to commercial speech, as it has to fighting words. In *44 Liquormart, Inc.,* v. *Rhode Island* (1996), for instance, the Court struck down a law forbidding the advertising of the price of alcoholic drinks.[61] It now appears that states may forbid and punish only false and misleading advertising, along with advertising the sale of anything illegal—for example, narcotics. Although the Supreme Court has not specifically removed it from the nonprotected category, the Court has interpreted the First, Fifth, and Fourteenth Amendments so as to provide considerable constitutional protection for commercial speech.

Protected Speech

Apart from these four categories of nonprotected speech, all other expression is constitutionally protected, and courts strictly scrutinize government regulation of such speech. The Supreme Court uses the following doctrines to measure the limits of governmental power to regulate speech.

Virginia's Attorney General, Jerry Kilgore (right), *speaks to reporters outside the U.S. Supreme Court building in Washington, D.C., where the justices heard a First Amendment challenge to Virginia's cross-burning law on December 11, 2002.*

fighting words
Words that by their very nature inflict injury on those to whom they are addressed or incite them to acts of violence.

commercial speech
Advertisements and commercials for products and services; they receive less First Amendment protection, primarily to discourage false and misleading ads.

IN COMPARATIVE PERSPECTIVE

HATE SPEECH IN CANADA

Although the Supreme Court of Canada, in interpreting the nation's Charter of Rights, generally follows the rulings on freedom of speech of the Supreme Court of the United States, it refused to do so with respect to hate speech. Whereas the U.S. Supreme Court held that the First Amendment bars making hate speech a crime,* the Canadian Supreme Court upheld a law making it a crime to express "hatred against any identifiable group . . . distinguished by colour, race, religion, or ethnic origin."

James Keegstra, a high school teacher, was convicted of communicating anti-Semitic teachings to his students. His conviction, however, was overturned by an appeals court on the ground that the law punishing hate speech violated the Charter's guarantee of freedom of expression. In reversing the lower court and upholding Keegstra's conviction and Canada's hate speech law, the Supreme Court observed:

> The international commitment to eradicate hate propaganda and, most importantly, the special role given equality and multiculturalism in the Canadian Constitution necessitate a departure from the view, reasonably prevalent in America at present, that the suppression of hate propaganda is incompatible with the guarantee of free expression. . . .

> At the core of freedom of expression lies the need to ensure that truth and the common good are attained, whether in scientific and artistic endeavors or in the process of determining the best course to take in our political affairs. . . . Nevertheless, the argument from truth does not provide convincing support for the protection of hate propaganda. Taken to its extreme, this argument would require us to permit the communication of all expression, it being impossible to know with *absolute* certainty which factual statements are true, or which ideas obtain the greatest good. . . . There is very little chance that statements intended to promote hatred against an identifiable group are true, or that their vision of society will lead to a better world. To portray such statements as crucial to truth and the betterment of the political and social milieu is therefore misguided.†

*R.A.V. v. St. Paul, 505 U.S. 377 (1992).
†Regina v. Keegstra, 3 S.C.R. 697 (1990).

PRIOR RESTRAINT   Of all the forms of governmental interference with expression, judges are most suspicious of those that impose **prior restraint**—censorship before publication. Prior restraints include governmental review and approval before a speech can be made, before a motion picture can be shown, or before a newspaper can be published. Most prior restraints are unconstitutional, as the Court has said: "Any system of prior restraints of expression comes to this Court bearing a heavy presumption against its constitutional validity."[62] About the only prior restraints approved by the Court relate to military and national security matters—such as the disclosure of troop movements[63]—and to high school authorities' control over student newspapers.[64] Student newspapers at colleges and universities receive the same protections as other newspapers because they are independent and financially separate from the college or university.

VOID FOR VAGUENESS   Laws must not be so vague that people do not know whether their speech would violate the law and hence are afraid to exercise protected freedoms. Laws must not allow the authorities who administer them so much discretion that they may discriminate against people whose views they dislike. For these reasons, the Court strikes down laws using the void for vagueness doctrine.

LEAST DRASTIC MEANS   Even for an important purpose, a legislature may not pass a law that impinges on First Amendment freedoms if other, less drastic means are available. To illustrate, a state may protect the public from unscrupulous lawyers, but it may not do so by forbidding attorneys from advertising their fees for simple services. The

prior restraint
Censorship imposed before a speech is made or a newspaper is published; usually presumed to be unconstitutional.

state could adopt other ways to protect the public from such lawyers that do not impinge on their freedom of speech; it could, for example, provide for the disbarment of lawyers who mislead their clients.

CONTENT AND VIEWPOINT NEUTRALITY Laws concerning the time, place, or manner of speech that regulate some kinds of speech but not others or that regulate speech expressing some views but not others are much more likely to be struck down than those that are content-neutral or viewpoint-neutral, that is, laws that apply to *all* kinds of speech and to *all* views. For example, the Constitution does not prohibit laws forbidding the posting of handbills on telephone poles. Yet laws prohibiting only religious handbills or only handbills advocating racism or sexism would in all probability be declared unconstitutional because they would relate to the kinds of handbills or what is being said rather than to all handbills regardless of what they say.

The lack of viewpoint neutrality was the grounds for the Court's striking down a St. Paul, Minnesota, ordinance that prohibited the display of a symbol that would arouse anger on the basis of race, color, creed, religion, or gender. The ordinance was not considered viewpoint-neutral because it did not forbid displays that might arouse anger for other reasons, for example, because of political affiliation.[65]

FREEDOM OF THE PRESS

Courts have carefully protected the right to publish information, no matter how journalists get it. But some reporters, editors, and others argue that this is not enough. They insist that the First Amendment gives them the right to ignore legal requests and to withhold information. They also contend that the First Amendment gives them a *right of access*, a right to go wherever they need to go to get information.

Does the Press Have the Right to Withhold Information?

Although most reporters have challenged the right of public officials to withhold information, they claim the right to do so themselves, including the right to keep information from grand juries and legislative investigating committees. Without this right to withhold information, reporters insist, they cannot assure their sources of confidentiality, and they will not be able to get the information they need to keep the public informed.

The Supreme Court, however, has refused to acknowledge that reporters, and presumably scholars, have a constitutional right to ignore legal requests such as subpoenas and to withhold information from governmental bodies.[66] It is up to Congress and the states to provide such privileges for news reporters, and many states have passed *press shield laws* providing some protection for reporters from state court subpoenas.

Does the Press Have the Right to Know?

The press has argued that if reporters are excluded from places where public business is conducted or are denied access to information in government files, they are not able to perform their traditional function of keeping the public informed. In similar fashion, some reporters argue that they may enter facilities such as food markets, child care centers, and homes for the mentally ill, even using false identities, to expose racial discrimination, employment discrimination, and financial fraud. The Supreme Court, however, has refused to acknowledge a constitutional right of the press to know, although it did concede that there is a First Amendment right for the press, along with the public, to be present at criminal trials.[67]

Although they have no constitutional obligation to do so, many states have adopted *sunshine laws* requiring government agencies to open their meetings to the public and the press. Congress requires most federal executive agencies to open hearings and meetings of advisory groups to the public, and most congressional committee meetings are open to the public. Federal and state courtroom trials are also open, but judicial conferences, in which the judges discuss how to decide the cases, are not.

Congress has authorized the president to establish a classification system to keep some public documents and governmental files secret, and it is a crime for any person to divulge such classified information. So far, however, although they have been threatened, no newspapers have been prosecuted for doing so.

The Freedom of Information Act (FOIA) of 1966, since amended, liberalized access to nonclassified federal government records. This law makes the records of federal executive agencies available to the public, with certain exceptions, such as private financial transactions, personnel records, criminal investigation files, interoffice memorandums, and letters used in internal decision making. If federal agencies fail to act promptly on requests for information, applicants are entitled to speedy judicial hearings. The burden is on an agency to explain its refusal to supply material, and if the judge decides the government has improperly withheld information, the government has to pay the legal fees. Since the inception of FOIA, more than 250,000 people have requested information, and more than 90 percent of these requests have been granted.

President Bill Clinton issued an executive order requiring the automatic declassification of almost all government documents after 25 years. Any person who wants access to documents that are not declassified can appeal to an Interagency Security Classification Appeals panel, which has a record of ruling in favor of releasing documents. The Electronic Freedom of Information Act of 1996 requires most federal agencies to put their files online and to establish an index of all their records. The National Aeronautics and Space Administration (NASA) has done the most of the federal agencies (see www.nasa.gov). One of the most frequent requests to NASA's Electronic Reading Room is for documents relating to unidentified flying objects (UFOs).

Free Press Versus Fair Trials

When newspapers and television report in vivid detail the facts of a crime, interview prosecutors and police, question witnesses, and hold press conferences for defendants and their attorneys—as in the O. J. Simpson murder trial and Oklahoma City bombing cases—they may so inflame the public that finding a panel of impartial jurors and conducting a fair trial is difficult. In England, strict rules determine what the media may report, and judges do not hesitate to punish newspapers that comment on pending criminal proceedings. By contrast, in the United States free comment is protected. Yet the Supreme Court has not been indifferent to protecting persons on trial from inflammatory publicity. Judges may impose "gag orders" on lawyers and jurors, but not reporters, restraining them from talking about an ongoing trial, and new trials may be ordered as a remedy for prejudicial publicity. Trials may, on rare occasions, be closed to the press and the public. Although federal rules of criminal procedure forbid radio or photographic coverage of criminal cases in federal courts, most states permit televising courtroom proceedings, and court TV programs have become very popular.

OTHER MEDIA AND COMMUNICATIONS

When the First Amendment was written, freedom of "the press" referred to leaflets, newspapers, and books. Today the amendment protects other media as well—the mails, motion pictures, billboards, radio, television, cable, telephones, fax machines, and the Internet. Because each form of communication entails special problems, each needs a different degree of protection.

The Mails

More than 80 years ago, Justice Oliver Wendell Holmes Jr. wrote in dissent, "The United States may give up the Post Office when it sees fit, but while it carries it on, the use of the mails is almost as much a part of free speech as is the right to use our tongues."[68] In 1965, the Court adopted that view by striking down an act that had directed the postmaster general to detain foreign mailings of "communist political propaganda" and to deliver these materials only upon the addressee's request.[69] The Court has also set aside federal laws authorizing postal authorities to exclude from the mails materials they consider obscene.

Although government censorship of mail is unconstitutional, household censorship is not. The Court has sustained laws giving householders the right to ask the postmaster to order mailers to delete their names from certain mailing lists and to refrain from sending any advertisements that they believe to be "erotically arousing or sexually provocative."[70] Moreover, Congress may forbid—and has forbidden—the use of mailboxes for any materials except those sent through the United States mails.

Handbills, Sound Trucks, and Billboards

Religious and political pamphlets, leaflets, and handbills have been historic weapons in the defense of liberty, and their distribution is constitutionally protected. So, too, is the use of their contemporary counterparts, sound trucks and billboards. A state cannot restrain the distribution of leaflets merely to keep its streets clean,[71] but it may impose reasonable restrictions on their distribution so long as they are neutrally enforced, without regard to the content.

Motion Pictures and Plays

Prior censorship of films to prevent the showing of obscenity is not necessarily unconstitutional; however, laws calling for submission of films to a government review board are constitutional only if there is a prompt judicial hearing. The burden is on the government to prove to the court that the particular film in question is obscene. Prior censorship of films by review boards was once common, but no longer. Live performances, such as plays and revues, are also entitled to constitutional protection.[72]

Broadcast and Cable Communications

Television remains an important means of distributing news and appealing for votes, though the Internet has gained popularity. Yet of all the mass media, broadcasting receives the least First Amendment protection. Congress has established a system of commercial broadcasting, supplemented by the Corporation for Public Broadcasting, which provides funds for public radio and television. The Federal Communications Commission (FCC) regulates the entire system by granting licenses and making regulations for their use.

The First Amendment would prevent censorship if the FCC tried to impose it. The First Amendment does not, however, prevent the FCC from imposing sanctions on stations that broadcast indecent or filthy words, even if they are not legally obscene.[73] The FCC did precisely that when it fined Infinity Broadcasting for indecent remarks by "shock jock" Howard Stern. Nor does the First Amendment prevent the FCC from refusing to renew a license if, in its opinion, a broadcaster does not serve the public interest.

The Supreme Court allows more governmental regulation of broadcasters than of newspaper and magazine publishers because space on the airwaves was limited. However, technological advances such as cable television, videotapes, and satellite broadcasting have opened up new means of communication and brought competition to the electronic media. Recognizing these changes, Congress passed the Telecommunications Act of 1996, allowing telephone companies, broadcasters, and cable TV stations to compete with one another. In adopting the act, Congress did not abandon all government regulation of the airways. On the contrary, the act calls for many new regulations—for example, requiring that all new television sets sold in the United States be equipped with V-chips that allow viewers to block programs containing violent or sexual material.

The Court has upheld a congressional requirement that cable television stations must carry the signals of local broadcast television stations.[74] The Court has also held that Congress may authorize cable operators to refuse access to leased channels for "patently offensive" programs. The Court, however, struck down congressional requirements that if a cable operator allows such offensive programming, it must be blocked and unscrambled through special devices. In *United States* v. *Playboy Entertainment Group* (2000), the Court underscored the greater protection for cable than for broadcast television. Whereas broadcast television may be required to provide programming for

At a press conference, Howard Stern defends his use of raunchy language and subject matter that led to the FCC fining the Infinity Broadcasting network. Stern subsequently decided to leave the network to work on a satellite radio station.

children and not air violence at certain times, the Court held that such rules do not apply to cable television because unwanted programming can be blocked by homeowners.[75]

Telecommunications and the Internet

Millions of Americans log on to the Internet to buy books, clothing, jewelry, airplane tickets, stocks, and bonds. Because the Internet has become a commercial marketplace and a major channel for communication, Congress is struggling with issues raised by cyberspace communication. Although Congress has imposed a moratorium on state taxation of commercial transactions on the Internet, debate continues over whether the national government should preempt state taxation. How do existing laws against copyright piracy apply to the World Wide Web? Should there be national regulation of junk e-mail, or can state laws take care of the problem? In what ways may Congress regulate indecent and obscene communications on the Web? Should Congress try to protect the privacy of those who use the Web? (For more information about privacy and developments on the Web, go to the Electronic Privacy Information Center at www.epic.org.)

As Congress and the state legislatures begin to deal with these and other new problems, legislators and judges will have to apply traditional constitutional principles to new technologies and means of communication. The Court distinguishes between a limited ban on indecent messages on radio and broadcast television and those on telephones, cable television, and the Internet. Radio and broadcast messages are readily available to children and can intrude into the privacy of the home without prior warning. By contrast, telephone messages may be blocked, and access by minors is more readily restricted.[76]

In its first ruling on First Amendment protection for the Internet, *Reno* v. *American Civil Liberties Union* (1997), the Court struck down provisions of the Communications Decency Act of 1996 that had made it a crime to send obscene or indecent messages to anyone under 18 years of age. In doing so, the Court emphasized the unique character of the Internet, holding that it is less intrusive than radio and broadcast television.[77] In response to *Reno* v. *ACLU,* Congress passed the Child Online Protection Act of 1998 (COPA), which made it a crime for a commercial Web site to knowingly make available to anyone under the age of 17 sexually explicit material considered "harmful to minors" based on "community standards." But in 2004 the Supreme Court held that the law was unenforceable because imposing criminal penalties was not the least drastic means of achieving Congress's goals; Internet filters and adult checks could be used to block minors' access to sites with sexually explicit material.[78] In addition, the Court struck down the Child Pornography Prevention Act of 1996, which made it a federal crime to create or distribute "virtual child pornography" generated by computer images of young adults rather than actual children. The law went beyond punishing child pornography, which is a crime because actual children are involved, the Court ruled, and had the potential to chill clear artistic and literary expression.[79]

FREEDOM OF ASSEMBLY

In 1998, Khallid Abdul Muhammad, a known racist and anti-Semite, organized what he called a "Million Youth March" in New York City. Mayor Rudolph Giuliani denied a permit for the march on grounds that it would be a "hate march." A federal appeals court upheld a lower court ruling that denial of the permit was unconstitutional; however, the three-judge panel placed restrictions on the event, limiting its duration to four hours and scaling it back to a six-block area. The march proceeded, surrounded by police in riot gear who broke up the demonstration after Muhammad delivered a vitriolic speech against police, Jews, and city officials.[80]

It took judicial authorities to defend the rights of these unpopular speakers and marchers, but it is not always the "bad guys" whose rights have to be protected by the courts. It also took judicial intervention in the 1960s to preserve for Martin Luther King Jr. and those who marched with him the right to demonstrate in the streets of southern cities on behalf of civil rights for African Americans.

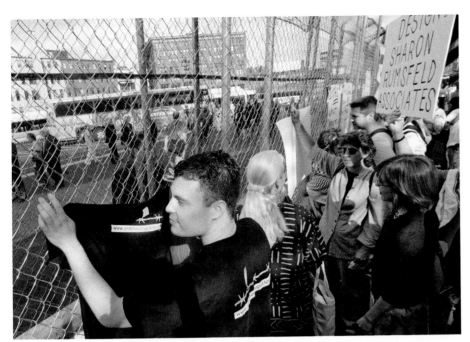

Although the First Amendment affirms the right of the people to peacefully assemble, demonstrations are often highly regulated affairs, involving an elaborate process on the part of organizers to obtain permits for rallies and marches and often resulting in a large, intimidating police presence at these events. Some cities even go so far as to establish "free speech zones," where protesters are forced to remain in designated areas surrounded by police barricades and even barbed wire.

Such incidents present a classic free speech problem. It is almost always easier, and certainly politically more prudent, to maintain order by curbing public demonstrations by unpopular groups. However, if police did not have the right to order groups to disperse, public order would be at the mercy of those who resort to street demonstrations to create tensions and provoke street battles.

A recent controversy surrounds Attorney General John Ashcroft's decision in 2002 to allow law enforcement agents to go undercover to monitor activities and assemblies in any public place—including mosques, churches, and chat rooms on the Internet—in combating international terrorism. He thereby abandoned the Department of Justice's guidelines adopted in 1976 after Congress discovered that FBI agents were conducting surveillance and had infiltrated the civil rights movement and other groups engaged in lawful activities, as well as closely monitored King and other leaders. In response to criticisms that the new guidelines infringed on the freedoms of assembly and association, Ashcroft stressed that FBI agents would be limited to investigating terrorist activities.

Public Forums and Time, Place, and Manner Regulations

The Constitution protects the right to speak, but it does not give people the right to communicate their views to everyone, in every place, at every time they wish. No one has the right to block traffic or to hold parades or make speeches in public streets or on public sidewalks whenever he or she wishes. Governments may not censor what can be said, but they can make "reasonable" *time, place,* and *manner* regulations for protests or parades. The Supreme Court has divided public property into three categories: public forums, limited public forums, and nonpublic forums. The extent to which governments may limit access depends on the kind of forum involved.

Public forums are public places historically associated with the free exercise of expressive activities, such as streets, sidewalks, and parks. Courts look closely at time, place, and manner regulations that apply to these traditional public forums to ensure that they are being applied evenhandedly and that action is not taken because of what is being said rather than how and where or by whom it is being said.

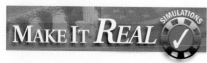

CIVIL LIBERTIES: THE GREAT BALANCING ACT

The war against international terrorism has highlighted the politics of rights in balancing freedom and security. In this simulation, you judge the constitutionality of state and local policies affecting civil rights and civil liberties and find out the political implications as well as how liberals, conservatives, and centrists would decide.

Go to Make It Real "Civil Liberties: The Great Balancing Act."

civil disobedience
Deliberate refusal to obey a law or comply with the orders of public officials as a means of expressing opposition.

Other kinds of public property, such as rooms in a city hall or in a school after hours, may be designated as *limited public forums,* available for assembly and speech for limited purposes, for a limited amount of time, and even for a limited class of speakers (such as only students, only teachers, or only employees), provided the distinctions between the people allowed access and those excluded are not biased.

Nonpublic forums include public facilities such as libraries, courthouses, prisons, schools, swimming pools, and government offices that are open to the public but are not public forums. As long as people use such facilities within the normal bounds of conduct, they may not be constitutionally restrained from doing so. However, people may be excluded from such places as a government office or a school if they engage in activities for which the facilities were not created. They have no right to interfere with programs or try to take over a building—especially facilities such as a university president's office—in order to stage a political protest.

Does the right of peaceful assembly include the right to violate a law nonviolently but deliberately? We have no precise answer, but in general, **civil disobedience**, even if peaceful, is not a protected right. When Martin Luther King Jr. and his followers refused to comply with a state court's injunction forbidding them to parade in Birmingham without first securing a permit, the Supreme Court sustained their conviction, even though there was serious doubt about the constitutionality of the injunction and the ordinance on which it was based.[81]

More recently, the First Amendment right of antiabortion protesters to picket in front of abortion clinics has come into conflict with a woman's right to go to an abortion clinic. Protesters have often massed in front of clinics, shouting at employees and patrons and blocking entrances to the clinic. The Supreme Court has struck down provisions that prohibit protesters from expressing their views. But the Court has upheld injunctions that keep antiabortion protesters outside of a buffer zone around abortion clinics and also upheld injunctions that were issued because of prior unlawful conduct by the protesters. The proper constitutional test for such injunctions is "whether the challenged provisions . . . burden no more speech than necessary to serve a significant government interest," such as public safety or the right of women to go into such a clinic.[82]

The combination of First Amendment guarantees for rights and freedoms and their judicial enforcement is one of the fundamental features of our government and political system. As Supreme Court Justice Robert H. Jackson wrote:

> The very purpose of [the] Bill of Rights was to withdraw certain subjects from the vicissitudes of political controversy, to place them beyond the reach of majorities and officials and to establish them as legal principles to be applied by the courts. One's right to life, liberty, and property, to free speech, a free press, freedom of worship and assembly, and other fundamental rights may not be submitted to vote: they depend on the outcome of no elections.[83]

The connection between constitutional limitations and judicial enforcement is an example of the "auxiliary precautions" James Madison believed were necessary to prevent arbitrary governmental action. Citizens in other free nations rely on elections and political checks to protect their rights; in the United States, we also appeal to judges when we fear our freedoms are in danger.

S U M M A R Y

1. The Constitution protects our right to seek a writ of habeas corpus and forbids *ex post facto* laws and bills of attainder.

2. First Amendment freedoms—freedom of religion, of speech, of the press, and of assembly and association—are at the heart of a healthy constitutional democracy.

3. Since World War I, the Supreme Court has become the primary branch of government for giving meaning to these constitutional restraints. And since 1925, these constitutional limits have been applied not only to Congress but to all governmental agencies—national, state, and local.

4. The First Amendment forbids the establishment of religion and also guarantees the free exercise of religion. These two freedoms, however, are often in conflict with each other and represent conflicting notions of what is in the public interest.

5. The Supreme Court holds that there are only four categories of nonprotected speech—libel, obscenity, fighting words, and commercial speech. All other speech is protected under the First Amendment, and government may regulate that speech only when it has a compelling reason and does so in a content-neutral way.

6. Over the years, the Supreme Court has taken a pragmatic approach to First Amendment freedoms. It has refused to make them absolute rights above any kind of governmental regulation, direct or indirect, or to say that they must be preserved at whatever price. But the justices have recognized that a constitu-

tional democracy tampers with these freedoms at great peril. They have insisted on compelling justification before permitting these rights to be limited. How compelling the justification is, in a free society, will always remain an open question, but is especially difficult during times of war.

KEY TERMS

writ of habeas corpus
ex post facto law
bill of attainder
due process clause
selective incorporation

establishment clause
vouchers
free exercise clause
bad tendency test
clear and present danger test

preferred position doctrine
nonprotected speech
libel
sedition
obscenity

fighting words
commercial speech
prior restraint
civil disobedience

FURTHER READING

STUART BIEGEL, *Beyond Our Control? Confronting the Limits of Our Legal System in the Age of Cyberspace* (MIT Press, 2001).

STEVEN P. BROWN, *Trumping Religion: The Christian Right, The Free Speech Clause, and the Courts* (University of Alabama Press, 2002).

JAMES MACGREGOR BURNS AND STEWART BURNS, *A People's Charter: The Pursuit of Rights in America* (Knopf, 1991).

JESSE CHOPER, *Securing Religious Liberty: Principles for Judicial Interpretation of Religion Clauses* (University of Chicago Press, 1995).

LOUIS FISHER, *Religious Liberty in America: Political Safeguards* (University Press of Kansas, 2002).

MIKE GODWIN, *Cyber Rights: Defending Free Speech in the Digital Age* (MIT Press, 2003).

ROBERT JUSTIN GOLDSTEIN, *Flag Burning and Free Speech: The Case of Texas v. Johnson* (University Press of Kansas, 2002).

NAT HENTOFF, *Living the Bill of Rights: How to Be an Authentic American* (HarperCollins, 1998).

LAWRENCE LESSIG, *Code and Other Laws of Cyberspace* (Basic Books, 2000).

LEONARD W. LEVY, *Emergence of a Free Press* (Oxford University Press, 1985).

ANTHONY LEWIS, *Make No Law: The Sullivan Case and the First Amendment* (Random House, 1991).

CATHARINE A. MACKINNON, *Only Words* (Harvard University Press, 1993).

ALEXANDER MEIKLEJOHN, *Political Freedom: The Constitutional Powers of the People* (Harper & Row, 1965).

JOHN STUART MILL, *Essay on Liberty*, in *The English Philosophers from Bacon to Mill*, ed. Arthur Burtt (Random House, 1939), pp. 949–1041.

JOHN T. NOONAN JR., *The Lustre of Our Country: The American Experience of Religious*

Freedom (University of California Press, 1998).

DAVID M. O'BRIEN, *Animal Sacrifice and Religious Freedom:* Church of the Lukumi Babalu Aye *v.* City of Hialeah (University Press of Kansas, 2004).

DAVID M. O'BRIEN, *Constitutional Law and Politics: Civil Rights and Civil Liberties,* 6th ed. (Norton, 2005).

SHAWN FRANCIS PETERS, *Judging Jehovah's Witnesses: Religious Persecution and the Dawn of the Right Revolution* (University Press of Kansas, 2002).

J. W. PELTASON AND SUE DAVIS, *Understanding the Constitution,* 16th ed. (Harcourt, 2004).

NADINE STROSSEN, *Defending Pornography: Free Speech, Sex, and the Fight for Women's Rights* (Scribner, 1995).

RIGHTS TO LIFE, LIBERTY, AND PROPERTY

16

We have had to rethink the balance between liberty and security since the terrorist attacks of September 2001. Neither is likely to be taken for granted again. We are all affected by measures to strengthen homeland security—whether in schools; at concerts; traveling in airports, on trains, or on public streets; or in our homes. Yet we are still the freest people in the world. And we need to remember how fortunate we are to live in a society that values *due process*—established rules and regulations that restrain persons in government who exercise power. Such procedures are not available to citizens in China, much of Africa and South America, and elsewhere in the world.

Public officials in the United States have great power. Under certain conditions, they can seize our property, put us in jail, and—in extreme circumstances—even take our lives. The framers of our Constitution recognized it is necessary—but dangerous—to give power to those who govern. It is so dangerous that we do not depend on the ballot box alone to keep our officials from becoming tyrants. Because political power may threaten our liberty, we parcel it out in small chunks and surround it with restraints. No single official can decide to take our lives, liberty, or property. Officials must act according to the rule of law. If they act outside the scope of their authority or contrary to law, they can be restrained, dismissed, or punished. These rights to due process are the precious rights of all who live under the American flag—rich or poor, young or old, man or woman, and regardless of race, religion, or color.

In this chapter, we look at the rights of all persons to due process, but before we do, let us look at the precious freedoms and rights that flow from citizenship.

TIME LINE

RIGHTS TO LIFE, LIBERTY, AND PROPERTY

1873	*Slaughterhouse Cases* differentiate between state and federal citizenship and therefore rights
1961	*Mapp* v. *Ohio* applies the Fourth Amendment exclusionary rule to the states
1965	*Griswold* v. *Connecticut* proclaims a constitutional right to privacy
1966	*Miranda* v. *Arizona* holds that police must inform defendants of their rights
1968	*Terry* v. *Ohio* authorizes police pat-downs for weapons
1973	*Roe* v. *Wade* extends a woman's right to privacy to decide whether to have an abortion
1976	Capital Punishment reinstated after a ten-year moratorium
1992	*Planned Parenthood* v. *Casey* reaffirms *Roe* v. *Wade* and a woman's right to choose
2001	USA PATRIOT Act enacted in response to September 11, 2001 terrorist attacks
2003	*Lawrence* v. *Texas* strikes down a law making homosexual sodomy a crime
2004	*Rasul* v. *Bush* holds that "enemy combatants" are entitled to a review of the charges against them by an independent tribunal

Proud naturalized citizens are sworn in at an emotional ceremony.

naturalization
A legal action conferring citizenship on an alien.

dual citizenship
Citizenship in more than one nation.

right of expatriation
The right to renounce one's citizenship.

CITIZENSHIP RIGHTS

Every nation has rules that determine nationality and define who is a member of, owes allegiance to, and is a subject of the nation. But in a constitutional democracy, citizenship is an *office*, and like other offices, it carries with it certain powers and responsibilities. How citizenship is acquired and retained is therefore a matter of considerable importance.

How Citizenship Is Acquired and Lost

The basic right of citizenship was not given constitutional protection until 1868, when the Fourteenth Amendment was adopted; prior to that, each state determined citizenship. The Fourteenth Amendment states, "All persons born or naturalized in the United States, and subject to the jurisdiction thereof, are citizens of the United States and of the State wherein they reside." This means that all persons born in the United States, except children born to foreign ambassadors and ministers, are citizens of this country regardless of the citizenship of their parents. (Congress has defined the United States for this purpose to include Puerto Rico, Guam, the Northern Marianas, and the Virgin Islands.) A child born to an American citizen living abroad or who has an American citizen as a grandparent is an American citizen if either the parent or grandparent has lived in the United States for at least five years, including two of which were after age 14. Although the Fourteenth Amendment does not make Native Americans citizens of the United States and of the states in which they live, Congress did so in 1924.

NATURALIZATION Citizenship may also be acquired by **naturalization**, a legal action conferring citizenship on an alien. Congress determines naturalization requirements. Today, with minor exceptions, nonenemy aliens over age 18 who have been lawfully admitted for permanent residence and who have resided in the United States for at least five years and in the state for at least six months are eligible for naturalization. Any state or federal court in the United States or the Immigration and Naturalization Service (INS) can grant citizenship. The INS, with the help of the Federal Bureau of Investigation (FBI), makes the necessary investigations.

Any person denied citizenship after a hearing before an immigration officer may appeal to a federal district judge. Citizenship is granted if the judge is satisfied that the applicant has met all the requirements after reviewing the FBI check that no disqualifying felony conviction has been found. The applicant renounces allegiance to his or her former country, swears to support and defend the Constitution and laws of the United States against all enemies, and promises to bear arms on behalf of the United States when required to do so by law. Those whose religious beliefs prevent them from bearing arms are allowed to take an oath swearing that if called to duty, they will serve in the armed forces as noncombatants or will perform work of national importance under civilian direction. The court or INS then grants a certificate of naturalization.

Naturalized citizenship may be revoked by court order if the government can prove that citizenship was secured by deception. But citizenship cannot be taken from people because of what they have done—for example, for committing certain crimes, voting in foreign elections, or serving in foreign armies. In addition, citizenship, however acquired, may be renounced voluntarily. Even so, the government must prove that the citizen "not only voluntarily committed the expatriating act prescribed in the statute, but also intended to relinquish his citizenship."[1]

DUAL CITIZENSHIP Because each nation has complete authority to decide for itself the definition of nationality, it is possible for a person to be considered a citizen by two or more nations. **Dual citizenship** is not unusual, especially for people from nations that do not recognize the right of individuals to renounce their citizenship, called the **right of expatriation**. (One of the issues of the War of 1812 was that England did not recognize sailors born in England as having abandoned their English citizenship on becoming naturalized American citizens.) Children born abroad to American citizens may also be citizens of the nation in which they were born. Children born in the United States of parents from a foreign nation may also be citizens of their parents' country.

Among the nations that allow dual citizenship are Canada, Mexico, France, and the United Kingdom. One expert estimates that based on the number of American children born to foreign-born parents, the number of Americans eligible to hold citizenship in another country grows by about 500,000 a year.[2] Moreover, with more than 7 million Mexican-born immigrants in the United States and their American-born children now becoming eligible to apply for Mexican citizenship, the number of dual citizens in the United States is on the rise. Dual citizenship carries negative as well as positive consequences; for example, a person with dual citizenship may be subject to national service obligations and taxes in both countries.

Rights of American Citizens

An American becomes a citizen of one of our states merely by residing in that state. *Residence* as understood in the Fourteenth Amendment means the place one calls home. The legal status of residence should not be confused with the fact of physical presence. A person may be living in Washington, D.C., but be a citizen of California—that is, consider California home and vote in that state.

Most of our most important rights flow from *state* citizenship. In the *Slaughter-House Cases* (1873), the Supreme Court carefully distinguished between the privileges of U.S. citizens and those of state citizens.[3] It held that the only privileges of national citizenship are those that "owe their existence to the Federal Government, its National Character, its Constitution, or its laws." These privileges have never been completely specified, but they include the right to use the navigable waters of the United States and to protection on the high seas, to assemble peacefully and petition for redress of grievances, to vote if qualified to do so under state laws and have one's vote counted properly, and to travel throughout the United States.

In times of war, the rights and liberties of citizenship are tested and have been curbed. Although the Supreme Court overruled President Abraham Lincoln's use of military courts to try civilians during the Civil War,[4] it upheld the World War II internment of Japanese Americans in "relocation camps" and never questioned their loyalty or the government's argument that they posed a threat to national security. The Supreme Court drew a distinction between the rights of citizenship during peacetime and wartime, observing that, "hardships are part of war, and war is an aggregation of hardships. All citizens alike, both in and out of uniform, feel the impact of war in greater or lesser measure. Citizenship has it responsibilities as well as its privileges, and in time of war the burden is always heavier."[5] The Supreme Court also approved the use of military tribunals to try captured foreign saboteurs[6] but held that citizens may not be subject to courts-martial or denied the guarantees of the Bill of Rights.[7] For that reason, John Walker Lindh, the young American captured fighting with the Taliban in Afghanistan, was accorded the assistance of counsel and tried in court. However, in his war against international terrorism, President George W. Bush issued orders declaring U.S. citizens "enemy combatants," for plotting with the Al-Qaeda network, and authorized their and other captured foreign nationals' detention in military compounds, without counsel or access to a court of law. His orders were controversial and the Supreme Court ruled in 2004 that U.S. citizens and foreign nationals may not be detained indefinitely without the opportunity to consult an attorney and to contest the basis for their detention before an independent tribunal.[8]

THE RIGHT TO LIVE AND TRAVEL IN THE UNITED STATES This right, which is not subject to any congressional limitation, is perhaps the most precious aspect of American citizenship. Aliens have no such right. They may be stopped on the high seas or at the borders and turned away if they fail to meet the terms and conditions stipulated by Congress for admission. Today millions of people around the world yearn to come and live in the United States, but only American citizens have a constitutionally guaranteed right to do so.

THE RIGHT TO TRAVEL ABROAD The right to international travel can be regulated within the bounds of due process. Under current law, it is unlawful for citizens to leave or enter the United States without a valid passport (except as otherwise provided by the president, as has been done for travel to Mexico, Canada, and parts of the Caribbean). Travel to Cuba is forbidden unless special permission is granted, as has increasingly been done for journalists, artists, scholars, and politicians; however, the Bush administration tightened restrictions on Cuban Americans who want to visit their families in Cuba.

Rights of Aliens

During periods of suspicion and hostility toward aliens, the protections of citizenship are even more precious. Congress enacted the Enemy Alien Act of 1798, which remains in effect, authorizing the president during wartime to detain and expel citizens of a country with which we are at war. Citizens may not be expelled from the country, but aliens may be expelled for even minor infractions.[9] The Supreme Court also upheld 1996 amendments to the Immigration and Naturalization Act that require mandatory detention during deportation hearings of aliens accused of certain crimes,[10] though they may not be held longer than six months.[11]

Still, the Constitution protects many rights of *all persons,* not just of American citizens. Only citizens may run for elective office and their right to vote may not be denied, but all other rights are not so literally restricted. Neither Congress nor the states can deny to aliens the right of freedom of religion or the right of freedom of speech. Nor can any government deprive any person of the due process of the law or equal protection under the laws.[12]

However, Congress and the states may deny or limit welfare and many other kinds of benefits to aliens. Congress has denied most federally assisted benefits to illegal immigrants and has permitted states to deny them many other benefits, making an exception only for emergency medical care, disaster relief, and some nutrition programs. The Court has also upheld laws barring the employment of aliens as police officers, schoolteachers, and probation officers.[13] While states have considerable discretion over what benefits they give to aliens, the Supreme Court has held that states cannot constitutionally exclude children of undocumented aliens from the public schools or charge their parents tuition.[14]

Admission to the United States

President Franklin Roosevelt, reminding us of our heritage as a haven for people fleeing religious and political persecution, opened his address to a convention of the Daughters of the American Revolution with the salutation, "Fellow immigrants and revolutionaries." Some Americans, however, are concerned that admitting so many people from abroad will dilute American traditions and values.[15] Throughout our history, debates have flared among those wishing to open our borders and those wishing to close them.

Aliens do not have a constitutional right to enter the United States. Congress has wide discretion in setting the numbers, terms, and conditions under which aliens can enter and stay in the United States. The Immigration Act of 1965, as amended in 1990 and 1996, sets an annual ceiling of 675,000 nonrefugee aliens allowed to come here as permanent residents, but when refugees and other exempt categories are added, about 800,000 people enter the United States each year. The law also sets an annual limit on immigrants from any single country. Preference is given for family reunification and to people who have special skills or who are needed to fill jobs for which U.S. workers are not available. Another provision allows for the admission of "millionaire immigrants" who are willing and able to invest a substantial sum to create or support a business in the United States that will provide jobs for Americans. There have been few takers for admission under this provision. There is also a "diversity" category to provide visas for 55,000 immigrants from 34 countries whether or not they have relatives living in the

Immigrants arriving at Ellis Island in 1900 came with high hopes but few material possessions.

United States. These visas are drawn annually by lottery from a pool of qualified applicants.

In addition to regularly admitted aliens, political refugees are admitted. In recent years, more than 100,000 were admitted annually, but the Bush administration decreased the number to 70,000.[16] *Political refugees* are people who have well-founded fears of persecution in their own countries based on their race, religion, nationality, social class, or political opinion. People admitted as political refugees can apply to become permanent residents after one year. The attorney general, acting through the Immigration and Naturalization Service, may also grant *asylum* to applicants who have well-founded fears of persecution in the country to which they would be returned, based on their race, religion, nationality, membership in a particular social group, or political opinion. It is not enough, however, that applicants face the same terrible conditions that all other citizens of their country face or that they wish to escape bad economic conditions. They must show specific danger of persecution.

The Immigration and Naturalization Service may turn back at the border persons seeking asylum if it considers their requests insubstantial; it may even hold them in detention camps. The president may order the Coast Guard—as Presidents George H. W. Bush and Bill Clinton did with respect to Haitian and Cuban refugees—to stop people on the high seas before they enter the territorial waters of the United States and return them to the country from which they have fled without determining whether they qualify as refugees.[17] Nonetheless, many people are still willing to risk great danger to get here and suffer detention once they arrive, just for the chance of being granted asylum. According to the 2000 census, an estimated 115,000 immigrants from the Middle East alone are here illegally.[18]

Once in the United States, aliens are subject to the full range of obligations, including the payment of taxes. Aliens are counted in the census for the purpose of apportioning seats in the U.S. House of Representatives. Legally admitted aliens may be detained and deported for a variety of reasons—for example, conviction of crimes involving immoral acts, turpitude, incitement of terrorist activity, illegal voting in elections, and conviction of domestic violence. In the months following the September 2001 terrorist attacks, over 1,100 people were detained for questioning and their identities not disclosed, and approximately 5,000 more people of Middle Eastern descent were questioned voluntarily.[19]

HOW SHOULD THE UNITED STATES GOVERNMENT DEAL WITH UNDOCUMENTED ALIENS?

An estimated 2.3 to 2.4 million undocumented aliens—mostly from Mexico and other nations in Central and South America and a few from Canada—illegally cross our borders, not because they fear political persecution, but because they see greater economic opportunity in the United States. Even though most undocumented immigrants from Mexico return to Mexico after only two years and well over half return within ten years, undocumented aliens present a big political problem. How should the United States government deal with this problem?

property rights
The rights of an individual to own, use, rent, invest in, buy, and sell property.

contract clause
Clause of the Constitution (Article I, Section 10) originally intended to prohibit state governments from modifying contracts made between individuals; for a while interpreted as prohibiting state governments from taking actions that adversely affect property rights; no longer interpreted so broadly and no longer constrains state governments from exercising their police powers.

police powers
Inherent powers of state governments to pass laws to protect the public health, safety, and welfare; the national government has no directly granted police powers but accomplishes the same goals through other delegated powers.

eminent domain
Power of a government to take private property for public use; the U.S. Constitution gives national and state governments this power and requires them to provide just compensation for property so taken.

regulatory taking
Government regulation of property so extensive that government is deemed to have taken the property by the power of eminent domain, for which it must compensate the property owners.

PROPERTY RIGHTS

Constitutional Protection of Property

Property does not have rights. People do. People have the right to own, use, rent, invest in, buy, and sell property. Historically, the close connection between liberty and ownership of property, between property and power, has been emphasized in American political thinking and American political institutions. A major purpose of the framers of the Constitution was to establish a government strong enough to protect people's rights to use and enjoy their property. At the same time, the framers wanted to limit government so it could not endanger that right. As a result, the framers included in the Constitution a variety of clauses protecting **property rights**.

Of special concern to the framers were the efforts of some state legislatures to protect debtors at the expense of their creditors by issuing paper currency and setting aside private contracts. To prevent these practices, the legal tender and contract clauses in the Constitution forbid states from making anything except gold or silver legal tender for the payment of debts and from passing any "Law impairing the Obligation of Contracts."

The **contract clause** (Article I, Section 10) was designed to prevent states from extending the period during which debtors could meet their payments or otherwise get out of contractual obligations. The framers had in mind an ordinary contract between private persons. However, beginning with Chief Justice John Marshall (1801–1835), the Supreme Court expanded the coverage of the clause to prevent states from taking away privileges previously conferred on corporations. In effect, the contract clause was used to protect property and to maintain the status quo at the expense of a state's power.

In the late nineteenth century, however, the Supreme Court gradually began to restrict the coverage of the contract clause and to subject contracts to what in constitutional law are known as **police powers**—the powers of states to protect the public health, safety, and welfare of their residents. By 1934, the Supreme Court actually held that even contracts between individuals—the very ones the contract clause was intended to protect—could be modified by state law to avert social and economic catastrophe.[20] Although the contract clause is still invoked occasionally to challenge state regulation of property, it is no longer a significant limitation on governmental power.

What Happens When the Government Takes Our Property?

Both the national and state governments have the power of **eminent domain**—the power to take private property for public use—but the owner must be fairly compensated. This limitation, contained in the Fifth Amendment, was the first provision of the Bill of Rights to be enforced as a limitation on state governments as well as on the national government.[21]

What constitutes a "taking" for purposes of eminent domain? Ordinarily, but not always, the taking must be direct, and a person must lose title and control over the property. Sometimes, especially in recent years, the courts have found that a governmental taking has gone "too far," and the government must pay compensation to its owners, even when title is left in the name of the owners.[22] These are called **regulatory takings**. Thus if a government creates landing and takeoff paths for airplanes over property adjacent to an airport, making the land completely unsuitable for its original use (say, raising chickens), compensation is warranted.[23] The government may, however, impose land use and environmental regulations, temporarily prohibiting the development of a property, without compensating the owners.[24]

"Just compensation" is not always easy to define. When there is a dispute over compensation, the courts make the final resolution based on the rule that "the owner is entitled to receive what a willing buyer would pay in cash to a willing seller at the time of the taking."[25] An owner is not entitled to compensation for the personal value of an old, broken-down house that is loved dearly—just the value of the old, broken-down house.

DUE PROCESS RIGHTS

Perhaps the most difficult parts of the Constitution to understand are the clauses in the Fifth and Fourteenth Amendments forbidding the national and state governments to deny any person life, liberty, or property without "due process of law." Cases involving these guarantees have resulted in hundreds of Supreme Court decisions. Even so, it is impossible to explain *due process* precisely. In fact, the Supreme Court has refused to give due process a precise definition and has emphasized that "due process, unlike some legal rules, is not a technical conception with a fixed content unrelated to time, place and circumstances."[26] We define **due process** as rules and regulations that restrain those in government who exercise power. There are, however, basically two kinds of due process: procedural and substantive.

Procedural Due Process

Traditionally, **procedural due process** refers not to the law itself but to the *way in which a law is applied.* To paraphrase Daniel Webster's famous definition, the due process of law requires a procedure that hears before it condemns, proceeds upon inquiry, and renders judgment only after a trial or some kind of hearing. Originally, procedural due process was limited to criminal prosecutions, but it now applies to most kinds of governmental proceedings. It is required, for instance, in juvenile hearings, disbarment proceedings, proceedings to determine eligibility for welfare payments, revocation of drivers' licenses, and disciplinary proceedings in state universities and public schools.

A law may also violate the procedural due process requirement if it is too vague or if it creates an improper presumption of guilt. A vague statute fails to provide adequate warning and does not contain sufficient guidelines for law enforcement officials, juries, and courts.

The liberty that is protected by due process includes "the right of the individual to contract, to engage in any of the common occupations of life, to acquire useful knowledge, to marry, to establish a home and bring up children, to worship God according to the dictates of his own conscience, and generally to enjoy those common law privileges long recognized as essential to the orderly pursuit of happiness by free men."[27] The property protected by due process includes a variety of rights that may be conferred by state law, such as certain kinds of licenses, protection from being fired from some jobs except for just cause (for example, incompetence) and according to certain procedures, and protection from deprivation of certain pension rights.

Substantive Due Process

Procedural due process places limits on *how* governmental power may be exercised; **substantive due process** places limits on *what* a government may do. Procedural due process mainly limits the executive and judicial branches because they apply the law and review its application; substantive due process mainly limits the legislative branch because it enacts laws. Substantive due process means that an "unreasonable" law, even if properly passed and properly applied, is unconstitutional. It means that there are certain things governments *should not be allowed to do.*

Before 1937, substantive due process was used primarily to protect the right of employers to make contracts with employees freely, without government interference.[28] During this period, the Supreme Court was dominated by conservative jurists who considered almost all social welfare legislation unreasonable. They used the due process clause to strike down laws setting maximum hours of labor, establishing minimum wages, regulating prices, and forbidding employers to fire workers because they joined a union.

Since 1937, the Supreme Court has largely refused to apply the doctrine of substantive due process in reviewing laws regulating business enterprises and economic

---

★★ THINKING IT THROUGH

The inability to keep illegal aliens out of the country is not a question of constitutional power, for Congress has complete power over the admission of aliens. Rather, the problems are political and practical. Although Congress has authorized an increase in the number of border patrol guards and funded additional fencing of the California–Mexico border, there are thousands of miles of borders. Moreover, it is difficult to track down undocumented aliens once inside the United States and then expel them in a fashion consistent with the practices and policies of a free society.

Congress faces conflicting pressures: from Hispanic groups concerned that making it illegal to hire undocumented workers will make employers hesitate to hire any Hispanics, from employers who do not want to keep costly records and investigate the legal status of everybody they hire, from employers of farm workers who want to be sure they will have enough laborers to pick seasonal crops, from American workers who do not want undocumented workers being used to keep wages low, and from city and local governmental officials who have to find the funds to provide social services for undocumented aliens.

The United States government tends to consider immigration policy a purely internal matter. In California and some other states, there are strong anti-immigration pressures. Immigration policy clearly affects our relations with other nations, especially with Mexico, as the lengthy negotiations over the North American Free Trade Agreement (NAFTA) demonstrated. Although we view immigration policy as a matter of national sovereignty, Mexicans see it as a matter that directly affects them and have advocated "open borders."

---

due process
Established rules and regulations that restrain people in government who exercise power.

procedural due process
Constitutional requirement that governments proceed by proper methods; places limits on how governmental power may be exercised.

substantive due process
Constitutional requirement that governments act reasonably and that the substance of the laws themselves be fair and reasonable; places limits on what a government may do.

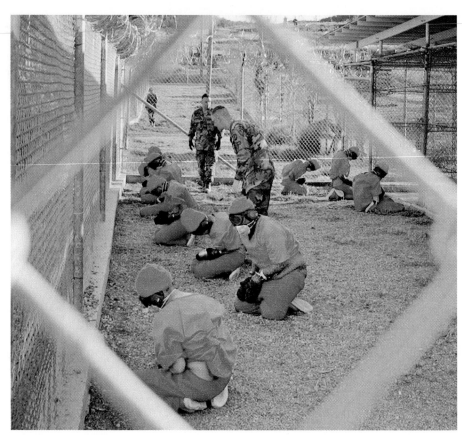

The USA PATRIOT Act, passed in the wake of the September 11, 2001 attacks, removes those designated by the president as "enemy combatants" from many of the procedural due process protections that are the cornerstone of the U.S. legal system. Both U.S. citizens and noncitizens alike can be designated as "enemy combatants" at the president's discretion.

interests. The Court now believes that deciding what constitutes reasonable regulation of business and commercial life is a legislative, not a judicial, responsibility. As long as the justices find a conceivable connection between a law regulating business and the promotion of the public welfare, the Supreme Court will not interfere with laws passed by Congress or state legislatures.

This does not mean, however, that the Court has abandoned substantive due process. On the contrary, substantive due process has taken on new life as a protector of civil liberties, especially the right of privacy. Substantive due process has deep roots in concepts of natural law and a long history in the American constitutional tradition. For most Americans most of the time, it is not enough merely to say that a law reflects the wishes of the popular or legislative majority. We also want our laws to be just, and we continue to rely heavily on judges to decide what is just.

PRIVACY RIGHTS

The most important extension of substantive due process in recent decades has been its expansion to protect the right of privacy, especially marital privacy. Although there is no mention of the right of privacy in the Constitution, in *Griswold* v. *Connecticut* (1965), the Supreme Court pulled together elements of the First, Third, Fourth, Fifth, Ninth, and Fourteenth Amendments to recognize that personal privacy is one of the rights protected by the Constitution.[29]

There are three aspects of this right: (1) the right to be free from governmental surveillance and intrusion, especially with respect to intimate decisions on sexuality; (2) the right not to have private affairs made public by the government; and (3) the right to be free in thought and belief from governmental regulations.[30]

PEOPLE & POLITICS *Making a Difference* ★★★

ESTELLE GRISWOLD

Estelle Trébert Griswold was born in 1900 and, after working as a singer in France and, later, during World War II as a medical technologist in Washington, D.C., she became the executive director of the Planned Parenthood League of Connecticut (PPLC) in 1953. In that position, Griswold led a fight for the legalization of birth control in Connecticut that resulted in a landmark Supreme Court ruling on the right of privacy and the Constitution's protection for intimate decisions on human sexuality.

Connecticut had prohibited the use of contraceptives in an 1879 law and had also made it a crime to "assist, abet, or counsel" someone on birth control. By the 1950s, contraceptives were nonetheless widely sold in drug stores and the law was generally ignored. But Griswold and some doctors and advocates of women's rights contended that the law had a chilling effect. Griswold and the

PPLC lobbied the state legislature to repeal the law, but the legislation was repeatedly blocked by the Catholic-dominated Connecticut state senate. Attempts to have courts strike down the law also failed.

Griswold and Dr. Lee Buxton decided to open a birth control clinic and create a test case challenging Connecticut's law. After opening the clinic, they held a press conference and a few days later police arrived and, after receiving PPLC literature, they arrested Griswold and Buxton, who were tried, convicted, and fined $100 each for violating the law.

On appeal in *Griswold* v. *Connecticut* (1965),* the Supreme Court struck down Connecticut's law for violating a constitutionally-protected right of privacy. The decision remains controversial because a right of privacy is not specifically enumerated in the Bill of Rights. But the ruling laid the basis for other landmark

decisions on a woman's right to choose, in *Roe* v. *Wade* (1973),† and on constitutional protection for private consensual sexual activities in *Lawrence* v. *Texas* (2003),‡ which struck down Texas's law making homosexual sodomy a crime.

* *Griswold* v. *Connecticut,* 381 U.S. 479 (1965).
† *Roe* v. *Wade,* 410 U.S. 113 (1973).
‡ *Lawrence* v. *Texas,* 539 U.S. 558 (2003).

Abortion Rights

The most controversial aspect of constitutional protection of privacy relates to the extent of state power to regulate abortions. In *Roe* v. *Wade* (1973), the Supreme Court ruled that (1) during the first trimester of a woman's pregnancy, it is an unreasonable and therefore unconstitutional interference with her liberty and privacy rights for a state to set any limits on her choice to have an abortion or on her doctor's medical judgments about how to carry it out; (2) during the second trimester, the state's interest in protecting the health of women becomes compelling, and a state may make a reasonable regulation about how, where, and when abortions may be performed; and (3) during the third trimester, when the fetus becomes capable of surviving outside the womb, the state's interest in protecting the unborn child is so important that the state can prohibit abortions altogether, except when necessary to preserve the life or health of the mother.[31]

The *Roe* decision led to decades of heated public debate and attempts by Presidents Ronald Reagan and the first George Bush to select Supreme Court justices who might be expected to reverse it. Nonetheless, *Roe* v. *Wade* was reaffirmed in *Planned Parenthood* v. *Casey* (1992). A bitterly divided Rehnquist Court, by a five-person majority (O'Connor, Kennedy, Souter, Blackmun, and Stevens), upheld the view that the due process clause of the Constitution protects a woman's liberty to choose an abortion prior to viability. The Court, however, held that the right to have an abortion prior to viability may be subject to state regulation that does not "unduly burden" it. In other words, states may make "reasonable regulations" on how a woman exercises her right to an abortion so long as they do not prohibit any woman from making the ultimate decision on whether to terminate a pregnancy before viability.[32]

The battle over abortion has been fought in the courts and on the streets, and has been a key issue in recent presidential elections.

Applying the undue burden test, the Court has held, on the one hand, that states can prohibit the use of state funds and facilities for performing abortions; states may make a minor's right to an abortion conditional on her first notifying at least one parent or a judge; and states may require women to sign an informed consent form and to wait 24 hours before having an abortion. On the other hand, a state may not condition a woman's right to an abortion on her first notifying her husband. The Court also struck down Nebraska's ban on "partial birth" abortions in *Stenberg* v. *Carhart* (2000) because it completely forbade one kind of medical procedure and provided no exception for when a woman's life is at stake and thus imposed an "undue burden" on women.[33] Nonetheless, in 2003 Congress passed and President George W. Bush signed into federal law a similar ban on "partial birth" abortions that was immediately challenged in the courts, and which will be appealed to the Supreme Court.

Sexual Orientation Rights

Although there is general agreement on how much constitutional protection is provided for marital privacy, in *Bowers* v. *Hardwick* (1986), the Supreme Court refused to extend such protection to private relations between homosexuals[34]; a bare majority of the Court also held that homosexuals may be excluded from the Boy Scouts of America.[35] By a 5-to-4 vote in *Bowers,* the Court refused to declare unconstitutional a Georgia law that made consensual sodomy a crime. But a number of state supreme courts, including that in Georgia, later found greater privacy protection in their state constitutions than the U.S. Supreme Court found in the U.S. Constitution. Finally, in *Lawrence* v. *Texas* (2003),[36] the Court struck down Texas's law making homosexual sodomy a crime. Writing for the Court and noting the trend in state court decisions that did not follow *Bowers,* Justice Kennedy held the law to violate personal autonomy and the right of privacy. Dissenting Justice Scalia, along with Chief Justice Rehnquist and Justice Thomas, warned that the decision might lead to overturning laws barring same-sex marriages, as some state courts and Canadian courts had already done.

In addition, the U.S. Supreme Court, in *Romer* v. *Evans* (1996),[37] struck down an initiative amending the Colorado constitution that prohibited state and local governments from protecting homosexuals from discrimination. Although the Court did not rule on the basis of substantive due process, it held this provision to violate the equal protection clause because it lacked a rational basis and simply represented a prejudice toward a particular group of people.

Because of the strong emotions on both sides of this issue, the right of privacy as an element of substantive due process is one of the developing edges of constitutional law, one about which people both on and off the Court have strong disagreements. How the Supreme Court handles privacy issues has become front-page news.

RIGHTS OF PERSONS ACCUSED OF CRIMES

Despite what you sometimes see in television police dramas, law enforcement officers have no general right to break down doors and invade homes. They are not supposed to search people except under certain conditions, and they have no right to arrest them except under certain circumstances. They also may not compel confessions, and they must respect other procedural guarantees aimed at ensuring fairness and the rights of the accused. Persons accused of crimes are guaranteed these and other rights under the Fourth, Fifth, Sixth, Eighth, and Fourteenth Amendments.

Freedom from Unreasonable Searches and Seizures

According to the Fourth Amendment, "The right of the people to be secure in their persons, houses, papers, and effects, against unreasonable searches and seizures, shall not be violated, and no Warrants shall issue, but upon probable cause, supported by Oath or affirmation, and particularly describing the place to be searched, and the persons or things to be seized."

Protection from unreasonable searches and seizures requires police, if they have time, to obtain a valid **search warrant**, issued by a magistrate after the police indicate under oath that they have *probable cause* to justify its issuance. Magistrates must perform this function in a neutral and detached manner and not serve merely as rubber stamps for the police. The warrant must specify the place to be searched and the things to be seized. *General search warrants*—warrants that authorize police to search a particular place or person without limitation—are unconstitutional. A search warrant is usually needed to search a person in any place he or she has an "expectation of privacy that society is prepared to recognize as reasonable," for example, in a hotel room, a rented home, or a friend's apartment.[38] In short, the Fourth Amendment protects people, not places, from unreasonable governmental intrusions.[39]

Police may make reasonable *warrantless searches* in *public places* if the officers have probable cause, or at least a reasonable suspicion, that the persons in question have committed or are about to commit crimes. No later than two days after making such an arrest, the police must take the arrested person to a magistrate so that the magistrate—not just the police—can decide whether probable cause existed to justify the warrantless arrest.[40] Probable cause, however, does not, except in extreme emergencies, justify a warrantless arrest of people in their own homes.

Under the common law, police officers apprehending a fleeing suspected felon can use weapons that might result in the felon's serious injury or even death. But the Fourth Amendment places substantial limits on the use of what is called *deadly force.* It is unconstitutional to shoot at an apparently unarmed, fleeing suspected felon unless the officer has probable cause to believe that the suspect poses a significant threat of death or serious injury to the officer or others. Also, when feasible, the officer must first warn the suspect, "Halt or I'll shoot."

Not every time the police stop a person to ask questions or to seek that person's consent to a search is there a seizure or detention requiring probable cause or a warrant. If the police just ask questions or even seek consent to search an individual's person or possessions in a noncoercive atmosphere, there is no detention. "So long as a reasonable person would feel free 'to disregard the police and go about his business,' the encounter is consensual and no reasonable suspicion is required." But if the person refuses to answer questions or consent to a search, and the police, by either physical force or a show of authority, restrain the movement of the person, even though there is no arrest, the Fourth Amendment comes into play.[41] For example, if police approach people in airports and request identification, this act by itself does not constitute a detention. The same is true if police ask bus passengers for consent to search their luggage for drugs. But if the police do more, especially after consent is refused, then their actions require them to have some objective justification for the search beyond mere suspicion.[42]

The Supreme Court also upheld, in *Terry* v. *Ohio* (1968), a *stop and frisk* exception to searches of individuals when officers have reason to believe they are armed and dangerous or have committed or are about to commit a criminal offense. The *Terry* search is limited to a quick pat-down to check for weapons that might be used to assault the arresting officer, to check for contraband, to determine identity, or to maintain the status quo while obtaining more information.[43] If individuals who are stopped for questioning refuse to identify themselves, they may be arrested, though police must have a reasonable suspicion they are involved in criminal activities.[44] If an officer stops and frisks a suspect to look for weapons and finds criminal evidence that might justify an arrest, the officer can make a full search.[45] Police and border guards may also conduct *border* searches—searches of persons and the goods they bring with them at border crossings.[46] The border search exception also permits officials to open mail entering the country if they have "reasonable cause" to suspect it contains merchandise imported in violation of the law.[47]

There are several other exceptions to the general rule against warrantless searches and seizures of what is found by police and customs officials. The most important are the following:

1. *The Plain-View Exception.* The plain-view exception permits officers to seize evidence without a warrant if they are lawfully in a position from which the

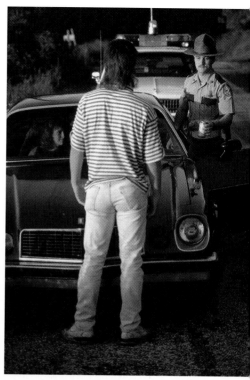

Police may detain and search cars and their passengers if they have reasonable suspicion to believe the passengers may be involved in criminal activity.

search warrant
A writ issued by a magistrate that authorizes the police to search a particular place or person, specifying the place to be searched and the objects to be seized.

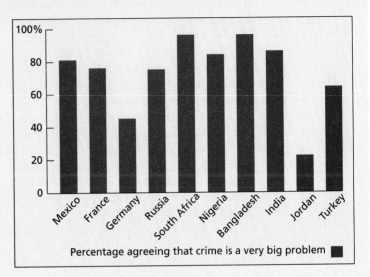

GLOBAL *Perceptions*

QUESTION: Do you think crime is a very big problem?

There is anxiety about crime in almost every country in the world. In virtually every region, except North America, majorities in nearly every country cite crime as a "very big problem." In the United States, only 48 percent of the public believe that crime is a very big problem, and only 26 percent in Canada. Some of the countries where public perceptions of crime as a big problem are the highest are Bangladesh and South Africa (96%), Guatemala and Honduras (93%), Argentina (88%), and India (86%). The lowest perceptions are in Jordan (22%), South Korea (35%), and Germany (45%). In most cases, though, crime is more of a *perceived* problem than an actual problem.

Source: The Pew Global Attitudes Project, *How Global Publics View Their Lives, Their Countries, the World, and America,* 2002, T-18.

evidence can be viewed, it is immediately apparent to them that the items they observe are evidence of a crime or are contraband, and they have probable cause to believe—a reasonable suspicion will not do—that the evidence uncovered is contraband or evidence of a crime.[48]

2. *Exigent Circumstances.* Searches are permissible when officers do not have time to secure a warrant before evidence is destroyed, when a criminal escapes capture, or when there is need "to protect or preserve life or avoid serious injury." An example is that firefighters and police may enter a burning building without a warrant and may remain there for a reasonable time to investigate the cause of the blaze after the fire has been extinguished. However, after the fire has been put out, the emergency is not to be used as an excuse to make an exhaustive, warrantless search for evidence.

3. *The Automobile Exception.* If officers have probable cause to believe that an automobile is being used to commit a crime, even a traffic offense, or that it contains persons who have committed crimes, or that it contains evidence of crimes, they may stop the automobile, detain the persons found therein, and search them and any containers or packages found inside the car.[49] Once an automobile has been lawfully detained, the police officers may order the driver and passengers to get out of the car without violating the Fourth Amendment[50]; if police arrest the driver, they may search the contents of the car.[51]

4. *Foreign Agents.* Although never directly sustained by the Supreme Court, Congress has endorsed the presidential claim that a president can authorize warrantless wiretaps and physical searches of agents of foreign countries. Congress created the Foreign Intelligence Surveillance Court to approve such requests; this court, consisting of federal district judges, meets in secret. The USA PATRIOT Act of 2001 expanded the size of this court and lowered the basis for its approval of warrants in cases involving terrorism and permits searches for intelligence and just evidence of terrorist activities.

In addition, various administrative searches by nonpolice government agents, such as teachers and health officials, do not require search warrants. Rules governing the conduct of such administrative searches are more lenient than those for searches by police investigating crimes. Administrative searches conducted without grounds for suspicion of particular individuals have been upheld in certain limited circumstances.[52]

One recent troublesome area relates to **racial profiling**—the police practice targeting members of certain racial groups for street questioning or traffic stops on the assumption that members of these groups are likely to be engaged in illegal activities. African Americans and civil rights organizations have complained for years about the practice because police do not need probable cause to stop someone and because it encourages racial discrimination.[53] In response, President George W. Bush issued guidelines governing 70 federal law enforcement agencies that bar the use of race and ethnicity in routine investigations; however, they may still be used to "identify terrorist threats and stop potential catastrophic attacks."[54]

Another controversial practice is the recent expansion of compulsory, random drug testing. The Supreme Court has upheld the constitutionality of blood and urine tests of rail employees involved in train accidents, of federal employees, and of high school students engaged in interscholastic athletic competitions. But it struck down a Georgia law requiring candidates for designated state offices to certify that they had taken and passed a drug test because Georgia failed to show why this invasion of personal privacy was necessary.[55] In 2002, however, the Court on a 5-to-4 vote held that schools may require students who participate in extracurricular activities of any kind to submit to random drug tests.[56]

THE EXCLUSIONARY RULE In *Mapp* v. *Ohio* (1961), the Supreme Court adopted a rule excluding from a criminal trial evidence that the police obtained unconstitutionally or illegally.[57] This **exclusionary rule** was adopted to prevent police misconduct. Critics of the exclusionary rule question why criminals should go free just because of police misconduct or ineptness,[58] but the Supreme Court has refused to abandon the rule. It has made some exceptions to it, however, such as cases in which police relied in "good faith" on a search warrant that subsequently turned out to be defective or granted improperly.[59]

THE RIGHT TO REMAIN SILENT During the seventeenth century, certain special courts in England forced confessions from religious dissenters. The British privilege against self-incrimination developed in response to these practices. Because they were familiar with this history, the framers of our Bill of Rights included in the Fifth Amendment the provision that persons shall not be compelled to testify against themselves in criminal prosecutions. This protection against self-incrimination is designed to strengthen the fundamental principle that no person has an obligation to prove innocence. Rather, the burden is on the government to prove guilt.

The privilege against self-incrimination applies literally only in criminal prosecutions. But it has always been interpreted to protect any person subject to questioning by any agency of government, such as a congressional committee. It is not enough, however, to contend that answers might be embarrassing or might lead to loss of a job or even to civil suits; persons must have a reasonable fear that their answers might support a criminal prosecution against them.

Sometimes authorities would rather have information from witnesses than prosecute them. Congress has established procedures so that prosecutors and congressional committees may secure a grant of **immunity** for such a witness. When immunity has been granted, a witness no longer has a constitutional right to refuse to testify, and the government cannot use the information derived directly from the compelled testimony in any subsequent prosecution, though the witness may still be prosecuted for crimes on the basis of other evidence.

THE *MIRANDA* WARNING Police questioning of suspects is a key procedure in solving crimes. Roughly 90 percent of all criminal convictions result from guilty pleas and never reach a full trial. Police questioning, however, can easily be abused. Police officers sometimes forget or ignore the constitutional rights of suspects, especially those who are frightened and ignorant. Unauthorized detention and lengthy interrogation to wring confessions from suspects, common practice in police states, were not unknown in the United States.

Use of metal detectors and locker searches at schools does not require search warrants and other protections applied to police searches.

racial profiling
Police targeting of racial minorities as potential suspects of criminal activities.

exclusionary rule
Requirement that evidence unconstitutionally or illegally obtained be excluded from a criminal trial.

immunity
Exemption from prosecution for a particular crime in return for testimony pertaining to the case.

The Miranda warning is read to a suspect by a police officer to inform him of his rights, such as the right to remain silent and the right to have an attorney present.

Federal and state laws require police officers to take people they have arrested before a magistrate promptly so that the magistrate may inform them of their constitutional rights and allow them to get in touch with friends and seek legal advice. Despite these requirements, police were often tempted to quiz suspects first, trying to get them to confess before a magistrate informed them of their constitutional right to remain silent.

To put an end to such practices, the Supreme Court, in *Miranda* v. *Arizona* (1966), announced that no conviction could stand if evidence introduced at the trial had been obtained by the police during "custodial interrogation" unless suspects were notified that they have a right to remain silent and that anything they say can and will be used against them; to terminate questioning at any point; to have an attorney present during questioning by police; and to have a lawyer appointed to represent them if they cannot afford to hire their own attorney.[60] If suspects answer questions in the absence of an attorney, the burden is on prosecutors to demonstrate that suspects knowingly and intelligently gave up their right to remain silent. Failure to comply with these requirements leads to reversal of a conviction, even if other evidence is sufficient to establish guilt.

Critics of the *Miranda* decision believe that the Supreme Court severely limited the ability of the police to bring criminals to justice. Over the years, the Court has modified the original ruling by allowing evidence obtained contrary to the *Miranda* guidelines to be used to attack the credibility of defendants who offer testimony at their trial that conflicts with their statements to the police. Congress tried to get around *Miranda* in the Crime Control and Safe Streets Act of 1968 by allowing confessions made in violation of *Miranda* to be used as evidence in federal courts. But in *Dickerson* v. *United States* (2000), the Court reaffirmed the constitutionality of the *Miranda* doctrine. In an opinion by Chief Justice William H. Rehnquist, the Court held that the *Miranda* warning is not merely a rule of evidence to enforce the constitutional guarantee but is itself constitutionally required and applies in both state and federal courts.[61]

Fair Trial Procedures

Many people consider the rights of persons accused of a crime to be less important than other rights. But as Justice Felix Frankfurter observed, "The history of liberty has largely been the history of observance of procedural safeguards." Further, these safeguards have frequently "been forged in controversies involving not very nice people."[62] Nonetheless, they guarantee that all persons accused of crimes will have the right to representation by counsel and to a fair trial by an impartial jury.

THE RIGHT TO COUNSEL If after questioning by police the suspect is arrested and charged with a crime, the Supreme Court has ruled that the accused has a constitutional right to counsel at every stage of the criminal proceedings—preliminary hearings, bail hearings, trial, sentencing, and first appeal. Communications between the accused and counsel are privileged. However, in cases of terrorism, under new guidelines issued by Attorney General John Ashcroft, police may listen in, undercover, on consultations between lawyers and detainees if "reasonable suspicion exists to believe that an inmate may use communications with attorneys or their agent to facilitate acts of terrorism."

INDICTMENT Except for members of the armed forces and foreign terrorists, the national government cannot require anyone to stand trial for a serious crime except on the basis of a grand jury indictment or its equivalent; states are not required to use grand juries, and those that do not vest prosecutors with the power to seek indictments. A **grand jury** is concerned not with a person's guilt or innocence but merely with whether there is enough evidence to warrant a trial. The grand jury has wide-ranging investigatory powers and "is to inquire into all information that might bear on its investigations until it is satisfied that it has identified an offense or satisfied itself that none has occurred."[63] The strict rules that govern jury proceedings do not apply. The grand jury may admit hearsay evidence, and the exclusionary rule to enforce the Fourth Amendment does not apply. If a majority of the grand jurors agree that a trial is justified, they return what is known as a *true bill,* or **indictment**.

grand jury
A jury of 12 to 23 persons who, in private, hear evidence presented by the government to determine whether persons shall be required to stand trial. If the jury believes there is sufficient evidence that a crime was committed, it issues an indictment.

indictment
A formal written statement from a grand jury charging an individual with an offense; also called a *true bill.*

The Constitution guarantees the accused the right to be informed of the nature and cause of the accusation so that he or she can prepare a defense. After indictment for an offense, prosecutors and the attorney for the accused usually discuss the possibility of a **plea bargain** whereby the defendant pleads guilty to a lesser offense that carries a shorter prison sentence. Prosecutors, facing more cases than they can handle, like plea bargains because they save the expense and time of going to trial. Likewise, defendants are often willing to "cop a plea" for a lesser offense to avoid the risk of more serious punishment.

When defendants plead guilty, they are usually forever prevented from raising objections to their conviction. That is why, before accepting guilty pleas, the judge questions defendants to be sure their attorneys have explained the alternatives and they know what they are doing.

TRIAL   After indictment and preliminary hearings that determine bail and what evidence will be used as evidence against the accused, the Constitution guarantees a *speedy and public trial.* Do not, however, take the word "speedy" too literally. Defendants are given time to prepare their defense and in fact often ask for delays because delays can work to their advantage. In contrast, if the government denies the accused a speedy trial, not only is the conviction reversed but the case must also be dismissed outright.

Under the Sixth Amendment, the accused has a right to trial before a **petit jury** selected from the state and district in which the alleged crime was committed. Although federal law requires juries of 12 members, the Supreme Court has held that states may try defendants before juries consisting of as few as six persons. Conviction in federal courts must be by unanimous vote, but the Court has ruled that state courts may render guilty verdicts by nonunanimous juries, provided that such juries consist of six or more persons.[64]

An *impartial jury*, one that meets the requirements of due process and equal protection, consists of persons who represent a fair cross section of the community. Although defendants are not entitled to juries on which there must be individuals of their own race, sex, religion, or national origin, government prosecutors cannot strike people from juries because of race or gender, and neither can defense attorneys use what are called *peremptory challenges* to keep people off juries because of race, ethnic origin, or sex.[65]

During the trial, the defendant has a right to obtain witnesses in his or her favor and to have the judge subpoena witnesses to appear at the trial and testify. Both the accused and witnesses may refuse to testify on the grounds that their testimony would tend to incriminate themselves. If they testify, the prosecution has the right to cross-examine them, just as the accused has the right to confront and to cross-examine witnesses.

Sentencing and Punishment

At the conclusion of the trial, the jury recommends a verdict of guilty or not guilty. If the accused is found guilty, the judge hands down the sentence. The Eighth Amendment forbids the levying of excessive fines and the inflicting of cruel and unusual punishment.

In federal courts, judges follow the sentencing guidelines set down by the United States Sentencing Commission. Such sentences are not considered cruel and unusual. Many states have also established guidelines for sentencing by state courts.

THREE STRIKES AND YOU'RE OUT   Although the crime rate has actually been going down in the past few years, public concern about crime remains high. At the national and state level, presidents, governors, and legislators vie with one another to show their toughness on crime. California, Virginia, Washington, and a number of other states have "three strikes and you're out" laws, requiring a lifetime sentence without the possibility of parole for anyone convicted of a third felony, even though for a minor offense. In some states, the felonies must be for violent crimes; in others, any three felonies will do. Scholars are skeptical that "three strikes and you're out" laws reduce crime, and constructing

"The court finds itself on the horns of a dilemma. On the one hand, wiretap evidence is inadmissible, and on the other hand, I'm dying to hear it."

plea bargain
Agreement between a prosecutor and a defendant that the defendant will plead guilty to a lesser offense to avoid having to stand trial for a more serious offense.

petit jury
A jury of 6 to 12 persons that determines guilt or innocence in a civil or criminal action.

more jails to take care of aging felons requires great expenditures of public funds. California's tough law for committing three felonies was nonetheless upheld by the Supreme Court, and a 25-years-to-life sentence for stealing three golf clubs, each valued at $399, was held not to violate the prohibition against cruel and unusual punishment.[66]

APPEALS AND DOUBLE JEOPARDY   After trial, conviction, and sentencing, defendants may appeal their convictions if they claim they have been denied some constitutional right or denied the due process and equal protection of the law. The Fifth Amendment also provides that no person shall be "subject for the same offense to be twice put in jeopardy of life or limb." **Double jeopardy** does not prevent punishment by the national and the state governments for the same offense or for successive prosecutions for the same crime by two states. Nor does the double jeopardy clause forbid civil prosecutions, even after acquittal in a criminal trial for the same conduct.[67]

THE DEATH PENALTY   Capital punishment remains controversial. Japan and the United States are the only two industrialized countries to retain the death penalty. The 25 members of the European Union have outlawed capital punishment, and courts in South Africa and several central and eastern European countries have declared it unconstitutional and a denial of human dignity.

After a ten-year moratorium on executions in the late 1960s and early 1970s, the U.S. Supreme Court ruled that the death penalty is not necessarily cruel and unusual punishment if it is imposed for crimes that resulted in a victim's death, if the procedures used by the courts "ensure that death sentences are not meted out wantonly or freakishly," and if these processes "confer on the sentencer sufficient discretion to take account of the character and record of the individual offender and the circumstances of the particular offense to ensure that death is the appropriate punishment in a specific case."[68]

The Rehnquist Court has made it easier to impose death sentences, cut back on appeals, and carry out executions. More states have added the death penalty (there are now 38), and the national government has increased the number of crimes for which the death penalty may be imposed. As a result, the number of persons on death row has increased dramatically. Since capital punishment was reinstated in 1976, more than 600 people have been executed nationwide, and more than 3,500 are on death row. As the number of executions has increased, however, concerns have also grown about the fairness of how capital punishment is imposed. These concerns have been fueled by DNA tests that have established the innocence of a sizable number of those convicted of murder.[69]

The prohibition against cruel and unusual punishment also forbids punishments grossly disproportionate to the severity of the crime. In 2002, the Supreme Court overruled a prior ruling[70] and held that it is excessive and disproportionate to execute mentally retarded convicted murderers because they are not capable of understanding the seriousness of their offense. The Court noted that in recent years there has been a movement to bar executions of mentally retarded death-row inmates. And because 18 of the 38 states imposing capital punishment exempt the mentally retarded, the Court concluded that there was an emerging "national consensus" against executing mentally retarded inmates.[71]

HOW JUST IS OUR SYSTEM OF JUSTICE?

Because the American system of criminal justice contains many guarantees for protecting the rights of the accused, critics often argue that due to these protections, justice is not done. Among the other criticisms are that the system is inefficient, biased, and unfair.

Too Many Loopholes?

Some observers argue that by overprotecting criminals and placing too much of a burden on the criminal justice system not to make any mistakes, we delay justice, encourage disrespect for the law, and allow guilty persons to go unpunished. Justice should be swift and certain without being arbitrary. But under our procedures, criminals may go

double jeopardy
Trial or punishment for the same crime by the same government; forbidden by the Constitution.

In Comparative Perspective

THE DEATH PENALTY AROUND THE WORLD

The United States and Japan are the only two industrialized countries that retain the death penalty. Most of the 78 countries that still impose capital punishment are in Africa, the Middle East, the Carribean, and Central America.

According to Amnesty International, 117 countries have abolished capital punishment for all or most crimes. In the last 30 years 65 countries joined this group, most recently Bhutan and Samoa (2004), Armenia (2003), and Cyprus and Yugoslavia (2002).

Among the 79 countries that abolished capital punishment for all crimes are the 25 countries in the European Union, other Western and Eastern European countries, Cambodia, and South Africa. Another 15 countries have abolished capital punishment for ordinary criminal offenses: Albania, Argentina, Armenia, Bolivia, Brazil, Chile, the Cook Islands, El Salvador, Fiji, Greece, Israel, Latvia, Mexico, Peru, and Turkey.

Another 23 countries retain the death penalty but have abolished it in practice by not carrying out executions in a decade or more. Among these countries are Algeria, Brunei, Congo, Kenya, the Russian Federation, Sri Lanka, and Tunisia.

Source: Amnesty International, "The Death Penalty" (as of May 1, 2004), at www.wen.amnesty.org/pages/deathpenalty-countries-eng.

---

unpunished because the police decide not to arrest them; the prosecutor decides not to prosecute them; the grand jury decides not to indict them; the judge decides not to hold them for trial; the jury decides not to convict them; the appeals court decides to reverse the conviction; the judge decides to release them on a writ of habeas corpus; or the president or governor decides to pardon, reprieve, or parole them if convicted. As a result, the public never knows whom to hold responsible when laws are not enforced. The police blame prosecutors, prosecutors blame the police, and they all blame the juries and judges.

Others take a different view and point out that there is more to justice than simply securing convictions. All the steps in the administration of criminal laws have been developed over centuries of trial and error, and each step has been constructed to protect ordinary persons from particular abuses by those in power. History warns against entrusting the instruments of criminal law enforcement to a single officer. For this reason, responsibility is vested in many officials.

Too Unreliable?

Critics who say that our system of justice is unreliable often point to trial by jury as the chief source of trouble. No other country relies as heavily on trial by jury as the United States. Jury trials are also time-consuming and costly. Trial by jury, critics argue, leads to a theatrical combat between lawyers who base their appeals on the prejudices and sentiments of the jurors. "Mr. Prejudice and Miss Sympathy are the names of witnesses whose testimony is never recorded, but must nevertheless be reckoned with in trials by jury."[72]

The jury system allows for what is called *jury nullification* when jurors ignore their instructions to consider only the evidence presented in court and vote for acquittal to express their displeasure with the law or the actions of prosecutors or police. Jury nullification has a long history. In colonial times, juries refused to convict colonists of political crimes against the king as a way to protest British rule. Before the Civil War, northern juries refused to convict people for helping runaway slaves. Before the 1970s, white southern juries sometimes refused to convict police for brutality against blacks.

Responding to growing public disenchantment with juries after a raft of unpopular verdicts, states have been rewriting the rules for the jury system. These changes include making it more difficult for people to be excused from jury service, allowing for nonunanimous decisions, limiting how long jurors can be sequestered, and exerting more control by judges over lawyers' statements to jurors in order to prevent appeals to jurors' emotions.

CHANGING FACE OF AMERICAN POLITICS

A RENEWED DEBATE OVER THE DEATH PENALTY

Although the number of individuals sentenced to death has grown in the last several decades, in recent years the number of death-row inmates and executions has declined (see below). While some groups, like the U.S. Conference of Catholic Bishops, oppose the death penalty on moral grounds, the renewed debate now focuses on the fairness of the entire process of administering capital punishment. The American Bar Association (ABA) has called for a halt to executions because the death penalty is administered in arbitrary and capricous ways that deny fundamental due process and the equal protection of the law. Prominent Republicans and Democrats also are questioning the system of imposing the death penalty.

The debate about the fairness of capital punishment was sparked by the increasing number of inmates who have been released because new DNA evidence proved their innocence—often after they had spent a decade or more on death row. Critics also point out the seeming randomness in imposing capital punishment. Public prosecutors seek the death penalty in less than 5 percent of all murder cases. Defendants often agree to plea bargains in return for life sentences. When murder trials are held, some juries refuse to impose the death sentence. And of the criminals sentenced to death, some receive clemency or are paroled. A study of more than 4,500 capital cases found that more than two-thirds of all death sentences are overturned. Why? The primary reasons are that defense lawyers were incompetent, important evidence was overlooked, witnesses lied, or prosecutors withheld evidence from the defense. In addition, racial discrimination in the imposition of capital punishment is a major concern. Blacks who murder whites are much more likely to receive death sentences than whites who murder blacks or blacks who kill blacks.

Persons Executed, 1930–2003

Number of Death Row Inmates, 1953–2003

SOURCE: Death Penalty Information Center. See also Hudo Bedau and Paul Cassell, eds., *Debating the Death Penalty* (Oxford University Press, 2004).

Defenders of the jury system reply that trial by jury provides a check by non-professionals on the actions of judges and prosecutors. There is no evidence that juries are unreliable; on the contrary, decisions of juries do not significantly differ from those of judges.[73] Moreover, the jury system helps educate citizens and enables them to participate in the application of their country's laws.

Too Discriminatory?

During the past several decades, the Supreme Court has worked particularly hard to enforce the ideal of equal justice under the law. Persons accused of crimes who cannot afford attorneys must be furnished them at government expense. If transcripts are required for appeals, such transcripts must be made available to those who cannot afford to purchase them. If appeals are permitted, the government must provide attorneys for at least one appeal of the decision of the trial court. Poor people cannot be imprisoned because of the inability to pay a fine. Nor, once sentenced, can poor people be kept in jail beyond the term of the sentence because they cannot afford to pay a fine. Even for civil proceedings—divorce proceedings, for example—fees cannot be imposed that deny poor people their fundamental rights, such as the right to obtain a divorce.

Tribune Media Services.

Unfair to Minorities?

One of the acute problems of our society is the tension between the police and the African American, Hispanic, and Middle Eastern communities congregated in inner cities. Many members of minorities believe they do not have equal protection under the law and that they are targeted by law enforcement officers. "Whether the stated belief is well founded or not," one political scientist observed, "is at least partly beside the point. The existence of the belief is damaging enough."[74]

Some blacks consider the police to be enforcers of white law. Studies proving prejudice on the part of some white police officers and examples of rough, even brutal, police treatment of blacks are ample evidence to support this viewpoint. One study in California found that "the rate of unfounded arrest was four times higher for African Americans than Anglos. Latino rates were double those of Anglos."[75] Police use of racial profiling, already a concern of blacks and Hispanics, has also became a concern of Muslims and whites.[76]

In recent decades, action has been taken to recruit more African Americans, Hispanics, and women as police officers, including appointment to command posts. In larger cities, there are now oversight boards including civilians to which complaints about police misconduct can be brought. **Community policing** is also being substituted in some cities for traditional police procedures. Police departments work with churches and other local community groups and take police out of patrol cars to walk the beat and work in neighborhoods. Community policing, when combined with working with community organizations to sponsor crime prevention programs, appears not only to reduce crime but also to improve minorities' confidence in the police.[77]

THE SUPREME COURT AND CIVIL LIBERTIES

Judges play a major role in enforcing constitutional guarantees. Such reliance on judicial protection of our civil liberties focuses public attention on the Supreme Court. Yet only a small number of controversies are actually carried to the Supreme Court, and a Supreme Court decision is not the end of the judicial process. Lower court judges as well as police, superintendents of schools, local prosecutors, school boards, state legislatures, and thousands of others clarify the Court's doctrines.

Moreover, the Supreme Court can do little unless its decisions over time reflect a national consensus. As Supreme Court Justice Robert H. Jackson observed, "The attitude of a society and of its organized political forces, rather than its legal machinery, is the controlling force in the character of free institutions. Any court that undertakes by its

community policing
Assigning police to neighborhoods where they walk the beat and work with churches and other community groups to reduce crime and improve relations with minorities.

legal processes to enforce civil liberties needs the support of an enlightened and vigorous public opinion."[78] Thus the Bill of Rights—and the other procedural and substantive liberties of our Constitution—cannot rest on a foundation merely of tradition. The preservation of these rights depends on wide, continuing, and knowledgeable public support.

S U M M A R Y

1. One of the basic distinctions between a free society and a police state is that in a free society, there are effective restraints on the way public officials, especially law enforcement officials, perform their duties. In the United States, the courts enforce these constitutional restraints.

2. The Constitution protects the acquisition and retention of citizenship. It protects the basic liberties of citizens as well as aliens, although in times of war, foreign saboteurs and terrorists may be detained and tried without the rights accorded citizens and other aliens.

3. The Constitution protects our property from arbitrary governmental interference, although debates about which interferences are reasonable and which are arbitrary are not easily settled. If private property is taken or rendered worthless by the government, just compensation must be paid to the owner.

4. The Constitution imposes limits not only on the procedures government must follow but also on the ends it may pursue. Some actions are out of bounds no matter what procedures are followed. Legislatures have the primary role in determining what is reasonable and what is unreasonable. However, the Supreme Court continues to exercise its own independent and final review of legislative determinations of reasonableness, especially on matters affecting civil liberties and civil rights.

5. The Supreme Court has pulled together elements from the First, Fourth, Fifth, Ninth, and Fourteenth Amendments to recognize a constitutionally protected right to personal privacy, especially with regard to marital privacy, including the right of a woman to choose an abortion.

6. The framers knew from their own experiences that in their zeal to maintain power and to enforce the laws, especially in wartime, public officials are often tempted to infringe on the rights of persons accused of crimes. To prevent such abuse, the Bill of Rights requires federal officials to follow detailed procedures in making searches and arrests and in bringing people to trial.

7. The Supreme Court continues to play a prominent role in developing public policy to protect the rights of the accused, to ensure that the innocent are not punished, and to guarantee that the public is protected against those who break the laws. The Court's decisions influence what the public believes and how police officers and others involved in the administration of justice behave. But the Court alone cannot guarantee fairness in the administration of justice.

K E Y   T E R M S

naturalization
dual citizenship
right of expatriation
property rights
contract clause
police powers

eminent domain
regulatory taking
due process
procedural due process
substantive due process
search warrant

racial profiling
exclusionary rule
immunity
grand jury
indictment
plea bargain

petit jury
double jeopardy
community policing

F U R T H E R   R E A D I N G

JEFFREY ABRAMSON, *We, the Jury: The Jury System and the Ideal of Democracy* (Harvard University Press, 2000).

LIVA BAKER, *Miranda: Crime, Law and Politics* (Atheneum, 1983).

STUART BANNER, *The Death Penalty: An American History* (Harvard University Press, 2002).

ROBERT P. BURNS, *A Theory of the Trial* (Princeton University Press, 1999).

DAVID COLE, *Enemy Aliens: Double Standards and Constitutional Freedoms in the War on Terrorism* (The New Press, 2003).

JOHN DENVIR, *Democracy's Constitution: Claiming the Privileges of American Citizenship* (University of Illinois Press, 2001).

LOUIS FISHER, *Nazi Saboteurs on Trial: A Military Tribunal and American Law* (University Press of Kansas, 2003).

GEORGE P. FLETCHER, *Basic Concepts of Criminal Law* (Oxford University Press, 1998).

DAVID J. GARROW, *Liberty and Sexuality: The Right to Privacy and the Making of* Roe *v.* Wade (Macmillan, 1994).

ROGER HOOD, *The Death Penalty: A Worldwide Perspective,* 3d ed. (Oxford University Press, 2002).

RANDALL KENNEDY, *Race, Crime, and the Law* (Pantheon, 1997).

ANTHONY LEWIS, *Gideon's Trumpet* (Random House, 1964).

JOHN R. LOTT JR., *More Guns, Less Crime: Understanding Crime and Gun Control Laws* (University of Chicago Press, 2000).

DAVID M. O'BRIEN, *Constitutional Law and Politics: Vol. 2, Civil Rights and Civil Liberties,* 6th ed. (Norton, 2005).

J. W. PELTASON AND SUE DAVIS, *Understanding the Constitution,* 15th ed. (Harcourt, 2001).

WILLIAM H. REHNQUIST, *All the Laws but One: Civil Liberties in Wartime* (Knopf, 1998).

BARRY SCHECK, PETER NEUFELD, AND JIM DWYER, *Actual Innocence: Five Days to Execution, and Other Dispatches from the Wrongly Convicted* (Doubleday, 2000).

MARY E. VOGEL, *Coercion to Compromise: Plea Bargaining, the Courts, and the Making of Political Authority* (Oxford University Press, 2001).

WELSH S. WHITE, *Miranda's Waning Protections: Police Interrogation Practices After Dickerson* (University of Michigan Press, 2001).

EQUAL RIGHTS UNDER THE LAW

17

The Declaration of Independence proclaims the precious rights of *equality* and *liberty:* "We hold these truths to be self-evident, that all men are created equal, that they are endowed by their Creator with certain unalienable Rights, that among these are Life, Liberty, and the pursuit of Happiness." Although the Declaration does not specify equality of white, Christian, or Anglo-Saxon men (at that time "all men" meant white, property-owning Anglo-Saxon men), it took almost 200 years for that definition to be expanded to include all races, all religions, and all women as well as men. This creed of individual dignity and equality is nonetheless older than our Declaration of Independence; its roots go back into the teachings of Judaism and Christianity.

The Constitution, however, does not make any reference to "equality" (the word never appears in the Constitution or in the Bill of Rights). But we know the framers believed that all men—at least all white adult men—were equally entitled to life, liberty, and the pursuit of happiness. But like the Declaration, the Constitution refers only to "person," "people, "citizens," and "he," but not to women, and none of its lofty sentiments applied to slaves, who enjoyed neither liberty nor equality.

The framers resolved their ambiguity about what kind of equality and for whom by creating a system of government designed to protect what they called *natural rights.* (Today we speak of *human rights,* but the idea is basically the same.) By **natural rights** the framers meant that every person has an equal right to protection against arbitrary treatment and an equal right to the liberties guaranteed by the Bill of Rights. These rights

SAVE
Brown
vs.
Board of
Education
BUILD
THE NEW
CIVIL RIGHTS
MOVEMENT
www.bamn.c

TIME LINE

EQUAL RIGHTS UNDER THE LAW

1865–1877	Reconstruction Era leads to freedom for former slaves
1896	*Plessy* v. *Ferguson* upholds "separate but equal" doctrine
1942	FDR orders internment of Japanese Americans in internment camps
1948	Truman desegregates the military
1954	*Brown* v. *Board of Education* declares school segregation unconstitutional
1963	March on Washington held to demand equal rights for African Americans
1964	Civil Rights Act forbids racial discrimination in public accomodations
1967	Age Discrimination Act creates the first legal protections based on age
1972	Title IX prohibits sex discrimination in education
1978	*University of California Regents* v. *Bakke* upholds affirmative action programs in higher education aimed at achieving diverse student bodies
1991	Americans with Disabilities Act is the first expansion of civil rights since the 1970s
2003	*Grutter* v. *Bollinger* reaffirms *Bakke* on the permissibility of affirmative action programs

natural rights
The rights of all people to dignity and worth; also called *human rights.*

affirmative action
Remedial action designed to overcome the effects of past discrimination against minorities and women.

do not depend on citizenship; they are not granted by governments. They are the rights of *all people.*

The terms *civil liberties* and *civil rights* are often used interchangeably to refer to rights that are protected by constitutional democracies. *Civil liberties* is sometimes used more narrowly to refer to freedom of conscience, religion, and expression. *Civil rights* is used to refer to the right not to be discriminated against because of race, religion, gender, or ethnic origin. Our Constitution provides two ways of protecting civil rights. First, it ensures that government officials do not discriminate against us; second, it grants national and state governments the power to protect these civil rights against interference by private individuals.

This chapter is concerned with both the protection of our rights from abuse *by government* and the protection *through government* of our right to be free from abuse by our *fellow citizens.* Here, we focus on the struggles of African Americans, women, Hispanics, Asian Americans, and Native Americans to secure the basic civil rights to the vote, to an education, to a job, and to a place to live on equal terms with their fellow citizens.

EQUALITY AND EQUAL RIGHTS

Americans are committed to equality. "Equality," however, is an elusive term. The concept for which there is the greatest consensus and that is most clearly written into the Constitution is that everybody should have *equality of opportunity* regardless of race, ethnic origin, religion, and, in recent years, gender and sexual orientation. Advancing the equality of opportunity has led to the historic struggles for civil rights.

A variation of the concept of equal opportunity is *equality of starting conditions.* There is not much equal opportunity if one person is born into a well-to-do family, lives in a safe suburb, and receives a good education, while another is born into a poor, broken family, lives in an inner-city neighborhood, and attends inferior schools. Thus, it is argued, if we are to have equality of opportunity in a meaningful sense, special opportunities must be provided for the disadvantaged through federal programs such as Head Start, which provides children from poor families with preschool experiences that prepare them for elementary school.

Traditionally, we have emphasized *individual* achievement, but in recent decades, some politicians and civil rights leaders have focused attention on the concept of *equality between groups.* When large disparities in wealth and advantage exist between groups—as between blacks and whites or between women and men—equality becomes a highly divisive political issue. Those who are disadvantaged tend to emphasize economic and social factors that exclude them from the mainstream. They champion programs like **affirmative action** that are designed to provide special help to people who have been disadvantaged due to their group memberships. Those who are advantaged, however, often act to maintain the status quo and downplay socioeconomic disparities. As a result, whether such programs promote or deny equality remains one of the most controversial current debates.

Finally, equality can also mean *equality of results.* A perennial debate, especially among college students, is whether social justice and genuine equality can exist in a nation in which people of one class have so much and others have so little and where the gap between them grows ever wider.[1] There is considerable support for guaranteeing a minimum floor—a "safety net"—below which no one should be allowed to fall. Yet Americans generally do not support an equality of results—that everybody should have the same amount of material goods—but instead tend to take the view that regardless of current economic status, a person should be able to expect that things will get better and that hard work and an entrepreneurial spirit will be rewarded.

THE QUEST FOR EQUAL JUSTICE

To gain some perspective on the court decisions, laws, and other governmental actions relating to civil rights for women and minorities, we review here the political history and social contexts in which these constitutional issues arise. These issues involve not only court decisions, laws, and constitutional amendments, however. They encompass the entire social, economic, and political system. And although the struggles of all groups are interwoven, they are not identical, so we deal briefly and separately with each.

Racial Equality

Americans had a painful confrontation with the problem of race before, during, and after the Civil War (1861–1865). As a result of the northern victory, the Thirteenth, Fourteenth, and Fifteenth Amendments became part of the Constitution. During Reconstruction, Congress passed a series of civil rights laws to implement these amendments and established programs to provide educational and social services for the freed slaves. But the Supreme Court struck down many of these laws, and it was not until the 1960s that progress was again made toward ensuring African Americans their civil rights.

"*When my distinguished colleague refers to the will of the 'people,' does he mean his 'people' or my 'people'?*"

SEGREGATION AND WHITE SUPREMACY Before Reconstruction programs had any significant effect, the white southern political leadership was restored to power, and by 1877, Reconstruction was ended. Northern political leaders abandoned African Americans to their fate at the hands of their former white masters; presidents no longer concerned themselves with the enforcement of civil rights laws, and Congress enacted no new ones. The Supreme Court either declared old laws unconstitutional or interpreted them so narrowly that they were ineffective. The Court also gave such a limited construction to the Thirteenth, Fourteenth, and Fifteenth Amendments that they failed to accomplish their intended purpose of protecting the rights of African Americans.[2]

White supremacy went unchallenged in the South, where most African Americans lived. They were kept from voting; they were forced to accept menial jobs; they were denied educational opportunities; they were segregated in public facilities.[3] African Americans were lynched on an average of one every four days, and few whites raised a voice in protest.

During World War I, African Americans began to migrate to northern cities to seek jobs in war factories. Their relocation was accelerated in the 1930s by the Great Depression and in the 1940s by World War II. Although discrimination continued, more jobs became available, and social gains resulted. As migration of African Americans out of the rural South into southern and northern cities shifted the racial composition of cities, the African American vote became important in national elections. These changes created an African American middle class opposed to segregation as a symbol of servitude and a cause of inequality. By the middle of the twentieth century, urban African Americans were active and politically powerful citizens. There was a growing demand for the abolition of color barriers.

SLOW GOVERNMENT RESPONSE By the 1930s, African Americans were resorting to lawsuits to challenge the doctrine of segregation. And after World War II, this civil rights litigation began to have a major impact. In the years that followed, the Supreme Court, beginning with the landmark 1954 ruling in *Brown* v. *Board of Education,* outlawed racially segregated public schools[4] and subsequently struck down most of the devices that had been used by state and local authorities to keep African Americans from voting.[5]

Presidents Harry S Truman and Dwight D. Eisenhower used their executive authority to fight segregation in the armed services and the federal bureaucracy. They directed the Department of Justice to enforce whatever civil rights laws were on the books, but Congress still held back. In the late 1950s, an emerging national consensus in favor of governmental action to protect civil rights plus the political clout of African Americans in the northern states began to have some influence on Congress. In 1957, Congress

Rosa Parks decision not to give up her seat on the bus in Montgomery, Alabama, sparked a boycott by African Americans who, for more than a year, refused to ride the segregated city buses.

overrode a southern filibuster in the Senate and enacted the first federal civil rights laws since Reconstruction.

A TURNING POINT   Even after the Supreme Court declared racially segregated public schools unconstitutional, most African Americans still went to segregated schools, and there was widespread resistance to integration in the South. Many legal barriers in the path of equal rights had fallen, yet most African Americans still could not buy houses where they wanted, secure the jobs they needed, find educational opportunities for their children, or eat in a restaurant or walk freely on the streets of "white neighborhoods."

But times were changing. What had once been deemed a "southern problem" was finally recognized as a national challenge. A massive social, economic, and political movement began to supplement the struggles in the courtrooms. It began in Montgomery, Alabama, on December 1, 1955, when Rosa Parks refused to give up her seat to a white man in the front of a bus and as required by law was removed from the bus. The black community responded by boycotting city buses.

The boycott worked. It also produced a charismatic national civil rights leader, the Reverend Martin Luther King Jr. Through his doctrine of nonviolent resistance, King gave a new dimension to the struggle. By the early 1960s, new organizational resources came into existence in almost every city to support and sponsor "sit-ins," "freedom rides," "live-ins," and other nonviolent demonstrations. These measures were often met with violence, and some state and local governments failed to protect the victims or to prosecute the parties responsible for the violence.[6]

The simmering forces of social discontent boiled over in the summer of 1963. A peaceful demonstration in Birmingham, Alabama, was countered with fire hoses, police dogs, and mass arrests. More than a quarter of a million people converged on Washington, D.C., to hear King and other civil rights leaders speak while countless millions more watched them on television. By the time the summer was over, there was hardly a city, North or South, that had not had demonstrations, protests, or sit-ins; some also had violence.

This direct action had some effect. Many cities enacted civil rights ordinances, more schools were desegregated, and President John F. Kennedy urged Congress to enact a comprehensive civil rights bill. Late in 1963, the nation's grief over the assassination of President Kennedy, who had become identified with civil rights goals, added political fuel to the drive for decisive federal action to protect civil rights.[7] President Lyndon B. Johnson made civil rights legislation his highest priority, and on July 2, 1964, after months of

Firefighters in Birmingham, Alabama, turned their hoses full blast on civil rights demonstrators in the 1960s. At times the water came with such force, even on children, that it literally tore the bark off fully-grown trees.

debate, he signed into law the Civil Rights Act of 1964, forbidding discrimination on the basis of race, color, religion, sex, or nationality.[8]

RIOTS AND REACTION   By the early 1970s, the legal phase of the civil rights movement had largely come to a close, but as things got better, discontent grew. Millions of impoverished African Americans demonstrated growing impatience with the discrimination that remained. This volatile situation gave way to racial violence and disorders. In 1965, a brutal riot took place in Watts, a section of Los Angeles. In 1966 and 1967, the disorders spread in scope and intensity. The Detroit riot in July 1967, the worst such disturbance up to that time in modern American history, made clear the deep divisions between the races and the urgency of taking corrective action.[9]

President Johnson appointed the special Advisory Commission on Civil Disorders in 1967 to investigate the origins of the riots and to recommend measures to prevent such disasters in the future. When the commission (called the Kerner Commission after its chair, Illinois Governor Otto Kerner) issued its report, it said in stark, clear language: "What white Americans have never fully understood—but what the Negro can never forget—is that white society is deeply implicated in the ghetto. White institutions created it, white institutions maintain it, and white society condones it." The basic conclusion of the commission was this: "Our nation is moving toward two societies, one black, one white—separate and unequal" and that "only a commitment to national action on an unprecedented scale" could change this trend.[10]

The commission made sweeping recommendations on jobs, education, housing, and the welfare system. But other events diverted attention from these recommenda-

PEOPLE & POLITICS   *Making a Difference*

MARTIN LUTHER KING, JR.

Martin Luther King, Jr., a Baptist minister and civil rights leader, was born January 25, 1929, in Atlanta, Georgia. After graduating from high school, he entered Morehouse College in 1944 and majored in sociology, but in his junior year he decided to enter the ministry. After Morehouse, King entered the Crozer Theological Seminary in Pennsylvania and there he became a follower of Indian pacifist Mohandas Gandhi. Following graduation, King earned a doctorate from Boston University in 1955. He then became pastor of the Dexter Avenue Baptist Church in Montgomery, Alabama.

In 1957, King and Ralph Abernathy founded the Southern Christian Leadership Conference in order to advance the cause of civil rights. In that year, King's home and church were bombed and violence against black protesters began to escalate. In March 1963, King was jailed in Birmingham, Alabama, for leading a protest parade without a permit. Subsequently, he led the March on Washington, on August 28, 1963, at which hundreds of thousands of civil rights activists demonstrated and focused national attention on the racial problems in the country. The March contributed to building support for the passage of the Civil Rights Act of 1964.

Speaking at the March from the steps of the Lincoln Memorial, King delivered his famous "I Have A Dream" speech, in which he said he dreamed of the day when "my four little children . . . will not be judged by the color of their skin but by the content of their character," and concluded with the memorable line, "Free at last! Thank God Almighty, we are free at last!"

In 1963 King became *Time* magazine's Man of the Year, and in 1964 he was awarded the Nobel Peace Prize for his leadership in the civil rights movement and advocacy of nonviolent protest.

King was assassinated on April 4, 1968, outside his Memphis, Tennessee, motel room.

Susan B. Anthony and Elizabeth Cady Stanton were the two most influential leaders of the women's suffrage movement in the nineteenth century.

tions: the Vietnam War; Watergate; the elections of Ronald Reagan and George H. W. Bush, who were reluctant to take governmental actions to enforce civil rights; and a growing skepticism about the effectiveness of governmental action generally.

The Clinton administration was more sympathetic toward the use of governmental power to deal with issues of inequality than its immediate predecessors, but because of budgetary constraints and Republican opposition to "big government" programs, it was largely unable to promote any major initiatives directly aimed at the problems of the inner cities. The administration of George W. Bush pursued more race-neutral policies like the No Child Left Behind program aimed at raising educational standards across the nation. Still, civil rights leaders like the Reverend Jesse Jackson continue efforts to eliminate the vestiges of past racial discrimination through boycotts and lawsuits aimed at persuading businesses and corporations to reach out and hire and promote more African Americans.

Women's Rights

The struggle for equal rights for women was intertwined with the battle to secure equal rights for African Americans. The Seneca Falls Women's Rights Convention (1848), which launched the women's movement, involved men and women who actively campaigned to abolish slavery and to secure the rights of African Americans and women. But as the Civil War approached, women were urged to abandon their cause and devote their energies to getting rid of slavery.[11] The Civil War brought the women's movement to a halt, and the temperance movement to prohibit the sale of liquor diverted attention away from women's rights as well. The Fourteenth and Fifteenth Amendments did not advance voting rights for women, even as they guaranteed that right to freed male slaves.

By the turn of the twentieth century, however, a vigorous campaign was under way for **women's suffrage**—the right to vote. The first victories came in western states, where Wyoming led the way. As a territory, Wyoming had given women the right to vote. When members of Congress in Washington grumbled about this "petticoat provision," the Wyoming legislators replied they would stay out of the Union 100 years rather than come in without women's suffrage. Congress gave in and admitted Wyoming to the Union. By the end of World War I, more than half the states had granted women the right to vote in some or all elections.

To many suffragists, this state-by-state approach seemed slow and uncertain. They wanted a decisive victory—a constitutional amendment that would force all states to allow qualified women to vote. Finally, in 1919, Congress proposed the Nineteenth Amendment. Opposition to granting voting rights to women was intertwined with opposition to granting voting rights to African Americans. Many southerners opposed the amendment because it gave Congress enforcement power, which might bring federal officials to investigate elections to ensure that the amendment was being obeyed—an interference that might call attention to how blacks were being kept from voting.

With the ratification of the Nineteenth Amendment in 1920, women won the right to vote, but they were still denied equal pay and equal rights, and they suffered numerous legal disabilities imposed by both national and state laws. In the 1970s and 1980s, the unsuccessful struggle to secure the adoption of the Equal Rights Amendment occupied much of the attention of the women's movement. But there are now other goals, and the political clout of women is mobilized behind issues that range from equal pay to world peace, sexual harassment, abortion rights, and election to office.[12]

Since the late 1980s, the Supreme Court has been reluctant to expand the Fourteenth Amendment's protection against gender discrimination, though it did hold that Virginia could not create a separate military academy for women instead of admitting them into the all-male Virginia Military Institute, a 150-year-old state-run institution.[13]

The courts, however, have increasingly enforced the prohibition against sex discrimination in the 1964 Civil Rights Act and expanded it to forbid sexual harassment in the workplace. Ironically, that prohibition was put into the act in an effort by members of the House of Representatives to defeat passage of the legislation, which aimed primarily at ending racial discrimination.[14] As a result, it was initially not taken very seriously, and not until the 1980s did it apply to "quid pro quo" sexual harassment, in which an employer makes a person provide sexual favors as a condition of employment (in

women's suffrage
The right of women to vote.

hiring, promotions, and firing).[15] Sexual harassment was then brought to national attention in 1991 by accusations made against Justice Clarence Thomas by Anita Hill, a law professor and former colleague, at the time of his Senate confirmation. Subsequently, the Supreme Court ruled that the law also applies to situations in which employees experience discrimination because they are forced to work in a "hostile environment." A hostile environment is defined as a workplace "permeated" with intimidation, ridicule, and insult that is severe and pervasive, and this includes same-sex harassment.[16]

Some women still complain of a "glass ceiling" in large corporations, preventing their advancement. But there is no denying that major progress has been made, with more and more women going to college and professional schools and into the media and business. Indeed, during the past three decades, the percentage of women graduating from colleges and universities has outpaced that of men (see Figure 17–1).

Hispanics

The struggle for civil rights has not been limited to women and African Americans. Each new wave of immigrants has been considered suspect by those who arrived earlier—all the more so if its members were not white or English-speaking. Formal barriers of law and informal barriers of custom combined to deny equal rights. But as groups established themselves—first economically and then politically—most of these barriers were swept away, and constitutionally guaranteed rights were asserted.

As we discussed in Chapter 5, most Hispanics—many of whose ancestors have been Americans for generations—are bilingual, speaking English as well as Spanish. However, because English may not be their first language, it has been difficult for some Hispanics to establish themselves educationally or to advance into the ranks of executives and professionals. Although not as visible as African Americans, Hispanics have suffered the same kinds of discrimination in employment, education, and accommodations.

Hispanic political clout has been unrealized because of internal political differences and because many Hispanics are not citizens or registered to vote. However, after California adopted Proposition 187 in 1994, which denied medical, educational, and social services to illegal immigrants, and Congress amended the federal welfare laws to curtail benefits to noncitizens, many immigrants rushed to become naturalized. Half of all Hispanic Americans live in two states: in 2001, California became the first big state in which whites are in the minority; Texas, the second most populous state, became the second majority-minority state in 2004.[17]

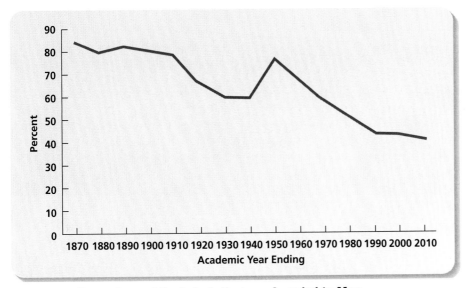

FIGURE 17–1 Percentage of Bachelor's Degrees Awarded to Men.
*Percentage for 2010 is projected by the Pell Institute for the Study of Opportunity in Higher Education, National Center for Education Statistics.
SOURCE: Michael A. Fletcher, "Degrees of Separation," *The Washington Post,* June 25, 2002, p. A1.

Asian Americans

The term "Asian American" describes approximately 10 million individuals from many different countries and many different ethnic backgrounds. Most do not think of themselves as Asians but as Americans of Chinese, Japanese, Indian, Vietnamese, Cambodian, Korean, or other specific ancestry. They live chiefly in the western states, but their number has been increasing rapidly in New York and Texas.

Although Asian Americans are often considered a "model minority" because of their general success in education and business, the U.S. Civil Rights Commission found that "Asian-Americans do face widespread prejudice, discrimination and barriers to equal opportunity" and that racially motivated violence against them "occurs with disturbing frequency."[18]

CHINESE AMERICANS   The Chinese were the first Asians to come to the United States. Beginning in 1847, when young male peasants came here to get away from poverty and to work in mines, on railroads, and on farms, the Chinese encountered economic and cultural fears of the white majority, who did not understand them or their culture. In response, the Chinese seldom tried to assimilate but instead gravitated to "Chinatowns." Discriminatory immigration and naturalization restrictions, imposed beginning in 1882, were strengthened in later years and were not removed until the end of World War II.

Since that time, the Chinese have moved into the mainstream of American society, and they are beginning to run for and win local political offices. Gary Locke, a Democrat and a graduate of Yale and Boston University Law School, was elected in 1996 and re-elected in 2000 governor of Washington, the first Chinese American to become governor of a continental state.

JAPANESE AMERICANS   The Japanese first migrated to Hawaii in the 1860s and then to California in the 1880s. Most Japanese immigrants remained in the West Coast states. By the beginning of the twentieth century, they faced overt hostility. In 1905, labor leaders organized the Japanese and Korean Exclusion League, and in 1906, the San Francisco Board of Education excluded all Chinese, Japanese, and Korean children from neighborhood schools. Some western states passed laws denying the right to own land to aliens who were ineligible to become citizens—meaning aliens of Asian ancestry.

During World War II, anti-Japanese hysteria provoked the internment of West Coast Japanese—most of whom were loyal American citizens guilty of no crimes—in prison camps in California, Colorado, and some other states. During this time, the property of

In the war hysteria following the outbreak of World War II, Japanese Americans were rounded up and transported to internment camps.

Japanese Americans was often sold at confiscatory rates, and many lost their businesses, jobs, and incomes. Following the war, the exclusionary acts were repealed. In 1988, President Ronald Reagan signed a law providing $20,000 restitution to each of the approximately 60,000 surviving World War II internees.

OTHER ASIAN AMERICANS   Like other Asian Americans, Koreans faced overt discrimination in jobs and housing, but a Korean middle class has been growing, with many Korean Americans becoming teachers, doctors, and lawyers. Others operate small family businesses such as dry cleaners, florist shops, service stations, and small grocery stores, often in inner cities.[19]

When Filipinos first came to the United States in the early part of the twentieth century, they were considered American nationals because the Philippine Islands were an American possession. Nonetheless, they were denied rights to full citizenship and faced discrimination and even violence, including anti-Filipino riots in the state of Washington in 1928 and later in California, where nearly one-third of the over 1.5 million Filipinos live.[20] Their economic status has improved, but their influence in politics remains as small as their numbers.

The newest Asian arrivals consist of more than a million refugees from Vietnam, Laos, and Cambodia, who first came to the United States in 1975 and settled mostly in California. Although this group included middle-class people who left during the fall of Saigon following the end of the Vietnam War, it also consisted of large numbers of "boat people" who came to our shores without any financial resources. In a relatively short time, most established themselves economically. Although they are starting to have political influence, some remain socially and economically segregated.

Native Americans

Almost half of the more than 2 million Native Americans live on or near a *reservation*—a tract of land given to the tribal nations by treaty—and are enrolled as members of one of the 550 federally recognized tribes, including 226 groups in Alaska.[21] About 200 different Native American languages are spoken.

Native Americans speak of their tribes as "nations," yet they are not possessed of the full attributes of sovereignty. Rather, they are a separate people with power to regulate their own internal affairs, subject to congressional supervision. States are precluded from regulating or taxing the tribes or extending the jurisdiction of their courts over the tribes unless authorized to do so by Congress.[22] In recent years, Congress has stepped in to mediate growing tensions between Indian tribes who have used their sovereignty over reservations to operate gambling casinos and the states in which these reservations are located.

By acts of Congress, Native Americans are citizens of the United States and of the states in which they live. They have the right to vote. Native Americans living off reservations and working in the general community pay taxes just like everybody else; off reservations they have the same rights as any other Americans. If they are enrolled members of a recognized tribe, they are entitled to certain benefits created by law and by treaty. The Bureau of Indian Affairs of the Department of the Interior administers these benefits.

During the period of assimilation that began in 1887 and lasted until 1934, tribal governments were weak, some reservations were dissolved, and more than 100 tribes had their relationship with the federal government severed.[23] The civil rights movement of the 1960s created a more favorable climate for the concerns of Native Americans. Their goals were to reassert treaty rights and secure greater autonomy for the tribes. Under the leadership of the Native American Rights Fund (NARF), more Indian law cases were brought in the past several decades than at any time in our history.[24]

As a result of the efforts of Native American leaders and a greater national consciousness of the concerns of minorities, most Americans are now aware that many Native Americans live in poverty. Native Americans "are in far worse health than the rest of the population, dying earlier and suffering disproportionately from alcoholism, accidents, diabetes, and pneumonia."[25] Although in recent years the rest of the United States has enjoyed about 4 percent unemployment, many reservations continue to experience 50 to 60 percent unemployment. Some reservations lack adequate health care facilities,

MAJOR CIVIL RIGHTS LAWS

- **Civil Rights Act, 1957** Makes it a federal crime to prevent persons from voting in federal elections.
- **Civil Rights Act, 1964** Bars discrimination in employment or in public accommodations on the basis of race, color, religion, sex, or national origin; created the Equal Employment Opportunity Commission.
- **Voting Rights Act, 1965** Authorizes the appointment of federal examiners to register voters in areas that have been discriminating.
- **Age Discrimination in Employment Act, 1967** Prohibits job discrimination against workers or job applicants aged 40 through 65 and prohibits mandatory retirement.
- **Fair Housing Act, 1968** Prohibits discrimination on the basis of race, color, religion, or national origin in the sale or rental of most housing.
- **Title IX, Education Amendment of 1972** Prohibits discrimination on the basis of sex in any education program receiving federal financial assistance.
- **Rehabilitation Act, 1973** Requires that recipients of federal grants greater than $2,500 hire and promote qualified handicapped individuals.
- **Fair Housing Act Amendments, 1988** Gave the Department of Housing and Urban Development authority to prohibit housing bias against the handicapped and families with children.
- **Americans with Disabilities Act, 1991** Prohibits discrimination based on disability and requires that facilities be made accessible to those with disabilities.
- **Civil Rights Act, 1991** Requires that employers justify practices that negatively affect women and minorities as job-related or show that no alternative practices would have a lesser impact. Also established a commission to examine the "glass ceiling" that keeps women from becoming executives and to make recommendations on how to increase promotion of women and minorities to management positions.

CHANGING FACE OF AMERICAN POLITICS

RACIAL AND ETHNIC IDENTIFICATION

Since 1860, the U.S. census has changed its classifications of race and ethnicity in light of the nation's growing diversity and political developments. The classifications have changed several times and continue to provoke controversy. The classification "Hispanic," for example, was picked by an ad hoc government committee over "Latino" in 1975 to identify Spanish-speaking and Spanish-surnamed individuals. The term was chosen because it connotes the cultural diasporas of centuries-old conquests by Spain. But some prefer "Latino" because it refers to the Latin-based Romance languages of

1860	1870	1880	1890	1900	1910	1920	1930	1940	1950
White	White	White	White	White	White	White	White	White	White
Black	Black	Black	Black	Black	Black	Black	Black	Black	Negro
Mulatto	Mulatto	Mulatto	Mulatto		Mulatto	Mulatto			
	Chinese	Chinese	Chinese	Chinese	Chinese	Chinese	Chinese	Chinese	Chinese
	Indian	Indian	Indian	Indian	Indian	Indian	Indian	Indian	American Indian
			Quadroon						
			Octoroon						
			Japanese	Japanese	Japanese	Japanese	Japanese	Japanese	Japanese
						Filipino	Filipino	Filipino	Filipino
						Hindu	Hindu	Hindu	
						Korean	Korean	Korean	
							Mexican		
					Other	Other	Other	Other	Other

Tiger Woods, the prize-winning golfer, is proud of his diverse heritage. He is both African American and Asian (Thai). He feels that ethnic background should not make a difference. It doesn't to him. As Woods says, "I am an American and proud of it."

equal protection clause
Clause in the Fourteenth Amendment that forbids any state to deny to any person within its jurisdiction the equal protection of the laws. By interpretation, the Fifth Amendment imposes the same limitation on the national government. This clause is the major constitutional restraint on the power of governments to discriminate against persons because of race, national origin, or sex.

educational opportunities, decent housing, and jobs. Congress has started to compensate Native Americans for past injustices and to provide more opportunities for the development of tribal economic independence, and judges are showing greater vigilance in the enforcement of Indian treaty rights.

In 1986, Ben Nighthorse Campbell became the first Native American to be elected to Congress. He was elected as a Democrat from Colorado but became a Republican after being elected to the Senate in 1992, and then was reelected in 1998; he retired in 2005.

Spain, France, Italy, and Portugal, as well as Portuguese-speaking Brazilians. In recent years "Latino" has become a more popular term, but many still prefer "Hispanic" because it connotes a history of imperialism and does not include the French and Italians.[*]

Below are the categories used in the decennial counts from 1860 to 2000. Each new category is boldfaced at its first inclusion. For more information, see AmeriStat's Web site, at www.ameristat.org.

1960	1970	1980	1990	2000
White	**White**	**White**	**White**	**White**
Negro	**Negro/Black**	**Black/Negro**	**Black/Negro**	**Black/African American/Negro**
Chinese	Chinese	Chinese	Chinese	Chinese
American Indian	American Indian	Indian	Indian	American Indian or Alaska Native
Japanese	Japanese	Japanese	Japanese	Japanese
Filipino	Filipino	Filipino	Filipino	Filipino
		Asian Indian	Asian Indian	Asian Indian
	Korean	Korean	Korean	Korean
Aleut		Aleut	Aleut	
Eskimo		Eskimo	Eskimo	
Hawaiian	Hawaiian	Hawaiian	Hawaiian	Native Hawaiian
Part Hawaiian				
		Vietnamese	Vietnamese	Vietnamese
		Guamanian	Guamanian	Guamanian or Chamorro
		Samoan	Samoan	Samoan
			Other Asian	**Other Asian**
			Pacific Islander	**Pacific Islander**
Other	**Other**	**Other**	**Other race**	**Some other race**
E	Mexican	Mexican American	Mexican/Mexican American	Mexican/Mexican American
T				
H				
N		**Chicano**	Chicano	Chicano
I	**Puerto Rican**	Puerto Rican	Puerto Rican	Puerto Rican
C	**Central/South American**			
I	**Cuban**	Cuban	Cuban	Cuban
T	**Other Spanish**	Other Spanish/Hispanic	Other Spanish/Hispanic	Other Spanish/Hispanic/Latino
Y	**(None of these)**	Not Spanish/Hispanic	Not Spanish/Hispanic	Not Spanish/Hispanic/Latino

[*] Darrly Fears, "The Roots of 'Hispanic'," *The Washington Post,* October 15, 2003, p. A21.

EQUAL PROTECTION OF THE LAWS: WHAT DOES IT MEAN?

The **equal protection clause** of the Fourteenth Amendment declares that no state (including any subdivision thereof) shall "deny to any person within its jurisdiction the equal protection of the laws." Although there is no parallel clause explicitly limiting the national government, the Fifth Amendment's **due process clause**, which states that no person shall "be deprived of life, liberty, or property, without due process of law," has

due process clause
Clause in the Fifth Amendment limiting the power of the national government; similar clause in the Fourteenth Amendment prohibiting state governments from depriving any person of life, liberty, or property without due process of law.

been interpreted to impose the same restraints on the national government as the equal protection clause imposes on the states.

The equal protection clause applies only to the actions of *governments*, not to those of private individuals. If a discriminatory action is performed by a private person, it does not violate the Constitution, although it may violate federal and state laws. The equal protection clause does not, however, prevent governments from creating various classifications of people in its laws. What the Constitution forbids is *unreasonable* classifications. In general, a classification is unreasonable when there is no relation between the classes it creates and permissible governmental goals. A law prohibiting redheads from voting, for example, would be unreasonable. In contrast, laws denying persons under 18 the right to vote, to marry without the permission of their parents, or to apply for a license to drive a car appear to be reasonable (at least to most persons over 18).

Constitutional Classifications and Tests

One of the most troublesome constitutional questions is how to distinguish between constitutional and unconstitutional classifications. The Supreme Court uses three tests for this purpose: the *rational basis* test, the *strict scrutiny* test, and the *heightened scrutiny* test.

THE RATIONAL BASIS TEST   The traditional test to determine whether a law complies with the equal protection requirement places the burden of proof on the parties attacking the law. They must show that the law has no rational or legitimate governmental goals. Traditionally the rational basis test applied only to legislation affecting economic interests and, with two exceptions in the last 70 years,[26] the Court upheld the legislation and deferred to legislative judgments. But recently the Court has applied the test to challenges to legislation affecting noneconomic interests.[27] Notably, in *Roemer* v. *Evans* (1996) the Court struck down an amendment to Colorado's constitution that barred local governments from adopting laws that forbid discrimination against homosexuals.[28] The Court held that the law lacked a rational basis and was based on animus and bias against gays and lesbians.

 # GLOBAL *Perceptions*

QUESTION: Do you agree that "homosexuality is a way of life that should be accepted by society"?

Public perceptions of homosexuals vary widely around the world. In the United States a bare majority (51%) think homosexuality should be accepted, a smaller percentage than in Canada (69%) and West European countries, such as Germany (83%), France (77%), Great Britain (74%), and Italy (74%). The lowest public acceptance appears in African countries, with the exception of South Africa (33%); and in Middle Eastern countries; as well as most Asian countries, with the exception of Japan (54%) and the Philippines (64%).

SOURCE: The Pew Global Attitudes Project, 2003, p. T-65.

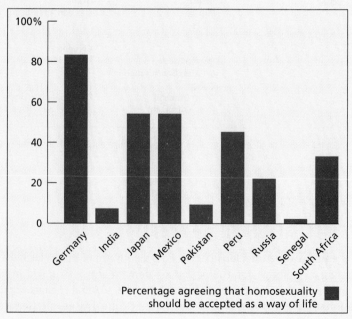

Percentage agreeing that homosexuality should be accepted as a way of life

SUSPECT CLASSIFICATIONS AND STRICT SCRUTINY When a law is subject to strict scrutiny, the courts must be persuaded that there is both a "compelling governmental interest" to justify such a classification and no less restrictive way to accomplish this compelling purpose. The Court applies the strict scrutiny test to suspect classifications. A *suspect classification* is a class of people deliberately subjected to such unequal treatment in the past or relegated by society to a position of such political powerlessness as to require extraordinary judicial protection.[29]

Classifications based on race or national origin are always suspect. It does not make any difference if the laws are designed for supposedly benign purposes—that is, to help persons of a particular race or national origin. For example, the Supreme Court has held that laws that give preference for public employment based on race are subject to strict scrutiny.

QUASI-SUSPECT CLASSIFICATIONS AND HEIGHTENED SCRUTINY To sustain a law under this test, the burden is on the government to show that its classification serves "important governmental objectives." Classifications based on gender are subject to heightened scrutiny. Not until 1971 was any classification based on gender declared unconstitutional. Before that time, many laws provided special protection for women—such as a Michigan law forbidding any woman other than the wife or daughter of a tavern owner to serve as a barmaid. As Justice William J. Brennan Jr. wrote for the Court, "There can be no doubt that our nation has had a long and unfortunate history of sex discrimination. Traditionally such discrimination was rationalized by an attitude of 'romantic paternalism' which in practical effect put women, not on a pedestal, but in a cage."[30]

Today the Court's view is that treating women differently from men (or vice versa) is forbidden when supported by no more substantial justification than "the role-typing society has long imposed upon women."[31] If the government's objective is "to protect members of one sex because they are presumed to suffer from an inherent handicap or to be innately inferior," that objective is illegitimate, and the government must have "an exceedingly persuasive justification" for discriminating between men and women.[32] In recent years, the Supreme Court has struck down most laws brought before it that were

IN COMPARATIVE PERSPECTIVE

CANADIAN COURTS FORBID DISCRIMINATION AGAINST HOMOSEXUALS

Within months of the Massachusetts state supreme court's ruling that its state constitution forbids discrimination against same-sex marriages and the U.S. Supreme Court's decision striking down laws making homosexual sodomy a crime,[*] the Ontario High Court ruled that the government had to recognize same-sex marriages. In doing so the court extended a series of rulings barring discrimination against homosexuals in Canada.

The Supreme Court of Canada in 1995 held that sexual orientation was embraced by the equality guarantee of Section 15(1) of Canada's Charter of Rights and Freedom, which provides: "Every individual is equal before and under the law and has the right to the equal protection and equal benefit of the law without discrimination and, in particular, without discrimination based on race, national or ethnic origin, colour, religion, sex, age or mental or physical disability."[†]

Subsequent decisions further expanded protection for gays and lesbians in holding, for example, that they may not be discriminated against in employment.[‡] On the basis of those rulings, courts in Quebec and British Columbia invalidated prohibitions against same-sex marriages. And in *Halpern* v. *Attorney General of Canada* (2003), the Court of Appeal for Ontario held that Canada's Charter of Rights and Freedoms bars discrimination against same-sex marriages. The high court rejected the government's arguments that it had compelling interests in barring same-sex marriages. Specifically, the court ruled that interests in uniting the opposite sexes, encouraging the birth and rearing of children of the marriage, and promoting companionship, were not compelling justifications for discrimination against homosexuals and same-sex marriages.

The full text of the opinion in *Halpern* v. *Attorney General of Canada* is available on the Web site of the Court of Appeal of Ontario at www.ontariocourts.on.ca/decisions.

[*]*Lawrence* v. *Texas,* 539 U.S. 558 (2003).
[†]*Egan* v. *Canada,* 2 S.C.R. 513 (1995).
[‡]*Vriend* v. *Albert,* 1 S.C.R. 493 (1998); and *M.* v. *H.,* 2 S.C.R. 3 (1999).

alleged to discriminate against women but has tended to do so on the basis of federal statutes like the 1964 Civil Rights Act.

POVERTY AND AGE Just as racial minorities and women are entitled to special constitutional protection, it is argued, so should the poor and the elderly be protected. But the Supreme Court rejected the argument "that financial need alone identifies a suspect class for purposes of equal protection analysis."[33] However, state supreme courts in Texas, Ohio, and elsewhere have ruled that unequal funding for public schools as a result of "rich" districts spending more per pupil than "poor" districts violates their state constitutional provisions for free and equal education.[34]

Age is not a suspect class. Many laws commonly make distinctions based on age: to obtain a driver's license, to marry without parental consent, to attend schools, to buy alcohol, and so on. Many governmental institutions have age-specific programs: for senior citizens, for adult students, for midcareer persons. The Supreme Court has repeatedly refused to make age a suspect classification requiring extra judicial protection. As Justice Sandra Day O'Connor observed, "States may discriminate on the basis of age without offending the Fourteenth Amendment if the age classification in question is rationally related to a legitimate state interest."[35]

Congress, however, responding to "gray power," frequently treats age as a protected category. Congress has made it illegal for most employers to discriminate on the basis of advancing age. Except for a few exempt occupations, employers may not impose mandatory retirement requirements. Congress also attempted to extend the protections against age discrimination to cover state employees, but the Supreme Court ruled that Congress lacks the constitutional authority to open the federal courts to suits by state employees for alleged age discrimination. State employees are limited to recovering monetary damages under state laws in state courts.[36]

FUNDAMENTAL RIGHTS AND STRICT SCRUTINY The Court also strictly scrutinizes laws impinging on *fundamental rights*. What makes a right fundamental in the constitutional sense? It is not the importance or the significance of the right that makes it fundamental but whether it is explicitly or implicitly *guaranteed by the Constitution*. Under this test, the rights to travel and to vote have been held to be fundamental, as well as First Amendment rights such as the right to associate for the advancement of political beliefs. Rights to an education, to housing, or to welfare benefits have not been deemed fundamental.

There is a continuing legal debate on whether or not schools in poorer districts deny the right to equal education because these districts are not able to fund their public schools as successfully as wealthier districts.

Important as these rights may be, there are no constitutional provisions specifically protecting them from governmental regulation.

Proving Discrimination

Does the fact that a law or a regulation has a differential effect—what has come to be known as *disparate impact*—on persons of a different race or sex by itself establish that the law is unconstitutional? In one of its most important decisions, *Washington* v. *Davis* (1976), the Supreme Court said no.[37] "An unwavering line of cases" from the Supreme Court "hold that a violation of the Equal Protection Clause requires state action motivated by discriminatory intent; the disproportionate effects of state action are not sufficient to establish such a violation."[38] Or, as the Court said in another case, "the Fourteenth Amendment guarantees equal laws, not equal results."[39]

What do these rulings on disparate impact mean in practical terms? They mean, for example, that even when city ordinances permit only single-family residences and thus make low-cost housing projects impossible, they are not unconstitutional—even if their effect is to keep minorities from moving into the city—unless it can be shown that they were adopted with the *intent* to discriminate against minorities. For another example, preference for veterans in public employment does not violate the equal protection clause, even though its effect is to keep many women from getting jobs; the distinction between veterans and nonveterans was not adopted deliberately to create a sex barrier.

What is constitutional can nonetheless be illegal. For example, state laws creating legislative districts with no intent to discriminate against African Americans that in effect dilute their voting power are not unconstitutional. But in the Voting Rights Act of 1965, Congress made such laws illegal if the result is to dilute the voting power of African Americans, regardless of the laws' intent. The Voting Rights Act of 1965 tests the legality of state voting laws and practices by their *effects* rather than by the *intentions* of the legislatures that passed them.

VOTING RIGHTS

Under our Constitution, it is the states, not the federal government, that regulate elections and voting qualifications. However, Article I, Section 4, gives Congress the power to supersede state regulations as to the "Times, Places and Manner" of elections for representatives and senators. Congress has used this authority, along with its authority under Article II, Section 2, to set the date for selection of electors, to set age qualifications and residency requirements to vote in national elections, to establish a uniform day for all states to hold elections for members of Congress and presidential electors, and to give American citizens who reside outside the United States the right to vote for members of Congress and presidential electors in the states in which they previously lived.

Limitations on the states' power to set voting qualifications are contained in the Fourteenth Amendment (forbidding qualifications that have no reasonable relation to the ability to vote), the Fifteenth Amendment (forbidding qualifications based on race), the Nineteenth Amendment (forbidding qualifications based on sex), and the Twenty-Sixth Amendment (forbidding states to deny citizens 18 years of age or older the right to vote on account of age). These amendments also empower Congress to enact the laws necessary to enforce their provisions.

Protecting Voting Rights

In the 1940s, the Supreme Court began to strike down one after another of the devices that had been used to keep African Americans from voting. In the one-party South of the early decades of the twentieth century, the Democratic party would hold whites-only primaries, effectively disenfranchising black voters. In *Smith* v. *Allwright* (1944), the Court declared the **white primary** unconstitutional.[40] In 1960, the Court held that **racial gerrymandering**—the drawing of election districts to ensure that African Americans would be a minority in all districts—was contrary to the Fifteenth Amendment.[41] In 1964, the

white primary
Primary operated by the Democratic party in southern states that, before Republicans gained strength in the "one-party South," essentially constituted an election; ruled unconstitutional in *Smith* v. *Allwright* (1944).

racial gerrymandering
The drawing of election districts so as to ensure that members of a certain race are a minority in the district; ruled unconstitutional in *Gomillion* v. *Lightfoot* (1960).

Twenty-Fourth Amendment eliminated the **poll tax**—payment required as a condition for voting—in presidential and congressional elections. In 1966, the Court held that the Fourteenth Amendment forbade the poll tax as a condition in any election.[42]

Officials seeking to deny African Americans the right to vote were forced to rely on registration requirements. On the surface, such requirements appeared to be perfectly proper, but it was the way they were administered that kept blacks from the polls. White election officers confronted African Americans trying to register while white police stood guard; white judges heard appeals of decisions made by registration officials. Officials often seized on the smallest error on an application form as an excuse to disqualify a black voter. In one parish in Louisiana, after four white voters challenged the registration of some black voters on the grounds that those voters had made an "error in spilling" [sic] in their applications, registration officials struck 1,300 out of approximately 1,500 black voters from the rolls.[43]

In many southern areas, **literacy tests** were used to discriminate against African Americans. Some states required applicants to demonstrate that they understood the national and state constitutions and that they were persons of good character. Although poor whites often avoided registering out of fear of embarrassment from failing a literacy test, the tests were more often used to discriminate against African Americans.[44] Whites were often asked simple questions; blacks were asked questions that would baffle a Supreme Court justice. "In the 1960s southern registrars were observed testing black applicants on such matters as the number of bubbles in a soap bar, the news contained in a copy of the *Peking Daily*, the meaning of obscure passages in state constitutions, and the definition of terms such as *habeas corpus*."[45] In Louisiana, 49,603 illiterate white voters were able to persuade election officials they could understand the Constitution, but only two illiterate black voters were able to do so.

The Voting Rights Act of 1965

For two decades after World War II, under the leadership of the Supreme Court, many limitations on voting were declared unconstitutional, but this approach still did not open the voting booth to African Americans. Finally Congress acted. The Civil Rights Act of 1964 had hardly become law when events in Selma, Alabama, dramatized the inadequacy of depending on the courts to prevent racial barriers in polling places. Led by Martin Luther King Jr., a voter registration drive in Selma sparked arrests, marches on the state capital, and the murder of two civil rights workers. Still there was no dent in the color bar at the polls. Responding to events in Selma, President Lyndon Johnson made a dramatic address to Congress and the nation calling for federal action to ensure that no person would be deprived of the right to vote in any election for any office because of color or race. Congress responded with the Voting Rights Act of 1965.

Section 2 of the Voting Rights Act prohibits voting qualifications or standards that result in a denial of the right of any citizen to vote on account of race and color. Section 5 requires that states with a history of denying African Americans or Hispanic citizens the right to vote must clear with the Department of Justice changes in voting practice or laws that might dilute the voting power of these groups.[46] What precisely constitutes "dilution" and how it is to be measured are the subject of much litigation. Examples include changes in the location of polling places, changes in candidacy requirements and qualifications, changes in filing deadlines, changes from ward to at-large elections, changes in boundary lines of voting districts, and changes that affect the creation or abolition of an elective office and imposition by state political parties of fees for delegates to nominating conventions.[47]

Following the 1990 census, the Department of Justice pressured southern state legislatures to draw as many districts as possible in which minorities would constitute a majority of the electorate. Most of these districts tended to be Democratic, leaving the other congressional districts in these states heavily white and Republican. The lower federal courts sustained the Department of Justice's interpretation. As a result, there was a considerable increase in the number of congressional districts represented by minorities and Republicans.

poll tax
Payment required as a condition for voting; prohibited for national elections by the Twenty-Fourth Amendment (1964) and ruled unconstitutional for all elections in *Harper* v. *Virginia Board of Elections* (1966).

literacy test
Literacy requirement imposed by some states as a condition of voting, generally used to disqualify blacks from voting in the South; now illegal.

The Supreme Court, however, in a series of cases beginning with *Shaw* v. *Reno* (1993), announced that although it was a legitimate goal for state legislatures to take race into account when they drew electoral districts in order to increase the voting strength of minorities, they could not make race the sole or predominant reason for drawing district lines. The Department of Justice, said the Supreme Court, was wrong in forcing states to create as many **majority-minority districts** as possible. A test case involved the North Carolina legislature's creation of a majority-minority district 160 miles long and in some places only an interstate highway wide. "If you drove down the interstate," said one legislator about this district, "with both car doors open, you'd kill most of the people in the district." North Carolina's reapportionment scheme, the Supreme Court declared, was so "irrational on its face that it can be understood only as an effort to segregate voters into separate voting districts because of their race." To comply with the Voting Rights Act, the Supreme Court explained, states must provide for districts roughly proportional to the minority voters' respective shares in the voting-age population.[48]

Since then the Court has expanded *Shaw* by clarifying that it was not meant to suggest that a "district must be bizarre on its face before there is a constitutional violation." Legislatures may take racial considerations into account when they draw district lines, but when race becomes the overriding motive, the state violates the equal protection clause.[49] Even though many southern states had to redraw legislative districts, when African American incumbents ran in the newly drawn districts, with majority white electors, they were reelected.[50]

Problems with voting irregularities remain. After the 2000 presidential election, some black voters in several counties in Florida complained that they were discouraged from voting or that their votes were not counted. Also, in some states, like Florida, felons are denied the right to vote but in not in other states. In the 2004 presidential election, both parties, as well as international observers, monitored and contested processes for violations of voting procedures.

EDUCATION RIGHTS

Until the Supreme Court struck down such laws in the 1950s, southern states had made it illegal for whites and blacks to ride in the same train cars, attend the same theaters, go to the same schools, be born in the same hospitals, or be buried in the same cemeteries. **Jim Crow laws**, as they came to be called, blanketed southern life. How could these laws stand in the face of the equal protection clause? This was the question raised in *Plessy* v. *Ferguson* (1896).

In the *Plessy* decision, the Supreme Court endorsed the view that governmentally imposed racial segregation in public transportation, and presumably in public education, did not necessarily constitute discrimination if "equal" accommodations were provided for the members of both races.[51] But the "equal" part of the formula was meaningless. African Americans were segregated in unequal facilities and lacked the political power to protest effectively. The passage of time did not lessen the inequalities. Beginning in the late 1930s, African Americans started to file lawsuits challenging the doctrine. They cited facts to show that in practice "separate but equal" was not equal and always resulted in discrimination against African Americans.

The End of "Separate but Equal": *Brown* v. *Board of Education*

At first, the Supreme Court was not willing to upset the separate but equal doctrine, but in *Brown* v. *Board of Education of Topeka* (1954), the Court finally reversed the *Plessy* doctrine as it applied to public schools by holding that "separate but equal" is a contradiction in terms. *Segregation is itself discrimination.*[52] A year later, the Court ordered school boards to proceed with "all deliberate speed to desegregate public schools at the earliest practical date."[53]

But many school districts moved very slowly, and in the 1960s, Congress and the president joined even more directly in the battle against school segregation. Title VI of the Civil Rights Act of 1964, as subsequently amended, stipulated that federal dollars under any

majority-minority district
A congressional district created to include a majority of minority voters; ruled constitutional so long as race is not the main factor in redistricting.

Jim Crow laws
State laws formerly pervasive throughout the South requiring public facilities and accommodations to be segregated by race; ruled unconstitutional.

Thurgood Marshall (center), George C.E. Hayes (left), and James Nabrit Jr. (right) argued and won Brown v. Board of Education of Topeka *before the Supreme Court in 1954.*

grant program or project must be withdrawn from an entire school or institution of higher education that discriminates "on the ground of race, color, or national origin," gender, age, or disability, in "any program or activity receiving federal financial assistance."

From Segregation to Desegregation—but Not Yet Integration

School districts that had operated two kinds of schools, one for whites and one for blacks, now had an obligation to develop plans and programs to move from segregation to integration. For such school districts, desegregation would not be enough; they would have a duty to bring about integration. If they failed to do so on their own initiative, federal judges would supervise the school districts to ensure that they were doing what was necessary and proper to overcome the evils of segregation.

But since most whites and most African Americans continued to live in separate neighborhoods, merely removing legal barriers to school integration did not by itself integrate the schools. To overcome this residential clustering by race, some federal courts mandated busing across neighborhoods, moving white students to once predominantly black schools and vice versa. Busing students was not popular and triggered protests in many cities.

The Supreme Court sustained busing only if it was to remedy the consequences of *officially* sanctioned segregation, **de jure segregation**. The Court refused to permit federal judges to order busing to overcome the effects of **de facto segregation**, segregation that arises as a result of social and economic conditions such as housing patterns.

Following *Brown* v. *Board of Education*, the federal government intervened in more than 500 school desegregation cases. As a result, many southern cities now have more integrated schools than large northern cities do. However, in both North and South, many school districts in central cities today are predominantly African American or

de jure segregation
Segregation imposed by law.

de facto segregation
Segregation resulting from economic or social conditions or personal choice.

Hispanic. This segregated pattern of schools is partly the result of "white flight" to the suburbs in the 1970s and 1980s and the transfer of white students to private schools to escape court-ordered busing. In more recent years, it is also due to higher birthrates and immigration among African Americans and Hispanics.

After a period of vigorous federal court supervision of school desegregation programs, the Supreme Court in the 1990s restricted the role of federal judges.[54] It instructed some of them to restore control of a school system to the state and local authorities and to release districts from any busing obligations once a judge concludes that the authorities "have done everything practicable to overcome the past consequences of segregation."[55]

Political support for busing and for other efforts to integrate the schools also faded.[56] Many school districts eliminated mandatory busing, with the result that *Brown*'s era of court-ordered desegregation drew to a close. The percentage of southern blacks attending white-majority schools fell from over 40 percent to 30 percent, or about the level in 1969.[57] Some African American leaders, while still supporting desegregation efforts, are now more concerned about improving the quality of inner-city schools than desegregating them. They are turning to state courts and state constitutions, which mandate equal public education, in order to force increases in public school financing and to make adequate educational resources available to all on equal terms.[58]

RIGHTS OF ASSOCIATION, ACCOMMODATIONS, JOBS, AND HOMES

Association

As we have noted, the Fifth and Fourteenth Amendments apply only to governmental action, not to private discriminatory conduct. As Justice William O. Douglas said, our Constitution creates "a zone of privacy which precludes government from interfering

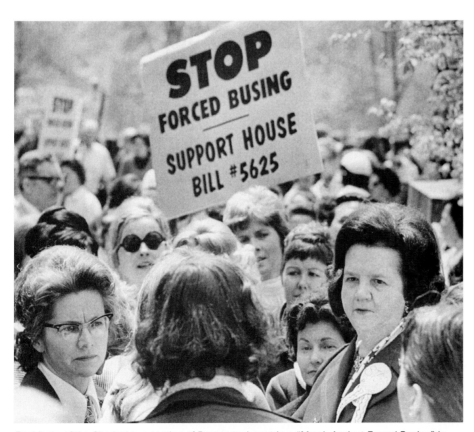

Residents of the Charlestown section of Boston took part in a "March Against Forced Busing" in May 1976.

with private clubs or groups. The associational rights which our system honors permit all-white, all-black, all-brown, and all-yellow clubs to be established. They also permit all-Catholic, all-Jewish, or all-agnostic clubs. . . . Government may not tell a man or a woman who his or her associates must be. The individual may be as selective as he desires."[59]

Families, churches, or private groups organized for political, religious, cultural, or social purposes are constitutionally different from large associations organized along other lines. For example, the Supreme Court has upheld the application of laws forbidding sex or racial discrimination by organizations such as the Jaycees, the Rotary Club, and large (in this case, more than 400 members) private eating clubs. Such associations and clubs are not small, intimate groups. Nor were they able to demonstrate that allowing women or minorities to become members would change the content or impact of their purposes.[60] In *Boy Scouts of America* v. *Dale* (2000), however, the Court held that the Boy Scouts may exclude homosexuals because it is a private association and because of its overall mission.[61]

Accommodations

In 1883, the Supreme Court had declared unconstitutional an act of Congress that made it a federal offense for any operator of a public conveyance, hotel, or theater to deny accommodations to any person because of race or color on the grounds that the Fourteenth Amendment does not give Congress such authority.[62] Since the 1960s, however, the constitutional authority of Congress to legislate against discrimination by private individuals is no longer an issue because the Court has broadly construed the **commerce clause**—which gives Congress the power to regulate interstate and foreign commerce—to justify action against discriminatory conduct by individuals. Congress has also used its power to tax and spend to prevent not only racial discrimination but also discrimination based on ethnic origin, sex, disability, and age.

TITLE II: PLACES OF PUBLIC ACCOMMODATION   For the first time since Reconstruction, the Civil Rights Act of 1964 authorized the massive use of federal authority to combat privately imposed racial discrimination. Title II makes it a federal offense to discriminate against any customer or patron in a place of public accommodation because of race, color, religion, or national origin. It applies to any inn, hotel, motel, or lodging establishment (except establishments with fewer than five rooms and occupied by the proprietor—in other words, small boardinghouses); to any restaurant or gasoline station that serves interstate travelers or serves food or products that have moved in interstate commerce; and to any movie house, theater, concert hall, sports arena, or other place of entertainment that customarily hosts films, performances, athletic teams, or other sources of entertainment that are moved in interstate commerce. Within a few months after its adoption, the Supreme Court sustained the constitutionality of Title II.[63] As a result, public establishments, including those in the South, opened their doors to all customers.

TITLE VII: EMPLOYMENT   Title VII of the 1964 Civil Rights Act made it illegal for any employer or trade union in any industry affecting interstate commerce and employing 15 or more people (and, since 1972, any state or local agency such as a school or university) to discriminate in employment practices against any person because of race, color, national origin, religion, or sex. Employers have an obligation to create workplaces that avoid abusive environments. Related legislation made it illegal to discriminate against persons with physical handicaps, veterans, or persons over 40.

There are a few exceptions. Religious institutions such as parochial schools may use religious standards. Age, sex, or handicap may be considered where occupational qualifications are absolutely necessary to the normal operation of a particular business or enterprise—for example, hiring only women to work in women's locker rooms.

The Equal Employment Opportunity Commission (EEOC) was created to enforce Title VII. The commission works together with state authorities to try to bring about compliance with the act and may seek judicial enforcement of complaints against private employers. The attorney general prosecutes Title VII violations by public agencies. Not only do aggrieved persons have a right to sue for damages for themselves, but they can also do so for other persons similarly situated in a **class action suit**. The vigor with

commerce clause
The clause of the Constitution (Article I, Section 8, Clause 3) that gives Congress the power to regulate all business activities that cross state lines or affect more than one state or other nations.

class action suit
Lawsuit brought by an individual or a group of people on behalf of all those similarly situated.

which the EEOC and the attorney general have acted has varied over the years, depending on the commitment of the president in office and the willingness of Congress to provide an adequate budget for the EEOC.[64]

Title VII was supplemented by a 1965 presidential executive order requiring all contractors doing work for the federal government, including universities, to adopt and implement affirmative action programs to correct "underutilization" of women and minorities. Such programs may not establish racial or ethnic quotas for minorities or women, but they may require contractors to establish timetables and goals; to follow open recruitment procedures; to keep records of applicants by race, sex, and national origin; and to explain why their labor force does not reflect the same proportion of persons in the appropriate labor market pools. Failure of contractors to file and implement an approved affirmative action plan may lead to loss of federal contracts or grants.

THE FAIR HOUSING ACT AND AMENDMENTS Housing is the last frontier of the civil rights crusade, the area in which progress is slowest and genuine change most remote.

> Segregated housing contributes mightily to a vicious circle that also includes educational and employment discrimination. . . . Because of poor schools for many minorities, they cannot find well-paying jobs. Without such jobs, they often cannot afford to live in nicer neighborhoods with decent housing. And because of their location in less desirable communities, good educational systems are less likely to be available.[65]

In 1948, the Supreme Court made racial or religious **restrictive covenants** (a provision in a deed to real property restricting its sale) legally unenforceable.[66] The 1968 Fair Housing Act forbids discrimination in housing, excluding from its protection what it called "Mrs. Murphy boardinghouses," housing owned by private individuals who own no more than three houses; dwellings that have no more than four separate living units in which the owner maintains a residence; and religious organizations and private clubs housing their own members on a noncommercial basis. For all other housing, the act forbids owners to refuse to sell or rent to any person because of race, color, religion, national origin, sex, or physical handicap or because a person has children. Discrimination in housing also covers efforts to deny loans to minorities.

The Department of Justice has filed hundreds of cases, especially those involving large apartment complexes, yet African Americans and Hispanics continue to face discrimination in housing. Some real estate agents continue to steer African Americans and Hispanics toward neighborhoods that are not predominantly white and to require larger rental deposits from minorities than from whites. Yet less than 1 percent of these discriminatory actions are complained about because they are so subtle that victims are often unaware that they are being discriminated against. However, the number of discrimination complaints received by the Department of Housing and Urban Development and local and state agencies has been increasing as the result of more aggressive enforcement.

Voluntary segregation obviously exists. "It's a fact of life that blacks like to live in black neighborhoods and whites like to live in white neighborhoods," according to Daniel Mitchell, who added, "Real estate agents generally like to bring customers to places they will like and where the agent can make a sale."[67] Whatever the reasons, housing segregation persists.

THE AFFIRMATIVE ACTION CONTROVERSY

When white majorities were using governmental power to discriminate against African Americans, civil rights advocates cited with approval the famous words of the first Justice John Marshall Harlan: "Our Constitution is color-blind and neither knows nor tolerates class among citizens."[68] But by the 1960s, there was a new set of constitutional and national policy debates. Many people began to assert that government neutrality is not enough. If governments, universities, and employers stopped discriminating but changed nothing else, individuals previously discriminated against would still be kept from equal participation in American life. Because they had been so disadvantaged by past discrimination,

restrictive covenant
A provision in a deed to real property prohibiting its sale to a person of a particular race or religion. Judicial enforcement of such deeds is unconstitutional.

they suffered disabilities not shared by white males in the competition for openings in medical schools, for skilled jobs, or for their share of government grants and contracts.

Remedies to overcome the consequences of past discrimination against African Americans, Hispanics, Native Americans, and women are known as *affirmative action* by supporters but as *reverse discrimination* by opponents. The Supreme Court's first major statement on the constitutionality of affirmative action programs came in a celebrated case relating to university admissions. Allan Bakke—a white male and a top student at Minnesota and Stanford universities, as well as a Vietnam War veteran—applied in 1973 and again in 1974 to the medical school of the University of California at Davis. In each of those years, the school admitted 100 new students, 84 in a general admissions program and 16 in a special admissions program created for minorities who had previously been underrepresented. Bakke's application was rejected each year while students with lower grade-point averages, test scores, and interview ratings were admitted under the special admissions program. After his second rejection, Bakke brought suit in federal court claiming he had been excluded because of his race, contrary to requirements of the Constitution and Title VI of the Civil Rights Act of 1964.

In *University of California Regents* v. *Bakke* (1978), the Supreme Court ruled the California plan unconstitutional.[69] The problem with the California plan was it created a *quota*—a set number of admissions from which whites were excluded solely because of race. But the Court also declared that affirmative action programs are not necessarily unconstitutional. A state university may properly take race and ethnic background into account as "a plus," as one of several factors in choosing students in order to achieve a diverse student body.

After *Bakke:* Refinements and Uncertainty

Following *Bakke,* the Court dealt with a variety of affirmative action programs in public and private employment, sustaining most but not all of them. As the justices continued to disagree on the application of the equal protection clause, opposition to such programs became more heated.

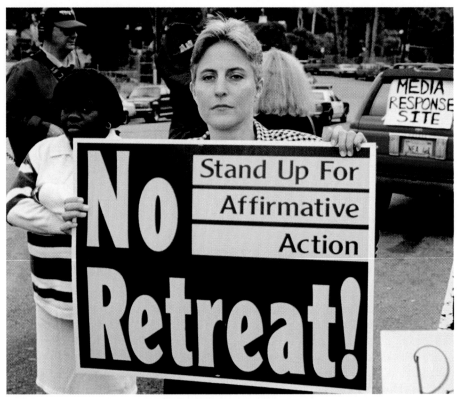

Many Americans believe that affirmative action is the best way to address the issue of past racial and ethnic quotas.

In *Richmond* v. *Croson* (1989), the Rehnquist Court struck down a regulation by the city of Richmond requiring nonminority city contractors to subcontract at least 30 percent of the dollar amount of their contracts to one or more minority business enterprises. Writing for the Court, Justice Sandra Day O'Connor called into question the validity of most government affirmative action plans and stated, "Race-sensitive remedial measures are to be justified only after a strong basis in evidence has established that remedial action is necessary to overcome the consequences of past discriminatory action."[70]

Since *Croson,* a bare majority of the Court has rejected the view that racial classifications, whether benign or hostile, should ever be subject to less than strict scrutiny by either the national or state and local governments.[71] And as we have noted, the Rehnquist Court is similarly opposed to the use of race as the sole criterion in the drawing of electoral district lines.[72] The only permissible programs in government employment and contracting are those that are narrowly tailored remedies for past discrimination.

California's Proposition 209 and Other Plans

In 1995, the Regents of the University of California voted to eliminate race or gender as factors in employment, purchasing, contracting, or admissions. The following year, Californians voted overwhelmingly for Proposition 209 to amend the state constitution to forbid state agencies—including schools, colleges, and universities—to discriminate against or grant preferential treatment to any individual or group on the basis of race, sex, color, ethnicity, or national origin in public employment, public education, or public contracting, except where necessary to comply with a federal requirement.

Although Proposition 209 clearly forbids universities and other state agencies to take race and gender into account, it did not make unconstitutional state-supported outreach programs designed to recruit more women and minorities to become scientists and engineers, nor does it prevent state universities from continuing outreach programs aimed at schools with large minority enrollments. Due to such outreach programs the percentage of students admitted to the University of California from "underrepresented groups"—African Americans, Native Americans, and Hispanics—gradually rebounded.[73] The University of California's board of regents also shifted policy to take into account the economic backgrounds and personal achievements, not just grades and SAT scores, of students applying for admission. As a result, the percentage of racial and ethnic minorities moved back to previous levels, though still low at Berkeley, where Asian Americans make up more than 40 percent of the student body.[74]

Opponents of affirmative action had hoped that the adoption of Proposition 209 in California would start a national movement to restrict or eliminate affirmative action programs, and some federal programs designed to give women- and minority-owned businesses greater access to federal contracts were cut back. Under pressure from the Office of Civil Rights, some universities stopped offering scholarships based solely on race or ethnicity. But Congress has not moved to limit other federal affirmative action programs.

California and six other states (Texas, Louisiana, Mississippi, Georgia, Florida, and Washington) abandoned affirmative action programs—some like California and Washington because of voter opposition and others like Texas and Georgia because federal courts held that they were unconstitutional.[75] They adopted the strategy of automatic admissions for a certain percentage of all high school graduates as a means of maintaining diversity in colleges and expanding educational opportunities for minorities. California offers admission to the top 4 percent of high school graduates, Texas offers admission to the top 10 percent, and Florida to the top 20 percent of every high school graduating class.

These programs, though, have been sharply criticized for taking students from poor inner-city and rural schools who are not prepared to compete effectively in college with students from wealthier and more advantaged school districts. Critics also complain that under the program some students from the top high schools are denied admission to state flagship universities. Texas Republican Governor Rick Perry and others argue that too many graduates of the most demanding high schools are leaving the state when they do not get into the University of Texas at Austin. In 2005, the Texas legislature will

★★ YOU DECIDE

Are affirmative action programs aimed at promoting diversity in education and employment legitimate and worthwhile?

The Supreme Court in *Grutter* v. *Bollinger* (2003) by a five-to-four vote upheld law schools' admissions policies aimed at achieving diverse student bodies through "special efforts" to recruit, but not fixed quotas for, students from groups that have historically been discriminated against, like African Americans, Hispanics, and Native Americans. Do you think affirmative-action programs aimed at promoting diversity in education and employment are legitimate and worthwhile?

consider modifying the program to give universities and colleges more discretion in admissions.[76]

Reaffirming the Importance of Diversity

The controversy and the conflicting lower court decisions on the permissibility of affirmative action in higher education resulted in confusion and uncertainty about the holding in *University of California Regents* v. *Bakke* that colleges and universities may pursue diverse student bodies. Finally, the Supreme Court clarified the matter in 2003, reaffirming *Bakke* in two companion cases challenging the admission policies of the University of Michigan undergraduate college and law school. Both sought to achieve diverse student bodies, but with different kinds of programs.

Jennifer Gratz, a white high school student with a 3.8 GPA, was denied admission to the undergraduate college. She challenged its admissions policy based on a "selection index" that ranked on a 150-point scale applicants' test scores and grades for up to 100 points, and allocated 40 points for other factors, including 4 points for children of alumni, 16 points for residents of rural areas, and 20 points for students from underrepresented minority groups or from socioeconomically disadvantaged familes. Writing for the Court in *Gratz* v. *Bollinger* (2003) over the dissent of Justices Stevens, Souter, and Ginsburg, Chief Justice Rehnquist struck down

Jennifer Gratz, (right) is the successful plaintiff in Gratz v. Bollinger, *a case that struck down the University of Michigan's undergraduate admissions policy that awarded points to applicants based on various factors including racial and ethnic background. Barbara Grutter (left) is the unsuccessful plaintiff in* Grutter v. Bollinger, *a case that challenged the admissions policy of the University of Michigan's law school. Unlike the undergraduate admissions policy, the law school took an applicant's racial and ethnic background into account when considering that applicant's qualifications but did not award points based on this information.*

the policy as too mechanical and not narrowly tailored to giving applicants "individualized consideration" as *Bakke* required.[77]

In *Grutter* v. *Bollinger* (2003), however, a bare majority upheld the law school's affirmative-action policy that made "special efforts" to achieve racial and ethnic diversity.[78] Unlike the undergraduate program, the law school did not use a point system based in part on race. Writing for the Court, Justice O'Connor held that law school admissions were based on a "highly individualized, holistic review of each applicant's file" and did not use race as a factor in a "mechanical way." For that reason, it was consistent with *Bakke*'s holding that race may be used as a "plus factor" in achieving a diverse student body.

Justice O'Connor reaffirmed the importance of diversity, observing: "In order to cultivate a set of leaders with legitimacy in the eyes of the citizenry, it is necessary that the path to leadership be visibly open to talented and qualified individuals of every race and ethnicity." But she also added that, "We expect 25 years from now, the use of racial preferences will no longer be necessary." Chief Justice Rehnquist and Justices Scalia, Kennedy, and Thomas dissented, maintaining that race may never be used as a consideration in college admissions.

The Court thus reaffirmed the importance of diversity in education and employment. Public support for affirmative action as measured in public opinion polls varies by race, social class, education, and life experience, but close inspection suggests that "whites and blacks are not separated by unbridgeable gaps on affirmative action issues, at least not insofar as college admissions decisions are concerned."[79] People's responses seem to depend to a significant degree on how the survey question is put. If the question asked is something like "Are you in favor of abolishing preferences in hiring or college admissions based on race or gender?" most people say yes. But if the question is something like "Do you favor affirmative action programs to increase the number of minorities in colleges or in jobs?" there is general support for such programs.

EQUAL RIGHTS TODAY

Today, legal barriers have been lowered, if not removed, by civil rights legislation, executive orders, and judicial decisions. Important as these victories are, according to civil rights leader James Farmer, "They were victories largely for the middle class—those who could travel, entertain in restaurants, and stay in hotels. Those victories did not change life conditions for the mass of blacks who are still poor."[80]

As prosperous middle-class African Americans have moved out of inner cities, the remaining *underclass,* as they are coming to be called, has become even more isolated from the rest of the nation.[81] There are similar trends in Hispanic communities in Los Angeles, Dallas, and Houston.[82] Children are growing up on streets where drug abuse and crime are everyday events. They live in "separate and deteriorating societies, with separate economies, diverging family structures and basic institutions, and even growing linguistic separation within the core ghettos. The scale of their isolation by race, class, and economic situation is much greater than it was in the 1960s, with impoverishment, joblessness, educational inequality, and housing insufficiency even more severe."[83]

One of the difficulties is that as conditions have become better for many African Americans and Hispanics, the less fortunate see themselves as getting worse off, while most Americans see conditions for minorities as improving. "Both perceptions will be correct. And the fact that both are correct in arriving at opposite perceptions of what is going on will itself lead to further misunderstanding."[84]

> Despite the lack of improvement in social conditions, the push for integration has lessened: In fact, power on both sides of the color line is based to some extent on acceptance of segregation. On the black side of the color line, it is advantageous to keep African Americans within black electoral areas and keep black-controlled resources within black institutions; integrationist policies are often viewed as posing larger

TRAVEL THE CIVIL RIGHTS TIMELINE

This simulation lets you travel through a timeline of significant events in the struggles for civil rights of Native Americans, African Americans, Hispanic Americans, women, and the disabled. It provides links to speeches and biographies of leaders of each of those movements.

Go to Make it Real "Travel the Civil Rights Timeline."

threats than they actually do. On the white side of the line, . . . some residents in outlying suburbs see critical advantages in their almost all-white and all middle-class status.[85]

Some contend that attention should be paid to the plight of the underclass and that instead of focusing on issues of race, what is needed is a focus on class differences and policies that provide jobs and improve education.[86] Others say there has to be a revival of the civil rights crusade, a restoration of vigorous civil rights enforcement, job training, and, above all, an attack on residential segregation.[87] In any event, it is clear that questions as to how best to provide equal opportunities for all citizens remain high on the national agenda.

SUMMARY

1. Americans are committed to "equality," an elusive term, with most support for equality of opportunity, some for equality of starting conditions, and some for equality of results.

2. Progress in securing civil rights for African Americans was a long time coming. After the Civil War, the national government briefly tried to secure some measure of protection for the freed slaves and to enforce the Thirteenth, Fourteenth, and Fifteenth Amendments and the civil rights laws passed to implement them. But when federal troops withdrew from the South in 1877, the national government withdrew from the field, and blacks were left to their own resources. Not for nearly a century did the national government take action to prevent racial segregation and discrimination against blacks.

3. The crusade for women's rights was born partly out of the struggle to abolish slavery. Similarly, the modern women's movement learned and gained power from the civil rights movements of the 1950s and early 1960s. The fate of these two social movements has long been intertwined. Women secured the right to vote in the Nineteenth Amendment.

4. Concern for equal rights under the law continues today for African Americans and women. Hispanics, Asian Americans, and Native Americans have also experienced discrimination.

5. The Supreme Court uses a three-tiered approach to evaluate the constitutionality of laws challenged as violating the equal protection clause. Laws touching economic concerns are sustained if they are rationally related to the accomplishment of a legitimate government goal. Laws that classify people because of gender or sexual orientation are subject by the courts to heightened scrutiny and are sustained only if they serve important governmental objectives. Strict scrutiny is used to review laws that touch fundamental rights or classify people because of race or ethnic origin. Such laws will be sustained only if the government can show a compelling public purpose.

6. A series of constitutional amendments, Supreme Court decisions, and laws passed by Congress have now secured the right to vote to all Americans aged 18 and over. Following the Voting Rights Act of 1965, the Justice Department can oversee practices in locales with a history of discrimination. Recent Supreme Court decisions have refined the lengths to which legislatures can go, or are obliged to go, in creating minority-majority districts.

7. *Brown* v. *Board of Education of Topeka* (1954) struck down the "separate but equal" doctrine that had justified segregated schools in the South, but school districts responded slowly. The Supreme Court demanded compliance, and some federal courts mandated busing children across neighborhoods to comply. Still, full integration has proved elusive, as "white flight" has left many inner cities, and their schools, predominantly black or Hispanic.

8. Discrimination in public accommodations was outlawed by the Civil Rights Act of 1964. This act also provided for equal employment opportunity. The Fair Housing Act of 1968 and its 1988 amendments prohibited discrimination in housing.

9. The desirability and constitutionality of affirmative action programs that provide special benefits to members of groups subjected to past discrimination divide the nation and the Supreme Court. Remedial programs tailored to overcome specific instances of past discrimination are likely to pass the Supreme Court's suspicion of classifications based on race, national origin, and gender. The Court has also reaffirmed the importance of achieving diversity in education and employment.

KEY TERMS

natural rights
affirmative action
women's suffrage
equal protection clause

due process clause
white primary
racial gerrymandering
poll tax

literacy test
majority-minority district
Jim Crow laws
de jure segregation

de facto segregation
commerce clause
class action suit
restrictive covenant

FURTHER READING

TAYLOR BRANCH, *Parting the Waters: America in the King Years, 1954–1963* (Simon & Schuster, 1988).

TAYLOR BRANCH, *Pillar of Fire: America in the King Years, 1963–65* (Simon & Schuster, 1998).

GORDON H. CHANG, ED., *Asian Americans and Politics* (Stanford University Press, 2001).

IRIS CHANG, *The Chinese in America: A Narrative History* (Viking, 2003).

CLARE CUSHMAN, ED., *Supreme Court Decisions and Women's Rights* (CQ Press, 2000).

ARLENE M. DAVILA, *Latinos, Inc.: The Marketing and Making of a People* (University of California Press, 2001).

DAVID DENT, *In Search of Black America: Discovering the African American Dream* (Simon & Schuster, 2000).

JANET DEWART, ED., *The State of Black America* (National Urban League, published annually).

WILLIAM N. ESKRIDGE JR., *Gaylaw: Challenging the Apartheid of the Closet* (Harvard University Press, 2000).

JONATHAN GOLDBERG-HILLER, *The Limits to Union: Same-Sex Marriage and the Politics of Civil Rights* (University of Michigan Press, 2002).

ANDREW HACKER, *Two Nations: Black and White, Separate, Hostile, Unequal* (Scribner, 1992).

RANDALL KENNEDY, *Race, Crime, and the Law* (Pantheon, 1997).

PHILIP A. KLINKER AND ROGER M. SMITH, *The Unsteady March: The Rise and Decline of Racial Equality in America* (University of Chicago Press, 2000).

RICHARD KLUGER, *Simple Justice: The History of Brown v. Board of Education* (Knopf, 1976).

DAVID M. O'BRIEN, *Constitutional Law and Politics: Civil Rights and Civil Liberties*, 6th ed. (Norton, 2005).

GARY ORFIELD, AND CHUNGMEI LEE, *Brown at 50: King's Dream or Plessy's Nightmare* (The Civil Rights Project, Harvard University, 2004).

J. W. PELTASON, *Fifty-Eight Lonely Men: Southern Federal Judges and School Desegregation* (University of Illinois Press, 1971).

RUTH ROSEN, *The World Split Open: How the Modern Women's Movement Changed America* (Viking, 2000).

JOHN DAVID SKRENTNY, ED., *Color Lines: Affirmative Action, Immigration, and Civil Rights Options for America* (University of Chicago Press, 2001).

GIRARDEAU A. SPANN, *The Law of Affirmative Action: Twenty-Five Years of Supreme Court Decisions on Race and Remedies* (New York University Press, 1999).

PHILIPPA STRUM, *Women in the Barracks: The VMI Case and Equal Rights* (University Press of Kansas, 2002).

ROBERTO SURO, *Strangers Among Us: How Latino Immigration Is Transforming America* (Knopf, 1998).

SUSAN F. VAN BURKLEO, *"Belonging to the World": Women's Rights and Constitutional Culture* (Oxford University Press, 2001).

MAKING ECONOMIC AND REGULATORY POLICY

18

Congress and the president received some stunning news in the summer of 1999: For the first time in two decades, the federal government's budget was balanced. Although Congress and the president had set the process in motion with budget agreements in 1990, 1993, and 1997, the news came nearly three years ahead of schedule and showed a much larger surplus in the future than anyone had predicted. Suddenly, the federal government was looking at almost $6 trillion in surpluses over the next ten years.

The balanced budget and projected surplus was the product of three events. Defense spending fell dramatically with the end of the cold war, spending for domestic programs did not rise as fast, largely because the economy was growing, and tax revenues increased more than expected. Practically everything that could go right did go right, and the budget forecast became brighter with each passing month.

Just as surprisingly, perhaps, the budget surplus was gone within three years, in part because just about everything that could go wrong with the economy and the world did go wrong, and in part because Congress and the new Bush administration decided to give $1.3 trillion of the projected surpluses back to the American public in the 2001 tax cuts, subtracted another $300 billion for further tax cuts in 2003 and $400 billion for a new prescription drug plan for the elderly in 2004, and allocated $200 billion for the wars in Afghanistan and Iraq. Suddenly, the $6 trillion in projected surpluses became $3 trillion in projected deficits.

The disappearing surplus shows just how sensitive federal budgets are to unexpected events such as wars and economic downturns, as well as legislative decisions.

TIME LINE

MAKING ECONOMIC AND REGULATORY POLICY

1890	Sherman Antitrust Act seeks to control monopolies
1906	Congress enacts the Pure Food and Drug Act establishing the first regulations of food and drug safety
1913	Federal Reserve Board created
1913	Sixteenth Amendment allows federal income tax
1921	Budget and Accounting Act
1938	Fair Labor Standards Act establishes a 40-hour work week
1947	World Trade Organization is created to facilitate free trade among nations
1967	Clean Air Act begins decades of improving air quality
1970	Occupational Safety and Health Administration regulates safety in the workplace
1974	Congressional Budget Office is created to provide budgetary expertise to Congress
1987	Alan Greenspan is selected as chair of the Federal Reserve
1999	First balanced budget in 30 years

public policy
A specific course of action taken by government to achieve a public goal.

policy agenda
The informal list of issues that Congress and the president consider most important for action.

Having worked for twenty years to get the budget balanced, Congress and the president subtracted much of the money away over a three-month span, leading some critics to argue that Republicans were hoping to "strangle the beast" of big government by denying it the money to create new programs such as national health insurance.

Although there may be some truth to the charge, Congress and the president did not stop spending. Moreover, as the budget deficit increases, so does the national debt and the interest payments the federal government must make to its lenders. Like credit-card debt for individuals, the federal government must pay interest on its bills, too. In 2005, for example, the federal government will spend almost $170 billion in interest, or almost five times as much as aid to college students and their schools.

The preceding chapters concentrated on the structure of our federal system and how government institutions are organized and operate. In this chapter and the two that follow, we focus on what the national government *does*—how voters, interest groups, and institutions (Congress, the White House, the executive branch, the courts) interact to promote the general welfare and provide for the common defense. We will be talking about making and implementing three different kinds of *public policy:* economic, social, and foreign policy.

MAKING PUBLIC POLICY

When government decides to act, it mostly does so through a **public policy**, which is a specific course of action that government takes to address a problem such as the federal budget deficit. A public policy can be conveyed to the public in the laws passed by Congress and signed by the president, opinions issued by the Supreme Court, and/or rules written by the executive branch. But whatever form it takes, a public policy tells the public who is about to get what, when, and how from government.

The Policy Making Process

Every policy reflects a series of separate decisions leading to final implementation and action. The process involves six steps: (1) making assumptions about the world, (2) identifying the problem to be solved, (3) deciding whether to act at all, (4) deciding how much to do, (5) choosing a tool for solving the problem, and (6) making rules for implementation.

The process does not always follow these seven steps in order. Making public policy is an often unpredictable process in which problems and solutions are loosely connected. It can start anywhere in the circle and skip back and forth at will. The result is a policy-making process that is often unpredictable and almost always in flux.[1]

1. *Making Assumptions about the World.* Every government decision involves assumptions about the future. Is the economy going to get stronger? If so, perhaps employment will go up and the costs of supporting the unemployed will go down. Is teenage pregnancy going to increase? If so, perhaps childhood poverty, which increases as more single teenagers have children, will also increase. Is world terrorism going to increase? If so, perhaps the United States needs to strengthen its border security or build an antimissile defense.

   Because there is no sure way to choose among competing assumptions about such a distant future, policy makers often make choices that help sell their particular views of the world. They are often pessimistic about the future when they define problems, but optimistic when they announce specific proposals to fix the problems. The result is that problems may look much worse than they truly are, while solutions may seem likely to work better than they possibly could.

2. *Picking the Problem.* Choosing the problem to be solved is the essential decision in setting the **policy agenda**. The policy agenda, as John Kingdon defines

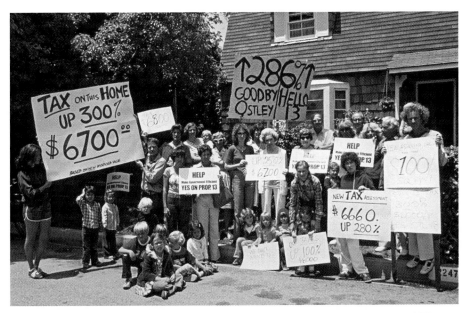

Antitax protests erupted all over the country after Californians passed Proposition 13 in 1978, which placed strict limitations on state government revenues. California voters later enacted limits on state spending.

it, "is the list of subjects or problems to which governmental officials, and people outside of government closely associated with those officials, are paying some serious attention at any given time."[2]

Problems reach the list of possible agenda items from a variety of sources. Some arise from events such as the September 11 terrorist attacks; others because of newspaper or television stories about a controversial issue such as gay marriage; and still others because of interest group pressure. The government monitors a battery of assumptions on the state of the economy, for example, that can show the beginnings of an economic slowdown through the number of jobless claims, the rise of inflation through the consumer price index, or problems in credit through rising or falling interest rates. Readers need only visit www.fedstats.gov to see the range of information government provides to policy makers in search of problems.

3. *Deciding Whether to Act at All.* The fact that a problem exists does not automatically mean Congress and the president will try to solve it. Nothing forces presidents, members of Congress, or judges to act unless doing so will further some goal that they value such as reelection or a place in history. Some problems help policy makers achieve their personal or political goals, in which case they will decide to act, while others do not, in which case they pick other problems to solve.

    Policy makers clearly understand that public pressure for action ebbs and flows over time. In fact, writes political scientist Anthony Downs, "American public attention rarely remains sharply focused upon any one domestic issue for very long—even if it involves a continuing problem of crucial importance to society." According to Downs, attention to problems follows an issue-attention cycle in which each problem "suddenly leaps into prominence, remains there for a short time, and then—though still largely unresolved—gradually fades from the center of public attention."[3]

4. *Deciding How Much to Do.* Once the federal government decides that it wants to do something about a problem, one of its most difficult decisions is how much to do. It can launch a comprehensive program such as Social Security or Medicare, or an incremental program that can be expanded bit by bit over time.

RAISING REVENUE

In the federal budget for fiscal year 2005 (see Figure 18-1), federal receipts include six basic sources of revenue:

1. *Individual income taxes.* Taxes on individual Americans account for more than 40 percent of the federal government's tax revenue. Over the years, the income tax has grown increasingly complex as Congress responded to claims for differing kinds of exemptions and rates. Some members of Congress have advocated simplification or even elimination of the income tax in favor of a national sales tax.

2. *Corporate income taxes.* These taxes account for just under 10 percent of the national government's tax revenues. As late as 1943, revenue from corporate income taxes exceeded that from individual income taxes.

3. *Payroll receipts.* Payroll taxes are the second-largest and most rapidly rising source of federal revenue, accounting for 33.2 percent of all federal revenue, not including borrowing. Most people pay more in Social Security taxes than in federal income taxes. These are highly **regressive taxes**, meaning that low-income people generally pay larger fractions of their income than high-income people do.

4. *Excise taxes.* These taxes on liquor, tobacco, gasoline, telephones, air travel, and other so-called "luxury items" account for roughly 4 percent of federal revenue.

5. *Customs duties and tariffs.* Although no longer the main source of federal income, in recent years these taxes provided an annual yield of almost $20 billion.

6. *Borrowing.* Since World War II, the government has regularly resorted to borrowing money through the sale of federal securities such as savings bonds and treasury bills to private investors, many of whom are located in other nations. The government must pay interest rates on the money it borrows, which in turn becomes a significant cost in the annual federal budget.

distributive policy
A type of policy that provides benefits to all Americans.

redistributive policy
A type of policy that takes benefits (usually through taxes) from one group of Americans and gives them to another (usually through spending).

regressive tax
A tax whereby people with lower incomes pay a higher fraction of their income than people with higher incomes.

The first involves the size of the proposed solution. Will it be an incremental proposal or a major policy reform? Will it involve a slight change in existing regulations or a new federal program? Although major policy reforms are generally much more difficult to pass, in part because they involve more federal spending and/or produce greater regulation, such initiatives allow Congress and the president to claim much greater credit for solving a problem.

The second decision involves the way in which government benefits are to be distributed across the various groups in society. Federal programs that offer new benefits to all groups in society and are funded by all citizens equally are usually described as **distributive policy**. National parks, air traffic control, the interstate highway system, education funding, national defense, and Social Security are all defined as distributive in nature.

In contrast, federal programs that take resources (usually through taxes) from one or more groups in society so that another group can benefit (usually in the form of an entitlement program) are described as **redistributive policy**. Such programs tend to provide benefits to the less fortunate in society, often provoking conflict between the haves and have nots. Welfare, poverty programs, Head Start for poor preschool children, and special programs to help minority groups are often characterized as redistributive. Some political scientists call these programs zero-sum games, meaning that one group's gain (the program's benefits) is another's loss (the program's cost in taxes).

5. *Choosing a Tool.* Public policy scholars generally argue that the federal government has four basic tools available to solve most public problems: (1) spending money, (2) providing goods or services directly, (3) providing protection against risk, and (4) enforcing restrictions and penalties.[4]

Outright money payments are made either directly to individuals or to agencies that provide services to them. Social Security is a direct payment to individuals; Head Start, which provides early-childhood education for disadvantaged children, is funded by the federal government and delivered by local agencies.

Goods and services are provided either completely free to the public or for a price. National parks such as Yosemite and the Grand Canyon generally charge an admission fee; the National Air and Space Museum on the Washington Mall is open to the public for free; and Americans do not pay anything directly for national defense. Ultimately, of course, nothing the government does is completely free—the National Air and Space Museum is supported by general taxes, as is defense.

Protections against risk involve a range of devices to encourage activities where the private sector might otherwise not go. The most familiar protections are federal loan guarantees, under which the government promises to cover the losses in the event that a student, farmer, small business, or other borrower fails to repay a debt. The federal government also provides protection against risk in the form of special exemptions from certain laws. Major league baseball, for example, is exempted from federal antitrust law. The exemption was designed to encourage the expansion of the national pastime, but was never given to professional football, hockey, or basketball.

Restrictions and penalties are designed to encourage or discourage certain behaviors. The list of laws and regulations that limit what individual citizens, associations, and businesses can do is seemingly endless, and includes everything from criminal laws to requirements that all cigarette packages carry the surgeon general's warning that smoking can be dangerous to your health. The violation of a particular law usually results in a government sanction of some kind, usually a fine or imprisonment.

6. *Making Rules for Implementation.* As we shall see later in this chapter, almost everything the federal government does involves a rule. Technically, a government **rule** is a precise legal statement that implements a law. It is issued through a

formal process that tells the public exactly who will get what, when, and how from government, whether, for example, by specifying the amount of sulfur dioxide that can be released from a smokestack, the required height of a wheelchair ramp in a private building, or the number of life jackets that must be on a ferryboat. As such, rules are essential for turning even the most detailed legislation into action, and rule making is the central device used to execute the laws.

Technically, rule making comes at the very end of the policy-making process and is almost invisible to most Americans. Nevertheless, it is the essential step in converting the abstract ideas and language of laws, presidential orders, and court rulings into precise rules governing what individual members of the public, companies, or agencies can or must do.

Policy Making Alliances

Although formal decisions about public policy are made by Congress, the president, and/or the courts, most decisions involve collections of political leaders and interest groups that join together on behalf of a specific cause. Some of these collections exist for decades, while others come together for a specific cause, then disband. The former are often called **iron triangles**, while the latter are labeled **issue networks**.

IRON TRIANGLES By definition, an iron triangle has three sides that hold together over long periods of time: (1) a federal department or agency, (2) a set of loyal interest groups, and (3) a House and/or Senate authorizing committee. Each side supports the other two. Congress gives money to the agency, for example, and gets campaign money and endorsements from the interest groups in return; the interest groups give money and endorsements to Congress and gets special services from the agency in return; the agency gives special services to the interest groups and gets money from Congress in return.

ISSUE NETWORKS As the number of interest groups has increased, iron triangles have been replaced by much looser collections of participants. As political scientist Hugh Heclo has argued, the notion that iron triangles make all policy was "not so much wrong as it was disastrously incomplete" in today's complicated policy environment.[5] Although iron triangles can exist for decades, even centuries, the increasing number of small, highly specialized interest groups makes an iron triangle almost impossible to create, if only because Congress and federal agencies can no longer identify a steady occupant for the third corner of the triangle. They have to find temporary allies, depending on the issue. There is nothing "iron" about such coalitions of smaller groups: They last only as long as a given issue is hot.

Issue networks tend to concentrate power in the relatively small number of individuals that organize and maintain the networks. Like the promoters of rock concerts, these individuals make the key decisions about who participates and what they say. As such, some political scientists refer to the rise of well-financed issue networks such as the ones used to promote prescription drugs for older Americans or tax cuts for business as a form of elitism, not pluralism, in which a very small number of leaders gain significant influence from delaying action as a way to maintain power.

ECONOMIC POLICY

The federal government has been involved in economic policy since the end of the Revolutionary War. The framers wanted a government strong enough to promote free trade, protect patents and trademarks, and enforce contracts between individuals and businesses. And they wanted a government with enough funding so that it could build the postal roads, bridges, railroads, and canals that would allow the young economy to grow.

Much as they worried about the state of the economy, the framers did not concentrate economic policy in any branch. Instead, they divided economic policy-making control between the the legislative and executive branches and between the House and the Senate. Article I, Section 8, of the Constitution gives Congress the power to borrow, coin, and print money yet requires that all bills for raising revenue originate in the House, while Article

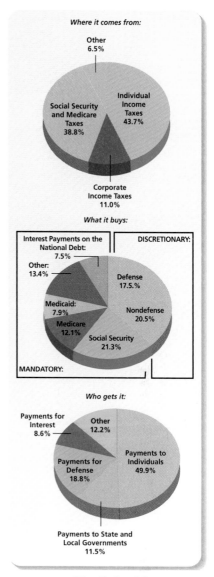

FIGURE 18–1 The Federal Government Dollar, 2005.
SOURCE: Summary Tables, *Budget of the United States, Fiscal Year 2005,* Washington: D.C., U.S. Government Printing Office, February, 2004

rule
A precise legal definition of how government will implement a policy.

iron triangle
A policy making alliance that involves very strong ties among a congressional committee, an interest group, and a federal department or agency.

issue network
A policy making alliance among loosely connected participants that comes together on a particular issue, then disbands.

II, Section 2, gives the president the power to appoint the officers of government who would actually do the borrowing, coining, spending, and taxing yet requires that all officers be confirmed by the Senate. In a similar vein, Article I gives Congress the power to regulate commerce with foreign nations, among the states, and with Native American tribes, while Article II gives the president authority to negotiate the treaties and enforce the laws. Finally, Article I gives Congress the power to establish post offices and build postal roads, which were as important to the free movement of commerce in the 1700s as the highways, rails, and Internet are today, yet Article II gives the president the power to appoint executive officials such as the postmaster general of the United States.

By creating a national government of limited powers and providing constitutional guarantees to protect property from excessive regulation, the framers succeeded in protecting capitalism. More than two centuries later, the U.S. economy is the strongest in the world, and the federal government continues to safeguard the basic conditions needed for capitalism to thrive. Part of the government's role is to stay out of the way as individuals and businesses create wealth through new ideas and hard work, but part is to promote the national welfare through **fiscal policy**, which uses federal spending and taxation to stimulate or slow the economy, and **monetary policy**, which manipulates the supply of money that individuals and businesses have in their hands to keep the economy from swinging wildly from boom to bust. In addition, the federal government promotes economic growth and trade and controls many economic decisions through regulations against certain kinds of business, labor, and environmental practices.

These tools are designed to smooth the ups and downs of the normal *business cycle*. Economists tend to focus on four discrete stages of the cycle: (1) expansion, in which the economy produces new jobs and growth; (2) contraction, as the economy starts to slow down; (3) recession, in which the economy reaches a trough of low growth; and (4) recovery, in which the economy rebounds. The goal of effective economic policy today is to make sure the peaks are not too high and the troughs are not too low. In general, **inflation** is considered the primary policy problem during expansion and recovery, while **unemployment** is considered the greatest problem during contraction and recession.

Inflation is usually measured by the Consumer Price Index (CPI), which shows how much more or less consumers are paying for the same "basket of goods" over time. The major components of the CPI are food, shelter, fuel, clothing, transportation, and medical care. In turn, unemployment is measured simply by the percentage of able-bodied workers who are looking for jobs but cannot find them. It does not measure the number of able-bodied workers who have given up looking for work or who have taken jobs below their skill levels with lower pay.

The federal government exercises less control over the national economy than it does over social or foreign policy. Nevertheless, it keeps a firm hand on many of the gears and levers that guide not only the economy's general direction but the rate at which it moves. These controls are taxes, spending, and borrowing.

FISCAL POLICY

Congress and the president make fiscal policy by taxing, borrowing, and spending money. Nothing reflects the growth of federal programs and the rise of big government more clearly than the increased spending by the national government. In 1933, the federal government spent only $4 billion, about $30 per capita. In 2005, the figure was $2.4 trillion, or more than $8,000 per person.

The Federal Budget

Today federal, state, and local governments spend an amount equal to about one-third of the income of all Americans. The national government is the biggest spender of all—it spends more than all state and local governments combined. Annual spending by the national government accounts for some 23 percent of the gross domestic product (GDP), or nearly one dollar out of every four spent in the U.S. economy. The national debt is approaching $7 trillion, and the United States paid almost $180 billion in 2005 in interest payments on that debt.

fiscal policy
Government policy that attempts to manage the economy by controlling taxing and spending.

monetary policy
Government policy that attempts to manage the economy by controlling the money supply and thus interest rates.

inflation
A rise in the general price level (and decrease in dollar value) owing to an increase in the volume of money and credit in relation to available goods.

unemployment
The number of Americans who are out of work but actively looking for a job. The number does not usually include those who are not looking.

Figure 18–2 The Disappearing Federal Budget Deficit

SOURCE: *Congressional Quarterly Weekly,* January 17, 2004, p. 172.

WHERE THE MONEY COMES FROM "In this world," Benjamin Franklin once said, "nothing is certain but death and taxes." Tax collecting is one of the oldest activities of government. Today the federal government gets most of its funds from payroll taxes for Social Security and Medicare, personal and corporate income taxes, admission fees to federal parks, import taxes, fines, and revenues from the sale of federal products such as maps and data (see Figure 18–1 on page 463).

Putting power over taxation into the hands of the people was a major achievement in the development of self-government. "No taxation without representation" has been a battle cry the world over. The Constitution clearly provided that Congress "shall have Power to lay and collect Taxes, Duties, Imposts, and Excises." **Tariffs** (import duties) and **excise taxes** (consumer taxes on specific kinds of merchandise) have to be levied uniformly throughout the United States.

Raising money is only one objective of taxation. Regulation and, more recently, promoting economic growth are other objectives. In a broad sense, all taxation regulates human behavior. For example, a **progressive tax**—under which people with high incomes pay larger fractions of their incomes than people with low incomes—has a leveling tendency on people's wealth.

Ordinary people borrow money when they face emergency expenses. The same is true of governments. The **deficit** is the difference between the annual revenues raised and the expenditures of government, including the interest on past borrowing. Deficits and surpluses affect the **national debt**, which is the cumulative total of all deficits, minus surpluses, over the years.[6] The debt began growing again in 2002 as revenues fell because of an economic slowdown and tax cuts, while spending increased dramatically with the September 11 relief effort and new measures for homeland security, followed by the wars in Afghanistan and Iraq and their aftermath, and later with prescription drug coverage for the elderly (see Figure 18–2).[7]

Borrowing costs money. The federal government borrows from investors who buy Treasury notes, Treasury bills, and U.S. savings bonds. These investors include individuals (foreign and domestic), U.S. government accounts, banks, and other institutions.

Americans might not be as troubled by the size of the debt if they understood two characteristics of federal borrowing. First, the government owes roughly 90 percent of the money to its own citizens rather than to foreign governments or investors, although the amount owed to foreigners is growing. Second, the economic strength and resources of the country are more significant than the size of the debt.

tariff
Tax levied on imports to help protect a nation's industries, labor, or farmers from foreign competition. It can also be used to raise additional revenue.

excise tax
Consumer tax on a specific kind of merchandise, such as tobacco.

progressive tax
A tax graduated so that people with higher incomes pay a larger fraction of their income than people with lower incomes.

deficit
The difference between the revenues raised annually from sources of income other than borrowing and the expenditures of government, including paying the interest on past borrowing.

national debt
The total amount of money the federal government has borrowed to finance deficit spending over the years.

WHERE THE MONEY GOES   Much of the money the federal government takes in is spent on benefit payments to individuals and national defense. Measured in absolute dollars spent in 2005, almost half of federal spending went to required benefit payments for individuals such as Social Security, Medicare, Medicaid, and other major social programs (again, see Figure 18–1 on page 463).

The proportions do not change when spending is measured as a percentage of the nation's **gross domestic product (GDP)**, which is an estimate of the total output of all U.S. economic activity. Spending on domestic **entitlement** programs, such as Social Security, Medicare, and unemployment insurance, to which qualified citizens are "entitled" by national legislation runs at about 11 percent of the GDP. Spending for defense is a little more than 3 percent of GDP, payments on the deficit make up another 3 percent of GDP, and nondefense discretionary spending comes to just over 3 percent.

Years ago, revenues and outlays were so small that federal tax and spending decisions had little impact on the overall economy. In today's $2.4 trillion federal budget, even small changes in taxes and spending can alter the direction of the economy. However, because many federal programs are open to all eligible citizens, much of the federal budget is "uncontrollable." The most uncontrollable parts of the budget are Social Security, Medicare, unemployment benefits, health benefits for the poor through Medicaid, and interest on the national debt.

The Budget Process

Before Congress enacted the Budget and Accounting Act of 1921, each executive agency dealt with Congress on its own, requesting that Congress appropriate funds for its activities with little or no presidential coordination. In 1921, the Bureau of the Budget (changed to the Office of Management and Budget in 1970) was created in the Treasury Department, and for the first time, the executive branch presented one budget to Congress.

THE EXECUTIVE BRANCH   The federal government's fiscal year begins on October 1. The budget process begins nearly two years in advance, when the various departments and agencies estimate their needs and propose their budgets to the president.[8] While Congress is debating the budget for the coming fiscal year, the agencies are making estimates for the year after that (see Table 18–1). Agency officials take into account not only their needs as they see them but also the overall presidential program and the probable reactions of Congress. Departmental budgets are detailed; they include estimates of expected needs for personnel, supplies, office space, and the like.

The **Office of Management and Budget (OMB)**, a staff agency of the president, handles the next phase. OMB budget examiners review each agency's budget and reconcile

gross domestic product (GDP)
The total output of all economic activity in the nation, including goods and services.

entitlements
Government programs, such as unemployment insurance, disaster relief, and disability payments, that provide benefits to all eligible citizens.

Office of Management and Budget (OMB)
Presidential staff agency that serves as a clearinghouse for budgetary requests and management improvements for government agencies.

TABLE 18–1   STEPS IN THE BUDGET PROCESS, FISCAL YEAR 2006

February–December 2004	Executive branch agencies develop requests for funds, which are reviewed by the Office of Management and Budget and forwarded to the president for final decision.
December 2004	The formal budget documents are prepared.
January–February 2005	The budget is transmitted to Congress as a formal message from the president.
March–September 2005	Congress reviews the president's proposed budget, develops its own budget, and approves spending and revenue bills.
October 1, 2005	Fiscal year 2006 begins.
October 1, 2005–September 30, 2006	Executive branch agencies execute the budget provided in law.
October–November 2006	Data on actual spending and receipts for the completed fiscal year become available.

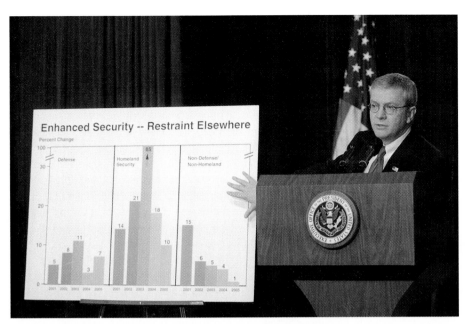

White House budget director Josh Bolton discussing President Bush's 2005 budget proposal. The proposed budget called for an increase in spending on the military and on homeland security and cuts in spending on domestic programs.

it with the president's overall plans. OMB then holds informal hearings with every department and agency to give each one a chance to clarify and defend its estimates.

Once this give-and-take is over, the OMB director gives the president a single, consolidated set of estimates of both revenue and expenditures—the product of perhaps a year's work. The president takes several days to review these figures and make adjustments. The budget director also helps the president prepare a budget message that will stress key aspects of the budget and tie it to broad national goals. The president must submit the budget recommendations and accompanying message to Congress between the first Monday in January and the first Monday in February. The president's budget recommendations cover thousands of pages.

THE LEGISLATIVE BRANCH Presidential submission of a budget proposal is only the beginning. Under our Constitution, Congress must appropriate the funds and raise the taxes. But the president also plays a role, since all appropriations and tax proposals are subject to a presidential veto. Thus the White House is an active participant in the congressional budget battles. When Congress acts on the budget, it does so by first approving the overall budget resolution. Then the actual appropriation of funds is detailed in 13 different bills, each of which is presented to the president for approval.

Congress adopted the Budget and Impoundment Control Act of 1974 to enhance its role in the budget process. This act specifies that the president must include proposed changes in tax laws, estimates of amounts of revenue lost through existing preferential tax treatments, and five-year estimates of the costs of new and continuing federal programs. The act also calls on the president to seek authorizing legislation for a program a year before asking Congress to fund it.

The 1974 Budget Act also created the **Congressional Budget Office (CBO)**, which gave Congress its own independent agency to prepare budget data and analyze budgetary issues. By February 15 of each year, CBO furnishes its analysis of the presidential recommendations to the House and Senate budget committees. CBO also provides Congress with biannual forecasts of the economy, analyzes alternative fiscal policies, prepares five-year cost estimates for bills proposed by congressional committees, and undertakes studies requested by committees. CBO also monitors the results of congressional action on individual appropriations and revenues against the targets or ceilings specified by legislation.

Such budget reform efforts did not by themselves balance the budget, but they did set in place a discipline and a mind-set that moved toward balancing the budget. Equally

Congressional Budget Office (CBO)
An agency of Congress that analyzes presidential budget recommendations and estimates the costs of proposed legislation.

IN COMPARATIVE PERSPECTIVE

TAXING POLICY IN THE UNITED STATES AND DENMARK

One way to compare nations is to ask how much citizens pay in income taxes. The higher the amount paid, the larger the national government is likely to be. Because income taxes are progressive in nature, they allow for the redistribution of income from wealthier households to low-income households.

Much as Congress and the president complain that Americans are overtaxed, the United States actually ranks well down the list of Western democracies in its income tax rates. Although it makes up the difference through an across-the-board Social Security and Medicare tax on all workers, as well as state and local sales taxes, its overall tax rate is roughly half as high as that in Denmark and other Scandinavian countries.

The difference is in what Denmark provides in government services. Whereas the United States provides help for needy and older Americans on a more selective basis, Denmark has a universal system of support that covers every citizen regardless of their income. The Danish government provides free health care, retirement pensions, and free college education, including some living expenses, for all of its citizens. It also pro-

vides child care, paid maternity leave, and unemployment support and welfare for those who qualify. Families also receive a government allowance for each child under the age of 18.

The Danish government also runs nursing homes, homeless shelters, children's homes, and alcohol and drug treatment centers, which are often provided in the United States through charitable institutions. These benefits are not only guaranteed for Danish citizens, they are often provided in government-run facilities such as hospitals and clinics.

Although the United States provides health coverage to older Americans and poor families and children, its coverage is less generous and often requires co-payments by participants. Moreover, the United States generally gives its citizens cash assistance to purchase health care and other services from private, not government, providers and sets time limits on how long needy Americans can receive services. In general, Denmark imposes few, if any, time limits.

As a result, Denmark's government spends more money on each citizen and must raise more money through taxes, hence the significant difference between what U.S. and Danish citizens pay each year to their governments.

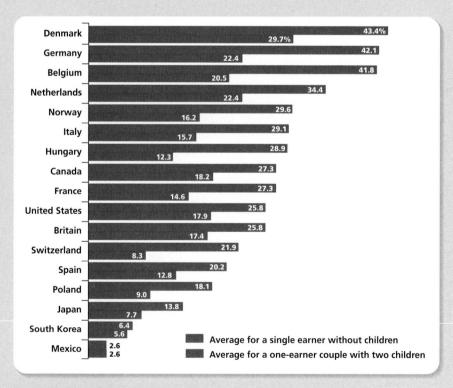

Percentage of Wages Full-Time Workers Pay in Income Taxes in Selected Countries.

NOTE: The rates include contributions to social insurance and retirement funds, less cash benefits paid, such as child allowances.

SOURCE: "Tax Burdens," *The Washington Post,* September 30, 2000, p. A14.

if not more important was the economic boom of the 1990s, which generated huge tax revenues that helped achieve the first budget surpluses in 30 years.

The Politics of Taxing and Spending

In addition to raising funds to run the government, taxes also promote economic growth and reward certain types of behavior, such as owning a home, contributing to charities, and investing in high-risk but desirable (from a national standpoint) energy or housing ventures. Cynics suggest, too, that from a member of Congress's point of view, tax legislation has the additional and important function of raising campaign funds. As long as tax legislation is under consideration, lobbyists will be more inclined to contribute.[9]

Among people outside government, no one likes taxes, but nearly everyone realizes how necessary they are. There is considerable disagreement about the best type of tax. Some say a *progressive income tax* (also called a *graduated income tax*) is best because it is relatively easy to collect, hits hardest those who are most able to pay, and hardly touches those at the bottom of the income ladder. Others argue that *excise taxes* are the fairest because they are paid by people who spend money for luxury goods and thus obviously have money to spare. In addition, by discouraging people from buying expensive goods, excise taxes occasionally have a deflationary effect when prices are on the rise. However, excise taxes are more expensive to collect than income taxes. In some cases, such as the tax on tobacco, they may hit the poor the hardest. Excise taxes also face strong resistance from affected industries—tobacco, liquor, and airlines, for example.

The most controversial tax is a general **sales tax**, which is levied by all but a few states on the sale of most goods, sometimes exempting food and drugs. Labor and liberal organizations see sales taxes as *regressive:* Because a sales tax is the same for all persons, these taxes are not related to a taxpayer's ability to pay, and poor persons pay a higher percentage of their income in sales taxes for the goods and services they buy than rich people do. Proponents of a national sales tax stress its potential anti-inflationary effect and point to its successful use in a number of states.

The sales tax is exclusively a state and local tax in the United States, but in Europe a similar tax, a **value-added tax (VAT)**, is used to raise revenues for central governments. The VAT differs from a sales tax in that it collects a tax on the increased value of a product *at each stage of production and distribution* rather than just at the point of sale, as with a sales tax. A loaf of bread would thus have value added several times: The farmer would pay a value-added tax on the grain before selling to the miller, who would be taxed before selling to the baker, and so forth. The value-added tax is seen by some as a way to infuse a large amount of new revenue into the federal government. Opponents of the tax see it as regressive and increasing the tax burden. States see a federal VAT as invading their turf. Since it taxes consumption and not savings, a VAT could encourage savings and investment, both of which are vital to economic growth.

Tax Expenditures

Tax expenditures are a final type of fiscal policy that uses the tax code to provide special tax incentives or benefits to individuals and businesses for economic goals such as home ownership, retirement savings, and college education. These benefits, which now total more than $400 billion each year, come from special exclusions, exemptions, or reductions from gross income or from special credits, preferential tax rates, or deferrals of tax liability.

Tax expenditures are one means by which the national government carries out public policy objectives. For example, the government encourages investment in research and development by allowing such costs to be deducted from a company's taxes. Federal grants could also achieve this objective.

Critics assert that the rich get their "welfare" through such loopholes. This form of "welfare" does not require a visible appropriation of money plainly identified in the budget. However meritorious the objectives of tax expenditures are—encouraging home ownership, research and development, retirement savings—these tax benefits do not benefit all levels of society. In many instances, they lead investors to put their money into low-yield investments to obtain large tax benefits, which in turn pulls money out of more productive parts of the economy.

sales tax
General tax on sales transactions, sometimes exempting food and drugs.

value-added tax (VAT)
A tax on increased value of a product at each stage of production and distribution rather than just at the point of sale.

tax expenditure
Loss of tax revenue due to federal laws that provide special tax incentives or benefits to individuals or businesses.

MONETARY POLICY

Monetary policy is the second way the national government manages the economy. The core element of **monetarism** is the idea that prices, incomes, and economic stability reflect growth in the amount of money that circulates through the economy at any one time. Monetarists contend that money supply is the key factor affecting the economy's performance and that restrained yet steady growth in the money supply will encourage solid economic growth but not inflation.

The Federal Reserve System

Monetary policy is not made by either Congress or the president but by the Board of Governors of the **Federal Reserve System** (often simply called "the Fed"), specifically its Federal Open Market Committee. The members of the committee, some of the most powerful people in the United States, have a lot to say about how much interest you pay on the car you are buying and whether you refinance your home because of lower interest rates. They can stimulate the economy so that it could be easier for you to find a job or slow it down so that it could be harder. Who are these people with so much power, and how do they influence economic policy?

The Fed's Board of Governors consists of a chair and six other members who are appointed by the president with the consent of the Senate to 14-year terms, with one member's term expiring every two years. These long, staggered terms are intended to insulate members from politics as much as possible. They supervise 12 regional Federal Reserve banks, each headed by a president and governed by a nine-member board of directors chosen from the private banking business in that region.

The 12 members of the Fed's Open Market Committee are all professional economists or bankers. Though their names are unfamiliar to most people, this group, which meets every six to eight weeks, decides how much money will be allowed to enter the economy, manages foreign currency operations, and regulates banks. It does this by buying and selling government securities, which can encourage either lower or higher interest rates. Other lenders closely watch the decisions of the Fed and typically make their interest rates consistent with Fed decisions. Because lenders make it either more or less expensive to borrow money, they influence a wide range of economic activity.

The chair of the Board of Governors, by tradition an economist, is appointed by the president to a four-year term. The current chair, Alan Greenspan, is one of the most influential national public policy officials. Greenspan was first appointed by President Ronald Reagan in 1987 and reappointed by Presidents George H. W. Bush and Bill Clinton. Greenspan's leadership had helped foster economic growth and was widely respected by financial leaders, factors that influenced Clinton's decision to reappoint him. The staff of the Fed reports directly to the chair, not to the board, and the chair is the one who appears before Congress and the country to explain the policies of the Federal Reserve System. The chair heads the Federal Open Market Committee and is credited or blamed for the decisions made by the Fed.

The Fed has three basic tools for influencing the economy. First, it can change the discount rate that determines how much banks must pay for borrowing money. Raising rates slows down the economy by increasing costs for money and credit; lowering rates stimulates the economy by making money more easily available for investment and growth.

Second, the Fed buys and sells federal debt. Selling federal debt to the public tends to slow down the economy by taking dollars out of circulation that could have been used for investment or growth, while buying federal debt back from the public tends to free up money that can be used for new activities, thereby stimulating the economy.

Third, the Fed determines how much money nationally chartered banks must keep in their reserves. Raising the requirement tends to slow down the economy by reducing the funds banks have available to lend to the public for investment and growth, while decreasing the requirement injects more money into the economy.

monetarism
A theory that government should control the money supply to encourage economic growth and restrain inflation.

Federal Reserve System
The system created by Congress in 1913 to establish banking practices and regulate currency in circulation and the amount of credit available. It consists of 12 regional banks supervised by the Board of Governors. Often called simply *the Fed.*

PEOPLE & POLITICS *Making a Difference* ★★★

ALAN GREENSPAN, INFLATION BUSTER

Already regarded as one of the most important economic policy makers of the late twentieth century, Federal Reserve Board chair Alan Greenspan may well be remembered more for stopping inflation than promoting growth. Appointed to his post in 1987 by Ronald Reagan, Greenspan is best described as a monetarist who used the Fed to promote his view that the economy can only grow so fast before it ignites inflation.

Greenspan is best known for using interest rates to either stimulate or slow down the economy. As the economy worsened in late 2000 and early 2001, for example, the Fed began cutting interest rates to stimulate demand. In all, the Fed cut its federal funds rate 11 times in 2001, dropping the amount banks charge each other to borrow money from 6.5 percent in January to just 1.75 by December. When the economy did not respond, the Fed lowered the rate again to 1.25 percent in Novem-

ber 2002, and to just 1.0 pecent in June 2003, where it remained through most of 2004. Worried about inflation, the Fed raised the rate to 1.25 in June 2004, 1.50 in August 2004, 1.75 in September 2004, 2.0 in November 2004, and 2.25 in December 2004.

Whether as an inflation fighter or a recession breaker, Greenspan is now one of the world's most watched economic leaders. Although he once joked that he had learned "to mumble with great incoherence" early on at the Fed, he also knew the power of words to slow the economy. In December 1996, for example, he wondered out loud whether the stock market was suffering from what he called "irrational exuberance," which prompted an immediate 145-point drop in the Dow Jones Industrial Average, the most widely followed stock indicator.

Greenspan finished his doctorate in economics in 1977, after leaving the Ford

administration. He starts each day with a 2½-hour hot bath to soothe his ailing back. It is time he uses to read memos and analyze the latest economic data. "The unsung hero at the Fed is the assistant who has to read his waterlogged scribblings," says his wife, Andrea Mitchell, an NBC News correspondent. How interesting to think that the major architect of contemporary economic policy makes some of his toughest choices in the bathtub.

Government and Economic Policy

Depression is a hard teacher, and the 1930s had a tremendous impact on American thinking about the role of government in the economy. The Great Depression that began in 1929 brought mass misery. "One vivid, gruesome moment of those dark days we shall never forget," wrote one observer. "We saw a crowd of some fifty men fighting over a barrel of garbage which had been set outside the back door of a restaurant. American citizens fighting for scraps of food like animals!"[10]

The Depression continued despite Franklin D. Roosevelt's New Deal economic agenda, which pumped new money into the economy, created hundreds of thousands of federally subsidized jobs, and established new regulations governing the financial markets. Faint signs of recovery could be seen in the mid-1930s, but a new recession in 1937 and 1938 indicated that the country was by no means out of the woods. Between 8 and 9 million people were jobless in 1939. Then came World War II, and unemployment seemed cured. Millions of people had more income, more security, and higher standards of living. Lord Beveridge in England posed a question that bothered many thoughtful Americans: "Unemployment has been practically abolished twice in the lives of most of us—in the last war and in this war. Why does war solve the problem of unemployment which is so insoluble in peace?"[11]

There were several theories about what the federal government could do to stimulate the economy at the time. Some economists urged the government to reduce spending, lower taxes, curb the power of labor, and generally leave business and the economy alone. This first theory is called **laissez-faire economics**.

laissez-faire economics
Theory that opposes governmental interference in economic affairs beyond what is necessary to protect life and property.

GLOBAL *Perceptions*

QUESTION: Does the phrase "there is economic prosperity" describe your country very well, somewhat well, not too well, or not well at all?

Economic prosperity is a very important goal for citizens around the world, but many countries are far from the goal. But whether the citizens of a country believe their nation is actually prosperous varies in part by the degree to which their economies are getting better in a relative sense. Thus, even though their nations are poor by comparison with the United States, the citizens of Honduras, Vietnam, Pakistan, and Uzbekistan are actually the most likely to say their countries are the most prosperous. In turn, some of the world's most prosperous nations have the least satisfied citizens, in part because they have come to expect better economic performance.

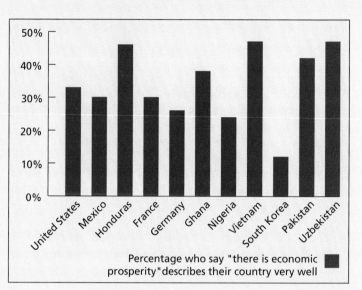

Percentage who say "there is economic prosperity" describes their country very well

SOURCE: Pew Global Attitudes Project, 2003, p. 81.

Another group, deeply influenced by the work of English economist John Maynard Keynes,[12] recommended that when consumer spending and investment decline, government spending and investing should increase. Government must do the spending and investing during a recession because private enterprise will not or cannot. This second theory is called **Keynesian economics**. Roosevelt embraced Keynesian economics and pushed for much greater spending by the federal government as the answer to continued hard times.

Keynesian economics influences government management of the economy to this day. Yet politically, Keynesian economics presents a problem. It is much easier to increase spending and government programs than it is to curb them. As a result, deficit spending became a habit in this country for 50 years. To stimulate demand, the government spent more money than it took in. For many years, this policy was thought to be beneficial to the economy. It was also convenient politically. However, when the national debt soared, both Congress and the president searched for ways to balance the budget.

PROMOTING ECONOMIC GROWTH

Federal economic policy involves more than the effort to smooth the ups and downs of the business cycle. It also involves efforts to promote economic growth, often measured by the number of new jobs or businesses created. In doing so, it helps create jobs for individual Americans, which in turn produces higher revenues, which in turn produces either greater savings or more federal spending.

Promoting Business

The national government promotes a prosperous economy through its monetary and fiscal policies. It also provides various services to business and industry through an economic development infrastructure composed of several dozen departments and agencies, including the Departments of Agriculture and Commerce and the Small Business Administration.

The Department of Commerce is the most visible business promoter within the federal bureaucracy and is sometimes known as the nation's "service center for business." Its cabinet secretary, usually a person with an extensive business background, is

Keynesian economics
Economic theory based on the principles of John Maynard Keynes stating that government spending should increase during business slumps and be curbed during booms.

a spokesperson for business interests. Historically, the department has been at the center of the government's efforts to promote economic growth and encourage business research and development.

The Department of Commerce also encourages innovation through the protection of intellectual property. Its Patent and Trademark Office (PTO) administers the patent system that Congress established "to promote the Progress of Science and useful Arts" under Article I of the Constitution. Each year, the PTO issues more than 100,000 patents to cover new and useful inventions that provide their owners certain exclusive rights for 17 years. The number of patents issued annually almost doubled during the economic expansion of the 1990s, but fell back during the 2001–2002 economic downturn.

The Department of Agriculture continues to provide ample support for farmers, including federal subsidies for corn, barley, oats, wheat, soybeans, cotton, and rice. Under a mix of programs that cost more than $15 billion in 2005 alone, the federal government either guarantees farmers a minimum price for their crops or pays a fee for not planting their fields. The department also provides a host of services to farmers, from education on how to generate higher yields to research on everything from blueberries to forest management. Although these payments were originally designed to help small family farmers, research by the Environmental Working Group, a Washington, D.C., advocacy group, showed that two-thirds of all payments from 1996 to 2000 went to just 10 percent of farmers, most of whom owned large tracts of land.[13]

Speaking at the Chinese University of Finance and Economics in Beijing, U.S. Trade Representative Robert Zoellick makes a point while answering a student's question.

Promoting International Trade

The United States experienced its first **trade deficit** in in more than a century when the amount of imports exceeded the value of exports in 1971. Since then, the nation has had trade deficits in the billions of dollars every year. Congress and the president are under continuing pressure from industry, unions, and regional political leaders to protect American jobs, companies, and communities from foreign competition. These pressures come not only from the textile and auto industries but also from glass, steel, shoes, lumber, electronics, book publishing, aluminum, farming, and domestic wine and spirit coalitions, to name just a few. These leaders claim that the trade deficit justifies the imposition of trade sanctions.

The problem, however, is not that the United States is importing too much but that it is exporting too little. German cars, Japanese technology, and Indonesian textiles are fine products; if other countries produce better cars or shoes at a lower price, free traders argue, the United States should buy from them and direct our labor and capital to areas in which it can do better.

The question is also whether U.S. products are given fair treatment by other nations. American agricultural products are denied entry into some countries and are subject to high tariffs in others. American automobile manufacturers complain of unfair restrictions imposed by the Japanese on our cars. Finally, some countries exploit the U.S. advantage in technology by slavishly copying our products and then selling them back to us or to other countries at a profit.

Another unfair trade practice is *dumping*—selling products below the cost of manufacturing or below their domestic price with the intention of driving other producers out of the market and then raising prices to profitable levels. Another practice is government *subsidizing* of certain industries. Some countries, for example, subsidize steel for export. Others require lengthy inspection procedures for imported goods. Japan has protected several of its industries—producers of automobiles, baseball bats, and even chopsticks, for example—by setting standards that are virtually impossible for U.S. manufacturers to meet. Japan also sets limits on rice imports.

In 1947, a group of countries formed a trade organization to negotiate free trade by lowering tariffs (taxes on imports that raise their price) and quotas (limits on the quantity of a particular product that may be imported) and other disadvantages countries face when trading. Today the **World Trade Organization (WTO)**, based on the **General Agreement on Tariffs and Trade (GATT)**, includes more than 130 countries, and its membership accounts for four-fifths of the world's trade. The WTO has negotiated agreements through eight rounds of trade negotiations (the most recent was called the Uruguay Round, named after the site of the initial conference).

trade deficit
An imbalance in international trade in which the value of imports exceeds the value of exports.

World Trade Organization (WTO)
International organization derived from the General Agreement on Tariffs and Trade (GATT) that promotes free trade around the world.

General Agreement on Tariffs and Trade (GATT)
An international trade organization with more than 130 members, including the United States and the People's Republic of China, that seeks to encourage free trade by lowering tariffs and other trade restrictions.

★ ★ YOU DECIDE

SHOULD THE UNITED STATES PROHIBIT OUTSOURCING?

Free trade has many economic benefits, not the least of which is access to inexpensive goods made in other countries. But it also carries costs, most notably in the loss of jobs in the United States. Between 2004 and 2015, the United States will export, or outsource, more than 3.3 million jobs to other nations, including hundreds of thousands of computer programming, accounting, data entry, and customer service jobs that used to be held by American workers. Concerns about the job losses have led some labor leaders to call for penalties on companies that convert higher-paying U.S. jobs into much lower-paying jobs abroad.

The United States has tried to focus WTO and GATT negotiations on trade in agricultural items, foreign investment, and protection of technological innovations and intellectual property. Although U.S. imports and those of other countries still face many trade restrictions, the WTO and GATT have greatly helped lower tariffs and quotas and increase fair trade throughout the world. Many analysts maintain that GATT is one of the most successful innovations in the history of international relations and one of the contributing factors to the United States' economic success since the end of the cold war.[14]

Not everyone believes that free trade should be unlimited, however. Labor unions, environmentalists, and human rights advocates argue that U.S. trade policies spur the creation of low-wage jobs abroad and encourage child labor, pollution, and worker abuse.

THE NORTH AMERICAN FREE TRADE AGREEMENT In 1992, the United States, Canada, and Mexico signed the **North American Free Trade Agreement (NAFTA)**, which formed the largest geographical free trade zone in the world, even surpassing the European Community's 15-country conglomerate. Although President George Bush signed NAFTA near the end of his presidency, the agreement could not become law until ratified by Congress. President Bill Clinton promoted NAFTA, even though many members of his own party were its most vigorous opponents. Congress passed NAFTA by a thin margin in a bipartisan vote in which the Democrats were the minority.

Though trade among the United States, Canada, and Mexico is not absolutely "free" or unimpeded, the agreement has had a tremendous impact on the economies of all three countries. Today Mexico is the United States' third most important trading partner, and the United States is Mexico's most important trading partner. Critics of NAFTA remain concerned because Mexican antipollution laws are significantly less stringent than those in the United States, and Mexican workers work for considerably lower wages. Both of these factors make relocation to Mexico attractive to many U.S. companies seeking to lower labor and pollution control costs.

Recent reports suggest that many of those lower-paid jobs in Mexico have moved to China. Hourly wages in Tijuana, Mexico, range from $1.50 to $2.00, well below the U.S. minimum wage of $5.15 per hour but well above the 25 cents per hour paid in China. More than 500 low-wage assembly line factories in Mexico closed between 2000 and 2002, due largely to the migration of jobs in the global economy to Asia.[15]

REMOVING BARRIERS TO FREE TRADE Worries about the migration of jobs often leads to calls for **protectionism**, which can take the form of special taxes, or tariffs, placed on imported goods. Most economists oppose protectionism because it prevents efficient use of resources and because consumers pay much more for protected products than they otherwise would in the world economy. Tariffs merely divert attention from real solutions like increased productivity and capital investments and inevitably invite retaliation from foreign countries.

In the 1930s, many nations experienced high unemployment, low production, and general economic misery. The United States was no exception. In an effort to aid ailing American industries, Congress passed the Smoot-Hawley tariff, the highest general tariff the United States had ever had. Supporters hoped high tariffs on imported goods would increase the demand for goods produced in the United States and thus help get the country out of the Great Depression. The exact opposite occurred. Other nations retaliated with high tariffs on American goods. Demand fell, intensifying the Depression.

Later, Congress gave the president power to negotiate mutual tariff reductions with other nations, subject to certain restrictions, and by the early 1970s, tariffs on industrial products had been substantially reduced. Trade barriers are less severe today than they were back in the 1930s. But restrictions still exist. Certain tariffs, quotas on imported goods, and import regulations limit American consumption of foreign products. Most exist to protect American farmers, businesses, or workers in certain industries. Thus we have restrictions on clothing and textile imports, and these restrictions cost U.S. consumers a lot more than they benefit workers' wages.

The United States has generally supported increased trade and fewer trade barriers, yet many Americans worry that globalization will hurt the country. Free trade and

North American Free Trade Agreement (NAFTA)
Agreement signed by the United States, Canada, and Mexico in 1992 to form the largest free trade zone in the world.

protectionism
Policy of erecting trade barriers to protect domestic industry.

globalization policies do not confer equal benefits on everyone. Inevitably, some workers will be worse off as a result of a freer international flow of goods and capital. All told, trade barriers cost U.S. consumers approximately $80 billion a year—equal to more than $1,200 per family.[16] At least some of these barriers helped save U.S. jobs, however, while protecting the environment and promoting human rights abroad.

U.S. economic policy in the future will probably be a combination of free trade and selective protectionism. Though protectionism shields highly visible industries from competition at home or abroad, such measures often constitute a kind of subsidy that protects one industry at the expense of another—and always at high cost to American consumers.

Even free trade advocates can occasionally find a reason, often political, for protectionism. In March 2002, for example, President George W. Bush imposed 30 percent tariffs on a range of products made with imported steel in an effort to protect the ailing U.S. steel industry. In doing so, he honored a campaign promise he had made in Ohio, Pennsylvania, and West Virginia, which were key battleground states in his 2000 campaign.

There is no question that steel imports hurt the U.S. industry. Nearly 50,000 jobs were lost between 1997 and 2002 because of bankruptcies and factory closings, and more than 300,000 jobs were at risk. As European steel makers complained to the World Trade Organization, however, the international economy was merely working its will by rewarding more efficient foreign steelmakers with a bigger market. The WTO agreed that the U.S. tariffs violated free trade rules, forcing the United States to drop the tariffs or face international retaliation on a range of products from Florida oranges to North Carolina tobacco. In December 2003, the Bush administration dropped the tariffs.

REGULATING THE ECONOMY

The Constitution explicitly authorizes Congress to regulate commerce among the states and with foreign nations. In our earliest years, Congress used this regulatory power to impose or suspend tariffs on imports from other nations. In the nineteenth century, the federal government created a number of agencies to regulate the conduct of citizens and commercial enterprises with an eye toward promoting economic development. Among these were the Army Corps of Engineers (1824), the Patent and Trademark Office

★★ THINKING IT THROUGH

Although outsourcing clearly hurts U.S. workers in the short term, most economists agree that efforts to stop the movement would hurt the economy in the longer term. "Protectionism will do little to create jobs," Federal Reserve Board Chairman Alan Greenspan said in 2004, "and if foreigners retaliate, we will surely lose jobs. We need to discover the means to enhance the skills of our work force and to further open markets here and abroad." Liberals tend to agree, but argue that the federal government should provide greater help for workers who lose their jobs to foreign nations. "The answer is not to try to stop outsourcing," says former Clinton administration Secretary of Labor Robert Reich, "but we do have to get serious about job retraining, lifetime learning, extended unemployment insurance, and wage insurance."

Outsourcing may make perfect economic sense in the long term, but has very harsh consequences in the short term. Workers whose jobs move abroad often face years of unemployment, which is why the issue became so central early in the 2004 campaign.

SOURCE: Jyoti Thottam, "Is Your Job Going Abroad?" *Time*, March 1, 2004, pp. 26–30.

United Steelworkers of America President Leo Gerard addresses steelworkers who came to Washington, D.C., to protest the problems globalization and free trade have created in their industry.

(1836), the Steamboat Inspecting Service (1837), and the Copyright Office of the Library of Congress (1870). In 1887, Congress created the Interstate Commerce Commission to deal with the widespread dissatisfaction over the practices of railroads.

Additional regulations were created to break up monopolies, to clean up meat-packing conditions such as those exposed in Upton Sinclair's *Jungle* (1906), to prevent the kind of pesticide contamination described in Rachel Carson's *Silent Spring* (1962), to correct the lack of auto safety documented in Ralph Nader's *Unsafe at Any Speed* (1965), and to prevent employment discrimination on the basis of race, color, national origin, religion, sex, and age. More recently, government has created regulations to protect citizens from raw sewage in rivers; lead in paint and gasoline; toxins in the air; radon gas in homes; and asbestos, cotton dust, and hazardous products in the environment. Federal regulations for environmental, health, and safety are estimated at about $200 billion in higher product cost.[17]

The Role of Regulation

In a broad sense, *regulation* is any attempt by the government to control the behavior of corporations, other governments, or citizens. **Regulation** is commonly defined as any method the government uses to alter the natural workings of the open market to achieve some desired goal. Regulation by government interjects political goals and values into the economy in the form of rules that direct behavior in the marketplace. These rules have the force of law and are backed by the government's police powers. (See the discussion of rules earlier in this chapter.)

There are no unregulated economies in the world. The United States operates in a competitive market economy in which wages, prices, the allocation of goods and services, and the employment of resources are generally regulated by the laws of supply and demand. The nation relies on private enterprise and market incentives to carry out most of our production and distribution.

Nevertheless, market economies have imperfections. Even opponents of regulation recognize that the market does not always solve every problem. Consider pollution. For a long time, no price was imposed on a business for using air and water to discharge toxic wastes. Therefore, market forces did not consider the social costs of its air and water pollution. When the market fails to set appropriate costs and benefits, pressures develop for the government to step in. The government can, for example, create regulations imposing penalties for air pollution. Market forces also do not encourage taking a bus instead of a car to work. If government enacted higher taxes on gasoline, our fuel costs would be brought more in line with Europe's. Such a policy would also reduce our dependence on Middle East oil and promote domestic energy production.

In 1935, there were 4,000 pages of regulations in the *Code of Federal Regulations*, which lists all federal rules; today, there are more than 70,000 pages of regulations.[18] Both political parties say regulatory overkill threatens to overwhelm entrepreneurs and divert them from building vital, innovative companies. Although some economists estimate that regulations can add as much as $3,000 to the cost of a new car, the regulations also purchase important benefits such as cleaner air and safer cars, which, in turn, reduce accidents and improve the overall quality of life.[19] The question is not whether there are both costs and benefits from regulation but whether the balance is right. Conservatives tend to overstate the costs of many regulations and understate the benefits, while liberals tend to overstate the benefits and understate the costs.

Types of Regulation

There are two general categories of regulation: economic and social regulation.

Economic regulation generally refers to government controls on the behavior of businesses in the marketplace: the entry of individual firms into particular lines of business, the prices that firms may charge, and the standards of service they must offer.

Although the national government has been regulating interstate commerce since 1789, it was generally reluctant to regulate private businesses until the industrial revolution of the late 1800s. As the U.S. economy grew, so did the need for rules governing business and labor. Congress created the Interstate Commerce Commission in 1887

Regulation
Efforts by government to alter the free operation of the market to achieve social goals such as protecting workers and the environment.

as the first of what would become many independent regulatory commissions. The ICC was established to regulate the railroads and other transporation industries, but was abolished in the late 1970s as part of the deregulation movement discussed later in this chapter (see Table 18–2 for a list of key government regulatory agencies).

The second type of regulation, *social regulation,* refers to government attempts to correct a wide variety of side effects, usually unintended, brought about by economic activity. Concern for worker health and safety and for environmental hazards has led to much social regulation. Social regulation also includes efforts by government to ensure equal rights in employment, education, and housing. Whereas economic regulation is usually organized along industry lines, social regulation cuts across these lines.

The Environmental Protection Agency, the Consumer Product Safety Commission, and the Occupational Safety and Health Administration are regulatory agencies engaged in social regulation. In economic terms, producers regulated by social regulation must now pay for external costs that once were free, such as using rivers, landfills, or the atmosphere for waste disposal. These costs, however, are then passed along to the consumer, so the true cost of the product is more accurately reflected in its price. Some goods subsequently become too costly, and demand drops. Others become more popular (for instance, safe toys), and demand increases. The final goal of social regulation is the socially beneficial allocation of resources.

Congress has created two types of regulatory agencies: those within the executive branch and those that have a degree of independence from Congress and the president. Members of executive branch agencies serve at the pleasure of the president. Executive

TABLE 18–2 KEY REGULATORY AGENCIES AND THEIR MISSIONS

Agency	Year Established	Primary Functions
Federal Trade Commission (FTC)	1914	Administers certain antitrust laws concerning advertising, labeling, and packaging to protect consumers from unfair business practices
Food and Drug Administration (FDA)	1931	Establishes regulations concerning purity, safety, and labeling accuracy of certain foods and drugs; issues licenses for manufacturing and distribution
Securities and Exchange Commission (SEC)	1934	Oversees the activities of the stock markets and assures that all publicly-reported information is honest
National Labor Relations Board (NLRB)	1935	Guarantees the right of employees to organize and oversees complaints about unfair practices by employers and unions
Federal Communications Commission (FCC)	1934	Licenses civilian radio and television communication; licenses and sets rates for interstate and international communication
Animal and Plant Health Inspection Service	1953	Sets standards; inspects and enforces laws relating to meat, poultry, and plant safety
Environmental Protection Agency (EPA)	1970	Develops environmental quality standards; approves state environmental plans
Occupational Safety and Health Administration (OSHA)	1970	Develops and enforces worker safety and health regulations
Bureau of Alcohol, Tobacco and Firearms (ATF)	1972	Enforces laws and regulates legal flow of these materials
Consumer Product Safety Commission (CPSC)	1972	Establishes mandatory product safety standards and bans sales of products that do not comply
Nuclear Regulatory Commission (NRC)	1974	Licenses the construction and operation of nuclear reactors and similar facilities and regulates nuclear materials; licenses the export of nuclear reactors and the export and import of uranium and plutonium
National Nuclear Security Administration	2000	Monitors the nation's nuclear bomb-building laboratories; oversees the military's stockpile of nuclear weapons; protects the secrecy of U.S. weapons research
Transportation Security Administration (TSA)	2001	Controls passenger and baggage screening; regulates what passengers can carry; requires airlines to check bags through electronic screens; oversees all airport, land, and maritime security

CHANGING FACE OF AMERICAN POLITICS

WOMEN AND MINORITIES IN THE BOARDROOM

Boards of directors wield great power in directing the activities of their companies—they oversee executive salaries and compensation, approve major decisions such as mergers and acquisitions of other companies, and are responsible for the honesty of corporate financial reports.

Although women and minorities now constitute a significant percentage of the U.S. workforce, they occupy relatively few of the seats on the boards of America's largest corporations. As of 2003, just 10.6 percent of board members at the nation's 1,500 largest companies were women, and 9.5 percent were minorities. These percentages have grown slightly over the past decade, but they still remain well below the representation of women and minorities in the workforce and among mangers and executives.

These percentages may increase in coming years as corporations seek to add more board members under new federal rules adopted in the wake of the accounting scandals at Enron, WorldCom, and other leading corporations. The problem is not a lack of names for nomination—in May 2002, for example, the New American Alliance, a nonprofit association of Latino business leaders, and the Hispanic Association for Corporate Responsibility joined together to create a database of more than 1,000 Hispanic candidates for board openings. If the numbers do not grow, advocacy groups have promised to pressure the Securities and Exchange Commission for a rule requiring greater diversity.

Percentage of Women and Minorities in the Workforce and Board Room, 2003

	Percent Women	Percent Racial Minorities
U.S. Workforce	47.2%	29.7%
Executives and Managers	34.2	14.9
Seats on the Boards of the 1,500 Largest Companies	10.6	9.5

SOURCE: Data from Susan Williams, "Board Diversity," Investment Responsibility Resource Center, Background Report A, February 9, 2004.

---

branch regulatory agencies include the Food and Drug Administration, the Office of Surface Mining, and the National Highway Traffic Safety Administration. Commissioners of independent regulatory agencies are appointed by the president and confirmed by the Senate, and they cannot be removed by a president except for cause. Independent agencies, usually headed by a board composed of seven members, include the Federal Communications Commission, the Equal Employment Opportunity Commission, and the Nuclear Regulatory Commission.

Regulating Business

During most of the nineteenth century, our national policy was to leave business pretty much alone. However, four major waves of regulatory legislation occurred in the twentieth century: at its start, in the 1910s, in the 1930s, and in the late 1960s through 1980. In each case, changing circumstances gave rise to the legislation.

Perhaps the number one responsibility of government regulation in our free market system is to maintain competition. When one company gains a **monopoly**, or several create an *oligopoly,* the market system operates ineffectively. The aim of **antitrust legislation** is to prevent monopolies, break up those that exist, and ensure competition. In the past, so-called natural monopolies, such as electric utilities and telephone companies, were protected by the government because it was assumed that in these fields competition would be grossly inefficient.

In the late nineteenth century, social critics and populist reformers believed that consumers were being cheated, especially in the oil, sugar, whiskey, and steel industries, where large monopolies, called **trusts**, stifled competition. People began to have mixed feelings about big business. Americans, who have often been impressed by bigness—the tallest skyscraper, the largest football stadium, the biggest steel mill—and the efficiency that often goes with bigness, became skeptical about giant enterprises.

In 1890, Congress responded by passing the Sherman Antitrust Act, which was designed "to protect trade and commerce against unlawful restraints and monopolies."

monopoly
Domination of an industry by a single company; also the company that dominates the industry.

antitrust legislation
Federal laws (starting with the Sherman Antitrust Act of 1890) that try to prevent a monopoly from dominating an industry and restraining trade.

trust
A monopoly that controls goods and services, often in combinations that reduce competition.

Henceforth, persons making contracts, combinations, or conspiracies in restraint of trade in interstate and foreign commerce could be sued for damages, required to stop their illegal practices, and subjected to criminal penalties. However, the Sherman Antitrust Act had little immediate impact; presidents made few attempts to enforce it, and the Supreme Court's early interpretation of the act limited its scope.[20]

Congress added the Clayton Act to the antitrust arsenal in 1914. This act outlawed such specific abuses as charging different prices to different buyers in order to destroy a weaker competitor, granting rebates, making false statements about competitors and their products, buying up supplies to suppress competition, and bribing competitors' employees. In addition, *interlocking directorates* (having an officer or director in one corporation serve on the board of a competitor) were banned, and corporations were prohibited from acquiring stock in competing concerns if such acquisitions substantially lessened interstate competition. That same year, Congress established the Federal Trade Commission (FTC), run by a five-person board, to enforce the Clayton Act and prevent unfair competitive practices. The FTC was to be the "traffic cop" for competition.[21]

Regulating Labor

Government regulation of business is essentially restrictive. Most laws and rules curb business practices and steer private enterprise into socially useful channels. But regulation cuts two ways. In the case of American workers, most laws in recent decades have tended not to restrict labor but to confer rights and opportunities on it. Actually, many labor laws do not touch labor directly; instead they regulate relations with employers.

Federal regulations protect workers in the following important areas, among others:

1. *Public contracts.* The Walsh-Healy Act of 1936, as amended, requires that no worker employed under contracts with the national government in excess of $10,000 be paid less than the prevailing wage and that he or she be paid overtime for all work in excess of eight hours per day or 40 hours per week.

2. *Wages and hours.* The Fair Labor Standards Act of 1938 set a maximum workweek of 40 hours for all employees engaged in interstate commerce or in the production of goods for interstate commerce (with certain exemptions). Work beyond that amount must be paid for at $1\frac{1}{2}$ times the regular rate.

3. *Child labor.* The Fair Labor Standards Act of 1938 prohibits child labor (under 16 years of age, or under 18 in hazardous occupations) in industries that engage in or produce goods for interstate commerce.

4. *Industrial safety and occupational health.* The Occupational Safety and Health Act of 1970 created the first comprehensive federal industrial safety program. It gave the secretary of labor broad authority to set safety and health standards for companies engaged in interstate commerce.

Federal regulations also protect employee rights to organize unions. Under the 1935 National Labor Relations Act (usually called the Wagner Act), for example, the federal government gave workers significant new rights to organize unions, while prohibiting businesses from discriminating against union members or refusing to bargain in good faith with union representatives.

Congress passed a major modification of the labor laws in 1947, the Labor-Management Relations Act, commonly called the Taft-Hartley Act. The act outlawed the **closed shop** (a company that requires an employer to hire and retain only union members in good standing) and permits the **union shop** (a company in which new employees are obligated to join the union within a stated period of time), prohibits employers from refusing to bargain with employees, allows courts to issue **labor injunctions** forbidding specific individuals or groups to perform acts considered harmful to the rights or property of an employer or community, and structures the process of **collective bargaining** between unions and employers to set wages, benefits, and working conditions.

closed shop
A company with a labor agreement under which union membership is a condition of employment.

union shop
A company in which new employees must join a union within a stated time period.

labor injunction
A court order forbidding specific individuals or groups from performing certain acts (such as striking) that the court considers harmful to the rights and property of an employer or a community.

collective bargaining
Method whereby representatives of the union and employer determine wages, hours, and other conditions of employment through direct negotiation.

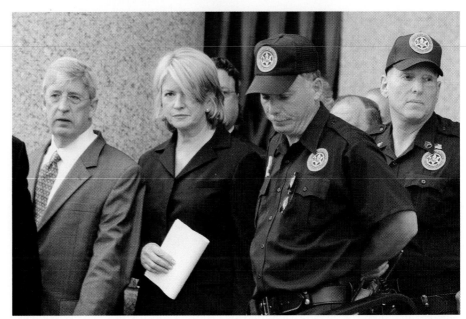

Martha Stewart was tried and convicted in 2004 for misleading federal investigators about why she sold her stock in a drug company called ImClone Systems. Her decision to sell was based on inside information she received about a failed cancer drug trial before this information was made public.

Regulating Markets

The stock market crash of 1929 did more than devastate the American economy and usher in the Great Depression. It also revealed deep problems in how stocks were sold to investors. Millions of new investors entered the stock market in the 1920s only to find out that the companies in which they had invested were virtually worthless.

Prior to 1934, when the Securities and Exchange Commission (SEC) was created, investors had to determine whether a company was telling the truth about its stock. Since 1934, that responsibility has fallen to the SEC. Under the Securities Exchange Act of 1934 and a long list of later laws, companies that offer their stock for sale to the public must tell the truth about their businesses, which means full disclosure of all financial statements, as well as the stocks they are selling and the risks involved in investing.

At the same time, the act also required that anyone in the business of selling stocks, including brokers, dealers, and stock exchanges such as the New York Stock Exchange and NASDAQ, must treat investors fairly and honestly, putting investors' interests first. That means, for example, that individuals who know about a new stock offering in advance or have other inside information on events that might increase or decrease the value of a given stock are prohibited from using that information to benefit themselves.

Congress added to the long inventory of other laws to protect investors when it passed a corporate reform bill in 2002. The law was designed to prevent the kind of deceptive accounting games that led to the Enron collapse earlier in the year. The law strengthened the SEC, created a new oversight board to monitor accounting practices, and set new disclosure requirements on how corporations treat certain expenditures. Despite the public's concern about Enron, the bill was stalled in the Senate until the WorldCom scandal broke in June. The bill passed the Senate almost immediately after by a 97-to-0 vote.

Regulating and Protecting the Environment

Air and water pollution vividly illustrates the regulatory dilemma. Critics of strict controls on air, water, and noise pollution say the pursuit of a clean environment increases the costs of products and causes unemployment. They call attention, for example, to the disastrous economic consequences of the shutdown of companies for pollution violations. Until relatively recently, governments at all levels did little to protect the environment, and what little was done was by state and local governments. In recent decades, however, the national government has taken on new responsibilities, primarily because local governments failed to act.

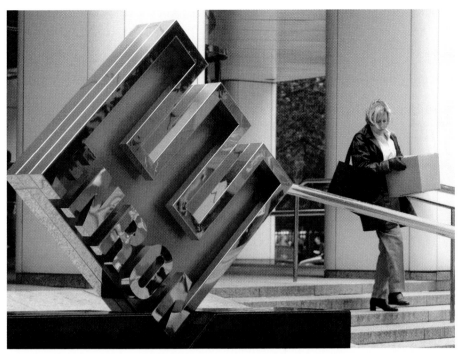

The fall of Enron, the nation's largest energy trading company, caused thousands of employees to lose their jobs as well as their pensions.

Perhaps the most controversial environmental regulation involves **environmental impact statements**, which are used to assess the potential effects of new construction or development on the environment. Most projects using federal funds must file such statements. Since 1970, thousands of statements have been filed. Supporters contend that such statements point out major flaws in projects and can lead to cost savings along with greater environmental awareness. Critics claim that environmental impact reviews simply represent more government interference, paperwork, and delays in the public and private sectors.

Environmental impact statements are only one form of environmental regulation, however. The 1990 Clean Air Act was designed to tighten controls on automobiles and the fuel they use. Building on regulations established under the 1967, 1970, and 1977 acts of the same name, the 1990 act required automakers to install pollution controls to reduce emissions of hydrocarbons and nitrogen oxides and set stiff standards for the kinds of gasoline that can be sold. The 1990 act also required power companies to cut pollution from coal-burning power plants, phased out the use of certain chemicals that harm the earth's protective ozone layer and may contribute to global warming, and set new limits on a long list of cancer-causing pollutants.

The act also promoted further use of the profit motive to encourage self-regulation by private business. Under new rules issued by the Environmental Protection Agency, businesses are allowed to generate a certain amount of pollution. If they cut the amount of pollution below their allotment, they can sell the balance to other companies that are polluting more. By setting overall caps for certain regions of the country, this "cap-and-trade" system encourages individual companies to reduce the total amount of pollution they would have produced under traditional regulations. Initial efforts along these lines have been successful, while saving billions.

Protecting the Global Environment

As globalization has expanded, so have the environmental challenges and hazards associated with that growth. Global temperatures are on the rise, suggesting the possibility that economic development and the burning of carbon-based fuels that goes with it may have created a blanket of carbon dioxide "greenhouse gases" that traps heat in the earth's atmosphere.

Concerns about the consequences of global warming led to negotiation of the Kyoto Protocol in 1997. Named for the Japanese city in which it was negotiated, this treaty

environmental impact statement
A statement required by federal law from all agencies for any project using federal funds to assess the potential effect of the new construction or development on the environment.

required participating countries to make substantial cuts in greenhouse gas emissions year by year until 2012. Because not all nations participated in the negotiations and because the effort to control carbon-based fuels would slow the growth of less developed nations, the Kyoto Protocol immediately divided the world between North (developed countries) and South (less developed countries). Moreover, because the United States would be required to spend billions of dollars reducing the greenhouse gases from its cars and coal-fired electric plants, the Senate signaled its reluctance to participate, too. As of 2005, the Kyoto Protocol has yet to be fully embraced by the world, while nations in both North and South continue to pump carbon dioxide into their skies.

Global warming is only one of several environmental problems the world faces, however. Greenhouse gases may be on the rise, but the world's ozone layer, which protects humans from cancer-causing ultraviolet radiation, is thinning. Unlike global warming, the world has made considerable progress in limiting the major chemicals that have contributed to the "ozone hole" in the atmosphere.

THE DEREGULATION MOVEMENT

One solution to criticisms of government regulation has been **deregulation**, the reduction or complete abolition of federal regulation in a particular sector of the economy. Deregulation began in 1977 with the airline, trucking, and railroad industries, and has continued with banking and telecommunications.

At the same time the federal government has been working to deregulate certain industries, it has also created new procedures to limit the amount of regulation the federal government can impose. In 1993, for example, President Bill Clinton issued an executive order prohibiting agencies from issuing regulations unless the benefits of the regulations (in lives saved, for example) outweighed the costs. In 2001, President George W. Bush followed suit by imposing a 60-day hold on all regulations published by the Clinton administration until his administration could ensure that the regulations met the benefit/cost test.

Deregulating Transportation

No industry has undergone more extensive deregulation than the transportation industry. Over the past generation, airlines, trucking, and railroads have been granted considerable freedom in conducting their operations. No deregulation effort was more visible to individual consumers than airline deregulation.

deregulation
A policy promoting cutbacks in the amount of federal regulation in specific areas of economic activity.

Meeting of the United Nations Global Warming Conference in Kyoto, Japan, in December 1997, which constructed the treaty known as the Kyoto Protocol.

The federal government began regulating aviation when the Civil Aeronautics Board (CAB) was established by the federal government in 1938 to protect airlines from unreasonable competition by controlling rates and fares. Critics charged that airlines competed only in the frequency of flights and in the services they offered, forcing consumers to pay higher fares than needed.

After years of debate, Congress abolished the CAB in 1978, allowing the market to set fares through competition. Although many fares fell, some medium-sized cities lost service because carriers found it more profitable to use their aircraft in busier markets. Airlines were raising fares on routes over which they had monopolies in order to subsidize lower fares on more competitive routes. Critics charged that safety precautions and maintenance suffered as a result of cutthroat competition and the ease with which new airlines could enter the market.

Although problems have been associated with airline deregulation, it has resulted in generally lower fares, greater choice of routes and fares in most markets, and more efficient use of assets by the industry.[22] Some airlines have been driven into bankruptcy and others have merged, but deregulation of the airlines has been judged a success by the surviving airlines and most observers of the industry. If an airline is overcharging passengers, a competitor will eventually steal those travelers away. Southwest Airlines is an example of a discount airline that took advantage of deregulation to take on larger airlines.[23] Deregulation has strengthened the industry by forcing companies to streamline their operations in order to survive in a competitive market. But recent mergers of major airlines have worsened the problems caused by deregulation and cancellation of service to rural and medium-sized cities in parts of states in the West, while the post–September 11 collapse in travel has pushed several airlines toward bankruptcy, which in turn prompted Congress to provide loans to many airlines to help them through the crisis.

Deregulating Telecommunications

Airline deregulation may have been the most visible to consumers, but the deregulation of telecommunications may eventually have a greater impact on how Americans live, whether in the form of lower phone bills, easier access to the Internet, or better cellular technology. Unlike the deregulation of transportation, which came in a number of steps over time, deregulation of telecommunications came in a single, massive bill called the Telecommunications Act of 1996.

The act opened up large areas of telecommunications to companies that once were regulated both in the services they could provide and the prices they could charge. The main objective of the new law was to increase competition among phone, cable, and other communications companies. Telephone companies that were once divided into seven local "baby Bells" were allowed to offer services outside their defined regions. Local telephone companies won the freedom to provide long-distance service, manufacture communications equipment, and offer video service in competition with cable television.

At the same time, local telephone companies opened their networks to competition for local telephone service from cable television and long-distance companies. In short, restrictions were removed so that cable television and local and long-distance telephone companies could effectively compete with one another.

The Telecommunications Act also contained two highly controversial provisions: new regulation on Internet content and a requirement that all television makers install a "V-chip" to allow parents to block out television shows with objectionable content. However, the Supreme Court struck down the provisions making it a crime for any person knowingly to make indecent material accessible to minors on the Internet. The Court found the provision too vague and held that the Internet receives full protection under the First Amendment.[24] Although the debate continues on who will decide what is deemed violent or offensive, most surveys suggest that parents are unwilling or unable to use the V-chip to control their family viewing habits.[25]

BALANCING THE NATION'S BUDGET: WHAT CAN YOU GET FOR $4 TRILLION?

Imagine for a moment that you are the director of the Office of Management and Budget and have been directed to recommend budget cuts that are equal to the amount of revenue lost through the president's tax cuts. Each budget cut carries more than a dollar cost, of course. Each has some political impact on the president's approval and reelection. If the damage is too high, you will be out of a job long before the next election.

Go to Make It Real "Balancing the Nation's Budget: What Can You Get for $4 Trillion?"

The Cost of Regulation

Although the need for regulation, especially in areas affecting health and safety, is widely accepted, there are concerns about the negative consequences of regulation. A marked decrease in lead paint poisonings, the use of childproof bottle tops, and the banning of many cancer-producing pesticides are all positive outcomes. On the negative side, regulations generally increase the cost of products and may hamper some industries:

- *Regulation disrupts the operation of the market.* Some governmental intervention upsets the normal adjustment processes of the market and thus encourages higher prices, misallocation of resources, and inefficiency.

- *Regulation may discourage competition.* Some forms of regulation (often the kind desired by industry) actually have the reverse of their desired effect. This is especially true when the government grants operating licenses and charters to maintain a certain level of quality or stability in the market. Regulatory red tape has also been charged with discouraging entry into industries and driving small businesses out.

- *Regulation may discourage technological development.* If the reward for innovation is a new set of rules and a struggle for permission to use a new product, business may not find it worth the effort to innovate.

- *Regulation increases costs to industry and consumers.* Some critics estimate that government regulations cost every U.S. household $8,000 to $10,000 annually, while advocates argue that regulations return even more in health and safety.

The mere fact that the national government stops regulating an industry does not mean that the industry will be unregulated, however. Sometimes the states take over, making it even more difficult for an industry to operate on a large scale. California, for example, has much tougher automobile emission rules than the national government. Variations in state regulations are the reason businesspeople themselves sometimes call for more, not less, national regulation; they would prefer one set of national guidelines to 50 different state ones.

In sum, the federal government is heavily involved in making economic and regulatory policies. It collects taxes, regulates the money supply, tries to prevent monopolies that would hurt consumers, and seeks to promote free trade. It does all this while trying to let the market, not government bureaucrats, shape the demand and price of products and services. Most Americans want their government to play only a limited role in the economy, but competing values such as fairness, equality, protecting the environment, and encouraging healthy competition inevitably encourage elected officials to take on certain balancing or referee responsibilities in order to promote the common good.

SUMMARY

1. The policy-making process involves a variety of choices made by Congress, the president, and the courts, including (1) making assumptions about the world, (2) identifying the problem to be solved, (3) deciding whether to act at all, (4) deciding how much to do, (5) choosing a tool for solving the problem, and (6) making rules for implementation.

2. The national government influences how wealth is produced and distributed primarily via fiscal policy (taxing and spending), monetary policy (control of the money supply), and regulatory policy.

3. Fiscal policy is implemented by the federal budget, which is annually negotiated between the president and Congress. Monetary policy is primarily under the control of the Federal Reserve System, which has considerable independence from both Congress and the president as it works to supply sufficient amounts of money and credit so that the economy will grow but not so much that it will lead to inflation.

4. Government's role in promoting growth and jobs is not new. It is as old as the Republic itself. The federal government has long been involved in promoting agriculture and concerned about the health of producers and consumers of farm commodities. Working through the Department of Commerce, it also promotes business. The national government is also involved in promoting trade and commerce with other nations. Our ability to buy from other nations and sell them our goods and services has much to do with the health of our economy.

5. Regulation, now a major activity of government, involves altering the natural workings of the open market to achieve some desired goal. Economic regulation aims to control the behavior of business in the marketplace. Social regulation aims to correct the unintended side effects of economic activity and to ensure

equal rights in employment, education, and housing.

6. Regulation is a means of eliminating some of the abuses and problems generated by the private economy while avoiding government ownership and the risks of too much centralization. Regulation is an inevitable byproduct of a complex, industrialized, high-technology society.

7. The federal government regulates the economy in five ways. It maintains competition by preventing monopoly and oligopoly. It regulates labor to give workers the right to organize into unions. It regulates markets to protect investors. It regulates the environment to protect the public. And it is increasingly involved in regulating the global environment. A deregulation movement designed to get the government out of the regulation of certain businesses has taken form over the past 30 years. Liberals sometimes favor deregulation if they believe it will foster more competition. Conservatives generally favor deregulation that will get federal regulators off their backs in areas such as safety, health, and environmental and consumer protection standards.

K E Y   T E R M S

public policy
policy agenda
distributive policy
redistributive policy
rule
iron triangle
issue network
fiscal policy
monetary policy
inflation
unemployment
tariff
excise tax

progressive tax
regressive tax
deficit
national debt
gross domestic product (GDP)
entitlements
Office of Management and Budget (OMB)
Congressional Budget Office (CBO)
sales tax
value-added tax (VAT)

tax expenditure
monetarism
Federal Reserve System
laissez-faire economics
Keynesian economics
trade deficit
World Trade Organization (WTO)
General Agreement on Tariffs and Trade (GATT)
North American Free Trade Agreement (NAFTA)

protectionism
regulation
monopoly
antitrust legislation
trust
closed shop
union shop
labor injunction
collective bargaining
environmental impact statement
deregulation

F U R T H E R   R E A D I N G

JEFFREY H. BIRNBAUM AND ALAN S. MURRAY, *Showdown at Gucci Gulch: Lawmakers, Lobbyists, and the Unlikely Triumph of Tax Reform* (Vintage, 1988).

STEPHEN G. BREYER, *Breaking the Vicious Circle: Toward Effective Risk Regulation* (Harvard University Press, 1993).

GARY BRYNER, *Blue Skies, Green Politics: The Clean Air Act of 1990 and Its Interpretation,* 2d ed. (CQ Press, 1995).

GARY BURTLESS, ROBERT J. LAWRENCE, ROBERT E. LITAN, AND ROBERT J. SHAPIRO, *Globaphobia: Confronting Fears About Open Trade* (Brookings Institution Press, 1998).

THOMAS W. CHURCH AND ROBERT T. NAKAMURA, *Cleaning Up the Mess: Implementation Strategies in Superfund* (Brookings Institution Press, 1993).

ROBERT W. CRANDALL AND HAROLD FURCHTGOTT-ROTH, *Cable TV: Regulation or Competition?* (Brookings Institution Press, 1996).

ROBERT W. CRANDALL AND LEONARD WAVERMAN, *Who Pays for Universal Service? When Telephone Subsidies Become Transparent* (Brookings Institution Press, 2000).

ROBERT W. CRANDALL ET AL., *An Agenda for Federal Regulatory Reform* (American Enterprise Institute/Brookings Institution, 1997).

ROBERT M. ENTMAN, *Competition, Innovation, and Investment in Telecommunications* (Aspen Institute, 1998).

THOMAS L. FRIEDMAN, *The Lexus and the Olive Tree: Understanding Globalization* (Anchor Books, 2000).

AL GORE, *Earth in the Balance: Ecology and the Human Spirit* (Houghton Mifflin, 1992).

WILLIAM GREIDER, *Secrets of the Temple: How the Federal Reserve Runs the Country* (Simon & Schuster, 1987).

PHILIP K. HOWARD, *The Death of Common Sense: How Law Is Suffocating America* (Random House, 1994).

CORNELIUS M. KERWIN, *Rulemaking: How Government Agencies Write Law and Make Policy,* 2d ed. (CQ, 1998).

ROBERT KUTTNER, *Everything for Sale: The Virtues and Limits of Markets* (Knopf, 1997).

LAWRENCE LESSIG, *Code and Other Laws of Cyberspace* (Basic Books, 2000).

CALVIN MACKENZIE AND SARANNA THORTON, *Bucking the Deficit: Economic Policy-Making in America* (Westview Press, 1996).

STEVEN A. MORRISON AND CLIFFORD WINSTON, *The Evolution of the Airline Industry* (Brookings Institution Press, 1995).

PETER G. PETERSON, *Facing Up: Paying Our Nation's Debt and Saving Our Children's Future* (Simon & Schuster, 1994).

ALLEN SCHICK, *The Federal Budget: Politics, Policy, Process,* rev. ed. (Brookings Institution Press, 2000).

JOSEPH E. STIGLITZ, *Globalization and Its Discontents* (Norton, 2002).

JOHN WARGO, *Our Children's Toxic Legacy: How Science and Law Fail to Protect Us from Pesticides* (Yale University Press, 1997).

BOB WOODWARD, *Maestro: Greenspan's Fed and the American Boom* (Simon & Schuster, 2000).

JEFFREY WORSHAW, *Other People's Money: Policy Changes, Congress, and Bank Regulation* (Westview Press, 1997).

DANIEL YERGIN AND JOSEPH STANISLAW, *The Commanding Heights: The Battle Between Government and the Marketplace That Is Remaking the Modern World* (Simon & Schuster, 1998).

Although the Preamble to the Constitution promises that the federal government will promote the general welfare, liberals and conservatives often differ sharply on just what the promise means. Liberals tend to believe that the federal government should take the lead in helping needy Americans, while conservatives tend to believe that the free market and state and local governments should be the source of support for those in need.

These differences came to a head at 3 A.M. early Saturday morning, November 22, 2003, when the House held its final vote on prescription drug coverage for older Americans. Although most members of Congress wanted to add drug coverage to the 1965 Medicare program, Democrats and Republicans disagreed sharply on how much the government should provide and who should deliver the coverage. Democrats wanted the federal government to provide more coverage and run the program, while Republicans wanted to provide limited coverage and allow private insurance companies to compete against each other to run the program.

But Republicans controlled a majority in the House, and neither party was sure how conservative members would vote on the $400 billion bill. If enough conservative Republicans voted to defeat their party's proposal, Democrats might have a chance to offer their own version of prescription drug coverage.

With members eager to adjourn for the Thanksgiving recess, most House members hurried to the floor to cast their votes and leave town. With all but one member voting and constrained by the customary 15-minute period, Democrats and a handful of conservative Republicans defeated the bill, 216 to 219. All that remained was the bang of the gavel bringing the vote to a close.

MAKING SOCIAL POLICY

TIME LINE

MAKING SOCIAL POLICY

1862	Morrill Land Grant Act helps create state universities
1933	FDR's New Deal creates dozens of federal agencies that employ many people during the Great Depression
1935	Social Security system is created
1935	Aid to Families with Dependent Children nationalizes welfare
1944	GI Bill allows World War II vets to attend college
1946	School Lunch Act finances school lunches for children around the country
1964	Food Stamp Act is the first federal program to provide food directly
1965	Medicare and Medicaid are created to provide health care for the elderly and disabled
1965	Department of Housing and Urban Development is created to promote urban renewal

Unfortunately for the Democrats, the Speaker of the House, J. Dennis Hastert, refused to let the gavel drop at the 15-minute deadline. Instead, he kept the vote open for another 158 minutes as the Republican leadership lobbied members to change their votes on the biggest vote of Hastert's career. With his whips working the aisles and President Bush working the phones, Hastert concentrated his fire on the six conservative Republicans who had voted against the bill.

Just before 6:00 A.M., C. L. "Butch" Otter of Idaho and Trent Franks of Arizona switched their votes from nay to aye, turning the 216 to 219 defeat into what would become a 220 to 215 victory as a handful of other members switched from one side to the other, too. Although Democrats complained bitterly about the outcome, the extended vote was perfectly legal under House rules, which only *recommend* a 15-minute limit. "A vote is a pressure cooker sometimes," Hastert said later. "It just took that amount of time to get people to change their minds.[1]

With the victory in hand, the bill moved quickly through the legislative process and to the president's desk on December 8 for a signature. In return for a $35 monthly premium, the federal government will cover 75 percent of all yearly drug costs between $250 and $2,250, thereby helping all participants regardless of need. In addition, the federal government will cover 95 percent of all drug costs above $3,600, thereby protecting participants who face extremely high, or catastrophic, drug costs.

Athough the new program will certainly help older Americans, it did nothing to help the 60 million Americans who have no health insurance at all in any given year, let alone those who have no prescription drug coverage. Moreover, it did not address rising drug costs for Americans of any age. The faster drug costs rise, the less valuable will be the new Medicare benefit for older Americans, and the more all Americans will need help.

More important perhaps, Congress and the president did nothing to address the long-term financial problems facing Medicare. According to the latest projections, the Medicare program will start to run a deficit in 2019, which means that the federal government will have to either raise taxes or cut benefits to cover the total cost. Unless something is done soon to control costs, Congress may yet have another tight vote to cut the prescription drug program it just enacted.

This chapter will explore how the federal government promotes the general welfare today, how that promise has expanded over the past century, and what remains to be done to protect the needy. It will also examine three areas of social policy that are likely to be active over the next few years: health, education, and crime control.

THE ROLE OF GOVERNMENT IN SOCIAL POLICY

The nation has been debating the federal government's role in promoting the general welfare from the beginning of the Republic. Some Americans ask whether government should be involved at all in social policies such as child care, help for the needy, and job training, all of which were once thought of as purely private, religious, or charitable responsibilities. Others ask which level of government should be involved in specific issues such as education, welfare distribution, and crime control, all of which were once thought to be solely state and local responsibilities. Today, these responsibilities are a large part of the agenda of our national government.

Who Is Responsible for the Needy?

Americans are sharply divided on whether and how much the government at all levels should do to care for the less fortunate. Conservative Americans believe that people are responsible for their own lot in life even if that means they must live in poverty. They doubt government's ability to provide effective, efficient protection against misfortune and put their faith in the free market instead. They believe that the economy will provide opportunities for those who are willing to work hard. Many also believe that charities and religious institutions, not government, should help the less fortunate.

Orphanages run by religious orders provided for needy children. These orphans attended the Sisters of Charity of the Incarnate World Orphanage in Galveston, Texas, in the late 1890s.

Liberal Americans believe that government must step in to help the needy through social programs such as job training, child care assistance, public housing, and other forms of aid. Although they too may doubt the efficiency of public solutions, they believe that the free market is often unfair, leaving some Americans behind because of their race, sex, lack of access to education, and so forth. They believe that government should provide a safety net against poverty, joblessness, and prejudice.

The two political parties tend to divide sharply in this debate along these ideological lines. Republicans believe that the national government is part of the problem, not the solution, to poverty and other social ills because it gets in the way of the free market. They tend to favor programs that create incentives for people to pull themselves out of poverty through hard work.

In contrast, Democrats are more likely to believe that only the national government has the resources and jurisdiction to provide adequate Social Security, help local governments improve the quality of education, and ensure that all Americans, rich and poor, have access to proper medical attention. They tend to favor programs that make sure all Americans are protected from the occasional failures of the free market system. They believe that the national government must provide a safety net for individuals and a minimum standard of living—a job, an education, health care, housing, and basic nutrition—for all citizens.

These differences are clear in recent public opinion surveys. Just 20 percent of Republicans interviewed in 2003 mostly or completely agreed that success in life is pretty much determined by forces outside our control, compared to 36 percent of Democrats. Similarly, just 46 percent of Republicans mostly or completely agreed that government should guarantee every citizen enough to eat and a place to sleep, compared to 81 percent of Democrats.[2]

Which Level of Government Should Take Care of the Needy?

Americans also disgree on whether the federal government should care for the needy. Some Americans argue that state and local governments should solve social policy problems such as poverty, in part because states and localities know more about the specific needs in their communities. Others believe that only the national government can ensure that every American is protected against misfortune, in part because poor states and localities do not have the resources to provide as much help as their richer neighbors.

In recent years, Democrats and Republicans have resolved the debate in part by setting national standards that require all states and localities to provide minimum levels of help. In turn, state governors have been increasingly critical of *unfunded mandates* such as the annual student testing required under the No Child Left Behind Act of 2002 that require state action with little or no federal funding for implementation. The tendency of Congress to impose unfunded mandates forces state governments to raise taxes or reduce funding for other state programs. Governors argue that if Congress inaugurates a new program requiring states to take action, Congress should provide the federal funds to help pay for the state's costs to administer that program.

THE EARLY HISTORY OF SOCIAL POLICY IN THE UNITED STATES

Most Western governments expanded their social programs long before the United States did. Americans generally believed that people who could not succeed in a nation as big, rich, and open as the United States simply were not working hard enough. This commitment to *rugged individualism* meant that government, be it local, state, or national, played only a limited role in people's lives. Rather grudgingly, state governments in the early twentieth century extended relief to needy groups, especially the old, the blind, and the orphaned. But government aid was limited, and much reliance was placed on private charity.[3]

This is not to suggest that the national government ignored domestic policy, however. From its founding, the national government took care of its military veterans. Indeed, with the Revolutionary War barely over, the Continental Congress established the nation's first programs to help soldiers who had been disabled in battle, as well as

GLOBAL *Perceptions*

QUESTION: Please indicate whether you completely agree, mostly agree, mostly disagree, or completely disagree with the following statement: Success in life is pretty much determined by forces outside our control.

Citizens around the world differ greatly on who is responsible for individual success. Americans tend to believe that success is determined more by the individual, while citizens in countries with relatively weak economies tend to blame forces beyond their control. Only 32 percent of Americans completely or mostly agree that success in life is pretty much determined by events outside our control, compared with 55 percent of Brazilians, 56 percent of Polish, 58 percent of the citizens of India, 63 percent of South Africans, 71 percent of Kenyans, 76 percent of the Turkish, and 75 percent of South Koreans. The Japanese and Canadians come closest to the U.S. view at 43 and 35 percent, respectively.

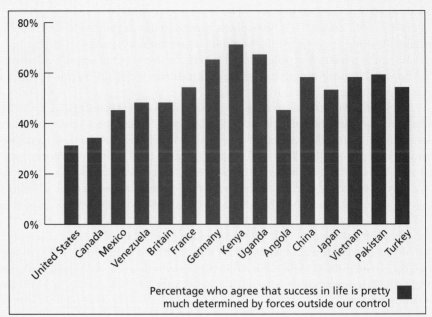

Percentage who agree that success in life is pretty much determined by forces outside our control

SOURCE: Pew Global Attitudes Project, 2003, p. T7.

general retirement pensions for officers. Thus, contrary to those who argue that government did little to care for older Americans until it created the Social Security system in 1935, the Continental Congress actually provided care for older veterans well before the new government was even created.

Once established in the 1780s, the financial security system for veterans expanded slowly but steadily as the soldiers aged into disability and poverty. Americans could not stand to see their veterans in tattered clothing and felt obliged to provide support for the less fortunate. In 1818, for example, Congress expanded retirement benefits to cover all veterans of the Revolutionary War, whether officers or not, and created the first old soldiers' homes for poor veterans. In 1840, Congress expanded the veterans program again to provide financial relief to the widows of soldiers killed in battle.[4]

These early programs set two important precedents for contemporary domestic policy. First, they established the notion that some Americans would be automatically entitled to certain government benefits on the basis of an eligibility requirement such as service in the nation's armed forces. Thus veterans' relief was the nation's first **entitlement**, under which the government provides benefits to any citizen who is eligible. In the original program, only military officers met the eligibility requirement.

Second, these early programs also established government's right to restrict some benefits only to those citizens who could actually prove their need for help. Thus veterans' programs were early examples of what are now called **means-tested entitlements**, under which citizens must prove they are poor enough to deserve the government's help. In the original program, only poor veterans could go to old soldiers' homes.

Veterans' benefits are also important because they eventually came to cover huge numbers of Americans. As political scientist Theda Skocpol has noted, the Civil War triggered a massive expansion in veterans' benefits. The war involved 2.2 million Union

entitlements
Programs such as unemployment insurance, disaster relief, or disability payments that provide benefits to all eligible citizens.

means-tested entitlements
Programs such as Medicaid and welfare under which applicants must meet eligibility requirements based on need.

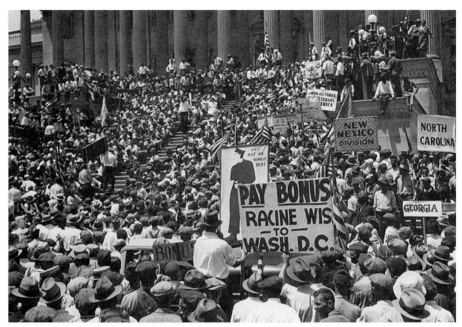

On July 4, 1932, over 20,000 war veterans marched to the Capitol in Washington, D.C. to demand the passage of the Bonus Bill, which allowed the immediate payment of the Soldiers' Bonus.

soldiers who would later qualify for veterans' benefits. "By 1910, about 28 percent of all American men aged 65 or more, more than half a million of them, received federal benefits averaging $189 a year," writes Skocpol. "Over three hundred thousand widows, orphans, and other dependents were also receiving payments from the federal treasury."[5]

Because so many men served in the Civil War and because veterans' benefits were even more generous toward Spanish-American War and World War I veterans, veterans' benefits accounted for one-quarter of all federal spending by 1932. The numbers would have been even higher if Confederate soldiers had been entitled to benefits. However, Congress decided to leave their care to the former Confederate states.

TYPES OF SOCIAL POLICY

Having entered the twentieth century with only a handful of federal domestic programs, most of which were built around helping veterans, the federal government left the century with a deep inventory of domestic programs. According to the *Catalog of Federal Domestic Assistance,* which lists every one of the federal government's 1,425 domestic funding programs in a searchable database (at www.cfda.gov), there are at least 38 separate programs for farmers, another 142 for colleges and their students, 148 for women, and 257 for children.

The Goals of Social Policy

Because most of these programs are restricted to one group of citizens only, they are often described as *categorical* aid. One only needs to type in a search term on the Internet such as "students," "elderly," "children," "disabled," "workers," "farmers," "women," or "veterans" to see just how much help the federal government provides in each category. But regardless of category, federal domestic policy focuses on two broad goals.

The first goal is to protect citizens against poverty and personal misfortune, whether by providing relief for unemployed workers, health care for the elderly, emergency shelter for the homeless, or school lunches for poor children, almost all of which are available to citizens only on the basis of a means test. Although almost all Americans are covered by federal unemployment insurance through a payroll tax, only workers who have been laid off from their jobs through no fault of their own can qualify for benefits, and only then for a relatively brief period of time. (For an inventory of federal programs for helping workers, visit the Department of Labor Web site at www.workers.gov.)

The second goal of federal domestic policy is to raise the quality of life for all Americans, whether by improving air and water quality, building roads and bridges, regulating air traffic, fighting crime, or strengthening local schools through federal aid, almost all of which are available to all communities regardless of need. Almost all federal aid to the states is distributed on the basis of formula grants that allocate money on the basis of population, not need.

Most scholars trace the federal government's effort to protect citizens against economic and personal hard times to the Great Depression and the Social Security Act of 1935. Although there is no question that Franklin Roosevelt's New Deal agenda stimulated a remarkable expansion in the federal government's domestic policy role, there is also no question that federal, state, and local governments were helping citizens long before the Depression began.

Until about a century ago, the poor were divided into two groups: the worthy poor, meaning people who were in poverty through no fault of their own, and the unworthy poor, meaning people who were in poverty because of idleness or the unwillingness to work, which was deemed the source of most unemployment at the time. As historian Joel Handler writes, this categorization emerged in the early 1800s as states began to place the worthy poor into separate government institutions such as schools for the blind and disabled. This movement was driven by a clear recognition that "those who were dependent by misfortune did not deserve the stigma of the unworthy poor."[6]

Types of Protection

By the early 1900s, however, public attitudes toward the poor had begun to change. Although the nation continued to distinguish between the worthy and unworthy poor, Congress and the president soon invented two very different types of federal programs to protect Americans against hardship, both of which continue to exist today.

The first type of help for the less fortunate is called **public assistance**, a term that is often used interchangeably with the word "welfare" to label government aid for the poor. The first public assistance programs were actually created in the late 1800s when states established aid programs to help single, poor mothers and their children. Although these programs were often described as "mothers' pensions" to create the impression that the beneficiaries had earned the benefits through some contribution, they created a precedent for many of the federal government's later antipoverty programs.

Most of this assistance flows through noncontributory programs, meaning that recipients do not have to pay anything in advance to receive benefits. Most federal assistance programs also impose a means test on all applicants. As noted earlier, these tests require applicants to disclose all financial assets and income to prove that they fall below the poverty line, which is generally calculated as three times the amount of money an individual or family needs to purchase the food for a nutritious diet. Defined as such, the poverty level changes with the size of the family. The poverty line for participation in federal assistance programs is set by the Department of Health and Human Services. In 2004, the line was drawn at $9,310 of pretax income for an individual, while the level for a four-person family was set at $18,850.[7]

The U.S. Bureau of the Census uses a somewhat different measure of income to determine how many Americans are poor at any given time. According to its measure, which runs a year or two behind the Department of Health and Human Services, 12 percent, or 35 million Americans were poor in 2002. The poverty rate was 16.7 percent among children, 10.3 among Asian Americans, 24.1 percent among African Americans, and 21.8 percent among Hispanics.[8]

Public assistance in the United States today incorporates elements of job training, transportation subsidies, housing subsidies, free school lunches, food aid for poor families and pregnant mothers with young children, and tax credits for low-income people. The national government also provides what some opponents label as "corporate welfare" to favored industries such as agriculture and steel, as well as "middle-class welfare" to college students, home buyers, and the citizenry as a whole in the form of college loans, tax deductions for home mortgages, and access to national parks and forests

public assistance
Aid to the poor; "welfare."

(supported by taxpayers but rarely used by poor people). However, the term "welfare" is generally used for public assistance to the needy, including the following forms:

- Direct payments to single parents with young children, the unemployed, and the disabled
- Vouchers that can be exchanged for food
- Low-cost and/or public housing
- Reduced cost or free access to public transportation, higher education, or job training
- Free or low-cost medical care

In absolute numbers, most poor people are white. As a percentage within their own population, however, a larger proportion of African Americans and Hispanics are poor. Moreover, in both absolute and proportional terms, more women than men are poor. Indeed, some scholars refer to the relatively recent rise in poverty among women as the "feminization of poverty."[9] Although women tend to take jobs in lower-paying occupations than men, they earn less than men even when they are in the same jobs. They also save money over their lifetimes less than men, in part because they often take time off from their careers to care for their children and parents.

The second type of protection against hardship is called **social insurance**, a term that refers to government programs that provide benefits to anyone who is eligible either because of past service (veterans, miners, merchant marines) or payments of some kind (payroll taxes for Social Security and Medicare, insurance premiums). Some social insurance programs, such as unemployment and disability insurance, provide benefits only to those in need, thereby acting like private automobile and life insurance, which pay off only when an accident or death occurs. Other social insurance programs, such as Social Security and Medicare, pay benefits regardless of wealth, thereby acting more like a private savings program or annuity, which pays off at a set point in time.

Many federal assistance programs involve partnerships with state governments. There are two reasons for the connection. First, except for veterans' policy, states have been responsible for protecting their citizens against hardship since the United States was formed. Second, states and local governments have the administrative agencies to stay in touch with recipients of aid, whether to make sure they are actually eligible for support or to provide services such as job training or school lunches.

Because states vary greatly in their generosity, most federal assistance is designed to set a minimum floor of support that individual states can raise on their own. The most generous states in the country tend to be located in the Northeast and West, where living costs tend to be higher and legislatures more liberal, while the least generous tend to be found in the South. In this way, states act as a check on the federal government's ability to raise benefits too far, frustrating those who believe that the federal government should set a uniform level of benefits for all citizens while ensuring the consent of the governed for helping those in need. (Table 19–1 shows the amount of federal payments to individuals in 2005.)

TABLE 19–1 FEDERAL PAYMENTS TO INDIVIDUALS, 2005	
Major Public Assistance Programs	
Medicaid	$182 billion
State Children's Health Insurance	5.2 billion
Supplemental Security Income	35.5 billion
Food stamps	30.7 billion
Child nutrition	11.6 billion
Family support payments to states	22.6 billion
Low Income Tax Credit	33.7 billion
Social Insurance Funding	
Social Security	$428 billion
Medicare	325 billion
Disability insurance	82 billion
Unemployment insurance	41 billion

SOURCE: Summary Tables, *Budget of the United States, Fiscal Year 2005*, Washington, D.C., U.S. Government Printing Office, February 2004.

THE EXPANSION OF SOCIAL POLICY IN THE TWENTIETH CENTURY

The federal government's commitment to helping the poor and improving the quality of life expanded rapidly during the Great Depression that followed the stock market crash of 1929. The "social safety net" built by state and local governments and private charities simply could not meet the needs of the huge increase in the homeless, unemployed, and poor.

social insurance
Programs in which eligibility is based on prior contributions to government, usually in the form of payroll taxes.

The WPA, part of President Roosevelt's New Deal, created jobs for thousands of workers during the Great Depression of the 1930s.

The New Deal

The most significant expansion of federal social policy occurred in the five years that followed Franklin Roosevelt's inauguration in 1933. That year, as part of Roosevelt's New Deal agenda, the federal government began making loans to states and localities to help the poor, and soon it launched a long list of programs to help older Americans (Social Security), the jobless (unemployment insurance), and the poor (Aid to Families with Dependent Children).

THE FIRST 100 DAYS   Before creating these signature New Deal programs, however, the Roosevelt administration moved quickly to help the needy. The first 100 days of the administration produced the most significant list of legislation ever passed in American history, including the Federal Emergency Relief Administration (FERA), established in May 1933 to give unemployed workers cash grants to get them through the summer, and the Civil Works Administration (CWA), created in November 1933 to provide millions of public jobs to help many of those same workers make it through the winter.

The list of "alphabet agencies" grew longer as the administration created a host of new programs to help the poor, including the Works Progress Administration (WPA), which was created in 1935 to provide work for millions of unemployed Americans, and the Civilian Conservation Corps (CCC), which put millions of young Americans to work clearing trails and building roads in the national forests and parks. Between 1933 and 1945, for example, the WPA put 8.5 million Americans to work at a cost of $10 billion. All told, the WPA built 650,000 miles of roads, 125,000 public buildings, 8,200 parks, and 850 airports. The wages were hardly generous, however. The average WPA worker received just $55 a month, far below the $100 the federal government deemed a subsistence wage. The WPA was abolished during World War II when the economy finally rebounded.

Together, these and other New Deal programs created a national safety net to catch those in need. It is little wonder, therefore, that scholars would describe the New Deal as the "big bang" of domestic policy.[10] Although the distinction between the worthy and unworthy poor still remained, joblessness was no longer defined as merely a problem of individual idleness or the unwillingness to work.

HELP FOR OLDER AMERICANS   Once past the immediate crisis, the Roosevelt administration began designing the flagship programs of the New Deal. First on the list was **Social Security**, which was enacted in 1935 and stands today as the federal government's most popular social program. Social Security was designed to meet two goals: (1) to provide a minimum income floor for poor beneficiaries and (2) to ensure that benefits bear a relationship to the amount of payroll taxes a beneficiary actually paid. Supported by equal contributions from employers and employees, the program now covers more than 90 percent of the American work force.[11] The universal nature of Social Security is one reason it is politically so popular: Everyone benefits, regardless of need. In 2004, the Social Security Administration issued checks to almost 50 million Americans every month, and three times that many working people contribute to the fund.

Social Security was expanded in 1939 to include financial support for survivors of workers covered by Social Security when the retired worker died, and in 1954, the program was again expanded to include support for disabled workers and the children of deceased or disabled workers. Benefit levels were raised repeatedly during the first 40 years of the program, often just before an election. The increases became so frequent and so costly that Congress finally indexed benefits to rise with inflation in 1975. Under legislation enacted in 1983, the Social Security retirement age started to rise in 2003 and will reach 67 years of age by the year 2027. In 2005, for example, workers who retire at age 65 years and 6 months are eligible for full benefits, while workers who retire early at age 62 are eligible for a reduced amount. The average benefit in 2004 was $922, while the maximum benefit for a worker retiring at full retirement age was $1,850.[12]

Until the 1970s, growth in Social Security benefits was relatively uncontroversial, largely because "the costs were initially deceptively low," while the benefits increased steadily, making the system politically painless.[13] Since Social Security began, the program has experienced steady growth and is now the world's largest insurance program for retirees, survivors, and people with disabilities. In 2005, Social Security and Medicare expenditures totaled nearly $753 billion.

Social Security, unlike many welfare programs, is financed not from general taxes but from a trust fund into which taxes on employees and employers are paid under the Federal Insurance Contribution Act, commonly known as FICA. Over the years, Congress added benefits to the Social Security system without adding enough money to the trust fund to cover the added expense. In 1983, Congress tried to solve the problem by raising the retirement age at which one qualifies for Social Security benefits, increasing Social Security taxes, imposing the first-ever tax on the Social Security payments of

The Gray Panthers, an activist group made up of elderly Americans, often marches in support of numerous social issues, not only those causes that relate specifically to their needs.

Social Security
A combination of entitlement programs, paid for by employer and employee taxes, that includes retirement benefits, health insurance, and support for disabled workers and the children of deceased or disabled workers.

upper-income individuals, and imposing a one-time cut in the annual cost-of-living increase in benefits.

Social Security taxes are now the largest tax paid by most Americans, and for three-quarters of Americans, their Social Security tax now exceeds their income tax. Employees paid a 6.2 percent FICA tax on all wages up to $87,900 in 2004, and an additional 1.45 percent on all wages up to any amount for Medicare. All employee taxes are matched dollar for dollar by employers, meaning that self-employed Americans must pay 15.3 percent total.

Although Social Security has been enormously successful in lowering the poverty rate among older Americans, it is under increasing pressure as Americans get older. In 1990, for example, the average American was 33 years old; by 2020, the average age will be 38 years. The average age is rising in part because Americans are having fewer children, and in part because of medical advances that have increased the lifespan. Medical advances have been particularly important in increasing the number of very old Americans—the number of Americans over the age of 85 is expected to grow from roughly 3 million in 2000 to 17 million in 2050, which means increased Social Security and Medicare costs.

These increases would not be a problem if the payroll taxes coming into Social Security and Medicare from today's workers were put away for their eventual retirement.

PEOPLE & POLITICS *Making a Difference* ★ ★ ★

LUCILLE ROYBAL-ALLARD

Having served Los Angeles's Hispanic community in the California legislature for six years, Lucille Roybal-Allard entered the U.S. Congress in 1992 as the first Mexican-American woman elected to the House. Six years later, she became the first Mexican-American woman to head the Hispanic Congressional Caucus, which had been founded by her father and two other Hispanic House members in 1976. In 1998, she was elected chair of the entire California congressional delegation, another first for a Mexican-American woman.

Although Roybal-Allard is proud of her father's work, she represents a new generation of Hispanic Caucus members who are trying to broaden the debate about Hispanic issues. "People need to understand that Latino issues are American issues and American issues are Latino issues," she says. "We all care about the same thing."*

As the number of Hispanic Americans has grown steadily over the past three decades, Roybal-Allard and other leaders have worked hard to educate the rest of the country that the term "Hispanic" cov-

ers a wide range of groups such as Mexicans, Cubans, Puerto Ricans, and Central and South Americans who care just as much about jobs, education, and health care as the rest of the nation.

Indeed, Roybal-Allard is careful to note that she was not the first Hispanic woman elected to Congress. That honor belongs to Ileana Ros-Lehtinen, who was born in Havana, Cuba, in 1952, immigrated to the United States in 1959, and was elected to Congress in 1988.

Whatever their country of origin, many of today's Hispanic members of Congress have a broader agenda than their predecessors. "The era that my father grew up in, in which his principles and values were formed, was totally different than my own," says San Antonio Democratic Representative Charles Gonzalez, who replaced his father, Henry B. Gonzalez, in Congress in 1999. "He was a product of a time when discrimination was open and obvious. We are products of a different process."†

New Jersey Representative Bob Menendez agrees. A Cuban-American who has served as vice-chair of the entire

House Democratic Caucus, Menendez says that "I'd like to think that we as Latinos are just as interested in health care, retirement security and our place in the world as any other American. We should be going beyond the issues we're forced to deal with by necessity, and into other issues where we can make a difference. We are coming into our own."

*Roxanne Roberts, Janelle Erlichman, "Politics with a Latin Beat: Hispanic Caucus Celebrates a Major Minority," *The Washington Post,* September 21, 2000, p. C-1.
†Gregory Rodriguez, "From Minority to Mainstream: Latinos Find Their Voice," *The Washington Post,* January 24, 1999, p. B1.

But much of the revenue actually goes to payments for today's retirees. Social Security is thus a "pay-as-you-go" system, in which today's young workers finance the retirement of today's elderly. At some point in the not-too-distant future, there will not be enough workers paying into the two programs to cover all the benefits. Under current projections, Medicare is expected to start running deficits in 2019, and Social Security in 2029. Sooner or later, Congress will have to decide whether to raise taxes on workers, cut benefits for older Americans, increase the retirement age, or some combination of all three.

The Social Security system is still running a surplus, meaning that the amount of revenue collected through Social Security taxes is still greater than the amount of money going out in benefits. The surpluses are invested in Treasury bonds, with the promise that they will be repaid with interest later. As the baby boomers retire and begin to collect Social Security, however, the bonds must be redeemed to pay benefits, and the program will start running annual deficits. Experts differ on when the next Social Security funding crisis will come, but there is little disagreement that something will have to be done to ensure the viability of Social Security for young people now paying into the system.[14]

HELP FOR THE UNEMPLOYED   Social Security was not the only strand of economic protection woven during the New Deal. The New Deal also produced the federal government's first unemployment insurance program, which was enacted as part of the 1935 Social Security Act. Under the program, which is administered by state governments but funded in part with federal unemployment taxes, eligible workers can receive benefits for up to 26 weeks in most states. In periods of high unemployment, the federal government also provides funds for extended benefits for a maximum of 39 weeks in most states.

HELP FOR THE POOR   The federal government became involved in protecting women and children against poverty when Congress passed the Infancy and Maternity Protection Act of 1921. Supported by many of the same women's groups that had just won ratification of the Nineteenth Amendment, which gave women the right to vote, the act gave the newly created federal Children's Bureau funds to encourage states to create new maternal, infant, and early childhood health programs. Although the act was allowed to expire in 1929, it set a precedent for future federal involvement in protecting families against poverty.

Congress also established the school lunch program during the New Deal as both a way to help feed the hungry and to strengthen the ailing farm economy. The Federal Surplus Relief Corporation began purchasing surplus agriculture products for needy families in 1935 and launched the nation's first school lunch programs for poor children shortly thereafter. By 1941, more than 5 million children were receiving free school lunches, consuming more than 450 million pounds of surplus pork, dairy products, and bread. Although the program was disbanded during World War II because of food shortages, it was restored under the 1946 National School Lunch Act. As President Harry Truman said at the signing ceremony, "No nation is any healthier than its children." He could have added that many draftees had been rejected for service in World War II because of malnutrition.

Congress moved even further to help the needy when it passed the Aid to Families with Dependent Children (AFDC) program in 1935.[15] By its very name, AFDC tried to shift the focus away from what the mother had or had not done to deserve poverty and onto the children who suffered whatever the cause, thereby reducing public opposition to expanded benefits. Under the program, states were given federal money to establish cash grants for poor families under two conditions: (1) States had to match the federal funds with some contribution of their own, and (2) states had to establish a means test for all families receiving benefits. AFDC was abolished in 1996 when Congress and the president created an entirely new program that required states to set time limits on public assistance, thereby creating a greater incentive for welfare recipients to find work.

The Great Society

The second major expansion of social policy came in the 1960s with what became known as the Great Society. At a commencement speech at the University of Michigan in May 1964, President Lyndon Johnson described his vision of the Great Society:

THE FEDERAL GOVERNMENT'S SAFETY NET FOR OLDER AMERICANS

Social Security and Disability—established 1935

Provides *retirement* benefits starting at age 65 and 4 months in 2004 (with reduced benefits available as early as age 62), and *disability* benefits payable at any age to people with a severe physical or mental impairment that prevents them from doing "substantial" work for a year or more or who have a condition that is expected to result in death. Other members of the family of persons eligible for retirement or disability benefits may be entitled to *family* benefits. The Old Age, Survivors, and Disability Insurance Trust Fund (OASDI) also provides *survivors'* benefits for certain family members of deceased persons who earned enough Social Security credits while working.

Medicare—established 1965

Provides hospital insurance (Part A) and medical insurance (Part B) to individuals who are also entitled to Social Security. Part A is funded by a portion of the Social Security taxes paid by people still working and pays for inpatient hospital care, skilled nursing care, and other services. Part B is funded by monthly premiums paid by enrollees and from general revenues and pays for a portion of doctors' fees, outpatient hospital visits, and other medical services and supplies.

Supplemental Security Income (SSI)—established 1972

Provides monthly payments to disabled persons or those over age 65 who meet an income test. Levels of SSI support vary by state to reflect cost-of-living differences. SSI recipients also qualify for Medicaid, food stamps, and other assistance. SSI benefits are financed by general tax revenues.

SOURCE: Social Security Administration, at www.ssa.gov/pubs/10006.html.

President Lyndon Johnson's vision of a Great Society relied on the principle of government action to solve economic and social problems.

The Great Society rests on abundance and liberty for all. It demands an end to poverty and racial injustice. . . . But that is just the beginning. The Great Society is a place where every child can find knowledge to enrich his mind and to enlarge his talents. . . . It is a challenge constantly renewed, beckoning us toward a destiny where the meaning of our lives matches the marvelous products of our labors.[16]

Johnson's agenda was as broad as his rhetoric, and Congress enacted much of it in a fairly short period of time. Great Society programs dramatically increased the role of the federal government in education through a number of programs that exist today:

- *Food stamps.* The food stamp program gives poor families coupons that can be used to purchase the basics of a healthy, nutritious diet. The average benefit is about $75 per person per month.

- *Head Start.* Head Start is a preschool program designed to help poor children get ready for kindergarten. The program serves more than 900,000 children each year at a cost of roughly $7,000 per child. Almost 30 percent of Head Start teachers and staff are parents of Head Start children or were Head Start children themselves.

- *Medicaid.* **Medicaid** was created in 1965 to provide basic health services for poor families. The program is administered by state governments, which are responsible for determining eligibility, and covers everything from hospital care to family planning.

- *Supplemental Security Income.* The SSI program was created in 1972, to provide an extra measure of support for the elderly poor and the blind or disabled. The program provides monthly benefit checks ranging from just $1 to roughly $800 and is administered by the Social Security Administration.

- *Housing assistance.* The Department of Housing and Urban Development, which was created in 1965, administers a number of programs designed to help low-income families find affordable, safe housing, in part by giving property owners subsidies to make up the difference between what tenants can pay and what the local housing market will bear.

The Great Society also produced a vast new social insurance program to cover all hospital and most other health care costs for older Americans. Under the **Medicare** program, the federal government pays all of the reasonable costs of all inpatient hospital care, including drugs, surgery, and postoperative care, regardless of the beneficiary's personal wealth. Like Social Security, this insurance is "purchased" through payroll taxes, which are set aside solely for Medicare expenditures. Medicare beneficiaries are also entitled to purchase additional federal health insurance to cover the costs of outpatient care, physician visits, and laboratory fees, but not prescription drugs.[17] Medicare beneficiaries must also pay a deductible on all hospital stays and a monthly premium for the additional insurance.

The Great Society also produced a long list of important changes in other social policies, including the following:

- *Civil Rights Act of 1964*—set forth the most comprehensive civil rights protections since Reconstruction

- *Food Stamp Act of 1965*—expanded the New Deal program to improve nutrition among the poor

- *Elementary and Secondary Education Act of 1965*—established federal funding and programs in public education for disadvantaged children

- *Higher Education Act of 1965*—established federal funding for colleges and college students

- *Department of Housing and Urban Development Act of 1965*—created a new department with responsibility for low-rent housing and urban renewal programs

- *Child Nutrition Act of 1966*—expanded federal programs to reduce childhood hunger

Medicaid
Federal program that provides medical benefits for low-income persons.

Medicare
National health insurance program for the elderly and disabled.

- *Fair Packaging and Labeling Act of 1966*—expanded federal oversight of consumer labeling
- *Age Discrimination Act of 1967*—prohibited discrimination based on age
- *Housing and Urban Development Act of 1968*—expanded federal housing and urban development programs
- *Open Housing Act of 1968*—prohibited discrimination in housing
- *Omnibus Crime Control and Safe Streets Act of 1968*—provided federal aid for local law enforcement, crime prevention, and corrections programs

Although Great Society programs such as Medicare, Head Start, and food stamps remain essential threads in the social safety net today, they were enacted during a period of enormous domestic unrest over race relations and the Vietnam War. Unable to win public support for his "guns and butter" agenda, and unsure that he could even win his own party's presidential nomination, Johnson eventually decided not to seek reelection in 1968.

Reforming Welfare

Republicans have not been the only critics of the New Deal and Great Society welfare programs. President Bill Clinton made welfare reform a centerpiece of his reelection agenda in 1996, having promised to "end welfare as we know it."[18]

Working with the new Republican congressional majority, Clinton won passage of the Personal Responsibility and Work Opportunity Reconciliation Act in 1996, which replaced AFDC with Temporary Assistance for Needy Families (TANF). Its name captures two themes of the new act—individuals should take more responsibility for themselves, and work, not welfare, is the goal of public assistance.

The burden of administering the new program was shifted entirely to the states. The federal government now gives *block grants* of money to the states and generally requires that the states match those funds. Under the new rules, federally funded public assistance is limited to five years over a person's lifetime, and all recipients must enter some kind of work training program within two months of receiving initial benefits. Although states can exempt up to 20 percent of cases from the work requirements and lifetime limits—an exemption intended for blind and disabled persons, the message to recipients is clear: find work soon.

The law originally excluded legal immigrants from many welfare programs, but at the strong urging of the governors, most welfare benefits were later restored to legal immigrants. To discourage persons on welfare from moving to states with more generous assistance payments, the law gave states the option of limiting welfare to newcomers from other states. This provision was declared unconstitutional by a federal district court judge, who said it "denies 'equal protection of the laws' to indigent families moving from one state to another."[19]

There are several ways to measure the success of the 1996 welfare reform. One is simply to ask whether the number of welfare recipients has declined. By 2002, the number of welfare recipients was lower than it had been in more than three decades. As the authors of a 2002 study of welfare reform argue, "The welfare rolls have declined greatly, more mothers than ever are working, the average income of female-headed families is increasing, and poverty has dropped substantially."[20] The number continued to fall in 2003 despite the economic downturn. As of March 2003, the total number of Americans who received federal welfare benefits had fallen to 4.9 million, 60 percent fewer than in August 1996 when the reforms were enacted.

Yet merely reducing the number of welfare recipients is no guarantee that they either have good-paying jobs or are moving out of poverty. It is one thing to remove a recipient from the welfare rolls and quite another to get the person into a good job with decent benefits. Research suggests that most mothers who leave welfare make $7 to 8 per hour, well above the minimum wage. However, most mothers who leave welfare have other expenses, such as transportation and child care, that may or may not be covered

★★ YOU DECIDE

SHOULD THE FEDERAL GOVERNMENT ENCOURAGE WELFARE RECIPIENTS TO GET MARRIED?

Although the 1996 welfare reform focused most on replacing welfare with work, it also ordered the federal government to promote marriage. Advocates argue that marriage improves the lives of both children and parents. Married adults, whether women or men, are happier, healthier, and wealthier than their unmarried peers and are more likely to give their children a healthier start. Some advocates even argue that more marriages would reduce health costs by reducing depression and crime. None of these advocates supports same-sex marriage, however.

The federal government can promote marriage in two ways. First, it can reduce the penalties it imposes on welfare recipients who get married. Under current law, for example, a single mother working full time at a minimum-wage job who marries stands to lose as much as $8,000 a year in cash and noncash benefits. Second, it can promote marriage through advertising, counseling, or even providing cash grants for getting married to be paid out over a period of years.

by state or local assistance, and many who go to work lose their food stamps and Medicaid, which means they are more dependent on food banks and have to go without preventive health care.

Besides confirming the fundamental American belief in rugged individualism, the 1996 welfare bill has significant ramifications for our federal system. This *devolution* of power to the states in the area of welfare is seen as a testing ground for other transfers of responsibility to the states with and without federal funding.

SOCIAL POLICY CHALLENGES FOR THE FUTURE: HEALTH, EDUCATION, AND SAFETY

Even if states take on a greater social policy role, the federal government is sure to remain the greatest source of funding for the safety net. As Table 19–2 shows, human resource spending for programs such as Social Security, Medicare, Medicaid, and child nutrition has more than doubled since 1950. Spending is almost certain to rise in coming years as the baby boom generation enters retirement and starts to draw down the Social Security surplus and use Medicare. Moreover, the federal social policy agenda will almost certainly expand as Congress and the president respond to public pressure for action on health care, education, and crime control.

The Federal Role in Health Care

Medicare is just one of the federal government's many health programs. It has been involved in reducing disease since 1887, when the federal government opened a one-room laboratory on Staten Island, New York, to study infectious diseases carried to the United States on passenger ships. In time, that one-room laboratory expanded into the National Institutes of Health (NIH), a conglomeration of 37 separate institutes on a 300-acre campus in Bethesda, Maryland.

The surgeon general of the United States is arguably the most visible health care official in government. As head of the Public Health Service (PHS), the surgeon general works closely with the NIH. Researchers in these institutes, working closely with experts in private laboratories, study causes and seek cures for serious diseases. Fellowships for health research are granted to able scientists and physicians. The NIH administers billions of dollars in grants each year to support the research of university and other scientists and physicians. The PHS also administers grants to states and local communities to help improve public health. Another federal agency promoting health is the Food and Drug Administration (FDA).

There are dozens of other federal agencies that work to improve public health. The Centers for Disease Control and Prevention (CDC) in Atlanta is also intimately involved in preventing disease. The CDC and its 7,800 "disease detectives" have been at the forefront of identifying a host of mystery illnesses, including the respiratory disease that attacked attendees at an American Legion convention in 1976 (Legionnaire's disease), toxic shock syndrome in 1980, and hepatitis C in 1989, while tracking down the causes of major health disasters, including the outbreak of the SARS upper-respiratory virus in 2003 and 2004.

TABLE 19–2　CHANGING PRIORITIES IN THE FEDERAL BUDGET

Function	1950	1960	1970	1980	1990	2000	2005
National defense	32%	52%	42%	23%	24%	15%	19%
Human resources	33	28	39	53	49	64	65
Physical resources	7	9	8	11	10	5	5
Interest on the debt	11	8	8	10	15	13	7

SOURCE: Summary Tables, *Budget of the United States, Fiscal Year 2005*, Washington, D.C., U.S. Government Printing Office, February 2004.

Despite its success in improving the nation's health, the federal government faces two major health care challenges in the future: containing costs and expanding coverage.

THE RISING COST OF HEALTH CARE   Health care costs in the United States have nearly quadrupled, after controlling for inflation, since 1970.[21] Although they slowed with the rest of the economy in 2001, costs are expected to escalate rapidly as the nation ages over the next two decades.

All Americans pay for the increasing costs (see Figure 19–1). Employers directly pay a large share of the costs of health insurance; about 6 percent of employee compensation is the cost of health care.[22] Consumers also pay more for health care, whether through increased private insurance premiums, deductibles, or copayments for services. Finally, taxpayers pay for the increases through federal dollars that might otherwise go to other programs such as homeland security, college loans, or highway construction.

The good news is that costs have risen in part because people live longer. Life expectancy increased by more than five years between 1970 and 1995. Most experts believe it will rise another year by 2015, in part because of advanced treatments, including new drugs for battling HIV-AIDS.[23] In 1900, only one out of every 25 Americans was over the age of 65. By 1950, the number was one in 12 and by 1985, one in nine. According to experts, the number will rise to one in five by 2030. In 1900, the average American lived to age 47; by 2000, the average had increased to 79. Again according to experts, the number will rise into the mid-80s by 2030.

As people live longer, of course, they place greater demands on the health care system, as well as on the Social Security program. New and advanced medical technology—life-support systems, ultrasound, sophisticated x-ray equipment, and genetic counseling—have all increased the costs of health care. They also place greater demands on other social policies.

The bad news is that some costs have nothing to do with saving lives or preventing disease. Some physicians claim that they have to perform procedures that may be medically unnecessary but are legally essential to reduce the risk of being sued by patients. These procedures are alleged to add up to billions in unnecessary costs, but they do not necessarily improve the quality of care provided to patients.[24] Physicians also complain about the high cost of malpractice insurance, nine times more costly in the United States than in Canada. Malpractice insurance costs for all physicians have more than doubled in a decade. A physician's insurance coverage routinely costs as much as $60,000 a year.[25] For specialists like obstetricians, premiums are 400 percent higher than for internists.[26]

Trial lawyers who represent people whose health was damaged or families of those whose lives were lost due to medical malpractice defend the huge punitive awards. They argue that physicians, like all professionals, have a responsibility to exercise sound professional judgment in their jobs, and when they do not, they should provide restitution to their victims.

Moreover, at least part of the cost crisis is avoidable. Medicare alone spends billions of dollars each year treating smoking-related diseases, and over the next 20 years the costs to treat such diseases will continue to rise.[27] Other illnesses at least partly related to lifestyle include heart disease, liver disease, HIV/AIDS, and the epidemic of health disorders created by obesity.

COVERING THE UNINSURED   Despite passage of the Medicare program, the nation has yet to develop a comprehensive insurance program for the approximately 60 million Americans who are uninsured at some point in any given year.[28] Although some rely on public clinics, emergency room care, or charity, many people go without any health or dental care.[29] Many of the uninsured have jobs, but their employers do not provide health insurance, and because their incomes are above the poverty line, they do not qualify for Medicaid. Uninsured individuals usually seek care in hospital emergency rooms only when their illness has reached a critical stage. Postponing medical care drives up costs because critical care is much more expensive than preventive medicine or early treatment.

★★ **THINKING IT THROUGH**

Although the federal government has long engaged in activities designed to promote good social behavior, such as early childhood vaccinations, campaigns against smoking, the use of seat belts, and the 55-mile-an-hour speed limit, not all Americans believe that marriage is the answer to welfare. They note that domestic violence and child abuse occur almost as frequently in married as in unmarried households. They also worry that government grants for marriage would promote a rash of false marriages designed to get the cash.

Most important, opponents believe that the best way to encourage marriage among welfare recipients is to find them good-paying jobs. They look to states such as Minnesota that have created strong welfare-to-work programs that do not punish married women for getting a job. Married women who entered Minnesota's Family Investment Program were a third more likely to still be married three years later than married women who stayed in the old welfare system. In theory, good-paying jobs lead to higher self-esteem, which leads to a sustainable marriage.

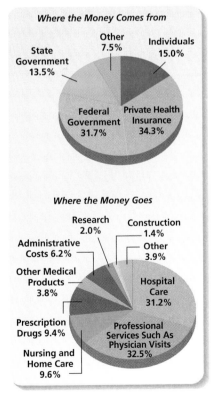

FIGURE 19–1 The Health Care Dollar, 2000.

Source: Centers for Medicare and Medicaid Services, at www.cms.bhs.gov/statistics/nhe.

IN COMPARATIVE PERSPECTIVE

HEALTH CARE IN THE UNITED STATES AND CANADA

Advanced industrial democracies like Canada, Germany, Japan, the Netherlands, and the United Kingdom provide health care for their entire population either through national health insurance or a national health service. Although the United States outspends all these countries in terms of health expenditures as a percentage of gross domestic product (see chart), this high level of spending on health care does not mean that the United States has a healthier population. The nation's infant mortality rates, for instance, are among the worst of all industrialized countries, and the United States ranks below average for industrialized nations in male and female life expectancy at birth.

The United States also differs from other countries in the extent to which health care costs are paid by public funds. Central or local governments fund approximately three-quarters of the cost of health care in most advanced industrial democracies.

In Canada, about 9 percent of the nation's GDP is devoted to health care spending, and all Canadians are covered by provincial health insurance. Canada's administration of health care is based on a publicly funded system, whereas the program in the United States is divided among public and private insurers. Canada's administrative costs per patient are only one-fourth the size of ours, and companies in the United States often pay three to five times more than Canadian companies to fund employee health and social benefits, including taxes collected by governments to pay for some of these benefits.

The Canadian health care system is not without its faults. Canadians are taxed at a much higher rate than Americans, in part to pay for the publicly funded system. In addition, patients may face delays in receiving services, especially for routine health problems and elective surgery. Doctors and nurses are also paid less in Canada, and thousands of them have moved to the United States, where salaries are much higher. Costs for health care are also increasing faster than the rate of inflation, and the Canadian federal and provincial governments have begun to cut back on funding certain services. Nevertheless, most Canadians express satisfaction with their health care system, and Canada manages to insure all of its people while spending far less per capita than the United States.

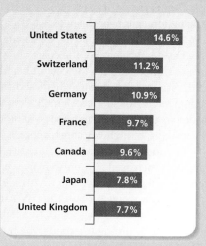

Total Health Care Expenditures as a Share of Gross Domestic Product, 2002.
SOURCE: Organization for Economic Cooperation and Development, Health Data, 2004.

But it is not just the poor who are uninsured. People who change jobs may often go without coverage for several months before their new insurance takes effect. And people with serious medical conditions may find the insurance company unwilling to cover their expenses, claiming that the illness is a "preexisting condition." Some insurance companies set caps on their coverage, meaning that families coping with very expensive illnesses end up essentially uninsured.

Although there are many different proposals for health care reform, the essential approaches include a single-payer system, prepaid health plans, employer-mandated coverage, spending caps, individual responsibility, and medical savings accounts.

Single Payer. Under a single-payer system, the national government, using broad-based taxes, covers the costs of health care and hospitalization and sets the rates. Like the system in Canada, such a plan would provide universal coverage and benefits to *all* Americans. No longer would people need to worry about the costs of catastrophic illnesses or a change in jobs that would exclude them from coverage. Proponents claim that the single-payer system would save billions of dollars in administrative expenses by reducing the number of insurers from about 1,200 to 1. Opponents of the single-payer system claim it would lead to a bureaucratic mess, with little incentive for innovation, cost control, or diversity of coverage. They further claim that the government would be put in the position of deciding which procedures to pay for and how to ration access to these procedures. As a result, they contend, Americans would lose not only quality in their health care but their freedom of choice as well.

It takes banks of computers for HMO employees to organize and run the bureaucracy of managed health care.

Business leaders generally oppose single-payer coverage out of concern for costs and what the program would do to taxes and the federal budget. The American Medical Association, U.S. Chamber of Commerce, Health Insurance Association of America, and other interest groups representing health care providers oppose the single-payer system. Labor unions, some senior citizens groups, and most consumer groups advocate this type of plan.

Prepaid Health Plans. Cost containment has been a frequent refrain of large corporations and consumer groups. In the 1970s and 1980s, business owners reduced benefits, increased payments by employees, and encouraged employees to join managed care plans called **health maintenance organizations (HMOs)** in which individuals or their employees pay a set amount for each person covered each year in return for health care and hospital coverage. During the 1980s and 1990s, HMO enrollment increased fourfold, from just under 10 million in 1980 to almost 80 million Americans in 2004. Most HMOs guarantee access, but many do not guarantee that a patient can see the same physician.

Because there are no national standards of heath care quality, consumer groups are pressing HMOs to improve treatment of specific conditions and are urging Congress and the president to enter the battle.[30] HMOs counter that they provide adequate care at reasonable costs and that national standards would drive up costs. Consumers want the reduced costs associated with HMOs but do not like the limitations on choice of physicians and the right to sue health plans or the lack of coverage for some procedures.[31]

The quality of HMO care and limitations on patient choice became political issues in the 2000 elections. Both parties endorsed competing variations of what they call a "patient's bill of rights." Such a bill of rights would permit a woman to see a gynecologist as her primary care physician, allow for review of the need for medical procedures, leave it to the doctor to determine the length of stay in the hospital, require coverage of emergency care a "prudent layperson" would deem necessary, and remove rules that deny doctors permission to talk to patients. George W. Bush called for granting HMO patients the right to appeal denials of care to an independent review panel, providing report cards on HMOs, giving women direct access to their obstetrician-gynecologist, and in some cases being able to sue HMOs. Even though both presidential nominees called for expanded rights for HMO consumers, legislation on this matter after the election consistently stalled in both houses, due in part to an aggressive advertising campaign against the reforms that was funded by insurance companies and HMOs.

health maintenance organization (HMO)
Alternative means of health care in which people or their employers are charged a set amount and the HMO provides health care and covers hospital costs.

Employer-Mandated Coverage. Currently more than 161 million Americans get some form of medical insurance from their employers.[32] But many small businesses contend that they cannot afford to provide this benefit and stay in business. Some have estimated that the costs of health care for small businesses may be 10 to 40 percent higher than for large businesses. In businesses with fewer than 25 employees, only about one-third of the workers receive coverage directly from their employer.[33] Mandating coverage does not solve this problem, nor does it take care of individuals who do not have jobs.

Proponents counter that the negative consequences can be mitigated through tax credits and government subsidies. They also point out that if all small businesses provide health insurance, none of them will be put at a disadvantage compared to other small businesses. As noted, the federal government allows businesses to deduct what they pay in health benefits to employees as a business expense and gives tax credits to low-income families to purchase coverage for their children.

Spending Caps. Because the cost of providing health care each year consumes a larger and larger share of our gross domestic product, some have proposed that the national government impose an overall expenditure cap on health care that applies not only to public expenditures but to private ones as well. Supporters of a cap include some prominent Democrats. The American Hospital Association, American Medical Association, and Pharmaceutical Manufacturers Association vigorously oppose the idea. They argue that spending caps would limit research and development in medicine and deter talented young people from pursuing medical careers. However, the costs associated with an ever-older population may yet lead to some form of spending caps and the health rationing that would clearly go with them.

Individual Responsibility for Coverage. Another reform proposal is to apply a free market approach to health care by abolishing *all* employer-provided benefits and encouraging individuals to buy health insurance on their own, in much the same way that individuals are responsible for purchasing their own automobile insurance. Those with low incomes, including people not now insured, would have tax credits or vouchers to assist in the purchase of insurance.

Advocates of such a market solution say that if individuals purchased their own insurance, they might pay more attention to costs and more closely monitor doctor and hospital fees. When higher wages are combined with tax credits, some individuals could end up with improved benefits tailored to their individual needs. Such a plan would also eliminate the need to impose price controls or pay for a large health care bureaucracy. It is unlikely, however, that employees would recover all they now spend on health care from their employers, so costs to individual consumers might increase. It is also unlikely that all uninsured persons who need government assistance could be taken care of without a tax increase to pay for it. Perhaps most important, such a proposal would run into so much political opposition that it presents an unlikely alternative.

Medical Savings Accounts. In 1996, Congress authorized an experiment with **medical savings accounts**. As of 2004, individuals may make tax-deductible contributions of roughly $2,600 a year ($5,150 for a family) to a special medical savings account that can be used to pay medical expenses not covered by insurance or government.[34] Withdrawals for other purposes are taxable and subject to an early withdrawal penalty.

Supporters of medical savings accounts say that they will eventually lower health care costs by giving people the incentive to spend their own money more carefully. They also allow people to go to a doctor of their own choosing without prior approval from their insurance company. Opponents of medical savings accounts say that they amount to nothing more than a tax break for the wealthy and the healthy. Because of high deductibles, people may decide not to seek needed services and preventive care. Opponents also argue that because healthier people are more likely to sign up for medical savings accounts, sicker people pay higher insurance premiums. Older and less wealthy people will not be able to afford to invest in medical savings accounts, critics charge, and will be forced to depend on more expensive insurance.

medical savings account
Alternative means of health care in which individuals make tax-deductible contributions to a special account that can be used to pay medical expenses.

The Federal Role in Education

The federal government has been involved with education at least since the Northwest Ordinance of 1785, in which Congress set aside one section in each township for support of a public school. In 1862, the Morrill Land Grant Act provided grants of land to states for universities specializing in the mechanical or agricultural arts. The U.S. Office of Education was established in 1867 to oversee these programs, but the scope of federal involvement was modest by today's standards. Even the G.I. Bill, which helped provide a college education for approximately 20 million World War II veterans, was seen more as an employment program than educational one.

During the cold war, however, education became one part of the national defense. When the Soviet Union launched *Sputnik*—the first man-made satellite to orbit the earth—in 1957, Congress responded in 1958 by passing the National Defense Education Act to upgrade science, language, and mathematics courses.

ELEMENTARY AND SECONDARY EDUCATION Kindergarten through high school education is generally seen as a state and local responsibility. Most children go to public schools run by local school boards and funded, at least partly, by property taxes. Because school districts vary greatly in the wealth of their residents, children from poor districts are much more likely to have lower-quality public schools than those from wealthier districts. As a result, public schools vary in the quality of teacher preparation, student performance, dropout rates, and educational opportunities provided to minority students.

Although the federal government has been reluctant to make direct investments in poor school districts, it has tried to help the children those districts serve. In 1964, for example, Congress created the Head Start program for preschool children. Under the program, needy children get help learning to read and understand numbers. Head Start centers also provide healthy meals and snacks and monitor child health care. Many also work with parents to encrourage greater involvement and literacy.

Recent evaluations of the program suggests that Head Start increases learning, but they have also revealed the need for improvement. In 2004, Head Start provided funding to 19,000 child-care centers with almost 50,000 classrooms, some of which reported chronic shortages of well-trained teachers. In addition, the student–teacher ratio varied significantly across the centers. Moreover, the program is not an entitlement, meaning that funding only covers roughly a third of all eligible children. When the dollars run out, Head Start centers stop enrolling participants.

Head Start is not the federal government's only education program, however. In 1965, Congress passed the Elementary and Secondary Education Act (ESEA), which supplied educational materials for underprivileged public school students and provided funding for research on how to assist children from disadvantaged backgrounds. Over the years, the act was amended to provide federal support for special education, as well as additional funding for textbooks, teacher training, and other support for poor schools. In 2005, the federal government spent $38 billion on local education, or barely 9 percent of total school spending.

As concerns about the quality of public education increased during the 1990s, however, the federal government became more involved in local education, first by setting national goals for student achievement, then by passing the No Child Left Behind Act in 2001. In return for federal funding, states were required to annually test at least 95 percent of all third and eighth graders in reading and math. In addition, states were required to grade schools as passing or failing, set higher standards for teachers, and give students in failing schools the option to move to higher-performing schools. Schools must either improve test scores each year or risk being labeled "in need of improvement." Under the act, all students are supposed to be proficient in reading and math by 2014.

Although the new law set higher standards, it increased federal spending for education by only a tiny percentage. By 2005, many states were complaining that they did not have enough funding to test every student every year, nor enough to meet the law's requirement for teacher training and certification. In addition, schools with many disabled or special-needs-type students can be unfairly categorized as "failing" because they cannot meet the test-score requirement.

Americans ask more of their schools than just to educate their children. Schools have become one-stop social policy centers and are now a major means by which basic nutrition is provided to millions of poor children. Schools screen at-risk children and attempt to get them medical and psychological assistance; they seek to socialize students into acceptable behaviors, often in the face of increasing violence in the surrounding neighborhoods; and they often reach out to families to provide basic help in parenting.

HIGHER EDUCATION   The federal government also provides help to college and universities. In 2005, the federal government provided roughly 70 percent, or $23 billion, of the financial aid that college students receive. Pell grants for low-income students and low-interest guaranteed student loans continue to be the most available and most used subsidies for college expenses. In 1998, Congress added three new programs to improve the odds that needy children will make it to college. GEAR-UP, which supports early interventions to help students complete high school, the Learning Anytime Anywhere Partnerships (LAAP), which provide federal funding for distance-learning through the Internet, and a new initiative designed to improve teacher quality in primary and elementary schools. Although the three programs account for less than 1 percent of federal spending for education, they acknowledge the link between the quality of primary and elementary education and college success, as well as the need to act early to increase the odds of success for needy students.

CHANGING FACE OF AMERICAN POLITICS

ACCESS TO COLLEGE

Federal aid to education has increased access to college for all Americans, but it has had a particularly significant effect on women and students of color. The effect has been pronounced at both the community college and four-year college levels, where women now earn the majority of associate and bachelor degrees, and where students of color have more than doubled over the decades. Under the 1998 Higher Education Act, the number of students of color should increase even faster as the federal government puts more dollars into preparing students for college.

	1976–77	2000–01
Associate Degrees		
Men	51.8%	40.0%
Women	48.2	60.0
White	84.5	71.0
Black, non-Hispanic	8.2	11.0
Hispanic	4.1	9.9
Asian/Pacific Islander	1.7	4.9
American Indian/Alaska Native	0.6	1.1
Nonresident alien	0.8	2.0
Bachelor's Degrees		
Men	53.8%	42.7%
Women	46.2	57.3
White	88.0	73.8
Black, non-Hispanic	6.4	10.3
Hispanic	2.0	6.5
Asian/Pacific Islander	1.5	6.0
American Indian/Alaska Native	0.4	0.7
Nonresident alien	1.7	2.6

SOURCE: U.S. Department of Education, National Center for Education Statistics: *Postsecondary Institutions in the United States: Fall 2001 Degrees and Other Awards Conferred: 2000–01* (Washington, D.C., 2003), accessed at nces.edu.gov/fastfacts.

The Federal Role in Crime Control

Controlling crime is also considered primarily a state and local matter. The federal government usually acts more as a banker than a police officer, providing grants to states and local governments to hire their own police officers, build more prisons, improve drug enforcement, and prosecute organized crime.

Crime is hardly unimportant to national politics, however. The federal government must enforce its own laws against everything from counterfeiting to pollution while protecting its borders and preventing drugs from flowing into the country.

Congress has intervened on such matters as gun control. Because guns are manufactured and transported across state lines, Congress has the power to regulate sales under the Constitution's commerce clause and has used it to ban the sale and ownership of semiautomatic weapons and assault rifles and set age minimums for the purchase of handguns (21 years of age) and long guns such as rifles and shotguns (18 years of age).

In 1993, for example, Congress passed landmark legislation imposing a waiting period on the purchase of handguns. Under the Brady Handgun Violence Prevention Act, federally licensed firearms dealers have five days to check with local law enforcement officials regarding the background of a potential purchaser. If local law enforcement officials fail to respond within five business days, the handgun can be sold. The National Rifle Association has been powerful enough to stop most other antigun legislation, even though such legislation has had the support of most police chiefs and most of the general public. The debate over gun control at the local, state, and national levels remains intense.

In 1994, Congress passed an omnibus anticrime bill that authorized over $30 billion in spending on federal crime initiatives. The money funded the hiring of as many as 100,000 new police officers and the construction of new prisons and "boot camps" for juvenile offenders. The bill also added new assault rifle restrictions, made a long list of federal offenses punishable by death, imposed federal penalties and programs aimed at curbing domestic violence, and, with its "three strikes and you're out" provision, mandated life imprisonment upon conviction for a third violent felony.

The federal government enforces its laws primarily through the Department of Justice, which contains the Federal Bureau of Investigation (FBI). The FBI was created in 1908 and charged with gathering and reporting evidence in matters relating to federal criminal laws. In addition, the FBI provides investigative services on a cooperative basis to local law enforcement in fingerprint identification and laboratory services. Other law enforcement agencies of the federal government include the Drug Enforcement Agency

Sarah Brady campaigned tirelessly to win passage of the Brady Handgun Violence Prevention Act. She became a vocal advocate for gun control after her husband, James Brady, President Ronald Reagan's White House Press Secretary, was shot on March 30, 1981. Brady was shot by John Hinckley Jr. during his failed assassination attempt on President Reagan.

Legislation has been proposed to require purchasers of guns at gun shows to undergo an identity check on whether they have a record of criminal activity.

(DEA), which is responsible for preventing the flow of illegal narcotics into the United States, patrolling U.S. borders, and conducting joint operations with countries where drugs are produced, and the Bureau of Alcohol, Tobacco and Firearms, which monitors the sale of destructive weapons and guns inside the United States, regulates alcoholic beverage production, and oversees the collection of taxes on alcohol and tobacco.

Although the number of violent crimes decreased through the 1990s, it began rising in 2001, reinforcing the widespread perception that crime and violence are increasing and the federal government needs to step in. As a result, Congress has made more and more crimes federal ones and increased the severity of punishments for them. As more people are put in prisons, the costs for building and running them has increased dramatically.

Terrorism is clearly the federal government's top crime priority today. Only weeks after the September 11, 2001, terrorist attacks on New York City and Washington, D.C., Congress passed a massive antiterrorism law in October 2001 and created the new Department of Homeland Security the following summer. For his part, the president created the Office of Homeland Security within the White House in October and ordered a complete reorganization of the Federal Bureau of Investigation in early 2002 to create a stronger focus on preventing terrorism. Under the USA PATRIOT Act of 2001 (the letters stand for Uniting and Strengthening America by Providing Appropriate Tools Required to Intercept and Obstruct Terrorism), for example, the federal government was given sweeping authority to conduct secret investigations of suspected terrorists, use "roving wiretaps" to intercept conversations on any phones that a suspect might use, and detain any noncitizens believed to be a national security risk for up to seven days without being charged with a crime.

Although the USA PATRIOT Act is not scheduled to expire until December 31, 2005, the Bush administration made its renewal a centerpiece of the president's 2004 State of the Union Address. "Key provisions of the Patriot Act are set to expire next year," the president told Congress. "The terrorist threat will not expire on that schedule. Our law enforcement needs this vital legislation to protect our citizens." The administration also asked Congress to expand authority to investigate what it called "lone-wolf" terrorists who are not affiliated with a foreign government or known terrorist organization such as Al-Qaeda, which planned the September 11 attacks.[35]

THE POLITICS OF SOCIAL POLICY

Despite the nation's current focus on terrorism and homeland security, social policy still dominates the agenda of American politics. Welfare, health care, education, and crime—and their costs—are today's political battleground between the parties and between contending interest groups. Education reform was at the forefront of the 2000 presidential election, while the war on terrorism was part of the 2004 campaign.

The nation long ago answered questions about whether the national government has a role in providing decent housing, adequate health care, and a solid education for all of its citizens. The question is not whether the nation will provide a safety net for its needy citizens, but how strong the net will be and who will be responsible for providing it. Although the vast majority of Americans support Social Security and Medicare, for example, they are sharply divided over how much the nation should do for its poorest citizens. They are also increasingly divided about reforms such as the No Child Left Behind Act and its mandatory testing.

Nevertheless, social policy will be part of the federal agenda far into the future. Although Presidents and Congress cannot always know what Americans will support and how much they are willing to pay, they can be sure that most Americans want government to take care of citizens who are needy through no fault of their own.

Summary

1. Conservatives advocate private solutions for most social problems, while liberals argue that it is the responsibility of government to provide a minimum standard of living—including a job, an education, health care, housing, and nutrition—for all citizens. Since the New Deal, some national government involvement in social programs has been widely accepted, although the extent of involvement has waxed and waned. Conservatives generally prefer state and local government action over federal programs.

2. Social Security, inaugurated in 1935 as part of the New Deal, is perhaps the most significant social legislation in U.S. history. Through a system of employee and employer taxes, retired workers and disabled individuals receive monthly payments and health benefits. With the country's aging population, strains on the system are likely to increase.

3. Welfare takes many forms, including direct payments to the poor, the unemployed, and the disabled; food stamps; job training; housing subsidies; free school lunches; tax credits; and subsidized medical care. Public assistance programs began with the New Deal and have grown ever since.

4. Welfare has long been criticized as creating disincentives to work, and many proposals have been put forward to make programs more effective and efficient. The most recent welfare reform, which became law in August 1996, transferred the administrative burden to the states, giving them more discretion over recipients and benefits while helping to fund welfare programs through block grants of federal money.

5. The federal government supports medical research and has increased its role in health care cost control and access as the country's mostly private health care system is beset by rising costs, increasing numbers of uninsured Americans, unnecessary procedures, endless paperwork, high litigation costs, avoidable illnesses, and limited access. A variety of proposals for reform are under consideration, including a single-payer system, prepaid health plans, employer-mandated coverage, spending caps, individual responsibility for coverage, and medical savings accounts.

6. Education continues to be primarily a state and local government function in the United States. The federal government plays an important role in funding public schools and pushing national goals for better education, and is also heavily involved in helping finance college and university education.

7. Crime control has been part of the national agenda for decades, especially related to drugs, but has become much more visible as part of the war on terrorism.

Key Terms

entitlements	social insurance	Medicare	medical savings account
means-tested entitlements	Social Security	health maintenance	
public assistance	Medicaid	organization (HMO)	

Further Reading

ANNE MARIE CAMMISA, *From Rhetoric to Reform? Welfare Policy in American Politics* (Westview Press, 1998).

BARBARA EHRENREICH, *Nickled and Dimed: On (Not) Getting By in America* (Metropolitan Books, 2001).

FRANK FISCHER, *Evaluating Public Policy* (Nelson-Hall, 1995).

LAURENE A. GRAIG, *Health of Nations: An International Perspective on U.S. Health Care Reform* (CQ Press, 1993).

CHRISTOPHER JENCKS, *The Homeless* (Harvard University Press, 1994).

PAUL C. LIGHT, *Still Artful Work: The Continuing Politics of Social Security Reform* (McGraw-Hill, 1995).

THOMAS E. MANN AND NORMAN J. ORNSTEIN, EDS., *Intensive Care: How Congress Shapes Health Policy* (Brookings Institution Press, 1995).

DANIEL PATRICK MOYNIHAN, *Miles to Go: A Personal History of Social Policy* (Harvard University Press, 1996).

CHARLES MURRAY, *Losing Ground: American Social Policy, 1950–80* (Basic Books, 1984).

B. GUY PETERS, *American Public Policy: Promise and Performance*, 4th ed. (Chatham House, 1996).

PAUL E. PETERSON AND MARTIN R. WEST, EDS., *No Child Left Behind: The Politics and Practice of School Accountability* (Brookings Institution Press, 2004).

FRANCES FOX PIVEN AND RICHARD A. CLOWARD, *Regulating the Poor: The Functions of Public Welfare* (Vintage, 1993).

THEDA SKOCPOL, *Social Policy in the United States: Future Possibilities in Historical Perspective* (Princeton University Press, 1995).

R. KENT WEAVER, *Ending Welfare as We Know It* (Brookings Institution Press, 2001).

MARGARET WEIR, ED., *The Social Divide: Political Parties and the Future of Activist Government* (Brookings Institution Press, 1998).

BOB WOODWARD, *Agenda: Inside the Clinton White House* (Simon & Schuster, 1994).

MAKING FOREIGN AND DEFENSE POLICY

20

The Bush administration entered office facing a long list of foreign policy challenges. North Korea and Iran were continuing to develop nuclear weapons, Israel and the Palestinians were embroiled in violence, the global economy was entering a deep downturn, HIV-AIDS was spreading rapidly through Africa and Asia, and terrorism was on the rise.

Iraq and its brutal dictator, Saddam Hussein, were also on the foreign policy agenda. "From the very beginning, there was a conviction, that Saddam Hussein was a bad person and that he needed to go," Bush's former Treasury Secretary Paul O'Neill told CBS News in 2004. "From the very first instance, it was about Iraq. It was about what we can do to change this regime. Day one, these things were laid and sealed." No one ever questioned the basic assumption that Hussein had to go. "It was all about finding a way to do it," O'Neill recalled. "That was the tone of it. The president saying 'Go find me a way to do this.'"[1]

The Bush administration was particularly concerned about Iraq's interest in developing **weapons of mass destruction** (WMD)—a term that refers to chemical, biological, and/or nuclear weapons that can be used to inflict massive casualties on an enemy. Hussein had used chemical weapons against his own citizens in the 1980s, but he had promised to destroy his inventory of biological and chemical agents at the end of the Gulf War in 1991, which followed Iraq's invasion of its oil-rich neighbor, Kuwait. As President Bush warned in his first press conference in mid-February 2001, "the primary goal is to make it clear to Saddam that we expect him to be a peaceful neighbor in the region and we expect him not to develop weapons of mass destruction. And if we find him doing so, there will be a consequence."

Despite these concerns, Iraq was hardly the top foreign policy issue early in the Bush administration. The president did not mention Iraq once when he outlined his domestic

TIME LINE

MAKING FOREIGN AND DEFENSE POLICY

1862	First military draft provokes riots
1917	United States enters World War I
1941	Pearl Harbor bombed, United States enters World War II
1945	Nuclear bombing of Hiroshima and Nagasaki ends World War II
1945	United Nations Charter signed in San Francisco
1947	National Security Agency and CIA created
1949	North Atlantic Treaty Organization created
1950	Start of the Korean War
1961	Kennedy seeks to motivate idealist youth through the Peace Corps
1964	Gulf of Tonkin resolution authorizes expansion of war in Vietnam
1972	Biological and Chemical Weapons treaty
1975	End of Vietnam War
1989	Cold war ends with the collapse of the Soviet Union
1993	World Trade Center is bombed but survives
2001	Attacks on World Trade Center and Pentagon

weapons of mass destruction
Biological, chemical, and nuclear weapons that can inflict massive casualties in a single event.

and foreign policy agenda before Congress in late February 2001, for example, nor did he ask for any new authority to remove Hussein from power.

Iraq moved rapidly up the list of priorities in the days and weeks following the terrorist attacks on New York City and Washington, D.C., on September 11 of that year, however. The war on terrorism was now the nation's top priority, and Iraq a potent enemy. Convinced that Iraq was ready and willing to use weapons of mass destruction against the United States, Bush ordered the military to start planning for a possible invasion on September 17, only six days after the terrorist attacks.[2] He also began building the case for action with the American public, arguing in his 2002 State of the Union Address that Iraq was part of an "axis of evil" that threatened the peace of the world.

On September 12, 2002, one year and one day after the terrorist attacks, Bush took the case to the United Nations. Iraq was not only "expanding and improving facilities that were used for the production of biological weapons," he said, it also had made several attempts to buy the equipment required to enrich uranium for a nuclear weapon. Bush also made the case for removing Hussein from power: "The United States has no quarrel with the Iraqi people; they've suffered too long in silent captivity. Liberty for the Iraqi people is a great moral cause, and a great strategic goal. The people of Iraq deserve it; the security of all nations requires it. Free societies do not intimidate through cruelty and conquest, and open societies do not threaten the world with mass murder. The United States supports political and economic liberty in a unified Iraq."

Three weeks later, on October 1, the Central Intelligence Agency gave members of Congress its 90-page National Intelligence Estimate on Iraq, which provided the evidence for war and formed the backbone of the president's October 7 address to the nation making the case for war. Three days later, on October 10, the House voted 296 to 133 in favor of a joint resolution authorizing the use of force in Iraq; the next day, the Senate voted 77 to 23 for the same resolution. The votes clearly indicated bipartisan, if not unified, support for action. Future Democratic presidential candidate John Kerry (D.-Mass.) voted in favor of the resolution, as did his running mate, John Edwards (D.-N.C.), and Senators Joseph Biden (D.-Del.), Hillary Clinton (D.-N.Y.), and Joseph Lieberman (D.-Conn.).

Meanwhile, the U.S. military continued planning for a possible war, moving thousands of troops and supplies into position in the Persian Gulf region. On March 20, 2003, the war began. U.S. troops reached the outskirts of Baghdad on April 6, secured the city over the next two days, and helped topple Hussein's statue at the center of the city on April 9. On May 1, President Bush stood on the deck of the USS *Abraham Lincoln* underneath a banner that read "MISSION ACCOMPLISHED" and told the nation that "Major combat operations in Iraq have ended."

Unfortunately, many of the assumptions on which the war was fought turned out to be wrong. Planners assumed, for example, that the Iraqi people would greet U.S. troops as liberators and accept a long, quiet occupation as the country returned to normalcy. Instead, the streets were soon filled with looting, followed by armed conflict between U.S. troops and religious militias. Having disarmed the Iraqi army and disbanded the local police, U.S. troops found themselves in charge of everything from directing traffic to protecting supply convoys.

Planners also assumed the Iraqi economy would make a quick recovery based on revenues from its oil fields, which in turn would help pay for the reconstruction of hospitals, schools, and other civic institutions. Instead, the Iraqi economy was on the verge of complete collapse. Although the oil fields emerged from the war intact, pipelines were damaged, roads and bridges were destroyed, sewer and water systems had collapsed, and few Iraqis were willing to risk their lives to help in the rebuilding.

Finally, planners assumed that U.S. troops would quickly find the weapons of mass destruction that had been so important to the case for war. Eighteen months after entering Baghdad, no such weapons had been found. As the Senate Select Committee on Intelligence reported in July 2004, most of the key judgments embedded in warnings about Iraq's weapons of mass destruction were "either overstated, or were not supported by, the underlying intelligence reporting."[3] Moreover, the highly critical Senate report concluded that the intelligence community "did not accurately or adequately explain to policy makers the uncertainties behind the judgments" that underpinned the conclusion that Iraq still had an active weapons program.

As these and other assumptions failed, and casualties mounted, public support for the war declined. The number of Americans who approved of the president's handling of the situation in Iraq fell from 73 percent just after the fall of Baghdad in April 2003 to just 42 percent by mid-June 2004, while the number who said the war was going "not too well" or "not well at all" rose from just 6 percent to 39 percent during the same period.[4] Although the United States did transfer some control to an interim government in late June 2004, it was clearly preparing for a long stay as the president entered the fall election campaign. Serious fighting continued.

This chapter will ask how choices are made in planning and executing foreign policy. We will first examine the foreign policy challenges before the nation today, including the new war against terrorism, then turn to the key actors in making foreign and defense policy, appraise the politics of making foreign and defense policy, and inventory the range of foreign and defense policy options. We will conclude with a more detailed assessment of defense policy.

President Bush on the deck of the USS Abraham Lincoln *on May 1, 2003, declares an end to major combat operations in Iraq. Since that time, thousands of injuries and deaths have occurred on both sides of the conflict.*

VITAL INTERESTS IN THE TWENTY-FIRST CENTURY

The framers of the U.S. Constitution did not have a grand strategy for using the basic tools of foreign and defense policy to preserve the nation and protect U.S. interests across the globe. Rather, they worried first about protecting the nation long enough to survive. Although the framers generally believed in free trade and hoped to protect their young nation from foreign threats, their general focus was on keeping the nation out of harm's way in Europe as it addressed its economic and domestic problems.

Toward these ends, the framers made three basic decisions that guide foreign policy to this day. First, they declared that foreign policy was a national, not state, responsibility. Even as the Constitution divided power between the president and Congress, Article I, Section 10 declares that no state shall enter into a treaty, alliance, or confederation with another nation, meaning that only the national government can conduct foreign policy.

Second, the framers concentrated the authority to make foreign and defense policy in the presidency. They gave the president sole authority to command the army and navy, make treaties, appoint ambassadors, and oversee the departments of government, thereby making the president both commander and diplomat in chief. The framers recognized that foreign policy could not be conducted by a collection of interests. The nation needed a single point of contact for representing what was then a very clearly defined national interest: survival.

Finally, having given the president authority to implement policy, the framers checked that power by giving Congress as a whole the power to declare war, raise an army and a navy, and make the rules of war and by giving the Senate the power to ratify all treaties by a two-thirds vote and confirm all ambassadors by a majority vote. Even as they made sure the national government could protect the United States against foreign threats through the use of armed force, they worried that a president might exploit that power to deny basic liberties. As John Jay argued in *The Federalist*, No. 4, "Absolute monarchs will often make war when their nations are to get nothing by it, but for purposes and objects merely personal, such as, a thirst for military glory."

Defining Vital U.S. Interests

In the broadest sense, the primary goal of U.S. foreign and defense policy is to protect the nation from harm, whether from other nations or individual terrorists, nuclear missiles, or suicide bombings. Over the past several generations, the United States has become involved in world affairs to a degree unprecedented in its history. Although much of this activity was due to the cold war against communism from 1945 to 1990, the

IMPORTANT FOREIGN POLICY CONCEPTS

- **Internationalism:** A foreign policy that recognizes that concern for trade, human rights, and international peace requires not only a strong military but also the willingness to intervene where vital U.S. interests are at stake.
- **Isolationism:** A foreign policy that curtails U.S. military aid and intervention abroad as much as possible. It was the dominant policy in this country during the nineteenth century and to some degree in the 1920s and 1930s.
- **Realpolitik:** A foreign policy based on practical and self-interest factors rather than on moral, idealistic, or theoretical considerations. Realists say the United States should intervene in world affairs only if its vital interests are in jeopardy or if a dispute involves overt outside aggression, not simply internal rebellion.
- **Containment:** A foreign policy aimed at halting the spread of communism, especially the influence of the former Soviet Union. This was the underlying foreign and national security policy of the United States between 1947 and 1990.
- **Deterrence:** Effective deterrence is commonly measured by a nation's ability to survive a nuclear attack with enough of its own weapons to inflict massive casualties on its enemy. This strategy of *mutual assured destruction* (MAD) is still at the core of American nuclear policy.
- **New World Order:** A vague and often confusing label pinned on the post–cold war period in which the United States presumably plays a vital role as the only remaining superpower in preserving peace, encouraging economic opportunity, and promoting human rights throughout the world.
- **Multilateralism:** A view of foreign policy that stresses cooperation between the United States and other nations in efforts to solve problems such as global warming, terrorism, disease, and the spread of weapons of mass destruction. It is often contrasted with *unilateralism,* which argues that the United States is free to pursue foreign policy goals such as removing Saddam Hussein from power without international support.
- **Preemption:** A foreign policy approach articulated by the Bush administration in 2002 based on the notion that the United States should initiate war if it concludes that a foreign nation constitutes an immediate threat to the United States.

sheer size and wealth of the United States makes it both a natural world leader and a target for criticism. There are other reasons as well. U.S. security and economic interests are inevitably tied to what happens in the rest of the world. Whether Americans like it or not, events far from home affect their life, liberty, and pursuit of happiness.

Balancing political, economic, and social values is critical in defining vital U.S. interests. Americans want peace, but not if it means that they must give up basic freedoms. Americans favor human rights, but not if it means less trade and fewer jobs. Americans support the general concept of a United Nations that represents all the nations of the world, but not if the United States must give up command of its own troops in U.N. missions. They want the United States to protect weaker nations against aggression, as long as not too many U.S. soldiers are put in harm's way. Where possible, they want to improve the standard of living in less-developed nations and protect the global environment, but they also want new markets for U.S. products, inexpensive imports, and adequate supplies of energy. The task of defining our interests requires extensive balancing of sometimes competing goals.

This balancing continues to involve a mix of long-standing goals such as stopping the spread of HIV-AIDS, enhancing human rights, addressing global warming and other environmental threats, reducing hunger and illiteracy, finding a lasting peace in the Middle East, and closing the gap between rich and poor nations. But it has also expanded in recent years to include the war on terrorism and a much more aggressive effort to control the spread of weapons of mass destruction.

The War on Terrorism

September 11 clearly changed the U.S. foreign policy agenda radically. As the 9/11 Commission argues, the foreign policy agenda used to be determined by national boundaries, industrial strength, and military strength. "Threats emerged slowly, often visibly, as weapons were forged, armies conscripted, and units trained and moved into place."[5] (See Table 20–1 for examples of how public opinion changed after September 11.)

Today's threats know no borders—they emerge quickly and without respect for power, prestige, or military might. Driven by their hatred of America and its allies such as Spain, terrorists do not distinguish between politics and religion, nor between governments and civilians. "It is not a position with which Americans can bargain or negotiate," the Commission argues. "With it there is no common ground—not even respect for life—on which to begin a dialogue."

EARLY WARNINGS   The 9/11 Commission also notes that the September 11 attacks were a shock, but should not have been a surprise to the U.S. government. After all, terrorist activity increased dramatically during the 1990s. Terrorists had tried and failed to destroy the World Trade Center in New York City with a truck bomb in 1993; planned but failed to destroy a dozen U.S. airliners over the Pacific in 1995; killed 19 U.S. soldiers and wounded hundreds in Saudi Arabia with a truck bomb in 1996; killed 224 people, including 12 Americans, in truck bomb attacks on U.S. embassies in Nairobi, Kenya, and Dar es Salaam, Tanzania, in 1998; planned, but failed, to bomb Los Angeles International Airport on New Year's Eve, 1999; and killed 17 U.S. sailors on the USS *Cole* in 2000.

Yet, the U.S. government was still unprepared for September 11, in part because the nation's intelligence agencies missed a number of key warning signs, and in part because this attack involved such a massive loss of human life. As the 9/11 Commission reported, the most important failure leading to the tragedy was one of imagination: Americans and their leaders never thought it could happen here.

THE WAR IN AFGHANISTAN   Days after the September 11 attacks, the United States put the international community on notice that it would pursue terrorists wherever they found comfort. Speaking before a joint session of Congress on September 20, 2001, President Bush announced, "From this day forward, any nation that continues to harbor or support terrorism will be regarded by the United States as a hostile regime. Every nation in every region now has a decision to make. Either you are with us, or you are with the terrorists."

The war in Afghanistan was the first major action against a nation that clearly harbored terrorism. The United States quickly linked the attacks to Osama bin Laden and his Al-Qaeda terrorist network, and Bin Laden to Afghanistan's extremist Taliban government. "The Taliban must act and act immediately," Bush told Congress. "They will hand over the terrorists or they will share in their fate." Two weeks later, Bush demanded bin Laden's arrest again, warning the Taliban that "Full warning has been given. For those nations that stand with the terrorists, there will be a heavy price."

The war began the next morning, October 7, and was effectively over on December 7 when Taliban forces withdrew from the southern city of Kandahar. Afghan's interim leader, Hamid Karzai, took control of the new government two weeks later.

Although the war was quick, and U.S. casualties were light, the Afghan government is still unstable, the economy weak, and drug trafficking still robust. Moreover, as the 9/11 Commission warned, Taliban and Al-Qaeda fighters have regrouped in the south, warlords control much of the country, relief workers refuse to operate in many regions, and guns and ammunition are easily available.

TABLE 20–1 CHANGING FOREIGN POLICY GOALS BEFORE AND AFTER SEPTEMBER 11, 2001			
	Before	*After*	*Change*
Reduce spread of AIDS	73%	59%	−14%
Deal with world hunger	47	34	−13
Combat drug trafficking	64	55	−9
Promote U.S. business interests	37	30	−7
Ensure adequate energy supplies	74	69	−5
Promote democracy	29	24	−5
Help reduce world poverty	25	20	−5

SOURCE: Pew Research Center for the People and the Press, *Public Opinion in a Year for the Books* (Pew Research Center, 2002), p. 12.

Still, there is at least some cause for hope. More than 90 percent of the Afghanistan public registered for the nation's first democratic elections in October, 2004, 40 percent of whom were women. Moreover, the current government appeared to be initially tolerant of competition—two dozen candidates announced their intention to enter the presidential campaign, for example, which required copies of at least 10,000 voter registration cards from supporters. The election was held on October 9, 2004, with reports of heavy turnout despite threats of violence. Interim President Hamid Karzai emerged with 55 percent of the votes among a field of candidates.

PREVENTING FUTURE ATTACKS   The war in Afghanistan was the first phase of what will be a very long war against terrorism. In many ways, terrorists have the advantage in an open society such as the United States. Short of curbing basic freedoms, there is only so much the nation can do to tighten its borders, police its streets, and prevent attacks. Even in Afghanistan, where the United States secured a quick victory in overthrowing the fundamentalist Taliban government that had provided a safe haven for Al Qaeda, the United States could not be sure that it destroyed even a fraction of the network that planned the attacks on New York City and Washington, D.C.

Unlike a traditional war, in which great armies mass against each other in battle, the war on terrorism must be fought against a highly agile adversary that will use all means at its disposal, including suicide bombings, to create terror. Doing so involves more than hunting down terrorists before they strike, however. "The U.S. government must define what the message is, what it stands for," the 9/11 Commission argues. "We should offer an example of moral leadership in the world, committed to treat people humanely, abide by the rule of law, and be generous and caring to our neighbors. . . . To Muslim parents, terrorists like bin Laden have nothing to offer their children but visions of violence and death. America and its friends have a crucial advantage—we can offer these parents a vision that might given their children a better future."[6]

Unfortunately, the 2004 reports of Iraqi prisoner abuse by U.S. military police did little to reinforce America's reputation for treating people humanely. As of July 2004, the Army had identified 94 cases of abuse, including 40 deaths, in the 16 prisons it has used to detain suspected terrorists and prisoners of war. (See the People and Politics: Making a Difference box later in this chapter for a profile of the army general who led the first investigation of abuse.)

Weapons of Mass Destruction

The international community has been working to reduce the threat of biological, chemical, and nuclear war for decades, starting with the nuclear disarmament talks between the United States and the Soviet Union in the 1970s. With the cold war over in 1989, the United States and Russia began to look for new ways of reducing their nuclear arsenals and agreed in 2002 to reduce the number of nuclear warheads dramatically.

Indian and Pakistani troops patrol the border in escalating numbers as religious and territorial differences over ownership of Kashmir bring the two countries closer to war. Tensions were reduced in part due to interventions by U.S. corporations that are dependent on India's high-tech workforce.

The world is still threatened by weapons of mass destruction, however. A handful of nations continue to maintain biological weapons, and at least nine have declared that they have developed chemical weapons, including Russia, China, Ethiopia, India, Iran, Pakistan, South Korea, and Vietnam. Still others may have biological and chemical weapons programs that they have not declared. Moreover, several other nations have or intend to develop nuclear weapons, including India, Iran, North Korea, and Pakistan. Israel is said to have nuclear weapons as well.

THE BUSH DOCTRINE   Increased worries about the use of weapons of mass destruction against the United States following September 11 led to the **Bush Doctrine**, which the president announced at the U.S. Military Academy at West Point in June 2002. "If we wait for threats to materialize," Bush told the class of '02, "we will have waited too long."[7]

Under the doctrine, the United States reserves the right to attack any nation or group that threatens to use weapons of mass destruction against the United States and its interests. The doctrine supports the use of **preemption**, under which the United States promises to take action *before* an adversary could use its weapons.

The Bush Doctrine was central to the administration's case for war in Iraq. As already noted in the introduction to this chapter, the administration had discussed the need to remove Saddam Hussein from power at the very first meeting of the National Security Council on January 30.

The discussions became much more serious after September 11. The president reportedly asked the White House's senior counterterrorism officer, Richard Clarke, to investigate the possibility that Iraq had been involved in the terrorist attacks. "Go back over everything, everything," Bush allegedly told Clarke. "See if Saddam did this." When Clarke answered, "But Mr. President, Al-Qaeda did this," Bush reportedly replied, "I know, I know, but . . . see if Saddam was involved. Just look. I want to know any shred." Although Clarke insisted that the CIA, FBI, and White House had already concluded that there were no such links, the president nevertheless insisted that Clarke "Look into Iraq, Saddam."[8]

THE CASE FOR WAR   Convinced that Iraq continued to be a great threat to U.S. security regardless of its role in September 11, the Bush administration decided to force Iraq to disarm, while making the argument for war if Iraq refused. Despite cautions from U.N. inspectors who argued that Iraq had dismantled its biological and chemical weapons program and abandoned its quest for nuclear weapons after the war in 1991, the Bush administration was convinced that the weapons not only existed, but constituted a clear and present danger to the United States.

The administration was sharply divided on how to disarm Iraq, however. The president's national security adviser, Condoleezza Rice, argued that the United States had a moral obligation to remove Hussein from power, even if doing so meant war. "This is an evil man who, left to his own devices, will wreak havoc again on his own population, his neighbors, and, if he gets weapons of mass destruction and the means to deliver them, on all of us," Rice told the British Broadcasting Corporation in August 2002. "There is a very powerful moral case for regime change. We certainly do not have the luxury of doing nothing."[9] Her position was strongly supported by Secretary of Defense Donald Rumsfeld and Vice President Dick Cheney.

In contrast, Secretary of State Colin Powell argued that the United States needed to consider the impact of such an attack on other foreign and defense policy goals, as well as on the war on terrorism itself. Although he also believed the world would be better off without Hussein in power, he worried about both the cost and impact of war. Having overseen the first war with Iraq as the U.S. Army's most senior officer in 1991, Powell knew that U.S. military power would win any war against Iraq, but he also believed that a prolonged war in Iraq, especially one waged with minimal international support, might increase hostility toward the United States, while giving terrorist organizations more targets for violence.

THE WAR IN IRAQ   On September 20, 2002, the Bush administration resolved the debate by asking Congress for the authorization to use armed force to defend the United States from the Iraqi threat and enforce the terms of all past U.N. resolutions regarding disarmament and ongoing inspections. As noted at the start of this chapter, Congress granted the authority on October 10.

Bush Doctrine
A policy adopted by the Bush administration in 2001 that asserts America's right to attack any nation that has weapons of mass destruction that might be used against U.S. interests at home or abroad.

preemption
Associated with the Bush Doctrine, a belief that a nation is justified in attacking another nation to prevent possible attacks on itself.

After six more months of international negotiation and further preparation for war, the Bush administration used the authority. With Britain as its only major military ally, the United States launched a massive bombing campaign on March 20, 2003, followed by a ground assault through southern Iraq on March 21. With the Air Force in close support using precision-guided bombs, the Army and Marine Corps moved quickly up the road to Baghdad. One hundred thirty-nine soldiers had been killed in combat as of May 1 when the president announced an end to the war.

The battle for Iraq was only beginning, however. Another 613 soldiers died during the year that followed, including 150 at the height of the internal uprising against the U.S. military in April 2004. The mounting death toll has led some analysts to ask whether there are enough troops in Iraq to provide needed security. According to one estimate by the RAND Corporation, a Santa Monica, California, think tank, winning the peace in Iraq would take roughly 500,000 troops at any one time, or more than three times the number of foreign troops assigned to the effort in 2004. Assuming a 24-month rotation cycle, the world would need to draw upon a force of 2.5 million troops, or almost double the total number of troops now in the U.S. military alone.[10]

Terrorism has also increased as opponents of the U.S. engagement have turned to kidnapping, beheadings, and suicide bombings against governments and private companies that are involved in the campaign. Both Spain and the Philippines withdrew their troops from Iraq following terrorist attacks on their citizens. Spain removed its 1,300 troops after 200 citizens were killed in a series of Madrid train bombings just days before national elections.

As the war continued to take its toll on U.S. forces, the Bush administration finally returned to the United Nations in the spring of 2004 to ask for help in rebuilding Iraq. In June 2004, the United Nations helped select an interim Iraqi government headed by Prime Minister Iyad Allawi, but has been unwilling to commit a peacekeeping force until Iraq becomes less dangerous. Despite hopes to the contrary, the war continued to intensify even after the United States transferred authority to the new Iraqi government two days ahead of schedule on June 30, 2004. By the end of September 2004, more than 1,000 U.S. troops had been killed in battle and the number continued to rise through October and November.

More importantly, violence against both the United States and the new Iraqi government escalated dramatically. On October 25, 2004, for example, 49 newly-trained Iraqi troops were executed; on October 28, another 11 were executed; and on October 30, just three days before the presidential election, nine U.S. Marines were killed in a suicide attack on their convoy, marking the worst day in the war in six months.

THE MISSING WEAPONS OF MASS DESTRUCTION   Although the case for war was based almost entirely on allegations that Iraq was ready to use weapons of mass destruction against the United States., the weapons have never been found. According to a U.S. Intelligence Committee report released in July 2004, most of the key judgments in the intelligence community's assessment of Iraq's weapons programs were "either overstated, or were not supported by, the underlying intelligence reporting."[11]

Equally important for making foreign policy, the intelligence community "did not accurately or adequately explain to policy makers the uncertainties behind the judgments" contained in a key October 2002 assessment that the Central Intelligence Director, George Tenet, had called a "slam dunk case" that Iraq had the weapons.[12] Tenet resigned three weeks before the report was released and was replaced by a former CIA intelligence officer and member of Congress, Porter Goss (R.-Fla.) three months later.

Continued Priorities

Although the war on terrorism has occupied the headlines since September 11, the United States still has a deep inventory of other foreign policy goals that require ongoing attention, including efforts to promote democracy around the world; prevent the spread of infectious diseases such as HIV-AIDS, tuberculosis, and polio; address global climate change; and provide humanitarian aid. The United States has also pursued three other priorities we will discuss next: (1) finding a Middle East peace, (2) promoting free trade, and (3) encouraging international understanding.

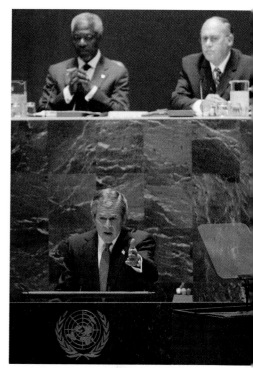

President Bush addresses the General Assembly at the United Nations on September 12, 2002, seeking approval for military action against Iraq. The U.N. Security Council ultimately did not grant its approval and in 2004, U.N. Secretary General Kofi Annan (left) charged that the U.S. war against Iraq was in violation of international law because it did not have the backing of the U.N. Security Council.

The U.S. war against Iraq began on March 20, 2003, with a bombing campaign designed to produce "shock and awe" within Iraq and thereby assure the collapse of military resistance.

An increase in suicide bombings by Palestinians is a violent indication of the distance Palestine and Israel still have to travel to find a lasting peace. Israel responded with its own attack on terrorist bases in Palestine.

MIDDLE EAST PEACE   Progress toward a lasting Middle East peace is particularly important in reducing international terrorism. However, despite decades of U.S. effort, the region remains locked in a violent struggle between Israel and the Palestinians who live in occupied territory called the West Bank. Although the United States has made some progress in designing a road map to peace, much of the past progress toward that goal was lost in the wave of suicide bombings that began on Passover in October 2001, and Israel's subsequent decision to build a 225-mile wall separating itself from Palestine.

The rising tide of attack and counterattack put the United States in an extraordinarily difficult position. As a longtime ally of Israel, the United States supported Israel's use of force against the camps that sheltered the militants. Moreover, Israel Prime Minister Ariel Sharon used the language of the Bush Doctrine to justify his actions. However, the United States could not condone a renewed Israeli occupation of the Palestinian territories without weakening support for the war on terrorism among key Arab nations. The United States eventually resolved its dilemma by calling for Israel to withdraw while encouraging the Palestinian people to remove their leader, Yasser Arafat, from power, but found itself no closer to resolving the Palestinian question.

INTERNATIONAL TRADE   Even as the world has become more dangerous, it has become more interdependent and competitive economically. The United States has generally responded to this globalization with a basic policy of free trade, meaning a commitment to the free movement of goods across international borders. It does not allow the export of technologies that can be used to build nuclear weapons, however, and has long protected certain defense industries that would be essential should it ever be forced into another world war. It has also used trade as a tool to promote human rights and democratic reform.

The United States pursued a mix of goals in the battle over free trade with mainland China. On the one hand, China has a long history of violating basic human and democratic rights. On the other hand, China has one of the fastest-growing economies in the world. U.S. exports to China have tripled over the past decade, and imports from China have grown rapidly. This balancing effort reached a crescendo over President Clinton's request for **permanent normal trade relations (PNTR) status** for China, granting China the same favorable trade concessions and tariffs that its best trading partners receive.

The debate over China trade was so controversial that Congress refused to give President Clinton an extension of past "fast-track," or accelerated congressional action on trade agreements. Under fast-track authority, which had been given to every president since Nixon but expired in 1994, Congress limited its own debate about trade agreements to a simple yes-or-no vote with no amendments. In 1998, however, Congress finally granted PNTR status to China. Four years later, it restored fast-track authority under the Trade Act of 2002, giving the Bush administration the opportunity to open new rounds of trade talks with Chile, Singapore, and South Africa.

ECONOMIC DEVELOPMENT AND INTERNATIONAL UNDERSTANDING   The United States has long promoted these twin goals through foreign aid, which is discussed later in this chapter, and programs such as the Peace Corps, which was established in 1961 as one of the top priorities of the Kennedy administration.

Advertised on its Web site as "the toughest job you'll ever love," Peace Corps volunteers are expected to serve in another nation for two years and become part of the community they are serving. Volunteers work on a variety of projects, such as teaching math and science, doing community development work, and improving water and sanitation systems. Most volunteers either have a college degree, specific international experience, or a combination of both. About 10 percent of the 7,300 current volunteers are over 50 years old. The Peace Corps picks up the expenses and typically trains each volunteer in language and job skills for about three months prior to service abroad.[13]

The Peace Corps operates in about 80 nations and has had funding of about $260 million a year. More than 170,000 Americans have been Peace Corps volunteers. Eight Peace Corps alumni have served in Congress. The Peace Corps is wholly separate from the State and Defense Departments and the intelligence agencies.

permanent normal trade relations (PNTR) status

Trade status granted as part of an international trade policy that gives a nation the same favorable trade concessions and tariffs that the best trading partners receive.

THE FOREIGN AND DEFENSE POLICY BUREAUCRACY

Even in troubled times, the president does not have absolute authority to act. Congress has the power to declare war, to appropriate funds for the armed forces, and to make rules that govern the armed forces. But the president is commander in chief of the armed forces and is authorized to negotiate treaties and receive and send ambassadors—that is, to recognize or refuse to recognize other governments. The Senate confirms U.S. ambassadorial appointments and gives consent (by a two-thirds vote) to treaty ratification. The courts have the power to interpret treaties, but by and large they have ruled that relations with other nations are matters for the executive to decide. The primacy of the executive in foreign policy is a fact of political life of all nations, including constitutional democracies.

Officially, the president's principal foreign policy adviser is the secretary of state, although others, such as the national security adviser or the vice president, are sometimes equally influential. The secretary of state administers the State Department, receives visits from foreign diplomats, attends international conferences, and usually heads the U.S. delegation in the General Assembly of the United Nations. The secretary also serves as the administration's chief coordinator of all governmental actions that affect our relations with other nations. In practice, the secretary of state delegates the day-to-day responsibilities for running the State Department and spends most of the time negotiating with the leaders of other countries.

The interdependence of foreign, economic, and domestic policies requires more than just one or two advisers. The conduct of foreign affairs is now the business of several major departments and agencies, including State, Defense, Treasury, Agriculture, Commerce, Labor, Energy, the Central Intelligence Agency (CIA), and the new Department of Homeland Security. The need for immediate reaction and full preparedness has transferred many responsibilities directly to the president and to a great extent to the senior White House aides who assist in coordinating information and advice. Yet no matter what the system for advice and coordination, there are always overlaps of responsibilities, redundancy, and competition among agencies.

The National Security Council

The key coordinating agency for the president is the National Security Council (NSC). Created by Congress in 1947, it is intended to help presidents integrate foreign, military, and economic policies that affect national security. The NSC serves directly under the president. By law, it consists of the president, vice president, secretary of state, and secretary of defense. Recent presidents have sometimes included the director of the CIA, the White House chief of staff, and the national security adviser as nonstatutory members of the NSC.

The national security adviser, appointed by the president, has emerged as one of the most influential foreign policy makers, sometimes rivaling the secretary of state in influence. Presidents come to rely on these White House aides both because of their proximity (down the hall in the West Wing of the White House) and because they owe their primary loyalties to the president, not to any department or program. Each president has shaped the NSC structure and adapted its staff procedures to suit his personal preferences, but over the years, the NSC, as both a committee and a staff, has taken on a major role in making and implementing foreign policy. For her part, Condoleezza Rice has generally sided with the Bush administration's neoconservatives against the State Department and Colin Powell. In doing so, she has followed a time-honored path in which the NSC adviser can be more of an adversary of the State Department than an ally.

The State Department

The State Department is responsible for the diplomatic realm of foreign and defense policy. The department is organized around a series of "desks" representing different parts of the world and foreign policy missions. The State Department is also responsible for negotiating treaties with other nations and international organizations, protecting U.S. citizens abroad, promoting U.S. commercial interests in other nations, and granting visas to foreign visitors.

National Security Advisor Condoleezza Rice meets with President George W. Bush at the presidential retreat at Camp David. President Bush chose Rice to be secretary of state during his second term.

The State Department also plays a significant role in homeland security. Many of the September 2001 attackers had entered the United States on student visas granted by the State Department's Bureau of Consular Affairs. Although their movements once in the United States were supposed to be monitored by the Justice Department's Immigration and Naturalization Service, the State Department was criticized for being too lax in granting visas to almost anyone with enough income to purchase an airline ticket.

The State Department's budget of about $6 billion (not counting foreign aid) is the lowest of all the cabinet departments—only a fraction of the Department of Defense's much larger budget.[14] Considering the State Department's role and prestige, its staff of 25,000 worldwide is small, especially compared with the more than 2 million civilian and military personnel in the Department of Defense.

Its role is particularly impressive given recent cutbacks. The United States has closed at least 30 consulates and embassies over the past two decades, and many operate with obsolete technology and in antiquated and unsafe buildings. These cutbacks help explain the breakdowns in the visa issuance process. The State Department simply did not have enough employees to interview every applicant for a visa.

STAFFING THE DIPLOMATIC SYSTEM   American embassies are staffed largely by members of the U.S. Foreign Service. Although part of the State Department, the service represents the entire government and performs jobs for many other agencies. Its main duties are to carry out foreign policy as expressed in the directives of the secretary of state; gather political, economic, and intelligence data for American policy makers; protect Americans and American interests in foreign countries; and cultivate friendly relations with host governments and foreign peoples.

The Foreign Service is composed of highly-trained civil servants who are comparable to army officers in the military. They are a select, specially trained group expected to take assignments anyplace in the world on short notice. There are approximately 4,000 such officers; in recent years, fewer than 225 junior officers have won appointment each year. Approximately two-thirds of our U.S. ambassadors to about 160 nations come from the ranks of the Foreign Service. The others are usually political appointees, large donors, or friends of the president.

The Foreign Service is one of the most prestigious yet most criticized career services of the national government. Criticism sometimes comes as much from within as from outside. Critics claim that the organizational culture of the Foreign Service stifles creativity; attracts officers who are, or at least become, more concerned about their status than their responsibilities; and requires new recruits to wait 15 years or more before being considered for positions of responsibility. Like other federal agencies, most notably the Central Intelligence Agency and the Federal Bureau of Investigation, the Foreign Service has had great difficulty recruiting officers with significant Arabic-language skills, which clearly weakens the ability to interpret, let alone collect, intelligence on the terrorist networks that have emerged in the Middle East and central Asia.

Perhaps the greatest challenge for Foreign Service diplomats is how to function effectively in a high-tech world. Some have even suggested that diplomats posted in foreign countries are no longer needed to gather intelligence or to speak for the United States and that they should be replaced altogether and most of their work be conducted by e-mail, fax, and videoconferencing from Washington. Yet having a diplomat on the scene in Iran or Saudi Arabia who speaks Farsi and Arabic and who knows a country's major leaders personally is often a better method than relying on even the most sophisticated technologies, especially when making subtle judgments about a nation's political, economic, and military policies.[15]

The Central Intelligence Agency and the Intelligence Community

As the Senate Intelligence Committee and 9/11 Commission both noted, effective foreign policy is dependent on accurate, timely information. Before our foreign policy makers can act on important issues, they have to know as much as possible about other countries: their possible reactions to a particular policy, their strengths and weaknesses, the character of their leaders, and, if possible, their strategic plans and intentions. The people who gather and analyze intelligence data are therefore among the most important advisers to policy makers.[16]

The Central Intelligence Agency, an outgrowth of the World War II Office of Strategic Services, was created in 1947 to coordinate the gathering and analysis of information that flows into various parts of the U.S. government from all over the world. In recent years, the CIA has had about 20,000 employees, who both collect information and shape the intelligence estimates that policy makers use to set priorities.

Although most of the information the CIA gathers comes from open sources, the term "intelligence" conjures up visions of spies and undercover agents. Secret intelligence occasionally does supply crucial data. But it is not all glamour; much is routine. Intelligence work involves three basic operations: reporting, research, and dissemination. *Reporting* is based on the close and rigorous observation of developments around the world; *research* is the attempt to detect meaningful patterns out of what was observed in the past and to understand what appears to be going on now; *dissemination* means getting the right information to the right people at the right time.

FBI Agent Coleen Rowley's testimony before the Senate Judiciary Committee on June 6, 2002, exposed communication problems between FBI field offices and FBI headquarters in Washington, D.C. Agent Rowley outlined how the FBI headquarters hindered the field office in Minneapolis in its investigation of a suspected terrorist before September 11, 2001.

The CIA is only one of 15 intelligence agencies in the federal government, including the State Department's Bureau of Intelligence and Research; the Defense Department's Defense Intelligence Agency (which combines the intelligence operations of the Army, Navy, Air Force, and Marine Corps); the Federal Bureau of Investigation; the Treasury Department's Office of Terrorism and Finance Intelligence; the Energy Department's Office of Intelligence; the Homeland Security Department's Directorate of Information Analysis and Infrastructure Protection and Directorate of Coast Guard Intelligence; and the National Security Agency (which specializes in electronic reconnaissance and code breaking), National Reconnaissance Office (which runs the U.S. satellite surveillance programs), and National Geospatial-Intelligence Agency (which collects and analyzes photographic imagery). Together, the 15 agencies constitute the *intelligence community.*

Because each of these agencies was created to collect unique information (imagery, electronic intelligence, and so forth) for a unique client (the president, the secretary of defense, or others), they rarely share information with each other. The lack of cooperation clearly affected the government's ability to prevent the September 11 attacks. "Many dedicated officers worked day and night for years to piece together the growing body of evidence on Al Qaeda and to understand the threats," the 9/11 Commission concluded. "Yet, while there were many reports on bin Laden and his growing Al-Qaeda organization, there was no comprehensive review of what the intelligence community knew and what it did not know, and what that meant."[17] Although the Commission noted merit in keeping the agencies separate, not the least of which is the need for competing sources of information, it did recommend the creation of a single cabinet-level National Intelligence Director, or czar, to oversee the community. Congress was unable to reach agreement on how much power to give the czar. The legislation stalled before the 2004 presidential election.

The Department of Defense

The president, Congress, the National Security Council, the State Department, and the Defense Department all make overall defense policy and attempt to integrate U.S. national security programs, but the day-to-day work of organizing for defense is the job of the Defense Department. Its headquarters, the Pentagon, houses within its 17.5 miles of corridors 23,000 top military and civilian personnel. The offices of several hundred generals and admirals are there, as is the office of the secretary of defense, who provides civilian control of the armed services.

Although the Department of Defense has existed for more than half a century, its leaders are still working to ensure both strategic vision and practical coordination among the military services. Prior to 1947, there were two separate

The Pentagon, headquarters for the Defense Department, is the world's largest building. It has 17.5 miles of corridors and houses nearly 23,000 workers, who tell time by 4,200 clocks, consume 30,000 cups of coffee daily, and place 200,000 calls a day on 87,000 phones connected by 100,000 miles of cable.

Its significance as the center of U.S. defense policy made the Pentagon a prime target in the attacks on September 11, 2001. More than 150 civilian and military personnel were killed in the early morning attack.

military departments—War and Navy. The difficulty of coordinating them during World War II led to demands for unification. In 1947, the Air Force, already an autonomous unit within the War Department, was made an independent department, and all three military departments—Army, Navy, and Air Force— were placed under the general supervision of the secretary of defense. The Unification Act of 1947 was a bundle of compromises between the Army, which favored a tightly integrated department, and the Navy, which wanted a loosely federated structure, but the act at least brought the military services onto a common organizational chart.

The committee known as the Joint Chiefs of Staff serves as the principal military adviser to the president, the National Security Council, and the secretary of defense. It includes the heads of the three armed services, plus the commandant of the Marine Corps, and the chair and vice chair of the Joint Chiefs. The president, with the consent of the Senate, appoints all the service chiefs to four-year nonrenewable terms. Note that the twice-renewable two-year term of the chair of the Joint Chiefs is part of the process of ensuring civilian control over the military.

Before 1986, the members of the Joint Chiefs of Staff were, collectively, very powerful. They advised the president and the secretary of defense. Because they functioned as a committee and could not act until unanimous agreement was reached, however, they often produced overly broad decisions. Critics therefore viewed much of the work of the Joint Chiefs as wasteful and even dangerous.

The Department of Defense Reorganization Act of 1986 shifted considerable power to the chair. Reporting through the secretary of defense, the chair now advises the president on military matters, exercises authority over the forces in the field, and is responsible for overall military planning. In theory, the chair of the Joint Chiefs can even make a military decision that the chiefs of the other services oppose. On paper at least, these other chiefs now serve the chair merely as advisers, and even the chair's deputy, the vice chair, outranks the other service chiefs. The chair has a mandate to encourage "jointness" in military education and in other spheres to integrate the

GLOBAL Perceptions

QUESTION: How important is it to you to live in a country where the military is under the control of civilian leaders?

Civilian control of the military is considered essential for preventing tyranny. Although the U.S. military has always been under the control of elected, civilian leaders, many nations are led by military officers who stay in power solely through the threat of force. Citizens in nations that have recently broken free of military control were particularly likely to say it is very important to have civilian control of the military. Thus, 58 percent of Nigerians, 55 percent of Ugandans, and 48 percent of Argentineans say it is very important to maintain civilian control.

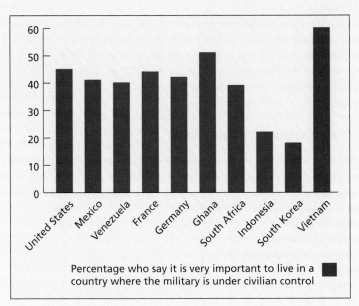

Percentage who say it is very important to live in a country where the military is under civilian control

SOURCE: Pew Global Attitudes Project, 2003, p. T-69.

services for maximum effectiveness. The chair of the Joint Chiefs today is the most powerful peacetime military officer in U.S. history. These changes clearly contributed to military success in the Afghanistan and Iraq wars, where special operations forces and U.S. Marines worked closely with Navy and Air Force pilots to target precision-guided weapons on enemy positions.

It is crucial to recognize, however, that the chair of the Joint Chiefs is *not* the head of the military. The chair and the Joint Chiefs are advisers to the secretary of defense and the president, but the president can, and on occasion has, disregarded their advice. A president must weigh military action or inaction against the larger foreign and security interests of the nation.

UNDERSTANDING THE DEFENSE BUREAUCRACY   The defense bureaucracy is best understood—as is any bureaucracy—as something less than a monolith. Insiders often stress that this policy-making structure is best thought of as a *confederation* or a bargaining arena rather than a tight chain-of-command hierarchy. In fact, in recent years, strong sentiment has emerged for more centralized control and direction of the nation's defense bureaucracy.

CHANGING FACE OF AMERICAN POLITICS

DIVERSITY IN THE MILITARY

The U.S. military has become much more diverse over the past three decades, in part due to much more aggressive recruiting of women and minorities. In 1973, for example, just 2 percent of all recruits were women, while 23 percent were people of color. By 2002, 17 percent were women, and 35 percent were people of color.

Year	Percentage of White Recruits	Percentage of Women Recruits
1973	77%	2%
1983	76	12
1993	73	24
2002	67	17

SOURCE: Department of Defense, *Population Characteristics in the Military Services, 2002*, U.S. Government Printing Office, 2003, Appendix D.

Former Secretary of State Colin Powell.

The four armed services—Army, Navy, Marine Corps, and Air Force—vary greatly in terms of diversity, however. As of 2004, roughly 42 percent of the Army, 37 percent of the Navy, 32 percent of the Marine Corps, and 26 percent of the Air Force were African American, Hispanic, Asian American, or another minority group. At the same time, 19 percent of the Air Force, 16 percent of the Army, 14 percent of the Navy, and just 6 percent of the Marine Corps were women.

There are several reasons why the armed forces have done better recruiting people of color than recruiting women. First, the military has worked hard to improve its reputation as an equal opportunity employer. Colin Powell's rise to the highest post in the armed services has often been used to show recruits of color that anything is possible in the military. Powell entered the military as a second lieutenant in 1958, served two tours of duty in Vietnam, and eventually became the first African American officer to chair the Joint Chiefs of Staff.

Second, the military has long focused on recruiting high school graduates who are not college-bound, which is a group that contains more people of color. The military has also developed several new programs that set aside substantial amounts of funding for future college tuition, which has also been effective in recruiting people of color.

Disputes among the military services involve more than professional jealousies. The technological revolution in warfare has rendered obsolete many concepts about military missions, thereby threatening the traditional roles of some of the services. In the past, it made sense to divide command among land, sea, and air forces. Today, defense research and development are constantly altering formerly established roles and missions, yet the individual services are reluctant to give up their traditional functions or to serve each other's crucial needs. The Navy, for example, is interested in waging sea warfare, not in running a freight service for the Army. Interservice rivalries erupt when the Army and Air Force quarrel over who should provide air support for ground troops. Each branch also supports weapons that bring it prestige. The Air Force and Navy dispute, for example, the effectiveness of land-based versus sea-based missiles.[18]

Whether strategic policies are worked out by the Defense Department, the White House, or Congress, the decisions result from a political process in which some measure of consensus is essential. The Joint Chiefs engage in the same type of vote trading used in Congress. On budget issues, the chiefs often endorse all the programs desired by each service. When forced to choose on an issue of policy, the chiefs have traditionally compromised among the different service positions rather than attempt to develop a position based on a unified military point of view.

The Department of Homeland Security

The new Department of Homeland Security plays a small but important role in foreign policy by policing U.S. borders. Created in late 2002, the department is composed of 22 agencies and a work force of 170,000 full-time civil servants. It includes the Border Patrol, the Coast Guard, the Customs Service, the Secret Service, the Immigration Service, and the Transportation Security Administration.

The department has three basic goals: to prevent the entry of terrorists into the country, reduce the chances of a terrorist attack, and help the nation recover from an attack if and when it occurs. Toward these goals, it is responsible for screening all passengers and baggage on U.S. domestic flights (Transportation Security Administration), checking all cargo (Customs Service, Coast Guard) and visitors entering the United States (Immigration Service), patrolling the borders (Border Patrol, Coast Guard), and providing aid and assistance to communities affected by human and natural disasters (Federal Emergency Management Administration). Although the Bureau of Consular Affairs remains in the State Department, the secretary of homeland security now has primary responsibility for making sure that visas are not issued to potential terrorists.

Despite making significant progress toward tighter airport security over its first three years, it still needs time to develop similar programs for the nation's seaports and so-called "soft targets" such as nuclear power plants, chemical factories, sports facilities, and shopping malls. The 9/11 Commission recommended that the department move as quickly as possible to create a biometric screening system that uses fingerprints and digital photographs to identify U.S. citizens and visitors alike.

PARTICIPANTS IN FOREIGN AND DEFENSE POLICY

Foreign policy flows through the same institutional and constitutional structures as domestic policy. Public opinion, interest groups, foreign countries, political parties, and Congress all affect the making of foreign policy. Yet these structures operate somewhat differently from the way they do in domestic affairs.

The Public

In crisis situations such as the new war against terrorism, presidents and their military and intelligence advisers make the key decisions, often operating from a high-tech operations center in the basement of the White House. Yet even in these situations, presidents and their advisers know that their decisions will ultimately require support from the public and from Congress.

At first glance, many Americans appear indifferent or uninformed about foreign and defense policy. Foreign affairs issues are more remote than domestic issues. Most Americans have a poor sense of world geography and an even weaker grasp of geopolitics. However, Figure 20–1 shows that many Americans, whether ill-informed or not, have strong opinions about which nations are vital to U.S. interests. They also had strong reactions to the September 11 terrorist attacks. Three months before the attacks, for example, 64 percent of Americans said that international terrorism was a "major threat" to the well-being of the United States; one month before the attacks, 53 percent said the world was a "more dangerous place" than it had been a decade earlier.[19]

Americans also had clear preferences for action. Interviewed only days after the attacks, 77 percent said the United States should go to war with Afghanistan even if it meant taking heavy casualties, and 44 percent said military action to attack terrorism abroad was a wiser investment than building up the nation's defenses at home. As for the aims of military intervention, 57 percent said the United States should use military force to prevent terrorism. As Table 20–2 shows, Americans became much more concerned about making foreign policy with the nation's allies in mind, in making sure the United States was in charge, and increasing defense spending.

Individual Americans have also been deeply involved in the war on terrorism, whether by attending rallies and protests for and against the Iraq war, donating blood and money to the victims of the September 11 attacks, or writing letters to their members of Congress or the president. Many Americans have also joined together to create new organizations such as MoveOn.org, which opposes the Iraq war, while the families

Sergeant First Class Nathan Ross Chapman, 31, was the first American casualty in Afghanistan after the start of the war on terrorism. Deaths, such as Chapman's, affect the general public more than specific foreign policy issues.

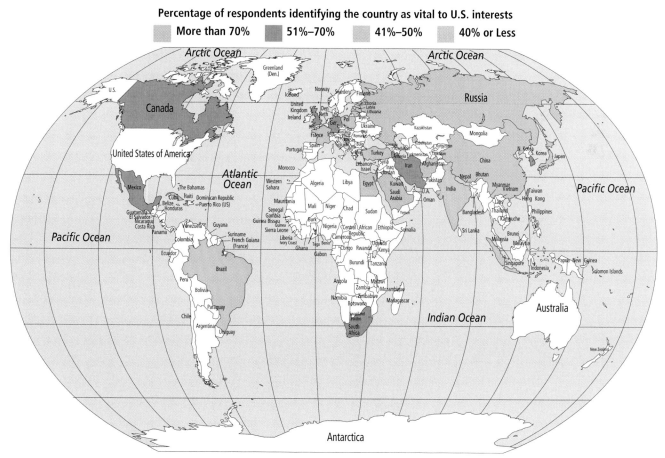

FIGURE 20–1 Public Views of U.S. Interests.
Source: John E. Reilly, ed., *American Public Opinion and U.S. Foreign Policy, 1999* (Chicago Council on Foreign Relations, 1999), p. 13.

SHOULD THE UNITED STATES BUILD A MISSILE SHIELD?

The United States has been trying to design a missile shield for more than 20 years. First proposed by President Ronald Reagan, the goal of his "Star Wars" system was simple: identify, intercept, and destroy incoming ballistic missiles before they enter the atmosphere above the United States. The idea mostly languished after the end of the cold war but regained momentum with the possibility that China, North Korea, and Iran were all developing long-range missiles capable of reaching the United States.

The idea also gained added support following the terrorist attacks on New York City and Washington, D.C. According to the Pew Research Center for the People and the Press, 35 percent of Americans favored a missile defense system before the attacks, compared with 49 percent after.

of the September 11 victims also created a charitable organization to put pressure on Congress to create the 9/11 Commission and have remained a powerful voice in demanding implementation of the Commission's report.

Interest Groups

It is difficult to generalize about the impact of interest groups on American foreign policy. At times of international crisis, the president is usually able to mobilize public support so that interest groups find it difficult to exert much influence. As a general rule, special-interest groups with other than major economic interests rarely have a decisive role in the formulation of foreign policy.

Ethnic interest groups, however, sometimes play an important role in foreign and defense policy decisions. As a nation of immigrants and the children and grandchildren of immigrants, our citizens often retain a special bond with their country of origin. Thus Irish Americans, Jewish Americans, Cuban Americans, African Americans, Asian Americans, Polish Americans, Greek Americans, Arab Americans, and Mexican Americans take a keen interest in decisions affecting Ireland, Israel, Cuba, South Africa, China, Japan, Vietnam, the Philippines, South Korea and other Pacific Rim nations, Poland, Greece, the Middle East, and Mexico. Such groups sometimes exert great pressures on policy makers to support (or in the case of Cuba, contest) the country to which they are emotionally linked.

Business groups also play a role in foreign and defense policy decisions. Defense contractors are heavily involved in decisions about defense spending and contribute large amounts of campaign money to presidential and congressional candidates. They also lobby hard on behalf of their projects before Congress and the executive branch, which can and does raise questions of conflicts of interest and special favors.

In July 2004, for example, executives of Houston-based Halliburton, Inc., were called before Congress to address allegations of waste and abuse in administering more than $8 billion in defense contracts that had been awarded without competition from other potential contractors. The charges were particularly visible because the company had been led by Vice President Dick Cheney during the 1990s, which created the appearance of favoritism in the contracting process.

TABLE 20–2 VIEWS OF FOREIGN POLICY BEFORE AND AFTER SEPTEMBER 11, 2001

	Before	*After*
The United States should formulate foreign policy based on		
Mostly U.S. interests	38%	30%
Interests of allies	48	59
Neither or both	8	7
The U.S. leadership role should be		
Single leader or first among equals	38	45
Just one of leading nations	50	46
No leadership role	8	3
National defense spending should be		
Increased	32	50
Kept the same	44	41
Cut back	20	7

SOURCE: Pew Research Center for the People and the Press, *Public Opinion in a Year for the Books* (Pew Research Center, 2002), p. 12.

Defense contractors are not the only business interests involved in foreign and defense policy. Agricultural interests have lobbied successfully for expanded grain and food exports, the steel industry has lobbied successfully for import quotas on foreign steel, the entertainment industry has campaigned against piracy of music and film abroad, and the high-tech industry has pressed Congress to allow the immigration of more computer programmers.

Businesses may even have their own foreign policies. *New York Times* reporter Thomas L. Friedman wrote in August 2002 that General Electric played a major role in reducing the nuclear tension between Pakistan and India over the disputed Kashmir region. According to Friedman, the U.S. high-tech economy has become dependent on millions of English-speaking, low-wage workers in India for everything from computer programming to troubleshooting. Not surprisingly, U.S. companies were angered when the State Department urged U.S. citizens to leave India because of the nuclear tension. They warned India that they would move their operations to other countries if the nation continued to threaten nuclear war. As Friedman wrote, "This was a real education for India's leaders in New Delhi, but, officials conceded, they got the message: loose talk about war or nukes could be disastrous for India. This was reinforced by another new lobby: the information technology ministers who now exist in every Indian state to drum up business."[20]

Foreign Nations

Most countries have embassies that lobby for their interests in Washington. In addition, some countries like Japan have built up a powerful network of lawyers, lobbyists, and Washington-based publicists who are retained by Japanese companies and trade associations, as well as by the Japanese government, to defend their extensive economic interests in the United States.[21] Lobbyists representing industrialized countries like South Korea, Taiwan, Singapore, Brazil, and Mexico have also expanded their Washington lobbying efforts to fight U.S. protectionism and import quotas on textiles, shoes, and other products. Such lobbying is legal, provided that the lobbyists register and report their activities to Congress.

Foreign nations have occasionally tried to influence U.S. policy through less visible means. In 1996, for example, the fact that China and Indonesia had made large contributions to the Clinton–Gore reelection campaign came to light. Although the president vigorously denied any connection between the contributions and administration policy, the Democratic National Committee returned the money. George W. Bush's inaugural committee returned a $100,000 gift in early 2001 to a donor who had questionable ties to foreign leaders.[22]

Political Parties

Political parties do not usually play a major role in shaping foreign and defense policy, for two reasons: (1) Many Americans still prefer to keep partisan politics out of foreign policy, and (2) parties usually take less clear and candid stands on foreign policy than they do on domestic policy. Party platforms often obscure the issues instead of highlighting them, and many members of Congress fail to follow any strict party line when it comes to foreign policy.

At the end of World War II, sentiment grew strong for a bipartisan approach to foreign policy. An ambiguous concept, **bipartisanship** in foreign affairs generally means (1) collaboration between the executive and the congressional leaders of both parties, (2) support of presidential foreign policies by both parties in Congress, and (3) downplaying major foreign policy differences in national elections and in presidential debates. Overall, bipartisanship is an attempt to remove the issues of foreign policy from partisan politics.

Not everybody agrees that bipartisanship is desirable. There is virtue, critics say, in debating contending ideas—such as foreign aid or the missile shield.

★★ THINKING IT THROUGH

There are three potential problems with a missile shield. First, it would be extremely expensive to build. Some experts predict that an effective shield would cost $100 billion or more to design, test, and implement. Second, experts argue that a shield could be easily defeated by launching thousands of decoys, all of which would have to be identified or destroyed to find the real missiles. Third, a missile shield could undermine the nuclear stability created by the concept of mutual assured destruction. Finally, a shield does nothing to protect the United States against the kind of low-tech terrorist attacks that have become so frequent around the world. Some advocates of the shield have responded to these concerns by supporting a limited shield that could be used to destroy enemy missiles immediately after launch.

---

bipartisanship
A policy that emphasizes a united front and cooperation between the major political parties, especially on sensitive foreign policy issues.

The spirit of bipartisanship is reflected in the report of the 9/11 Commission, issued on July 22, 2004. The commission was made up of both Democrats and Republicans who managed to put their ideological differences aside and to ultimately issue a report that is critical of both the Clinton and Bush administrations in their handling of terrorism. Shown here are 9/11 Commission Chairman Thomas Kean and Vice Chairman Lee Hamilton.

Congress

Although Congress seldom initiates foreign policy on its own, it has taken the lead on some trade and economic assistance questions and, of course, controls the power of the purse. In addition, Congress is authorized to define the limits of presidential war powers.[23]

Congress is a crucial link between policy makers and the public. Regardless of their party, members of Congress want a voice in foreign policy, or at least what some members call "meaningful consulation." After all, they represent the constituents who must fight the wars, pay the taxes, and bear the burdens of wartime. Congress also represents a check on presidential power through its spending and oversight power.

To date, however, Congress has not been a significant check in the Iraq War. With U.S. troops at risk, Congress has approved the president's requests for additional spending, including an additional $25 billion in 2004 on top of the $65 billion already approved and spent on the wars in Afghanistan and Iraq.

Making Foreign Policy in a Democracy

A democratic foreign policy is presumably one in which policy makers are known and are held accountable to the people. This is a tough test for any policy, yet it is especially tough for foreign policy because of the frequent need to act with speed and sometimes with secrecy, the generally low level of information among the general public, the anonymity of most foreign policy leaders, and the complexity of most international issues and strategic policy options. Still, the American public wants to be consulted and informed, and it wants its leaders held accountable.[24]

A constitutional democracy may not be able to keep leaders from making mistakes, but it can make sure that policy mistakes eventually become public. It is then that the safeguarding agencies of democracy—the opposition party, the press, and public opinion—play a crucial role in demanding accountability. The public's opposition to the Vietnam War eventually forced the United States to withdraw, for example, and its outrage over the genocide in Kosovo eventually forced the United States to intervene.

The temptation during times of crisis is to rally around the president and the flag in support of the country. But as noted elsewhere in this book, dissent is an essential element of maintaining accountability during such moments.

FOREIGN AND DEFENSE POLICY OPTIONS

The United States has a number of tools for achieving foreign policy success, not the least of which is military might. But military might is no longer enough to ensure success, or even deter foreign threats. Absent conventional diplomacy to send its message clearly, foreign aid to help nations in need, economic sanctions to isolate its adversaries, and public diplomacy to help other nations understand its agenda, no amount of military might will succeed.

Conventional Diplomacy

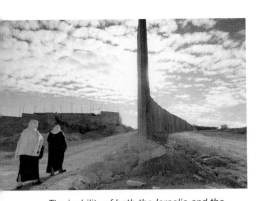

The inability of both the Israelis and the Palestinians to reach an agreement on Israeli settlements in the West Bank by means of conventional diplomacy has led to the use of violence on both sides of the issue and ultimately to Israel's construction of a "separation wall" that it believes will protect Israeli settlers from further violence.

Much of U.S. foreign policy is conducted by the Foreign Service and ambassadors in face-to-face discussions in Washington and other capitals, at the United Nations in New York and Geneva, at North Atlantic Treaty Organization or World Trade Organization meetings, and elsewhere around the world in regional or international organizations and world conferences. International summit meetings, with their high-profile pomp and drama, are another form of conventional diplomacy. Even though traditional diplomacy appears more subdued and somewhat less vital in this era of personal leader-to-leader communication by telephone, fax, and teleconferencing, it is still an important, if slow, process by which nations can gain information, talk about mutual interests, and try to resolve disputes.

Much of the conventional diplomacy carried out by the State Department may not produce important breakthroughs, yet it is difficult to measure the value of diplomatic representation. No price tag can be placed on close personal relations with foreign officials or on information gathered and arguments made to promote American interests around the world. Surely the closing of one embassy or the withdrawal from an international organization is unlikely to cause major setbacks for the United States, yet a less active diplomatic corps could mean a less effective foreign policy.

When relations between nations become strained, diplomatic relations are sometimes broken as a means of political coercion. When the United States breaks diplomatic ties, the consequences are more than merely symbolic. Doing so greatly restricts tourist and business travel to a country and in effect curbs economic as well as political relations with the nation.

Breaking diplomatic relations, however, is a next-to-last resort (force is the last resort), for such action undermines the ability to reason with a nation's leaders or to use other diplomatic strategies to resolve conflicts. The act also undermines our ability to get valuable information about what is going on in a nation and to have a presence there.

Kofi Annan, secretary general of the United Nations. Annan came under intense criticism in late 2004 for his role in managing the Iraqi oil accounts during the 1900s when Iraq was allowed to sell oil to purchase medical supplies and food.

THE ROLE OF THE UNITED NATIONS The United Nations is one of the most important arenas for traditional diplomacy. Established in 1945 by the victors of World War II, the United Nations now has 189 nation members.

Despite its promise as a forum for world peace, the United Nations was mostly ineffective during its first 45 years. Critics contend that it either ducked crucial global issues or was politically unable to tackle them. During much of that time, the U.N. General Assembly, dominated by a combination of Third World and communist nations, was hostile to many U.S. interests. The General Assembly often became a talk shop, passing vague resolutions. More recently, the five permanent members of the U.N. Security Council—the United States, China, Russia (which replaced the Soviet Union), Britain, and France—have usually worked in harmony. Moreover, the United Nations' assumption of responsibilities in the Persian Gulf War and its extensive peacekeeping missions in Cyprus and Lebanon won it respect. U.N. efforts in Cambodia and Somalia were less successful.

In addition, several of the specialized agencies of the United Nations—including the World Health Organization, the United Nations High Commission for Refugees, and the World Food Program—are considered major successes. But the review is much more mixed with respect to the United Nations' peacekeeping efforts, of which it has conducted more than 50. Such a review suggests that these operations are plagued by inadequate and often under-prepared personnel. "First-world countries with first-rate armies are usually unwilling to put their troops at risk," writes former United States Ambassador Dennis Jett. "Thus these operations are often left to third-world countries, and the United Nations sends some of the worst soldiers in the world off to situations where it can only hope they are not called on to actually do anything."[25]

Foreign Aid

The United States offers aid to more than 100 countries directly and to other nations through contributions to various U.N. development funds. Since 1945, the United States has provided about $400 billion in economic assistance to foreign countries. In recent years, however, foreign aid spending has amounted to around $15 billion per year, or less than 50 percent of what it spent in inflation-adjusted dollars back in 1985.[26]

Most foreign aid goes to a few countries that the United States deems to be of strategic importance to our national security: Israel, Egypt, Ukraine, Jordan, India, Russia, South Africa, and Haiti. That list is sure to change in the future as the nation reallocates its budget to nations central to the war on terrorism. However, regardless of which nation receives the aid, most foreign aid is actually spent in the United States, where it pays for the purchase of American services and products being sent to those countries. It thus amounts to a hefty subsidy for American companies and their employees.

Many Americans and members of Congress oppose foreign aid. A recent poll of American citizens found that only 9 percent supported increasing foreign aid, while 47 percent favored reducing it. Another 40 percent would keep it pretty much at the same level.[27] Few powerful interest groups or constituencies back foreign aid initiatives. State Department officials are invariably the biggest advocates of foreign aid. Presidents also recognize the vital role foreign aid plays in advancing U.S. interests. Successive presidents have all wanted to maintain the leverage with key countries that economic and military assistance provides. One of the major debates today is how much debt relief to provide for the world's poorest nations, some of which spend up to 50 percent of their budgets to service debt on old loans. The problem is particularly severe in Central and South America, where international debt has brought high inflation, unemployment, and civil unrest.

Despite these arguments, Congress invariably trims the foreign aid budget, responding in part to polls that show most Americans believe the United States spends more on foreign aid than it does on Medicare and other domestic priorities. Members of Congress often criticize foreign aid as a "Ghana versus Grandma" case. How, they say, can you give away taxpayers' money to some foreign country when we have poor older people who can't afford their prescription drugs and decent medical help?[28]

Critics also note that U.S. foreign aid has subsidized the most autocratic and most corrupt of dictators. And there are plenty of instances in which foreign aid money has been stolen or misspent. Defenders counter that some corruption is inevitable. "You can't engage in bone-poor countries that lack laws and independent journalists and elections, and expect American standards of transparency," writes *Washington Post* editorial writer Sebastian Mallaby. "Yes, many aid programs fail and will continue to do so. But you don't give up trying to educate and house people just because it's hard. And you don't give up on international engagement just because it's as daunting as it is important."[29]

Economic Sanctions

The United States has frequently applied economic pressure in response to a nation's unwillingness to abide by what we perceive to be international law or proper relations. Indeed, the United States has employed economic sanctions more than any other nation—over 100 times in the past 50 years. **Economic sanctions** entail a denial of export, import, or financial relations with a target country in an effort to change that country's policies. Economic sanctions imposed on South Africa doubtless helped end apartheid and encourage democracy in that nation, while sanctions on Libya helped end its nuclear weapons program. But sanctions imposed on Cuba have not had much effect in dislodging that nations' dictatorial regime. The United States imposed sanctions on India and Pakistan in 1998 when both nations began a round of nuclear testing, but because of economic distress both in Pakistan and among U.S. wheat growers, Congress and the president lifted most of the sanctions within months of imposing them.

The popularity of economic sanctions has risen and fallen over the years. They are especially unpopular among farmers and corporations that have to sacrifice part of their overseas markets to comply with government controls, and they rarely work as effectively as intended. Brookings Institution scholar Richard Haass claims, "Sanctions have caused humanitarian suffering (Haiti), weakened friendly governments (Bosnia), bolstered tyrants (Cuba), and left countries with little choice but to develop nuclear weapons (Pakistan)."[30] They can also be costly to U.S. businesses and workers while intensifying anti-American sentiment.

Senator Richard Lugar believes that sanctions seldom work unless they are multilateral rather than imposed by the United States alone.[31] Scholars suggest that when dealing with authoritarian regimes, the United States should direct sanctions at rulers, not the populace at large. "Iraqis are not our enemies. Nor are the Cubans," writes Gary Hufbauer. "Where the president imposes comprehensive sanctions on an authoritarian regime, he should view those sanctions as a prelude to the exercise of military force, not as a substitute for force. Unless we are prepared to remove bad governments with military force, we have no business heaping prolonged punishment on innocent people."[32]

Military Intervention

economic sanctions
Denial of export, import, or financial relations with a target country in an effort to change that nation's policies.

War is not merely an extension of diplomacy but rather the complete and total breakdown of diplomatic efforts. The United States has used military force in other nations on the average of almost once a year since 1789, although usually in short-term initiatives

IN COMPARATIVE PERSPECTIVE

FOREIGN AID IN THE NETHERLANDS

Wealthy nations can do many things to help other countries around the world, not the least of which is provide direct foreign aid. According to the Organization for Economic Cooperation and Development, which monitors international governance, the United States was the largest foreign aid contributor in the world in 2003, giving $15 billion to a variety of projects around the globe. The United States is far from the most generous, however. Although the Netherlands gives less foreign aid in absolute dollars, it contributes a much greater amount measured against its gross national income. By that measure, it is nearly six times more generous than the United States.

The Netherlands is more generous than the United States and most other nations in other ways, too. According to the Center for Global Development, a nonpartisan Washington, D.C., think tank, the Netherlands is also open to free trade with other nations, willing to invest its own money in less-developed economies, welcoming to immigrants, helpful in improving environmental protection and technological innovation in less-developed economies, and ready to contribute troops in peacekeeping missions. When all its contributions are added up into a single index of commitment to helping poorer nations, the Netherlands emerges as the most committed nation in the world, followed by Denmark, Portugal, New Zealand, and Switzerland.* By these same measures, the U.S. ends up number 20 on the list of the world's 21 richest nations.

Foreign Aid Spending, 2003

Nation	Total Spending (billions of U.S. dollars)	Percentage of Gross National Income
Norway	$2.04	0.92%
Denmark	1.24	0.84
Netherlands	4.07	0.81
Sweden	2.10	0.70
France	7.34	0.41
Switzerland	1.23	0.38
United Kingdom	6.17	0.34
Germany	6.7	0.28
Canada	2.21	0.26
Spain	2.03	0.25
Japan	8.91	0.20
Italy	2.39	0.16
United States	15.79	0.14

SOURCE: Organization for Economic Cooperation and Development, 2003. *The rankings come from the Center for Global Development, www.cgd.org.

such as NATO's military activities in Bosnia and Kosovo. Although presidential candidate John Kerry argued that the Iraq war was the first time in history that the United States had gone to war because it chose to, not because it had to, it has actually sent forces into combat many times without a clear threat. It did not have to go to war against Spain in 1898 or send troops to Cuba, Haiti, the Dominican Republic, Lebanon, Mexico, Nicaragua, Somalia, South Vietnam, or even Europe in World War I.[33] (See Table 20–3 for the number of Americans killed in the nation's major wars.)

Experts tend to agree that the use of force is most successful when it is used in small and even medium-sized countries for short engagements (Grenada, Panama, Kuwait, Kosovo, and Afghanistan). They also agree that it "often proves ineffective in the context of national civil wars (the United States in Vietnam; Israel in Lebanon)."[34] Lessons from past interventions are one reason Americans were reluctant to support, if not opposed to, U.S. military intervention in Haiti, Bosnia, and Kosovo. It also helps explain the public's weakening support for the Iraq war.

U.S. military efforts with its NATO allies in Kosovo sought to put an end to "ethnic cleansing" in that area. After an extensive air campaign, ground troops were able to force the withdrawal of Serbian military and police, permit the safe return of refugees, and secure stability in the province. President Clinton had been hesitant to use the military in a decisive way in Kosovo in large part because of the apparent opposition of the American people and Congress. And many in the military were also reluctant to commit forces to what they viewed as primarily a humanitarian initiative rather than a defense of America's vital national security interests. These opposing views prompted renewed debates about the conditions under which the United States should resort to military intervention.[35]

TABLE 20–3   THE COSTS OF WAR

Number killed

Revolutionary War	4,435
War of 1812	2,260
Civil War	214,939
Spanish-American War	385
World War I	53,402
World War II	291,557
Korean War	35,516
Vietnam War	58,516
Persian Gulf War	382
Afghanistan War	74[*]
Iraq war	937[*]

SOURCE: *The Washington Post*, May 26, 2003; figures updated by authors.

[*]Figures as of July 25, 2004.

Not all military action is visible to the public or even the intended target. Covert activities are planned and executed to conceal the identity of the sponsor. The United States repeatedly engaged in covert operations during the cold war, including early intervention in Vietnam and Central America, as well as in Afghanistan, where it supported rebels fighting the Soviet invasion. But covert activities in Cuba, Chile, and elsewhere have backfired, and support for this strategy has cooled in the post–cold war era.[36] Ironically, U.S. covert aid to the Afghan rebels eventually led to the Soviet withdrawal, which in turn led to the establishment of the Taliban, which allowed Osama bin Laden and his followers to establish training bases in its territory.

Public Diplomacy

In July 2002, President George W. Bush created the White House Office of Global Communications to address the question he asked before a joint session of Congress only a week after the terrorist attacks on New York City and Washington, D.C.: "Why do they hate us?" The office is designed to enhance America's image abroad, thereby countering the image of the United States as the "Great Satan," as some of its enemies describe it.[37]

Bush was not the first president to worry about the U.S. image abroad. President Franklin Roosevelt created the Office of War Information early in World War II, which in turn established the Voice of America program to broadcast pro-American information into Nazi Germany. President Harry Truman followed suit early in the cold war with the Soviet Union by launching the Campaign of Truth, which eventually led to the creation of the United States Information Agency under President Dwight Eisenhower. Both agencies exist today and are being strengthened as part of the "new public diplomacy." In this case, the word "public" refers to citizens of other nations, not the United States.

Public diplomacy is a blend of age-old propaganda techniques and modern information warfare. It has three basic goals: (1) to cast the enemy in a less favorable light among its supporters, (2) to mold the image of a conflict such as the war in Afghanistan, and (3) to clarify the ultimate goals of U.S. foreign policy. The United States has tried to convince the people of Afghanistan that Osama bin Laden is the true enemy of the people, the war is not between Muslims and Western democracies, and the war is about preventing the deaths of innocent women and children in both Afghanistan and the United States. Public diplomacy is not a substitute for traditional information warfare such as jamming enemy radio broadcasts, destroying radio and television towers, and disseminating misleading information about the enemy. But it does strike at the heart of the hate that fuels terrorism.

SPECIAL PROBLEMS IN DEFENSE POLICY

The United States has a long history of military involvement in world affairs. Since 1945, more than 100,000 U.S. military personnel have died in undeclared wars; more than 400,000 have suffered battle injuries.[38] But Congress has formally declared war on only a few occasions. The war in Afghanistan was never formally declared, nor was the air war over Kosovo or the Iraq war. Although Congress passed joint resolutions supporting both engagements, the president moved military forces into position well before passage.

Americans believe that the United States should use its military power carefully. As noted earlier in this chapter, almost three out of five Americans said the United States should use military force to prevent future terrorism, compared to just one out of five who said it should use force to punish the terrorists. Even after the events of September 11, 2001, substantial numbers of Americans continued to believe that the United States should not send forces into regional conflicts when other means are available to achieve our objectives. Many also continued to believe that the United States should not intervene in conflicts without a broad public consensus at home and an alliance of nations abroad.

These views eventually led to the Powell Doctrine, formulated by General Colin Powell, the future secretary of state, when he served as chair of the Joint Chiefs of Staff in the late 1980s. The Powell Doctrine reflects the concerns of both average Americans and

In the first major offensive of the war on terrorism, American troops invaded Afghanistan.

many senior military leaders. "When the United States goes to war," he said, "it should be for a clear purpose, only when our vital national security interests are threatened, and our goal should be overwhelming victory." Powell pointed out that "halfhearted warfare for half-baked reasons" is misguided defense policy.[39] As one analyst explained Powell's reasoning: "He argues that the people he calls 'K-mart parents'—working class Americans who tend to be the parents of soldiers—should understand why their children are being put at risk and should never doubt that the country will back them to the hilt."[40]

This doctrine involves far more than a simple contest between internationalism and isolationism; it raises issues about human rights and moral leadership as well as about military effectiveness. The Powell Doctrine has widespread support. Still, most Americans believe it would be a mistake to forsake our unique leadership position and abandon responsibilities to encourage peace and human rights at this time of incredible global change.[41]

The All-Volunteer Force

The Constitution authorizes Congress to do what is "necessary and proper" in order to "raise and support Armies," "to provide and maintain a Navy," and "to provide for calling forth the Militia." The problem is that the role of the United States in the world has changed dramatically since 1789, as have the nation's military needs. Although our boundaries once defined our major national interest, U.S. interests now reach around the globe.

Military conscription (the draft) was first instituted in 1862, during the Civil War. It was used during World War I, when Congress passed the Selective Service Act. This act called for a draft of males between the ages of 21 and 30, with exemptions for certain public officials and for clergy. In both instances, conscription ended when the conflicts ended. The first peacetime draft began in 1940, with the Selective Service and Training Act. By the time of Pearl Harbor, in late 1941, men between the ages of 18 and 35 were eligible for the draft. When World War II ended, however, the draft continued, in various forms, for almost three decades.

Shortly before the Vietnam War ended, Congress replaced the draft with an *all-volunteer force*, which is composed entirely of citizens who choose to serve. The armed services offer a variety of benefits to make sure they meet their annual recruiting targets, including college loans, signing bonuses, special training, and even job placement with private employers after tours of duty are completed. The all-volunteer concept has worked well during peacetime, particularly when the quality of recruits is measured by the educational achievement and performance on standardized intelligence tests.

However, it is not yet clear that the all-volunteer force will able to recruit enough Army troops to fight the wars in Afghanistan and Iraq. "I worry about this every single day—recruiting and retention," said the Army's top personnel officer in July 2004. "We are recruiting a volunteer force during a time of war. We've never done that before."[42] Although the Air Force and Navy continue to meet their annual recruiting targets, the Army failed to meet its targets in the spring of 2004, in part because of the increased death toll in Iraq, and in part because of the prison abuse scandal.

The Army is far from a crisis point, however, and expects to meet its targets by increasing recruitment and retention bonuses—soldiers now receive a one-time $10,000 bonus for reenlisting at the end of their two-year tour. But the Army could easily use a draft if necessary. Because males must register with the Selective Service at age 18, the list of potential draftees is already on file.

Women in Combat

As the number of women in the armed forces has increased, so has the number of women who serve in combat zones. Whereas women constituted 6 percent of U.S. forces in the first war in Iraq in 1991, they constituted 14 percent of forces in the second war in 2002–2004, during which they protected supply convoys, flown transport and supply aircraft, medical helicopters, fired Patriot antimissile systems, and worked as tank mechanics and military police guarding Iraqi prisoners of war. They have also borne the ultimate sacrifice of

PEOPLE & POLITICS *Making a Difference* ★★★

GEN. ANTONIO TAGUBA

In March 2004, Americans were shocked to read that some U.S. military police had abused Iraqi prisoners held in Baghdad's notorious Abu Ghraib prison, which had once been used by Saddam Hussein's secret police. Much of the information involved an internal Army report by Major General Antonio M. Taguba, who cited "egregious acts and grave breaches of international law" by prison guards, including sleep deprivation, intimidation by military guard dogs, and sexual humiliation.

Taguba is the son of a Philippine resistance fighter in World War II, who was captured by the Japanese in 1943 and escaped from the Bataan Death March. Born in Manila in 1950, Taguba moved to the United States with his family when he was 11 years old. Taguba later worked his way up through the Army to become the second highest ranking Filipino-American in uniform.

Taguba was assigned to the Abu Ghraib investigation in January 2004 to conduct an "informal investigation" into allegations of mistreatment raised by military officers and the International Red Cross. Taguba earned the assignment because of his reputation for absolute integrity. "If you want the truth, he's going to tell you the truth," said one Army general who was quoted in a *New York Times* profile of Taguba. "He's not bullied; he's a stand up guy."*

Taguba brought a deep love of country to the difficult task, which exposed the Army to intense criticism and further investigation. "I am proud to serve in the world's best Army," he once said. But "if we are to remain the best, the well-being of its soldiers and families must be its principal focus." It was not until 1999,

he remembers, that the Army finally recognized the service of his father with a Bronze star and a letter of recognition. "It took over 54 years to gain my parents their due recognition. They sought not to be recognized, only to be appreciated."

*Douglas Jehl, "Head of Inquiry on Iraq Now in Spotlight," *The New York Times,* May 11, 2004, p. A1.

---

service—22 women were killed in the line of duty between March 2003 and July 2004, starting with Army private Lori Piestewa, a member of the Hopi Indian Tribe, who was killed in the same ambush in which private Jessica Lynch was captured.

Federal law already allows women to fly Air Force and Navy combat aircraft, and the Pentagon has now opened thousands of combat-related positions in the military services to women. The military is redesigning its assignments to ensure that equal opportunity exists within its ranks but has yet to assign women to specific combat roles.

Despite their accomplishments in battlefield support positions, women have faced significant barriers to advancement in the armed services, most notably sexual harassment.[43] In March 2003, for example, the Air Force removed the senior leadership at the Air Force Academy in Colorado Springs following repeated allegations of sexual abuse. Further congressional investigation found 142 specific complaints of verbal and physical abuse between 1993 and 2003, many of which had been received with indifference or retribution. Most of the Academy's senior leadership was removed in the wake of the scandal, including the superintendent, commandant and vice commandant of cadets, and dean of the faculty.

The Politics of Defense Spending

The U.S. defense budget reached more than $440 billion in 2005, a figure that covers everything from weapons and ammunition to salaries for soldiers, sailors, pilots, and civil servants, and pensions for more than 1.5 million retired Defense Department personnel. The defense budget also includes more than $12 billion dedicated to nuclear

Women now make up approximately 14 percent of the total enlistment in the U.S. armed forces.

weapons research and maintenance and environmental cleanup projects that are actually run by the Department of Energy.[44]

Defense spending fell dramatically at the end of the cold war as weapons systems were canceled or postponed, bases closed, ships retired, and large numbers of troops brought home from Germany, the Philippines, and elsewhere. The Army was cut by over 30 percent, and the National Guard and the military reserve were cut back about 25 percent. As a result, defense spending has also fallen, dropping from 25 percent at the height of the cold war in the mid-1980s to 15 percent in 2000.

The defense budget has been rising ever since, however, and will hit 19 percent of the budget in 2005. Most of the increase involves the purchase of new equipment such as the Joint Strike Fighter, which will serve the Air Force, Navy, and Army, and will be used for the wars in Afghanistan and Iraq.[45] The budget also included the combined costs of the wars in Afghanistan and Iraq, which are expected to hit a $90 billion total by 2005.

Even as defense spending rises, some experts argue that the nation needs a much lighter, highly mobile force to combat terrorism and that further spending on "cold war legacy" systems such as nuclear attack submarines and heavy tanks is wasteful.[46] They argue that the United States cannot have it all—meaning old cold war systems, high-tech space defenses, decent military pay, and the kind of expensive precision weaponry used in Afghanistan. Nor do they believe that the United States should continue spending money on weapons systems, such as the Comanche helicopter or V-22 tilt-rotor aircraft, that simply fail to perform as promised.

Despite the logic, Congress can rarely muster the will to kill a weapons system. Cutting defense spending means cutting jobs, and cutting jobs, especially those in the home districts of powerful members of Congress, is politically painful.[47]

The B-2 Stealth bomber is often used as a notable example. The Pentagon has not asked for more of these billion-dollar planes, yet Congress often approves funds for them because cuts in weapons systems and plant closings mean not only that people in the Defense Department and on bases lose their jobs but also that local shopkeepers, bankers, lawyers, doctors, contractors, housekeepers, baby-sitters—the list goes on and on—are put out of work.

Weapons are, in fact, a major American industry, one that members of Congress work hard to promote and protect. As former World War II hero Dwight Eisenhower warned in his presidential Farewell Address in 1960, the United States must be wary of the *military-industrial complex* that supports increased defense spending as a way to protect jobs. Eisenhower's words are well-worth rereading today:

> This conjunction of an immense military establishment and a large arms industry is new in the American experience. The total influence—economic, political, even spiritual—is felt in every city, every State house, every office of the Federal government. We recognize the imperative need for this development. Yet we must not fail to comprehend its gave implications. Our toil, resources and livelihood are all involved; so is the very structure of our society.
>
> In the councils of government, we must guard against the acquisition of unwarranted influence, whether sought or unsought, by the military industrial complex. The potential for the disastrous rise of misplaced power exists and will persist.[48]

The military-industrial complex has become even more significant as the U.S. military has privatized many of the jobs that are essential for war. Private contractors were responsible for building the bases and feeding U.S. troops in Iraq, for example, as well as maintaining and repairing military equipment, providing security for foreign diplomats, and even interrogating prisoners. As of August 1, 2004, at least 110 contractors had been killed in the Iraq war.[49]

The military is also dealing with the dramatic number of mergers and acquisitions in the defense industry. In the 1950s, for example, 11 different companies were building fighter aircraft; by 2004, just three companies remained: Boeing, Lockheed-Martin, and Northrop Grumman. As the consolidation has increased, the amount of competition between firms has declined, while making the U.S. more dependent on a handful of firms to build the next generation of weapons.[50]

FIGURE 20–2 Defense Expenditures, 2003.

SOURCE: Michael O'Hanlon, "Protecting the American Homeland," *Brookings Review* 20 (Summer, 2002), p. 15.

Although Secretary of Defense Donald Rumsfeld asked Congress to cancel the Crusader mobile cannon in the spring of 2002, members of Congress were able to salvage funding for continued development.

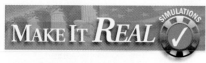

THE IMPACT OF FOREIGN AID

U.S. policy makers have at least three choices to make in giving foreign aid to a country. First, they must decide whether to give any funding at all. The decision depends in part on the strategic value of the recipient nation to U.S. foreign policy goals such as fighting the war on terrorism or reducing the flow of illegal drugs. Second, they must decide what kind of aid to give. Third, they must decide how much to give. Because the foreign aid budget is limited, these decisions determine which nations will be helped or hurt, which in turn determines whether the United States is able to achieve its policy goals. This simulation challenges readers to make the key decisions in distributing a fixed foreign aid budget. Where should the money go, and in what form?

Go to make it Real "The Impact of Foreign Aid."

PROSPECTS FOR THE FUTURE

The world has become a much more uncertain place since the end of the cold war. The Internet has rendered borders virtually meaningless for controlling the flow of information; the global economy has increased the number and size of multinational corporations; and terrorism appears to be spreading rapidly.

The United States is clearly struggling to address this uncertainty without frustrating the public or compromising basic democratic principles. On the one hand, for example, Americans favor open borders, easy movement of imports and exports, short lines at airports, quick access to information, and protection of their privacy. On the other hand, they want government to monitor terrorists, detect dangerous cargo, ensure airport security, keep secrets from the enemy, and make sure that no one slips through the border to bring harm to the nation.

Although the goals are not necessarily contradictory, they do require a careful balance of individual liberty and national interest. They also involve an effort to prevent the spread of terrorism by promoting global peace and understanding. The war on terrorism will not be won in a single battle with a single adversary, nor will weapons of mass destruction disappear without a broad international commitment to action. As the United States has learned over the hard months of combat in Iraq, coalition building may be difficult, frustrating, and most certainly time-consuming, but, ultimately, it may be the only option available.

S U M M A R Y

1. The United States has adopted many, sometimes competing foreign policy goals over the years, from promoting peace in the Middle East to addressing the spread of HIV-AIDS. It is putting its greatest emphasis today on three primary goals: winning the war on terrorism, controlling weapons of mass destruction, and promoting U.S. trade in an increasingly competitive global economy.

2. The president has the primary responsibility to shape foreign and defense policy. The principal foreign policy adviser is the secretary of state, although other cabinet secretaries, including the secretary of defense, are also influential. The National Security Council and the intelligence agencies also play key roles. Public opinion, interest groups, foreign countries, political parties, and Congress also affect the making of foreign policy.

3. Presidents, Congress, and the American people all become involved in defining our vital national security interests, but they often have contradictory views. Presidents must sometimes act swiftly and decisively. Plainly, the role of the president in foreign affairs was strengthened during the cold war years as the United States developed an enormous standing military capability and an extensive intelligence network. Presidents are often in a good position to see the nation's long-term interests above the tugging of bureaucratic and special interests. But in our constitutional democracy, presidents and their advisers must consult with Congress and inform the American people. The media and special interests also play a role.

4. U.S. foreign policy interests are advanced by one or a combination of the following strategies: diplomacy, foreign aid, eco-

nomic sanctions, political coercion (including the breaking off of diplomatic relations), covert action, and military intervention. Traditional diplomacy is often augmented by the U.S. role in the United Nations.

5. The U.S. military is an all-volunteer force. Although the military does provide enormous opportunities for women and minorities, women have yet to play a significant role in combat.

6. Although the past decade witnessed major reductions in the size of the military and major cuts in military spending, some critics say the defense budget can be cut much further. Critics on the right, however, claim that we have weakened our defense preparedness. The nature of warfare and the preventing of wars are changing in ways that are hard to predict.

K E Y   T E R M S

weapons of mass destruction
Bush Doctrine
preemption

permanent normal trade
relations (PNTR) status

bipartisanship

economic sanctions

FURTHER READING

GEORGE H. W. BUSH AND BRENT SCOWCROFT, *A World Transformed* (Knopf, 1998).

WARREN CRISTOPHER, *In the Stream of History: Shaping Foreign Policy for a New Era* (Stanford University Press, 1998).

IVO H. DAALDER AND MICHAEL E. O'HANLON, *Winning Ugly: NATO's War to Save Kosovo* (Brookings Institution Press, 2000).

JOSEPH G. DAWSON III, ED., *Commanders-in-Chief: Presidential Leadership in Modern Wars* (University Press of Kansas, 1993).

LOUIS FISHER, *Presidential War Power* 2nd ed. (University Press of Kansas, 2004).

JOHN LEWIS GADDIS, *The United States and the End of the Cold War* (Oxford University Press, 1992).

RICHARD N. HAASS, *The Reluctant Sheriff: The United States After the Cold War* (Council on Foreign Relations, 1997).

RICHARD N. HAASS AND MEGHAN L. O'SULLIVAN, EDS., *Honey and Vinegar: Incentives, Sanctions, and Foreign Policy* (Brookings Institution Press, 2000).

OLE HOLSTI, *Public Opinion and American Foreign Policy* (University of Michigan Press, 1996).

SAMUEL HUNTINGTON, *The Clash of Civilization and the Remaking of World Order* (Simon & Schuster, 1996).

LOCH K. JOHNSON, *Secret Agencies: U.S. Intelligence in a Hostile World* (Yale University Press, 1996).

HAROLD HONGJU KOH, *The National Security Constitution: Sharing Power After the Iran-Contra Affair* (Yale University Press, 1990).

STEVEN KULL AND I. M. DESTLER, *Misreading the Public: The Myth of a New Isolationism* (Brookings Institution Press, 1999).

THOMAS W. LIPPMAN, *Madeleine Albright and the New American Diplomacy* (Westview Press, 2000).

ROBERT LITAN, *Globalphobia* (Brookings Institution Press, 2002).

ROBERT S. LITWAK, *Rogue States and U.S. Foreign Policy: Containment After the Cold War* (Johns Hopkins University Press, 2000).

NATIONAL COMMISSION ON TERRORIST ATTACKS ON THE UNITED STATES, *The 9/11 Commission Report* (W.W. Norton, 2004).

MICHAEL E. O'HANLON, *How to Be a Cheap Defense Hawk* (Brookings Institution Press, 2002).

WILLIAM PERRY, *Preventive Defense: A New Security Strategy for America* (Brookings Institution Press, 1999).

JOHN PRADOS, *Keepers of the Keys: A History of the National Security Council from Truman to Bush* (Morrow, 1991).

ROSEMARY RIGHTER, *Utopia Lost: The United Nations and World Order* (Twentieth Century Fund, 1995).

JOSEPH ROMM, *Defining National Security: The Nonmilitary Aspect* (Council on Foreign Relations, 1993).

GEORGE SHULTZ, *Turmoil and Triumph: My Years as Secretary of State* (Scribner, 1993).

RONALD STEEL, *Temptations of a Superpower* (Harvard University Press, 1995).

STEPHEN R. WEISSMAN, *A Culture of Deference: Congress's Failure of Leadership in Foreign Affairs* (Basic Books, 1995).

GEORGE C. WILSON, *This War Really Matters: Inside the Fight for Defense Dollars* (CQ Press, 2000).

BOB WOODWARD, *Plan of Attack* (Simon & Schuster, 2004).

STATE AND LOCAL POLITICS
WHO GOVERNS?

21

Many of the most critical domestic and economic issues facing the United States are decided by our state and local officials. Elected and appointed officials in our states and localities decide how our schools are run, how welfare policy is shaped, who goes to prison or gets probation, and how much property and sales taxes we pay. Such challenging responsibilities as overseeing the transition from welfare to work, maintaining prisons and jails (over 90 percent of the people incarcerated in America are in state and local facilities, not federal prisons), and bringing the residents of the inner cities in our large metropolitan areas into the economic mainstream require leadership and thoughtful public policy making at the state and local levels of government as well as in Washington, D.C.

State and local governments are beginning to recover from the economic downturn of the early 2000s. States had to raise income and sales taxes as well as fees on all kinds of services, from fishing and marriage licenses to divorce filings and college tuition fees. Over a three-year period, the University of Arizona, the University of Virginia, and the California State University system, for example, all increased tuition by over 30 percent.[1] States also had to make deep cuts in spending on health care and other programs, along with turning to one-time gimmicks such as borrowing against pension funds.[2] The budget crisis in California led to the recall of Governor Gray Davis and the election of Arnold Schwarzenegger, who vowed not to raise taxes, proposing instead a referendum to authorize a $15 billion bond sale order to deal with the state's $14 billion shortfall.

Actor Arnold Schwarenszenegger was elected governor of California in a special election held because of the state's budget crisis and his promise not to raise taxes.

State and local governments flourished long before there was a national government. Indeed, the framers of our Constitution shaped the national government largely according to their practical experience with colonial and state governments. What happens today in state and local governments continues to influence the policies of the national government. The reverse, of course, is also true: The national government and its policies have an important impact on local and state government. The national government's activities—such as the war against international terrorism, key Supreme Court decisions, and major congressional investigations and legislation—receive such great publicity that we often overlook the countless ways governments closer to home affect our lives.

Studying state and local governments to find out how they operate and who governs them is also a challenge. It is one thing to study our national system, vast and complex as it is; it is something else to study 50 separate state governments, each with its own legislature, executive, and judiciary and each with its own intricate politics and political traditions.

Moreover, state and local governments are only part of a much larger picture. To discuss the government of the state of Mississippi or the city of Detroit without mentioning race, the government of New York City or Los Angeles without noting the politics of ethnic groups, or the government of Texas without referring to the cattle and oil industries would be to ignore the real dynamics of the political process. State and local governments, like the national government, are more than organizational charts. They are systems of politics and people with their own unique histories that affect how and what public policies are enacted. The great variations among the states and localities—in population, economic resources, and environment—make comparisons and generalizations difficult.

Still, every government system is part of a larger social system. A government is a structure and a process that resolves, or at least manages, conflicts. It regulates, distributes, and sometimes redistributes property and wealth. It is also a means for achieving certain goals and performing services desired both by those who govern and by the governed. It operates in the context of an economic system, class structure, and lifestyle that are often more important than the structure of the government itself or even the nature of its political processes. The interrelations among the economic, social, and political systems are complex and difficult to unscramble, and it is hard to decide which is cause and which is effect.[3]

This already complex picture is complicated further by the fact that almost 88,000 cities, counties, towns, villages, school districts, water control districts, and other governmental units are piled one on top of another within the states.[4] If all states or cities or towns were alike, the task might be manageable. But of course they are not. Each city, like each state, has distinct characteristics.

WHO HAS THE POWER?

How can we grasp the operations and problems of state and local government without becoming bogged down in endless detail? We can do so by focusing on the core components of democratic governance: citizen participation, liberty, constitutional checks and balances, representation, and responsible leadership. Further, we can address several questions that throw light on all these problems: Who governs? How much influence or control is in the hands of the business community? Does political power tend to gravitate toward a relatively small number of people? If so, who are these people? Do they work closely together, or do they oppose each other? Do the same people or factions shape the agenda for public debate and dominate all decision making? Or do some sets of leaders decide certain questions and leave other questions to other leaders or simply to chance?

In 1924, two sociologists from Columbia University, Robert and Helen Lynd, decided to study a typical American city as though they were anthropologists investigating a tribe in Africa or Indonesia. For two years, they lived in Muncie, Indiana—at that time a city of 38,000 residents—asking questions and watching how people made their living, raised their children, used their leisure time, and joined in civic and social associations. The Lynds reported that despite the appearance of democratic rule, a social and economic elite actually ran things.[5] Their work stimulated studies in all kinds of communities to find out whether power is concentrated in the hands of the few, is dispersed among the many, or operates in some other way.

Relying on a mix of research methods, social scientists since the Lynds' time have studied patterns of power in communities and arrived at a variety of findings. Floyd Hunter, a sociologist who analyzed Atlanta in the 1950s, found a relatively small and stable group of top policy makers drawn largely from the business class. This elite operated through secondary leaders who sometimes modified policy, but the power of the elite was almost always important.[6] In contrast, Robert Dahl and his graduate students at Yale studied New Haven at the same time and concluded that although some people had a great deal of influence, there was no permanent elite. Instead, there were shifting coalitions of leaders who sometimes disagreed among themselves but who always had to keep in mind what the public would accept when making decisions.[7]

Rule by a Few or Rule by the Many?

One group of investigators, chiefly sociologists such as Hunter, have been concerned with **social stratification** in the political system—how politics is affected by divisions among socioeconomic groups or classes in a community. These social scientists assume that political influence is a function of social stratification. They try to find out who governs particular communities by asking various citizens to identify the people who are most influential. Then they study those influential people to determine their social characteristics, their roles in decision making, and the interrelations among them and between them and the rest of the citizens. Using this technique, they find that the upper socioeconomic groups make up the *power elite,* that elected political leaders are subordinate to that elite, and that the major conflicts within the community are between the upper and the lower socioeconomic classes.

Other investigators question these findings and raise objections to the research techniques used. They contend that the evidence in social stratification studies does not support the conclusion that communities are run by a power elite. Rather, the notion of a power elite is merely a reflection of the techniques used and the assumptions made by stratification theorists. Instead of studying the activities of those who are thought to have "clout," these researchers insist, one should study how decisions are actually made.

Researchers conducting *community power* studies analyzing the making of decisions usually find a relatively open, pluralistic power structure. Some people do have more influence than others, but that influence is shared among many people and tends to be limited to particular issues and areas. For example, those who decide how the public schools are run may have little influence over other economic policies. In many communities and for many issues, there is no identifiable group of influential people. Policies emerge not from the actions of a small group but rather from the unplanned and unanticipated consequences of the behavior of a relatively large number of people, especially from the countless contending groups that form and win access to those who make the important decisions. According to community power theorists, the social structure of the community is certainly one factor, but not the determining factor in how goods and services are distributed.

social stratification
Divisions in a community among socio-economic groups or classes.

Comparing power elite and community power studies highlights the fact that how we ask questions often influences the answers we get. If we ask highly visible and actively involved citizens for their opinions of who is powerful, we find that they name a relatively small number of people as the real brokers of power. But if we study dozens of local events and decisions, we find that a variety of people are actually involved—different people in different policy areas.

Other studies of local politics suggest that local values, traditions, and the structure of governmental organizations also determine which issues get on the local agenda.[8] Thus tobacco, mining, or steel interests may be so dominant in some areas that tax, regulation, or job safety policies are kept off the local policy agenda for fear of offending the "powers that be." Those "powers" may indeed go to great lengths to prevent what they deem to be adverse policies. This type of research alerts us to weigh carefully the possibility that defenders of the status quo can mobilize power resources in such a way that nondecisions may be more important than decisions. In effect, these researchers tell us not only to study who governs but also to study the procedures and rules of the game. They urge us to determine which groups or interests would gain and which would lose by political decisions.[9]

On many economic policy matters, local corporations and business elites are involved. Studies of cities in Michigan and of Atlanta employing refined and contextual analysis of political decision making concluded that business elites are indeed important, but they are not necessarily the controlling factor in city governance:

> There is, then, no controlling hand in community politics. No conspiracy of business and government exists. Business interests do not invariably dominate government policy even where a single industry dominates the community. However, the giant industrial companies do provide the backdrop against which the public policy process operates in the industrial city. They are always there, seldom intervening in specific policy matters but never far from the calculations of policy makers.[10]

Studies of states and communities have now produced enough findings that we can see how formal government institutions, social structure, economic factors, and other variables interact in a working political system.

THE STAKES IN THE POLITICAL STRUGGLE

The national government has become the driving force behind the nation's economic strength and security. It assumes major responsibility for protecting civil rights, fighting inflation and unemployment, regulating sectors with great economic power, and subsidizing weaker sectors of the economy—not to mention matters of war and peace. State and local governments cannot claim so central a role. Yet the role of states and localities is increasing over a range of domestic policies, even though they diverge in their priorities and policies as a result of the maze of interests in each state. In response to health concerns and budget deficits, for example, seven states charge more than $1 per pack of cigarettes in taxes, while about half charge just 33 cents or less, and some cities, like New York, impose additional taxes both to discourage smoking and to raise revenue.

Since World War II, state and local government activities have increased much faster than the nondefense activities of the federal government. In the past decade, the federal government has been downsizing while state and local governments have been growing. About six times as many people work for state and local governments—15 million—than work for the federal government, which has fewer than 3 million civilian employees.[11] Most state and local employees work in education (8.2 million), hospitals (917,000), law enforcement (887,000), and corrections (702,000).[12]

State and local governments deal more directly with the average person than the national government does, because neighborhood, school, and housing problems are closely regulated at the state and local levels. States have had to assume greater responsibilities for raising taxes, setting economic and social priorities, and administering most welfare and job creation programs as a result of cutbacks in federal funds and devolution of responsibilities to the states.

The points at which people come into contact with government services and officials most often concern schools, streets and highways, parks and playgrounds, police and fire protection, zoning, and health care. But even in these areas, the mix of national, state, and local programs and responsibilities is such that it is often hard to isolate which level of government does what to or for whom. Also, there are some national-to-individual relationships that bypass state and local governments altogether, such as the Internal Revenue Service, the U.S. Postal Service, and Social Security.

The Maze of Interests

Special-interest groups can be found in varying forms in every state and locality. For example, industrial Rhode Island has farm organizations, and rural Wyoming has trade unions. Influential economic pressure groups and political action committees, organized to raise and disburse campaign funds to candidates for public office, operate in the states much as they do nationally. They try to build up the membership of their organizations, they lobby the state capitals and city halls, they educate and organize the voters, and they support their political friends in office and oppose their enemies. They also face the same internal problems all groups face: maintaining unity, dealing with subgroups that break off in response to special needs, and balancing democracy with discipline.

One great difference, however, is that group interests can be concentrated and highly influential in states and localities, whereas their strength tends to be diluted in the national government. Big business does not really run things in Washington, D.C., any more than Wall Street, the Catholic Church, or the American Legion does. But in some states and localities, certain interests clearly dominate because they represent the social and economic majorities of the area. Few politicians in Wisconsin will attack dairy farmers, few candidates for office in Florida will oppose benefits for senior citizens, and few officeholders in Idaho will support gun control. In other areas, industries such as timber or energy are influential because of their role in the local economy.

It is the range and variety of these local groups that give American politics its special flavor, excitement, and challenge: auto unions and manufacturers in Michigan, corn and hog farmers in Iowa, gas and oil dealers in Texas, gun owners in New Hampshire and Idaho, tobacco farmers in North Carolina and Virginia, poultry growers in Arkansas, Boeing and Microsoft in the Seattle area, coal miners in West Virginia, and sheep ranchers in Utah. However, the power of these groups should not be exaggerated.

We have to be cautious about lumping all workers, all businesspeople, all teachers, all Hispanics, or all African Americans together. The union movement is sometimes sharply divided among the truckers, building trades, machinists, auto workers, and so on. The business community is often divided between big industrial, banking, and commercial firms on the one hand and small merchants on the other. In New England, Irish and Italian fraternal societies express the opinions of their respective groups on public issues; other organizations speak for people of French Canadian or Polish descent. New England politicians fear the power of ethnic groups to influence elections, especially primaries, yet there are plenty of examples of "Yankees" winning in heavily ethnic areas. Similarly, Asian American, Latino, and African American communities are playing an increasingly important role in elections in states such as California, Florida, and Texas.

Compared to the other considerations affecting voters' choices, the ethnic factor may be small. Still, even a small percentage of the populace voting according to their ethnic interests can have a decisive effect on an election. Much depends on the character of the candidates and their personal appeal. Any group, no matter how strong, must cope with a variety of cross pressures, including a general sense that the voter does not vote for "one of our own" on that ground alone.

Other interests that are more specialized may also have a close relationship with local government. Many businesspeople sell products to the state or perform services for it: milk dealers, printers, contractors, parking meter manufacturers, computer and communications technology firms, makers of playground equipment, textbook

Government reaches into many trivial aspects of our lives, such as restrictions on our pets.

TOP TEN ISSUES FACING STATE LEGISLATURES

State legislatures are confronting a range of controversial issues. The top ten state legislative issue are:

■ Dealing with budget shortfalls
■ Providing for health coverage
■ Raising educational standards
■ Lowering the cost of prescription drugs
■ Providing tax incentives for attracting and retaining businesses
■ Reforming tax laws
■ Regulating energy production and delivery
■ Addressing the rising cost of medical malpractice liabilities and insurance premiums
■ Improving air quality
■ Deciding whether to recognize same-sex marriages

SOURCE: Melissa Conradi, "Ten Issues to Watch," *Governing* (January 2004), available at www.governing.com/articles/lissues.htm.

publishers, and so on. They often organize formally or informally to improve their relations with purchasing officials. At the local level, developers and home builders and their lawyers press for zoning and planning commission action. Millions of dollars are often at stake, and the resulting action or inaction frequently shapes both the economic growth and the environmental quality of a community.

Business interests are inevitably involved in city and county politics and policy making. As one study of Atlanta found, the business elite is rarely a passive or reluctant partner in setting local priorities. "Atlanta's postwar political experience is a story of active business-elite efforts to make the most of their economic and organizational resources in setting the terms on which civic cooperation occurs."[13] Businesses everywhere depend on local governments for parking, good roads and transportation, safety, urban renovations, and much more. Business elites get involved in long-range community planning, are keenly interested in who gets elected, and are ever watchful of changes in taxation structures.

Another type of interest group intimately concerned with public policy is the professional association. States license barbers, beauticians, architects, lawyers, doctors, teachers, accountants, dentists, and many other occupational groups. You will find representatives from the Beauticians Aid Association, the Funeral Directors and Embalmers Association, the Institute of Dry Cleaning, and the Association of Private Driver-Training Schools lobbying at the statehouse. Associations representing such groups are concerned with the nature of the regulatory laws and the makeup of the boards that do the regulating. They are especially concerned about the rules for admission to their profession or trade and about the way in which professional misconduct is defined and punished. Stiffening licensing requirements for physicians will decrease the supply of new doctors, for example, and thereby raise the incomes of those in practice. Bar associations, for the same reason, closely monitor licensing standards for the legal profession and the appointment of state and local judges.

Today, other groups of citizens are also likely to organize to influence decisions in the state capital: those who are pro-life and those who are pro-choice, those who want stiffer sentences for drunken driving, and those who favor three-strikes-and-you're-out legislation to send repeat criminals to jail for life. Right to Life groups, Planned Parenthood, antismoking groups, animal rights activists, and prison guards are also well organized. Increasingly significant are environmental groups such as the Sierra Club, both in forging public policies and as forces in election contests.

Professions and occupations of various types are regulated by the government through licensing and standards.

Lobbyists at the Statehouse

Many businesses, especially larger corporations, employ lobbyists, public relations specialists, political consultants, or law firms to represent them.[14] One of the growth businesses in state politics is consulting, usually by specialized lawyers or former state legislators. For a fee, lobbyists push desired bills through the legislature or block unwanted ones. This kind of activity again raises the question of who has clout or who governs. Clearly, those who can hire skilled lobbyists and other experts to shape the public agenda often wield more influence than unorganized citizens, who rarely even follow state and regional governmental decision making.

Lobbyists are present in every state capital, and they are there to guide through the legislature a small handful of bills their organization wants passed or to stop those their organization wants defeated.[15] Legislators process hundreds or even thousands of bills each year, in addition to doing casework on behalf of constituents and worrying about reelections. Shrewd lobbyists usually get a chance—sometimes several chances—to influence the fate of their few bills.

There is a widespread impression that lobbyists have freer rein in state legislatures than they do in the U.S. Congress and, what is more, that bribes or informal payoffs by lobbyists are cruder and more obvious in state legislatures. Certainly lobbying restrictions in the states are more relaxed than at the federal level, although in some of the larger states they may be even more stringent. There is less media coverage of state politics in many states than is focused on national politics in Washington, D.C. Corruption of legislators and state officials is usually hard to prove. Exposure of scandals in several states pushed many legislatures to curb election abuses and pass ethics codes with stringent conflict-of-interest provisions.[16] Several legislatures have enacted comprehensive financial disclosure laws, and today most state governments are more open, professional, and accountable than in the past.[17] Former President Jimmy Carter, who served in the Georgia Senate and then became governor, recalled that only a "tiny portion" of the 259 members of the Georgia legislature were not good or honest people. But Carter found that "it is difficult for the common good to prevail against the intense concentration of those who have a special interest, especially if the decisions are made behind locked doors."[18]

In a few states, one corporation or organization may exercise considerable influence; in others, a "big three" or "big four" dominate politics. But in most states, there is competition among organizations; no single group or coalition of groups stands out. In no

CHANGING FACE OF AMERICAN POLITICS

THE GROWING DIVERSITY OF STATE POPULATIONS

The 2000 Census showed significant changes in both the number and location of minority Americans. The percentage of whites declined from 76 percent of the population in 1990 to 69 percent in 2000, while the percentage of Hispanics increased from 9 percent to 12.5 percent, blacks from 11.7 percent to 12.1 percent, and Asian-Pacific Islanders from 2.8 percent to 3.7 percent.

America's growing minority population is not equally distributed across the states and cities, however. Roughly three-quarters of all Hispanics live in the West or South, accounting for a quarter of the population in the West and 12 percent of the population in the South. In turn, just over half of all blacks live in the South, making up 20 percent of the total population; while half of the Asian-Pacific Islander population live in just three states, California, New York, and Hawaii; and two-fifths of all Native Americans live in the West.

Although Hispanics are counted as a single minority group, almost 60 percent of Hispanics actually identified themselves in the 2000 Census as Mexican, another 10 percent as Puerto Rican, and 4 percent as Cuban. Similarly, the Asian-Pacific Islander population includes Asian Indians, Chinese, Filipinos, Japanese, Koreans, Native Hawaiians, and Samoans; while Native Americans include members of six American Indian tribes—Cherokee, Navajo, Latin American Indian, Choctaw, Sioux, and Chippewa—as well as Eskimo.

By 2025, the U.S. Census Bureau predicts that the percentage of white Americans will decline to 62 percent. By then, four states and the District of Columbia will be "majority minority," and several others will be closing in on the 50 percent mark.

Top Ten States by Minority Population in 2000	Top Ten States by Minority Population Projected in 2025
District of Columbia 72%	Hawaii 77%
Hawaii 71	District of Columbia 74
New Mexico 52	California 66
California 50	New Mexico 60
Texas 44	Texas 54
Mississippi 38	New York 47
Louisiana 36	Maryland 46
Maryland 35	New Jersey 45
New York 35	Alaska 43
Georgia 33	Louisiana 43

SOURCE: U.S. Census Bureau, "State Projections by Single Year of Age, Sex, Race, and Hispanic Origin, 1995–2025," accessed online at www.census .gov/population/www/projections/stproj.html on February 15, 2004.

Don Wright/Don Wright, Inc.

state does only one organization control legislative politics, although the powerful Anaconda Company once came close in Montana. For example, some 400 lobbyists are registered in Arkansas. Of these, 125 represent utilities; more than 200 represent individual businesses, industry, or professions; nine represent labor interests; eight work on behalf of senior citizens; and three lobby for environmental interests. The Arkansas Power and Light Company, the railroads, the poultry and trucking industries, the teachers, and the state Chamber of Commerce are the most effective lobbyists. "It is still true that ordinarily those with greater economic resources, greater numbers, and higher status have far more impact than those who lack these attributes," writes political scientist Diane Blair. "Nevertheless, an increasingly complex economy has produced many more actors in the political system, and especially when there is division among the economic elite, some of the lesser voices can be heard."[19]

In Michigan, about 1,250 lobbyists are registered with the state, including representatives of the "big three" automakers, the United Auto Workers, the AFL-CIO, the Michigan Education Association, the Michigan Manufacturers Association, the city of Detroit, the Michigan Chamber of Commerce, certain conservation and environmental groups, and various antitax groups.[20]

As a result of the influence and growing number of lobbyists, states have adopted ethics laws that regulate their activities. Seven states completely ban lobbyists from contributing to campaign contributions at any time, for instance; 23 states prohibit lobbyists from making contributions during a legislative session. Half of the states restrict the monetary value of gifts that public employees may receive.

Not to be overlooked are the growing number of groups and media outlets that view themselves as "watchdogs" of the public policy process. Groups such as the League of Women Voters, Common Cause, and various citizens' groups regularly monitor state politics for questionable fund-raising or lobbying practices. Their "watchdog" efforts are sometimes aided by reporters who cover state capitals.

PARTICIPATION PATTERNS IN SMALL AND MEDIUM-SIZED CITIES

Although it is widely believed that citizens feel "closer" to city and county governments than they do to the more remote national government in Washington, D.C., citizens generally take less interest in, vote less often in, and are less informed about their local governments than they are about the national government. There are understandable reasons for the lower involvement in local government. Although issues about where to locate a garbage dump or a prison or how to deal with police brutality can arouse considerable heat, most of the time local governments are preoccupied with relatively noncontroversial routine matters, such as keeping the roads in shape, providing fire and police service, attracting businesses that can create more jobs, or applying for state and federal financial assistance.

Local communities want to keep their tax rates down and promote their cities as "nice places" in which to live, work, and raise families. Mayors and city officials generally try to avoid controversy and the kind of criticism that will divide a community. Although they do not always succeed, they go to considerable lengths to be reasonable and work for the good of the community. Few aggressively seek to alter the status quo. They do not, as a rule, try to promote equality by redistributing various resources to needier citizens. **Redistributive policies** are programs to shift wealth or benefits from one segment of the population to another, usually from the rich to the poor. Local officials tend to believe that this is the task of the national or state authorities—if they think it should be done at all. Typically, they say their communities do not have the funds for such programs. They might add, "Go see the governor" or "Go talk to your member of Congress." This may be good advice, because various programs (educational loans, unemployment

redistributive policies
Governmental tax and social programs that shift wealth or benefits from one segment of the population to another, often from the rich to the poor.

compensation, disability assistance, and so on) explicitly designed to help the less fortunate are administered at the state or federal level.

Neighborhood groups sometimes become involved in protecting their neighborhoods and petitioning for improvements. One concern that often activates neighborhood groups is the possibility that "undesirable" facilities might be located in their neighborhood, such as drug rehabilitation clinics, prisons, dumps, or homeless shelters. Although attendance at local government meetings is usually low, the announcement of a landfill area or a prison construction project often stimulates the reaction that local officials call NIMBY, an acronym for "Not In My Back Yard!"

The Role of Local Media

Most communities have only one newspaper, and in small communities it is often a weekly. Some newspapers and local radio and television stations do a good job of covering city and county politics, but this is the exception rather than the rule. Reporters assigned to cover local politics are often inexperienced beginners, yet they provide the only news that citizens get about their city council or zoning board. Even the best of them have difficulty conveying the full complexities of what is going on in a column or two of newsprint.

Some local newspapers enjoy a cozy relationship with elected local officials. Sometimes the owners or editors are social friends or golfing buddies of local officials. Friendships and mutual interests develop, and close scrutiny of what goes on in city hall takes a back seat to city boosterism. In effect, "newspapers boost their hometown, knowing that its prosperity and expansion aid their own. Harping on local faults, investigating dirty politics, revealing unsavory scandals, and stressing governmental inefficiencies only provide readily available documentary material to competing cities."[21]

Editors and station managers recognize that their readers or listeners are more interested in state or national news, and especially in sports, than in what is going on at municipal planning meetings or county commission sessions. Much of what takes place in local government is rather dull. It may be important to some people, yet it strikes the average person as decidedly less exciting than what goes on at the White House or whether Congress has finally solved the Social Security problem or whether their stocks have gone up or down or whether the New York Jets or the Los Angeles Lakers won last night. We have dozens of ways to find out about Congress and the White House, but we usually have only one source for stories about the mayor or sheriff or school board. Of course, we could attend board meetings or even talk with our mayor, but that is not what most people are likely to do.

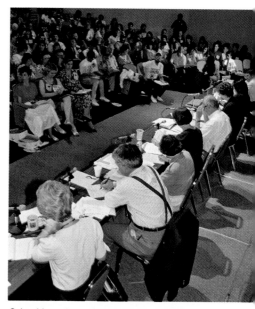

School board meetings in Austin, Texas, do not usually draw a crowd, but when the topic of sex education was discussed, a vocal and concerned crowd turned out.

Apathy in Grassroots America

Voter apathy in local elections is summed up in the bumper sticker "DON'T VOTE. IT ONLY ENCOURAGES THEM." Many important political and economic transactions in communities are ignored by the press and citizens. Charter revision and taxation often galvanize only those directly affected by the new taxes or regulations. Even New England town meetings have difficulty getting people to participate—despite the fact that decisions made at these meetings have major consequences for local tax rates and the quality of the schools, the police force, and the parks and recreational areas. Thomas Jefferson once proclaimed the town meeting to be the noblest, wisest instrument yet devised for the conduct of public affairs, but today most towns find that only about 2 or 3 percent of the population cares enough to come.[22]

The major reason for grassroots apathy is that local politics simply does not interest the average person. Most people are content to leave politics and political responsibilities to a relatively small number of activists while they pursue their own private concerns—their bowling leagues, their children's Little League or soccer games, golf, or fishing. In a healthy democracy, we can expect that most people will be involved with their families and jobs; other than voting occasionally, they tend to leave civic responsibilities to a relatively small number of their fellow citizens. This is probably a reasonable choice. It may also be an indication of satisfaction with the state of the community.

Cynicism about the effectiveness and fairness of local political processes is sometimes reflected in the politics of protest—mass demonstrations, economic boycotts, even civil disorders—to make demands on government. When certain issues become intense, people become politically active. African Americans, Hispanics, gays, and others form political organizations to present their grievances and marshal votes. Neighborhood organizations work for better housing and enforcement of inspection ordinances and to prevent crime and drug dealing.

Civic Initiatives in Local Governments

Just as there will always be indifference toward politics and apathy about government, so too will there always be creative, entrepreneurial people who are willing to step forward and find new ways of solving problems. States such as Oregon and Minnesota seem to encourage a climate of innovation and civic enterprise, and a wider look at the United States finds buoyant, optimistic, creative problem solvers in nearly every corner of the nation.

Enterprising local activists have advocated and implemented cost-saving energy programs, environmental cleanup campaigns, recycling and solar energy initiatives, job training centers, AIDS prevention efforts, housing for the elderly, tutoring for the illiterate, housing for the poor, and hundreds of other problem-solving and opportunity-enhancing community efforts.[23] In almost every case, they create partnerships with elected officials at city hall, sometimes with the Urban League or Chamber of Commerce, and often with local foundations and business corporations.

Sometimes it takes a tragedy to get community groups mobilized. Such a tragic event happened in Boston when gang members burst into the funeral of a young man.

PEOPLE & POLITICS *Making a Difference* ★★★

T. WILLARD FAIR

Urban League leader T. Willard Fair is a committed problem solver for his Liberty City community in Miami. He is recognized as a one-man force trying to rid Liberty City of drug dealers. In the late 1980s, Fair started a private–public collaboration to improve the quality of life in this inner-city community. Among many other results, his efforts led to 3,500 arrests, the breakup of 27 crack houses, the towing of many abandoned vehicles, and the trimming of trees to expose shaded areas where drug deals were made. But above all, Fair was able to get his neighbors in Liberty City to band together and have faith that their neighborhood could be rid of its pushers.

Fair started the program after reading about a young woman who had been shot. Residents were too fearful of drug dealers to cooperate with police. Fair became a catalyst for change, enlisting the help of government and school officials, police and fire officers, churches, residents, and local businesses. He also persuaded the national drug program to share some funds, and he raised other funds by whatever means he could. By the 1990s, he could declare, along with the Liberty City residents, that their 70-square-block, drug-free zone was "off limits" to what he calls "the drug boys."

Along with Governor Jeb Bush, Fair co-founded the Liberty City Charter School, the first charter school in Florida.

Fair has received over 100 awards, including Florida's Outstanding Citizen Award, for his dedication and efforts in

community building, combating crime, and promoting education among inner-city children. He remains the president of the Urban League of Greater Miami, with which he has worked for 40 years.

SOURCE: www.baco.org/about/board/fair.htm.

"In the presence of the mourners, the gang killed one of those in attendance," writes the Reverend Eugene Rivers of the Azusa Christian Community:

> That brazen act told us we had to do more. Now. That young man's death galvanized us, and soon the Ten Point Coalition was reaching out to at-risk youth. Our mission was to pair the holy and the secular, to do whatever it took to save our kids. The black churches worked hand-in-hand with the schools, courts, police, and social service agencies. We called on anyone and everyone who had the means to help our children. We formed programs for teens, neighborhood watches, and patrols. . . . We established ourselves in the neighborhood, standing on the same street corner where the drug dealers once stood. We tracked down the thieves, dealers, and gangs. We tried to give people a chance, but if they wouldn't take it, we staked our claim and ran them out of our neighborhood.[24]

There are persistent debates about how to solve social, economic, and racial problems in our large metropolitan areas. Some people contend that government can't undertake this task and that private initiatives can be more effective. Others insist that state and local governments are best suited to deal with these challenges. Still others contend that imaginative public–private collaboration is needed to fashion the strategies and mobilize the resources to revive our cities and bring about greater opportunity. Whatever the merits of such contending interpretations, it is clear that neighborhood organizations and spirited civic renewal are critical to the vitality of local government.[25]

CHALLENGES FOR STATE AND LOCAL GOVERNMENTS

Most states and communities are confronting testing times. Virtually all of the states and major cities face serious budget problems and increasing demands for services. People don't like tax increases, but they want better schools, a clean environment, and safe roads. About one-third of our inner-city governments and school systems are in financial distress. The cycle of poverty in the inner cities remains one of the greatest threats to the economic health of the country. Cities, though, often cannot raise enough funds through local taxes to create jobs and to provide adequate educational opportunities and housing. Federal and state initiatives have attempted to create economic opportunities for inner-city residents. Community development banks, "empowerment zones," Head Start, charter schools, and national service (Americorp) programs have all been tried in an attempt to bring residents of depressed inner cities into the economic mainstream. But these efforts have been inadequate and must compete with other demands on financially pressed states and localities.

The following central issues in the states and local communities command the attention of the country. They vary depending on location, of course, yet these urgent challenges are part of the unfinished business of a government by the people:

- *People want more services* yet at the same time would like to see their taxes cut. City and state officials are constantly trying to do more with less and introduce efficiencies into city and state operations. Voters in many communities have enacted spending limits that constrain growth in public budgets.

- *Racism still exists in many communities.* As our nation has become more diverse, most Americans have learned to appreciate the strength that comes from multiple cultures and races. Yet racist groups still thrive in some areas, and bigotry and discrimination persist.

- *Drugs, gangs, and drug-related crime impose tough policy challenges.* The costs of corrections and prisons have skyrocketed in recent years, yet gangs, drugs, and crime are still a menace in some urban and even rural areas.

- *The Costs of Homeland Security.* Due to the continuing threat of international terrorism, states and localities must assume a greater role in safeguarding

★★ THINKING IT THROUGH

Residents of the District of Columbia do not have the same opportunity to vote for representatives in Congress. They have no representation in the Senate and only symbolic representation in the House of Representatives, one nonvoting delegate. In 1790, when the district was created from land from Maryland and Virginia, residents could continue to vote for congressional representatives from their former states. In 1800, however, Congress took over complete control and representation of D.C. residents in Congress ended. During the last 30 years, residents have campiagned for "home rule" and statehood.

Arguments for Statehood

1. Statehood would give residents the power of self-governance.
2. Residents are disenfranchised, and the principle of "no taxation without representation" is fundamental to the country.
3. Statehood would give residents and neighborhoods greater power to address problems in improving educational opportunities, health care, and other social services.

Arguments Against Statehood

1. If the District of Columbia became a state, then why not New York City, Philadelphia, or Boston?
2. Statehood is impractical for economic reasons.
3. Congress already gives the district considerable control over its self-governance.

Not all citizens are apathetic. These young people are spending their free time rehabilitating a community center.

Local residents often form groups to handle and discuss issues that are important to their neighborhood, as illustrated by this gathering of Neighborhood Watch volunteers.

airports and other public places, as well as assume the role of "first responders" in the event of an attack. Mayors of major cities and some governors, however, complain that the national government has failed to provide and deliver the funding necessary for these expanded responsibilities.

■ *Poverty in the inner cities persists.* We have extremes of rich and poor within metropolitan regions, and often the wealthier suburbs turn their backs on the problems and poverty of the older cities. Indifference to these inequalities and lack of opportunities may undermine a sense of community and fairness in America.

■ *We need to guarantee the best possible education for all our young people.* Parents are demanding better education and more parental involvement. Communities have been experimenting with educational choice and competition, school vouchers, and charter schools. Improving the public schools is necessary, but their resources and the salaries of teachers are often too low to attract and retain the best-qualified teachers. State and local governments have the responsibility to pay for public education, so educational reform and the search for excellent teachers and learning processes will remain a top state and local priority. Many states, though, object to the Bush administration's push for national standards, under its No Child Left Behind program, as an intrusion on the states and too costly in the current economic environment. Utah decided to forgo federal funds and declined to partipate in the program, and some other states may do likewise.

■ *Environmental regulation, land use, and recycling are also major challenges at the local level.* Every city and state wants economic growth and economic opportunities for its workers and businesses, but many forms of economic development impose costs in terms of the quality of air, water, landscapes, and health. Local officials face tough decisions about the need to balance economic and environmental concerns.

■ *Health care costs and delivery are challenges to all levels of government.* Health care reform has been an important policy issue for many years. Some states, like Maine, have experimented with universal health care; others have worked to control costs. Many of the uninsured end up obtaining health care in emergency rooms in local public hospitals, which in turn seek funding from the local and state governments.

For more information on these and other issues confronting state and local governments, go to our home page at www.prenhall.com/burns, or to the Web site of the Council of State Governments at www.csg.org, or that of the National Conference of State Legislatures at www.ncsl.org.

S U M M A R Y

1. Many of the most critical domestic and economic issues facing the United States today are decided at the state and local levels of government.

2. Studies of states and communities have investigated how formal government institutions, social structure, economic factors, and local traditions interact to create a working political system. Some studies find that a power elite dominates, whereas community power studies find pluralism and diverse interest groups competing for influence over a range of policy areas. Special-interest groups operate in every state and locality, but their influence varies.

3. Although it is widely believed that local governments are "closer to the people" than the national government, voting and other forms of participation at the local level are low.

4. Innovative programs at the local level address problems in education, the environment, crime and violence, and ways to improve community life. Local civil action is one of the most important forms of citizen participation in politics.

K E Y   T E R M S

social stratification   redistributive policies

F U R T H E R   R E A D I N G

JOHN R. BAKER, ED., *The Lanahan Readings on State and Local Government* (Lanahan Press, 2001).

THAD L. BEYLE, ED., *State Government: CQ's Guide to Current Issues and Activities, 2004–2005* (CQ Press, 2004).

BUZZ BISSINGER, *A Prayer for the City* (Random House, 1997).

ALLAN CIGLER AND BURDETT LOOMIS, EDS., *Interest Group Politics,* 6th ed. (CQ Press, 2002).

FRANK J. COPPA, *County Government* (Praeger, 2000).

THOMAS E. CRONIN AND ROBERT D. LOEVY, *Colorado Politics and Government: Governing the Centennial State* (University of Nebraska Press, 1993).

E. J. DIONNE JR., ED. *Community Works: The Revival of Civil Society in America* (Brookings Institution Press, 1998).

THOMAS D. DYE AND SUSAN A. MACMANUS, *Politics in States and Communities,* 11th ed. (Prentice Hall, 2003).

ROBERT S. ERIKSON, GERALD C. WRIGHT, AND JOHN P. MCIVER, *Statehouse Democracy: Public Opinion and Policy in the American States* (Cambridge University Press, 1993).

STEPHEN GOLDSMITH, *The Twenty-First Century City* (Regnery, 1997).

VIRGINIA GRAY, RUSSELL HANSON, AND HERBERT JACOB, EDS., *Politics in the American States,* 8th ed. (CQ Press, 2003).

VALERIE C. JOHNSON, *Black Power in the Suburbs* (State University of New York Press, 2002).

DANIEL KEMMIS, *The Good City and the Good Life* (Houghton Mifflin, 1995).

MADELEINE KUNIN, *Living a Political Life* (Vintage, 1995).

JOHN O. NORQUIST, *The Wealth of Cities* (Addison-Wesley, 1998).

DOUGLAS W. RAE, *City: Urbanism and Its End* (Yale University Press, 2003).

ALAN ROSENTHAL, *The Third House: Lobbyists and Lobbying in the States,* 2d ed. (CQ Press, 2001).

JON C. TEAFORD, *The Rise of the States* (Johns Hopkins University Press, 2002).

JOSEPH F. ZIMMERMAN, *The New England Town Meeting: Democracy in Action* (Praeger, 1999).

See also the *State Politics and Policy Quarterly* and the Web site of the Council of State Governments at www.csg.org.

STATE CONSTITUTIONS
CHARTERS OR STRAITJACKETS?

22

I n response to the Massachusetts supreme court's ruling that discriminating against same-sex marriages violated the state constitution, the legislature convened in 2004 a convention to propose an amendment banning same-sex marriages. The convention met in February and again in March to approve an amendment barring same-sex marriages, but recognizing "civil unions" that confer the same benefits, rights, and privileges on same-sex couples that legally married couples enjoy. But under Massachusetts's constitution, the amendment must be resubmitted in the next legislative session for its approval, and then submitted to the voters for ratification in a statewide vote. The matter will therefore not come before voters until November 2006.

Massachusetts is not alone in considering constitutional reforms growing out of the controversy over same-sex marriages. In response to similar state supreme court decisions, Alaska, Hawaii, Nebraska, and Nevada adopted constitutional amendments prohibiting the marriage of same-sex couples. Constitutional amendments are likewise now under consideration in more than a dozen other states.[1]

Constitutional conventions are nonetheless rarely successful, and constitutional amendments in most (though not all) states are often very difficult to achieve. New York,

for example, has had only four constitutions since 1777. Yet, by constitutional mandate, every 20 years the people of New York are asked on a general election ballot if they want to convene a constitutional convention to propose a new constitution. In addition, the legislature—with the concurrence of the governor—put the question before the voters in 1965; the voters approved, and a convention was held in 1967, but its work was rejected. When voters were asked in 1977 if they wanted to convene another convention, they said no. The question came before them again in 1997, as it will in 2017.

In preparation for the 1997 vote, the Temporary Commission on Constitutional Revision was set up to identify issues and to inform voters about the need for a new constitution. The commission called for a convention of ordinary citizens and suggested that New Yorkers take advantage of new technology such as cable television and electronic town meetings to observe convention proceedings. The commission targeted the budget process, state–local relations, education, and public safety as being of special importance.[2] A constitutional convention, commission members argued, could then write a new constitution in clear English, simplify voter registration, improve voting rules and ballot access, regulate campaign finance and lobbying, reform the legislative process, restore confidence in the courts, reform the tax structure, and improve protection for the environment.[3]

But opposed to calling a constitutional convention were the American Federation of Labor–Congress of Industrial Organizations (AFL-CIO), the Conservative party, the Sierra Club, the National Abortion Rights Action League (NARAL), some antitax groups, and some legislative leaders from both parties. They saw a convention as a threat to their right to organize; trial lawyers worried about limits on lawsuits; environmentalists feared that a convention might jeopardize provisions protecting open spaces; some women's groups were fearful that the convention might restrict abortion rights; and some conservatives feared that liberal interests would control the convention.

There was little public interest in the campaign for a constitutional convention, however. Two weeks before the election, polls indicated that voters, upset by the apparent inability of the state government to get anything done, were overwhelmingly in favor of calling for a constitutional convention to make government work better. But opponents of constitutional revision got busy. Unions and other anticonvention groups launched television advertisements, direct-mail operations, and phone banks, arguing that the convention was a waste of money and would open the door to dangerous changes. On November 5, 1997, 62 percent of New York voters rejected the call for the convention.[4]

New York's experience is not unusual. In recent years, voters in several states have rejected calls for a constitutional convention. For example, in 1994 Michigan voters rejected the call for a convention by almost 3 to 1 in all 183 counties; Arkansas voters in December 1995 rejected the call by 4 to 1 in all 75 counties.[5] No constitutional conventions have been held since Rhode Island had one in 1986, and it won approval of the voters for only eight of 14 proposed revisions.

Now, you might give some thought to your own state constitution. Like the U.S. Constitution, state constitutions are both instruments of government and limitations on government. Unlike the federal constitution, however, state constitutions are not popular symbols. On a trip to your state capitol, you are unlikely to find the state constitution "displayed [like] the federal Constitution, in a setting similar to a Shinto shrine."[6]

In this chapter, we examine the roots of state constitutions and some of the ways we work around constitutional rigidity. Then we look at methods of amending state constitutions, ending with a few case studies of states that have tried, for the most part unsuccessfully, to adopt new constitutions.

THE ROOTS OF STATE CONSTITUTIONS

The first state constitutions were outgrowths of colonial charters. Massachusetts and New Hampshire can boast of charters still in effect that are older than the federal Constitution. Virginia added a bill of rights to its constitution in 1776—13 years before the national one was proposed by Congress. In 1787, the framers of the U.S. Constitution drew heavily on their experience with these state charters. "What is the Constitution of the

United States but that of Massachusetts, New York, and Maryland!" remarked John Adams. "There is not a feature in it," he said, "which cannot be found in one or the other."[7]

Subject only to the broad limitations of the U.S. Constitution, the people of each state are free to create whatever kind of republican government they wish. All state constitutions are similar in general outline (see Figure 22–1). A state constitution typically consists of a preamble, a bill of rights, articles providing for the separation of powers (although the supreme court of Rhode Island ruled that there is no separation of powers in that state),[8] a two-house legislature, an executive branch, an independent judiciary with the power of judicial review, a description of the form and powers of local units of government, an article on how to amend the constitution, and miscellaneous provisions dealing with election procedures, corporations, railroads, finances, education, and other specific topics.

The bills of rights in state constitutions are, in general, similar to the federal Bill of Rights, although they sometimes use different language and cover different rights. For example, "Twenty-seven states have speech and press guarantees quite different from the First Amendment's, thirty-eight have equality guarantees dissimilar to the equal protection clause, and thirty-nine have guarantees of a separation of church and state that differ from the federal establishment clause."[9] Fourteen states adopted the Equal Rights Amendment even though it was never ratified to become part of the U.S. Constitution.

Constitutional Rigidity and Evasion

State constitutions contain more details than the U.S. Constitution does. They are longer and less flexible, and they require more frequent amendment[10] (see Figure 22–2). Louisiana has had 11 constitutions; Georgia has had ten; South Carolina, seven; and

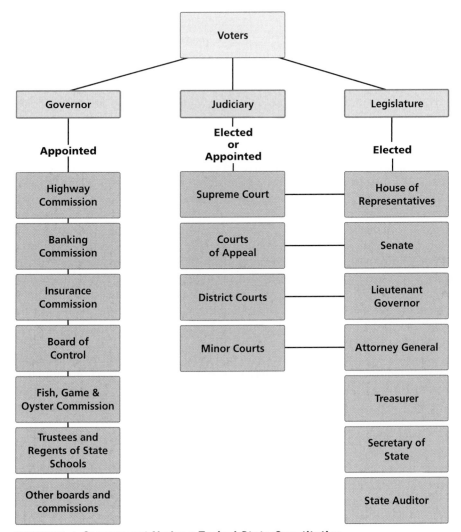

FIGURE 22–1 Government Under a Typical State Constitution.

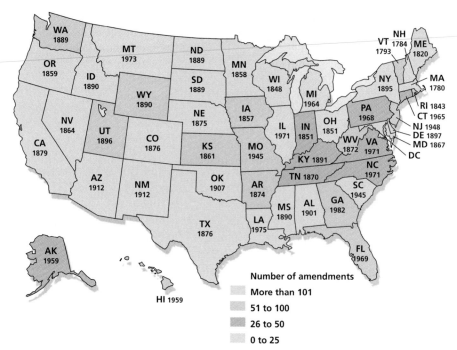

Number of amendments
More than 101
51 to 100
26 to 50
0 to 25

FIGURE 22–2 Amending State Constitutions.

Alabama, Florida, and Virginia, six.[11] Only 29 states have their original constitution. The average state constitution is over 100 years old and has been amended about 120 times.[12] State constitutions vary in length—from the 8,295 words of Vermont's (the only state constitution shorter than the Constitution of the United States as amended) to the longest, the 310,296 words of Alabama's. Alabama's constitution is almost 40 times as long as the U.S. Constitution, which has only 7,400 words; most state constitutions have around 26,000.[13]

Although most state constitutional provisions deal with matters of significance, some also deal with seemingly trivial subjects. California's much-amended constitution (over 500 amendments since it was adopted in 1879) goes into great detail about the taxation of fish and the internal organization of various departments.[14] The Oklahoma constitution proclaims, "Until changed by the Legislature, the flash test for all kerosene oil for illuminating purposes shall be 115 degrees Fahrenheit; and the specific gravity test for all such oil shall be 40 degrees."[15] The South Dakota constitution declares that providing hail insurance is a public purpose and authorizes the legislature to levy a tax to provide for it.[16] The Alabama constitution authorizes the legislature to indemnify peanut farmers for losses incurred as a result of *Aspergillus flavus* (a fungus) and freeze damage in peanuts.[17] In 2000, Florida voters approved an amendment declaring the development of high-speed ground transportation in the public interest of reducing traffic congestion. And in 2003 Wisconsin voters approved one guaranteeing the people's right to fish, hunt, trap, and take game.

In addition to the inclusion of these statute-like details, state constitutions and their more frequently adopted amendments tend to be longer than the U.S. Constitution because their bills of rights cover, in addition to the traditional rights, more recently emerging protections, such as the right to an equal public education and the rights of victims of crimes. Finally, state constitutions have to deal with a much wider range of functions, educational provisions, and criminal codes than the U.S. Constitution, which created a national government of intentionally limited powers to deal with a limited range of functions.[18] It has long been asserted that the length and detail of state constitutions account for the fact that many of them have not had the longevity of the national Constitution. However, a careful empirical study shows that "longer and more detailed design of state constitutions actually enhances rather than reduces their longevity."[19]

Constitutions as Roadblocks

The earliest state constitutions granted authority to the legislatures without much restriction on how their powers should be exercised. But after many legislatures gave special privileges to railroads, canal builders, and other interests, constitutional amendments were adopted to prevent such abuses. Distrusting the legislatures, reform groups began to insist that certain controls be incorporated into state constitutions. In time, state constitutions became encrusted in layer upon layer of procedural detail.

What does this mean for democratic government? It means that state constitutions—intended as charters of self-government—are often like straitjackets imposed on the present by the past. Some outdated provisions do no harm, but more often they are roadblocks to effective government. For example, fixed salaries do not reflect changing economic conditions, and a rigidly organized administrative structure is incapable of adjusting to new needs. When a constitution allocates revenues, elected officials are deprived of discretion to deal with budget difficulties as they arise. Under such conditions, the legislature cannot act, and voters then turn to constitutional amendments.

Getting Around the Constitution

Can state constitutions forever prevent the wishes of the people from being carried out? Not necessarily. The constitutional system of the states, like that of the national government, includes more than the formal written document. Unwritten rules, practices, political parties, and interest groups also shape events. When people see a need for change, they usually find ways to overcome formal barriers.

One device for constitutional change is **judicial interpretation**, whereby judges modify a constitutional provision by a new interpretation of its meaning. The more complex and detailed the constitution, the easier it is for judges to redefine meanings. Actually, one reason for the growing length of some constitutions is that amendments are often required to reverse judicial interpretations. In addition, some sections of state constitutions have been invalidated by federal action, especially in the area of civil rights and suffrage.

The New Judicial Federalism

In what is called **new judicial federalism**, state constitutions have taken on greater importance. For decades, state judges tended to look only to the U.S. Constitution and Bill of Rights and how these were interpreted by the U.S. Supreme Court. But since the 1970s, as the Supreme Court has become more conservative, some state supreme courts have been relying on their own state constitutions and state bills of rights in overruling state laws and the actions of state and local officials. In recent years, state supreme courts have refused to follow the U.S. Supreme Court's rulings and on the basis of their state constitutions have held unconstitutional sobriety checkpoints for drivers,[20] the random drug testing of public employees,[21] and restrictions on minors who seek abortions.[22]

This trend takes its inspiration from the U.S. Supreme Court, which sent clear messages to state supreme court judges that they are free to interpret their own state constitutions to impose greater restraints than the U.S. Constitution does. The U.S. Supreme Court and the U.S. Constitution set the floor, not the ceiling, for the protection of rights.[23] As a result, some state judges are now using their constitutions to require state legislatures to provide better schools for children living in poor neighborhoods, build low-income housing, provide public financing of abortions for poor women, and regulate business enterprises to protect the environment.[24]

When state judges rely on their own state constitutions to protect rights beyond those required by the U.S. Constitution, they do so at some political peril, since most judges are dependent on voter approval to keep their office. This risk has increased now that the Supreme Court requires state judges who wish to escape a review of their decisions by the Supreme Court to make it clear they have decided a case on adequate and independent state constitutional grounds.[25]

judicial interpretation
A method by which judges modify the force of a constitutional provision by reinterpreting its meaning.

new judicial federalism
The practice of some state courts using the bill of rights in their state constitutions to provide more protection for some rights than is provided by the Supreme Court's interpretation of the Bill of Rights in the U.S. Constitution.

CHANGING FACE OF AMERICAN POLITICS

SAME-SEX MARRIAGES AND STATE CONSTITUTIONS

State legislatures around the country are considering proposed amendments to their state constitutions that would ban same-sex marriages. The firestorm was set off by the Massachusetts supreme court's ruling that its state constitution forbids discrimination against same-sex marriages. Subsequently, local government officials, from New Paltz, New York, to San Francisco, California, and Portland, Oregon, issued thousands of marriage licenses to same-sex couples, in some cases in violation of state law.

Thirty-nine states already prohibit same-sex marriages with state laws modeled after the federal Defense of Marriage Act of 1996, which bars federal recognition of same-sex marriages and permits states to ignore those marriages performed in other states. But in New York, Washington, and elsewhere, the constitutionality of those laws is being challenged in courts. Only four states—Alaska, Hawaii, Nebraska, and Nevada—have already amended their constitutions to bar same-sex marriages.

In the November 2004 elections, voters in 11 states adopted ballot initiatives that define marriage as a union between a man and a woman: Arkansas, Georgia, Kentucky, Michigan, Mississippi, Montana, North Dakota, Ohio, Oklahoma, Oregon, and Utah.

Several states, though, have enacted laws, not constitutional amendments, that confer health, inheritance, and other benefits on same-sex couples. In response to a decision of its state supreme court, in 2000 Vermont enacted a law recognizing "civil unions" and providing same-sex couples with state-level marriage benefits. California, Hawaii, and New Jersey recognize "domestic partnerships" that confer most benefits of marriage. Bills to recognize same-sex marriages have also been introduced in the legislatures of Connecticut and New York.

AMENDING STATE CONSTITUTIONS

Amendments may be proposed by the state legislature, citizen-initiated ballot petitions, or constitutional conventions. After an amendment has been proposed, it must be ratified. In all states except Delaware, where the legislature can ratify as well as propose amendments, ratification is by the voters. In most states, an amendment becomes part of the constitution when approved by a majority of those voting on the amendment. In a 2003 special election in New Mexico, voters approved constitutional amendments that created a cabinet-level secretary of education and authorized more spending for public education by just 195 votes (92,198 to 92,003).[26] In some other states—such as Minnesota—approval by a majority of all those voting in the election is required. This provision makes ratification difficult, because some people who vote for candidates do not vote on amendments. Slightly more than three-quarters of all constitutional amendments proposed by legislatures have been adopted in recent years.[27]

Legislative Proposals

All states permit their legislature to propose amendments; in fact, this is the most commonly used method. Although provisions vary, the general practice is to require the approval by two-thirds of each chamber of the legislature. Some states, however, permit proposal of an amendment by a simple majority in two successive legislatures.

A legislature may appoint a **revision commission** to make recommendations for constitutional change that, except in Florida, have no force until acted on by the legislature and approved by the voters. The legislature creates a commission of a relatively small number of people—some selected by the governor and some by the legislature—and charges it with presenting proposals for constitutional revision. A commission is less expensive than a full-blown constitutional convention, does not require initial voter approval, and gives the legislature final control of what is presented to the electorate.

California, for instance, turned to a revision commission to overcome its budgetary gridlock after its senate rejected a 1992 proposal asking voters if they wanted a constitutional convention (the first in 113 years). California's constitution has been so

revision commission
A state commission that recommends changes in the state constitution for action by the legislature and vote by the voters.

frequently amended that about 85 percent of the state's annual revenues are allocated before the governor and legislature even start working on the budget! Eventually, *all* state revenues could be allocated constitutionally if the trend continued, and there would be no state funds available for programs such as higher education and health care. A 23-member revision commission was created in 1993 to examine the budget process and the configuration of state and local duties. Two years later, the commission made its recommendations. But the legislature failed to act on any of them, in part because it was an election year. Also, because the state senate was Democratic and the state assembly Republican, it proved impossible to work out any compromise.

Constitutional commissions are in fact infrequently used. The recommendations of revision commissions are also seldom implemented quickly, perhaps because the commissioners have not been responsive to political currents or are not representative of broad enough interests. Still, a commission may provide less partisan consideration of amendments and be more resistant to single-interest groups than either the legislature or a convention. Mississippi has tried, so far unsuccessfully, to use a commission for changing its 1890 constitution, which was designed to keep African Americans out of the political process.[28]

Nonetheless, Florida, Virginia, and Louisiana have used the commission procedure to bring about significant constitutional change. Utah's Constitutional Revision Commission is a permanent body, required by law to submit recommendations for constitutional revision to the legislature 60 days before each regular session.[29] It has initiated revisions relating to the rights of crime victims as well as to changes in revenue and taxation. Florida has a Taxation and Budget Reform Commission that is called into session every ten years. Unlike other such commissions, in addition to making recommendations to the legislature, it may propose constitutional amendments directly to the voters. In 1998, the commission recommended nine amendments; Florida voters approved eight of them.

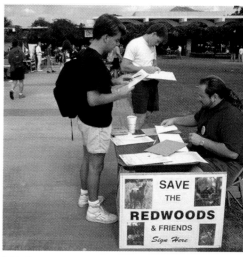

Initiative petitions deal with a great variety of reforms.

Initiative Petitions

At the end of the nineteenth century, revelations of corruption diminished the prestige of state governments, especially state legislatures. Out of this disillusionment came a variety of reforms as part of the Progressive movement. Among them was the **constitutional initiative petition**, a device that permits voters to place specific constitutional amendments on the ballot by petition. Eighteen states allow amendments to their constitutions to be proposed by initiative petitions.

The number of signatures required on petitions varies from 4 to 15 percent of either the total electorate or the number of voters who voted in the last election.[30] Although it takes more signatures to propose a constitutional amendment than to place other kinds of initiatives on the ballot, "the higher threshold is no longer a significant impediment to well-financed special-interest groups."[31]

Once the appropriate state official (attorney general or secretary of state) approves the precise wording of a petition, the amendment is placed on the ballot at the next general election. (California allows initiatives to appear even on primary election ballots.) The number of votes required to approve a constitutional amendment is typically a majority vote, although a few states have a more demanding requirement. Illinois requires a majority of those voting in the election or three-fifths of those voting on the amendment, and Nevada requires a majority vote on the same measure in two successive elections.

In some states, initiative proposals are limited to *amending* the state constitution, not to *revising* it. The distinction between revision and amendment is that revision refers to a comprehensive change to the basic governmental plan, a substantial alteration in the basic governmental framework, or a substantial alteration of the entire constitution, rather than to a less extensive change in one or more of its provisions.[32] Some states exclude certain subjects from amendment by initiative. Massachusetts, for example, does not allow amendments by popular initiative that concern religion, the judiciary, or judicial decisions; that are restricted to a particular town, city, or political division; that

constitutional initiative petition
A device that permits voters to place specific amendments to a state constitution on the ballot by petition.

★★ YOU DECIDE

**WHO SHOULD PROPOSE
CONSTITUTIONAL AMENDMENTS?**

Of the 24 states that have the popular initiative,
only 18 permit constitutional amendments by
initiative. Are states well served by having
citizens propose amendments, or is it a bad
idea? Should all states be required to permit
constitutional alteration by the initiative process?
What do you think?

appropriate money from the state treasury; or that restrict rights such as freedom of speech.

In recent years, voters have approved about 50 percent of amendments proposed by initiative petitions. This figure compares with a slightly more than 75 percent approval rate for amendments proposed by state legislatures.[33] A variety of factors may account for the lower adoption rate of initiative measures. Initiatives tend to be used for controversial issues that have already been rejected by the legislature and engender an organized opposition. Initiatives are also often proposed by narrow-based groups or by reform-minded elites who lack broad support for their views. Sometimes initiatives are proposed in order to launch educational campaigns rather than to actually win adoption.

People anxious to limit the power of state and local governments are using the initiative process in more states. Since California in 1978 adopted Proposition 13, which limited the state government's right to raise property taxes, other states have followed suit. In addition, these "new reformers" have produced "a series of state constitutional amendments that, taken together, fundamentally altered the character and powers of state governments by limiting the tenure of governmental officials, reducing their powers, and transferring policy making responsibilities to the people."[34] In addition, "the focus of constitutional initiatives . . . has shifted from questions of governmental structure . . . to questions of substantive policy," such as initiatives on tort liability, the rights of gays, affirmative action, and the rights of immigrants.[35]

Constitutional Conventions

Americans love constitutional conventions (or at least we used to); we have had 233 of them—144 in the nineteenth century but only 63 in the twentieth century.[36] One scholar noted that calling conventions of the people is a uniquely American idea, emphasizing that legislators cannot be trusted and that the supreme power belongs to the people.[37]

PEOPLE & POLITICS *Making a Difference* ★ ★ ★

WARD CONNERLY

Ward Connerly emerged on the national political scene by spearheading a drive to amend California's constitution with a ballot initiative, Proposition 29, the California Civil Rights Initiative, which forbids state agencies from discriminating against or granting preferential treatment to any individual or group on the basis of race, gender, color, ethnicity, or national origin in public education and employment, except when necessary to comply with federal law. Californians overwhelmingly appoved Proposition 29 and it became a model for ballot initiatives in other states.

A successful land developer, Connerly was appointed to the University of California Board of Regents for a 12-year term (1993–2005). Following his leadership, the Regents ended the University's affirmative-action program for admissions. Connerly founded and remains chairman of the American Civil Rights Institute, a nonprofit organization promoting a "colorblind society."

Most recently, Connerly sponsored another ballot initiative to amend California's constitution, Proposition 54, known as the Racial Privacy Initative, which would have barred state agencies from collecting information on a person's race, ethnicity, and national origin. But in the 2003 special election that unseated Governor Gray Davis and elected Arnold Schwarzenegger, voters defeated Proposition 54 by a margin of 64 to 36.*

*See Ward Connerly, "Not a Chance: The Electoral Journey of Proposition 54," National Review online (October 15, 2003), at www.nationalreview.com/comment/connerly20031015818.asp; and Ward Connerly, *Creating Equal: My Fight Against Race Preference* (Encounter Books, 2002).

Forty-one state constitutions authorize their legislature to submit the calling of a convention to the voters; the other states assume that the legislature has the power to do so. Fourteen state constitutions require the legislature to question voters about a convention at fixed intervals, varying from every 9 to every 20 years. For example, Missouri is required to submit the question to the voters every 20 years; Hawaii raises the issue every 9 years; Michigan, every 16 years.

If the voters approve, the next step is to elect delegates to a convention. Some state constitutions contain elaborate procedures governing the number of delegates, the method of election, and the time and place of the convention. Others leave the details to the legislature. The way convention delegates are selected seems to affect the kind of document the convention proposes. Selection by nonpartisan, multimember districts is more likely to result in a reform convention that makes major changes than one in which political parties play a major role.[38]

After delegates have been chosen, they usually assemble at the state capital. When the convention has prepared a draft of the new constitution, the document is submitted to the voters. But first the convention delegates have to make a difficult choice: Should the voters be asked to accept or reject the new constitution as a whole? Or should they vote on each section separately?

The advantage of the first method is that each provision of a constitution ties in with another, and to secure all the advantages of revision, the entire constitution should be adopted. The disadvantage is that those who oppose a particular provision may vote against the entire constitution. When convention delegates know that a particular provision is controversial, they may decide to submit that provision separately. Whichever method they choose, the supporters of change must rally their forces to gain voter approval of their work.

THE POLITICS OF CONSTITUTIONAL REVISION

Constitutions are not a neutral set of rules perched above the world of everyday politics. Rather, they significantly affect who gets what from government. Therefore, how a constitution is changed can help or hinder various groups.

Although recently there have been campaigns for constitutional reform under way in Alabama, Oklahoma, and Texas, most people simply do not care.[39] It is difficult to work up enthusiasm for revising a state constitution except among people with special interests, and they are more likely to oppose than to favor adoption. Supporters of the status quo thus have a built-in advantage, which, combined with obstacles to the amending process in the constitution, helps explain the lack of action. "Revision is time-consuming, requiring sophisticated legal and drafting skills of the highest order, and involves negotiation and compromise. To be successful, revision requires gubernatorial as well as legislative leadership. . . . An effective political campaign is essential. . . . Success at the polls is not assured. Constitutional revision can be a high-risk endeavor and will continue to be."[40] Following are some case studies that illustrate the risky nature of constitutional revision.

Rhode Island Amends Its Constitution

Rhode Island's constitutional convention produced 14 separate propositions for amending its 1843 constitution. On November 4, 1986, voters approved eight of the 14 provisions, rejecting attempts to increase compensation of state legislators, to provide for merit selection of judges, and to create a "paramount right to life without regard to age, health, function, or condition of dependency," which would have banned abortions or public funding of them. The voters approved provisions strengthening free speech, due process, equal protection rights, and expanding fishing rights and access to the shore, as well as a statement that the rights protected by the Rhode Island constitution "stand independent of the U.S. Constitution."

★ ★ THINKING IT THROUGH

Critics charge that when several complex initiatives are on the ballot, voters are asked to make decisions for which they are not well prepared. Others contend that the use of the initiative petition prevents elected representatives from exercising their proper authority. Still others hold that the initiative process encourages detailed and frequent amendment of a constitution, which should be a blueprint of enduring principles and not be too specific about how government operates on a day-to-day basis. Critics also charge that the initiative process has recently become the tool of well-organized single-interest groups that present voters with simplistic choices of yes or no on complex matters.

Defenders of the constitutional initiative petition contend that it is a valuable safety valve against an unresponsive legislature. When a legislature is tied so closely to special interests that it refuses even to acknowledge the real needs of a majority of citizens, the initiative process can be a corrective. Defenders also contend that voters are much smarter than critics think they are and that they have in fact acted rather prudently when asked to decide most constitutional questions.

The Rhode Island constitution calls for voters to be asked every ten years if they want to convene a constitutional convention. In November 1994, the voters rejected a convention by a vote of 173,693 to 118,545.[41] There nonetheless remained considerable public pressure in the form of a 2-to-1 vote in November 2001 in favor of a nonbinding ballot question for a constitutional convention focused on separation of powers issues in order to reverse a decision of the Rhode Island supreme court to the effect that the Rhode Island constitution allows the state legislature to both make and execute state laws. After years of debate and continued pressure from Common Cause and 30 other organizations, in 2003 Rhode Island's legislature approved a constitutional amendment strengthening the separation of powers and placed it on the 2004 ballot for voters' approval.[42]

Louisiana Revises Its Constitution

The Louisiana Constitutional Revision Commission set out during 1973 and 1974 to write a streamlined "people's constitution"—one the average person could understand.[43] The AFL-CIO, National Association for the Advancement of Colored People, League of Women Voters, Committee for a Better Louisiana, National Municipal League, and many other lobbying groups became involved in shaping the new constitution. It took well over a year to write, and it cost the taxpayers approximately $4 million. In the end, a readable 26,000-word document replaced the existing 265,000-word document that contained some 536 amendments. In April 1974, Louisiana voters approved the new charter by a large margin.

The Louisiana constitution can no longer be cited as the prime example of an unworkable state constitution, although over 100 amendments have been added since 1974 and the length has inched back up to about 54,112 words. "Indeed," according to one commentator, constitutional amendment in Louisiana is "sufficiently continuous to justify including it with Mardi Gras, football, and corruption as one of the premier components of state culture."[44]

Changing the Hawaii Constitution

More than 800 proposals for constitutional changes were submitted to the Hawaii state constitutional convention of 1978. The League of Women Voters and other groups conducted extensive information and discussion meetings, and the convention held many public hearings on key issues. The 102 delegates to the convention met for nearly three months. After extensive debate, the convention narrowed the proposals to 34 questions to be placed on the fall ballot. Convention delegates rejected proposals for the initiative, referendum, and recall; for a unicameral legislature; and for an elected (instead of an appointed) attorney general.

The delegates were not opposed to all government reforms, for they endorsed a two-term limit for governor and lieutenant governor, moved to make Hawaii party primaries more open by allowing voters to cast ballots without declaring party preference, and authorized the state legislature to provide partial public funding for election campaigns and establish spending limits. The convention reflected concern over government spending by setting tougher overall debt and spending limits for the state. It also strengthened environmental safeguards and gave further constitutional and financial protection to the special status of native Hawaiians. In November 1978, 74 percent of the voters went to the polls; all 34 amendments were adopted; 20 percent of the voters had accepted the amendments as a package.

However, in 1986, Hawaiians rejected the periodic question of whether to call a convention by a vote of 173,977 to 139,236. Again in 1996, the question of calling a convention was put to the voters, and the vote was 163,869 in favor and 160,153 against, but 45,245 people left the question unanswered. Blank ballots were tallied as a no, in response to a decision of the state supreme court that the Hawaii constitution required approval by a majority of all ballots cast. The Ninth U.S. Circuit Court of Appeals, which refused to order a new election, sustained this decision.

Other proposals for a convention had been backed by several interests, including those who wanted to overturn a decision of the Hawaii supreme court favoring the legalization of same-sex marriages, by those who wanted to impose term limits, and by those who wanted to limit the power of state courts to restrict police searches.

Hawaii's experiences with the revision process are reminders that constitution making is not just an exercise in abstract argument or logical reasoning but flows directly from a state's political life.

Texas Keeps Its Old Constitution

Texas has a lengthy constitution. Adopted in 1876, it has been amended more than 370 times. The most recent effort to thoroughly revise it was in 1972, after political scandals brought in a new governor, Dolph Briscoe, and a reform-oriented state legislature. After pushing through a variety of reforms dealing with the ethics of officeholders, campaign practices, and registration of lobbyists, the legislature did an unconventional thing by calling into being a constitutional convention consisting of members of the legislature rather than a specially elected body.

After working for 17 months, the legislator-delegates came up with a much revised and shortened document intended to modernize many obsolete governmental practices. The convention deadlocked, however, over whether to give constitutional status to the state's right-to-work law, which prohibits labor contracts that require union membership as a condition of employment, so this issue was referred to the voters. In the end, neither the AFL-CIO nor Governor Briscoe supported all of the convention's recommendations. The governor was especially opposed to the proposal that legislative sessions be held annually, rather than every two years, which he argued would cause higher taxes. Advocates of the revised constitution tried to salvage their work by offering substantial parts of the new charter to the voters as amendments to the existing constitution.

Conservatives praised the old constitution, claiming it had served Texas well for 100 years. Progressives complained that the old constitution was elitist, permitted only the narrowest governmental objectives, and made real change nearly impossible. In November 1975, amid charges and countercharges, Texas voters rejected the amendments by a 2-to-1 margin.[45] Since then, Texans have approved 143 amendments and rejected 33 but have not held another convention.

After three years of preparations and deliberation, the proposed Texas constitution of 1974 failed by three votes in the final hectic session of the constitutional convention.

The Arkansas Constitution

Arkansas's eighth constitutional convention was a protracted affair. The 100 delegates who were elected in 1978 held their organizational session in the winter of that year but did not get down to work until the spring of 1979. Having reconvened in June 1980 to revise the final draft, they submitted the proposed constitution to the voters in November 1980.

Opposition developed to a provision in the new constitution allowing the legislature, by a two-thirds vote, to set interest rates rather than limit them, as in the current constitution. Other groups opposed a provision enlarging the taxing powers of local governments. Even though then Governor Bill Clinton, the Democratic party, and the Arkansas Education Association endorsed the new constitution, the voters rejected it, 2 to 1.

The question of a constitutional convention was again put to Arkansas voters in December 1995. Those planning the 1995 convention structured the convention call in such a way that the convention would avoid addressing "issues which were not critical to state government but which would inflame folks" and would concentrate on "issues of pure governance."[46] Nonetheless, the call for the convention was decisively rejected.

Alabama Considers a New Constitution

Alabama has had six constitutions. The most recent, written in 1901 and adopted in 1902, was "a document of the Old South,"[47] unashamedly and openly designed to keep African Americans segregated in public schools and from voting or participating in governmental matters.[48] It has been amended more than 740 times and there have been many unsuccessful attempts to modernize and replace it.

The issue of constitutional reform remains on Alabama's agenda. A 21-member, independent commission called the Alabama Citizens for Constitutional Reform has been pushing the idea for years.[49] It proposed that the legislature put the issue of whether a constitutional convention should be held to a statewide vote and if voters approved, they would select in a special election delegates from each of the 105 House districts, who would convene to propose a new constitution, which then would be presented to the people for approval or rejection. One poll showed that 61 percent of the state's residents favor constitutional reform.[50]

The proposal for putting the issue of calling a constitutional convention before the voters in November 2002 was nonetheless defeated in the House of Representatives by a vote of 33 to 105.[51] However, both of the Democratic and Republican candidates for governor supported constitutional reforms and a statewide vote on the matter, though Republican candidate Bob Riley opposed holding a citizens' constitutional convention. Shortly after his inauguration as governor in 2003, Riley instead addressed the matter by establishing a 35-member Alabama Citizens' Constitutional Commission to propose constitutional reforms in five areas: strengthening the governor's line-item veto power, giving more home rule back to counties, requiring more than a simple majority of the legislature to raise taxes, changing provisions that earmark 90 percent of all tax revenues for specific purposes, and studying how the constitution might be shortened and reformed. The commission's recommendations went to the legislature for approval and they must be ratified by the voters. The legislature proposed amendments eliminating language in the constitution that requires segregated schools and poll taxes, which remain even though they were invalidated by federal courts over forty years ago.[52] But in 2004 voters defeated that amendment by just 1850 votes out of the more than 1.3 million cast.

S U M M A R Y

1. State constitutions spell out the fundamental laws of the states. Although they vary considerably in detail, each outlines the organizational framework of the state, vesting powers in the legislature and other departments. Each includes a bill of rights, sets procedures for holding elections, provides for local governments, and contains a variety of provisions dealing with finances, education, and other state issues.

2. Most state constitutions are cumbersome documents containing much more detail than the U.S. Constitution. Although reformers may have introduced such detail to prevent abuse, most constitutional scholars believe such matters are better left to statutory law.

3. In the past 20 years, there has been a flurry of renewed interest in state constitutions as they have been discovered to be additional instruments for protecting and expanding rights in what is known as the new judicial federalism.

4. State constitutions can be amended by ratification by the voters of proposals submitted by the legislature, by popular initiative petitions, or by constitutional conventions. Conventions tend to revise the entire constitution rather than just amend portions of it.

5. In recent decades, there has been an expanded use of the initiative process in several states to bring about narrowly targeted constitutional reforms.

6. Despite the considerable constitutional change brought about during the last half-century through amendments, voters have often been resistant to sweeping constitutional revision.

K E Y   T E R M S

judicial interpretation   **new judicial federalism**   **revision commission**   **constitutional initiative petition**

F U R T H E R   R E A D I N G

The Greenwood Publishing Group has commissioned reference guides for the constitution of each state, written by an expert on the state. As of 2004, guides for 38 states have been published, including Alabama, Alaska, Arizona, Arkansas, California, Colorado, Connecticut, Delaware, Florida, Hawaii, Idaho, Indiana, Iowa, Kansas, Kentucky, Louisiana, Maine, Michigan, Minnesota, Mississippi, Montana, Nebraska, Nevada, New Hampshire, New Jersey, New Mexico, New York, North Carolina, North Dakota, Oklahoma, Tennessee, Texas, Utah, Vermont, Washington, Wisconsin, West Virginia, and Wyoming.

WILLI PAUL ADAMS, *The First American Constitutions: Republican Ideology and the Making of State Constitutions in the Revolutionary Era* (Rowman & Littlefield, 2001).

PAUL FINKELMAN AND STEPHEN E. GOTTLIEB, EDS., *Toward a Usable Past: Liberty Under State Constitutions* (University of Georgia Press, 1991).

RICHARD J. ELLIS, *Democratic Delusions: The Initiative Process in America* (University Press of Kansas, 2003).

JENNIFER FREISEN, *State Constitutional Law* (Michie, 1996).

SANFORD LEVINSON, ED., *Responding to Imperfection: The Theory and Practice of Constitutional Amendment* (Princeton University Press, 1995).

CHARLES LOPEMAN, *The Activist Advocate: Policy Making in State Supreme Courts* (Praeger, 1999).

ROBERT L. MADDEX, *State Constitutions of the United States* (CQ Press, 1998).

JAMES T. McHUGH, *Ex Uno Plura: State Constitutions and Their Political Cultures* (State University of New York, 2003).

LAURA J. SCALIA, *America's Jeffersonian Experiment: Remaking State Constitutions, 1820–1850* (Northern Illinois University Press, 1999).

G. ALAN TARR, *Understanding State Constitutions* (Princeton University Press, 2000).

ROBERT F. WILLIAMS, *State Constitutional Law: Cases and Materials* (Michie, 1993).

See also the quarterly review *State Constitutional Commentaries and Notes,* published by the Edward McNail Burns Center for State Constitutional Studies at Rutgers University.

PARTIES AND ELECTIONS IN THE STATES

23

The chaos in the counting of ballots in Florida in the 2000 election surprised many Americans, who assumed that vote counting is simple and precise. They were wrong. The problems were not isolated to Florida's clogged voting machines, defective punch cards, and inconsistent standards for dealing with problems. Ballots were misplaced in New Mexico; voting machines broke down in several states; people's names were incorrectly purged from voting lists; and long lines of people waiting to vote led to court challenges in many states. In the weeks and months following the election, at least half the states launched efforts to study the problems and propose solutions; in addition, national commissions, advisory groups, and experts undertook extensive analyses of our voting procedures.

Most people agree that many communities need new voting equipment and that the antiquated and flawed punch-card technology used by "roughly 30 percent of the nation's voters" needed to be replaced.[1] As a result of the widespread problems in election administration in 2000, Congress passed the Help America Vote Act (HAVA) in 2002. HAVA provides federal funds to help states replace antiquated punch-card and lever voting machines. By accepting the funding, states were to have these new machines in place by the November 2004 election or apply for a waiver to delay implementation until 2006. In as many as 42 states, new voting machines were in place in 2004. Nevertheless, of the 30 states that applied for federal funds to replace punch-card and/or lever voting machines, 24 applied for a waiver."[2] Despite widespread concerns before the election, there were no major problems

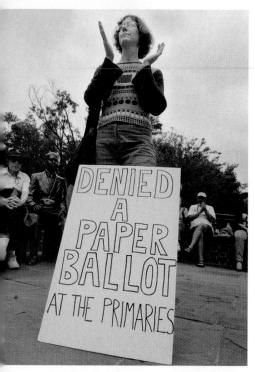

Antiquated punch-card and lever voting machines received considerable notoriety during the 2000 presidential election. These machines were blamed for many of the problems that plagued certain precincts in Florida, leading to the controversy over recounts and disqualified ballots. The new touch-screen voting machines, however, come with their own problems, among them no legal requirement that they provide a paper record of each vote cast in case verification should become necessary and a potential vulnerability to hackers who may wish to disrupt the election results.

with voting technology in the 2004 election. Had the election been closer in any one of several states, then more concerns would likely have surfaced.

Some of this technology prompted debates about the accuracy of computerized voting machines, especially if the machines were paperless and did not allow voters to know if their votes had been tallied correctly. Those working the polls in 2004 were required by the 2002 legislation to demand identification from first-time voters who registered by mail but did not provide identification with their registration.

The National Association of Secretaries of State—the state officials charged with election administration—issued recommendations that included better pay for poll workers; aggressive voter education on matters like how to ask for a second ballot if the first is spoiled; equal access to balloting for minorities, the poor, and elderly voters; maintaining up-to-date voter lists; ensuring the integrity of absentee ballots; and providing federal money to local communities to upgrade their voting systems.[3] The 2002 elections saw no repeats of the troubled recounts in Florida in 2000. There was, however, some controversy in South Dakota about the registration drives among Native Americans. Charges of fraud in Native American voter registration surfaced before the election but were dismissed by the South Dakota attorney general. The 2000 election and its aftermath taught us to not take election administration for granted. The states have the responsibility to manage elections and to ensure the right of participation to every citizen. The central role of states in our electoral democracy is the subject of this chapter.

ELECTORAL POLITICS IN THE STATES AND LOCALITIES

The U.S. Constitution provides only the most general guidelines to the states concerning the regulation of elections for members of the U.S. Congress. Article I, Section 4, says, "The Times, Places and Manner of holding Elections for Senators and Representatives shall be prescribed in each State by the Legislature thereof; but the Congress may at any time by Law make or alter such Regulations, except as to the Places of choosing Senators." The constitutional language regarding presidential elections also defers to state law: "Each State shall appoint, in such Manner as the Legislature thereof may direct, a Number of Electors."

Amendments to the U.S. Constitution relating to elections do not alter the central role of state constitutions and state law regarding voting rights. Rather, these amendments expressly forbid the states to restrict the right to vote in any election, for state and local as well as for national offices, to certain kinds of people. States cannot deny the franchise on the basis of "race, color, or previous condition of servitude" (Fifteenth Amendment), gender (Nineteenth Amendment), failure to pay a poll tax (Twenty-Fourth Amendment), or age for persons over age 18 (Twenty-Sixth Amendment).

Federalism and Elections

Political federalism in this country is noteworthy. Most elected officials, including even the president, are elected in a process that reinforces the importance of states. State identities are important to both politicians and voters. We think of ourselves as citizens of a particular state as well as of the United States. States have distinctive political traditions and political cultures. Because of these strong state identities and differences between the states in laws and practices, it should not be surprising that state parties are in many ways more important than national parties. Indeed, national parties, aside from their congressional campaign committees, are largely federations of state parties. And since our national parties as electoral organizations have never been strong, the activities they undertake usually end up being carried out by the state parties. The independence of state parties also helps explain why, for instance, Democratic voters in one state can be so different from those in another and why Republicans from different states can come down on opposite sides of some major issues.

The electoral process in the United States is *decentralized* in its rules and administration. Elections in the United States are administered by state and local governments, not by the national government. Even the president is chosen in state elections conducted according to state rules. Because of the electoral college and the winner-take-all system, presidential politics focuses not on getting the most popular votes but instead on getting a plurality of votes in as many states as possible. State elections also determine who will serve as members of Congress, as governor, and as other statewide officials like attorney general, as well as the outcome of many ballot measures.

Most states prescribe the organization of the state parties, the means by which their officers are elected, and the nomination process for president and other offices.[4] In states that have some form of public financing of elections or parties, such as Maine and Arizona, the state also regulates the distribution of public funds to the parties and the reporting of how those funds are spent.

States differ in the hours the polls are open, how close to the voting place campaigning may be conducted, and whether they require voter registration. Largely because of overriding federal legislation, differences between the states in how long you must have lived in the state before voting and how you may register to vote have diminished in recent years.

As we learned in the 2000 presidential election in Florida, there is great variation in the way people vote, even from county to county. Some Florida counties used ballots read by optical scanners, and others used punch-card ballots. Other states use these same types of ballots as well as paper ballots, voting machines, and even the Internet. Following the 2000 election, Florida mandated that voting in statewide elections be by computerized touch screens or ballots read by optical scanning machines.[5] Some of these devices malfunctioned in the 2002 Florida primary election. Despite these mishaps, a substantial amount of variation in voting systems continued through the 2004 election. In nearly half of the states (22), some voters continued to have punch card ballots, for example.[6] Delays in funding the 2002 legislation delayed implementation of new voting technologies in 2004 in many states. For a state by state summary of election reforms, see www.electionline.org.

Along with the variation in ballots, we have many types of elections, including *general elections* to determine who holds office and *primary elections* to determine who will run in the general elections. Most statewide elections are partisan, whereas most local elections for school boards, water districts, and city governments are nonpartisan. State legislative elections are partisan except in Nebraska, where the legislature is nonpartisan. Voters in all states but Delaware must ratify changes to the state constitution in a referendum. Roughly half of the states allow votes on initiatives and referendums put on the ballot by petition. The initiative and referendum are also found in many local governments.

THE ROLE OF POLITICAL PARTIES

Although political parties are not mentioned in the U.S. Constitution, they are vital not only to our national government but also to the functioning of the electoral system within the states. Parties organize the competition by recruiting and nominating candidates, function as the loyal opposition when out of power, unify and organize the electorate, and provide a link between the people and their government. The existence of political parties is acknowledged in many state constitutions.

Election rules in general favor the two major parties over minor parties. The Republican and Democratic parties have a "preferred position"—that is, their candidates will definitely be placed on the ballot. Ballot access for minor party and independent candidates is less certain. State laws typically require minor parties to garner a minimum number of votes in the previous election or submit a prescribed number of signatures of registered voters in order to appear on the ballot. States vary in the difficulty of ballot access for minor parties, depending on three factors: the number of signatures

CHANGING FACE OF AMERICAN POLITICS

A DEMOGRAPHIC PROFILE OF LOCAL GOVERNMENT OFFICIALS

Number of Local Elected Officials	494,093

Gender	
Male	76.3%
Female	23.7

Race	
White	96.7
Black	2.8
American Indian or Alaskan Native	0.4
Asian or Pacific Islander	0.1
Hispanic	1.4

SOURCE: U.S. Bureau of the Census, "Popularly Elected Officials in 1992," *1992 Census of Governments* (U.S. Government Printing Office, 1992). Note: This is the most recent census of elected officials and these proportions may have changed somewhat since the data were collected.

required, the time allowed to collect them, and whether signatures must be distributed across several counties.

State election ballots are of two kinds. The **party column ballot** (also known as the *Indiana ballot*), which encourages party-line voting, is organized by parties, with the party name and symbol at the top of a column that lists all the party's candidates running for offices in that election (see Figure 23–1). Typically, there is an option at the top of the ballot column that allows voters to cast votes for all candidates of that party. When voters choose such an option, they cast a **straight ticket** vote. Voters may also have to work their way through state constitutional amendments, referendums, and initiatives on the ballot.

Partly to discourage straight ticket voting, some states use the **office block ballot** (also known as the *Massachusetts ballot*), which lists all the candidates running for an office together in one block or on one screen, all those running for another office in another block/screen, and so on (see Figure 23–2). If voters want to cast a straight ticket vote, they have to hunt through each block/screen for their preferred candidate. Office block ballots encourage **split ticket** voting, or voting for candidates from more than one party. One consequence of computerized ballots will be a shift to office block formats.

Party Organization and Officers

AN EARLIER ERA: MACHINES AND BOSSES   In the nineteenth century, political *machines* became established in a number of American cities. Typically, these were organizations in which one political party dominated the political life of the city, often by recruiting new immigrants as supporters and voters by offering them patronage jobs and social welfare benefits. For many years, the epitome of a political machine in the United States was Tammany Hall, the building where the Tammany Society (named after a Delaware Indian chief) met and ran New York City politics. Tammany Hall was closely identified with Democrats and was ruled by William Tweed, the boss of New York City politics.

A *boss* is a party leader who uses patronage, government contracts, and access to power to dictate policy. Some bosses, like Tweed, were never elected to office but were powers behind the scene who told the mayor and other city officials what to do. Party bosses were common after the Civil War and well into the twentieth century. Other cities with powerful political machines were Chicago, Los Angeles, Boston, Pittsburgh, Cincinnati, Philadelphia, Indianapolis, San Francisco, and Baltimore.

The principal objective of the urban reform movement in the early twentieth century was to overthrow the bosses and the political machines. Reformers advocated nonpartisan local elections, competitive bids for projects, and civil service in place of

party column ballot
Type of ballot that encourages party-line voting by listing all of a party's candidates in a column under the party name.

straight ticket
A vote for all of one party's candidates.

office block ballot
Ballot on which all candidates are listed under the office for which they are running.

split ticket
A vote for some of one party's candidates and some of another party's.

Official Ballot for Piute County, Utah, November 2, 2004

FIGURE 23–1 A Sample Party Column Ballot.

FIGURE 23–2 A Sample Office Block Ballot.

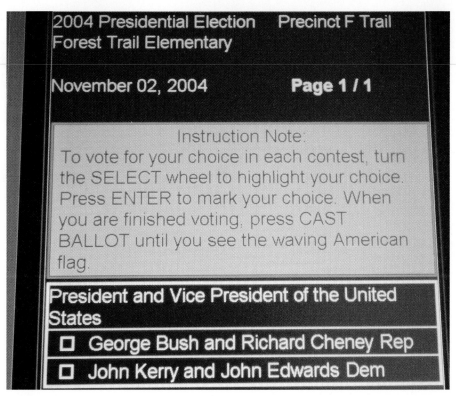

Modern voting machines, such as the touch-screen model shown here, tend to favor the office block ballot over the party column ballot.

patronage. They achieved most of their goals, although it is not clear whether the power of political machines was reduced by these reforms or by other social and economic forces.

PARTY ORGANIZATIONS TODAY Although state party organizations are not all alike, most organize themselves along the same lines as the national parties. In all states, there is a *party chair* who is elected by the party's central committee or delegates to a party convention. Other statewide party officers include the *vice chair,* who by state law or party bylaws often must be of the opposite gender from the party chair,[7] plus officers like treasurer and secretary. Party leaders generally answer to a *central committee,* which consists of 20 or more persons who are elected or otherwise chosen for specified terms.

The state party chair is the spokesperson for the party, especially when the party does not control the governorship. He or she raises money for the party and its candidates. When the party controls the governorship, the central committee defers to the governor in the selection of the chair. Because overt expressions of partisanship are thought to be unbecoming of elected officials, it is often the party chair who defends the party and, when necessary, goes on the offensive against the opposition party.

The day-to-day operations of the party are usually carried out by the party's *executive director,* a full-time employee who oversees the staff, assists the chair, and coordinates the work of the central committee and other party officials. The executive director schedules functions and serves as a liaison with the national organizations.

At the local level, political parties generally have a structure patterned after the state party organization. In some counties, party organizations are fully staffed and functioning, but in most counties, they are run by volunteers and are mostly inactive until just before an election. Local parties provide opportunities for ordinary citizens to become involved in politics, a first step that can eventually lead to running for office. Some states, like Minnesota, have congressional district parties as well.[8]

Although party bosses and strong party machines are a thing of the past, local politics is still organized on a partisan basis in many of our largest cities. More typically, as noted, local politics is nonpartisan with three-quarters of U.S. cities having nonpartisan elections.[9]

Party Activities in Elections

American politics is candidate-centered. Candidates create their own campaign organizations. Yet parties serve important secondary roles in elections. They provide the structure for elections; in some places, they recruit candidates, register voters, mobilize voters on election day, and supply resources and campaign help to their candidates.

STRUCTURE FOR ELECTIONS Our election system would function in a dramatically different way if we had no political parties to organize the competition. Parties narrow the field of candidates through a primary election or convention process, providing voters with relatively few choices in the general election. Candidates, to one degree or another, must secure the support of fellow partisans to win a place on the ballot as the party's nominees for the offices they are seeking.

CANDIDATE RECRUITMENT Party officials often seek out candidates to run for office, help train them in how to run, and occasionally provide modest financial support. One sign of the weakness of our parties is that many offices go uncontested, including some members of Congress. The number of unopposed candidates increases as you go down the ballot. To be sure, some incumbents have done such a good job that to oppose them would be an exercise in futility. Yet lack of competition in elections violates American assumptions about democracy and is reminiscent of politics in the former communist states, where party officers ran unopposed. One important characteristic of American parties at all levels is that they are extremely open to would-be candidates. Virtually anybody can run for the state legislature. Generally speaking, the greater the likelihood that a party nomination will help with winning the general election, the more competition there is for that nomination.

VOTER REGISTRATION All states except North Dakota require citizens to register before permitting them to vote. In California, you can register online, at www.ss.ca.gov/elections/elections.htm, and some states, like Wisconsin, allow registration at the polls on election day. Voter registration became easier when Congress passed the National Voter Registration, or Motor Voter, Act in 1993. People are now able to register to vote when they apply for or renew their driver's license or visit certain public agencies. The half-dozen states that permit election day registration or do not require voter registration are exempt from the law. The idea behind Motor Voter is to ease the registration process, thereby increasing the number of registered voters and turnout.

What difference has Motor Voter made? "During the 2002 election cycle, over 16 million people were added to the voter registration rolls via the Motor Voter, or just under 43 percent of all new registrants.[10] Many of the new Motor Voter registrants are registering as Independents. In terms of party balance, Motor Voter does not appear to have made much difference, contrary to expectations that it would result in a bias in favor of Democrats.[11]

At the time of registration, some states ask voters to register with a political party; in other states, party registration is optional. Most states do not register voters by party. To see what your state requires, visit the voter registration section of the Federal Election Commission Web site at www.fec.gov. Even in states that require party registration, voters have the option to decline to state their party at the time of registration. For example, in California in 2002, 15 percent of the registered voters declined to state their party preference.[12] Opting out of party registration often means voters may not vote in a party primary, which in some states may be the election that effectively decides the officeholder. An excellent data bank on voter registration and turnout is maintained by the National Conference of State Legislatures at www.ncsl.org.

Helping register sympathetic voters is important to candidates, parties, and interest groups. These efforts are typically aimed at citizens they anticipate will vote for their party's candidate. Voter registration drives targeted at African Americans helped Democrats in key states and congressional districts. Both parties worked to register Hispanic voters in 2002. Interest groups with active voter registration efforts include organized labor, business groups, and groups concerned about the environment and abortion.

Political parties favor laws requiring voters to disclose their party preference at the time they register. First, this requirement permits parties to limit participation in their primaries to registered party members in states that have a closed primary system. Second, party registration creates voter registration lists, which parties find extremely useful for campaigning and fund raising. In addition, *list vending*—selling voter lists with addresses, phone numbers, and party preferences—is a multimillion-dollar industry. Third, voter registration helps the parties in the redistricting process because state legislators, using party registration, voting, and other data, can draw new congressional and state legislative district boundaries in ways that give their party an advantage. Examples of states where partisanship was a major factor in the 2001–2002 redistricting are Georgia for the Democrats and Utah for the Republicans.[13]

VOTER MOBILIZATION   Just over three-quarters of eligible voters are registered, and of that number, only about two-thirds vote in presidential elections, meaning that *only half the voting-age population bothers to vote* in a presidential election and fewer still in a midterm election.[14] Get-out-the-vote drives are therefore a major activity of candidates and parties. Elections are often decided by which party does better at turning out its supporters. Party workers, through telephone or door-to-door canvassing, identify registered voters who are likely to support their party and then contact those voters personally on election day, perhaps more than once, to encourage them to go to the polls. Where resources permit, the parties may even provide transportation to the polls or baby-sitting services.[15]

In states that permit registration by mail or by roving registrars, volunteers register voters at the same time they find voters who will support their party's candidates in the election. When absentee or mail ballots are options, voter mobilization efforts help voters fill out the form requesting an absentee ballot and then mail the form for them. A few weeks later, a party volunteer checks to make sure a ballot has arrived and has been filled out and returned. Because most voters prefer one party over another, it makes sense for candidates from the same party to consolidate their efforts.

CAMPAIGN RESOURCES   American political parties, with some notable exceptions, are organizationally weak. In better-organized states, parties often provide campaign funds and campaign help. They raise funds for their party organization and finance voter registration and mobilization efforts, often with the help of national parties. As at the national level, control of the governorship helps in fund raising because interest groups are much more likely to contribute to the governor's party. Texas Governor George W. Bush not only tapped into his base of affluent Texans but also won the support of other gov-

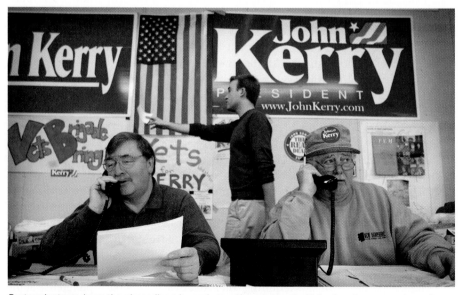

Party volunteers keep the phone lines humming as they urge potential voters to come out on election day and support their candidate.

ernors to finance much of his 2000 presidential campaign. He built on this network to raise record-setting amounts as a candidate in his 2004 reelection campaign.

In states with well-organized parties, the parties train the candidates they have recruited. Wisconsin and New York have strong state legislative campaign committees that distribute resources to candidates, as the national party committee does to congressional candidates.[16] Sometimes the state parties provide polling data to state and local candidates, help establish campaign themes, or prepare generic advertising that can be used in several state legislative districts.

Until 2004, parties also channeled money from the national congressional and senatorial campaign committees to local candidates for U.S. Senate or U.S. House involved in competitive races. This **soft money**, which could come in disclosed but unlimited amounts, was banned at the national level by the Bipartisan Campaign Reform Act (BCRA) in 2002.[17] State parties operate under their own rules, and all but Connecticut permit soft money for state and local candidates. Moreover, the 2002 reforms permit limited amounts of soft money, $10,000, to go to state and local parties for voter registration and mobilization.[18] Between 1996 and 2002, Republican and Democratic national party committees, including the congressional and senatorial campaign committees, raised and distributed large amounts of soft money. Because state parties largely spend the soft money for the national parties, this expenditure has not generally made state parties stronger.

One reason parties raised soft money was to respond to **issue advocacy**, in which an interest group attacks some political candidates or supports others but carefully avoids specifically telling voters to vote for or against that individual. Though much of the soft money and issue advocacy advertising focuses on presidential and congressional elections, both parties have also devoted these resources to gubernatorial, judicial,[19] and state legislative races.[20]

Issue advocacy, which aims to defeat or elect a particular candidate, has been important since the 1996 elections and was again significant in 2002.[21] One notable example was again the pharmaceutical industry, which in 2000 provided substantial funding for a group named Citizens for Better Medicare. In 2002, their money was directed to another group—United Seniors. In both instances, the issue advocacy was important in reshaping the debate on the prescription drug issue for senior citizens. The pharmaceutical industry did not mount major issue ads in 2004. Tort reform was a more important topic for issue ads in 2004.

Voting Choices

Voters generally base their election decisions on three factors, listed in decreasing order of importance: political party identification, candidate appeal, and issues. But in many local elections, since party labels are absent from the ballot, voters rely more on candidate appeal, issues, and factors like incumbency, media endorsements, and name recognition.

PARTY IDENTIFICATION Party identification is the most important predictor of voting behavior. Parties provide a party label that guides voters in making their decisions. Party labels are especially important in elections in which voters have little information about candidates, as in contests for attorney general, state senator, state representative, or county commissioner. The simplifying device of party labels helps voters sort through the many candidate choices they encounter on election day.

People who identify themselves as strong Democrats and strong Republicans are remarkably loyal to their party when voting for governor and other state and local offices. Independent-leaners have clear partisan preferences in the direction of one party or the other. Pure Independents have no party preference and are most inclined to vote for one party and then another with changing circumstances, but there are few Pure Independents in the total electorate.[22]

CANDIDATE APPEAL Although party identification is important, it is not decisive. Candidate appeal can be crucial. For example, in the 2003 California recall election, voters not only viewed governor Gray Davis negatively,[23] they were positive about Arnold Schwarzenegger's success in business, his independence from special interests because

soft money
Unlimited contributions to political parties for party-building purposes.

issue advocacy
Promoting a particular position on an issue, often funded by interest groups and designed to influence voters' choices on election day.

of his personal wealth, and his sponsorship of a ballot initiative that provided for after-school programs.[24] In some respects the 2003 California recall election resembled the 1998 Minnesota gubernatorial election, in which Reform party candidate Jesse Ventura was elected largely because his style and approach generated interest among voters, and a plurality preferred him over the established candidates in the major parties. Minnesota's system of public financing helped Ventura become visible, and he worked hard to become credible. In the end, he won in a stunning upset. As governor, he remained unconventional, abandoned the Reform Party for the Independent party, found working with the state legislature difficult, and took exception to media scrutiny of his family.[25] He decided not to run for reelection in 2002.

In state and local elections, name identification and the advantages of incumbency are important. Incumbents generally have an advantage in candidate appeal because of greater name recognition and access to campaign resources. Candidates sometimes use creative means to generate positive name recognition. For example, when Bob Graham was governor of Florida, he often worked one day a week in different jobs around the state to demonstrate his desire to relate to his constituents.

ISSUE VOTING   Issues can be very important to the outcome of elections. Economic conditions are an important factor in state and local elections, as they are in national ones. William Weld, a Republican, was able to win his first Massachusetts gubernatorial election in 1990, despite the fact that Massachusetts is a very strong Democratic state, because the economy was so bad. Former New Jersey Governor Christine Todd Whitman won election in part because her incumbent opponent had raised state taxes and she promised a 30 percent tax cut. Mitt Romney campaigned successfully in 2002 for governor of Massachusetts on the theme of an outsider being able to restore economic growth and fiscal discipline. His success as a businessman and as head of the 2002 Salt Lake City Winter Olympics reinforced this message. Democratic candidate Kathleen Sebelius won her 2002 gubernatorial election in a heavily Republican state by emphasizing her support for public education and her opponent's view that schools in Kansas "can make it with 1 or 2 or 3%" less funding. "Sebelius' stance on this issue appealed to enough moderate Republicans to win her the election."[26] Although issues are important in state and local elections, it is fair to say that they are probably less important than at the national level.[27]

JUDICIAL ELECTIONS.   Judicial elections in some states are partisan and resemble campaigns for other offices in intensity. In 2000, the Michigan Democratic party ran ads attacking incumbent candidates for the Michigan supreme court who had been appointed by a former Republican governor. One of the ads showed an insurance executive sitting at his desk searching through papers and asking the secretary, "Where are my judges?" She replies, "Just where they've always been, right in your pocket." The executive looks in his suit coat pocket to see three justices frolicking in handfuls of money. Three pictures appear on the screen and a voice says, "Justices Markman, Taylor, and Young have accepted hundreds of thousands from insurance and big business. Justice should not be for sale."[28]

Ads attacking judicial candidates like this were not unique to Michigan in 2000. Ohio, Illinois, Alabama, and Idaho had races in which similar ads were used by political parties or interest groups[29]; this occurred again in several states in 2002. A 2002 Supreme Court decision, *Republican Party of Minnesota* v. *White,* allowes judicial candidates to state their views on disputed legal and political issues. One potential consequence of this will be more position taking on issues by judicial candidates. Substantial spending by political parties and interest groups in judicial elections has prompted criticism by good-government groups and led the American Bar Association to form a task force on this topic.

NONPARTISAN LOCAL ELECTIONS   Nonpartisan elections were intended to weaken political parties in local elections, and they have been successful. Arguing that political parties had little to contribute to the administration of local government, reformers during the first half of the twentieth century introduced nonpartisan elections. The two parties were, in effect, blocked from exerting an open influence on local politics.

Some observers contend that nonpartisan local elections make it more difficult for poor persons, minorities, and the less educated to participate effectively. For such people, the party label serves to identify politicians who share their values and perspectives on government. Well-educated and wealthy voters know more about who is running and what they stand for, even without party labels. Nonpartisan elections sometimes help Republican candidates, especially in cities with populations of more than 50,000, because Republican voters tend to vote more in low-turnout elections and are more likely to know which candidates are Republicans.[30] Others have found that there is not generally an advantage to Republican candidates in nonpartisan elections.[31]

Parties in State Government

PARTIES IN THE EXECUTIVE BRANCH   Just as winning the presidency is the big prize at the national level, so is winning the governorship at the state level. The party that controls the governorship has the power to appoint executive department officials and some state judges. Governors are usually perceived as the leaders of their party, and they establish the political agenda and help define the party for their state. They customarily win office with the help of fellow partisans, and they know from the day they take office that the other party is planning ways to defeat them and their party in the next election.

Governors often assist in recruiting candidates for the state legislature; they usually campaign on behalf of their party, even when they are not on the ballot for reelection. Presidential candidates often seek the help of governors. Governors raise money for campaigns as well as for the state party. They have wide latitude in appointing boards, commissions, judges, and state administrators, and they almost always take party affiliation and activity into account when making appointments.

PARTIES IN THE LEGISLATURE   Like Congress, state legislatures (excluding Nebraska, which is nonpartisan) are organized largely along party lines. The *speaker of the house or assembly* and the *president of the senate* are elected by the majority party in most states. They preside over floor proceedings and make key assignments to standing committees and study committees. Most state legislatures have floor leaders, called *majority leaders* and *minority leaders* and majority and minority *whips*.

In most states, parties sit on different sides of the aisle in the legislative chambers and are separated in committee meetings as well. Committee chairs in most state legislatures go to members from the majority party in that chamber, with the leaders of the majority party wielding great power in the final decision. The **party caucus** is often important in state legislatures. The caucus is a meeting of party leaders and legislators to discuss party policy. Because some state legislatures meet for only a few months a year, the party caucus can help hammer out agreements rapidly.

One area in which legislatures are predictably partisan is **redistricting**. Each decade, following the national census, state legislatures are constitutionally required to realign congressional and state legislative district boundaries to make them equal in population and reflect population changes. The 2001–2002 redistricting was especially important because the two parties were so evenly divided in numbers of legislative chambers controlled. Going into the 2004 elections, the Democrats controlled 43 chambers, the Republicans 51, and three were tied.[32]

How district lines are drawn can help or hurt a party. Where one party controls both houses and the governorship or has a veto-proof majority in the legislature, the majority party can do pretty much what it wants with district boundaries, so long as it keeps the districts equal in population and respects the rights of racial minorities. Where power is divided between the parties, the result is often a redistricting that protects incumbents.

Typically, after redistricting occurs, several U.S. House incumbents retire rather than face the uncertainty of an election in a newly drawn district or the prospect of running against another incumbent. This was less the case in 2002 because to a very large extent, state legislatures drew district boundaries to protect incumbents. California, with its 53 congressional districts, emerged from redistricting with only one or two districts considered competitive in 2002 and 2004. Three notable exceptions to this are the partisan gerrymandering carried out in Utah and Texas by Republicans and in Georgia by Democrats. In these cases, the parties controlled the process and sought to create districts more favorable to their party, even if it gave incumbents from their party districts that were less safely partisan.

party caucus
A meeting of the members of a party in a legislative chamber to select party leaders and develop party policy. Called a *conference* by the Republicans.

redistricting
The redrawing of congressional and other legislative district lines following the census, to accommodate population shifts and keep districts as equal as possible in population.

In five states, commissions rather than the legislature do the redistricting. Commissions tend to be more neutral and often create more competitive districts. This was the case in Arizona with the last redistricting. Arizona's new congressional district, the First District, had nearly equal numbers of registered Democrats and Republicans and was seen as a toss-up by political prognosticators.

Parties in Local Government

Political parties are still important in the politics of many cities, especially the larger ones, although they are in a much weaker position now than they were 25 or 50 years ago. Mayors often lead city party organizations and play a role in the campaigns of presidents, senators, and governors. The mayor's office is sometimes a stepping-stone to other offices. Former Governor Jesse Ventura began his political career as mayor of Brooklyn Park, Minnesota; U.S. Senator Richard Lugar was once mayor of Indianapolis; George Voinovich was mayor of Cleveland and became governor of Ohio before going on to the U.S. Senate; and U.S. Senator Dianne Feinstein was mayor of San Francisco. In 2002, former St. Paul mayor Norm Coleman was elected to the U.S. Senate from Minnesota.

Parties rarely get involved in initiative and referendum elections at the local or state level, but some nonpartisan local elections have partisan overtones as candidates may be identified with the parties, or the parties may want to advance the career of a local nonpartisan candidate.

PARTY BALANCE AND IMBALANCE

State politics may be classified according to how the parties share public offices. In a **two-party state**, the Republican and Democratic parties regularly assemble winning majorities. Two-party states include Indiana, Illinois, and Missouri. In a **one-party state**, one party wins all or nearly all the offices, and the second party usually receives only one-third or less of the popular vote. One-party Republican states currently include Utah, Idaho, and Kansas. Massachusetts is an example of a Democratic one-party state. Democrats occasionally win in Utah, and the same is true for Republicans in Massachusetts, but the more predictable tendency is to support the predominant party.

Since the end of World War II, there has been an accelerating trend toward two-party politics. The Democratic party lost its previously solid support in the South as more and more white southerners moved over to the Republican party. At first, Republican resurgence in the South was mainly evident in presidential and congressional elections, but in recent years, Republicans have regularly been elected to southern state legislatures. Since the mid-1970s, the number of Republicans in southern state legislatures has increased from about 12 percent to near parity.[33]

Republican gains have also been evident in contests for governor. Since 1966, all southern states have at least once elected a Republican governor, and in 2005, seven southern states were led by Republican governors. In terms of the popular vote for president, the South has voted more Republican than the country as a whole in nine of the last 11 presidential elections.[34] In 2004, all eleven former confederate states went to George W. Bush. Even with southerner Al Gore on the ballot, the Democrats carried no southern state in 2000.

Outside the South, there has also been a gradual spread of two-party politics, with the rise of Democratic strength in the formerly solid Republican states of Iowa, Maine, and New Hampshire. Democrats have lost strength in parts of the Rocky Mountain area; however, the Democratic party has been gaining loyalists in the Northeast and Pacific Coast states.

What are the consequences of party balance? When parties and their candidates compete on an equal basis, they are more likely to be sensitive to public opinion, for the loss of even a fraction of the voters can tip the scales to the other side in the next election. Party competition tends to push leaders within each party to work together, at least as elections draw near. Any defection may throw a race to the opponents, so

two-party state
A state in which the two major parties alternate in winning majorities.

one-party state
A state in which one party wins all or nearly all the offices and the other party receives only a small proportion of the popular vote.

competition generally produces more teamwork and efficiency in government. It may also generate more service to constituents by legislators.

In a one-party state, party imbalance may have a serious effect on the accountability that is part of electoral competition. Competition that otherwise would occur *between* the major parties occurs *within* the majority party. The most important contests in some states like Massachusetts are generally not between Democrats and Republicans but among Democrats in the primary; the same is true for Republicans in Utah. In these intraparty fights, personalities dominate the campaign. Voters do not participate as much as they do in two-party contests.

If party imbalance disorganizes the dominant party, it pulverizes the minority party. With faint hope of winning, minority party leaders do not put up much of a fight. They find it difficult to raise money for campaigns and to persuade people to become candidates. They have no state or local patronage to give out. Volunteers are slow to come forward. Young people wishing to succeed in politics drift into the dominant party. The second party is likely to be concerned only with national politics, where it may win an election, and the patronage that could come its way if its candidate wins the White House.

Party imbalance can be found in more extreme forms in cities and towns than at the state level. Republicans hardly ever carry Chicago, Boston, Washington, Baltimore, Albany, Hartford, Pittsburgh, and many other cities throughout the industrial North. But party balance is not always a determining factor. In heavily Democratic New York City, for example, voters elected a Republican, Michael Bloomberg, as mayor in 2001. Bloomberg had been a Democrat but ran for mayor as a Republican with the strong endorsement of outgoing Republican mayor Rudolph Giuliani.

ELECTIONS AT THE STATE AND LOCAL LEVELS

Each year, there are thousands of state and local elections. Europeans, who are used to voting for one or two candidates at the national and local levels and voting only once every two or three years, are flabbergasted to learn that we engage in elections almost continuously. Selection of town and local officials in the late winter may be followed in the spring by primaries to choose delegates to conventions, then primaries to choose party candidates, then general elections in the fall in which the actual officeholders are chosen—all interspersed with special elections, special town or state referendums, and even, in some states, recall elections to throw officials out of office as happened in California in 2003 when voters removed Gray Davis from the governorship and replaced him with Arnold Schwarzenegger.

Even more bewildering to some is the number of offices we vote on, from president to probate judge, from senator to sheriff, from governor to library board member. This is the *long ballot.* Europeans are more accustomed to electing a handful of key officials, who in turn appoint career officials. Given this volume of election activity, it is fair to conclude that Americans like elections, even though most of them choose not to vote in most of those elections.

Differences in Who May Vote

Subject to constitutional constraint, states can regulate who may vote. Most, for example, do not permit prison inmates to vote. If a state wanted to permit 16-year-olds to vote, it could do so. Voter registration rules can discourage people from participating in elections. States differ in the length of their residency requirement, as well as in whether they permit roving registrars, postcard registration, online registration, or election day registration. Most states require a periodic purge of the voter registration list to remove people who have moved or died.

A common reason why people do not register is that they have moved and have not registered at their new address. Fifteen percent of Americans change their residence every year.[35] After moving, they may not realize that they need to register at their new address until only a few days before the election, and then it is too late. Maryland, North

Carolina, and the District of Columbia allow college students who have moved within a city or county to vote without registering if they notify election officials of their move. All told, a state's registration rules can lower turnout by as much as 9 percent.[36]

Differences in How We Vote

Although millions of Americans carry cell phones, own computers, and shop on the Internet, as a nation we still vote in an antiquated way. One of the surprises of the 2000 presidential election was the extent to which we are still using outdated technology. Nearly one in five counties in the United States use punch-card ballots, which are subject to problems like dangling or dimpled chads that do not clearly indicate the voter's intent. Another two in five communities use optically scannable ballots on which the voter uses a pencil to mark the ballot and a scanner records the vote.[37] Although much more reliable than punch cards, scanned ballots are also subject to problems if voters mark outside the box or do not use a pencil.

Voting machines with levers are used in 15 percent of counties, and paper ballots are used in 12 percent. Unlike punch cards, optical scanners, and paper ballots, voting machines do not permit an audit of the vote.[38]

Surprisingly, fewer than 10 percent of counties use electronic or computer voting systems. Such voting could be facilitated by the fact that many high school computer labs are connected to the Internet and could provide voting locations for those that do not have Internet access at home. The costs for these types of reforms are estimated to be around $3.5 billion over five years.[39] One concern will be the secrecy of voting by computer, and another will be how to do a recount. The issue of some audit device, perhaps a paper print-out of each person's vote, was seen by some as a necessary precauton in the move to electronic voting. Most observers agree that voting processes and machinery are in need of an overhaul. Despite these concerns, significant changes in how we vote are certain to occur.

The biggest voting problem in 2004 was long lines in several states. This was more the result of insufficient voting machines and booths than a breakdown in voting technology. The margin of victory for President Bush was large enough that the process was not as contested as in 2000.

Voting by Mail and by Absentee Ballot

Modern technology makes it possible to vote by other means than appearing in person at a voting place on election day. Cities like San Diego, Berkeley, and Vancouver first experimented with holding *elections by mail*. Voters are mailed a pamphlet that describes the questions to be decided in the election and gives instructions on how to complete the ballot and return it by mail. Voters sign the return envelope, and their signature is compared against their signature on the voter registration form. There have been no major problems in administering these local mail ballot elections, and the response has been considerably higher than the norm for in-person special elections.[40]

In January 1996, Oregon voters elected a U.S. senator in a special election through the mail rather than in person. Oregonians had 20 days from the date the ballots were mailed to return them to county clerks, and two-thirds of those who received ballots returned them. Now all Oregon elections are conducted through the mail, including the 2000 and 2002 general elections. There appear to have been few instances of fraud, and the Oregon election officials are strong advocates of vote-by-mail elections in the future.

Opponents of the vote-by-mail system worry about fraud and that voters might be pressured to vote a certain way. A husband might press his wife to vote a certain way, or parents might try and direct the vote of their young adult children still living at home. Another problem might be if supporters of a candidate might visit voters at home soon after the ballots are delivered and pressure people to vote on the spot, perhaps offering to mail the ballot. Supporters point to the higher turnout and lower costs in administering vote-by-mail elections. They also point to the absence of fraud or abuse in the vote-by-mail elections.

A less dramatic reform of election laws is the *absentee ballot*. In most of the country, voters may request a ballot by mail, often without having to state a reason for doing so.[41] Absentee balloting is especially useful for initiative measures. In states like California

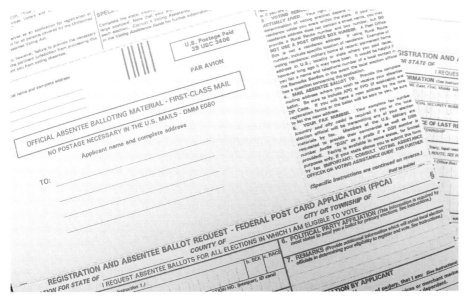

These absentee ballots will be sent to voters in Missouri as an alternative to the conventional practice of going to the polls to vote.

or Washington, where voters may face 20 or more complicated ballot questions, those who vote by absentee ballot can take their time researching and pondering how they are going to vote and do not have to decide within the few minutes they would have in a voting booth.

Increased ease in obtaining ballots has significantly expanded the rate of absentee voting in California. It has been used especially by Republicans to activate retirees and other voters who find it difficult to get from their homes to the polling places. Absentee ballots made up nearly half of all ballots in Washington in 1998.[42] Other states have also liberalized their absentee voting provisions. Oklahoma and Texas, for instance, have *early voting,* whereby voters may vote for several days before an election at several locations in each county.

Absentee ballots also figured in the controversy in the Florida 2000 presidential voting. In two counties, absentee ballot request forms had incorrect voter identification numbers, but the county clerk permitted the Republican party to correct the mistake after the forms were returned to the county. In other Florida counties, some absentee ballots from military personnel did not have postmark dates or were otherwise technically not in compliance with the law. Initially, some counties did not count these ballots, but eventually, most military ballots were counted.

Differences in Nomination Processes

State law establishes the process by which party nominees are selected. Most states use a *primary election,* but some permit the parties to nominate their candidates through a *caucus* or *convention.* In the caucus system, party delegates who are elected in local voting district meetings decide on the party nominee. In some states, a convention narrows the field to two candidates if no candidate gets a set percentage of delegate votes at the party convention.

The dynamics of winning a nomination in states with a caucus system are different from those in states with a primary. In a caucus system, having a grassroots organization that can mobilize voters to attend a neighborhood meeting is essential for candidates. The state best known for the caucus system is Iowa, whose party caucuses yield the first decision in our presidential election system and are covered extensively by the media. Some form of the caucus or convention system is used in about a dozen states.

There are two kinds of party primaries, closed and open. In a **closed primary**, only voters registered in a party may vote in that party's primary. Such a primary discourages **crossover voting**—allowing voters from outside the party to help determine the

closed primary
Primary election in which only persons registered in the party holding the primary may vote.

crossover voting
Voting in another party's primary.

party's nominee—which is why partisans prefer closed primaries. In an **open primary**, any voter can participate in any party's primary. Wisconsin has long had open primaries.

Some states, like Montana, Washington, and California, allowed voters to vote for more than one party in the same primary election; this is called a **blanket primary**. Thus a voter could choose a Democratic nominee for governor and Republican nominees for U.S. senator and attorney general. The blanket primary, according to those who advocated it, encouraged voters to select the best nominees regardless of party and was thought to help moderate candidates. Opponents said it further weakened parties, made our system even more candidate-driven, and gave voters from one party the opportunity to choose the weakest candidate from the opposing party. However, research shows that less than 5 percent of voters actually vote for the weakest candidate from the opposing party.[43] In July 2000, the Supreme Court ruled that blanket primaries are unconstitutional because they violate the right to political association under the First Amendment.[44]

In a primary election, when all the candidates are from the same party, voters make their choices based on candidate appeal and issues. They may also vote for the candidate they perceive has the best chance of winning the general election.[45] California voters rejected an initiative to establish an open primary in 2004.

Louisiana has a unique system. All candidates, regardless of party, run in a single election. If no candidate gets a majority of the votes, there is a runoff election to determine the winner. It is not uncommon for both candidates in a runoff to be from the same party.

Differences in Timing and Frequency of Elections

Federal law sets the date of the presidential election as "the Tuesday next after the first Monday in November, in every fourth year," with similar language applying to elections for the House and Senate. States are free to determine the dates of all other elections, but for ease of administration, they usually consolidate gubernatorial and state general elections on the first Tuesday after the first Monday in November. Two states elect their governor every two years. Five states conduct their elections (primary and general) for governor, other state officials, and the state legislature in odd-numbered years, leaving the even-numbered years for federal elections. Two-thirds of the states (including the two-year states) elect governors in presidential midterm years, halfway between presidential elections.

Separating state elections from presidential or federal elections permits voters to focus more closely on state issues than if they had to vote for state and federal candidates at the same time. Separating elections also means that state and local officials are not as likely to be hurt by an unpopular presidential candidate at the top of the ticket. The passage of campaign finance reform at the federal level may prompt some states to consider off-year state elections. Having state elections in a different year from federal elections may reduce federal oversight and encourage soft money donors to contribute more to state parties.

Some states hold their primaries in late spring, others in mid-September. Primary elections are under the control of state law. Some states have two primaries in presidential years, one for the presidency in the spring and one for other contests in the fall.

State law establishes the rules for local elections but often allows cities and towns some discretion in setting the dates of elections. Many municipal elections are held in the spring of odd-numbered years, again to avoid any positive or negative carryover from candidates running for federal or statewide office. Counties usually conduct their elections at the same time state officials are elected.

State governments can also hold *special elections* to vote on a ballot initiative, a statewide constitutional change, or even a whole new constitution or to replace a U.S. senator who has died or resigned. Participation in special elections varies greatly, depending on what is being decided, but turnout is generally lower than in midterm general elections. Before states hold special elections to fill a vacated U.S. Senate seat, they often have a special primary election to determine the party nominees for that election. In these primaries, turnout is even lower than in the special general election.

open primary
Primary election in which any voter, regardless of party, may vote.

blanket primary
Primary election open to all voters, who may vote for a candidate from any party for each office.

The frequency of our elections and the range of choices sometimes make it hard for voters to pay enough attention to cast informed votes. For this reason, some reformers have proposed consolidating elections to once or twice every couple of years.

Participation

What are the consequences of holding so many elections at so many different times? One is that Americans pick and choose which elections, if any, they participate in. States vary significantly in their rate of **turnout**, the proportion of the voting-age public that votes. Note that political scientists do not calculate turnout on the basis of voter registration because there is such variability in state registration rules that it is unfair to compare the turnout in a state with difficult registration laws with the turnout in a state whose laws make voting registration much more accessible. Rather, turnout is calculated on the Census Bureau's estimate of the voting-age population in each state.

Primaries usually draw fewer voters than general elections, and sometimes the turnout is quite low. Low turnout raises concerns about whether voters in primary elections reflect the general public. Primary voters are generally better educated, earn more money, and are more likely to be white than voters in general elections, who themselves are not representative of the voting-age population.[46] Primary election turnout is also related to strength of partisan identification, ease of voter registration, and the issues in the campaign.

Campaign Finance

In the early 1970s, many states enacted campaign finance disclosure laws, a few instituted partial public financing of elections, and others provided partial underwriting of the costs of parties. **Disclosure** is a common element of campaign finance legislation at the state and local levels. Candidates are typically asked to file disclosure statements specifying where the money came from to finance their campaign. Interest groups are often required to file reports on how they distribute their campaign contributions. Once elected, most state and local officials are required to file a different kind of disclosure form, one that indicates their personal wealth, investments, and other financial matters that may reveal conflicts of interest.

Roughly three-fourths of the states have enacted campaign finance reforms that limit individual contributions, and several states provide some form of public financing. State laws are often patterned after federal law, but states have experimented with lower contribution limits than those allowed in federal elections.[47] Other states have experimented with tax credits to encourage small contributions. In 1996, Maine voters passed a ballot initiative that provided what supporters call a "clean money" option of public financing.[48] Under this system, candidates who agree to raise a limited amount of private money and accept spending limits receive public funds for their campaigns.

Voting on Ballot Questions

Voting on ballot questions is heavily influenced by campaign spending. Presumably, greater expenditures make the most difference when there is a low level of information, as is the case with many ballot propositions. And opinions on ballot propositions are more volatile because voters' views on such matters are not deeply rooted in party affiliation, feelings toward an incumbent, or party appeal.[49]

Because many initiatives are supported by well-funded interests and because a vote in one state can start a national movement on an issue, initiative campaigns can attract large sums of money. Some examples of heavy spending include a 1988 election in Maryland in which the National Rifle Association and other groups spent a record $6.8 million in an unsuccessful attempt to defeat a handgun registration referendum. The tobacco industry spent more than $21 million in California in 1988 to defeat an initiative raising the

---

★ ★ THINKING IT THROUGH

One reason not to vote via the Internet is that not all Americans have access to computers or the Internet. Less-educated and poorer Americans, some of the groups who already turn out to vote less frequently than others, could be further discouraged from participation in elections if this became the means of voting. For example, in 2004, Al Sharpton, a Democrat running in the presidential primaries, criticized Internet voting, calling it a "high-tech poll tax."[*] Conversely, younger people, who tend to vote least often, are the most interested in the Internet, and this may be a means to reach and involve them.

A second reason for not switching to Internet voting is ballot security. How would election officials know if a voter was actually casting someone else's ballot? In 2004 the Pentagon dropped its plans to experiment with Internet voting for American military personnel living overseas. The decision came after a group of academics deemed the Internet so insecure that the integrity of the entire election could be undermined by online voting.[†] The obvious answer is a personal identification number, or PIN, much like what is used for banking purpose. Although such processes are technically possible, they would impose costs on election officials to maintain lists of PINs, to be able to remind voters who forget their PIN, and to create software that handles electronic ballot submissions.

[*]Adam Liptak, "The Nation; Is Internet Voting a 'High-Tech Poll Tax'?" *The New York Times*, January 18, 2004, sec. 4, p. 3.

[†]Dan Keating, "Pentagon Drops Plan to Test Internet Voting; Security Fears Derail $22 Million Experiment," *The Washington Post*, March 31, 2004, p. A23.

Despite all this, many groups still advocate Internet voting. Some Web sites also offer sample Internet voting systems and plans for implementing the process. Some of these sites are www.internetvoting.com, www.safevote.com, and www.election.com. Some groups, like People for Internet Responsibility, maintain that states like Arizona, which have experimented with Internet voting, were too hasty, especially in light of large-scale releases of credit card numbers retrieved from major Internet vendors. To see their statement on Internet voting, go to www.pfir.org.

---

turnout
The proportion of the voting-age public that votes.

disclosure
A requirement that candidates specify where the money came from to finance their campaign.

To encourage voter participation, election signs and ballots are often printed in several languages.

cigarette tax. More than $101 million was spent in California in that year on five initiatives that dealt with automobile insurance reform. A decade later, in what remains one of the most expensive initiative battles in U.S. history, over $92 million was spent for and against a successful initiative to permit casinos on Native American lands in California.[50]

Voting on ballot questions is different from voting for candidates because voters do not have such simplifying factors as party identification and candidate appeal to rely on. More people vote for candidates than vote on ballot questions. Voters who are confused tend to vote no. "Ballot fatigue," tiring from too many contests and questions on the ballot, also makes people more likely to vote no.[51]

Voting in Recall Elections

Recall elections permit citizens to attempt to remove elected public officials from office before the end of their term of office. As with initiatives and referendums, recalls require sufficient petition signatures from registered voters to meet a preestablished threshold. Recall elections have been relatively rare at the statewide level. For example, before the successful 2003 recall of Governor Gray Davis there had been 31 unsuccessful attempts started to recall California governors, none of which made it to the ballot.[52] Only two governors in American history have ever been recalled, including Davis.[53] Some argue that Davis was recalled largely because of his failing political character, which resulted in a lack of goodwill and trust with voters.[54]

The 2003 California recall ballot consisted of two questions: the first asking whether or not to remove Governor Davis from office, and the second asking who should replace Davis if he were recalled.[55] If a majority had voted no on the first question, the results of the second question would not have mattered. Because a majority voted yes on the first question, the person who got the most votes on the second question became the new governor. Other states divide the questions, first having an election to decide whether to recall the official and if a majority votes yes, a second election to determine the replacement.

Recall elections have been more common at the local level, including in elections for school board.

THE FUTURE OF GRASSROOTS DEMOCRACY

Political parties are vital to the operation of our democracy. Many political scientists believe that our system would be strengthened if we had stronger political parties. The first step in the renewal of the parties would be to change their negative image and persuade citizens that political activity is essential to a healthy constitutional democracy. The next would be to give people who support parties a greater say in choosing the candidates who run under their party's label. Although our candidate-centered tradition will certainly remain, it is important to moderate it with strengthened parties that can discipline candidates, at least by withholding resources that candidates cannot easily acquire elsewhere. We would do well to make ballots and elections more voter-friendly. The proliferation of elections, including special elections, turns off even the most committed citizens. Why not, many reformers argue, consolidate elections so that voters might exercise their vote only once or twice, rather than three or four times, a year?

Getting qualified people to run for office is another challenge. The spiraling cost of campaigns and the advantages enjoyed by incumbents have deterred many good potential candidates. Others are repelled by the nasty and negative tone of recent elections. But unless a democracy produces able citizens who are willing to run for office, it loses its ability to hold incumbents accountable.

One of the advantages of 50 states and thousands of communities is that they afford citizens a multitude of opportunities for participation, making involvement less intimidating. The fact that our states do not all have the same approach to elections, parties, or voting also provides valuable data for states considering changing their process. One disadvantage of so many governmental units and so many different elected officials is that they make politics seem more complicated. Citizens willing to become involved, however, often find they can have more influence than they expected.

S U M M A R Y

1. In the United States, there are no national elections, only state elections. Even the presidential election is really a set of 51 different elections to choose electors who will in turn cast their ballots for president. Elections for U.S. senators and representatives are conducted largely under state law.

2. Political parties are essential to the functioning of democracy at all levels, but they are principally organized at the state, congressional district, or county levels. This arrangement makes state parties vitally important. Routinely, they are patterned after the national party organization and include a chair, a vice chair, and a central committee. State parties are often run by full-time party administrators called executive directors.

3. Political parties play important roles in candidate recruitment, voter registration, voter mobilization, and fund raising, and they provide a link between people and government. Parties are also important to the operation of most state legislatures. The governor is the head of his or her party. Governors consider party loyalty when appointing people to executive and judicial openings.

4. Voters usually vote along party lines in state and local elections, although candidate appeal and issues can also influence them.

5. Political parties were once strong and well organized at the local level; in some cities, these organizations were called machines and were led by party bosses. Reaction to the abuses of these machines led to reform efforts. One of these reforms was to make most local politics officially nonpartisan.

6. States vary in whether the two parties are competitive. In one-party states, elections are generally won by one party, while in two-party states, the parties alternate in holding power.

7. State election law is important in defining who may vote, when elections will be held, how party nominees are chosen, and which candidates will appear on the ballot. State election law also establishes a framework for ensuring fair elections.

8. State registration laws make voting more or less difficult, depending on their requirements. States may require persons to register by party to vote in primary elections; when voting is thus limited, the primaries are called closed primaries. Over the course of U.S. history, states have gradually eased registration requirements.

9. Turnout varies by type of election; it is higher in general than primary elections and higher in presidential than midterm elections. Turnout is higher in state than local elections, and regularly scheduled elections typically have higher turnout than special elections. Turnout in vote-by-mail elections is also higher than in in-person elections in most cases. More people vote for major candidate races than vote on ballot questions.

K E Y   T E R M S

party column ballot	**soft money**	**two-party state**	**open primary**
straight ticket	**issue advocacy**	**one-party state**	**blanket primary**
office block ballot	**party caucus**	**closed primary**	**turnout**
split ticket	**redistricting**	**crossover voting**	**disclosure**

F U R T H E R   R E A D I N G

BRUCE E. CAIN AND ELISABETH R. GERBER, EDS., *Voting at the Political Fault Line: California's Experiment with the Blanket Primary* (University of California Press, 2002).

THOMAS M. CARSEY, *Campaign Dynamics: The Race for Governor* (University of Michigan Press, 2000).

THOMAS E. CRONIN, *Direct Democracy: The Politics of Initiative, Referendum, and Recall* (Replica Books, 2000).

PAUL S. HERRNSON, *Party Campaigning in the 1980s* (Harvard University Press, 1988).

MALCOLM E. JEWELL AND SARAH M. MOREHOUSE, *Political Parties and Elections in American States,* 4th ed. (CQ Press, 2001).

V. O. KEY JR., *American State Politics: An Introduction* (Knopf, 1956).

NORMAN R. LUTTBEG, *The Grassroots of Democracy* (Lexington Books, 1999).

DAVID B. MAGLEBY, *Direct Legislation: Voting on Ballot Propositions in the United States* (Johns Hopkins University Press, 1984).

L. SANDY MAISEL AND KARA Z. BUCKLEY, *Parties and Elections in America: The Electoral Process,* 4th ed. (Rowman & Littlefield, 2005).

A. JAMES REICHLEY, ED., *Elections American Style* (Brookings Institution Press, 1987).

ALAN ROSENTHAL, *Governors and Legislators: Contending Powers* (CQ Press, 1990).

ALAN ROSENTHAL, *Legislative Life: People, Process, and Performance in the States* (Harper & Row, 1981).

BYRON E. SHAFER, *The Two Majorities and The Puzzle of Modern American Politics* (University Press of Kansas, 2003).

LINDA WITT, KAREN M. PAGET, AND GLENNA MATTHEWS, *Running as a Woman: Gender and Politics in American Politics* (Free Press, 1994).

JOSEPH FRANCIS ZIMMERMAN, *The Initiative: Citizen Lawmaking* (Greenwood Press, 1999).

STATE LEGISLATURES

24

S tate legislatures existed long before the Continental Congress was formed in 1776 and exerted great power under the Articles of Confederation. Having existed as the primary form of government even under British colonial rule, state legislatures were reluctant to give up their power to either the national government or their own governors. Most states had relatively weak executives, and several had no executive at all. Indeed, the creation of the Constitution was in part a reaction against the excessive power of the state legislatures, which is why the framers of the Constitution imposed limits on the powers of the state legislatures (see especially Article I, Section 9).

The Tenth Amendment to the U.S. Constitution makes it clear that any power not given to the national government or denied to the states lies with the states or with the people. State constitutions, in turn, give some of this reserved power exclusively to nonlegislative agencies and specifically deny some to the legislature. What is left is inherited by the state legislatures.

Although state legislatures today do not dominate state policy making the way they did in 1787, they do play a vital role in state politics and policy. State legislators strive to solve problems and provide services—and do so, whenever possible, without raising taxes or creating larger bureaucracies. Legislators these days seek to make the legislature a counterbalance to powerful governors and powerful state bureaucracies.

In recent years, legislatures have been involved in a remarkable variety of activities:

- Colorado's legislature adopted stronger gun control legislation.

- New Hampshire legislators voted to prevent the use of death penalty sentencing.

- Vermont voted to recognize "civil unions" between same-sex couples, granting them virtually all the benefits, protections, and responsibilities given to married couples.

- Mississippi legislators overrode their governor's veto of a major Medicaid program.

- South Carolina legislators voted, by a narrow margin, to remove the Confederate flag over their statehouse dome but allowed it to fly over a monument on the capitol grounds.

- Hawaii's legislature approved the medical use of marijuana.

- The Tennessee legislature overrode the governor's veto and enacted an $18.3 billion budget without a state income tax their governor had demanded.

- New York adopted legislation banning hand-held cell phone use while driving.

- By enacting large penalties for "excessive prices," Maine has attempted to force down drug prices.

- Many states have adopted some form of election reform, including new ballots, a ban on punch cards, and new computer voting systems.

- Many states launched new homeland security programs in the wake of September 11.

In short, legislatures everywhere make or modify policies on all kinds of issues by balancing conflicting political pressures, while facilitating compromises between political factions or different parts of the state. They also make laws and modify and approve budgets. Legislatures perform countless constituency services and, along with the governor and the courts, help keep state agencies accountable to both the laws and the citizens. Legislators must constantly reconcile pressures among competing interest groups. Representing local views at the state level, they dramatize issues and bring them into the open. A state legislature serves as a lightning rod to which most of the conflicting pressures of American society are drawn.

This chapter will examine state legislatures in greater detail by asking what they do, how they are organized, and how they have adapted to a much more complex world. As they have grown into more professional bodies, state legislatures are claiming a greater role in how government works and are important partners in both state policy and federal action.

THE LEGISLATIVE BRANCH

The 50 state legislatures share many characteristics—all states except Nebraska have a two-house **bicameral legislature**. Nebraska has a one-house **unicameral legislature**.[1] The larger chamber is generally called the house of representatives. (In a few states, it is called the assembly or house of delegates.) It contains from as few as 40 members in Alaska and 41 in Delaware to as many as 400 members in New Hampshire and 203 in Pennsylvania; the average number is around 100. In all but five states, representatives serve two-year terms; in Alabama, Louisiana, Maryland, Mississippi, and North Dakota, representatives serve for four years. The smaller chamber, known as the senate, is typically composed of about 40 members. State senators serve four-year terms in most states.

But state legislatures also differ in important ways, not the least of which is their basic level of professionalism, generally defined as having full-time legislators, more staff, and higher pay, which in turn may draw more ambitious candidates for office and longer service.

How Do Legislatures Compare?

Legislative professionalism sometimes, but not always, correlates with the number of seats in the legislature. The professional nature of state legislatures is in part a product of population but also a product of how many representatives the state has chosen to

bicameral legislature
A two-house legislature.

unicameral legislature
A one-house legislature.

have. Certain states, such as New Hampshire and Wyoming, have part-time "citizen leg-islatures," whereas New York and California are sometimes characterized as full-time professional legislatures.

In the New Hampshire House of Representatives, for example, legislators are es-sentially volunteers. These "citizen-legislators" represent districts of about 3,000 people. They earn just $200 for the two-year term and meet for no more than 45 days a year. In contrast, the California Assembly has 80 members, each representing a district of about 450,000 people. California legislators earn $99,000 a year in addition to expense al-lowances, meet nearly all year long, and consider their legislative work a full-time oc-cupation (see Table 24–1).

Legislative salaries are most often set by the legislature. Most legislators are reluc-tant to increase their salaries, and as a result, lawmakers' salaries lag well behind the rate of inflation and increases in the cost of living. Most people run for the legislature for reasons other than compensation. "No one goes into politics to get rich," notes

---

TABLE 24–1   THE DIVERSITY OF STATE LEGISLATURES

State legislatures across the country vary greatly in many respects. The National Confer-ence of State Legislatures grouped them into three types based on their length of session.

RED: Full- or Near-Full-Time, High-Pay, Large-Staff "Professional Legislatures"

Alaska	New York
California	New Jersey
Florida	Ohio
Illinois	Pennsylvania
Massachusetts	Wisconsin
Michigan	

WHITE: In-Between Hybrid

Alabama	Minnesota
Arkansas	Missouri
Arizona	Nebraska
Colorado	North Carolina
Connecticut	Oklahoma
Delaware	Oregon
Hawaii	South Carolina
Iowa	Tennessee
Kansas	Texas
Kentucky	Virginia
Louisiana	Washington
Maryland	

BLUE: Part-Time, Low-Pay, Small-Staff "Citizen Legislatures"

Georgia	New Mexico
Idaho	North Dakota
Indiana	Rhode Island
Maine	South Dakota
Mississippi	Utah
Montana	Vermont
Nevada	West Virginia
New Hampshire	Wyoming

Source: National Conference of State Legislatures, "Full-Time and Part-Time Legislatures," www.ncsl.org/programs/legman/about/partfulllegis.htim, accessed April 27, 2004.

Massachusetts state Senator Tom Birmingham. "But you can't have a system where only the rich get into politics."[2]

Legislatures also differ by the level of activity. Forty-three state legislatures meet every year from January through May or June. Legislatures in seven states, including Arkansas, Montana, Nevada, and Texas, meet only every other year. Some state constitutions limit their legislatures to regular sessions of a fixed number of days, usually 60 or 90. Such restrictions reflect distrust of government and the feeling that "the faster we get it over with, the better." *Special sessions* have been developed to get around these limitations. The governor has the power to call the legislature into special session and in some states to determine the issues that may be discussed in the special session—a power governors frequently use. The trend in many states has been to somewhat longer annual legislative sessions and higher salaries.

How Are Legislatures Organized?

State legislatures look very very much like the United States Congress, or vice versa. A s*peaker,* usually chosen by the majority party, presides over the lower house. In many states, speakers have more power to control proceedings than their national counterpart has. For example, most state speakers have the right to appoint committees and thus play a key role in determining policy. But the power of speakers varies greatly: Speakers have great powers in West Virginia, New Hampshire, and Arizona but minimal powers in Alaska, Mississippi, Hawaii, and Wyoming.[3] In 26 states, lieutenant governors preside over the senate, though they are usually mere figureheads; in other states, the presiding officer is chosen by the majority party in the senate.[4]

As in the U.S. Congress, the committee system prevails. In several states, such as Maine and Massachusetts, *joint committees* are used to speed up legislative action. However, state legislative committees usually do not have the same power over bills as their national counterparts: Some still lack adequate professional assistance, the seniority system is not as closely followed as in Congress, and membership turnover is somewhat higher, especially where term limits have taken effect.

Every legislature has committees on education, transportation, agriculture, and energy or natural resources. Most also have important committees on rules, appropriations, and taxes (sometimes called the Ways and Means Committee). Legislators generally specialize and become experts on one or two substantive matters, such as education, crime, taxation, or the budget process. As in any organization or large assembly, an individual earns respect and influence primarily by developing specialized knowledge about either policy or procedural matters.

Once again, however, there are striking differences among state legislatures. Some have excellent staff and splendid information technology and are well-run professional organizations. The New York legislature has nearly 3,100 permanent staffers, for example, Pennsylvania has nearly 3,000, and California has 2,300. Others have not changed in decades.[5] North Dakota has just 31 permanent staff for the entire legislature, for example, while New Mexico has 49, Idaho has 75, and Delaware has 84. These and other differences sometimes stem from historical or ethnic traditions. They can also arise from urban-rural or east-west factional splits and sometimes from regional differences, as is the case with the "Hill people" versus the "Delta people" in Mississippi. Here is how one expert on state politics viewed some of the more distinctive characteristics shaping state politics in the United States:

> In New York professional politics, political wheeling and dealing and frantic activity are characteristic. In Virginia, one gets a sense of tradition, conservatism, and gentility. . . . Louisiana's politics are wild and flamboyant. By contrast, moderation and caution are features of Iowa. A strong disposition of compromise pervades Oregon, with politicians disposed to act as brokers and deal pragmatically rather than dogmatically. In Kansas, hard work, respect for authority, fiscal prudence, and a general conservatism and resistance to rapid social change are pervasive features of the state environment. Indiana is intensely partisan. Wyoming is mainly individualistic, and Ohio is fundamentally conservative. In Hawaii, the relatively recent political dominance of Japanese

and the secondary status of Chinese, native Hawaiians, and Haoles (whites) makes for tough ethnic politics. Yankee Republicans used to run Massachusetts, but now the Irish dominate. Their personalized style, which blends gregariousness and political loyalty, results in a politics of the clan. Mormonism of course dominates Utah.[6]

Who Serves in the State Legislature?

Like members of the U.S. Congress, the vast majority of state legislators run for reelection and win. Indeed, about one-third of state legislative elections are uncontested; this is especially true in smaller, one-party states and in the South.[7]

An incumbent seeking reelection has many advantages over a challenger: name recognition, better access to campaign funds, experience in running campaigns, and a record of helping with constituent problems. Also like members of the U.S. Congress, few legislators feel politically secure, even when they have not been opposed in the last election.

In an incumbent's mind, there is seldom such a thing as a "safe district" and a sure reelection. "Whatever their margins of victory in prior elections, however 'safe' their district may appear to the analyst, incumbents know that lightning can strike. . . . They have seen colleagues relax their efforts and subsequently lose their seats. They live in perpetual danger of casting a roll-call vote that upsets their constituency or mobilizes a key interest group to seek their defeat."[8] Incumbents also worry about scandals in their party or having to run with an unpopular candidate at or near the top of their party ticket.

THE DEMOGRAPHIC PROFILE The typical American state legislator is a 48-year-old white male, well educated and well off, often a businessman or lawyer of Anglo-Saxon origin who has had some type of previous political experience—not always elective— at the city or county level. Some have worked as a staff member in the legislature or in state government.[9] Most state legislators have held some type of local party position and have been active in political campaigns. Surprisingly, about one-third were born in some other state, a reflection of our increasingly mobile population.

State legislators tend to have more education and higher incomes than other citizens in their states. They are usually hardworking, public-spirited citizens who believe being in the legislature is a good opportunity for service. Yet state legislators enjoy less prestige than members of Congress, especially in states that have large legislatures. Discouraged by modest salaries and long hours, many serve a few terms and then either retire voluntarily or run for higher office. Some leave after just a couple of terms because they get bored listening to matters that do not interest them. As one one-termer explained, "A great deal in the political process does not—repeat, does not—involve the glamorous policy issues. Most of the work is sheer routine and hardly awe-inspiring."[10] And, of course, some are now leaving because of term limits in their states that prevent more than two or three terms.

PARTY AFFILIATION At the start of 2004, the state legislatures were almost evenly divided between the two parties. Democrats occupied 2,676 of the 5,411 House seats, while Republicans occupied 2,715; similarly, Democrats held 950 of the 1,971 Senate seats, while Republicans held 969. Only 70 of the nation's state legislators consider themselves Independents or nonpartisan, including all 49 members of Nebraska's unicameral legislature.[11] Given these margins, a change of just three seats would alter party control of 25 legislative chambers, House or Senate, in 22 states.

Party control was even tighter following the 2004 elections. Democrats picked up one legislature, giving them a 20 to 20 tie with Republicans, with 10 states divided.

OCCUPATION Lawyers continue to be the largest occupational group in most state legislatures, yet the percentage of attorneys has leveled off; today attorneys constitute only about 17 percent of state legislators nationwide. There has been an increase in those who consider themselves full-time legislators, and there has been a slight increase as well of teachers, homemakers, retirees, and students.[12] Real estate and insurance dealers and sales representatives are also commonly found in legislatures (see Figure 24–1).

CHANGING FACE OF AMERICAN POLITICS

WOMEN IN THE STATEHOUSE

In the late 1960s, state legislatures were dominated by men and often had the look of a "good old boys' club." This has changed in recent years as more women have been elected, bringing the national average up from just 4.5 percent in 1971 to 22 percent in 2004. Thirty-nine percent of the Washington State legislative seats are occupied by women, followed by Colorado at 34 percent, Maryland at 33 percent, New Mexico at 31 percent, and California at 30 percent. In South Carolina, by contrast, only 9 percent of the lawmakers are women.

As women have won more legislative seats, their influence has grown, particularly as more women win election to key legislative posts. In addition, women increasingly occupy key committee positions and often meet to plan strategies on women's issues.

It is not clear if the election of women to state legislatures has made a significant difference in how women are represented. Although some analysts believe female legislators are more likely to offer leadership on women, family, and children's policy issues,* other scholars have found little or no difference in how men and women deal with gender policy issues.†

Although more women and African Americans are winning election to state legislatures, both groups are still notably in the minority. Of the 7,382 state legislators in 2004, 22 percent were women, 9 percent were African American, and just 3 percent were Hispanic.

Female members of the Washington legislature constitute the highest percentage of women in any legislature in the nation's history.

Current Percentage of Women in State Legislatures.
SOURCE: Center for the American Women and Politics; reprinted from *The New York Times*, January 4, 1999, p. A18. Updated by the authors.

*See Sue Thomas, *How Women Legislate* (Oxford University Press, 1996). See also Kathleen Bratton and Kerry L. Haynie, "Agenda Setting and Legislative Success in State Legislatures: The Effects of Gender and Race," *Journal of Politics* 61 (August 1999), pp. 658–679.
†Beth Reingold, *Representing Women: Sex, Gender, and Legislative Behavior in Arizona and California* (University of North Carolina Press, 2000).

SOURCE: National Conference of State Legislatures, "Legislator Demographics," www.ncsl.org/programs/legman/about/demographic_overview.htm, accessed April 27, 2004.

The number of farmers continues to fall as redistricting continues to shift power away from rural areas and as the number of farms declines. Moreover, longer sessions of the legislatures make it less possible to be both a farmer and a legislator. When legislatures used to meet for just a few months in winter, farmers were able to fit their schedules to the legislative cycle.

Because legislators must have flexible schedules, the job often attracts retired people and those whose businesses or professional practices have been so successful that they can afford to take time off. Legislators used to identify themselves by their occupations outside the legislature, but this is less the case now; many refer to their occupation as legislator.

What State Legislators Do

The nation's 7,382 state legislators engage in many of the same lawmaking and oversight activities as members of the U.S. Congress: They enact laws that create state parks; specify salaries for state officials; draw up rules governing state elections; fix state tax rates; set workers' compensation policies; determine the quantity and quality of state correctional, mental health, and educational institutions; and oversee welfare programs. State legislators approve all appropriations and thereby confirm or modify a governor's proposed budget. Legislators in most states are also responsible for overseeing the administration of public policy. Although they do not administer programs directly, legislators can and do determine whether programs are being carried out according to legislative intentions through hearings, investigations, audits, and the budgetary process. Bill passage rate varies greatly from state to state, depending on a variety of factors, including procedural necessities, constitutional requirements, and local culture. Figure 24–2 outlines the steps involved in passing state laws.

State legislatures perform various functions within the larger federal system, such as ratifying proposed amendments to the U.S. Constitution, exercising the right to petition Congress to call for a constitutional convention in order to propose an amendment to the U.S. Constitution, and approving interstate compacts on matters affecting state policies and their implementation. The national government has recently turned back many health and welfare responsibilities to the states.

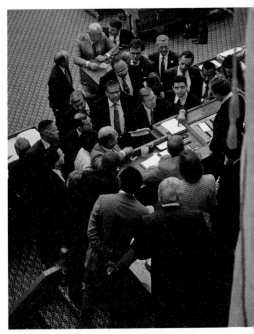

FIGURE 24–1 A Profile of State Legislators.
Source: National Conference of State Legislatures.

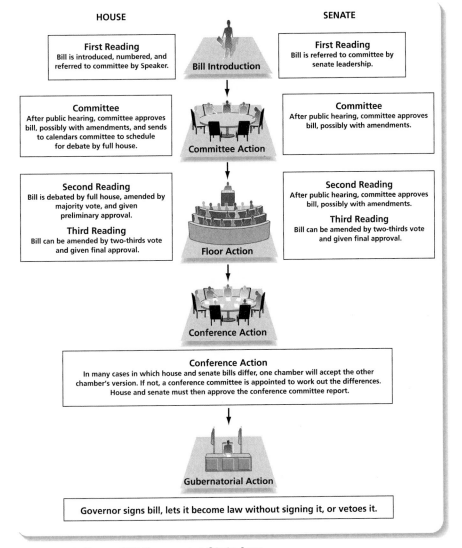

FIGURE 24–2 How a Bill Becomes a State Law.

Members of the Texas House of Representatives gather around the speaker's podium to iron out a disputed point.

Each state's constitution prescribes the procedures its legislatures must follow and sets limits on the rate of taxation, the kinds of taxes, the subjects that may be taxed, and the purposes of taxation. State legislatures participate in amending their states' constitutions by proposing amendments for voter ratification. Legislatures also have authority to impeach and try state officials, and they also are involved in the appointive process.

State legislators help translate public wants and aspirations into laws and regulations. In addition to their lawmaking functions, they also try to be ombudsmen—to listen, learn, and find solutions to problems. Invariably, state legislators wind up doing a lot of favors: getting a merchant a license to sell lottery tickets, persuading some state agency to look into safety standards at the local hospital, pushing for funds to repair county roads, arranging for a campaign supporter to be appointed to the state labor commission, and so on. State legislators are accessible. Citizens and students can nearly always contact their legislators directly and communicate with them in person, by telephone, or via e-mail.

With the growth of state functions, legislators are spending increasing amounts of time on casework or constituency services. Constituent relations are often the most time-consuming aspect of a legislator's job. Local city and school officials always need the help of legislators, and interest groups back home are always pressing their views. Legislators usually try hard to perform constituent casework because they recognize its political value. The more help they give to home-district citizens and businesses, they

PEOPLE & POLITICS *Making a Difference* ★ ★ ★

GARNET F. COLEMAN

Garnet F. Coleman entered the Texas state legislature in 1991 at age thirty representing Houston's urban center. Ten years later, he was named one of *Governing* magazine's top public officials of the year, largely for his work to expand health insurance coverage for uninsured children and poor families in Texas. Given the state's low-tax, limited-government history, the task has been difficult at best.

Yet, as *Governing* reports, he was able to build support slowly but surely over time until he finally convinced his colleagues in the legislature to simplify access for the state's nearly 600,000 children who were eligible for government health care but had not been enrolled by their parents or guardians.[*]

As Coleman had discovered, the state not only required parents and guardians to fill out as many as 14 different forms to enroll but also demanded regular recertification. Coleman's legislation shortened the form to just four pages and helped give one-third of the state's uninsured children access to coverage. Cole-

man was also a key sponsor of Texas welfare reform and pushed hard for expanded funding for children's services as a member of the House Committee on Public Health.

Inside the legislature, Coleman is known as a workaholic who never gives up. Outside the legislature, he is equally well known for his public battle with depression. In 1994, he was hospitalized for depression following his father's death. Instead of hiding his mental illness, he opened up to the public and his constituents about the need to increase access to mental health care, and cosponsored legislation to require private insurance companies to offer mental health coverage alongside more traditional physical health coverage and emergency care.

Like most state legislators, Coleman also works hard for his district. He was responsible for designing the funding mechanisms to cover the cost of Houston's new baseball and basketball stadiums, and he expanded funding for Texas Southern University, the University of

Houston, and Prairie View A & M. He worked to provide more than $200 million in special scholarship money to cover the Toward Excellence, Access and Success (TEXAS) scholarship program for disadvantaged students, which includes funding for Coleman's Teach for Texas program. Under the program, public school teachers receive scholarship support in return for a commitment to teach for at least three years in an underserved community.

[*]Alan Greenblatt, "Garnet F. Coleman: Health Crusader," *Governing*, November 2001, p. 37.

reason, the more they will earn respect, win reelection, or perhaps gather support for election to higher office.

What Legislative Committees Do

A legislative committee is where bills get drafted, hearings are held, and the general policy making and preliminary lawmaking takes place. Committees vary in power and influence from state to state. In general, however, the influence of committees has increased in recent decades. They used to be pale shadows of their counterparts in the U.S. Congress, and they often still are in the less populous states because of short sessions, limited staffing, and turnover of both staff and legislators. Still, legislative committees process and shape hundreds or even thousands of bills and resolutions every year.[13]

Committees do the legislature's work. They consider and amend legislation, oversee the implementation of the laws, interview judges, and serve as the major access point for citizens, interest groups, and lobbyists. The functions of a legislative committee are advisory; all of its proposals are subject to review, approval, or rejection by the legislative body of which it is a part.

Some of the functions of standing committees or interim committees include:

- Studying pending legislation
- Conducting public hearings on proposed bills and resolutions
- Debating and modifying initial proposals
- Grading legislation in terms of desirability
- Screening, eliminating, or burying undesirable legislation
- Confirming key administrative personnel
- Monitoring or overseeing administrative practices and regulations

The committee system allows members to concentrate their energies on specific areas of governmental operations. Over time, legislative committees and their members develop extensive knowledge about particular activities and provide greatly valued information about the content and desirability of proposed bills to their colleagues. Since it is impossible for everybody to be an expert on all aspects of state government, properly staffed and run committees can evaluate the merits and faults of a proposed law more effectively than any individual legislator can.

How State Legislators Decide

State legislators are influenced by many of the same factors that affect members of the U.S. Congress, including personal ideology and policy positions. For part-time, less professionalized legislatures, however, party membership and interest group pressure are much more important to legislative outcomes.

POLITICAL PARTIES Except in Nebraska, candidates for state legislatures are nominated by political parties in primaries or by party conventions and caucuses, and they are elected *as party members*. Although the official party organization is sometimes not a dominant influence in recruiting state legislative candidates, a candidate nonetheless has to go through the party to gain the nomination. Figure 24–3 shows the current party control of the state legislatures.

The role of political parties in the governance of legislatures and in policy making varies widely from state to state. In nearly half the states—especially in the urban, industrialized states and in the Northeast—the political party is a key factor in decision making. In other states—in the Southwest, for example—parties appear less significant. Coalitions there tend to form along rural-urban, conservative-liberal, or regional lines.

Parties in most states are less influential than they used to be. Candidates welcome what help they can get from the parties, but that is often not much. However, in some states, party leaders in the legislature raise and allocate campaign contributions that prove helpful to those running for the first or second time, particularly in competitive races. Party organizations and political action committees are major sources of money

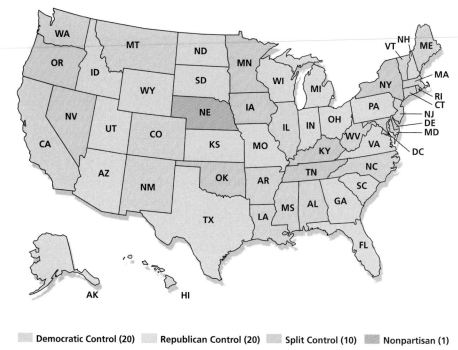

Democratic Control (20)   Republican Control (20)   Split Control (10)   Nonpartisan (1)

FIGURE 24–3 Party Control of State Legislatures, 2005.

for many legislative candidates. Still, legislative candidates almost always have to form their own personal organization, separate from the local party apparatus, to wage a winning campaign.

In nearly every state where there are two active parties, the political party selects legislative leaders and assigns members to committees. Party leaders in many state legislatures distribute sought-after perks, ranging from committee assignments to parking spaces. **Party caucuses**—meetings of all the members of one party in the chamber— also distribute campaign funds to their members and to specifically targeted districts.

Party unity on policy matters is typically found in states with a highly competitive two-party system. In those states, party caucuses develop party positions, and party members are expected to support them in the legislative chambers. In a few states, binding votes in party caucuses virtually (although not legally) force party members to vote as a unified bloc on the floor of their chamber. Binding caucus votes are taken on relatively few issues, however. Voting regularly with the party and being a member of the majority party can help legislators win discretionary grants or other favors for their districts.

The party caucus is a principal instrument for legislative decision making in about half the states, including Colorado, Delaware, Idaho, Montana, California, and Utah. In states where a party holds a slim majority of the seats in a legislative chamber, representatives are more likely to feel pressure to "toe the party line" than where a party commands a large majority.[14] Similarly, legislators are more likely to vote with their party in states where the political party plays an important role in recruiting and nominating candidates.

In legislatures in which a single party has had long-standing dominance or control, as used to be in some southern states, parties are less important in conducting and shaping legislative business. Because of the recent rise of the Republican party in the South and Southwest, however, parties and partisanship are gradually increasing in strength in such states as Florida, Texas, and North Carolina. A rebirth of partisanship and growing attention to elections of legislators are apparently making the parties more important than they have been in the past.

INTEREST GROUPS   Interest groups are a significant and growing source of influence on state legislatures. Teacher organizations, trade associations, labor groups, trial attorneys, taxpayer associations, insurance, mining, real estate, road builders, and banking interests are often the most visible single-interest groups. In states with an obvious

party caucus
A meeting of the members of a party in a legislative chamber to select party leaders and develop party policy.

major economic interest, such as agriculture, mining, lumbering, or fishing, legislators pay close attention to the needs of that interest, regardless of whether the group employs lobbyists. The legislatures in these states seldom pass legislation hostile to their own state's principal economic interests.

Most state interest groups use lobbying as a major tool of influence. **Lobbying** is attempting to influence the decisions of public officials, especially legislators. The right to lobby is secured by the First and Fourteenth Amendments to the Constitution, which protect the right of the people to petition the government for redress of grievances. State constitutions provide similar protections.

Anyone can try to influence how a state legislator votes. States usually define a professional **lobbyist** as someone who is paid to influence legislators on behalf of a client or clients. States now require lobbyists to register annually, either with the secretary of state's office or with an election or lobbyist commission. In most states, lobbyists must pay a fee for lobbying. In Texas, for example, professional lobbyists pay a $300 fee, although lobbyists for tax-exempt public interest groups pay only $100.

Hundreds of lobbyists openly ply their trade in the committee rooms and corridors of the state capitols. The more populated states register thousands of lobbyists. In one recent year, Texas and New York each registered as many as 1,800 professional lobbyists. At least 1,200 lobbyists work the state capitol in California. Even less-populated Vermont had more than 600 lobbyists registered with the secretary of state.

Most lobbyists are regular employees of corporations, unions, or trade associations. Many are members of law firms; others are former state employees. Effective lobbyists are specialists in both subject matter and legislative procedure. Lobbyists for organized interests know the schedule of general hearings, committee meetings, floor debates, and social events. They also know as much as possible about the legislators, their electoral support, their values, their hobbies, and who has their "ear." They are present and prepared when their interests are affected. Veteran lobbyists know how to influence legislators. Lobbyists live by two important rules: First, it's a lot easier to kill a bill than to pass it. And second, work in such a way that you have no permanent allies and no permanent enemies. Today's opponent may be your supporter on the next issue for which you are lobbying.[15]

Some of the most effective lobbyists are retired state legislators. They not only have good contacts with their former colleagues, they know where the leverage points are in the legislative process. "If you happen to know the four people on a certain senate committee," said one Colorado legislator, "it's pretty damn easy to kill a bill."[16]

Lobbyists have two sources of influence: (1) information and (2) campaign support. Information is usually the key ingredient in gaining or losing a vote. Lobbyists are useful providers of such information to anyone who can influence state policy making. "Lobbyists are strategists, tacticians, builders of coalitions among groups, experts and communicators. They testify in committees, buttonhole lawmakers one-on-one, organize meetings between their members and legislators, stage rallies and demonstrations, and try to put a favorable 'spin' on media coverage of their issues."[17] Plainly, however, lobbyists recognize that information and statistics are malleable and can be used to either support or oppose a bill.

In addition, interest groups are usually the major financial backers of incumbent legislators, and in return the lobbyists for those groups get unusual access. As the costs of state legislative races climb, so does the dependence of legislators, legislative leaders, and political parties on organized interests.[18]

Illegal use of lobbying techniques, primarily bribery, has been found in some states. Scandals have been exposed in Arkansas, Arizona, Kentucky, Massachusetts, New Mexico, and South Carolina, among others, in recent years.

Still, bribery is not a widespread problem in most states. Writing about his own experiences in the Vermont Senate, Frank Smallwood observed that as a general rule, most of the lobbyists "were articulate, hard-working, and extremely well informed in their particular areas of expertise. This last attribute—information—represented their chief weapon and gave them real clout. As far as I could find out, the lobbyists didn't offer legislators any money or other direct inducements, at least, they never offered me anything, not even a sociable drink. Instead they relied on information."[19]

State representatives often meet with local constituents to discuss local concerns.

lobbying
Engaging in activities aimed at influencing public officials, especially legislators, and the policies they enact.

lobbyist
A person who is employed by and acts for an organized interest group or corporation to influence policy decisions and positions in the executive and legislative branches.

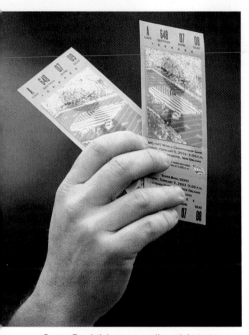

Super Bowl tickets as well as tickets to other major sports events are sometimes used as bribes by individuals who want to influence specific state or federal representatives.

In recent years, states have sought to regulate lobbying activities, conflicts of interest, and the financing of political campaigns. Wisconsin and Minnesota ban such favors as buying meals for a legislator. In the wake of a 1992 Federal Bureau of Investigation sting, lawmakers in Kentucky are now barred from taking anything from a lobbyist except $100 per year in meals and drinks. State senators in New York voluntarily declined the meals and gifts worth more than $25 that interest groups had routinely lavished on them.[20]

Not all these reforms have been easy to implement, nor have they all worked according to the original intentions. Laws that control lobbying and regulate how much individuals may spend to influence either elections or the legislative process are difficult to enforce. It is sometimes unclear, too, whether they infringe on the constitutional right of persons to petition their government and to spend their own money for political purposes.[21]

OTHER INFLUENCES ON STATE LEGISLATORS   A legislator's personality, leadership style, and conception of responsibilities influence how he or she will vote and perform constituent service.

Much as they promise to clean up state government and cut wasteful spending, many legislators fight hard to see that their own district gets a fair share of state government construction projects and subsidies. Voting for one's home district makes sense to many legislators. Former state legislator John E. Brandl writes that state legislators understand that on election day, their constituents who are grateful for favors received "are more apt to express positive sentiments on the ballot than those not receiving benefits from the capitol. . . . A former colleague of mine in the Minnesota House of Representatives seemed bewildered when he heard the suggestion that his first responsibility as a legislator might not be to look out for his district but rather to be concerned for the good of the whole state. 'Nobody who thinks like that could ever get elected from my district,' he maintained."[22]

But if state legislators are elected to represent the people and their views at the statehouse, few lawmakers think they should merely mirror or "re-present" the views of their district's constituents. Most legislators like to consider themselves **trustees** of their constituents, claiming to rely on their own conscience or on their considered judgments in making decisions. Legislators who view themselves as **delegates**, by contrast, adhere more closely to instructions from their constituents. Not surprisingly, the trustee role is not only more popular but also easier and more realistic to practice. Given the complexity of government and the difficulty of finding out where citizens stand on a wide variety of issues, the trustee role is a more workable one in the day-to-day decision making of a legislator during legislative sessions.

Views of constituents back home are influential on matters such as taxes and major construction on highway projects, yet on most issues, the people back home have little direct influence on lawmaking. On issues that are of keen local interest, legislators certainly do take their constituents into account when they vote. In other words, state lawmakers act as trustees on some issues and delegates on others. Yet conscience and personal philosophy are seldom the only, or even the most important, guide. Colleagues, committee recommendations, party leadership, staff counsel, and lobbying by the affected interests are also influential.

Newly elected legislators soon learn it makes sense to depend on friendly colleagues to inform them about issues. According to a Pennsylvania legislator, "Very early in the session, you try to find other representatives who sit on other committees and who are similar to you in their outlook politically. When a bill comes to the floor for a vote, you have to look to that person, you have to trust him."[23]

Another aspect of state politics that often fuels legislation is action taken by other states. Legislators frequently ask their staffs, "What is California, Minnesota, or Oregon doing on this problem?" Legislators are always on the lookout for innovative tax, educational, or welfare policies implemented elsewhere. Legislators are keenly interested in how their state compares to others in certain areas—on sales taxes, for example, high school dropouts, clean air, or federal moneys coming to the state. The press often uses such rankings in headlines and editorials.

The National Conference of State Legislatures, a nonpartisan professional organization funded by all 50 state legislatures, acts as an effective clearinghouse for new ideas

trustee
An official who is expected to vote independently, based on his or her judgment of the circumstances; one interpretation of the role of a legislator.

delegate
An official who is expected to represent the views of his or her constituents even when personally holding divergent views; one interpretation of the role of a legislator.

(www.ncsl.org). With about 180 staff members located mainly in Denver, Colorado, it distributes studies to legislators across the country. A rival yet smaller and more conservative group, the American Legislative Exchange Council, has developed in recent years (www.alec.org). The Council of State Governments (www.csg.org) and the State Legislative Leaders Foundation (www.sllf.org) are two groups that also help serve state legislative leaders.

Actions taken by the federal government also influence state laws and regulations. Over the past 30 years, state legislatures have been burdened by **federal mandates**, which require states to allocate state funds to match federally stipulated programs such as Medicare. Funding for federal mandates was often the fastest-growing part of a state's budget, a sore point with state legislators. In the 1990s, Congress began to place some mild restraints on the growth of federal mandates.

MODERNIZATION AND REFORM

As states are asked to take on increasing responsibility, their legislatures face greater pressure to modernize: Lobbying is more intense than ever, campaign costs have increased, and fewer members follow the old folkways that used to make for an almost clubhouse collegiality in most legislatures. The greater participation of women, minorities, and more independent-minded legislators has meant a broader mix of agendas and ideas. The influence of legislative leaders has decreased, and that of the media and staff has grown.[24] According to state legislative scholar Alan Rosenthal, "Earlier, leaders were truly in command, and power was tightly held. Partly as a consequence of modernization and reform, legislatures have been democratized. Resources are more broadly distributed, and the gap between leaders and other legislators is narrower."[25]

State legislatures in the past were criticized as inefficient, ineffective, poorly staffed, boss-ridden, secretive, sexist, unrepresentative, and often dominated by rural interests. Most legislatures had little or no staff and high rates of turnover among members. Legislators had to rely primarily on information that came to them from lobbyists or the governor's office. Legislatures were often run by factions that could not be held accountable, and parliamentary procedures and inadequate committee systems either prevented action or served narrow or specially favored interests.

> Given the goals of members, the demands of groups, and the heavy workload, deliberation gives way to expediency. Members frequently are unwilling to say no to their colleagues, lest their colleagues say no to them. They also are averse to saying no to constituents, lest their constituents withdraw support. The process has become porous; much seeps through that probably should not. Standing committees do not screen the wheat from the chaff as diligently as they might.[26]

Most state legislatures have adopted internal reforms to address these perceived shortcomings. Thus most legislatures now have longer annual sessions, expanded and more competent staffs, more effective committee systems, streamlined procedures such as automated bill status and statute retrieval systems, higher salaries, and modern information systems.[27] In 1979, for example, state legislatures had 16,930 permanent staffers; by 2003, the number had climbed to 28,067.

Legislatures have also become more sensitive to new technologies. Every legislature now has a colorful Web site with detailed information about the workings of the lawmaking body. Hawaii has a fully equipped and staffed "public access room," making it easy for citizens to lobby their state legislators.[28] Virginia is considered a leader in e-government technology for its commitment to citizen–legislator communication through e-mail.[29] And most important, prodded by federal court rulings, legislative districts are now approximately equal in population and thus more representative of the people.

In short, the largely amateur, part-time state legislatures are a thing of the past in most states. The new professionalism reflects a determination on the part of most legislators—especially the leaders—to take charge of their own branch as major players in shaping state public policy.

federal mandate
A requirement imposed by the federal government as a condition for the receipt of federal funds.

"Yes, I think some officials should be limited to one or two terms, and others to none."

The movement to encourage full-time professional legislatures with substantial staffs, however, has not been universally praised. In fact, in recent years, some political scientists and some citizens have contended that we were better off when we had part-time citizen-legislators. The groundswell in the early 1990s to enact term limits was in many ways a voters' protest against professionalized legislators who appeared to be making their job of representation into a career.

Legislative Term Limits: Problem or Solution?

Although the complexity of state problems may well require professional legislators who devote full-time attention to legislative issues, this professionalism "runs counter to the traditional theory of American politics in which citizens come together, conduct the public's business and return to their other occupations."[30] In the 33 states where there are no term limits, many legislators are now viewed as career politicians—and hence less like the people they represent.

Term limits were the most talked-about legislative "reform" in the 1990s. It began in 1990 when voters in California, Colorado, and Oklahoma approved the first term-limit restrictions through citizen-instigated ballot initiatives. Two years later, another 11 states enacted voter initiatives along the same lines. Several more approved term-limit provisions of some type for their constitutions, while voters in three states rejected them. In addition, state legislators in Utah and Louisiana voted to impose term limits on themselves. State supreme courts in four states—Massachusetts, Nebraska, Oregon, and Washington—have struck down term limits as unconstitutional. Note, however, that Nebraska voters in 2000, four years after their court nullified voter-approved limits, voted to reinstate them.

There is some evidence that the term-limit movement has run out of energy. In 2002, Idaho legislators voted to repeal term-limit provisions that had been approved on several occasions by Idaho voters. Term-limit supporters complained that this legislative repeal constituted "a slap in the face to all Idaho voters. The arrogance of the Legislature to repeal an issue that has been supported by four separate votes is unconscionable."[31] But Idaho legislative leader Bruce Newcomb responded that term limits won approval only because out-of-state money influenced the votes: "We were a cheap state to buy; it was not in the public interest. . . . There was never a real debate. . . . They had no opposition."[32] In 2003, the Utah legislature followed suit, repealing the limits it had imposed on itself only five years earlier.[33]

Nevertheless, term-limit provisions exist in 17 states (see Table 24–2). These provisions limit state legislators to legislative service of six to twelve years. In some states, lawmakers are barred from serving in the same office beyond a set number of years. In 11 other states, they must skip one term (more in some states) before running again for office. In 2002, for example, 71 percent of Michigan's legislators were forced out of office under term limits.

Voters in California went even further and enacted a measure that slashed legislative staffs and curbed legislative pension benefits as well as limited the number of terms legislators could serve. This citizen-sponsored and citizen-enacted law also prohibited legislators from ever running again for the legislature.

Voters can, of course, dispatch legislators from office by voting for challengers. But voters seem to want the added constitutional device of doing for them what most voters do not do themselves—throw the rascals out! All the drama about term limits diverts attention from other serious problems, including weak parties, too many safe-seat districts where one party virtually always wins, and neglect of educational investment and economic development in the states.

Term limits have serious consequences for state legislative activity. In California, novice lawmakers now chair committees and hold leadership positions, and there are signs in California and elsewhere that term limits discourage legislative cooperation, decrease institutional expertise, and generally weaken legislatures relative to governors, bureaucrats, and lobbyists.

However, term limits thus far have changed the general profile of state legislators.[34] Indeed, opponents contend correctly, it takes several years for new legislators to become

TABLE 24–2 TERM LIMITS IN THE STATES

State	House			Senate		
	Year Enacted	Limit (years)	Year of Impact	Limit (years)	Year of Impact	Popular Vote in Favor
Maine	1993	8	1996	8	1996	67.6%
California	1990	6	1996	8	1998	52.2
Colorado	1990	8	1998	8	1998	71.0
Arkansas	1992	6	1998	8	2000	59.9
Michigan	1992	6	1998	8	2002	58.8
Florida	1992	8	2000	8	2000	76.8
Missouri*	1992	8	2002	8	2002	75.0
Ohio	1992	8	2000	8	2000	68.4
South Dakota	1992	8	2000	8	2000	63.5
Montana	1992	8	2000	8	2000	67.0
Arizona	1992	8	2000	8	2000	74.2
Oklahoma	1990	12	2004	12	2004	67.3
Nevada	1996	12	2008	12	2008	70.4
Utah	1994	12	2006	12	2006	—†
Wyoming	1992	12	2006	12	2006	77.2
Louisiana	1995	12	2007	12	2007	76.0
Nebraska†	2000	8	2008	—	—	55.8

SOURCE: National Conference of State Legislatures, "The Term Limited States," www.ncsl.org/programs/legman/about/states.htm, accessed April 27, 2004.

*Because of special elections, term limits became effective in 2000 for eight current members of the House and one senator in 1998.

†Passed by the legislature.

‡Nebraska has a unicameral legislature.

acquainted with rules, procedures, and regulations; therefore, to jettison politicians just as they begin to feel comfortable, confident, and knowledgeable is to lose a wealth of accumulated experience.

THE POLITICS OF DRAWING LEGISLATIVE DISTRICT LINES

State legislatures are required by their state constitutions, by federal laws, and by court rulings to draw district boundaries for both their state legislature and U.S. House of Representative seats after each population census. The 2000 census once again triggered redistricting of congressional and state legislative lines.

Redistricting is the action of a state legislature or other body in redrawing legislative electoral district lines. About a dozen states delegate these responsibilities to independent redistricting or reapportionment commissions. In Alaska, the governor's office draws the legislative districts. Most legislatures, however, consider these once-a-decade responsibilities so important that they are unwilling to turn control of this task over to anybody else.

The drawing of legislative district boundaries has always been controversial, in large part because redistricting decisions are made by partisan majorities in legislatures. The highly political nature of the undertaking is usually reflected in the results. "Redistricting is the political equivalent," says one observer, "of moving the left field fence for a right-handed pull hitter. By changing the boundaries, redistricting helps some, hurts others—and leaves just about everyone else scrambling."[35]

The politics and debate about redistricting are most intense in the years immediately after a census is taken. Drawing district boundaries to benefit a party, group, or

redistricting
The redrawing of congressional and other legislative district lines following the census, to accommodate population shifts and keep districts as equal as possible in population.

★★ YOU DECIDE

SHOULD TERM LIMITS BE IMPOSED ON STATE LEGISLATORS?

Proponents of term limits contend that the principle of rotation is an old and cherished one in the United States and that we should encourage citizen-legislators and discourage career politicians. Supporters also say incumbents have voted too many perks and advantages for themselves and that term limits may be the only way to restore real competition to legislative races. They argue that *permanent incumbency*—legislators and state officials staying on for multiple terms spanning decades—is creating a kind of professional ruling class that is out of touch with ordinary citizens. The term-limit movement is a manifestation of public frustration with what is viewed as a failure of government. Would placing limits on how long legislators can serve solve the problem?

incumbent is called **gerrymandering**. The term was first used in 1811 to describe a strange, salamander-shaped legislative district drawn in northeastern Massachusetts when Elbridge Gerry was governor. A district does not need to be odd in shape, however, to be gerrymandered.

As a result of huge differences in population among the districts, state legislative districts used to face problems of **malapportionment.** State legislatures for decades had given rural and small-town voters more votes in the legislature than they were entitled to on the basis of their declining share of the population. In Georgia, for instance, the 1960 reapportionment gave the largest county, with 556,326 inhabitants, no more representation than the three smallest counties, whose combined population was 6,980.[36] City officials complained bitterly that small-town and farmland-dominated legislators were unsympathetic to their problems and had different legislative priorities.

But no matter how much they protested, people who were underrepresented in the state legislatures made little progress. Legislators from small towns and farm areas naturally did not wish to reapportion themselves out of jobs, and their constituents did not wish to lose their influence. Even though the failure of state legislatures to reapportion often violated express provisions of state constitutions and raised serious questions under the U.S. Constitution, state and federal judges took the position that issues having to do with legislative districting were "political questions" and outside the scope of judicial authority.

Finally, the U.S. Supreme Court stepped in. In 1962, in *Baker* v. *Carr,* the Court held that voters do have standing to challenge legislative apportionment and that such questions should be considered by the federal courts. Arbitrary and capriciously drawn districts deprive people of their constitutional rights of representation, and federal judges may take jurisdiction over such cases.[37]

One Person, One Vote

In *Wesberry* v. *Sanders* (1964), the U.S. Supreme Court announced that as far as congressional representation is concerned, "as nearly as practicable one man's vote in a congressional election is to be worth as much as another's."[38] The Court extended this principle to representation in the state legislatures, although it subsequently modified this decision allowing for somewhat more population discrepancies among state legislative districts than for congressional districts.

In *Reynolds* v. *Sims* (1964), the Court held that "the fundamental principle of representative government in this country is one of equal representation for equal numbers of people, without regard to race, sex, economic status, or place of residence within a state." In the Court's view, this principle applied not only to the more numerous house of the state legislature, which was usually based on population, but also to the state senate, where representation was often based on area, such as the county or some other governmental unit. Defenders of this pattern had argued that as long as the more numerous chamber represented population, the senate could represent geographical units. Look at the federal system embodied in the U.S. Constitution, they said. Isn't representation in the U.S. Senate based on area? Although many thought this a compelling argument, a majority of the Court did not. Chief Justice Earl Warren explained: "Legislators represent people, not trees or acres. Legislators are elected by voters, not farms or cities or economic interests. . . . The right to elect legislators in a free unimpaired fashion is a bedrock of our political system."[39] The U.S. Senate analogy, in short, did not hold.

The Supreme Court has been especially strict about how states draw districts for the U.S. House of Representatives. A state legislature must justify any variance from mathematical equality by showing it made a good-faith effort to come as close as possible to the standard. The Supreme Court is, however, less insistent on absolute equality for state legislative districts. Thus the Court in 1983 upheld a Wyoming plan that allocated at least one state legislative seat per county, saying that Wyoming's policy was rational and appropriate to the special needs of that sparsely populated state.[40] This ruling was a rare exception to the general principle of allowing at most a 10 percent deviation between

gerrymandering
The drawing of legislative district boundaries to benefit a party, group, or incumbent.

malapportionment
Having legislative districts with unequal populations.

state legislative districts. Nevertheless, the requirement that the districts be established in accordance with the one-person, one-vote principle still remains.

New Rules for Redrawing the Districts

Even though the one-person, one-vote principle is firmly established, many issues affecting the nature of legislative representation continue to be hotly debated. In northern metropolitan areas, for instance, the general pattern has been for the center city to be Democratic and the outlying suburbs Republican. If legislative district lines in these areas are drawn like spokes from the center city to the suburbs, fewer Republicans will probably be elected than if the district lines are drawn in concentric circles.

In recent decades, African Americans and Hispanics have begun to charge that state legislatures have an obligation under the Voting Rights Act of 1965 to redraw legislative districts to avoid dilution of the influence of minorities at the ballot box. They have gone to court to force legislators to create **majority-minority districts**. The U.S. Supreme Court, however, has put restraints on implementation of the act. The Court has held that although legislatures may take race into account in drawing state and federal legislative district lines and must act to avoid diluting the voting strength of minorities, a legislature violates the constitutional rights of white voters if race becomes the overriding motive.[41]

Controversy continues to surround reapportionment, no matter what processes are used. No one ever doubts the ability of incumbents in the majority to rig elections through reapportionment. In the words of the old-time politicians, "You tell me the results you want, and I'll draw the district map to do it." Today, computers are shaping the districts, and the people who control the computers, their programming, and their data can influence the outcome.

Neither the courts nor the two major parties have adequately addressed the competitive integrity of the electoral process as a constitutional issue. But a case can be made that the vast majority of state legislative elections offer little meaningful competition. Whether designed by legislative party leaders or redistricting commissioners, those who carve up legislative districts every ten years do so primarily with the intent to protect incumbents or create districts that at least leave their party no worse off than it was before.

"Real competition, where a challenger to an incumbent might have some actual chance of winning, is evident in elections that are won by margins of less than 10 percent of the vote," writes Columbia University law professor Samuel Issacharoff.[42] But this is rarely the case in state after state. The wonder is "that anyone bothers to participate at all in such hollow elections."[43] And this was, in part, the reason that the term-limit crusade gained support in the first place.

DIRECT LEGISLATION: POLICY MAKING BY THE PEOPLE?

Many states, mostly in the West, believe that citizens should have the power to create legislation through the initiative, referendum, and recall. This "direct democracy" movement began with populist reformers in Utah in 1900 and spread quickly to Oregon in 1902, Montana in 1904, Maine and Michigan in 1908, and Arizona and Colorado in 1910. Of the nearly 2,500 initiatives that the public has placed on the ballot in the 24 states that allow this form of direct democracy, more than 1,000 have been in five states: Oregon, California, Colorado, North Dakota, and Arizona.

Reformers had good reason to bypass their legislatures in the early 1900s—legislatures in several states were either incompetent or under the domination of the political

---

★★★ THINKING IT THROUGH

Support for term limits comes from both Republicans and Democrats, yet organized support and financial aid have generally come from conservative antitax and antigovernment groups. *The Wall Street Journal* has frequently editorialized in support of term limits. Consumer activist and Green party presidential candidate Ralph Nader has also been among their most vocal supporters. He and like-minded populists on the left believe that only the bludgeon of term limits will motivate legislators to give reforms like public funding of political campaigns a serious chance. Many term limits were aimed at the U.S. Congress as the primary target, but that restriction was struck down by the U.S. Supreme Court.

Legislators and most political scientists have opposed this reform. They contend that term limits are a solution in search of a problem that does not exist. Most state legislators, they note, stay in the legislature for only three or four terms anyway. Indeed, most states have more of a problem nurturing and retaining experienced leaders than they have bringing in new blood. The expertise and institutional memory once available from veteran members and longtime leaders, critics say, will be diminished by term limits.[*] In addition, term limits deprive voters of their freedom to choose their elected officials.

Critics of term limits think this reform will have the unintended consequence of increasing the power of various unelected officials, such as lobbyists, legislative staffers, and bureaucrats. Power resides somewhere, critics say, and you don't get rid of it so much as shift it. "I calculate that term limits is costing the legislature 694 years of collective experience," complained Ohio state legislator Jo Ann Davidson. "Now the institutional memory vote will be in the hands of the lobbyists and the legislative staff when it should rest with the elected policy makers."[†]

[*]See David S. Broder, *Democracy Derailed: Initiative Campaigns and the Power of Money* (Harcourt, 2000), p. 223.

[†]Jo Ann Davidson, quoted in Francis X. Clines, "Term Limits Bring Wholesale Change into Legislatures," *The New York Times,* February 14, 2000, p. A19. See also the criticism in Peter Schrag, *Paradise Lost: California's Experience, America's Future* (New Press, 1998), p. 3. See also John M. Carey, Richard G. Niemi, and Lynda W. Powell, *Term Limits in the State Legislatures* (University of Michigan Press, 2000).

---

majority-minority district
A legislative district created to include a majority of minority voters; ruled constitutional so long as race is not the main factor in redistricting.

machines. For example, the Southern Pacific Railroad's political machine in California had dominated the selection of state legislators, governors, and U.S. senators for years.[44] The Progressives placed enormous trust in the wisdom of the people, assuming that voters would inform themselves about issues and make responsible decisions on a variety of policy questions put before them.

Initiative

The **initiative** permits a designated minimum number of voters to propose a law or constitutional amendment by petition. It becomes law if approved by a majority of the voters at a subsequent election. Twenty-four states, mostly in the West, authorize the making of laws by means of the initiative petition (see Figure 24–4). In California, Oregon, Washington, North Dakota, Arizona, Colorado, Michigan, and Massachusetts, the initiative has become an important feature of state political life.

In some states, the *direct initiative* applies to constitutional amendments and to legislation; in others, it can be used only for one or the other. Thus in Florida, the direct initiative can be used only to change the state constitution, while in Idaho, direct initiative can be used only for statutory lawmaking. In a state that permits the direct initiative, any individual or interest group may draft a proposed law and file it with a designated state official, usually the secretary of state. Supporters have only to secure a certain number of signatures (between 2 and 15 percent of the vote in the last election) to place the measure on the next general election ballot. Only California permits initiatives on primary election ballots.

The *indirect initiative* is used in a few states, including Alaska, Maine, and Massachusetts. After a certain number of petition signatures have been collected, the state legislature is given an opportunity to act on the measure without alteration; if approved, the law simply goes into effect. If not approved, the proposed legislation is then placed on the ballot, although in some states, additional signatures are required before the proposal can be placed before the voters.

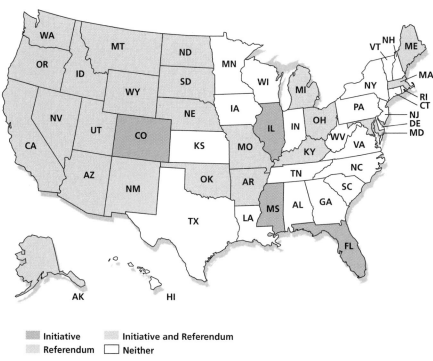

initiative
Procedure whereby a certain number of voters may, by petition, propose a law or constitutional amendment and have it submitted to the voters.

Legend:
- Initiative
- Referendum
- Initiative and Referendum
- Neither

FIGURE 24–4 Citizen-Initiated Initiative and Referendum at the State Level, 2005.

Referendum

A **referendum** permits voters to vote on, and possibly overturn, recently passed laws or legislatively proposed amendments to a state's constitution. A majority vote is required to overturn legislatively approved laws. The referendum, it should be noted, is required in every state except Delaware for the ratification of constitutional amendments.

Legislation may be subject to mandatory or optional referendums. The *mandatory referendum* calls for a waiting period, usually 60 to 90 days, before legislation goes into effect. If during this period a prescribed number of voters sign a referendum petition requesting that the act be referred to the voters, the law does not go into effect unless a majority of the voters give their approval at the next election. The *optional referendum* permits the legislature, at its discretion, to provide that a measure shall not become law until it has been approved by the voters at an election. This second kind is the more common.

Although statewide initiatives and referendums get the most attention, the same processes also flourish at the local level in many states. The annual volume of measures presented to voters in school districts, cities, and counties runs to several thousand, and covers a wide range of issues: bonds for school buildings, fluoridation of water, banning of glass bottles, restrictions on nuclear power facilities, and approval or rejection of convention facilities or sport stadiums.

Recall

Recall is the means by which voters may remove elected public officials before the end of their term. Eighteen states, mostly in the West, provide for the recall of state officers, but many others permit the recall of local officials (see Figure 24–5). Recall also requires a petition, but it needs more signatures (typically 25 percent of voters in the last election for the position in question) than the initiative or referendum.

The most famous recall in recent history involved the removal of California Governor Gray Davis and the election of former bodybuilder and movie star Arnold Schwarzenegger. In California and five other states, the recall election for the office-holder was held on the same ballot with the election of a successor—hence, the recall of Davis and election of Schwarzenegger occurred at the same time. In eight states, the recall election is held first and is followed by a special election for a successor at a later time. And in four states the recall election is held first and the successor is appointed by either a special board or the governor.

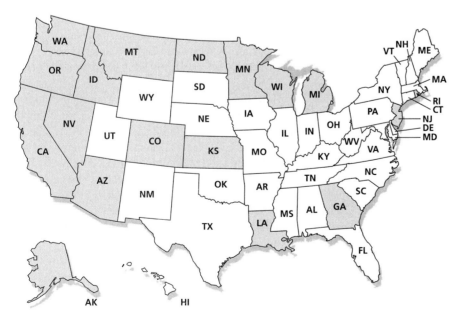

FIGURE 24–5 States That Provide for Citizen-Initiated Recall of Elected State Officials.

referendum
Procedure for submitting to popular vote measures passed by the legislature or proposed amendments to a state constitution.

recall
Procedure for submitting to popular vote the removal of public officials from office before the end of their term.

There are various kinds of recall elections. In some, the official must run and try to win reelection in a yes-or-no vote of confidence election; in others, candidates are permitted to file and run against the incumbent, making it, in effect, a new election. If in the former case an incumbent is voted out of office, a new election is required.

Recall is akin to impeachment by the public. But unlike impeachment, formal charges of wrongdoing against the incumbent are not required. Rather, recall permits throwing people out of office merely because of policy differences. For recall, voters need only circulate petitions and obtain the required number of signatures. Recall is seldom used at the state level, although one governor and several state legislators have been recalled. Although the recall is rarely used successfully in the 18 states that now permit it, even the threat of a recall serves to remind legislators and other state officials of their obligations to the voters.

Recall is also used surprisingly often against local officials—although only 18 states allow recall of statewide officials, 36 allow recall of local officials such as mayors, county commissioners, and school board superintendents. From 1977 to 2001, nearly 10 percent of all U.S. cities held a recall election of a mayor or city council member.[45]

A few years ago, New Jersey voters were asked to approve the right to recall local, state, and federal elected officials. Taxpayer and antipolitician groups argued passionately in favor of passage. *The New York Times* vigorously opposed the recall, saying it would discourage public officials from making unpopular decisions that nevertheless bring about long-term public benefits. The *Times* also editorialized that the recall authority was unnecessary: "If voters are unhappy with someone they have elected, they can vote that person out the next time! If an official breaks the law, prosecutors can deal with it."[46] But over 70 percent of New Jersey voters voted in favor of adopting the recall.

THE DEBATE OVER DIRECT DEMOCRACY

Hundreds of issues have been placed on state election ballots by citizen initiative in recent years. Citizens have turned to the initiative process to try to regulate handguns in California, to protect the moose in Maine, to encourage the death penalty in Massachusetts, to approve the sale of wine in grocery stores in Colorado, to abolish daylight savings time in North Dakota, and in several states to allow marijuana to be used for specific medicinal purposes.

In 2004, voters in 34 states cast ballots on 163 initiatives and referendums, including $3 billion for stem cell research in California (approved), education reform in five states (three approved, two rejected), legalized gambling in Washington State (rejected), relaxation of term limits on state legislators in Arkansas and Montana (rejected), legalization of marijuana for any usage in Alaska (rejected), and bans on same-sex marriage in 11 states (all approved).

Of the 163 ballot measures, 50 were initiatives and the rest were referendums of some kind. Nebraska voters actually faced four ballot choices on gambling, including one referendum from the legislature and three initiatives from the voters (all four failed).[47]

Contrary to election-night hunches, the gay-marriage initiatives did not bring large numbers of voters to the polls in hotly contested battleground states such as Michigan and Ohio—voters in the battleground states were already engaged by the campaigns. However, the bans appear to have boosted turnout in states that were not hotly contested by the two presidential campaigns. According to an analysis by the Brookings Institution's Michael McDonald, the same-sex marriage ban in Kentucky may have provided the margin of victory for the embattled Republican Senate incumbent, Jim Bunning.

Political scientists, law professors, and lawmakers are often critical of direct legislation.[48] Early opponents had argued that such measures would undermine the legitimacy of representative government and open the way for radical or special-interest legislation. Critics of the initiative and the referendum believe that the Progressives who advocated direct legislation were naively idealistic and that these mechanisms are more likely to be used by special interests. Only well-organized interests can gather the appropriate number of signatures and mount the required media campaigns to gain victory. Critics of direct democracy say that this is indeed what has happened in California, Oregon, and elsewhere.[49]

In addition to giving advantages to well-organized interests, direct legislation often introduces confusion because some petitions are worded not so much for clarity but to win votes. Moreover, the 30-second ads that support or oppose many initiatives also tend to confuse rather than clarify.

The results of direct democracy have been both positive and negative. Historically, direct legislation by initiative has resulted in progressive victories on many consumer and economic issues and conservative victories on social issues. Direct democracy has not weakened our legislatures; seats in state legislatures are still valued, sought after, and competed for by able citizens. However, direct democracy has clearly had a considerable impact on state taxes and spending, especially in states that have enacted budget and tax limits. These measures have pleased many conservatives, upset liberals, and made life difficult for governors and state legislators.

Another serious problem has arisen in western states. Political consulting firms, for a price, will gather signatures and put nearly anything you want on the ballot. Deceptive pitches are sometimes made to get people to sign petitions. It takes a small fortune to do this, and only well-organized, well-financed, single-interest groups can afford it.[50]

Still another problem with the initiative process is that it can be used to target minorities, as California's limitations on illegal immigrants in 1994 and affirmative action in 1996 did. Similarly, Colorado's controversial Measure 2 in 1992 targeted gays and lesbians. How far can the majority go in using the initiative process against minorities? The courts have generally reversed part or all of discriminatory initiatives that were successful at the polls, yet such reversals put the courts in the awkward position of opposing a vote of the people.

The initiative process has become a powerful tool used by interest groups, politicians, and ideologues. "A vote on an issue in a single state can propel an issue onto the national agenda because of the widespread media attention given to some controversial initiatives."[51] Interest groups have set state policy by means of the initiative and have used it to reduce local government options in taxing, zoning and planning, and related matters. "One reason for this tendency to take on matters that were previously local and decide them at the statewide level is interest group efficiency. It is easier to restrict local taxing powers, strike local rent control laws, and eliminate ordinances protecting gays and lesbians by mobilizing a single statewide vote" rather than by campaigning to reverse or defeat local initiatives.[52]

Viewed from another perspective, most of the perceived flaws of the populist processes of direct democracy are also the flaws of democracy. When we vote in an election, we often wish we had more information about issues and candidates. Delegates at constitutional conventions or national party conventions frequently have similar misgivings when they are forced to render yes-or-no votes on complicated issues. So, too, members of state legislatures—especially in those frantic days near the end of their sessions—yearn for more information, more clarity about consequences, and more discussion and compromise than time will permit.

Critics lament the rise in what they call "public policy making by bumper sticker." Opponents of direct legislation fear that the very fabric of legislative processes and representative government is at stake. To be sure, lack of faith in legislative bodies has sometimes prompted the use of direct legislation devices, but the best way to restore faith in the legislature is not to bypass it but to elect better people to it.

Supporters of populist democracy say they have not given up on the legislative process. Rather, they wish to use direct legislation primarily when legislatures prove unresponsive. If our legislature will not act, they say, give us the opportunity to debate our proposals in the open arena of election politics. Supporters further contend that the people are capable of making decisions on complex matters.

Voters throughout the country say that citizens ought to have the right, at least occasionally, to vote directly on policy issues. Surveys find that both voters and nonvoters say they would be more likely to become interested in politics and vote if some issues appeared along with candidates on their ballots.[53] Moreover, Californians, who have had to deal with more ballot issues than voters in any other state, continue to say statewide ballot propositions elections are overall "a good thing for California" (74 percent), even as they acknowledge limits to their own grasp of the process.[54]

The legislative process is never perfect. Even with larger professional staffs, hearings, new technologies, bicameralism, and other distinctive features of constitutional democracy, mistakes are made and defective bills are enacted into law in our legislatures. The Supreme Court has overturned hundreds of laws passed by state legislatures as unconstitutional, and state legislatures often spend much of their time amending or otherwise improving measures they passed in previous years. As a practical matter, however, Americans should be at least as skeptical and questioning of the initiative and referendum process as they already are of their state legislators.

S U M M A R Y

1. State legislatures were the most powerful institutions in the nation during the Revolutionary War, and remain powerful to this day. Although some state legislatures still rely on part-time legislators with little or no staff, many now elect full-time legislators who receive significant pay and staff support. In many ways, state legislatures are becoming more like the U.S. Congress every day.

2. The nation's 7,387 state legislators are called on to represent diverse views, help formulate state public policy, oversee the administration of state laws, and mediate political conflicts that arise in the state. State legislatures have become more diverse in recent decades as population changes have improved the election prospects of women and minority candidates.

3. The main influences on a state legislator's voting decisions are political parties, lobbyists and interest groups, district considerations, constituent views, colleagues, committee recommendations, the party leaders, the media, and actions taken by other states and the federal government. State legislators use many of the same tools for making decisions as members of the U.S. Congress.

4. State legislators are constantly subjected to intense lobbying by organized interests. Although lobbyists and interest group representatives are important sources of information, legislatures have become increasingly concerned about potential conflicts of interest and ethical conduct. Many states have created special rules covering campaign contributions and lobbying activities in the wake of scandals in their own legislatures.

5. As a result of legislative reform efforts, most states now have longer annual sessions, larger and more competent staffs, open-meeting laws, and a variety of electronic-age information systems. As they have become more professionalized, they have also become more capable of producing legislative impacts in a variety of policy areas such as the environment, education, and crime control.

6. Seventeen states have limited the number of terms legislators can serve. Most state legislators and political scientists oppose term limits for a variety of reasons, yet voters in many states have viewed them as a way of keeping their representatives accountable and encouraging the notion of citizen representation.

7. The politics of redistricting, or redrawing legislative boundaries, heats up every ten years after the census is taken. Redistricting is never easy; political careers can be ruined by redrawn boundaries. Major controversies have arisen over partisan and racially motivated drawing of legislative district lines, and the federal courts are increasingly asked to establish guidelines that will limit such outcomes.

8. Direct legislative procedures, especially the initiative petition, are a prominent part of the legislative process, particularly in the West. Other direct mechanisms, such as the referendum and the recall, are also available to voters in many states.

K E Y   T E R M S

bicameral legislature	**lobbyist**	**redistricting**	**initiative**
unicameral legislature	**trustee**	**gerrymandering**	**referendum**
party caucus	**delegate**	**malapportionment**	**recall**
lobbying	**federal mandate**	**majority-minority district**	

FURTHER READING

SHAWN BOWLER AND TODD DONOVAN, *Demanding Choices: Opinions, Voting, and Direct Democracy* (University of Michigan Press, 1998).

SHAWN BOWLER, TODD DONOVAN, AND CAROLINE J. TOLBERT, EDS., *Citizens as Legislators: Direct Democracy in the United States* (Ohio State University Press, 1998).

DAVID S. BRODER, *Democracy Derailed: Initiative Campaigns and the Power of Money* (Harcourt, 2000).

WILLIAM M. BULGER, *While the Music Lasts: My Life in Politics* (Houghton Mifflin, 1996).

BRUCE E. CAIN, *The Reapportionment Puzzle* (University of California Press, 1984).

JOHN M. CAREY, RICHARD G. NIEMI, AND LYNDA W. POWELL, *Term Limits in the State Legislatures* (University of Michigan Press, 2000).

THOMAS E. CRONIN, *Direct Democracy: The Politics of the Initiative, Referendum, and Recall* (Harvard University Press, 1989).

RICHARD J. ELLIS, *Democratic Delusions: The Initiative Process in America* (University Press of Kansas, 2002).

VIRGINIA GRAY, RUSSELL HANSON, AND HERBERT JACOB, EDS., *Politics in the American States, 7th ed.* (CQ Press, 1999).

JOHN J. KENNEDY, *The Contemporary Pennsylvania Legislature* (University Press of America, 1999).

TOM LOFTUS, *The Art of Legislative Politics* (CQ Press, 1994).

BURDETT A. LOOMIS, *A Legislative Year: Time, Politics, and Policies* (University Press of Kansas, 1994).

DAVID B. MAGLEBY, *Direct Legislation: Voting on Ballot Propositions in the United States* (Johns Hopkins University Press, 1984).

JAY MICHAEL AND DAN WALTERS, *The Third House: Lobbyists, Money, and Power in Sacramento* (Berkeley Public Policy Press, 2002).

GARY MONCRIEF, PEVERILL SQUIRE, AND MALCOLM E. JEWELL, *Who Runs for the Legislature?* (Prentice Hall, 2001).

NATIONAL CONFERENCE OF STATE LEGISLATURES AND AMERICAN SOCIETY OF LEGISLATIVE CLERKS AND SECRETARIES, *Inside the Legislative Process* (National Council of State Legislatures, 1998).

ALBERT J. NELSON, *Emerging Influentials in State Legislatures: Women, Blacks, and Hispanics* (Praeger, 1991).

BETH REINGOLD, *Representing Women: Sex, Gender, and Legislative Behavior in Arizona and California* (University of California Press, 2000).

JAMES RICHARDSON, *Willie Brown: A Biography* (University of California Press, 1996).

ALAN ROSENTHAL, *Drawing the Line: Legislative Ethics in the States* (University of Nebraska Press, 1996).

ALAN ROSENTHAL, *The Decline of Representative Democracy* (CQ Press, 1998).

PETER SCHRAG, *Paradise Lost: California's Experience, America's Future* (New Press, 1998).

FRANK SMALLWOOD, *Free and Independent: The Initiation of a College Professor into State Politics* (Stephen Greene Press, 1976).

JOHN A. STRAAYER, *The Colorado General Assembly*, 2d ed. (University Press of Colorado, 2000).

SUE THOMAS, *How Women Legislate* (Oxford University Press, 1994).

SUE THOMAS AND CLYDE WILCOX, EDS., *Women and Elective Office* (Oxford University Press, 1998).

JOEL A. THOMPSON AND GARY F. MONCRIEF, EDS., *Campaign Finance and State Legislative Elections* (CQ Press, 1998).

See *State Legislatures,* published ten times a year by the National Conference of State Legislatures. *Legislative Studies Quarterly* often has articles on state legislatures; it is published by the Legislative Studies Section of the American Political Science Association. *Governing,* published monthly by Congressional Quarterly, Inc., regularly covers state politics and state legislative issues. *Spectrum: The Journal of State Government* is a useful quarterly published by the Council of State Governments.

STATE GOVERNORS

25

The job of governor is one of the most important and exacting in American political life. Over the past two decades, Congress and the White House have transferred, or devolved, many activities to the states that were for a time considered national responsibilities, such as welfare assistance. This transfer has meant governors now have to be even more effective managers. They have to ask the right questions and consider the long-term implications and side effects of their policies more carefully than ever.

In good economic times, governors, with the concurrence of the state legislatures, get to spend vast sums of new money on state priorities such as education, economic development, transportation, health, and environmental protection. Such was the case during the boom times of the 1990s. Then came the recession of the early 2000s, which brought dramatic revenue shortfalls in more than 40 states. This put governors in a difficult position. To balance state budgets, they had to recommend cuts in services, project delays, state employee layoffs, pay raise postponements, and in some cases, higher taxes. In good economic times and bad, governors are invariably at the center of public policy developments.

Governors are also frequently involved in national politics and often viewed as national leaders. Seventeen governors have gone on to serve as U.S. presidents, and at least 17 members of the current U.S. Senate served earlier as governors in their states. Presidents usually pick two or three current or former governors for their cabinets, as George W. Bush did in selecting Christine Todd Whitman of New Jersey, Tom Ridge of Pennsylvania, and Tommy Thompson of Wisconsin. Moreover, as California's 2003 recall election proved, gubernatorial campaigns can generate enormous national attention. Arnold Schwarzenegger's successful campaign to unseat Governor Gray Davis was one of the top news stories of the year.

In this chapter, we look at how governors come into and keep office, a typical governor's power and influence, efforts to bring modern management techniques to the governor's office, ways that governors interact with other elected state officials, and the rewards of being governor. But first, we examine the rising expectations we have for governors.

RISING EXPECTATIONS FOR GOVERNORS

Although the constitutional powers of governors vary from state to state, Americans evaluate and rate their governors using many of the same critieria for rating presidents.[1] Governors in the large and even medium-sized states are responsible for running complex enterprises that are at least as complicated as *Fortune* 500 corporations. Lamar Alexander, former governor of Tennessee, said that a governor needs to "see the state's few most urgent needs, develop strategies to address them, and persuade at least half the people that he or she is right."[2] An effective governor also has to perform countless symbolic and ceremonial functions and win the respect of the people and the legislature in order to exercise fully the executive functions of the office.

Today, a governor is expected to be, among other things, the state's chief policy maker, shaper of the state budget, a savvy political party leader, chief recruiter of the best available advisers and administrators, and an inspiring renewer of confidence in state programs. The governor must also champion the state's interests against the encroachments of federal or local governments and be the state's chief booster to attract business and tourism. In order to be effective, governors are expected to take trips abroad to encourage foreign investment in their states and promote their local products.[3] Thirty-eight states even operate some form of overseas office, including trade mission posts in Harare and Kuala Lumpur.[4] Governors also work with their legislatures to raise revenues for such programs as welfare, education, and economic development. Governors act as crucial links among the states and between the local and the national governments.

BECOMING AND REMAINING GOVERNOR

Each state's constitution and laws spell out the rules of eligibility, tenure, and salary for its governor. Most states require their governors to be at least 30 years of age and a state resident for at least five years immediately preceding the election. Although California, Ohio, South Dakota, Washington, and Wisconsin set the minimum age at 18, the odds against election at age 18 are staggering. In theory, any qualified voter of the state who meets a state's age qualification is eligible for the office of governor; in practice, there are well-traveled career paths to the governor's office.

Most governors are white males about 40 to 55 years old, and a substantial minority hold law degrees. As the number of women legislators has grown, so has the number of women governors. Most governors were state legislators or held statewide elective office, and some have had law enforcement experience. Of the governors in office in 2004, for example, 9 were former members of Congress, 26 had served in their state legislatures, and 10 had been mayors.

One of the most common paths upward is election to the state legislature, followed by election to a statewide office such as lieutenant governor, secretary of state, or attorney general, followed by a run for governor. Illinois Governor George Ryan spent nearly 30 years in state politics, first as a state legislator, then as Speaker of the state house, then as a two-term lieutenant governor, and finally as a two-term secretary of state before becoming governor. Mayors often run for governor; the mayors of Albuquerque; Phoenix; Indianapolis; Lincoln, Nebraska; and Las Vegas have all run for governor in their states in recent years. Former Minnesota Governor Jesse Ventura, who is remembered by many people mainly as a professional wrestler, had also served four years as mayor of a suburban community.

Although elective service is certainly helpful for building a political base, it is hardly essential. Eleven governors in 2004 had not held elected or appointed office at all,

Governor Gary Locke, the first Chinese American governor in U.S. history, came to the office after years of public service. He was elected to the Washington State House of Representatives in 1982, served on both the House Judiciary and Appropriations Committees, and in his last five years was chairman of the House Appropriations Committee. In 1993 he became the chief executive of King County.

CHANGING FACE OF AMERICAN POLITICS

WOMEN GOVERNORS

Arizona Governor Janet Napolitano.

Montana Governor Judy Martz.

Kansas Governor Kathleen Sebelius.

There have been only 27 women governors of the states in all of U.S. history. But of the 27, 21 were elected to office since 1975, 16 since 1990, and 9 since 2000. A tenth entered the governor's office in Connecticut after the governor resigned. As women have occupied increasingly powerful positions in state legislatures and in lower-level state-wide offices such as lieutenant governor, attorney general, and secretary of state, they have become much more visible as potential candidates for the governorship. African Americans and Hispanics have not made similar gains, however. As of 2004, there was only one Hispanic governor in office, Bill Richardson of Nevada, and no African Americans.

Women Governors Elected Since 1975

Governor	State	Term of Office	Governor	State	Term of Office
Ella Grasso	Connecticut	1975–1980	Jane Dee Hull	Arizona	1998–2002
Dixie Lee Ray	Washington	1977–1981	Judy Martz	Montana	2001–
Martha L. Collins	Kentucky	1983–1987	Ruth Ann Minner	Delaware	2001–
Madeleine Kunin	Vermont	1985–1991	Jane Swift	Massachusetts	2001–2002
Kay Orr	Nebraska	1987–1991	Janet Napolitano	Arizona	2003–
Rose Mofford	Arizona	1988–1991	Linda Lingle	Hawaii	2003–
Joan Finney	Kansas	1991–1995	Kathleen Sebelius	Kansas	2003–
Ann Richards	Texas	1991–1995	Jennifer Granholm	Michigan	2002–
Barbara Roberts	Oregon	1991–1995	Olene Walker	Utah	2003–
Christine Todd Whitman	New Jersey	1994–2001	Kathleen Blanco	Louisiana	2004–
Jeanne Shaheen	New Hampshire	1997–2002	M. Jodie Rell	Connecticut	2004–

SOURCE: National Governors Association, www.nga.org/governors, accessed on April 27, 2004.

including Massachusetts Governor Mitt Romney, Mississippi Governor Haley Barbour, and Nevada Governor Kenny Guinn. Former Texas Governor George W. Bush was a businessman and baseball executive who enjoyed widespread name recognition as the son of a former president, as did his younger brother, Jeb Bush, who also went from a business career to the Florida governorship.

Two hundred years ago, most states had one- or two-year terms for their governors. Today, all states except New Hampshire and Vermont have four-year terms, and all states except Virginia allow governors to run for more than one term. Some governors, such as

Jim Thompson in Illinois, Roy Romer in Colorado, Cecil Andrus in Idaho, Mario Cuomo in New York, Jim Hunt in North Carolina, and Tommy Thompson in Wisconsin, were elected to three or four terms as governors, but 37 states now have a two-term limit on governors, and Utah has a three-term limit.

Governors under Pressure

Once elected, governors enjoy high visibility in their states. Governors earn more than $100,000 in most states; salaries range from $179,000 in New York to $65,000 in Nebraska.[5] In addition, governors receive an expense allowance; all but four are provided an executive mansion; 42 of them have regular access to a state plane or helicopter or both.

But just as governors have become increasingly important in recent decades, they have also had to deal with the twin problems of rising aspirations and scarcity of resources. People want better schools, highways that do not spoil the environment, adequate welfare programs, protections for civil rights, safe streets, and clean air and water. But citizens seldom, if ever, want higher taxes.

Former New York Governor Mario Cuomo (who served from 1983 until 1995) used to say he was always running into people who wanted him to expand programs. He would look them in the eye and say, "Now what are you going to give me so that I can pay for it? Do you want to wait longer in line at the Motor Vehicle office to get your license renewed? Do we stop paving the road in front of your home? Do you mind if we plow the snow less often?" Typically, of course, he heard that the people requesting additional spending did not want to forgo any of those things, which prompted him to say, "Well, then, I don't understand. Where do I get what I need to do what you want?" His point is simple. Given limited resources, choices must be made. Elected officials cannot afford to do everything people would like. Politicians are elected to negotiate trade-offs. You must "give to get."[6]

Governors and state legislators face the challenge of administering federally mandated welfare programs with fewer federal dollars. They have campaigned for the federal government to give more dollars to the states—without strings. The Republican-controlled U.S. Congress in the late 1990s responded by terminating some underfunded federally mandated programs and shifting a few other federal programs to the states. Governors and state legislators now face the challenge of reworking old federal welfare programs as state welfare programs with cutbacks in federal grants.

Reelection and Raising Taxes

About 75 percent of incumbent governors who run for reelection are reelected.[7] Nearly three-quarters of elections for governor are scheduled for nonpresidential or midterm election years (for example, 2006); Kentucky, Louisiana, Mississippi, New Jersey, and Virginia elect governors in odd-numbered years. Reformers have successfully argued that presidential and gubernatorial elections should be separated so that governors are not subject to the tides of national politics. In 2004, 11 governorships were up for election. (See Figure 25–1 for the party affiliations of the governors who held office in 2004.)

Incumbency is not always an advantage for reelection. Governors have to make tough decisions, which can antagonize major interests and arouse public criticism. Governors in Arizona, Alabama, Arkansas, and Oklahoma left office in recent years because of personal scandals. Governors in Oregon and Kansas left because they had such low approval ratings in the polls that they chose not to run again. Incumbents sometimes lose because of a depressed state economy or because they increased state taxes and became unpopular.

Public anger over taxes and budgets was clearly behind the 2003 California recall election. Gray Davis was widely criticized for having tripled the registration fee, or "car tax," that motorists paid on their vehicles. As future governor Arnold Schwarzenegger said repeatedly in his campaign, "I feel Californians have been punished enough. From the time they get up in the morning and flush the toilet they're taxed. When they go get a coffee they're taxed. When they get in their car they're taxed. When they go to the gas

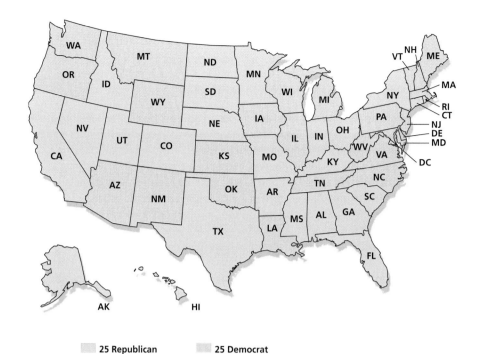

25 Republican   25 Democrat

FIGURE 25–1 Party Control of the Governor's Office, 2005.

California Governor Gray Davis (top) enjoyed serving as governor during the boom times of the late 1990s but faced staggering state deficits after his reelection in 2002. Davis was recalled in 2003 and replaced by Arnold Schwarzennegger (bottom).

station they're taxed. When they go to lunch they're taxed. This goes on all day long. Tax. Tax. Tax. Tax. Tax."[8]

Similarly, in New Jersey in 1993, Governor James Florio was narrowly defeated by Christine Todd Whitman due in part to a recession but mostly because Florio had recommended, and the legislature had enacted, a major tax increase. That tax increase came back to haunt Florio when he ran for U.S. senator in the New Jersey Democratic primary in 2000. His opponent, Jon Corzine, ran ads stressing Florio's role as a big spender and won the primary.

Circumstances often dictate what a governor can or cannot do. The health of the state's economy and the public's attitude toward proposed programs are critical factors. The good economic times in the late 1990s plainly helped most governors who ran for reelection while bad economic times hurt them in the early 2000's. In November 2004, only three incumbent governors won reelection, four were defeated in the primary or general election and four retired.

Some candidates for governor effectively campaign on promises to cut taxes. Republican James Gilmore in Virginia won a landslide victory in his 1998 race for governor by repeatedly saying "No Car Tax"—a reference to a highly unpopular personal property tax on cars, trucks, and motorcycles. George Pataki became governor in New York in 1994 by pledging a property tax reduction, and was reelected twice in part because he kept taxes low.[9]

Because voters reward frugality and sometimes punish elected officials for tax increases, most governors go to considerable lengths to avoid having to raise taxes, especially with an election approaching. Indeed, many politicians believe that a governor who proposes new taxes will face defeat in the next election, although some studies cast doubt on this fear.[10] Voters and legislatures often go along with governors who can make a compelling case for new revenues and new investments. When governors request a tax increase targeted for a specific worthy cause (for example, improving the schools), voters often support them. This is especially true if "political leaders are candid about why they need the money, sensible and fair in how they intend to spend it and courageous enough to lead the fight themselves. Americans are neither selfish nor short-sighted on taxes—they just want assurance that their money will be spent wisely."[11] Several governors around the country have proposed and campaigned for *investment taxes* (that is, taxes that could be invested in building better highways or increasing teachers' salaries) and became popular because of their targeted efforts to improve their state.

A GOVERNOR'S FORMAL POWERS

Before the American Revolution, royal governors, appointed by and responsible to the British crown, had broad powers, including extensive veto power over the voter-elected colonial legislatures. As anti-British sentiment increased, royal governors became more and more unpopular. The position of state governor in the new Republic was born in this atmosphere of distrust. In the 1770s and 1780s, state legislatures elected state governors, a method that ensured that governors would remain under the control of the people's representatives. The early state constitutions also limited governors to few powers and terms of just a year or two.

Gradually, however, the office of governor grew in importance. In New York, the position of chief executive was sufficiently developed and effective by 1787 that it became one of the main models for the proposed American presidency. If we compare the formal sources of authority in the U.S. Constitution and in a typical state constitution, we see significant differences. "The executive Power," says the Constitution, "shall be vested in a President of the United States of America." Compare this statement with its counterpart in a typical state constitution: "The executive department shall consist of a Governor, Lieutenant Governor, Secretary of State, Treasurer, Attorney General," and perhaps other officials. Unlike the president, the governor *shares* executive power with other elected officials. Most state constitutions go on to say, however, that "the supreme executive power shall be vested in the Governor, who shall take care that the laws be faithfully executed." Thus the public looks to the governor for law enforcement and the management of bureaucracies. In some states, the governor has been given authority to supervise the activities of local prosecutors.

Twenty-four states have strengthened the governorship by making the lieutenant governor run with the governor as a team so that the chief executive is less likely to be paired with a hostile lieutenant governor. In 39 states, the lieutenant governor, like the U.S. vice president, takes over executive office responsibilities if for any reason the governor cannot fulfill the duties of the office. Most important, in almost all states, the governor presents the state budget to the legislature and controls spending after the budget has been approved. Thus state officials must look to the governor as well as the legislature for funds.

The constitutional powers of governor vary from state to state (see Table 25–1). Yet regardless of a governor's formal constitutional authority, a governor's actual power and influence depend on his or her ability to persuade.[12] This power, in turn, usually depends on the governor's reputation, popularity, knowledge of what should be done, and, of course, ability to communicate. Governors must have political skills as well as constitutional authority if they are to provide leadership.

To supplement their formal constitutional powers, governors may hold town meetings around the state, appear on radio and television talk shows, or invite legislators and other influential party and policy leaders to the executive mansion for lobbying and consultation sessions. Remember, however, that not all states vest great constitutional power in the governor. Whether the state constitution defines a strong role is just one of the factors in determining the effectiveness of a governor.

Most governors have the following constitutional authority:

- To make appointments
- To prepare the state budget
- To veto legislation and to exercise an item veto over appropriations measures
- To issue executive orders
- To command the state National Guard
- To pardon or grant clemency
- To help establish the legislature's agenda

TABLE 25–1   RANKINGS OF STATES ACCORDING TO THE FORMAL
                    POWERS OF THE GOVERNOR

Strong

Maryland	Ohio
New Jersey	Pennsylvania
New York	Utah

Moderately Strong

Alaska	Nebraska
Colorado	North Dakota
Connecticut	South Dakota
Iowa	Tennessee
Kansas	West Virginia
Michigan	Wisconsin
Minnesota	Wyoming
Montana	

Moderate

Arizona	Louisiana
California	Maine
Delaware	Massachusetts
Florida	Missouri
Hawaii	Nevada
Idaho	New Mexico
Illinois	Oregon
Indiana	Texas
Kentucky	Virginia

Weak

Alabama	Oklahoma
Arkansas	Rhode Island
Georgia	South Carolina
Mississippi	Vermont
North Carolina	Washington
New Hampshire	

Source: Adapted from Thad L. Beyle, "The Governors," in *Politics in the American States: A Comparative Analysis*, 7th ed., eds. Virginia Gray, Russell Hanson, and Herbert Jacob (CQ Press, 1999), pp. 210–211.

Note: Rankings are based on budget powers, appointive and organizational powers, tenure potential, veto powers, and party control.

Appointive Power

Perhaps a governor's most important job is to recruit talented leaders and managers to head the state's departments, commissions, and agencies.[13] Through recruitment of effective people and prudent delegation of responsibilities to them, a governor can provide direction for the state government.

In most states, the governor is one executive among many, with only limited authority over elected officials, whom the governor can neither appoint nor dismiss. And if these officials are from a different political party than the governor, they are likely to oppose the governor's recommendations. Governors have greater, yet still limited, power over officials they appoint. Some governors appoint hundreds of key officials; others, such as those in Mississippi, South Carolina, and Texas, have severe restrictions on their appointive power. Moreover, in most states, governors must share their appointive power with the state senate and may remove people only when they have violated the law or failed in their legal duties. State administrators whose programs are supported by federal funds also have a measure of independence from the governor.

But along with the appointive power comes a host of challenges. First, salaries for cabinet and agency administrators are modest in many states, especially in the smaller ones, and it is often hard to get people to leave better-paying jobs in private industry. The situation is even worse when the state capital is in a remote or rural section of the state. Second, powerful politicians may demand that their friends be appointed to certain top posts, and they may threaten to be uncooperative if the governor does not go along with their "suggestions." Finally, relatively high turnover in many state positions often hampers a governor's efforts to carry out programs.

Fiscal and Budgetary Power

A governor's financial planning and budgetary powers are key weapons in getting programs passed. Purchasing, budgeting, and personnel matters are centralized under the governor. When implemented by a strong staff and backed by a strong political base, a governor's fiscal powers are extremely important.

In almost all states, the governor has responsibility for preparing the budget and presenting it to the state legislature. This takes place every year in 30 states and every second year in 20 states. The art of budget making involves assessing requests from various departments and agencies and balancing them against available resources. Governors and their staffs have to calculate the costs of existing and newly proposed programs and weigh those costs against estimated revenues for the state.

The budget process is similar in most states. In May and June, the governor's budget office, which may be called Office of Management and Budget or Department of Administration, sends request forms to the various executive agencies. From July to October, the agencies complete their detailed requests and send them back for consideration. Their requests are invariably 10 to 15 percent higher than what is available and also much higher than the governor's proposed guidelines. The governor's budget chief evaluates all requests, sometimes holds internal administrative hearings, and then makes recommendations to the governor. Finally, the governor presents the recommendations to the legislature at the beginning of the new year.

Although the governor and chief budget officials may appear to control the budgetary process, considerable budgeting influence remains in the hands of the executive branch agencies. Further, a governor's budget reflects to a very high degree budgetary decisions made over the years (costs such as prisons or state universities that will not be shut down), so what governors end up doing in practice is tinkering or adjusting at the edges of the overall budget.

The final budget document is presented to the legislature for adoption as an *appropriations measure.* State moneys cannot be spent without legislative appropriations. Legislators can, and usually do, make a number of alterations in a governor's budget. In theory, a legislature controls all state activities through the budget process because it has the final say in approving the budget. In practice, however, most legislatures do not review every budgetary item; they merely trim or make additions at the margins. Hence budgets reflect the policy views of those responsible for their preparation—namely, the governor and the governor's budget office. A governor who has control over the budget and uses this power effectively has an important asset.

Most states spend at least 40 percent of their state's budget on education. Welfare assistance, highways, prisons and criminal justice programs, health and rehabilitation efforts, and state parks and recreation consume other large portions of the budget. Fifty percent of a state's revenue usually comes from taxes; another 20 percent comes from federal sources. When state revenues do not match expenses, governors have to cut or delay programs, since state constitutions as a rule require a balanced budget, and states cannot print money as the federal government can. In addition, states spend roughly 9 percent of their funds implementing federal mandates, such as student testing under the No Child Left Behind Act.[14]

Veto Power

Among the most useful gubernatorial powers is the **veto**, the power to conditionally reject legislative bills, especially appropriations measures. Michigan Governor Jennifer Granholm vetoed more than 30 bills in her first eighteen months in office, including one that would have banned late-term abortions, another that would have created a process for creating specialty license plates, and another that would have given suburbs more control over the Detroit Water and Sewer Board, even though the board sets their rates. Her veto activity led the *Detroit Free Press* to title a story on her tenure "Granholm stars in her own 'Kill Bill.' "[15]

In all but eight states, governors have the **item veto**, which permits them to veto individual items in an appropriations bill while signing the remainder of the bill into law. Thus they can influence the flow of funds to the executive departments and thereby attempt to control their activities. In April 2004, for example, Colorado Governor Bill Owens vetoed an 8 percent increase in college tuition as one of about 85 items he struck down in the state's $14.2 annual budget.

In several states, a governor can reduce particular appropriations; this power is called the **reduction veto**. In 19 states, governors can exercise what is called an **amendatory veto**, which allows the governor to return a bill to the state legislature with suggested language changes, conditions, or amendments. In this last case, legislators must decide to accept the governor's recommendations or approve the bill in its original form, which in some cases requires a majority vote and in other cases a three-fifths or supermajority vote.

State legislatures can override a governor's veto; in most states, it takes a two-thirds majority of both legislative chambers. Some governors, like Wisconsin's Tommy Thompson, vetoed thousands of legislative measures. New York Governor George Pataki vetoed 1,379 provisions the legislature sent him in 1998.[16] Governors on average veto about 4 percent of the bills sent to them, but only about 2 percent of gubernatorial vetoes are overridden by legislatures.[17] Most governors believe the veto power should be used sparingly. Indeed, some observers think too frequent use of the veto is a sign of gubernatorial weakness because an effective governor usually wins battles through negotiations rather than by confronting state legislators.[18]

Legislators in several states have established a *veto session*—a short session following adjournment—so they can reconsider any measures vetoed by their governor. This is clearly an effort to reassert the legislature's check-and-balance authority in relation to the governor. Most states using veto sessions have legislatures that meet for a limited time; in full-time legislatures, a veto session would be unnecessary.

Executive Orders

One long-standing power of governors is their authority to issue **executive orders** that have the force of law. Even though executive orders differ from statutes or formal acts passed by the legislature, they have almost the same binding effect. Depending on the state, governors get their authority to issue executive orders from implied powers as chief executive, from specific constitutional grants, or from delegations of authority by their state legislatures. Executive orders supplementing a law are both more detailed and more important than the general guidelines contained in legislation. Governors have issued executive orders during such emergencies as natural disasters and energy crises, in compliance with federal rules and regulations, and to create advisory commissions. State legislators are sometimes angered by sweeping executive orders. They insist that they, not the governors or the courts, should be the primary lawmakers in a state.

In 1996, Governor Kirk Fordice of Mississippi issued an executive order banning same-sex marriages in his state. The intended effect of Fordice's executive order was to prevent county clerks from issuing marriage licenses for gays or lesbians after a similar measure had failed to win passage in the state's legislature.[19] Gay rights activists, joined by the Mississippi American Civil Liberties Union, criticized the governor, saying he was trying to circumvent the state legislature, adding that the state's constitution makes it

veto
Rejection by a president or governor of legislation passed by a legislature.

item veto
Right of an executive to veto parts of a bill approved by a legislature without having to veto the entire bill.

reduction veto
The power of governors in a few states to reduce a particular appropriation.

amendatory veto
The power of governors in a few states to return a bill to the legislature with suggested language changes, conditions, or amendments. Legislators then decide either to accept the governor's recommendations or to pass the bill in its original form over the veto.

executive order
Directive issued by a president or governor that has the force of law.

plain that it is the legislature, not the governor, that defines the authority and duty of county clerks. In this instance, this governor's executive order brought about what the state legislature had not been able to approve.

Governors do not have to issue executive orders to make an impact on state and local government, however. Even though he opposed same-sex marriages, Governor Mitt Romney of Massachusetts reminded local officials in 2004 they had to follow the state's Supreme Judicial Court decision allowing same-sex marriage of state residents. At the same time, however, he also said he intended to use a 1913 law to prohibit the marriage of same-sex couples from other states. Such marriages would be null and void under his interpretation, he argued, thereby preventing Massachusetts from drawing same-sex couples from across the United States.[20]

Commander in Chief of the National Guard

Emergencies enhance the authority of an executive because they call for decisive action. As commander in chief of the state's National Guard when it is not in federal service, a governor may use this force when local authorities are inadequate—in case of riots, floods, and other catastrophes. The National Guard has played a role in the aftermath of floods in midwestern states, riots and earthquakes in California, fires in Florida, and hurricanes throughout the southeastern states. In most states, the state police are also available for emergencies.

Congress provides most of the money to operate the National Guard. This fact, along with the supremacy clause of the U.S. Constitution, gives Congress and the president the power to take charge of a state's National Guard even against the wishes of a governor. In 1990, the Supreme Court ruled unanimously that Congress can authorize the president to call National Guard units to active duty and send them outside the United States despite the objections of the governors, several of whom had tried to keep President Ronald Reagan from calling their respective National Guards to training exercises in Honduras.[21] States could if they wish provide and maintain from their own funds a defense force exempt from being drafted into the armed forces of the United States, but none has done so.

Although governors are technically in charge of their state's National Guard, the president can call their troops into service during national emergencies. By the spring of 2004, approximately 42 percent, or 144,000 soldiers, of the states' 345,000 Army National Guard were either deployed in Iraq or preparing for deployment. The heavy deployment was of particular concern in states such as Idaho, Montana, and Colorado, where National Guard troops play an important role in fighting summer forest fires, and in Gulf states such as Florida and Texas, where they play a critical role in disaster relief and policing in the wake of hurricanes.[22]

Pardon Power

In half the states, governors may pardon violators of state law; in the other states, they share this duty with a pardoning board. Except in cases of impeachment or certain specified crimes, the governor may pardon the offender, commute a sentence by reducing it, or grant a reprieve by delaying the punishment. The governor is normally assisted by pardon attorneys or pardon boards that hold hearings and determine whether there are sufficient reasons for a pardon.

A Tennessee governor, Ray Blanton (1975–1979), caused considerable controversy and sparked a federal investigation when he pardoned or paroled several dozen convicts just before leaving office in 1979. Critics charged that some of these convicts allegedly "purchased" their releases. Blanton's misuse of his pardon powers created such a ruckus that his elected successor, Lamar Alexander, was sworn in early and the locks to the governor's office were quickly changed so Blanton was not able to enter the office, let alone grant any additional pardons. Seldom, however, is the pardon power the subject of such controversy, because it is generally administered with appropriate care.

Similar to the governor's pardon power is the authority for a governor to grant a stay of execution in death penalty cases. This is one of the most controversial aspects of

As commander in chief of the state's National Guard when it is not in federal service, a governor may use this force to handle state emergencies such as fires, floods, earthquakes, and other disasters. The war in Iraq necessitated the deployment of National Guard troops from all over the country to aid in the fighting. Here, Governor Arnold Schwartzenegger provides a morale boost for a California National Guard unit.

Former Illinois Governor George Ryan. A conventional politician in most ways, Ryan was plagued by various scandal accusations. Yet he will be remembered mostly for his bold and controversial review of death penalty practices in Illinois and for his criticism of state-sponsored executions. He commuted the death sentences of 163 men and 4 women to prison sentences of life or less.

executive power in states that provide for the death penalty.[23] Texas Governor George W. Bush came under attack during the 2000 presidential campaign for allowing more than 130 executions during his time in office, in part because another Republican governor, George Ryan of Illinois, had imposed a moratorium on executions earlier in the year. Ryan had long been a death penalty supporter, but he became persuaded that too many mistakes had been made by the courts in sentencing innocent people to death row. Indeed, 13 Illinois inmates in the past generation had been exonerated. "A series in *The Chicago Tribune* found that of 266 capital cases that had been appealed, fully half have been reversed for a new trial or sentencing hearing. In more than 30 cases, lawyers representing death row inmates were disbarred or suspended."[24] During the moratorium, Ryan established a special committee to make recommendations regarding Illinois death penalty procedures. The Ryan Commission report recommended a series of reforms aimed at creating a more just system of capital punishment.[25] Before leaving office in early 2003, Ryan commuted all Illinois death sentences to prison terms of life or less.

Policy-Making Influence

A governor's policy influence in the legislature depends in part on his or her popularity and formal powers. Obviously, governors can send detailed policy and program messages to their legislature and argue for their programs. In some states, they can trade appointive jobs for legislative support, and they can also use their veto power to trade for votes. They can attract more public attention to their views than any single legislator can. Much depends on a governor's ability, political base, and personal popularity, as well as on the political situation in which he or she operates.

Some states have a long tradition of strong executive leadership, while others give their governors relatively weak powers. On paper at least, the governors of Pennsylvania and New York, for example, have strong constitutional powers, and usually have strong party organizations behind them, which enhance close ties with followers in their respective legislatures.[26]

On paper again, the governors of Nevada and Texas have much less formal power and preside over relatively independent departments and agencies. Yet governors of rural and smaller states generally have few other competing institutions or interests when it comes time to exercise policy leadership, while governors in large states face a number of competitors. "Power governors in large urbanized states have many others with whom they must compete—heads of major industries, media personalities, mayors of large cities, and even presidents of prestigious universities," comments political scientist Thad Beyle. "There are lots of big fish in a larger pond, which can mean that a governor may not be as powerful as it might first appear."[27]

Consider these two contrasting evaluations of the governorships in New York and Mississippi:

> The office of governor of the Empire State is surely not small. On the contrary, because of substantial grants of formal power in the state constitution, the historical exercise of such power by formidable incumbents, and widespread expectations that the governor provide leadership, the New York governor is one of the strongest in the nation.[28]

> Mississippi's governor remained less powerful than the state legislature. The large number of independent boards and commissions and independently elected executive officials limits his ability to effectively manage the executive branch. It is easy for agency heads to "go native" and reflect the views of their co-workers and clients rather than those of the chief executive. . . . The office of governor in Mississippi has nevertheless become more influential in recent years.[29]

Balanced against a governor's formal powers are great obstacles, which may include a hostile legislature, cutbacks in federal funding, a depressed state economy, corrupt party or administrative officials, regional tensions in the state (downstate versus upstate, east versus west, urban versus rural), special interests and lobbyists, a cynical press, an indifferent or apathetic public, the sheer inertia of a vast bureaucracy, antiquated civil service systems, and the reluctance of most citizens to get involved.[30]

Some western governors complain that many of their states' problems are caused by absentee landlords or the national government, which together control much land in the West. The federal government owns 83 percent of Nevada, 68 percent of Alaska, 65 percent of Utah, and 53 percent of Oregon. This land is managed, regulated, and overseen by a score of federal agencies, such as the National Park Service, the Forest Service, the Bureau of Land Management, the Fish and Wildlife Service, and the Department of Defense. Governors of western states find they must constantly negotiate with these many federal agencies. In contrast, states east of the Rockies have only small amounts of land owned by the federal government. In Kansas and Maine, for example, less than 1 percent of the land is owned by the federal government.[31]

Governors also find they must become preoccupied with daily housekeeping tasks, and this focus often collides with their efforts to define long-range priorities. Former Vermont Governor Madeleine Kunin recalls she had to fix problems as they happened and yet simultaneously had to define her policy vision for the future. "Finding the time, energy, and perspective to carry out a dual strategy was to be the physical and mental challenge of governing."[32] Even though management duties occupy a fair amount of time, many governors consider these the least glamorous of their responsibilities (see Table 25–2).

Although governors come to office hoping to introduce new programs and reforms, they often spend most of their time raising money just to keep things going; hence some governors are viewed as merely budget balancers rather than as leaders or shapers of a state's future. The governor's role as leader of his or her political party also has an important impact on policy. The coalitions that governors form within their political parties help them put into effect the policies they desire. A governor's power increases in a state that has a competitive two-party system. In such a state, legislators of the governor's party are likely to work more closely with the governor to produce a successful legislative record.

Recent years have witnessed the election of a new breed of well-educated and able governors who have been effective in enlarging their policy-making roles: Jennifer Granholm in Michigan, Bill Richardson in New Mexico, Frank Murkowsi in Alaska, and Jeb Bush in Florida. Because many governors come to office with impressive legislative and administrative experience, they are more likely to be real executive heads of government, not mere figureheads. Some have initiated experimental welfare and job-training programs that have become models for others to emulate. Because states are

---

TABLE 25–2   HOW GOVERNORS SAY THEY SPEND THEIR TIME

Activity	Percentage of Time Spent*
Managing state government	29%
Working with the legislature	16
Meeting the general public	14
Performing ceremonial functions	14
Working with press and media	9
Working with federal government	7
Working with local governments	7
Carrying out political activities	6[†]
Recruiting and appointing	6
Doing miscellaneous activities (staff, interstate, reading, phoning)	16

SOURCE: Thad L. Beyle, "The Governor as Chief Legislator," *State Government,* Winter 1978, p. 3.

*Totals do not add to 100 percent but are averages of the governors' estimates of the time they devoted to the particular activities. Percentages based on responses from those scheduling gubernatorial time in 40 states.

†Plainly, some governors understate time spent campaigning for reelection.

now playing a larger role in planning and administering a wide range of social and economic programs, the managerial and planning ability of a governor is clearly important.

Governors and Media Relations

Governors often attempt to shape their influence through aggressive media outreach. Many worked effectively with the media during their gubernatorial campaign and therefore understand their potential. Once in office, however, governors are thrust into a defensive role rather than the offensive role they played during the election. Instead of running aggressive advertisements for their campaign, they are now under the media's magnifying glass, subject to scrutiny and dirt digging by reporters. They are quickly evaluated in light of campaign promises and in comparison with previous governors.[33]

Past governors have been very aware of the media, with a handful having professional backgrounds in reporting or public relations. For example, former governors Tom McCall of Oregon and Thomas Kean of New Jersey both had prior experience in public relations positions—McCall as a journalist and radio announcer and Kean as a state campaign chair for President Ford and a television reporter during the Reagan campaign. Governor Kean notes the importance of communication with the media: "The most important power the governor has is the power of communicating. If that isn't done properly, you lose your power very fast."[34]

But not all governors are effective in dealing with the media, nor do they necessarily enjoy it. As Minnesota's former Governor Jesse Ventura says of the media: "The American media are suffering from very serious problems, and now I've seen them first-hand. They have the most twisted set of biases I've ever seen. As their whipping-boy-of-choice, I've been in a unique position to see what the media have become. There are a few honorable exceptions, but for the most part, they're corrupt, shameless, and irresponsible as hell."[35]

Each governor tends to have a personal style in dealing with the media. Some are very vocal, preferring to host daily radio or television talk shows, while others prefer to avoid the spotlight unless necessary. To capitalize on the media's ability to disseminate information, governors have been known to request special time on television attempting to explain and make an argument for policy changes, especially tax increases. Others become visible by attending community functions such as building dedications or opening ceremonies or even crowning beauty queens. It is especially important for governors to be publicly active as a calming influence during an emergency situation. During a disaster, such as an earthquake, hurricane, or terrorist action, governors have the ability to call out the National Guard and organize official aid groups. To visit, show concern for, and help ameliorate the suffering of involved families can do wonders for a governor's public opinion ratings. Governors must face public scrutiny, yet they can use the media to set and gain support for the state's agenda.[36]

Governor Jeb Bush meets with one of the many Florida residents whose homes were damaged or destroyed by the strong hurricanes that swept through the state in 2004.

MANAGING THE STATE

Governors and their senior staffs are also responsible for managing their state's executive branch, whether by providing strategic planning and vision, initiating policy, settling disputes among different agencies, promoting the state (attracting tourism, exports, and investment), recruiting top state administrative and judicial officials, developing the budget, or negotiating disputes with the federal government and with nearby states.

Much recent federal legislation turning programs over to the states specifically designates the governor as the chief planning and administrative officer. This role has given governors both more flexibility and more headaches. On one hand, governors can now dispense federal funds as a form of patronage, supporting services and programs for influential professional and local communities. On the other hand, this new intergovernmental relations role requires more time, more staff, and constant negotiations both with the "feds" and with local interest group leaders vying for the money or services involved.

Some reformers have suggested that all state agencies should be accountable to the governor all the time, but others believe politics should be kept out of the day-to-day

SHOULD GOVERNORS BE INVOLVED IN POLICY DECISIONS AT A UNIVERSITY?

State universities are usually run by a president or chancellor who reports to a board of trustees appointed by the governor. However, there have been instances when governors have intervened to impose policies that clashed with the judgment of education professionals. State colleges and universities are dependent on funds appropriated by state legislatures, following recommendations by the governor. Universities and colleges are generally governed by appointed or elected boards of trustees that serve to buffer and protect them from political parties and interest groups. With advice from search committees consisting of representatives of the faculty, staff, alumni, and students, these boards appoint professional university presidents and delegate to them the responsibility for recommending and carrying out university policies.

Former California Governor Pete Wilson persuaded the California Board of Regents to reject the recommendations of the university president, the chancellors, and the academic senate to continue affirmative action policies. The governor wanted the board to remove gender and race as factors that might be considered in recruitment and admission policies. The board followed his recommendation. Was he right or wrong to intervene?

operations of a state agency. For example, how much influence should a governor have over the running of the department of corrections in a state? Should public agencies respond to fluctuations in public opinion or to a governor's political mood? Which policy decisions should be made by professionals and experts, and which should be controlled by elected officials or by partisan appointees?

Modernizing State Government

Governors in recent years have had more managerial control over their states as a result of the use of modern management techniques: strategic planning, systems analysis, and sophisticated information technology and budgeting systems. In fact, a modern system of professional management has gradually replaced the old "buddy system" in which governors relied on political pals to get things done.

In urban states with competitive party systems, such as New York, Illinois, New Jersey, Pennsylvania, Washington, and California, governors have considerable formal constitutional authority to organize their administrations as they see fit. Even in more rural states, such as South Dakota, scores of agencies have been consolidated into a few comprehensive units as the result of executive orders from the governors.

A few years ago, in the wake of highly publicized scandals, the South Carolina legislature agreed to abolish 75 state boards, folding them into 17 larger executive agencies. This restructuring also gave the governor the authority to hire and fire the directors of most of these agencies.[37]

During the past several decades, various reformers have urged that the governor be made the true manager of the executive branch, whether by consolidating agencies into a smaller number of more tightly controlled departments, giving the governor greater power to hire and fire senior executives, or modernizing state government through better information technology.

However, attempts to reorganize state governments have not received universal praise. In some states, reorganization commissions have submitted reports that were filed away and forgotten. Groups that profit from the existing structure can be counted on to resist change. So, too, can officials who fear loss of job or prestige. Also, legislators are sometimes reluctant to approve recommendations that might make a governor too powerful.

Many critics oppose not so much the idea of reorganization as the basic principle of strengthening executive power and responsibility, which has dominated the reorganization movement. Often, they say, there is little evidence to support the adoption of these reforms, and there is a real danger that reorganizers are overlooking basic values in their concern with saving money. Intent on efficiency and economy, reformers often fail to foresee the risks involved in creating a powerful chief executive where no effective party or legislative opposition exists to keep a strong governor in check.

Reformers agree that no one size of reform is right for every state. However, they maintain that the basic ideas—integrated authority, centralized direction, simplified structure, clear responsibility—are sound. In fact, it is more likely that narrow special interests not responsible to the voters will take over government when the administrative structure is cumbersome, confusing, and too spread out. The legislature can more effectively supervise an administration integrated under the governor's control than one in which responsibility is split.

Effects of Reorganization

Although large savings have been realized through centralized purchasing and the adoption of modern money management practices, it is difficult to measure the results of consolidating departments, strengthening the governor's control over the executive branch, or establishing an ombudsman office to handle citizen complaints. However, the best-governed states do seem to be those in which the administrative structure has been closely integrated under the governor.

Overall formal reorganization is not the only way states modify and modernize their governmental structures. Often they change in stages, copying innovations from other states. Certain states, in fact, serve as exporters of innovations. So does the federal government. When the federal government creates, say, the Department of Housing and Urban Development, states often respond by creating similar departments; when the federal government establishes the Department of Transportation, so do several of the states; and when the federal government creates a special White House–level office for trade, many governors set up their own offices for trade and export responsibilities.

Although governors are more powerful today than they have ever been, vigorous gubernatorial direction of a state's bureaucracy is still more the exception than the rule. Some governors fail to exploit their powers of appointment or budget setting. "Governors also have other tasks than functioning as chief bureaucrat. . . . Bureaucratic complexity also discourages involvement. Given these realities, involvement with state bureaucracies is very much a matter of governors picking their spots."[38]

Several former governors, including Mario Cuomo of New York and Pete Wilson of California, experimented with private sector reforms such as total quality management (TQM) and performance-based pay initiatives, but these reforms were opposed by public employee labor unions. Such proposals have also been viewed as impractical: "From TQM to vision statements to performance measurements to virtual organizations, the management theories and trends come thick and fast—faster than a lot of government employees can keep up with them."[39] Moreover, management reform often gets cast aside when one governor takes over from another, as when Republican Governor George Pataki replaced Democratic Governor Mario Cuomo in New York.

"Although the analogy between a governor and a private sector chief executive is apt," writes political scientist Thad Beyle, "governors have a distance to go before possessing comparable power of appointment and removal."[40] Many governors don't have the flexibility in hiring and firing personnel that business executives have, and they must share control with various boards, commissions, and elected officials.

In sum, governors can be influential in leading certain reforms and introducing management improvements, but they are rarely as influential and as effective as most citizens assume is the case. All kinds of constitutional, legal, and political restraints put brakes on their attempts to bring about fundamental change. Still, in good economic times, governors are generally able to begin new programs and improve the performance of existing state operations.

OTHER STATEWIDE ELECTED OFFICIALS

Other executive officials elected by the people in most states include the lieutenant governor, secretary of state, attorney general, treasurer, and auditor. (See Table 25–3 for an inventory of state elected officials.)

Lieutenant Governor

Forty-two states have a lieutenant governor, a post similar to vice president at the national level. In nearly half the states, the lieutenant governor is elected on the same ticket as the governor, and in those states, the job is indeed like that of the vice president—the job and its influence depend very much on the mood of the governor. In 26 states, the lieutenant governor presides over the state senate. In 39 states, the lieutenant governor becomes governor or acting governor in case of the death, disability, or absence of the governor from the state. Doubtless for this reason, more governors have sprung from this office than from other statewide elective offices. For example, in 2000, two lieutenant governors were elected governor: Judy Martz of Montana and Ruth Ann Minner of

TABLE 25–3	STATES WITH ELECTED OFFICIALS
Governor	50
Attorney general	44
Lieutenant governor	42*
State treasurer	40
Secretary of state	36
Superintendent of education	14
Agriculture commissioner	13
Comptroller	13
Insurance commissioner	11

SOURCE: *The Book of the States, 2000–2001* (Council of State Governments, 2000), p. 33. Copyright by the Council of State Governments. Reprinted with permission.

*In Alaska, Hawaii, and Utah, one elected official serves as both lieutenant governor and secretary of state. In Tennessee, there is no lieutenant governor, but the Speaker of the state senate has the additional statutory title of lieutenant governor.

Delaware. And the lieutenant governor in Texas, Rick Perry, became governor there when George W. Bush moved to the White House. Perry won his own election in 2002. In 2004, Connecticut's lieutenant governor. M. Jodi Rell, became governor when Governor John Rowland resigned in the wake of allegations that he accepted special gifts from state contractors. Rowland almost certainly would have been impeached by the state legislature if he had not resigned.

In states where the governor and lieutenant governor are elected on the same ticket, the lieutenant governor is likely to be given some significant responsibilities. Still, many lieutenant governors have no statutory duties, and in some smaller states, being lieutenant governor is really a part-time job. In the states where the lieutenant governor is elected independently of the governor, the lieutenant governor can sometimes be a member of the opposition party, and he or she can become a thorn in the side of the chief executive. In states like Texas, where the lieutenant governor is elected separately, the lieutenant governor is sometimes as politically powerful as the governor.[41]

There is some reason to question whether lieutenant governors are really necessary. After all, eight states, including Arizona, Georgia, and New Jersey, run perfectly well without one. If their only job is to stand in waiting in case the governor dies, resigns, or is impeached, the replacement function could be performed by a state's attorney general, secretary of state, or the ranking member of the governor's party in the legislature.

Although the position of lieutenant governor has worked well in some states, the view persists that lieutenant governors are often in search of job assignments that make them look important. The staffs and cabinets that are currently growing up around governors make the governor's chief of staff more of a deputy governor than most lieutenant governors. Moreover, many candidates for lieutenant governor appear to seek the post primarily for the name recognition and statewide experience to advance their political careers. In sum, the value to the state of the often obscure office of lieutenant governor is debatable.[42]

Attorney General

The attorney general—the state's chief lawyer—gives advice to state officials, represents the state before the courts, and in some states supervises local prosecutors. Some state attorneys general have real authority over local prosecutors and may prosecute cases on their own initiative, although in most states, criminal prosecution remains under the control of the local county prosecutor. In many states, attorneys general have taken the lead as champions of the consumer and protectors of the environment. They have launched major investigations into the insurance industry and into business practices. They have also led the fight against the tobacco companies and have waged antitrust investigations against corporations such as Microsoft.[43] New York State's attorney general, Eliot Spitzer, became a nationally recognized figure and *Time* magazine's 2002 Crusader of the Year through his investigations of Wall Street fraud, and he used that visibility to build a formidable campaign for governor in 2006.

An additional power of the attorney general is to make sure the state's laws are implemented properly. Attorneys general work in narcotics enforcement, investigate illegal activities, and often concentrate on laws that affect public safety. For example, Florida's attorney general, Bob Butterworth, recently set up a hot line to help eliminate Medicaid fraud.[44] In California, due to power companies' recent noncompliance with laws and allegations of gouging of California citizens, Attorney General Bill Lockyer has filed complaints against four major power companies.[45]

Disputes between attorneys general and governors can be partisan if they belong to different parties or have conflicting ambitions, but disputes can also be issue-oriented. Thus governors in many states have their own staff lawyers to represent them in contests with attorneys general. The office is sometimes a stepping-stone to the governorship—indeed, the acronym AG is often said to stand for both Attorney General and Almost Governor.

Secretary of State

The secretary of state publishes the laws, supervises elections, and issues certificates of incorporation. In some states, the secretary issues automobile licenses and registers corporate securities. Voters in 36 states elect secretaries of state. In eight states, governors appoint people to this position. In three states, secretaries of state are elected by the legislature. And three states don't have this position at all.

Although all secretaries of state have some election function, their responsibilities differ greatly from state to state. However, all share a general commitment to increasing voter education and turnout. In 1998, the National Association of Secretaries of State launched the "New Millennium Project" to encourage greater participation among young Americans. Several states now send birthday cards with voter registration forms to every 18-year-old, while others have created challenges that pit colleges against each other in registration contests.

Treasurer and Auditor

The treasurer is the guardian of the state's money. Although in some states the job is largely ministerial, state treasurers generally have the responsibility of ensuring that cash is available to meet the obligations of the state and that all available funds are invested to maximize interest return.

The auditor in most states has two major jobs: to authorize payments from the state treasury and to make periodic audits of officials who handle state money. In Montana,

PEOPLE & POLITICS *Making a Difference* ★ ★ ★

CATHY COX

Even as Florida's Secretary of State, Katherine Harris, was still counting votes during the 2000 election impasse that led to the Supreme Court battle in *Bush* v. *Gore*, Georgia's Secretary of State, Cathy Cox, was committing her state to creating a model voting system for the rest of the country. In 2002, she was named one of *Governing* magazine's top officials of the year for her efforts.

Cox entered office in 1999 and soon realized that her state's voting technology was among the worst in the nation. The state's 159 counties had every kind of voting system imaginable, from paper ballots to punch cards to old machines, almost none of which was particularly reliable. According to Cox, Georgia's antiquated voting system "spoiled" 94,000 ballots in 2000, almost twice the national average and thousands more than Florida's.[46]

Cox made Georgia history almost overnight. She started her first term by leading one of the largest bureaucratic overhauls in Georgia's history by moving the Secretary of State's vote-counting division from Atlanta to Macon, shaving millions off her budget at a time of great budget stress in the state, and modernizing her agency's own technology. More importantly, she promised to install touch-screen voting machines in every Georgia voting precinct by 2002, when she would stand for reelection herself.

"They told me that I was out of my mind," Cox remembers of her request for the $54 million in state funding to install the 19,000 new voting machines. But the former state legislator and lawyer could not be denied. She had already made history by becoming the first woman ever elected to state-wide office, and had a reputation as a street fighter who got what she wanted in the budget process.

In November 2002, she was reelected to office by winning 146 out of 159 counties and 61 percent of the votes cast, all of which were recorded on the new systems. "I wouldn't try to do this with my name on the ballot unless I was 1,000 percent sure of it," she later said. "We will show the rest of the nation that this is the way to vote."

the state auditor serves as insurance commissioner. Before money can be spent, the auditor must sign a *warrant* certifying that the expenditure is authorized by law and that the money is available in the treasury. This job is more accurately called the *preaudit* and is increasingly being assigned to a comptroller appointed by and responsible to the governor. Auditing *after* money has been spent, however, is a job most observers believe should be given to an officer responsible to the legislature. Even advocates of much more centralized administration believe that the auditor should not be responsible to the governor.

Other Officials

Such positions as superintendent of public education, agriculture commissioner, public utilities commissioner, comptroller, and insurance commissioner are less likely to be elected than treasurers or auditors. Putting positions like these on the ballot results in a longer ballot and voter fatigue; in one election, fully half the people who went to the polls failed to vote for superintendent of public instruction. The proliferation of elected officials also makes it more difficult for governors to manage and lead state government.

As part of the trend toward integrated administration, the duties of elected state officials have generally been limited to those specified in the state constitution. Some important functions have been given to officials appointed by the governor. In many states, the budget director appointed by the governor has a more important role than the elected treasurer or secretary of state. Yet elected officers can often control patronage, attract a following, and thus develop a political base from which to attack the governor's program and administration.

Sometimes progressive and controversial initiatives in state governments come from elected officials. An attorney general in Texas helped design and pass the Texas Open Records Act, one of the broadest and most strictly enforced freedom-of-information statutes in the country. A secretary of state in Massachusetts modernized election laws, helped enact campaign finance laws, and championed conflict-of-interest reforms. A state treasurer in Colorado battled to transfer some of his state's revenue deposits from a few large Denver banks to smaller banks around the state and devised incentives for these banks to lend money to students and small businesses and to support low-income housing and family farms.

GOVERNOR OF TEXAS AND THE VETO

Constitutional restrictions make the Texas governor one of the weakest in the nation. The Texas Constitution sets up a plural executive system, in which the executive officeholders are elected independently of the governor and this fragments authority. The governor has no appointed cabinet and the heads of some of the most important state agencies are independently elected. Such discord makes the coordination of policy difficult and severely limits gubernatorial power. However, the Texas governor has one of the strongest veto powers in the nation. He/she has ten days after passage to sign, veto, or allow legislation to become law without his/her signature.

Go to Make It Real "Governor of Texas and the Veto."

THE REWARDS OF BEING A GOVERNOR

No one thinks governors have an easy job. Most governors earn praise for their leadership, and most governors enjoy solid public approval ratings.[47] Recent governors—Zell Miller of Georgia, Marc Racicot of Montana, Thomas J. Vilsack of Iowa, Gary Locke of Washington, Frank O'Bannon of Indiana, Mike Foster Jr. of Louisiana—became popular despite the political "heat" and the need to make tough decisions. "A governor achieves his personal best by being honest and by staying in touch with the people who elected him to serve them," says former Governor Lamar Alexander of Tennessee.[48] Former Governor Tom Kean of New Jersey echoed similar thoughts: "I have tried to show during my political career, and especially my years as governor, that responsible government can meet people's needs and bring them together, that government can make a difference in the way we live."[49]

Ultimately, the best governors are ones who have a keen sense of history and their own circumstance. A popular former governor of Utah, the late Scott Matheson, wrote that they have been the men and women who have the right combination of values "for quality service, the courage to stick to their convictions, even when in the minority, integrity by instinct, compassion by nature, leadership by perception, and the character to admit wrong, and when necessary, to accept defeat."[50]

S U M M A R Y

1. The job of governor is one of the most important and exacting in American political life. Governors are usually white male lawyers in their forties or fifties. At least three out of four governors who run again win reelection.

2. Today, a governor is expected to be the state's chief policy maker, the architect of the state budget, the chief manager of the state administration, and the political and symbolic leader of the state. The governor also plays an increasingly complex role as the crucial link between the national and local governments.

3. Governors have many formal powers. The most important are their appointive and budgetary powers. Governors also have veto and pardon powers and the power to issue executive orders. They are commanders in chief of the National Guard. But a governor's formal powers mean little if he or she is not a persuasive communicator with good judgment and the capacity to focus simultaneously on daily tasks and long-range priorities. Governors who are effective with the media find this an additional source of informal power. Governors help set the policy agenda and frame the debate on important public issues. Yet governors, as a general rule, have more responsibility than power.

4. Over the past generation, reforms in management and organization have strengthened most governorships. Most governors have gained powers that enable them to achieve more of their goals. But constitutional, legal, and political restraints continue to limit their efforts. Thus few governors have an easy tenure, and it is generally agreed that public demands and expectations on governors today are higher than ever.

5. In addition to a governor, the voters in most states also elect other statewide officials such as a lieutenant governor, secretary of state, attorney general, and state treasurer. In about half of the states, the governor and lieutenant governor run as a team ticket, but elsewhere this is not the case, and all other statewide elected officials run separately. Many of the officials play important political and policy roles in their states, and many current governors previously served in some other statewide elected capacity.

K E Y   T E R M S

veto	item veto	reduction veto	amendatory veto	executive order

F U R T H E R   R E A D I N G

LAMAR ALEXANDER, *Steps Along the Way: A Governor's Scrapbook* (Nelson, 1986).

CECIL ANDRUS AND JOEL CONNELLY, *Cecil Andrus: Politics Western Style* (Sasquatch Books, 1998).

THAD L. BEYLE, ED., *Governors and Hard Times* (CQ Press, 1992).

THOMAS M. CARSEY, *Campaign Dynamics: The Race for Governor* (University of Michigan Press, 2000).

THOMAS E. CRONIN AND ROBERT D. LOEVY, *Colorado Politics and Government* (University of Nebraska Press, 1993).

ROBERT S. ERIKSON ET AL., *Statehouse Democracy: Public Opinion and Policy in the American States* (Cambridge University Press, 1993).

EARL H. FRY, *The Expanding Role of State and Local Governments in U.S. Foreign Affairs* (Council on Foreign Relations Press, 1998).

VIRGINIA GRAY, RUSSELL HANSON, AND HERBERT JACOB, EDS., *Politics in the American States: A Comparative Analysis*, 7th ed. (CQ Press, 1999).

MADELEINE M. KUNIN, *Living a Political Life* (Vintage, 1995).

GERALD C. LUBENOW AND BRUCE E. CAIN, EDS., *Governing California* (Institute of Governmental Studies Press, 1997).

SARAH M. MOREHOUSE, *The Governor as Party Leader* (University of Michigan Press, 1998).

DAVID OSBORNE, *Laboratories of Democracy: A New Breed of Governor Creates Models for National Growth* (Harvard Business School Press, 1988).

GEORGE PATAKI WITH DANIEL PAISNER, *Pataki: An Autobiography* (Viking, 1998).

ALAN ROSENTHAL, *Governors and Legislatures: Contending Powers* (CQ Press, 1990).

SUE THOMAS AND CLYDE WILCOX, *Women and Elective Office* (Oxford University Press, 1998).

TOMMY G. THOMPSON, *Power to the People: An American State at Work* (HarperCollins, 1996).

JESSE VENTURA, *Do I Stand Alone?* (Pocket Books, 2000).

JESSE VENTURA, *I Ain't Got Time to Bleed* (Signet, 2000).

See also the quarterly *Spectrum: The Journal of State Government; Governing; State Policy Reports;* and *State Government News;* see also the valuable University of Nebraska Press series on state politics in the individual states, each of which has a chapter on governors.

The National Governors' Association publishes a variety of surveys, reports, and studies, including the weekly *Governors' Bulletin* and the *Proceedings of the National Governors' Association* annual meetings. These and related documents can be purchased by writing to the National Governors' Association, 444 N. Capitol Street NW, Washington, D.C., 20001.

JUDGES AND JUSTICE IN THE STATES

26

Although we hear more about federal judges than about their state counterparts, most of the nation's judicial business is conducted by the 29,000 state and municipal judges. Put into perspective: federal courts have almost 2 million annual criminal, civil, and bankruptcy filings, whereas state courts confront over 92 million cases, most of which are traffic related (over 55 million).[1] Most state judges are white males, but this imbalance is changing rapidly. Nationwide there are about 5,000 female state court judges, about one in five, and they are now represented on all but one state supreme court (Indiana).[2] State judges preside over most criminal trials, settle most lawsuits between individuals, and administer most estates. They have a vital role in determining who gets what, where, when, and how. Thus they have a crucial role in making public policy.

State judges have the final say—most of the time. Through **writs of habeas corpus**—petitions to federal courts alleging that petitioners are being held by a state as the result of a proceeding that denies them due process of law in violation of the U.S. Constitution—criminal defendants may occasionally get federal district judges to review the actions of state courts. Or if state judges have to interpret the meaning of the U.S. Constitution, a national law, or a national treaty—that is, if the case raises a *federal question*—the losing party may request that the U.S. Supreme Court review the decision of the highest state court to which it may be taken under state law. Of the hundreds of thousands of decisions by state judges each year, very few are reviewed by the U.S. Supreme Court.

In recent decades, state courts have become more prominent in the political life of their state. In many states, a **new judicial federalism** has emerged, with judges interpreting the bill of rights in their state constitutions more broadly than the U.S. Supreme Court has in applying the national Bill of Rights, in such areas as the right of privacy, public school financing, and equal protection of the law.[3] There has also been a revolution in **tort law**—law relating to compensation for injuries to person, reputation, or property. This "tort revolution" has flooded state courts as more people sue more often about more disputes. For example, *product liability suits* are brought by people who believe they have been injured as the result of faulty products, and *malpractice suits* are brought by people who believe they have been injured as the result of mistakes by doctors, hospitals, lawyers, and other professionals. And there have been notable increases in cases relating to property rights and breaches of contract. However, this has triggered a backlash against the explosion of tort filings, and many states have instituted legislative tort reforms making it more difficult to bring lawsuits.

There has also been a significant increase in criminal cases as people press for tougher action against criminals. About half of the states have passed so-called three-strikes-and-you're-out laws, which prescribe a mandatory life sentence after three felony convictions.[4] These felony cases are threatening to overwhelm our courts and our prisons.

As state courts have become more active in our political life, state judges have become embroiled in controversial issues. And as the public has grown more sophisticated about the importance of judges as policy makers, judicial politics in the states is becoming a significant feature of the political landscape.

THE STRUCTURE OF STATE COURTS

Each state has its own court system. Because the 50 systems vary, it is difficult to generalize about them. For convenience, we categorize and discuss state courts as (1) minor courts of limited jurisdiction, (2) trial courts of general jurisdiction, and (3) appellate courts (see Figure 26–1).

writ of habeas corpus
Court order requiring explanation to a judge why a prisoner is being held.

new judicial federalism
The practice of some state courts using the bill of rights in their state constitutions to provide more protection for some rights than is provided by the Supreme Court's interpretation of the Bill of Rights in the U.S. Constitution.

tort law
Law relating to injuries to person, reputation, or property.

CALIFORNIA SUPREME COURT
Highest state court; seven justices

COURTS OF APPEAL
Intermediate court; reviews decisions of Superior Courts; divided into six districts

SUPERIOR COURT
One in each county; 58 in the state.
Each court may have many departments.
Decide questions of fact and law

SMALL CLAIMS	CRIMINAL	CIVIL	JUVENILE
Claims of $2,500 or less.	Felonies: crimes punishable by imprisonment in state facilities.	Disputes where the claim is over $2,500 and cases involving wills, land titles, divorce, child custody, etc.	Correction of offenders under age 18. Protection of abused and neglected minors.

FIGURE 26–1 The California State Courts.
SOURCE: Guide to California Courts, at www.courtinfo.ca.gov/reference/guide.

Minor Courts

In most states, minor courts handle **misdemeanors**—relatively minor violations of state and local laws—as well as traffic cases and civil suits involving small amounts of money. In some places, they also hold preliminary hearings and set bail for more serious charges. **Felonies** are serious crimes tried in trial courts; the penalty for which can range from imprisonment in a penitentiary for more than a year to death. Decisions of the minor courts may be appealed and in most instances tried *de novo*—that is, tried all over again without reference to what happened in the minor courts. In most places, these courts are financed and administered by the local unit of government—the township, city, or county. In cities, these minor courts are known as *municipal courts* and are often divided into traffic courts, family courts, small claims courts, and police courts. Paid *magistrates* trained in the law preside over most of these courts.

Although traditional justice of peace courts are being phased out, the *justice of the peace* system survives in some states (Arizona, Arkansas, Delaware, Louisiana, Montana, Texas, and Wyoming) and in rural areas; in New York, these civil authorities are called *town justices.* Justices of the peace are elected for short terms, usually two to six years. They need not be trained in the law, and their authority is limited to performing marriages, notarizing papers, handling traffic violations, and hearing misdemeanors, usually those involving fines of less than $200. They also hear minor civil disputes. Because plaintiffs can often choose among several justices of the peace in a county, they may pick the one most likely to decide in their favor. Thus it has been said that the initials for *justice of the peace*, JP, stand for "judgment for the plaintiff."

Courts handling minor crimes are often so crowded that cases are "processed" with little time for individual attention. While many critics of the legal system contend that judges are too lenient and criminals are back on the streets too quickly, others charge that poor and ignorant defendants often spend days in jail waiting for their cases to go to trial. A new and apparently effective reform is the establishment of *court-watching groups.* In some cities, these groups are sponsored by organizations concerned with seeing that the courts treat fairly those charged with crimes. In other cities, groups are sponsored by organizations concerned that judges are too easy on defendants. Prosecutors, public defenders, and judges, it is alleged, become a comfortable work group, with little or no public scrutiny. Court watchers make these professionals more sensitive to the views of the general public.

Trial Courts of General Jurisdiction

Trial courts where cases first appear **(original jurisdiction)** are called county courts, circuit courts, superior courts, district courts, and common pleas courts. They administer common, criminal, equity, and statutory law. Some states maintain separate courts for criminal and civil matters. States generally also have special *probate courts* to administer estates and handle related matters. These courts are all *courts of record* in which trials take place, witnesses are heard, and juries render verdicts, although most cases are heard and decided by a judge. *Appellate courts* may review decisions of trial courts; however, most decisions of trial judges are not reviewed and are final. There is a growing recognition that these courts do more than apply the law; they also participate in the never-ending process of shaping the law and public policy.[5]

Appellate Courts

In a few states—Delaware, Montana, New Hampshire, Nevada, North Dakota, Rhode Island, West Virginia, and Vermont—trial court decisions are appealed directly to the state supreme court. (In North Dakota, the supreme court can assign cases to a court of appeals composed of three judges chosen from among the trial judges.) Most states, however, have intermediate appeals courts that fit into the system in much the same way that the United States courts of appeals fit into the federal structure.

All states have a *court of last resort,* usually called the supreme court. In Maine and Massachusetts, the court of last resort is called the supreme judicial court; in Maryland

Family court judges deal with the legal issues of minors—children under the age of 18.

"Due to an overcrowded prison system, I'm sentencing you to stand in that corner for the next six months."
The Wall Street Journal.

misdemeanor
A minor crime; the penalty is a fine or imprisonment for a short time, usually less than a year, in a local jail.

felony
A serious crime, the penalty for which can range from imprisonment in a penitentiary for more than a year to death.

original jurisdiction
The authority of a court to hear a case "in the first instance."

PEOPLE & POLITICS *Making a Difference* ★ ★ ★

NEW YORK CHIEF JUDGE JUDITH S. KAYE

Chief Judge Judith S. Kaye is the first woman to serve as chief judge on New York's highest court, the New York State Court of Appeals. Chief Judge Kaye is a leading advocate of judicial reforms and of justice for children and combating domestic violence.

Chief Judge Kaye graduated from Barnard College and earned her law degree from the New York University School of Law. After practicing commercial law for 15 years, she was appointed to the court of appeals by Democratic Governor Mario Cuomo in 1983. In 1993, Governor Cuomo elevated her to chief judge.

Besides serving as president of the Conference of Chief Justices (2004–2005) and as chair of the Board for the National Center for State Courts (2002–2003), Chief Judge Kaye has lectured and written widely on the legal process, state constitutional law, women in the law, professional ethics, and judicial reform.*

*See, e.g., Judith S. Kaye, "State Courts at the Dawn of a New Century: Common Law Courts Reading Statutes and Constitutions," in David M. O'Brien, ed., *Judges on Judging: Views from the Bench* (C.Q. Press, 2004), pp. 295–304.

and New York, this court is called the court of appeals; in West Virginia, it is the supreme court of appeals. And if that is not confusing enough, in New York, the trial courts are called supreme courts. Texas and Oklahoma have two courts of last resort—a supreme court that handles civil matters and a court of criminal appeals.

Unless a federal question is involved, state supreme courts are the highest tribunal to which a case may be appealed. State courts of last resort have five to nine judges; most have seven. Each state court has developed its own method of operating, with the pattern and practices varying widely among the states. Of the more than 60,000 decisions by state supreme courts, only 2 percent are appealed to the U.S. Supreme Court, which reviews less than 1 percent of all appeals.[6]

All state judges of all state courts take an oath to uphold the supremacy of the U.S. Constitution, and all state judges have the power of **judicial review**. That is, they may refuse to enforce, and may restrain state and local officials from enforcing, state laws or regulations or actions if they conclude that these conflict with the state constitution or the U.S. Constitution. State judges may also declare actions of federal officials or federal laws or regulations to be in conflict with the U.S. Constitution, subject to final review by the U.S. Supreme Court.

State supreme courts have also led the way in making judicial decisions available on the Internet. All have Web sites, and about 98 percent provide access to written opinions and decisions, along with other information, and 10 percent make oral arguments available.[7] The Web site of the National Center for State Courts (www.ncsconline.org) provides links to state court Web sites.

State Courts and State Politics

Judges are a much more prominent part of the American political scene, at both the national and state levels, than in other countries. But state courts differ from federal courts in several ways:

judicial review
The power of a court to refuse to enforce a law or a government regulation that in the opinion of the judges conflicts with the U.S. Constitution or, in a state court, the state constitution.

1. State judges are more likely to decide cases involving their legislative and executive branches than the U.S. Supreme Court is with respect to congressional and presidential matters.[8] State judges are likely to be part of the state's legal culture, since most of them have been educated in the state's law schools.[9]

2. State judges are unconstrained by the doctrine of federalism in dealing with local units of government.

3. State judges are much less constrained than federal courts from hearing cases brought by taxpayers. In federal courts, persons lack *standing to sue*—the legal right to sue—unless they show some immediate personal injury. Furthermore, in nine states, the state supreme court can give advisory opinions at the request of the governor or state legislature. An **advisory opinion** is an opinion unrelated to a particular case that gives a court's view about a constitutional or legal issue.

4. Unlike federal judges, most state judges serve for limited terms and stand for election, so they can claim to be representatives of the people. "As elected representatives, like legislators, they feel less hesitant to offer their policy views than do appointed judges."[10] In addition, if there is dissatisfaction with a decision of a state supreme court, it can be more readily set aside than a decision of the U.S. Supreme Court can.[11]

HOW JUDGES ARE CHOSEN

Judges are selected in four different ways (see Figure 26–2): appointment by the governor, election by the legislature, popular election, or a modified appointment plan known as the Missouri Plan.

Appointment by the Governor and Election by the Legislature

In Delaware, Hawaii, Maine, New Jersey, New York, and Vermont, judges are appointed by the governor and confirmed by the state senate. In Delaware and Massachusetts, governors select appointees from names submitted by judicial nominating commissions. Election by the legislature is the constitutional practice in Connecticut, Rhode Island, South Carolina, and Virginia. However, we need to look beyond the formal election procedures. "A majority of the judges serving in states utilizing an elective judiciary . . . are in fact initially appointed by the governor to fill mid-term vacancies, usually

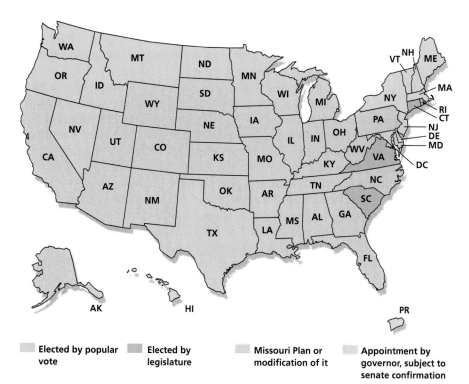

Elected by popular vote   Elected by legislature   Missouri Plan or modification of it   Appointment by governor, subject to senate confirmation

FIGURE 26–2 Method for Selection of Judges of the Court of Last Resort.
SOURCE: *The Book of the States, 2000–2001* (Council of State Governments, 2002), p. 53.

advisory opinion
An opinion unrelated to a particular case that gives a court's view about a constitutional or legal issue.

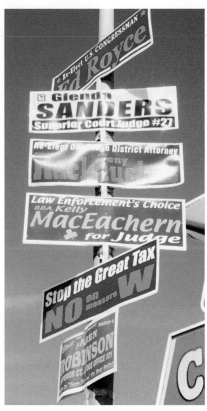

In states with elected judges, campaigns can become very competitive.

occasioned by the retirement or death of sitting judges . . . and these appointed judges are overwhelmingly favored in their first electoral bids following appointment."[12]

In addition to the formal process of nomination and selection, there are several informal processes. Lawyers interested in becoming judges may make their interest known either directly or indirectly to party officials; leaders of the local bar associations may promote favored members; various members of the bar may seek out candidates and recruit them. Political leaders and interest groups also participate. Following such suggestions, the names go through the formal appointment process.[13]

Popular Election

In nearly half the states, judges are chosen in elections. Over 85 percent of all state and local judges face elections, far more than the number of elected state legislators and executive officials. Appellate court judges in eight state face partisan elections, 13 states hold nonpartisan elections, and another 19 states have retention elections for state judges.[14]

Some states, mostly in the West and upper Midwest, hold *nonpartisan* primaries for nominating judicial candidates and elect them on nonpartisan ballots. But nonpartisan judicial elections do not necessarily mean that political parties are not involved. In at least half of the states with nonpartisan judicial elections, parties actively campaign on behalf of candidates. Some states try to isolate judicial elections from partisanship by holding them separately from other elections.

In 1986, California amended its constitution to forbid political parties from endorsing candidates for judicial office. However, federal courts declared the proposition unconstitutional, and California political parties are once again endorsing judicial candidates. Apparently the prevailing view, as Justice Thurgood Marshall observed, is that "the prospect that voters might be persuaded by party endorsements is not a *corruption* of the democratic political process; it *is* the democratic political process."[15]

In recent years, most states have adopted provisions similar to the American Bar Association's code of judicial conduct that bar judicial candidates from telling the electorate anything about their views on legal and political matters—whether they are in favor, for example, of punishing criminals harshly or of expanding privacy rights. A "chief justices' summit" was convened in 2000 by the chief justices of the 17 most populous states with judicial elections and recommended reforms, including public funding for judicial elections and closer monitoring of judicial campaigns. Some states have gone further; the Minnesota Supreme Court, for instance, prohibited judicial candidates from soliciting campaign contributions, declaring their party affiliation, or publicly voicing their positions on controversial issues. But the U.S. Supreme Court struck down Minnesota's ban on judicial candidates' announcing their position on controversial legal and political matters as a violation of the First Amendment guarantee of free speech.[16] State and federal courts in Alabama, Georgia, Michigan, Ohio, and other states have also handed down decisions that are "a roadblock for efforts to curb the increasingly raucous nature of judicial politics."[17]

Until recently, there was little interest in judicial elections, and voter turnout tended to be low. But judicial elections are becoming increasingly costly and spirited. In the 2000 elections, candidates for state supreme courts raised an unprecedented $45 million, over 60 percent more than in 1998 and double that spent in 1994. Interest groups in five states with the most hotly contested judicial races raised an additional $16 million.[18] Special-interest groups focus attention on judges whose decisions they find objectionable. The issues vary from election to election and from state to state. In some states, the issue has been the death penalty. In Texas and California, efforts to limit liability lawsuits and damage awards have led to campaign clashes over judicial candidates, with trial lawyers, consumers, and union groups on one side and business interests on the other. In Idaho, one candidate for the supreme court campaigned on a platform that the theory of evolution could not be true—and won. In Wisconsin, the chief justice won reelection, although she had to fight for her seat and felt compelled to explain why she had once allowed an aerobics class in the court's hearing room. An Illinois judge was unseated because of his decisions in abortion cases. Judges now have to act like politicians and "feel they are under increasing pressure to be accountable to public opinion."[19] The image of impartial courts may well become a casualty of the increasingly heated politics of judicial campaigns and elections.

The costs of judicial elections are escalating. Critics charge that the need to raise large sums for their campaigns compromises the impartiality of judges and judicial candidates. Judicial campaigns have been especially expensive in Alabama, Illinois, Michigan, Mississippi, and Ohio, in which almost $35 million was spent on state supreme court candidates in those five states alone.[20] In many states that elect judges, it is increasingly clear that judicial candidates are dependent on a small number of law firms, businesses, or special-interest groups, such as the U.S. Chamber of Commerce and the Business Roundtable, for their campaign funds.[21]

In response to the growing cost of state judicial elections, the American Bar Association, the American Judicature Society, and other organizations are promoting the public financing of state judicial campaigns and elections.[22] Two states, Wisconsin and North Carolina, provide public financing for some judicial elections. Wisconsin has had publicly financed elections for state supreme court justices since the 1970s; candidates are eligible for $97,000 in state money if they agree to a $215,000 spending limit. The system is paid for through a one dollar check-off contribution on income tax returns, and has been historically underfinanced. In 2004, North Carolina's Judicial Campaign Reform Act went into effect. Under it all, appellate-level judicial races are nonpartisan, and candidates who agree to fund-raising and spending limits receive public financing in the general election. The public financing of judicial elections is also under consideration in a number of other states, including Idaho, Illinois, New York, and Texas.

MINORITY REPRESENTATION   The one-person, one-vote rule that applies to legislative elections does not apply to judicial elections.[23] States may create judicial districts so that one judge "represents" many more voters than another judge. However, although there is no requirement that states elect judges, if they choose to do so, the federal Voting Rights Act of 1965 applies to these judicial elections.[24]

Because the Voting Rights Act of 1965 forbids any practice or procedure that dilutes the voting power of minorities, it raises a question about the constitutionality of at-large judicial elections. When judges are elected at large for a city or a state, African American and Hispanic candidates sometimes find it difficult to get elected. African American and Hispanic voters tend to be concentrated in the inner cities or in certain geographical areas; thus their impact is diluted in citywide or statewide elections. For example, in a state in which the population consists of 20 percent African American voters, 20 percent Hispanic voters, and 60 percent Anglo voters, with five judges to be elected on a statewide basis, few if any African American judges or Hispanic judges will be elected. Some Hispanics and African Americans argue that the solution is to divide such a state into five districts, with one judge elected in each district, and draw district lines in such a way that African Americans and Hispanics make up a majority of voters in as many districts as possible, giving them a chance to elect at least one of their own.

Merit Selection: The Missouri Plan

Many lawyers and political scientists have argued in favor of some kind of selection procedure in which there is a screening process before judges are appointed or elected to ensure that only candidates of merit will be considered. Merit systems are used in 16 states.

One of the oldest merit plans is the Missouri Plan.[25] The **Missouri Plan**, as used in most states, provides that when a judicial vacancy occurs, a special *nominating commission* (usually composed of three lawyers elected by the bar, three citizens appointed by the governor, and the chief justice) nominates three candidates.[26] The governor selects one, who then serves as a judge for at least a year. At the next general election, the voters are asked, "Shall Judge X be retained in office?" If a majority of the voters agree, the judge serves a new full term (typically six to 12 years); if not, another person is

Since the passage of the Voting Rights Act of 1965, minorities have had greater opportunities to be elected judges.

Missouri Plan
A system for selecting judges that combines features of the appointive and elective methods. The governor selects judges from lists presented by panels of lawyers and laypersons, and at the end of their term, the judges may run against their own record in retention elections.

CHANGING FACE OF AMERICAN POLITICS

WOMEN AND MINORITIES ON STATE SUPREME COURTS

State supreme courts were once composed overwhelmingly of white males. But women and minorities now constitute over 30 percent of the judges on state supreme courts. In 2003–2004, there were 92 women on state courts of highest resort, and in two states—New York and Washington—they made up over 50 percent of the bench. The New Mexico state supreme court has the largest number of Hispanic judges (60 percent of the bench). African American judges now sit in more than 20 percent of state high courts in Florida, Georgia, Indiana, Tennessee, and Texas. Asian and Pacific Islander judges sit on two state supreme courts, in California and Hawaii.

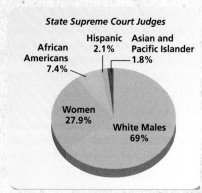

State Supreme Court Judges

- African Americans 7.4%
- Hispanic 2.1%
- Asian and Pacific Islander 1.8%
- Women 27.9%
- White Males 69%

SOURCE: American Judicature Society at www.ajs.org/js/select.htm; American Bar Association, *The Directory of Minority Judges of the United States*, 3d ed. (American Bar Association, 2001).

SOURCE: American Judicature Society at www.ajs.org/js/select.htm; American Bar Association, *The Directory of Minority Judges of the United States*, 3d ed. (American Bar Association, 2001).

selected by the same procedure. At the end of his or her term, the judge may ask to have his or her name placed on the ballot, and the voters are again asked whether they want to retain that judge in office.[27] These uncontested elections, in which judges run against their own record, are called *retention elections,* and some require a supermajority vote.

California has a slightly different form of merit selection. The governor appoints judges to the supreme court and the appellate court for 12-year terms, with the approval of the Commission on Judicial Appointments. The commission consists of the attorney general, chief justice, and senior appellate presiding justice for supreme court appointments or the senior presiding justice in the appellate district for appellate court appointments. In the next statewide election, the judge runs against his or her own record. The governor appoints trial judges to six-year terms; they may be challenged when seeking reelection, but their names do not appear on the ballot if they are running unopposed.

Even more of a hybrid is the system used in New Mexico, where a judicial nominating commission sends names to the governor, who selects a judge. At the next general election, an opponent nominated in the other party's primary may challenge the judge in a partisan election. If no opponent is nominated, the incumbent gets a "free ride." Whoever wins that election then serves one term and thereafter runs against his or her own record in a retention election.

Until recently, retention elections generated little interest and low voter turnout.[28] In all, of the almost 4,600 judicial retention elections since 1960, fewer than 60 judges have been removed by voters, although a few judges have decided not to run when they realized they might fail to be retained.[29] Recently, some state supreme court justices have been vigorously challenged in retention elections, especially when their decisions differed appreciably from the mainstream of public opinion and aroused the hostility of significant special interests. Frequently, the charge was that the judge was "soft on crime." Interest groups have learned that it is relatively easy to target incumbents, but because of constraints on the way judicial candidates are expected to campaign, it is "difficult for targeted judges to defend themselves."[30]

Most voters know little about judges, and what information they get comes from interested parties and persons, especially those who dislike what the judges have done. To provide a more balanced picture, a few states—Alaska, Utah, Colorado, Arizona, Tennessee—have tried to supply more neutral information about judicial performance. In Colorado, an *evaluation committee* in each judicial district—jointly appointed by the chief justice, governor, president of the senate, and speaker of the house—disseminates information through newspaper supplements, including a final recommendation of "retain" or "do not retain."[31] In Alaska, a judicial council composed of three lawyers, three nonlawyers, and the chief justice provides evaluations that are widely publicized.[32] In Utah, the Judicial Council—consisting of the chief justice, another justice, an appellate court judge, five district court judges, two juvenile court judges, three other lower court judges, a state bar representative, and the state court administration—certifies incumbents, and this certification, or lack of it, is indicated on the ballot.

Even though contested retention elections are the exception, sitting judges are aware that if they make decisions that offend organized interest groups, they may face opposition the next time their names are placed on the ballot. Whether these pressures threaten the independence of the courts or are necessary to ensuring judicial accountability within our political system in which judges play such an important role remains a matter of the political debate.[33]

The Appointive Versus the Elective System

For more than 200 years, people have debated the merits of an appointive versus an elective system for the selection of judges. Those who favor the appointive method contend that voters are generally uninformed about candidates and are not competent to assess legal learning and judicial abilities. Popular election, they claim, puts a premium on personality, requires judges to enter the political arena, and discourages many able lawyers from running for office. They also contend that the elective process conceals what is really going on. Absent name recognition, voters go for party labels, which are increasingly less significant as indicators of ideology.[34] In addition, because retirement and death create many vacancies, it is often the governor who selects the judges. The governor makes an interim appointment until the next election, and the temporary appointee usually wins the election.

Those who favor judicial elections counter that judges should be directly accountable to the people. When judges are appointed, they may lose touch with the general currents of opinion of the electorate. Moreover, the appointive process gives governors too much power over judges. And even if judicial elections do not result in the defeat of many sitting judges, elections serve to foster accountability because judges do not want to be defeated and will try to maintain popular support. In general, bar associations, corporate law firms, and judges themselves tend to favor some kind of merit selection system; plaintiffs, attorneys, women's associations, minority associations, and labor groups are skeptical or opposed.

How Judges Are Judged

Unlike federal judges who hold office during "good behavior"—essentially for life—most state judges are selected for fixed terms, typically six to 12 years. In Massachusetts, New Hampshire, and Puerto Rico, judges serve to age 70; in Rhode Island, they serve for life. Thirty-seven states and the District of Columbia mandate the retirement of judges at a certain age, usually 70.[35]

The states, rather than the national government, have taken the lead in establishing procedures to judge judges. Because impeachment has proved to be an ineffective means to remove judges, today each of the 50 states has a board, commission, or court to handle allegations of judicial misbehavior. Despite the objections of many judges, these commissions are most often composed of both nonlawyers and lawyers. They

★ ★ **YOU DECIDE**

SHOULD JUDGES BE ELECTED OR APPOINTED?

Which method produces better judges? The first problem is to define a "good judge." Most people define a good judge as one who makes decisions they like. Even if the desirable features are defined more precisely—ability to maintain neutrality between parties, knowledge of the law, writing ability, personal integrity, physical and mental health, and ability to handle judicial power sensibly—these are still factors that are hard to measure.

Are judges selected by appointment more likely to make decisions of a certain kind than judges chosen by election? Are judges of greater legal knowledge and probity more likely to be selected by one method rather than by another?

investigate complaints and hold hearings for judges who have been charged with improper performance of their duties or unethical or unfair conduct. Establishment of these commissions appears to have helped restore public confidence in the state judicial systems.[36]

For developments in the states and efforts to establish standards of conduct for judicial candidates, go to www.constitutionproject.org, the Web site of a nonpartisan group dedicated to protecting the independence of courts from partisan political attacks. See also the site of the Brennan Center's Project on Judicial Independence at the New York University Law School, www.brennancenter.org. You can also subscribe to its biweekly e-mail list to get summaries of news stories relating to judicial independence, judicial elections, and judicial appointments. Another valuable site for information about courts is that of the American Judicature Society, at www.ajs.org.

THE JUDICIAL REFORM MOVEMENT

Many reforms—court unification, centralized management, state financing, and merit selection—have been adopted, but waste and delay continue to plague our courts. We are, many charge, a "litigious society." Dockets are crowded, relief is costly, and inordinate delays are common.[37]

Proposed reforms for improving the administration of justice include the following:

- Judges should be selected by some kind of merit system that screens candidates in terms of their qualifications.

- Judges should be paid adequately so that they have the financial independence to concentrate on their work and so that successful lawyers will be willing to serve on the bench. In most states, judges' salaries are considerably less than the average incomes of practicing attorneys of the same age and experience. Judges are unable to earn anything beyond their salaries, and they must be cautious about investments in order to avoid conflicts of interest.

- Judges should serve for long terms so that they can make decisions without fear of losing their jobs.

- Rule-making powers should be given to the state supreme court or its chief justice. States are permitting judges to adopt procedural rules and codes of professional conduct. Most require lawyers to continue their education by taking refresher courses.

- Although no person should be appointed or elected to a court solely because of race, sex, or ethnic background, our courts need to become more representative of the communities they serve.[38]

- States should provide for alternative dispute resolution.

Alternative dispute resolution (ADR) refers to procedures that serve as alternatives to formal trials. These procedures include mediation, arbitration, conciliation, private judging, and advisory settlement conferences. From time to time, Congress has made grants to encourage states and localities to develop alternative dispute resolution mechanism, especially for domestic relations issues. ADRs can be part of the established court system or separate from it in neighborhood justice centers or arbitration and mediation forums. Half the states operate arbitration programs as part of their court system.

Despite the trendy nickname "rent-a-judge," the rather old practice of hiring private decision makers has been revived. These decision makers, often retired judges and lawyers, are paid by the parties to the dispute, who agree in advance to abide by the outcome. In some states, appeals courts can review these decisions. There is some concern that these alternative practices are drawing the best lawyers into the private system, resulting perhaps in one system for the rich, a private one, and one for the poor, a public one.

The judicial reform movement has been successful, but like most reform movements, it has its critics and skeptics. Some observers maintain that court delay is not as serious a problem as has been charged and that the remedies may undercut our system of checks and balances. Delay, for example, often works to the advantage of defendants and their attorneys, who wish to postpone trials. At other times, prosecutors want delays in order to put pressure on defendants to accept guilty pleas. Lawyers may seek delays so that they can accept more clients.

No matter how "modernized" the management of court business, the flow of legal business grows continuously. Some people have proposed that traffic violations, automobile injury cases, and so-called victimless crimes be handled by some procedure other than a court trial. New York has led the way in removing from the courts minor traffic offenses that do not involve serious moving violations; other states are following its lead. No-fault insurance programs could reduce the large number of cases stemming from automobile accidents. Because half the people in prison, as well as half the trials that are held, involve victimless crimes such as using marijuana, *decriminalization* could substantially reduce the load on the courts. Six states, for example, have already repealed statutes on public drunkenness and now consider alcoholism a disease rather than a crime.

The reform of state judicial systems is enmeshed in partisan, ideological, and issue politics. Judges are but one part of the total justice system, and their operations are best studied in the context of the entire justice system.

THE JUSTICE SYSTEM

Justice is handled in the United States by a series of institutions that are only loosely connected to each other. In addition to judges, there are juries, prosecutors, defense counsels, public defenders, victims, and defendants. Parole, probation, and prison officials are also part of the justice system.

The Jury

Although most of us will never be judges or serve as professionals in the administration of justice, all adult citizens have an opportunity—even an obligation—to be jurors. Trial by jury in civil disputes is used less often these days; people make settlements prior to trial, elect to have their cases decided by a judge alone, or have their cases referred to a mediator or arbitrator. Furthermore, only a small fraction of criminal cases are actually disposed of by a trial before a jury. Still, jury trials, or the threat of them, remain a key feature of our justice system.

We have moved from a jury system in which service was restricted to white male property owners to one in which jury duty is the responsibility of *all* adult citizens. Today more time and energy are spent in trying to persuade (or coerce) people to serve on juries than in trying to exclude them. Because jury service may be time-consuming and burdensome, many busy people do their best to avoid serving. In the past, judges were often willing to excuse doctors, nurses, teachers, executives, and other highly skilled persons who pleaded that their services were essential outside the jury room. As a result, juries were often selected from panels consisting in large part of older people, those who were unemployed or employed in relatively low-paying jobs, single people, and others who were unable to be excused from jury service. Most states have reacted to these problems by making it more difficult to be excused. In addition, many states have adopted a "one-day, one-trial" policy, which makes jury service less frequent and less onerous. Because jury trials take more time than bench trials (trials before judges) and cost more, some states use juries of fewer than 12 people for some criminal trials. A few states also permit verdicts by less than a unanimous vote. The U.S. Supreme Court has approved these practices, provided the juries consist of at least six persons.[39]

Only a handful of those accused of committing a crime actually stand trial, and only 10 to 15 percent of those who are convicted are declared guilty as the result of a

---

★ ★ THINKING IT THROUGH

Some studies point to judicial elections as working against women and minorities. One study found that judicial elections "have a built-in bias for men. . . . Few women, blacks, Hispanics, or Asians have the political connections, financial resources, and campaign sophistication to overcome the stereotype that has the blindfolded woman holding the scales of justice, but a white man sitting at the bench dispensing it."* Other studies show that more women are chosen by gubernatorial appointment and merit methods but that African Americans fare as well in judicial elections and nearly as well in legislative ones. Another study found that merit systems tend to produce higher proportions of Protestant judges, in contrast to Catholic and Jewish judges.

There is some evidence that elected judges are more likely to impose the death sentence than either appointed judges or juries.† Democratic judges tend to make more liberal decisions than their Republican colleagues do.‡ And courts to which judges are nominated and elected on a nonpartisan ballot show less partisan division than those whose judges are nominated by party conventions and elected in partisan elections.

*John H. Culver, "Politics and the California Plan for Choosing Appellate Judges," *Judicature* 66 (September–October 1982), p. 158.

†Stuart Taylor Jr., "Taking Politics for a Fatal Ride," *Recorder*, October 30, 1995, p.6. See also Justice John Paul Stevens, dissenting in *Harris* v. *Alabama*, 513 U.S. 504 (1995).

‡Sheldon Goldman, "Voting Behavior on the U.S. Courts of Appeals Revised," *American Political Science Review* 69 (June 1975), pp. 491–506.

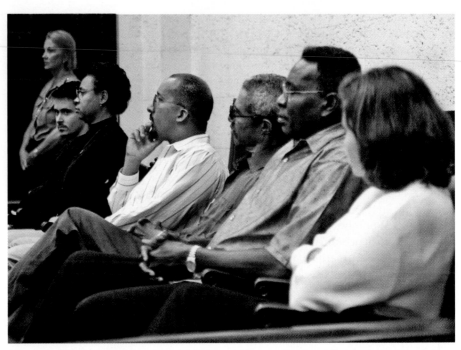

All citizens have an obligation to serve on juries, and lawyers develop skills in selecting people they think may be sympathetic to their client.

formal trial before either a judge or a jury. Most people who go to prison or who have to pay a criminal fine do so because they plead guilty.

The Prosecutor

The prosecutor is largely an American invention, one of the few governmental positions we did not inherit from England. The 18,000 prosecutors in the United States are usually county officials; most are locally elected and subject to little supervision by state authorities. In Connecticut, however, they are appointed by judges, in the Virgin Islands by the attorney general, and in New Jersey by the governor with the consent of the state senate. A prosecutor has "more control over life, liberty, and reputation than any other person in America."[40]

When presented with a case by the police, the prosecutor must decide first whether to file formal charges. He or she may (1) divert the matter out of the criminal justice system and turn it over to a social welfare agency; (2) dismiss the charges; (3) take the matter before a grand jury, which almost always follows the prosecutor's recommendation; or (4) in most jurisdictions, file an **information affidavit**, which serves the same function as a grand jury **indictment**.

A prosecutor who decides not to charge a person accused of some notorious crime is often subject to political pressure and public criticism. But for routine crimes, the prosecutor is politically in a better position to dismiss a charge than the police are. Police are supposed to enforce every law all the time. Of course, it is impossible for them to do so, and they must exercise discretion.[41] But officers who fail to arrest a person alleged to have committed a crime could well be charged with failing in their duty. The prosecutor, however, has more leeway. In fact, the prosecutor is less likely to be criticized for dropping a case because of insufficient evidence than for filing a charge and failing to get a conviction.

Defense Counsel, Public Defenders, and Others

Many defendants cannot afford the legal counsel to which they are constitutionally entitled. The **assigned counsel system** is the oldest system to provide such defendants with an attorney, and it continues to be used, especially in rural areas. Judges appoint

information affidavit
Certification by a public prosecutor that there is evidence to justify bringing named individuals to trial.

indictment
A formal written statement from a grand jury charging an individual with an offense; also called a *true bill.*

assigned counsel system
Arrangement whereby attorneys are provided for persons accused of crimes who are unable to hire their own attorneys. The judge assigns a member of the bar to provide counsel to a particular defendant.

attorneys to represent defendants who cannot afford them. Most such attorneys are paid from the public treasury, but sometimes they are expected to do the work ***pro bono***—for the public good. Seldom are they given funds to do any investigatory work on behalf of their clients. Often judges pick young lawyers just beginning their careers or old ones about to retire. Some less scrupulous lawyers make their living as assigned counsel; because it is often to their financial advantage to do so, they are quick to plead their clients guilty. They are known contemptuously as members of the "cop-out bar."[42]

Dissatisfaction with the assigned counsel system led to the creation of the **public defender system**, first started in Los Angeles in 1914 and now used in most big cities. Under this system, the government provides a staff of lawyers whose full-time job is to defend individuals who cannot pay. This system provides experienced counsel and relieves the bar of an onerous duty. Critics—including some defendants—protest that because public defenders are paid employees of the state, they are not likely to work as diligently on behalf of their clients as they would if they were specifically assigned to those clients. But most observers consider the defender system superior to the assigned counsel system. Steps are being taken to increase the pay of public defenders, protect their independence, and see that they win the confidence of the defendants they represent.

Victims and Defendants

When we talk about our criminal justice system, we sometimes forget the two most important parties in any criminal case—the victim of the crime and the person accused of it.

A disproportionate number of prisoners tend to be young, poorly educated, black males.

> The rights of victims or potential victims are not of the same order as the rights of the accused; the rights of the accused are constitutional rights spelled out in amendments, but nowhere in the Constitution is there any mention of the rights of victims or the public. The framers of the Constitution apparently were much more worried about protecting citizens against the government than about protecting citizens from each other.[43]

In general terms, defendants are likely to be "younger, predominantly male, disproportionately black, less educated, seldom fully employed, and typically unmarried. By the time the sorting process has ended, those sent to prison will consist of an even higher proportion of young, illiterate, black males."[44] Victims, too—compared to the rest of the population—tend to be young, black or another minority, and uneducated. A substantial number of victims—either because of lack of knowledge of what to do or fear of doing it, or because, as in the case of rape victims, they believe they have little chance of proving their attackers to be guilty—never report crimes to police and prosecutors.

Our system puts the responsibility for prosecuting criminals on the government. In most instances, victims have no role other than as witnesses. They are not consulted about what the charge should be or asked what they think might be an appropriate penalty. The matter is strictly between the state, represented by the prosecutor, and the accused, represented by an attorney.

As a result, in recent decades a victims' rights movement has emerged. The movement originated with liberals (chiefly feminists concerned about the difficulty of winning prosecutions for rape and about the harsh treatment of female witnesses), but has gained the support of conservatives who consider the judicial system unfair to victims. In the 1984 Victims of Crime Act, Congress authorized federal funds, which are distributed by the Office of Crime Victims in the Department of Justice, to support state programs compensating victims and providing funds to some victims of federal crimes as well.

About 30 states have amended their constitutions to provide for a "victims' bill of rights," which makes it easier for victims to recover stolen property held in police custody, among other things. Many also give victims a chance to be heard when prosecutors file formal charges, when judges set bail and impose sentences, and when parole boards consider releasing prisoners. These victims' bills of rights are not without constitutional problems. The introduction of "victim-impact statements" by prosecutors seeking the death penalty, for instance, has been controversial. The U.S. Supreme Court,

pro bono
To serve the public good; term used to describe work that lawyers (or other professionals) do for which they receive no fees.

public defender system
Arrangement whereby public officials are hired to provide legal assistance to those persons accused of crimes who are unable to hire their own attorneys.

after first holding to the contrary, has upheld the right of prosecutors to make "victim-impact statements" to a jury in murder trials about the personal qualities of the victim and to allow the jury to consider evidence relating to the murder victim's personal characteristics and the emotional impact of the crime on the victim's family.[45]

Plea Bargaining

Although most criminal cases end with a guilty plea, common practice is for the prosecution to offer to reduce the seriousness of the charge and sentence if a defendant will enter a plea of guilty to a lesser crime. This practice is called a **plea bargain**. At one time, this practice was universally condemned. Many people still consider there is something improper about it, like bartering away justice.

Critics say that plea bargaining forces people to give up their rights; moreover, defendants often do not get off much more leniently by pleading guilty to lesser offenses than if they stood trial.[46] Defenders of plea bargaining contend it works, producing "a result approximating closely, but informally and more swiftly, the results which ought to ensue from a trial, while avoiding most of the undesirable aspects of that ordeal."[47] Many experts and investigators who have looked into the matter have endorsed plea bargaining.

Plea bargaining offers something to all involved. Prosecutors are able to dispose of cases quickly, avoid long and drawn-out trials, eliminate the risk of losing cases, and build up better "election-worthy" conviction records. The accused avoid the danger of being sentenced for more serious charges by pleading guilty to lesser offenses. Defense attorneys avoid "the dilemma of either incurring the expense of going to trial with a losing case or appearing to provide no service whatever to their clients."[48] By being able to handle more clients, they can also make more money. Judges are able to dispose of cases on their dockets more rapidly. In fact, were every case tried, it would overwhelm the judicial system.

Once the bargain between the prosecutor and the defendant's attorney has been accepted, the matter is taken before a judge. The judge goes through a series of questions to the defendant: "Are you pleading guilty because you are guilty? Are you aware of the maximum sentence for the crime to which you are entering a guilty plea? Were you coerced into pleading guilty or offered anything in return for it? Are you satisfied with the representation afforded by your attorney?" Following appropriate responses, the plea is accepted.[49] As long as defendants know what they are doing and enter into the bargain intelligently, they waive their constitutional rights to trial by pleading guilty and may not subsequently back out of the arrangement. Prosecutors must also live up to their side of the bargain.[50]

Sentencing

Due process must be observed in sentencing, which takes place in open court. The prisoner must be present and represented by counsel. In many places, social workers are assigned to help the judge determine the proper sentence. The judge also receives recommendations from the prosecution (and in some jurisdictions from the victim as well), hears the arguments of the defense, and then sets the sentence within the limits prescribed by the state.

The judge sets the sentence, but concerns about sentencing permeate the judicial system. One writer has put it this way:

> Because police and prosecutors screen out a large proportion of the doubtful cases, most left to be dealt with by the courts are those in which there is no serious dispute over the guilt or innocence of the defendant. . . . This fact sets the tone for the process. . . . Everyone concerned—the defense lawyers, the prosecutor, the judge, the probation officer—becomes aware of the fact that he or she is involved in a process where the primary focus is on deciding what to do with the people who are in fact guilty.[51]

Early in our national history, retribution, deterrence, and protection of society were the primary purposes of sentencing. Then rehabilitation became the major goal, and many people thought it was a more humane approach. The indefinite sentence became popular, motivated by the idea that each prisoner should be considered an individual suffering from an "illness." Each prisoner should be diagnosed, a course of treatment

plea bargain
Agreement between a prosecutor and a defendant that the defendant will plead guilty to a lesser offense to avoid having to stand trial for a more serious offense.

should be prescribed, and if and when such experts as psychologists and social workers could certify a "cure," the prisoner should be released.

Most political leaders and many scholars have become disillusioned about our ability to bring about "cures."[52] Others are disillusioned about the deterrent effect of imprisonment. A comprehensive study of rehabilitative efforts inside prisons, although rejecting the conclusion that "nothing works," nonetheless stated: "We do not know of any program or method of rehabilitation that could be guaranteed to reduce the criminal activity of released offenders.[53]

Moreover, judges may enjoy considerable discretion in sentencing, and they frequently give different sentences to defendants convicted of the same crime.[54] To reduce such disparities in sentencing, several reforms have been suggested, including establishing more precise legislative standards, creating advisory sentencing councils, and adopting the British practice of allowing appellate courts to modify sentences.

Disillusionment with rehabilitation and disparate sentencing by judges, combined with growing concerns about crime in the streets and mounting criticism about alleged judicial leniency, has fueled legislative action for mandatory minimum sentencing requirement and for narrowing judicial discretion.[55] State after state has adopted mandatory prison terms—also known as *determinate sentencing*—for more and more crimes. As noted earlier, a three-strikes-and-you're-out requirement has been adopted by many states.

Probation and Prisons

Prison populations in the United States are skyrocketing. Including juvenile facilities, the United States has over 2 million people behind bars, over 1.3 million in state and federal prisons, 621,000 in local jails, and more than 100,000 in juvenile facilities[56] (see Table 26–1). (*Prisons* are for committed criminals serving long sentences; *jails* are for short-term stays for persons awaiting trial and those with sentences of a year or less.) More people are imprisoned in the United States than in any other country. "The American inmate population has grown so large that it is difficult to fathom: imagine the combined population of Atlanta, St. Louis, Pittsburgh, Des Moines, and Miami behind bars."[57]

In addition to those in prison or jails, there are almost 4.5 million adult men and women on probation or parole. (*Probationers* are offenders courts have placed in community supervision rather than putting them in prison; *parolees* are people released after serving a prison term who are under supervision and are subject to being returned to prison for rule violations or other offenses.)

State and federal prison populations in the United States actually declined during the 1960s, but public demands for tougher sentences caused them to climb after 1969. The prison population has more than tripled since 1980 (see Figure 26–3), though declining slightly for the first time in 30 years in 2000.

The increase in prison population has resulted in serious overcrowding. In some states, conditions are so bad that in recent years federal judges have issued orders calling for either immediate improvement or the release of persons being held in conditions

---

TABLE 26–1 PRISONERS UNDER THE JURISDICTION OF STATE AND FEDERAL CORRECTIONAL AUTHORITIES

State and federal prisons	1,312,354
Local jails	621,149
Juvenile facilities	108,965
Territorial prisons	16,130
Immigration and Naturalization Service facilities	8,894
Military facilities	2,420
Indian country jails	1,775

SOURCE: U.S. Department of Justice, Bureau of Justice Statistics, "Nation's State Prison Population Falls in Second Half of 2000—First Such Decline Since 1972," press release, August 12, 2001.

FIGURE 26–3 Incarceration Rates in Federal and State Jurisdictions.
SOURCE: U.S. Department of Justice, Bureau of Justice Statistics, "The Incarceration Rate Has More than Tripled Since 1980," at www.ojp.usdoj.gov/bjs/glance/incrt.htm.

that violate the Eighth Amendment prohibition against cruel and unusual punishment. Most states are responding to judicial intervention by spending millions to build new prisons and renovate old ones. It costs over $60,000 to build each cell, and an average of $20,000 a year must be spent to guard and feed each prisoner.

Relatively few people commit most violent crimes. One out of every three persons let out of prison returns in three years. If we could identify these "career criminals" (**recidivists**) and keep them in prison, while at the same time releasing offenders who are not likely to commit other crimes, we might be able to cut down on the overcrowding in the prisons and better protect the public. The trouble with this idea is that it is not easy to determine in advance who is a career criminal and who is not. For this reason, some people argue that requiring every criminal convicted of a second offense to stay in prison for five years would cut the crime rate significantly.

Some cities and counties have even resorted to **privatization**, turning over the responsibility for operating jails to private firms on a contractual basis. Prison facilities have been privatized in New Jersey, Wisconsin, and the District of Columbia, as well as in many southern and western states, with Texas and California having the largest number. Correctional peace officers strongly oppose privatization and have become a potent interest group making major contributions to gubernatorial elections.

The high cost of correction is leading some states to rethink the wisdom of mandatory sentencing and to reconsider the need to create such alternatives for nonviolent offenders as halfway houses, intensive probation, work release programs, and other community corrections facilities, even home confinement, first pioneered in New Mexico in 1983, whereby prisoners are observed by a variety of monitoring devices.[58] The problem is that these alternative solutions are subject to political attack for being "soft on criminals." Even so, pressure to find places to hold prisoners is so great that correction officials believe that these alternatives, including home confinement, will become an increasingly important part of the criminal justice system.[59]

COURTS IN CRISIS

Crime is a national issue, confronting everyone. The public's attention has been focused on terrorist attacks, drive-by shootings, random killings—especially in schools—and other forms of violence. Yet courts are already overwhelmed by a huge volume of cases. As the American Bar Association observed, "Justice in the United States takes too long, costs too much and is virtually inaccessible and unaffordable for too many Americans. . . . Our courts are grossly overburdened . . . and woefully underfunded. . . . The justice system is no longer a 'court of last resort' . . . but is becoming an emergency room for every social trauma."[60]

There is widespread agreement that our justice system, on both the civil and the criminal side, is in recurring crisis. There is less agreement on what to do about it. The problems are complex, and the issues are political in the best sense of the word: each suggested reform—alternative dispute resolution, mandatory sentencing, or decriminalization, for instance—has costs and benefits. Change and reform are likely to come slowly, and perhaps this is as it should be, for our justice system has been created over the centuries, built on the accumulated wisdom of the past. How best to administer justice is likely to remain on our political agenda.

recidivist
A repeat offender.

privatization
Contracting public services to private organizations.

S U M M A R Y

1. State and local courts are important forums for the making and carrying out of public policy. As they have become more active in political life, state judges have become embroiled in controversial issues, and the public has recognized their importance as policy makers. A new judicial federalism has emerged with state courts interpreting their state bills of rights more broadly than the U.S. Supreme Court applies the national Bill of Rights.

2. Each state has its own court system. Although the systems vary, they generally include minor courts of limited jurisdiction, trial courts of general jurisdiction, and appellate courts.

3. Judges are selected in four different ways: through appointment by the governor, election by the legislatures, popular election, or a merit system modeled along the lines of the modified appointment plan known as the Missouri Plan. Most legal reformers and political scientists appear to favor either the Missouri Plan or some merit selection system over judicial elections.

4. Judicial reforms are aimed at eliminating the waste and delay that plague courts. Among those suggested are alternative dispute resolution mechanisms, mandatory sentencing, and the decriminalization of some nonviolent crimes. Other reforms include merit systems that screen candidates for judgeships, higher pay and longer terms for judges to increase their judicial independence, rule-making powers for state supreme courts, and the appointment of judges more representative of the communities they serve.

5. Judges, together with jurors, prosecutors, defense counsel, public defenders, and correction officials, make up a loosely interrelated justice system. Many observers believe that this system is not properly dispensing justice to individual defendants or protecting the public from career criminals.

6. In recent years, more attention has been paid to the rights of victims at both the national and state levels, including amendments to state constitutions giving victims and their families the right to participate in the trial and providing for compensation to victims and their families.

7. There are over 2 million persons in our prisons. Prisons are overcrowded. Imprisonment has been justified as retribution, deterrence, protection of society, and rehabilitation. Disillusionment with rehabilitation and the disparate sentencing by judges has led to the enactment of mandatory minimum sentencing requirements, including three-strikes-and-you're-out legislation.

K EY T ERMS

writ of habeas corpus
new judicial federalism
tort law
misdemeanor
felony

original jurisdiction
judicial review
advisory opinion
Missouri Plan

information affidavit
indictment
assigned counsel system
pro bono

public defender system
plea bargain
recidivist
privatization

F URTHER R EADING

STEPHEN J. ADLER, *The Jury: Trial and Error in the American Courtroom* (Times Books, 1994).

LAURENCE BAUM, *American Courts: Process and Policy,* 5th ed. (Houghton Mifflin, 1998).

MATTHEW BOSWORTH, *Courts as Catalysts: State Supreme Courts and Public School Finance Equity* (State University of New York Press, 2001).

DAVID COLE, *No Equal Justice: Race and Class in the American Criminal Justice System* (New Press, 1999).

GEORGE F. COLE AND CHRISTOPHER SMITH, *Criminal Justice in America,* 3d ed. (Wadsworth, 2001).

NORMAN J. FINKEL, *Commonsense Justice: Jurors' Notions of the Law* (Harvard University Press, 1995).

SUSAN P. FINO, *The Role of State Supreme Courts in the New Judicial Federalism* (Greenwood Press, 1987).

JULIA FIONDA, *Public Prosecutors and Discretion* (Oxford University Press, 1995).

JOHN B. GATES AND CHARLES A. JOHNSON, *The American Courts: A Critical Assessment* (CQ Press, 1991).

JOSEPH R. GRODIN, *In Pursuit of Justice: Reflections of a State Supreme Court Justice* (University of California Press, 1989).

DAVID HEILBRONE, *Rough Justice: Days and Nights of a Young D.A.* (Pantheon Books, 1990).

RANDOLPH JONAKAIT, *The American Jury System* (Yale University Press, 2003).

LAURA LANGER, *Judicial Review in State Supreme Courts: A Comparative Study* (State University of New York Press, 2002).

CHARLES LOPEMAN, *The Activist Advocate: Policymaking in State Supreme Courts* (Praeger, 1999).

MARILYN D. McSHANE AND FRANK P. WILLIAMS III, EDS., *Encyclopedia of American Prisons* (Garland Press, 1996).

DAVID W. NEUBAUER, *America's Courts and Criminal Justice System,* 7th ed. (Wadsworth, 2001).

DAVID M. O'BRIEN, ED., *Judges on Judging: Views from the Bench* (CQ Press, 2004).

ELLIOT E. SLOTNICK, ED., *Judicial Politics: Readings from Judicature,* 3d ed. (American Judicature Society, 2005).

MICHAEL SOLIMINE AND JAMES WALKER, *Respecting State Courts: The Inevitability of Judicial Federalism* (Greenwood Press, 2000).

HARRY P. STUMPF AND JOHN H. CULVER, *The Politics of State Courts* (Longman, 1992).

G. ALAN TARR AND MARY CORNELIA ALDIS PORTER, *State Supreme Courts in State and Nation* (Yale University Press, 1988).

PAUL B. WICE, *Court Reform and Judicial Leadership* (Praeger, 1995).

See also Judicature, *The Journal of the American Judicature Society,* published bimonthly, and its Web site at www.ajs.org. The National Center for State Courts does not publish a regular journal but is an independent, nonprofit organization dedicated to the improvement of justice. Its materials can be obtained from its headquarters at 300 Newport Avenue, Williamsburg, VA 23185; its home page is www.ncsconline.org.

LOCAL GOVERNMENTS AND METROPOLITICS

Local government is big, costly, and overlapping, and it affects every one of us every day. Counties, cities, suburban communities, school districts, townships, metropolitan planning agencies, water control districts—all are crowded together and piled on top of one another. We typically live under several layers of government, pay taxes to nearly all of them, and also elect most of their leaders. The complex and fragmented arrangements of metropolises also exacerbate the ills of inner cities and limit the options for addressing urban problems. In short, "where we live has a powerful effect on the choices we have and our capacity to achieve a high quality life."[1]

Local governments in the United States employ about 11.5 million people in almost 88,000 different jurisdictions (see Table 27–1). North Carolina, for example, has 960 units of local government, including 102 counties, 541 municipalities, and 319 special districts.[2] Illinois has 6,903 units of local government, made up of 102 counties, 1,291 municipalities, 1,433 townships, 3,145 special districts, and 934 school districts.

Why is there such a labyrinth of government in this country? The basic pattern was imported from England, as were many of our governmental forms. Over time, new governments were created to take on new jobs when existing units proved either too small or unequal to the task. Also, people kept moving into, or at least near, the large cities. The past three generations have seen millions of Americans moving from the cities to the suburbs, and a steady migration to urban and suburban areas continues from rural areas as well. Decades of compromise and struggle among conflicting groups have given us our present system. It creaks and groans. It costs a lot of money. People claim it is inefficient. But these local governments are democratically accountable and encourage experimentation in making public policy.

TABLE 27–1   GROWTH OF GOVERNMENTS IN THE UNITED STATES

Type of Government	1972	1982	1992	2002
U.S. government	1	1	1	1
State governments	50	50	50	50
Local governments	78,218	81,780	84,955	87,849
County	3,044	3,041	3,043	3,034
Municipal	18,517	19,076	19,297	19,431
Township	16,991	16,734	16,656	16,506
School district	15,781	14,851	14,422	13,522
Special district	23,885	25,078	33,555	35,356
Total	**78,269**	**81,831**	**85,006**	**87,900**

SOURCE: U.S. Bureau of the Census, *Statistical Abstract of the United States: 2002,* available at www.census.gov/prod/2003pubs/02statab/stlocgov.pdf.

THE NATURE OF STATE AND LOCAL RELATIONS

Local governments vary in structure, size, power, and relation to one another. But in a *constitutional* sense, they all rely on power "borrowed" from the state. Most state constitutions create a **unitary system** in which power is vested in the *state* government, and local units exist only as agents of the state.[3] Local government is not mentioned in the U.S. Constitution. Local units exercise only those powers expressly given to them by their respective state governments. Most local units of government, unlike states, do not have constitutional status. State-local relations are generally unitary in nature, in contrast to the federal nature of nation-state relations.

Because local governments are typically created by the state legislatures and usually have no constitutional authority in their own right, there are fewer obstacles to state interference in local matters than there are to national interference in state matters. State officers participate in local government to a much greater extent than federal officers do in state politics. When doubts arise about the authority of local governments, courts generally decide against them.

Initially, state legislatures had almost unlimited authority over their local governments and ran them pretty much at will. They granted, amended, and repealed city charters; established counties; determined city and county structure; set debt limits; and passed laws for the local units.

But by the end of the nineteenth century, voters amended or adopted state constitutions that curtailed the power of state legislatures. Many state constitutions forbade state legislatures from passing laws dealing with local governments, and constitutional provisions determined the structure, and in some cases even the process, of local governments.

Constitutional home rule granted constitutional independence to some local units, primarily larger cities, giving them constitutional authority over their form of government and a wide range of other matters. With the protection of constitutional home rule, state legislatures no longer determined the structure and powers of local units.

The extent of state control over local units today varies from state to state and also among the different kinds of local government within each state. At one extreme, local officials merely have to file reports with specified state officials. At the other extreme, state officials have the authority to appoint and remove some local officials, thus exerting considerable control over local affairs. When local governments prove ineffective, state officials may offer local governments financial assistance with certain strings attached or may even take over responsibilities previously handled by local people. In an unusual move in 2002, for instance, a Pennsylvania school reform commission, created to improve Philadelphia's public school system, decided take over from the city and privatize 42 of the city's failing schools, the largest experiment yet in the privatization of

unitary system
Constitutional arrangement in which power is concentrated in a central government.

constitutional home rule
State constitutional authorization for local governments to conduct their own affairs.

public schools.[4] By contrast, after the September 11, 2001, terrorist attacks, governments took responsibility from private companies for screening airline passengers.

State officials are genuinely conscious of local problems. That is in part because problems once thought to be local have come to be viewed as involving the entire state, especially problems relating to law enforcement, the environment, finance, and welfare. This heightened concern is acknowledged by mayors and city managers, who regularly work with both state and federal officials. In recent years, the direct ties between national and local officials, especially in the larger urban areas—ties that used to ally them against state officials—have weakened as federal assistance has been cut back. Municipalities have also become more outspoken in opposing policies of the national government. New York City and over 240 other municipalities and counties, for instance, have enacted resolutions formally opposing the expanded investigatory powers granted to law enforcement agencies under the USA Patriot Act.[5]

COUNTIES IN THE UNITED STATES

Counties are the largest jurisdiction within a state. Yet they get a lot less attention from citizens and the media than do cities or school districts. There are two major types of counties: large urban ones and rural ones. Urban counties have many of the same structures as their rural counterparts, but they are more intertwined with their urban centers. A few counties are better known than the cities or local municipalities within them: for example, Westchester County, New York; Montgomery County, Maryland; Marin and Orange Counties, California; and Cook County, Illinois (which includes Chicago). Some cities, such as Boston, Denver, Baltimore, Philadelphia, San Francisco, and Honolulu, are simultaneously cities and counties; New York consists of five counties—New York, Kings, Queens, the Bronx, and Richmond.

States are divided into counties (in Louisiana they are called *parishes,* and in Alaska they are known as *boroughs*). With a few exceptions (such as Connecticut and Rhode Island, where counties have lost their governmental function), county governments exist everywhere in the United States. There are 3,034 of them, and they vary in size, population, and functions. Loving County, Texas, for example, has fewer than 150 inhabitants; Los Angeles County, California, has nearly 10 million. Besides Los Angeles County, the most populated counties are Cook County, Illinois; Harris County, Texas; Maricopa County, Arizona; and Orange County, California.[6] (Table 27–2 lists the 15 largest counties.)

Counties were originally organized on the idea that a county seat would be no more than a day's journey for anyone within the county's borders. Farm families could pile into their wagons and head for the county seat, and while farmers were attending to business, their families could shop and pick up the local gossip. Then they could all get home in time to do the evening chores. Today, of course, we can drive across a whole state or several states in a day.

The traditional functions of counties are law enforcement, highway construction and maintenance, tax collection and property assessment, recording of legal papers, and welfare. Until recently, counties were convenient subdivisions that largely carried out policies established elsewhere. Over the past generation, however, counties have taken on more tasks than they have lost. Counties in a few states have given up some of their responsibilities, but in most other states, especially in the South, they are taking over from the states such urban functions as transportation, water and sewer operation, and land use planning.[7] Elsewhere, cities are contracting with counties to provide such joint services as personnel training, law enforcement, and correctional facilities. County governments are least active in the New England states, where the county is little more than a judicial and law-enforcement district; county officials do some road building but not much else.

County Government

Most counties have little legislative power. The typical county has a central governing body, variously titled but most frequently called the *county commission* or *board of supervisors.* Most boards have from three to seven members, with a median size of six.

TABLE 27–2 THE 15 LARGEST U.S. COUNTIES BY POPULATION
1. Los Angeles Co., Calif.
2. Cook Co., Ill.
3. Harris Co., Tex.
4. Maricopa Co., Ariz.
5. Orange Co., Calif.
6. San Diego Co., Calif.
7. Kings Co., N.Y.
8. Miami-Dade Co., Fla.
9. Queens Co., N.Y.
10. Dallas Co., Tex.
11. Wayne Co., Mich.
12. King Co., Wash.
13. San Bernardino Co., Calif.
14. Santa Clara Co., Calif.
15. Broward Co., Fla.

SOURCE: U.S. Bureau of the Census, *Statistical Abstract of the United States, 2001* (U.S. Government Printing Office, 2001).

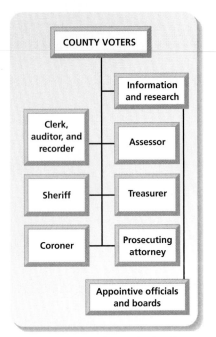

FIGURE 27–1 The Commission Form of County Government.

FIGURE 27–2 The Council with Elected Executive Form of County Government.

They administer state laws, levy taxes, appropriate money, issue bonds, sign contracts on behalf of the county, and handle whatever jobs the state laws and constitution assign to them (see Figure 27–1).

County boards are of two types. The larger boards are usually composed of township supervisors or other township officials. The smaller boards are usually, though not always, elected in at-large elections. At-large elections make it difficult for minorities to be elected to office, especially when they are concentrated in a few areas. Minorities usually win more seats in a district election than in an at-large system.

The county board shares its powers with a number of other officials, most commonly the sheriff, the county prosecutor or district attorney, the county clerk, the coroner, and the auditor, who are generally elected rather than appointed. Sometimes county treasurers, health officers, and surveyors are also found on the ballot.

In general, counties are administered by an unwieldy collection of relatively independent agencies, and until recently, there was seldom a single executive responsible for coordinating such activities. However, today about 800 counties appoint a chief administrative officer who serves at the pleasure of the county commissioners. Approximately 400 counties now elect a *county executive* who is responsible for most administrative functions (see Figure 27–2).

County Performance

How well do counties perform? The picture is mixed. The existence of counties adds to the fragmentation of authority and responsibility among a variety of elected officials, often producing needless jurisdictional conflicts, inefficiencies in purchasing, duplication of costs, and resistance to developing modern personnel systems.

Although counties have often been the forgotten government within the states, this is changing. Their jurisdictional boundaries give them great potential for solving complex problems that are difficult to solve at the city level or have been decentralized to local levels of government by the states. The growing professionalization of county workforces and the trend of electing or appointing professional county executives are improving efficiency. "City-county functional consolidation in areas such as emergency medical services and natural-disaster planning is growing throughout the United States. . . . Increasing cooperation is likely to occur in the future as cities and counties struggle to provide more services to a tax-resistant public."[8]

TOWNS, CITIES, SUBURBS

The number of towns has been declining (see Table 27–1). But, the New England town meeting remains a celebrated institution. The traditional picture of independent citizens coming together to settle public affairs and speak their minds is a stirring one. The New England town is sometimes pointed to as the one place in the United States where there is no elite and where participatory democracy really exists. The town meeting is our most obvious example of *direct democracy;* voters participate directly in making rules, passing new laws, levying taxes, and appropriating money. At least 1,000 New England towns, especially those with populations under 20,000, still hold annual town meetings. Maine has nearly 400 towns that use the town meeting system of democracy, and Vermont has about 200.

Despite this idealized picture, it is generally a veteran group of activists that provides political and policy-making leadership. The assemblies at town meetings usually choose a board of executive officers, historically called *selectmen*. These boards, which generally have three to five members, carry on the business of the town between meetings. The selectmen are in charge of town property; they also grant licenses, supervise other town officials, and call special town meetings. A town treasurer, assessor, constable, and the school board, as well as others, are elected by the voters or appointed by the selectmen. A town administrator often functions as a city manager and reports to the board of selectmen.

Some state and local officials in New England say the town meeting is on the decline. Derry, New Hampshire, for example, held its last town meeting in 1985; then it switched to a mayor-council system. The town meeting had served Derry well for most of its 158-year history, but it proved unable to deal with rapid growth and an influx of people who commute long distances to work. In the 1990s, nearly 60 communities or school districts in New Hampshire modified their town meeting process so that meetings are for discussion purposes only, with final decisions made by the voters at the polls one week later. In Rhode Island, 13 towns abandoned the town meeting, and 18 towns use the meeting only to adopt the town budget.

Many larger communities in New England with populations of more than 25,000 have modified the town meeting by moving to a *representative* town meeting. At representative town meetings, between 50 and 300 local residents from various town precincts are elected to serve three-year terms representing their neighborhoods at their annual town meetings. This is a popular format in many suburbs of Boston with 25,000 to 50,000 residents. Yet the open town meeting, at least in small towns in New England, still proves to be a vital way for people to participate in the policy making of their communities.

During the last half century, the areas around the cities have been the fastest-growing places in the United States (see Figure 27–3). At least 50 percent of Americans now live in suburban communities. Suburbs have grown up at the expense of towns and cities for a variety of reasons: inexpensive land, lower taxes, cleaner air, more open space for recreational purposes, less crime, better highways, and the changing character of the inner cities. There is no one explanation for the exodus to the suburbs. In part it was because people wanted to escape the deteriorating central cities. Resistance to mandatory busing to achieve integrated schools in the 1960s and 1970s also contributed to so-called white flight. But it was just as much a matter of class as of race, with middle- and upper-middle-income-level whites, Asians, and African Americans moving to the suburbs to escape urban crime and to seek more attractive environments in terms of class, religion, race, and lifestyle.[9]

In addition, suburbs have grown because industries have moved from the central cities in search of cheaper land, lower taxes, and less restrictive building and health

The New England town meeting, like this one in Sandwich, New Hampshire, has long been a celebrated American institution.

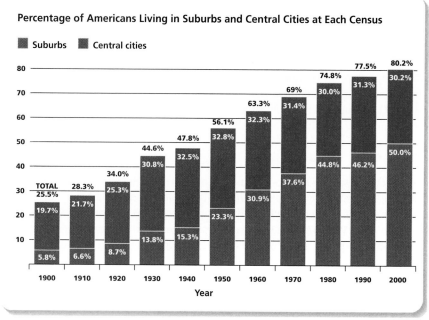

Percentage of Americans Living in Suburbs and Central Cities at Each Census

■ Suburbs ■ Central cities

FIGURE 27–3 **Moving to the Suburbs.**

Sixty miles outside Los Angeles, California, the town of Palmdale is in the midst of a housing construction boom as more people want to live near, but not in, the vast metropolis of L.A.

codes. Other businesses followed the people and the industries, and a myriad of shopping centers grew in outlying communities. Much of this exodus was accelerated by federal policies promoting interstate highways and mortgages insured by the Federal Housing Administration. Most of the new jobs created in the United States continue to be located in the suburbs or newer cities on the fringes of the central cities.

The major tasks of suburban government are often bound together with those of the metropolis.[10] Larger cities usually maintain an elaborate police department with detective bureaus, crime detection laboratories, and communications networks, but its jurisdiction stops at the city line. Criminals, however, seldom stop at the city line. Suburbs have fewer police, and they are often untrained in criminology, so they call on urban police expertise. Cities and suburbs are also tied together by highways, all of which have local access roads. In matters of health, too, there are often wide differences in services between city and suburb, but germs, pollution, and smog do not notice city signposts.

Older suburbs from Long Island to the San Francisco Bay Area are now experiencing some of the problems long associated with disinvestment and population decline. Some suburbs, too, are challenged by sprawling growth that creates crowded schools, traffic congestion, loss of open spaces, and a lack of affordable housing. Many people believe there is a need for collaborative city-suburb strategies to address sprawl and the structural challenges facing older suburbs and inner cities. We'll return to this topic later in this chapter.

The Rise of "Edge Cities"

In recent decades, cities have been built on the edges of older cities. Writer Joel Garreau calls these "edge cities" and suggests that virtually every expanding American city grows in the fashion of Los Angeles, with multiple urban cores.[11] Thus we have Tysons Corner, Virginia, outside Washington, D.C.; the Perimeter Center at the northern tip of Atlanta's Beltway; the Galleria area west of downtown Houston; and the Schaumburg area northwest of Chicago.

Edge cities are defined as places with 5 million or more square feet of office space, 600,000 or more square feet of retail space, and more jobs than bedrooms. More often than not, these edge cities were empty spaces or farmland just 30 years ago. New freeways appeared first, then a shopping mall or two, and then industrial parks.

Some of the problems of the inner city have caught up with edge cities, just as they have with suburbs: traffic congestion, parking problems, crime, pollution, and urban blight. Political problems have cropped up as well. Most edge cities are in unincorporated areas of counties and are subject in varying degrees to control by county governments. These edge cities are sometimes run by "shadow governments"—private owners who set the fees for policing, transportation, and various other services that are normally financed by taxes. There is not much room for government by the people in a community that is essentially a business.

CITY GOVERNMENT TODAY

What does the word "city" call to mind? Bright lights and crowded streets? A city is not merely improved real estate; it is also people—men and women living and working together. Aristotle observed that people came together in the cities for security, but they stayed there for the good life.

The "good life" is defined differently by different people, yet it often includes these attractions:

- Employment opportunities
- Cultural centers, museums, performing arts centers, theaters
- Diverse educational institutions
- Entertainment and night life
- Professional sports teams
- Wide variety of stores and specialty shops
- Good restaurants
- Diversity of people, architecture, and lifestyles

Although a few cities existed when the U.S. Constitution was written, the nation was overwhelmingly rural in 1787, and seven out of ten people worked on farms. People clustered mainly in the villages and small towns scattered throughout the 13 states and adjacent territories. The villages and towns were the indispensable workshops of democracy, the places where democratic skills were developed, where grand issues were debated, and above all, where the people resolved to fight the British to secure their fundamental rights.

The United States is now a nation of about 19,429 cities, and although some cities have just a few hundred people, others have millions. Three American supercities and their suburbs (New York, Los Angeles, and Chicago) have populations larger than the total population of the Republic in the 1780s.

Every municipality has two major purposes. One is to provide government within its boundaries: to maintain law and order, keep streets clean, educate children, purify water, create and maintain parks, and make the area a good place in which to live.[12] As an instrument of the state, the city has a second major purpose: to carry out state functions.

A **charter** is to a city what a constitution is to a national or state government. It outlines the structure of the government, defines the authority of the various officials, and provides for their selection. Although charters are good sources of information on how the people in our cities are governed, they can be misleading. Different structures are not neutral in their impact, for different forms encourage different kinds of participation and responsiveness. In short, power and clout and who gets what, where, and how can definitely be shaped by a city's structural arrangements.

The Mayor-Council Charter

The **mayor-council charter** is the oldest and most popular charter (see Figure 27–4). Under this type of charter, the city council is usually a single chamber. The size of the

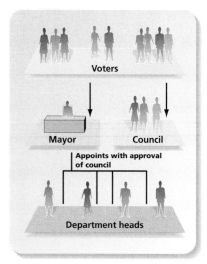

FIGURE 27–4 The Mayor-Council Form of City Government.

charter
City "constitution" that outlines the structure of city government, defines the authority of the various officials, and provides for their selection.

mayor-council charter
The oldest and most common form of city government, consisting of either a weak mayor and a city council or a strong mayor elected by voters and council.

council varies from as few as two members to as many as fifty, though seven is the median size in cities with more than 5,000 people.

Many methods are used to select council members: nonpartisan and partisan elections, elections by large and small wards, or elections from the city at large. Large cities that elect members affiliated with political parties generally choose them by small districts or wards rather than at large. This arrangement tends to support strong party organizations. Nonpartisan at-large elections make party influence difficult. The larger the election districts, the more likely citywide considerations will affect the selection of council members, and the greater the influence of citywide institutions such as local newspapers.

The difference between at-large citywide elections and elections based on small, single-member districts within a city can be significant for racial and ethnic representation on the city council. The at-large system tends to produce councils made up of the city's elite and middle classes. The small district gives minorities and the less advantaged a somewhat better chance for representation where neighborhoods may have high concentrations of one minority.

The Voting Rights Act of 1965 forbids states and cities with a past history of discrimination against minority voters from adopting the at-large system for electing council members if the effect would be to dilute the voting strength of these minorities. In fact, no local government in regions spelled out in this act can make a change in its voting system without the approval of the U.S. attorney general. But what of cities or counties that have long had at-large elections? Can they be forced to give them up because at-large elections virtually ensure that minorities will never be elected? The mere fact that no African American is elected under a certain system does not by itself constitute a violation of the Fourteenth or Fifteenth Amendment. The Constitution forbids only practices adopted or maintained *with the intent to discriminate.*

When Congress debated the extension of the Voting Rights Act in 1982, civil rights advocates urged it to outlaw at-large systems. They contended that city officials are not so foolish as to admit that they want to keep minorities from being elected. Others argued that cities should be free to adopt whatever election system they wished; after all, the Constitution guarantees that no person will be denied the right to vote because of race, not that candidates of the voter's own race will win an election.

The Voting Rights Act as interpreted by the Supreme Court has made it easier to prove that at-large systems violate civil rights. Discriminatory intent need not be proved by direct evidence; it may be inferred if a city or county has a past history of discrimination designed to keep minorities from voting, minorities make up a large majority of the population, and no member of a minority has ever been elected to office under an at-large system.[13]

Weak Mayor Councils and Strong Mayor Councils

The powers of the mayor-council form of government vary from charter to charter and even more widely from city to city and mayor to mayor. There are, however, two basic variations of the mayor-council form: the weak mayor council and the strong mayor council.

weak mayor-council form
Form of local government in which the members of the city council select the mayor, who then shares power with other elected or appointed boards and commissions.

strong mayor-council form
Form of local government in which the voters directly elect the city council and the mayor, who enjoys almost total administrative authority and appoints the department heads.

In cities with the **weak mayor-council form,** mayors are often chosen from members of the elected city council rather than elected directly by the people. The mayor's appointive powers are usually restricted, and the city council as a whole generally possesses both legislative and executive authority. The mayor must usually obtain the council's consent for all major decisions. Often weak mayor-council cities permit direct election by the voters of a number of department heads, such as police chief or controller. In weak mayor-council cities, there is no single administrative head for the city, and power is fragmented. The weak mayor-council plan was designed for an earlier era, when cities were smaller and government was simpler. It is ill-suited to large cities, where political and administrative leadership is vital.

Under the **strong mayor-council form,** the mayor is elected directly by the people and given fairly broad appointment powers. The mayor, often with the help of his or her staff, prepares and administers the budget, enjoys almost total administrative authority, and has the power to appoint and dismiss department heads. This system obviously calls for a mayor to be both a good political leader and an effective administrator—qualities not always found in the same person.

Many people believe the strong mayor-council system is the best form of government for large cities because it gives the cities strong political leaders and makes responsive administration possible. Further, by centering authority in the hands of a few individuals, it makes less likely the growth of "invisible government" by people who have power but are not publicly accountable for its use.

The Council-Manager Charter

Reformers in the early 1900s acclaimed the **council-manager plan** (also known as the *city-manager plan*), in which the city council hires a professional administrator to manage city affairs. It was indeed a significant governmental innovation. In 1908, the small city of Staunton, Virginia, appointed a general manager to oversee the city's work. Little note was taken of the step, but the council-manager plan soon became the darling of both reformers and the business elite. They liked the idea that the council would serve as a sort of "board of directors" in the business sense of setting broad policies, while a professional executive would see that these policies were carried out with businesslike efficiency (see Figure 27–5).

Under the council-manager charter, the council is usually elected in nonpartisan primaries and elections, either on a citywide basis or by election districts much larger than the wards in mayor-council cities. The council appoints a city manager and supervises the manager's activities. The council still makes the laws and approves the budget, and although it is not supposed to interfere in administration, the council often supervises city government through the manager. The mayor is expected to preside over the council and represent the city on ceremonial occasions, but many mayors in fact do a good deal more than this. Contrary to what some textbooks imply, the mayor in council-manager cities can sometimes be a strong policy and political leader as well as a dominant influence in exercising political power.[14] This has surely been the case in cities as different as Cambridge, Massachusetts; San Antonio, Texas; and Colorado Springs, Colorado.

The city manager advises the council on policy and supervises the administration of city business. Because council-manager cities try to attract the best available persons, few of their charters require the councils to select managers from among local citizens, nor do they prescribe detailed qualifications. Although city-manager charters seem to call for a nonpolitical city manager who merely carries out policies adopted by the council and for council members who refrain from interfering with the administration of city affairs, it is often difficult to distinguish clearly between making and applying policy.

Today more than 2,700 cities, located in virtually every state, operate under a council-manager charter. It has, in fact, become the most popular form of local government in medium-sized cities of more than 10,000 citizens. It is especially popular in California, where about 98 percent of the cities use it, as well as in other western and Sun Belt cities. The largest cities operating under a city manager are Dallas, San Antonio, San Diego, Phoenix, Kansas City, Cincinnati, Oakland, and Fort Worth.

How has the city-manager plan worked? In cities characterized by low social diversity and high consensus about community goals, the council-manager form has met with success. Such cities have generally enjoyed improved standards of public employment, reduced costs, and better services. But some observers say this plan has also weakened political leadership in these cities and has confused citizens as to who really provides policy leadership.

In an effort to become more responsive, some council-manager cities have expanded the size of their councils and have abandoned at-large elections for district elections. More than 60 percent of the city-manager cities now also directly elect their mayors in an effort to provide greater political accountability and leadership.[15]

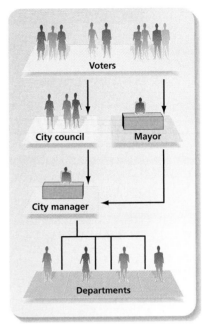

FIGURE 27–5 The Council-Manager Form of City Government.

council-manager plan
Form of local government in which the city council hires a professional administrator to manage city affairs; also known as the *city-manager plan*.

CHANGING FACE OF AMERICAN POLITICS

CITY COUNCILS ARE BECOMING MORE DIVERSE

America's city councils are becoming more racially and ethnically diverse, with the number of people of color serving almost doubling in the last two decades, in all categories of cities (small, medium, and large), from 7 percent to 13 percent.

Percentage of Council Members

Year	White	African American	Hispanic	Asian	Native American	Other
1979	92	5	1			
1989	86	10	1	3		1
2001	87	8	3	1	1	1

Over the last decade, Hispanic council membership has increased the most in medium cities, with populations of 70,000 to 199,999—jumping from zero to six percent—and in large cities, with populations over 200,000, growing from 1 percent to 11 percent. During the same time, the percentage of Asian Americans declined from 3 percent to 1 percent.

The representation of women on city councils increased as well. The proportion of women grew from 21 percent to 25 percent in small cities, from 25 percent to 36 percent in medium-sized cities, and from 33 percent to 36 percent in large cities.

SOURCE: National League of Cities, *Research Brief on America's Cities: The Faces of America's City Councils* (September 2003), available at www.nlc.org.

THE ROLE OF THE MAYOR

Two hundred years ago, the notion of a strong mayor providing vigorous leadership was nonexistent. The need for strong mayoral leadership developed in the late nineteenth century as a means to deal with the social revolution brought on by urbanization, massive waves of immigration, and mounting economic problems of growing cities. In the larger cities, gradually and often grudgingly, the office of mayor became a key position for political leadership.

The typical mayor is a college graduate, an experienced grassroots politician, a business or legal professional, and between 40 and 50 years old. Mayors in the largest cities earn $90,000 to $170,000 and in middle-sized cities between $40,000 and $80,000. City managers, chief city administrators, and top appointees sometimes make more than the mayors.

Although most mayors are male, several of the nation's largest cities have had female mayors, including Pittsburgh; Houston; Dallas; San Diego; San Antonio; and Portland, Oregon. In fact, about 20 percent of municipal governments in the United States with a population of 30,000 or more are headed by women, and the number is growing. Many of them worked their way up through service on school boards and city councils and in the League of Women Voters. An increasing number of African Americans also serve as mayors. More than 300 cities have had African American mayors, including Atlanta, Philadelphia, Denver, Detroit, Houston, San Francisco, Newark, Richmond, and Washington, D.C.

The main job of the mayor is administrative in the broadest sense of the term. Mayors supervise the line agencies—police, fire, public safety, traffic, health, sanitation—as well as a host of special agencies, such as the board of elections, the city planning agency, and commissions that regulate particular occupations and professions. Big-city mayors usually have staffs that carry out typical executive office functions such as personnel, management, budgeting, scheduling, and public relations. In this respect, mayors face the same tasks as corporate executives: coordinating a variety of activities, assigning responsibilities, checking that projects are carried out, finding the ablest people to take charge, and allocating money through control of the budget.

Usually mayors become involved with the private sector in an effort to promote economic opportunities. They try to secure additional jobs, increase the tax base, make

PEOPLE & POLITICS *Making a Difference* ★ ★ ★

SAN FRANCISCO MAYOR GAVIN NEWSOM

A month after being sworn into office as San Francisco's 42nd mayor, 36-year old Democrat Gavin Newsom directed the county clerk's office to permit the issuance of marriage licenses to same-sex couples. He did so in opposition to President George W. Bush's disparaging of same-sex marriages in his State of the Union address in January 2004. Newsom countered that California's state constitution barred discrimination against same-sex marriages and several lawsuits were filed in support of and in opposition to Newsom's action.

In the weeks that followed, over 4,000 marriage licenses were issued to same-sex couples. Moreover, Mayor Newsom's decision had a ripple effect across the country as other cities and counties started doing likewise, and state legislatures in turn became embroiled in debates over adopting constitutional amendments to bar legal recognition of same-sex marriages. California's state attorney general sued to stop the city from issuing the licenses, and attorneys for San Franscisco sued the state, contending that denial of same-sex marriages violated the state constitution's equal protection clause. The California state supreme court initially halted the issuing of marriage licenses to same-sex couples while it considered the matter further.

New York City Mayor Michael Bloomberg (center) with former Mayor Rudolph Giuliani (left) and New York Governor George Pataki (right). A successful businessman, Mayor Bloomberg used his own money to finance his election campaign in 2001 and it was his success in business that convinced voters that he could effectively run New York City.

the city more attractive to certain kinds of businesses, and coordinate public service expansion with private sector requirements. The private sector becomes involved in economic development because its success depends on having an educated labor base with appropriate skills, a constant consumer population, stable communities, and increasing property values.

Many mayors, such as those in New York, San Francisco, Seattle, Atlanta, Chicago, and Miami, have their own "foreign policies." That is, they play host to foreign dignitaries and business delegations and travel abroad seeking foreign investments as they sing the praises of local exportable goods.[16]

Sometimes a mayor must depend on the party organization to ensure support in the council, as in Chicago, where the huge city council consists of 50 members. Other mayors may have to deal with smaller councils, but they are likely to be weak unless they have enough political support to win cooperation.

Although partisan politics is waning as a feature of city government, mayors as party leaders still often dominate the party's city organizations. Mayors help recruit candidates for office, deal with revolts and opposition within their parties, and represent their parties in Washington or the state capitals. As chief legislator, mayors draw up proposed legislation and also make many specific policies. As chief fund-raisers, mayors bargain for more money for their cities before state and national legislatures. Mayors often climb the political ladder to run for governor or sometimes even president. For example, Ohio's former governor and now U.S. senator, George Voinovich, had previously been mayor of Cleveland, and former California governor Pete Wilson had been mayor of San Diego. U.S. Senator Richard Lugar of Indiana had been mayor of Indianapolis.

Mayors are expected to help revitalize the economy and attract investors, sports teams, tourists, and conventions. It takes courage and missionary zeal to overcome the pessimism and decay that beset most inner cities. But several recent mayors—including Rudolph Giuliani in New York City and both Richard J. Daley and his son Richard M. Daley in Chicago—succeeded in reducing crime, increasing economic opportunities, and revitalizing downtown businesses and residential areas.

In recent decades, mayors, like presidents and governors, have grown in power and importance. Most cities have altered their charters to give their mayors power to appoint and remove heads of departments, investigate departmental activities, send legislative messages to the city councils, prepare budgets, and veto council ordinances. In other words, mayors have been given a share in policy making, and city administration has been centralized under the mayor's direction.

WHO INFLUENCES LOCAL POLICY MAKING?

Most Americans, most of the time, leave the responsibility of running the cities and counties to local officials and people willing to serve on boards and in local civic organizations. This does not mean that Americans rave about the quality of services received from local governments. Although they generally respond favorably to the services they get from city government and local public transportation agencies, they often rate them less favorably than they do the services provided by commercial organizations.

But if most people do not choose to be leaders in their communities, that does not mean they do not care about tax rates, the quality of schools in the community, and the availability of services. Hundreds of local people can be mobilized quickly if city hall mishandles local affairs or makes unpopular decisions. Indeed, activism has increased in recent years. It is now common for people to form groups to protect their communities from landfills, toxic dumps, shopping malls, and highways. With dogged perseverance and shoestring budgets, grassroots protest groups have often successfully taken on city hall or won victories for their neighborhoods in the courts.

A sure way to involve people in city government is to propose a policy that threatens the value or safety of the homes of middle- or upper-middle-class taxpayers. The slightest hint that a correctional facility, a freeway, a garbage dump, or a toxic disposal site is coming to their neighborhood will swiftly mobilize citizens who are otherwise happy to be passive spectators in local government. Similarly, the firing of a popular school principal, the closing of a neighborhood school, or a major increase in the property tax will produce a volley of citizen protests that can change the policy-making process at city hall.

Elected and appointed officials try to sense the mood of the local citizenry. They want to avert marches on city hall, recall elections, and citizen dissatisfaction. Their desire to be reelected and respected keeps them reasonably accountable.[17]

Interest Groups in Cities

The stakes and prizes in city politics are considerable: city jobs and commissioner posts, tax breaks, city contracts, regulations, licenses, and much more. Local politicians must deal with the kinds of interest groups found in any industrial society: organized workers, business leaders, neighborhood associations, professional associations, good government associations, home builders and developers, consumers, taxpayers, environmentalists, and various racial and ethnic groups.

The most powerful groups in most cities are typically business groups. Employers provide the economic base for taxes and for jobs, and mayors know they will win or lose the next election in large part on how well they promote the local economy.

Investors and businesses are free to locate wherever they please. Thus they may move from a central city to a nearby suburb or from one city to another. City policy makers, therefore, must follow an "economic logic" that requires them to adopt policies that persuade businesses and investors to remain as participants in the local economy, either by keeping tax rates relatively low or by increasing the quality of service and amenities. If successful, this kind of growth politics enhances the prospects of city officials for reelection because economic growth, especially business investment, boosts the tax base and increases economic opportunities.[18]

But business groups have to share political power and influence with unions, environmentalists, ethnic groups, and many others. Most business officials learn that they can influence city political decision making by cultivating allies.[19] City politics generally involves informal alliances of public officials working together with private sector individuals and institutions.[20]

Police, firefighters, street cleaners, teachers, and other public employees are organized into unions, many of which are affiliated with national unions. Such unions are often a major influence in larger cities. They fight for improved pay, better working conditions, and job security. Although strikes by city employees providing vital services are prohibited by law in most states, enforcement is difficult. Teachers and municipal workers use the strike, or the threat of a strike, to force cities to increase wages and provide better benefits. Mayors complain that public employee unions are sometimes so powerful that they make the old-fashioned political machine look tame.

In addition, nonprofit groups such as the League of Women Voters, cultural foundations, local nonpartisan civic city clubs, independent local planning groups, and arts leagues exist in most urban areas, and they, too, want to be heard in the policy-making discussions of their cities.

Americans would like to believe that every citizen has a say in local government. Prominent families and local business leaders, however, often have more influence than the rest of us. Nursing home residents, the unemployed, migratory workers, young drifters, and the homeless are unlikely to have much influence. Participation in community affairs is often a middle-class and upper-middle-class practice. Low-income residents and the homeless are often ignored when mayors and business elites pursue aggressive economic development policies. "For renters and low-income residents, . . . a booming economy with rising land values may put affordable housing out of reach."[21] This is true in New York City as well as in places like Aspen, Colorado. There are costs as well as benefits to urban growth. Economic development can destroy neighborhoods and drive cities into debt.

THE CENTRAL CITY AND ITS POLITICS

Today most Americans live in *metropolitan areas*, which include large cities and their suburbs, rather than in the small towns so beloved in American fact and fiction. A metropolitan area is, in the minds of most people, a big city and its suburbs. But the Census Bureau, which counts 280 metro areas, down from 284 in 1990, uses a more formal definition:

> A metro area is built around one or more central counties containing an urban area of at least 50,000 people. It also includes outlying counties with close ties—economic and social—to the central counties. To be considered part of the metro area, the outlying counties must meet certain criteria, including numbers of commuters, population density and growth, and urban population.[22]

About 80 percent of Americans (226 million) live in metropolitan areas, 55 percent live within 60 miles of a coastal shoreline (Atlantic, Pacific, Gulf of Mexico, Great Lakes, or St. Lawrence River), and 30 percent live in central cities. The five fastest-growing metropolitan areas are in the South and the West: Las Vegas, Nevada; Naples, Florida; Yuma, Arizona; McAllen–Edinburg–Misson, Texas; and Austin–San Marcos, Texas.[23]

In the nineteenth century, masses of new immigrants arrived in the cities from Europe. In the twentieth century, migrants came from the rural areas, especially from the South. More recently, this country experienced waves of newcomers from Cuba, Korea, Vietnam, the Philippines, Nicaragua, Haiti, Mexico, and other Latin American countries. The majority of newcomers settled first in the inner cities—usually in the poorest and most decayed sections—which inevitably put great stress on the schools and sometimes on community safety as well. Overcrowding and substandard housing in these areas increased health and fire hazards.

The picture of central cities as composed exclusively of huddled, starving, homeless youth gangs and unemployed masses, however, is misleading. Nor is it fair to say simply that central cities have all the problems and suburbs have all the resources. Central cities do have more "high-cost citizens" (truly needy, handicapped, and senior citizens), and most aging cities have been losing population. They have lost businesses, too, because land, rents, utilities, and taxes are often less expensive in the outer suburbs, and businesses move to lower their operating costs. But their departure means that

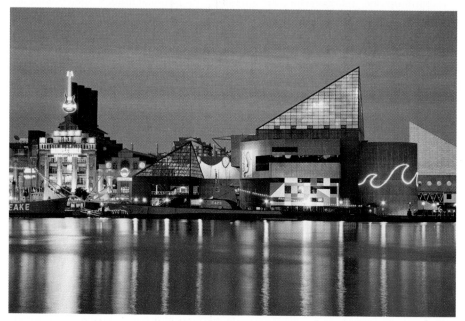

Urban renewal has brought new life to the Inner Harbor in Baltimore, Maryland. Development and renewal projects such as this bring jobs and business to communities that were at one time ravaged by neglect and decay.

cities have smaller tax bases. Higher operating costs in the cities also result from aging public works.

As the income gap between city and suburban residents widens, central cities find it hard to raise new revenues or to force suburbanites to pay a larger share of the bill for the city services they use. This is the economic problem. The legal problem is that most of the states have not permitted their cities to raise funds in any meaningful way with a local income tax.[24]

In an effort to recapture part of the tax base that escapes to the suburbs in the evenings, some cities have imposed local payroll or other types of *commuter taxes* to obtain revenue from people who work in the central cities and make frequent use of city facilities yet live in the suburbs. Some city officials say the payroll or commuter tax is an effective way to shift some of the burden to those who benefit from the city but live beyond its borders. But others say it is unlikely to provide significant long-term revenue growth, and they think it encourages even more businesses to leave the city.

Recently, though, many of the once down-and-out central cities have shown signs of rejuvenation and gentrification. Cities such as Boston, Cleveland, Newark, and Washington, D.C., which were losing population a decade or two ago, are now gaining new residents. Gentrification and "yuppie" development have attracted some suburbanites to come back to central cities. The reasons for the rebound of many central cities varies from city to city, yet the sustained economic boom in the 1990s increased local tax revenues, which were then invested heavily in local infrastructure to make cities more appealing. The boom and investment in cities also helped create more jobs.[25]

However, there has also been a growing sentiment against trying to strengthen metropolitan structures and instead to move in the opposite direction. Perhaps the strongest movement in that direction is in Los Angeles, where there are serious attempts to have the San Fernando Valley withdraw from Los Angeles and create its own city. The issue is extremely controversial, especially among the large Hispanic populations in the area, and even though the vote on secession failed in 2002, the matter will continue to be debated.

MEETING THE CHALLENGES OF GROWTH AND ECONOMIC DEVELOPMENT

Until recently, almost everybody wanted to see his or her city grow. Everybody was a city booster. The local newspaper, television stations, radio stations, Chamber of Commerce, union leaders, business community, developers, teachers, and proud citizens worked together to attract new industries. Such industries would bring, they hoped, new jobs, more amenities, increased land values, and more opportunities for the young. The consensus was that a city with a growing population was a healthy one; one with a decreasing population was a sick one.

Local politicians found it risky to oppose economic development and economic growth; those who did feared that they would not be reelected. However, beginning two decades ago, an *antigrowth* movement developed in many cities. There had always been restraints in the wealthy suburbs outside of the central cities; in fact, many suburbs were created to escape the growth taking place in central cities. These suburbs adopted building and zoning codes and land use regulations to make it difficult, if not impossible, for industries to be located there and to keep out people who could not afford large houses on large lots. New suburbs were carefully planned to ensure that they would not become too crowded. These zoning regulations were attacked in the courts as strategies to keep the poor and minorities out, but as long as they were racially neutral on their face, the courts left them undisturbed.

In the last two decades, environmental awareness spread, and coalitions formed to fight unregulated growth. Disturbed by noise, pollution, and traffic jams and fearful that developers would build too many houses too close together and overload the infrastructure of roads, sewage disposal, and schools in the community, opponents of growth joined together.

Strategies to Govern Metro Regions

Divided executive authority, fragmented legislative power, splintered and noncompetitive political parties, the absence of strong central governments, and the necessity to bargain with national, state, and local officials—all these factors suggest that metro regions, where about 80 percent of Americans now live, are shapeless giants with nobody in charge. Metro regions, of course, typically encompass many cities, counties, towns, and suburbs, so they too are complicated and often splintered.

At the turn of the twentieth century, reformers were afraid of domination by political bosses. But in the modern metropolis, political machines do not run the central city. Urban bureaucracies may wield a lot of power, but they do not offer metropolitan leadership. Special interests seldom really control the metropolis, nor does a business elite. Who, then, governs the metropolis? It's typically a "nobody's in charge" arrangement.

Growing fragmentation of government in large metropolitan areas has brought about a variety of reform movements and structural innovations aimed at improving efficiency, effectiveness, and performance. Political scientists and public administration specialists have never been bashful about proposing remedies. Here are the better-known ideas, all of which have been tried somewhere, yet none of which has been adopted nationwide.

ANNEXATION   In the South, West, and Southwest, large central cities have absorbed adjacent territories. Oklahoma City, for example, added almost 600 square miles. Houston; Phoenix; San Antonio; El Paso; Colorado Springs; and Kansas City, Missouri, also expanded their boundaries. The now-extended cities serve almost as regional governments.[26]

But annexation has not proved helpful to cities in the Northeast and Midwest because these cities are ringed by entrenched suburban communities that seldom want to be annexed, and state laws make it difficult for the central city to do so against the wishes of the suburbs. Even in such places as the Houston metropolitan area, the annexation option is plagued by legal obstacles and political jealousies.

AGREEMENTS TO FURNISH SERVICES   The most common solution to the problems of overlapping and duplicating jurisdictions is for the units of government to contract for services. This reform is applauded by many economists, who say it comes close to providing a market that operates according to laws of supply and demand. Most of these agreements involve a few cities sharing a single activity. For example, a city may provide hospital services to its neighbors or contract with the county for law enforcement. Especially popular in the Los Angeles area, the contract system is used with increasing success in many parts of the country.

PUBLIC AUTHORITIES   Public authorities such as the Port Authority in the New York City area or the Tennessee Valley Authority in the South were established to undertake specialized functions in their regions. They have a legal mandate granted to them by the state (or states) to raise money, hire experts, and take over some city services, such as transportation, water, and housing. The Port Authority of New York and New Jersey built the Twin Towers of the World Trade Center, which were destroyed by the terrorist attacks. It is now responsible for redeveloping the area and for overseeing the operation and security of the bridges and tunnels connecting New York and New Jersey. For more information, go to the Web site at www.panynj.gov.

Why public authorities? In part because state legislatures are sometimes hostile to mayors and prefer to place important functions outside the reach of mayors and political machines and in part because such authorities have financial flexibility (for example, they might be able to incur debt outside the limits imposed on the city by the state). But most important, many problems are simply too big or cover too wide a geographical area to be handled properly by a city or a group of cities.

Public authorities pose a special problem for mayors. Not only are many of the vital functions of metropolitan government removed from the mayors' direct control, but even worse, public authorities and special districts constantly come into conflict with local agencies dealing with the same problems in the city.

But if public authorities are a problem for mayors, they are also a temptation. By sponsoring these independent agencies, mayors can sometimes cut down on their administrative load. They can tap other sources of funds and keep city tax rates lower than they would otherwise be. If things go wrong, mayors can say they did not have authority over a certain function and hence cannot be held responsible.

SPECIAL DISTRICTS   Special districts are units of government typically established to provide one or more specific services, such as sewage disposal, fire protection, water supply, or pollution control for a local or regional area. They are often created to enable an existing unit of government to evade tax and debt limits and to spread the tax burden over a wider area than individual municipalities or counties. Many smaller special districts are formed in suburban areas to obtain urban services without having to create a city government or be annexed by one.

Special districts usually have governing boards appointed by officials of other governments or elected by the general public. Special districts are useful for dealing with urgent problems that overlap boundaries of existing governmental units. Many urban and regional problems defy city and county boundaries, and special districts offer economies of scale that make sense. But critics charge that the rapid increase in the number of special districts over the last 30 years has prevented comprehensive planning. They also lament that few citizens know who runs these special districts, and even fewer know how these officials make decisions.

REGIONAL COORDINATING AND PLANNING COUNCILS   Almost all metro regions have some kind of *council of government* (COG). COGs began in the 1950s and were encouraged by the national government. Congress, in fact, mandated that certain federal grants be reviewed by regional planning groups. In essence, these councils bring locally elected officials together. They devote most of their time and resources to physical planning; rarely do they tackle problems of race, poverty, and financial inequities in metro regions. Councils are set up, moreover, in such a way as to give suburbs a veto over virtually any project that would threaten their autonomy. In a few regions, the councils assume operating responsibilities over such regional activities as garbage collection, transportation, and water supply. Critics say these councils rarely provide for creative areawide governance, yet they serve as an important common ground for elected officials to talk about mutual problems, and they help solve some problems in many of the regions.

CITY-COUNTY CONSOLIDATIONS   One traditional means of overcoming the fragmentation of metro regions is to merge the city with the county. This is a pet reform of business elites, the League of Women Voters, and Chambers of Commerce. It is viewed as a rational, efficient way to simplify administration, cut costs for taxpayers, and eliminate duplication.

About 30 city-county mergers have taken place. Occasionally, one city joins with another, as Sacramento and North Sacramento did in the 1960s. Such mergers can usually be brought about only by a referendum approved by the citizens of the region. Although efforts have been made to consolidate cities with counties, few have been successful in recent decades. Other than St. Louis, Nashville, Jacksonville, and Indianapolis, most consolidations have occurred in a handful of smaller urban areas. One recent success of a regional coalition, after decades of failure, is the consolidation of the City of Louisville and Jefferson County, Kentucky.[27]

What happened in Indianapolis is typical of these consolidations, most of which are in the South and West. In 1970, Indianapolis combined with Marion County to create UNIGOV. This merger required special permission by the legislature. UNIGOV provides many services, but the school systems remain separate, as do the police and sheriff departments.

The era of city-county consolidation appears over. Only about ten consolidations have taken place since 1970, and only one—Athens and Clark Counties in Nevada—

After September 11, 2001, the New York Port Authority and the Lower Manhattan Development Corporation began to search for appropriate ways to rebuild the World Trade Center site. Shown here is Architect Daniel Libeskind's winning design for a complex that will include not only office space but a memorial for the victims of the tragedy as well.

occurred in the 1990s. Proposed mergers are usually defeated by county voters. But it is no longer unusual to find counties running what used to be city jails, zoos, libraries, and similar services. Formal and informal agreements abound as cities and counties remedy overlap and fragmentation by shifting responsibilities for providing specific services among themselves.

FEDERATED GOVERNMENT   This strategy attempts to take political realities into account by building on existing governments but assigning some crucial functions to an areawide metro government.[28] One of the few attempts—and there have been only a few—to create a federated government is the Twin Cities Metropolitan Council for the Minneapolis–St. Paul region. This regional organization, established by the legislature in 1967, consists of a 17-member council. Sixteen members are appointed by the governor to represent equal-population districts, and the seventeenth is a full-time executive who serves at the pleasure of the governor.

Today the Metropolitan Council, in essence a new layer of government superimposed on top of existing units, serves as a metropolitan planning and policy-making as well as policy-coordinating agency. It reviews applications for federal funds from the region. It guides regional planning and development and opposes local actions that would endanger the overall welfare of the region. It also has taxing authority for the region. The Twin Cities model appears to be a ready candidate for transfer elsewhere, yet this has happened only in Portland, Oregon.

Portland adopted a bold new charter for the Portland Metropolitan Services District. It is a directly elected regional government serving three counties and 24 cities. Its nonpartisan commission members and elected executive officer have an impressive budget and more than 1,200 employees. They oversee waste collection, a zoo, recycling, waste disposal, transportation planning, and regional air and water quality programs, and they constructed Portland's new Convention Center. They have also created a greenbelt around the metro area that preserves extensive open areas.

COMMUNITY SELF-HELP   The problems of governing urban and metro regions have also been addressed by community self-help organizations. Countless people are coming together in their own neighborhood to tackle common problems or to form neighborhood cooperatives. Some of these self-help groups simply handle baby-sitting arrangements or organize charity events or golf tournaments; others are involved in neighborhood crime watches or Little League field construction. Local nonprofit groups in New York have built award-winning apartment complexes amid burned-out inner-city tenements. Other groups have mobilized to bring about storefront revitalization, street improvement, and area beautification programs by initiating farmers' markets, mini-parks, and gardens.[29]

The contemporary self-help movement is rooted in an American past that has long been marked by volunteerism and local associations. In former times, the whole community often rallied when a neighbor's barn burned down; volunteer fire departments emerged out of this tradition. But as the nation has become more mobile and impersonal, we have drifted away from these traditions. Today, most Americans shop at shopping malls rather than on Main Street or in the old downtown area. At the same time, they resent the fact that public institutions have become remote and overly professionalized. Thus people across the country are joining together to do in an informal and decentralized way what extended families or small villages of the past used to do. Simply, they come together to lend a hand.

Many local groups seeking help from city hall or from county officialdom give up after running into a maze of building codes, zoning rules, and countless regulations that inhibit innovation in local government. The alternative to despair is to do it yourself. And this is exactly what is happening at the grassroots level right now. The more successful experiments are watched carefully by the professionals at city hall, and some of the innovations are copied by those in office.

Sometimes progress or justice comes about because some activists take issues to court. Such was the case in bringing in alternative housing for lower-income residents in Mount Laurel, New Jersey. And it was also the case in addressing the fatal effects of toxic dumping by businesses in Woburn, Massachusetts.[30]

THE POLITICS OF METROPOLITAN REORGANIZATION

In most metropolitan regions, to combine city and suburbs would be to shift political power to the suburbs. In most northern centers, this would give suburban Republicans more control of city affairs. In other cases, it would enable Democrats to threaten the one-party Republican systems in the suburbs. Under these circumstances, neither Democratic leaders in the central cities nor Republicans in the suburbs show much enthusiasm for metropolitan schemes. African Americans and Hispanics often oppose area consolidation or similar reform proposals that would invariably dilute their political power, often severely.

Some people believe that solutions to metropolitan problems are beyond the capacity of the metropolis itself. They favor a strengthened role for the national government, with special emphasis on ensuring "equity" or on relating services directly to needs. Some advocate reviving federal revenue sharing. Others believe that the job must be done by the states, which hold the fundamental constitutional power. Still others put forward bold proposals to establish regional planning and governance arrangements that would embrace "citistate" areas that include two or more metropolitan clusters, like Baltimore and Washington, D.C.[31]

Today's aging central cities unquestionably face problems: congestion, smog, tension, loss of community, drugs, unsafe streets, neglected children, and visual pollution. They live with racial and ethnic tensions, not just white–black rivalry but rivalry among Latinos, Koreans, and a host of other racial and ethnic groups. Gangs, poverty, broken families, drive-by shootings, and drug-related crimes make life miserable for many who live in the inner cities. Yet is this new? Writers and critics since Thomas Jefferson have projected an unflattering image of the city as a cold, impersonal, and often brutal environment in which crime flourishes and people lose their dignity.

Supporters contend, however, that the big city is not just a place of smog and sprawl; it is the center of innovation, excitement, and vitality. In the last couple of decades, many

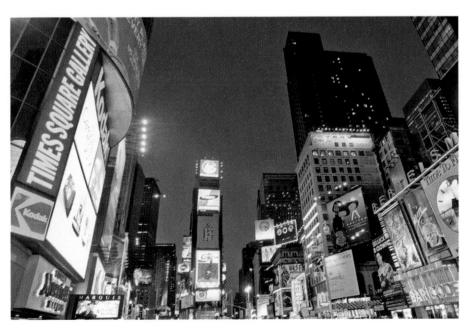

The Times Square area of New York City has undergone major redevelopment, with new theaters and hotels replacing porno movie houses and rundown buildings.

major cities, including Boston; New York; and Washington, D.C., have promoted the gentrification of run-down areas. The city offers social diversity and puts less community pressure on the individual to conform. The large community is a meeting place for talent from all over the nation and the world: dancers, musicians, writers, scholars, actors, and business leaders.

Some observers dismiss the notion of an "urban crisis." They contend that most city dwellers live more comfortably than ever before, with more and better housing, schools, and transportation. By any conceivable measure of material welfare, the present generation of urban Americans is better off than other large groups of people anywhere at any time. Most cities, especially in the West and South, are thriving, and older cities such as Boston, Pittsburgh, and Indianapolis are generally viewed as revived and vital, not decaying.

Throughout history, cities have been threatened by political, social, and environmental catastrophes. Urban decay, in one form or another, has always been with us.[32] Cities thrive because over time they respond to crises and because they are an economic necessity. The economy, transportation systems, past investments, and cultural contributions all make cities inevitable. How well cities survive, and with what mix of people, will depend on the tides of the national economy, the way our regions are organized, the way our social and economic policies are designed, the vision and leadership individual cities muster to build their future, and the degree to which our national leaders promote policies that can help our central cities.[33]

S UMMARY

1. Local government is big, costly, and overlapping. Local governments in the United States come in a variety of shapes and structures and perform various functions. However, since constitutional power is vested in the states, most counties, cities, towns, and special districts are agents of the state.

2. The most common governmental form at the county level is a board of county commissioners, although larger urban counties are moving to council-administrator or council-elected executive plans.

3. There is no typical suburb. Although many suburbs are homogeneous, the suburban United States is highly heterogeneous. Suburbs are confronting the same problems as the urban areas they surround. In fact, big cities and their suburbs are now referred to as metropolitan areas and are growing fastest in the South and West.

4. The most common governmental forms at the city level are the mayor-council

and the council-manager (city-manager) plans. Mayor-council governments generally have a strong mayor elected by voters, though some plans have a weak mayor elected by the council. Council-manager plans appoint a professional administrator. In general, council-manager plans are found in medium-sized to large cities and in cities in the West, especially in the Sun Belt. Mayors and managers are key political leaders.

5. Although local governments are run by officials, business interests and interest group activism also influence policy.

6. The standard of living in the central cities of the United States may be much better than it was 50 years ago, but the inequalities between many central cities and their middle and outer rings of affluent suburbs are increasing. Central cities often face economic hardships, intense racism, and drug-related gangs and criminals. Fragmentation and dispersal of political authority in the metropolitan areas and even in many of the central

cities themselves often make it difficult not only to govern the big cities but also to respond with adequate policies and funds to treat the problems of the metropolis.

7. Cities, suburbs, and metro areas all face problems related to growth, uneven tax bases, environmental concerns, and fragmented authority. A variety of strategies have been used in an effort to solve these problems—annexation, agreements to furnish services, public authorities, special districts, regional coordinating and planning councils, city-county consolidations, federated government, and community self-help programs. Almost all of the strategies for meeting the challenges of growth and economic development involve shifts in political power.

K EY T ERMS

unitary system	charter	weak mayor-council form	council-manager plan
constitutional home rule	mayor-council charter	strong mayor-council form	

FURTHER READING

BARBARA ACKERMANN, *"You the Mayor?" The Education of a City Politician* (Auburn House, 1989).

ROGER BILES, *Richard J. Daley: Politics, Race, and the Governing of Chicago* (Northern Illinois University Press, 1996).

BUZZ BISSINGER, *A Prayer for the City* (Random House, 1997).

MICHAEL BRIAND, *Practiced Politics: Five Principles for a Community That Works* (University of Illinois Press, 1999).

FRANK M. BYRAN, *Real Democracy: The New England Town Meeting and How It Works* (Cambridge University Press, 2004).

PETER DREIER, JOHN MOLLENKOPF, AND TODD SWANSTROM, *Place Matters: Metropolitics for the Twenty-first Century* (University Press of Kansas, 2001).

ALAN EHRENHALT, *The Lost City: Discovering the Forgotten Virtues of Community in the Chicago of the 1950s* (Basic Books, 1995).

JOEL GARREAU, *Edge City* (Doubleday, 1991).

STEPHEN GOLDSMITH, *The Twenty-First Century City: Resurrecting Urban America* (University Press of America, 1999).

JOHN J. HARRIGAN AND ROGER VOGEL, *Political Change in the Metropolis,* 7th ed. (Longman, 2000).

DENNIS R. JUDD AND TODD SWANSTROM, *City Politics: Private Power and Public Policy,* 4th ed. (Longman, 2003).

DAVID L. KIRP ET AL., *Our Town: Race, Housing, and the Soul of Suburbia* (Rutgers University Press, 1997).

SUZANNE M. LELAND AND KURT THURMAIER, EDS., *Case Studies of City-County Consolidation* (M. E. Sharpe, 2004).

PAUL G. LEWIS, *Shaping Suburbia: How Political Institutions Organize Urban Development* (University of Pittsburgh Press, 1996).

DONALD C. MENZEL, ED., *The American County: Frontiers of Knowledge* (University of Alabama Press, 1996).

JOHN O. NORQUEST, *The Wealth of Cities: Revitalizing the Centers of American Life* (Addison-Wesley, 1998).

MYRON ORFIELD, *Metropolitics: A Regional Agenda for Community and Stability* (Brookings Institution Press, 1997).

DAVID RUSK, *Inside Game/Outside Game: Winning Strategies for Saving Urban America* (Brookings Institution Press, 1999).

MICHAEL H. SHUMAN, *Going Local: Creating Self-Reliant Communities in a Gobal Age* (Routledge, 2000).

CLARENCE N. STONE, *Regime Politics: Governing Atlanta, 1946–1988* (University Press of Kansas, 1989).

JON C. TEAFORD, *Post-Suburbia: Government and Politics in the Edge Cities* (Johns Hopkins University Press, 1996).

HEATHER ANN THOMPSON, *Whose Detroit? Politics, Labor, and Race in a Modern American City* (Cornell University Press, 2002).

ROBERT J. WASTE, *Independent Cities: Rethinking U.S. Urban Policy* (Oxford University Press, 1998).

WILLIAM JULIUS WILSON, *When Work Disappears: The World of the New Urban Poor* (Harvard University Press, 1996).

See also *Governing: The Magazine of States and Localities,* published monthly by Congressional Quarterly, Inc.; *The National Civic Review,* published by the National Civic League; *The Municipal Yearbook,* published annually by the International City Management Association; and the Web site of the U.S. Conference of Mayors at www.usmayorsorg/uscm/home.asp.

MAKING STATE AND LOCAL POLICY

28

S tate and local officials constantly wrestle with policy decisions and controversies. What is the best way to attract business and increase the number of jobs yet encourage environmental quality? How should our state deal with the soaring costs of providing Medicaid? What can be done about frustrating peak-hour gridlock on our highways? Should a community close one of its hospitals? Will voters approve a bond issue to construct a needed new high school? Should states approve or ban marriage licensing or civil unions for same-sex couples? And what role should the states play in helping to reduce CO_2 emissions that are increasing global warming? State and local authorities also puzzle about how much they can do about terrorism threats.

Mayors, governors, state legislators, county commissioners, judges, union officials, developers, Chambers of Commerce, political party leaders, and many others strive to come up with public policy compromises to such dilemmas. These deliberations receive little media attention compared to the attention paid to decisions made in Washington, D.C., yet the effect of these choices on our day-to-day lives is often equally or perhaps even more important.

This chapter will examine some of the policy areas that consume much of the attention of state and local officials and the budgets of state and local governments. State and local governments spend most of their budgets on educating people, on welfare and health-related matters, on highway and transportation systems, and on safety and law enforcement issues. We will discuss them as well as the issues of planning and regulation.

PUBLIC EDUCATION

In ancient Greece, Plato and Aristotle saw education as a vital task of government. Thomas Jefferson, too, was convinced that an educated citizenry was essential to democratic government. But only in the twentieth century did the idea that government should provide tax-supported education for everyone become generally accepted.

For a long time, many people opposed "free" education. They feared it would lead to social unrest, undermine the family, give government control over the minds of the young, require huge bureaucracies, and result in a fatal mixture of education and politics. And was it fair, they asked, to make people who could afford to educate their own children in private schools pay taxes to educate other people's children? Despite these objections, today free public education for grades 1 through 12 is an established practice in the United States.

Education is now the number one policy priority for most states. State and local governments have the primary responsibility for education and put up most of the funds. In recent years, there has been a decline in the federal contribution to education; however, this has not deterred the federal government from pushing federal goals for education. An excellent example of this was the George W. Bush–sponsored and congressionally approved No Child Left Behind Act of 2001, a reauthorization of an earlier law that required greater school district accountability, more testing, and increased emphasis on reading, especially for younger children. One of the most intriguing educational reforms in decades, this national legislation used a combination of national standards and comprehensive testing to measure students' progress. If too many children in a public school fail to meet the desired standard, then parents there have the right to move them elsewhere.

Approximately one-third of all state and local government expenditures are for education—more than for any other function of government (see Figure 28–1). The federal government's contribution to education is fairly constant across states, but since 1979, overall state funding has surpassed that of local governments, with the exception of a few states in which revenues for education continue to come primarily from local government. The state role in financing education has increased over the last generation as a result, at least in part, of pressure from the courts to equalize expenditures on education across local school districts. There is also wide variation between states in the total amount of state and local spending per student, from a high of over $11,000 in New York and Connecticut to a low of about $5,000 in Utah, with an average of almost $8,000.[1]

Administration

Unlike most other democracies, which typically administer and fund education at the national level, the basic unit responsible for public elementary and secondary education in the United States is the local school district, and there are nearly 15,000 of them. In almost all districts, voters elect a board of education that sets the school tax rate, appoints a superintendent of schools and other personnel, hires teachers, and runs the schools from kindergarten or grade 1 through grade 12. Each state has a state superintendent of public instruction or commissioner of education. In about a third of the states, this official is popularly elected; in almost all states, he or she shares authority with a state board of education.

Although actual operation of the public schools is the responsibility of the local community, state officers have important supervisory powers and distribute financial assistance to the communities. State money is distributed according to many formulas, but as noted, the trend is toward giving more money to poorer communities to equalize education spending. Many policies are established at the state level, and it is up to local authorities to enforce them. Local authorities must ensure that new school buildings meet the minimum specifications set by the state. In some states, officials have the authority to set the course of study in schools—that is, to determine what must be taught and what may not be taught. In several states, especially in the South and Southwest, state authorities determine which textbooks will be used as well.

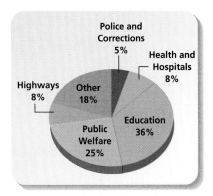

FIGURE 28–1 Typical State Government Expenditures.

Source: *The Book of the States, 2002* (Council of State Governments, 2002), p. 282.

The Role of the National Government

After the former Soviet Union's successful launch of *Sputnik,* the first satellite put into orbit, in 1957, Congress responded by increasing federal funding for education to strengthen math and science education. The national government's share in financing local education rose from about 2 percent in 1940 to about 9 percent in 1980. Since then, however, the trend has reversed, and the federal share of spending on local education declined and has stabilized at 6 percent.

Through the national Department of Education, created in 1979, and other agencies, the federal government makes grants to the states for facilities, equipment, scholarships, loans, research, model programs, and general aid at the elementary, secondary, and higher education levels. But federal control over how the money may be spent comes with these federal dollars. Today federal regulations cover school lunch programs, employment practices, admissions, record keeping, care of experimental animals, and many other matters. Indeed, local school authorities regularly complain that there are more regulations than dollars.

Educational Issues

What shall be taught and who shall teach it are hotly contested matters. Schools are favorite targets for groups eager to have children taught the "right" things. Religious groups want family values and morality emphasized, and some want constraints imposed on the teaching of evolution. Others want the schools to teach facts only, without regard for values, especially in areas like sex education. Labor leaders want students to get the right impression about labor and its role in society. Business leaders are eager for children to see the free enterprise system in a favorable light and want high school graduates who will be well prepared for increasingly technical jobs. Minorities and women's groups want textbooks to present issues from the perspective they consider correct. Professional educators and civil libertarians try to isolate schools from the pressures of all outside groups—or at least the ones with which they disagree. They say decisions regarding what textbooks should be assigned, what books should be placed in school libraries, and how curricula should be designed are best left to professionals.

It has long been an American tradition that education should be kept free from partisan political influences. The separation of schools from politics is strongly supported. Local school boards are usually nonpartisan and are often elected when no partisan races are on the ballot. Elaborate attempts have been made to isolate educational agencies from the rest of government. This separation is strongly supported by parent–teacher associations, the National Education Association, the American Federation of Teachers, and other educational groups. Most citizens also believe education should be kept out of the hands of mayors and city councils. However, education is of such concern to so many people, and there are so many different ideas about how schools should be run, that it cannot be divorced from politics.

PUBLIC SCHOOL INTEGRATION   During the 1970s and 1980s, battles were fought in many cities over how to overcome racial segregation in the public schools. One method, which became contentious, was to bus students from one neighborhood to another to achieve racial balance in the schools and overcome the effects of past segregation. By the 1990s, battles over school busing were ending, but despite the efforts of the federal courts, racial segregation is still the pattern for the inner-city schools of most large cities in parts of the North, South, and West. Indeed, over the last 15 years there has been a substantial slippage toward segregation in most of the states that had experienced solid desegregation.[2]

EDUCATIONAL REFORM   Over the past two decades, a series of reports on education helped focus national attention on educational reform.[3] A 1990 meeting between President George H. W. Bush and many of the nation's governors laid the foundation for the Goals 2000: Educate America Act, which sought to achieve many of the goals identified as important since the 1960s. With the aid of federal money, states were encouraged to set educational standards in order to achieve a number of goals, including these:

In many poorer communities, classes are conducted in overcrowded, poorly equipped buildings.

- All children will start school ready to learn.

- The high school graduation rate will be at least 90 percent.

- Students will have mastered a challenging curriculum by grades 4, 8, and 12.

- Teachers will have access to professional development opportunities.

- U.S. students will rank first in the world in science and math achievement.

- All adults will be literate.

- Schools will be free of drugs, violence, and firearms.

- Every school will promote parental involvement in education.[4]

Several states initially objected to Washington's setting goals and standards for public education, which had traditionally been a local function. Further, some observers thought it unfair to "hold students to nationwide standards if they have not had the equal opportunity to learn" due to unequal resources among communities.[5] These concerns, however, did not deter states from setting goals and standards. The autonomy of local and state authorities is also protected, with the federal government's role defined in terms of general goals.

Education has been a key theme in recent elections, with candidates from both major parties and all ideologies insisting that we must improve the quality of public education. However, there are differences about how that should be done. Proposed reforms debated are vouchers, charter schools, national student testing, and more emphasis on reading. Some of these found their way into the Elementary and Secondary Education Act of 2001 (also called the "No Child Left Behind Act"). And all of them were debated in the 2004 elections at various levels.

VOUCHERS   Some reformers contend we will not see real progress in public education until we inject competition into the system by permitting parents to shop for schools the way they shop for goods and services in the economy. One way to do this would be to provide parents with a set amount of money—**vouchers**—that they could use to pay for part or all of their children's education in a public or private school of their choice. This reform has been labeled "choice in education" because it would give parents the freedom to choose where to send their children to school.[6]

This reform has proved divisive. Voucher advocates say it could help the neediest students escape failed schools and get the valuable academic preparation at private or religious schools. Yet opponents contend it will badly injure financially struggling public schools by diverting much needed money.

vouchers
Money provided by the government to parents for payment of their children's tuition in a public or private school of their choice.

Voucher programs have been tried since the mid-1980s in New York, Indianapolis, San Antonio, and Milwaukee. Some programs were directed at low-income students, a plan that, according to one observer, meant some poor families formed political alliances with conservative Republicans, not their more natural liberal Democratic allies. Political scientist and voucher advocate Terry Moe argues:

> In the new politics of education, the conservatives have become the progressives, pushing for major change, promoting the causes of the disadvantaged, and allying themselves with the poor. The progressives of yesteryear, meantime, have become the conservatives of today, resisting change, defending the status quo against threats from without, and opposing the poor constituents they claim to represent.[7]

Among the vigorous opponents of vouchers are teachers' unions, including the National Education Association (NEA) and the American Federation of Teachers (AFT), which, understandably, see vouchers as a threat to jobs and benefits because the use of vouchers could drain off financial support from the public schools.

Some proponents have proposed that voucher programs should include religious schools. Well over 80 percent of the students receiving vouchers in places like Milwaukee and San Antonio attend religious schools, most of them Catholic schools. Opponents of vouchers for religious schools argue that such an arrangement violates the constitutional separation of church and state. They fear too that in some parts of the country, vouchers would be used for schools that practice racial segregation.

Other people oppose the voucher system, even for public schools, on the grounds that such a system would have a negative impact on efforts to reform the public schools. Some argue that it would promote "skimming," meaning that the higher-achieving students would opt out of public schools, leaving behind the underachievers and the discipline problems and creating an increasingly negative atmosphere in public schools. In rural areas, where few private schools exist, some people fear that vouchers might encourage parents to keep the money under the guise of providing "private" home schooling.

Proposals for school vouchers that have been put before the voters have been defeated in Oregon, Colorado, and Washington. In recent years, California and Michigan voters have turned down initiatives that would have established vouchers, in spite of well-financed campaigns supporting their adoption. The political movement pushing vouchers lost some of its steam because of these defeats, the opposition of the teachers' unions, and court rulings that said poor families do not have the right to demand vouchers from state and local governments to allow their children to attend better schools.

In 2002, a divided U.S. Supreme Court ruled that poor children could be granted public money (vouchers) to attend religious schools without violating the separation of church and state provisions in the Bill of Rights. Chief Justice William Rehnquist wrote that his majority opinion was "not an endorsement of religious schooling" but merely a means "to assist poor children in failed schools."[8]

Colorado enacted a law in 2003 that provides for students in certain "low" or "unsatisfactory" performance schools to get out of public schools at the request of the parents. "Students qualify if they do badly on state tests and come from poor families living within one of the 11 desegregated districts."[9] A lawsuit was almost immediately filed to block this new Colorado law. The lawsuit claims this voucher program would force taxpayers in many instances to support religion, takes away funding from public schools, undermines our tradition of "full" public schools, and removes local control from school boards.

In 2004, a Florida appeals court ruled that a voucher program in that state violated Florida's constitution because it sent public money to religious institutions.[10]

CHARTER SCHOOLS   One educational reform that does not go as far as vouchers yet still provides publicly funded alternatives to standard public schools is the **charter school**. Some states now grant charters to individuals or groups to start schools and receive public funds if they can meet standards specified by law. Unlike vouchers, which provide funds to the parents, charter schools are under the direct authority of local school

charter school
A publicly funded alternative to standard public schools in some states, initiated when individuals or groups receive charters; charter schools must meet state standards.

CHARTER SCHOOLS

In East Los Angeles sits Vaughn Street School, California's first charter school, established in 1992. Most of the children at this elementary school speak English as their second language and live in dangerous neighborhoods. Once the children had to step around a dead body as they approached the school's entryway. It was not a healthy learning environment.

In 1992, Vaughn Street's pupils ranked in the 9th percentile in reading (91 percent of public school students in America could read better than they) and the 14th percentile in math. Now their reading and math scores rank in the 47th and 59th percentile, respectively. Today these students experience hands-on learning about computers in the $1.6 million learning center, and parents from more wealthy neighborhoods want to send their kids to Vaughn. Principal Yvonne Chan attributes these changes to freedom from bureaucracy.

During the past decade, the number of charter schools has grown steadily because of concerns about students' poor academic performance and high dropout rate. About a fifth of all high school students do not graduate. For more state-by-state information, visit the Web site of the Center for Education at www.edreform.com/pubs/chglance.htm.

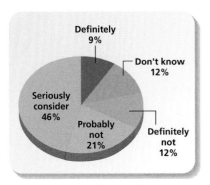

Would Parents Choose Charter Schools?

Source: Public Agenda, reported in "Issues 2000: Education," *The Economist*, September 30, 2000, p. 20.

boards. There are a few thousand charter schools, with more than 700,000 students. "The vast majority of the schools are operated by local nonprofit organizations, and the educational theories that guide them are as various as the communities they serve."[11]

As with privatization in other government services, charter schools are intended to interject the competition of the marketplace into elementary and secondary education. Charter schools generally have more flexibility to hire and fire teachers and are not subject to the collective bargaining arrangements that prevail in many public school systems. Proponents of charter schools want to remove these schools from state and local regulation as much as possible. Some of their teachers may not have extensive training as education majors, yet proponents of charter schools maintain that classroom performance is more important than the undergraduate major of the teacher.

Teacher unions are concerned about the charter movement, because they might lose their collective bargaining position with school boards if charter schools multiply. Other opponents contend that in school systems already strapped for money, it does not make sense to divert funds to such untested experiments. Concerns about what will be taught in charter schools and the level of teacher competence are often expressed. Also at issue is whether religious schools should qualify for public funds as charter schools.

Charter schools are the fastest form of choice in K–12 education, and they got a big boost from the federally enacted "No Child Left Behind" law that holds out conversion to charter schools as a possible solution for ineffective traditional public schools.

There is much to admire in the charter school movement. Two "Teach For America" alumni launched a series of charter schools under the name of Knowledge Is Power Programs or KIPP. With elementary schools in Houston, New York City, North Carolina, and elsewhere, they have demonstrated effective results. The key to their success is a strict and strong initial commitment by parents and pupils to a philosophy of hard work, longer hours of class time and homework, and no short cuts. That coupled with carefully recruited, dedicated teachers has proven successful.[12]

Yet charter schools vary widely in quality across the country. Indeed, initial test results run in California and by the U.S. Department of Education find that economically disadvantaged students are making more rapid progress in traditional public schools rather than in the new charter schools.[13] This leads critics of the charter movement to say there is no credible evidence that deregulating public education leads to higher student achievement. Supporters contend that the vast majority of charter schools serve students with academic and family problems who are poorly served by traditional public schools. Plainly, there are some excellent and some below average charter schools. Opponents and supporters alike agree that quality schools must be constructed—one at a time.

NATIONAL STUDENT TESTING Standardized testing is neither new nor controversial. What is new and controversial is *statewide* standardized testing. In 1990, only 14 states had standards for their core curriculum, but 49 states have now adopted standards. After adopting standardized testing for students, Oregon rejected a ballot initiative that would have amended the state constitution to require annual testing of math and verbal skills of public school students in grades 4 through 12.

Even more controversial are *national* tests and *national* norms or goals. Such tests would be administered to students periodically to permit parents, administrators, and legislators to assess how individual students, classes, schools, school districts, and states compare with one another. Moreover, once such testing is established, it could be expanded to include year-to-year measurement of individual students as they progress through the public schools.

Some critics of standardized national tests contend it is unfair and misleading to use such tests to measure learning. Minority students and students in districts in impoverished areas may not do well on these tests, and their low scores will reinforce cultural bias. Other critics worry that the use of such tests will force teachers to "teach to the test." Sensitive to the fact that their students will be compared with students in other classes, teachers will attempt to "beat the test" by emphasizing certain topics and ignoring others. This strategy might work for some students but would limit the learning of others. The main contention of the opponents of national testing, however, is that such measurement will not produce positive changes in education.

State and local policymakers continue to wrestle with how best to fund and implement the standardized testing that is mandated by the federal "No Child Left Behind" Act. While the general goals have been embraced, policymakers and educators hate to have their local schools labeled as "in need of improvement." And local authorities complain that state and national standards often measure factors that are beyond the control of a particular school and its staff. "It's really not fair to judge a school whose kids come without having ever read a book, and compare it to a school where kids go to the library and have libraries in their home," says Lynn Stockleg, a middle school teacher in Tulsa, Oklahoma. "It's rather discouraging when you're one of those schools. You know you're working very, very hard and yet your scores are consistently low."[14]

State and local officials have certainly discovered as well that complying with the "No Child Left Behind" Act is proving far more expensive than anyone had expected.

HIGHER EDUCATION

Until the 1950s, most local school districts provided only elementary and secondary education, although some larger cities also supported junior colleges and universities. Since the end of World War II, however, there has been a major expansion of *community colleges.* Now students may attend the first two years of college or receive a technical education right in their own communities. The trend is to create separate college districts to operate and raise funds for these local colleges.

Administration

States support many kinds of universities and colleges, including land-grant universities such as Michigan State University, created by the Morrill Act of 1862. State colleges and universities are governed by boards appointed by the governor in some states and elected by the voters in others. These boards are designed to give public institutions of higher education some independence, even though they greatly depend on their state legislature and governor for funding.

With about 80 percent of our more than 15 million college students now attending publicly supported institutions, the control and support of higher education have become significant political issues. States spend between 8 and 15 percent of their budgets on higher education, thus making it the third largest allocation of state funds after K–12 spending and Medicaid. States have created boards with varying degrees of control over operations and budgets. In addition, governors have tried to impose controls on universities and colleges that many university administrators insist are inappropriate. Yet institutions of higher education have greater independence from political oversight than other tax-supported institutions. Publicly funded colleges and universities usually can control teaching loads, internal procedures, areas of teaching emphasis, hiring and promotion, and the allocation of funds among internal units.

Funding Higher Education

In the twenty-first century, we face questions of access and funding for our colleges and universities due to increasing enrollments. Who should go? Only those who can afford it? What about minorities who are underrepresented in our colleges and universities? Access to colleges and universities for all students who wish to go has long been the declared goal in many states, but is this goal realistic? Should students be required to pay higher tuition to cover the cost of their education?

Tuition at state universities has gone up, often at two or three times the rate of inflation. Professors' salaries have not kept pace with tuition increases and have grown only slightly more than the rate of inflation. Although many people agree we need an infusion of new money to update college laboratories, improve libraries, and recruit and keep first-rate college professors, there is little consensus about who should pay for

This charter school in Jersey City, New Jersey, provides a computer lab for its science classes.

HOPE SCHOLARSHIPS

During the past decade, several states have established HOPE scholarships, modeled after Georgia's Helping Outstanding Pupils Educationally (HOPE) program. Georgia, in 1993, instituted HOPE scholarships providing any high school graduate with a B average or better full tuition, all mandatory fees, plus a book allowance of $100 a quarter or $150 a semester if he or she attends a state public college, university, or technical institute. The program was later expanded to provide up to $3,000 per year for students meeting the same standards who attend a private Georgia university. Students can keep their scholarship so long as they maintain their B average.

At least thirteen states currently have versions of HOPE scholarship programs.

For more state-by-state information, go to the Web site of the Education Commission of the States at www.ecs.org.

these efforts. The federal government is the chief supplier of student financial aid, and many states are now making major efforts to expand their programs of student aid. Many states, such as Georgia, California, Washington, and Alaska, are investing in programs aimed at keeping top students in their states at state-run as well as independent colleges.

Most institutions of higher education—both independent and state-run—receive some kind of government subsidy, through a variety of devices, so that students do not pay the full cost of their education. The national government and most states provide need-based financial assistance in the form of loans and grants, with students in the greatest financial need at the higher-cost institutions eligible for the most aid. Thus higher education has what is in effect a limited voucher system; students receive funds and can choose the kind of college or university that best serves their needs. It also means that in the United States, we have avoided a *two-track system*—one set of colleges and universities for the poor and another for the rich. Poor students can be found in most high-cost independent colleges and universities along with students from higher-income families. Funding for the public universities must compete with the rising costs of other state services, notably Medicaid, transportation, the criminal justice system, and prisons.

Many states are currently experimenting with new ways to fund higher education. As state funds for higher education have gone down in many states, public colleges and universities have been given the okay to raise tuition levels. Gradually the burden of paying for college is being shifted from the state to students and their parents.[15]

Colorado passed a law in 2004 that creates a voucher system for paying for higher education. If this plan survives current court challenges, Colorado will become the first state to fund undergraduate education primarily through grants to individual students. The state's three independent colleges are also entitled to these funds as the law currently stands. Other states will watch whether Colorado has found a better way to fund higher education or whether this mainly masks continued state investments in its higher education institutions.[16]

SOCIAL SERVICES

What role should state and local governments play in making sure all citizens have basic housing, health, and nutritional needs met? How important are these social services compared to government's obligation to provide police and fire protection, education, parks and recreation, and other services? For much of our history, human service needs were left to private charities that ran orphanages, old-age homes, hospitals, and other institutions. Philosophically, this reliance on private charity fit well with the American notions of limited government and self-reliance. That view changed dramatically during the Great Depression of the 1930s, when poverty, unemployment, and homelessness affected such large numbers of people that the government could no longer act as if these were private matters. Then in the mid-1960s, with President Lyndon Johnson's Great Society agenda, the nation embarked on a second major wave of social service programs, which Johnson called the War on Poverty. Today we continue to debate whether such programs accomplish their goals and whether alternatives would prove more successful.

Welfare

Pressure to reform the welfare system increased among both Democrats and Republicans in the last decades of the twentieth century. The number of Americans on welfare soared from about 2 million households in 1950 to close to 6 million in the early 1990s.[17] Why such growth? Some said that this country had finally recognized its obligation to care for the truly poor. Others charged that "government handouts" robbed recipients of the self-confidence they need to go to work and succeed; in this sense, dependence on welfare becomes a curse.

Welfare policy has been a complex web of federal, state, and local programs that shared or matched financial responsibilities. Until recently, the federal government picked up the lion's share of welfare costs. Most of the administrative burden, however, fell on state and local governments. Every state had a department of human services or welfare that either administered welfare programs directly or supervised local officials who administered these programs. County welfare departments determined who was entitled to assistance and dealt directly with recipients.

In 1996, fundamental changes were made in the role of the federal government in providing welfare. Most of the responsibility for welfare was shifted to the states, with national guidelines for administration. The landmark legislation that ended the Aid to Families with Dependent Children (AFDC) program was named Temporary Assistance for Needy Families (TANF).[18] States now receive federal block grants that require state matching funds. Each state files a plan with the secretary of health and human services every two years that (1) explains how it will ensure that recipients engage in work activities within two months of receiving benefits, (2) establishes goals to prevent and reduce out-of-wedlock pregnancies, (3) describes treatment of families moving into the state, and (4) explains whether it intends to provide aid to noncitizens. Money is distributed to states based on the highest amount of federal funding they received in the previous three fiscal years. To continue receiving federal funds, states must spend at least 75 percent of the amount they spent in 1994. Federal money is disbursed through state legislatures, not controlled by the governors. Additional federal funds are available to states as incentives for high performance and as loans in times of financial hardship for the state.

States are encouraged to experiment with welfare programs. Their experiments are evaluated by the federal government in order to ensure that they meet policy goals. Some states had previously started to cut back on welfare payments. For example, Wisconsin's governor, Tommy Thompson (who later served as George W. Bush's Secretary of Health and Human Services), proposed capping welfare payments for unwed teenage mothers, regardless of the number of children they have. Larger grants were paid to those who were married.[19] This provision is now included in national law. Previously, federal laws had unintentionally encouraged fathers to leave the family by making it easier for single-parent families to receive benefits. Current law seeks to overcome this disincentive by offering higher benefits to two-parent families.

Other states have developed **responsibility contracts**, requiring recipients to sign a written agreement specifying their responsibilities and outlining a plan for them to obtain work and achieve self-sufficiency. Some states provide child care and Medicaid benefits beyond the federal one-year extension for families who lose benefits due to unemployment.

About half of the states, including Massachusetts, New York, Wisconsin, and California, have experimented with **workfare** programs designed to help welfare recipients develop the self-confidence, skills, and habits necessary for regular employment. Workfare gives able-bodied adults who do not have preschool-aged children the opportunity to learn job skills that can lead to employment. Another government program creates **enterprise zones** in large cities that give tax incentives to companies that provide job training for the unemployed in depressed neighborhoods.[20]

As a result of the 1996 welfare reform, the percentage of people on welfare was reduced by more than half—from close to 6 million families in the early 1990s to less than half that in recent years. Initially, federal and state welfare expenditures declined significantly, though the booming economy of the late 1990s doubtless helped create a lot of jobs and thus contributed to this decline.

At first glance, the 1996 welfare reform seemed a successful policy; however, the program has had its shortcomings. One critic who worked closely with the bill, Georgetown University Law Center's Peter Edelman, says: "The main lesson of the 1996 law is that having a job and earning a livable income are two different things."[21] It is true that many of the recipients who found jobs through the 1996 law found low-income or part-time jobs. While these jobs technically removed names from the poverty list, they did not decrease the very real difficulty of finding grocery money each week. A survey conducted

This welfare-to-work trainee is learning skills that will enable her to find employment at a steady, well-paid job.

responsibility contract
A welfare strategy adopted by some states in which recipients sign a written agreement specifying their responsibilities and outlining a plan for obtaining work and achieving self-sufficiency.

workfare
A welfare strategy adopted by some states that gives able-bodied adults who do not have preschool-aged children the opportunity to learn job skills that can lead to employment.

enterprise zone
Inner-city area designated as offering tax incentives to companies that invest in plants there and provide job training for the unemployed.

Public health clinics provide free vaccinations and other health services to children whose families cannot afford medical insurance.

by the National Governors' Association found that most governors believe the plan requires more contrived community service jobs and costs far more money than allotted.[22] In times of recession, and because many of those left on welfare after the 1996 law are the hard cases—people with little education, no work experience, and tenuous personal backgrounds—creating even more stringent work requirements does not even begin to address the individual needs of those on welfare.

States are now the prime laboratories for making and implementing social policy. The federal government originally became involved in welfare programs because states had been unwilling or unable to tackle these problems on their own. When confronted with competing demands in other policy areas, will states give the needs of poor people a lower priority? And what happens when good economic times turn bad? How will the states cope with larger numbers of needy people?

State welfare expenditures fell again because the recession of 2001 and 2002 forced just about every state to lower payments, tighten eligibility requirements, and shorten the time limits on recipients. Yet several states continue to experiment, sometimes successfully, with reducing poverty, promoting work, and encouraging marital stability.[23]

Health

During the hot summer of 1794, a yellow fever epidemic ravaged Philadelphia. The streets were deserted. All who could afford to do so had fled with their families to the country. Every night, the sounds of the death cart echoed through the nearly empty city. Most families that remained behind lost a child, a father, or a mother. Only when cool weather returned did the city resume normal activity.

Yellow fever, dysentery, malaria, and other diseases periodically swept American cities in the eighteenth and nineteenth centuries. As late as 1879, yellow fever struck hard in the South. Memphis was nearly depopulated. Following the lead of Louisiana and Massachusetts, state after state established a board of health to deal with such epidemics. Spurred by the medical discoveries of Louis Pasteur and other scientists, authorities undertook additional efforts to protect public health. Open sewers were covered, and hygienic measures were instituted.

Prevention and disease control are still major public health activities today. Doctors are required to report cases of communicable disease. Health department officials then investigate to discover the source of the infection, isolate the afflicted, and take whatever action is called for. Most state health departments give doctors free vaccine and serum, and many local departments give free vaccinations to those who cannot afford private physicians. Mobile units take free x-rays of schoolchildren, teachers, and the general public; county health departments provide free or low-cost inoculations, vision tests, and hearing tests. Public health officials also try to protect water supplies and ensure the safe disposal of waste and sewage. They protect the community's food supply by inspecting hotels, restaurants, and food markets.

Today the overwhelming public health issues are pollution, AIDS, smoking, drug abuse, depression, and obesity. Issues such as "mad cow" disease and the West Nile virus also demand state as well as national attention. Like the contagious and infectious disease issues of prior times, they require concerted efforts and public health policies. Thousands of local governments—counties, cities, townships, and special health districts—have some kind of public health program. Every state has an agency, usually called a department of health, that administers the state program and supervises local health officials. At the national level, the U.S. Public Health Service conducts research, assists state and local authorities, and administers federal grants to encourage local agencies to expand their programs. Every state also administers various federally funded medical benefit programs for the needy, such as Medicaid, not to be confused with Medicare—the Social Security health care program for people over 65. Medicaid is the second largest item in overall state budgets.

The current health care crisis in the United States involves access and cost. Wealthy people can afford the costs and gain access; poor people on welfare have somewhat less access to health care, and the quality of their care is often lower. Also, the people in the

GOING UP IN SMOKE

One cause of rising health care costs has been treating illnesses related to the use of tobacco. The battle to recover some of the costs incurred by government has gone on for years, but in 1998, the state attorneys general worked out a $206 billion settlement of the Medicare lawsuit against tobacco companies, the money to be used to offset the costs incurred by the states for treating sick smokers. A part of the money may also go to Medicaid. Smoking prevention programs and a ban on billboard advertising were also included in the deal. Under the terms of the settlement, states may pass additional legislation, further taxing the tobacco industry at the state level.

In 1998, California voters narrowly approved Proposition 10, which provided for a 50-cent-per-pack increase in the tax on cigarettes and a $1.00 increase per pack on other forms of tobacco. The money generated by this tax will be used to establish a new county commission to create and oversee early childhood smoking prevention programs.*

*Alan K. Ota, "Multi-State Agreement Renews Democrats' Interest in Pushing Tobacco Legislation," *Congressional Quarterly Weekly,* November 21, 1998, p. 3178.

middle regularly worry about whether their personal insurance will be adequate to cover their health care needs. Programs such as Medicaid seek to fill the health insurance gaps for low-income persons. The larger goal of Medicaid is to improve the health of those who might otherwise go without health care.

Medicaid continues to be a huge concern for state governments nationwide. The increasing number of Medicaid-eligible citizens, coupled with the rising cost of prescription drugs, long-term health care, and HMOs—all far beyond the rate of inflation—add up to a Medicaid program in need of help. Further, the program was expanded during strong financial times, often to include low-income children as well as parents, but when state fiscal conditions are less than perfect, Medicaid is in danger.[24] "That's the irony of Medicaid: The program has a difficult time doing its job when its services are most needed. A sour economy increases demand for coverage and spending, at the same time revenues are eroding and putting heavy pressure on state budgets," notes Trinity Tomsie, who covers Medicaid issues for the National Conference on State Legislator's Fiscal Affairs Program.[25]

State policy makers now face tough questions about whether or not to maintain coverage and if so, how: Should reforms limiting the number of people eligible be implemented to cut costs? Can drug manufacturers be leaned on for rebates? Should a preferred-drug list, based on cost and efficacy, be established? The program is enormous, covering the health care needs for over 40 million Americans and taking an average of at least 13 percent of annual state funds.

Governors around the country pressed President George W. Bush and Congress to increase the federal share of Medicaid's costs, to no avail. Many were frustrated when the president advocated a large farm bill appropriating money for farm subsidies, seemingly ignoring what many think a more pressing financial issue, Medicaid funding. State officials acknowledge nowadays that soaring Medicaid spending threatens recent state goals such as reducing public school class size, increasing public transportation infrastructure, and funding innovative environmental programs. Some states "have reached into the funds received in settling their suits with tobacco companies, or tapped public employee pension funds, or drained their rainy day reserves in order to meet the requirement in state constitutions that they balance their budgets."[26] Other state officials proposed imposing premiums, copayments, and enrollment caps on Medicaid clients as a way to cut costs and raise revenues.

LAW ENFORCEMENT

Many state and local government powers stem from their **police powers**, the inherent power of states to use physical force if necessary to protect the health, safety, and welfare of their citizens. This power is among those not delegated to the federal government by the Constitution and reserved to the states. It is on this basis that mayors or governors impose curfews, as they have in some urban riots. But the police power extends to other activities of government, such as regulating public health, safety, and morals.

The State Police

In 1835, the famous Texas Rangers were organized as a small border patrol. In 1865, Massachusetts appointed a few state constables to suppress gambling, a job the local police had proved unable or, more probably, unwilling to do. But not until 1905, with the organization of the Pennsylvania State Constabulary, did a state police system come into being. It was so successful that other states soon followed.

The establishment of the Pennsylvania State Constabulary marked a sharp break with traditional police methods. This was a mounted and uniformed body organized on a military basis; centralized control was given to a superintendent directly responsible to the governor. The Pennsylvania pattern was followed by other states.

State police became a part of our law enforcement system for a variety of reasons. The growth of urban and metropolitan areas, the coming of the automobile (and the resulting demand for greater protection on the highways and the creation of a mobile

police powers
Inherent powers of state governments to pass laws to protect public health, safety, and welfare; the national government has no directly granted police powers but accomplishes the same goals through other delegated powers.

RACIAL PROFILING

Racial profiling—state police stopping and arresting minorities—made news in New Jersey but was also found to occur in other states as well. An extensive review based on interviews with troopers, state officials, and victims revealed a pattern of selective enforcement that had gone on for more than a decade.

The story begins in the mid-1980s, when the federal Drug Enforcement Administration (DEA) responded to the street violence of the crack epidemic by enlisting local police forces to catch smugglers who were importing drugs from Latin America, often to Florida, and moving them to major American cities by car.

By 1989, the New Jersey State Police had become such a successful part of "Operation Pipeline" that DEA officials hailed the troopers as exemplary models for most other states.

But on New Jersey roadways, black and Hispanic drivers were subjected to such frequent and unjustified traffic stops and searches that they complained of a new violation in the state's traffic code: "DWB—driving while black." In state police barracks, some black and Hispanic troopers bitterly acknowledged that even though the state officially prohibited racial profiling, senior troopers trained them to single out drivers on the basis of their ethnicity or race.

On April 22, 1998, troopers shot and wounded three unarmed black and Hispanic men during a traffic stop on the New Jersey Turnpike, propelling the controversy to the center of the state's political stage. State officials, including Governor Christine Todd Whitman, at first clung to their insistence that there was no pattern of profiling. But under pressure from civil rights leaders and the federal Justice Department's Civil Rights Division, the Whitman administration ultimately acknowledged racial profiling, revamped its narcotics strategy, and agreed to let a federal judge monitor the force.

A 2001 court decision wiped out most of these arrests and paid compensation to the victims.

SOURCE: Adapted from David Kocieniewski and Robert Hanley, "An Inside Story of Racial Bias and Denial," *The New York Times*, December 3, 2000, pp. 53, 56.

force for catching fleeing criminals), and the need for a trained force to maintain order during strikes, fires, floods, and other emergencies all promoted the creation of state police.

Other Police Forces

State police are not the only law enforcement agencies maintained by state governments. There are liquor law enforcement officials, fish and game wardens, fire wardens, detective bureaus, and special motor vehicle police. This dispersion of functions has been criticized, yet each department insists it needs its own law enforcement agency to handle its special problems.

At the local level, almost every municipality maintains its own police force; the county has a sheriff and deputies, and some townships have their own police officers. In fact, there are more than 40,000 separate law enforcement agencies in the United States, employing more than 600,000 men and women.

With crime continuing to be an important issue to many voters, crime control is always on the minds of elected officials. State and local governments spend more than $50 billion on police protection and correctional or prison institutions. Local governments pay for over 70 percent of all law enforcement costs, including such routine activities as controlling traffic and patrolling neighborhoods but also maintaining court security and preventing juvenile crime. The number of police officers increased by 10 percent during the 1990s and may increase even more with recent state and federal homeland security legislation. The federal government in the 1990s provided grants for recruiting and temporarily paying for nearly 100,000 new local police officers throughout the country. But when these grants later expired, many local governments experienced fiscal budget shortfalls. Local governments now struggle to pay for these recently added police officers.

Federal–State Action

The national government has gradually moved into law enforcement, a field traditionally reserved for state and local governments, although the main cost of local law enforcement is still borne by local governments. Today, for example, it is a federal offense to transport kidnapped individuals or stolen goods across state lines. Taking firearms, explosives, or even information across state lines for illegal purposes is also a federal offense. Federal law enforcement agencies include the Federal Bureau of Investigation (FBI), the Bureau of Alcohol, Tobacco, and Firearms (ATF), and the Drug Enforcement Administration (DEA).

Crime rates have been declining. Despite positive trends, politicians in both parties continue to press for government to do more about crime. Some advocate stricter laws regulating guns, while others favor more police on the street or more prisons. Because politicians fear appearing "soft on crime," taking action on crime is almost always a high priority at all levels of government.

Since the September 11, 2001, terrorist attacks on New York City and the Pentagon, every state has designated a homeland security coordinator. These state officials are working with the new federal Department of Homeland Security to beef up preparedness and training efforts aimed at preventing and dealing with future terrorist attacks. The national government approved federal funds in 2002 that were to be used to train and equip "so-called first responders, along with grants to prevent bioterrorism, which have increasingly become the focus of many state officers."[27] While there is a clear need for new and expanded homeland security efforts, few states have the resources to do so. Many local and state officials have complained that most new federal funds are being redirected toward new homeland security concerns such as bioterrorism preparedness while ignoring many of the traditional and basic public safety systems. This has added to budget shortfalls in most states and has led state and local officials to insist on greater federal funds and greater flexibility in how states and localities decide what their priorities are.[28]

PLANNING THE URBAN COMMUNITY

Are our cities good places in which to live and work? Crime, pollution, garbage, crowded shopping areas, dented fenders, slums and blighted areas, inadequate parks, challenging traffic patterns, and shattered nerves—are these the inevitable costs of urban life?

For at least the first century of the United States' existence, American cities were allowed to grow unchecked. Industrialists were permitted to erect factories wherever they wished; developers were allowed to construct towering buildings that prevented sunlight from reaching the streets below; commuters, bicyclists, and pedestrians ended up with transportation systems that rarely met their needs.

Zoning Laws

The most common method of ensuring orderly growth is *zoning*—creating specific areas and limiting property usage in each area. A community may be divided into designated areas for single-family, two-family, or multifamily dwellings; for commercial purposes; and for light or heavy industry. Regulations restrict the height of buildings or require that buildings be located a certain distance apart or a certain distance from the boundaries of the lot.

Zoning regulations attempt to enable the city or county government to coordinate services with land use and to stabilize property values by preventing, for example, garbage dumps from being located next to residential areas. Day-to-day enforcement is usually the responsibility of a building inspector, who ensures that a projected construction project is consistent with building, zoning, fire, and sanitary regulations before granting a building permit. A zoning ordinance, however, is no better than its enforcement. In most cases, a zoning or planning commission or the city council can amend ordinances and make exceptions to regulations, and these officials are often under tremendous pressure to grant exceptions. But if they go too far in permitting special cases, the whole purpose of zoning is defeated.

Zoning is only one kind of community planning. Until recently, city planners were primarily concerned with streets and buildings. Today most are also concerned with the quality of life. Consequently, planning covers a broad range of activities, including methods to avoid air pollution, improve water quality, and provide for better parks. Planners collect all the information they can about a city and then prepare long-range plans. Can smaller-scale communities be devised within urban centers? Can downtown areas be revitalized, and if so, how? Where should main highways or mass-transit facilities be constructed to meet future needs? Will the water supply be adequate for the population 10, 20, or 50 years from now? Are hospitals and parks accessible to all? Does the design of public buildings encourage crime or energy waste?

Controlling Growth

Critics of urban and state planning are skeptical whether governors, mayors, or state and local legislators can prevent what they sometimes call the "Los Angelization" of the United States, by which they mean urban growth without much planning for transportation, environmental protection, or management of water and other resources. Unregulated market forces can cause severe harm to residents, and "politics as usual" does not ensure sensible growth patterns or protect the air, water, and beauty of most states and communities.

Seattle and San Francisco residents voted to limit the height and bulk of downtown buildings in an effort to protect these cities from excessive growth. Maryland and many other states have passed "smart growth" laws aimed at preserving large blocks of contiguous land and ensuring that the necessary roads, sewers, and schools are in place before development proceeds. This legislation is implemented in two ways. The state gives priority funding to development in areas designated by counties as having the proper infrastructure and meeting other guidelines; state funds are also allocated to local governments and private land trusts to purchase the development rights to land "rich in agricultural, forestry, natural, and cultural resources."[29]

Repair of deteriorating infrastructure, although a nuisance to residents, is necessary to maintain the quality of life in cities and also to attract businesses and consumers.

The population of the United States will soar by 50 to 60 million by 2025. A few urban planners recommend looking at European cities such as Paris, where choice neighborhoods in the heart of the city combine elegant six- and seven-story apartment buildings above neighborhood retail stores. Most Americans would reject this dense, crowded lifestyle devoid of driveways, grassy front lawns, and backyard pools. But a closer look at European cities often finds a great number of interior gardens within apartments and meticulously groomed neighborhood parks. Columnist Neal Peirce writes that "density and mixed use aren't bad; they're just different—and sometimes better" and notes the discussion and advocacy of a U.S. version of Parisian greenery in a group called Community Greens: Shared Parks in Urban Blocks (www. communitygreens.org).[30]

Obviously, planning and sensible growth depend on public support. They also depend on market forces. No plan will be effective, however, unless it reflects the interests and values of major groups within the community. Planning is clearly a political activity. Different groups view the ends and means of planning differently, and agreements on tough policy options are often hard to reach. Moreover, one of the barriers to successful planning is the general fear of government power. Effective planning therefore requires imaginative collaboration among planners, community leaders, and the popularly elected officials who must bear the responsibility for implementing the plans.[31]

Environmental Regulation

State and local governments have long been concerned about managing land use and protecting the environment. In such heavily polluted places as Pittsburgh, smoke abatement ordinances were enacted as early as 1860, but aggressive action on air pollution did not come until after World War II.[32] By the 1950s, states had established agencies to deal with resource management issues, but it was the federal legislation of the early 1970s that pushed environmental protection onto their agendas.[33] One important reason for the expanded federal role is the reality that pollution does not recognize state boundaries. Air and water pollution are particular examples of the interstate nature of environmental problems.

In the 1950s and 1960s, the federal government provided grants to state and local governments for research and assistance in developing and implementing their own environmental standards. The key piece of legislation in the transition to a greater role for the federal government was the Federal Environmental Protection Act, passed in 1970, which created the Environmental Protection Agency (EPA). Other acts dealing with specific environmental problems followed: the Clean Air Act of 1970, the Clean Water Act of 1972, the Safe Drinking Water Act of 1974, the Toxic Substances Control Act of 1976, and Superfund (the federal Comprehensive Environmental Response, Compensation and Liability Act) of 1980. Most of these acts have been amended one or more times. Subsequent to the passage of the Superfund Act in 1980, which was created in response to public outcry regarding the most contaminated toxic dump sites across the United States, several state and local policies have been established to cover the toxic sites that do not qualify as Superfund sites but still warrant cleanup action.[34]

As states became more involved in toxic waste regulation and air pollution in the 1960s and 1970s, pressure on the national government to develop national environmental standards increased. Part of the pressure for federal legislation was due to the inconsistent state policies being considered and enacted. Not surprisingly, states tend to have different environmental concerns. For example, swine and poultry regulations are more important in the Midwest and Plains states, whereas nuclear cleanup is important in the West and Southwest, and timber regulation is of concern to the Pacific Northwest. Not only did environmental activists want a single national approach to the overarching problems of air and water pollution, but so did many of those who were being regulated. Automobile manufacturers, for instance, preferred one national standard for automobile emissions rather than dozens of differing state standards. Businesses operating in several states also pressed for uniform federal environmental standards.[35]

The basic model of environmental regulation has been for the federal government to set national standards for water and air quality. State and local governments are typically put in charge of both implementing standards and monitoring compliance. Typically, too, states complain that federal regulations and unfunded mandates impose a heavy financial burden on them.

Another area in which states are increasingly responsible for environmental policy is waste management. Not unexpectedly, states where the economy is growing have regulated waste management more aggressively than states where this is not the case. Economically hard-pressed states fear driving industries away. Fears about nuclear waste, acid rain, and hazardous wastes have sparked extensive efforts at regulation

These wind turbines near Palm Springs, California, constitute an alternative source of energy.

To encourage residents to purchase vehicles that use clean-burning fuel, Utah has issued these special license plates that allow people to drive in the carpool lane of I-15 without a passenger. Those with energy-efficient vehicles are also eligible to receive tax credits.

within states, as well as court battles with nearby states over the export of unwanted byproducts of energy development.

Although the EPA gets lots of headlines, state and local governments have more people working to control pollution. States can and do experiment with ways to improve air quality. California, for instance, has been a leader in testing automobile emissions. One innovation being considered is *remote sensing,* which uses roadside devices that shoot an infrared beam across a road to detect the emissions of passing cars. This device also has a video camera that records the license plates of vehicles in violation of emission standards. Such a system could replace the periodic state inspections now required for all vehicles.

Many states have been using alternative renewable energy both to cut down on energy costs and to rejuvenate dwindling rural economies. Large-scale wind-energy projects, for example, have been started in New York, Pennsylvania, Colorado, Iowa, Kansas, Texas, and Washington, among other states. Most of these were begun in the 1990s or more recently. As fossil fuel costs became increasingly unpredictable, states started to diversify their approach by investing in biomass, wind, hydroelectric, solar, and geothermal projects. Some states have even implemented innovative tax incentives and "net metering" programs (a practice allowing customers who have solar panels or other personal energy-generating capital to sell their energy back to the overall grid) in order to encourage more individual responsibility. Although none of these tactics have yet become widely accepted, nor is renewable energy expected to soon replace traditional energy sources, they are evidence of active state and local environmental efforts (Figure 28–2). Many states have also taken the lead in regulating cold-fired power plants, unsafe mercury pollution levels and greenhouse gas emissions.[36]

Environmental interest groups continue to press for stronger state and local environmental regulation, cars that go more miles on a gallon of gas and "smart" hybrid cars, and continue to demand that stiff penalties be imposed for violations of environmental laws. Further, some of the effort has shifted to individual action—recycling, conservation, saving and planting trees, and using public transportation. As the need for environmental regulation becomes more and more pressing, many state and local

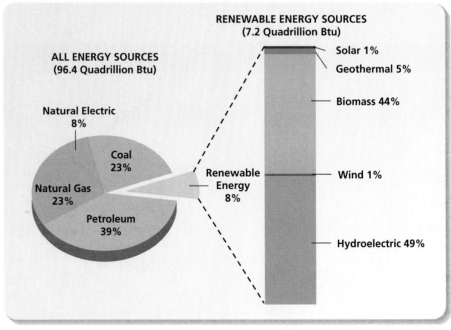

FIGURE 28–2 U.S. Energy Consumption by Source, 1999.
From 1998 to 1999, electricity generated from wind power increased 50 percent and geothermal use increased 14 percent.
SOURCE: Energy Information Administration.

governments continue to react by expanding existing legislation and appropriating money for research and regulatory agency staff.[37]

Transportation

Before the automobile, long-distance commercial travel was mainly by canal and railroad. Local roads were built and repaired under the direction of city, township, and county officials. Able-bodied male citizens were required either to put in a certain number of days working on the public roads or to pay taxes for that purpose. By the 1890s, bicycle clubs began to urge the building of hard-surfaced roads, but it was not until the early 1900s and the growing popularity of the automobile that road building became a major industry. This function was gradually transferred from the township to larger units of government, but counties and townships still have important building and maintenance functions.

Although much of the money comes from the federal government, it is the state and local governments that build the highways, public buildings, airports, parks, and recreational facilities. State and local governments, in fact, spend more money on transportation than on anything else except education and welfare. Because highways and bridges around the nation are aging, a federal tax on gasoline was levied to help rebuild these public facilities.

The national government has supported state highway construction since 1916, and through various federal highway laws passed since then, federal aid has increased. States do the planning, estimate the costs, and arrange for the construction work, even when they receive federal assistance. In order to receive support, however, states must submit their plans to, and have their work inspected by, the U.S. Department of Transportation (DOT). All federally funded highways must meet DOT standards governing the engineering of the roadbed, employment conditions for construction workers, and weight and load conditions for trucks.

Under the Federal Highway Act of 1956, states planned and built the National System of Interstate and Defense Highways. The interstate system consists of 43,000 miles of superhighways linking almost all cities with a population of 50,000 or more. The federal government paid 90 percent of the cost of this system, with most of the money coming from taxes on gasoline, tires, and trucks that are placed in a trust fund designated for that purpose.

In 1998, Congress passed a $216 billion, six-year surface transportation bill that included $173 billion in funding for highways as well as $2 billion for highway safety. The bill funds repairing cracked asphalt, increasing safety reinforcements on bridges, and expanding the network of highways. One billion dollars is dedicated to state programs to increase the percentage of drivers who use safety belts and to prevent drunk driving. The legislation also provided $41 billion for mass transit.[38] This massive federal investment is funded by continuing the 18.3 cents-per-gallon tax on gas.

Traffic has become a major problem in recent years—especially in older cities such as Boston; Denver; Los Angeles; Seattle; San Francisco; Washington, D.C.; and New York. In addition to a growing population and an increasing number of car owners, drivers are driving more each year. As a result, traffic and congestion have become pressing issues for state governments. Increasing road space, building public transportation systems, or establishing staggered work hours should help; however, transportation policy makers have not found it that simple. Adding roads or lanes often leads more people to use them and may ultimately result in new traffic patterns that are no better than the old ones. Public transportation is an option, but Americans love their vehicles, illustrated by the fact that cities with public transportation often have more traffic problems than those without. Staggering work hours is also difficult because businesses work most effectively through collaboration—both with other businesses and within a firm—and so, it is most efficient for workers to be on the job at the same time each day. Consequently, as population and car ownership continue to rise and the traffic solution remains elusive, automobile congestion will continue to be a pressing state public policy issue.[39]

Economic Development

Another central priority for governors and mayors, as well as other state and local officials, is providing jobs for their citizens. Governors commonly spend a significant amount of time encouraging companies to relocate within their borders, courting corporate officials, going on trade missions to other countries to promote their state's products, and negotiating favorable tax and other incentives with new businesses. This interest is not new. What is new is the international scope of these activities. Former Utah Governor Norman Bangerter was fond of saying, "The one thing you will always see on an economic development trip to Tokyo is another governor."

States compete with one another because economic development is the key to increasing the tax base that funds government services. But states face a dilemma, because satisfying the demands of new businesses can be expensive, and tax incentives can reduce the tax return the new companies will generate. Competition among states has intensified to the point that localities are worried about keeping the jobs they have, not just persuading new companies to move to their area. New York City has offered billions of dollars in incentives to influence several companies not to leave. Critics of these "bidding wars" believe that states should spend tax money on rebuilding infrastructure and strengthening education rather than offering public funds to selected large private companies.

REGULATION

States and local communities adopt safety regulations on the assumption (sometimes mistaken) that the benefits to the general public will outweigh the costs to the individuals and groups being regulated. Thus laws requiring drivers' licenses, compelling motorists to stop at red lights, mandating seat-belt use, or imposing severe penalties on

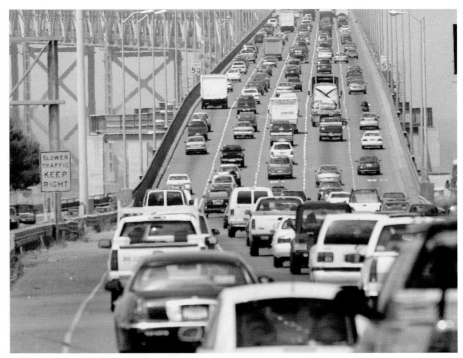

The San Francisco-bound Oakland–San Francisco Bay Bridge. The Texas Transportation Institute's annual study of 75 urban areas found that rush hours are more common and their delays are more extensive than in the past. The average urban motorist in recent years spends 62 hours a year stalled in traffic.

people caught driving under the influence of alcohol or drugs are intended to protect the safety and freedom of innocent pedestrians or occupants of other motor vehicles. Most such laws are accepted as both necessary and legitimate. States have raised the drinking age and stiffened the punishments for drunk driving, in most cases because the federal government tied federal funds to the passage of such legislation. An interest group, Mothers Against Drunk Driving (MADD), also lobbied effectively to force the issue.

Public Utilities

Corporations receive their charters from the states. Banks, insurance companies, securities dealers, doctors, lawyers, teachers, barbers, and various other businesses and professions are licensed by the states, and their activities are supervised by state officials. Farmers and industrial and service workers are also regulated. But of all businesses, public utilities are the most closely monitored.

It is easier to list than to define public utilities. They include water plants, electric power and natural gas distribution companies, telephone companies, railroads, and bus lines. Public utilities are distinguished from other businesses because government gives them special privileges, such as the power of **eminent domain** (the right to take private property for public use), the right to use public streets, and a certain amount of protection from competition (monopoly). In return, utilities are required to give the public adequate service at reasonable rates.

Public utilities supply essential services in fields in which market competition may be counterproductive. In the United States, private enterprise—subject to public regulation rather than public ownership—has been the usual method of providing essential services. Nevertheless, more than two-thirds of our cities own their own waterworks, about 100 operate their own gas utilities, and many are taking over the operation of their transit systems. But other services—intercity transportation, airlines, telephone, and the supply of natural gas—are almost everywhere provided by private enterprises subject to government regulation.

Every state has a utilities commission (usually called the Public Utilities Commission, or PUC) to ensure that utilities operate in the interest of the public. In 36 states, utility commissioners are appointed by the governor with the consent of the state senate. In Virginia and South Carolina, they are chosen by the legislature, and in eleven other states, they are elected by the voters.[40] PUC posts were once considered political plums, and commissioners used them as stepping-stones to higher elective office. This is less true these days.

PUCs must strike a balance between fair rates for consumers and adequate profits for the utility companies. "The tremendous work load on these commissions," writes one observer, "finds commissioners constantly walking a tightrope between helping a regulated industry get a decent return on investment, and making sure consumers get good service at a fair price."[41] Utility commissioners raise or lower utility rates—perhaps the most visible part of their job—but they are also involved in toxic waste disposal, nuclear power, and truck regulation, as well as telephone, cable television, and other energy-related disputes. The average tenure for commissioners is only about three and a half years, a statistic that suggests the burnout involved in the job.

Utility commissioners operate under the assumption that their decisions are not political, yet nearly every decision they make comes under political attack or stirs political reaction. Several states have enacted laws prohibiting conflicts of interest, limiting commissioners' affiliations with the utilities they regulate and, for at least a year after they resign from the PUC, prohibiting them from accepting employment with any company that was under their regulation. Other states have established a separate office of consumer advocate to encourage even greater responsiveness to consumer needs.

Technology and innovation are driving the deregulation of utilities across the nation. The deregulation of utilities is a controversial topic in virtually every state legislature, as telephone and power companies seek to influence the new rules for competition.

With only one exception, federal and state taxes on motor fuels (gasoline and diesel) go directly to pay for highway construction. The exception is a gasoline tax that was part of President Bill Clinton's 1993 deficit reduction package. The trucking industry and others strongly objected to the tax because it broke with the tradition of gasoline taxes paying for highway construction and maintenance. Republican congressional leaders vowed to repeal the tax, which was done in 1998.*

Not everyone is pleased by the heavy commitment of public funds to highways. These roads, some say, are a massive subsidy for automobile users and makers; without highways, autos would not be so popular or so widely used, and mass transit would be used more. Some people use the highways far more than others, yet everyone must contribute to the taxes that pay for highway construction. Why not tax people in proportion to their actual use of the highways? Some people advocate installing a meter in every vehicle at a cost of less than $20 to measure usage of roadways in order to extract adequate federal user fees. Others favor incentives or restrictions on employers to encourage mass transit and car pools, such as limiting parking space as part of a building permit for a new business.

*Alissa J. Rubin and Andrew Taylor, "GOP Goes for a Gas Tax Repeal," *Congressional Quarterly Weekly,* May 11, 1996, p. 1276.

eminent domain
Power of a government to take private property for public use; the U.S. Constitution gives national and state governments this power and requires them to provide just compensation for property so taken.

The San Onofre nuclear plant at San Onofre Beach, approximately 60 miles south of Los Angeles, California.

Telephone communication is no longer limited to transmissions over telephone lines but now includes cellular and satellite communications. Gas turbines now make it possible for some consumers to generate their own electricity rather than depend on power from public utility companies. Much of the political pressure for deregulation of utilities comes from businesses as well as from consumers.[42]

State legislatures and utility regulators are adopting a marketplace model in which competition between providers is encouraged rather than restricted. In the past, state utility regulators structured rate systems to provide a subsidy to rural and low-income consumers of telephone and electricity services. It is likely that these subsidies will continue, but it is more difficult to identify who pays the subsidy with so many firms now providing telephone and electricity services.

The politics of regulation, especially regulation of public utilities, is of growing interest to citizens and consumers. In many areas, citizens' groups make presentations to the PUC and regularly monitor PUC operations. There has been an increasing interest in PUC activity all across the country, especially in regulating nuclear power and monitoring the cost of energy. For example, after many years of citizen concern over the environmental impact of the San Onofre Nuclear Generating Station, the California Coastal Commission adopted a plan that would mitigate, but not prevent, the destruction of fish and kelp.[43] In Virginia, the water in Chesapeake Bay was found to contain high levels of pollutants that cause an increased risk of cancer, and that discovery led the public utilities director to impose a strict monitoring program and stiff fines for violations.

Employers and Employees

Despite the expanded regulations of the national government, state and local governments still have much to say about working conditions.

- *Health and safety legislation:* States require proper heating, lighting, ventilation, fire escapes, and sanitary facilities in work areas. Machinery must be equipped with safety guards. Some standards have also been established to reduce occupation-related diseases. Health, building, and labor inspectors tour industrial plants to ensure compliance with the laws.

- *Workers' compensation:* Today all states have workers' compensation programs based on the belief that employees should not have to bear the cost of accidents or illnesses incurred because of their jobs. The costs of accidents and occupational diseases are borne by employers and passed on to consumers in the form of higher prices. In the past, employees had to prove that their employers were at fault if they suffered an accident on the job. Today if people are injured or contract a disease in the ordinary course of employment, they are entitled to compensation set by a prearranged schedule. Workers' compensation is a controversial issue, with employers arguing that employee claims of workplace stress are excessive and will make American firms uncompetitive.

- *Child labor:* All states forbid child labor, yet state laws vary widely in their coverage and in their definition of child labor. Many states set the minimum age for employment at 14. Higher age requirements are normal for employment in hazardous occupations and during school hours. Many of these regulations have been superseded by stricter federal laws.

- *Consumer protection:* This movement, which became prominent in the 1960s and 1970s, believes that consumers should be provided with adequate safety information and should have their complaints heard. Most states have offices to hear consumer complaints, including lawyers working in the offices of the state attorney general. State governments often establish professional standards and handle complaints about legal and medical services or insurance practices.

Recent state activity to protect consumers has focused on fraud, especially "guaranteed prize schemes," which are mailed to more than 50 million Americans and to which millions respond. When the prize is not exactly what was promised or the method for selecting winners is deceptive, people often complain to their state government. Other areas in which state governments have been active in attempting to protect consumers include charitable solicitations by telephone, long-distance phone service promotions, credit and promotions, and auditing irregularities and fraud in corporations.

THE IMPORTANCE OF STATE AND LOCAL POLICY

All 50 state governments and more than 86,000 local governments are on the front lines of trying to solve community and regional social problems. They must often work closely with one another and the national government, and this is a frequent source of frustration.[44]

Divided government in Washington in recent years has meant neither political party could have its way with domestic policy. Bill Clinton and George W. Bush had different priorities, and the generally divided U.S. Senate in recent years has usually taken a cautious approach on such issues as health care and environmental regulation.

State officials continue to be frustrated with national legislation such as the "No Child Left Behind" and homeland security legislation in recent years that mandate extensive federal requirements into core areas of state and local policy responsibilities yet provide inadequate federal funds to assist in the achievement of these goals.

Innovative governors and state legislators have sponsored important changes in welfare reform, educational testing, transportation, urban planning, and insurance regulation. But the challenges facing state and local officials never let up.

SUMMARY

1. We ask our state and local governments to do many things for us, and what we request in the areas of education, public welfare, health and hospitals, public safety, and transportation are the most costly, accounting for most state and local expenditures.

2. In addition, we ask states and communities to keep our streets safe, protect our natural resources, provide parks and recreation, encourage job opportunities, and protect consumers. There are, of course, great differences in how states and communities set their priorities in these areas. Some communities are so concerned about environmental quality that they are settling for selective growth at the expense of job opportunities. Other communities favor attracting jobs and industry despite environmental costs.

3. Education has been a major area of state and local government activity and concern. It moved to center stage because of a growing concern that our system was not keeping pace with our needs or our global competitors. Several reform efforts have sought to improve our system.

4. Concern about the U.S. system of higher education has also grown as states attempt to balance budgets and meet pressing demands in corrections, health, welfare, and other areas. Few people question the need for a major investment in laboratories, computer instruction, and libraries at colleges and universities, yet the federal government has not offered to pay for these things, and most states do not have the resources to do more than stay afloat in this policy area.

5. The huge national welfare overhaul legislation in 1996 eliminated any federal implementation of programs, transferring all responsibility to the states, supported with block grants of federal money. It was prompted by a desire to trim the federal budget and to eliminate disincentives for self-sufficiency and responsibility that the former welfare system seemed to create. Before the national legislation was passed, many states had experimented with limiting their caseload, placing time limits on welfare, implementing a work requirement, and placing special requirements on teenage mothers. Most of these ideas were then included in the 1996 federal law.

6. States play an important role in setting policies relating to public health. States have long sought to eradicate disease and foster practices conducive to a healthy population. The challenges for states today include the administration of federal outlay programs such as Medicaid, reforming health care services, and controlling the AIDS epidemic. Soaring Medicaid costs have posed an additional challenge to state governments.

7. Law enforcement is a traditional responsibility of state and local governments. After several decades of rising crime rates, that trend has recently been reversed, in part because of increased national and state expenditures.

8. Some state and local governments have taken the lead in protecting the environment, but more generally it has been the federal government that sets the policy standard in environmental matters. Busi

nesses operating in several states are often most involved in pressing for national standards of air and water quality and policies on toxic wastes. The federal government typically sets environmental standards; the states enforce them.

9. Transportation is a major area of state and local government activity. Although the federal government provides some financial assistance with the construction of roads and highways as well as urban mass transit, the responsibility of planning, building, and maintaining these transportation systems lies with the states. Federal and local fuel taxes have been used to help pay for transportation.

10. States openly compete with one another in the area of economic development by offering tax incentives, waiving environmental regulations, and giving other enticements to businesses to locate or stay within their boundaries.

11. The primary purpose of regulation is to protect the health and safety of individuals and to promote fairness in the marketplace. Among the most regulated industries are public utilities because they enjoy a monopoly. Government usually gives these companies special privileges, specifically eminent domain—the power to take private property for public use. Public utilities, like other industries, are being deregulated as state and federal governments permit competition in these areas. States regulate other economic activities by conducting inspections, granting licenses, and limiting land uses.

KEY TERMS

vouchers
charter school

responsibility contract
workfare

enterprise zone
police powers

eminent domain

FURTHER READING

BURT S. BARNOW, THOMAS KAPLAN, AND ROBERT A. MOFFITT, EDS., *Evaluating Comprehensive State Welfare Reforms* (Brookings Institution Press, 2000).

JOHN D. DONAHUE, *Disunited States* (Basic Books, 1997).

DENNIS DRESANG AND JAMES GOSLING, *Politics and Policy in American States and Communities*, 2d ed. (Prentice Hall, 1998).

R. KENNETH GODWIN AND FRANK KEMERER, *School Choice and Tradeoffs: Lib-*

erty, Equity, and Diversity (University of Texas Press, 2002).

VIRGINIA GRAY AND RUSSELL HANSON, *Politics in the American States: A Comparative Analysis*, 8th ed. (CQ Press, 2003).

DAVID HAGE, *Reforming Welfare By Rewarding Work: One State's Successful Experiment* (University of Minnesota Press, 2004).

JOHN J. HARRIGAN, *Politics and Policy in States and Communities,* 6th ed. (HarperCollins, 1997).

NORMAN R. LUTTBEG, *The Grassroots of Democracy: A Comparative Study of Competition and Its Impact in American Cities in the 1990s* (Lexington Books, 1999).

DAVID C. NICE, *Policy Innovation in State Government* (Iowa State University Press, 1994).

GARY ORFIELD AND CHUNGMEI LEE, *Brown at 50: King's Dream or Plessy's Nightmare* (Harvard Civil Rights Project, 2004).

MICHAEL A. PAGANO AND ANN O. M. BOWMAN, *Cityscape and Capital: The Politics of Urban Development* (Johns Hopkins University Press, 1997).

DENISE SCHEBERLE, *Federalism and Environmental Policy,* 2d ed. (Georgetown University Press, 2004).

MARK SCHNEIDER, PAUL TESKE, AND MELISSA MARSHALL, *Choosing Schools: Consumer Choice and the Quality of American Schools* (Princeton University Press, 2002).

C. EUGENE STEUERLE, VAN DOORN OOMS, GEORGE PETERSON, AND ROBERT D. REISCHAUER, EDS., *Vouchers and the Provision of Public Services* (Brookings Institution Press, 2000).

SANDRA VERGARI, ED., *The Charter School Landscape* (University of Pittsburg Press, 2002).

R. KENT WEAVER, *Ending Welfare as We Know It* (Brookings Institution Press, 2000).

JOHN F. WITTE, *The Market Approach to Education: An Analysis of America's First Voucher Program* (Princeton University Press, 1999).

See also *Governing: The Magazine of States and Localities,* published monthly by Congressional Quarterly, Inc., and the series of excellent books on state government public policy making published by the University of Nebraska Press.

STAFFING AND FINANCING STATE AND LOCAL GOVERNMENTS

29

State and local government workers are American government's first responders. New York City police and firefighters were the first to arrive at the World Trade Center on September 11, 2001; city paramedics were the first to treat the victims; city social workers were on the scene almost immediately to deal with the grief and shock; and virtually every city worker was involved in some way in the recovery.

The nation's state and local employees are more than first responders to disaster, however. Six million are public school teachers; 1.2 million work as police and firefighters; 700,000 work as prison guards and correction officers; 600,000 work in social welfare; 450,000 work in state, county, and city hospitals; and 200,000 work in parks and recreation.

State and local employees have some of the most challenging jobs in the nation. They help families move from welfare to work; provide shelter for the homeless; keep the streets and sidewalks clean; drive the subways and buses; provide vaccinations for poor children; pave the streets and purify the water; build and run affordable housing; enroll families and children for Medicaid coverage; provide unemployement insurance and counseling; and even take the tickets at National League Baseball games. The federal government may design the economic regulation and social policy, but state and local government employees are the ones who often deliver on the promises.

This chapter will examine the role of state and local employees in more detail, while asking how states and localities raise the money to pay for such a large workforce. The chapter will also review the increasing financial pressure states and local governments face as needs increase and funding gets tighter.

THE ROLE OF PUBLIC EMPLOYEES

State and local governments are responsible for many policy goals, including greater accountability in public education, greater access to health care for uninsured children, and economic development for poor communities; but they do most of that work by hiring state and local government employees to actually deliver the goods and services. Unlike the federal government workforce, which actually has relatively few employees who work directly with citizens, almost all state and local employees have contact with the citizens.

As of 2002, roughly 19 million people worked for state and local governments, roughly ten times the number that worked for the federal government. And according to the U.S. Bureau of Labor Statistics, state and local governments will continue growing well into the next decade—by 2012, over 21 million Americans will work in the nation's roughly 87,000 state and local governments, a growth rate of almost 20 percent. During the same period, the federal government is expected to stay the same size.[1]

Merit Systems

More than one-third of the cost of state and local government is for people. How are these people chosen? A few of them are elected. The rest are generally hired through some kind of **merit system** in which selection and promotion depend on demonstrated performance (merit) rather than on political patronage. Although in many jurisdictions it still helps to know the right people and belong to the right party, patronage is not as prevalent as it once was. Affirmative action requirements call for recruitment through open procedures. The fact that many public employees now belong to unions has also reduced patronage.

Throughout much of the nineteenth century, governments at all levels were dominated by political patronage, a political **spoils system** in which employment was a reward for partisan loyalty and active political support in campaigns and elections. However, in 1939, Democratic Senator Carl Hatch of Arizona pushed through Congress the first Hatch Act, which promoted the merit principle and limited the political activities of federal, state, and local employees whose salaries were supported with federal funds. Subsequently, state and local governments enacted "little Hatch Acts" that enforced merit principles and restricted the political activities of their employees. Merit testing is now used in 30 states for hiring or promoting employees.[2] Moreover, under a 1976 Supreme Court decision, states cannot dismiss civil servants for political reasons.[3]

Merit systems are generally administered by an office of state personnel, which prepares and administers examinations, provides lists of job openings, establishes job classifications, and determines salary schedules. It also serves as a board of appeal for employees who are discharged. State personnel offices are concerned with training the already employed, bargaining with labor unions, administering affirmative action programs, and filling top-level executive positions.

Critics complain that state personnel offices take too much time to fill job vacancies, in part because they are hampered by red tape and clumsy rules, and in part because job lists are not kept up-to-date. Some critics also complain that hiring and firing rules deprive responsible officials of authority over their subordinates. It is argued that there is so much emphasis on insulating public employees from political coercion that employees enjoy too much job security. Administrators cannot get rid of incompetents; sometimes it takes months and several elaborate hearings to dismiss public employees unwilling or unable to do their jobs. Although merit systems are supposed to emphasize ability and minimize political favoritism, they sometimes discourage able people from seeking public sector jobs.

Public Employee Unions

Public employee unions grew rapidly over the past generation as government workers organized to demand better wages, hours, working conditions, and pensions. These unions now wield considerable political clout in most states and cities. In places such

merit system
A system of public employment in which selection and promotion depend on demonstrated performance rather than on political patronage.

spoils system
A system of public employment based on rewarding party loyalists and friends.

CHANGING FACE OF AMERICAN POLITICS

THE STATE AND LOCAL WORKFORCE

Like the federal government, state and local governments have become more diverse over the past two decades and will become even more diverse as they add new jobs. Excluding school teachers, who are overwhelmingly white and female, the U.S. Census Bureau reports that the state and local workforce is becoming an employer of choice for both women and minorities. The increasing percentage of Hispanics is largely due to population growth in states such as California, Florida, and Texas, where Hispanic workers are moving into state and local government jobs at high rates.[*]

Although the percentages of women and minority workers have increased over the past two decades, both groups remain underpaid relative to males and whites. In 2001, males made an average of $39,800 a year, compared with $32,100 for females, $31,500 for African Americans, and $33,500 for Hispanics. Among high-paid professional jobs, men made almost $9,000 a year more than females, in part because men tend to concentrate in the higher-paying professions such as law, finance, and health administration, while women tend to concentrate in historically underpaid professions in human services such as child welfare.

	1981	2001
Male	59%	55%
Female	41	45
White	79%	69%
African American	16	19
Hispanic	4	8

[*]See U.S. Census Bureau, *Statistical Abstract of the United States, 2003* (U.S. Census Bureau, 2004), table no. 470.

as New York City, they are viewed as one of the most powerful forces in political life. In dealing with unions, state and local governments participate in **collective bargaining**—negotiating disputes between unions and management—and **binding arbitration**—settling disputes by agreeing to adhere to the decision of an arbitrator.

Thirty-five percent of state employees and 46 percent of local employees are represented by unions, compared with less than 10 percent of private-sector employees.[4] Indeed, national employee unions see state and local government as a significant growth area.

The American Federation of State, County, and Municipal Employees (AFSCME), is the largest state and local government union, representing over 1.4 million members, followed by the Service Employees International Union (SEIU), with more than 600,000 state and local government members. In addition, National Education Association (NEA) represents roughly 2.5 million of the nation's 6 million public-school teachers, followed by the American Federation of Teachers (AFT), which represents another 1 million.

Many police offers and firefighters are also union members. The firefighters' union is often considered one of the most effective political organizations among public employee unions, and the union sometimes engages in door-to-door and telephone campaigning to elect city officials. Unions often raise funds for candidates and sponsor letter-writing campaigns to influence local and national elections. Union pressure in the 1970s and 1980s was a major reason the average pay of public employees, including benefits, rose faster than that of workers in private industry. However, since 1995, employees in private businesses have done better than public employees.

The failure of the merit system to meet many of the needs of public employees encouraged the growth of public sector unions. Growth was also spurred by the example of the success of collective bargaining in the private sector (see Table 29–1). But much

collective bargaining
Method whereby representatives of the union and the employer determine wages, hours, and conditions of employment through direct negotiation.

binding arbitration
A collective bargaining agreement in which both parties agree, in case of dispute over the terms of the union contract, to adhere to the decision of an arbitrator.

★★ YOU DECIDE

SHOULD PEOPLE ON THE PUBLIC PAYROLL BE ENTITLED TO STRIKE?

Deeply embedded in our civic ethic is the idea that civil servants should not strike, especially those (like police and firefighters) on whom the public depends for vital services. Many state and local elected officials, and certainly many ordinary citizens, believe it is wrong and dangerous for police, firefighters, and hospital workers to strike. In 1919, Massachusetts Governor Calvin Coolidge became famous for opposing the Boston police strike with these words: "There is no right to strike against the public safety by anybody, anywhere, anytime."

At the national level, Ronald Reagan's decision to fire all 11,000 air traffic controllers who engaged in an illegal strike in 1981 was supported by most of the public. When serious problems arise, like the summer wildfires in the West, residents don't want their local firefighters to be in the middle of a public employee strike.

Should public employees be allowed to strike? If you would limit the right of public employees to strike, would you limit all public employees? Would you feel differently if you were a public employee yourself?

outsourcing
Contracting of government services to private firms.

of the success of public employee unions has come about because government workers learned how to become a political force in government. Most public employees are educated, intelligent people who can deliver two of the most valuable components of campaigns: money and labor (not to mention the votes of their members, members' families, and friends).

Many people think that public workers have more job security and better wages and fringe benefits than people working in the private sector. Critics point out that public employees seem to have the best of both worlds: job protection coupled with the bargaining power of a labor union. Although collective bargaining and unionization have been generally accepted in the private sector, these rights were not as widely accepted in the public sector.

Because the public sector provides services almost everyone wants and perceives as necessities, demand is relatively constant. Also, public employee unions are an effective political force, so they can influence crucial decisions that affect taxation and the allocation of revenue. Some analysts believe these two factors may result in policies that favor public employees. Awareness of this political clout of the unions has stiffened the spines of some city and state officials. Today it is not uncommon for mayors in large cities to fight the unions and win support from taxpayers and business groups who think the unions have overstepped their bounds.

Should Public Services Make a Profit?

To make government more efficient and curb the growing influence of public employee unions, many communities have "contracted out" certain public services to the private sector. This practice, called **outsourcing**, can mean that governments save money while the private sector providers still make a profit.[5] Because state and local governments retain the power to raise the revenue for outsourced activities, they maintain control of how the private firms perform through very precise contracts. Today virtually every community service is contracted out somewhere in the United States, and this trend is expected to continue.[6]

In Texas, for example, any citizen who seeks public assistance can call a toll-free help number answered by private employees who have instant computer access to an array of state and local government benefits, as well as the caller's own financial information. Using the information, these telephone operators can tell each caller whether he or she qualifies for a variety of programs, from food stamps to health insurance for their children.

TABLE 29–1 COMPARISON OF MERIT AND COLLECTIVE BARGAINING SYSTEMS

	Merit System	Collective Bargaining
Management rights	Extensive	Minimal
Employee participation and rights	Union membership not required	Union membership required
Recruitment and selection	Open competitive exam; open at any level	Union membership and/or occupational license
Promotion	Competitive on basis of merit (often including seniority)	On basis of seniority
Classification of position	Based on objective analysis	Classification negotiable
Pay	Based on balanced pay plan or subject to prevailing rates	Negotiable and subject to bargaining power of union
Hours, leave, conditions of work	Based on public interest as determined by legislature and management	Negotiable
Grievances	Appeal through management with recourse to civil service agency	Appeal by union representation to impartial arbitrators

SOURCE: From *Democracy and the Public Service*, 2d ed. by Frederick C. Mosher, © 1982. Used by permission of Oxford University Press, Inc.

Texas is also poised to outsource its entire human service bureaucracy. In 2004, the state consolidated twelve separate human services agencies into four, then asked private contractors to run the entire operation. Although state employees will still make the final decision about who actually gets the benefits, private firms will actually run the administrative side of the new departments, from hiring employees to buying computers.[7]

Many state and local governments have also given private companies complete control of certain activities such as garbage collection through full **privatization**. Privatization involves the complete severance of a function from government—private firms are responsible for both performing a service and also for collecting the revenues through regular billing. Although states and localities vary widely in the extent to which they privatize, public–private partnerships have grown during the past two decades in order to reduce the costs of government services and to improve economic development. One frequently cited example of privatization is Indianapolis; under the leadership of former Mayor Stephen Goldsmith, the city claimed to have saved $230 million over a decade through outsourcing and full privatization.[8]

As cities and states have become pressed for cash, efforts to encourage entrepreneurs to provide public services at a profit have increased. Delegation of emergency and police powers to profit-making corporations, however, raises questions of liability and protection of individual rights. It also raises fears that private contractors will hire transient help at less pay, undermining merit systems and public employee morale.

For successful privatization to occur, the contract between the government and the private company providing the service must define that service to the satisfaction of both parties. On one hand, because of the wide range of services provided by local police departments or health departments, it may be difficult to word such a contract. On the other hand, garbage collection and snow removal can easily be defined and specified in a contract, making these services attractive for privatization, so the trend toward outsourcing municipal services like these will continue.[9]

PAYING FOR STATE AND LOCAL GOVERNMENT

John Shannon, an authority in the field of public finance, has written that there were three "R's" that shocked state and local governments in the recent past. The first "R" was the *revolt* of the taxpayers, which started with California's Proposition 13 and quickly became a national phenomenon. The second "R" was the *recession* of the late 1980s and early 1990s, which placed demands on state and local governments to care for the unemployed and needy. And the third "R" was the *reduction* in federal grants, which meant state and local governments were on their own.[10] States had to search for ways to make ends meet and to live within their revenue projections.

The three "R's" returned with a vengeance in the late 1990s and early 2000s. Taxpayers continue to protest against tax increases, especially property and income taxes; recession returned in 2001 with a devastating impact on state budget revenues; and the federal government continued to tighten grants. Although federal grants to the states did go up from $285 billion in 2000 to nearly $400 billion in 2004, three-quarters of the increase was due to increased spending for health care under the Medicaid program for poor citizens and for food stamps. With unemployment payments surging with the recession, most states found themselves with little or no leeway to meet their budget needs. As of 2003, the 50 states found themselves with a combined $21.5 billion budget shortage, which they closed through budget cuts. By 2005, however, the economy had started to recover, and state revenues rose as a result. According to the National Conference of State Legislatures, the total budget gap in 2004 was just $720 million total. Although 20 states still faced budget deficits, 30 actually reported surpluses.

★★ THINKING IT THROUGH

Strikes by all public unions are illegal in most states, and even states that permit them prohibit strikes by those who provide "vital and essential services." Nevertheless, such strikes do occur, and in most instances, local and state officials are more concerned with getting people back to work than with sending them to jail for violating the law. Thus amnesty for the strikers has usually been the rule. Union organizers, for their part, refuse to consider such strikes as defying the law; instead, they believe the strike is a legitimate and useful weapon in a labor dispute. Still, the strike is generally viewed as a weapon of last resort, to be used only under intolerable conditions.

Moreover, striking has political risks for the public employee unions. Adverse public reaction may strengthen the hand of governors, mayors, or other politicians who oppose the unions. Many union leaders now favor compulsory arbitration over the strike, and more than 20 states have enacted laws providing for some form of arbitration. In binding arbitration, a neutral third party or mediating board hears the arguments of both sides in the dispute and devises what it considers to be a fair settlement. The arbitrator's verdict is final. Union leaders who favor arbitration hope that it will gain them something they might not get at the bargaining table, but without arousing the public backlash that usually accompanies strikes. Binding arbitration is used in several states, mostly in such public safety areas as police and fire protection.

Although binding arbitration does not always prevent employee strikes, the number of such strikes has been reduced in states where it is practiced. However, the settlements that result from binding arbitration are often expensive. Each decision in a binding arbitration case has a ripple effect on the rest of a city or state administration. A pay raise for one group sets the standard for other public workers.

privatization
Full release of government to private firms, including the power to collect revenues.

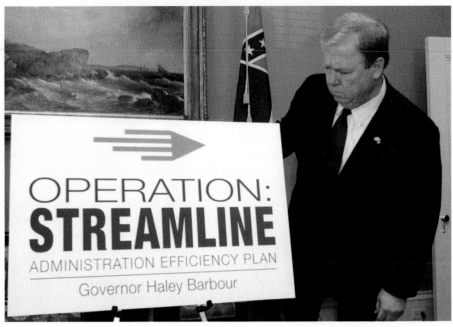

Mississippi Governor Haley Barbour unveils "Operation: Streamline," a plan designed to eliminate the state's $709 million in a year's time. Some of the efficiency measures outlined in the plan include removing civil service protection from some state jobs, which would allow several hundred state employees to be fired, and changing the health insurance plan for state employees and teachers by possibly making them pay for some of their own coverage.

Florida, Nevada, Oklahoma, South Dakota, and Wyoming actually reported surpluses larger than 5 percent of their total spending. "But this breathing room comes after three consecutive years of fiscal crisis, when states had to cut funding in such core areas as education, health care and corrections," writes the National Conference of State Legislatures.[11]

States are far from healthy, however. Most had to cut spending or raise taxes to balance their budgets for 2005. Most also faced increased spending pressure as the federal government continued to trim its own spending.

Sources of Revenue

State and local governments get most of their money from taxes.[12] Yet unlike the federal government, they are more likely to share control of the process of raising taxes with the voters through referendums, which are sometimes required before they can levy new or higher taxes. In addition, state and local governments frequently have to meet responsibilities mandated by higher levels of government, which do not always provide the funding for those mandates.

The politics of reducing the federal budget deficit and the antitax mood of the public in recent decades have meant that Congress and the president often enacted policies and expected state and local governments to pick up the tab. At the same time, citizens had high expectations for services provided by their state and local governments—and wanted even more services. This combination of increasing demand and decreasing federal funding made state and local governments the fiscal "stress joints" of American government. When the economy is thriving, states often have surplus revenue and enact tax cuts, but when times are not as good, they have to raise taxes and cut spending. Because most states are constitutionally forbidden to use deficit spending for general government programs, they have to balance their budgets and respond to shortfalls by strengthening and diversifying their revenue bases.[13]

The overlapping layers of government in the United States complicate the tax picture. Tax policies at different levels of government often conflict. While the federal government is reducing taxes, states may be raising them. Indeed, when the federal government cuts both taxes and federal grants, state and local governments have little choice but to raise taxes or cut spending. This is precisely what happened in the late 1970s and early 1980s, and in the economic slow-down of 2002.[14] But the ability of states to respond to changing economic circumstances has been hampered by the tax revolt of the late 1970s, which lowered taxes and brought forth constitutional amendments that make it harder to raise them. Many states also enacted spending limits, which reduced the discretion of state and local elected officials.

The ability of different levels and units of government to make their own tax policy has made tax collection more complicated and expensive. For example, national officials, state officials, and some local officials collect taxes on gasoline, and each level of government maintains its own tax-collecting office. Taxpayers are allowed to deduct certain business expenses and state income taxes from their federal income tax. Texas, Florida, South Dakota, New Hampshire, Nevada, Washington, and Wyoming have no personal income tax and rely primarily on sales taxes. In those states, taxpayers lose the deduction for state income taxes on their federal tax returns. By contrast, in Alabama, Iowa, Louisiana, Missouri, Montana, North Dakota, Oklahoma, Oregon, and Utah, taxpayers may deduct their federal income tax from their state taxes.[15] Thus changes in state laws can affect the amount of federal and state taxes a person must pay. Although there is little coordination in setting tax policy, there is cooperation between state and federal tax administrators.

No matter who collects the taxes, all the money comes out of a single economy. Although each level of government has a different tax base and each tax hits some groups rather than others, all taxes ultimately depend on the productivity of the American people. And that productivity is affected by many of the activities of government.

Who Pays the Taxes?

Who bears the cost of state and local services is decided in the United States by politics. State and local governments are free to extract whatever taxes they wish from whomever they wish, as long as their taxing practices meet the stipulations of the U.S. Constitution and, in most cases, unless the tax is in conflict with federal laws. The Constitution has been interpreted to prohibit states from taking the following actions:

1. Taxing exports or imports or levying tonnage duties without the consent of Congress
2. Using their taxing power to interfere with federal operations
3. Discriminating against interstate commerce, unduly burdening it, or taxing it directly
4. Using their taxing power to deprive persons of equal protection of the law
5. Depriving individuals of their property without due process

Constitutional lawyers and judges spend much of their time applying these principles to concrete situations. Out of hundreds of disputes, courts have decided that states may collect sales taxes from interstate sales and income taxes from persons and corporations within the states, even if the income was earned from interstate business. However, states may not tax the privilege of engaging in interstate commerce or the profits made through interstate transactions that cannot be apportioned to a single state. Congress has placed a moratorium on state sales taxes on Internet sales, to the anguish of most state officials and traditional firms competing with Internet commerce.

State constitutions also restrict state legislatures' taxing power. Certain kinds of property, such as that used for educational, charitable, and religious purposes, are exempt from taxation. State constitutions frequently list the kinds of taxes that may be collected and stipulate the amount of tax that may be collected from various sources.[16]

General Property Tax

Widely criticized as "one of the worst taxes known to the civilized world," the **general property tax** is a chief revenue source for local governments. The property tax is difficult to administer, leads to favoritism and inequities, and takes little account of ability to pay.[17]

general property tax
Tax levied by local and some state governments on real property or personal, tangible property, the major portion of which is on the estimated value of one's home and land.

Third grade students at Green Bay Elementary School in North Chicago, Illinois, which has the highest poverty level in its district. There is a continuing debate as to whether funding for such schools should come primarily from local property taxes.

Forty years ago, it provided 45 percent of the revenues for state governments and an even higher percentage of the revenues for local governments. But during the past two decades, reliance on property taxes has declined. Today they provide less than one-third of total state and local government revenues. But some states remain acutely dependent on property taxes. New Hampshire, for instance, raises nearly two-thirds of its state and local revenues from the property tax. At the other end of the scale, Alabama and New Mexico raise only about one-tenth of their state and local tax dollars from the property tax.[18]

ADMINISTRATION OF THE PROPERTY TAX   A hundred years ago, wealth was primarily *real property*—land and buildings—that was relatively easy to value. Assessors could guess the value of the property a person owned, and that assessment was a good indicator of his or her ability to pay taxes. Today wealth takes many forms. People own varying amounts of personal property—both *tangible* (furniture, jewels, washing machines, rugs, paintings) and *intangible* (stocks, bonds, money in the bank). It is possible to concentrate a large amount of wealth in a small rented apartment. The nature of real property has also changed. It no longer consists mainly of barns, houses, and land but rather of large industrial plants, huge retail stores, and office buildings whose values are hard to measure. In addition, property ownership is less likely these days to reflect ability to pay taxes. An elderly couple with a large house valued at $300,000 may be living on Social Security payments and a small allowance provided by their children. But they have to pay higher property taxes than a young couple with two healthy incomes who live in a rented apartment.

Although many communities stipulate that the general property tax be imposed on all property, this is not what actually happens. Significant amounts of real property are exempted from property taxes because they are owned by tax-exempt groups, such as churches and charitable organizations. Local governments often waive the tax as an economic development inducement or for other reasons. As a result, two taxpayers may own similar property, but one is assessed at a higher rate, and the principle of horizontal equity is violated. Intangible personal property is also seldom taxed. Some communities deliberately impose a lower rate on intangible property to induce owners to declare ownership. In addition, tangible personal property such as watches, rings, and other jewelry often escapes taxation or is grossly undervalued.

The general property tax is hard to adjust to changing circumstances. This tax is typically administered by an assessor, who attempts to place a value on property—an **assessment**. The assessment may or may not reflect the real market value of the property. In some states, the assessment is legally required to be a percentage of market value—say, 25 percent. The property tax rate is usually a tax per $100 or $1,000 of assessed valuation or some other such measure. Local and state governments can do very little to change the assessment, but they can raise or lower the tax rates.

During times of rising prices, assessed values increase much more slowly than the general price level does. So when governments need more money, the lagging tax bases fail to provide it. When prices fall, valuations do not drop at the same rate. When people cannot pay taxes, property may be sold on the market to cover tax delinquency, but such occurrences are rare. In some areas, property taxes are already so high that to increase them may discourage businesses and lower-income families from moving into the locality.

A property tax bill typically includes fees or taxes charged by three, four, or more governmental units, such as the city, county, school board, water utility, and other special districts. The lump-sum payment aspect of the property tax is one reason for its widespread unpopularity and has prompted some places to permit taxpayers to pay their taxes in installments, often collected with their mortgage payments.

PROPERTY TAXES AND PUBLIC EDUCATION   Local reliance on the property tax to support public schools has generated increasing controversy in recent years. The amount of money available to finance education varies tremendously from area to area; rich suburban areas with a high property valuation per pupil are able to spend much more

assessment
The valuation a government places on property for the purposes of taxation.

than poor areas like the central cities, which need the money most. Reformers have urged the states to take over the financing of public education, or at least to assume a greater share of the burden, in order to equalize differences from community to community. Although this is not a popular idea, most states do distribute funds to local districts in an attempt to ensure more equitable expenditures.

Those hoping for greater state support for the public schools have often turned to the courts. Several state courts have ruled that wide differences between school districts in per-pupil expenditures are inconsistent with the equal protection clause of the Fourteenth Amendment.[19] The California Supreme Court, for example, saw such differences as violating the California constitution.[20] However, in 1973, the U.S. Supreme Court held that there is no federal constitutional requirement that the amount spent per pupil in each school district must be the same.[21] The Court's 1973 decision temporarily slowed the push toward equalization of school expenditures, but the controversy and the issues remain. Several state courts have now handed down rulings similar to that of the California Supreme Court. Kentucky, New Hampshire, New Jersey, New York, Ohio, Texas, and Wyoming courts, for example, have held that their state constitutions require that education be financed in a way that avoids differences in funding due to differences in wealth among local school districts.[22]

Despite its weaknesses, the general property tax remains an important source of revenue for local government. Supporters of the tax say it is a practical and suitable tax because real rather than personal property is the chief beneficiary of many local services, such as fire protection. Alternatives are few, and each has disadvantages. Moreover, some of the bad features of the general property tax can be corrected by improving assessment and administration methods.

One effort to reform the general property tax is the *circuit-breaker exemption* (sometimes called a *negative income tax*) by which most states and certain cities give a form of tax relief to lower-income families and the elderly. The idea is to protect family income from property tax overload in the same way an electrical circuit breaker protects

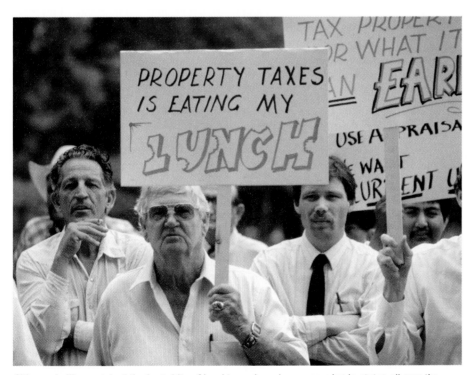

Citizen rebellions against the large bite of local taxes have been occurring in states all over the country.

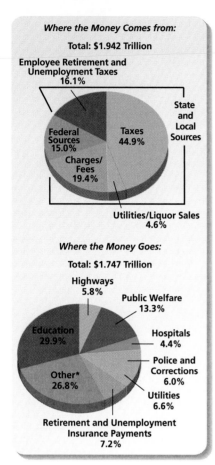

FIGURE 29–1 State and Local Revenues and Expenditures, 2003.
*Includes administration, parks and recreation, housing, transportation, etc.
SOURCE: U.S. Bureau of the Census, *Statistical Abstract of the United States, 2003* (U.S. Census Bureau, 2004), table no. 443.

indexing
Providing automatic increases to compensate for inflation.

sales tax
General tax on sales transactions, sometimes exempting food and drugs.

a family home from an electrical current overload: "When the property tax burden of an individual exceeds a predetermined percentage of personal income, the circuit breaker goes into effect to relieve the excess financial pressure."[23] The circuit-breaker property tax exemption seems to be most popular in the Great Lakes and Plains states and least popular in the Southeast, where property tax burdens are low.

TAX REFORM AND REVOLT Hostility to the property tax spawned the tax revolts of the last three decades of the twentieth century. The watershed event in the politics of tax cutting was the passage in 1978 of California's Proposition 13, which limits increases in property taxes to a maximum 2 percent each year. Throughout the 1970s, California property taxes had risen dramatically, spurring voters to pass this initiative to cut them.

Such direct citizen involvement in making fiscal policy is not uncommon in the United States, and there has been a resurgence of initiative and referendum activity in recent decades.[24] Passage of Proposition 13 made tax reduction an important issue nationwide. Heralded as the start of a modern tax revolt, it triggered taxing and spending limits in more than a dozen states and helped launch movements for constitutional amendments setting federal spending limits, requiring a balanced federal budget, and **indexing** income tax brackets (automatically adjusting income tax rates to rise with inflation so that, in effect, they remain constant). Tax reduction was not limited to ballot initiatives but spread to state legislatures, most of which reduced income, sales, or property taxes.

State and local tax cuts are only one way of attempting to limit government spending. States and localities have also adopted various limits on government spending. In their simplest form, such limitations restrict future spending to current levels; more typically, they provide for an annual increase in spending that is either limited to a fixed percentage or tied to increases in personal income or inflation. Spending limitations can be enacted without tax cuts and, unlike tax cuts, can incur few political costs since no services are being reduced in the short run. New Jersey was the first state to enact spending limits that applied to both state and local governments. Passed in 1976, the New Jersey law limited the growth in state expenditures to the annual percentage increase in per capita personal income and restricted localities to increases of no more than 5 percent without voter approval. Nearly half of the states have followed New Jersey's example and imposed limits on state expenditures.[25]

One consequence of the tax revolt is that the property tax has become a less significant part of the tax base of local governments. As a result, local governments have had to develop other sources of funding.

Other Taxes

State and local governments also raise revenues through a wide range of other taxes that have become increasingly popular since the property tax revolts of the 1970s and 1980s (see Figure 29–1). States and localities seek to diversify their taxes to "spread the pain" of taxes as much as possible.

SALES TAXES Born during the Great Depression, the **sales tax** is the most important source of revenue for states, which annually collect over $170 billion. Almost all states impose some kind of general sales tax, normally on retail sales, with Washington State (64 percent of all revenues comes from the sales tax), Florida (59 percent), Tennessee (57 percent), Nevada (54 percent), and South Dakota (53 percent) all well above the national average of 32 percent.

Local sales taxes were uncommon until after World War II, but now 34 states also allow cities to impose sales taxes. Sales taxes are unpopular with local merchants, who fear they drive business away. In most cases, this is a minor issue that arises only along state borders where consumers can drive into another state with a lower sales tax to make purchases. Most consumers do not pay that much attention to the sales tax on most items.

Sales taxes are easy to administer and produce large amounts of revenue. Many consumers consider sales taxes relatively painless because paying a small amount every day avoids having to pay a large tax bill all at one time. But labor groups and low-income consumers remain opposed to sales taxes, favoring wider use of the income tax instead. They argue that people with small incomes spend a larger percentage of their budgets on food and clothing than the wealthy do, so sales taxes fall heaviest on those least able to pay. That is why many states exempt necessities—primarily food and drugs—from the sales tax.

States continue to search for ways to tax services, both because the states are under acute pressure to find new revenues and because the service sector of the economy continues to expand. All states tax some services, but none has a broad-based tax on services. Among the kinds of services taxed are cable television, landscaping, income tax preparation, pest control, videotape rental, laundry and dry cleaning, and photocopying.

State and local officials listen with concern to talk about the federal government's imposing a **value-added tax (VAT)** like that used in many western European countries. This tax is imposed on the value added to a product at *each stage* of production and distribution. Should the federal government impose such a tax, state and local officials fear that their ability to use the sales tax will be reduced.

There is a running battle about whether states can tax mail-order catalog and Internet sales. Opponents contend that taxing such sales violates the constitutional provisions governing interstate commerce. The Supreme Court has generally left the issue to Congress, and Congress has imposed a moratorium on all Internet taxes until 2007 while it sorts out the pros and cons. Under the moratorium, nine states are allowed to tax Internet sales, while another six allow local governments to tax Internet sales as well.[26]

Although Internet taxes only account for $80 to 120 million today, the future stakes are high. Online retail sales are estimated to reach $130 billion by 2006.[27] By 2005, 10 to 12 percent of apparel, accessory, and toy sales and 20 to 25 percent of book, music, software, video, and consumer electronics sales could be by Internet.[28] Billions in revenues could go to states and localities if they taxed these purchases at the same rate they tax merchants operating within their states.

But there is a question of fairness. Local merchants who have to collect sales taxes are at a disadvantage if mail-order and internet firms can escape these taxes. Mail-order merchants and their lobbyists claim it would be an administrative nightmare to collect and reimburse all the sales taxes, and they argue that they should not be obligated to collect taxes for a state in which they do not have a physical presence. But this position does not reduce complexity. It means if there is an Eddie Bauer store in your state and you buy a shirt from the Eddie Bauer catalog, you are charged sales tax, while a similar shirt from a Lands' End catalog would escape the tax in every state where it has no stores.

The large volume of commerce now conducted electronically suggests that some more sensible and consistent policy will have to be developed. Congress enacted the Internet Tax Freedom Act of 1998, creating the Advisory Commission on Electronic Commerce to study the matter. In the meantime, the federal government imposed a moratorium on state and local taxes on e-commerce. State and local governments contend that the moratorium unfairly preempts their authority and will erode the tax base of many governments. The issue of taxation of e-commerce is becoming more controversial and significant as the size of e-commerce grows. On one hand, how can retailers avoid multiple taxation, overregulation, and conflicting state regulations? On the other hand, is it fair to require bricks-and-mortar firms to collect sales taxes but not their electronic competitors? And as e-commerce grows and is exempted from state taxes, state sales tax revenues will decline, and schools and other institutions supported by such taxes will suffer, or other taxes will have to be increased.

INCOME TAXES   The state income tax has been one of the fastest-growing revenue sources for most states, with Oregon (income taxes account for 74 percent of its

value-added tax (VAT)
A tax on increased value of a product at each stage of production and distribution rather than just at the point of sale.

PEOPLE & POLITICS *Making a Difference* ★★★

MAKING A DIFFERENCE: DIANE L. HARDT

As Wiconsin's state income, sales, and excise tax administrator Diane L. Hardt knows, the sales tax may be simple to explain, but it is extraordinarily complex to administer. As a tax administrator, Hardt understood that complexity is the enemy of saving money—every dollar lost to administrative confusion is a dollar unavailable for a public purpose.

Much of the complexity comes from other states, however. Before she and several tax administrators from other states began work on the Streamlined Sales Tax Project in 2000, every state had its own rules and definitions regarding the tax, and often applied the rules differently to residents and nonresidents. Some states defined grape juice as a fruit, making it exempt from sales tax, while others defined it as a soft drink, making it fully taxable; some states made residents and nonresidents alike pay

sales tax on clothing, while others made clothing exempt for their residents but not for visitors. The complexity not only confused citizens, it made it impossible for states to agree on a common method for taxing internet sales when and if Congress abolishes the moratorium.

A career civil servant with an MBA from the University of Wisconsin, Hardt led the national effort to create common definitions of what gets taxed, at what rates, and for whom. Although the 20 state legislatures that adpoted the project's recommendations in law can always change their position, they have agreed on a basic framework that helps businesses collect their sales tax more efficiently, while discouraging residents from using the internet to evade taxes that they might not even have to pay. "Nobody got everything they wanted," she says of the negotiations that produced

the rules. "But we had the right people at the table from the business side and the government side and just kept talking through the issues with an eye on the big picture."

She might have added that nobody likes to pay taxes, but they like it even less when it is confusing and costly to do.

---

revenues), New York (59 percent), Massachusetts (58 percent), Virginia (55 percent), and Colorado (52 percent) well above the national average of 37 percent.

Several states impose a tax on personal income, and income tax revenue is higher than general sales tax revenue in more than 20 states. Personal income taxes are generally mildly **progressive taxes**; that is, the rate goes up with the size of the income. State income tax rates, however, do not rise as sharply as the federal income tax and seldom go above 8 percent of taxable income. Corporation incomes are frequently taxed by states at a flat rate. In some states, exemptions are generous.

States generally do not allow local governments to levy income taxes. However, some cities—following the lead of Philadelphia and Toledo—now collect a *wage tax*, and most cities in Ohio and cities, towns, and school districts in Pennsylvania levy a similar *payroll tax* on all persons. For instance, visiting professional athletes who compete in Philadelphia are subject to the city's earned-income tax. The Toledo tax also applies to corporate profits. A municipal income tax enables hard-pressed cities to collect money from citizens who use city facilities but live in the suburbs. Similar taxes are collected by New York City, Detroit, and Louisville.

EXCISE TAXES   Almost all states tax gasoline, alcohol, and cigarettes; taxes on specific items are known as **excise taxes**. Because many cities also tax these items, the combined local, state, and federal levies often double the cost of these "luxury" items to the consumer. Gasoline taxes are sometimes combined with the funds collected for automobile and driver's licenses and are earmarked for highway construction and maintenance. Liquor taxes often consist of both license fees to manufacture or sell alcoholic beverages

progressive tax
A tax graduated so that people with higher incomes pay a larger fraction of their income than people with lower incomes.

excise tax
Consumer tax on a specific kind of merchandise, such as tobacco.

and levies on their sale or consumption; they are often used for general government spending.

Some states own liquor stores, with the profits going to the state treasury. High taxation of liquor is justified on the grounds that it reduces the amount of alcohol consumed, falls on an item that is not a necessity of life, and eases the task of law enforcement. Some states, like North Carolina, set aside part of their alcohol taxes for mental health programs and the rehabilitation of alcoholics. If the tax is raised too high, however, liquor purchases tend to be diverted into illegal channels, and tax revenues fall off.

The rationale for taxing cigarettes is similar. High tobacco taxes in states like Alaska, New Jersey, and Hawaii, which do not grow tobacco, and low tobacco taxes in tobacco-growing states like Virginia and the Carolinas, have led to interstate smuggling. Some states levy a general sales tax on top of the excise tax, especially on tobacco products.

Governments impose an excise tax on cigarettes to generate revenue but also to discourage smoking and to fund the cost of treating smokers.

SEVERANCE TAXES In several states, **severance taxes** have been a key source of revenue. These are taxes on the privilege of "severing" or removing such natural resources as coal, oil, timber, and gas from the land. In recent years, severance taxes accounted for more than 20 percent of tax collections in eight states: Alaska, Louisiana, Montana, New Mexico, North Dakota, Oklahoma, Texas, and Wyoming. Although more than 30 states rely on some type of severance tax, significant revenues from this tax are not available to most states. Tax revenues from severance taxes go up and down with the price of oil, gas, and coal.

The state and local taxes described here do not begin to exhaust the kinds of taxes collected by state and local governments. Admission taxes, stock transfer taxes, inheritance taxes, parimutuel taxes, corporate franchise taxes, and taxes on utilities and insurance are common.

Other Revenues

In addition to taxation, states derive revenue from fees and special service charges. At least 10 percent of the money collected by state and local governments comes from inspecting buildings, recording titles, operating courts, licensing professions, disposing of garbage, and other services. Parking meters have become an important revenue source for some cities. Municipal governments frequently operate water supply and local transit systems. City-operated liquor stores are administered by, and turn a profit in, certain cities in Alaska, Minnesota, North Carolina, and South Dakota. The city of Dallas owns and operates an FM radio station (WRR), which plays classical music. Some states and cities run other business enterprises, such as cable television services, from which they make money (and sometimes lose it, too). North Dakota, for example, operates a state-owned bank. Municipally owned gas and power companies often contribute to city treasuries. In some cases, utility profits are large enough to make other city taxes unnecessary.

LEGALIZED GAMBLING Recent years have seen a dramatic increase in legalized gambling in the United States. Only Hawaii and Utah do not permit some form of legalized gambling. For many years, only Nevada permitted legalized casino gambling, but now 37 states, the District of Columbia, and Puerto Rico have legalized gambling, including lotteries, and 20 states allow casinos. This increase occurred because Native American tribes asserted their right to self-rule on reservations and brought casinos to states like California, Michigan, Connecticut, and South Dakota. In addition, gambling companies asserted that prohibitions against land-based casinos did not apply to floating ones, and they promoted gambling on riverboats and dockside casinos. A casino is estimated to be within a four-hour drive for 95 percent of all Americans. "The Bible Belt might as well be renamed the Blackjack Belt, with floating and land-based casinos."[29]

Over time, states have become some of the largest sponsors of gambling, most notably through state lotteries, which are used in states as well as Canadian provinces and

User fees, like the tolls collected at this tunnel entrance in New York City, contribute to the maintenance of such facilities.

severance tax
A tax on the privilege of "severing" such natural resources as coal, oil, timber, and gas from the land.

generate net profits in excess of $37.8 billion. Many of the state lotteries were adopted as a result of statewide referendums, which sometimes promised to provide funding for education or other important state services. New York State provides an explanation of how the lottery benefits public education at www.nylottery.org. Not surprisingly, there is now a North American Association of State and Provincial Lotteries, and its Web site (www.naspl.org) provides a broad range of information on gambling in the United States.

More recently, video poker and other forms of gambling have been spreading to more states. As improvements have been made in data encryption, it is now technologically possible for people to engage in virtual gambling in the privacy of their homes. What does this technology do to state laws limiting or banning gambling? The possibility of betting online also raises the issue of whether those who take bets can be prosecuted for permitting underage gambling.

The federal government has tried to play a role in restricting gambling in various forms, such as betting on college or high school sports and underage gambling. Many coaches of college sports have requested that limitations be placed on betting on their games. The American Gaming Association (www.americangaming.org) provides media updates on government efforts to restrict gambling. Or you can refer to the links and resources provided by the North American Gaming Regulators Association at www.nagra.org.[30]

LOTTERIES Lotteries are a special form of state-sponsored and state-administered gambling that are used to raise money for public purposes. Along with the District of Columbia and Puerto Rico, 37 states operate lotteries to generate revenue without raising taxes. Lotteries are not entirely new; the Continental Congress ran a lottery to help finance the Revolutionary War. Indeed, all 13 original states used lotteries as a form of voluntary taxation in the 1780s. Lotteries also helped establish some of the nation's earliest colleges, notably Princeton, Harvard, and Yale. In 1964, New Hampshire was the first state to revive the practice in modern times to help balance its budget.

In recent decades, state lotteries have increased in popularity, in part because they increase revenues without raising taxes. Although state-run lotteries provide less than 3 percent of all state revenues, they provide essential revenues that would have to be replaced by other sources, all of which are less politically popular. States pay out between 50 and 70 percent of their gross receipts from lotteries in prizes and roughly 6 percent to cover administration costs. The remaining revenues are used for public purposes.

These Pennsylvania lottery winners collected over $110 million dollars. States rely on lotteries, among other methods, to raise revenue for various state functions.

Revenues from lotteries are used for a variety of purposes. About half of the states with lotteries earmark most or all of their proceeds for education; a significant number of the remaining states commit their proceeds to the state general fund. Some states, like Kansas and Oregon, designate lottery profits for economic development; Minnesota commits part of what it makes through the lottery to the environment; Pennsylvania and West Virginia designate senior citizens' programs to receive lottery profits.

Proponents of lotteries identify a popular cause like education, the environment, or senior citizens as the beneficiaries of lottery profits in hopes of getting popular support for passage of the lottery. Opposition to the lottery often comes from church groups, which contend that state lotteries are immoral because they are a form of legalized gambling. Proponents counter that churches often raise funds through raffles, bingo, and other games of chance. Opponents also argue that lotteries are a bad investment because they yield a poor rate of return. Proponents respond that tickets are purchased more for their entertainment value than as an investment.

GRANTS Grants from states to local governments have become increasingly important during the past several decades. The national government once allocated large sums to cities, but has largely stopped providing such direct support. Local governments now go to the states to get more than $300 billion in assistance. State officials return revenues collected from certain taxes to local governments, often without specifying the purposes for which the money should be used. Local governments receive state and federal grants in a wide range of areas, including education, transportation, corrections, law enforcement, housing, welfare, community development, and health care. One reason local governments receive so much money in the form of grants is that they are the unit of government closest to the people and most experienced at providing services.

Local governments often see state and federal grants as enhancing the services they provide. In return for a modest investment of local tax revenue, local governments can get grant money from state or federal governments. But grant money may not be available for some pressing local priorities, or the strings attached to the money may permit state and federal governments to set local priorities. In such cases, are local governments wise to pursue the grants, or should they put their money into their most pressing priorities? Local governments also worry about depending on grant money if state or federal money should dry up in the future.

Borrowing Money

State and local governments collect large sums of money to pay for current operating expenses—garbage collection, police protection, and social services. To fund long-term projects—so-called *capital expenditures*—cities and states often have to borrow money. This long-term borrowing is necessary for building schools, constructing roads, and clearing slums—projects whose costs are so large that it is not feasible to pay for them out of current revenue. Moreover, because these improvements have long lives and add to the wealth of the community, it is reasonable to pay for them over time. For this purpose, governments issue bonds, most often with voter approval.

During the early years of the nineteenth century, states and cities subsidized railroad and canal builders. The money for these and other public improvements came from bonds issued by the cities or states and purchased by investors. Provision for payment of these debts was inadequate, and citizens were burdened with debts long after the improvements had lost their value. As a result, default on obligations was frequent. Aroused by the legislatures' abuse of their authority, voters insisted on constitutional amendments restricting legislative discretion to borrow money. The power to borrow money for the long term now routinely requires voter approval.

Increasingly important since the passage of the National Tax Reform Act are special-purpose governments or special districts: airport authorities, bridge and highway authorities, water and wastewater districts, public transit authorities, and community college districts. Their creation has resulted in turning more and more to *revenue bonds* to help finance their operations. The repayment and dividends due investors come from tolls and fees charged by the facility. In most cases, revenue bonds do not require voter approval, making it much easier to issue this kind of debt and also to spend more on services like public transportation.[31]

State and local bonds are attractive to investors because the interest is exempt from federal income tax. State and local governments can borrow money at a lower interest rate than private businesses can, and although credit ratings differ sharply according to economic health, the credit of most cities and states is good. Hence they can easily find buyers for their bonds. Because governments are often permitted to issue bonds beyond the limitations on their general indebtedness, they use them whenever possible. However, as New York City learned in the 1970s, excessive reliance on bonds can be detrimental to the fiscal health of a state or city.

INTERGOVERNMENTAL COMPETITION

State and local governments exist in a competitive environment in which they seek to enhance their own economy and overall reputation. They have become more competitive in courting business and economic growth because of the increasing mobility of business and the stagnant growth in some sectors of the economy and in some regions of the country. One way governments compete in this marketplace is through the use of *tax incentives* that offer reduced tax rates to promote business investment in the local community. Government officials assume that a progrowth policy is good politics because voter confidence increases when new jobs and businesses move into a community or state.

Local governments that are successful in luring businesses to locate within their boundaries also assume that in the long run these new businesses will add to the tax base by stimulating sales taxes and property taxes. In the case of large shopping malls that attract shoppers from surrounding communities, the revenues from the sales tax may actually lower the tax burden for residents of the city because of sales taxes paid by nonresidents.

Developers of shopping malls or office complexes who are thinking about relocating often play one local government against another in an effort to drive down their tax

Safeco Field in Seattle, Washington, home to the Seattle Mariners, is one of the country's new sports stadiums built with a combination of state, local, and private funding.

burden. Established businesses in the community then cry foul about the tax incentives offered to attract new businesses or keep those who threaten to leave. Economists are skeptical about how important these incentives really are. Some believe that such factors as space availability, cost of land, cost of labor, and quality of life are at least as important in decisions about where businesses locate.[32]

Sports teams, stadiums, and arenas provide another example of intergovernmental competition for tax incentives. In recent years, competition between cities, especially larger cities, has drawn them into funding the construction of major sports facilities for professional football, basketball, hockey, or baseball teams. Because the teams are identified with the city or state and are perceived to enhance the community's reputation, local and state governments have been responsive to the demands of team owners. Some cities have offered team owners "sweetheart deals" to keep the team or build them a new stadium.[33] The New York Yankees threatened to leave their historic location in the Bronx for New Jersey's Meadowlands but agreed to stay put after winning concessions from local government. Often the building of new facilities requires a referendum, but other arrangements, such as the proceeds from parking and vendors, are open to negotiations between the owners and government officials.[34]

Finally, local governments are also competing to build prisons and other correctional facilities. As the number of people in prison has soared from 218,000 in 1974 to 1.3 million in 2000, the number of prisons has grown from from 600 to more than 1,000. In small counties and poor areas of the country, a new prison can provide a variety of economic benefits, from jobs to construction income. In Texas, which has the largest number of state prisons in the country, the number of counties with a prison increased from just 3 percent in 1979 to 28 percent in 2000; in Florida, which has the second largest number, the number surged from 45 percent to 78 percent.[35]

Competing for businesses, baseball teams, and prisons can have negative impacts on a state or local government, not the least of which is the uneven distribution of income on the basis of bidding wars. A dollar spent on prison construction and employment in one county means a dollar not spent in another—some experts estimate that Cook County, Illinois, will lose $88 million in federal benefits from 2000 to 2010 because thousands of its residents were counted in the county in which they were imprisoned rather than the county in which they originally lived.

ASSESSING STATE AND LOCAL PERFORMANCE

As the old saying goes, states and localities are where the rubber meets the road. They are often responsible for delivering on the promises that the federal government makes, whether in health care, homeland security, economic development, or welfare reform. As the federal budget deficit continues to grow, and Social Security and Medicare spending grows, states can expect even greater pressure to fill the gap created by dwindling federal spending for discretionary programs.

Unfortunately, state and local governments vary greatly in their administrative capabilities. According to *Governing* magazine, which rates states, counties, and cities, on overall management, only 10 states won an A or A− grade for their financial management in 2001, just three got an A or A− for managing their employees effectively, five received an A or A− for their ability to measure and manage the results of their programs, and six earned an A or A− for information technology. Alabama got the worst report card in 2001, with a C+ in financial management, a D+ in employee management, a D+ in managing for results, a C− in information technology, and a C− overall; while Michigan, Utah, and Washington came out on top with enough A's and B's to earn an A− overall.[36]

Although many state and local governments are getting better every year, they still have a long way to go to meet public expectations. They also tend to cut budgets for management improvement during the lean years, which contributes to future performance problems.

S U M M A R Y

1. Wages for public employees constitute more than one-third the cost of state and local government. These public employees, who are the first point of contact for many Americans, are hired through merit systems.

2. One of the most controversial aspects of state and local government in recent years has been the unionization of over 50 percent of public employees at the state and local levels. Public employee unions have been increasingly successful in recruiting new members and bargaining for better wages, hours, working conditions, and pensions. Their success has caused some public backlash.

3. One response to growing costs has been the outsourcing of public services to the private sector. Garbage collection, recreation, and even emergency services are now contracted out in some cities. Arguments in favor of privatization include lower cost and better services. But others argue that this movement reduces government accountability and may lead to corruption in the awarding of contracts.

4. State and local governments get most of their money from taxes. Decreasing federal funding has made state and local governments the "stress joints" of American government.

5. The general property tax, despite its unpopularity, remains the most important source of revenue for many local governments. Property is generally thought of as real estate but can include other personal property like automobiles or boats. Administration of the tax is generally handled at the local level, but several states provide oversight. The property tax is a major revenue source for public schools.

6. Tax revolts in the 1970s and 1980s resulted in limits on property taxes in several states and often made it more difficult to raise property taxes. The property tax is now a less significant part of the tax base of local governments.

7. State and local governments have traditionally received revenues primarily from property taxes but also from sales taxes, income taxes, excise taxes, and severance taxes. Recently, they have diversified their revenue sources by turning to such devices as lotteries, legalized gambling, user fees, other fees and special service charges, and taxes not previously used at the state and local levels. This diversification was made necessary by economic downturns and by cutbacks in federal support. Intergovernmental grants from states to cities and school districts have increased in importance as local governments have had to deal with rising costs and expectations but limited revenues. In addition, the growth in special-district governments has led to greater reliance on revenue bonds to finance local services.

8. States and local governments have also become more competitive in courting business and economic growth, especially through tax incentives and subsidies.

K E Y   T E R M S

merit system	outsourcing	indexing	progressive tax
spoils system	privatization	sales tax	excise tax
collective bargaining	general property tax	value-added tax (VAT)	severance tax
binding arbitration	assessment		

F U R T H E R   R E A D I N G

J. RICHARD ARONSON, ELI SCHWARTZ, AND DAVID S. ARNOLD, *Management Policies in Local Government Finance*, 4th ed. (International City/County Management Association, 1996).

DAVID BRUNORI, ED., *The Future of State Taxation* (University Press of America, 1998).

TERRY N. CLARK AND LORNA C. FERGUSON, *City Money: Political Processes, Fiscal Strain, and Retrenchment* (Columbia University Press, 1983).

RONALD C. FISHER, *Intergovernmental Fiscal Relations* (Kluwer, 1997).

KATHRYN A. FOSTER, *The Political Economy of Special-Purpose Government* (Georgetown University Press, 1997).

M. DAVID GELFAND, ED., *State and Local Taxation and Finance in a Nutshell*, 2d ed. (West, 2000).

STEVEN D. GOLD, ED., *The Fiscal Crisis of the States: Lessons for the Future* (Georgetown University Press, 1995).

CHARLES T. GOODSELL, *The Case for Bureaucracy*, 3d ed. (Chatham House, 1994).

ROY T. MEYERS, ED., *Handbook of Government Budgeting* (Jossey-Bass, 1999).

National Conference of State Legislatures, Legislative Budget Procedures in the 50 States (National Conference of State Legislatures, 1998).

DAVID ALAN NIBERT, *Hitting the Lottery Jackpot: State Governments and the Taxing of Dreams* (Monthly Review Press, 2000).

MICHAEL PAGANO AND RICHARD MOORE, *Cities and Fiscal Choices* (Duke University Press, 1985).

B. GUY PETERS, *The Politics of Taxation: A Comparative Perspective* (Blackwell, 1991).

JOHN E. PETERSEN AND DENNIS R. STRACHOTA, EDS., *Local Government Finance: Concepts and Practices* (Government Finance Officers Association, 1991).

HENRY J. RAIMONDO, *Economics of State and Local Government* (Praeger, 1992).

HARVEY S. ROSEN, *Public Finance,* 6th ed. (McGraw-Hill, 2002).

E. S. SAVAS, *Privatization: The Key to Better Government,* 2d ed. (Chatham House, 1998).

RONALD SNELL, ED., *Financing State Government in the 1990s* (National Conference of State Legislatures and National Governors' Association, 1993).

THOMAS R. SWARTZ AND JOHN E. PECK, EDS., *The Changing Face of Fiscal Federalism* (Sharpe, 1990).

Also, the U.S. Bureau of the Census regularly publishes reports on state and municipal finances.

SUSTAINING CONSTITUTIONAL DEMOCRACY

America's founding generation fought an eight-year revolution to secure its rights and liberty. First at the Constitutional Convention in
1787 and later in the first Congress, they confronted the challenges
of creating a government, writing a Constitution, and drafting a Bill
of Rights that would protect rights to life, liberty, and self-government for themselves and subsequent generations. But they knew, as we also know, that passive
allegiance to ideals and rights is never enough. Every generation must see itself
as responsible for nurturing these ideals by actively renewing the community
and nation of which it is a part.

The framers knew about the rise and decline of ancient Athens. They were familiar with
Pericles's funeral oration, which states that the person who takes no part in public affairs is
a useless person, a good-for-nothing.[1] According to Pericles and many Athenians, the city's
business was everyone's business. Athens had flourished as an example of what a civilized
city might be, but it collapsed when greed, self-centeredness, and complacency set in. As
time went on, the Athenians wanted security more than they wanted liberty, comfort more
than freedom. In the end they lost it all—security, comfort, and freedom. "Responsibility
was the price every man must pay for freedom. It was to be had on no other terms."[2]

If we are to be responsible citizens of the United States in the truest meaning of the
term, our dreams must transcend personal ambition and the accumulation of material
goods. Our responsibilities as citizens include speaking up for what we believe, such as
support for or opposition to particular policies like the War in Iraq, same-sex unions, health
care reform, or less regulation of the economy. Such a discourse of opinion helps produce
more representative policy and informed citizens. Our country needs citizens who

understand that our well-being is tied to the well-being of our neighbors, community, and country. This spirit was evident in the days and weeks following the September 11, 2001, terrorist attacks on New York City and Washington, D.C. All across the country, people contributed to relief efforts. In an address to the nation in the evening of the day of the attacks, President Bush said, "Terrorist attacks can shake the foundations of our biggest buildings, but they cannot touch the foundation of America. These acts shatter steel, but they cannot dent the steel of American resolve."[3] As the war on terrorism was waged, what also became clear was the tremendous contrast between the freedom of citizens in the United States and the repression that had been part of the Taliban regime in Afghanistan and the reign of Saddam Hussein in Iraq.

More people today live under conditions of political freedom than under authoritarian governments than at any previous time. The transition from living under authoritarian rule to political freedom is often difficult, as evidenced by the efforts to form democratic governments in Afghanistan and Iraq. Throughout history, most people have lived in societies in which a small group at the top imposed its will on others. Authoritarian governments justify their actions by saying that people are too weak to govern themselves; they need to be ruled. Thus neither in Castro's Cuba nor in the military regime of North Korea, neither in the People's Republic of China nor in Saudi Arabia, do ordinary people have a voice in the type of decisions we Americans routinely make: Who should be admitted into college or serve in the military? Who should be allowed to immigrate into the country? How much money should be spent for schools, economic development initiatives, health care, or environmental protection? In America, we take the freedom to make such decisions for granted.

The theme in this epilogue is simple: elected leadership and constitutional structures and protections are important, but an active, committed citizenry is equally important. Freedom and obligation go together. Liberty and duty go together. The answer to a nation's problems lies not in producing a perfect constitution or a few larger-than-life leaders. The answer lies in encouraging a nation of attentive and active citizens who will, above and beyond their professional and private ambitions, care about the common concerns of the Republic and strive to make democracy work.

THE CASE FOR GOVERNMENT BY THE PEOPLE

The essence of our Constitution is that it both grants power to government and withholds power from it. Fearing a weak national government and popular disorder, the framers wanted to strengthen the powers of the national government so that it could carry out its responsibilities, such as ensuring domestic order and maintaining national defense. They also wanted to limit state governments in order to keep them from interfering with interstate commerce and property rights. Valuing above all the principle of individual liberty, the framers wanted to protect the people from too much government. They wanted a limited government—yet one that would work. The solution was to divide up the power of the national government, to make it ultimately responsive, if only indirectly, to the voters.

Most Americans want a government that is efficient and effective but that also promotes social justice. We want to maintain our commitment to liberty and freedom. We want a government that acts for the majority yet also protects minorities. We want to safeguard our nation and our streets in a world full of change and violence. We want to protect the rights of the poor, the elderly, and minorities. Do we expect too much from our elected officials and public servants? Of course we do!

Constitutional democracy is a system of checks and balances. It balances values against competing values. Government must balance individual liberties against the collective security and needs of society. The question always is, which rights of which people are to be protected by what means and at what price to individuals and to the whole society? These questions arose again and again in the war on terrorism following the terrorist attacks of September 2001. Following these attacks, the USA PATRIOT Act became law, allowing greater government surveillance. Both conservatives and liberals have criticized the USA PATRIOT

GLOBAL *Perceptions*

QUESTION: Please indicate if you have a very favorable, somewhat favorable, somewhat unfavorable, or very unfavorable opinion of the United States?

A merican's like to think of their country as leading the free world and point to our long history of constitutional democracy. Over our history we have attempted to export our views of good government to other countries, or to "make the world safe for democracy." How realistic are these self-assessments? How does the rest of the world view the United States?

The Pew Global Attitudes Project asked random samples of adults all over the world about their views of the United States. In both surveys, majorities in most countries had a favorable view of the United States with a range from 10 percent favorable (Pakistan in 2002) to a high of 94 percent (Kenya in 1999/2000). In most countries public opinion was less favorable toward the United States in 2002 than in 1999/2000.

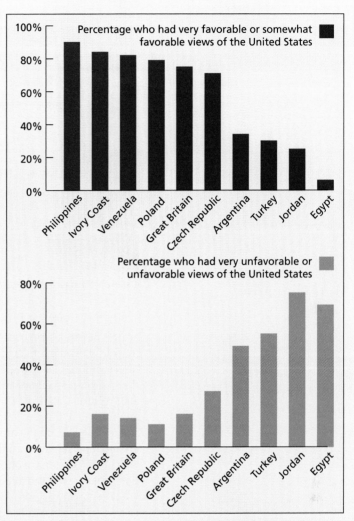

SOURCE: Pew Global Attitudes Project, *What the World Thinks in 2002* (Washington, D.C.: The Pew Research Center for the People and the Press, 2002), pp. 4, T-45.

Act. The Supreme Court also rebuffed the Bush administration's position that it could hold "enemy combatants" indefinitely and without access to the courts.

PARTICIPATION AND REPRESENTATION

No political problem is more complicated than working out the proper relationship between voters and elected officials. It is not just a simple issue of being sure that elected officials do what the voters want them to do. Every individual has a host of conflicting desires, fears, hopes, and expectations, and no government can represent them all. But even if millions of voters could be represented in their many interests, the question of how they would be represented would remain. Through direct representation, such as a traditional New England town meeting or ballot initiatives and referendums? Through economic or professional associations, such as labor unions or political action committees? Through a coalition of minority groups? All of these and other alternatives can be defended as proper forms of representation in a constitutional democracy. Yet all also have limitations.

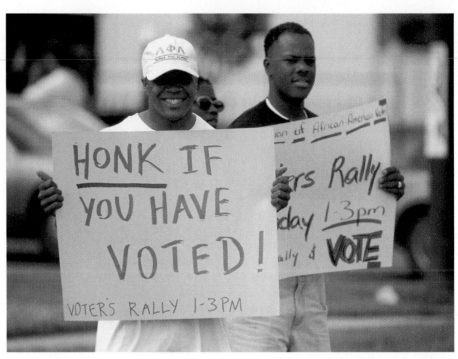

These participants in a voter's rally urge citizens to accept responsibility for perpetuating democracy.

Some propose to bypass this thorny problem of representation by vastly increasing the role of direct popular participation in decision making.[4] An example of an expanded direct popular participation in governmental decision making is the recall, a process that removes office holders from office based on a petiton process and election. The 2003 recall of California Governor Gray Davis and election of Arnold Schwarzenegger is an example of the recall in action. The use of the recall has been relatively rare at the statewide level, but the process has the potential to alter the relationship between voters and representatives. If the process were to become a means for people who disagree with policy positons of office holders to remove those persons from office between elections, representatives might hesitate to say or do much.

What many people regard as the most perfect form of democracy would exist when every person has a full and equal opportunity to participate in all decisions and in all processes of influence, persuasion, and discussion that bear on those decisions. Direct participation in decision making, its advocates contend, will serve two major purposes. First, it will enhance the dignity, self-respect, and understanding of individuals by giving them responsibility for the decisions that shape their lives. Second, direct participation will act as a safeguard against undemocratic and antidemocratic forms of government and prevent the replacement of democracy by dictatorship or tyranny. This idea rests on a theory of self-protection that says interests can be represented, furthered, and defended best by the people they concern directly.

New technologies as well as new uses of old technologies present ways in which governments can appeal directly to voters and voters can speak directly to public officials. We now have voting by mail in Oregon and other places, and some people advocate voting on the Internet. Digital town halls may be next. Some applaud these developments; others are appalled by them.

But we still need institutions such as elected legislatures, which can take the time to digest complicated information and conduct impartial hearings to air competing points of view. The average citizen rarely has the time or experience to evaluate all the available information. Experience with many forms of participatory democracy also suggests its limitations as a form of decision making. In an age of rapidly growing population, increasingly complex economic and social systems, and enormously wide-ranging decision-making units of government, direct participation works best in small communities or at the neighborhood level. As a practical matter, people simply cannot spend endless hours taking part in every decision that affects their lives.

Participatory democracy can still play an important role in smaller units—in neighborhood associations, local party committees, and the like. But much of the work of government at all levels requires elected representatives. Since we must have representatives, who shall represent whom? By electing representatives in a multitude of districts, it is possible to build into representative institutions—the U.S. Congress, for example—most minority interests and attitudes. In the United States, we generally have election processes in which only the candidate receiving the greatest number of votes wins. But there are other ways. For example, one way widely used in European nations like Austria and Denmark is proportional representation—a system in which each party running receives the proportion of legislative seats corresponding to its proportion of votes.[5]

Representation can also be influenced by whether there is only one party, two, or several. Ours is generally a strong two-party system that knits local constituencies into coalitions that can elect and sustain national majorities. A major factor in maintaining our two-party system is that single-member legislative districts such as those for the U.S. Congress and state legislatures tend to lead to two-party systems. This regularity, called *Duverger's law*, is generally seen as helping moderate our politics.[6] In contrast, when countries adopt proportional representation, minor parties have greater influence.

Which is better, elected officials who represent coalitions of minorities or officials who represent a relatively clear-cut majority and have little or no obligation to the minority? The answer depends on what you expect from government. A system that represents coalitions of minorities usually reflects the trading, competition, and compromising that must take place in order to reach agreement among the various groups. Such a government has been called *broker rule:* Elected officials act essentially as a go-between or mediator among organized groups that have definite policy goals. Under broker rule, leaders cannot get too far ahead of the groups; they must talk back and forth, shifting in response to changing group pressures. Instead of acting for a united popular majority with a fairly definite program, either liberal or conservative, the government tries to satisfy all major interests by giving them a voice in decisions and sometimes a veto over actions. In the pushing and hauling of political groups, the government is continually involved in delicate balancing acts, and no one wins all the time.

Some critics argue that fair representation has not been achieved in the American system. In the U.S. Congress and many state legislatures, for example, we still have relatively few women and minorities. Critics also point to the extent of nonvoting and other forms of nonparticipation in politics; the fact that low-income persons are less well organized than upper-income persons; the bias of strong organized groups toward the status quo; the domination of television and the press by a few corporations; and the virtual monopoly of party politics by the two major parties, which do not always offer the voters meaningful alternatives. Critics are concerned that our system of government builds in procedures designed to curtail legislative majorities—for example, the filibuster in the Senate or the power of the Supreme Court to declare laws unconstitutional. The use of the filibuster to block judicial nominees from President George W. Bush is an example of the filibuster curtailing legislative majorities. The Supreme Court overturns laws enacted by Congress or state legislatures, as it did when it declared the Texas sodomy law unconstitutional in *Lawrence* v. *Texas*.[7]

Such charges may be exaggerated, but they cannot be denied. Those who believe that governments should be more directly responsive to political majorities can point to steady improvement in recent years. Election laws have been changed to simplify voter registration, expand and improve voting procedures, and enforce one-person, one-vote standards. Efforts to limit the ability of rich people and well-financed interests to influence elections were cited by Congress as a motivation for passage of campaign finance reform in 2002 and by the Supreme Court in upholding that legislation in 2003.[8] Pressure has also been building to streamline voting systems and simplify voter registraton processes.

Over the course of U.S. history, there has been a shift toward greater direct democracy, and this trend is likely to continue. The founders designed a system with direct representation limited to the House of Representatives. Today both the House and Senate are directly elected. Moreover, with the advent of direct primaries, voters decide the nominees for federal office. The initiative and referendum process provides a direct way for citizens to enact or overturn laws, or even recall those in government. Who may vote in our elections has also been dramatically expanded from white male property owners to all citizens over 18 years of age.

In the age of the Internet, pressures to expand the role of citizens in making laws and voting on candidates or recalling officeholders via petition are examples of how direct democracy may be further expanded. Some states in recent elections have allowed voters to cast their ballots via the Internet. Arizona did so in the 2000 Democratic presidential primary and Michigan did the same in 2004. In the 2004 general election the Pentagon will use an internet voting program for overseas voters. The Internet also has become a means to help organize and inform volunteers, raise funds, and learn about current events.[9]

By this point, you undoubtedly appreciate that democracy has to mean much more than popular government and unchecked majority rule. A democracy needs competing politicians with differing views about the public interest. A vital democracy, living and growing, places its faith in the participation of citizens as voters, faith that they will elect not just people who will mirror their views but leaders who will exercise their best judgment—"faith that the people will not condemn those whose devotion to principle leads them to unpopular courses, but will reward courage, respect honor, and ultimately recognize right."[10]

The Role of the Politician

Americans today have decidedly mixed views about elected officials. They realize that at their best, politicians are skillful at compromising, mediating, negotiating, and brokering—and that governing often requires these qualities. But they also suspect politicians of being ambitious, conniving, unprincipled, opportunistic, and corrupt. Americans hold politicians in low esteem compared with people in other professions.

Still, we often find that individual officeholders are bright, hardworking, and friendly (even though we may suspect they are simply trying to win our vote). And our liking sometimes turns into reverence after these same politicians die. George Washington, Abraham Lincoln, Dwight D. Eisenhower, and John F. Kennedy are acclaimed today. Harry Truman liked to joke that "a statesman is a politician who has been dead for about ten or fifteen years."[11] Of course, we must put the problem in perspective. In all democracies, the public probably expects too much from politicians. Further, people naturally distrust those who wield power. Public officeholders, after all, tax us, regulate us, and conscript us. We dislike political compromisers and ambitious opportunists—even though we may need such people to get things done.[12]

Yet as we have demonstrated with numerous examples in this book, individuals can and do make a difference in public life. Individuals can make a difference in shaping policy on the local, state, national, and international levels, whether the policy be drunk driving, early childhood medical care, land mines, or using the courts to influence a policy agenda.

Politics is a necessity. Politics is a vital and at times a noble leadership activity. Politicians are essential for running the American Republic, whose fragmented powers require them to mediate among factions, build coalitions, and compromise among and within branches of government to produce policy and action.

Leadership in a Constitutional Democracy

While the need for leadership in government is easily recognized, defining what leadership is and how it operates in a constitutional democracy is more challenging. Leadership can be understood only in the context of both leaders and followers. A leader without followers is a contradiction in terms. Leadership is also situational and contextual; a person is often effective in only one kind of situation. Leadership is not necessarily transferable. James Madison, for example, was a brilliant political and constitutional theorist; he was also a superb politician. Yet he was not a brilliant president.[13] The leadership required to lead a marine platoon up a hill in battle is different from the leadership needed to change racist or sexist attitudes in city governments. The leadership required of a campaign manager differs from that required of a candidate.

Although leaders are often skilled managers, they need more than just managerial skills. Managers are concerned with doing things the right way; leaders are concerned with doing the right thing. Managers are concerned with efficiency and process, especially routines and standard operating procedures. Leaders, by contrast, concentrate on goals, purposes, and a vision of the future. Some leaders have indispensable qualities of contagious self-confidence, unwarranted optimism, and dogged idealism that attract and mobilize others to undertake tasks they never dreamed they could accomplish. In short, they empower others and enable many of their followers to become leaders in their own right. Most of the significant breakthroughs in our nation, as well as in our communities, have been made or shaped by people who, while seeing all the complexities and obstacles ahead of them, believed in themselves and in their purposes so much that they refused to be overwhelmed and paralyzed by self-doubts. They were willing to gamble, to take risks, to look at things in a fresh way, and often to invent new rules.

Must a politician gain public office by denouncing the profession of politics? From the tone of many recent congressional and presidential races, it would appear that this may be so. Presidential candidates who have denounced Washington politics include Jimmy Carter, Ronald Reagan, Bill Clinton, and Howard Dean. In 2004 Dean said that if he was elected, members of Congress were "going to be scurrying for shelter, just like a giant flashlight on a bunch of cockroaches."[14] Political Scientist Richard Fenno's landmark study of congressional candidates found that incumbents often run against Washington in general and Congress in particular when at home in their districts.[15] Journalist Charles McDowell of the *Richmond Times-Dispatch* noted this trend on the PBS series *The Lawmakers* and suggested that such a tactic "demeans an honorable and essential profession—that of the politician." McDowell proposed that every member of Congress be required to take the following oath:

> I affirm that I am a politician. That I am willing to associate with other known politicians. That I have no moral reservations about committing acts of politics. Under the Constitution, I insist that politicians have as much right to indulge in politics as preachers, single-issue zealots, generals, bird-watchers, labor leaders, big business lobbyists, and all other truth-givers.
> I confess that, as a politician, I participate in negotiation, compromise, and trade-offs in order to achieve something that seems reasonable to a majority. And although I try to be guided by principle, I confess that I often find people of principle on the other side, too.
> So help me God.

Politics and politicians, including those who work in Washington, are necessary and important to our freedom, security, and prosperity. While people will disagree about particular policies and processes, there is no disputing the need for government. It is also the case that the vast majority of politicians are smart, honorable, and deserve our respect and admiration. Political leaders recognize the fundamental—unexpressed as well as expressed—wants and needs of potential followers. By bringing followers to a fuller consciousness of their needs, they help convert their hopes and aspirations into practical demands on other leaders, especially leaders in government. A leader in a democracy consults and listens while educating followers and attempting to renew the goals of an organization.

RECONCILING DEMOCRACY AND LEADERSHIP

Americans are fond of saying, "It is all politics, you know." This greatly oversimplified insight is offered as profound. More important, it is intended as a negative judgment, as if things somehow would be improved if we did not have politics and politicians.

But politics is the lifeblood of democracy, and without politics, there is no freedom. To conclude that politicians are interested in winning elections is about as profound as to conclude that businesspeople are interested in profits. Of course they are! We do not expect our economy to operate because the shoe store owner is motivated only by a desire to see that people have dry, warm feet. Rather, we harness the store owner's desire to make a living as a way to see to it that the largest number of people get the shoes they want at the lowest possible price. Similarly, we harness the elected official's desire for re-election as the way to ensure that elected officials do what most of the voters want them to do. It is the politician's need to serve and please the voters that is the indispensable link in making democracy work.[16]

One of our major political challenges is to reconcile democracy and leadership. In the past, we often have held a view of leaders as all-powerful. Yet a nation of subservient followers can never be a democratic one. A democratic nation requires educated, skeptical, caring, engaged, and conscientious citizens. It also requires citizens who will recognize when change is needed and have the courage to bring about necessary reforms and progress.[17] Such citizens provide the leaders that enable constitutional democracy to survive and thrive. Constitutional democracy requires citizens who are willing to run for office and then serve with integrity. It is understandable that good people shy away from seeking office, with the ensuing loss of privacy and other burdens of public office. But no matter how brilliant our Constitution or strong our economy, ultimately our system depends on individuals willing to compete for office.

Experience teaches that power wielded justly today may be wielded corruptly tomorrow. It is right and necessary to protest when a policy is wrong or when the rights of other citizens are diminished. Democracy rests solidly on a realistic view of human nature. Criticism of official error is not unpatriotic. Our capacity for justice, as theologian and philosopher Reinhold Niebuhr observed, makes democracy possible. But our "inclination to injustice makes democracy necessary."[18] Democratic politics is the forum where, by acting together, citizens become and remain free.[19]

Leadership thought of as an engagement among equals can empower people and enlarge their opinions, choices, and freedoms. The answer for our republic lies not in producing a handful of great, charismatic, Mount Rushmore-type leaders but in educating a citizenry who can boast that we are no longer in need of superheroes because we have become a nation of citizens who believe that each of us can make a difference and that all of us should regularly try to do so.[20]

Leaders will always be needed. However, our system of government is, in many ways, designed to prevent strong and decisive action, lest too much political power be placed in the hands of too few people. Thus, although we have emphasized the role of leadership in constitutional democracies in these last few pages, the potential for abuse is checked not only by an involved citizenry but also by the very structure of our constitutional system—separation of powers, checks and balances, federalism, bicameral legislatures, and the rule of law.

The ultimate test of a democratic system is the legal existence of an officially recognized opposition. A cardinal characteristic of a constitutional democracy is that it not only recognizes the need for the free organization of opposing views but also positively encourages this organization. Freedom for political expression and dissent is basic—even freedom for nonsense to be spoken so that good sense not yet recognized gets a chance to be heard.[21]

THE DEMOCRATIC FAITH

Crucial to the democratic faith is the belief that a constitutional democracy cherishes the free play of ideas. Only where the safety valve of public discussion is available and where almost any policy is subject to perpetual questioning and challenge can there be the assurance that both minority and majority rights will be served. To be afraid of public debate is to be afraid of self-government. "Rulers always have and always will find it dangerous to their security to permit people to think, believe, talk, write, assemble, and

Louisiana Governor Kathleen Babineaux Blanco at her inauguration on January 12, 2004. The peaceful transfer of power is a sign of a mature and successful democracy.

particularly to criticize the government as they please," said former Supreme Court Justice William J. Brennan, "but the language of the First Amendment indicates the framers weighed the risk involved in such freedoms and deliberately chose to stake this government's security and life upon preserving liberty to discuss public affairs intact and untouched by government."[22]

Thomas Jefferson once said, "Were it left to me to decide whether we should have a government without newspapers or newspapers without a government, I should not hesitate for a moment to prefer the latter." This is reflective of the high importance he placed on informing the citizenry. Jefferson also had boundless faith in education. He believed that people are rationally endowed by nature with an innate sense of justice; the average person has only to be informed to act wisely. In the long run, said Jefferson, only an educated and enlightened democracy can hope to endure.

Education is one of the best predictors of voting, participation in politics, and knowledge of public affairs. People may not be equally involved or equally willing to invest in democracy, but the attentive public—frequently people like yourself who have gone to college—has the willingness and self-confidence to see government and politics as necessary and important. An educated public has an understanding of how government works, how individuals can influence decision makers, and how to elect like-minded people.

As college students who are studying American government, you have knowledge of ways to influence public policy and the political process. You have gained an appreciation for the ways individuals and groups can both push and block an agenda. You also know that many people choose not to participate in elections or politics, enhancing the power of those who do. Finally, you should also have an appreciation that when knowledge is combined with political activity, the influence of the individual participant is expanded.

Does political participation by committed individuals bring about constructive change? It is important to recall that in the last half-century, restaurants, motels, and landlords once openly discriminated against individuals on the basis of race. Racial segregation in education was commonplace in several states; segregated neighborhoods were a fact of life in others and in some places remains so. Finally, in some sections of the country, discriminatory practices denied blacks and poor whites access to voting. Women were discriminated against in the workplace and in government. The significant changes toward more freedom and equality that have resulted from civil rights legislation and court cases are remarkable. This is not to say that we have erased the legacies

Education fosters self-confidence in dealing with bureaucracy, is a strong predictor of voting, and provides a knowledge base important to political influence.

of racism and other kinds of discrimination from our national life. But as historian Arthur M. Schlesinger Jr. writes, "The genius of America lies in its capacity to forge a single nation from peoples of remarkably diverse racial, religious, and ethnic origins." Schlesinger acknowledges that our government and society have been more open to some than to others, "but it is more open to all today than it was yesterday and it is likely to be even more open tomorrow than today."[23]

We are a restless, dissatisfied, and searching people. We are often our own toughest critics. Our political system is far from perfect, but it still is an open system and one that has become more and more democratic over time. People *can* fight city hall. People who disagree with policies in the nation can band together and be heard. We know only too well that the American dream is never fully attained. It must always be pursued.

Millions of Americans visit the great monuments in our nation's capital each year. They are always impressed by the memorials to Washington, Jefferson, Lincoln, Franklin D. Roosevelt, and the Vietnam, Korean, and World War II veterans. They are awed by the beauty of the Capitol, the Supreme Court, and the White House. The strength of the nation, however, resides not in these official buildings and monuments but in the hearts, minds, and behavior of citizens. If we lose faith, stop caring, stop participating, and stop believing in the possibilities of self-government, the monuments "will be meaningless piles of stone, and the venture that began with the Declaration of Independence, the venture familiarly known as America will be as lifeless as the stone."[24]

The future of democracy in America will be shaped by citizens who care about preserving and extending our political rights and freedoms. Our individual liberties will never be ensured unless there are people willing to take responsibility for the progress of the whole community, people willing to exercise their determination and democratic faith. Carved in granite on one of the long corridors in a building on the Harvard University campus are these words of American poet Archibald MacLeish: "How shall freedom be defended? By arms when it is attacked by arms, by truth when it is attacked by lies, by democratic faith when it is attacked by authoritarian dogma. Always, in the final act, by determination and faith."

FURTHER READING

DEREK BOK, *The Trouble with Government* (Harvard University Press, 2001).

RICHARD D. BROWN, *The Strength of a People: The Idea of an Informed Citizenry in America, 1650–1870* (University of North Carolina Press, 1996).

JAMES MACGREGOR BURNS, *Leadership* (Harper & Row, 1978).

ROBERT COLES, *Lives of Moral Leadership: Men and Women Who Have Made a Difference* (Random House, 2000).

AMY GUTMANN AND DENNIS THOMSON, *Democracy and Discontent: Why Moral Conflict Cannot Be Avoided in Politics, and What Should Be Done About It* (Belknap Press, 1996).

APPENDIX

The Declaration of Independence

Drafted mainly by Thomas Jefferson, this document adopted by the Second Continental Congress, and signed by John Hancock and fifty-five others, outlined the rights of man and the rights to rebellion and self-government. It declared the independence of the colonies from Great Britain, justified rebellion, and listed the grievances against George the III and his government. What is memorable about this famous document is not only that it declared the birth of a new nation, but that it set forth, with eloquence, our basic philosophy of liberty and representative democracy.

IN CONGRESS, JULY 4, 1776
(The unanimous Declaration of the Thirteen United States of America)

PREAMBLE

When, in the course of human events, it becomes necessary for one people to dissolve the political bands which have connected them with another, and to assume, among the powers of the earth, the separate and equal station to which the laws of nature and of nature's God entitle them, a decent respect to the opinions of mankind requires that they should declare the causes which impel them to the separation.

New Principles of Government

We hold these truths to be self-evident; that all men are created equal, that they are endowed by their Creator with certain unalienable rights, that among these are life, liberty, and the pursuit of happiness.

That, to secure these rights, governments are instituted among men, deriving their just powers from the consent of the governed.

That whenever any form of government becomes destructive of these ends, it is the right of the people to alter or to abolish it, and to institute new government, laying its foundation on such principles, and organizing its powers in such form, as to them shall seem most likely to effect their safety and happiness. Prudence, indeed will dictate that governments long established should not be changed for light and transient causes; and accordingly all experience hath shown that mankind are more disposed to suffer while evils are sufferable, than to right themselves by abolishing the forms to which they are accustomed. But when a long train of abuses and usurpations, pursuing invariably the same object, evinces a design to reduce them under absolute despotism, it is their right, it is their duty, to throw off such government, and to provide new guards for their future security.

Reasons for Separation

Such has been the patient sufferance of these colonies; and such is now the necessity which constrains them to alter their former systems of government. The history of the present king of Great Britain is a history of repeated injuries and usurpations, all having in direct object the establishment of an absolute tyranny over these states. To prove this, let facts be submitted to a candid world.

He has refused his assent to laws, the most wholesome and necessary for the public good.

He has forbidden his governors to pass laws of immediate and pressing importance unless suspended in their operation till his assent should be obtained; and when so suspended, he has utterly neglected to attend to them.

He has refused to pass other laws for the accommodation of large districts of people, unless those people would relinquish the right of representation in the legislature, a right inestimable to them, and formidable to tyrants only.

He has called together legislative bodies at places unusual, uncomfortable, and distant for the depository of their public records, for the sole purpose of fatiguing them into compliance with his measures.

He has dissolved representative houses repeatedly, for opposing, with manly firmness, his invasions on the rights of people.

He has refused, for a long time after such dissolutions, to cause others to be elected; whereby the legislative powers incapable of annihilation, have returned to the people at large for their exercise; the state remaining, in the meantime, exposed to all the dangers of invasion from without and convulsions within.

He has endeavored to prevent the population of these states; for that purpose obstructing the laws of naturalization of foreigners, refusing to pass others to encourage their migration hither, and raising the conditions of new appropriations of lands.

He has obstructed the administration of justice, by refusing his assent to laws for establishing judiciary powers.

He has made judges dependent on his will alone for the tenure of their offices, and the amount and payment of their salaries.

He has erected a multitude of new offices, and sent hither swarms of officers to harass our people and eat out their substance.

He has kept among us, in times of peace, standing armies, without the consent of our legislature.

He has affected to render the military independent of, and superior to, the civil power.

He has combined with others to subject us to jurisdiction foreign to our constitution and unacknowledged by our laws, giving his assent to their acts of pretended legislation:

For quartering large bodies of armed troops among us;

For protecting them, by a mock trial, from punishment for any murders which they should commit on the inhabitants of these states;

For cutting off our trade with all parts of the world;

For imposing taxes on us without our consent;

For depriving us, in many cases, of the benefits of trial by jury;

For transporting us beyond seas, to be tried for pretended offenses;

For abolishing the free system of English laws in a neighboring province, establishing therein an arbitrary government, and enlarging its boundaries, so as to render it at once an example and fit instrument for introducing the same absolute rule into these colonies;

For taking away our charters, abolishing our most valuable laws, and altering, fundamentally, the forms of our governments;

For suspending our own legislatures, and declaring themselves invented with power to legislate for us in all cases whatsoever.

He has abdicated government here, by declaring us out of his protection and waging war against us.

He has plundered our seas, ravaged our coasts, burned our towns, and destroyed the lives of our people.

He is at this time transporting large armies of foreign mercenaries to complete the works of death, desolation, and tyranny already begun with circumstances of cruelty and perfidy scarcely paralleled in the most barbarous ages and totally unworthy of the head of a civilized nation.

He has constrained our fellow-citizens, taken captive on the high seas, to bear arms against their country, to become the executioners of their friends and brethren, or to fall themselves by their hands.

He has excited domestic insurrections among us, and has endeavored to bring on the inhabitants of our frontiers the merciless Indian savages, whose known rule of warfare is an undistinguished destruction of all ages, sexes, and conditions.

In every stage of these oppressions we have petitioned for redress in the most humble terms; our repeated petitions have been answered only by repeated injury. A prince whose character is thus marked by every act which may define a tyrant is unfit to be the ruler of a free people.

Nor have we been wanting in attention to our British brethren. We have warned them, from time to time, of attempts by their legislature to extend an unwarrantable jurisdiction over us. We have reminded them of the circumstances of our emigration and settlement here. We have appealed to their native justice and magnanimity; and we have conjured them, by the ties of our common kindred, to disavow these usurpations, which would inevitably interrupt our connections and correspondence. They, too, have been deaf to the voice of justice and of consanguinity. We must, therefore, acquiesce in the necessity which denounces our separation, and hold them, as we hold the rest of mankind, enemies in war, in peace, friends.

We, therefore, the representatives of the United States of America, in General Congress assembled, appealing to the Supreme Judge of the world for the rectitude of our intentions, do, in the name and by authority of the good people of these colonies, solemnly publish and declare, that these united colonies are, and of right ought to be, free and independent states; that they are absolved from all allegiance to the British crown, and that all political connection between them and the state of Great Britain is, and ought to be, totally dissolved; and that, as free and independent states, they have full power to levy war, conclude peace, contract alliances, establish commerce, and do all other acts and things which independent states may of a right do. And, for the support of this declaration, with a firm reliance on the protection of Divine Providence, we mutually pledge to each other our lives, our fortunes, and our sacred honor.

The Federalist, No. 10, James Madison

The Federalist, No. 10, *written by James Madison soon after the Constitutional Convention, was prepared as one of several dozen newspaper essays aimed at persuading New Yorkers to ratify the proposed constitution. One of the most important basic documents in American political history, it outlines the need for and the general principles of a democratic republic. It also provides a political and economic analysis of the realities of interest group or faction politics.*

To the People of the State of New York: Among the numerous advantages promised by a well-constructed union, none deserves to be more accurately developed than its tendency to break and control the violence of faction. The friend of popular governments, never finds himself so much alarmed for their character and fate, as when he contemplates their propensity of this dangerous vice. He will not fail, therefore, to set a due value on any plan which, without violating the principles to which he is attached, provides a proper cure for it. The instability, injustice, and confusion introduced into the public councils, have, in truth, been the mortal diseases under which popular governments have everywhere perished; as they continue to be the favorite and fruitful topics from which the adversaries to liberty derive their most specious declamations. The valuable improvements made by the American constitutions on the popular models, both ancient and modern, cannot certainly be too much admired; but it would be an unwarrantable partiality, to contend that they have as effectually obviated the danger on this side, as was wished and expected. Complaints are everywhere heard from our most considerate and virtuous citizens, equally the friends of public and private faith, and of public and personal liberty, that our governments are too unstable; that the public good is disregarded in the conflicts of rival parties; and that measures are too often decided, not according to the rules of justice, and the rights of the minor party, but by the superior force of an interested and overbearing majority. However anxiously we may wish that these complaints had no foundation, the evidence of known facts will not permit us to deny that they are in some degree true. It will be found, indeed, on a candid review of our situation, that some of the distresses under which we labor have been erroneously charged on the operations of our governments; but it will be found, at the same time, that other causes will not alone account for many of our heaviest misfortunes; and, particularly, for that prevailing and increasing distrust of public engagements, and alarm for private rights, which are echoed from one end of the continent to the other. These must be chiefly, if not wholly, effects of the unsteadiness and injustice, with which a factious spirit has tainted our public administrations.

By a faction, I understand a number of citizens, whether amounting to a majority of the whole, who are united and actuated by some common impulse of passion, or of interest, adverse to the rights of other citizens, or to the permanent and aggregate interests of the community.

There are two methods of curing the mischiefs of faction: the one, by removing its causes; the other, by controlling its effects.

There are again two methods of removing the causes of faction: the one, by destroying the liberty which is essential to its existence; the other, by giving to every citizen the same opinions, the same passions, and the same interests.

It could never be more truly said, than of the first remedy, that it was worse than the disease. Liberty is to faction what air is to fire, an aliment without which it instantly expires. But it could not be a less folly to abolish liberty, which is essential to political life, because it nourishes faction, than it would be to wish the annihilation of air, which is essential to animal life, because it imparts to fire its destructive agency.

The second expedient is as impracticable, as the first would be unwise. As long as the reason of man continues fallible, and he is at liberty to exercise it, different opinions will be formed. As long as the connection subsists between his reason and his self-love, his opinions and his passions will have a reciprocal influence on each other; and the former will be objects to which the latter will attach themselves. The diversity in the faculties of men, from which the rights of property originate, is not less an insuperable obstacle to an uniformity of interests. The protection of these faculties is the first object of government. From the protection of different and unequal faculties of acquiring property, the possession of different degrees and kinds of property immediately results; and from the influence of these on the sentiments and views of the respective proprietors, ensues a division of the society into different interests and parties.

The latent causes of faction are thus sown in the nature of man; and we see them everywhere brought into different degrees of activity, according to the different circumstances of civil society. A zeal for different opinions concerning religion, concerning government, and many other points, as well of speculation as of practice; an attachment to different leaders ambitiously contending for preeminence and power; or to persons of other descriptions whose fortunes have been interesting to the human passions, have, in turn, divided mankind into parties, inflamed them with mutual animosity, and rendered them much more disposed to vex and oppress each other, than to cooperate for their common good. So strong is this propensity of mankind, to fall into mutual animosities, that where no substantial occasion presents itself, the most frivolous and fanciful distinctions have been sufficient to kindle their unfriendly passions and excite their most violent conflicts. But the most common and durable source of factions, has been the various and unequal distribution of property. Those who hold, and those who are without property, have ever formed distinct interests in society. Those who are creditors, and those who are debtors, fall under a like discrimination. A landed interest, a manufacturing interest, a mercantile interest, a moneyed interest, with many lesser interests, grow up of necessity in civilized nations, and divide them into different classes, actuated by different sentiments and views. The regulation of these various and interfering interests forms the principal task of modern legislation, and involves the spirit of the party and faction in the necessary and ordinary operations of the government.

No man is allowed to be a judge in his own cause; because his interest will certainly bias his judgment, and, not improbably, corrupt his integrity. With equal, nay, with greater reason, a body of men are unfit to be both judges and par-

ties at the same time; yet what are many of the most important acts of legislation, but so many judicial determinations, not indeed concerning the right of single persons, but concerning the rights of large bodies of citizens? And what are the different classes of legislators, but advocates and parties to the causes which they determine? Is a law proposed concerning private debts? It is a questions to which the creditors are parties on one side, and the debtors on the other. Justice ought to hold the balance between them. Yet the parties are, and must be, themselves the judges; and the most numerous party, or, in other words, the most powerful faction, must be expected to prevail. Shall domestic manufacturers be encouraged, and in what degree, by restrictions on foreign manufacturers? Are questions which would be differently decided by the landed and the manufacturing classes; and probably by neither with a sole regard to justice and the public good. The apportionment of taxes, on the various descriptions of property, is an act which seems to require the most exact impartiality; yet there is, perhaps, no legislative act, in which greater opportunity and temptation are given to a predominant party to trample on the rules of justice. Every shilling, with which they overburden the inferior number, is a shilling saved to their own pockets.

It is in vain to say, that enlightened statesmen will be able to adjust these clashing interests, and render them all subservient to the public good. Enlightened statesmen will not always be at the helm, nor, in many cases, can such an adjustment be made at all, without taking into view indirect and remote considerations, which will rarely prevail over the immediate interest which one party may find in disregarding the rights of another, or the good of the whole.

The inference to which we are brought is, that the causes of faction cannot be removed; and that relief is only to be sought in the means of controlling its effects.

If a faction consists of less than a majority, relief is supplied by the republican principle, which enables the majority to defeat its sinister views, by regular vote. It may clog the administration, it may convulse the society; but it will be unable to execute and mask its violence under the forms of the Constitution. When a majority is included in a faction, the form of popular government, on the other hand, enables it to sacrifice to its ruling passion or interest, both the public good and the rights of other citizens. To secure the public good, and private rights, against the danger of such a faction, and at the same time to preserve the spirit and the form of popular government, is then the great object to which our inquiries are directed. Let me add, that it is the great desideratum, by which alone

this form of government can be rescued from the opprobrium under which it has so long laboured, and be recommended to the esteem and adoption of mankind.

By what means is this object attainable? Evidently by one of two only. Either the existence of the same passion or interest in a majority, at the same time, must be prevented; or the majority, having such coexistent passion or interest, must be rendered, by their number and local situation, unable to concert and carry into effect schemes of oppression. If the impulse and the opportunity be suffered to coincide, we well know that neither moral nor religious motives can be relied on as an adequate control. They are not found to be such on the injustice and violence of individuals, and lose their efficacy in proportion to the number combined together; that is, in proportion as their efficacy becomes needful.

From this view of the subject, it may be concluded, that a pure democracy, by which I mean a society consisting of a small number of citizens, who assemble and administer the government in person, can admit of no cure for the mischiefs of faction. A common passion or interest will, in almost every case, be felt by a majority of the whole; a communication and concert, results from the form of government itself; and there is nothing to check the inducements to sacrifice the weaker party, or an obnoxious individual. Hence, it is, that such democracies have ever been spectacles of turbulence and contention; have ever been found incompatible with personal security, or the rights of property; and have in general been as short in their lives, as they have been violent in their deaths. Theoretic politicians, who have patronized this species of government, have erroneously supposed, that by reducing mankind to a perfect equality in their political rights, they would, at the same time be perfectly equalized and assimilated in their possessions, their opinions, and their passions.

A republic, by which I mean a government in which the scheme of representation takes place, opens a different prospect, and promises the cure for which we are seeking. Let us examine the points in which it varies from pure democracy, and we shall comprehend both the nature of the cure and the efficacy which it must derive from the union.

The two great points of difference, between a democracy and a republic, are, first, the delegation of the government, in the latter, to a small number of citizens, elected by the rest; secondly, the greater number of citizens, and greater sphere of country, over which the latter may be extended.

The effect of the first difference is, on the one hand, to refine and enlarge the public views, by passing them through the medium of a chosen body of citizens, whose wisdom may best discern the true interest of their country, and whose patriotism and love of justice, will be least likely to sacrifice it to temporary or partial considerations. Under such a regulation, it may well happen, that the public voice, pronounced by the representatives of the people, will be more consonant to the public good, than if pronounced by the people themselves, convened for the purpose. On the other hand the effect may be inverted. Men of factious tempers, of local prejudices, or of sinister designs, may by intrigue, by corruption, or by other means, first obtain the suffrages, and then betray the interest of the people. The question resulting is, whether small or extensive republics are most favourable to the election of proper guardians of the public weal; and it is clearly decided in favour of the latter by two obvious considerations.

In the first place, it is to be remarked that, however small the republic may be, the representatives must be raised to a certain number, in order to guard against the cabals of a few; and that however large it may be, they must be limited to a certain number, in order to guard against the confusion of a multitude. Hence, the number of representatives in the two cases not being in proportion to that of the constituents, and being proportionally greatest in the small republic, it follows, that if the proportion of fit characters be not less in the large than in the small republic, the former will present a greater option, and consequently a greater probability of a fit choice.

In the next place, as each representative will be chosen by a greater number of citizens in the large than in the small republic, it will be more difficult for unworthy candidates to practice with success the vicious arts, by which elections are too often carried; and the suffrages of the people being more free, will be more likely to centre in men who possess the most attractive merit, and the most diffusive and established characters.

It must be confessed, that in this, as in most other cases, there is a mean, on both sides of which inconveniences will be found to lie. By enlarging too much the number of electors, you render the representatives too little acquainted with all their local circumstances and lesser interests; as by reducing it too much, you render him unduly attached to these, and too little fit to comprehend and pursue great and national objects. The federal constitution forms a happy combination in this respect; the great and aggregate interests being referred to the national, the local and particular to the state legislatures.

The other point of difference is, the greater number of citizens, and extent of territory, which may be brought within the compass of republican, than of democratic government; and it is this circumstance principally which renders factious combinations less to be dreaded in the former, than in the latter. The smaller the society, the fewer probably will be the distinct parties and interests composing it; the fewer the distinct parties and interests, the more frequently will a majority be found of the same party; and the smaller the number of individuals composing a majority, and the smaller the compass within which they are placed, the more easily will they concert and execute their plans of oppression. Extend the sphere, and you take in a greater variety of parties and interests; you make it less probable that a majority of the whole will have a common motive to invade the rights of other citizens; or if such a common motive exists, it will be more difficult for all who feel it to discover their own strength, and to act in unison with each other. Besides other impediments, it may be remarked, that where there is a consciousness of unjust or dishonourable purposes, communication is always checked by distrust, in proportion to the number whose concurrence is necessary.

Hence, it clearly appears, that the same advantage, which a republic has over a democracy, in controlling the effects of faction, is enjoyed by a large over a small republic—is enjoyed by the union over the states composing it. Does this advantage consist in the substitution of representatives, whose enlightened views and virtuous sentiments render them superior to local prejudices, and to schemes of injustice? It will not be denied that the representation of the union will be most likely to possess these requisite endowments. Does it consist in the greater security afforded by a greater variety of parties, against the event of any one party being able to outnumber and oppress the rest? In an equal degree does the increased variety of parties, comprised within the union, increase the security? Does it, in fine, consist in the greater obstacles opposed to the concert and accomplishment of the secret wishes of an unjust and interested majority? Here, again, the extent of the union gives it the most palpable advantage.

The influence of factious leaders may kindle a flame within their particular states, but will be unable to spread a general conflagration through the other states; a religious sect may degenerate into a political faction in a part of the confederacy; but the variety of sects dispersed over the entire face of it, must secure the national councils against any danger from that source: a rage for paper money, for an abolition of debts, for an equal division of property, or for any other improper or wicked project, will be less apt to pervade the whole body of the union than a particular member of it; in the same proportion as such a malady is more likely to taint a particular county or district, than an entire state.

In the extent and proper structure of the union, therefore, we behold a republican remedy for the diseases most incident to republican government. And according to the degree of pleasure and pride we feel in being republicans, ought to be our zeal in cherishing the spirit, and supporting the character of federalists.

The Federalist, No. 51, James Madison

The Federalist, *No. 51, also written by Madison, is a classic statement in defense of separation of powers and republican processes. Its fourth paragraph is especially famous and is frequently quoted by students of government.*

To what expedient, then, shall we finally resort, for maintaining in practice the necessary partition of power among the several departments as laid down in the Constitution? The only answer that can be given is that as all these exterior provisions are found to be inadequate the defect must be supplied, by so contriving the interior structure of the government as that its several constituent parts may, by their mutual relations, be the means of keeping each other in their proper places. Without presuming to undertake a full development of this important idea I will hazard a few general observations which may perhaps place it in a clearer light, and enable us to form a more correct judgment of the principles and structure of the government planned by the convention.

In order to lay a due foundation for that separate and distinct exercise of the different powers of government, which to a certain extent is admitted on all hands to be essential to the preservation of liberty, it is evident that each department should have a will of its own; and consequently should be so constituted that the members of each should have as little agency as possible in the appointment of the members of the others. Were this principle rigorously adhered to, it would require that all the appointments for the supreme executive, legislative, and judiciary magistracies should be drawn from the same fountain of authority, the people, through channels having no communication whatever with one another. Perhaps such a plan of constructing the several departments would be less difficult in practice than it may in contemplation appear. Some difficulties, however, and some additional expense would attend the execution of it. Some deviations, therefore, from the principle must be admitted. In the constitution of the judiciary department in particular, it might be inexpedient to insist rigorously on the principle: first, because peculiar qualifications being essential in the members, the primary consideration ought to be to select that mode of choice which best secures these qualifications; second, because the permanent tenure by which the appointments are held in that department must soon destroy all sense of dependence on the authority conferring them.

It is equally evident that the members of each department should be as little dependent as possible on those of the others for the emoluments annexed to their offices. Were the executive magistrate, or the judges, not independent of the legislature in this particular, their independence in every other would be merely nominal.

But the great security against a gradual concentration of the several powers in the same department consists in giving to those who administer each department the necessary constitutional means and personal motives to resist encroachments of the others. The provision for defense must in this, as in all other cases, be made commensurate to the danger of attack. Ambition must be made to counteract ambition. The interest of the man must be connected with the constitutional rights of the place. It may be a reflection on human nature that such devices should be necessary to control the abuses of government. But what is government itself but the greatest of all reflections on human nature? If men were angels, no government would be necessary. If angels were to govern men, neither external nor internal controls on government would be necessary. In framing a government which is to be administered by men over men, the great difficulty lies in this: you must first enable the government to control the governed; and in the next place oblige it to control itself. A dependence on the people is, no doubt, the primary control on the government; but experience has taught mankind the necessity of auxiliary precautions.

This policy of supplying, by opposite and rival interests, the defect of better motives, might be traced through the whole system of human affairs, private as well as public. We see it particularly displayed in all the subordinate distributions of power, where the constant aim is to divide and arrange the several offices in such a manner as that each may be a check on the other—that the private interest of every individual may be a sentinel over the public rights. These inventions of prudence cannot be less requisite in the distribution of the supreme powers of the State.

But it is not possible to give to each department an equal power of self-defense. In republican government, the legislative authority necessarily predominates. The remedy for this inconveniency is to divide the legislature into different branches; and to render them, by modes of election and different principles of action, as little connected with each other as the nature of their common functions and their common dependence on the society will admit. It may even be necessary to guard against dangerous encroachments by still further precautions. As the weight of the legislative authority requires that it should be thus divided, the weakness of the executive may require, on the other hand, that it should be fortified. An absolute negative on the legislature appears, at first view, to be the natural defense with which the executive magistrate should be armed. But perhaps it would be neither altogether safe nor alone sufficient. On ordinary occasions it might not be exerted with the requisite firmness, and on extraordinary occasions it might be perfidiously abused. May not this defect of an absolute negative be supplied by some qualified connection between this weaker department and the weaker branch of the stronger department, by which the latter may be led to support the constitutional rights of the former, without being too much detached from the rights of its own department?

If the principles on which these observations are founded be just, as I persuade myself they are, and they be applied as a criterion to the several State constitutions, and to the federal Constitution, it will be found that if the latter does not perfectly correspond with them, the former are infinitely less able to bear such a test.

There are, moreover, two considerations particularly applicable to the federal system of America, which place that system in a very interesting point of view.

First. In a single republic, all the power surrendered by the people is submitted to the administration of a single government; and the usurpations are guarded against by a division of the government into distinct and separate departments. In the compound republic of America, the power surrendered by the people is first divided between two distinct governments, and then the portion allotted to each subdivided among distinct and separate departments. Hence a double security arises to the rights of the people. The different governments will control each other, at the same time that each will be controlled by itself.

Second. It is of great importance in a republic not only to guard the society against the oppression of its rulers, but to guard one part of the society against the injustice of the other part. Different interests necessarily exist in different classes of citizens. If a majority be united by a common interest, the rights of the minority will be insecure. There are but two methods of providing against this evil: the one by creating a will in the community independent of the majority—that is, of the society itself; the other, by comprehending in the society so many separate descriptions of citizens as will render an unjust combination of a majority of the whole very improbable, if not impracticable. The first method prevails in all governments possessing an hereditary or self-appointed authority. This, at best, is but a precarious security; because a power independent of the society may as well espouse the unjust views of the major as the rightful interests of the minor party, and may possibly be turned against both parties. The second method will be exemplified in the federal republic of the United States. Whilst all authority in it will be derived from and dependent on the society, the society itself will be broken into so many parts, interests and classes of citizens, that the rights of individuals, or of the minority, will be in little danger from interested combinations of the majority. In a free government the security for civil rights must be the same as that for religious rights. It consists in the one case in the multiplicity of interests, and in the other in the multiplicity of sects. The degree of security in both cases will depend on the number of interests and sects; and this may be presumed to depend on the extent of country and number of people comprehended under the same government. This view of the subject must particularly recommend a proper federal system to all the sincere and considerate friends of republican government, since it shows that in exact proportion as the territory of the Union may be formed into more circumscribed Confederacies, or States, oppressive combinations of a majority will be facilitated; the best security, under the republican forms, for the rights of every class of citizen, will be diminished; and consequently the stability and independence of some member of the government, the only other security, must be proportionally increased. Justice is the end of government. It is the end of civil society. It ever has been and ever will be pursued until it be obtained, or until liberty be lost in the pursuit. In a society under the forms of which the stronger faction can readily unite and oppress the weaker, anarchy may as truly be said to reign as in a state of nature, where the weaker individual is not secured against the violence of the stronger; and as, in the latter state, even the stronger individuals are prompted, by the uncertainty of their condition, to submit to a government which may protect the weak as well as themselves; so, in the former state, will the more powerful factions or parties be gradually induced, by a like motive, to wish for a government which will protect all parties, the weaker as well as the more powerful. It can be little doubted that if the State of Rhode Island was separated from the Confederacy and left to itself, the insecurity of rights under the popular form of government within such narrow limits would be displayed by such reiterated oppressions of factious majorities that some power altogether independent of the people would soon be called for by the voice of the very factions whose misrule had proved the necessity to it. In the extended republic of the United States, and among the great variety of interests, parties, and sects which it embraces, a coalition of a majority of the whole society could seldom take place on any other principles than those of justice and the general good; whilst there being thus less danger to a minor from the will of a major party, there must be less pretext, also, to provide for the security of the former, by introducing into the government a will not dependent on the latter, or, in other words, a will independent of the society itself. It is no less certain that it is important, notwithstanding the contrary opinions which have been entertained that the larger the society, provided it lie within a practicable sphere, the more duly capable it will be of self-government. And happily for the *republican cause,* the practicable sphere may be carried to a very great extent by a judicious modification and mixture of the *federal principle.*

The Federalist, No. 78, Alexander Hamilton

The Federalist, *No. 78, written by Alexander Hamilton, explains and praises the provisions for the judiciary in the newly drafted Constitution. Notice especially how Hamilton asserts that the courts have a key responsibility in determining the meaning of the Constitution as fundamental law. Hamilton is outlining here the doctrine of judicial review as we now know it.*

We proceed now to an examination of the judiciary department of the proposed government.

In unfolding the defects of the existing Confederation, the utility and necessity of a federal judicature have been clearly pointed out. It is the less necessary to recapitulate the considerations there urged as the propriety of the institution in the abstract is not disputed; the only questions which have been raised being relative to the manner of constituting it, and to its extent. To these points, therefore, our observations shall be confined.

The manner of constituting it seems to embrace these several objects: 1st. The mode of appointing the judges. 2nd. The tenure by which they are to hold their places. 3rd. The partition of the judiciary authority between different courts and their relations to each other.

First. As to the mode of appointing the judges: this is the same with that of appointing the officers of the Union in general and has been so fully discussed in the two last numbers that nothing can be said here which would not be useless repetition.

Second. As to the tenure by which the judges are to hold their places: this chiefly concerns their duration in office, the provisions for their support, the precautions for their responsibility.

According to the plan of the convention, all judges who may be appointed by the United States are to hold their offices *during good behavior;* which is conformable to the most approved of the State constitutions, and among the rest, to that of this State. Its propriety having been drawn into question by the adversaries of that plan is no light symptom of the rage for objection which disorders their imaginations and judgments. The standard of good behavior for the continuance in office of the judicial magistracy is certainly one of the most valuable of the modern improvements in the practice of government. In a monarchy it is an excellent barrier to the despotism of the prince; in a republic it is a no less excellent barrier to the encroachments and oppressions of the representative body. And it is the best expedient which can be devised in any government to secure a steady, upright, and impartial administration of the laws.

Whoever attentively considers the different departments of power must perceive that, in a government in which they are separated from each other, the judiciary, from the nature of its functions, will always be the least dangerous to the political rights of the Constitution; because it will be least in a capacity to annoy or injure them. The executive not only dispenses the honors but holds the sword of the community. The legislature not only commands the purse but prescribes the rules by which the duties and rights of every citizen are to be regulated. The judiciary, on the contrary, has no influence over either the sword or the purse; no direction either of the strength or of the wealth of the society, and can take no active resolution whatever. It may truly be said to have neither FORCE NOR WILL but merely judgment; and must ultimately depend upon the aid of the executive arm even for the efficacy of its judgments.

This simple view of the matter suggests several important consequences. It proves incontestably that the judiciary is beyond comparison the weakest of the three departments of power; that it can never attack with success either of the other two; and that all possible care is requisite to enable it to defend itself against their attacks. It equally proves that though individual oppression may now and then proceed from the courts of justice, the general liberty of the people can never be endangered from that quarter; I mean so long as the judiciary remains truly distinct from both the legislature and the executive. For I agree that "there is no liberty if the power of judging be not separated from the legislative and executive powers." And it proves, in the last place, that as liberty can have nothing to fear from the judiciary alone, but would have everything to fear from its union with either of the other departments, that as all the effects of such a union must ensue from a dependence of the former on the latter, notwithstanding a nominal and apparent separation; that as, from the natural feebleness of the judiciary, it is in continual jeopardy of being overpowered, awed, or influenced by its co-ordinate branches; and that as nothing can contribute so much to its firmness and independence as permanency in office, this quality may therefore be justly regarded as an indispensable ingredient in its constitution, and, in a great measure, as the citadel for the public justice and the public security.

The complete independence of the courts of justice is peculiarly essential in a limited Constitution. By a limited Constitution, I understand one which contains certain specified exceptions to the legislative authority; such, for instance, as that it shall pass no bills of attainder, no *ex post facto laws,* and the like. Limitations of this kind can be preserved in practice no other way than through the medium of courts of justice, whose duty it must be to declare all acts contrary to the manifest tenor of the Constitution void. Without this, all the reservations of particular rights or privileges would amount to nothing.

Some perplexity respecting the rights of the courts to pronounce legislative acts void, because contrary to the Constitution, has arisen from an imagination that the doctrine would imply a superiority to the judiciary to the legislative power. It is urged that the authority which can declare the acts of another void must necessarily be superior to the one whose acts may be declared void. As this doctrine is of great importance in all the American constitutions, a brief discussion of the grounds on which it rests cannot be unacceptable.

There is no position which depends on clearer principles than that every act of a delegated authority, contrary to the tenor of the commission under which it is exercised, is void. No legislative act, therefore, contrary to the Constitution, can be valid. To deny this would be to affirm that the deputy is greater than his principal; that the servant is above his master; that the representatives of the people are superior to the people themselves; that men acting by virtue of powers do not authorize, but what they forbid.

If it be said that the legislative body are themselves the constitutional judges of their own powers and that the construction they put upon them is conclusive upon the other departments it may be answered that this cannot be the natural presumption where it is not to be collected from any particular provisions in the Constitution. It is not otherwise to be supposed that the Constitution could intend to enable the representatives of the people to substitute their *will* to that of their constituents. It is far more rational to suppose that the courts were designed to be an intermediate body between the people and the legislature in order,

among other things, to keep the latter within the limits assigned to their authority. The interpretation of the laws is the proper and peculiar province of the courts. A constitution is, in fact, and must be regarded by the judges as, a fundamental law. It therefore belongs to them to ascertain its meaning as well as the meaning of any particular act proceeding from the legislative body. If there should happen to be an irreconcilable variance between the two, that which has the superior obligation and validity ought, of course, to be preferred; or, in other words, the Constitution ought to be preferred to the statute, the intention of the people to the intention of their agents.

Nor does this conclusion by any means suppose a superiority of the judicial to the legislative power. It only supposes that the power of the people is superior to both, and that where the will of the legislature, declared in its statutes, stands in opposition to that of the people, declared in the Constitution, the judges ought to be governed by the latter rather than the former. They ought to regulate their decisions by the fundamental laws rather than by those which are not fundamental.

This exercise of judicial discretion in determining between two contradictory laws is exemplified in a familiar instance. It not uncommonly happens that there are two statutes existing at one time, clashing in whole or in part with each other and neither of them containing any repealing clause or expression. In such a case, it is the province of the courts to liquidate and fix their meaning and operation. So far as they can, by any fair construction, be reconciled to each other, reason and law conspire to dictate that this should be done; where this is impracticable, it becomes a matter of necessity to give effect to one in exclusion of the other. The rule which has obtained in the courts for determining their relative validity is that the last in order of time shall be preferred to the first. But this is a mere rule of construction, not derived from any positive law but from the nature and reason of the thing. It is a rule not enjoined upon the courts by legislative provision but adopted by themselves, as consonant to truth and propriety, for the direction of their conduct as interpreters of the law. They thought it reasonable that between the interfering acts of an equal authority that which was the last indication of its will should have the preference.

But in regard to the interfering acts of a superior and subordinate authority of an original and derivative power, the nature and reason of the thing indicates the converse of that rule as proper to be followed. They teach us that the prior act of a superior ought to be preferred to the subsequent act of an inferior and subordinate authority; and that accordingly, whenever

a particular statute contravenes the Constitution, it will be the duty of the judicial tribunals to adhere to the latter and disregard the former.

It can be of no weight to say that the courts, on the pretense of a repugnancy, may substitute their own pleasure to the constitutional intentions of the legislature. This might as well happen in the case of two contradictory statutes; or it might as well happen in every adjudication upon any single statute. The courts must declare the sense of the law; and if they should be disposed to exercise WILL instead of JUDGMENT, the consequence would equally be the substitution of their pleasure to that of the legislative body. The observation, if it prove anything, would prove that there ought to be no judges distinct from that body.

If, then, the courts of justice are to be considered as the bulwarks of a limited Constitution against legislative encroachments, this consideration will afford a strong argument for the permanent tenure of judicial offices, since nothing will contribute so much as this to that independent spirit in the judges which must be essential to the faithful performance of so arduous a duty.

This independence of the judges is equally requisite to guard the Constitution and the rights of individuals from the effects of those ill humors which the arts of designing men, or the influence of particular conjunctures, sometimes disseminate among the people themselves, and which, though they speedily give place to better information, and more deliberate reflection, have a tendency, in the meantime, to occasion dangerous innovations in the government, and serious oppressions of the minor party in the community. Though I trust the friends of the proposed Constitution will never concur with its enemies in questioning that fundamental principal of Republican government which admits the right of the people to alter or abolish the established Constitution whenever they find it inconsistent with their happiness; yet it is not to be inferred from this principle that the representatives of the people, whenever a momentary inclination happens to lay hold of a majority of their constituents incompatible with the provisions in the existing Constitution would, on that account, be justifiable in a violation of those provisions; or that the courts would be under a greater obligation to connive at infractions in this shape than when they had proceeded wholly from the cabals of the representative body. Until the people have, by some solemn and authoritative act, annulled or changed the established form, it is binding upon themselves collectively, as well as individually; and no presumption, or even knowledge of their sentiments, can warrant their representatives in a departure from it prior to such an act. But it is easy to see that it would require an uncommon portion of fortitude in the judges to do their duty as faithful guardians of the Constitution, where legislative invasions of it had been instigated by the major voice of the community.

But it is not with a view to infractions of the Constitution only that the independence of the judges may be an essential safeguard against the effects of occasional ill humors in the society. These sometimes extend no farther than to the injury of the private rights of particular classes of citizens, by unjust and partial laws. Here also the firmness of the judicial magistracy is of vast importance in mitigating the severity and confining the operation of such laws. It not only serves to moderate the immediate mischiefs of those which may have been passed but it operates as a check upon the legislative body in passing them; who, perceiving that obstacles to the success of iniquitous intention are to be expected from the scruples of the courts, are in a manner compelled, by the very motives of the injustice they mediate, to qualify their attempts. This is a circumstance calculated to have more influence upon the character of our governments than but a few may be aware of. The benefits of the integrity and moderation of the judiciary have already been felt in more States than one; and though they may have displeased those whose sinister expectations they may have disappointed, they must have commanded the esteem and applause of all the virtuous and disinterested. Considerate men of every description ought to prize whatever will tend to beget or fortify that temper in the courts; as no man can be sure that he may not be tomorrow the victim of a spirit of injustice, by which he may be a gainer today. And every man must now feel that the inevitable tendency of such a spirit is to sap the foundations of public and private confidence and to introduce in its stead universal distrust and distress.

That inflexible and uniform adherence to the rights of the Constitution, and of individuals, which we perceive to be indispensable in the courts of justice, can certainly not be expected from judges who hold their offices by a temporary commission. Periodical appointments, however regulated, or by whomsoever made, would, in some way or other, be fatal to their necessary independence. If the power of making them was committed either to the executive or legislature there would be danger of an improper complaisance to the branch which possessed it; if to both, there would be an unwillingness to hazard the displeasure of either; if to the people, or to persons chosen by them for the special purpose, there would be too great a disposition to consult popularity to justify a reliance that nothing would be consulted by the Constitution and the laws.

There is yet a further and a weighty reason for the permanency of the judicial offices which is deducible from the nature of the qualifications they require. It has been frequently remarked with great propriety that a voluminous code of laws is one of the inconveniences necessarily connected with the advantages of a free government. To avoid an arbitrary discretion in the courts, it is indispensable that they should be bound down by strict rules and precedents which serve to define and point out their duty in every particular case that comes before them; and it will readily be conceived from the variety of controversies which grow out of the folly and wickedness of mankind that the records of those precedents must unavoidably swell to a very considerable bulk and must demand long and laborious study to acquire a competent knowledge of them. Hence it is that there can be but few men in the society who will have sufficient skill in the laws to qualify them for the stations of judges. And making the proper deductions for the ordinary depravity of human nature, the number must be still smaller of those who unite the requisite integrity with the requisite knowledge. These considerations apprise us that the government can have no great option between fit characters; and that a temporary duration in office which would naturally discourage such characters from quitting a lucrative line of practice to accept a seat on the bench would have a tendency to throw the administration of justice into hands less able and less well qualified to conduct it with utility and dignity. In the present circumstances of this country and in those in which it is likely to be for a long time to come, the disadvantages on this score would be greater than they may at first sight appear; but it must be confessed that they are far inferior to those which present themselves under the other aspects of the subject.

Upon the whole, there can be no room to doubt that the convention acted wisely in copying from the models of those constitutions which have established *good behavior* as the tenure of their judicial offices in point of duration, and that so far from being blamable on this account, their plan would have been inexcusably defective if it had wanted this important feature of good government. The experience of Great Britain affords an illustrious comment on the excellence of the institution.

Presidential Election Results, 1789–2004

Year	Candidates	Party	Popular Vote	Electoral Vote
1789	George Washington			69
	John Adams			34
	Others			35
1793	George Washington			132
	John Adams			77
	George Clinton			50
	Others			5
1796	John Adams	Federalist		71
	Thomas Jefferson	Democratic-Republican		68
	Thomas Pinckney	Federalist		59
	Aaron Burr	Democratic-Republican		30
	Others			48
1800	Thomas Jefferson	Democratic-Republican		73
	Aaron Burr	Democratic-Republican		73
	John Adams	Federalist		65
	Charles C. Pinckney	Federalist		64
1804	Thomas Jefferson	Democratic-Republican		162
	Charles C. Pinckney	Federalist		14
1808	James Madison	Democratic-Republican		122
	Charles C. Pinckney	Federalist		47
	George Clinton	Independent-Republican		6
1812	James Madison	Democratic-Republican		128
	DeWitt Clinton	Federalist		89
1816	James Monroe	Democratic-Republican		183
	Rufus King	Federalist		34
1820	James Monroe	Democratic-Republican		231
	John Quincy Adams	Independent-Republican		1
1824	John Quincy Adams	Democratic-Republican	108,740(30.5%)	84
	Andrew Jackson	Democratic-Republican	153,544(43.1%)	99
	Henry Clay	Democratic-Republican	47,136(13.2%)	37
	William H. Crawford	Democratic-Republican	46,618(13.1%)	41
1828	Andrew Jackson	Democratic	647,231(56.0%)	178
	John Quincy Adams	National Republican	509,097(44.0%)	83
1832	Andrew Jackson	Democratic	687,502(55.0%)	219
	Henry Clay	National Republican	530,189(42.4%)	49
	William Wirt	Anti-Masonic		7
	John Floyd	National Republican	33,108(2.6%)	11
1836	Martin Van Buren	Democratic	761,549(50.9%)	170
	William H. Harrison	Whig	549,567(36.7%)	73
	Hugh L. White	Whig	145,396(9.7%)	26
	Daniel Webster	Whig	41,287(2.7%)	14
1840	William H. Harrison	Whig	1,275,017(53.1%)	234
	Martin Van Buren	Democratic	1,128,702(46.9%)	60
1844	James K. Polk	Democratic	1,337,243(49.6%)	170
	Henry Clay	Whig	1,299,068(48.1%)	105
	James G. Birney	Liberty	63,300(2.3%)	
1848	Zachary Taylor	Whig	1,360,101(47.4%)	163
	Lewis Cass	Democratic	1,220,544(42.5%)	127
	Martin Van Buren	Free Soil	291,163(10.1%)	
1852	Franklin Pierce	Democratic	1,601,474(50.9%)	254
	Winfield Scott	Whig	1,386,578(44.1%)	42
1856	James Buchanan	Democratic	1,838,169(45.4%)	174
	John C. Fremont	Republican	1,335,264(33.0%)	114
	Millard Fillmore	American	874,534(21.6%)	8
1860	Abraham Lincoln	Republican	1,865,593(39.8%)	180
	Stephen A. Douglas	Democratic	1,381,713(29.5%)	12
	John C. Breckinridge	Democratic	848,356(18.1%)	72
	John Bell	Constitutional Union	592,906(12.6%)	79
1864	Abraham Lincoln	Republican	2,206,938(55.0%)	212
	George B. McClellan	Democratic	1,803,787(45.0%)	21
1868	Ulysses S. Grant	Republican	3,013,421(52.7%)	214
	Horatio Seymour	Democratic	2,706,829(47.3%)	80
1872	Ulysses S. Grant	Republican	3,596,745(55.6%)	286
	Horace Greeley	Democratic	2,843,446(43.9%)	66
1876	Rutherford B. Hayes	Republican	4,036,571(48.0%)	185
	Samuel J. Tilden	Democratic	4,284,020(51.0%)	184
1880	James A. Garfield	Republican	4,449,053(48.3%)	214
	Winfield S. Hancock	Democratic	4,442,035(48.2%)	155
	James B. Weaver	Greenback-Labor	308,578(3.4%)	
1884	Grover Cleveland	Democratic	4,874,986(48.5%)	219
	James G. Blaine	Republican	4,851,931(48.2%)	182
	Benjamin F. Butler	Greenback-Labor	175,370(1.8%)	
1888	Benjamin Harrison	Republican	5,444,337(47.8%)	233
	Grover Cleveland	Democratic	5,540,050(48.6%)	168

Presidential Election Results, 1789–2004

Year	Candidates	Party	Popular Vote	Electoral Vote
1892	Grover Cleveland	Democratic	5,554,414(46.0%)	277
	Benjamin Harrison	Republican	5,190,802(43.0%)	145
	James B. Weaver	Peoples	1,027,329(8.5%)	22
1896	William McKinley	Republican	7,035,638(50.8%)	271
	William J. Bryan	Democratic; Populist	6,467,946(46.7%)	176
1900	William McKinley	Republican	7,219,530(51.7%)	292
	William J. Bryan	Democratic; Populist	6,356,734(45.5%)	155
1904	Theodore Roosevelt	Republican	7,628,834(56.4%)	336
	Alton B. Parker	Democratic	5,084,401(37.6%)	140
	Eugene V. Debs	Socialist	402,460(3.0%)	0
1908	William H. Taft	Republican	7,679,006(51.6%)	321
	William J. Bryan	Democratic	6,409,106(43.1%)	162
	Eugene V. Debs	Socialist	420,820(2.8%)	0
1912	Woodrow Wilson	Democratic	6,286,820(41.8%)	435
	Theodore Roosevelt	Progressive	4,126,020(27.4%)	88
	William H. Taft	Republican	3,483,922(23.2%)	8
	Eugene V. Debs	Socialist	897,011(6.0%)	0
1916	Woodrow Wilson	Democratic	9,129,606(49.3%)	277
	Charles E. Hughes	Republican	8,538,211(46.1%)	254
1920	Warren G. Harding	Republican	16,152,200(61.0%)	404
	James M. Cox	Democratic	9,147,353(34.6%)	127
	Eugene V. Debs	Socialist	919,799(3.5%)	0
1924	Calvin Coolidge	Republican	15,725,016(54.1%)	382
	John W. Davis	Democratic	8,385,586(28.8%)	136
	Robert M. La Follette	Progressive	4,822,856(16.6%)	13
1928	Herbert C. Hoover	Republican	21,392,190(58.2%)	444
	Alfred E. Smith	Democratic	15,016,443(40.8%)	87
1932	Franklin D. Roosevelt	Democratic	22,809,638(57.3%)	472
	Herbert C. Hoover	Republican	15,758,901(39.6%)	59
	Norman Thomas	Socialist	881,951(2.2%)	0
1936	Franklin D. Roosevelt	Democratic	27,751,612(60.7%)	523
	Alfred M. Landon	Republican	16,681,913(36.4%)	8
	William Lemke	Union	891,858(1.9%)	0
1940	Franklin D. Roosevelt	Democratic	27,243,466(54.7%)	449
	Wendell L. Willkie	Republican	22,304,755(44.8%)	82
1944	Franklin D. Roosevelt	Democratic	25,602,505(52.8%)	432
	Thomas E. Dewey	Republican	22,006,278(44.5%)	99
1948	Harry S Truman	Democratic	24,105,812(49.5%)	303
	Thomas E. Dewey	Republican	21,970,065(45.1%)	189
	J. Strom Thurmond	States' Rights	1,169,063(2.4%)	39
	Henry A. Wallace	Progressive	1,157,172(2.4%)	0
1952	Dwight D. Eisenhower	Republican	33,936,234(55.2%)	442
	Adlai E. Stevenson	Democratic	27,314,992(44.5%)	89
1956	Dwight D. Eisenhower	Republican	35,590,472(57.4%)	457
	Adlai E. Stevenson	Democratic	26,022,752(42.0%)	73
1960	John F. Kennedy	Democratic	34,227,096(49.9%)	303
	Richard M. Nixon	Republican	34,108,546(49.6%)	219
1964	Lyndon B. Johnson	Democratic	43,126,233(61.1%)	486
	Barry Goldwater	Republican	27,174,989(38.5%)	52
1968	Richard M. Nixon	Republican	31,783,783(43.4%)	301
	Hubert H. Humphrey	Democratic	31,271,839(42.7%)	191
	George C. Wallace	American Independent	9,899,557(13.5%)	46
1972	Richard M. Nixon	Republican	46,632,189(61.3%)	520
	George McGovern	Democratic	28,422,015(37.3%)	17
1976	Jimmy Carter	Democratic	40,828,587(50.1%)	297
	Gerald R. Ford	Republican	39,147,613(48.0%)	240
1980	Ronald Reagan	Republican	42,941,145(51.0%)	489
	Jimmy Carter	Democratic	34,663,037(41.0%)	49
	John B. Anderson	Independent	5,551,551(6.6%)	0
1984	Ronald Reagan	Republican	53,428,357(59%)	525
	Walter F. Mondale	Democratic	36,930,923(41%)	13
1988	George Bush	Republican	48,881,011(53%)	426
	Michael Dukakis	Democratic	41,828,350(46%)	111
1992	Bill Clinton	Democratic	38,394,210(43%)	370
	George Bush	Republican	33,974,386(38%)	168
	H. Ross Perot	Independent	16,573,465(19%)	0
1996	Bill Clinton	Democratic	45,628,667(49%)	379
	Bob Dole	Republican	37,869,435(41%)	159
	H. Ross Perot	Reform	7,874,283(8%)	0
2000	George W. Bush	Republican	50,456,169(48%)	271
	Al Gore	Democratic	50,996,116(48%)	266
	Ralph Nader	Green	2,767,176(3%)	0
2004	George W. Bush	Republican	60,608,582(51%)	286
	John Kerry	Democratic	57,288,974(48%)	252
	Ralph Nader	Independent	400,924(.35%)	0

Presidents and Vice Presidents

1. George Washington (1789)
   John Adams (1789)

2. John Adams (1797)
   Thomas Jefferson (1797)

3. Thomas Jefferson (1801)
   Aaron Burr (1801)
   George Clinton (1805)

4. James Madison (1809)
   George Clinton (1809)
   Elbridge Gerry (1813)

5. James Monroe (1817)
   Daniel D. Tompkins (1817)

6. John Quincy Adams (1825)
   John C. Calhoun (1825)

7. Andrew Jackson (1829)
   John C. Calhoun (1829)
   Martin Van Buren (1833)

8. Martin Van Buren (1837)
   Richard M. Johnson (1837)

9. William H. Harrison (1841)
   John Tyler (1841)

10. John Tyler (1841)

11. James K. Polk (1845)
    George M. Dallas (1845)

12. Zachary Taylor (1849)
    Millard Fillmore (1849)

13. Millard Fillmore (1850)

14. Franklin Pierce (1853)
    William R. King (1853)

15. James Buchanan (1857)
    John C. Breckinridge (1857)

16. Abraham Lincoln (1861)
    Hannibal Hamlin (1861)
    Andrew Johnson (1865)

17. Andrew Johnson (1865)

18. Ulysses S. Grant (1869)
    Schuyler Colfax (1869)
    Henry Wilson (1873)

19. Rutherford B. Hayes (1877)
    William A. Wheeler (1877)

20. James A. Garfield (1881)
    Chester A. Arthur (1881)

21. Chester A. Arthur (1881)

22. Grover Cleveland (1885)
    T. A. Hendricks (1885)

23. Benjamin Harrison (1889)
    Levi P. Morton (1889)

24. Grover Cleveland (1893)
    Adlai E. Stevenson (1893)

25. William McKinley (1897)
    Garret A. Hobart (1897)
    Theodore Roosevelt (1901)

26. Theodore Roosevelt (1901)
    Charles Fairbanks (1905)

27. William H. Taft (1909)
    James S. Sherman (1909)

28. Woodrow Wilson (1913)
    Thomas R. Marshall (1913)

29. Warren G. Harding (1921)
    Calvin Coolidge (1921)

30. Calvin Coolidge (1923)
    Charles G. Dawes (1925)

31. Herbert C. Hoover (1929)
    Charles Curtis (1929)

32. Franklin D. Roosevelt (1933)
    John Nance Garner (1933)
    Henry A. Wallace (1941)
    Harry S Truman (1945)

33. Harry S Truman (1945)
    Alben W. Barkley (1949)

34. Dwight D. Eisenhower (1953)
    Richard M. Nixon (1953)

35. John F. Kennedy (1961)
    Lyndon B. Johnson (1961)

36. Lyndon B. Johnson (1963)
    Hubert H. Humphrey (1965)

37. Richard M. Nixon (1969)
    Spiro T. Agnew (1969)
    Gerald R. Ford (1973)

38. Gerald R. Ford (1974)
    Nelson A. Rockefeller (1974)

39. James E. Carter Jr. (1977)
    Walter F. Mondale (1977)

40. Ronald W. Reagan (1981)
    George H. W. Bush (1981)

41. George H. W. Bush (1989)
    James D. Quayle III (1989)

42. William J. B. Clinton (1993)
    Albert Gore (1993)

43. George W. Bush (2001)
    Richard Cheney (2001)

GLOSSARY

527 groups Interest groups organized under Section 527 of the Internal Revenue Service Code that may advertise for or against candidates. If the source of funding is corporations or unions, they have some restrictions on broadcast advertising. 527 groups were important in the 2000 and 2004 elections.

absentee (or early) voting Period before the regularly scheduled election date, during which voters are allowed to cast ballots. With recent changes in election law, a person does not have to offer a reason for voting absentee.

administrative discretion Authority given by Congress to the federal bureaucracy to use reasonable judgment in implementing the laws.

adversary system A judicial system in which the court of law is a neutral arena where two parties argue their differences.

advisory opinion An opinion unrelated to a particular case that gives a court's view about a constitutional or legal issue.

affirmative action Remedial action designed to overcome the effects of past discrimination against minorities and women.

agriculture commissioner The elected official responsible for administering laws and programs that benefit agriculture.

amendatory veto The power of governors in a few states to return a bill to the legislature with suggested language changes, conditions, or amendments. Legislators then decide either to accept the governor's recommendations or to pass the bill in its original form over the veto.

American dream The widespread belief that the United States is a land of opportunity and that individual initiative and hard work can bring economic success.

amicus curiae **brief** Literally, a "friend of the court" brief, filed by an individual or organization to present arguments in addition to those presented by the immediate parties to a case.

Annapolis Convention A convention held in September 1786 to consider problems of trade and navigation, attended by five states and important because it issued the call to Congress and the states for what became the Constitutional Convention.

annexation powers Authority of cities to add territory, subject to restrictions set by state law.

Antifederalists Opponents of ratification of the Constitution and of a strong central government generally.

antitrust legislation Federal laws (starting with the Sherman Act of 1890) that try to prevent a monopoly from dominating an industry and restraining trade.

appellate jurisdiction The authority of a court to review decisions made by lower courts.

appraisal district Local agency that determines the value of pieces of property in a county. All local governments are required to use its evaluations, or appraisals, for tax purposes.

appropriations bill Bill that authorizes the expenditure of money for a public program or purpose. In Texas, the general appropriations bill approved by the legislature every two years is the state budget.

Articles of Confederation The first governing document of the confederated states, drafted in 1777, ratified in 1781, and replaced by the present Constitution in 1789.

assessment The valuation a government places on property for the purposes of taxation.

assigned counsel system Arrangement whereby attorneys are provided for persons accused of crimes who are unable to hire their own attorneys. The judge assigns a member of the bar to provide counsel to a particular defendant.

at-large district Legislative or other political district, sometimes called a multimember district because two or more officials are elected from it, that includes an entire county, city, or other political subdivision.

at-large elections Election systems under which officeholders are elected by voters in the entire city, school district, or single-purpose district.

attentive public Those citizens who follow public affairs carefully.

attorney general The state's chief legal officer, who represents Texas in lawsuits and is responsible for enforcing the state's antitrust, consumer protection, and other civil laws.

Australian ballot A secret ballot printed by the state.

bad tendency test Interpretation of the First Amendment that would permit legislatures to forbid speech encouraging people to engage in illegal action.

bicameral legislature A two-house legislature.

bicameralism The principle of a two-house legislature.

bifactionalism Presence of two dominant factions organized around regional, economic, or ideological differences within a single political party. For much of the twentieth century, Texas functioned as a one-party system with two dominant factions.

bifurcated court system Existence of two courts at the highest level of the state judiciary. The Texas Supreme Court is the court of last resort in civil cases, and the Texas Court of Criminal Appeals has the final authority to review criminal cases.

bill of attainder Legislative act inflicting punishment, including deprivation of property, without a trial, on named individuals or members of a specific group.

binding arbitration A collective bargaining agreement in which both parties agree, in case of dispute over the terms of the union contract, to adhere to the decision of an arbitrator.

bipartisanship A policy that emphasizes a united front and cooperation between the major political parties, especially on sensitive foreign policy issues.

blanket primary Primary election open to all voters, who may vote for a candidate from any party for each office.

bloc Group of legislators who act together for a common goal regardless of party affiliation.

bundling A tactic of political action committees whereby they collect contributions from like-minded individuals (each limited to $2,000) and present them to a candidate or political party as a "bundle," thus increasing their influence.

bureaucracy A form of organization that operates through impersonal, uniform rules and procedures.

bureaucrat A career government employee.

Bush doctrine A policy adopted by the Bush administration in 2001 that asserts America's right to attack any nation that has weapons of mass destruction that might be used against U.S. interests at home or abroad.

cabinet Advisory council for the president, consisting of the heads of the executive departments, the vice president, and a few other officials selected by the president.

calendar Agenda or the list of bills to be considered by the house or the senate on a given day.

Calendars Committee Special procedural committee that schedules bills that already have been approved by other committees for floor debate in the house.

candidate appeal How voters feel about a candidate's background, personality, leadership ability, and other personal qualities.

capital murder Murder committed under certain circumstances for which the death penalty or life in prison must be imposed. p. 38

capitalism An economic system characterized by private property, competitive markets, economic incentives, and limited government involvement in the production and pricing of goods and services.

caucus A meeting of local party members to choose party officials or candidates for public office and to decide the platform.

central clearance Review of all executive branch testimony, reports, and draft legislation by the Office of Management and Budget to ensure that each communication to Congress is in accordance with the president's program.

centralists People who favor national action over action at the state and local levels.

charter school A publicly funded alternative to standard public schools in some states, initiated when individuals or groups receive charters; charter schools must meet state standards.

charter City "constitution" that outlines the structure of city government, defines the authority of the various officials, and provides for their selection.

checks and balances Constitutional grant of powers that enables each of the three branches of government to check some acts of the others and therefore ensure that no branch can dominate.

chief of staff The head of the White House staff.

city commission Form of city government in which elected commissioners collectively serve as a city's policy-making body and individually serve as administrative heads of different city departments.

civil disobedience Deliberate refusal to obey a law or comply with the orders of public officials as a means of expressing opposition.

civil lawsuit Noncriminal legal dispute between two or more individuals, businesses, governments, or other entities.

civil service system System under which public employees are hired and promoted on their abilities. It features competitive examinations and offers job security from one election to another.

class action suit Lawsuit brought by an individual or a group of people on behalf of all those similarly situated.

clear and present danger test Interpretation of the First Amendment that holds that the government cannot interfere with speech unless the speech presents a clear and present danger that it will lead to evil or illegal acts. To shout "Fire!" falsely in a crowded theater is Justice Oliver Wendell Holmes's famous example.

closed primary Primary election in which only persons registered in the party holding the primary may vote.

closed rule A procedural rule in the House of Representatives that prohibits any amendments to bills or provides that only members of the committee reporting the bill may offer amendments.

closed shop A company with a labor agreement under which union membership is a condition of employment.

cloture A procedure for terminating debate, especially filibusters, in the Senate.

coattail effect The boost that candidates may get in an election because of the popularity of candidates above them on the ballot, especially the president.

collective bargaining Method whereby representatives of the union and employer determine wages, hours, and other conditions of employment through direct negotiation.

commerce clause The clause of the Constitution (Article I, Section 8, Clause 1) that gives Congress the power to regulate all business activities that cross state lines or affect more than one state or other nations.

commercial speech Advertisements and commercials for products and services; they receive less First Amendment protection, primarily to discourage false and misleading ads.

commissioners court Principal policy-making body for county government. It sets the county tax rate and supervises expenditures.

committee In the legislature, a group of lawmakers who review and hold public hearings on issues or bills they are assigned by the presiding officer. Committees that specialize in bills by subject matter are designated as standing committees. A bill has to win committee approval before it can be considered by the full house or senate. Most bills die in committees, which perform as a legislative screening process.

community policing Assigning police to neighborhoods where they walk the beat and work with churches and other community groups to reduce crime and improve relations with minorities.

comptroller The state's primary tax administrator, accounting officer, and revenue estimator.

concurrent powers Powers that the Constitution gives to both the national and state governments, such as the power to levy taxes.

concurring opinion An opinion that agrees with the majority in a Supreme Court ruling but differs on the reasoning.

confederation Constitutional arrangement in which sovereign nations or states, by compact, create a central government but carefully limit its power and do not give it direct authority over individuals.

conference committee Committee appointed by the presiding officers of each chamber to adjust differences on a particular bill passed by each in different form.

Congressional Budget Office (CBO) An agency of Congress that analyzes presidential budget recommendations and estimates the costs of proposed legislation.

Connecticut Compromise Compromise agreement by states at the Constitutional Convention for a bicameral legislature with a lower house in which representation would be based on population and an upper house in which each state would have two senators.

conservatism A belief that limited government ensures order, competitive markets, and personal opportunity.

constable Elected law enforcement officer who is primarily responsible for executing court judgments, serving subpoenas, and delivering other legal documents.

constitution Legal structure of a political system, establishing government bodies and defining their powers.

Constitutional Convention The convention in Philadelphia, May 25 to September 17, 1787, that framed the Constitution of the United States.

constitutional county court County court created by the Texas Constitution, presided over by the county judge.

constitutional democracy A government that enforces recognized limits on those who govern and allows the voice of the people to be heard through free, fair, and relatively frequent elections.

constitutional home rule State constitutional authorization for local governments to conduct their own affairs.

constitutional initiative petition A device that permits voters to place specific amendments to a state constitution on the ballot by petition.

constitutionalism The set of arrangements, including checks and balances, federalism, separation of powers, rule of law, due process, and a bill of rights, that requires leaders to listen, think, bargain, and explain before they act or make laws. We then hold them politically and legally accountable for how they exercise their powers.

contract clause Clause of the Constitution (Article I, Section 10) originally intended to prohibit state governments from modifying contracts made between individuals; for a while interpreted as prohibiting state governments from taking actions that adversely affect property rights; no longer interpreted so broadly and no longer constrains state governments from exercising their police powers.

council of government (COG) Council comprised of representatives of other governments in a defined region of the state.

council-manager plan Form of local government in which the city council hires a professional administrator to manage city affairs; also known as the *city-manager plan*.

county attorney Elected official who is the chief legal officer of some counties. He or she also prosecutes lesser criminal offenses, primarily misdemeanors, in county courts.

county auditor Appointed officer who is primarily responsible for reviewing every bill and expenditure of a county to assure it is correct and legal.

county chair Presiding officer of a political party's county executive committee. He or she is elected countywide by voters in the party primary.

county clerk Chief record-keeping officer of a county.

county executive committee Panel responsible on the local level for the organization and management of a political party's primary election. It includes the party's county chair and each precinct chair.

county judge Presiding officer of a county commissioners court. This office also has some judicial authority, which is assumed by separate county courts-at-law in most urban counties.

county treasurer Elected officer who is responsible for receiving and disbursing county funds.

court of appeals A court with appellate jurisdiction that hears appeals from the decisions of lower courts.

cross-cutting cleavages Divisions within society that cut across demographic categories to produce groups that are more heterogeneous or different.

crossover voting Voting by a member of one party for a candidate of another party.

de facto segregation Segregation resulting from economic or social conditions or personal choice.

de jure segregation Segregation imposed by law.

de novo In a civil lawsuit or criminal trial, evidence is presented again before an appellate court because no record was kept of the evidence presented to the trial court.

dealignment Weakening of partisan preferences that points to a rejection of both major parties and a rise in the number of Independents.

decentralists People who favor state or local action rather than national action.

defendant In a criminal action, the person or party accused of an offense.

deficit The difference between the revenues raised annually from sources of income other than borrowing and the expenditures of government, including paying the interest on past borrowing.

delegate An official who is expected to represent the views of his or her constituents even when personally holding different views; one interpretation of the role of the legislator.

democracy Government by the people, either directly or indirectly, with free and frequent elections.

democratic consensus Widespread agreement on fundamental principles of democratic governance and the values that undergird them.

demographics The study of the characteristics of populations.

department Usually the largest organization in government; also the highest rank in federal hierarchy.

deregulation A policy promoting cutbacks in the amount of federal regulation in specific areas of economic activity.

devolution revolution The effort to slow the growth of the federal government by returning many functions to the states.

Dillon rule Principle holding that local governments are creations of state government and that their powers and responsibilities are defined by the state.

direct democracy Government in which citizens vote on laws and select officials more directly.

direct primary Election in which voters choose party nominees.

discharge petition Petition that, if signed by a majority of the members of the House of Representatives, will pry a bill from committee and bring it to the floor for consideration.

disclosure A requirement that candidates specify where the money came from to finance their campaign.

dissenting opinion An opinion disagreeing with the majority in a Supreme Court ruling.

distributive policy A type of policy that provides benefits to all Americans.

district attorney Elected official who prosecutes more serious criminal offenses, usually felonies, before state district courts.

district clerk Elected county official who maintains custody of state district court records.

district court Primary trial court in Texas. It has jurisdiction over criminal felony cases and civil disputes.

divided government Governance divided between the parties, as when one holds the presidency and the other controls one or both houses of Congress.

division votes Votes taken on the computerized voting boards in the Texas house but erased without being permanently recorded.

double jeopardy Trial or punishment for the same crime by the same government; forbidden by the Constitution.

dual citizenship Citizenship in more than one nation.

due process clause Clause in the Fifth Amendment limiting the power of the national government; similar clause in the Fourteenth Amendment prohibiting state governments from depriving any person of life, liberty, or property without due process of law.

economic diversification Development of new and varied business activities. New businesses were encouraged to relocate or expand in Texas after the oil and gas industry, which had been the base of the state's economy, suffered a major recession in the 1980s.

economic sanctions Denial of export, import, or financial relations with a target country in an effort to change that nation's policies.

electoral college The electoral system used in electing the president and vice president, in which voters vote for electors pledged to cast their ballots for a particular party's candidates.

elite Small group of people who exercise disproportionate power and influence in the policy-making processes.

elitism Political system in which power is concentrated in the hands of a relatively small group of individuals or institutions.

eminent domain Power of a government to take private property for public use; the U.S. Constitution gives national and state governments this power and requires them to provide just compensation for property so taken.

enterprise zone Inner-city area designated as offering tax incentives to companies that invest in plants there and provide job training for the unemployed.

entitlement programs Government programs, such as unemployment insurance, disaster relief, and disability payments, that provide benefits to all eligible citizens.

enumerated powers The powers explicitly given to Congress in the Constitution.

environmental impact statement A statement required by federal law from all agencies for any project using federal funds to assess the potential effect of the new construction or development on the environment.

environmentalism An ideology that is dominated by concern for the environment but also promotes grassroots democracy, social justice, equal opportunity, nonviolence, respect for diversity, and feminism.

equal protection clause Clause in the Fourteenth Amendment that forbids any state to deny to any person within its jurisdiction the equal protection of the laws. By interpretation, the Fifth Amendment imposes the same limitation on the national government. This clause is the major constitutional restraint on the power of governments to discriminate against persons because of race, national origin, or sex.

establishment clause Clause in the First Amendment that states that Congress shall make no law respecting an establishment of religion. It has been interpreted by the Supreme Court as forbidding governmental support to any or all religions.

ethnicity A social division based on national origin, religion, language, and often race.

ethnocentrism Belief in the superiority of one's nation or ethnic group.

ex post facto **law** Retroactive criminal law that works to the disadvantage of an individual; forbidden in the Constitution.

excise tax Consumer tax on a specific kind of merchandise, such as tobacco.

exclusionary rule Requirement that evidence unconstitutionally or illegally obtained be excluded from a criminal trial.

executive agreement A formal but often secret agreement between the U.S. president and the leaders of other nations that does not require Senate approval.

Executive Office of the President The cluster of presidential staff agencies that help the president carry out his responsibilities. Currently the office includes the Office of Management and Budget, the Council of Economic Advisers, and several other units.

executive order Directive issued by a president or governor that has the force of law.

executive privilege The power to keep executive communications confidential, especially if they relate to national security.

express powers Powers specifically granted to one of the branches of the national government by the Constitution.

extradition Legal process whereby an alleged criminal offender is surrendered by the officials of one state to officials of the state in which the crime is alleged to have been committed.

extraterritorial jurisdiction Power of an incorporated city to control development within nearby unincorporated areas.

faction A term used by the founders of this country to refer to political parties and special interests or interest groups.

fairness doctrine Federal Communications Commission policy that required holders of radio and television licenses to ensure that different viewpoints were presented about controversial issues or persons; largely repealed in 1987.

federal mandate A requirement imposed by the federal government as a condition for the receipt of federal funds.

Federal Register Official document, published every weekday, that lists the new and proposed regulations of executive departments and regulatory agencies.

Federal Reserve System The system created by Congress in 1913 to establish banking practices and regulate currency in circulation and the amount of credit available. It consists of 12 regional banks supervised by the Board of Governors. Often called simply *the Fed*.

federalism Constitutional arrangement whereby power is distributed between a central government and subdivisional governments, called states in the United States. The national and the subdivisional governments both exercise direct authority over individuals.

Federalists Supporters of ratification of the Constitution whose position promoting a strong central government was later voiced in the Federalist party.

felony A serious crime, the penalty for which can range from death to imprisonment in a penitentiary for more than a year.

fighting words Words that by their very nature inflict injury on those to whom they are addressed or incite them to acts of violence.

filibuster A procedural practice in the Senate whereby a senator refuses to relinquish the floor and thereby delays proceedings and prevents a vote on a controversial issue.

first reading Introduction of a bill in the house or the senate and its referral to a committee by the presiding officer.

fiscal policy Government policy that attempts to manage the economy by controlling taxing and spending.

free exercise clause Clause in the First Amendment that states that Congress shall make no law prohibiting the free exercise of religion.

free rider An individual who does not join a group representing his or her interests yet receives the benefit of the influence the group achieves.

full faith and credit clause Clause in the Constitution (Article IV, Section 1) requiring each state to recognize the civil judgments rendered by the courts of the other states and to accept their public records and acts as valid.

gender gap The difference between the political opinions or political behavior of men and of women.

General Agreement on Tariffs and Trade (GATT) An international trade organization with more than 130 members, including the United States and the People's Republic of China, that seeks to encourage free trade by lowering tariffs and other trade restrictions.

general law cities City allowed to exercise only those powers specifically granted to it by the legislature. General law cities have fewer than 5,000 residents.

general obligation bonds Method of borrowing money to pay for new construction projects, such as prisons, mental hospitals, or school facilities. The bonds, which require voter approval, are repaid with tax revenue.

general property tax Tax levied by local and some state governments on real property or personal, tangible property, the major portion of which is on the estimated value of one's home and land.

gerrymandering The drawing of legislative district boundaries to benefit a party, group, or incumbent.

globalization of the economy Increased interdependence in trade, manufacturing, and commerce as well as most other business activities between the United States and other countries.

government corporation A government agency that operates like a business corporation, created to secure greater freedom of action and flexibility for a particular program.

grand jury A jury of 12 to 23 persons who, in private, hear evidence presented by the government to determine whether persons shall be required to stand trial. If the jury believes there is sufficient evidence that a crime was committed, it issues an indictment.

Grange Organization formed in the late nineteenth century to improve the lot of farmers. The Grange influenced provisions in the Texas Constitution of 1876 limiting taxes and government spending and restricting big business, including banks and railroads.

Green party A minor party dedicated to the environment, social justice, nonviolence, and a foreign policy of nonintervention. Ralph Nader ran as the Green party's nominee in 2000.

gross domestic product (GDP) The total output of all economic activity in the nation, including goods and services.

hard money Political contributions given to a party, candidate, or interest group that are limited in amount and fully disclosed. Raising such limited funds is harder than raising unlimited funds, hence the term "hard" money.

Hatch Act Federal statute barring federal employees from active participation in certain kinds of politics and protecting them from being fired on partisan grounds.

health maintenance organization (HMO) Alternative means of health care in which people or their employers are charged a set amount and the HMO provides health care and covers hospital costs.

hold A procedural practice in the Senate whereby a senator temporarily blocks the consideration of a bill or nomination.

home rule City with a population of more than 5,000, which can adopt any form of government residents choose, provided it does not conflict with the state constitution or statutes.

homestead exemption Reduction in property taxes that some local governments grant on a taxpayer's residence.

honeymoon Period at the beginning of a new president's term during which the president enjoys generally positive relations with the press and Congress, usually lasting about six months.

horse race A close contest; by extension, any contest in which the focus is on who is ahead and by how much rather than on substantive differences between the candidates.

ideology A consistent pattern of beliefs about political values and the role of government.

immunity Exemption from prosecution for a particular crime in return for testimony pertaining to the case.

impeachment Formal accusation against the president or other public official; the first step in removal from office.

implementation The process of putting a law into practice through bureaucratic rules or spending.

implied powers Powers inferred from the express powers that allow Congress to carry out its functions.

impoundment A decision by the president not to spend money appropriated by Congress; now prohibited under federal law.

incumbents The current holders of elected office.

independent agency A government entity that is independent of the legislative, executive, and judicial branches.

independent expenditure The Supreme Court has ruled that individuals, groups, and parties can spend unlimited amounts in campaigns for or against candidates as long as they operate independently from the candidates. When an individual, group, or party does so, they are making an independent expenditure.

independent regulatory commission A government agency or commission with regulatory power whose independence is protected by Congress.

independent school district Specific form of special district that administers the public schools in a designated area.

indexing Providing automatic increases to compensate for inflation.

indictment A formal written statement from a grand jury charging an individual with an offense; also called a *true bill*.

individualism Attitude, rooted in classical liberal theory and reinforced by the frontier tradition, that citizens are capable of taking care of themselves with minimal governmental assistance.

individualistic subculture View that government should interfere as little as possible in the private activities of its citizens while assuring that adequate public facilities and a favorable business climate are available to permit individuals to pursue their self-interests.

inflation A rise in the general price level (and decrease in dollar value) owing to an increase in the volume of money and credit in relation to available goods.

information affidavit Certification by a public prosecutor that there is evidence to justify bringing named individuals to trial.

information Document formally charging a person with a misdemeanor.

infrastructure Streets, waste disposal systems, libraries, and other public facilities built and operated by governments.

inherent powers The powers of the national government in the field of foreign affairs that the Supreme Court has declared do not depend on constitutional grants but rather grow out of the very existence of the national government.

initiative Procedure whereby a certain number of voters may, by petition, propose a law or constitutional amendment and have it submitted to the voters.

inquest Examination by a justice of the peace or a medical examiner of unusual circumstances under which someone has died.

Institutionalization In the context of political science, the development of a legislative body into a formally structured system with stable membership, complex rules, expanded internal operations, and the delineation of staff functions.

intent calendar Daily list of bills eligible for debate on the floor of the Texas senate, if the sponsor is recognized by the lieutenant governor.

interest group A collection of people who share some common interest or attitude and seek to influence government for specific ends. Interest groups usually work within the framework of government and employ tactics such as lobbying to achieve their goals.

interested money Financial contributions by individuals or groups in the hope of influencing the outcome of an election and subsequently influencing policy.

interims Periods between legislative sessions.

interstate compact An agreement among two or more states. The Constitution requires that most such agreements be approved by Congress.

iron triangle A mutually dependent relationship among interest groups, congressional committees and subcommittees, and government agencies that share a common policy concern.

issue advocacy Promoting a particular position or an issue paid for by interest groups or individuals but not candidates. Much issue advocacy is often electioneering for or against a candidate and until 2004 had not been subject to any regulation.

issue network A policy making alliance among loosely connected participants that comes together on a particular issue, then disbands.

item veto Right of an executive to veto parts of a bill approved by a legislature without having to veto the entire bill.

Jim Crow laws State laws formerly pervasive throughout the South requiring public facilities and accommodations to be segregated by race; ruled unconstitutional.

joint committee A committee composed of members of both the House of Representatives and the Senate; such committees oversee the Library of Congress and conduct investigations.

judicial activism Philosophy proposing that judges should interpret the Constitution to reflect current conditions and values.

judicial interpretation A method by which judges modify the force of a constitutional provision by reinterpreting its meaning.

judicial review The power of a court to refuse to enforce a law or a government regulation that in the opinion of the judges conflicts with the U.S. Constitution or, in a state court, the state constitution.

judicial self-restraint Philosophy proposing that judges should interpret the Constitution to reflect what the framers intended and what its words literally say.

justice of the peace court Low-ranking court with jurisdiction over minor civil disputes and criminal cases.

justiciable dispute A dispute growing out of an actual case or controversy and that is capable of settlement by legal methods.

Keynesian economics Economic theory based on the principles of John Maynard Keynes, stating that government spending should increase during business slumps and be curbed during booms.

labor injunction A court order forbidding specific individuals or groups from performing certain acts (such as striking) that the court considers harmful to the rights and property of an employer or a community.

laissez-faire economics Theory that opposes governmental interference in economic affairs beyond what is necessary to protect life and property.

land commissioner The elected official who manages the state's public lands and administers the Veterans Land Program, which provides low-interest loans to veterans for the purchase of land and houses.

Legislative Budget Board The panel that makes budgetary recommendations to the full legislature. It is chaired by the lieutenant governor and includes the speaker of the house and eight other key lawmakers.

Legislative Redistricting Board A board created by constitutional amendment charged to redistrict the Texas legislature if it is not accomplished in the regular session following the release of the census.

libel Written defamation of another person. Especially in the case of public officials and public figures, the constitutional tests designed to restrict libel actions are very rigid.

liberalism A belief in the positive uses of government to bring about justice and equality of opportunity.

Libertarian party A minor party that believes in extremely limited government. Libertarians call for a freemarket system, expanded individual liberties such as drug legalization, and a foreign policy of non-intervention, free trade, and open immigration.

libertarianism An ideology that cherishes individual liberty and insists on a sharply limited government, promoting a free market economy, a noninterventionist foreign policy, and an absence of regulation in the moral and social spheres.

lieutenant governor The presiding officer of the senate. This officeholder would become governor if the governor were to die, be incapacitated, be removed from office, or leave office voluntarily in midterm.

limited government Constitutional principle restricting governmental authority and spelling out personal rights.

line item veto Presidential power to strike, or remove, specific items from a spending bill without vetoing the entire package, declared unconstitutional by the Supreme Court.

literacy test Literacy requirement imposed by some states as a condition of voting, generally used to disqualify blacks from voting in the South; now illegal.

lobbying Engaging in activities aimed at influencing public officials, especially legislators, and the policies they enact.

lobbyist A person who is employed by and acts for an organized interest group or corporation to try to influence policy decisions and positions in the executive and legislative branches.

logrolling Mutual aid and vote trading among legislators.

magistrate judge An official who performs a variety of limited judicial duties.

majority leader The legislative leader selected by the majority party who helps plan party strategy, confers with other party leaders, and tries to keep members of the party in line.

majority rule Governance according to the expressed preferences of the majority.

majority The candidate or party that wins more than half the votes cast in an election.

majority-minority district A congressional district created to include a majority of minority voters; ruled constitutional so long as race is not the main factor in redistricting.

malapportionment Having legislative districts with unequal populations.

mandate A president's claim of broad public support.

manifest destiny A notion held by nineteenth-century Americans that the United States was destined to rule the continent, from the Atlantic to the Pacific.

maquiladora program Policies initiated by Mexico in 1964 to stimulate economic growth along the U.S.-Mexico border.

mass media Means of communication that reach the mass public, including newspapers and magazines, radio, television (broadcast, cable, and satellite), films, recordings, books, and electronic communication.

mayor-council charter The oldest and most common form of city government, consisting of either a weak mayor and a city council or a strong mayor elected by voters and council.

means-tested entitlements Programs such as Medicaid and welfare under which applicants must meet eligibility requirements based on need.

Medicaid Federal program that provides medical benefits for low-income persons.

medical examiner Appointed official who is responsible for determining the cause of death of murder victims or others who die under suspicious or unusual circumstances.

medical savings account Alternative means of health care in which individuals make tax-deductible contributions to a special account that can be used to pay medical expenses.

Medicare National health insurance program for the elderly and disabled.

merit selection Proposal under which the governor would appoint state judges from lists of potential nominees recommended by committees of experts. Appointed judges would have to run later in retention elections to keep their seats but would not have opponents on the ballot. Voters would simply decide whether a judge should remain in office or be replaced by another gubernatorial appointee.

merit system A system of public employment in which selection and promotion depend on demonstrated performance rather than political patronage.

metro government Local government in which city and county governments consolidate to avoid duplication of public services.

minor party A small political party that rises and falls with a charismatic candidate or, if composed of ideologies on the right or left, usually persists over time; also called a *third party*.

minority leader The legislative leader selected by the minority party as spokesperson for the opposition.

***Miranda* ruling** Far-reaching decision of the U.S. Supreme Court that requires law enforcement officers to warn a criminal suspect of his or her right to remain silent and have an attorney present before questioning.

misdemeanor A minor crime; the penalty is a fine or imprisonment for a short time, usually less than a year, in a local jail.

Missouri Plan A system for selecting judges that combines features of the appointive and elective methods. The governor selects judges from lists presented by panels of lawyers and laypersons, and at the end of their term, the judges may run against their own record in retention elections.

monetarism A theory that government should control the money supply to encourage economic growth and restrain inflation.

monetary policy Government policy that attempts to manage the economy by controlling the money supply and thus interest rates.

monopoly Domination of an industry by a single company by fixing prices and discouraging competition; also, the company that dominates the industry by these means.

moralistic subculture View that government's primary responsibility is to promote the public welfare and that it should actively use its authority and power to improve the social and economic well-being of its citizens.

movement A large body of people interested in a common issue, idea, or concern that is of continuing significance and who are willing to take action. Movements seek to change attitudes or institutions, not just policies.

municipal court   Court of limited jurisdiction that hears cases involving city ordinances and primarily handles traffic tickets.

national debt   The total amount of money the federal government has borrowed to finance deficit spending over the years.

national party convention   A national meeting of delegates elected in primaries, caucuses, or state conventions who assemble once every four years to nominate candidates for president and vice president, ratify the party platform, elect officers, and adopt rules.

national supremacy   Constitutional doctrine that whenever conflict occurs between the constitutionally authorized actions of the national government and those of a state or local government, the actions of the federal government prevail.

natural law   God's or nature's law that defines right from wrong and is higher than human law.

natural rights   The rights of all people to dignity and worth; also called *human rights*.

naturalization   A legal action conferring citizenship on an alien.

necessary and proper clause   Clause of the Constitution (Article I, Section 8, Clause 3) setting forth the implied powers of Congress. It states that Congress, in addition to its express powers, has the right to make all laws necessary and proper for carrying out all powers vested by the Constitution in the national government.

New Jersey Plan   Proposal at the Constitutional Convention made by William Paterson of New Jersey for a central government with a single-house legislature in which each state would be represented equally.

new judicial federalism   The practice of some state courts using the bill of rights in their state constitutions to provide more protection for some rights than is provided by the Supreme Court's interpretation of the Bill of Rights in the U.S. Constitution.

news media   Media that emphasizes the news.

nolo contendere   Plea of "no contest" to a criminal charge.

nonpartisan election   A local or judicial election in which candidates are not selected or endorsed by political parties and party affiliation is not listed on ballots.

nonprotected speech   Libel, obscenity, fighting words, and commercial speech, which are not entitled to constitutional protection in all circumstances.

North American Free Trade Agreement (NAFTA)   Agreement signed by the United States, Canada, and Mexico in 1992 to form the largest free trade zone in the world.

obscenity   Quality or state of a work that taken as a whole appeals to a prurient interest in sex by depicting sexual conduct in a patently offensive way and that lacks serious literary, artistic, political, or scientific value.

office block ballot   Ballot on which all candidates are listed under the office for which they are running, making split-ticket voting easier.

Office of Management and Budget (OMB)   Presidential staff agency that serves as a clearinghouse for budgetary requests and management improvements for government agencies.

Office of Personnel Management (OPM)   Agency that administers civil service laws, rules, and regulations.

one-party system   Domination of elections and governmental processes by a single party, which may be split into different ideological, economic, or regional factions. In Texas, the phrase is used to describe the period from the late 1870s to the late 1970s, when the Democratic Party claimed virtually all elected, partisan offices.

open primary   Primary election in which any voter, regardless of party, may vote.

open rule   A procedural rule in the House of Representatives that permits floor amendments within the overall time allocated to the bill.

open shop   A company with a labor agreement under which union membership cannot be required as a condition of employment.

opinion of the court   An explanation of a decision of the Supreme Court or any other appellate court.

ordinances   Local laws enacted by a city council.

original jurisdiction   The authority of a court to hear a case "in the first instance."

outsourcing   Contracting of government services to private firms.

override   An action taken by Congress to reverse a presidential veto, requiring a two-thirds majority in each chamber.

oversight   Legislative or executive review of a particular government program or organization. Can be in response to a crisis of some kind or part of routine review.

parliamentary system   A system of government in which the legislature selects the prime minister or president.

parole   Early release of an inmate from prison, subject to certain conditions.

party caucus   A meeting of the members of a party in a legislative chamber to select party leaders and to develop party policy. Called a *conference* by the Republicans.

party column ballot   Type of ballot that encourages party-line voting by listing all of a party's candidates in a column under the party name.

party convention   A meeting of party delegates to vote on matters of policy and in some cases to select party candidates for public office.

party identification   An informal and subjective affiliation with a political party that most people acquire in childhood.

party registration   The act of declaring party affiliation; required by some states when one registers to vote.

patronage   The dispensing of government jobs to persons who belong to the winning political party.

pay-as-you-go   Constitutional requirement that prohibits the legislature from borrowing money for the state's operating expenses.

penal code   Body of law that defines most criminal offenses and sets a range of punishments that can be assessed.

permanent normal trade relations (PNTR) status   Trade status granted as part of an international trade policy that gives a nation the same favorable trade concessions and tariffs that the best trading partners receive.

petit jury   A jury of 6 to 12 persons who determine guilt or innocence in a civil or criminal action.

petition for review   Petition to the Texas Supreme Court claiming that legal or procedural mistakes were made in the lower court.

place system   Form of at-large election in which candidates run for specific positions, or places, on a city council or other governing body.

plaintiff   Individual or party who initiates a lawsuit.

plea bargain   Agreement between a prosecutor and a defendant that the defendant will plead guilty to a lesser offense to avoid having to stand trial for a more serious offense.

plural executive   A fragmented system of authority under which most statewide executive officeholders are elected independently of the governor.

pluralism   Political system in which power is distributed among multiple groups.

plurality   Candidate or party with the most votes cast in an election, not necessarily more than half.

pocket veto   A veto exercised by the president after Congress has adjourned; if the president takes no action for ten days, the bill does not become law and is not returned to Congress for a possible override.

police powers   Inherent powers of state governments to pass laws to protect the public health, safety, and welfare; the national government has no directly granted police powers but accomplishes the same goals through other delegated powers.

policy agenda   The informal list of issues that Congress and the president consider most important for action.

political action committee (PAC)   The political arm of an interest group that is legally entitled to raise funds on a voluntary basis from members, stockholders, or employees in order to contribute funds to favored candidates or political parties.

political culture   The widely shared beliefs, values, and norms concerning the relationship of citizens to government and to one another.

political ideology   A consistent pattern of beliefs about political values and the role of government.

political party   An organization that seeks political power by electing people to office so that its positions and philosophy become public policy.

political patronage   The hiring of government employees on the basis of personal friendships or favors rather than ability or merit.

political predisposition   A characteristic of individuals that is predictive of political behavior.

political question   A dispute that requires knowledge of a nonlegal character or the use of techniques not suitable for a court or explicitly assigned by the Constitution to Congress or the president; judges refuse to answer constitutional questions that they declare are political.

political socialization   The process, most notably in families and schools, by which we develop our political attitudes, values, and beliefs.

poll tax   Payment required as a condition for voting; prohibited for national elections by the Twenty-Fourth Amendment (1964) and ruled unconstitutional for all elections in *Harper* v. *Virginia Board of Elections* (1966).

popular consent   The idea that a just government must derive its powers from the consent of the people it governs.

popular sovereignty   A belief that ultimate power resides in the people.

population density   Number of residents living within the boundaries of a city, county, or state in relationship to the land area. Population density is a significant factor in determining the level of local public services.

precinct chair   Local officer in a political party who presides over the precinct convention and serves on the party's county executive committee. Voters in each precinct elect a chair in the party's primary election.

precinct convention   Meeting held by a political party in each precinct on the same day as the party primary. In presidential election years, the precinct conventions and the primaries are the first steps in the selection of delegates to the major parties' national nominating conventions.

precincts   Specific local voting areas created by county commissioners courts. The state election code provides detailed requirements for drawing up these election units.

preemption   Associated with the Bush doctrine, a belief that a nation is justified in attacking another nation to prevent possible attacks on itself. Also, the right of a federal law or regulation to preclude enforcement of a state or local law or regulation.

preferred position doctrine   Interpretation of the First Amendment that holds that freedom of expression is so essential to democracy that governments should not punish persons for what they say, only for what they do.

president pro tempore   Officer of the Senate selected by the majority party to act as chair in the absence of the vice president.

presidential ticket   The joint listing of the presidential and vice presidential candidates on the same ballot as required by the Twelfth Amendment.

prior restraint   Censorship imposed before a speech is made or a newspaper is published; usually presumed to be unconstitutional.

privatization   Contracting public services to private organizations, including the power to collect revenues.

pro bono   To serve the public good; term used to describe work that lawyers (or other professionals) do for which they receive no fees.

probation   Procedure under which a convicted criminal is not sent to prison if he or she meets certain conditions, such as restrictions on travel and associates.

procedural due process   Constitutional requirement that governments proceed by proper methods; places limits on how governmental power may be exercised.

progressive tax   A tax graduated so that people with higher incomes pay a larger fraction of their income than people with lower incomes.

property rights   The rights of an individual to own, use, rent, invest in, buy, and sell property.

proportional representation   An election system in which each party running receives the proportion of legislative seats corresponding to its proportion of the vote.

prosecution   Conduct of legal proceedings against an individual charged with a crime.

protectionism   Policy of erecting trade barriers to protect domestic industry.

public assistance   Aid to the poor; "welfare."

public defender system   Arrangement whereby public officials are hired to provide legal assistance to people accused of crimes who are unable to hire their own attorneys.

public improvement district   Specific area of a city in which property owners pay special taxes in return for improvements to streets and other public facilities in their neighborhood.

public opinion   The distribution of individual preferences for or evaluations of a given issue, candidate, or institution within a specific population.

public policy   A specific course of action taken by government to achieve a public goal.

quid pro quo   Something given with the expectation of receiving something in return.

quorum   Required number of the members of a governing body who must be present so that official business, such as voting, can be conducted. In Texas, a quorum of the house and the senate is two-thirds of the membership. For committees, it is a majority of the members.

race   A grouping of human beings with distinctive characteristics determined by genetic inheritance.

racial gerrymandering   The drawing of election districts so as to ensure that members of a certain race are a minority in the district; ruled unconstitutional in *Gomillion* v. *Lightfoot* (1960).

racial profiling   Police targeting of racial minorities as potential suspects of criminal activities.

Radical Reconstructionists   The group of Republicans who took control of the U.S. Congress in 1866 and imposed hated military governments on the former Confederate states after the Civil War.

Railroad Commission   A three-member, elected body that has some oversight over rail safety but now primarily regulates oil and natural gas production in Texas.

rally point   A rise in public approval of the president that follows a crisis as Americans "rally 'round the flag" and the chief executive.

realigning election   An election during periods of expanded suffrage and change in the economy and society that proves to be a turning point, redefining the agenda of politics and the alignment of voters within parties.

realignment   Major shift in political party support or identification that usually occurs around a critical election. In Texas, realignment took place as a gradual transformation from a one-party system dominated by Democrats to a two-party system in which Republicans became competitive in elections.

reapportionment   The assigning by Congress of congressional seats after each census. State legislatures reapportion state legislative districts.

recall   Procedure for submitting to popular vote the removal of public officials from office before the end of their term.

recidivist   A repeat offender.

record vote   Vote taken in the house or the senate of which a permanent record is kept, listing how individual legislators voted.

redistributive policies   Governmental tax and social programs that shift wealth or benefits from one segment of the population to another, often from the rich to the poor.

redistricting   The redrawing of congressional and other legislative district lines following the census, to accommodate population shifts and keep districts as equal as possible in population.

reduction veto   The power of governors in a few states to reduce a particular appropriation.

referendum   Procedure for submitting to popular vote measures passed by the legislature or proposed amendments to a state constitution.

Reform party   A minor party founded by Ross Perot in 1995. It focuses on national government reform, fiscal responsibility, and political accountability. It has recently struggled with internal strife and criticism that it lacks an identity.

regressive tax   A tax whereby people with lower incomes pay a higher fraction of their income than people with higher incomes.

regular session   140-day period in the odd-numbered years in which the legislature meets and can consider and pass laws on any issue or subject.

regulation   Efforts by government to alter the free operation of the market to achieve social goals such as protecting workers and the environment.

regulations   The formal instructions that government issues for implementing laws.

regulatory taking   Government regulation of property so extensive that government is deemed to have taken the property by the power of eminent domain, for which it must compensate the property owners.

reinforcing cleavages   Divisions within society that reinforce one another, making groups more homogeneous or similar.

Religious Right   Political movement, based primarily in evangelical Protestant churches, that has played an increasingly prominent role in Texas and national politics.

representative democracy   Government that derives its powers indirectly from the people, who elect those who will govern; also called a *republic*.

republic   Form of government in which representatives of the people, rather than the people themselves, govern.

responsibility contract   A welfare strategy adopted by some states in which recipients sign a written agreement specifying their responsibilities and outlining a plan for obtaining work and achieving self-sufficiency.

restrictive covenant   A provision in a deed to real property prohibiting its sale to a person of a particular race or religion. Judicial enforcement of such deeds is unconstitutional.

retention elections Elections in which judges run on their own records rather than against other candidates. Voters cast their ballots on the question of whether the incumbent judge should stay in office.

revenue bonds Bonds that are used to finance construction of a public facility and are repaid with income produced by the facility.

revision commission A state commission that recommends changes in the state constitution for action by the legislature and vote by the voters.

revolving door Employment cycle in which individuals who work for governmental agencies regulating interests eventually end up working for interest groups or businesses with the same policy concern.

rider A provision attached to a bill—to which it may or may not be related—in order to secure its passage.

right of expatriation The right to renounce one's citizenship.

right-to-work law Law prohibiting the requirement of union membership in order to hold or get a job.

rollback election Election in which local voters can nullify a property tax increase that exceeds 8 percent in a given year.

rule A precise legal definition of how government will implement a policy.

rule-making process The formal process for making regulations.

runoff elections Elections that are required if no candidate receives an absolute majority of the votes cast in a city council, school district, or party primary race. The runoff is between the two top vote-getters.

safe seat An elected office that is predictably won by one party or the other, so the success of that party's candidate is almost taken for granted.

sales tax General tax on sales transactions, sometimes exempting food and drugs.

school board Governing body of a school district. Its responsibilities include the development or approval of educational policies, approval of the budget, hiring of the superintendent, and other personnel matters.

school superintendent Top administrator of a school district. He or she is hired by the elected school board to direct the district's daily operations.

search warrant A writ issued by a magistrate that authorizes the police to search a particular place or person, specifying the place to be searched and the objects to be seized.

second reading Initial debate by the full house or senate on a bill that has been approved by a committee.

secretary of state The official who administers state election laws, grants charters to corporations, and processes the extradition of prisoners to other states. This officeholder is appointed by the governor.

sedition Attempting to overthrow the government by force or to interrupt its activities by violence.

selective exposure The process by which individuals screen out messages that do not conform to their own biases.

selective incorporation The process by which provisions of the Bill of Rights are brought within the scope of the Fourteenth Amendment and so applied to state and local governments.

selective perception The process by which individuals perceive what they want to in media messages.

senatorial courtesy Presidential custom of submitting the names of prospective appointees for approval to senators from the states in which the appointees are to work.

Senior Executive Service Established by Congress in 1978 as a flexible, mobile corps of senior career executives who work closely with presidential appointees to manage government.

seniority rule A legislative practice that assigns the chair of a committee or subcommittee to the member of the majority party with the longest continuous service on the committee.

separation of powers Constitutional division of powers among the legislative, executive, and judicial branches, with the legislative branch making law, the executive applying and enforcing the law, and the judiciary interpreting the law.

severance tax A tax on the privilege of "severing" such natural resources as coal, oil, timber, and gas from the land.

Shays' Rebellion Rebellion by farmers in western Massachusetts in 1786–1787, protesting mortgage foreclosures; led by Daniel Shays and important because it highlighted the need for a strong national government just as the call for the Constitutional Convention went out.

sheriff Elected official who is the chief law enforcement officer of a county.

single-member district An electoral district in which voters choose one representative or official.

social capital Democratic and civic habits of discussion, compromise, and respect for differences, which grow out of participation in voluntary organizations.

social insurance Programs in which eligibility is based on prior contributions to government, usually in the form of payroll taxes.

Social Security A combination of entitlement programs, paid for by employer and employee taxes, that includes retirement benefits, health insurance, and support for disabled workers and the children of deceased or disabled workers.

social stratification Divisions in a community among socio-economic groups or classes.

socialism An economic and governmental system based on public ownership of the means of production and exchange.

socioeconomic status (SES) A division of population based on occupation, income, and education.

soft money Money raised in unlimited amounts by political parties for party-building purposes. Now largely illegal except for limited contributions to state and local parties for voter registration and get-out-the-vote efforts.

Speaker The presiding officer in the House of Representatives, formally elected by the House but actually selected by the majority party.

special or select committee A congressional committee created for a specific purpose, sometimes to conduct an investigation.

special purpose districts Units of local government created by the state to perform specific functions not met by cities or counties, including the provision of public services to unincorporated areas.

special session A legislative session that can be called at any time by the governor. This session is limited to thirty days and to issues or subjects designated by the governor.

special, or select, committees Special panels appointed to study major policy issues.

split ticket A vote for some of one party's candidates and some of another party's.

spoils system A system of public employment based on rewarding party loyalists and friends.

staggered terms Terms that begin on different dates, a requirement for members of state boards and commissions appointed by the governor.

standing committee A permanent committee established in a legislature, usually focusing on a policy area.

stare decisis The rule of precedent, whereby a rule or law contained in a judicial decision is commonly viewed as binding on judges whenever the same question is presented.

State Board of Education An elected panel that oversees the administration of public education in Texas.

state chair and vice chair Two top state leaders of a political party, one of whom must be a woman. They are selected every two years by delegates to the party's state convention.

state convention Meeting held in June of even-numbered years by each of the two major political parties. Delegates to this convention elect the party's state leadership and adopt a party platform. In presidential election years, the state convention selects the delegates to the party's national nominating convention.

state executive committee Statewide governing board of a political party. It includes a man and a woman from each of the thirty-one state senatorial districts and the state chair and vice chair, who are selected by delegates to the party's biennial state convention.

State of the Union Address The president's annual statement to Congress and the nation.

state treasurer This elective office was created by the Constitution of 1876 to manage state funds. It was abolished by the voters in 1995, and its duties were transferred to the comptroller's office.

states' rights Powers expressly or implicitly reserved to the states and emphasized by decentralists.

statism The idea that the rights of the nation are supreme over the rights of the individuals residing in that nation.

statutes Laws enacted by a legislative body.

statutory county court Court that exercises limited jurisdiction over criminal and/or civil cases. The jurisdiction of these courts varies from county to county.

statutory law Law enacted by a legislative body.

straight ticket A vote for all of one party's candidates.

strong mayor-council form Form of local government in which the voters directly elect the city council and the mayor, who enjoys almost total administrative authority and appoints the department heads.

subcommittee A few members of a larger committee appointed to review a particular bill and make recommendations on its disposition to the full committee.

subpoenas Court orders requiring people to testify in court or before grand juries or to produce certain documents.

substantive due process Constitutional requirement that governments act reasonably and that the substance of the laws themselves be fair and reasonable; places limits on what a government may do.

sunset The process under which most state agencies have to be periodically reviewed and recreated by the legislature or go out of business.

tag Rule that allows an individual senator to postpone a committee hearing on any bill for at least forty-eight hours, a delay that can be fatal to a bill during the closing days of a legislative session.

take care clause The constitutional requirement (in Article II, Section 3) that presidents take care that the laws are faithfully executed, even if they disagree with the purpose of those laws.

tariff Tax levied on imports to help protect a nation's industries, labor, or farmers from foreign competition. It can also be used to raise additional revenue.

tax abatements Exemptions from property taxes granted to certain businesses, usually to encourage them to move to or expand their operations in a city or county. The exemptions are granted for specific periods.

tax assessor-collector Elected official who determines how much property tax is owed on the different pieces of property within a county and then collects the tax.

tax expenditure Loss of tax revenue due to federal laws that provide special tax incentives or benefits to individuals or businesses.

Texas Court of Criminal Appeals Nine-member court with final appellate jurisdiction over criminal cases.

Texas Supreme Court Nine-member court with final appellate jurisdiction over civil lawsuits.

"The Establishment" In the days of one-party Democratic politics in Texas, the Establishment was a loosely knit coalition of Anglo business and oil company executives, bankers, and lawyers who controlled state policy making through the dominant conservative wing of the Democratic Party.

The Federalist Series of essays promoting ratification of the Constitution, published anonymously by Alexander Hamilton, John Jay, and James Madison in 1787 and 1788.

theocracy Government by religious leaders, who claim divine guidance.

third reading Final presentation of a bill before the full house or senate.

three-fifths compromise Compromise agreement between northern and southern states at the Constitutional Convention that three-fifths of the slave population would be counted for determining direct taxation and representation in the House of Representatives.

tort law Law relating to injuries to person, reputation, or property.

tort reform Changes in state law to put limits on personal injury lawsuits and damage judgments entered by the courts.

trade deficit An imbalance in international trade in which the value of imports exceeds the value of exports.

traditionalistic subculture View that political power should be concentrated in the hands of a few elite citizens who belong to established families or influential social groups. Public policy basically serves the interests of this small group.

transnational regionalism Expanding economic and social interdependence of South Texas and Mexico.

treaty A formal, public agreement between the United States and one or more nations that must be approved by two-thirds of the Senate.

trust A monopoly that controls goods and services, often in combinations that reduce competition.

trustee An official who is expected to vote independently, based on his or her judgment of the circumstances; one interpretation of the role of a legislator.

turnout The proportion of the voting-age public that votes, sometimes defined as the number of registered voters that vote.

two-party state A state in which the two major parties alternate in winning majorities.

two-party system Political system that has two dominant parties, such as that of the United States.

two-thirds rule Procedure under which the Texas senate has traditionally operated that requires approval of at least two-thirds of senators before a bill can be debated on the senate floor. It allows a minority of senators to block controversial legislation.

uncontrollable spending The portion of the federal budget that is spent on programs, such as Social Security, that the president and Congress are unwilling to cut.

unemployment The number of Americans who are out of work, but actively looking for a job. The number does not usually include those who are not looking.

unicameral legislature A one-house legislature.

union shop A company in which new employees must join a union within a stated time period.

unitary system Constitutional arrangement in which power is concentrated in a central government.

urbanization Process by which a predominantly rural society or area becomes urban.

value-added tax (VAT) A tax on increased value of a product at each stage of production and distribution rather than just at the point of sale.

veniremen Members of a panel from which a petit, or trial, jury is chosen.

veto Rejection by a president or governor of legislation passed by a legislature.

Virginia Plan Initial proposal at the Constitutional Convention made by the Virginia delegation for a strong central government with a bicameral legislature, the lower house to be elected by the voters and the upper chosen by the lower.

voter registration System designed to reduce voter fraud by limiting voting to those who have established eligibility by submitting the proper form.

Voting Rights Act Federal law designed to protect the voting rights of minorities by requiring the Justice Department's approval of changes in political districts and certain other electoral procedures. The 1965 act, as amended, has eliminated most of the restrictive practices that limited minority political participation.

vouchers Money provided by the government to parents for payment of their children's tuition in a public or private school of their choice.

ward politics Term, often with negative connotations, that refers to partisan politics linked to political favoritism.

weak mayor-council form Form of local government in which the members of the city council select the mayor, who then shares power with other elected or appointed boards and commissions.

weapons of mass destruction Biological, chemical, and nuclear weapons that can inflict massive casualties in a single event.

whip Party leader who is the liaison between the leadership and the rank-and-file in the legislature.

whistleblower A public employee who reports illegal activities or "blows the whistle" on agency wrongdoing.

white primary Primary operated by the Democratic party in southern states that, before Republicans gained strength in the "one-party South," essentially constituted an election; ruled unconstitutional in *Smith* v. *Allwright* (1944).

winner-take-all system An election system in which the candidate with the most votes wins.

women's suffrage The right of women to vote.

workfare A welfare strategy adopted by some states that gives able-bodied adults who do not have preschool-aged children the opportunity to learn job skills that can lead to employment.

World Trade Organization (WTO) International organization derived from the General Agreement on Tariffs and Trade (GATT) that promotes free trade around the world.

writ of certiorari A formal writ used to bring a case before the Supreme Court.

writ of habeas corpus Court order requiring explanation to a judge why a prisoner is being held in custody.

writ of mandamus Court order directing an official to perform an official duty.

Notes

Chapter 1

1. George W. Bush, "President Discusses War on Terrorism," Office of the Press Secretary, 8 November 2001. At www.whitehouse.gov/news/releases/2001/11/20011108-13, 24 November 2003.
2. Robert A. Dahl, *On Democracy* (Yale University Press, 1998), p. 145.
3. Harold Stanley and Richard Niemi, *Vital Statistics on American Politics, 2001–2002* (CQ Press, 2001), pp. 25–29.
4. For a major theoretical work on the principle of majority rule, see Robert A. Dahl, *Democracy and Its Critics* (Yale University Press, 1989).
5. *Reitman v. Mulkey*, 387 U.S. 369 (1967).
6. David B. Magleby, *Direct Legislation: Voting on Ballot Propositions in the United States* (Baltimore: Johns Hopkins University Press, 1984), p. 119.
7. Seymour Martin Lipset, "The Social Requisites of Democracy Revisited," *American Sociological Review* 59 (1994), pp. 1–22.
8. For a discussion of the importance for democracy of such overlapping group memberships, see David Truman's seminal work, *The Governmental Process,* 2d ed. (Knopf, 1971).
9. Joyce Appleby, "The American Heritage: The Heirs and the Disinherited," *Journal of American History* 74 (December 1987), p. 808.
10. Kevin Butterfield, "What You Should Know About the Declaration of Independence," *St. Louis Post-Dispatch,* July 4, 2000, p. F1.
11. Richard L. Hillard, "Liberalism, Civic Humanism and the American Revolutionary Bill of Rights, 1775–1790," paper presented at the annual meeting of the Organization of American Historians, Reno, Nevada, March 26, 1988.
12. Quoted in Charles L. Mee Jr., *The Genius of the People* (Harper & Row, 1987), p. 51.
13. Seymour Martin Lipset, "George Washington and the Founding of Democracy," *Journal of Democracy* 9 (October 1998), p. 31.
14. See the essays in Thomas E. Cronin, ed., *Inventing the American Presidency* (University Press of Kansas, 1989). See also Richard J. Ellis, ed., *Founding the American Presidency* (Rowman & Littlefield, 1999).
15. Charles A. Beard and Mary R. Beard, *A Basic History of the United States* (New Home Library, 1944), p. 136.
16. See Herbert J. Storing, ed., abridgment by Murray Dry, *The Anti-Federalist: Writings by the Opponents of the Constitution* (University of Chicago Press, 1985).
17. On the role of the promised bill of rights amendments in the ratification of the Constitution, see Leonard W. Levy, *Constitutional Opinions* (Oxford University Press, 1986), chap. 6.

Chapter 2

1. Max Lerner, *Ideas for the Ice Age* (Viking, 1941), pp. 241–242.
2. Sanford Levinson, *Constitutional Faith* (Princeton University Press, 1988), pp. 9–52.
3. Richard Morin, "We Love It—What We Know of It," *Washington Post National Weekly Edition,* September 22, 1997, p. 35.
4. Thomas Jefferson, quoted in Alpheus T. Mason, *The Supreme Court: Palladium of Freedom* (University of Michigan Press, 1962), p. 10.
5. Alexander Hamilton, James Madison, and John Jay, *The Federalist Papers,* ed. Clinton Rossiter (New American Library, 1961), p. 301.
6. Justice Brandeis dissenting in *Myers v. United States,* 272 U.S. 52 (1926).
7. James L. Sundquist, "Needed: A Political Theory for the New Era of Coalition Government in the United States," *Political Science Quarterly* 103 (1988), pp. 613–635; Robert A. Godwin and Art Kaufman, eds., *Separation of Powers: Does It Still Work?* (AEI Press, 1986).
8. Charles O. Jones, "The Separate Presidency," in Anthony King, ed., *The New American Political System,* 2d ed. (AEI Press, 1990), p. 3.
9. Morris P. Fiorina, "An Era of Divided Government," *Political Science Quarterly* 107 (1992), p. 407.
10. David R. Mayhew, *Divided We Govern: Party Control, Lawmaking, and Investigations, 1946–1990* (Yale University Press, 1991), p. 4. See also James A. Thurber, ed., *Divided Democracy: Presidents and Congress in Cooperation and Conflict* (CQ Press, 1991).

11. Charles O. Jones, *Separate but Equal Branches: Congress and the Presidency* (Chatham House, 1995).
12. Judith A. Best, *The Choice of the People? Debating the Electoral College* (Rowman & Littlefield, 1996).
13. See Alec Stone Sweet, Wayne Sandholtz, and Neil Fligstein, *The Institutionalization of Europe* (Oxford University Press, 2001); Alec Stone Sweet, *Governing with Judges: Constitutional Politics in Europe* (Oxford University Press, 2000); and Anne-Marie Slaughter, Alec Stone Sweet, and J. H. H. Weiler, *The European Court and National Courts—Doctrine, Jurisprudence: Legal Change in Its Social Context* (Hart, 1998).
14. *Marbury* v. *Madison,* 1 Cranch 137 (1803).
15. Dumas Malone, *Jefferson the President: First Term, 1801–1805* (Little, Brown, 1970), p. 145.
16. J. W. Peltason, *Federal Courts in the Political Process* (Random House, 1955).
17. See Eleanore Bushnell, *Crimes, Follies, and Misfortunes: The Federal Impeachment Trials* (University of Illinois Press, 1992), and Michael J. Gerhardt, *The Federal Impeachment Process: A Constitutional and Historical Analysis* (Princeton University Press, 1996).
18. Richard E. Neustadt, *Presidential Power* (Free Press, 1990), pp. 180–181.
19. See John R. Vile, ed., *Proposed Amendments to the U.S. Constitution: 1787–2001* (The Lawbook Exchange, 2003).
20. Ann Stuart Diamond, "A Convention for Proposing Amendments: The Constitution's Other Method," *Publius* 11 (Summer 1981), pp. 113–146; Wilbur Edel, "Amending the Constitution by Convention: Myths and Realities," *State Government* 55 (1982), pp. 51–56.
21. Russell L. Caplan, *Constitutional Brinksmanship: Amending the Constitution by National Convention* (Oxford University Press, 1988), p. x. See also David E. Kyvig, *Explicit and Authentic Acts: Amending the U.S. Constitution, 1776–1995* (University Press of Kansas, 1996), p. 440.
22. Samuel S. Freedman and Pamela J. Naughton, *ERA: May a State Change Its Vote?* (Wayne State University Press, 1979).
23. Kyvig, *Explicit and Authentic Acts,* p. 286; *Dillon* v. *Gloss,* 256 U.S. 368 (1921).
24. Gregory A. Caldeira, "Constitutional Change in America: Dynamics of Ratification Under Article V," *Publius* 15 (Fall 1985), p. 29.
25. Mark R. Daniels, Robert Darcy, and Joseph W. Westphal, "The ERA Won—at Least in the Opinion Polls," *P.S.: Political Science and Politics* (Fall 1982), p. 583.
26. Janet K. Boles, *The Politics of the Equal Rights Amendment: Conflict and Decision-Making Powers* (Longman, 1979), p. 4.
27. Gilbert Y. Steiner, *Constitutional Inequality: The Political Fortunes of the Equal Rights Amendment* (Brookings Institution Press, 1985), p. 64. See also Mary Frances Berry, *Why the ERA Failed: Politics, Women's Rights, and the Amending Process of the Constitution* (Indiana University Press, 1986).

Chapter 3

1. Quoted in Elisabeth Bumiller, "Marriage Amendment Backed," *The New York Times,* December 17, 2003, p. A30.
2. See Nicol C. Rae, "A Right too Far? The Congressional Politics of DOMA and ENDA," in Colton C. Campbell and John F. Stack, Jr., eds., *Congress and the Politics of Emerging Rights* 65 (Rowman & Littlefield, 2002).
3. John P. Feldmeler, "Federalism and Full Faith and Credit: Must States Recognize Out-of-State Same-Sex Marriages?" *Publius* 25 (Fall 1995), p. 126.
4. See Jeremy D. Mayer and Louis-Philippe Rochon, "Gay Rights in the USA: The States Lead the Way," *Federations* 2 (November 2001).
5. *Lawrence* v. *Texas,* 539 U.S. 558 (2003).
6. For background, see Samuel H. Beer, *To Make a Nation: The Rediscovery of American Federalism* (Harvard University Press, 1993).
7. The term "devolution revolution" was coined by Richard P. Nathan in testimony before the Senate Finance Committee; quoted in Daniel Patrick Moynihan, "The Devolution Revolution," *The New York Times,* August 6, 1995, p. B15.
8. See Michael Burgess, *Federalism and the European Union: The Building of Europe, 1950–2000* (Routledge, 2000), and Kalypso Nicolaidis and

Robert Howse, eds., *The Federal Vision: Legitimacy and Levels of Governance in the United States and the European Union* (Oxford University Press, 2001).

9. *United States* v. *Lopez*, 514 U.S. 549 (1995).

10. *Alden* v. *Maine*, 527 U.S. 706 (1999); *Kimel* v. *Florida Board of Regents*, 528 U.S. 62 (2000); *Vermont Agency of Natural Resources* v. *United States ex rel. Stevens*, 529 U.S. 765 (2000).

11. *Saenz* v. *Roe*, 526 U.S. 489 (1999).

12. *Reno* v. *Condon*, 528 U.S. 141 (2000).

13. Martha Derthick, "American Federalism: Half-Full or Half-Empty?" *Brookings Review* (Winter 2000), pp. 24–27.

14. William H. Stewart, *Concepts of Federalism* (Center for the Study of Federalism/University Press of America, 1984). See also Preston King, *Federalism and Federation*, 2d ed. (Cass, 2001).

15. Morton Grodzins, "The Federal System," in *Goals for Americans: The Report of the President's Commission on National Goals* (Columbia University Press, 1960).

16. Thomas R. Dye, *American Federalism: Competition Among Governments* (Lexington Books, 1990), pp. 13–17.

17. Michael D. Reagan and John G. Sanzone, *The New Federalism* (Oxford University Press, 1981), p. 175.

18. Gregory S. Mahler, *Comparative Politics: An Institutional and Cross-National Approach* (Prentice Hall, 2000), p. 31.

19. Frederick K. Lister, *The European Union, the United Nations, and the Revival of Confederal Governance* (Greenwood Press, 1996); Daniel J. Elazar, "The United States and the European Union: Models for their Epochs," in Nicolaidis and Howse, *The Federal Vision*, pp. 31–52.

20. William H. Riker, *The Development of American Federalism* (Academic, 1987), pp. 14–15. Riker contends not only that federalism does not guarantee freedom but also that the framers of our federal system, as well as those of other nations, were animated not by considerations of safeguarding freedom but by practical considerations of preserving unity.

21. The Court, however, ruled in several recent cases that Congress exceeded its power to regulate interstate commerce. See *Printz* v. *United States*, 521 U.S. 898 (1997); *United States* v. *Lopez*, 514 U.S. 549 (1995); *New York* v. *United States*, 505 U.S. 144 (1992); and *United States* v. *Morrison*, 529 U.S. 598 (2000).

22. *Gibbons* v. *Ogden*, 9 Wheaton (22 U.S.) 1 (1824).

23. *Champion* v. *Ames*, 188 U.S. 321 (1907).

24. *Caminetti* v. *United States*, 242 U.S. 470 (1917).

25. *Federal Radio Commission* v. *Nelson Brothers*, 289 U.S. 266 (1933).

26. *Heart of Atlanta Motel* v. *United States*, 379 U.S. 241 (1964).

27. See *United States* v. *Morrison*, 529 U.S. 598 (2000), striking down the Violence Against Women Act.

28. See *New York* v. *United States*, 505 U.S. 144 (1992), and *Printz* v. *United States*, 521 U.S. 898 (1997).

29. Ibid.

30. *Seminole Tribe of Florida* v. *Florida*, 517 U.S. 44 (1996); *Alden* v. *Maine*, 527 U.S. 706 (1999); *Kimel* v. *Florida Board of Regents*, 528 U.S. 62 (2000).

31. See *Franchise Tax Board of California* v. *Hyatt*, 538 U.S.488 (2003).

32. *California* v. *Superior Courts of California*, 482 U.S. 400 (1987).

33. David C. Nice, "State Participation in Interstate Compacts," *Publius* 17 (Spring 1987), p. 70. See also Council of State Governments, *Interstate Compacts and Agencies* (1995), for a list of compacts by subject and by state with brief descriptions.

34. *McCulloch* v. *Maryland*, 4 Wheaton 316 (1819).

35. Joseph F. Zimmerman, "Federal Preemption Under Reagan's New Federalism," *Publius* 21 (Winter 1991), pp. 7–28.

36. Oliver Wendell Holmes Jr., *Collected Legal Papers* (Harcourt, 1920), pp. 295–296.

37. *U.S. Term Limits, Inc.* v. *Thornton*, 514 U.S. 779 (1995).

38. *Garcia* v. *San Antonio Metro*, 469 U.S. 528 (1985).

39. See, for example, *United States* v. *Lopez*, 514 U.S. 549 (1995).

40. *U.S. Term Limits, Inc.* v. *Thornton*, 514 U.S. 779 (1995).

41. *Seminole Tribe of Florida* v. *Florida*, 517 U.S. 44 (1996).

42. *Alden* v. *Maine*, 527 U.S. 706 (1999); *Kimel* v. *Florida Board of Regents*, 528 U.S. 62 (2000); *Vermont Agency of Natural Resources* v. *United States ex rel. Stevens*, 529 U.S. 765 (2000).

43. George Will, "A Revival of Federalism?" *Newsweek*, May 29, 2000, p. 78.

44. *United States* v. *Morrison*, 529 U.S. 598 (2000).

45. John E. Chubb, "The Political Economy of Federalism," *American Political Science Review* 79 (December 1985), p. 1005.

46. Paul E. Peterson, *The Price of Federalism* (Brookings Institution Press, 1995), p. 127.

47. Donald F. Kettl, *The Regulation of American Federalism* (Johns Hopkins University Press, 1987), pp. 154–155.

48. See Paul J. Posner, *The Politics of Unfunded Mandates: Whither Federalism?* (Georgetown University Press, 1998).

49. Joseph Zimmerman, "Congressional Regulation of Subnational Governments," *PS: Political Science and Politics* 26 (June 1993), p. 179.

50. See Jerome J. Hanus, ed., *The Nationalization of State Government* (Heath, 1981).

51. Advisory Commission on Intergovernmental Relations, *Restoring Confidence and Competence* (Advisory Commission on Intergovernmental Relations, 1981), p. 30.

52. Cynthia Cates Colella, "The Creation, Care and Feeding of the Leviathan: Who and What Makes Government Grow," *Intergovernmental Perspective* (Fall 1979), p. 9.

53. Aaron Wildavsky, "Bare Bones: Putting Flesh on the Skeleton of American Federalism," in *The Future of Federalism in the 1980s* (Advisory Commission on Intergovernmental Relations, 1981), p. 79.

54. Peterson, *Price of Federalism*, p. 182.

55. John Kinkaid, "Devolution in the United States: Rhetoric and Reality," in Nicolaidis and Howse, *The Federal Vision*, p. 144.

56. Eliza Newlin Carney, "Power Grab," *National Journal*, April 11, 1998, p. 798.

57. Luther Gulick, "Reorganization of the States," *Civil Engineering* (August 1933), pp. 420–421.

58. David E. Osborne, *Laboratories of Democracy* (Harvard Business School Press, 1988), p. 363.

59. Dye, *American Federalism*, p. 199.

60. Richard A. Oppel and Christopher Drew, "States Planning Their Own Suits on Power Plants: Battle that E.P.A. Quit," *The New York Times*, November 9, 2003, p. A1; and Scott Richards and Yvette Hurt, "States Sue the Federal Environmental Agency," *Federations* 11 (November, 2003).

61. Edward Felsenthal, "Firms Ask Congress to Pass Uniform Rules," *Wall Street Journal*, May 10, 1993, p. B4.

62. John J. DiIulio Jr. and Donald F. Kettl, *Fine Print: The Contract with America, Devolution, and the Administrative Realities of American Federalism* (Brookings Institution Press, 1995), p. 60.

63. Kincaid, "Devolution in the United States," p. 148.

Chapter 4

1. Robert D. Putnam, "Bowling Alone: America's Declining Social Capital," *Journal of Democracy* 6 (January 1995), pp. 65–78. See also Robert D. Putnam, *Bowling Alone: The Collapse and Revival of American Community* (Simon & Schuster, 2000), and Robert D. Putnam, "Bowling Together," *American Prospect* 13 (February 11, 2002), pp. 20–22.

2. See Pippa Norris, "Does Television Erode Social Capital? A Reply to Putnam," PS: *Political Science and Politics* 29 (September 1996), pp. 474–479. See also Everett Carl Ladd, *The Ladd Report* (Free Press, 1999), and Michael Schudson, *The Good Citizen: A History of American Civic Life* (Harvard University Press, 1998).

3. Putnam, "Bowling Together."

4. Clinton Rossiter, *Conservatism in America* (Vintage, 1962), p. 72.

5. Bernard Bailyn, *The Ideological Origins of the American Revolution* (Belknap Press, 1967); Gordon S. Wood, *The Creation of the American Republic, 1776–1787* (University of North Carolina Press, 1969).

6. See Ronald Dworkin, *Taking Rights Seriously* (Harvard University Press, 1977).

7. *Marbury* v. *Madison*, 1 Cranch 137 (1803).

8. "A Nation Challenged: Excerpts from President's Speech: 'We Will Prevail' in War on Terrorism," *The New York Times*, November 9, 2001, p. B1.

9. Robert Coles, *The Political Life of Children* (Atlantic Monthly Press, 1986).

10. Fred I. Greenstein, *Children and Politics* (Yale University Press, 1965).

11. Raymond E. Wolfinger and Steven Rosenstone, *Who Votes?* (Yale University Press, 1980).

12. Franklin Boudotte, "Education for Citizenship," *Public Opinion Quarterly* (Summer 1942): 269–279.

13. Rachel X. Weissman, "The Kids Are All Right—They're Just a Little Converged," *American Demographics* 20, no. 12 (December 1998), pp. 30–32.

14. www.commoncause.org/laundromat/stat/top50.htm.

15. Floyd Norris and Joseph Kahn, "Enron's Many Strands: The Overview; Rule Makers Take On Loopholes That Enron Used in Hiding Debt," *The New York Times*, February 14, 2002, p. A1.

16. www.opensecrets.org/races/summary.asp?ID=NJSI&Cycle=2000.

17. Glen Justice, "Advocacy Groups Reflect on Their Role in the Election," *The New York Times*, November 5, 2004, p. A1.

18. See Michael B. Katz, *The "Underclass" Debate* (Princeton University Press, 1993); Theodore Dalrymple, *Life at the Bottom: The Worldview That Makes the Underclass* (Dee, 2001); and Charles A. Murray, *The Underclass Revisited* (AEI Press, 1999).

19. When adjusted using the consumer price index (CPI), the percentage of households earning over $75,000 a year has risen from 10.1 percent in 1970 to 22.6 percent in 1999. U.S. Bureau of the Census, *Statistical Abstracts of the United States, 2001* (Government Printing Office, 2001), tab. 661.

20. Bailyn, *Ideological Origins*.

21. Robert A. Dahl, "Liberal Democracy in the United States," in William Livingston, ed., *A Prospect of Liberal Democracy* (University of Texas Press, 1979), p. 64.

22. Ibid., pp. 59–60.

23. Franklin D. Roosevelt, State of the Union Address, January 11, 1944, in *The Public Papers of the President of the United States, 1944* (Government Printing Office, 1962), pp. 371–394.

24. Harry S Truman, State of the Union Address, 1949, in *The Public Papers of the President of the United States, 1949* (Government Printing Office, 1964), pp. 1–7.

25. E. J. Dionne Jr., *They Only Look Dead: Why Progressives Will Dominate the Next Political Era* (Simon & Schuster, 1996), p. 13.

26. Quoted in David Brooks, "Need a Map? The Right," *The Washington Post*, October 31, 1999, p. B1.

27. David B. Magleby, *The Outside Campaign* (Rowman & Littlefield, 2001).

28. www.people-press.org/reports/display.php3?PageID=751.

29. Warren B. Rudman, *Combat: Twelve Years in the U.S. Senate* (Random House, 1996), p. 270.

30. David B. Magleby, "Issue Advocacy in the 2000 Presidential Primaries," in David B. Magleby, ed., *Getting Inside the Outside Campaign* (Center for the Study of Elections and Democracy, Brigham Young University, 2000), p. 13. Also at www.byu.edu/outsidemoney.

31. Jonathan Rauch, "The Accidental Radical," *National Journal*, 26 July 2003, 2404–2410.

32. Kathleen Day, *S&L Hell: The People and the Politics Behind the $1 Trillion Savings and Loan Scandal* (Norton, 1993).

33. Sylvia Nasar, "Even Among the Well-Off, the Rich Get Richer," *The New York Times*, March 5, 1992, p. A1.

34. Irving Howe, *Socialism and America* (Harcourt, 1985); Michael Harrington, *Socialism: Past and Future* (Arcade, 1989).

35. Daniel Yergin and Joseph Stainslaw, *The Commanding Heights: The Battle Between Government and the Marketplace That Is Remaking the Modern World* (Simon & Schuster, 1998).

36. www.gp.org/platform/2000/index.html#call.

37. Charles Murray, *What It Means to Be a Libertarian* (Broadway Books, 1997).

38. Center for Political Studies, University of Michigan, *American National Election Study, 1990: Post-Election Survey*, April 1991.

39. Michael Kranish, "Discord Replaced by Desire to Win," *The Boston Globe*, July 31, 2000, p. A10.

40. Earl Black and Merle Black, *The Rise of Southern Republicans* (Belknap Press, 2002).

41. Herbert McClosky and Alida Brill, *Dimensions of Tolerance: What Americans Believe About Civil Liberties* (Russel Sage Foundation, 1983).

42. Nat Hentoff, "Liberal Trimmers of the First Amendment," *The Washington Post*, January 17, 1998, p. A25.

43. Dinesh D'Sousa, *Illiberal Education: The Politics of Race and Sex on Campus* (Free Press, 1991), p. 313.

Chapter 5

1. Franklin Delano Roosevelt, quoted in William Safire, *Lend Me Your Ears: Great Speeches in History* (Norton, 1997), p. 646.

2. Mark Hyman, "Sure, He's Latino. But Don't Expect Salsa at the Park," *BusinessWeek* 3835 (June 2, 2003): 85.

3. Martin Gross, "Homeland Security—Flying High," *The Washington Times*, February 1, 2002, p. A18.

4. "Islam Is Peace, Says President," press release, September 17, 2001, at www.whitehouse.gov/news/releases/2001/09/print/20010917-11.html.

5. Elisabeth Bumiller, "Bush Would Give Illegal Workers Broad New Rights," *The New York Times*, January 6, 2004, p. A1.

6. Albert Einstein, quoted in Laurence J. Peter, *Peter's Quotations* (Morrow, 1977), p. 358.

7. Alexis de Tocqueville, *Democracy in America*, ed. J. P. Mayer, trans. George Lawrence (Doubleday, 1969), p. 278. Originally published 1835 (*Volume 1*) and 1840 (*Volume 2*).

8. "Global Agricultural Trade," at www.ers.usda.gov/BRIEFING/AgTrade/commoditytrade.htm.

9. de Tocqueville, *Democracy in America*, trans. Henry Reeve, eBook at www.netlibrary.com, p. 153.

10. U.S. Bureau of the Census, *Statistical Abstract of the United States, 2003* (Government Printing Office, 2003), p. 269.

11. V. O. Key Jr., *Politics, Parties, and Pressure Groups*, 5th ed. (Crowell, 1964), p. 232.

12. Earl Black and Merle Black, *The Vital South: How Presidents Are Elected* (Harvard University Press, 1992), p. 4.

13. Arthur C. Paulson, *Realignment and Party Revival: Understanding American Electoral Politics at the Turn of the Twenty-First Century* (Westport, 2000), p. 46.

14. Joseph A. Pika and Richard A. Watson, *The Presidential Contest*, 5th ed. (CQ Press, 1996), pp. 80–81.

15. Colbert I. King, "Dean's Faith-Based Folly" January 10, 2004. *The Washington Post*, p. A19.

16. National Governor's Association, *Governor's Political Affiliations*, at www.nga.org/cda/files/GOVLIST2004.PDF.

17. www.cnn.com/ELECTION/2004/results/.

18. U.S. Bureau of the Census, at www.census.gov/population/cen2000/tab01.pdf.

19. www.polstate.com/archives/004713.html.

20. Robert S. Erikson, Gerald C. Wright, and John P. McIver, *Statehouse Democracy: Public Opinion and Policy in the American States* (Cambridge University Press, 1993).

21. U.S. Bureau of the Census, *Statistical Abstract of the United States, 2003* (Government Printing Office, 2003), p. 21.

22. Holly Idelson, "Count Adds Seats in Eight States," *Congressional Quarterly Weekly Report* 48 (December 29, 1999), p. 4240.

23. John M. Broder, "Term Waning, Gov. Davis Reflects on the Battle Lost," *The New York Times*, November 12, 2003, p. A12.

24. *Statistical Abstract, 2003*, p. 28.

25. Ibid., p. 34.

26. U.S. Census Bureau, Current Population Survey, March 2002, Racial Statistics Branch, Population Division. From www.census.gov/population/socdemo/race/black/ppl-164/tab21.pdf.

27. Ibid.

28. *Statistical Abstract, 2003*, pp. 38–39.

29. U.S. Bureau of the Census, *Statistical Abstract of the United States, 2003* (Government Printing Office, 2003) p. 16.

30. Ibid.

31. Ibid.

32. Robert D. Ballard, "Introduction: Lure of the New South," in *In Search of the New South: The Black Urban Experience in the 1970s and 1980s*, ed. Robert D. Ballard (University of Alabama Press, 1989), p. 5; *Statistical Abstract, 2003*, p. 27.

33. Ibid., p. 458.

34. Ibid., p. 463.

35. Ibid.

36. Ibid., p. 458.

37. U.S. Bureau of the Census, at www.census.gov/prod/2003pubs/p70-88.pdf.

38. *Statistical Abstract, 2003*, p. 154.

39. *Statistical Abstract, 2003*, p. 179.

40. *Statistical Abstract, 2003*, p. 15.

41. Jeremy D. Mayer, *Running on Race*, (Random House, 2002) pp. 4, 297. See also Mark R. Levy and Michael S. Kramer, *The Ethnic Factor: How America's Minorities Decide Elections* (Simon & Schuster, 1973). See also Mark Stern, "Democratic Presidency and Voting Rights," in *Blacks in Southern Politics*, ed. Lawrence W. Mooreland, Robert P. Steed, and Todd A. Baker (Praeger, 1987), pp. 50–51.

42. Harold W. Stanley and Richard G. Niemi, *Vital Statistics on American Politics, 2000–2001* (CQ Press, 2001), p. 122.

43. *Statistical Abstract, 2003*, p. 25.

44. See Earl Black, "Presidential Address: The Newest Southern Politics," *The Journal of Politics*, August, 1998, pp. 595–607.

45. "Black Elected Officials: A Statistical Summary 2001," Joint Center for Political and Economic Studies, at www.jointcenter.org/publications/BEO/BEO-01.pdf.

46. Ibid.

47. Rodolfo O. de la Garza, Louis De Sipio, F. Chris Garcia, John Garcia, and Angelo Falcon, *Latino Voices: Mexican, Puerto Rican, and Cuban*

Perspectives on American Politics (Westview Press, 1992), p. 14. See also Richard E. Cohen, "Hispanic Hopes Fade," *National Journal*, February 2, 2002.

48. *Statistical Abstract, 2003*, p. 26.

49. *Statistical Abstract, 2003*, p. 48.

50. Rodney Hero, F. Chris Garcia, John Garcia, and Harry Pachon, "Latino Participation, Partisanship, and Office Holding," *P.S.: Political Science and Politics* 33 (September 2000), p. 529. See also de la Garza et al., *Latino Voices*, p. 14.

51. U.S. Bureau of the Census, at www.census.gov/prod/2001pubs/c2kbr01-3.pdf.

52. Tom Squitieri, "Redistricting Falls Short of Hispanics' Hopes," *USA Today*, August 27, 2002, p. 11A.

53. *Statistical Abstract, 2003*, p. 25.

54. U.S. Bureau of the Census, *Profile of the Foreign-Born Population in the United States, 2000* (Government Printing Office, 2001), at www.census.gov/prod/2002pubs/p23-206.pdf.

55. *Statistical Abstract, 2003*, p. 153.

56. Ibid., p. 9.

57. *Statistical Abstract, 2003*, p. 50.

58. James West Davidson, William E. Gienapp, Christine Leigh Heyrman, Mark H. Lytle, and Michael B. Stoff, *Nation of Nations* (McGraw-Hill, 1990), pp. 833–834.

59. G. Thomas Edwards, *Sowing Good Seeds: The Northwest Suffrage Campaigns of Susan B. Anthony* (Oregon Historical Society Press, 1990), p. 136.

60. Paul Kleppner, *Continuity and Change in Electoral Politics, 1893–1928* (Greenwood Press, 1987), p. 172.

61. Margaret C. Trevor, "Political Socialization, Party Identification, and the Gender Gap," *Public Opinion Quarterly* 63 (Spring 1999), p. 62.

62. *Statistical Abstract, 2003*, p. 269; Sue Tolleson-Rinehard and Jyl J. Josephson, eds., *Gender and American Politics* (Sharpe, 2000), pp. 77–78.

63. U.S. Bureau of the Census, "Voting and Registration in the Election of November 2000," at www.census.gov/prod/2002pubs/p20-542.pdf.

64. Tolleson-Rinehard and Josephson, *Gender and American Politics*, (M.E. Sharpe, 2000) pp. 232–233. See also Cindy Simon Rosenthal, ed., *Women Transforming Congress.* (University of Oklahoma Press, 2002), pp. 128–139.

65. Barbara C. Burrell, *A Woman's Place Is in the House: Campaigning for Congress in the Feminist Era* (University of Michigan Press, 1994).

66. Marjorie Connelly, "The Election; Who Voted: A Portrait of American Politics, 1976–2000," *The New York Times*, November 12, 2000, p. D4.

67. Diane L. Fowlkes, "Feminist Theory: Reconstructing Research and Teaching About American Politics and Government," *News for Teachers of Political Science* (Winter 1987), pp. 6–9. See also Sally Helgesen, *Everyday Revolutionaries: Working Women and the Transformation of American Life* (Doubleday, 1998); Karen Lehrman, *The Lipstick Proviso: Women, Sex, and Power in the Real World* (Anchor/Doubleday, 1997); Tanya Melich, *The Republican War Against Women: An Insider's Report from Behind the Lines* (Bantam Books, 1998); and Virginia Valian, *Why So Slow? The Advancement of Women* (MIT Press, 1998).

68. Arlie Russell Hochschild, "There's No Place like Work," *The New York Times*, April 20, 1997, p. 51.

69. The Pew Research Center. *Gay Marriage a Voting Issue, but Mostly for Opponents.* February 27, 2004. www.people-press.org/reports/display.php3?ReportID=204; and Alexis Simendinger, "Why Issues Matter," *National Journal*, April 1, 2000, based on data from a Pew Center Poll conducted March 15–19, 2000.

70. *Statistical Abstract, 2003*, p. 461.

71. U.S. Census Bureau, "Poverty Rate Rises, Household Income Declines, Census Bureau Reports," *United States Department of Commerce News*, September 24, 2002. At www.census.gov/PressRelease/www/2002/cb02-124.html.

72. Wendy Margolis, Bonnie Gordon, Joe Puskarz, and David Rosenlieb, eds., *ABA LSAC Official Guide to ABA-Approved Law Schools, 2005 Edition* (Law School Admissions Council and the American Bar Association, 2004).

73. Anna Quindlen, "Some Struggles Never Seem to End," *The New York Times*, November 14, 2001, p. H24.

74. Elsa Brenner, "The Invisible Population," *The New York Times*, November 14, 1999. See also www.census.gov/population/www/documentation/twps0034.html.

75. Erica Goode. "Sunday Q & A," *The New York Times*, September 2, 2001, p. 16.

76. Rose Arce, "Massachusetts Court Upheld Same-Sex Marriage," see www.cnn.com/2004/LAW/02/04/gay.marriage/.

77. Rachel Gordon, Newsom's Plan for Same-Sex Marriages; Mayor Wants to License Gay and Lesbian Couples, *The San Francisco Chronicle*, February 11, 2004.

78. Adam Clymer, "Senate Expands Hate Crimes Law to Include Gays," *The New York Times*, June 21, 2000, p. A1.

79. *Boy Scouts of America* v. *Dale*, 120 S. Ct. 2446 (2000).

80. David Masci, "The Future of Marriage," *The CQ Researcher Online*, Vol. 14, No. 17 (May 7, 2004), pp. 397–420.

81. *Statistical Abstract, 2003*, p. 76.

82. Laura Vanderkam, "Cities Covet Young Urban Single Professionals," *USA Today*, December 17, 2003, p. 25A.

83. *Statistical Abstract, 2003*, p. 100.

84. Ibid., p. 75.

85. *General Social Survey (GSS) 1972–2000 Cumulative Codebook*, at www.icpsr.umich.edu/GSS/index.html.

86. See Leni Yahil, *The Holocaust: The Fate of European Jewry* (Oxford University Press, 1990).

87. Stephen C. LeSuer, *The 1838 Mormon War in Missouri* (University of Missouri Press, 1987), pp. 151–153.

88. John Conway, "An Adapted Organic Tradition," *Daedalus* 117 (Fall 1988), p. 382. For an extended comparison of the impact of religion on politics in the United States and Canada, see Seymour Martin Lipset, *Continental Divide: The Values and Institutions of the United States and Canada* (Routledge, 1990), pp. 74–89.

89. www.whitehouse.gov/news/releases/2004/01/20040120-7.html.

90. Wesley, Charles. "A Charge to Keep I Have." Text, 1778. Music by Lowell Mason, 1832.

91. "Address of Senator John F. Kennedy to the Greater Houston Ministerial Association," September 12, 1960, at www.cs.umb.edu/jfklibrary/j091260.htm.

92. Jodi Wilgoren, "The 2004 Campaign: Stem-Cell Research," *The New York Times*, January 10, 2004, p. A9.

93. Taylor Branch, *Parting the Waters: America in the King Years, 1954–63* (Simon & Schuster, 1988), p. 3.

94. Douglas Usher, "Strategy, Rules and Participation: Issue Activists in Republican National Convention Delegations 1976–1996," *Political Research Quarterly*, Vol. 53, No. 4. (December, 2000), p. 888.

95. Ronald Inglehart and Wayne E. Baker, "Looking Forward, Looking Back: Continuity and Change at the Turn of the Millennium," *American Sociological Review*, February, 2000, pp. 29, 31.

96. Roper Center for Public Opinion Research, February 27, 2004, at www.ropercenter.uconn.edu/cgi-bin/hsrun.exe/Roperweb/pom/StateId/CYk00u7Ih9k-52Swcm-ofACuZP3lA-.34Ik/HAHTpage/Summary_Link?qstn_i

97. William H. Flanigan and Nancy H. Zingale, *Political Behavior of the American Electorate*, 10th ed. (CQ Press, 2002), p. 131.

98. The Gallup Organization, at www.gallup.com/poll/focus/sr040302.asp.

99. Ibid.

100. *Statistical Abstract, 2003*, p. 67.

101. *Statistical Abstract, 2003*, pp. 21, 67. Also: American Religion Data Archive, at www.thearda.com.

102. Ibid.

103. Ibid.

104. American Religion Data Archive, at www.thearda.com.

105. CNN, at www.cnn.com/ELECTION/2000/results.

106. *2000 American National Election Study* (Center for Political Studies, 2000).

107. Ibid.

108. Lyman A. Kellstedt and John C. Green, "Is There a Culture War? Religion and the 1996 Election," paper presented at the annual meeting of the American Political Science Association, Washington, D.C., 1997, at www.wheaton.edu/polsci/kellstedt.

109. CNN, at www.cnn.com/ELECTION/2000/results.

110. Organization for Economic Cooperation and Development (OECD), at www.oecd.org/dataoecd/48/5/2371372.pdf.

111. Raymond E. Wolfinger, Fred I. Greenstein, and Martin Shapiro, *Dynamics of American Politics*, 2d ed. (Prentice Hall, 1980), p. 19.

112. Thomas Jefferson, "Autobiography," in *The Life and Selected Writings of Thomas Jefferson*, ed. Adrienne Koch and William Peden (Modern Library, 1944), p. 38.

113. Laura D'Andrea Tyson, "Needed: Affirmative Action for the Poor," *BusinessWeek*, July 7, 2003, p. 24.

114. *Statistical Abstract, 2003*, p 189.

115. "Plans to Tackle College Costs Risk Tripping Up Students," *USA Today*, January 5, 2004, p. 12A.

116. Harold W. Stanley and Richard G. Niemi, *Vital Statistics on American Politics, 2003–2004* (CQ Press, 2003), p. 363–364.

117. Stanley Fischer, "Symposium on the Slowdown in Productivity Growth," *Journal of Economic Perspectives* 2 (Fall 1988), pp. 3–7.

118. Robert Gavin, "Q&A Boston Fed Chief Cathy Minehan, On Soaring Productivity Rate," *The Boston Globe*, December 21, 2003, p. E2.

119. Alan B. Krueger. "After 40 Years, What Are Some Results and Lessons of America's War on Poverty?" *The New York Times*, January 8, 2004, p. C2.

120. U.S. Bureau of the Census, at www.census.gov/hhes/poverty/threshld/thresh03.html.

121. U.S. Bureau of the Census, at www.census.gov/prod/2003pubs/p60-222.pdf.

122. *Statistical Abstract, 2003*, p. 465.

123. Ibid., p. 442.

124. "Would You Like Your Class War Shaken or Stirred, Sir?" *The Economist*, September, 6, 2003, p. 46.

125. Ibid.

126. *Statistical Abstract, 2003*, p. 438. "Real" means that inflation has already been taken into account.

127. Daniel Bell, *The Coming of Post-Industrial Society: A Venture in Social Forecasting* (Basic Books, 1973), p. xviii.

128. *Statistical Abstract, 2003*, p. 404.

129. Ibid., p. 438.

130. Ibid., p. 404.

131. Mattei Dogan and Dominique Pelassy, *How to Compare Nations: Strategies in Comparative Politics*, 2d ed. (Chatham House, 1990), p. 47.

132. *Index to International Public Opinion, 1996–97* (Greenwood Press, 1997), p. 397.

133. Seymour Martin Lipset, *Continental Divide: The Values and Institutions of the United States and Canada* (Routledge, 1990), p. 170.

134. U.S. Bureau of Labor Statistics, at www.bls.gov/csx/1999/Aggregate/age.pdf.

135. *Statistical Abstract, 2001*, p. 433, *Statistical Abstract, 2003*, p. 466.

136. CNN, at www.cnn.com/election/2000/results/index.epolls.html.

137. Jose Antonio Vargas, "Vote or Die? Well, They Did Vote," *The Washington Post*, November 9, 2004, p. C1.

138. Seymour Martin Lipset, *Political Man* (Doubleday, 1963), pp. 283–286.

139. Thomas Jefferson to P. S. du Pont de Nemours, April 24, 1816, in *The Writings of Thomas Jefferson*, ed. Paul L. Ford (Putnam, 1899), vol. 10, p. 25.

140. *Statistical Abstract, 2003*, p. 151.

141. Ibid., p. 155.

142. Ibid., p. 154.

143. Herbert McClosky and John Zaller, *The American Ethos: Public Attitudes Toward Capitalism and Democracy* (Harvard University Press, 1984), p. 261.

144. John Gunther, *Inside U.S.A.* (Harper, 1947), p. 911.

145. Carl N. Degler, *Out of Our Past: The Forces That Shaped Modern America*, 3d ed. (Harper & Row, 1984), p. 322.

Chapter 6

1. John E. O'Neill and Jerome R. Corsi, *Unfit for Command: Swift Boat Veterans Speak Out Against John Kerry* (Regnery, 2004).

2. Kate Zernike and Jim Rutenberg, "Friendly Fire: The Birth of an Attack on Kerry," *The New York Times*, August 20, 2004, p. 1.

3. Elisabeth Bumiller and Kate Zeernike, "President Urges Outside Groups to Halt All Ads: But Doesn't Single Out Swift Boat Claims," *The New York Times*, August 24, 2004, p. A1.

4. Zernike and Rutenberg, "Friendly Fire."

5. Jim Rutenberg and Kate Zernike, "Veterans' Group had G.O.P. Lawyer," *The New York Times*, August 25, 2004, p. 1; Zernike and Rutenberg, "Friendly Fire."

6. Bill Sammon, "Bush Raps Anti-Kerry Ads on Vietnam; Rival Urged to Condemn Attacks Funded by Soros," *The Washington Post*, August 24, 2004, p. A1.

7. www.opensecrets.org/softmoney/softcomp1.asp?txtName=wal-mart.

8. www.opensecrets.org/softmoney/softcomp1.asp?txtName=microsoft $$$period.

9. U.S. Bureau of Labor Statistics, at www.bls.gov/cps/cpsaat40.pdf.

10. Michael Podhorzer, Department of Political Research, AFL-CIO, personal communication, June 14, 2002.

11. Brian C. Mooney, "Nation's Two Biggest Unions to Wait on Presidential Endorsement," *The Boston Globe*, September 11, 2003, p. A3.

12. Herbert B. Asher et al., *American Labor Unions in the Electoral Arena* (Rowman & Littlefield, 2001).

13. James MacGregor Burns and Stewart Burns, *A People's Charter: The Pursuit of Rights in America* (Knopf, 1991).

14. William R. Donohue, *The Politics of the American Civil Liberties Union* (Transaction Books, 1985).

15. David B. Magleby, ed., *The Other Campaign: Soft Money and Issue Advocacy in the 2000 Congressional Elections* (Rowman & Littlefield, 2002). See also David B. Magleby, ed., *Outside Money: Soft Money and Issue Advocacy in 1998 Congressional Elections* (Rowman & Littlefield, 2000); and Clyde Wilcox, *Onward Christian Soldiers: The Religious Right in American Politics* (Westview Press, 2000).

16. National Education Association, at www.nea.org/aboutnea.

17. Sam Dillon and Diana Jean Schemo, "Union Urges Bush to Replace Education Chief Over Remark," *The New York Times*, February 25, 2004, p. A15.

18. Robert Salisbury, "Interest Representation: The Dominance of Institutions," *American Political Science Review* 78 (March 1984), p. 66.

19. Ceci Connelly, "Democratic Candidates Criticize AARP," *The Washington Post*, November 19, 2003, p. A12.

20. V. O. Key Jr., *Public Opinion and American Democracy* (Knopf, 1961), pp. 504–507.

21. Jill Lawrence and Susan Page, "Top Candidates Strategize to Pin Down Nomination," *USA Today*, January 5, 2004, p. 1A.

22. "Inside the 2004 Campaign Tool Chest: Blogs and Online Voting," *The Los Angeles Times*, January 5, 2004, p. A10.

23. Joyce Purnick, "One-Doorbell-One-Vote Tactic Re-emerges in Bush–Kerry Race," *The New York Times*, April 6, 2004, p. A1; Glen Justice, "Bush Spent a Record on His Race in March," *The New York Times*, April 21, 2004, p. A18.

24. R. Kenneth Godwin, *One Billion Dollars of Influence: The Direct Marketing of Politics* (Chatham House, 1988).

25. Lucius J. Barker, "Third Parties in Litigation: A Systemic View of the Judicial Function," *Journal of Politics* 29 (February 1967), pp. 41–69; Jethro K. Lieberman, *Litigious Society*, rev. ed. (Basic Books, 1983).

26. Gregory A. Calderia and John R. Wright, "Organized Interests and Agenda Setting in the U.S. Supreme Court," *American Political Science Review* 82 (December 1988), pp. 1109–1127. See also Gregory A. Calderia and John R. Wright, "*Amici Curiae* Before the Supreme Court: Who Participates, When, and How Much?" *Journal of Politics* 52 (August 1990), pp. 782–806.

27. Karen O'Connor, *Women's Organizations' Use of the Courts* (Lexington Books, 1980).

28. Steven P. Brown, *Trumping Religion: The New Christian Right, Religious Liberty, and the Courts* (University of Alabama Press, October 2002), Ph.D. diss.

29. Lee Epstein and C. K. Rowland, "Debunking the Myth of Interest Group Invincibility in the Courts," *American Political Science Review* 85 (March 1991), pp. 205–217.

30. Sam Howe Verhovek, "Police Chief Resigns in Aftermath of Protests," *The New York Times*, December 8, 1999, p. A16.

31. Sam Howe Verhovek, "Talks and Turmoil: The Hosts," *The New York Times*, December 2, 1999, p. A16.

32. See Kenneth Klee, "The Siege of Seattle," *Newsweek*, December 13, 1999, p. 30.

33. David B. Magleby and Kelly D. Patterson, "Campaign Consultants and Direct Democracy: Politics of Citizen Control," in *Campaign Warriors: The Role of Political Consultants in Elections*, eds. James E. Thurber and Candice J. Nelson (Brookings Institution Press, 2000).

34. www.bipac.org/home.asp.

35. For a discussion of the 1998 New Mexico race, see Lonna Rae Atkeson and Anthony C. Coveny, "The 1998 New Mexico Third Congressional District Race," in Magleby, *Outside Money*, pp. 135–152.

36. Ethan Bronner, *Battle for Justice: How the Bork Nomination Shook America* (Norton, 1989), pp. 50–55.

37. Hugh Heclo, "Issue Networks and the Executive Establishment," in *The New American Political System*, ed. Anthony King (American Enterprise Institute, 1978).

38. David Mayhew, *Congress: The Electoral Connection* (Yale University Press, 1974), p. 45.

39. John R. Wright, "Contributions, Lobbying, and Committee Voting in the U.S. House of Representatives," *American Political Science Review* 84 (June 1990), pp. 417–438.

40. www.opensecrets.org/softmoney/softcomp1.asp?txtName=wal-mart.

41. www.clubforgrowth.org/what.php.

42. David B. Magleby and Jonathan W. Tanner, "Interest Group Electioneering in the 2002 Congressional Elections," in *The Last Hurrah*, eds. David B. Magleby and J. Quin Monson (Brookings Institution Press, 2004), p. 81. See also Thomas B. Edsall, "Drug Industry Financing Fuels Pro-GOP TV

Spots; Spending Swamps Donations for Liberal Ads by 3–1 Margin," *The Washington Post*, October 23, 2002, p. A11.

43. Christopher Rowland, "That Spoonful of Sugar Medicare Bids Mollify Makers on a Key Point: No Price Controls," *The Boston Globe*, June 29, 2003, p. H1.

44. Dana Milbank, "Conservatives Criticize Bush on Spending; Medicare Bill Angers Some Allies," *The Washington Post*, December 6, 2003, p. A1.

45. Dana Milbank and Claudia Deane, "President Signs Medicare Drug Bill; Supporters, Opponents Jockey for 2004 Edge," *The Washington Post*, December 9, 2003, p. A1.

46. *McConnell v. Federal Elections Commission*, 124 S.Ct. 621 (2003).

47. For evidence of the impact of PAC expenditures on legislative committee behavior and legislative involvement generally, see Richard L. Hall and Frank W. Wayman, "Buying Time: Moneyed Interests and the Mobilization of Bias in Congressional Committees," *American Political Science Review* 84 (September 1990), pp. 797–820.

48. Edwin M. Epstein, "Business and Labor Under the Federal Election Campaign Act of 1971," in *Parties, Interest Groups, and Campaign Finance Laws*, ed. Michael J. Malbin (American Enterprise Institute for Public Policy Research, 1980), p. 112. See also Gary Jacobson, *Money in Congressional Elections* (Yale University Press, 1980).

49. Open Secrets, at www.opensecrets.org/pacs/index.asp.

50. Kelly Huff, Ron Harris, and Ian Stirton, "FEC Issues Semi-Annual PAC Count," at www.fec.gov/press/20020120124pacno.html and www.fec.gov/press/paccnt_grph.html.

51. Federal Election Commission, at www.fec.gov/press/082101pac.html.

52. Amy Keller, "Leadership PACs 'Not Sinister,' FEC Told," *Roll Call*, February 27, 2003.

53. Federal Election Commission, at www.fec.gov.

54. Ruth Marcus, "Labor Spent $119 Million For '96 Politics, Study Says; Almost All Contributions Went to Democrats," *The Washington Post*, September 10, 1997, p. A19.

55. *Buckley* v. *Valeo*, 96 S.Ct. 647 (1976).

56. David B. Magleby and J. Quin Monson, eds., *The Last Hurrah: Soft Money and Issue Advocacy in the 2002 Congressional Elections*, p. 90; David B. Magleby, ed., *The Other Campaign: Soft Money and Issue Advocacy in the 2000 Congressional Election*, p. 53; David B. Magleby, ed., *Outside Money*, p. 41.

57. David B. Magleby, and J. Quin Monson, eds., *The Last Hurrah*, p. 3; David B. Magleby, ed., *The Other Campaign*, p. 1; David B. Magleby, ed., *Outside Money*, p. 212.

58. David B. Magleby, ed., *The Other Campaign*, p. 149.

59. Ibid.

60. *FEC v. Mass. Citizen's for Life, Inc.*, 479 U.S. 238; 107 S.Ct. 616 (1986).

61. America Coming Together, at http://actforvictory.org/.

62. Ibid.

63. Nicholas Confessore, "Bush's Secret Stash," *Washington Monthly* 36 (May 2004), pp. 17–23.

64. E. J. Dionne Jr., "Fear of McCain-Feingold," *The Washington Post*, December 3, 2002, p. A25.

65. www.campaignlegalcenter.org/press-814.html.

66. Hall and Wayman, "Buying Time," pp. 797–820. A different study of the House Ways and Means Committee found campaign contributions to be part of the representatives' policy decisions, but even more important was the number of lobbying contacts; see Wright, "Contributions, Lobbying, and Committee Voting."

67. Ronald Reagan, "Remarks to Administration Officials on Domestic Policy," December 13, 1988, *Weekly Compilation of Presidential Documents*, vol. 24 (December 1988), pp. 1615–1620.

68. Sylvia Tesh, "In Support of Single-Interest Politics," *Political Science Quarterly* 99 (Spring 1984), pp. 27–44.

69. Howard Dean also turned down the federal matching funds in the 2004 primaries.

70. Ross Sneyd, "Dean First Democrat to Forgo Public Funds," *Associated Press Online*, November 9, 2003.

71. California Commission on Campaign Financing, *The New Gold Rush: Financing California's Legislative Campaigns* (Center for Responsive Government, 1985), pp. 177–197. For a study of state lobby regulation, see Cynthia Opheim, "Explaining the Differences in State Lobby Regulation," *Western Political Quarterly* 44 (June 1991), pp. 405–421.

72. Adam Clymer, "Congress Sends Lobbying Overhaul to Clinton," *The New York Times*, December 16, 1995, p. A36.

73. Legislative Resource Center's Lobbying Section, telephone interview, April 7, 2004.

74. David B. Magleby, *Financing the 2000 Election* (Brookings Institution Press, 2002) p. 11; See also Susan B. Glasser, "George W. Bush's Dash for Cash," *The Washington Post*, April 19, 1999, p. A10.

75. Greg Hitt, "Democrats Move Ahead in Soft-Money Race," *The Wall Street Journal*, August 17, 2000, p. A24.

76. Open Secrets at www.opensecrets.org/industries/indus.asp?Ind+H04.

77. Marianne Holt, "Stealth PAC's Revealed: Interest Group Profiles." Press release, Center for Public Integrity, February 5, 2001.

78. David B. Magleby, ed., *Election Advocacy: Soft Money and Issue Advocacy in the 2000 Congressional Elections* (Center for the Study of Elections and Democracy, 2001), at www.byu.edu/outsidemoney.

79. David B. Magleby and Candice J. Nelson, *The Money Chase: Congressional Campaign Finance Reform* (Brookings Institution Press, 1990), pp. 72–97.

80. Factors that predict the formation of PACs include company size and the degree of regulation for corporations. See Craig Humphries, "Corporations, PACs, and the Strategic Link Between Contributions and Lobbying Activities," *Western Political Quarterly* 44 (June 1991), pp. 353–372.

81. Paul Krugman, "Toward One-Party Rule," *The New York Times*, June 27, 2003, p. A27.

Chapter 7

1. John E. Mueller, "Choosing Among 133 Candidates," *Public Opinion Quarterly* 34 (Fall 1970), pp. 395–402.

2. E. E. Schattschneider, *Party Government* (Holt, Rinehart and Winston, 1942), p. 1.

3. See Scott Mainwaring, "Party Systems in the Third Wave," *Journal of Democracy* (July 1998), pp. 67–81.

4. Joseph A. Schlesinger, *Political Parties and the Winning of Office* (University of Michigan Press, 1994).

5. James A. Thurber and Candice J. Nelson, eds., *Campaign Warriors: The Role of Political Consultants in Elections* (Brookings Institution Press, 2000).

6. Nick Anderson and Jonathan Peterson, "China Trade Vote: House OK's China Trade Bill," *The Los Angeles Times*, May 25, 2000, p. A1.

7. Elizabeth A. Palmer, "Bill to Extend Residency Program Passes House After Six-Month Wait," *Congressional Quarterly*, March 16, 2002, p. 706.

8. Gary W. Cox and Mathew D. McCubbins, *Legislative Leviathan: Party Government in the House* (University of California Press, 1993).

9. David B. Magleby and J. Quin Monson, eds. *The Last Hurrah? Soft Money and Issue Advocacy in the 2002 Congressional Elections* (Brookings Institution Press, 2004).

10. John Bart and James Meader, "The More You Spend, the Less They Listen: The South Dakota U.S. Senate Race," in *The Last Hurrah*, eds. David B. Magleby and J. Quin Monson, pp. 159–179.

11. See three books edited by David B. Magleby: *Outside Money: Soft Money and Issue Advocacy in the 1998 Congressional Elections* (Rowman & Littlefield, 2000); *The Other Campaign: Soft Money and Issue Advocacy in the 2000 Congressional Elections* (Rowman & Littlefield, 2002); and *Financing the 2000 Election* (Brookings Institution Press, 2002).

12. Amy Keller, "FEC Offers Post-BCRA Legislative Ideas," *Roll Call*, April 29, 2004.

13. Federal Election Commission, "The Biennial Contribution Limit," at www.fec.gov/pages/brochures/biennial.htm#Biennial%20Limit, February 2004; and Paul S. Herrnson, *Congressional Elections: Campaigning at Home and in Washington* (CQ Press, 2004), p. 16.

14. *Federal Election Commission v. Colorado Republican Federal Campaign Committee*, 116 S.Ct. 2309 (1996).

15. Federal Election Commission (ftp.fec.gov/FEC/[July 27,2004]).

16. David W. Brady and Craig Volden, *Revolving Gridlock: Politics and Policy from Carter to Clinton* (Westview Press, 1998); James A. Thurber, ed., *Divided Democracy: Cooperation and Conflict Between the President and Congress* (CQ Press, 1991); James A. Thurber, ed., *Rivals for Power: Presidential-Congressional Relations* (CQ Press, 1996); Charles O. Jones, *Separate but Equal Branches: Congress and the Presidency* (Chatham House, 1995), chaps. 5 and 6; and Jon R. Bond and Richard Fleisher, *The President in the Legislative Arena* (University of Chicago Press, 1990).

17. *California Democratic Party et al. v. Jones*, 120 S.Ct. 2402 (2000).

18. Bruce E. Cain and Elisabeth R. Gerber, eds., *Voting at the Political Fault Line: California's Experiment with the Blanket Primary* (University of California Press, 2002), pp. 341–342.

19. "Iowans Flock to Caucuses," *The Associated Press State & Local Wire,* January 20, 2004. Section: "Political News."

20. Arthur Sanders and David Redlawsk, "Money and the Iowa Caucuses," in *Getting Inside the Outside Campaign,* ed. David Magleby (Center for the Study of Elections and Democracy, 2000), pp. 20–29.

21. *The Book of the States, 2000–2001* (Council of State Governments, 2000), pp. 164–165.

22. For an analysis of the potential effects of different electoral rules in the United States see Todd Donovan and Shawn Bowler, *Reforming the Republic: Democratic Institutions for the New America.* Prentice Hall, 2004.

23. William H. Riker, "The Two-Party System and Duverger's Law: An Essay on the History of Political Science," *American Political Science Review* 76 (December 1982), pp. 753–766. For a classic analysis, see Schattschneider, *Party Government.*

24. Robin Toner, "The 1992 Elections: The World–News Analysis; At Dawn of New Politics, Challenges for Both Parties," *The New York Times,* November 5, 1992, p. B1.

25. See Paul S. Herrnson and John C. Green, eds., *Multiparty Politics in America,* 2d ed. (Rowman & Littlefield, 2002); and J. David Gillespie, *Politics at the Periphery: Third Parties in Two-Party America* (University of South Carolina Press, 1993).

26. L. Sandy Maisel and John F. Bibby, *Two Parties—or More? The American Party System* (Westview Press, 1998).

27. Ted G. Jelen, ed., *Ross for Boss* (State University of New York Press, 2001), p. 88.

28. Steven J. Rosenstone, Roy L. Behr, and Edward H. Lazarus, *Third Parties in America: Citizen Response to Major Party Failure,* 2d ed. (Princeton University Press, 1996). See also Xandra Kayden and Eddie Mahe Jr., *The Party Goes On: The Persistence of the Two-Party System in the United States* (Basic Books, 1985), pp. 143–144.

29. Dean Lacy and Quin Monson. "The Origins and Impact of Voter Support for Third-Party Candidates: A Case Study of the 1998 Minnesota Gubernatorial Election," *Political Research Quarterly* 55(2):409–437, 2002.

30. On the impact of third parties, see Howard R. Penniman, "Presidential Third Parties and the Modern American Two-Party System," in *The Party Symbol,* ed. William J. Crotty (Freeman, 1980), pp. 101–117. See also Frank Smallwood, *The Other Candidates: Third Parties in Presidential Elections* (University Press of New England, 1983).

31. Libertarian Party, at www.lp.org/campaigns/candidates.php.

32. Benjamin Franklin, George Washington, and Thomas Jefferson, quoted in Richard Hofstadter, *The Idea of a Party System* (University of California Press, 1969), pp. 2, 123.

33. For concise histories of the two parties, see two studies by Robert A. Rutland, *The Democrats: From Jefferson to Clinton* (University of Missouri Press, 1996), and *The Republicans: From Lincoln to Bush* (University of Missouri Press, 1996).

34. See V. O. Key Jr., "A Theory of Critical Elections," *Journal of Politics* 17 (February 1955), pp. 3–18; Walter Dean Burnham, *Critical Elections and the Mainsprings of American Politics* (Norton, 1970), pp. 1–10; and E. E. Schattschneider, *The Semisovereign People: A Realist's View of Democracy in America* (Holt, Rinehart and Winston, 1975), pp. 78–80.

35. William E. Gienapp, *The Origins of the Republican Party, 1852–1856* (Oxford University Press, 1987).

36. David W. Brady, "Election, Congress, and Public Policy Changes, 1886–1960," in *Realignment in American Politics: Toward a Theory,* eds. Bruce A. Campbell and Richard Trilling (Texas University Press, 1980), p. 188.

37. L. Sandy Maisel, *Parties and Elections in America: The Electoral Process* (Rowman & Littlefield, 2002), pp. 48–49.

38. Gerald Pomper, "Classification of Presidential Elections," *Journal of Politics* 29 (August 1967), p. 538.

39. CNN, at www.cnn.com/ELECTION/2000/results/.

40. V. O. Key Jr., *Political Parties and Pressure Groups,* 5th ed. (International Publishing, 1964). See also Paul Allen Beck and Marjorie Randon Hershey, *Party Politics in America,* 10th ed. (Longman, 2003).

41. "Party Fundraising Escalates," *Federal Elections Commission,* November 3, 2000, at www.fecweb1.fec.gov/press/pty00text.htm.

42. Paul Allen Beck and Marjorie Randon Hershey, *Party Politics in America,* 10th ed. (Longman, 2003).

43. Virginia Sapiro, "It's the Context, Situation, and Question, Stupid: The Gender Basis of Public Opinion," in *Understanding Public Opinion,* 2d ed., eds. Barbara Norrander and Clyde Wilcox (CQ Press, 2001), p. 41.

44. At www.bluedogdemocrats.com/.

45. Zell Miller, "George Bush vs. the Naïve Nine," *The Wall Street Journal,* November 3, 2003, p. A14.

46. GOP.com, "RNC Chairman Ed Gillespie," at www.gop.com/GOPDirectory/LeaderBio.aspx?ID=8, June 15, 2004.

47. Democratic National Committee, "Current DNC Leadership: Terry McAuliffe DNC Chairman," at www.democrats.org/about/bios/mcauliffe.html, June 15, 2004.

48. See L. Sandy Maisel, *From Obscurity to Oblivion: Running in the Congressional Primary,* rev. ed. (University of Tennessee Press, 1986).

49. The early Republican efforts and advantages over the Democrats are well documented in Thomas B. Edsall, *The New Politics of Inequality* (Norton, 1984); and Gary C. Jacobson, "The Republican Advantage in Campaign Finances," in *New Direction in American Politics,* eds. John E. Chubb and Paul E. Peterson (Brookings Institution Press, 1985), p. 6.

50. David C. King, "The Polarization of American Political Parties and Mistrust of Government," in *Why People Don't Trust Government,* eds. Joseph S. Nye, Philip Zelikow, and David C. King (Harvard University Press, 1997); and National Election Study, "Important Difference in What Democratic and Republican Parties Stand For, 1952–2000," at www.umich.edu/~nes/nesguide/toptable/tab2b_4.htm, July 2004.

51. Tom Shales, "Bush, Bringing the Party to Life; From the New Nominee, a Splendid Acceptance Speech," *The Washinton Post,* August 19, 1988, p. C1.

52. Kelly D. Patterson, *Political Parties and the Maintenance of Liberal Democracy* (Columbia University Press, 1996), pp. 30–31.

53. John F. Bibby, *Politics, Parties, and Elections in America,* 4th ed. (Nelson-Hall, 1999). For further data on these roles, see Cornelius P. Cotter, James L. Gibson, John F. Bibby, and Robert J. Huckshorn, *Party Organizations in American Politics* (Praeger, 1984).

54. See James L. Gibson, Cornelius P. Cotter, John F. Bibby, and Robert J. Huckshorn, "Assessing Party Organizational Strength," *American Journal of Political Science* 27 (May 1983), pp. 193–222. See also Cotter et al., *Party Organizations in American Politics.*

55. Paul S. Herrnson, *Party Campaigning in the 1980s: Have the National Parties Made a Comeback as Key Players in Congressional Elections?* (Harvard University Press, 1988), p. 122.

56. Jonathan S. Krasno and Daniel E. Seltz, *Buying Time: Television Advertising in the 1998 Congressional Elections,* report of a grant funded by the Pew Charitable Trusts (1998).

57. On the influence of local parties, see Kayden and Mahe, *The Party Goes On.* See also John C. Green and Daniel M. Shea, eds., *The State of the Parties: The Changing Role of Contemporary Parties,* 3d ed. (Rowman & Littlefield, 1999), which presents recent case studies of parties at the local level.

58. J. Quin Monson, "Get on Television vs. Get on the Van: GOTV and the Ground War in 2002," *The Last Hurrah? Soft Money and Issue Advocacy in the 2002 Congressional Elections,* eds. David B. Magleby and J. Quin Monson, pp. 90–112.

59. Jill Newell, White House staff, personal communication, July 2, 2002. A list of many of these positions appears in *Policy and Supporting Positions* (Government Printing Office, November 9, 1988). For a general discussion of presidential appointments, see G. Calvin Mackenzie, "Partisan Presidential Leadership: The President's Appointees," in L. Sandy Maisel, ed., *Parties Respond: Changes in American Parties and Campaigns,* 3d ed. (Westview Press, 1998), pp. 316–337.

60. *Marbury* v. *Madison,* I Cranch 137 (1803).

61. See Angus Campbell, Philip E. Converse, Warren E. Miller, and Donald E. Stokes, *The American Voter* (University of Chicago Press, 1960); Norman A. Nie, Sidney Verba, and John R. Petrocik, *The Changing American Voter,* enlarged ed. (Harvard University Press, 1979); and Warren E. Miller and J. Merrill Shanks, *The New American Voter* (Harvard University Press, 1996).

62. Angus Campbell et al., *The American Voter,* pp. 121–128.

63. Bruce E. Keith et al., *The Myth of the Independent Voter* (University of California Press, 1992).

64. See Byron E. Shafer, *The End of Realignment: Interpreting American Electoral Eras* (University of Wisconsin Press, 1991).

65. Michael F. Meffert, Helmut Norpoth, and Anirudh V. S. Ruhil, "Realignment and Macropartisanship," *American Political Science Review* 95 (December 2001), pp. 953–962.

66. Hedrick Smith, *The Power Game: How Washington Works* (Random House, 1988), p. 671.

67. Nine percent of all voters were Pure Independents in 1956 and 1960; Keith et al., *The Myth of the Independent Voter,* p. 51. In 1992, the figure was also 9 percent; *1992 National Election Study* (Center for Political Studies, University of Michigan, 1992).

68. Earl Black and Merle Black, *The Rise of Southern Republicans* (Harvard University Press, 2002).

69. Ibid.
70. For the "optimistic view," see Ralph M. Goldman, *Search for Consensus: The Story of the Democratic Party* (Temple University Press, 1979), pp. 366–373; Kayden and Mahe, *The Party Goes On;* Larry J. Sabato, *The Party's Just Begun: Shaping Political Parties in America's Future* (Scott, Foresman, 1988); Joseph A. Schlesinger, "The New American Political Party," *American Political Science Review* 79 (December 1985), pp. 1152–1169; and David E. Price, *Bringing Back the Parties* (CQ Press, 1984).
71. "Party Unity Background," *Congressional Quarterly Weekly Report* 60 (January 12, 2002), p. 142.
72. Barbara Sinclair, "Evolution or Revolution?" in Maisel, *Parties Respond,* pp. 263–285.
73. Paul S. Herrnson, *Party Campaigning in the 1980s* (Harvard University Press, 1988), pp. 80–81.
74. See Magleby, *Outside Money and The Other Campaign.*
75. *McConnell* v. *FEC,* 124 S.Ct. 516 (2003).
76. See David B. Magleby, "Dictum Without Data: The Myth of Issue Advocacy and Party Building," p. 11 at www.csed.byu.edu/Publications/Dictum.doc.

Chapter 8

1. WisPolitics Press Release, "UW-Madison, BYU: Few Differences Between Voters in Battleground, Other States, Major Study Finds," July 14, 2004, at www.wispolitics.com/printerfriendly.iml?Article=19985.
2. Robert Coles, *The Political Life of Children* (Atlantic Monthly Press, 2000), 24–25. See also Stephen M. Caliendo, *Teachers Matter: The Trouble with Leaving Political Education to the Coaches* (Greenwood, 2000).
3. Robert Coles, *The Political Life of Children* (Atlantic Monthly Press, 2000), pp. 59–60.
4. Pamela Johnston Conover, "The Influence of Group Identifications on Political Perception and Evaluation," *Journal of Politics* 46 (August 1984), pp. 760–785; and Henry E. Brady and Paul M. Sniderman, "Attitude Attribution: A Group Basis for Political Reasoning," *American Political Science Review* 79 (December 1985), pp. 1061–1078.
5. Caliendo, *Teachers Matter,* pp. 16–17.
6. James Garbarino, *Raising Children in a Socially Toxic Environment* (Jossey-Bass, 1995).
7. Russell J. Dalton, "Reassessing Parental Socialization: Indicator Unreliability Versus Generational Transfer," *American Political Science Review* 74 (June 1980), pp. 421–431.
8. Suzanne Koprince Sebert, M. Kent Jennings, and Richard G. Niemi, "The Political Texture of Peer Groups," in *The Political Character of Adolescence,* M. Kent Jennings and Richard G. Niemi (Princeton University Press, 1974), p. 246. See also Richard G. Niemi and M. Kent Jennings, "Issues and Inheritance in the Formation of Party Identification," *American Journal of Political Science* 35 (November 1991), pp. 970–988.
9. National Association of Secretaries of State, *New Millennium Project, Part I: American Youth Attitudes on Policies, Citizenship, Government and Voting* (Washington, D.C.: National Association of Secretaries of State, 1999). See also, "Political Interest on the Rebound Among the Nation's Freshmen." After 3 decades of plummeting political interest among freshmen, political interest has been on the rise since 2001. www.gseis.ucla.edu/heri/03 press release.pdf.
10. Margaret Stimmann Branson, "Making the Case for Civic Education: Educating Young People for Responsible Citizenship," paper presented at the Conference for Professional Development for Program Trainers, Manhattan Beach, Calif., February 25, 2001.
11. Kenneth Feldman and Theodore M. Newcomb, *The Impact of College on Students,* vol. 2 (Jossey-Bass, 1969), pp. 16–24, 49–56. See also David O. Sears and Nicholas A. Valentino, "Politics Matters: Political Events as Catalysts for Preadult Socialization," *American Political Science Review* 91 (March 1997), pp. 45–65.
12. Robert D. Putnam, "Bowling Together," *American Prospect* 13 (February 11, 2002), pp. 20–22.
13. Robert D. Putnam, "Bowling Together," in *United We Serve,* eds. E.J. Dionne Jr., Kayla Meltzer Drogosz, and Robert E. Litan (Brookings Institution Press, 2003), p. 19. The Putnam data is available at www.ksg.harvard.edu/saguaro/.
14. Benjamin I. Page and Robert Y. Shapiro, *The Rational Public* (University of Chicago Press, 1992), p. 267.
15. Quoted in Hadley Cantril, *Gauging Public Opinion* (Princeton University Press, 1944), p. viii.
16. John G. Geer, *From Tea Leaves to Opinion Polls: A Theory of Democratic Leadership* (Columbia University Press, 1996).
17. Everett C. Ladd and John Benson, "The Growth of News Polls in American Politics," in *Media Polls in American Politics,* eds. Thomas Mann and Gary Orren (Brookings Institution Press, 1992), pp. 19–31.
18. Benjamin I. Page and Robert Y. Shapiro, *The Rational Public: Fifty Years of Trends in Americans' Policy Preferences* (University of Chicago Press, 1992), p. 237.
19. George J. Church, "What in the World Are We Doing?" *Time,* October 18, 1993, p. 42.
20. "Do you approve or disapprove of the way George W. Bush is handling the situation with Iraq?" CBS News/New York Times Poll, May 3, 2003, and May 20, 2004, at www.pollingreport.com/iraq.htm.
21. Jacobs and Shapiro, *Politicians Don't Pander* (University of Chicago Press, 2000), p. 3.
22. David R. Mayhew, *Congress: The Electoral Connection* (Yale University Press, 1974); Richard F. Fenno Jr., *Home Style: House Members in Their Districts* (Longman, 1978).
23. Robert S. Erikson and Kent L. Tedin, *American Public Opinion: Its Origins, Content and Impact,* 6th ed. (Longman, 2001), pp. 272–273.
24. For a general discussion of political knowledge, see Michael Delli Carpini and Scott Keeter, *What Americans Know About Politics and Why it Matters* (Yale University Press, 1996).
25. The 2000 National Election Study, Center for Political Studies, University of Michigan. See the NES Guide to Public Opinion and Electoral Behavior at www.umich.edu/~nes/nesguide/nesguide.htm.
26. Robert S. Erikson and Kent L. Tedin, *American Public Opinion: Its Origins, Content and Impact,* 6th ed. (Longman, 2001), p. 304.
27. Neil S. Newhouse and Christine L. Matthews, "NAFTA Revisited: Most Americans Just Weren't Deeply Engaged," *Public Perspective* 5 (January–February, 1994), pp. 31–32.
28. Center for the Study of Elections and Democracy and Center for the Study of Politics, "2004 Election Panel Study Data," at www.csp.polisci.wisc.edu/byu uw/.
29. *2002 National Election Study* (Center for Political Studies, University of Michigan, 2002).
30. *2002 National Election Study* (Center for Political Studies, University of Michigan, 2002).
31. Federal Election Commission, "Presidential Election Campaign Fund," at www.fec.gov.
32. For a discussion of the relationship between civic skills and participation, see Sidney Verba, Kay Lehman Schlozman, and Henry E. Brady, *Voice and Equality: Civic Voluntarism in American Politics* (Harvard University Press, 1995).
33. John Balz, "Iorio pushes for national voting reform," *St. Petersburg Times,* May 11, 2001, p. 3B.
34. Juliet Eilperin, "Federal Aid Helps States Fund Election Reform," *The Washington Post,* March 16, 2003, p. A5.
35. Frank R. Parker, *Black Votes Count: Political Empowerment in Mississippi After 1965* (University of North Carolina Press, 1990), p. 3.
36. Bernard Grofman and Lisa Handley, "The Impact of the Voting Rights Act on Black Representation in Southern State Legislatures," *Legislative Studies Quarterly* 16 (February 1991), pp. 111–128.
37. International Institute for Democracy and Electoral Assistance, "Voter Turnout from 1945 to Date: A Global Report on Political Participation," at www.idea.int/voter turnout/index.html.
38. Raymond E. Wolfinger and Steven J. Rosenstone, "The Effect of Registration Laws on Voter Turnout," *American Political Science Review* 72 (March 1978), p. 41.
39. Raymond E. Wolfinger and Steven J. Rosenstone, "The Effect of Registration Laws on Voter Turnout," *American Political Science Review* 72 (March 1978), p. 24.
40. Raymond E. Wolfinger and Steven J. Rosenstone, *Who Votes?* (Yale University Press, 1980), pp. 78, 88.
41. Federal Election Commission, "The Impact of the National Voter Registration Act on Federal Elections 1999–2000," at www.fec.gov.
42. See Raymond E. Wolfinger and Ben Highton, "Estimating the Effects of the National Voter Registration Act of 1993," *Political Behavior* (June 1998), pp. 79–104; and Raymond E. Wolfinger and Jonathan Hoffman, "Registering and Voting with Motor Voter," *PS: Political Science and Politics* (March 2001), pp. 85–92.
43. For a discussion of the differences in the turnout between presidential and midterm elections, see James E. Campbell, "The Presidential Surge

and Its Midterm Decline in Congressional Elections, 1868–1988," *Journal of Politics* 53 (May 1991), pp. 477–487.

44. David E. Rosenbaum, "Democrats Keep Solid Hold on Congress," *The New York Times*, November 9, 1988, p. A24; and Louis V. Gerstner, "Next Time, Let Us Boldly Vote as No Democracy Has Before," *USA Today*, November 16, 1998, p. A15.

45. Data from Curtis Gans, "President Bush, Mobilization Drives Propel Turnout to Post-1968 High; Kerry, Democratic Weakness Shown," *Center for Voting and Democracy*, November 4, 2004 at www.fairvote.org/reports/csae2004electionreport.pdf.

46. Raymond E. Wolfinger and Steven J. Rosenstone, *Who Votes?* (Yale University Press, 1980), p. 102.

47. Howard W. Stanley and Richard G. Niemi, *Vital Statistics on Politics, 1999–2000* (CQ Press, 2000), pp. 120–121; CNN, at www.cnn.com/ELECTION/2000/results/index.my.html.

48. The Vanishing Voter, "Election Interest Among Young Adults Is Up Sharply From 2000," March 12, 2004, available at www.vanishingvoter.org/Releases/release031104.shtml.

49. See the classic book on this topic, Angus Campbell, Philip E. Converse, Warren E. Miller, and Donald E. Stokes, *The American Voter* (Wiley, 1960). This volume is a foundation of modern voting analysis despite much new evidence and reinterpretation. See also Warren E. Miller and J. Merrill Shanks, *The New American Voter* (Harvard University Press, 1996); and Eric R.A.N. Smith, *The Unchanging American Voter* (University of California Press, 1989).

50. www.census.gov/prod/2002pubs/p20-542.pdf.

51. Austin Ranney, "Nonvoting Is Not a Social Disease," *Public Opinion*, October–November 1983, pp. 16–19.

52. Thomas Byrne Edsall, *The New Politics of Inequality* (Norton, 1984), p. 181.

53. Steven J. Rosenstone and John Mark Hansen, *Mobilitzation, Participation, and Democracy in America* (Longman, 2003).

54. Frances Fox Piven and Richard A. Cloward, "Prospects for Voter Registration Reform: A Report on the Experiences of the Human SERVE Campaign," *PS: Political Science and Politics* 18 (Summer 1985), p. 589.

55. Ibid., p. 589.

56. Raymond E. Wolfinger and Steven J. Rosenstone, *Who Votes?* (Yale University Press, 1980), p. 109.

57. E. E. Schattschneider, *The Semisovereign People* (Dryden Press, 1975), p. 96.

58. Stephen Earl Bennett and David Resnick, "The Implications of Nonvoting for Democracy in the United States," *American Journal of Political Science* 84 (August 1990), pp. 771–802.

59. Bruce E. Keith, David B. Magleby, Candice J. Nelson, Elizabeth Orr, Mark C. Westlye, and Raymond E. Wolfinger, *The Myth of the Independent Voter* (University of California Press, 1992), pp. 60–75; and 2000 National Election Study, Center for Political Studies, University of Michigan, Ann Arbor.

60. Martin P. Wattenberg, *The Rise of Candidate Centered Politics: Presidential Elections of the 1980s* (Harvard University Press, 1991).

61. David Menefee-Libey, *The Triumph of Campaign-Centered Politics* (Chatham House/Seven Bridges Press, 2000).

62. Barry Goldwater, quoted in Theodore H. White, *The Making of the President, 1964* (Athenaeum, 1965), p. 217.

63. William H. Flanigan and Nancy H. Zingale, *Political Behavior of the American Electorate*, 8th ed. (CQ Press, 1994), p. 173.

64. Tim Graham, "Media-Powered Howard," National Review Online, January 30, 2004.

65. www.cnn.com/ELECTION/2004/pages/results/states/US/P/OO/epolls.O.html.

66. J. Merrill Shanks and Warren E. Miller, "Policy Direction and Performance Evaluation: Complementary Explanations of the Reagan Elections," *British Journal of Political Science* 20 (1990), pp. 143–235; and Warren E. Miller and J. Merrill Shanks, "Policy Direction and Performance Evaluation: Comparing George Bush's Victory with Those of Ronald Reagan in 1980 and 1984," paper presented at the annual meeting of the American Political Science Association, Atlanta, August 31–September 2, 1989.

67. Amihai Glazer, "The Strategy of Candidate Ambiguity," *American Political Science Review* 84 (March 1990), pp. 237–241.

68. Robert S. Erikson and David W. Romero, "Candidate Equilibrium and the Behavioral Model of the Vote," *American Political Science Review* 84 (December 1990), p. 1122.

69. Morris P. Fiorina, *Retrospective Voting in American National Elections* (Yale University Press, 1981).

70. www.cnn.com/ELECTION/2000/results/index.epolls.html.

71. Gerald H. Kramer, "Short-Term Fluctuations in U.S. Voting Behavior, 1896–1964," *American Political Science Review* 65 (March 1971),

pp. 131–143. See also Edward R. Tufte, "Determinants of the Outcomes of Midterm Congressional Elections," *American Political Science Review* 69 (September 1975), pp. 812–826; and Andrew E. Busch, *Horses in Midstream: U.S. Midterm Elections and Their Consequences* (University of Pittsburgh Press, 1999).

72. John R. Hibbing and John R. Alford, "The Educational Impact of Economic Conditions: Who Is Held Responsible?" *American Journal of Political Science* 25 (August 1981), pp. 423–439; and Morris P. Fiorina, "Who Is Held Responsible? Further Evidence on the Hibbing-Alford Thesis," *American Journal of Political Science* (February 1983), pp. 158–164.

73. Robert M. Stein, "Economic Voting for Governor and U.S. Senator: The Electoral Consequences of Federalism," *Journal of Politics* 52 (February 1990), pp. 29–53.

74. www.cnn.com/ELECTION/2004/pages/results/states/US/P/OO/epolls.O.html.

Chapter 9

1. *1994 Census of Governments* (U.S. Government Printing Office, 1995), vol. 1, no. 2, p. 1.

2. United States Senate, at www.senate.gov/general/contact_information/senators_cfm.cfm.

3. See U.S. Term Limits, at www.termlimits.org.

4. In the 1992 and 1994 National Election Studies, approximately 78 percent of Americans favored term limits. *1992 National Election Study and 1994 National Election Study* (Center for Political Studies, University of Michigan, 1992, 1994).

5. *U.S. Term Limits Inc.* v. *Thornton*, 514 U.S. 799 (1995).

6. For an insightful examination of electoral rules, see Bernard Grofman and Arend Lijphart, eds., *Electoral Laws and Their Political Consequences* (Agathon Press, 1986).

7. Arend Lijphart, "The Political Consequences of Electoral Laws, 1945–85," *American Political Science Review* 84 (June 1990), pp. 481–495. See also David M. Farrell, *Electoral Systems: A Comparative Introduction* (Macmillan, 2001).

8. www.fairvote.org/e_college/faithless.htm.

9. As noted, one of Gore's electors abstained, reducing his vote from 267 to 266; CNN, at www.cnn.com/2001/ALLPOLITICS/stories/01/06/electoral.vote/index.html.

10. Paul D. Schumaker and Burdett A. Loomis, *Choosing a President: The Electoral College and Beyond* (Seven Bridges Press, 2002), p. 60. See also George Rabinowitz and Stuart Elaine MacDonald, "The Power of the States in U.S. Presidential Elections," *American Political Science Review* 80 (March 1986), pp. 65–87; and Dany M. Adkison and Christopher Elliott, "The Electoral College: A Misunderstood Institution," *PS: Political Science and Politics* 30 (March 1997), pp. 77–80.

11. See, for example, David R. Mayhew, *Congress: The Electoral Connection* (Yale University Press, 1974); Richard F. Fenno Jr., *Home Style: House Members in Their Districts* (Little, Brown, 1978); and James E. Campbell, "The Return of Incumbents: The Nature of Incumbency Advantage," *Western Political Quarterly* 36 (September 1983), pp. 434–444.

12. Gary King and Andrew Gelman, "Systemic Consequences of Incumbency Advantage in U.S. House Elections," *American Journal of Political Science* 35 (February 1991), pp. 110–137.

13. Alan I. Abramowitz, "Economic Conditions, Presidential Popularity, and Voting Behavior in Midterm Congressional Elections," *Journal of Politics* 47 (February 1985), pp. 31–43. See also Gary C. Jacobson, *The Politics of Congressional Elections*, 5th ed. (Addison-Wesley, 2001), pp. 146–153.

14. See Edward R. Tufte, *Political Control of the Economy* (Princeton University Press, 1978); see also his "Determinants of the Outcomes of Midterm Congressional Elections," *American Political Science Review* 69 (September 1975), pp. 812–826. For a more recent discussion of the same subject, see Jacobson, *Politics of Congressional Elections*, pp. 123–178.

15. Alan I. Abramowitz and Jeffrey A. Segal, "Determinants of the Outcomes of U.S. Senate Elections," *Journal of Politics* 48 (1986), pp. 433–439.

16. This includes the postelection switch of Alabama Senator Richard Shelby to the Republican Party.

17. Paul S. Herrnson, *Congressional Elections: Campaigning at Home and in Washington*, 4th ed. (CQ Press, 2004), pp. 45, 48.

18. Linda L. Fowler and Robert D. McClure, *Political Ambition: Who Decides to Run for Congress* (Yale University Press, 1989); Paul S. Herrnson, *Congressional Elections: Campaigning at Home and in Washington*, 4th ed. (CQ Press, 2004), p. 45.

19. Kathleen Hall Jamieson, *Everything You Think You Know About Politics... and Why You're Wrong* (Basic Books, 2000), p. 38.

20. For a discussion of different explanations of the impact of incumbency, see Keith Krehbiel and John R. Wright, "The Incumbency Effect in Congressional Elections: A Test of Two Explanations," *American Journal of Political Science* 27 (February 1983), p. 140.

21. Roll Call, "Roll Call Casualty List," *Roll Call Politics*, November 5, 1998, p. 15; "Senate, House, Gubernatorial Results," *Congressional Quarterly Weekly*, November 11, 2000, pp. 2694–2703.

22. "Financial Activity of Senate and House General Election Campaigns," Federal Election Commission at www.ftp.fec.gov/fec.

23. Albert D. Cover, "One Good Term Deserves Another: The Advantages of Incumbency in Congressional Elections," *American Journal of Political Science* 21 (August 1977), pp. 523–542; Morris P. Fiorina, *Congress: Keystone of the Washington Establishment* (Yale University Press, 1978); and David Mayhew, *Congress: The Electoral Connection* (Yale University Press, 1974), pp. 52–53.

24. Mayhew, *Congress*, p. 61; Richard F. Fenno Jr., *Congressmen in Committees* (Little, Brown, 1973); and Steven S. Smith and Christopher J. Deering, *Committees in Congress*, 3d ed. (CQ Press, 1997).

25. Candice J. Nelson, "Spending in the 2000 Elections," in *Financing the 2000 Election* ed., David B. Magleby, (Brookings Institution Press, 2002), pp. 28–30.

26. Jonathan S. Krasno, *Challengers, Competition, and Reelection: Comparing Senate and House Elections* (Yale University Press, 1994), p. 2.

27. Alan I. Abramowitz, "Explaining Senate Election Outcomes," *American Political Science Review* 82 (June 1988), pp. 385–403.

28. David B. Magleby and J. Quin Monson, eds., *The Last Hurrah?: Soft Money and Issue Advocacy in the 2002 Congressional Elections* (Brookings Institution Press, 2004).

29. David B. Magleby, "More Bang for the Buck: Campaign Spending in Small State U.S. Senate Elections," paper presented at the annual meeting of the Western Political Science Association, Salt Lake City, March 30–April 1, 1989.

30. Associated Press writer, "Edwards Actions Doing Talking Over Possible Presidential Run," *Associated Press State and Local Wire* for North Carolina, June 18, 2001; and Christopher Graff, "Vermont Governor Takes First Step Toward Presidential Campaign," *The Associated Press State & Local Wire* of Vermont, November 19, 2001.

31. www.thegreenpapers.com/P04/tally.phtml.

32. Republican Delegate Selection and Voter Eligibility, at www.thegreenpapers.com/P04/R-DSVE.phtml.

33. The descriptions of these types of primaries are drawn from James W. Davis, *Presidential Primaries*, rev. ed. (Greenwood Press, 1984), chap. 3. See pp. 56–63 for specifics on each state (and Puerto Rico). This material is used with the permission of the publisher.

34. Paul T. David and James W. Caesar, *Proportional Representation in Presidential Nominating Politics* (University Press of Virginia, 1980), pp. 9–11.

35. See Rhodes Cook, *Race for the Presidency: Winning the 2004 Nomination* (CQ Press, 2004), p. 5. See also the Republican National Committee, at www.rnc.org.

36. Nelson W. Polsby and Aaron Wildavsky, *Presidential Elections: Strategies and Structures of American Politics*, 11th ed. (Rowman & Littlefield, 2004), p. 110.

37. The Green Papers, *The Green Papers, 2004 Presidential Primaries, Caucuses, and Conventions: New York Republican*, www.thegreenpapers.com/P04/NY-R.phtml.

38. Costas Panagopoulos, "Election Issues 2004 in Depth," *Campaigns & Elections*, May 2004, p. 48.

39. Jonathan Finer, "No Tea, but Democrats Get the Party Started," *The Washington Post*, July 29, 2003, p. A4.

40. National Association of Secretaries of State, at www.nass.org/issues.html#primaryplan.

41. Federal Elections Commission, "2004 Presidential Primary Dates and Candidates Filing Deadlines for Ballot Access," May 26, 2004, at www.fec.gov.

42. David Redlawsk and Arthur Sanders, "Groups and Grassroots in the Iowa Caucuses," in *Outside Money in the 2000 Presidential Primaries and Congressional Elections*, ed. David B. Magleby, in *PS Online* (June 2001), at www.apsanet.org/PS/june01/redlawsk.cfm.

43. Blake Morrison, "Dean Scream Gaining Cult-Like Status on Web," *USA TODAY*, January 22, 2004, p. 4A.

44. "A Useful Piece of Scream Therapy," *The Economist*, February 14, 2004, United States Section.

45. The viewership of conventions has declined as the amount of time devoted to conventions dropped. In 1988, Democrats averaged 27.1 million viewers and Republicans 24.5 million. By 1996, viewership for the Democrats was 18 million viewers on average and for the Republicans,

16.6 million. See John Carmody, "The TV Column," *The Washington Post*, September 2, 1996, p. D4. Viewership figures improved somewhat in 2000: Democrats averaged 20.6 million viewers and Republicans 19.2 million. See Don Aucoin, "Democrats Hold TV Ratings Edge," *Boston Globe*, August 19, 2000, p. F3.

46. Stephan J. Wayne, *The Road to the White House, 2004: The Politics of Presidential Elections* (Wadsworth, 2004), chap. 5.

47. Jeff Fishel, *Presidents and Promises* (CQ Press, 1984), pp. 26–28.

48. See White House, Education Reform: No Child Left Behind Act, at www.whitehouse.gov/infocus/education.

49. Adam Nagourney, "Kerry Camp Sees Edwards Helping with Rural Vote," *The New York Times*, July 9, 2004, p. 1.

50. John M. Glionna, "The Race to the White House; Nader Bid for Spot on Oregon's Ballot Fails; The State was the First Stop in the Populist Candidate's Quest to Qualify in all 50 States," *Los Angeles Times*, April 6, 2004, p. 14.

51. Arthur Kane, "Reform Party Endorsement Boosts Nader: The Liberal Activist is Now Eligible to Ease onto the Presidential Ballot in Seven States, Including Colorado," *The Denver Post*, May 13, 2004, p. A1.

52. Election Reform.org, at www.ballot-access.org.

53. CNN, "Burden of Proof," August 9, 2000; www.time.com/time/election2004/article/0,18471,641158,00.html.

54. Charles Babington, "Staggering Sum-Raising," *The Washington Post*, June 19, 2004, p. A6.

55. Lisa Getter, "GOP Can't Beat '3rd Party' Groups, So It Forms Them," *Los Angeles Times*, June 6, 2004, p. A20.

56. Sidney Kraus, *The Great Debates: Kennedy vs. Nixon, 1960* (Indiana University Press, 1962). See also Myles Martel, *Political Campaign Debates* (Longman, 1983).

57. "Televised Debate History, 1960–1996," at www.museum.tv/debateweb/html/history/1976/video.htm.

58. Stephen Koff, "VP Debate to Have Free-Flowing Exchange," *Plain Dealer* (Cleveland, Ohio), June 18, 2004, p. A21.

59. Commission on Presidential Debates, at www.debates.org/pages/news_040617_p.html.

60. Robert S. Erikson, "Economic Conditions and the Presidential Vote," *American Political Science Review* 83 (June 1989), pp. 567–575. Class-based voting has also become more important. See Robert S. Erikson, Thomas O. Lancaster, and David W. Romers, "Group Components of the Presidential Vote, 1952–1984," *Journal of Politics* 51 (May 1989), pp. 337–346.

61. David B. Magleby and Candice J. Nelson, *The Money Chase: Congressional Campaign Finance Reform* (Brookings Institution Press, 1990), pp. 13–14.

62. See Senate Committee on Governmental Affairs, "1997 Special Investigation in Connection with the 1996 Federal Election Campaigns," www.senate.gov/~gov_affairs/sireport.htm.

63. *Buckley* v. *Valeo*, 424 U.S. 1 (1976).

64. See Herbert E. Alexander and Monica Bauer, *Financing the 1988 Election* (Westview Press, 1991); & Frank J. Sorauf, *Inside Campaign Finance: Myths and Realities* (Yale University Press, 1992); and Herbert E. Alexander, *Financing Politics: Money, Elections, and Political Reform* (CQ Press, 1992).

65. Federal Election Commission, Public Disclosure Office, personal communication, July 23, 2004; see also Campaign Finance Institute, "Participation, Competition, Engagement: Reviving and Improving Public Financing for Presidential Nomination Politics," September 22, 2003, p. 52.

66. Beth Donovan, "Parties Turned Soft Money Law into Hard and Fast Spending," *Congressional Quarterly Weekly*, May 15, 1993, pp. 1196–1197; David E. Rosenbaum, "In Political Money Game, the Year of Big Loopholes," *The New York Times*, December 26, 1996, p. A1; and "Party Fundraising Escalates," at www.fec.gov.

67. David B. Magleby and J. Quin Monson, eds., 2004. *The Last Hurrah?: Soft Money and Issue Advocacy in the 2002 Congressional Elections* (Brookings Institution Press, 2004), pp. 82–83.

68. See Joseph A. Pika, "Campaign Spending and Activity in the 2000 Delaware U.S. Senate Race," in *Election Advocacy: Soft Money and Issue Advocacy in the 2000 Congressional Elections*, ed. David B. Magleby (Center for the Study of Elections and Democracy, Brigham Young University, 2001), pp. 51–61.

69. David B. Magleby, "Dictum Without Data: The Myth of Issue Advocacy and Party Building," at csed.byu.edu/publications/dictum.doc.

70. David B. Magleby and J. Quin Monson, "Campaign 2002: 'The Perfect Storm'" at www.apsanet.org/PS/july03/magleby.pdf.

71. David. B. Magleby, ed., *The Other Campaign: Soft Money and Issue Advocacy in the 2000 Congressional Elections* (Rowman & Littlefield, 2003); and

David B. Magleby and J. Quin Monson, *The Last Hurrah? Soft Money and Issue Advocacy in the 2002 Congressional Elections* (Brookings Institute Press, 2004), pp. 159–179.

72. Magleby and Monson, *The Last Hurrah?*, pp. 159–179.

73. Craig B. Holman and Luke P. McLoughlin, *Buying Time, 2000: Television Advertising in the 2000 Federal Elections* (Brennan Center for Justice, New York University School of Law, 2001), p. 33.

74. Nicholas Confessore, "Bush's Secret Stash: Why the GOP War Chest Is Even Bigger than You Think," *The Washington Monthly*, May 18, 2004, pp. 117–122.

75. Morton M. Kondracke, "McCain to Lead New Reform Fight for Free TV Time," *Roll Call*, May 30, 2002, at www.rollcall.com/pages/columns/kondracke/00/2002/kond0530.html.

76. Rick Hampson, "Former Banker Was Big Spender," *USA Today*, November 9, 2000, p. A9.

77. Federal Election Commission, "Disclosure Data Base: PAS200.ZIP," at www.fec.gov. See also David B. Magleby and Jason Richard Beal, "Independent Expenditures and Internal Communications," in *The Other Campaign*, ed., Magleby (Rowman & Littlefield, 2003), p. 83.

78. BCRA does allow candidates to pay themselves out of their campaign funds, something that helps less affluent candidates run. But given the high cost of campaign, such a strategy is often not going to be helpful to winning election.

79. Federal Election Commission, "2000–2001 Financial Activity of Senate and House General Election Campaigns," at www.fec.gov. Federal Election Commission, "1999–2000 Financial Activity of Senate and House General Election Campaigns," at www.fec.gov.

80. Federal Elections Commission, at herndon1.sdrdc.com/fecimg/srssea.html.

81. See Todd Donovan and Shawn Bowler, *Reforming the Republic: Democratic Institutions for a New America* (Prentice Hall, 2004).

82. Curtis B. Gans, Director, Committee for the Study of the American Electorate, facsimile to author, September 22, 2004.

83. The President's Commission for a National Agenda for the Eighties, *A National Agenda for the Eighties* (U.S. Government Printing Office, 1980), p. 97, proposed holding four presidential primaries, scheduled about one month apart.

84. Nelson W. Polsby, *Consequences of Party Reform* (Oxford University Press, 1983), p. 118.

85. Thomas E. Cronin and Robert Loevy, "The Case for a National Primary Convention Plan," *Public Opinion*, December 1982–January 1983, pp. 50–53.

86. Barbara Norrander and Greg W. Smith, "Type of Contest, Candidate Strategy, and Turnout in Presidential Primaries," *American Politics Quarterly* 13 (January 1985), p. 28.

87. Neal R. Peirce and Lawrence Longley, *The People's President: The Electoral College in American History and the Direct-Vote Alternative*, 2d ed. (Yale University Press, 1981), describe and advocate the direct-vote alternative. Nelson W. Polsby and Aaron B. Wildavsky, *Presidential Elections: Contemporary Strategies of American Politics*, 10th ed. (Chatham House, 2000), favor the present system.

88. Al Baker, "New York Risking the Loss of Ballot Equipment Money," *The New York Times*, April 29, 2004, p. B05.

89. Ibid.

90. Maha Al-Azar, "Broad Election Reforms Are Urged; Education Called As Crucial As Machines," *The Washington Post*, July 17, 2003, p. T04; Harris N. Miller, "Electronic Voting Is a Solution," *USA Today*, February 4, 2004, p. 14A.

Chapter 10

1. Donna Britt, "Janet's 'Reveal' Lays Bare an Insidious Trend, *The Washington Post*, February 4, 2004, p. B1.

2. Kelefa Sanneh, "During Halftime Show," *The New York Times*, February 2, 2004, p. D4.

3. Frank Ahrens, "Critics Blame Big Media for Sleaze Factor," *The Washington Post*, February 11, 2004, p. E1.

4. Frank Ahrens, "Critics Blame Big Media for Sleaze Factor," *The Washington Post*, February 11, 2004, p. E1.

5. www.cnn.com/2004/US/02/02/superbowl.jackson/.

6. Frank Rich, "My Hero, Janet Jackson," *The New York Times*, February 15, 2004, p. B1.

7. Barabara Meltz, "Kids May Need to Talk about a Revealing Halftime Show," *The Boston Globe*, February 5, 2004, p. D1.

8. Jube Shriver Jr., "FCC Rules Bono Remark Is Indecent," *Los Angeles Times*, March 19, 2004, p. C1.

9. Jonathon Krim, "Congress Acts to Curb Offensive Program; Senate Panel Proposes Fines, Delayed Media Consolidation," *The Washington Post*, March 10, 2004, p. E01.

10. Clear Channel Communications, *Howard Stern Show Taken Off Clear Channel Stations* (San Antonio, Texas: Corporate Communications, 2004).

11. William Rivers, *The Other Government* (Universe Books, 1982); Douglas Cater, *The Fourth Branch of Government* (Houghton Mifflin, 1959); Dom Bonafede, "The Washington Press: An Interpreter or a Participant in Policy Making?" *National Journal*, April 24, 1982, pp. 716–721; Michael Ledeen, "Learning to Say 'No' to the Press," *Public Interest* 73 (Fall 1983), p. 113.

12. Leslie G. Moeller, "The Big Four: Mass Media Actualities and Expectations," in *Beyond Media: New Approaches to Mass Communication*, eds. Richard W. Budd and Brent D. Ruben (Transaction Books, 1988), p. 15.

13. Pew Research Center for the People and the Press, "Far More Voters Believe Election Outcome Matters," questionnaire, March 25, 2004. people-press.org/reports/print.php3?PageID=802. One service that e-mails customized news and reminders to subscribers is infobeat.com.

14. U.S. Bureau of the Census, *Statistical Abstract of the United States, 2001* (Government Printing Office, 2001), tabs. 1125 and 1126.

15. Journalism.org, "Evening News Share," at www.stateofthenewsmedia.org/chartland.asp?id=210&ct=line&dir=&sort=&col1_box=1&col2_box=1&col3_box=1, March 15, 2004.

16. Journalism.org, "Cable TV," at www.stateofthenewsmedia.org/narrative_cabletv_audience.asp?cat=3&media=5, March 15, 2004.

17. David B. Magleby and J. Quin Monson, eds., *The Last Hurrah?* (Brookings Institution Press, 2004); David B. Magleby, ed., *The Other Campaign* (Rowman & Littlefield, 2003); David B. Magleby, ed., *Outside Money* (Rowman & Littlefield, 2000).

18. David B. Magleby, ed., *Dictum Without Data: The Myth of Issue Advocacy and Party Building* (Center for the Study of Elections and Democracy, 2000); David B. Magleby, "Party and Interest Group Electioneering in Federal Elections," in *Inside the Campaign Finance Battle*, eds., Anthony Corrado, Thomas E. Mann, and Trevor Potter (Brookings Institution Press, 2003), p. 147.

19. Magleby and Monson, eds., *The Last Hurrah?*; Magleby, ed., *The Other Campaign*; Magleby, ed., *Outside Money*.

20. Journalism.org, "Local TV," at www.stateofthenewsmedia.org/narrative_localtv_contentanalysis.asp?cat=2&media=6, March 15, 2004. See also, Marc Fisher, "TV Stations Offer a Clear Picture of Indifference," *The Washington Post*, September 26, 2000, p. B1.

21. Alliance for Better Campaigns, *Political Standard* 4 (March 2001), p. 6.

22. www.localnewsarchive.org/pdf/LocalTV2002.pdf.

23. David B. Magleby, "Direct Legislation in the American States," in *Referendums Around the World: The Growing Use of Direct Democracy*, eds. David Butler and Austin Ranney (AEI Press, 1994), pp. 218–257.

24. U.S. Bureau of the Census, *Statistical Abstract of the United States, 2003* (Government Printing Office, 2003), tab. 1126.

25. Leonard Wiener, "Radio's Future Shock," *U.S. News & World Report*, December 2, 2002, p. 40.

26. *Statistical Abstract of the United States, 2003*, p. 722.

27. Newspaper Association of America, at www.naa.org/marketscope/pdfs/ReaderTrendDaily_Age.pdf.

28. Audit Bureau of Circulations, at abcas1.accessabc.com/ecirc.

29. Elizabeth Weise, "With Dissidents on Board, Net Could See Revolutions," *USA Today*, October 31, 2000, p. 3D.

30. Inktomi, "Web Surpasses One Billion Documents," at www.inktomi.com/new/press/billion.html, January 18, 2000.

31. Pew Research Center for the People and the Press, at people-press.org/reports/print.php3?PageID=748.

32. Amy Poftak, Net-Wise Teens: Safety, Ethics, and Innovation, *Technology & Learning*, August 1, 2002, p. 36.

33. "Inside the 2004 Campaign Tool Chest: Blogs and Online Voting," *Los Angeles Times*, January 5, 2004, p. A10.

34. Mark Singer, "Running on Instinct. Howard Dean's Critics Say He Is Winging It. Can That Get Him to the White House?" *New Yorker*, January 12, 2004, pg. 43.

35. Pew Research Center for the People and the Press, "Web News Takes Off," press release, June 8, 1998, p. 1; Pew Research Center for the People and the Press, Survey Reports, "Public's News Habits Little Changed by September 11," June 9, 2002. See people-press.org/reports.

36. James Fallows, *Breaking the News: How the Media Undermine American Democracy* (Pantheon Books, 1996), p. 3.

37. Paul Starobin, "Heeding the Call," *National Journal,* November 30, 1996, pp. 2584–2589.

38. Howard Kurtz, "Jayson Blair, Continued; With a Story of Lies, The Fallen Writer Hopes to Turn a Page," *The Washington Post,* March 7, 2004, sec. D01.

39. Jacques Steinburg, "Editor of USA Today Resigns; Cites Failure Over Fabrications," *The New York Times,* April 21, 2004, p. A1.

40. See Robert A. Rutland, *Newsmongers: Journalism in the Life of the Nation, 1690–1972* (Dial Press, 1973).

41. Quoted in Frank Luther Mott, *American Journalism,* 3d ed. (Macmillan, 1962), p. 412.

42. During the 1930s, more than 1,000 speeches were made by members of Congress on one network alone. See Edward W. Chester, *Radio, Television, and American Politics* (Sheed & Ward, 1969), p. 62.

43. Frances Perkins, quoted in James MacGregor Burns, *Roosevelt: The Lion and the Fox* (Harcourt, 1956), p. 205.

44. Gannett Corp., at www.gannett.com/map/gan007.htm.

45. "California, Southland Focus; Tribune Gets Antitrust Approval in *Times* Deal," *Los Angeles Times,* April 7, 2000, p. C2.

46. www.pbs.org/wgbh/pages/frontline/shows/cool/giants.

47. Seth Schiesel, "FCC Rules on Ownership Under Review," *The New York Times,* April 3, 2002, p. C1.

48. Paul Davidson, "Spending Bill Settles Two Key Issues," *USA Today,* January 23, 2004, p. B3.

49. Stephen Labaton, "Court Orders FCC to Rethink New Rules on Growth of Media," *The New York Times,* June 25, 2004, p. 1.

50. Shanto Iyengar and Donald R. Kinder, *News That Matters* (University of Chicago Press, 1987).

51. Steven J. Simmons, *The Fairness Doctrine and the Media* (University of California Press, 1978).

52. "Political Fairness on TV," *Christian Science Monitor,* October 17, 2000, p. 10.

53. www.pewinternet.org/reports/chart/asp?. Accessed April 13, 2004.

54. Harvey G. Zeidenstein, "News Media Perception of White House News Management," *Presidential Studies Quarterly* 24 (Summer 1984), pp. 391–398.

55. Elihu Katz and Paul Lazarsfeld, *Personal Influence: The Part Played by People in the Flow of Mass Communications* (Free Press, 1955).

56. See Doris A. Graber, "Say It with Pictures: The Impact of Audiovisual News on Public Opinion Formation," paper presented at the annual meeting of the Midwest Political Science Association, Chicago, April 1987; and Benjamin I. Page, Robert Y. Shapiro, and Glenn R. Dempsey. "What Moves Public Opinion?" *American Political Science Review* 76 (March 1987), pp. 23–43.

57. See, for example, Jack Dennis, "Preadult Learning of Political Independence: Media and Family Communications Effects," *Communication Research* 13 (July 1987), pp. 401–433; and Olive Stevens, *Children Talking Politics* (Robertson, 1982).

58. See Angus Campbell, Philip E. Converse, Warren E. Miller, and Donald E. Stokes, *The American Voter* (Wiley, 1960).

59. Paul Lazarsfeld, Bernard Berelson, and Hazel Gaudet, *The People's Choice: How the Voter Makes Up His Mind in a Presidential Campaign,* 3d ed. (Columbia University Press, 1968); Bernard Berelson, Paul Lazarsfeld, and William McPhee, *Voting: A Study of Opinion Formation in a Presidential Campaign* (University of Chicago Press, 1954).

60. Pew Research Center for the People and the Press, "Scandal Reporting Faulted for Bias and Inaccuracy: Popular Policies and Unpopular Press Lift Clinton Ratings," press release, February 6, 1998, p. 1.

61. Gallup Organization, at www.gallup.com/poll-archives/980926.htm.

62. Stuart Oskamp, ed., *Television as a Social Issue* (Sage, 1988); James W. Carey, ed., *Media, Myths, and Narratives: Television and the Press* (Sage, 1988).

63. Doris A. Graber, *Processing the News: How People Tame the Information Tide,* 2d ed. (Longman, 1988), pp. 107–113.

64. Times Mirror Center for the People and the Press, "Times Mirror News Interest Index," press releases, January 16 and February 28, 1992.

65. John K. Robinson and Mark R. Levy, eds., *The Main Source: Learning from Television News* (Sage, 1986).

66. Graber, *Processing the News,* p. 115.

67. Tides Center, "Internet and American Life," at www.pewinternet.org/reports/reports.asp. Accessed April 13, 2004.

68. Rush Limbaugh, *See, I Told You So* (Pocket Books, 1993), p. 326.

69. See Nelson Polsby, *Consequences of Party Reform* (Oxford University Press, 1983), pp. 142–146. See also Stanley Rothman and S. Robert Lichter, "Media and Business Elites: Two Classes in Conflict!" *Public Interest* 69 (Fall 1982), pp. 119–125.

70. Michael Parenti, *Inventing Reality: The Politics of the Mass Media* (St. Martin's Press, 1986), p. 35.

71. Rick Lyman, "Multimedia Deal: The History; 2 Commanding Publishers, 2 Powerful Empires," *The New York Times,* March 14, 2000, p. C16.

72. David Broder, "Beware of the 'Insider' Syndrome: Why Newsmakers and News Reporters Shouldn't Get Too Cozy," *The Washington Post,* December 4, 1988, p. A21; see also Broder, "Thin-Skinned Journalists," *The Washington Post,* January 11, 1989, p. A21.

73. Daniel P. Moynihan, "The Presidency and the Press," *Commentary* 51 (March 1971), p. 43.

74. S. Robert Lichter, Stanley Rothman, and Linda S. Lichter, *The Media Elite* (Adler & Adler, 1986).

75. Larry J. Sabato, *Feeding Frenzy: How Attack Journalism Has Transformed American Politics* (Free Press, 1991).

76. See Thomas Patterson, *Out of Order* (Knopf, 1993); Paul Weaver, *News and the Culture of Lying* (Free Press, 1993); and Anthony Munro, "Yet Another Conspiracy Theory," *Columbia Journalism Review* 33 (November 1994), p. 71.

77. Maxwell McCombs and Donald Shaw, "The Agenda-setting Function of Mass Media," *Public Opinion Quarterly* 36 (1972) pp. 176–185.

78. Shanto Iyengar, Mark D. Peters, and Donald R. Kinder, "Experimental Demonstrations of the 'Not-So-Minimal' Consequences of Television News Programs," *American Political Science Review* 76 (December 1982), pp. 848–858.

79. Ibid.; Maxwell E. McCombs and Donald L. Shaw, "The Agenda-Setting Function of the Mass Media," *Public Opinion Quarterly* 36 (1972), pp. 176–187; Maxwell E. McCombs and Sheldon Gilbert, "News Influence on Our Pictures of the World," in *Perspectives on Media Effects,* eds. Jennings Bryant and Dolf Gillman (Erlbaum, 1986), pp. 1–15; and Iyengar and Kinder, *News That Matters.*

80. Quoted in Michael J. Robinson and Margaret A. Sheehan, *Over the Wire and on TV: CBS and UPI in Campaign '80* (Russell Sage Foundation, 1983), p. xiii.

81. ABC News, at abcnews.go.com/sections/us/DailyNews/WTC_MAIN010914.html.

82. David B. Magleby, *Direct Legislation: Voting on Ballot Propositions in the United States* (Johns Hopkins University Press, 1984).

83. Randal C. Archibold, "Edwards Tries Personal Touch to Gain in Iowa," *The New York Times,* December 3, 2003, p. A29; and Kathy Kiely, "Clark Catching On With Voters as Contests Near," *USA Today,* January 9, 2004, p. 4A.

84. Maureen Dowd, "Whence the Wince?" *The New York Times,* March 11, 2004, p. A29.

85. Mike Allen, "Ship Carrying Bush Delayed Return," *The Washington Post,* May 8, 2003, p. A29.

86. Paul T. David, Ralph M. Goldman, and Richard C. Bain, *The Politics of the National Party Conventions* (Brookings Institution Press, 1960), pp. 300–301.

87. Richard Davis, *The Press and American Politics: The New Mediator,* 2d ed. (Prentice Hall, 1996), p. 279.

88. Frank I. Lutz, *Candidates, Consultants, and Campaigns* (Blackwell, 1988), chap. 7.

89. www.pewinternet.org/reports/chart.asp?. Accessed April 13, 2004.

90. Larry J. Sabato, *The Rise of Political Consultants* (Basic Books, 1981).

91. See Sabato, *Rise of Political Consultants;* James David Barber, *The Pulse of Politics: Electing Presidents in the Media Age* (Norton, 1980); and Fred Barnes, "The Myth of Political Consultants," *New Republic,* June 16, 1986, p. 16.

92. Quoted in Sabato, *Rise of Political Consultants,* p. 144.

93. Thomas E. Patterson, *The Mass Media Election: How Americans Choose Their President* (Praeger, 1980), chap. 12.

94. John H. Aldrich, *Before the Convention* (University of Chicago Press, 1980), p. 65. See also Patterson, *Mass Media Election.*

95. John Foley et al., *Nominating a President: The Process and the Press* (Praeger, 1980), p. 39. For the press's treatment of incumbents, see James Glen Stovall, "Incumbency and News Coverage of the 1980 Presidential Election Campaign," *Western Political Quarterly* 37 (December 1984), p. 621.

96. Priscilla Southwell, "Voter Turnout in the 1986 Congressional Elections: The Media as Demobilizer?" *American Politics Quarterly* 19 (January 1991), pp. 96–108.

97. William Glaberson, "A New Press Role: Solving Problems," *The New York Times,* October 3, 1994, p. D6.

98. Patterson, *Mass Media Election,* pp. 115–117.

99. Raymond Wolfinger and Peter Linguiti, "Tuning In and Tuning Out," *Public Opinion* 4 (February–March 1981), pp. 56–60.

100. Marvin Kalb, "Financial Pressure Doomed Networks on Election Night," *Deseret News*, December 3, 2000, p. AA7.
101. Lewis Wolfson, *The Untapped Power of the Press* (Praeger, 1985), p. 79.
102. Stephen Hess, *The Government-Press Connection* (Brookings Institution Press, 1984), p. 106.
103. Lloyd Cutler, "Foreign Policy on Deadline," *Foreign Policy* 56 (Fall 1984), p. 114.
104. Michael B. Grossman and Martha Joynt Kumar, *Portraying the President* (Johns Hopkins University Press, 1981), pp. 255–263; and Fredric T. Smoller, *The Six o'Clock Presidency: A Theory of Presidential Press Relations in the Age of Television* (Praeger, 1990), pp. 31–49.
105. Susan Heilmann Miller, "News Coverage of Congress: The Search for the Ultimate Spokesperson," *Journalism Quarterly* 54 (Autumn 1977), pp. 459–465.
106. See Stephen Hess, *Live from Capitol Hill: Studies of Congress and the Media* (Brookings Institution Press, 1991), pp. 102–110.
107. Richard Davis, "Whither the Congress and the Supreme Court? The Television News Portrayal of American National Government," *Television Quarterly* 22 (1987), pp. 55–63.
108. For a discussion of the Supreme Court and public opinion, see Thomas R. Marshall, *Public Opinion and the Supreme Court* (Unwin Hyman, 1989); and Gregory Caldiera, "Neither the Purse nor the Sword: Dynamics of Public Confidence in the Supreme Court," *American Political Science Review* 80 (December 1986), pp. 1209–1228.
109. For a discussion of the relationship between the Supreme Court and the press, see Richard Davis, "Lifting the Shroud: News Media Portrayal of the U.S. Supreme Court," *Communications and the Law* 9 (October 1987), pp. 43–58; and Elliot E. Slotnick, "Media Coverage of Supreme Court Decision Making: Problems and Prospects," *Judicature* (October–November 1991), pp. 128–142.
110. Todd S. Purdam, "TV Political News in California Is Shrinking, Study Confirms," *The New York Times*, January, 13, 1999, p. A11.
111. Times Mirror Center, "Campaign '92," *Times Mirror*, January 16, 1992.
112. Quoted in Herbert Schmertz, "The Making of the Presidency," *Presidential Studies Quarterly* 16 (Winter 1986), p. 25.

Chapter 11

1. See Sarah A. Binder, "Going Nowhere: A Gridlocked Congress?" *The Brookings Review*, Winter, 2000, for an analysis of the growing distance between the two parties and the impact on the national policy agenda.
2. Charles Warren, *The Making of the Constitution* (Little, Brown, 1928), p. 195.
3. Congressional Quarterly, *Origins and Development of Congress* (CQ Press, 1982), pp. 53–54.
4. Richard F. Fenno Jr., *Home Style: House Members in Their Districts* (Little, Brown, 1978), p. 168.
5. *Bush* v. *Vera*, 517 U.S. 952 (1996).
6. *Hunt* v. *Cromartie*, 532 U.S. 234 (2001).
7. Frances E. Lee and Bruce I. Oppenheimer, *Sizing Up the Senate: The Unequal Consequences of Equal Representation* (University of Chicago Press, 1999).
8. Daniel Patrick Moynihan, introduction to Monica Friar and Herman Leonard, *The Federal Budget and the States: Fiscal Year 1994* (Kennedy School of Government, 1994).
9. See David M. Magleby, *Last Hurrah? Soft Money and Issue Advocacy in the 2002 Elections* (Brookings Institution Press, 2004).
10. R. P. Fairfield, *The Federalist Papers* (Doubleday, 1961), p. 160.
11. See Roger H. Davidson and Walter J. Oleszek, *Congress and Its Members*, 8th ed. (CQ Press, 2002).
12. Richard F. Fenno Jr., *The United States Senate: A Bicameral Perspective* (American Enterprise Institute, 1982), p. 1.
13. For discussion of the modern Speakership, see Barbara Sinclair, "House Majority Party Leadership in an Era of Legislative Constraint," in *The Postreform Congress*, ed. Roger H. Davidson (St. Martin's Press, 1992), pp. 91–111; and Ronald M. Peters Jr., ed., *The Speaker: Leadership in the U.S. House of Representatives* (CQ Press, 1995).
14. Newt Gingrich, quoted in Adam Clymer, "Firebrand Who Got Singed Says Being Speaker Suffices," *The New York Times*, January 22, 1996, p. 1.
15. Newt Gingrich, *To Renew America* (HarperCollins, 1995) and *Lessons Learned the Hard Way* (HarperCollins, 1998).
16. Dennis Hastert, quoted in Greg Hitt, "Hastert Is Tapped as House Speaker to Fill Vacuum Created by Livingston," *Wall Street Journal*, December 21, 1998, p. A20.
17. Richard E. Cohen and David Baumann, "Speaking Up for Hastert," *National Journal*, November 13, 1999, pp. 3298–3303.
18. For insightful memoirs by three recently retired U.S. senators, see Bill Bradley, *Time Present, Time Past: A Memoir* (Knopf, 1996); Warren B. Rudman, *Combat: Twelve Years in the U.S. Senate* (Random House, 1996); and Alan K. Simpson, *Right in the Old Kazoo: A Lifetime of Scrapping with the Press* (Morrow, 1997). See also the reflections of Joseph I. Lieberman, *In Praise of Public Life* (Simon & Schuster, 2000); and Adam Clymer, *Edward M. Kennedy: A Biography* (Morrow, 1999).
19. For an insightful set of essays on Senate leadership, see Richard A. Baker and Roger H. Davidson, eds., *First Among Equals: Outstanding Senate Leaders of the Twentieth Century* (CQ Press, 1991).
20. Barbara Sinclair, "Unorthodox Lawmaking in the Individualist Senate," *Extensions: A Journal of the Carl Albert Congressional Research and Studies Center*, vol. 3, no. 2 (Fall 1997), p. 11. See also Sinclair, *Unorthodox Lawmaking: New Legislative Processes in the U.S. Congress*, 2d ed. (CQ Press, 2000), chap. 3.
21. Nicol Rae and Colton Campbell, "The Changing Role of Political Parties in the U.S. Senate in the 104th and 105th Congresses," paper presented at the annual meeting of the American Political Science Association, Boston, September 3–6, 1998, p. 21.
22. Sarah A. Binder and Steven S. Smith, *Politics or Principles? Filibustering in the United States Senate* (Brookings Institution Press, 1997).
23. See David Nather, "Feud with Democrats over Judicial Nominees Keeps Frist's Cloture Score Down," *Congressional Quarterly Weekly*, November 29, 2003, p. 2949.
24. Helen Dewar, "Senate Filibuster Ends with Talk of Next Stage in Fight," *The Washington Post*, November 15, 2003, p. A9.
25. For a criticism of recent confirmation hearings and various reform proposals, see Stephen L. Carter, *The Confirmation Mess: Cleaning Up the Federal Appointments Process* (Basic Books, 1994). See also G. Calvin Mackenzie and Robert Shogan, eds., *Obstacle Course: The Report of the Twentieth Century Fund Task Force on the Presidential Appointment Process* (Twentieth Century Fund Press, 1996); and Michael Comiskey, *Seeking Justice: The Judging of Supreme Court Nominees* (University of Kansas, 2004).
26. Woodrow Wilson, *Congressional Government* (Houghton Mifflin, 1885; reprint, Johns Hopkins University Press, 1981), p. 69.
27. Christopher J. Deering and Steven S. Smith, *Committees in Congress*, 3d ed. (CQ Press, 1997).
28. Joel D. Aberbach, *Keeping a Watchful Eye: The Politics of Congressional Oversight* (Brookings Institution Press, 1990), p. 33. Aberbach's data exclude hearings by Appropriations, Administration, and Rules but do include Budget and the revenue committees.
29. Karen Foerstel, "Chairman's Term Limits Already Shaking Up House," *Congressional Quarterly Weekly*, March 24, 2000, p. 628.
30. Aberbach, *Keeping a Watchful Eye*.
31. "Résumé of Congressional Activity, 105th Congress," *Congressional Record*, Daily Digest, January 19, 1999, p. D29.
32. Ronald Reagan, quoted in Lawrence Longley and Walter Oleszek, *Bicameral Politics* (Yale University Press, 1989), p. 1.
33. For an example of intense bargaining on a major defense appropriation bill, see Pat Towell, "Camouflage-Green Defense Bill Poised for President's Signature," *Congressional Quarterly Weekly*, July 22, 2000, pp. 1819–1822.
34. Davidson and Oleszek, *Congress and Its Members*, p. 307.
35. For a history of the early Congresses, see James Sterling Young, *The Washington Community, 1800–1828* (Columbia University Press, 1966).
36. Davidson and Oleszek, *Congress and Its Members*, p. 30.
37. Polsby, "The Institutionalization of the U.S. House of Representatives," *American Political Science Association* (March 1968), pp. 144–168.
38. Norman J. Ornstein, Thomas Mann, and Michael Malbin, *Vital Statistics on Congress, 1999–2000* (AEI Press, 2000), p. 170.
39. Pew Research Center for the People and the Press, *Washington Leaders Wary of Public Opinion* (Pew Research Center, 1998), p. 30.
40. Herbert Asher, "The Learning of Legislative Norms," *American Political Science Review* 67 (June 1973), pp. 499–513.
41. See the case studies in Richard F. Fenno Jr., *Senators on the Campaign Trail: The Politics of Representation* (University of Oklahoma Press, 1996), p. 331. See also Benjamin Bishin, "Constituency Influence in Congress: Does Subconstituency Matter?" *Legislative Studies Quarterly* (August 2000), pp. 389–415.
42. Statistics from congressional Web sites (www.senate.gov; www.house.gov). See also the Library of Congress Web site (thomas.loc.gov).
43. For a fascinating comparison of two Rhodes scholars, one a liberal from Maryland and the other a conservative from Indiana, and what has

shaped their votes over several terms in the U.S. Senate, see Karl A. Lamb, *Reasonable Disagreement: Two U.S. Senators and the Choices They Make* (Garland, 1998).

44. See Richard Morrin, "Tuned Out, Turned Off: Millions of Americans Know Little About How Their Government Works," *The Washington Post National Weekly Edition*, February 5, 1996, pp. 6–7.

45. A 1999 CBS survey reported in "Poll Readings," *National Journal*, October 9, 1999, p. 2917.

46. Bradley, *Time Present, Time Past*, chap. 4.

47. Jackie Clames, "House Divided: Why Congress Hews to the Party Line on Impeachment," *Wall Street Journal*, December 16, 1998, p. 1.

48. Ornstein et al., *Vital Statistics on Congress, 1999–2000*, pp. 103–106.

49. Lieberman, *In Praise of Public Life*, p. 109.

50. Constance Ewing Cook, *Lobbying for Higher Education* (Vanderbilt University Press, 1998). See also Ken Kolman, *Outside Lobbying* (Princeton University Press, 1998).

51. Jill Barshay, "Bush Starts a Strong Record of Success with the Hill," *Congressional Quarterly Weekly*, January 12, 2002, p. 110.

52. See Jeffrey S. Peake, "Presidential Agenda Setting in Foreign Policy," paper presented at the annual meeting of the American Political Science Association, Boston, September 3–6, 1998.

53. Tim Penny, quoted in Lloyd Grove, "How a Bright Penny Just 'Wore Down,'" *The Washington Post National Weekly Edition*, August 30, 1993, p. 12.

54. Joseph P. Kennedy II, quoted in Clifford Krauss, "How Personal Tragedy Can Shape Public Policy," *The New York Times*, May 16, 1993, p. A16.

55. These figures come from the annual Resume of Congressional Activity, which is published in the Congressional Record at the end of each session of Congress; the 2003 resume was published in the *Congressional Record*, December 15, 2003, p. D1361.

56. See David Baumann, "The Heavy Reliance on Riders to the Must-Pass Appropriations Bills as a Crutch to Act on Significant Policy Issues," *National Journal*, January 10, 2004, p. 97.

57. See David W. Brady and Craig Volden, *Revolving Gridlock: Politics and Policy from Carter to Clinton* (Westview Press, 1998). For two case studies on the way bills get treated in Congress, see Janet M. Martin, *Lessons from the Hill: The Legislative Journey of an Education Program* (St. Martin's Press, 1993); and Steven Waldman, *The Bill—How Legislation Really Becomes Law: A Case Study of the National Service Bill* (Penguin, 1996).

Chapter 12

1. Pew Research Center on the People & the Press, "Different Faiths, Different Messages," March 19, 2003.

2. Charles O. Jones, *The Presidency in a Separated System* (Brookings Institution Press, 1994), p. 295. See also Jean Reith Schroedl, *Congress, the President, and Policymaking* (Sharpe, 1994).

3. Richard Pious, *The American Presidency* (Basic Books, 1978).

4. This history of presidential powers draws heavily on Sidney M. Milkis and Michael Nelson, *The American Presidency: Origins and Development, 1976–2000*, 4th ed. (CQ Press, 2003).

5. Letter from Abraham Lincoln to his Illinois law partner W. H. Herndon, February 15, 1848, in *Abraham Lincoln, Speeches and Writings, 1832–1858* (Library of America, 1989), p. 175.

6. Miles A. Pomper, "Bush Hopes to Avoid Battle with Congress over Iraq," *Congressional Quarterly Weekly*, August 31, 2002, p. 2251.

7. Leonard C. Meeker, "The Legality of U.S. Participation in the Defense of Vietnam," *Department of State Bulletin*, March 28, 1966, pp. 448–455.

8. Louis Fisher, *Congressional Abdication on War and Spending* (Texas A&M Press, 2000), p. 184.

9. Ibid., p. 170. See also Louis Fisher and David Gray Adler, "The War Powers: Time to Say Goodbye," *Political Science Quarterly* (Spring 1998), pp. 1–20.

10. Lee Hamilton, "The Role of the Congress in U.S. Foreign Policy," speech delivered to the Center for Strategic and International Studies, Washington, D.C., November 19, 1998.

11. Raoul Berger, *Executive Privilege: A Constitutional Myth* (Harvard University Press, 1974).

12. Mark J. Rozell, "The Law: Executive Privilege—Definition and Standards of Application," *Presidential Studies Quarterly* (December 1999), p. 924.

13. *United States* v. *Nixon*, 418 U.S. 683 (1974).

14. The president's executive orders can be reviewed on the White House Web site at www.whitehouse.gov.

15. *Clinton, et al.*, v. *New York City, et al.*, 524 U.S. 417 (1998).

16. For a recent biography of Washington, see Richard Brookhiser, *Founding Father: Rediscovering George Washington* (New York: Free Press, 1996).

17. See Bradley H. Patterson Jr., *The White House Staff: Inside the West Wing and Beyond* (Brookings Institution Press, 2000).

18. For the views on presidents and the White House staff of a highly placed White House aide in several administrations, see David Gergen, *Eyewitness to Power The Essence of Leadership, Nixon to Clinton* (New York: Touchstone, 2000).

19. See Irving Janis, *Groupthink* (Houghton Mifflin, 1982).

20. See Shelley Lynne Tomkins, *Inside OMB: Politics and Process in the President's Budget Office* (Sharpe, 1998).

21. See Thomas Cronin and Michael Genovese, *Paradoxes of the American Presidency*, 2d Edition (New York: Oxford University Press, 2004), chap. 9.

22. Letter from Kathryn Hughes, secretary of the cabinet in the Clinton White House, February 1997. See also Robert B. Reich, *Locked in the Cabinet* (Knopf, 1997).

23. Alexis Simendinger, James Kitfield, Peter H. Stone, and Kirk Victor, "Just the Ticket?" *National Journal* (February 14, 2004), p. 27.

24. Former Vice President Dan Quayle's views are of interest in *Standing Firm* (Harper, 1995). Three useful general treatments on the vice presidency are Jules Witcover, *Crapshoot: Rolling the Dice on the Vice Presidency* (Crown, 1992); Paul Light, *Vice Presidential Power* (Johns Hopkins University Press, 1984); and Joel Goldstein, *The Modern Vice Presidency* (Princeton University Press, 1982).

25. See Joseph G. Dawson III, ed., *Commanders in Chief: Presidential Leadership in Modern Wars* (University Press of Kansas, 1993).

26. See Paul C. Light, *The President's Agenda: Domestic Policy Choice from Kennedy Through Clinton* (Johns Hopkins University Press, 1999).

27. *United States* v. *Curtiss-Wright Export Corp.*, 299 U.S. 304 (1936).

28. For commentary by analysts who believe the *Curtiss-Wright* ruling was too sweeping, see Harold H. Koh, *The National Security Constitution* (Yale University Press, 1990); Louis Fisher, *Presidential War Power* (University Press of Kansas, 1995); and David Gray Adler and Larry N. George, eds., *The Constitution and the Conduct of American Foreign Policy: Essays on Law and History* (University Press of Kansas, 1996).

29. On the president's major involvement in the budget process, see Allen Schick, *The Federal Budget: Politics, Policy, Process* (Brookings Institution Press, 1995).

30. Richard E. Neustadt, *Presidential Power and the Modern Presidents* (Free Press, 1991).

31. Samuel Kernell, *Going Public: New Strategies of Presidential Leadership* (Congressional Quarterly, 3rd ed., 1997).

32. See the arguments in David Gray Adler and Michael A. Genovese, eds., *The Presidency and the Law: The Clinton Legacy* (University Press of Kansas, 2002); and Louis Fisher, *Congressional Abdication on War and Spending* (Texas A&M Press, 2000).

33. James A. Thurber, "An Introduction to Presidential-Congressional Rivalry," in *Rivals for Power: Presidential-Congressional Relations*, ed. James A. Thurber, (CQ Press, 1996), p. 6.

34. See, for example, former Republican Senator Warren G. Rudman's memoir, *Combat* (Random House, 1996), chaps. 2 and 3. See also former Democratic Congressman Timothy Penny and Major Garrett, *Common Cents* (Little, Brown, 1995).

35. See Paul C. Light, *The President's Agenda: Domestic Policy Choice from Kennedy to Clinton*, 3rd ed., for a discussion of the agenda-setting process.

36. The phrase "power to persuade" is from Richard Neustadt, *Presidential Power and the Modern Presidents: The Politics of Leadership from Roosevelt to Reagan*, (New York: The Free Press, 1990) p. 7.

37. See Paul Light, "The Focusing Skill and Presidential Influence in Congress," in C. Deering, *Congressional Politics* (Dorsey Press, 1989), p. 256.

Chapter 13

1. Andrew Kohut, *Deconstructing Distrust: How Americans View Government* (Pew Research Center for the People and the Press, 1998), p. 124.

2. See Paul C. Light, "To Give or Not to Give," *Reform Watch #7*, Washington, D.C.: Brookings Institution Press, 2003.

3. An exception is a book of essays in praise of innovations by federal agencies, John D. Donahue, ed., *Making Washington Work: Tales of Innovation in the Federal Government* (Brookings Institution Press, 1999).

4. Alexander Hamilton, James Madison, and John Jay, *The Federalist Papers* (New American Library), p. 427.

5. See Stanley Elkins and Eric McKitrick, *The Age of Federalism* (Oxford University Press, 1993), pp. 50–51.

6. See John A. Rohr, *To Run a Constitution: The Legitimacy of the Administrative State* (University of Kansas Press, 1986).

7. Dennis Palumbo and Steven Maynard-Moody, *Contemporary Public Administration* (Longman, 1991).

8. Donald Kettl, *Leadership at the Fed* (Yale University Press, 1986).

9. Tom Ridge, quoted in Maureen Shirhal, "Ridge Hints at Border Agency Consolidation," *Government Executive Daily Briefing*, February 26, 2002, at govexec.com/dailyfed/0202/022602td1.htm.

10. James Fesler and Donald Kettl, *The Politics of the Administrative Process* (Chatham House, 1991).

11. See Paul C. Light, *Thickening Government* (Brookings Institution Press, 1995).

12. See Terry M. Moe, "The Politics of Structural Choice: Toward a Theory of Public Bureaucracy," in *Organization Theory: From Chester Barnard to the Present and Beyond*, ed. Oliver E. Williamson (Oxford University Press, 1990), pp. 140–162.

13. Leonard White, *The Federalists* (Macmillan, 1956), p. 1.

14. For an analysis of the use and abuse of the civil service system in the early twentieth century, see Stephen Skowronek, *Building a New American State* (Cambridge University Press, 1982).

15. See Paul C. Light, "The State of the Federal Service," Brookings Institution Press, October 2001, and "The Troubled State of the Federal Service," Brookings Institution Press, May 2002.

16. See James Eccles, *The Hatch Act and the American Bureaucracy* (Vantage Press, 1981).

17. See Jeanne Ponessa, "The Hatch Act Rewrite," *Congressional Quarterly Weekly*, November 13, 1993, pp. 3146–3147.

18. Theodore J. Lowi Jr., *The End of Liberalism*, 2d ed. (Norton, 1979).

19. Eric Pianin, "EPA Aims to Change Pollution Rules," *Washington Post*, December 5, 2003, p. A2.

20. Kent Weaver, *Automatic Government: The Politics of Indexation* (Brookings Institution Press, 1988), p. 1; updated estimate provided by Paul C. Light.

21. James Q. Wilson, *Bureaucracy: What Government Agencies Do and Why They Do It* (Basic Books, 1989), p. 257.

22. See David E. Lewis, "The Presidential Advantage in the Design of Bureaucratic Agencies," paper presented at the annual meeting of the American Political Science Association, Boston, September 3–6, 1998.

23. Morris P. Fiorina, "Flagellating the Federal Bureaucracy," *Society* (March–April 1983), p. 73.

24. See Steven S. Smith, *The American Congress* (Houghton Mifflin, 1995); see also Joel D. Aberbach, *Keeping a Watchful Eye: The Politics of Congressional Oversight* (Brookings Institution Press, 1990).

25. See Matthew McCubbins and Thomas Schwartz, "Congressional Oversight Overlooked: Police Patrols Versus Fire Alarms," *American Journal of Political Science* 2 (February 1984), pp. 165–179.

Chapter 14

1. Alexis de Tocqueville, *Democracy in America*, ed. Phillips Bradley (Knopf, 1944), vol. 1, pp. 278–280.

2. Harold J. Laski, *The American Democracy* (Viking, 1948), p. 110.

3. See Carol Guarnieri and Patrizia Pederzoli, *The Power of Judges: A Comparative Study of Courts and Democracy* (Oxford University Press, 2002); and C. N. Tate and T. Vallinder, eds., *The Global Expansion of Judicial Power* (New York University Press, 1995).

4. Jerome Frank, *Courts on Trial: Myth and Reality in American Justice* (Princeton University Press, 1949), pp. 80–103. See also Martin Shapiro, *Courts* (University of Chicago Press, 1981), and Robert P. Burns, *A Theory of the Trial* (Princeton University Press, 1999).

5. *United States* v. *Students Challenging Regulatory Agency Procedures (SCRAP)*, 412 U.S. 669 (1973).

6. *Flast* v. *Cohen*, 392 U.S. 83 (1968); *Lujan* v. *Defenders of Wildlife*, 504 U.S. 555 (1992).

7. Philip J. Cooper, *Hard Judicial Choices: Federal District Court Judges and State and Local Officials* (Oxford University Press, 1988), p. 15.

8. *Bordenkircher* v. *Hayes*, 434 U.S. 357 (1978).

9. *Luther* v. *Borden*, 7 Howard 1 (1849).

10. *Bush* v. *Gore*, 531 U.S. 98 (2000).

11. John Roche, "Judicial Self-Restraint," *American Political Science Review* 49 (1955), pp. 762, 768.

12. See Charles Lopeman, *The Activist Advocate: Policymaking in State Supreme Courts* (Praeger, 2000).

13. Eleanore Bushnell, *Crimes, Follies, and Misfortunes: The Federal Impeachment Trials* (University of Illinois Press, 1992); and Mary L. Volcansek, *None Called for Justice: Judicial Impeachment* (University of Illinois Press, 1993).

14. Administrative Office of the U.S. Courts, *Judicial Facts and Figures* (Tables 2.11, 3.1, and 4.1), at www.uscourts.gov (as of February 5, 2004).

15. C. K. Rowland, "The Federal District Courts," in *The American Courts: A Critical Assessment*, eds. John B. Gates and Charles A. Johnson (CQ Press, 1991), pp. 61–80.

16. *Peretz* v. *United States*, 501 U.S. 923 (1991).

17. See Christopher P. Banks, *Judicial Politics in the D. C. Circuit* (Johns Hopkins University Press, 1999); Donald R. Songer and Susan B. Haire, *Continuity and Change in the United States Courts of Appeals* (University of Michigan Press, 2000); David Klein, *Making Law in the U.S. Courts of Appeals* (Cambridge University Press, 2002); and Jonathan Matthew, *Decision Making in the U.S. Courts of Appeals* (University of Michigan Press, 2002).

18. See *Anastasoff* v. *United States*, 223 F. 3d 898 (2000); and Jerome I. Braun, "Eighth Circuit Decision Intensifies Debate over Publication and Citation of Appellate Opinions," *Judicature* 83 (September–October 2000).

19. Neil D. McFeeley, *Appointment of Judges: The Johnson Presidency* (University of Texas Press, 1987), p. 1.

20. Harold W. Chase, *Federal Judges: The Appointing Process* (University of Minnesota Press, 1972); Sheldon Goldman, *Picking Federal Judges: Lower Court Selection from Roosevelt Through Reagan* (Yale University Press, 1997).

21. See David M. O'Brien, "Ironies and Disappointments: Bush and Federal Judgeships," in Colin Campbell and Bert A. Rockman, eds., *The George W. Bush Presidency* (CQ Press, 2004), pp. 133–157; and Brannon P. Denning, "The Judicial Confirmation Process and the Blue Slip," *Judicature* (March–April 2002), pp. 218–226.

22. Lisa M. Holmes and Roger E. Hartley, "Increasing Senate Scrutiny of Lower Federal Court Nominees," *Judicature* (May–June 1997), p. 275.

23. George Watson and John Stookey, "Supreme Court Confirmation Hearings: A View from the Senate," *Judicature* (December 1987–January 1988), p. 193. See also John Massaro, *Supremely Political: The Role of Ideology and Presidential Management in Unsuccessful Supreme Court Nominations* (State University of New York Press, 1990).

24. Barbara A. Perry and Henry J. Abraham, "A 'Representative' Supreme Court? The Thomas, Ginsburg, and Breyer Appointments," *Judicature* (January—February 1998), pp. 158–165.

25. Goldman, *Picking Federal Judges*, pp. 161, 327–336.

26. Sheldon Goldman, "Bush's Judicial Legacy: The Final Imprint," *Judicature* (April–May 1993), p. 291.

27. Eleanor Dean Acheson, quoted in David M. O'Brien, "Judicial Legacies: The Clinton Presidency and the Courts," in *The Clinton Legacy*, eds. Colin Campbell and Burt A. Rockman (Chatham House, 2000), p. 101.

28. As of July 23, 2004, based on data reported by the Federal Judicial Center at www.fjc.gov/newweb/jnetweb.nsf/hisj.

29. Robert A. Carp and C. K. Rowland, *Politics and Judgment in Federal District Courts* (University Press of Kansas, 1996).

30. Sheldon Goldman, "Reagan's Judicial Legacy: Completing the Puzzle and Summing Up," *Judicature* (April–May 1989), pp. 318–330.

31. Robert A. Carp, Donald Songer, C. K. Rowland, Ronald Stidham, and Lisa Richey-Tracey, "The Voting Behavior of Judges Appointed by President Bush," *Judicature* (April–May 1993), pp. 298–302.

32. David G. Savage, *Turning Right: The Making of the Rehnquist Supreme Court* (Wiley, 1992).

33. Naftali Bendavid, "Diversity Marks Clinton Judiciary," *Recorder* (December 30, 1993), p. 11.

34. O'Brien, "Judicial Legacies," pp. 96–117.

35. Helen Dewar, "Senate Democrats Block 3 More Bush Judicial Nominees," *The Washington Post*, July 23, 2004, at A5; Sheldon Goldman, "The Senate and Judicial Nominations," *Extensions* (Spring 2004), pp. 4–12.

36. Neil Lewis, "Deal Ends Impasse Over Judicial Nominees," *The New York Times*, May 18, 2004, p. A17.

37. Jeremiah Smith, quoted in Paul E. Freund, *Understanding the Supreme Court* (Little, Brown, 1949), p. 3.

38. Felix Frankfurter, letter to Justice Hugo Black, December 15, 1939, quoted in David M. O'Brien, *Constitutional Law and Politics*, 6th ed. (Norton, 2005), p. 74.

39. See Benjamin N. Cardozo, *The Nature of the Judicial Process* (Yale University Press, 1921), a classic.

40. William O. Douglas, quoted in David M. O'Brien, *Storm Center: The Supreme Court in American Politics,* 7th ed. (Norton, 2005), p. 184.

41. Ibid., p. 30 (figures as of the end of the 2003–2004 term).

42. William Howard Taft, letter to Horace Taft, November 14, 1929; quoted in Henry Pringle, *The Life and Times of William Howard Taft* (Farrar, 1939), vol. 2, p. 967.

43. See David N. Atkinson, *Leaving the Bench: Supreme Court Justices at the End* (University Press of Kansas, 1999).

44. David M. O'Brien, *Judicial Roulette: Report of the Twentieth Century Fund Task Force on Judicial Selection* (Priority Press Publications, 1988), pp. 10–11.

45. White Burkett Miller Center of Public Affairs, *Improving the Process of Appointing Federal Judges* (Miller Center, University of Virginia, 1996).

46. See Citizens for Independent Courts Task Force on Federal Judicial Selection, *Justice Held Hostage: Politics and Selecting Federal Judges* (Century Foundation, 2000).

47. Donald Santarelli, quoted in Jerry Landauer, "Shaping the Bench," *The Wall Street Journal,* December 10, 1970, p. 1.

48. Michael A. Kahn, "The Appointment of a Supreme Court Justice: A Political Process from Beginning to End," *Presidential Studies Quarterly* 25 (Winter 1995), pp. 26, 39.

49. Ex parte *McCardle,* 74 U.S. 506 (1869).

50. Barry Friedman, "Attacks on Judges: Why They Fail," *Judicature* (January–February 1998), p. 152.

51. William H. Rehnquist, quoted in John R. Vile, "The Selection and Tenure of Chief Justices," *Judicature* (September–October 1994), p. 98.

52. David Danelski, "The Influence of the Chief Justice in the Decisional Process of the Supreme Court," in *The Federal Judicial System: Readings in Process and Behavior,* eds. Thomas P. Jahnige and Sheldon Goldman (Holt, Rinehart and Winston, 1968), p. 148.

53. David M. O'Brien, "The Rehnquist Court's Shrinking Plenary Docket," *Judicature* (September–October 1997), p. 58.

54. O'Brien, *Storm Center,* p. 63.

55. See H. W. Perry Jr., *Deciding to Decide: Agenda Setting in the United States Supreme Court* (Harvard University Press, 1991).

56. Edward Lazarus, *Closed Chambers: The First Eyewitness Account of the Epic Struggles Inside the Supreme Court* (Times Books/Random House, 1998).

57. O'Brien, *Storm Center,* Chap. 3.

58. Lincoln Caplan, *The Tenth Justice: The Solicitor General and the Rule of Law* (Knopf, 1987); and Rebecca Mae Salokar, *The Solicitor General: The Politics of Law* (Temple University Press, 1992).

59. Charles Fried, *Order and Law: Arguing the Reagan Revolution—A First-hand Account* (Simon & Schuster, 1991). See also Rebecca Dean, Joseph Ignagni, and James Meernik, "The Solicitor General as Amicus, 1950–2000: How Influential? *Judicature* 87 (September–October, 2003), p. 60.

60. Jeffrey A. Segal and Robert M. Howard, "How Supreme Court Justices Respond to Litigant Requests to Overturn Precedent," *Judicature* (November–December 2001), pp. 148–157.

61. Gregory A. Caldeira and John R. Wright, "Organized Interest and Agenda Setting in the U.S. Supreme Court," *American Political Science Review* 82 (December 1988), p. 1110; and Donald R. Songer and Reginald S. Sheehan, "Interest Groups' Success in the Courts: *Amicus* Participation in the Supreme Court," *Political Research Quarterly* 46 (June 1993), pp. 339–354.

62. *Webster* v. *Reproductive Health Services,* 492 U.S. 490 (1989); *Roe* v. *Wade,* 410 U.S. 113 (1973); and Susan Behuniak-Long, "Friendly Fire: *Amici Curiae* and *Webster* v. *Reproductive Health Services,*" *Judicature* (February–March 1991), pp. 261–270.

63. *United States* v. *Lopez,* 514 U.S. 549 (1951).

64. Caldeira and Wright, "Organized Interest and Agenda Setting"; Songer and Sheehan, "Interest Groups' Success in the Courts," *American Political Science Review* 82 (December 1988), p. 1118.

65. Tony Mauro, "The Supreme Court as Quiz Show," *Recorder* (December 8, 1993), p. 10.

66. Joyce O'Connor, "Selections from Notes Kept on an Internship at the U.S. Supreme Court, Fall 1988," *Law, Courts, and Judicial Process* 6 (Spring 1989), p. 44.

67. Tony Mauro, "No Comfort for Counsel After Court Review," *Recorder* (November 10, 1997), p. 8.

68. Mauro, "Yipes! Stripes!" *Recorder,* February 8, 1995, p. 8.

69. Joan Biskupic, "Supreme Court Film Offers Glimpse Behind Justices' Closed Doors," *The Washington Post,* June 17, 1997, p. A15.

70. William H. Rehnquist, *The Supreme Court: A New Edition of the Chief Justice's Classic History* (Knopf, 2001), pp. 289–290.

71. Forrest Maltzman, James F. Spriggs III, and Paul Wahlbeck, *Crafting Law on the Supreme Court: The Collegial Game* (Cambridge University Press, 2000).

72. Daniel M. Berman, *It Is So Ordered: The Supreme Court Rules on School Segregation* (Norton, 1986), p. 114; and O'Brien, *Storm Center,* pp. 262–272.

73. Charles Evans Hughes, quoted in Donald E. Lively, *Foreshadows of the Law: Supreme Court Dissents and Constitutional Development* (Praeger, 1992), p. xx.

74. *Brown* v. *Board of Education of Topeka,* 347 U.S. 483 (1954).

75. *United States* v. *Nixon,* 418 U.S. 683 (1974).

76. Gerald N. Rosenberg, *Hollow Hope: Can Courts Bring About Sound Change?* (University of Chicago Press, 1991).

77. J. W. Peltason, *Fifty-Eight Lonely Men: Southern Federal Judges and School Desegregation* (University of Illinois Press, 1971); and Gary Orfield and Chungmei Lee, *Brown at 50: King's Dream or Plessy's Nightmare* (The Civil Rights Project, Harvard University, 2004).

78. See Shawn Francis Peters, *Judging the Jehovah's Witnesses* (University of Kansas Press, 2002); Clyde Wilcox, *Onward, Christian Soldiers? The Religious Right in American Politics* (Westview Press, 1996); Mark Tushnet, *The NAACP's Legal Strategy Against Segregated Education, 1925–1950* (University of North Carolina Press, 1987); and Karen O'Connor, *Women's Organizations' Use of the Court* (Lexington Books, 1980).

79. Cooper, *Hard Judicial Choices,* pp. 347–350.

80. Arthur S. Miller, "In Defense of Judicial Activism," in *Supreme Court Activism and Restraint,* eds. Stephen C. Halpern and Charles M. Lamb (Heath, 1982), p. 177.

81. *United States* v. *Carolene Products,* 304 U.S. 144 (1938). Variations on this basic position have been restated in dozens of books. Halpern and Lamb, *Supreme Court Activism and Restraint,* and Mark Tushnet, *Red, White, and Blue: A Critical Analysis of Constitutional Law* (Harvard University Press, 1988) provide analysis from all perspectives. See also Terri Jennings Peretti, *In Defense of a Political Court* (Princeton University Press, 1999).

82. J. W. Peltason, "The Supreme Court: Transactional or Transformational Leadership," in *Essays in Honor of James MacGregor Burns,* eds. Michael R. Beschloss and Thomas E. Cronin (Prentice Hall, 1988), pp. 165–180; and Valerie Hoeksta, *Public Reactions to Supreme Court Decisions* (Cambridge University Press, 2003).

83. *Planned Parenthood* v. *Casey,* 505 U.S. 833 (1992).

84. Thomas R. Marshall, *Public Opinion and the Supreme Court* (Unwin Hyman, 1989), p. 193. See also William Mishler and Reginald S. Sheehan, "The Supreme Court as a Counter-Majoritarian Institution: The Impact of Public Opinion on Supreme Court Decisions," *American Political Science Review* 87 (January 1993), pp. 87–101; and Helmut Norpoth and Jeffrey A. Segal, "Popular Influence on Supreme Court Decisions," *American Political Science Review* 88 (September 1994), pp. 711–724.

85. See John B. Gates, *The Supreme Court and Partisan Realignment* (Westview Press, 1992).

86. Rosenberg, *Hollow Hope,* p. 343.

87. Rehnquist, *Supreme Court,* p. 98.

88. Gallup Organization, "Confidence in Institutions," June 8–10, 2001, at www.gallup.com; and Herbert Kritzer, "The Impact of *Bush* v. *Gore* on Public Perceptions and Knowledge of the Supreme Court," *Judicature* (July–August 2001), pp. 32–38.

89. Edward White, "The Supreme Court of the United States," *American Bar Association Journal* 7 (1921), p. 341.

Chapter 15

1. Jeffrey Smith, *War and Press Freedom* (Oxford University Press, 1999); and David Cole, *Enemy Aliens: Double Standards and Constitutional Freedoms in the War on Terrorism* (The New Press, 2003).

2. *Felker* v. *Turpin,* 518 U.S. 651 (1996); *Winthrow* v. *Williams,* 507 U.S. 680 (1993); *McCleskey* v. *Zant,* 499 U.S. 467 (1991); and *Stone* v. *Powell,* 428 U.S. 465 (1976).

3. *Rasul* v. *Bush,* 124 S.Ct. 2686 (2004); and *Hamdi* v. *Rumsfeld,* 124 S.Ct. 2633 (2004).

4. *Stogner* v. *California,* 539 U.S. 607 (2003).

5. *United States* v. *Lovett,* 328 U.S. 303 (1946).

6. Neil H. Cogan, ed., *The Complete Bill of Rights: The Drafts, Debates, Sources, and Origins* (Oxford University Press, 1997); Robert A. Rutland,

The Birth of the Bill of Rights, 1776–1791 (University of North Carolina Press, 1955).

7. *Barron* v. *Baltimore,* 7 Peters 243 (1833).
8. *Gitlow* v. *New York,* 268 U.S. 652 (1925).
9. Richard C. Cortner, *The Supreme Court and the Second Bill of Rights: The Fourteenth Amendment and the Nationalization of Civil Liberties* (University of Wisconsin Press, 1981).
10. Dorothy Toth Beasley, "Federalism and the Protection of Individual Rights: The American State Constitutional Perspective," in *Federalism and Rights,* ed. Ellis Katz and G. Alan Tarr (Rowman & Littlefield, 1996); and Charles Lopeman, *The Activist Advocate: Policymaking in State Supreme Courts* (Praeger, 1999).
11. *Witters* v. *Washington Department of Services for the Blind,* 474 U.S. 481 (1986); and *Locke* v. *Davey,* 124 S.Ct. 1307 (2004).
12. *Everson* v. *Board of Education of Ewing Township,* 333 U.S. 203 (1947).
13. *Lemon* v. *Kurtzman,* 403 U.S. 602 (1971).
14. *Capital Square Review Board* v. *Pinette,* 515 U.S. 753 (1995).
15. *Lynch* v. *Donnelly,* 465 U.S. 669 (1984).
16. *Allegheny County* v. *Greater Pittsburgh ACLU,* 492 U.S. 573 (1989).
17. *Bowen* v. *Kendrick,* 487 U.S. 589 (1988); *Lee* v. *Weisman,* 505 U.S. 577 (1992); *Board of Education of Kiryas Joel Village School District* v. *Grumet,* 512 U.S. 687 (1994); and *Zelman* v. *Simmons-Harris,* 536 U.S. 629 (2002).
18. *Mitchell* v. *Helms,* 530 U.S. 793 (2000).
19. *Agostini* v. *Felton,* 521 U.S. 74 (1997).
20. *Lee* v. *Weisman,* 505 U.S. 577 (1992); and *Santa Fe Independent School District* v. *Doe,* 530 U.S. 290 (2000).
21. *Engel* v. *Vitale,* 370 U.S. 421 (1962).
22. *Edwards* v. *Aguillard,* 482 U.S. 578 (1987).
23. *Marsh* v. *Chambers,* 463 U.S. 783 (1983).
24. *Elk Grove Unified School District* v. *Newdow,* 124 S.Ct. 2301 (2004).
25. *Witters* v. *Washington Department of Services for the Blind,* 474 U.S. 481 (1986).
26. *Mueller* v. *Allen,* 463 U.S. 388 (1983); and *Zelman v. Simmons-Harris,* 536 U.S. 639 (2002).
27. *Zobrest* v. *Catalina Foothills School District,* 515 U.S. 1 (1993); *Agostini* v. *Felton,* 521 U.S. 74 (1997); *Mitchell* v. *Helms,* 530 U.S. 793 (2000).
28. *Zelman* v. *Simmons-Harris,* 536 U.S. 639 (2002).
29. Justice Blum, "D.C. School Voucher Applications Fall Short," *The Washington Post,* June 11, 2004, p. A1.
30. *Employment Division of Human Resources of Oregon* v. *Smith,* 494 U.S. 872 (1990).
31. *Church of Lukumi Babalu Aye* v. *City of Hialeah,* 508 U.S. 520 (1993).
32. *City of Boerne* v. *Flores,* 521 U.S. 507 (1997).
33. *Rosenberger* v. *University of Virginia,* 515 U.S. 819 (1995).
34. *Board of Regents of the University of Wisconsin System* v. *Southworth,* 529 U.S. 217 (2000).
35. Oliver Wendell Holmes Jr., in *Abrams* v. *United States,* 250 U.S. 616 (1919).
36. John Stuart Mill, *Essay on Liberty,* in *The English Philosophers from Bacon to Mill,* ed. Arthur Burtt (Random House, 1939), p. 961.
37. Robert Jackson, in *West Virginia State Board of Education* v. *Barnette,* 319 U.S. 624 (1943).
38. *Brown* v. *Hartlage,* 456 U.S. 45 (1982), reversing a decision of the Kentucky Court of Appeals based on the bad tendency test.
39. Oliver Wendell Holmes Jr., in *Schenck* v. *United States,* 249 U.S. 47 (1919).
40. *Dennis* v. *United States,* 341 U.S. 494 (1951).
41. *New York Times* v. *Sullivan,* 376 U.S. 254 (1964).
42. *Yates* v. *United States,* 354 U.S. 298 (1957).
43. *Brandenburg* v. *Ohio,* 395 U.S. 444 (1969).
44. *New York Times* v. *Sullivan,* 376 U.S. 254 (1964).
45. *Hustler Magazine* v. *Falwell,* 485 U.S. 46 (1988).
46. *Masson* v. *New York Magazine, Inc.,* 501 U.S. 496 (1991).
47. *Gertz* v. *Robert Welch, Inc.,* 418 U.S. 323 (1974).
48. Potter Stewart, concurring in *Jacobellis* v. *Ohio,* 378 U.S. 184 (1964).
49. John Marshall Harlan, in *Cohen* v. *California,* 403 U.S. 15 (1971).
50. *Miller* v. *California,* 413 U.S. 15 (1973).
51. *Young* v. *American Mini Theatres,* 427 U.S. 51 (1976); *Renton* v. *Playtime Theatres, Inc.,* 475 U.S. 41 (1986); and *City of Los Angeles* v. *Alameda Books, Inc.,* 535 U.S. 425 (2002).
52. *Barnes* v. *Glen Theatre, Inc.,* 501 U.S. 560 (1991); and *City of Erie* v. *Pap's A.M.,* 529 U.S. 277 (2000).
53. *New York* v. *Ferber,* 458 U.S. 747 (1982); and *Ashcroft* v. *Free Speech Coalition,* 535 U.S. 234 (2002).
54. *General Media Communications* v. *Cohen,* 524 U.S. 951 (1998).
55. See Catharine A. MacKinnon, *Only Words* (Harvard University Press, 1993); and compare another feminist, Nadine Strossen, *Defending Pornography: Free Speech, Sex, and the Fight for Women's Rights* (Scribner, 1995).
56. *Butler* v. *Her Majesty the Queen,* 1 S.C.R. 452 (1992).
57. *Chaplinsky* v. *New Hampshire,* 315 U.S. 568 (1942).
58. *Cohen* v. *California,* 403 U.S. 115 (1971).
59. *R.A.V.* v. *St. Paul,* 505 U.S. 377 (1992). See also *Wisconsin* v. *Mitchell,* 508 U.S. 476 (1993); and *Apprendi* v. *New Jersey,* 530 U.S. 466 (2000).
60. *Virginia* v. *Black,* 538 U.S. 343 (2003).
61. *44 Liquormart, Inc.,* v. *Rhode Island,* 517 U.S. 484 (1996); and *Thompson* v. *Western States Medical Center,* 535 U.S. 357 (2002).
62. *New York Times Company* v. *United States,* 403 U.S. 670 (1971).
63. *Near* v. *Minnesota,* 283 U.S. 697 (1930); ibid.
64. *Hazelwood School District* v. *Kuhlmeier,* 484 U.S. 260 (1988).
65. *R.A.V.* v. *St. Paul,* 505 U.S. 377 (1992). See also *Wisconsin* v. *Mitchell,* 508 U.S. 476 (1993).
66. *Branzburg* v. *Hayes,* 408 U.S. 665 (1972).
67. *Richmond Newspapers, Inc.,* v. *Virginia,* 448 U.S. 555 (1980). See also David M. O'Brien, *The Public's Right to Know: The Supreme Court and the First Amendment* (Praeger, 1981).
68. Oliver Wendell Holmes Jr., dissenting in *Milwaukee Publishing Co.* v. *Burleson,* 255 U.S. 407 (1921).
69. *Lamont* v. *Postmaster General,* 381 U.S. 301 (1965).
70. *Rowan* v. *Post Office Department,* 397 U.S. 728 (1970).
71. *McIntyre* v. *Ohio Election Commission,* 514 U.S. 334 (1995).
72. *Southeastern Promotions, Ltd.,* v. *Conrad,* 420 U.S. 546 (1975).
73. *Federal Communications Commission* v. *Pacifica Foundation,* 438 U.S. 726 (1978).
74. *Turner Broadcasting System* v. *Federal Communications Commission,* 518 U.S. 180 (1997).
75. *United States* v. *Playboy Entertainment Group,* 529 U.S. 803 (2000); and *Denver Area Educational Television* v. *Federal Communications Commission,* 518 U.S. 727 (1996).
76. See and compare *Federal Communications Commission* v. *Pacifica Foundation,* 438 U.S. 726 (1978); and *Sable Communications* v. *Federal Communications Commission,* 492 U.S. 115 (1989).
77. *Reno* v. *American Civil Liberties Union,* 521 U.S. 844 (1997).
78. *Ashcroft* v. *ACLU,* 124 S.Ct. 2783 (2004).
79. *Ashcroft* v. *Free Speech Coalition,* 535 U.S. 234 (2002).
80. Freedom Forum Online at www.freedomforum.org/assembly/1998/9/2/march.asp.
81. *Walker* v. *Birmingham,* 388 U.S. 307 (1967).
82. *Madsen* v. *Women's Health Center,* 512 U.S. 753 (1994); *Schenck* v. *Pro-Choice Network,* 519 U.S. 357 (1997); and *Hill* v. *Colorado,* 530 U.S. 703 (2000).
83. *West Virginia State Board of Education* v. *Barnette,* 319 U.S. 624 (1943).

Chapter 16

1. *Vance* v. *Terrazas,* 444 U.S. 252 (1980).
2. G. Pascal Zachary, "Dual Citizenship Is Double-Edged Sword," *The Wall Street Journal,* March 25, 1998, pp. B1, B15, quoting T. Alexander Aleinikoff of the Carnegie Endowment for International Peace.
3. *Slaughter-House Cases,* 83 U.S. 36 (1873).
4. *Ex Parte Milligan,* 71 U.S. 2 (1866).
5. *Korematsu* v. *United States,* 323 U.S. 214 (1944).
6. *Ex Parte Quirin,* 317 U.S. 1 (1942).
7. *Reid* v. *Covert,* 354 U.S. 1 (1957).
8. *Hamdi* v. *Rumsfeld,* 124 S.Ct. 2686 (2004); and *Rasul* v. *Bush,* 124 S.Ct. 2633 (2004).
9. *Mathews* v. *Diaz,* 426 U.S. 67 (1976); *Shaughnessy* v. *United States ex rel Mezei,* 345 U.S. 206 (1953).
10. *Demore* v. *Kim,* 538 U.S. 510 (2003).
11. *Zadvydas* v. *David,* 533 U.S. 678 (2001).
12. *Yick Wo* v. *Hopkins,* 118 U.S. 356 (1886); *Kwong Hai Chew* v. *Colding,* 344 U.S. 590 (1953); *Zadvydas* v. *Davis,* 533 U.S. 678 (2001); *Rasul* v. *Bush,* 124 S.Ct. 2686 (2004); and *Hamdi* v. *Rumsfeld,* 124 S.Ct. 2633 (2004).
13. *Foley* v. *Connelie,* 435 U.S. 291 (1978); *Ambach* v. *Norwick,* 441 U.S. 68 (1979); and *Cabell* v. *Chavez-Salido,* 454 U.S. 432 (1982).
14. *Plyler* v. *Doe,* 457 U.S. 202 (1982).
15. See Samuel Huntington, *Who Are We?* (Free Press, 2004).
16. Karen De Young, "Bush Lowers Refugee Quota to 70,000," *The Washington Post,* November 22, 2001, p. A45.
17. *Sale* v. *Haitian Centers Council, Inc.,* 509 U.S. 155 (1993).

18. Christopher Marquis, "Census Bureau Estimates 115,000 Middle Eastern Immigrants Are in the U.S. Illegally," *The New York Times*, January 23, 2002, p. A10.

19. Francis X. Clines, "Harsh Civics Lesson for Immigrants," *The New York Times*, November 11, 2001, p. B7.

20. *Chicago Home Building & Loan Association v. Blaisdell*, 290 U.S. 398 (1934).

21. *Chicago, Burlington & Quincy Railway Co. v. Chicago*, 166 U.S. 226 (1897).

22. *First English Evangelical v. Los Angeles County*, 482 U.S. 304 (1987). See Richard A. Epstein, *Taking: Private Property and the Power of Eminent Domain* (Harvard University Press, 1985).

23. *Lucas v. South Carolina Coastal Commission*, 505 U.S. 647 (1992).

24. *Tahoe-Sierra Council, Inc., v. Tahoe Regional Planning Agency*, 535 U.S. 302 (2002).

25. *United States v. 564.54 Acres of Land*, 441 U.S. 506 (1979).

26. *Mathews v. Eldridge*, 424 U.S. 319 (1976), restated in *Connecticut v. Doeher*, 501 U.S. 1 (1991).

27. *Meyer v. Nebraska*, 262 U.S. 390 (1923).

28. *Lochner v. New York*, 198 U.S. 45 (1905).

29. *Griswold v. Connecticut*, 381 U.S. 479 (1965).

30. Philip B. Kurland, *Some Reflections on Privacy and the Constitution* (University of Chicago Center for Policy Study, 1976), p. 9. A classic and influential article about privacy is Samuel D. Warren and Louis D. Brandeis, "The Right to Privacy," *Harvard Law Review*, December 15, 1890, pp. 193–220.

31. *Roe v. Wade*, 410 U.S. 113 (1973).

32. *Planned Parenthood of Southeastern Pennsylvania v. Casey*, 505 U.S. 833 (1992).

33. *Stenberg v. Carhart*, 530 U.S. 914 (2000).

34. *Bowers v. Hardwick*, 478 U.S. 186 (1986).

35. *Boy Scouts of America v. Dale*, 530 U.S. 640 (2000).

36. *Lawrence v. Texas*, 539 U.S. 558 (2003).

37. *Romer v. Evans*, 517 U.S. 620 (1996).

38. But see *Washington v. Chrisman*, 455 U.S. 1 (1982).

39. *Katz v. United States*, 389 U.S. 347 (1967).

40. *County of Riverside v. McLaughlin*, 500 U.S. 44 (1991).

41. *California v. Hodari D.*, 499 U.S. 621 (1991).

42. *Bond v. United States*, 529 U.S. 334 (2000).

43. *Terry v. Ohio*, 392 U.S. 1 (1968).

44. *Hiibel v. Sixth Judicial District of Nevada*, 124 S.Ct. 2451 (2004).

45. *Minnesota v. Dickerson*, 508 U.S. 366 (1993).

46. *Almeida-Sanchez v. United States*, 413 U.S. 266 (1973); *United States v. Ortiz*, 422 U.S. 891 (1975); *United States v. Arvizu*, 534 U.S. 161 (2002); and *United States v. Flores-Montano*, 124 S.Ct. 1582 (2004).

47. *United States v. Ramsey*, 431 U.S. 606 (1977).

48. *Coolidge v. New Hampshire*, 403 U.S. 443 (1971); and *Arizona v. Hicks*, 480 U.S. 321 (1987).

49. *United States v. Ross*, 456 U.S. 798 (1982).

50. *Pennsylvania v. Mimms*, 434 U.S. 110 (1977); and *Ohio v. Robinette*, 519 U.S. 33 (1997).

51. *Thorton v. United States*, 124 S.Ct. 2127 (2004).

52. *Chandler v. Miller*, 520 U.S. 305 (1997).

53. Randall Kennedy, *Race, Crime, and the Law* (Pantheon Books, 1997), pp. 136–168; and David Cole, *No Equal Justice: Race and Class in the American Criminal Justice System* (New Press, 1999).

54. Quoted in Eric Lichtblau, "Bush Limits Use of Race in Federal Investigations," *International Herald Tribune*, June 19, 2003, p. 5.

55. *Treasury Employees v. Von Raab*, 489 U.S. 656 (1989); *Skinner v. Railway Labor Executives' Association*, 489 U.S. 602 (1989); *Vernonia School District 47J v. Acton*, 515 U.S. 646 (1995); and *Chandler v. Miller*, 520 U.S. 305 (1997).

56. *Board of Education of Independent School District No. 2 of Pottawatomie City v. Earls*, 536 U.S. 822 (2002).

57. *Mapp v. Ohio*, 367 U.S. 643 (1961).

58. Senate Committee on the Judiciary, *The Jury and the Search for Truth: The Case Against Excluding Relevant Evidence at Trial: Hearing Before the Committee*, 104th Cong., 1st sess. (U.S. Government Printing Office, 1997).

59. *United States v. Leon*, 468 U.S. 897 (1984); and *Arizona v. Evans*, 514 U.S. 1 (1995).

60. *Miranda v. Arizona*, 384 U.S. 436 (1966), but see *Yarborough v. Alvarado*, 124 S.Ct. 2140 (2004).

61. *Dickerson v. United States*, 530 U.S. 428 (2000).

62. Justice Felix Frankfurter, dissenting in *United States v. Rabinowitz*, 339 U.S. 56 (1950).

63. *United States v. Enterprises, Inc.*, 498 U.S. 292 (1991).

64. *Williams v. Florida*, 399 U.S. 78 (1970); and *Burch v. Louisiana*, 441 U.S. 130 (1979).

65. *J.E.B. v. Alabama ex rel T.B.*, 511 U.S. 127 (1994); *Batson v. Kentucky*, 476 U.S. 79 (1986); *Powers v. Ohio*, 499 U.S. 400 (1991); *Hernandez v. New York*, 500 U.S. 352 (1991); and *Georgia v. McCollum*, 505 U.S. 42 (1990).

66. *Ewing v. California*, 538 U.S. 11 (2003).

67. *Benton v. Maryland*, 395 U.S. 784 (1969). See also *Kansas v. Hendricks*, 521 U.S. 346 (1997).

68. *Graham v. Collins*, 506 U.S. 461 (1993).

69. Barry Scheck, Peter Neufeld, and Jim Dwyer, *Actual Innocence: Five Days to Execution and Other Dispatches from the Wrongly Convicted* (Doubleday, 2000); and Timothy Kaufman-Osborn, *From Noose to Needle: Capital Punishment and the Late Liberal State* (University of Michigan Press, 2002).

70. *Penry v. Lynaugh*, 492 U.S. 302 (1989).

71. *Atkins v. Virginia*, 536 U.S. 304 (2002).

72. Jerome Frank, *Courts on Trial* (Princeton University Press, 1949), p. 122. See also Steven Brill, *Trial by Jury* (American Lawyer Books/Touchstone, 1989).

73. Harry Kalven Jr. and Hans Zeisel, *The American Jury* (University of Chicago Press, 1971), p. 57. See also Jeffrey Abramson, *We, the Jury: The Jury System and the Ideal of Democracy* (Harvard University Press, 2000).

74. George Edwards, *The Police on the Urban Frontier* (Institute of Human Relations Press, 1968), p. 28. See also Jerome G. Miller, *African-American Males and the Criminal Justice System* (Cambridge University Press, 1996).

75. Sandra Bass, "Blacks, Browns, and the Blues: Police and Minorities in California," *Public Affairs Report* 38 (November 1997), p. 10.

76. See David Cole, *No Equal Justice: Race and Class in the American Criminal Justice System* (New Press, 1999); and Randall Kennedy, *Race, Crime, and the Law* (Pantheon, 1997).

77. See "Understanding Community Policing" (Bureau of Justice Administration), at www.community_policy.org.

78. Robert H. Jackson, *The Supreme Court in the American System of Government* (Harvard University Press, 1955), pp. 81–82.

Chapter 17

1. Andrew Hacker, *Two Nations: Black and White, Separate, Hostile, Unequal* (Scribner, 1992).

2. *Slaughter-House Cases*, 83 U.S. 36 (1873); and *Civil Rights Cases*, 109 U.S. 3 (1883).

3. *Plessy v. Ferguson*, 163 U.S. 537 (1896).

4. *Brown v. Board of Education of Topeka*, 347 U.S. 483 (1954); and *Brown v. Board of Education of Topeka*, 349 U.S. 294 (1955).

5. *Gomillion v. Lightfoot*, 364 U.S. 339 (1960).

6. Michael R. Belknap, *Federal Law and Southern Order: Racial Violence and Constitutional Conflict in the Post-Brown South* (University of Georgia Press, 1987), pp. 128–204.

7. Taylor Branch, *Parting the Waters: America in the King Years, 1954–1963* (Simon & Schuster, 1988). See also Harris Wofford, *Of Kennedys and Kings: Making Sense of the Sixties* (Farrar, Straus & Giroux, 1980).

8. See Charles Whalen and Barbara Whalen, *The Longest Debate: A Legislative History of the 1964 Civil Rights Act* (Mentor, 1985); and Hugh Davis Graham, *The Civil Rights Era* (Oxford University Press, 1990).

9. Aldon D. Morris, *The Origins of the Civil Rights Movement: Black Communities Organizing for Change* (Free Press/Macmillan, 1985); James Farmer, *Lay Bare the Heart: An Autobiography of the Civil Rights Movement* (Arbor House, 1985).

10. National Advisory Commission on Civil Disorders, *The Kerner Report* (U.S. Government Printing Office, 1968), p. 1.

11. Ellen Carol Du Bois, *Feminism and Suffrage: The Emergence of an Independent Women's Movement in America, 1848–1869* (Cornell University Press, 1978); Joan Hoff-Wilson, "Women and the Constitution," *News for Teachers of Political Science* (Summer 1985), pp. 10–15.

12. Susan M. Hartmann, *From Margin to Mainstream: American Women and Politics Since 1960* (Temple University Press, 1989); and Susan Gluck Mezey, *In Pursuit of Equality: Women, Public Policy, and the Federal Courts* (St. Martin's Press, 1992).

13. *United States v. Virginia*, 518 U.S. 515 (1996). See also Philippa Strum, *Women in the Barracks: The VMI Case and Equal Rights* (University Press of Kansas, 2002).

14. David M. O'Brien, "Ironies and Unanticipated Consequences of Legislation: Title VII of the 1964 Civil Rights Act and Sexual Harassment," in

Congress and the Politics of Emerging Rights, eds. Colton C. Campbell and John F. Stack Jr. (Rowman & Littlefield, 2002), pp. 27–44.

15. *Meritor Savings Bank, FBD* v. *Vinson,* 477 U.S. 57 (1986).

16. *Oncale* v. *Sundowner Offshore Services,* 523 U.S. 75 (1998); and *Faragher* v. *City of Boca Raton,* 524 U.S. 775 (1998); and *Burlington Industries* v. *Ellerth,* 524 U.S. 742 (1998).

17. Gregory Rodriguez, "The Nation: Where Minorities Rule," *The New York Times,* February 10, 2002, p. WK6.

18. Celia W. Dugger, "U.S. Study Says Asian-Americans Face Widespread Discrimination," *The New York Times,* February 29, 1992, p. 1, reporting on U.S. Civil Rights Commission, *Civil Rights Issues Facing Asian Americans in the 1990s* (U.S. Government Printing Office, 1992).

19. Won Moo Hurh, *Korean Immigrants in America* (Fairleigh Dickinson University Press, 1984).

20. Antonio J. A. Pido, *The Filipinos in America: Macro/Micro Dimensions of Immigration and Integration* (Center for Migration Studies of New York, 1986).

21. Harold L. Hodgkinson, *The Demographics of American Indians: One Percent of the People, Fifty Percent of the Diversity* (Institute for Educational Leadership/Center for Demographic Policy, 1990), pp. 1–5.

22. Charles F. Wilkinson, *American Indians, Times, and the Law* (Yale University Press, 1987); and Vine Deloria Jr. and Clifford M. Lytle, *The Nations Within: The Past and Future of American Indian Sovereignty* (Pantheon Books, 1984).

23. *County of Yakima* v. *Yakima Indian Nation,* 502 U.S. 251 (1992).

24. Theodora Lurie, "Shattering the Myth of the Vanishing American," *Ford Foundation Letter* 22 (Winter 1991), p. 5.

25. Spencer Rich, "Native Americans: They Can Still Get Free Health Care If They're Indian Enough," *The Washington Post National Weekly Edition,* July 14, 1986, p. 34, quoting the Office of Technology Assessment.

26. *Morey* v. *Doud,* 354 U.S. 459 (1957); *Allegheny Pittsburgh Coal Co.* v. *County Commission,* 488 U.S. 336 (1989).

27. *City of Cleburne, Texas* v. *Cleburne Living Center,* 473 U.S. 432 (1985); *Heller* v. *Doe,* 509 U.S. 312 (1993); and *Roemer* v. *Evans,* 517 U.S. 620 (1996).

28. *Roemer* v. *Evans,* 517 U.S. 620 (1996).

29. *San Antonio School District* v. *Rodriguez,* 411 U.S. 1 (1973).

30. *Frontiero* v. *Richardson,* 411 U.S. 677 (1973).

31. *Califano* v. *Webster,* 430 U.S. 313 (1977).

32. *Mississippi University for Woman* v. *Hogan,* 458 U.S. 718 (1982); and *United States* v. *Virginia,* 518 U.S. 515 (1996).

33. *San Antonio School District* v. *Rodriguez,* 411 U.S. 1 (1973); Douglas Reed, *On Equal Terms: The Constitutional Politics of Educational Opportunity* (Princeton University Press, 2001).

34. Matthew Bosworth, *Courts as Catalysts: State Supreme Courts and Public School Finance Equity* (State University of New York Press, 2001).

35. Sandra Day O'Connor, in *Kimel* v. *Florida Board of Regents,* 528 U.S. 62 (2000).

36. Ibid.

37. *Washington* v. *Davis,* 426 U.S. 229 (1976). See also *Hunter* v. *Underwood,* 471 U.S. 522 (1985).

38. Sandra Day O'Connor, concurring in *Hernandez* v. *New York,* 500 U.S. 352 (1991).

39. *Personnel Administrator of Massachusetts* v. *Feeney,* 442 U.S. 256 (1979).

40. *Smith* v. *Allwright,* 321 U.S. 649 (1944).

41. *Gomillion* v. *Lightfoot,* 364 U.S. 339 (1960).

42. *Harper* v. *Virginia Board of Elections,* 383 U.S. 663 (1966).

43. *Report of the United States Commission on Civil Rights* (U.S. Government Printing Office, 1959), pp. 103–104.

44. Harold W. Stanley, *Voter Mobilization and the Politics of Race: The South and Universal Suffrage, 1952–1984* (Praeger, 1987).

45. Abigail M. Thernstrom, *Whose Votes Count? Affirmative Action and Minority Voting Rights* (Harvard University Press, 1987), p. 15.

46. Thernstrom, *Whose Votes Count?* For a contrary view, see Bernard Grofman, Lisa Handley, and Richard G. Niemi, *Minority Representation and the Quest for Voting Equality* (Cambridge University Press, 1992).

47. *Morse* v. *Republican Party of Virginia,* 517 U.S. 116 (1996).

48. *Shaw* v. *Reno,* 509 U.S. 630 (1993).

49. *Hunt* v. *Cromartie,* 532 U.S. 234 (2001).

50. Orlando Patterson, *The Ordeal of Integration: Progress and Resentment in America's "Racial" Crisis* (Civitas/Counterpoint, 1997), p. 67.

51. *Plessy* v. *Ferguson,* 163 U.S. 537 (1896).

52. *Brown* v. *Board of Education of Topeka,* 347 U.S. 483 (1954). See also J. W. Peltason, *Fifty-Eight Lonely Men: Southern Federal Judges and School Desegregation* (University of Illinois Press, 1971), p. 248.

53. *Brown* v. *Board of Education of Topeka,* 349 U.S. 294 (1955).

54. *Freeman* v. *Pitts,* 503 U.S. 467 (1992); and *Missouri* v. *Jenkins,* 515 U.S. 70 (1995).

55. See Gary Orfield, Susan E. Eaton, and the Harvard Project on School Desegregation, *Dismantling Desegregation: The Quiet Reversal of Brown v. Board of Education* (New Press, 1996).

56. Raymond Hernandez, "NAACP Suspends Yonkers Leader After Criticism of Usefulness of School Busing," *The New York Times,* November 1, 1995, p. A13.

57. Gary Orfield and Chungmei Lee, *Brown at 50: King's Dream or Plessy's Nightmare?* (The Civil Rights Project, Harvard University, 2004), available at www.civilrightsproject.harvard.edu.

58. See Douglas Reed, *On Equal Terms,* pp. 21–22.

59. William O. Douglas, dissenting in *Moose Lodge No. 107* v. *Irvis,* 407 U.S. 163 (1972).

60. *New York State Club Association* v. *New York City,* 487 U.S. 1 (1988).

61. *Boy Scouts of America* v. *Dale,* 530 U.S. 640 (2000).

62. *Civil Rights Cases,* 109 U.S. 3 (1883).

63. *Heart of Atlanta Motel* v. *United States,* 379 U.S. 421 (1964).

64. Darryl Van Duch, "Plagued by Politics, EEOC Backlog Grows," *Recorder,* August 18, 1998, p. 1; David Rovella, "EEOC Chairman Casellas: 'We Are Being Selective,'" *National Law Journal,* November 20, 1995, p. 1.

65. Charles M. Lamb, "Housing Discrimination and Segregation," *Catholic University Law Review* (Spring 1981), p. 370.

66. *Shelley* v. *Kraemer,* 334 U.S. 1 (1948).

67. Daniel Mitchell, quoted in CQ Researcher, *Housing Discrimination* 5 (February 24, 1995), p. 174.

68. John Marshall Harlan, dissenting in *Plessy* v. *Ferguson,* 163 U.S. 537 (1896).

69. *University of California Regents* v. *Bakke,* 438 U.S. 265 (1978). See Howard Ball, *The Bakke Case* (University Press of Kansas, 2000).

70. Sandra Day O'Connor, in *Richmond* v. *Croson,* 488 U.S. 469 (1989).

71. See *Adarand Constructors, Inc.,* v. *Pena,* 515 U.S. 2000 (1995).

72. *Shaw* v. *Reno,* 509 U.S. 630 (1993); *Miller* v. *Johnson,* 515 U.S. 900 (1995).

73. "Affirmative Action in California Passed," *The Economist,* April 8, 2000, p. 29.

74. "Affirmative Action," *The Economist,* April 20, 2002, p. 30; "Affirmative Action: Moving on, but Very Slowly," *The Economist,* October 4, 2003, p. 29.

75. *Hopwood* v. *Texas,* 518 U.S. 1016 (1996).

76. Jonathan D. Glater, "Diversity Plan Shaped in Texas Is Under Attack," *The New York Times,* June 13, 2004, p. E1.

77. *Gratz* v. *Bollinger,* 539 U.S. 244 (2003).

78. *Grutter* v. *Bollinger,* 539 U.S. 306 (2003).

79. Carol M. Swain et al., "When Whites and Blacks Agree: Fairness in Educational Opportunities," Institute of Governmental Studies, University of California at Berkeley, Working Paper 98–11, 1998, p. 6. See also Lee Sigelman and Susan Welch, *Black Americans' Views of Racial Inequality: The Dream Deferred* (Cambridge University Press, 1994); and Peter Skerry, "The Affirmative Action Paradox," *Society* 35 (September–October 1998), p. 11.

80. James Farmer, quoted in Rochelle L. Stanfield, "Black Complaints Haven't Translated into Political Organization and Power," *National Journal,* June 14, 1980, p. 465.

81. Gary Orfield and Chungmei Lee, *Brown at 50;* and Donald Kinder and Lynn M. Sanders, *Divided by Color: Racial Politics and Democratic Ideals* (University of Chicago Press, 1996).

82. Gregory Rodriguez, "Where the Minorities Rule," *The New York Times,* February 10, 2002, p. WK6.

83. Gary Orfield, "Separate Societies: Have the Kerner Warnings Come True?" in *Quiet Riots: Race and Poverty in the United States—The Kerner Report Twenty Years Later,* eds. Fred R. Harris and Roger W. Wilkins (Pantheon, 1988), p. 103. See also Nicholas Lehmann, *The Promised Land* (Knopf, 1991).

84. Patterson, *The Ordeal of Integration,* p. 54.

85. Gary Orfield and Carole Ashkinaze, *The Closing Door: Conservative Policy and Black Opportunity* (University of Chicago Press, 1991), p. 26.

86. William J. Wilson, *The Truly Disadvantaged: The Inner City, the Underclass, and Public Policy* (University of Chicago Press, 1987), esp. chap. 5; and Kevin Phillips, *The Politics of Rich and Poor* (Random House, 1995).

87. Orfield and Ashkinaze, *Closing Door,* pp. 221–234; and A. Leon Higginbotham Jr., *Shades of Freedom* (Oxford University Press, 1996).

Chapter 18

1. See John Kingdon, *Agendas, Alternatives, and Public Policies* (Boston: Little, Brown, 1984), for a description of the policy-making process.

2. Kingdon, *Agendas, Alternatives, and Public Policies,* p. 3.

3. Anthony Downs, "The 'Issue-Attention Cycle,' " *The Public Interest* 28 (Summer 1972), p. 38.

4. Lester Salamon and Michael Lund, "The Tools Approach: Basic Analytics," in L. Salamon, ed., *Beyond Privatization: The Tools of Government Action* (Washington, D.C.: Urban Institute Press, 1989).

5. Hugh Heclo, "Issue Networks and the Executive Establishment," in A. King, ed., *The New American Political System* (Washington, D.C.: American Enterprise Institute, 1978), pp. 87–124.

6. See "National Debt," at www.jeffords.senate.gov/debt.html.

7. Andrew Taylor, "With Half-Trillion in Red Ink, U.S. Inc. Looks Bad on Paper," *CQ Weekly*, January 17, 2004, p. 132.

8. For a discussion of the budgetary cycle, see Allen Schick, *The Federal Budget: Politics, Policy, Process*, rev. ed. (Brookings Institution Press, 2000).

9. Efforts at past tax reform are described in Jeffrey H. Birnbaum and Alan S. Murray, *Showdown at Gucci Gulch: Lawmakers, Lobbyists, and the Unlikely Triumph of Tax Reform* (Vintage, 1988). See also Timothy J. Conlan, Margaret T. Wrightson, and David R. Beam, *Taxing Choices: The Politics of Tax Reform* (CQ Press, 1990).

10. Quoted in Frederick Lewis Allen, *Since Yesterday* (Harper, 1940), p. 64.

11. W. H. Beveridge, *The Pillars of Security* (Macmillan, 1943), p. 51.

12. The debate over Keynes and his economic theories is still alive in the United States. See Donald E. Moggridge, *Maynard Keynes: An Economist's Biography* (Routledge, 1992).

13. Environmental Working Group, at www.ewg.org.

14. Gary Burtless, Robert J. Lawrence, Robert E. Litan, and Robert J. Shapiro, *Globaphobia: Confronting Fears About Open Trade* (Brookings Institution Press, 1998), p. 29. For more information about GATT and the World Trade Organization, go to www.wto.org.

15. Mary Jordan, "Mexican Workers Pay for Success," *The Washington Post*, June 20, 2002, p. A1.

16. Burtless et al., *Globaphobia*, p. 126.

17. See Robert W. Crandall et al., *An Agenda for Federal Regulatory Reform* (American Enterprise Institute/Brookings Institution, 1997), for a discussion of reasons for the increased activity.

18. Harold W. Stanley and Richard G. Niemi, *Vital Statistics in American Politics, 1999* (CQ Press, 1999), p. 258.

19. Stephen Moore, ed., *Restoring the Dream: The Bold New Plan by House Republicans* (Times Books, 1995), p. 156.

20. *United States v. E. C. Knight Co.*, 156 U.S. 1 (1895).

21. On the origins of the Federal Trade Commission and the role of Louis D. Brandeis, see Thomas K. McCraw, *Prophets of Regulation* (Belknap Press, 1984), chap. 3.

22. For a useful history of airline deregulation, see Steven A. Morrison and Clifford Winston, *The Evolution of the Airline Industry* (Brookings Institution Press, 1995).

23. On Southwest Airlines and its longtime chief executive Herb Kelleher, see Kevin Freiberg and Jackie Freiberg, *Nuts!* (Bard Press, 1996).

24. *Reno v. American Civil Liberties Union*, 521 U.S. 844 (1997).

25. See Robert W. Crandall and Harold Furchtgott-Roth, *Cable TV: Regulation or Competition?* (Brookings Institution Press, 1996); Richard Klinger, *The New Information Industry: Regulatory Challenges and the First Amendment* (Brookings Institution Press, 1996); and Lawrence Lessig, *Code and Other Laws of Cyberspace* (Basic Books, 2000).

Chapter 19

1. Jackie Koszczuk and Jonathan Allen, "Late-Night Medicare Vote Drama Triggers Some Unexpected Alliances," *Congressional Quarterly Weekly*, November 29, 2003, p. 2958.

2. The Pew Research Center for the People and the Press, *Evenly Divided and Increasingly Polarized: 2004 Political Landscape* (Pew Research Center, November 5, 2003), pp. 39–44.

3. Michael B. Katz, *In the Shadow of the Poorhouse: A Social History of Welfare in America* (Basic Books, 1986).

4. This history draws heavily on Theda Skocpol's wonderful work on the subject, starting with "America's First Social Security System: The Expansion of Benefits for Civil War Veterans," *Political Science Quarterly* 108 (Winter 1993), pp. 64–87.

5. Ibid., pp. 85–86.

6. Joel F. Handler, *The Poverty of Welfare Reform* (Yale University Press, 1995), p. 21.

7. The 2004 guidelines can be found at www.aspe.hhs.gov/poverty/figures-fed-reg.shtml.

8. See U.S. Census Bureau, "Poverty Highlights." www.census.gov/hhes/poverty/poverty-2/pov02hi.html.

9. Gertrude Schaffner Goldberg and Eleanor Kremen, eds., *The Feminization of Poverty: Only in America?* (Greenwood Press, 1990).

10. See, for example, Margaret Weir, "Political Parties and Social Policymaking," in *The Social Divide: Political Parties and the Future of Activist Government*, ed. Margaret Weir (Brookings Institution Press, 1998).

11. Self-employed workers must cover both amounts, and many state and local government workers are not required to participate.

12. These and other simple facts about Social Security can be found at www.ssa.gov.

13. Martha Derthick, "No More Easy Votes for Social Security," *Brookings Review* 10 (Fall 1992), pp. 50–53.

14. For a pessimistic view of the viability of Social Security, see Neil Howe and Richard Jackson, "The Myth of the 2.2 Percent Solution," at www.cato.org/pubs/sspslles.html. Robert D. Reischauer of the Brookings Institution testified before the House Committee on Ways and Means on November 19, 1998, that Social Security will start running deficits by 2021 and that by 2032, "reserves will be depleted."

15. See Theda Skocpol, *Protecting Soldiers and Mothers: The Political Origins of Social Policy in the United States* (Belknap Press, 1992), chap. 9, for a history of the act.

16. Lyndon Johnson, speech at the University of Michigan, May 1964, in *Congress and the Nation, 1965–1968: A Review of Government and Politics During the Johnson Years* (CQ Press, 1969), vol. 2, p. 650.

17. For a history of Medicare and other Great Society programs, see James L. Sundquist, *Politics and Policy: The Eisenhower, Kennedy, and Johnson Years* (Brookings Institution Press, 1968).

18. William J. Clinton, acceptance speech, Democratic National Convention, Chicago, July 6, 1992.

19. Robert Pear, "Judge Rules States Can't Cut Welfare," *The New York Times*, October 14, 1997, p. A1.

20. Isabel V. Sawhill, R. Kent Weaver, Ron Haskins, and Andrea Kane, eds., *Welfare Reform and Beyond: The Future of the Safety Net* (Brookings Institution Press, 2002), p. 19.

21. Centers for Medicare and Medicaid Services, "Health Accounts," at www.cms.hhs.gov/statistics/nhe.

22. U.S. Bureau of the Census, *Statistical Abstracts of the United States*, 1999 (U.S. Government Printing Office, 1999), p. 448.

23. Ibid., p. 93.

24. Laurene A. Graig, *Health of Nations: An International Perspective on U.S. Health Care Reform* (CQ Press, 1993), p. 20.

25. Michael D. Lemonick, "Doctors' Deadly Mistakes," *Time*, December 13, 1999, p. 74.

26. Jennifer Steinhauer, "At Beth Israel, Lapses in Care Mar Gains in Technology," *The New York Times*, February 15, 2000, p. B1.

27. "Medicare Funds Going Up in Smoke," *Deseret News*, May 17, 1994, p. A1.

28. Congressional Budget Office, *How Many People Lack Health Insurance and for How Long?* (Congressional Budget Office, May, 2003).

29. U.S. Bureau of the Census, at www.census.gov.

30. "Measuring the HMOs," *Los Angeles Times*, October 3, 1998, p. B7.

31. Mary Agnes Carey and Rebecca Adams, "Managed-Care Conferees Agree on Appeals Principles; Key Details Remian Unresolved," *Congressional Quarterly Weekly*, April 15, 2000, p. 903.

32. Congressional Budget Office, *How Many People Lack Health Insurance and for How Long?*

33. Institute of Medicine, Committee on Employer-Based Health Benefits, *Employment and Health Benefits: A Connection at Risk*, eds. Marilyn J. Field and Harold T. Shapiro (National Academy Press, 1993), p. 5.

34. The amount permitted for a medical savings account is 75 percent of the maximum total deduction for medical expenses for an individual or couple; see Internal Revenue Service, at www.irs.ustreas.bov/prod/forms_pubs/pubs/p96901.htm.

35. Martin Kady II, "America's Uneasy Mandate for Domestic Security," *Congressional Quarterly Weekly*, April 24, 2004, p. 950.

Chapter 20

1. The complete timeline for the Iraq war, including all links and citations to specific quotes in this section, can be found at www.cooperativeresearch.org.

2. See Glenn Kessler, "U.S. Decision On Iraq Has Puzzling Past Opponents of War Wonder When, How Policy Was Set," *The Washington Post*, January 12, 2003, p. A1, for a detailed history of the increasing interest in Iraq.

3. U.S. Select Committee on Intelligence, *Report on the U.S. Intelligence Community's Prewar Intelligence Assessments on Iraq: Conclusions*, no report number, July 7, 2004, p. 1.

4. Pew Research Center for the People and the Press, "Public Support for War Resilient," June 17, 2004, questions 2a and 52.

5. National Commission on Terrorist Attacks on the United States, *The 9/11 Commission Report,* Government Printing Office, 2004, p. 362.

6. National Commission on Terrorist Attacks on the United States, *The 911 Commission Report,* p. 376.

7. See the entire doctrine explained in *The National Security Strategy of the United States,* White House, September 7, 2002.

8. This reference is contained in the chronology as www.cooperativeresearch.org, which draws from Richard Clarke's *Against All Enemies: Inside America's War on Terror* (Free Press, 2004).

9. Condoleezza Rice, quoted in Glenn Kessler, "Rice Lays Out Case for War in Iraq," *The Washington Post,* August 16, 2002, p. A1.

10. James T. Quinlivan, "Burden of Victory: The Painful Arithmetic of Stability Operations," *RAND Review,* vol. 27, no. 2, 2003, pp. 28–29.

11. United States Senate Select Committee on Intelligence, *Report on the U.S. Intelligence Community's Prewar Intelligence Assessments on Iraq,* Committee print, reported July 7, 2004, Committee summary p. 1, available at www.intelligence.senate.gov/conclusions.pdf.

12. The "slam dunk case" story is reported in Bob Woodward's *Plan of Attack* (Simon & Schuster, 2004).

13. For more information, visit the Peace Corps Web site at www.peacecorps.gov. For a useful study of the Peace Corps, see Elizabeth Cobbs Hoffman, *All You Need Is Love: The Peace Corps and the Spirit of the 1960s* (Harvard University Press, 1998).

14. U.S. Department of Defense, at www.defenselink.mil; U.S. Department of State, at www.state.gov.

15. The case for continued reliance on vital U.S. embassies abroad is well made in Mary Locke and Casimir A. Yost, eds., *Who Needs Embassies? How U.S. Missions Abroad Help Shape Our World* (Georgetown University School of Foreign Policy, 1997).

16. For a fascinating history of U.S. intelligence operations, see Christopher Andrew, *For the President's Eyes Only: Secret Intelligence and the American Presidency from Washington to Bush* (HarperCollins, 1995). See also Rhodri Jeffreys-Jones, *The CIA and American Democracy,* 2d ed. (Yale University Press, 1998).

17. National Commission on Terrorist Attacks on the United States, *The 9/11 Commission Report,* p. 12.

18. See George C. Wilson, *This War Really Matters: Inside the Fight for Defense Dollars* (CQ Press, 2000).

19. Pew Research Center for the People and the Press, *Public Opinion in a Year for the Books* (Pew Research Center, 2002), p. 1.

20. Thomas L. Friedman, "India, Pakistan, and G.E.," *New York Times,* August 11, 2002, sec. 4, p. 13.

21. For an examination of how Japanese companies try to influence foreign policy and trade officials in Washington, see Pat Choate, *Agents of Influence* (Knopf, 1990).

22. "G.O.P. Returns $100,000 Gift," *The New York Times,* January 20, 2001, p. A8.

23. For a useful review of how Congress has occasionally challenged and even more often failed to challenge the White House when it comes to the war power, see Louis Fisher, *Presidential War Power* (University Press of Kansas, 1995).

24. For an analysis that asserts U.S. foreign policy is almost entirely shaped by self-appointed elites, see Eric Alterman, *Who Speaks for America? Why Democracy Matters* (Cornell University Press, 1998). More generally, see Ole Holsti, *Public Opinion and American Foreign Policy* (University of Michigan Press, 1996).

25. Dennis C. Jett, "The U.N.'s Failures Are Everyone's Fault," *The New York Times,* May 22, 2000, p. A23. See also Christopher S. Wren, "Era Waning: Holbrooke Takes Stock," *The New York Times,* January 14, 2001, p. 8.

26. "U.S. Foreign Aid Spending Since World War II," *Public Perspective* 8 (August–September 1997), p. 11.

27. Gallup Poll, May 2000, www.gallup.com.

28. See Sebastian Mallaby, "Why So Stingy on Foreign Aid?" *Washington Post National Weekly Edition,* July 3, 2000, p. 27.

29. Ibid. But see Doug Bandow, "The Case Against Foreign Aid," *Christian Science Monitor,* September 29, 1999, p. 9; and Eric Schmitt, "Helms Urges Foreign Aid Be Handled by Charities," *The New York Times,* January 12, 2001, p. A4.

30. Richard N. Haass, "Sanctions Almost Never Work," *The Wall Street Journal,* June 19, 1998, p. A14. See also Richard N. Haass and Meghan L. O'Sullivan, eds., *Honey and Vinegar: Incentives, Sanctions, and Foreign Policy* (Brookings Institution Press, 2000).

31. Richard Lugar, in Gerald F. Seib, "Capital Journal," *The Wall Street Journal,* June 17, 1998, p. A18.

32. Gary Hufbauer, "Foreign Policy on the Cheap," *Washington Post National Weekly Edition,* July 20, 1998, p. 22.

33. See Robert Kagan, "The Kerry Doctrine," *The Washington Post,* August 1, 2004, p. B7, for this argument.

34. Gary Hufbauer and Jeffrey J. Schott, "Economic Sanctions and Foreign Policy," *PS: Political Science and Politics* 18 (Fall 1985), p. 278.

35. See Ivo H. Daalder and Michael E. O'Hanlon, *Winning Ugly: NATO's War to Save Kosovo* (Brookings Institution Press, 2000), esp. chap. 6.

36. John Prados, *The President's Secret Wars: CIA and Pentagon Covert Operations Since World War II* (Morrow, 1986); Daniel Patrick Moynihan, *Secrecy: The American Experience* (Yale University Press, 1998).

37. P. W. Singer, "Winning the War of Words: Information Warfare in Afghanistan," *Brookings Analysis Paper No. 5,* October 2001.

38. Norman A. Graebner, "The President as Commander in Chief: A Study in Power," in *Commander-in-Chief: Presidential Leadership in Modern Wars,* ed. Joseph G. Dawson III (University Press of Kansas, 1993), p. 31.

39. Colin L. Powell, quoted in Steven Mufson, "From Soldier to Diplomat," *Washington Post National Weekly Edition,* December 25, 2000, p. 6.

40. Bill Keller, "The World According to Powell," *New York Times Magazine,* November 25, 2001, p. 14.

41. T. M. Destler and Steven Kull, *Misreading the Public: The Myth of a New Isolationism* (Brookings Institution Press, 1998).

42. Eric Schmitt and Thom Shanker, "Army to Call Up Recruits Earlier," *The New York Times,* July 22, 2004, p. A1.

43. Evan Thomas and Gregory L. Vistica, "Falling Out of the Sky," *Newsweek,* March 17, 1997, p. 26.

44. Office of Management and Budget, *Budget of the United States, Fiscal Year 2005* (U.S. Government Printing Office, 2004).

45. Ibid.

46. John Spratt and Hugh Brady, "National Security v. Social Security," *Brookings Review,* vol. 20, no. 3 (Summer 2002), p. 12.

47. See, for example, James Kitfield, "Ships Galore!" *National Journal,* February 10, 1996, pp. 298–302.

48. *Public Papers of the Presidents,* Dwight D. Eisenhower, 1960, pp. 1035–1040.

49. See Renae Merle, "Contract Workers Are War's Forgotten," *The Washington Post,* July 31, 2004, p. A1.

50. Michael Rich, John Birkler, and Mark Lorell, "Defense Industry Goliaths," *The Atlantic Monthly,* July/August, 2003, p. 89.

Chapter 21

1. Dale Russakoff and Amy Argetsinger, "States Plan Big Tuition Increases," *The Washington Post,* July 22, 2003, p. A1.

2. See Jon M. Broder, "Despite Rebound, States' Budgets Are Still Reeling," *The New York Times,* January 5, 2004, p. A1.

3. For a discussion of what factors improve economic performance and state policy effectiveness, see Paul Brace, *State Government and Economic Performance* (Johns Hopkins University Press, 1993); and Susan E. Clarke and Martin R. Saiz, "Economic Development and Infrastructure Policy," in *Politics in the American States,* eds. Virginia Gray, Russell Hanson, and Herbert Jacob, 7th ed. (CQ Press, 1999), pp. 540–543.

4. U.S. Bureau of the Census, *Statistical Abstract of the United States,* available at www.census.gov/prod/2003pubs/o2statab/stlocgov.pdf.

5. Robert S. Lynd and Helen M. Lynd, *Middletown* (Harcourt, 1929). See also their analysis of Muncie ten years later in *Middletown in Transition* (Harcourt, 1937).

6. Floyd Hunter, *Community Power Structure* (University of North Carolina Press, 1953). For a reassessment and rebuttal of Hunter's findings, see M. Kent Jennings, *Community Influentials: The Elites of Atlanta* (Free Press, 1964).

7. Robert A. Dahl, *Who Governs? Democracy and Power in an American City* (Yale University Press, 1961).

8. See the interesting study of San Jose, California, by Phillip J. Troustine and Terry Christensen, *Movers and Shakers: The Study of Community Power* (St. Martin's Press, 1982). See also Clarence N. Stone, *Regime Politics: Governing Atlanta, 1946–1988* (University Press of Kansas, 1989).

9. See, for example, Peter Bachrach and Morton S. Baratz, *Power and Poverty: Theory and Practice* (Oxford University Press, 1970); Matthew A. Crenson, *The Unpolitics of Air Pollution: A Study of Non-Decision Making in Two Cities* (Johns Hopkins University Press, 1971); and John Gaventa, *Power and Powerlessness: Quiescence and Rebellion in an Appalachian Valley* (University of Illinois Press, 1980).

10. Bryan D. Jones and Lynn W. Bachelor, *The Sustaining Hand: Community Leadership and Corporate Power*, 2d ed. (University Press of Kansas, 1993), p. 254. See also Stone, *Regime Politics*.

11. U.S. Census, *Statistical Abstract of the United States*, "Federal Government Civilian Employees" (December 31, 2002), at www.census.gov/govs/apes/02federalstate.txt; and "State Government Employment Data" (March 2002), at www.census.gov/govs/apes/02stlus.txt.

12. U.S. Census, *Statistical Abstract of the United States*, at www.census.gov/press-release/www/release/archives/governments/001531.html.

13. Stone, *Regime Politics*, p. 232.

14. For a detailed analysis of how the W. R. Grace Company and Beatrice Foods Company had to rely on law firms to fight legal actions surrounding their operations in Woburn, Massachusetts, see Jonathan Harr, *A Civil Action* (Vintage Books, 1996). See also Alan Rosenthal, *The Third House: Lobbyists and Lobbying in the States*, 2d ed. (CQ Press, 2001).

15. See Clive S. Thomas and Ronald J. Hrebenar, "Interest Groups in the States," in *Politics in the American States*, ed. Gray et al., pp. 122–158.

16. For a general discussion of ethics reform and enforcement efforts, see *Spectrum: The Journal of State Government* (Winter 1993).

17. On various efforts to improve ethical practices and professionalism in the state legislatures and the limits of these efforts, see Alan Rosenthal, *Drawing the Line: Legislative Ethics in the States* (University of Nebraska Press, 1996).

18. Jimmy Carter, *Why Not the Best?* (Bantam Books, 1976), p. 101. See also the memoir by Tom Loftus, a former speaker of the Wisconsin State Assembly, *The Art of Legislative Politics* (CQ Press, 1994), chap. 3.

19. Diane D. Blair, *Arkansas Politics and Government* (University of Nebraska Press, 1988), p. 118.

20. William P. Browne and Kenneth VerBurg, *Michigan Politics and Government* (University of Nebraska Press, 1995), pp. 241–245.

21. Paul Peterson, *City Limits* (University of Chicago Press, 1981), p. 124. See also the useful discussion of the challenge of covering state legislative politics in Browne and VerBurg, *Michigan Politics and Government*, pp. 242–245.

22. Joseph F. Zimmerman, *The New England Town Meeting: Democracy in Action* (Praeger, 1999).

23. See for example, Daniel Kemmis, *The Good City and the Good Life* (Houghton Mifflin, 1995); and David L. Kirp, John P. Dwyer, and Larry A. Rosenthal, *Our Town: Race, Housing, and the Soul of Suburbia* (Rutgers University Press, 1997).

24. Eugene F. Rivers III, "High-Octane Faith," in *Community Works: The Revival of Civil Society in America*, ed. E. J. Dionne Jr. (Brookings Institution Press, 1998), p. 61.

25. For the efforts of a big-city mayor and his team of advisers, see Buzz Bissinger, *A Prayer for the City* (Random House, 1997). See also the example of Milwaukee's mayor, John O. Norquist, *Wealth of Cities* (Addison-Wesley, 1998).

Chapter 22

1. Kavan Peterson, "50-State Rundown on Gay Marriage Laws," *Stateline* (February 25, 2004), available at www.stateline.org.

2. Temporary New York State Commission on Constitutional Revision, *Effective Government Now for the New Century* (Nelson A. Rockefeller Institute of Government, 1995).

3. Mario M. Cuomo, "Real Reform: It's Time for a People's State Constitutional Convention," *Rockefeller Institute Bulletin* (1993), pp. 41–46.

4. Richard Perez-Pena, "Voters Reject Constitutional Convention: Last-Minute Campaign Appears to Sway Ballot," *The New York Times*, November 5, 1997, p. B1.

5. Michigan Department of State, Bureau of Elections, at www.sos.state.mi.us/law; and Arkansas Government Relations, at www.uark.edu/~govinfo/PAGES/History/del.html.

6. Gerald Benjamin, "The Functions of State Constitutions in a Federal System," paper presented at the American Political Science Association Round Table, Washington, D.C., 1984.

7. John Adams, quoted in Judith S. Kaye, "Federalism's Other Tier," *Constitution* 3 (Winter 1991), p. 50.

8. *Providence Journal*, July 7, 2000, as reported at www.projo.com.

9. G. Alan Tarr, *Understanding State Constitutions* (Princeton University Press, 2000), p. 47.

10. Donald S. Lutz, "Toward a Theory of Constitutional Amendment," in *Responding to Imperfection: The Theory and Practice of Constitutional Amendment*, ed. Sanford Levinson (Princeton University Press, 1995), pp. 237–274.

11. *The Book of the States, 2002–2003* (Council of State Governments, 2002), p. 3; John Kincaid, "State Constitutions in the Federal System," *Annals of the American Academy of Political and Social Science* 496 (March 1988), p. 14.

12. See Richard J. Ellis, *Democratic Delusions: The Initiative Process in America* (University Press of Kansas, 2003).

13. *Book of the States, 2002–2003*, p. 14.

14. Steve Geissinger, "Changing the Constitution Is a Powerful Government-Reform Tool Avoided by Officials," *Alameda Times-Star*, November 9, 2003, p. C1.

15. Jack W. Strain, *An Outline of Oklahoma Government*, ed. Leroy Crozier and Carl F. Reherman (Bureau of Local Government Services, Department of Political Science, Central State University, 1984), p. 21.

16. South Dakota Constitution, Article XI, Section 8.

17. Alabama Constitution, Amendment 383 (1901).

18. Christopher W. Hammons, "State Constitutional Reform: Is It Necessary?" *Albany Law Review* 64 (2001), pp. 1328–1334.

19. Christopher W. Hammons, "Was James Madison Wrong? Rethinking the American Preference for Short, Framework-Oriented Constitutions," *American Political Science Review* 93 (December 1999), p. 838. See also ibid.

20. *Indiana* v. *Gerschoffer*, 763 N.E.2d 960 (Ind., 2002).

21. *Anchorage Police Department Employees Association* v. *Anchorage*, 24 P.3d 547 (Alaska, 2001).

22. *American Academy of Pediatrics* v. *Lungren*, 490 P.2d 797 (Calif. 1997).

23. Kaye, "Federalism's Other Tier," p. 54.

24. See, e.g., Matthew Bosworth, *Courts as Catalysts: State Supreme Courts and Public School Finances Equity* (State University of New York Press, 2001); and Charles Lopeman, *The Activist Advocate: Policy Making in State Supreme Courts* (Praeger, 1999).

25. *Michigan* v. *Long*, 463 U.S. 1032 (1983); "Our Judicial Federalism," *Intergovern-mental Perspective* 15 (Summer 1989), pp. 8–15; and William M. Wiecek, "Some Protection of Personal Liberty: Remembering the Future," and Kermit L. Hall, "Mostly Anchor and Little Sail: The Evolution of American State Constitutions," in *Toward a Usable Past: Liberty Under State Constitutions*, eds. Paul Finkelman and Stephen E. Gottlieb (University of Georgia Press, 1991), pp. 371–417.

26. Deborah Baker, "Canvassing Board Certifies Amendment Election," *Santa Fe New Mexican* (October 14, 2003), at A1.

27. According to the *Book of the States, 2002–2003*, p. 11, in 1998–1999, of the 266 legislative proposed amendments in the 49 states that require submission to the voters for ratification, 210, or 78.8 percent, were adopted.

28. Tip H. Allen Jr., "The Enduring Traditions of the State Constitutions," in Dale Krane and Stephen D. Shaffer, *Mississippi Government and Politics: Modernizers Versus Traditionalists* (University of Nebraska Press, 1992), pp. XX–XXV.

29. *Book of the States, 2002–2003*, p. 14.

30. David B. Magleby, "Direct Legislation in the American States," in *Referendums Around the World: The Growing Use of Direct Democracy*, eds. David Butler and Austin Ranney (American Enterprise Institute Press, 1994), p. 225.

31. California Commission on Campaign Financing, *Democracy by Initiative: A Summary of the Report and Recommendations of the California Commission on Campaign Financing* (Center for Responsive Government, 1992), p. 25.

32. *Amador Valley Joint Union High School District* v. *State Board of Equalization*, 22 Cal. 3d 208 (1978), quoted in Eugene C. Lee, "The Revision of California's Constitution," *CPS Brief: A Publication of the California Policy Seminar* 3 (April 1991), p. 1.

33. *Book of the States, 2002–2003*, p. 11. See also Magleby, "Direct Legislation," p. 251.

34. Tarr, *Understanding State Constitutions*, p. 158.

35. Ibid., pp. 160–61.

36. Gerald Benjamin and Thomas Gais, "Constitutional Conventionphobia," in *State Constitutions: Competing Perspectives*, eds. Burton C. Agata and Eric Lane (Hofstra Law and Policy Symposium, 1996), vol. 1, p. 69; and Tarr, *Understanding State Constitutions*, p. 25.

37. Caleb Nelson, "Majorities, Minorities, and the Meaning of Liberty: A Reevaluation of Scholarly Explanations for the Rise of the Elective Judiciary in Antebellum America," Yale Law School (1991), p. 51, elaborating the thesis of Gordon Wood, *The Creation of the American Republic, 1776–1787* (University of North Carolina Press, 1969), pp. 306–325.

38. Elder Witt, "State Supreme Courts: Tilting the Balance Toward Change," *Governing*, August 1988, p. 33.

39. G. Alan Tarr, Keynote Address, conference on State Constitutional Reform, May 4, 2000, at www.camlaw.rugers.edu/statecon/keynote.html.

40. Lee, "Revision of California's Constitution," p. 7. See also Lutz, "Toward a Theory of Constitutional Amendment," pp. 355–370.

41. Re Jan Ruggiero, Director of Elections, Elections Division, Office of the Secretary of State, Providence, R.I., at www.state.ri.us.

42. Common Cause of Rhode Island, "Separation of Powers," at www.commoncauseri.org/news.

43. Cecil Morgan, "A New Constitution for Louisiana," *National Civic Review*, July 1974, pp. 343–356.

44. Tarr, *Understanding State Constitutions*, p. 143.

45. Beryl E. Pettus and Randall W. Bland, *Texas Government Today* (Dorsey Press, 1979), pp. 34–36. See also Janice C. May, "Texas Constitutional Revision and Laments," *National Civic Review*, February 1977, pp. 64–69.

46. Andre Henderson, "Selling a Constitution: California Desperately Needs a New Charter, That Doesn't Mean It Will Get One," *Governance*, December 1995, pp. 30–31.

47. B. Drummond Ayres Jr., "Alabama Governor Set for Tough Race," *The New York Times*, February 27, 2002, p. A16.

48. Albert E. McKinley, "Two New Southern Constitutions," *Political Science Quarterly*, 18 (September 1903), pp. 480–511.

49. For more information go to the Web site of the Alabama Citizens for Constitutional Reform at www.constitutionalreform.org.

50. *Montgomery Advertiser*, December 11, 2002, the Associated Press, "Constitution Work May Come in 2003," at www.montgomeryadvertiser.com.

51. Editorial, "Constitutional Count, House Sending Clear Message: People Can't Be Trusted," *The Birmingham News*, March 21, 2002, p. A20.

52. David White, "Constitution Could Lose Segregation Provisions," *The Birmingham News*, April 16, 2003, p. A1.

Chapter 23

1. John Mintz, "It's Not as Easy as 1-2-3; Problems Exist with Both Hands, Machine Counts," *The Washington Post*, November 19, 2000, p. A1.

2. See electionline.org, the Electionline project started in the wake of the election administration problems in the 2000 presidential election. Funded by the Pew Charitable Trusts, the project is a nonpartisan clearinghouse on election reform.

3. Katharine Q. Seelye, "Panel Suggests Election Changes That Let States Keep Control," *The New York Times*, February 5, 2001, p. A16.

4. John F. Bibby, *Politics, Parties, and Elections in America*, 5th ed. (Wadsworth, 2003).

5. Florida Department of State, at election.dos.state.fl.us.

6. www.electionline.org.

7. According to Todd Taylor, executive director, Utah Democratic party, these requirements are intended to promote gender equity; personal communication, November 18, 1998.

8. See Cornelius P. Cotter, James L. Gibson, John F. Bibby, and Robert J. Huckshorn, *Party Organizations in America* (Praeger, 1984).

9. Ronald E. Weber, ed., *American State and Local Politics: Directions for the 21st Century* (Chatham House, 1999), p. 174.

10. Federal Election Commission, "National Voter Registration Act Report, 2002" at www.fec.gov.

11. Benjamin Highton and Raymond E. Wolfinger, *Political Behavior*, vol. 20, no. 2. (June, 1998), pp. 94–97.

12. California Secretary of State, at www.ss.ca.gov/elections/ror_021902.htm.

13. Mary Clare Jalonick, "Utah GOP Floats a Salt Lake Split-Up," *Congressional Quarterly Weekly*, May 5, 2001, p. 1032.

14. Federal Election Commission, at www.fec.gov/pages/2000turnout/reg&to00.htm.

15. For a discussion of coordinated campaigns, see Paul Herrnson, "National Party Organizations and the Postreform Congress," in *The Postreform Congress*, ed. Roger Davidson (St. Martin's Press, 1992), pp. 65–67.

16. See Cotter et al., *Party Organizations in America*.

17. Richard Perez-Pena, "A Federal Soft-Money Ban Could Benefit State Parties," *The New York Times*, March 22, 2002, p. B6.

18. Richard A. Oppel Jr., "Election Panel Rebuffs Effort to Weaken 'Issue Ad' Limits," *The New York Times*, June 20, 2002, p. A1.

19. David B. Magleby, ed., *Financing the 2000 Elections* (Washington, D.C.: Brookings Institution Press), p. 223.

20. Ibid., p. 203.

21. David B. Magleby and J. Quin Monson., *The Last Hurrah* (Washington, D.C.: Brookings Institution Press), p. 5.

22. See Bruce E. Keith, David B. Magleby, Candice J. Nelson, Elizabeth Orr, Mark C. Westlye, and Raymond E. Wolfinger, *The Myth of the Independent Voter* (University of California Press, 1992), p. 52.

23. The Field Poll, "Voters Very Dissatisfied with State Budget Negotiations. Blame Davis and Both Parties in the Legislature. Three in Four Fear the State Is Seriously Off on the Wrong Track," at www.field.com/fieldpollonline/subscribers/RLS2074.pdf, 15 July 2003.

24. The Field Poll, "How Schwarzenegger's History and Characteristics Helps and Hurts Him in His Bid to Become Governor," at www.field.com/fieldpollonline/subscribers/RLS2083.pdf, 17 August 2003.

25. Jodi Wilgoren, "Gov. Ventura Says He Won't Seek Reelection," *The New York Times*, June 19, 2002, p. A14.

26. Lawrence McQuillan, "Democrat Wins Republican State," *USA Today*, January 7, 2002, at www.usatoday.com/news/politicselections/2002-11-06-sebelius_x.htm.

27. William H. Flanigan and Nancy H. Zingale, *Political Behavior of the American Electorate*, 8th ed. (CQ Press, 1994), p. 171.

28. See BetterCampaigns.org at www.bettercampaigns.org/standard/display.php?StoryID=10.

29. William Glaberson, "Fierce Campaigns Signal a New Era for State Courts," *The New York Times*, June 5, 2000, p. A1.

30. Willis D. Hawley, *Nonpartisan Elections and the Case for Party Politics* (Wiley, 1973), pp. 81–82. See also Brian F. Schaffner, Matthew Streb, and Gerald Wright, "Teams Without Uniforms: The Nonpartisan Ballot in State and Local Elections," *Political Research Quarterly* 54 (March 2001), pp. 7–30.

31. Susan Welch and Timothy Bledsoe, "The Partisan Consequences of Non-Partisan Elections and the Changing Nature of Urban Politics," *American Journal of Political Science*, vol. 30, no. 1 (February, 1986), pp. 128–139.

32. Election Data Services, at www.electiondataservices.com/home.htm.

33. Terrel L. Rhodes, *Republicans in the South: Voting for the State House, Voting for the White House* (Praeger, 2000), p. 88.

34. Harvey L. Schantz, "Sectionalism in Presidential Elections," in *American Presidential Elections: Process, Policy, and Political Change*, ed. Harvey L. Schantz (SUNY Press, 1996), pp. 106–107. See also Zell Miller, "The Democratic Party's Southern Problem," *The New York Times*, June 4, 2001, p. A17.

35. U.S. Bureau of the Census, *Statistical Abstract of the United States, 2001* (U.S. Government Printing Office, 2001), p. 26.

36. Raymond E. Wolfinger and Steven J. Rosenstone, *Who Votes?* (Yale University Press, 1980), p. 130.

37. Election Data Service, at www.electiondataservices.com/home.htm.

38. Ibid.

39. Ibid.

40. David B. Magleby, "Participation in Mail Ballot Elections," *Western Political Quarterly* 40 (March 1987), pp. 79–91.

41. Absentee ballots for all states are available from www.justvote.org.

42. Diane Morgan, Office of the Washington Secretary of State, personal communication, March 22, 1999.

43. Bruce E. Cain and Elisabeth R. Gerber, eds., *Voting at the Political Fault Line: California's Experiment with the Blanket Primary* (University of California Press, 2002), p. 341.

44. *California Democratic Party et al. v. Jones, Secretary of State of California, et al.,* 530 U.S. 567 (2000); and Linda Greenhouse, "Split Decisions: The Court Rules, America Changes," *The New York Times*, July 2, 2000, sec. 4, p. 1.

45. Malcolm E. Jewell and David M. Olson, *Political Parties and Elections in American States*, 3d ed. (Dorsey Press, 1988), p. 121; Flanigan and Zingale, *Political Behavior of the American Electorate*, p. 195.

46. James I. Lengle, *Representation and Presidential Primaries: The Democratic Party in the Postreform Era* (Greenwood Press, 1981). For more on primary elections, see Larry M. Bartels, *Presidential Primaries and the Dynamics of Public Choice* (Princeton University Press, 1988); Jeane J. Kirkpatrick, *The New Presidential Elite: Men and Women in National Politics* (Basic Books, 1976); and Barbara Norander, "Ideological Representativeness of Presidential Primary Voters," *Journal of Politics* 51 (November 1989), pp. 977–992.

47. Federal Election Commission, at www.fec.gov.

48. Other "clean money" states are Vermont, Arizona, and Massachusetts. Edward Zuckerman, "Maine Campaign Reform: Were Voters 'Hoodwinked' by Outside Groups?" *Political Finance and Lobby Reporter*, December 24, 1996, pp. 1–4.

49. David B. Magleby, "Campaign Spending and Referendum Voting," paper presented at the annual meeting of the Western Political Science Association, Albuquerque, N.M., March 1994.

50. *Financing California's Statewide Ballot Measures: Receipts and Expenditures Through December 31, 1998* (California Secretary of State, 1998), p. 2.

51. David B. Magleby, *Direct Legislation: Voting on Ballot Propositions in the United States* (Johns Hopkins University Press, 1984), chaps. 7–9.

52. California Secretary of State Kevin Shelly, at www.ss.ca.gov/elections/elections_recall_faqs.htm#20.

53. US Department of State, "Schwarzenegger Wins California Gubernatorial Vote," at www.usinfo.state.gov/dhr/Archive/2003/Oct/09-562246.html.

54. See Larry Gerston and Terry Christensen, *Recall: California's Political Earthquake* (M. E. Sharpe, 2004).

55. California Voter Foundation, at www.calvoter.org/voter/elections/archive/recall/index.html.

Chapter 24

1. For a useful look at Nebraska's unique legislature, see Jack Rodgers, Robert Sittig, and Susan Welch, "The Legislature," in *Nebraska Government and Politics*, ed. Robert D. Miewald (University of Nebraska Press, 1984), pp. 57–86.

2. Tom Birmingham, quoted in Karen Hansen, "Legislator Pay: Baseball It Ain't," *State Legislatures* (July–August 1997), p. 20.

3. Richard A. Clucas, "Exercising Control: The Power of State House Speakers," paper presented at the annual meeting of the Western Political Science Association, Los Angeles, March 1998. See also Malcolm E. Jewell and Marcia Lynn Whicker, *Legislative Leadership in the American States* (University of Michigan Press, 1997).

4. *The Book of the States, 2000–2001* (Council of State Governments, 2000), p. 46.

5. See James D. King, "Changes in Professionalism in U.S. State Legislatures," *Legislative Studies Quarterly* 15 (May 2000), pp. 327–343.

6. Alan Rosenthal, *Legislative Life: People, Process, and Performance in the States* (Harper & Row, 1981), pp. 112–113.

7. See Peverill Squire, "Uncontested Seats in State Legislative Elections," *Legislative Studies Quarterly* 35 (February 2000), pp. 131–146.

8. Alan Rosenthal, "The Legislative Unraveling of Institutional Fabric," in *The State of the States*, 3d ed., ed. Carl E. Van Horn (CQ Press, 1996), p. 118.

9. Gary F. Moncrief, Peverill Squire, and Malcolm E. Jewell, *Who Runs for the Legislature?* (Prentice Hall, 2000).

10. Frank Smallwood, *Free and Independent: The Initiation of a College Professor into State Politics* (Stephen Greene Press, 1976), p. 223.

11. *Book of the States, 2000–2001*, p. 70.

12. See Sue Thomas, *How Women Legislate* (Oxford University Press, 1994). See also Lesley Dahlkemper, "Growing Accustomed to Her Face," *State Legislatures*, July–August 1996, pp. 37–45, and Kathleen Dolan and Lynne Ford, "Change and Continuity Among Women State Legislators," *Political Research Quarterly*, vol. 50 (March 1997), pp. 137–151.

13. For fascinating comparative data, see *Inside the Legislative Process: A Comprehensive Survey by the American Society of Legislative Clerks and Secretaries* (National Council of State Legislatures, 1998).

14. Keith E. Hamm and Gary F. Moncrief, "Legislative Politics in the States," in Virginia Gray et al., *Politics in the American States*, 7th ed. (CQ Press, 1999), p. 184.

15. Lobbying strategies are outlined in Jay Michael and Dan Walters, *The Third House: Lobbyists, Power, and Money in Sacramento*, (Berkeley Public Policy Press, 2001) Other lobbying realities are discussed in Loftus, *Art of Legislative Politics*, chap. 10, and Alan Rosenthal, *Drawing the Line: Legislative Ethics in the States* (University of Nebraska Press, 1996).

16. Thomas Frank, "Ex-Legislators Use Contacts," *The Denver Post*, July 5, 1996, p. 16A. See also Loftus, *Art of Legislative Politics*.

17. Samuel K. Gove and James D. Nowlan, *Illinois Politics and Government* (University of Nebraska Press, 1996), p. 53.

18. Joel A. Thompson and Gary F. Moncrief, eds., *Campaign Finance in State Legislative Elections* (CQ Press, 1998).

19. Frank Smallwood, *Free and Independent*, (S. Greene Press, 1976) p. 165. See also Alan Rosenthal, *The Third House: Lobbyists and Lobbying in the States* 2d ed. (CQ Press, 2001); but also "State Legislators Mix Public and Private Business, Study Says," *The New York Times*, May 21, 2000, p. 26.

20. Winnie Hu, "Lobbying Code Puts an End to Lawmakers' Gravy Train," *The New York Times*, April 11, 2000, pp. A1, A27. See also Christopher Swope, "Winning Without Food and Cigars," *Governing*, November 2000, pp. 40–46.

21. Charles Mahtesian, "The Ethics Backlash," *Governing*, October 1999, pp. 39–41.

22. John E. Brandl, *Money and Good Intentions Are Not Enough: Or, Why a Liberal Democrat Thinks States Need Both Competition and Community* (Brookings Institution Press, 1998), p. 58.

23. Quoted in David Ray, "The Sources of Voting Cues in Three State Legislatures," *Journal of Politics*, Vol. 44 (November 1982), p. 1081. See also John J. Kennedy, *The Contemporary Pennsylvania Legislature* (University Press of America, 1999).

24. Karl T. Kurtz, "The Old Statehouse, She Ain't What She Used to Be," *State Legislatures*, January 1994, pp. 20–23. See also Alan Rosenthal, *The Decline of Representative Democracy* (CQ Press, 1998).

25. Alan Rosenthal, "The Legislative Institution: In Transition and at Risk," in *The State of the States*, 2d ed., ed. Carl E. Van Horn (CQ Press, 1993), pp. 136–137. See also Alan Ehrenhalt, "An Embattled Institution," *Governing*, January 1992, pp. 28–33; and Karen Hansen, "Our Beleaguered Institution," *State Legislatures*, January 1994, pp. 12–17.

26. Rosenthal, "The Legislative Institution," p. 144.

27. See, for example, Christopher Conte, "Laptop Legislatures," *Governing*, November 1999, p. 36.

28. Carrie Koch, "A Room for a View," *State Legislatures*, May 1997, pp. 32–34.

29. Bette H. Dillehay, "E-Government as Virginia's Vision," in *Spectrum: The Journal of State Government* (Winter 2002), pp. 24–25.

30. Rich Jones, "The State Legislatures," in *The Book of the States, 1992–1993* (Council of State Governments, 1992), p. 125.

31. Michael Janofsky, "Idaho Legislature Repeals Term Limit Law, Undoing Voter Approved Measure," *The New York Times*, February 2, 2002, p. A11. See also Wayne Hoffman, "The Battle over Term Limits," *State Legislatures*, May 2002, pp. 25–29.

32. Janofsky, "Idaho Legislature," p. A11.

33. See Daniel B. Wood, "The Term-Limit Movement of the '90s Stalls," *Christian Science Monitor*, April 27, 2004, p. A1.

34. See John M. Carey, Richard G. Niemi, and Lynda W. Powell, *Term Limits in the State Legislatures* (University of Michigan Press, 2000).

35. Jack Quinn et al., "Redrawing the Districts, Changing the Rules," *Washington Post National Weekly Edition*, April 1, 1991, p. 23.

36. Gordon E. Baker, *The Reapportionment Revolution* (Random House, 1966), p. 47.

37. *Baker* v. *Carr*, 369 U.S. 186 (1962).

38. *Wesberry* v. *Sanders*, 376 U.S. 1 (1964).

39. *Reynolds* v. *Sims*, 377 U.S. 533 (1964).

40. *Brown* v. *Thomson*, 103 S.Ct. 2690 (1983).

41. *Shaw* v. *Reno*, 509 U.S. 630 (1993); *Abrams* v. *Johnson*, 138 L.Ed. 2d 285 (1997). For a summary of state and federal judicial cases on drawing legislative district lines, see *Redistricting Case Summaries from the '90s* (National Conference of State Legislatures, 1998); see also Ronald E. Weber, "Emerging Trends in State Legislative Redistricting," *Spectrum: The Journal of State Government*, Vol. 75 (Winter 2002), pp. 13–15; additional updates can be found at the National Conference of State Legislature Web site, www.ncsl.org.

42. Samuel Issacharoff, "In Real Elections, There Ought to Be Competition," *The New York Times*, February 16, 2002, p. A31.

43. Ibid.

44. See Spencer C. Olin, *California's Prodigal Sons: Hiram Johnson and the Progressives, 1911–1917* (University of California Press, 1968).

45. Alan Greenblatt, "Total Recall," *Governing*, September, 2003, p. 21.

46. Editorial, *The New York Times*, October 29, 1993, p. A16.

47. See National Conference of State Legislatures, "Voters Decide High-Profile Issues on State Ballots," November 3, 2004.

48. See, for example, Eugene C. Lee, "The Initiative Boom: An Excess of Democracy," in *Governing California*, eds. Gerald C. Lubenow and Bruce E. Cain (Institute of Governmental Studies, University of California, 1997), pp. 113–136. See also David S. Broder, *Democracy Derailed: Initiative Campaigns and the Power of Money* (Harcourt, 2000). But see Zolton L. Hajnul, Elisabeth R. Gerber, and Hugh Louch, "Minorities and Direct Legislation: Evidence from California Ballot Proposition Elections," paper presented at the annual meeting of the American Political Science Association, Washington, D.C., September 1–3, 2000. See also Elisabeth Gerber, *The Populist Paradox* (Princeton University Press, 1999).

49. See Peter Schrag, *Paradise Lost: California's Experience, America's Future* (New Press, 1998). See also the decidedly negative appraisal offered by

Richard Ellis, *Democratic Delusions: The Initiative Process in America* (University Press of Kansas, 2002).

50. David B. Magleby and Kelly D. Paterson, "Consultants and Direct Democracy," *PS: Political Science and Politics* 31 (June 1998), pp. 160–161. See also Broder, *Democracy Derailed.*

51. David B. Magleby, "Ballot Initiatives and Intergovernmental Relations," paper presented at the annual meeting of the Western Political Science Association, Los Angeles, March 1998, p. 2.

52. Ibid., p. 13.

53. Thomas E. Cronin, *Direct Democracy: The Politics of the Initiative, Referendum, and Recall* (Harvard University Press, 1989).

54. Michael G. Hagen and Edward L. Lascher Jr., "Public Opinion About Ballot Initiatives," paper presented at the annual meeting of the American Political Science Association, Boston, September 3–6, 1998.

Chapter 25

1. See Thad L. Beyle, "Enhancing Executive Leadership in the States," *State and Local Government Review* (Winter 1995), pp. 18–35, and Thad L. Beyle, "The Governors," in *Politics in the American States: A Comparative Analysis,* 7th ed., eds. Virginia Gray, Russell Hanson, and Herbert Jacob (CQ Press, 1999), pp. 191–231.

2. Lamar Alexander, *Steps Along the Way: A Governor's Scrapbook* (Nelson, 1986), p. 112. Similar views can be found in former Vermont Governor Madeleine M. Kunin's memoir, *Living a Political Life* (Vintage, 1995).

3. See Earl H. Fry, *The Expanding Role of State and Local Governments in U.S. Foreign Policy* (Council on Foreign Relations Press, 1998). See also, for example, Alan Johnson, "Taft Shows He's Up to the Job on Foreign Grounds," *Columbia Dispatch,* February 14, 2000.

4. *The Book of the States, 1998–1999* (Council of State Governments, 1998), p. xxiii.

5. Ibid., tab. 2.3, p. 18.

6. This story is adapted from Robert S. McElvaine, *Mario Cuomo: A Biography* (Scribner, 1988), pp. 337–338. See also the assessment of Governor Pete Wilson's turbulent first years as governor of California in Robert Reinhold, "The Curse of the Statehouse," *New York Times Magazine,* May 3, 1992, pp. 27–28, 54, 58–59.

7. Thad L. Beyle, "Governors," *The Book of the States, 2002* (Council of State Governments, 2002), p. 135.

8. Charlie LeDuff, "The California Recall: The Governor-Elect," *The New York Times,* October 9, 2003, p. A33.

9. James M. Perry, "Virginia's New Governor Joins a GOP Trend," *The Wall Street Journal,* February 11, 1998, p. A24.

10. Richard F. Winters, "The Politics of Taxing and Spending," in *Politics in the American States,* ed. Gray et al., p. 329.

11. Fred Branfman and Nancy Stefanik, "Who Says Raising Taxes Is Political Suicide?" *Washington Post National Weekly Edition,* February 13, 1989, p. 24. See also the excellent case studies of governors in Michigan, Massachusetts, Pennsylvania, Arizona, and elsewhere who pushed through economic development programs in the 1980s, in David Osborne, *Laboratories of Democracy: A New Breed of Governor Creates Models for National Growth* (Harvard Business School Press, 1988).

12. In some cases, a governor's style and strategy alienate legislators. See, for example, Charles Mahtesian's analysis of Minnesota's Jesse Ventura, "Can He Govern?" *Governing,* May 2000, pp. 36–42. In contrast, Governor Bruce Babbitt worked effectively even with a legislature controlled by the opposition party. See David R. Berman, *Arizona Politics and Government* (University of Nebraska Press, 1998), pp. 116–117.

13. For a lighthearted commentary by a member of Governor Pete Wilson's Electronic Commerce Advisory Council, see Stewart Alsop, "Helping the Governor Figure Out E-Commerce," *Fortune,* June 8, 1998, p. 269.

14. National Conference of State Legislatures, news release, April 7, 2004, www.ncsl.org/programs/press/2004/pr040407.htm, accessed on April 27, 2004.

15. Kathleen Gray, "Granholm Stars in Her Own 'Kill Bill,'" *Detroit Free Press,* April 26, 2004, p. A1.

16. Cited in a profile of New York in *Governing,* February 1999, p. 66.

17. Thad L. Beyle, "Being Governor," in *The State of the States,* 3d ed., ed. Carl E. Van Horn (CQ Press, 1996), p. 89. See also Beyle, "The Governors."

18. But see Governor Tommy Thompson's defense of using frequent vetoes, *Power to the People: An American State at Work* (HarperCollins, 1996), and the view of one of his main critics in the Wisconsin legislature, Tom Loftus, *The Art of Legislative Politics* (CQ Press, 1994), chap. 5. On the varied effectiveness of the line item veto as a tool for fiscal responsibility, see Glenn Abney and Thomas P. Lauth, "The Item Veto and Fiscal Responsibility," *Journal of Politics,* vol. 59 (August 1997), pp. 882–892. On

how a governor's rash use of the line item veto can infuriate legislators, see Mahtesian, "Can He Govern?" p. 40.

19. Ronald Smothers, "Mississippi Governor Bans Same-Sex Marriages," *The New York Times,* August 24, 1996, p. A6.

20. Katie Zezima, "Obey Same-Sex Marriage Law, Officials Told," *The New York Times,* April 25, 2004, p. A15.

21. *Perpich et al.* v. *Department of Defense,* 110 L.Ed. 312 (1990).

22. Kathleen Hunter, "Guard Deployments Spark State Security Concerns," Stateline.org, Tuesday, April 27, 2004, p. 1.

23. For background on this controversy, see Jonathan Alter, "The Death Penalty on Trial," *Newsweek,* June 12, 2000, pp. 26–34.

24. "Governor Ryan's Brave Example," *The New York Times,* July 3, 2000, p. A20. See also Judy Keen, "Death Penalty Issue Looms over Bush Campaign," *USA Today,* June 16, 2000, p. 17A.

25. The entire Ryan Commission report is available online at www.idoc.state.il.us/ccp/. See also Francis Clines, "Death Penalty Is Suspended in Maryland," *The New York Times,* May 10, 2002, p. A16.

26. For a scholarly analysis of the role political parties play in nominating and assisting governors, see Sarah McCally, *The Governor as Party Leader: Campaigning and Governing* (University of Michigan Press, 1998).

27. Beyle, "The Governors," p. 230.

28. Sarah F. Liebschutz et al., *New York Politics and Government* (University of Nebraska Press, 1998), p. 93.

29. Thomas Hardy, "The 'Weak' Governor," in *Mississippi Government and Politics,* eds. Dale Krane and Stephen Shaffer (University of Nebraska Press, 1992), p. 152.

30. See, for example, how hard it is for a governor to control the economic fortunes of a state, especially during a recession, in Paul Brace, *State Government and Economic Performance* (Johns Hopkins University Press, 1993).

31. *State Legislatures,* June 2000, p. 7.

32. Kunin, *Living a Political Life,* p. 382.

33. Beyle, "The Governors," pp. 224–226.

34. Thomas H. Kean, quoted in Barbara Salmore and Stephen Salmore, *New Jersey Politics and Government* (University of Nebraska Press, 1998), p. 136.

35. Jesse Ventura, *I Ain't Got Time to Bleed* (Signet Press, 2000), pp. 296–297.

36. Beyle, "The Governors," pp. 224–226.

37. Alan Ehrenhalt, "Reinventing Government in the Unlikeliest Place," *Governing,* August 1993, pp. 7–8.

38. Richard C. Elling, "Bureaucracy: Maligned Yet Essential," in *Politics in the American States: A Comparative Analysis,* 6th ed., eds. Virginia Gray and Herbert Jacob (CQ Press, 1996), p. 308.

39. Jonathan Walters, "Fad Mad," *Governing,* vol. 9, September 1996, p. 49.

40. Beyle, "Being Governor," p. 106.

41. See the discussion of Governor George W. Bush and his relationship with his lieutenant governor in Jonathan Walters, "The Taming of Texas," *Governing,* July 1998, p. 20. See also "The Future of the Texas Lieutenant Governor," *Comparative State Politics,* October 1995, pp. 21–24.

42. But see Charles N. Wheeler III, "Why Illinois Still Needs Lieutenant Governor's Position," *Illinois Issues,* September 1994, pp. 6–7.

43. On the recent fate of attorneys general who have aspired to become governors, see Charles Mahtesian, "Blocked Path to the Big Job," *Governing,* March 1996, p. 47.

44. Attorney General Bob Butterworth, at www.legal.firn.edu.

45. Office of the Attorney General, State of California, at www.caag.state.ca.us.

46. See Anya Sosetek, "Cathy Cox: Machine Politics," *Governing,* November 2002, p. 42.

47. Professor Thad L. Beyle at the University of North Carolina at Chapel Hill tracks state polls on governors' job performances and finds that Democratic, Republican, and Independent governors alike all averaged about 60 percent public approval in the 1990s.

48. Alexander, *Steps Along the Way,* p. 141.

49. Thomas H. Kean, *The Politics of Inclusion* (Free Press, 1988), p. 248.

50. Scott Matheson with James Edwin Kee, *Out of Balance* (Peregrine Smith Books, 1986), p. 186. See also the reflections of another popular western governor in Cecil Andrus and Joel Connelly, *Cecil Andrus: Politics Western Style* (Sasquatch Books, 1998).

Chapter 26

1. National Center for State Courts, *Overview of State Trial Court Caseloads* (National Center for State Courts, 2001), p. 13.

2. See Mark S. Hurwitz and Drew Noble Lanier, "Women and Minorites on State and Federal Appellate Benches," *Judicature* 85 (September–October 2001), p. 84; and Chris W. Bonneau, "The Composition of State Supreme Courts," *Judicature* 85 (July–August 2001), p. 26.

3. See Michael Solimine and James Walker, *Respecting State Courts: The Inevitability of Judicial Federalism* (Greenwood Press, 2000); and Matthew Bosworth, *Courts as Catalysts: State Supreme Courts and Public School Finance Equity* (State University of New York Press, 2001).

4. The Supreme Court upheld these laws in *Ewing* v. *California*, 538 U.S. 11 (2003).

5. Lynn Mather, "Policy Making in State Trial Courts," in *The American Courts: A Critical Assessment,* eds. John B. Gates and Charles A. Johnson (CQ Press, 1991), pp. 119–157.

6. Henry R. Glick, "Policy Making and State Supreme Courts," in ibid., pp. 87–88.

7. Patrick Schmidt and Paul Martin, "To the Internet and Beyond: State Supreme Courts on the World Wide Web," *Judicature* 84 (May–June 2001), pp. 314–325.

8. Robert F. Williams, "In the Supreme Court's Shadow: Legitimacy of State Rejection of Supreme Court Reasoning and Results," *South Carolina Law Review* 56 (Spring 1984), p. 353.

9. Harry P. Stumpf and John H. Culver, *The Politics of State Courts* (Longman, 1992), pp. 8–11.

10. Hans A. Linde, "Observations of a State Court Judge," in *Judges and Legislators: Toward Institutional Comity,* ed. Robert A. Katzmann (Brookings Institution Press, 1988), p. 118.

11. Peter J. Galie, "The Other Supreme Courts: Judicial Activism Among State Supreme Courts," *Syracuse Law Review* 33 (1982), pp. 731–793.

12. Philip L. Dubois, "State Trial Court Appointments: Does the Governor Make a Difference?" *Judicature* 68 (June–July 1985), pp. 20–21.

13. Charles H. Sheldon and Nicholas P. Lovrich Jr., "State Judicial Recruitment," in *The American Courts,* pp. 172–173.

14. See American Judicature Society at www.ajs.org/js/judicialselectioncharts. pdf.

15. Thurgood Marshall, in *Renne* v. *Geary,* 501 U.S. 312 (1991).

16. *Republican Party of Minnesota* v. *White,* 536 U.S. 765 (2002).

17. William Glaberson, "Court Rulings Curb Efforts to Rein in Judicial Races," *The New York Times,* October 7, 2000, p. A8.

18. Roy A. Schotland, "Financing Judicial Elections," in *Financing the 2000 Elections,* ed. David B. Magleby (Brookings Institution Press, 2002), p. 103.

19. "Judges Say Political Influence Threatens Independence of Judiciary," *Press and Dakotan,* at www.pressandakotan.com/stories/101797/ judges.html.

20. Schotland, "Financing Judicial Elections."

21. Michael Scherer, "The Making of the Corporate Judiciary," *Mother Jones,* November 2003, p. 72.

22. See Justice at Stake Campaign, the Brennan Center for Justice at New York University Law School and the National Institute on Money in State Politics, *The New Politics of Judicial Elections* (Justice at Stake Campaign, 2001); and American Bar Association, Standing Committee on Judicial Independence, *Public Financing of Judicial Campaigns: Report of the Commission on Public Financing of Judicial Campaigns* (American Bar Association, 2002).

23. *Wells* v. *Edwards,* 409 U.S. 1095 (1973).

24. *Chisom* v. *Roemer,* 501 U.S. 400 (1991); *Houston Lawyers' Association* v. *Texas Attorney General,* 501 U.S. 419 (1991). See also Tracy Thompson, "The New Front in the Battle for Civil Rights: Judgeships," *Washington Post National Weekly Edition,* December 18, 1989, p. 34.

25. J. W. Peltason, *The Missouri Plan for the Selection of Judges* (University of Missouri Studies, 1945). The plan was previously known as the Nonpartisan Plan for the Selection of Judges or the Kales Plan until called the Missouri Plan by this monograph.

26. Beth M. Henschen, Robert Moog, and Steven Davis, "Judicial Nominating Commissioners: A National Profile," *Judicature* 73 (April–May 1990), pp. 328–334.

27. Philip L. Dubois, "The Politics of Innovation in State Courts: The Merit Plan of Judicial Selection," *Publius* 20 (Winter 1990), p. 40.

28. Warren K. Hall and Larry T. Aspin, "What Twenty Years of Judicial Retention Elections Have Told Us," *Judicature* 70 (April–May 1987), pp. 340–347; Susan B. Caron and Larry C. Berkson, *Judicial Retention Elections in the United States* (American Judicature Society, 1980).

29. Larry T. Aspin, "Trends in Judicial Retention Elections, 1964–1968," *Judicature* 83 (September–October 1999), p. 79; "Evaluating the Performance of Judges Standing for Retention," *Judicature* 79 (January–February 1996), pp. 190–195.

30. Traciel Reid, "The Politicization of Retention Elections," *Judicature* 83 (September–October 1999), p. 68.

31. Thomas E. Cronin and Robert D. Loevy, *Colorado Politics and Government* (University of Nebraska Press, 1993), pp. 251–253.

32. "The Need for Judicial Performance Evaluations for Retention Elections," *Judicature* 75 (October–November 1991), p. 124.

33. Henry Weinstein, "Forum Airs Questions of Jurist Independence," *The Los Angeles Times,* November 22, 1998, p. A18.

34. Anthony Champagne and Greta Thielemann, "Awareness of Trial Court Judges," *Judicature* 74 (February–March 1991), p. 276.

35. Jeffrey Shaman, Steven Lubet, and James Alfini, *Judicial Conduct and Ethics,* 3d ed. (Lexis, 2000), sec. 15.07.

36. Jolanta Juskiewicz Perlstein and Nathan Goldman, "Judicial Disciplinary Commissions: A New Approach to the Discipline and Removal of State Judges," in *The Analysis of Judicial Reform,* ed. Phil Dubois (Lexington Books, 1982), pp. 93–106.

37. Franklin M. Zweig et al., "Securing the Future for America's State Courts," *Judicature* 73 (April–May 1990), pp. 297–298.

38. Beverly Blair Cook, "Women Judges in the Opportunity Structure," in *Women, the Courts, and Equality,* eds. Laura L. Crites and Winfred L. Hepperle (Sage, 1987), pp. 143–171.

39. *Burch* v. *Louisiana,* 441 U.S. 130 (1979); *Ballew* v. *Georgia,* 435 U.S. 223 (1978). See Reid Hastie, Steven D. Penrod, and Nancy Pennington, *Inside the Jury* (Harvard University Press, 1983), for a study showing that nonunanimous verdicts are more likely to bring convictions than those requiring unanimity. Federal courts often use juries of fewer than 12 for civil cases. For federal criminal trials, the Supreme Court still requires both the common law jury of 12 and unanimous verdicts.

40. Robert H. Jackson, quoted in Jack M. Kress, "Progress and Prosecution," *Annals of the American Academy of Political and Social Science* (January 1976), p. 100.

41. William K. Muir, *Police: Streetcorner Politicians* (University of Chicago Press, 1977).

42. Charles E. Silberman, *Criminal Violence, Criminal Justice* (Random House, 1978), p. 303.

43. Jay Livingston, *Crime and Criminology* (Prentice Hall, 1992), p. 474.

44. Silberman, *Criminal Violence,* p. 218. See also David Cole, *No Equal Justice: Race and Class in the American Criminal Justice System* (New Press, 1999).

45. *South Carolina* v. *Gathers,* 490 U.S. 805 (1989).

46. Thomas M. Uhlman and N. Darlene Walker, "A Plea Is No Bargain: The Impact of Case Disposition on Sentencing," *Social Science Quarterly* 60 (September 1979), pp. 218–234. See also Malcolm M. Feeley, *The Process Is the Punishment* (Russell Sage, 1979).

47. Thomas Church Jr., "Plea Bargains, Concessions and the Courts: Analysis of a Quasi-Experiment," *Law and Society Review* 14 (Spring 1976), p. 400. For a contrary view, see National Advisory Commission on Criminal Justice Standards and Goals, *Report of the Task Force* (U.S. Government Printing Office, 1979).

48. Church, "Plea Bargains," p. 400.

49. Jonathan D. Casper, *American Criminal Justice: The Defendant's Perspective* (Prentice Hall, 1972), pp. 52–53. Abraham S. Goldstein, *The Passive Judiciary: Prosecutorial Discretion and the Guilty Plea* (Louisiana State University Press, 1981), is critical of judges for not supervising plea bargains more actively.

50. *Santobello* v. *New York,* 404 U.S. 257 (1971).

51. Edward Barrett, "The Adversary Proceeding and the Judicial Process," lectures to the National College of State Trial Judges, quoted in Lynn M. Mather, "Some Determinants of the Method of Case Disposition: Decision-Making by Public Defenders in Los Angeles," *Law and Society Review* 12 (Winter 1974), pp. 187–188.

52. Henry N. Pontell, *A Capacity to Punish* (Indiana University Press, 1985).

53. Lee Sechrest, Susan O. White, and Elizabeth D. Brown, eds., *The Rehabilitation of Criminal Offenders: Problems and Prospects* (National Academy of Sciences, 1979), pp. 3–6.

54. John Hagan and Kristin Bumiler, "Making Sense of Sentencing: A Review and Critique of Sentencing Research," in *Research on Sentencing,* eds. Alfred Blumstein et al. (National Academy Press, 1983), vol. 2; Susan Welch, Michael Combs, and John Gruhl, "Do Black Judges Make a Difference?" *American Journal of Political Science* 32 (February 1988), pp. 126–135.

55. William B. Eldridge, "Shifting Views of the Sentencing Functions," *Annals of the American Academy of Political and Social Science* (July 1982), pp. 104–111.

56. Bureau of Justice Statistics, "The Nation's Prison Population Growth Rate Slows," press release, August 9, 2000.

57. Eric Schlosser, "The Prison-Industrial Complex," *Atlantic,* December 1998, p. 52.

58. Barbara Fink, "Opening the Door on Community Corrections," *State Legislatures,* September 1984, pp. 24–31.

59. Gary Enos, "Despite New Technology, Home Confinement Faces Risks, Public Opposition," *City and State,* May 21, 1990, p. 14.
60. Quoted in Associated Press, "ABA 'Public Jurist' Considers Reforms in Legal System," December 1993.

Chapter 27

1. Peter Dreier, John Mollenkopf, and Todd Swanstrom, *Place Matters: Metropolitics for the Twenty-first Century* (University Press of Kansas, 2001), p. 21.
2. Jack Fleer, *North Carolina Government and Politics* (University of Nebraska Press, 1994), p. 198.
3. *Hunter* v. *City of Pittsburgh,* 208 U.S. 161 (1907).
4. See Jacques Steinberg, "42 Failing Schools in Philadelphia to Be Privatized," *The New York Times,* April 18, 2002, p. A1.
5. Michelle Garcia, "N.Y. City Council Passes Anti-Patriot Act Measure," *The Washington Post,* February 5, 2004, p. A11.
6. U.S. Bureau of the Census, *Statistical Abstract of the United States, 2001* (U.S. Government Printing Office, 2001).
7. An excellent overview of counties is Donald C. Menzel, ed., *The American County: Frontiers of Knowledge* (University of Alabama Press, 1996).
8. Ellen Perlman, "Polite Tenacity," *Governing,* November 2000, pp. 34, 214.
9. For a history of suburban development, see Rosalyn Baxandall and Elizabeth Ewen, *Picture Windows: How the Suburbs Happened* (Basic Books, 2000).
10. See Paul G. Lewis, *Shaping Suburbia: How Political Institutions Organize Urban Development* (University of Pittsburgh Press, 1996).
11. Joel Garreau, *Edge City* (Doubleday, 1991).
12. For the views of three mayors on the good city, see Stephen Goldsmith, *The Twenty-First Century City* (Regnery, 1997); Daniel Kemmis, *The Good City and the Good Life* (Houghton Mifflin, 1995); and John O. Norquist, *The Wealth of Cities: Revitalizing the Centers of American Life* (Addison-Wesley, 1998).
13. *Rogers* v. *Lodge,* 458 U.S. 613 (1982); *Thornburg* v. *Gingles,* 478 U.S. 30 (1986).
14. For the experience of one mayor in a council-manager city, see the memoir by Cambridge, Massachusetts, Mayor Barbara Ackermann, *"You the Mayor?" The Education of a City Politician* (Auburn House, 1989).
15. See James II. Svara and Associates, *Facilitative Leadership in Local Government: Lessons from Successful Mayors and Chairpersons in the Council-Manager Form* (Jossey-Bass, 1994).
16. See Earl H. Fry, *The Expanding Role of State and Local Governments in U.S. Foreign Affairs* (Council on Foreign Relations, 1998), esp. chap. 4.
17. It is fascinating to examine how mayors of different cities view their roles and responsibilities. Excellent books about important mayors are Roger Biles, *Richard J. Daley: Politics, Race, and the Governing of Chicago* (Northern Illinois University Press, 1995); Adam Cohen and Elizabeth Taylor, *American Pharoah: Mayor Richard J. Daley: His Battle for Chicago and the Nation* (Little, Brown, 2000); and Robert A. Dahl, *Who Governs? Democracy and Power in an American City* (Yale University Press, 1961), a classic study of Mayor Richard Lee of New Haven. See also two reflective books by mayors in medium-sized or smaller cities: Kemmis, *The Good City and the Good Life;* and Ackermann, *"You the Mayor?"*
18. Dennis R. Judd and Todd Swanstrom, *City Politics: Private Power and Public Policy,* 2d ed. (Longman, 1998), p. 7.
19. See, for example, the analysis of other groups such as the African Americans in Atlanta in Clarence N. Stone, *Regime Politics: Governing Atlanta, 1946–1988* (University Press of Kansas, 1989). See also Bryan D. Jones and Lynn W. Bachelor, *The Sustaining Hand: Community Leadership and Corporate Power,* 2d ed. (University Press of Kansas, 1993).
20. For suggestions on how to form community groups and effective alliances seeking progress in cities, see Michael Briand, *Practical Politics: Five Principles for a Community That Works* (University of Illinois Press, 1999).
21. Judd and Swanstrom, *City Politics,* p. 7.
22. For greater detail, see U.S. Bureau of the Census, "Standards for Defining Metropolitan Areas," at www.census.gov.
23. U.S. Bureau of the Census, *Statistical Abstract of the United States, 2000* (U.S. Government Printing Office, 2000).
24. The legal constraints on Baltimore, for example, are outlined in David Rusk, *Baltimore Unbound: A Strategy for Regional Renewal* (Abell Foundation/Johns Hopkins University Press, 1996).
25. D'Vera Cohn, "A New Millennium for America's Cities," *Washington Post National Weekly Edition,* October 30, 2000, p. 34.

26. David Rusk, former mayor of Albuquerque, makes this case well in *Baltimore Unbound* and in *Cities Without Suburbs,* 2d ed. (Woodrow Wilson Center Press/Johns Hopkins University Press, 1995).
27. See Suzanne M. Leland and Kurt Thurmaier, eds., *Case Studies of City-County Consolidation* (M.E. Sharpe, 2004); and Jered B. Carr and Richard C. Feiock, eds., *City-County Consolidation and Its Alternatives* (M. E. Sharpe, 2004).
28. See Myron Orfield, *Metropolitics: A Regional Agenda for Community and Stability* (Brookings Institution Press, 1997); and Manuel Pastor, ed., *Regions That Work: How Cities and Suburbs Can Grow Together* (University of Minnesota Press, 2000).
29. See E. J. Dionne, Jr., ed., *Community Works: The Revival of Civil Society in America* (Brookings Institution Press, 1998).
30. See David L. Kirp, et al., *Our Town: Race, Housing, and the Soul of Suburbia* (Rutgers University Press, 1997); and Jonathan Harr, *A Civil Action* (Vintage, 1996).
31. See the recommendation often prescribed by a major proponent of regionalism, Neal R. Peirce, in Charles Mahtesian, "The Civic Therapist," *Governing,* September 1995, pp. 24–27. See also Dreier, Mollenkopf, and Swanstrom, *Place Matters,* ch. 7.
32. "The End of Urban Man? Care to Bet?" *The Economist,* December 31, 1999, pp. 25–26.
33. See the thoughtful recommendations in Robert J. Waste, *Independent Cities: Rethinking U.S. Urban Policy* (Oxford University Press, 1998). But also see Clarissa Rile Hayward, "The Difference States Make: Democracy, Identity, and the American City," *American Political Science Review* 97 (November 2003), p. 501.

Chapter 28

1. *Governing: State and Local Source Book* (Governing Magazine, 2004) p. 15.
2. See Gary Oldfield and Chungmei Lee, *Brown at 50: King's Dream or Plessy's Nightmare,* (The Harvard Civil Rights Project, 2004). Also see Gary Orfield, Susan E. Eaton, and the Harvard Project on School Desegregation, *Dismantling Desegregation: The Quiet Reversal of Brown* v. *Board of Education* (New Press, 1996).
3. National Commission on Excellence in Education, *A Nation at Risk: The Imperative for Educational Reform—An Open Letter to the American People* (U.S. Government Printing Office, 1983). Ernest L. Boyer, *High School: A Report on Secondary Education in America* (Harper & Row, 1983), based on observations of high schools, contains a detailed series of recommendations. See also the National Science Board Commission on Precollege Education, *Mathematics, Science, and Technology: Educating Americans for the 21st Century* (U.S. Government Printing Office, 1983), and Carnegie Forum on Education and the Economy, *A Nation Prepared: Teachers for the 21st Century* (Carnegie Forum, 1986).
4. James B. Steman and Wayne C. Riddle, *Goals 2000: Educate America Act Implementation Status and Issues* (Congressional Research Service, 1996), pp. 2–4.
5. Rochelle L. Stanfield, "Learning Curve," *National Journal,* July 3, 1993, pp. 1688–1691.
6. C. Eugene Steuerle, Van Doorn Ooms, George Peterson, and Robert D. Reischauer, eds., *Vouchers and the Provision of Public Services* (Brookings Institution Press, 2000). See also "Colorado Adopts Statewide School Vouchers," *State Legislatures,* July–August 2003, p. 7.
7. Terry M. Moe, "Private Vouchers," in *Private Vouchers,* ed. Terry M. Moe (Hoover Institution Press, 1996), p. 35. Yet see also John F. Witte, *The Market Approach to Education: An Analysis of America's First Voucher Program* (Princeton University Press, 1999).
8. William H. Rehnquist, quoted in Richard Rothstein, "Failed Schools? The Meaning Is Unclear," *The New York Times,* July 3, 2002, p. A14.
9. "Colorado Adopts Statewide School Vouchers," *State Legislatures,* July–August, 2003, p. 7.
10. Greg Winter, "Florida Court Rules Against Religious School Vouchers," *The New York Times,* August 17, 2004, p. A15.
11. Elizabeth Kolbert, "Unchartered Territory," *New Yorker,* October 9, 2000, p. 36. For the example of charter schools being initiated in Rhode Island, see Maureen Moakley and Elmer Cornwell, *Rhode Island Politics and Government* (University of Nebraska Press, 2001), pp. 189–190.
12. See, for example, Lynn Rosellini, "Closing the Gap," *U.S. News,* March 22–29, 2004, pp. 87–88.
13. See Diana Jean Schemo, "Charter Schools Lagging Behind, U.S. Data Reveal," *The New York Times,* August 17, 2004, pp. A1, A16. See also Richard

Lee Colvin, "What's Wrong With Our Schools?," *State Legislatures*, September, 2003, pp. 12–15.

14. Quoted in "Statewide Student Tests," *State Legislatures*, February 2004, p. 33. See also Dewayne Matthews, "No Child Left Behind: The Challenge of Implementation," *The Book of States* (Council of State Governments, 2004), pp. 493–496. See also, June Kronholz, "Bush's Education Law Gets an Incomplete," *The Wall Street Journal*, September 1, 2004, p. A6.

15. See Christine Walton and Julie Davis Bell, "New Ways to Fund Higher Ed," *State Legislatures*, December, 2003, pp. 28–31. See also John Buntin, "Setting Colleges Free," *Governing*, September, 2003, pp. 18–22.

16. See Alexander Russo, "Varsity Vouchers," *State Legislatures*, June 2004, p. 27.

17. Ed Lazere, "Welfare Balances After Three Years of TANF Block Grants," report, Center on Budget and Policy Priorities, January 12, 2000, p. 1.

18. R. Kent Weaver, *Ending Welfare as We Know It* (Brookings Institution Press, 2000).

19. See Tommy G. Thompson, *Power to the People: An American State at Work* (HarperCollins, 1996).

20. See Burt S. Barnow, Thomas Kaplan, and Robert Moffitt, eds., *Evaluating Comprehensive State Welfare Reforms* (Brookings Institution Press, 2000); Carol W. Weissert, ed., *Learning from Leaders: Welfare Reform Politics and Policy in Five Midwestern States* (Brookings Institution Press, 2000).

21. Peter Edelman, "The True Purpose of Welfare Reform," *The New York Times*, May 29, 2002, p. A21.

22. Robert Pear, "Study by Governors Calls Bush Welfare Plan Unworkable," *The New York Times*, April 4, 2002, p. A14.

23. See, for example, David Hage, *Reforming Welfare by Rewarding Work, One State's Successful Experiment* (University of Minnesota Press, 2004), and Courtney Jarchow and Jack Tweedie, "Welfare and Wedding Vows," *State Legislatures*, April 2003, pp. 24–28.

24. See Katherine Barrett, Richard Greene, and Michele Mariani, "A Case of Neglect: Why Health Care Is Getting Worse, Even Though Medicine Is Getting Better," *Governing*, February, 2004, pp. 22–24. See also other articles in this edition of *Governing*.

25. Trinity D. Tomsie, "Managing Medicaid in Tough Times," *State Legislators*, June 2002, p. 13.

26. David S. Broder, "States in Fiscal Crises," *Washington Post National Weekly Edition*, May 27, 2002, p. 4

27. Jodi Wilgoren, "New Terror Alert Brings No Change in States' Security," *The New York Times*, May 25, 2002, p. A11.

28. See Amy C. Hughes, "State Emergency Management: New Realities in a Homeland Security World," *The Book of States* (Council of State Governments, 2004), pp. 485–488.

29. Larry Morandi, "Growing Pains," *State Legislatures*, October–November 1998, pp. 24–28.

30. Neal Peirce, "Parisian Green: A Hint for Us," Washington Post Writers Group, at www.npeirce@citistates.com, June 2, 2002, p. 1.

31. See Robert B. Albritton, "Subsidies: Welfare and Transportation," in *Politics in the American States: A Comparative Analysis*, 7th ed., eds. Virginia Gray, Herbert Jacob, and Kenneth Vines (CQ Press, 1999), and E. J. Dionne Jr., ed., *Community Works: The Revival of Civil Society in America* (Brookings Institution Press, 2000).

32. For a discussion of the evolution of environmental policy in a particularly interesting place, see Charles O. Jones, *Clean Air: The Policies and Politics of Pollution Control* (University of Pittsburgh Press, 1973).

33. Jacqueline Vaughn Switzer and Gary Bryner, *Environmental Politics*, 2d ed. (St. Martin's Press, 1998), pp. 64–66.

34. Jeff Dale, "Realistic Redevelopment," *State Legislatures*, February 1999, pp. 28–31.

35. Bruce A. Williams, "Economic Regulation and Environmental Protection," in *Politics in the American States*, eds. Gray et al. (CQ Press, 1996), pp. 478–515.

36. See Larry Morandi, "Clearing the Air," *State Legislatures*, February, 2004, pp. 30–31. And Jeffrey Ball, "Governors of 3 West Coast States Join to Combat Global Warming," *The Wall Street Journal*, September 22, 2003, p. A4.

37. See Garry Boulard, "The Great Hydrogen Hope," *State Legislatures*, February 2004, pp. 12–15.

38. Alan K. Ota, "Congress Clears Huge Transportation Bill, Restoring Cut-Off Funding to States," *Congressional Quarterly Weekly*, May 23, 1998, pp. 1385–1386.

39. But see Michele Mariani, "Transit's High-Tech Route," *Governing*, May, 2004, pp. 60–67; and Rob Gurwitt, "Connecting the Suburban Dots," *Governing*, October, 2003, pp. 36–40.

40. *The Book of the States, 2003* (Council of State Governments, 2003), p. 466.

41. Nancy M. Davis, "Politics and the Public Utilities Commissioner," *State Legislatures*, May 1985, p. 20. See also William T. Gormley Jr., "Policy, Politics, and Public Utility Regulation," *American Journal of Political Science* 27 (February 1983), pp. 86–105.

42. See, for example, Rebecca Smith, "States Face Fights as Caps Expire on Electric Rates," *The Wall Street Journal*, August 17, 2004, p. 1 and p. 12.

43. Amy Wallace, "San Onofre Mitigation Plan Wins Approval," *The Los Angeles Times*, July 17, 1991, p. A3.

44. See Donald F. Kettl, "Federalism, Anyone?" *Governing*, February, 2004, p. 14.

Chapter 29

1. U.S. Bureau of Labor Statistics, "Table 1: Employment by major industry division, 1992, 2002, and projected 2012 employment," www.bls/gov/news.release/ecopro.to1.htm, accessed on May 2, 2004.

2. Ibid., p. 350.

3. *Elrod* v. *Burns*, 427 U.S. 347 (1976).

4. U.S. Census Bureau, "Table 3: Union Affiliation of Employed Wage and Salary Workers by Occupation," News release, www.bls.gov/news.release/union2.t03.htm, accessed on May 3, 2004.

5. Werner Z. Hirsch, "Factors Important in Local Government's Privatization Decisions," *Urban Affairs Review*, 31 (November 1995), pp. 226–243.

6. Edwin Blackstone and Simon Hakim, "Private Ayes: A Tale of Four Cities: New York, Philadelphia, Indianapolis, and Phoenix," *American City and County* 112 (February 1997), pp. 4–8.

7. See Jonathan Walters, "Going Outside," *Governing*, May, 2004, pp. 7–15.

8. Stephen Goldsmith, *The Twenty-First Century City* (Regnery, 1997), p. 10.

9. See Reason Public Policy Institute, a pro-privatization think tank, at www.privatization.org.

10. John Shannon, "The Deregulation of Fiscal Federalism," in *The Changing Face of Fiscal Federalism*, eds. Thomas R. Swartz and John E. Peck (Sharpe, 1990), p. 31.

11. National Conference of State Legislatures, "State Budget Gaps Shrink, NCSL Survey Finds," news release, April 28, 2004, www.ncsl.org/programs/press/2004/040428.htm, accessed on May 3, 2004.

12. See Henry S. Wulf, "Trends in State Government Finances," in *Book of the States, 2002*, (The Council of State Governments, 2002) pp. 269–277.

13. John Shannon, "The Deregulation of the American Federal System, 1789–1989," in *The Changing Face of Fiscal Federalism*, eds. Swartz and Peck, pp. 17–34.

14. Roy W. Bahl Jr., "Changing Federalism: Trends and Interstate Variations," in ibid., p. 59.

15. *Book of the States, 2002*, p. 290.

16. For a recent discussion of state and local tax issues, see Katherine Barrett, Richard Greene, Michele Mariani, and Anya Sostek, "The Way We Tax: A 50-state Report," *Governing*, February, 2003, pp. 11–40.

17. For a brief history of the property tax, see Dennis Hale, "The Evaluation of the Property Tax: A Study of the Relation Between Public Finance and Political Theory," *Journal of Politics* 47 (May 1985), pp. 382–404. See also C. Lowell Harris, ed., *The Property Tax and Local Finance* (Academy of Political Science, 1983).

18. *Critical Issues in State-Local Fiscal Policy: A Guide to Local Option Taxes* (National Conference of State Legislatures, 1997), p 10. See also *Statistical Abstract of the United States, 2001* (U.S. Government Printing Office, 2001), pp. 278 ff.

19. See Roy Bahl, David L. Sjoquist, and W. Loren Williams, "School Finance Reform and Impact on Property Taxes," *Proceedings of the Eighty-Third Annual National Tax Association Conference, 1990* (National Tax Association, Tax Institute of America, 1991), pp. 163–171.

20. *Serrano* v. *Priest*, 5 Cal.3d 487, 96 Cal. Rptr. 601 (1971).

21. *San Antonio Independent School District* v. *Rodriguez*, 411 U.S. 1 (1973).

22. David L. Kirp, "New Hope for Failing Schools: State Courts Are Remedying the Shame of Inadequate Education Funding," *Nation*, June 1, 1998, p. 20. See also *Board of Education, Levittown, Etc.* v. *Nyquist*, 439 N.E.2d 359 (1982); *Washakie County School District Number One* v. *Herschler*, 606 Pac.2d 310 (1980); and *Edgewood Independent School District* v. *Kirby*, 34 Tex. Sup.Ct. J. 386 (1991).

23. J. Richard Aronson and John L. Hilley, *Financing State and Local Governments*, 4th ed. (Brookings Institution, 1986), p. 138. See also U.S. Advisory Commission on Intergovernmental Relations, *Property Tax Circuit-Breakers: Current Status and Policy Issues* (U.S. Government Printing Office, 1975), and Steven D. Gold, "Circuit Breakers and Other Relief Measures," in *Property Tax and Local Finance*, ed. Harris, pp. 119–132.

24. David B. Magleby, *Direct Legislation: Voting on Ballot Propositions in the United States* (Johns Hopkins University Press, 1984), pp. 61–76.

25. *Survey of Legislative Fiscal Officers* (National Conference of State Legislatures, 1996); Mandy Rafool, NCSL tax specialist, personal communication, September 15, 1998.

26. Carl Hulse, "Senate Extends until 2007 Ban on Internet Access Tax," *The New York Times,* April 30, 2004, p. A-12.

27. Ken Park, *World Almanac and Book of Facts, 2002,* (World Almanac, 2001) p. 630.

28. Ernst & Young, "Global Online Retailing: A Special Report," p. 7, at www.ey.com.

29. James Popkin and Katia Hetter, "America's Gambling Craze," *U.S. News and World Report,* March 14, 1994, p. 43.

30. To find out more about lotteries go on the Web site of the Multi-State Lottery Association at www.musl.com or the North American Association of State and Provincial Lotteries at www.naspl.org. You may find more about the history of lotteries at www.scigames.com.

31. Kathryn A. Foster, *The Political Economy of Special-Purpose Government* (Georgetown University Press, 1997); Robert L. Bland and Wes Clarke, "Budgeting for Capital Improvements," in *Handbook of Government Budgeting,* ed. Roy T. Meyers (Jossey-Bass, 1999), pp. 653–677.

32. For a thorough discussion of issues related to intergovernmental competition in attracting business and related tax issues, see Robert L. Bland, *A Revenue Guide for Local Government* (International City Managers Association, 1989), chap. 9.

33. Charles Mahtesian, "The Stadium Trap," *Governing,* May 1998, p. 22.

34. See Mark Rosentraub, *Major League Losers: The Real Cost of Sports and Who's Paying for It* (Basic Books, 1997).

35. Sarah Lawrence and Jeremy Travis, *The New Landscape of Imprisonment: Mapping America's Prison Expansion* (Urban Institute, 2004), p. 14.

36. See "Grading the States, 2001," *Governing,* February, 2001.

Epilogue

1. Thucydides, *History of the Peloponnesian War,* trans. Benjamin Jowett (Prometheus Books, 1998).

2. Edith Hamilton, *The Echo of Greece* (Norton, 1957), p. 47.

3. The White House, at www.whitehouse.gov/news/releases/2001/09/20010911-16.html.

4. For a book advocating more direct democracy, see Ted Becker and Christa Daryl Slaton, *The Future of Teledemocracy* (Praeger 2000); for a contrary view, see Richard J. Ellis, *Democratic Delusions: The Initiative Process in America* (University Press of Kansas, 2002).

5. For an extensive list of countries that use some form of proportional representation, see ed.labonte.com/pr.html.

6. For more on the relationship between electoral institutions and party systems, see Maurice Duverger, *Political Parties: Their Organization and Activity in the Modern State* (Wiley, 1954).

7. *Lawrence* v. *Texas,* 539 U.S. 558 (2003).

8. Campaign Media Legal Center, at wwwcampaignlegalcenter.org/BCRA.html; *McConnell* v. *FEC,* 124 S.CT. 619 (2003).

9. Bruce Bimber and Richard Davis, *Campaigning Online: The Internet in U.S. Elections.* Oxford University Press, 2003.

10. John F. Kennedy, *Profiles in Courage* (Pocket Books, 1956), p. 108.

11. Harry S Truman, impromptu remarks before the Reciprocity Club, Washington, D.C., April 11, 1958, as reported by the *New York World-Telegram* April 12, 1958, p. 4. Found at www.bartleby.com/73/1405.html.

12. These three books will give you insight into the life of a politician: Bill Bradley, *Time Present, Time Past: A Memoir* (Knopf 1996); Warren B. Rudman, *Combat: Twelve Years in the U.S. Senate* (Random House, 1996); Mark Hatfield, *Against the Grain: Reflections of a Rebel Republican* (White Cloud Press, 2001).

13. For a contrary view of Madison's presidency, see Gary Rosen, *American Compact: James Madison and the Problem of the Founding* (University Press of Kansas, 1999).

14. Judy Wilgoren, "Dean Spares No Opponent as He Sprints Across Iowa," *The New York Times.* 15 October 2003, p. A17.

15. Richard F. Fenno, Jr., *Home Style: House Members in Their Districts* (Boston: Little, Brown and Company, 1978), pp. 162–169.

16. See Lawrence R. Jacobs and Robert Y. Shapiro, *Politicians Don't Pander* (University of Chicago Press, 2000); Christopher Beem, *The Necessity of Politics* (University of Chicago Press, 1999); and John E. McDonough, *Experiencing Politics* (University of California Press, 2000).

17. See Kareem Abdul-Jabar and Alan Steinberg, *Black Profiles in Courage* (Morrow, 1996).

18. Reinhold Niebuhr, *The Children of Light and the Children of Darkness* (Scribner, 1944), p. xi.

19. See Bernard Crick, *In Defense of Politics,* rev. ed. (Pelican Books, 1983); and Stimson Bullitt, *To Be a Politician,* rev. ed. (Yale University Press, 1977).

20. See Benjamin R. Barber, *A Passion for Democracy* (Princeton University Press, 1998).

21. See Nat Hentoff, *Free Speech for Me—but Not for Thee: How the American Left and Right Relentlessly Censor Each Other* (Harper Perennial, 1993).

22. William J. Brennan, commencement address, Brandeis University, May 18, 1986.

23. Arthur M. Schlesinger Jr., *The Disuniting of America* (Norton, 1993), p. 134.

24. John W. Gardner, *Self-Renewal,* rev. ed. (Norton, 1981), p. xiv.

PHOTO CREDITS

INDEX